KU-495-714

Contents

√ No new ed
2/90

WHO'S WHO
IN
ECONOMICS

A Biographical Dictionary
of Major Economists
1700–1981

WHO'S WHO IN ECONOMICS

A Biographical Dictionary of Major Economists 1700–1981

edited by

MARK BLAUG

*Professor of Economics of Education,
University of London Institute of Education*

and

PAUL STURGES

*Lecturer in Library and Information Studies,
Loughborough University of Technology*

Wheatsheaf
Books

A MEMBER OF THE HARVESTER PRESS GROUP

First published in Great Britain in 1983 by
WHEATSHEAF BOOKS LTD
A MEMBER OF THE HARVESTER PRESS GROUP
Publisher: John Spiers
Director of Publications: Edward Elgar
16 Ship Street, Brighton, Sussex

© Mark Blaug and Paul Sturges, 1983

British Library Cataloguing in Publication Data
Blaug, Mark
  Who's who in economics: a biographical
  dictionary of major economists 1700-1981.
  1. Economics – Biography
  I. Title II. Sturges, Paul
  330′.092′2   HB76

  ISBN 0-7108-0125-4

Typeset in Times & Set OCR Phototypeset
Printed in Great Britain by
Unwin Brothers Limited, The Gresham Press
Old Woking, Surrey

All rights reserved

131 5587

Preface

Our title begs two questions: What is an 'economist'? and, What is a 'major economist'? Neither is capable of being answered perfectly, but a stab at an answer is necessary if we are to justify our choice of whom we have included and excluded from this dictionary.

There are many economists in the world. There are few economists in the world. Both of these statements are perfectly true: it all depends on how we define an 'economist'. In America, the 1960 Census of Population classified 22,424 individuals as either prefessors, instructors, scientists, or practitioners in the area of 'economics'; however, the National Register of Scientific and Technical Personnel for 1964 included only 12,143 American scientists and technicians claiming professional competence in some branch of economics. Other definitions of an 'economist' are possible, such as having one's highest degree in economics, being a member of at least one professional association of economists, having work experience primarily in the field of economics, being currently employed in economics, and identifying oneself as an economist. Depending on which criterion is chosen, we can obtain 5000 or 17,000 economists in the United States in 1964 (Tolles and Melichar, 1968) and what is true of America is just as true of the rest of the world.

We have chosen to define an economist as one who publishes more or less regularly in one of the hundreds of learned journals of economics. This is unfair to the many dedicated teachers of economics who publish little if anything, to business and government economists whose writings are never published, and to economists working for international agencies whose writings frequently remain anonymous. Our choice of the publication criterion for the status of 'economist' was, however, dictated by our prior choice of a criterion of eminence in economics. The dictionary definition of 'eminence' is 'one who stands high as compared with others, especially in his own calling', for which near synonyms are 'distinguished', 'celebrated' and 'illustrious'. But who is to judge high standing as compared with others? Presumably, none other than the peer group, which is to say that eminent or major economists are those who receive prizes and honorary degrees, are nominated and elected to offices in professional associations of economists, and are frequently cited in the writings of other economists. In fact, we may virtually reduce the concept of eminence to frequency of citations, because the citation counts of particular economists (number of times they are footnoted in economic journals over a period of time) have been shown to be highly correlated with the award of Nobel prizes and with election to offices in such leading professional associations as the American Economic

Association and the Canadian Economic Association (Quandt, 1976; Bordo and Landlau, 1979; Grubel, 1979).

It hardly matters which criterion we adopt for the top fifty or so economists because they would appear under almost all the headings we can devise. It is only when we extend the list of major economists to several hundreds that we encounter difficulties in choosing a purely objective criterion that truly reflects majority opinion in economics rather than the invidious judgements of one or two individuals who happen to be editing a biographical dictionary. We were greatly tempted to forego all subjective opinion and to lean entirely on frequency of citations as the only criterion of eminence or importance. Unfortunately, all the existing data sources for citation analysis contain biases and, moreover, citation frequencies are a good but by no means flawless measure of recognition of scientific achievement. There are, of course, good reasons why scholars are committed to citing the works of others: nothing is as fundamental to science as the notion that scientific knowledge is public and freely available to all, implying that there is no such thing as an inalienable property right in new ideas. The practice of citing authorities must therefore be viewed as an attempt to provide incentives to intellectual pioneers by giving public recognition to their priority claims. For that reason scientific communities all develop informal mechanisms for penalising individuals who, in effect, infringe the property right of others by failing to acknowledge their influences and sources of inspiration. Nevertheless, this informal mechanism operates imperfectly and citation practices are frequently abused: witness the typical doctoral dissertation with endless citations of the works of the candidate's supervisors, the common habit of advertising one's own works by self-citations however irrelevant to the theme in question, the tendency of friends or members of a citation cartel to cite each other, and the general inclination to cite 'stars' in the profession to show that the author is knowledgeable (Grubel, 1979, p. 135).[1] However, despite all the shortcomings of defining 'eminence' by the number of times a scholar is cited, it is difficult to conceive of any other single indicator that is equally revealing of peer recognition. We have therefore selected almost all the living economists in this dictionary on the grounds that they have had the greatest impact on their colleagues as revealed by the high frequency with which they are cited. Nevertheless, we have added a sprinkling of other names whose works may be rarely cited but whose achievements in advice to policy-makers in business and government are generally recognised by their peers. What we have then is a list of 674 living economists from all over the world selected on grounds that are largely, but not entirely, objective. In addition, we describe the careers of 397 dead economists selected by a critical comparison of the names appearing in the indices of leading histories of economic thought.[2]

---

1 Even a statement about citation practices may require a citation.
2 The ratio of living to dead economists is, if anything, too favourable to dead economists. In economics, as in other branches of human knowledge, over 90 per cent of all the economists that have ever lived are alive now.

Our data source for citation frequencies is the Social Sciences Citation Index (SSCI), published tri-annually since 1966 by the Institute of Scientific Information (ISI) in Philadelphia, Pennsylvania. SSCI indices citations from a large number of English, French, German, Italian, Portuguese and Spanish journals, including 138 economic journals as well as some non-journal material, such as books, proceedings, symposia, and monographic series, treating each chapter as though it were an article appearing in a journal (ISI, 1979). Economists as such are not identified in SSCI but the type of journal in which the citations appear allows one to pick out economists from other social scientists in the rank order of citation frequencies over the ten year period 1970-80.

SSCI has no rivals on its own grounds. Nevertheless, it does have severe limitations. If we compare the 138 economic journals in SSCI with the larger set of 201 economic journals listed in the eighteen volumes of the AEA *Index of Economic Articles 1886-1976*, or the even larger set of 232 journals listed in the current *Journal of Economic Literature*, which is supplemented by some 200 collective volumes, it appears that the overlap is large, but that SSCI is somewhat thin on European journals, and even thinner on Asian journals. We have therefore supplemented SSCI by an informal count of citation frequencies in missing European and Asian journals of economics. We cut off our SSCI list of living economists at 640 because the name of the senior editor appeared as the 641st most frequently cited living economist in the years 1970-80. Clearly, 641 is the natural break between major and minor economists!

It is worth noting that our total number of 674 seems to be something like 5 per cent of all living economists, at least if an 'economist' is defined as one who publishes more or less regularly in an academic journal: vol. 18 of the AEA *Index of Economic Articles* lists about 9000 economists as having published at least one article in the year 1976; some 4000 additional names appear in the previous ten volumes covering the years 1965-75, indicating a total stock of living, publishing economists of 13,000 of whom 674 is just over 5 per cent. In short, the editors of this biographical dictionary appear to have made twenty times as many enemies as friends!

Our entries typically comprise the following elements:

1 full name,
2 year and place of birth,
3 title of current post, with name and location of current employer,
4 most recent previous posts,
5 degrees received,
6 professional affiliations, offices held, prizes won and honours received,
7 major fields of interest,
8 statement of principal contributions to economics (in 100 words or less),
9 chief publications (limited to five books and five articles).

The authors of the entries for living economists are the economists themselves: each was asked to supply the relevant information, including a statement of their principal contributions to economics as they – and not we – judged them. We obtained a 87 per cent response rate to our mailing, but we may have failed to contact some of the ninety economists from whom no reply was received (they are nevertheless entered below with the rubric: n.e. = no entry); until editing this volume, we never appreciated how rapidly some economists move about the world.[3] The entries for the 400 or so dead economists (marked with an asterisk) were written by ourselves on the basis of standard sources. We also include two country indices (by place of birth and by place of residence) and an index of major fields of interest.

We sincerely hope that this volume will fill an empty niche in the scanty reference shelf of fellow economists and students of economics. If successful in meeting a need, it will be followed by a second edition in the mid-1980s, bringing the information up to date and extending the coverage of names.

We are deeply indebted to Eugene Garfield and Calvin Mark Lee of ISI for assistance in extracting information on the most frequently cited economists in SSCI over the decade 1970-80. We also wish to express our thanks to Gustav Bombach, Roger Cardinal, Jean-Claude Eicher, Herbert Grubel, Fritz Machlup, Christian Morrisson, Dennis O'Brien, Pedro Schwartz and Sidney Weintraub for valuable advice on our selection procedures, and to Rita Tullberg, Rolf Henricksson, Bruce Larson, Ingrid Metzger-Buddenberg, Evert Schoorl, Claude Ménard, Mary Rowlatt and Mona McKay for providing vital information on some recently deceased economists. The efforts of Claire Sturges in struggling with the editors' handwriting and typing the manuscript are also gratefully noted.

3 Special problems were encountered in obtaining information about recently deceased economists: contact with friends and colleagues of the deceased were not always successful and this explains the absence of information about such well-known names as M.J. Farrell, C.E. Ferguson, S. Hymer, R.A. Kessel and J. Schmookler.

References

AEA (1979), *Index of Economic Articles*, Homewood, Ill., Richard D. Irwin, vols 1-18.

Bordo, M.D. and Landau, D. (1979), 'The pattern of citations in economic theory 1945-68: an exploration towards a quantitative history of thought', *History of Political Economy*, II, 2, Summer, pp. 241-53.

Grubel, H.G. (1979), 'Citation counts for leading economists', *Economic Notes* (Monte Dei Paschi de Siena Journal), 8, 2, pp. 134-45.

Institute of Scientific Information (1979), *Social Sciences Citation Index 1979. Guide and List of Source Publications*, Philadelphia, Penn., ISI.

Quandt, R.E. (1976), 'Some quantitative aspects of the economic journal literature', *Journal of Political Economy*, 84, 4, August, pp. 741-55.

Tolles, A.N. and Melichar, E. (1968), 'Who are the economists?', *Studies of the Structure of Economists' Salaries and Income, American Economic Review*, LVIII, 5, pt 2, December, pp. 123-53.

Mark Blaug
Paul Sturges
London, January 1982

Abbreviations

General

Admin	—	Administration
Amer.	—	America, American
Ass.	—	Assistant
Assoc.	—	Association, Associate
Bull.	—	Bulletin
Bus.	—	Business
Coll.	—	College
Comm.	—	Committee
Corp.	—	Corporation
Dept.	—	Department
Dir.	—	Director
Disting.	—	Distinguished
Div.	—	Division
Econ.	—	Economic, economics
Ed.	—	Editor, editorial
Edn.	—	Edition
Exec.	—	Executive
Fed.	—	Federal
Fin.	—	Financial, Finance
Grad.	—	Graduate
Hist.	—	History, Historical
Inst.	—	Institute, Institution
Internat.	—	International
J.	—	Journal
Jr	—	Junior
Maths	—	Mathematics
Nat.	—	National
Pol.	—	Policy
Polit.	—	Political
Pop.	—	Population
Prof.	—	Professor
Res.	—	Research
Soc.	—	Society
Sr	—	Senior
Stat.	—	Statistical
Stats	—	Statistics
Stud.	—	Studies
Suppl.	—	Supplement
Transl.	—	Translation
Univ.	—	University
Vis.	—	Visiting

Associations, Institutions, Publishers

AAA	—	American Accounting Association
AAAS	—	American Academy of Arts and Sciences
AAEA	—	American Agricultural Economics Association
AAUP	—	American Association of University Professors

AEA	—	American Economic Association
AFA	—	American Finance Association
AHA	—	American History Association
ANU	—	Australian National University
ASA	—	American Statistical Association
A & U	—	Allen & Unwin, London, UK
AUTE	—	Association of University Teachers of Economics, UK
BA	—	British Academy
BAAS	—	British Association for the Advancement of Science
BIT	—	Bureau International du Travail or ILO
CBE	—	Commander of the British Empire
CEA	—	Canadian Economic Association
CNRS	—	Centre National de la Recherche Scientifique, Paris, France
CUP	—	Cambridge University Press, Cambridge, UK
EEA	—	Eastern Economic Association, USA
EEC	—	European Economic Community
EHA	—	Economic History Association, USA
EHS	—	Economic History Society, UK
Em Soc	—	Econometric Society
FAO	—	Food and Agricultural Organisation, UN
HMSO	—	Her Majesty's Stationery Office, UK
IARIW	—	International Association for Research in Income and Wealth
IBRD	—	International Bank for Reconstruction and Development
IEA	—	International Economic Association
ILO	—	International Labour Office, UN
IMF	—	International Monetary Fund
IRRA	—	Industrial Relations Research Association
LASA	—	Latin America Studies Association
LSE	—	London School of Economics and Political Science, London, UK
MEA	—	Midwest Economics Association
MIT	—	Massachusetts Institute of Technology, Cambridge, Mass., USA
NAS	—	National Academy of Sciences, USA
NBER	—	National Bureau of Economic Research, New York, NY, USA
N-H	—	North-Holland Publishing Co., Amsterdam, The Netherlands
NIESR	—	National Institute of Economic and Social Research, London, UK
NSF	—	National Science Foundation
NTA	—	National Tax Association
NYU	—	New York University, NYC, New York, USA
OBE	—	Order of the British Empire
OECD	—	Organisation for Economic Co-operation and Development
ORSA	—	Operations Research Society of America
OUP	—	Oxford University Press, Oxford, UK
PAA	—	Population Association of America
RES	—	Royal Economic Society
RSA	—	Regional Science Association, USA
RSS	—	Royal Statistical Society
SEA	—	Southern Economic Association
SSRC	—	Social Science Research Council
TIAA	—	Teachers Insurance and Annuity Association

UCLA	—	University of California, Los Angeles, Calif., USA
UNCTAD	—	UN Conference on Trade and Development
UNECA	—	UN Economic Commission for Africa
UNECAFE	—	UN Economic Commission for Asia and the Far East
UNECLA	—	UN Economic Commission for Latin America
Univ. Camb.	—	University of Cambridge, Cambridge, UK
WEA	—	Western Economic Association, USA
WHO	—	World Health Organisation, UN
WRSA	—	Western Regional Science Association, USA

Journals

AEP	—	*Australian Economic Papers*
AER	—	*American Economic Review*
AJAE	—	*American Journal of Agricultural Economics*
Bell JE	—	*Bell Journal of Economics*
BJIR	—	*British Journal of Industrial Relations*
BNLQR	—	*Banca Nazionale del Lavoro Quarterly Review*
BOIS	—	*Bulletin of the Oxford Institute of Statistics*
Camb JE	—	*Cambridge Journal of Economics*
CJE	—	*Canadian Journal of Economics*
CSSH	—	*Comparative Studies in Society and History*
DE	—	*De Economist*
Ec	—	*Economica*
Econ App	—	*Economie Appliquêe*
Econ Int	—	*Economia Internazionale*
Econom	—	*The Economist*
EDCC	—	*Economic Development and Cultural Change*
EHR	—	*Economic History Review*
EI	—	*Economic Inquiry*
EJ	—	*Economic Journal*
Ekon Tids	—	*Ekonomisk Tidskrift*
Em	—	*Econometrica*
ER	—	*Economic Record*
ESQ	—	*Economic Studies Quarterly*
ESS	—	*Encyclopaedia of the Social Sciences*, E.R.A. Seligman and A. Johnson (eds) (Macmillan, 1930-5, 15 vols)
Europ ER	—	*European Economic Review*
For Aff	—	*Foreign Affairs*
HOPE	—	*History of Political Economy*
IESS	—	*International Encyclopedia of the Social Sciences*, D.L. Sills (ed.) (Macmillan and Free Press, 1968, 18 vols)
ILO Bull Lab Stat	—	*ILO Bulletin of Labour Statistics*
ILRR	—	*Industrial Labor Relations Review*
Int ER	—	*International Economic Review*
Int Lab Rev	—	*International Labour Review*
JASA	—	*Journal of the American Statistical Association*
J Bank Fin	—	*Journal of Banking and Finance*
J Bank Res	—	*Journal of Bank Research*
J Bus	—	*Journal of Business*
J Comp E	—	*Journal of Comparative Economics*
JDE	—	*Journal of Development Economics*
J Dev Stud	—	*Journal of Development Studies*
J Ec Behav	—	*Journal of Economic Behavior and Organization*
J Ec Dyn	—	*Journal of Economic Dynamics and Control*
JEH	—	*Journal of Economic History*
JEI	—	*Journal of Economic Issues*
JEL	—	*Journal of Economic Literature*

J Em	—	*Journal of Econometrics*
JET	—	*Journal of Economic Theory*
J Eur EH	—	*Journal of European Economic History*
JFE	—	*Journal of Farm Economics*
J Fin	—	*Journal of Finance*
J Fin Econ	—	*Journal of Financial Economics*
JHE	—	*Journal of Health Economics*
JHR	—	*Journal of Human Resources*
JI Bus Stud	—	*Journal of International Business Studies*
J Ind E	—	*Journal of Industrial Economics*
J Int E	—	*Journal of International Economics*
J Law E	—	*Journal of Law and Economics*
J Math E	—	*Journal of Mathematical Economics*
JMCB	—	*Journal of Money, Credit and Banking*
J Mon Ec	—	*Journal of Monetary Economics*
JMS	—	*Journal of Management Studies*
JNS	—	*Jahrbücher für Nationalökonomie und Statistik*
JPE	—	*Journal of Political Economy*
J Post Keyn E	—	*Journal of Post-Keynesian Economics*
J Pub E	—	*Journal of Public Economics*
J Reg S	—	*Journal of Regional Science*
JRSS	—	*Journal of the Royal Statistical Society*
JSW	—	*Jahrbüch für Sozialwissenschaften*
J Transp EP	—	*Journal of Transport Economics and Policy*
JUE	—	*Journal of Urban Economics*
LBR	—	*Lloyds Bank Review*
MBR	—	*Midland Bank Review*
MLR	—	*Monthly Labor Review*
MS	—	*Manchester School of Economic and Social Studies*
OBES	—	*Oxford Bulletin of Economics and Statistics*
OEP	—	*Oxford Economic Papers*
PDR	—	*Pakistan Development Review*
PF	—	*Public Finance*
Pol Meth	—	*Political Methodology*
QJE	—	*Quarterly Journal of Economics*
QREB	—	*Quarterly Review of Economics and Business*
RE	—	*Revue Economique*
REP	—	*Revue d'Economie Politique*
REStat	—	*Review of Economics and Statistics*
REStud	—	*Review of Economic Studies*
RISE	—	*Revista Internazionale di Scienze Economiche e Commerciali*
Riv Intern	—	*Rivista Internazionale*
RIW	—	*Review of Income and Wealth*
SAJE	—	*South African Journal of Economics*
Scand JE	—	*Scandinavian Journal of Economics*
SEJ	—	*Southern Economic Journal*
SJPE	—	*Scottish Journal of Political Economy*
Swed JE	—	*Swedish Journal of Economics*
Urb Stud	—	*Urban Studies*
WA	—	*Weltwirtschaftliches Archiv*
WD	—	*World Development*
WEJ	—	*Western Economic Journal*
YBESR	—	*Yorkshire Bulletin of Economic and Social Research*
YEE	—	*Yale Economic Essays*
ZGS	—	*Zeitschrift für die gesamte Staatswissenschaft*
ZN	—	*Zeitschrift für Nationalökonomie*

A

AARON, Henry J.

Born 1936, Washington, DC, USA.
Current Post Prof. Econ., Univ. Maryland, USA.
Recent Posts Sr Fellow, Brookings Inst.; Assoc. prof., Univ. Maryland, 1967–74; Ass. secretary, Planning Evaluation, US Dept Health, Education, Welfare, 1977–8.
Degrees BA (Polit. Science-Econ.) UCLA, 1958; MA (Russian Regional Stud.), PhD (Econ.) Harvard Univ., 1960, 1963.
Offices and Honours Phi Beta Kappa, 1958; Ass. R.A. Wallace, Ass. secretary, US Treasury, 1961; Sr staff economist, US President's Council Econ. Advisers, 1966–7; Member, Council Econ. Advisers, State of Maryland, 1969–75; Vis. prof., Harvard Univ., 1974; Member, Exec. Comm., AEA, 1978–; Member, Board Dirs, Abt Assoc., 1978–; Chairman, Advisory Council Social Security, 1978–9.
Principal Contributions Issues in the economics of taxation. Economic aspects of social security and health care. Questions of the provision of public goods.
Publications *Books:* 1. *The New View of Property Taxation* (Brookings Inst., 1975); 2. *Politics and the Professors: The Great Society in Transition* (Brookings Inst., 1978); 3. *On Social Welfare* (Abt Assoc., 1980); 4. *The Economics of Taxation*, ed. (with M. Boskin), (Brookings Inst., 1980); 5. *How Taxes Affect Economic Behavior*, ed. (with J.A. Pechman), (Brookings Inst., 1981).
Articles: 1. 'Structuralism versus monetarism: a note on evidence', *J Dev Stud*, 3, Jan. 1967; 2. 'The foundations of the "war on poverty" re-examined', *AER*, 57(5), Dec. 1967; 3. 'Perspectives on poverty 4: income transfer programs', *MLR*, 92(2) Feb. 1969; 4. 'Local public expenditures and the migration effect', *WEJ*, 7(4), Dec. 1969; 5. 'Public goods and income distribution' (with M.C. McGuire), *Em*, 38(6), Nov. 1970.

ABRAMOVITZ, Moses

Born 1912, New York City, NY, USA.
Current Post Managing ed., *JEL*.
Recent Posts Prof. Econ., Coe prof. Amer. Econ. Hist., Stanford Univ., 1948–77.
Degrees AB Harvard Univ., 1932; PhD Columbia Univ., 1939.
Offices and Honours Fellow, AAAS, ASA; Disting. Fellow, pres., 1980, AEA.
Principal Contributions Measurement of the importance of inventory investment fluctuations in business cycles; explanation of the different behaviour of inventories of raw materials, goods in process and finished goods; description and explanation of long swings (Kuznets cycles) in economic growth; measurement of total factor productivity growth and its importance as a source of long-term growth in industrialised economies; and description and explanation of rapid post-World War II growth of industrialised economies.
Publications *Books:* 1. *Price Theory for a Changing Economy* (Columbia Univ. Press, 1939); 2. *Inventories and Business Cycles* (NBER, 1950); 3. *The Trend of Public Employment in Great Britain* (with V. Eliasberg) (NBER, 1954); 4. *Evidences of Long Swings in Aggregate Construction Since the Civil War* (NBER, 1964).
Articles: 1. 'Resource and output trends in the United States since 1870', *AER/S*, 46(2), May 1956; 2. 'The nature and significance of Kuznets cycles', *EDCC*, 9, April 1961, reprinted in *Readings in Business Cycles*, R.A. Gordon and L.R. Klein (eds) (Richard D. Irwin, 1965); 3. 'Rapid growth potential and its realization: the experience of capitalist economies in the post-war period', in *Economic Growth and Resources*, E. Malinvaud (ed.), (Macmillan, 1979).

ACKLEY, Gardner

Born 1915, Indianapolis, Ind., USA.
Current Post Henry Carter Adams Univ. prof. Polit. Econ., Univ. Michigan, USA.

Recent Posts US Office Price Admin., 1941–6; Econ. adviser, Ass. dir., US Office Price Stabilization, 1951; Member, 1962–8, Chairman, 1964–8, US President's Council Econ. Advisers; US Ambassador Italy, 1968–9; Member, US Nat. Advisory Council Social Security, 1978–9.

Degrees BA, LLD Western Michigan Univ., 1936, 1964; MA, PhD, Univ. Michigan, 1937, 1940; LLD Kalamazoo Coll., 1967.

Offices and Honours Fulbright Res. Scholar, 1956–7; Board Eds., 1953–6, Comm. honours and awards, 1959–61, Chairman, Comm. Res. Publications, 1959–61, Vice-pres., 1962, Pres.-elect, 1981, AEA; Dir., US SSRC, 1959–61; Fellow, AAAS, 1968; Cavaliere del Gran Croce, Italy, 1969; Member, Amer. Philosophical Soc., 1972; Dir., NBER, 1971–80.

Principal Contributions Rigorous formulations of macro-economic principles. Contributions to the theory of inflation. Analysis of incomes policies and wage-price controls. Discussions of current macro-economic policy issues. Analysis of Italian economic problems and developments, 1947–65. Analyses of role of economists advising governments. Comparative analysis of stabilisation policies in Europe, N. America and Japan.

Publications *Books:* 1. *Macro-economic Theory* (Macmillan, 1961); 2. *Un Modello Econometico dello Sviluppo Italiano nel Dopoguerra* (Svimez, 1963); 3. *Stemming World Inflation* (Atlantic Inst., 1971); 4. *Macro-economics: Theory and Policy* (Macmillan, 1978); 5. *Asia's New Giant: How the Japanese Economy Works* (contributor), (Brookings Inst., 1978).

Articles: 1. 'Relative prices and aggregate consumer demand' (with D.B. Suits), *AER*, 40, Dec. 1950; 2. 'The wealth-saving relationship', *JPE*, 59, April 1951; 3. 'Administered prices and the inflationary process', *AER/S*, 49, May 1959; 4. 'An incomes policy for the 1970s', *REStat*, 54(3), Aug. 1972; 5. 'The costs of inflation', *AER*, 68(2), May 1978.

ADAMS, Francis Gerard

Born 1929, USA.

Current Post Prof. Econ., Fin.-Dir. Econ. Res. Unit, Univ. Pennsylvania, USA.

Recent Posts Consultant Forecasting, OECD, Paris, 1966–7; Sr staff economist, US President's Council Econ. Advisers, 1968–9.

Degrees BA, MA, PhD Univ. Michigan, 1949, 1951, 1956.

Principal Contributions Empirical research in income distribution, the utilisation of attitudinal data in macro-economic models, development of industrial models, models of primary commodity markets, models of regions, and models of world trade. An important focus has been the integration of commodity models into project LINK and, more generally, into models of developing economies.

Publications *Books:* 1. *An Econometric Analysis of International Trade* (with H. Eguchi and F.J.M. Meyer zu Schlochtern), (OECD, 1969); 2. *Econometric Models of World Agricultural Commodity Markets* (with J.R. Behrman), (Ballinger, 1976); 3. *Stabilizing World Commodity Markets: Analysis, Practice and Policy* (with S. Klein), (Heath-Lexington, 1978); 4. *Econometric Modeling of World Commodity Policy* (with J.R. Behrman), (Heath-Lexington, 1978); 5. *Modeling the Multi-regional Economic System: Perspectives for the Eighties*, ed. (with N.J. Glickman), (Heath-Lexington, 1980).

Articles: 1. 'The size of individual incomes: socio-economic variables and chance variation', *REStat*, 40, Nov. 1958; 2. 'Prediction with consumer attitudes: the time series-cross section paradox', *REStat*, 47, Nov. 1965; 3. 'An economic-linear programming model of the US petroleum refining industry' (with J.M. Griffin), *JASA*, 67, Sept. 1972; 4. 'Anticipations variables in an econometric model: performance of the anticipations versons of Wharton Mark III (with V.G. Duggal), *Int ER*, 15(2), June 1974, repr. in *Econometric Performance*, L.R. Klein and E. Burmeister (eds), (Univ. Penn. Press, 1976); 5. 'Integrating commodity models into

LINK', in *Modelling the International Transmission Mechanism*, J. Sawyer (ed.), (N-H, 1979).

ADAMS, Walter

Born 1922, Vienna, Austria.
Current Post Disting. univ. prof. Econ., Past-pres., Michigan State Univ., East Lansing, USA.
Recent Posts Vis. prof., Salzburg Seminar, 1959, 1960, Falkenstein Seminar, 1972; Vis. prof., Univ. Grenoble, 1966.
Degrees BA Brooklyn Coll., 1942; MA, PhD, Yale Univ. 1946, 1947; Hon. LLD Central Michigan Univ., 1973; Hon. LLD Michigan State Univ., 1979.
Offices AEA, 1947–; Pres., AAUP, 1972–4; Exec. Comm., Assoc. Evolutionary Econ., 1976–9; Pres., MEA, 1979–80; Pres., Assoc. Social Econ., 1980–1.
Principal Contributions Empirical studies of the link between industry structure, conduct and performance, emphasising the role of government as a promoter of monopoly. Demonstrated the baneful effects of import restraints on the performance of the US steel and automobile industries. Contributed case-studies on the industry-labour-government complex.
Publications *Books:* 1. *The Structure of American Industry* (Macmillan, 1950, 1982); 2. *Monopoly in America* (Macmillan, 1955); 3. *Is the World our Campus?* (Mich. State Univ. Press, 1960); 4. *The Brain Drain* (ed.) (Macmillan, 1968); 5. *The Test* (Macmillan, 1971).
Articles: 1. 'Competition, monopoly, and countervailing power', *QJE*, 67, Nov. 1953, 68, Aug. 1954; 2. 'The role of competition in the regulated industries', *AER/S*, 48, May 1958; 3. 'Steel imports and vertical oligopoly power', (with J.B. Dirlam), *AER*, 54, Sept. 1964, 56, March 1966; 4. 'Big steel, invention, and innovation' (with J.B. Dirlam), *QJE*, 80, May 1966; 5. 'The military-industrial complex and the new industrial state', *AER/S*, 58, May 1968.

ADELMAN, Irma

Born 1930, Romania.
Current Post Prof. Agric. Resource Econ., Prof. Econ., Univ. Cal., Berkeley, 1979–.
Recent Posts Prof. Econ., Northwestern Univ., 1966–72; Fellow, Center Advanced Study Behavioral Sciences, Stanford Univ., 1970–1; Sr economist, Development Res. Center, Internat. Bank Reconstruction Development, 1971–2; Prof. Econ., Univ. Maryland, 1972–9; Cleveringa Chair, Leiden Univ., Fellow, Netherlands Inst. Advanced Study, 1977–8.
Degrees BA, MA, PhD Univ. Cal., Berkeley, 1949, 1950, 1955.
Principal Contributions Analysis of economic distribution and growth; interactions among economic, social, and political forces in economic development; the development of computable general equilibria for development planning.
Publications *Books:* 1. *Theories of Economic Growth and Development* (Stanford Univ. Press, 1961, 1974), (Spanish transl. *Teorias del desarrollo economico*, 1964, Japanese transl., 1971); 2. *The Theory and Design of Economic Development*, ed. (with E. Thorbecke) (Johns Hopkins Univ. Press, 1966); 3. *Society, Politics, and Economic Development – A Quantitative Approach*, (with C.T. Morris) (Johns Hopkins Univ. Press, 1967); 4. *Economic Growth and Social Equity in Developing Countries*, (with C.T. Morris) (Stanford Univ. Press, 1973); 5. *Income Distribution Policy in Developing Countries: A Case-study of Korea*, (with S. Robinson) (Stanford Univ. Press, 1977).
Articles: 1. 'The dynamic properties of the Klein-Goldberger model' (with F.L. Adelman), *Em*, 27, Oct. 1959, repr. in *Readings in Business Cycles* (eds. R.A. Gordon and L. Klein) (Irwin, 1964), and in *Readings in Economic Statistics and Econometrics* (ed. A. Zellner) (Little, Brown & Co., 1968); 2. 'An econometric analysis of population growth', *AER*, 53, June 1963; 3. 'Foreign aid and economic development: the case of Greece' (with H.B. Chenery),

REStat, 48, April 1966, repr. in *Studies in Development Planning* (ed. H.B. Chenery) (Harvard Univ. Press, 1971); 4. 'Strategies for equitable growth', *Challenge*, May/June 1974; 5. 'Development economics – a reassessment of goals', *AER*, 65(2), May 1975.

ADELMAN, Morris Albert

Born   1917, New York City, NY, USA.
Current Post   Prof. Econ., MIT, USA.
Degrees   BSS City Coll., New York, 1938; PhD Harvard Univ., 1948.
Offices and Honours   AEA, RES, Internat. Assoc. Energy Economists (Pres. 1980–1), Mineral Economics award (Amer. Inst. Mining Metallurgical and Petroleum Engineers, 1979).
Principal Contributions   Long-term trends in industrial concentration; international oil and gas markets; scarcity and monopoly.
Publications   n.e.

AFTALION, Albert*

Dates and Birthplace   1874–1956, Bulgaria.
Posts Held   Prof., Univ. Lille, 1904–20, Univ. Paris, 1920–40.
Career   One of the professors appointed to chairs in economics in the law faculties of the universities of France after 1878 who questioned the free-trade *laissez faire* orthodoxy of the 'Paris group' and gradually introduced more scientific content into French economics. He is best known for his 'real' theory of business cycles, including the statement in 1909 of the 'acceleration principle' of derived demand (restated and named by J.M. Clark in 1917). Much of his later work dealt with the nature of the French inflation 1919–24 and the causes of international gold movements between the two world wars.
Publications   *Books:* 1. *L'oeuvre économique de Simonde de Sismondi* (1899); 2. *Essai d'une théorie des crises générales et périodiques* (1909); 3. *Les crises périodiques de surproduction*, 2 vols (1913); 4. *Les fondements du*

socialisme: étude critique (1923); 5. *La valeur de la monnaie dans l'économie contemporaine*, 2 vols (1927); 6. *L'or et la monnaie, leur valeur: les mouvements de l'or* (1938).
Secondary Literature   F. Perroux *et al.*, *L'oeuvre scientifique d'Albert Aftalion* (Domat-Montchrestien, 1945); D. Villey, 'Aftalion, Albert', *IESS*, vol. 1.

AIGNER, Dennis J.

Born   1937, Los Angeles, Cal., USA.
Current Post   Prof. Econ., Co-dir., Modelling Res. Group, 1976–, Chairman, Dept. Econ., Univ. Southern Cal., Los Angeles, USA, 1979–.
Recent Posts   Prof. Econ., 1970–7, Chairman, Social Systems Res. Inst., Univ. Wisconsin, Madison, 1971–6; Res. consultant, Rand Corp., 1976.
Degrees   BS (Agric. Econ.) MA (Stats.) PhD (Agric. Econ.), Univ. Cal., Berkeley, 1959, 1962, 1963.
Offices and Honours   Fellow, Em Soc; Fulbright Res. Scholar, Vis. prof., Center Operations Res. and Econometrics (CORE), Univ. Catholique Louvain, Belgium, 1970–1; ASA Vis. lecturer, Program Stats., 1980–3.
Principal Contributions   Econometric modelling with latent variables; frontier production functions, original contribution in 1968 and continued to the present; and experimental design, a recent interest, promoted by work in designing peak-load pricing experiments in electricity.
Publications   *Books:* 1. *Principles of Statistical Decision-making* (Macmillan, 1968); 2. *Basic Econometrics* (Prentice-Hall, 1971); 3. *Latent Variables in Socioeconomic Models*, ed. (with A.S. Goldberger), (N-H, 1977); 4. *Experimental Design in Econometrics*, ed. (with C. Morris), (N-H, 1979); 5. *Specification and Estimation of Frontier Production, Profit and Cost Functions*, ed. (with P. Schmidt), (N-H, 1980).
Articles: 1. 'On estimating the industry production function' (with S. Chu), *AER*, 58, Sept. 1968; 2. 'Estimation of Pareto's law from grouped observations' (with A.S. Goldberger), *JASA*, 65, June 1970; 3. 'A compendium on estimation

of the autoregressive-moving average model from time series data', *Int ER*, 12(3), Oct. 1971; 4. 'An appropriate econometric framework for estimating a labor supply function from the SEO file', *Int ER*, 15(1), Feb. 1974; 5. 'Formulation and estimation of stochastic frontier production functions' (with C.A.K. Lovell and P. Schmidt), *J Em*, 6 July 1977.

AKERLOF, George A.

Born 1940, New Haven, Conn., U.S.A.

Current Post Prof. Econ., Univ. Cal., Berkeley, USA.

Recent Posts Cassel prof., LSE, 1978–80.

Degrees BA Yale Univ., 1962; PhD MIT, 1966.

Offices and Honours n.e.

Principal Contributions n.e.

Publications *Articles:* 1. 'The market for "lemons"', *QJE*, 84(3), August 1970; 2. 'Irving Fisher on his head: the consequences of target-threshold monitoring for the demand for money', *QJE*, 93(2), May 1979; 3. 'Irving Fisher on his head II: the consequences of the timing of payments for the demand for money' (with R. Milbourne), *QJE*, 95, Aug. 1980; 4. 'Jobs as dam sites', *REStud*, 48, Jan. 1981; 5. 'The labor contract as partial gift exchange', *QJE*, forthcoming, 1982.

AKERMAN, Gustaf*

Dates and Birthplace 1888–1959 Vienna, Austro-Hungary.

Posts Held Civil servant, Swedish Foreign Affairs Dept, 1915–18; Ass. prof., Univ. Lund, 1923; Prof., Univ. Goteborg, 1931–53.

Degrees Jur. kand. Univ. Uppsala, 1913; Dr Univ. Lund, 1923.

Career Elder brother of Johann Henrik, an economist and historian in his own right, and a pupil of Wicksell, whose 1923–4 book on capital theory led Wicksell to reformulate his own theory of fixed capital formation. Like Böhm-Bawerk, Akerman was inspired by his reading of John Rae. He partially refor-

mulated his ideas in a 1931 book, and also worked on industrial rationalisation, price regulations, economic fluctuations and employment questions.

Publications *Books:* 1. *Real Kapital und Kapitalzins*, 2 vols (1923–4); 2. *Om den Industriella Rationaliseringen* (1931); 3. *Mjölleregleringen* (1937); 4. *Engelsk Arbetslöshet och Arbetslöshetspolitik* (1947).

Secondary Literature K. Wicksell, *Lectures on Political Economy*, vol. 1, App. 2 (Macmillan, 1934).

ALBACH, Horst

Born 1931, Essen, Rheinland, Germany.

Current Post Prof. Management Sciences, Univ. Bonn, 1961–.

Recent Posts Pres., 1969–72, Chairman Board, 1972–, Universitätsseminar der Wirtschaft; Council Experts Vocational Education, 1972–4; Nat. Science Council, 1974–7; Member, Council Econ. Experts, Fed. Republic Germany, 1978–.

Degrees Diplom-Kaufmann, Diplom-Volkswirt, Dr rer. pol. (Econ.), Univ. Cologne 1956, 1957, 1958; Hon. PhD (Econ.) Stockholm School Econ., 1976, Helsinki School Econ., 1976.

Offices and Honours Member, AEA, Em Soc, Management Sciences Inst.; Pres., German Operations Res. Soc.; Academy Science N. Rhine Westfalia, 1972–; Vice-pres., Gesellschaft Wirtschafts- und Sozialwissenschaften, 1975–8.

Principal Contributions Capital budgeting under certainty and uncertainty; tax incentives for business investment; theory of the growth of the firm; and transfer pricing.

Publications *Books:* 1. *Wirtschaftlichkeitsrechnung bei Unsicheren Erwartungen* (Cologne and Opladen, 1959); 2. *Optimale Wohngebietsplanung* (with O.M. Ungers), (Wiesbaden, 1969); 3. *Beiträge zur Unternehmensplanung* (Wiesbaden, 1969); 4. *Steuersystem und Unternehmerische Investitionspolitik* (Wiesbaden, 1970); 5. *Hochschulplanung* (with W. Schüler and G. Fandel), (Munich, 1977). *Articles:* 1. 'Capital budgeting and risk management', in *Quantitative Wirtschaftsforschung, Wilhelm Krelle zum 60. Geburtstag*, eds H. Albach *et al.* (J.C.B. Mohr, 1977); 2. 'Approaches to a theory of income distribution in the firm', in *Income Distribution and Economic Inequality*, Z. Griliches (ed), (Campus, 1978); 3. 'The capital structure of the firm, empirical investigations in the financing behavior of German industrial firms', *Liiketaluodillinen Aikakauskirja* (Finnish *J Bus. Econ.*), 28(2), 1979; 4. 'Market organization and pricing behavior of oligopolistic firms in the ethical drugs industry – an essay in the measurement of effective competition', *Kyklos*, 32(3), 1979; 5. 'Average and best practice production functions in German industry', *J Ind E*, 29, Sept. 1980.

ALCHIAN, Armen A.

Born 1914, Fresno, Cal., USA.
Current Post Prof. Econ., UCLA.
Recent Posts Economist, Rand Corp., 1947–64.
Degrees BA (Econ.), PhD (Econ.), Stanford Univ., 1936, 1944.
Offices Member, Mont Pelerin Soc.; Pres., WEA, 1974; Member, AAAS, 1978.
Principal Contributions Analysis of effects of inflation on common stock prices; effects of property rights systems; long-run implications of competitive processes.
Publications *Books:* 1. *University economics* (with W.R. Allen), (Wadsworth, 1964, 1972); 2. *Exchange and Production* (Wadsworth, 1964, 1967, 1977); 3. *Economic Forces at Work* (Liberty, 1978).
Articles: 1. 'Uncertainty, evolution and economic theory', *JPE*, 58, June 1950; 2. 'Costs and outputs', in *The Allocation of Economic Resources*, eds M. Abramovitz *et al.* (Stanford Univ. Press, 1959); 3. 'The meaning and validity of the inflation-induced lag of wages' (with R.A. Kessel), *AER*, 50, March 1960; 4. 'Information costs, pricing and resource unemployment', *WEJ*, 7(2), June 1969; 5. 'Vertical integration, appropriable rents and the competitive contracting process' (with B. Klein and R.G. Crawford), *J Law E*, 21(2), Oct. 1978.

ALDCROFT, Derek Howard

Born 1936, Abergele, N. Wales.
Current Post Prof. Econ. Hist., Head Dept, Univ. Leicester, England.
Recent Posts Reader, Econ. Hist., Univ. Leicester, 1970–3; Prof. Econ. Hist., Head Dept, Univ. Sydney, 1973–6.
Degrees BA (Econ.), PhD Manchester Univ, 1958, 1962.
Offices and Honours Member, EHA; Chairman, Ed. Board, *J Transport Hist.*, 1971–8; Member, Ed. Board, *Bus. Hist. Review*, 1971–3; British Academy Overseas Vis. Fellow, Australia, 1979.
Principal Contributions Growth and development in advanced economies and reinterpreting Britain's inter-war growth. Presently preparing a study on *Britain's economic growth failure, 1950–1980*, a macro-economic analysis of the reasons for Britain's sluggish growth performance in the post-war period.
Publications *Books:* 1. *The Interwar Economy: Britain 1919–1939* (Batsford, 1970); 2. *British Transport since 1914* (David & Charles, 1975); 3. *From Versailles to Wall Street: the International Economy, 1919–1929* (Allen Lane, Penguin Books, 1977); 4. *The East Midlands Economy* (Pointon York Publishing, 1979); 5. *The European Economy, 1914–1980* (Croom Helm, 1980).
Articles: 1. 'Economic growth in Britain in the inter-war years: a reassessment', *EHR*, 20, Aug. 1967; 2. 'Innovation on the railways: the lag in diesel and electric traction', *J Transp. EP*, 3(1), 1969; 4. 'A new chapter in transport history: the twentieth-century revolution', *J Transport Hist.*, 3, 1976; 5. 'The economy, management and foreign competition 1870–1914', in *Industry, Education and the Economy in the Nineteenth Century: did Britain go Wrong?*, eds G. Roderick and M. Stephens (Falmer Press, 1981).

ALEXANDER, Sidney Stuart

Born 1916, Forest City, Penn., USA.
Current Post Prof. Econ. Management, MIT, 1956–.
Recent Posts Economist, IMF, 1948–52; Econ. adviser, Columbia Broadcasting System, 1952–6.
Degrees BS, MS, PhD, Harvard Univ., 1936, 1938, 1946.
Principal Contributions Theory of effects of a devaluation on the trade balance; foundations of normative judgements in social policy; economics and politics of the Middle East; economics of energy and mineral supply.
Publications *Books:* 1. (principal contributor) *The Outlook for Key Commodities, The Outlook for Energy Sources,* in *Resources for Freedom: Report to the President by the President's Materials Policy Commission,* vols 2 & 3 (US Govt Printing Office, 1952).
Articles: 1. 'Effects of a devaluation on the trade balance', *IMF Staff Papers,* 2, April 1952; 2. 'Economics and business planning', in S.S. Alexander *et al., Economics and the Policy Maker* (Brookings Inst., 1959); 3. 'The impersonality of normative judgements', in *Essays in Honor of Sir Roy Harrod,* eds W.A. Eltis *et al.,* (OUP, 1970); 4. 'Social evaluation through notional choice', *QJE,* 88(4), Nov. 1974.

ALIBER, Robert Z.

Born 1930, Keene, New Hampshire, USA.
Current Post Prof. Internat. Econ. Fin., Univ. Chicago, USA.
Recent Posts Staff economist, Comm. Econ. Development, 1961–4; Sr econ. adviser, Agency Internat. Development, 1964; Lecturer, School Advanced Internat. Study., Johns Hopkins Univ., 1964; Assoc. prof., Grad. School Bus., Univ. Chicago, 1965–; Chairman, Comm. Public Pol. Stud., Univ. Chicago, 1978–81.
Degrees BA Williams Coll., 1952; BA, MA, Univ. Camb., 1954, 1957; PhD Yale Univ., 1962.
Offices AEA; Academy Internat. Bus.

Principal Contributions The microfoundations of international finance, including the pricing of exchange risk and of political risk as well as the other factors which segment national financial markets. Has explored the consequences of segmentation of these markets for international corporate financial management and national financial management. Also given attention to the evolution of international financial arrangements, and the expansion of the domain of national currency areas.
Publications *Books:* 1. *The International Money Game* (Basic Books, 1973, 1979); 2. *National Monetary Policies and the International Financial System* (Univ. Chicago Press, 1974); 3. *The Political Economy of Monetary Reform* ed., (Macmillan, 1977); 4. *Exchange Risk and Corporate International Finance* (Macmillan, 1978); 5. *Money, Banking, and the Economy* (with T. Mayer and J. Duesenberry), (Norton, 1981).
Articles: 1. 'The costs and benefits of the US role as a reserve currency country', *QJE,* 78, Aug. 1964; 2. 'The theory of the international corporation: a theory of direct foreign investment', in *The International Corporation,* ed. C.P. Kindleberger (MIT Press, 1970); 3. 'Uncertainty, currency areas, and the exchange rate system', *Ec,* N.S. 39, Nov. 1972; 4. 'Floating exchange rates: the twenties and the seventies', in *Flexible Exchange Rates and the Balance of Payments* (N-H, 1980); 5. 'The integration of offshore and domestic markets for national currencies', *J Mon E,* 6(3), Summer 1980.

ALLAIS, Maurice

Born 1911, Paris, France.
Current Post Prof. l'Ecole Nat. Supérieure des Mines de Paris, 1944–; Dir. Recherche au CNRS, 1954–.
Recent Posts Dir. Groupe de Recherches Econ. et Sociales, 1944–70; Dir. Centre d'Analyse Econ., CNRS, Ecole Nat. Supérieure des Mines de Paris, Univ. Paris X, 1946–; Prof. d'Econ. Théorique, Inst. Stat. Univ. Paris, 1947–68; Disting. Vis. Scholar, Univ. Virginia, 1958–9; Prof. d'Econ.

Inst. des Hautes Etudes Internat. Geneva, 1967–70.

Degrees Ancien élève de l'Ecole Polytechnique, 1931; Ancien élève de l'Ecole Nat. Supérieure des Mines de Paris, 1936; Ingénieur-Docteur de l'Univ. Paris, 1949; Dr Hon. Causa, Univ. Gröningen, 1964.

Offices and Honours Lauréat, l'Académie des Sciences, Prix Laplace, 1933; Académie des Sciences Morales et Politiques, Prix Charles Dupin, 1954, Prix Joseph Dutens, 1959; Officier, l'Ordre des Palmes Académiques, 1949; Lauréat, Johns Hopkins Univ., ORSA, 1958; Lauréat, Soc. Française d'Astronautique, Prix Galabert, 1959; Assoc. Française pour la Communauté Atlantique, 1960; Grand Prix André Arnoux, 1968; gold medal, Soc. d'Encouragement pour l'Industrie Nat., 1970; Officier, Légion d'Honneur, 1977; Hon. member, AEA, 1976; gold medal, CNRS, 1978; Commandeur, l'Ordre Nat. du Mérite, 1981.

Principal Contributions Reformulation of the theories of: general economic equilibrium, maximum efficiency, and the foundations of the economic calculus; new concepts: distributable surplus, the envelope-frontier in hyper-space for indices of preferences. Capital; new concepts: original income, characteristic function, optimal growth under capitalism (first demonstration of the 'golden rule of capital accumulation'). Consumers' choice; critique of neo-Bernouillian theories, Allais' paradox, empirical measure of cardinal utility. Monetary dynamics; new concepts: the function of required saving, psychological rate of interest, rate of 'forgetfulness', psychological time. Applied economics: mining research, management of nationalised coalmining, transport infrastructures, European economic integration.

Publications *Books:* 1. *A la recherche d'une discipline économique*, 2 vols (Imprimerie Nat., 1943); 2. *Economie et intérêt*, 2 vols (Imprimerie Nat., 1947); 3. *L'Europe unie, route de la prospérité* (Calmann-Lévy, 1959); 4. *L'Impôt sur le capital et la réforme monétaire* (Edns Hermann, 1977); 5. *Expected Utility Hypothesis and the Allais' Paradox: Contemporary Discussions on Rational Decisions under Uncertainty with Allais' Rejoinder*, ed. (with O. Hagen), (Reidel, 1979).

Articles: 1. 'The role of capital in economic development', in *Le rôle de l'analyse économétrique dans la formulation des plans de developpement* (Pontificiae Academiae Scientiarum Scripta Varia, Pontifica Academia Scientiarum, 1965); 2. 'Growth and inflation', *JMCB*, 1(3), Aug. 1969; 3. 'Les théories de l'équilibre économique général et de l'efficacité maximale – impasses récentes et nouvelles perspectives', *REP*, 3, 1971, ('Theories of general economic equilibrium and maximum efficiency'), in *Equilibrium and Disequilibrium in Economic Theory* (Reidel, 1977); 4. 'Forgetfulness and interest', *JMCB*, Pt I, 4(1), Feb. 1972.

ALLEN, Roy

Born 1906, Stoke-on-Trent, England.

Current Post Part-time lecturer, LSE.

Recent Posts Prof. Stats, LSE, 1944–73; (Prof. Emeritus, 1973–); Consultant, UK Royal Comission Civil Liability, 1974–8.

Degrees BA, MA, Univ. Camb. 1927, 1932; DSc. (Econ.) Univ. London, 1944; Hon. DSc. (Social Science) Univ. Southampton, 1970.

Offices and Honours Fellow, BA, 1952; CBE, 1954; Knight Bachelor, 1966; Hon. Fellow, Sidney Sussex Coll., Univ. Camb., 1971; Member of official UK committees: Retail prices index advisory comm., Civil Aviation Authority, Comm. Inquiry Decimal Currency, Impact Rates Comm., and others.

Principal Contributions Development of mathematical methods in economics. The theory of value: utility, preferences and consumer demand (e.g. income and substitution effects). Macro-economic theory and specifically models of cyclical growth. Index number theory. The design and calculation of index numbers in practice and specifically the retail prices index. Family expenditure surveys and the analysis of family budgets. The framework of the balance of payments and measures of the gain from trade. Development of the system of national accounts statistics.

Publications *Books:* 1. *Mathematical Analysis for Economists* (Macmillan, 1938); 2. *Statistics for Economists* (Hutchinson, 1949); 3. *Macro-economic theory* (Macmillan, 1967); 4. *Index Numbers in Theory and Practice* (Macmillan, 1975); 5. *Introduction to National Accounts Statistics* (Macmillan, 1980).

Articles: 1. 'The nature of indifference curves', *REStud*, 1, Feb. 1934; 2. 'A reconsideration of the theory of value' (with J.R. Hicks), *Ec*, N.S. 1–2, Feb., May 1934; 3. 'The supply of engineering labour under boom conditions' (with B. Thomas), *EJ*, 49, June 1939; 4. 'Index numbers of retail prices 1938–51', *Applied Stats*, 1, June 1952; 5. 'On official statistics and official statisticians', *JRSS*, 133, Pt 4, 1970.

ALMON, S

N.e.

ALONSO, W.

N.e.

AMEMIYA, Takeshi

Born 1935, Tokyo, Japan.

Current Post Prof. Econ., Stanford Univ., Cal., USA, 1974–.

Recent Posts Assoc. prof. Econ., Stanford Univ., 1968–74.

Degrees BA Internat. Christian Univ., Tokyo, 1958; MA (Econ.) Amer. Univ., Washington, DC, 1961; PhD, (Econ.) Johns Hopkins Univ., 1964.

Offices and Honours Fellow, ASA; Guggenheim Memorial Foundation Fellow, 1975–6; Fellow, Council member, Em Soc, 1980–2; Co-ed., *Em*, 1981–.

Principal Contributions Statistical analysis of time series models, non-linear simultaneous equation models, and cross-section models such as qualitative response models and censored regression models.

Publications *Articles:* 1. 'A comparative study of alternative estimators in a distributed-lag model' (with W.A. Fuller), *Em*, 35, July/Oct. 1967; 2. 'Regression analysis when the dependent variable is truncated normal', *Em*, 41(6), Nov. 1973; 3. 'The non-linear two-stage least-squares estimator', *J Em*, 2(2), July 1974; 4. 'The maximum likelihood and the non-linear three-stage least squares estimator in the general nonlinear simultaneous equation model', *Em*, 45(4), May 1977; 5. 'The m^{-2}-order mean squared errors of the maximum likelihood and the minimum logit chi-square estimator', *Annals of Stats*, 8, 1980.

AMOROSO, Luigi*

Dates and Birthplace 1886–1965, Naples, Italy.

Posts Held Prof. Polit. Econ., Univ. Rome; formerly Exec., Banco di Napoli and Istituto Naz. Assicurazioni; Dir. Banco Naz. del Lavoro.

Degree Dr Maths.

Offices and Honours Fellow, Em Soc.; Cavaliere Italian Republic.

Career A follower of Pareto, who was inspired by the desire to simplify the structure of economic theory. His proof in a 1928 *Annali de Economia* article of the 'existence' of Walrasian general equilibrium when utility functions are 'generalised' and not just 'additive' is one of his major achievements. During the Fascist period he was able, unlike some colleagues, to continue working in Italy. His *Principii*, written during this period, has discussions of money and equilibrium quite free from political implication and in the third part an economic theory of Fascism, stated in analytical terms, which remains within the mainstream of economic science.

Publications *Books:* 1. *Lezioni di Economia Matematica* (1921); 2. *Principii di Economica Corporativa* (1938); 3. *Meccanica Economica* (1942); 4. *Economica di Mercato* (1949).

ANDERSON, James*

Dates and Birthplace 1739–1808, Hermiston, Scotland.

Degree LLD Univ. Aberdeen, 1780.

Career Gentleman farmer and prolific writer on agriculture and corn law questions, chiefly in his periodical *The Bee*, and his series of *Recreations*. His discovery of the 'Ricardian' theory of rent arose from his agricultural studies. It is first stated in the *Observations*, where he concluded that the rent of land is a premium paid for the privilege of cultivating soils that are more fertile than others and that its payment equalises the profits of farmers tilling land of different qualities. The same idea is formulated more precisely in the *Enquiry. . .*

Publications *Books:* 1. *Observations on the Means of Exciting a Spirit of National Industry* (1777); 2. *An Enquiry into the Nature of the Corn Laws* (1777); 3. *Recreations in Agriculture, Natural History, Arts and Miscellaneous Literature*, 6 vols (1799–1802).

Secondary Literature E. Cannan, *A History of the Theories of Production and Distribution in English Political Economy* (Staples Press, 1898).

ANDO, Albert K.

Born 1929, Tokyo, Japan.
Current Post Prof. Econ. Fin., Univ. Pennsylvania, USA.
Recent Posts Assoc. prof. Econ., MIT.
Degrees BS (Econ.) Seattle Univ., 1951; MA (Econ.) St Louis Univ., 1953; MS (Econ.), PhD (Math. Econ.) Carnegie Inst. Technology (now Carnegie-Mellon Univ.), 1956, 1959.
Offices and Honours Ford Foundation Faculty Res. Fellow, 1966–7; Fellow, Em Soc.; Assoc. ed., *JASA*, 1966–9, *J Em*, 1972–6; Chairman, Subcomm. Monetary Res., US SSRC, 1967–; Guggenheim Memorial Foundation Fellow, 1970–1; Member, Board Eds, AEA, 1973–4; Alexander von Humboldt award Sr Amer. Scientists, 1977–8.
Principal Contributions Theoretical and empirical investigation of consumer behaviour. Theory of aggregation and partitions in dynamic systems. Macroeconomic models, with emphasis on interactions between growth and cyclical fluctuations. Monetary and financial aspects of the US economy.

Publications *Books:* 1. *Essays on Social Science Models* (with H.A. Simon and F.M. Fisher), (MIT Press, 1963); 2. *Studies in Stabilization Policies* (with E.C. Brown, *et al.*), (Brookings Inst. 1968); 3. *International Aspects of Stabilization Policies*, ed. (Fed. Reserve Bank Boston, 1975).

Articles: 1. 'The relative stability of monetary velocity and the investment multiplier' (with F. Modigliani), *AER*, 55, Sept. 1965; 2. 'Some aspects of stabilization policies, the monetarist controversy, and the MPS model', *Int ER*, 15(3), Oct. 1974; 3. 'Some reflections on describing structure of financial sectors', in *The Brookings Model: Perspective and Recent Developments*, eds L.R. Klein and G. Fromm (N-H, 1975); 4. 'Some stabilization problems of 1971–5, with an application of optimal control algorithms', in *Frontiers of Quantitative Economics*, ed. M. Intriligator (N-H, 1977); 5. 'On a theoretical and empirical basis of macroeconometric models', in *Proceedings of the Conference on Methodology of Large-scale Econometric Models*, ed. J. Kmenta (N-H, 1981).

ANGELL, James Waterhouse

Born 1898, Chicago, Ill., USA.
Posts Held Lecturer, prof., Columbia Univ., 1924–66.
Degrees BA, MA, PhD, Harvard Univ., 1918, 1921, 1924.
Offices and Honours Vice-pres., AEA, 1940; US Minister, Allied Commission on Reparations, Germany, 1945–6.
Career Monetary economist who also wrote on international prices and business cycles. The *Theory of International Prices* was a history of ideas relating to exchange rates, which was eclipsed by Jacob Viner's later researches. *The Behavior of Money* summarises much of Angell's empirical work on money, which again suffered neglect as a result of being published in the same year as Keynes's *General Theory*.
Publications *Books:* 1. *The Theory*

of International Prices – History, Criticism and Restatement (Harvard Univ. Press, 1926); 2. *The Recovery of Germany* (Prentice-Hall, 1929); 3. *Financial Policy of the United States* (Prentice-Hall, 1933); 4. *The behavior of Money* (Prentice-Hall, 1936); 5. *Investment and Business Cycles* (Prentice-Hall, 1941).

ANTONELLI, Etienne*

Dates and Birthplace   1879–1971, Valencia, Spain.
Posts Held   Prof. Conservatoire national des arts et métiers, Paris, 1932; Prof. Faculty of Law, Montpellier, 1934–52.
Degree   Dr Law, Univ. Paris.
Offices and Honours   Deputy, Haute-Savoie, 1924–32; Member, Conseil de la Fondation des Sciences Politiques, Paris; Commander, Légion d'Honneur; Croix de guerre (1914–18); Chevalier des Palmes Académiques.
Career   A follower, life-long friend and literary executor of Walras, he gave a course of lectures with a Walrasian structure at the Collège Libre des Sciences Sociales as early as 1912. This later appeared as *Principes* . . . in 1914. His earliest work had been on the state protection of viticulture and later work ranged widely, including specific studies of the social security system.
Publications   *Books:* 1. *Principes d'économie pure* (1914); 2. *Traité d'économie politique* (1927); 3. *L'économie pure du capitalisme* (1939); 4. *Manuel d'économie politique*, 2 vols, (1945–6); 5. *Etudes d'économie humaniste*, 2 vols, (1957–8); 6. *Structures des économies présentes* (1962).

ARCHIBALD, George Christopher

Born   1926, Glasgow, Scotland.
Current Post   Prof. Econ., Univ. British Columbia, Canada.
Recent Posts   Lecturer, LSE, 1950–64; Reader Econ., Univ. Essex 1964–7, Prof. Econ., 1967–71.
Degrees   BSc. (Econ.), MA, Univ. Camb., 1950, 1951.
Offices and Honours   Fellow, Em Soc., 1976, Royal Soc. Canada, 1979.

Principal Contributions   n.e.
Publications   *Books:* 1. *An Introduction to a Mathematical Treatment of Economics* (with R.G. Lipsey), (Weidenfeld & Nicolson, 1967, 1977) Portuguese transl. (Biblioteca de Ciencias Sociais, 1970), published in US as *Introduction to Mathematical Economics: Methods and Applications* (Harper & Row, 1976); 2. *The Theory of the Firm*, ed., (Penguin Books, 1971, 1974).
Articles: 1. 'Monetary and value theory: a critique of Lange and Patinkin' (with R.G. Lipsey), *REStud*, 26, Oct. 1958, reprinted in *Monetary Theory*, ed. R.S. Thorn (Random House, 1963), and *Readings in Monetary Theory*, ed. R.W. Clower (Penguin Books, 1976); 2. 'Chamberlin versus Chicago', *REStud*, 29, Oct. 1961, reprinted in *The Theory of the Firm*, ed. G.C. Archibald (Penguin Books, 1971), and in *Readings in Industrial Organization*, ed. C.K. Rowley (Macmillan, 1976); 3. 'The qualitative content of maximizing models', *JPE*, 73, Feb. 1965, reprinted in *Readings in Industrial Organization*, op. cit., and *The Theory of Demand: Real and Monetary*, ed. M. Morishima (OUP, 1973); 4. 'Excess demand for labour, unemployment and the Phillips curve: a theoretical and empirical study' (with R. Kemmiss and J.W. Perkins), in *Inflation and Labour Markets*, eds. D. Laidler and D. Purdy (Manchester Univ. Press, 1974); 5. 'Non-paternalism and the basic theorems of welfare economics' (with D. Donaldson), *CJE*, 9(3), Aug. 1976.

ARMSTRONG, W.E.

N.e.

ARNDT, Heinz Wolfgang

Born   1915, Breslau, Germany.
Current Post   Vis. Fellow, Development Stud. Centre, ANU, Australia.
Recent Posts   Prof. Econ., School General Stud., ANU, 1951–63; Prof. Econ., Res. School Pacific Stud., ANU, 1963–80.
Degrees   MA, BLitt. Univ. Oxford, 1938.

Offices and Honours Pres., Econ. Soc. Australia and New Zealand, 1957–9; Secretary, Australia SSRC, 1957–9; Member, Governing Council, UN Asian Development Inst., Bangkok, 1969–75; Deputy Dir. Country Studies Div., OECD, Paris, 1972.

Principal Contributions First economic history of inter-war period. First estimate of agricultural surplus population in underdeveloped regions. First proposal for generalised scheme of preferences for LDCs. First flow of funds analysis for India. Studies of macroeconomic policy, the capital market and banking in Australia; continuing study of economic development and policy in Indonesia.

Publications *Books:* 1. *The economic Lessons of the Nineteen-Thirties* (OUP, 1944, 1963); 2. *The Australian Trading Banks* (Longman, 1957, 1977); 3. *A Small Rich Industrial Country* (Longman, 1968, 1970); 4. *Australia and Asia* (ANU Press, 1972); 5. *The Rise and Fall of Economic Growth* (Longman, 1978).

Articles: 1. 'The concept of liquidity in international monetary theory', *REStud*, 15(1), 1947; 2. 'A suggestion for simplifying the theory of international capital movements', *Econ Int*, 7, Aug. 1954; 3. 'External economies in economic growth', *ER*, 31, Nov. 1955; 4. 'Overdrafts and monetary policy', *BNLQR*, 17, Sept. 1964; 5. 'Economic development: a semantic history', *EDCC*, 29(3), April 1981.

ARROW, H.J.

N.e.

ARROW, Kenneth Joseph

Born 1921, New York City, NY, USA.

Current Post Joan Kenney prof. Econ., Prof. Operations Res., Stanford Univ., Stanford, USA.

Recent Posts Prof. Econ., Stats, and Operations Res., Stanford Univ., 1953–68; Prof. Econ., Harvard Univ., 1968–74; James Bryant Conant Univ. Prof., Harvard Univ., 1974–9.

Degrees BSc. (Social Science) City Coll., NY, 1940; MA PhD, Columbia Univ. 1941, 1951; LLD Univ. Chicago, 1967, City Univ., NY 1972, Hebrew Univ., Jerusalem, 1975; Hon. degrees: Harvard Univ., 1968, Univ. Vienna, 1971, Columbia Univ., 1973, Yale Univ., 1974, Univ. René Descartes, 1975, Univ. Helsinki, 1976.

Offices and Honours Member, NAS, Amer. Philosophical Soc.; Fellow, AAAS; Foreign hon. member, Finnish Academy Sciences; Corresponding member, BA; Pres., Em Soc, 1956; John Bates Clark medal, AEA, 1957; Pres., Inst. Management Sciences, 1963; Nobel Prize for Econ. Science, 1972; Pres., AEA, 1973; Pres., WEA, 1980–1.

Principal Contributions Study of collective choice based on individual preferences and logical difficulties in aggregation. Properties of general equilibrium systems in economics: existence, stability and optimality. General equilibrium economics of uncertainty, including concept of contingent markets, measures of risk-aversion and their implications for demand for risky commodities, effect of differential information on economic behaviour, with its implications for medical economics and for social institutions more generally. Estimation of production functions, especially CES functions, and measurement of real value added. Optimal social investment policy; and optimal inventory policy.

Publications *Books:* 1. *Social Choice and Individual Values* (Wiley, 1951, Yale Univ. Press, 1963); 2. *Studies in the Mathematical Theory of Inventory and Production* (with S. Karlin and H. Scarf), (Stanford Univ. Press, 1958); 3. *Public Investment, the Rate of Return, and Optimal Fiscal Policy* (with M. Kurz), (Johns Hopkins Univ. Press, 1970); 4. *Essays in the Theory of Risk-bearing* (N-H, 1971); 5. *The Limits of Organisation* (Norton, 1971).

Articles: 1. 'Optimal inventory policy' (with T.E. Harris and J. Marschak), *Em*, 19, July 1951, 20, Jan. 1952; 2. 'Existence of equilibrium for a competitive economy' (with G. Debreu), *Em*, 22, July 1954; 3. 'Capital-labor substitution and economic efficiency' (with H.B. Chenery, *et al.*), *REStat*, 43, Aug.

1961; 4. 'The economic implications of learning by doing', *REStud*, 29, June 1962; 5. 'Optimal pricing, use, and exploration of uncertain natural resource stocks' (with S.L. Chang), in *Dynamic Optimization and Mathematical Economics*, ed. P.T. Liu, (N-H, 1980).

ARTIS, Michael J.

Born 1938, Croydon, England.
Current Post Prof. Econ., Univ. Manchester, England.
Recent Posts Sr res. officer, review ed., NIESR, 1967–72; Prof. Applied Econ., Swansea Univ. Coll., Wales, 1972–5.
Degree BA Univ. Oxford, 1959.
Offices Member, 1964–, Council member, 1977–81, RES; Ed., AUTE, 1975–7; Member, Bank of England Academic Panel, 1978–, HM Treasury Academic Panel, 1980–.
Principal Contributions The measurement of fiscal policy, the measurement of the demand for money and the design of monetary policy. Has also contributed to the theory (and its empirical application) of wage determination.
Publications *Books:* 1. *Foundations of British Monetary Policy*, contributor and joint ed. (Blackwell, 1964); 2. *British Economic Policy 1960–1974*, ed. F.T. Blackaby, contributor (CUP, 1978); 3. *Inflation, Development and Integration*, ed. J. Bowers, contributor (with M.H. Miller), (Leeds Univ. Press, 1979); 4. *Demand Management, Supply Constraints and Inflation*, joint ed. (Manchester Univ. Press, 1981); 5. *Macroeconomics* (OUP, 1981).
Articles: 1. 'Liquidity and the attack on the quantity theory', *OBES*, 23, Nov. 1961; 2. 'Two aspects of the monetary debate' (with A.R. Nobay), *Nat. Inst. Econ. Review*, 49, Aug. 1969; 3. 'The demand for money in the United Kingdom 1963–1973' (with M.K. Lewis), *MS*, 44, June 1976; 4. 'Monetary targets and the exchange rate: a case for conditional targets' (with D.A. Currie), *OEP*, 33, July 1981.

ASHENFELTER, Orley

Born 1942, San Francisco, Cal., USA.
Current Post Prof. Econ., Dir., Industrial Relations Section, Princeton Univ., USA.
Recent Posts Dir., Office Evaluation, US Dept. Labor, 1972–3; Vis. prof., Univ. Bristol, 1981.
Degrees BA (Econ.) Claremont Men's Coll., 1964; PhD (Econ.) Princeton Univ., 1968.
Offices and Honours Assoc. ed., *JUE*, 1975–; Guggenheim Memorial Foundation Fellow, 1976; Fellow, Em Soc, 1978.
Principal Contributions Work on the determinants of labour supply and unemployment, trying to separate the determinants of work-effort from the complex of constraints on work-effort that are an important part of the modern workplace. Work on trade unions has focused on the relationship between racial discrimination and trade union behaviour.
Publications *Books:* 1. *Discrimination in Labor Markets* (Princeton Univ. Press, 1974); 2. *Evaluating the Labor Market Effects of Social Programs* (Industrial Relations Section, Princeton Univ., 1976).
Articles: 1. 'Racial discrimination and trade unionism', *JPE*, 80(3), May/June 1972; 2. 'The estimation of income and substitution effects in a model of family labor supply' (with J.J. Heckman), *Em*, 42(1), Jan. 1974; 3. 'Estimating the effect of training programs on earnings', *REStat*, 60(1), Feb. 1978; 4. 'Unemployment and disequilibrium in a model of aggregate labor supply', *Em*, 48(3), April 1980.

ASHLEY, William James*

Dates and Birthplace 1860–1927, London, England.
Posts Held Chair, Dept Polit. Econ., Constitutional Hist., Univ. Toronto, 1888–92; Prof. Econ. Hist., Harvard Univ., 1892–1901; Prof. Commerce, Univ. Birmingham, 1901–25.
Degree BA Univ. Oxford, 1881.
Offices and Honours Vice-pres.,

RES; Pres., Econ. Section, BA, 1907, 1924; knighted, 1917.

Career Economic historian with direct ties to the German Historical School. At Oxford 1878–88 as a student and private tutor, he fell under the influence of Arnold Toynbee. He held that the principles of orthodox economics were not universally true and that modifications or fresh theories were needed for different societies and different times. Thus in the context of his own times, he favoured state action to assist trade unions and factory legislation, whilst supporting Joseph Chamberlain's imperial preference policies for trade. In *Economic Organisation . . .*, he wrote in favour of a corporativist system in which industry and labour both took on a corporative character and were regulated by the state in the interests of the whole community.

Publications *Books:* 1. *The Tariff Problem* (1903); 2. *The Bread of our Forefathers: an Inquiry into Economic History* (1928); 3. *An Introduction to English Economic History and Theory*, 2 vols (1931–6); 4. *The Economic Organisation of England: an Outline History* (3rd edn, 1949).

Secondary Literature A. Ashley, *William James Ashley: a Life* (King, 1932); B. Semmel, 'Ashley, William James', *IESS*, vol 1.

ASIMAKOPULOS, A.

N.e.

ATKINSON, Anthony Barnes

Born 1944, Caerleon, Monmouth, Wales.

Current Post Prof. Econ., LSE.

Recent Posts Prof. Econ., Univ. Essex, 1971–6; Prof. Polit. Econ., Univ. Coll. Univ. London, 1976–9.

Degrees BA, MA Univ. Camb., 1966, 1969.

Offices Ed., *J Pub E*, 1971–; Fellow, Em Soc, 1974–; Member, UK Royal Commission on the Distribution of Income and Wealth, 1978–9.

Principal Contributions Measurement and explanation of income inequality, with particular reference to the distribution and intergenerational transmission of wealth. Modern public economics and design of optimal taxation systems.

Publications *Books:* 1. *Poverty in Britain and the Reform of Social Security* (CUP, 1969); 2. *Unequal Shares* (Allen Lane, Penguin, 1972); 3. *The Economics of Inequality* (OUP, 1975); 4. *The Distribution of Personal Wealth in Britain* (with A.J. Harrison), (CUP, 1978); 5. *Lectures on Public Economics* (with J.E. Stiglitz), (McGraw-Hill, 1980).

Articles: 1. 'On the measurement of inequality', *JET*, 2, Sept. 1970; 2. 'The structure of indirect taxation and economic efficiency', *J Pub E*, 2, Feb. 1972; 3. 'The design of tax structure: direct versus indirect taxation' (with J.E. Stiglitz), *J Pub E*, 6, 1–2, July-Aug. 1976.

ATTWOOD, Thomas*

Dates and Birthplace 1783–1856, Birmingham, England.

Post Held Banker.

Career He and his brother Matthias (1779–1851), also a banker and able economist, first emerged as spokesmen for the distressed industrial areas of the West Midlands in the post-Napoleonic war period. He favoured a well-managed paper currency as a means of avoiding the deflation he associated with the gold standard then in force. His case was considered wildly unorthodox and his speech-making and pamphleteering activities in the Birmingham Union, though they mobilised local political sentiment, ultimately led to his arguments being ignored. Despite repeated mention in J.S. Mill's *Principles*, the name of Thomas Attwood practically disappeared from economics until modern times when Hawtrey and Viner drew attention to him once again.

Publications *Books:* 1. *The Remedy: or, Thoughts on the Present Distress* (1816); 2. *A letter to Nicholas Vansittart, on the Creation of Money and on its Action upon National Prosperity* (1817); 3. *Observations on Currency, Population, and Pauperism* (1818); 4.

Letter to the Earl of Liverpool (1819);
5. *The Scotch Banker* (1828).

Secondary Literature ed. F.W. Fetter, *Selected Economic Writings of Thomas Attwood* (LSE, 1964).

AUPETIT, Albert*

Dates and Birthplace   1876–1943, Sancerre, Cher, France.

Posts Held   Teacher, l'Ecole Pratique des Hautes Etudes, Paris, 1910–14; Secretary-general, Banque de France, 1920–6; Prof., l'Ecole des Sciences Polit., Paris, 1921; Businessman, 1926–43.

Offices and honours   Commander, Légion d'Honneur; Member, Inst. de France, 1936.

Career   One of Walras' few immediate followers, his *Essai . . .* is a brilliant and neglected product of his early years. It was both a significant step in the development of the theory of money and an early reformulation of Walrasian equilibrium theory.

Publications   *Books:* 1. *Essai sur la théorie générale de la monnaie* (1901); 2. *Les Grands marchés financiers: France* (1912).

Articles: 1. 'L'oeuvre économique de Cournot', *Revue de métaphysique et de morale*, 13, 1905.

Secondary Literature   G. Pirou, 'Nécrologie: Albert Aupetit', *REP*, 55, (3–4), 1945.

AUSPITZ, Rudolf*

Dates and Birthplace   1837–1906, Austro-Hungary.

Posts Held   Businessman, dealing in sugar, and member of Parliament.

Career   Joint author with Richard Lieben (1842–1919) of one of the outstanding early works in mathematical economics. The chief theoretical concern of their *Untersuchungen . . .* was partial equilibrium, which they discussed intensively in diagrammatic form, utilising total and marginal curves. In common with Jevons, they incorporated the idea of disutility of labour and they utilised the concept of consumer surplus. Their discussion of monopoly and partial monopoly is similar to that of Pareto, who along with Edgeworth and Irving Fisher was deeply influenced by their book.

Publications   *Books:* 1. *Untersuchungen über die Theorie des Preises* (with R. Lieben), (1889).

Secondary Literature   J.A. Schumpeter, 'Rudolf Auspitz', *ESS*, vol. 2; G. Turner, 'Auspitz, Rudolf, and Lieben, Richard', *IESS*, vol. 1.

AVERCH, H.

N.e.

AYRES, Clarence Edwin*

Dates and Birthplace   1891–1972, Lowell, Mass., USA.

Posts Held   Taught philosophy at Univs. Chicago. Amherst and Reed, 1917–30; Prof. Econ., Univ. Texas, 1930–68.

Degrees   BA Brown Univ., 1912, 1914; PhD Univ. Chicago, 1917.

Career   The leading representative of the institutional school in the years after World War II. He developed a theoretical system for institutionalism in which 'technological behaviour' is set alongside 'ceremonial behaviour' as determinants of economic progress. This method enabled him to assess the importance of institutions as agents for economic change. His policy prescriptions included a form of negative income tax. Although his influence inside the economics profession has proved limited, outside it his work has been well received.

Publications   *Books:* 1. *The Problem of Economic Order* (1938); 2. *The Theory of Economic Progress* (1944, 1978); 3. *The Divine Right of Capital* (1946); 4. *The Industrial Economy* (1952); 5. *Toward a Reasonable Society* (1961).

Secondary Literature   W. Breit, 'Ayres, Clarence E.', *IESS*, vol. 18.

B

BABBAGE, Charles*

Dates and Birthplace   1792–1871, Teignmouth, Devon, England.

Post Held Lucasian Chair Maths, Univ. Camb., 1828–39.

Degrees BA, MA, Univ. Camb., 1814, 1817.

Offices and Honours Co-founder Stat. Soc., Astronomical Soc., and BAAS; Fellow, Royal Soc., 1816.

Career Mathematician and, through his work on the 'difference engine' and the 'analytical engine', a pioneer of computer technology. The mechanical problems encountered in his own workshop during the government-financed work on his 'difference engine' led him to a general interest in manufacturing problems. *Economy of machinery* ... was the result of an investigative tour of British and European factories. It is his interest in the use of accurate mathematical and statistical work in various fields, including economics, which justifies his reputation as a forerunner of operations research.

Publications *Books:* 1. *On the Economy of Machinery and Manufactures* (1832); 2. *Passages from the Life of a Philosopher* (1864).

Secondary Literature P. and E. Morrison, 'Babbage, Charles', *IESS*, vol. 1.

BABEAU, André

Born 1934, Boulogne-Seine, France.

Current Post Prof., Univ. Paris X, Paris.

Recent Posts Dir. CREDOC, Paris, 1978–.

Degree Agrégé d'Econ. Univ. Paris, 1964.

Offices and Honours Member Comm., *RIW*; Member, Board Eds., *RE, Consommation*.

Principal Contributions Saving theory and wealth accumulation, particularly the transfers among economic agents related to inflation and relative price movements. Other results concern economies of scale in cash balances. Responsible in France for periodic sample surveys of saving behaviour.

Publications *Books:* 1. *Le profit. Collection que sais-je?* (Presse Univ. de France, 1969, 1979; Spanish transl., 1980); 2. *Analyse quantitative des décisions de l'entreprise: la décision de production* (with M. Desplas), (Bordas,

1973); 3. *Partage des surplus et inflation* (with A. Masson and D. Strauss-Kahn), (Cujas, 1975); 4. *Calcul économique appliqué: problèmes résolus de micro-économie* (Dunod, 1975); 5. *La richesse des Français: épargne, plus-value, héritage*, ed. P. Tabatoni, contributor (Presse Univ. de France, 1977).

Articles: 1. 'L'élasticité de substitution entre facteurs', *RE*, 4, 1964; 2. 'Economies of scales in households' cash balances: a series of empirical tests', *Europ ER*, 2, Aug. 1974; 3. 'La situation des ménages dans l'inflation, 1965–1974', *REP*, 5, 1976; 4. 'The price constant method and the determination of transfers related to inflation: the case of French households', *RIW*, 24(4), Dec. 1978; 5. 'La mobilisation de l'épargne dans les pays en voie de developpement' (with D. Kessler), *Consommation*, 4, 1980.

BACH, George Leland

Born 1915, Victor, Iowa, USA.

Current Post Frank E. Buck prof. Econ. Public Policy, Stanford Univ., Stanford, Cal., USA.

Recent Posts Dean, Grad. School Industrial Admin., 1949–63, Maurice Falk prof. Econ. Social Science, 1963–6, Carnegie-Mellon Univ.; Prof., Stanford Univ., 1966–81.

Degrees BA, Hon. LLD, Grinnell Coll., 1936, 1956; PhD Univ. Chicago, 1940; Hon. LLD Carnegie-Mellon Univ., 1967.

Offices and Honours Fellow, AAAS; Dir., NBER; Trustee, vice-chairman, Joint Council Econ. Education; Study Dir., Hoover Commission, 1949–50; Ford Foundation Faculty Fellow, 1960–1; Chairman, Nat. Task Force Econ. Education, 1960–3; Chairman, Board Dirs, Pittsburgh Branch, Fed. Reserve System, 1960–6; Chairman, AEA Comm. Econ. Education, 1962–76; Dow-Jones award for disting. service to bus. education, 1975; AEA-Joint Council Econ. Education award, 1977; Walter Gores award for excellence in teaching, 1978.

Principal Contributions Early analysis of federal reserve policymaking; early analysis of differential impact of inflation on different income groups, stressing combined interaction of economic, political and social forces; early analysis of differential effects of 'tight money' policy; earliest attempt to measure the effectiveness of different approaches to teaching economics, with new tests of economic understanding.

Publications *Books:* 1. *Federal Reserve Policy-making* (Alfred Knopf, 1950); 2. *Inflation: a Study in Economics, Ethics and Politics* (Brown Univ. Press, 1958); 3. *Making Monetary and Fiscal Policy* (Brookings Inst., 1971); 4. *The New Inflation* (Brown Univ. Press, 1973); 5. *Economics: an Introduction to analysis and Policy* (Prentice-Hall, 1980).

Articles: 1. 'Monetary-fiscal policy reconsidered', *JPE*, 57, Oct. 1949; 2. 'The redistributional effects of inflation' (with A. Ando), *REStat*, 39, Feb. 1957; 3. 'The differential effects of tight money' (with C.J. Huizenga), *AER*, 51(1), March 1961; 4. 'Economic education: aspirations and achievements' (with P. Saunders), *AER*, 55(3), June 1965; 5. 'Inflation and the redistribution of wealth' (with J. Stephenson), *REStat*, 56(1), Feb. 1974.

BAER, Werner

Born 1931, Offenbach, Germany.
Current Post Prof. Econ., Univ. Illinois, Urbana, USA.
Recent Posts Prof. Econ., Vanderbilt Univ., 1968–74.
Degrees BA Queens' Coll., 1953; MA, PhD, Harvard Univ., 1955, 1958.
Offices and Honours Member, AEA, RES, LASA.
Principal Contributions The study of the industrialisation process of Latin American countries and the impact of inflation on growth generally.
Publications *Books:* 1. *The Puerto Rican economy and US Economic Fluctuations* (Univ. Puerto Rico Press, 1962); 2. *Industrialization and Economic Development in Brazil* (Richard D. Irwin, 1965); 3. *The Development of the Brazilian Steel Industry* (Vanderbilt Univ. Press, 1969); 4. *The Brazilian Economy: its Growth and Development* (Grid Publishing, 1979).

Articles: 1. 'Employment and industrialization in developing countries' (with M.E.A. Hervé), *QJE*, 80, Feb. 1966; 2. 'Import substitution in Latin America', *Latin Amer. Res. Review*, Spring 1972; 3. 'The changing role of the state in the Brazilian economy' (with I. Kerstenetzky and A. Villela), *WD*, 2(5), 1973; 4. 'The trouble with index linking: reflections on the recent Brazilian experience' (with P. Beckerman), *WD*, 8(6), Sept. 1980.

BAGEHOT, Walter*

Dates and Birthplace 1826–77, Langport, Somerset, England.
Posts Held Banker; Ed., *The Economist*, 1861–77.
Degrees BA, MA, Univ. London, 1846, 1848.
Offices Called to the bar, 1852.
Career Chiefly known for his analysis of government in *The English Constitution* (1865–7). In his contributions to *The Economist* and in *Lombard Street* (1873), however, he developed a theory of central banking which highlighted the role of the Bank of England in maintaining confidence in the banking system. A posthumous volume of *Economic Studies* (1880) was all that existed of a projected treatise on political economy. His aim was to move away from the more abstract side of economics and to place emphasis on the importance of cultural and sociological factors in economic analysis.
Publications *Books:* 1. *Collected Works of Walter Bagehot*, ed. N. St John-Stevas, 11 vols (1966–78).
Secondary Literature N. St John-Stevas, *Walter Bagehot: a Study of His Life and Thought* (The Economist, 1959); H.S. Gordon, 'Bagehot, Walter. Economic contributions', *IESS*, vol. 1.

BAILEY, Elizabeth E.

Born 1938, New York City, NY, USA.
Current Post Commissioner, US Civil Aeronautics Board, 1977–.
Recent Posts Sr technical aide, Assoc. Member Technical Staff, Bell

Labs., 1960–73; Adjunct ass., adjunct assoc. prof. Econ., NYU, 1973–7; Supervisor, Econ. Analysis Group, Res. Head, Bell Labs., 1973–7.

Degrees BA (Econ.) Radcliffe Coll., 1960; MSc (Maths) Stevens Inst., 1966; PhD (Econ.) Princeton Univ., 1972.

Offices and Honours Member, Exec. Comm., Head, Comm. Status Women Econ., AEA; Board of Trustees, Princeton Univ.; Exec. Council, Federation Organisation Professional Women; Res. Advisory Comm., Amer. Enterprise Inst.; *Magna cum laude*, Radcliffe Coll., 1960.

Principal Contributions The subjects of regulation and de-regulation, pricing theory, the theory of innovation, and the theory of natural monopoly.

Publications *Books:* 1. *Economic Theory of Regulatory Constraint* (D.C. Heath, 1973); 2. *Selected Economic Papers of William J. Baumol*, ed. (NYU Press, 1976).

Articles: 1. 'Innovation and regulation', *J Pub E*, 3(3), Aug. 1974; 2. 'Weak invisible hand theorems on pricing and entry in a multi-product natural monopoly' (with W.J. Baumol and R.D. Willig), *AER*, 67(3), June 1977; 3. 'Economic gradient method' (with R.D. Willig), AER, 69(2), May 1979; 4. 'Contestability and the design of regulatory and anti-trust policy', *AER*, 71(2), May 1981.

BAILEY, Martin J.

Born 1927, Taft, Cal., USA.

Current Post Prof., Univ. Maryland, College Park, USA.

Recent Posts Economist, Inst. Defense Analyses, 1964–7; Assoc. Dean Management, Prof. Management, Prof. Econ., Univ. Rochester, 1968–73; Dep. ass. secretary (Tax Analysis), US Treasury, 1972–3.

Degrees BA (Econ.) UCLA, 1951; MA (Econ.), PhD (Econ.) Johns Hopkins Univ., 1953, 1956.

Offices Member, AEA.

Principal Contributions Put into a clear analytical framework the main features of ongoing, anticipated inflation, showing its effects on real income through changes in real cash balances.

Contributed to a renewed interest in the Ricardian equivalence theorem in public finance, and spelled out other similar implications of rational household responses to fiscal and monetary policy. Clarified and advanced the theory of the response of saving to changes in the rate of interest. Proved that the appropriate valuation of safety, *per* premature death avoided, exceeds the person's discounted future earnings. Proved that Arrow's 'general possibility theorem' of social choice is false.

Publications *Books:* 1. *National Income and the Price Level* (McGraw-Hill, 1962, 1971); 2. *The Taxation of Income from Capital*, ed. (with A.C. Harberger), (Brookings Inst., 1968); 3. *Reducing Risks to Life: Measurement of the Benefits* (Amer. Enterprise Inst., 1980).

Articles: 1. 'The welfare cost of inflationary finance', *JPE*, 64, April 1956; 2. 'Saving and the rate of interest', *JPE*, 65, Aug. 1957; 3. 'The possibility of rational social choice in an economy', *JPE*, 87(1), Feb. 1979; 4. 'The marginal utility of income does not increase: borrowing, lending, and Friedman-Savage gambles' (with M. Olson and P. Wonnacott), *AER*, 70(3), June 1980; 5. 'Positive time preference' (with M. Olson), *JPE*, 89(1), Feb. 1981.

BAILEY, Samuel*

Dates and Birthplace 1791–1870, Sheffield, England.

Posts Held Businessman.

Career Launched the first really effective analytical attack on Ricardo's system with *A Critical Dissertation* . . ., but the book only received a small part of the recognition it deserved. His ideas were too novel, and from his comparative isolation in Sheffied he was not equipped to push home his attack. He is particularly trenchant on Ricardo's labour theory of value, the defects in the concept of real value and Ricardo's theory of profits. Works which take a similar line include *Observations on Certain Verbal Disputes on Political Economy* (anon.) (1821), which has often been incorrectly attributed to Bailey himself.

Publications *Books:* 1. *A Critical*

Dissertation on the Nature, Measures and Causes of Value (1825, 1931); 2. *Letter to a Political Economist* (1826).

Secondary Literature R.M. Rauner, *Samuel Bailey and the Classical Theory of Value* (G. Bell & Sons, 1961).

BAIN, Joe S.

Born 1912, Spokane, Washington, USA.

Current Post Emeritus Prof., Univ. Cal., Berkeley, USA, 1975–.

Recent Posts Res. assoc., Public Admin. Harvard Univ., 1951–2; Ford res. prof., 1963–4, Prof. Econ., 1939–75, Univ. Cal., Berkeley.

Degrees BA UCLA, 1935; MA, PhD, Harvard Univ., 1939, 1940.

Offices and Honours Phi Beta Kappa, 1935; Board Eds., *AER*, 1951–4; Vis. lecturer, Univ. Washington, Seattle, 1966, Boston Coll., Mass., 1967; Vice-pres., AEA, 1968.

Principal Contributions Writing and teaching in the areas of price theory and industrial organisation, in which the latter augments and incorporates price theory, in so far as that explains and predicts market structure, conduct and performance – and their interrelationship. Most novel contribution has involved identifying and quantifying 'barriers to entry' as an important dimension of market structures, finding their sources, spinning a theory of the effects of these barriers on efficiency and pricing in monopolised and oligopoly industries, measuring such barriers, and testing for their predicted effects.

Publications *Books:* 1. *Pricing, Distribution and Employment: Economics of an Enterprise System* (Henry Holt, 1948, 1953); 2. *Barriers to New Competition: Their Character and Consequences in Manufacturing Industries* (Harvard Univ. Press, 1956); 3. *Industrial Organization* (Wiley, 1959, 1968); 4. *Northern California's Water Industry: the Comparative Efficiency of Public Enterprise in Developing a Scarce Natural Resource* (with R.E. Caves and J. Margolis), (Johns Hopkins Univ. Press, 1966); 5. *Essays on Price Theory and Industrial Organization* (Little, Brown & Co., 1972).

Articles: 'Pricing in monopoly and oligopoly', *AER*, 39, March 1949; 2. 'Relation of profit rate to industry concentration: American manufacturing, 1936–40', *QJE*, 65(3), Aug. 1951; 3. 'Conditions of entry and the emergence of monopoly', in *Monopoly and Competition and Their Regulation*, ed. E.H. Chamberlin (Macmillan, 1954); 4. 'Economies of scale, concentration, and the condition of entry in twenty manufacturing industries', *AER*, 44(1), March 1954; 5. 'Chamberlin's impact on micro economic theory', in *Monopolistic Competition Theory: Studies in Impact*, ed. R.E. Kuenne (Wiley, 1966).

Secondary Literature *Essays on Industrial Organization in Honor of Joe S. Bain*, eds R.T. Masson and P.D. Qualls (Ballinger, 1976).

BALASSA, Bela

Born 1928, Budapest, Hungary.

Current Post Prof. Polit. Econ., Johns Hopkins Univ., Baltimore, USA, 1967–, Consultant, World Bank, Washington, DC, 1966–.

Recent Posts Assoc. prof., Yale Univ., 1962–7.

Degrees Diplomkaufmann Hungary Academy Foreign Trade, 1948; Dr iuris Univ. Budapest, 1951; MA (Econ.), PhD (Econ.), Yale Univ., 1958, 1959.

Offices and Honours Assoc. ed., *REStat*; Pres., Assoc. Comparative Econ., 1970–1; Member, Ed. Board, *AER*, 1973–5; Pres., Assoc. Comparative Econ. Stud., 1979–80; Laureate Inst. France, 1980.

Principal Contributions Introduced several new concepts in economics, including the effective rate of protection (simultaneously with H.G. Johnson and W.M. Corden), 'revealed" comparative advantage, and the 'stages' approach to international specialisation. Also introduced new methods of analysis to examine trade creation and diversion, intra-industry versus inter-industry specialisation, as well as external shocks and policy responses to these shocks. Other contributions range from the study of central planning and its reform (with special regard to Hungary) to the dynamics of economic intergration, the purchasing-power parity doctrine, the analysis of factors contributing to economic growth, and alternative development strategies.

Publications *Books:* 1. *The Hungarian Experience in Economic Planning* (Yale Univ. Press, 1959); 2. *The Theory of Economic Integration* (Richard D. Irwin, 1961); 3. *The Structure of Protection in Developing Countries* (Johns Hopkins Univ. Press, 1971); 4. *European Economic Integration* (N-H, 1975); 5. *The newly Industrializing Countries in the World Economy* (Pergamon Press, 1981).

Articles: 1. 'The purchasing-power parity doctrine: a reappraisal', *JPE*, 72, Dec. 1964; 2. 'Tariff protection in industrial countries: an evaluation', *JPE*, 73, Dec. 1965; 3. 'Trade creation and trade diversion in the European Common Market', *EJ*, 77, March 1967; 4. 'The economic reform in Hungary', *Ec*, N.S. 37, Feb. 1970; 5. 'The changing pattern of comparative advantage in manufactured goods', *REStat*, 61(2), May 1979.

BALDWIN, Robert Edward

Born   1924, Niagara Falls, NY, USA.

Current Post F.W. Taussig res. prof. Econ., Univ. Wisconsin, Madison, USA.

Recent Posts   Chief economist, Office US Trade Representative, Exec. Office, US President, 1963–4; Res. prof., Brookings Inst., 1967–8; Consultant, US Dept. Labor, 1969–70, UN Trade and Development Conference, 1975, World Bank, 1978–9.

Degrees   BA Univ. Buffalo, 1945; PhD Harvard Univ., 1950.

Offices   Boards Eds., *J Int E, REStat, PDR.*

Principal Contributions   Has written extensively on trade theory in relation to welfare economics; discovered the so-called 'Baldwin envelope'; analysed the trade and employment effects of various policies, such as tariff cuts; further developed the political-economic model of trade policy; analysed long-run development forces and how they differ among countries; carried out special studies of Zambia and the Philippines.

Publications   *Books:* 1. *Economic*

Development: Theory, History, Policy (with G.M. Meier), (Wiley, 1957); 2. *Economic Development and Growth* (Wiley, 1966, 1980); 3. *Economic Development and Export Growth: a study of Northern Rhodesia, 1920–1960* (Univ. Cal. Press, 1966); 4. *Non-tariff Distortions of International Trade* (Brookings Inst., 1970); 5. *Foreign Trade Regimes and Economic Development: the Philippines* (NBER, 1975).

Articles: 1. 'MFN tariff reductions and developing country trade benefits under GSP' (with T. Murray), *EJ*, 87, March 1977; 2. 'International resource flows and patterns of trade and development', *Indian Econ. Review*, April 1978; 3. 'Determinants of trade and foreign investment: further evidence', *REStat*, 56(1), Feb. 1979; 4. 'Welfare effects on the United States of a significant multilateral tariff reduction' (with J. Mutti and J.D. Richardson), *J Int E*, 10(3), Aug. 1980; 5. 'The political economy of protectionism', in *Import Competition and Response* ed. J. Bhagwati (Univ. Chicago Press, 1981).

BALESTRA, P.

N.e.

BALL, Robert James

Born   1933, Saffron Walden, England.

Current Post   Prof. Econ., 1965–, Principal, 1972–, London Grad. Bus. School, London, UK.

Degrees   MA Univ. Oxford, 1955; PhD Univ. Pennsylvania., 1958.

Offices and Honours   Fellow, Em Soc, RES; Companion, British Inst. Management.

Principal Contributions   Development and practical usage of econometric forecasting and policy models relating to the UK economy. Continuous interest in matters relating to inflation, and general macro-economic policy. Ancillary contributions have been made to the determination of specific economic variables such as wage rates (1959), consumption (1963 and 1964), interest rates

(1965), employment (1966), inventories and investment (1963 and 1964), exports (1966) and prices (1972).

Publications *Books:* 1. *An Econometric Model of the United Kingdom* (with L.R. Klein, *et al.*), (Blackwell, 1961); 2. *Inflation and the Theory of Money* (A & U, 1964); 3. *Inflation*, ed. (with P. Doyle) (Penguin Books, 1969); 4. *The International Linkage of National Economic Models*, ed. (N-H, 1973); 5. *Money and Employment* (Macmillan, 1981).

Articles: 1. 'Some econometrics of the determination of absolute prices and wages' (with L.R. Klein), *EJ*, 69, Sept. 1959; 2. 'The relationship between aggregate consumption and wealth' (with P. Drake), *Int ER*, 5, Jan. 1964; 3. 'Short-term employment functions in British manufacturing industry' (with E.B.A. St Cyr), *REStud*, 33, July 1966; 4. 'The role of exchange-rate changes in balance of payments adjustment: the United Kingdom case' (with T. Burns and J. Laury), *EJ*, 87, March 1977; 5. 'Stabilisation policy in Britain 1964–81' (with T. Burns), in *Demand Management*, ed. M. Posner (Heinemann Educational Books, 1978).

BALOGH, Thomas

Born 1905, Budapest, Hungary.
Current Post Retired; Hon. Res. Fellow, Univ. Coll., London.
Recent Posts Emeritus Fellow, Balliol Coll., Univ. Oxford, 1945–73; UK Minister of Energy, 1974–5; Deputy chairman, British Nat. Oil Corp., 1976–9.
Degrees Dr Rer. Pol. Hon. DEcon. Budapest Univ., 1927, 1977; MA Univ. Oxford, 1945.
Principal Contributions International trade in an oligopolistic world. The futility of neo-classical economics. Reports to governments and international organisations on economic development of India and Mediterranean countries. Critique of monetarism. Recasting UK policy on North Sea oil.
Publications *Books:* 1. *Studies in Financial Organisation* (CUP, 1946); 2. *Unequal Partners* (Blackwell, 1963); 3. *Economics of Poverty* (Weidenfeld &

Nicolson, 1966); 4. *Labour and Inflation* (Fabian Soc., 1970); 5. *Fact and Fancy in International Economic Relations* (Pergamon Press, 1971).

Articles: 1. 'The apotheosis of the dilettante', in *The Establishment*, ed. H. Thomas (Blond, 1959).

BARAN, Paul Alexander*

Dates and Birthplace 1910–64, Ukraine, Russia.
Post Held Prof. Econ., Stanford Univ., 1948–64.
Degrees PhD Univ. Berlin, 1932; MA Harvard Univ., 1941.
Career Generally considered the intellectual founder of the 'dependency' school which holds that economic development in the advanced capitalist countries is functionally related to underdevelopment in the Third World. One of the foremost Marxist theorists in the West of the monopoly stage of capitalist development.
Publications *Books:* 1. *The Political Economy of Growth* (1957); 2. *Monopoly Capital*, (with P.M. Sweezy), (1966).
Articles: 1. *The longer view: essays toward a critique of political economy* (1969).

BARDHAN, Pranab Kumar

Born 1939, Calcutta, India.
Current Post Prof. Econ., Univ. Cal., Berkeley, USA.
Recent Posts Ass. prof. Econ., 1966–9, Vis. prof. Econ., 1971–2, MIT; Prof., Indian Stat. Inst., 1969–73; Prof., Delhi School Econ., 1973–6.
Degrees BA (Econ.), MA (Econ.) Univ. Calcutta, 1958, 1960; PhD (Econ.) Univ. Camb., 1966.
Offices and Honours Member, Board Eds., *AER*; Assoc. ed., *Int ER*; formerly co-ed., *Sankhya* (Indian Journal Stats.), Part C; Elected, nat. lecturer, Univ. Grants Commission, India, 1975; Stevenson prize, Univ. Camb., 1964.
Principal Contributions Integrating growth models in trade theory. Economic analysis of agrarian institutions in poor countries.

Publications   *Books:* 1. *Economic Growth, Development and Foreign Trade: a Study in Pure Theory* (Wiley, 1970); 2. *Poverty and Income Distribution in India*, ed. (with T.N. Srinivasan, (Stat. Publishing Soc., 1974).

Articles: 1. 'International trade theory in a vintage capital model', *Em*, 34, Oct. 1966; 2. 'Equilibrium growth in a model with economic obsolescence of machines', *QJE*, 83(2), May 1969; 3. 'Optimum growth and allocation of foreign exchange', *Em*, 39(6), Nov. 1971; 4. 'Wages and unemployment in a poor agrarian economy', *JPE*, 87(3), June 1979; 5. 'Interlocking factor markets and agrarian developments: a review of issues', *OEP*, 32(1), March 1980.

BARLOW, Robin

Born   1934, Blackburn, England.
Current Post   Prof. Econ., 1961–, Dir., Center Res. Econ. Development, Univ. Michigan, USA.
Degrees   BA Univ. Oxford, 1954; MBA, PhD, Univ. Michigan, 1958, 1961.
Offices and Honours   Member, AEA, RES, Nat. Tax Assoc.; Ford Foundation Foreign Area Training Fellow, 1959–61.
Principal Contributions   Health economics and public finance. Estimated the economic effects of malaria control in Sri Lanka by using a large-scale model to simulate the growth of per capita income with and without control and the cost-effectiveness of selected health programmes in Morocco. Used a median-voter model to estimate whether the property tax in Michigan led to an excessive or inadequate level of school expenditures. Collaborated in a survey of the working and investing behaviour of high-income Americans, and studied problems of comparing the national incomes of different countries.
Publications   *Books:* 1. *Economic Behavior of the Affluent* (with H.E. Brazer and J.M. Morgan), (Brookings Inst., 1966); 2. *The Economic Effects of Malaria Eradication* (Bureau Public Health Econ., Univ. Michigan, Res. Series no. 15, 1969).
Articles: 1. 'Efficiency aspects of local school finance', *JPE*, 78(5), Sept./Oct. 1970; 2. 'Policy analysis with a disaggregated economic-demographic model' (with G.W. Davies), *J Pub E*, 3(1), Feb. 1974; 3. 'Applications of a health planning model in Morocco', *Internat. J Health Services*, 6, 1976; 4. 'A test of alternative methods of making GNP comparisons', *EJ*, 87, Sept. 1977.

BARON, David P.

Born   1940, Kankakee, Ill., USA.
Current Post   Prof. Bus., Econ., and Environment, Grad. School Bus. Admin., Stanford Univ., Stanford, 1981–.
Recent Post   Prof., Grad. School Management, Northwestern Univ., 1968–81.
Degrees   BS Univ. Michigan, 1962; MBA Harvard Univ., 1964; DBA Indiana Univ., 1968.
Offices   Member, AEA; Em Soc; Board Eds., *AER*, 1975–8; Assoc. ed., *Decision Sciences*, 1978–.
Principal Contributions   The understanding of firm and industry behaviour under uncertainty in both the presence and absence of markets in which risks can be traded. Investigated the performance of regulatory systems when procedures or informational asymmetries create incentive problems that limit the achievement of regulatory objectives. Contributed to the theory of the capital structure of firms and to the investment banking function in corporate finance.
Publications   *Articles:* 'Price uncertainty. utility, and industry equilibrium in pure competition', *Int ER*, 2, Oct. 1970; 2. 'A model of regulation under uncertainty and a test of regulatory bias' (with R.A. Taggart Jr), *Bell JE*, 8, Spring 1977; 3. 'Investment policy, optimality, and the mean-variance model', *J Fin*, 34, March 1979; 4. 'Price regulation, quality, and asymmetric information', *AER*, 71(1), March 1981; 5. 'On the design of regulatory price adjustment mechanisms' (with R.R. De Bondt), *JET*, 1981.

BARONE, Enrico*

Dates and Birthplace   1859–1924, Italy.

Posts Held   Army officer, prof., War Coll., Turin; Prof., Istituto di Scienze Economiche, Rome, 1907.

Career   One of the outstanding early mathematical economists, whose chief contribution was made whilst serving as an army officer. Introduced to economics by Pantaleoni, his major achievements were in international trade theory, the theory of the firm, welfare economics and general equilibrium theory. In international trade theory, he used the concept of consumer surplus to demonstrate that protective tariffs tend to reduce economic welfare. His work on the theory of the firm, largely unpublished and now lost, used marginal productivity analysis as the basis of the firm's supply functions for output and demand functions for inputs. He then used this to refine the Walrasian analysis of general equilibrium. His demonstration that a ministry of production in a collectivist economy could plan production rationally is perhaps his best known contribution.

Publications   *Books:* 1. *Le Opera Economiche*, 3 vols (1936–7).

Secondary Literature   R.E. Kuenne, 'Barone, Enrico', *IESS*, vol. 2.

BARRO, Robert J.

Born   1944, New York City, NY, USA.

Current Post   John Munro prof. Econ., Univ. Rochester, USA.

Recent Posts   Ass. prof. Econ., Brown Univ., 1968–72; Assoc. prof. Econ., Univ. Chicago, 1973–5; Prof. Econ., Univ. Rochester, 1975–; Vis. Fellow, Hoover Inst., Stanford Univ., 1977–8; Res. assoc., NBER, 1978–.

Degrees   BS (Physics) Cal. Inst. Technology, 1965; PhD (Econ.) Harvard Univ., 1969.

Offices   Ed., *JPE*, 1973–5; NSF Review Panel Econ., 1976–8; Assoc. ed., *J Mon E*, 1976–80, *Em*, 1978–81; Fellow, Em Soc., 1980–.

Principal Contributions   Development of the 'new classical macro-economics'. Stressed the implications of incomplete information and rational expectations for understanding the business-cycle role of money and for evaluating monetary policy. Empirical work has sought to test the 'natural rate' hypothesis, with stress on the distinction between anticipated and unanticipated movements in monetary aggregates. Recent research involves the application of analogous approaches to the fiscal area, including analyses of public debt, government expenditures and tax rates. Conditions for the neutrality of deficits (the 'Ricardian theorem') have been studied, as has the relation of optimal taxation over time to a positive theory of debt creation. Earlier research concerned developments of the disequilibrium (Keynesian) approach to macro-analysis.

Publications   *Books:* 1. *Money, Employment and Inflation* (with H. Grossman), (CUP, 1976); 2. *The Impact of Social Security on Private Savings* (Amer. Enterprise Inst., 1978); 3. *Money, Expectations, and Business Cycles* (Academic Press, 1981).

Articles: 1. 'A general disequilibrium model of income and employment' (with H. Grossman), *AER*, 61(1), March 1971; 2. 'Are government bonds net wealth?', *JPE*, 82(6), Nov./Dec. 1974; 3. 'Rational expectations and the role of monetary policy', *J Mon E*, 2(1), Jan. 1976; 4. 'Unanticipated money growth and unemployment in the United States', *AER*, 67(3), March 1977; 5. 'On the determination of the public debt', *JPE*, 87(5), Pt 1, Oct. 1979.

BARTEN, Anton B

Born   1930, Amsterdam, The Netherlands.

Current Post   Prof. Econometrics, Catholic Univ. Louvain, Belgium.

Recent Posts   Vis. Prof., Grad. School Bus., Univ. Chicago, 1969–70; Special adviser, Commission European Communities, 1969–79.

Degrees   Dr (Econ.) Netherlands School Econ., 1966.

Offices and Honours   Kluwer award Social Sciences, 1968; Fellow, Em Soc, 1969–; Assoc. ed., *Em*, 1969–72; Res. Dir., Center Operations Res. and Econometrics, 1971–4, Chairman, Dept. Econ., 1979–82, Univ. Louvain; Officer Order of the Crown (Belgium), 1975;

Ordinary member, Internat. Stat. Inst., 1977–.

Principal Contributions Development of the Hicks-Allen approach to consumer theory into the direction of an empirical tool involving further elaboration of the theory, collection of data, model specification and statistical methodology of allocation systems. Also the construction of a multi-country macroeconomic model for the European Economic Community, with special emphasis on the linkage of the sub-models for each member country.

Publications *Articles:* 1. 'Consumer demand functions under conditions of almost additive preferences', *Em*, 32, 1964; 2. 'Family composition, prices and expenditure patterns', in *Econometric Analysis for National Economic Planning* (Butterworth, 1964); 3. 'Maximum likelihood estimation of a complete system of demand equations', *Eur ER*, 1, 1969; 4. 'COMET, a medium-term macro-economic model for the European Economic Community' (with G. d'Alcantara and G. Carrin), *Eur ER*, 7, 1976; 5. 'The systems of consumer demand functions approach: a review', *Em*, 45, 1977.

BARTOLI, Henri

Born 1918, Lyons, France.

Current Post Prof. Sciences Econ., Univ. Paris I, Panthéon-Sorbonne, 1971–.

Recent Posts Prof. Faculté de Droit et des Sciences Econ., Univ. Grenoble, 1945–59; Prof. Faculté de Droit et des Sciences Econ., Univ. Paris, 1959–71.

Degrees Dr Droit Univ. Lyons, 1943; Agrégation de sciences écon. de l'enseignement superieur, 1945.

Offices and Honours Officer, Médaille de la Résistance; Médaille forces françaises libres (au titre du BCRA); Chevalier, Légion d'Honneur; Officer, l'Ordre nat. du mérite; Officier, Palmes académiques; Chevalier, l'Ordre de la santé publique; Pres., section de sciences écon., Faculté de droit et des sciences écon. de Paris, 1966–71; Dir., l'UER d'analyse écon. de l'Univ. de Paris I, 1971–4; Vice-pres., conseil scientifique de l'Univ. Paris I, 1975–9;

Member, Conseil nat. de l'enseignement supérieur et de la recherche, 1972–7; Member, conseils d'admin., de direction, CNRS.

Principal Contributions History of economic thought (physiocrats, Marx, Proudhon, Italian economists). The epistemology of economics (economic time, determinism and non-determinism in economics, multi-dimensionality of variables, the rationality of decisions in political economy). General theory of economic and social systems. Labour economics (employment and unemployment, theory of the functioning of the labour market, manpower reserves and allocation, direct and indirect human costs of work); the politics of reducing the costs of work; and the origins of poverty.

Publications *Books:* 1. *Essai d'etude théorique de l'autofinancement de la nation* (These, 1943); 2. *La doctrine économique et sociale de Karl Marx* (Seuil, 1950); 3. *Science économique et travail* (Dalloz, 1957); 4. *Economie et création collective* (Economica, 1977).

Articles: 1. 'Emploi et industrialisation', *Econ App*, 1, 1968; 2. 'Relations économiques et rapports sociaux dans les pays occidentaux', in *Quelle économie? Quelle société?* (Semaine sociale, 1969, Chronique sociale de France, 1970); 3. 'Asynchronies et dominances', *Mélanges Demaria* (Milan, 1978); 4. 'La structure, la variable, l'évènement', *Mélanges Perroux* (Presses Universitaires, 1978); 5. 'La stratégie des besoins essentiels face aux situations d'extrême pauvreté', *Economies et sociétés*, Jan. 1980.

BARTON, John*

Dates and Birthplace 1789–1852, London, England.

Post Held Private income.

Career His fame arises from one incident. Ricardo's reading of Barton's *Observations* . . . caused him to change his mind on the question of whether the introduction of machines could ever harm the working class. The third (1821) edition of Ricardo's *Principles* includes a new chapter on machinery incorporating Barton's pessimistic analysis of the effects of machinery. Although Barton published several other pamphlets, his analysis never reached the same level of originality and his views were largely ignored. His attempts to influence opinion through his political correspondence with the Duke of Richmond and his membership of the Statistical Society, were similarly ineffective.

Publications *Books:* 1. *Observations on the Circumstances which Influence the Condition of the Labouring Classes of Society (1817, 1962).*

Secondary Literature *J. Barton, Economic Writings*, 2 vols, ed. G. Sotiroff (Regina, 1962); G. Sotiroff, 'Barton, John', *IESS*, vol. 2.

BASEVI, Giorgio

Born 1938, Genoa, Italy.

Current Post Prof. Internat. Econ., Univ. Bologna, Italy.

Recent Posts Prof. Internat. Econ., Catholic Univ. Louvain, Belgium, 1966–77.

Degrees Dottore Econ. e Commercio, Univ. Genoa, 1961; MA (Econ.), PhD (Econ.) Univ. Chicago., 1962, 1965.

Offices and Honours RES; AEA; Soc. Italiana degli Economisti; Vis. prof. Econ., Johns Hopkins Univ. Bologna Center, 1968–81; Econ. consultant, Commission of the Europ. Communities, 1975, 1976, 1980–1.

Principal Contributions Initial development of the theory of effective protection in the mid-1960s. One. of the early participants in Project Link directed by Lawrence Klein in relation to the Italian econometric model. Theory and policy design of monetary unions, being one of the signatories of the so-called 'All Saints Day Manifesto' and a co-author of the two OPTICA reports to the Commission of the EEC.

Publications *Books:* 1. *Teoria Pura del Commercio Internazionale* (Angeli, 1967); 2. *The International Linkage of National Economic Models*, ed. R.J. Ball, contributor (N-H, 1973); 3. *Higher oil prices and the World Economy*, eds E.R. Fried and C.L. Schultze, contributor (Brookings Inst., 1975); 4.

La Bilancia dei Pagamenti Italiani (Mulino, 1978); 5. *West Germany: A European and Global Power*, ed. (with W.L. Kohl), (Heath-Lexington, 1980).

Articles: 1. 'Vault cash and the shift in the desired level of free reserves', *JPE*, 71, Aug. 1963; 2. 'The United States tariff structure: estimates of effective protection of United States industries and industrial labor', *REStat*, 48, May 1966; 3. 'The restrictive effect of the US tariff and its welfare value', *AER*, 58(4), Sept. 1968; 4. 'Domestic demand and ability to export', *JPE*, 78(2), March/April 1970; 5. 'Vicious and virtuous circles. A theoretical analysis and a policy proposal for managing exchange rates', *Europ ER*, 10, 1977.

BASMANN, Robert Leon

Born 1926, Davenport, Iowa, USA.

Current Post Prof. Econ., Texas A & M Univ., College Station, USA.

Recent Posts Assoc. prof. Econ., Univ. Chicago, 1961–3; Vis. prof. Econ., Univ. Minnesota, 1963; Prof. Econ., Purdue Univ., 1963–9; J. Fish Smith prof. Econ., Brigham Young Univ., 1974; Adjunct prof. Econ., Univ. New Mexico, 1976.

Degrees BS, MS, PhD, Iowa State Univ., 1950, 1953, 1955; Post-doctoral Univ. Oslo, 1955–6.

Offices and Honours Consultant, US Fed. Govt agencies; Fellow, Em Soc, 1966–; *WEJ* best articles award, 1973.

Principal Contributions Pioneered development of econometric estimation and hypothesis testing for simultaneous economic equation systems. Pioneered development of exact distribution theory of econometric statistical estimators and test statistics for dynamic as well as non-dynamic models. Developed and tested intertemporal models of the empirical joint distribution of major components of income and major components of consumer expenditures for various sub-populations of US consumers.

Publications *Articles:* 1. 'A theory of demand with variable consumer preferences', *Em*, 24, Jan. 1956; 2. 'A generalized classical method of linear estimation of coefficients in a structural equation', *Em*, 25, Jan. 1957; 3. 'A note on the exact finite sample frequency functions of generalized classical linear estimators in a leading three-equation case', *JASA*, 58, March 1963; 4. 'The role of the economic historian in predictive testing of proffered "economic laws" ', *Explorations in Entrepreneurial Hist.*, 2(3), 1965; 5. 'Exact finite sample distributions for some econometric estimators and test statistics', in *Frontiers of Quantitative Economics*, vol. 2, eds M.D. Intriligator and D.A. Kendrick (N-H, 1974).

BASTABLE, Charles Francis*

Dates and Birthplace　1855–1945, Charleville, Cork, Ireland.
Posts Held　Chair Polit. Econ. Jurisprudence, Trinity Coll., Dublin, 1882–1932, Queens Coll., Galway, 1883–1903.
Degrees　MA, LLD, Trinity Coll.
Offices　Pres., Section F. BAAS, 1894; Fellow, BA.
Career　Best known for his work on international trade, restating in a more complete form the classical 'Ricardian' theory of trade. He was largely a follower of J.S. Mill, though not uncritically so, as when in a famous 1889 *QJE* article he exposed flaws in Mill's views on international payments. His *Public Finance* is generally descriptive, but does include some theoretical discussion of taxation.
Publications　*Books:* 1. *The Theory of International Trade* (1887); 2. *Public Finance* (1892).
Secondary Literature　J. Viner, *Studies in the Theory of International Trade* (Harper & Bros., 1937).

BASTIAT, Frederic*

Dates and Birthplace　1801–50, Bayonne, France.
Offices　Leading founder of *Associations pour la liberté des échanges*; Secretary, Paris Assoc.; Member, Constituent Assembly, 1848, subsequently Legislative Assembly.
Career　Inspired by the successes of the British Anti-Corn Law League, he became a lifetime campaigner for free trade. His brilliant first article in this vein in the *Journal des Economistes* (1844) was succeeded by his popular series of *Sophismes économiques*. These included the famous 'Petition of the candlemakers', a satirical attack on protectionism using the analogy of candlemakers who petition for the suppression of unfair competition from sunlight. He also directed controversial writings at Proudhon and the socialist writers. His *Harmonies économiques* of which a first volume appeared before his death, was an attempt at a systematic exposition of his economic ideas. His analysis is considerably inferior to his satirical powers, and his theory of value, rejecting the Ricardian emphasis on costs and sacrifices for a system based on the exchange of services, is perhaps the most interesting contribution.
Publications　*Books:* 1. *Oeuvres complètes*, 7 vols (1854–5).
Secondary Literature　L. Baudin, *Frédéric Bastiat* (Dalloz, 1862); H. Durand, 'Bastiat, Frédéric', *IESS*, vol. 2.

BATOR, Francis M.

Born　1925, Budapest, Hungary.
Current Post　Prof. Polit. Econ., Harvard Univ., Cambridge, USA.
Recent Posts　Sr econ. adviser, Agency Internat. Development, US Dept State, 1963–4; Sr staff, Nat. Security Council, White House, 1964–5; Dep. special ass., US President for Nat. Security Affairs, White House, 1965–7.
Degrees　BS, PhD, MIT, 1949, 1956; Hon. MA Harvard Univ., 1967.
Offices and Honours　AEA; RES; Inst. Strategic Stud.; Council Foreign Relations; Fellow, AAAS; Guggenheim Memorial Foundation Fellow, 1959; Consultant, Rand Corp., 1960–3, 1970–; US Member, UN Consultative Group on Econ. Projections, 1962; Special consultant, US Secretary Treasury, 1967–9; Member, US President's Advisory Comm. Internat. Monetary Arrangements, 1967–9; Consultant, US Under-secretary of State for Polit. Affairs, 1967–9; Disting. service award, US Treasury Dept, 1968; US Member,

UN Expert Group on Internat. Monetary Arrangements, 1969; Member, Foreign Affairs Task Force; Chairman, North Atlantic Study Group, Democratic Advisory Council Elected Officials, 1970–6.

Principal Contributions Early work dealt with welfare economics, externality theory, market failure, and the role of government; also with fiscal and monetary policy. While in government, worked on trade, aid, balance of payments, and international monetary reform (the SDRs), as well as on non-economic, defence and foreign policy issues. Recently: macro-economics and the US macro-economy, with special attention to energy and inflation.

Publications *Books:* 1. *The Question of Government Spending: Public Needs and Private Wants* (Harper & Bros., 1960, Collier Books, 1962; Spanish transl., 1964); 2. *Energy, the Next Twenty Years*, co-author (Ballinger, 1979).

Articles: 1. 'On capital productivity, input allocation and growth', *QJE*, 71, Feb. 1957; 2. 'The simple analytics of welfare maximization', *AER*, 47, March 1957, reprinted in D.R. Kamerschen, *Readings in Microeconomics* (Wiley, 1969), in W. Breit and H.M. Hochman, *Readings in Microeconomics* (Holt, 1971), in *Price Theory*, ed. H. Townsend (Penguin Books, 1971), and in Bobbs-Merril reprint series in Econ. (1974); 3. 'The anatomy of market failure', *QJE*, 72, Aug. 1958, reprinted in W. Breit and H.M. Hochman, *op. cit.*, in *The New Public Finance*, eds O.A. Davis and G. Tullock (Allyn & Bacon, 1970), and in Bobbs-Merril reprint series in Econ. (1974); 4. 'Budgetary reform: notes on principles and strategy', *REStat*, 45, May 1963, reprinted in R. Lindauer, *Macroeconomic Readings* (Free Press, 1968), and in H. Smith and R. Teigen, *Readings in Money, national Income and Stabilization Policy* (Richard D. Irwin, 1970); 5. 'The political economics of international of international money', *Foreign Affairs*, Oct. 1968, reprinted in S. Silver and N. Ginsberg, *Economics and society: readings and problems* (Appleton, Century-Crofts, 1982).

BAUER, Otto*

Dates and Birthplace 1881–1938, Vienna, Austro-Hungary.
Degrees Doctorat Law, Univ. Vienna, 1906.
Career Leading Marxist who challenged Kautsky on the question of agrarian policy. His work for the Austrian Social Democratic Party prevented him doing full justice to his analytical abilities. In addition to his work on agrarian policy, his earlier contribution on capital accumulation is also of outstanding quality. In the Marxist literature, however, he is best remembered for his analysis of the question of nationality.
Publications *Books:* 1. *Die Nationalitätenfrage und die Sozialdemokratie* (1907, 1924); 2. *Nationalkampf oder Klassenkampf?* (1911); 3. *Zwischen zwei Weltkriegen* (1936).
Articles: 'Die Akkumulation des Kapitals', *Die Neue Zeit*, 31, Bd 1, 1912–3.
Secondary Literature J. Braunthal (ed.), *Eine Auswahl aus seinem Lebenswerk mit einem Lebensbild Otto Bauers* (1961).

BAUER, Peter Thomas

Born n.e.
Current Post Prof. Econ., (with special reference to econ. development in underdeveloped countries), LSE, England, 1960–.
Recent Posts Smuts Reader, Univ. Camb., 1956–60; Fellow, Gonville and Caius Coll., Univ. Camb., 1946–60, 1968–.
Degree MA Univ. Camb.
Office Fellow, BA, 1975–.
Principal Contributions Critique of received opinion on various issues, including economic progress and occupational distribution, the vicious circle of poverty, the widening gap of income differences within and between countries; analysis of conceptual and practical problems of price and income stabilisation; discussion of the operation of marketing boards and commodity agreements in LDCs; role of cash crops in economic advance of LDCs; and systematic critique of the operation of foreign aid.

Publications *Books:* 1. *The Rubber Industry* (Harvard Univ. Press, 1948); 2. *West African Trade* (CUP, 1954, Routledge & Kegan Paul, 1963); 3. *Markets, Market Control and Marketing Reform* (with B.S. Yamey), (Weidenfeld & Nicolson, 1968); 4. *Dissent on Development* (Weidenfeld & Nicolson, 1972, Harvard Univ. Press, 1972, 1976); 5. *Equality, the Third World and Economic Delusion* (Weidenfeld & Nicolson, Harvard Univ. Press, 1981).

Articles: 1. 'The working of rubber regulations', *EJ*, 56, Sept. 1946; 2. 'Economic progress and occupational distribution' (with B.S. Yamey), *EJ*, 56, Dec. 1951; 3. 'Reduction in the fluctuations of incomes of primary producers' (with F.W. Paish), *EJ*, 62, Dec. 1952; 4. 'Economic history as theory', *Ec*, 38, May 1971; 5. 'East-West/North-South' (with B.S. Yamey), *Commentary*, 70(3), Sept. 1980.

BAUMOL, William

Born 1922, New York City, NY, USA.

Current Post Prof. Econ., Princeton Univ., NJ and NYU, USA, joint appointment 1971–.

Recent Post Prof., Princeton Univ., 1954–.

Degrees BSS Coll. City New York, 1942; PhD Univ. London, 1949; Hon. LLD Rider Coll., 1965; Hon. Dr Stockholm School Econ., 1971; Hon. LLD Knox Coll., 1973.

Offices and Honours Pres., AEA; Past Pres., EEA, Assoc. Environmental Resource Economists, Central New Jersey Chapter, ASA; Fellow, Em Soc; Guggenheim Memorial Foundation Fellow, 1957–8; Ford Foundation Faculty Research Fellow, 1965–6; Hon. Fellow, LSE, 1970; Member, AAAS, 1971.

Principal Contributions The first comprehensive theory of the endogenous determination of industry structure. Developed a model of the unbalanced growth of productivity in different economic sectors, which helps to explain economic problems of cities, education, arts, etc. Provided first analytic model

of behaviour of firms with objectives other than profit maximisation.

Publications *Books:* 1. *Welfare Economics and the Theory of the State* (Harvard Univ. Press, 1965); 2. *Performing Arts: the Economic Dilemma* (with W.G. Bowen), (Twentieth Century Fund, 1966); 3. *Business Behavior, Value and Growth* (Harcourt, Brace & World, 1966); 4. *The Theory of Environmental Policy* (with W.E. Oates), (Prentice-Hall, 1975).

Articles: 1. 'The transactions demand for cash: an inventory theoretic approach', *QJE*, 66, Nov. 1952; 2. 'Macro-economics of unbalanced growth: the anatomy of urban crisis', *AER*, 57(3), June 1967; 3. 'Optimal departures from marginal cost pricing' (with D.F. Bradford), *AER*, 60(3), June 1970; 4. 'Weak invisible hand theorems on the sustainability of multiproduct natural monopoly' (with E.E. Bailey and R.D. Willig), *AER*, 67(3), June 1977; 5. 'Cost-minimizing number of firms and determination of industry structure' (with D. Fischer), *QJE*, 92, Aug. 1978.

BECCARIA, Cesare Bonesana, Marquis of*

Dates and Birthplace 1738–94, Milan, Italy.

Posts Held Prof. Polit. Econ., Milan, 1768–70; Official, Austrian administration of Milan, 1770–94.

Career His early text on criminal law was an enormous international success and influenced the penal policies of many countries. His starting point was the utilitarian principle of the greatest happiness of the greatest number according to which the test of the seriousness of a crime, and hence the nature of the punishment, is always social injury and not private intention. His brief tenure of the Milan chair produced a set of lectures, published, posthumously which touched on all the main current fields of economic analysis, and which contain a surprising number of hints of theoretical developments to come.

Publications *Books:* 1. *An Essay on Crimes and Punishments* (1764); 2. *Elementi di Economia Pubblica* (1804).

Secondary Literature   C. Phillipson, *Three Criminal Law Reformers: Beccaria, Bentham, Romilly* (Dent, 1923); M.P. Mack, 'Beccaria', *IESS*, vol. 2.

BECKER, Gary Stanley

Born   1930, Pottstown, Penn., USA.
Current Post   Prof. Econ., Univ. Chicago, USA 1970–.
Recent Posts   Ass. prof. Econ., Univ. Chicago, 1954–7; Ass., assoc. prof. Econ., 1957–60, Prof. Econ., 1960–8, Arthur Lehman prof. Econ., 1968–9, Columbia Univ.; Ford Foundation Vis. prof. Econ., Univ. Chicago, 1969–70.
Degrees   BA Princeton Univ., 1951; MA, PhD, Univ. Chicago., 1953, 1955.
Offices and Honours   NAS; AAAS; ASA: Em Soc; Mont Pelerin Soc.; Founding member, Vice-pres., Nat. Academy Education, 1965–7; W.S. Woytinsky award, Univ. Michigan, 1965; John Bates Clark medal, 1967, Vice-pres., 1974, AEA; Professional achievement award, Univ. Chicago Alumni Assoc., 1968.
Principal Contributions   The first to provide a neo-classical analysis of discrimination in labour markets. Among the first to develop the implications of human capital theory. After analysing the allocation of time of economic agents, generalised the argument into the so-called 'new economics of the family', providing a standard explanation of such phenomena as marriage, divorce, the decision to have children, the decision to educate children, etc.
Publications   *Books:* 1. *The Economics of Discrimination* (Univ. Chicago Press, 1957, 1971); 2. *Human Capital (Columbia Univ. Press, 1964, 1975)*; 3. *Economic Theory* (Alfred A. Knopf, 1971); 4. *The Economic Approach to Human Behavior* (Univ. Chicago Press, 1976); 5. *A Treatise on the family* (Univ. Chicago Press, 1981).
Secondary Literature   J.R. Shackleton, 'Gary S. Becker: the economist as empire-builder', *Twelve Contemporary Economists*, eds J.R. Shackleton and G. Locksley (Macmillan, 1981).

BECKERMAN, Wilfred

Born   1925, Croydon, England.
Current Post   Fellow, Balliol Coll., Univ. Reader in Econ., Univ. Oxford.
Recent Posts   Fellow, Balliol Coll., Univ. Oxford, 1964–9; Econ. Adviser, UK Board of Trade, 1967–9; Prof. Polit. Econ., Univ. London, 1969–75.
Degrees   MA, PhD, Univ. Camb., 1951, 1951.
Offices   Member, UK Royal Commission Environmental Pollution, 1970–3; Pres., Section F (Econ.), BAAS, 1978.
Principal Contributions   Methods of analysis of factors contributing to economic growth and application to long-term forecasting (early 1960s); measurement of poverty (late 1970s); and economic policy analysis (early 1970s).
Publications   *Books:* 1. *The British Economy in 1975* (with others), (CUP, 1965); 2. *Introduction to National Income Analysis* (Weidenfeld & Nicolson, 1968, 1980); 3. *The Labour Government's Economic Record, 1964–70* (Duckworth, 1972); 4. *In Defence of Economic Growth* (Cape, 1974); 5. *Slow Growth in Britain: Causes and Consequences,* ed. and contributor (OUP, 1979).

BECKMANN, Martin Josef

Born   1924, Ratingen, Germany.
Current Post   Prof. Econ., Brown Univ., Providence, USA; Prof. Econ., Technical Univ., Munich, W. Germany.
Recent Posts   Fellow, Center Advanced Study Behavioral Sciences, 1955–6. Ass. prof., Yale Univ., 1956–9; Prof. Oekonometrie Unternehmensforschung Univ. Bonn, 1962–9.
Degree   Dr rer. pol. Univ. Frieburg, 1950.
Offices   Fellow, Em Soc; Founding member, Pres., RSA; Pres., WRSA; Member, Internat. Inst. Stat., AEA, ORSA.
Principal Contributions   Introduced linear and non-linear programming methods into location and transportation economics, and utility analysis into transportation planning. Used dynamic

programming to study intertemporal allocation problems. Also, economic analysis of rank structures in organisations.

Publications *Books:* 1. *Studies in the Economics of Transportation* (with C.B. McGuire and C.B. Winsten), (Yale Univ. Press, 1956); 2. *Location Theory* (Random House, 1968); 3. *Dynamic Programming of Economic Decisions* (Springer, 1969); 4. *Rank in Organizations* (Springer Lecture Notes in Econ., 1977).

BEESLEY, Michael E.

Born 1924, Birmingham, England.
Current Post Prof. Econ., London Grad. Bus. School, 1965–.
Recent Posts Chief econ. adviser, UK Ministry Transport, 1965–8, Consultant chief econ. adviser, UK Dept Environment, 1968–9; Faculty Dean, 1969–72, Dir., Small Bus. Unit, 1973, Dir., Inst. Public Sector Management, 1977, London Grad. Bus. School.
Degrees BCom., PhD, Univ. Birmingham, 1945, 1955.
Offices Managing ed., *J Transp EP*; Member, Ed. Advisory Board, *Applied Econ*; Member, UK Dept Transport, Standing Advisory Comm. Trunk Road Assessment; Dir., Transmark Ld.
Principal Contributions Development of cost-benefit analysis, as applied particularly to transport projects. The analysis of regulation and the relation between management requirements and the application of economic analysis.
Publications *Books:* 1. *Urban Transport: Studies in Economic Policy* (Butterworth, 1973); 2. *Corporate Social Responsibility – A Re-assessment* (with T.C. Evans), (Croom Helm, 1978); 3. *Liberalisation of the Use of British Telecommunications Network* (HMSO, 1981).
Articles: 1. 'The birth and death of industrial establishments', *J Ind E*, 4(1), Oct. 1955; 2. 'Estimating the social benefit of constructing an underground railway in London' (with C.D. Foster), *JRSS*, 126, Pt 1, 1963, reprinted in AEA *Readings in Welfare Economics*, eds K.J. Arrow and T. Scitovsky (Richard D. Irwin, Λ & U, 1969); 3.

'Urban form, car ownership and public policy', *Urb Stud*, 1(2), Nov. 1964; 4. 'The value of time spent in travelling: some new evidence', *Ec*, N.S. 32, May 1965; 5. 'Competition and supply in London taxis', *J Transp EP*, 13(1), Jan. 1979.

BEHRMAN, Jere Richard

Born 1940, Indianapolis, Ind., USA.
Current Post Prof. Econ., Univ. Pennsylvania, Philadelphia, USA.
Recent Posts Vis. lecturer Internat. Affairs, Princeton Univ., 1973; Hon. Fellow, Dept. Econ., Univ. Wisconsin, 1976–7; Res. assoc., Center Latin Amer. Devel. Stud., Boston Univ., 1978–9; Academic vis., LSE, 1979–80, 1981; Vis. scientist, Internat. Crop Res. Inst. Semi-Arid Tropics, Hyderabad, India, 1980, 1981.
Degrees BA Williams Coll., 1962; PhD (Econ.) MIT, 1966.
Offices and Honours Phi Beta Kappa, 1961; Carnegie Foundation Fellow, 1961; Nat. merit scholarships, 1962; NSF Fellow, 1962–3; Tyng Foundation Fellow, 1962–4; Danforth Foundation Fellow, 1962–6; AAEA award Merit Outstanding Res. Agricultural Econ., 1967; Ford Foundation Faculty Fellow, 1971–2; LASA, 1972–; Soc. Internat. Development, 1975–; PAA, 1976–; Guggenheim Memorial Foundation Fellow, 1979–80; Compton Foundation Fellow, 1980–1; Fellow, Em Soc, 1980.
Principal Contributions Pioneering extensions of modelling and econometric applications to situations in developing countries: agricultural supply response, market surpluses and risk aversion; analysis of macro-economic policies with extended model incorporating supply features and foreign sector constraints; investigation of international commodity markets, proposed commodity programmes, and impact on macro-goal attainment of developing countries; micro analysis of determinants of fertility, migration, health and nutrition, wages, income distribution and role of women. Secondary work on inter- and intra-generational earnings inequality in US. Extension of latent variable-vari-

ance components model to estimate bias in standard measures of returns to education. Incorporation of inequality aversion into intra-household investment decisions.

Publications   *Books:* 1. *Supply Response in Underdeveloped Agriculture: A Case Study of Four Major Annual Crops in Thailand 1937–1963* (N-H, 1968); 2. *Foreign Trade Regimes and Economic Development* (Columbia Univ. Press, 1976); 3. *Macroeconomic Policy in a Developing Country: the Chilean Experience* (N-H, 1977); 4. *Socioeconomic Success: a Study of the Effects of Genetic Endowments, Family Environment and Schooling* (with Z. Hrubec *et al.*), (N-H, 1980); 5. *The Commodity Problem and Goal Attainment in Developing Countries: An Integrated Econometric Examination of Basic Policy Issues* (with F.G. Adams), (Heath-Lexington, 1981).

Articles: 1. 'Sectoral elasticities of substitution between capital and labor in a developing economy: time series analysis in the case of post-war Chile', *Em*, 40(2), March 1972; 2. 'Short-run flexibility in a developing economy', *JPE*, 80(2), March/April 1972; 3. 'Sectoral investment determination in a developing economy', *AER*, 62(5), Dec. 1972; 4. 'Commodity agreements', in *Proposals for a New International Economic Order: An Economic Analysis of Effects on Rich and Poor Countries*, ed. W.R. Cline (Praeger, 1979); 5. 'Parental preferences and provision for progeny' (with R.A. Pollak and P. Taubman), *JPE*, 90(1), Feb. 1982.

BELL, Carolyn Shaw

Born 1920, Framingham, Mass., USA.

Current Post Katharine Coman Prof. Econ., Wellesley Coll., Mass., USA.

Recent Posts Dept. Econ., Wellesley Coll., 1951–.

Degrees BA Mount Holyoke Coll., 1941; PhD (Econ.) Univ. London, 1949.

Offices Board Overseers, Amos Tuck Grad. School Bus. Admin., Dartmouth, 1973–7; Exec. Comm., AEA, 1975–7; Chairwoman, Fed. Advisory Council Unemployment Insurance, 1975–7; Member, NAS, 1977–; Trustee, TIAA, 1977–; Pres., Eta of Mass. Chapter Phi Beta Kappa, 1978–9; Pres. AAUP Chapter.

Principal Contributions Identifying policy areas where basic data are insufficient, e.g. unemployment, income, economic hardship, and focusing attention on persistent need for revising models to fit realities of institutional change. Identifying consumer choice area beyond spending and saving decisions; retail distribution as an example of monopolistic competition; marketing as an information network. As teacher and activist, helping other economists to recognise sex bias within the profession, and work to overcome it. As a 'popularist', contributing to more public understanding of economics and what economists do.

Publications   *Books:* 1. *Consumer Choice in the US economy* (Bobbs-Merrill, 1964); 2. *Economics of the Ghetto* (Bobbs-Merrill, 1970); 3. *Coping in a Troubled Society*, co-author (Heath-Lexington, 1974).

Articles: 1. 'Liberty, property and no stams', *J Bus*, 40, April 1967; 2. 'Economics, sex and gender', *Social Science Quarterly*, 55(3), Dec. 1974; 3. 'Should every job support a family?', *Public Interest*, 1976; 4. 'Women in the labor force', *Encyclopedia Social Work*, 1977; 5. 'Economic data, policy-making, the law', *Boston Coll. Law Review*, forthcoming, 1982.

BEN-PORATH, Yoram

Born 1937, Ramat-Gan, Israel.

Current Post Prof., Hebrew Univ., Jerusalem; Dir., Maurice Falk Inst. Econ. Res. Israel.

Recent Posts Ass. prof., Univ. Chicago, 1966–7; Consultant, Rand Corp., 1972; Vis. lecturer, Harvard Univ., 1971–2; Vis. prof., UCLA, 1976–7.

Degrees BA, MA, Hebrew Univ., Jerusalem, 1961, 1963; PhD Harvard Univ., 1967.

Offices Member, Comm. Tax Reform, Israel, 1975; Fellow, Em Soc, 1976.

Principal Contributions An early paper on the life-cycle of earnings developed the implicit foundations of the theory of human capital. A series of papers in the 1970s was part of a broad effort to develop the micro aspects of economic demography and to link it up in a unified framework with labour economics. Recent work on the F-connection uses the concept of the identity of agents in transactions to understand the institutional structure of exchange. Most empirical work based on Israeli data.

Publications   *Books:* 1. *The Arab Labor Force in Israel* (Falk Inst., 1966).

Articles: 1. 'The production of human capital and the life-cycle of earnings', *JPE*, 75(4), Pt 1, Aug. 1967; 2. 'Economic analysis of fertility in Israel: point and counterpoint', *JPE*, 81(2), Pt 2, March/April 1973; 3. 'Labor-force participation rates and the supply of labor', *JPE*, 81, May/June 1973; 4. 'Fertility response to child mortality: micro data from Israel', *JPE*, 84(4), Pt 2, Aug. 1976; 5. 'The F-connection: families, friends, and firms, and the organization of exchange', *Pop. Development Review*, 6(1), March 1980.

BENTHAM, Jeremy*

Dates and Birthplace   1748–1832, London, England.

Post Held   Private income.

Degrees   BA, MA, Univ. Oxford, 1763, 1766.

Offices   Called to the bar, 1817.

Career   Bentham is remembered both as a pioneer of social science and as a tireless advocate of administrative, legal and parliamentary reform. He found in the principle of utility, and in particular in his notorious 'felicific calculus', an exact standard by which questions of reform could be settled. The reforms he pressed for were directed towards his four ends of good government: subsistence, abundance, security and equality. He interpreted the economics of Adam Smith in the light of the search for abundance and advocated a state which provided guaranteed employment, minimum wages and a variety of social benefits. Much of his influence on ideas and legislation was through a small but enthusiastic circle of pupils and disciples, amongst whom were many econo-

mists, including Ricardo and James and John Stuart Mill. Only a small portion of his vast literary output was published in his own lifetime, and a complete edition of his works projected in 36 volumes is even now in preparation. Even his strictly economic writings, a small part of the whole, contain many remarkable contributions that have only come to be properly appreciated in recent times.

Publications   *Books:* 1. *A Fragment on Government* (1776, 1891, 1951); 2. *An Introduction to the Principles of Morals and Legislation* (1780, 1823, 1948); 3. *Rationale of Judicial Evidence*, 5 vols, ed. J.S. Mill (1827); 4. *The Collected Works of Jeremy Bentham*, gen. ed. J. Burns (1968 – in progress).

Secondary Literature   W. Stark (ed.), *Jeremy Bentham's Economic Writings*, 3 vols (A & U, 1952); M.P. Mack, *Jeremy Bentham* (Heinemann, 1962); M.P. Mack, 'Bentham, Jeremy', *IESS*, vol. 2.

BERG, E.J.

N.e.

BERGMANN, Denis Raymond

Born   1919, Paris, France.

Current Post   Sr economist, Inst. Nat. Recherche Agronomique (INRA) Paris, 1963–.

Recent Posts   Asst to sr lecturer Agric. Econ., Inst. Nat. Agronomique (INA), Paris, 1947–63; Head, Econ. Dept., INRA, 1963–72; Member, 1964–79, Chairman, 1979–, Commission des Comptes de l'Agriculture de la Nation.

Degrees   Ingénieur agronome INA, 1940; MSc. Cornell Univ., 1947; Diplôme des Etudes Supérieures de Science Econ., Univ. Paris, 1953.

Offices   Internat. Assoc. Agric. Economists;   Corresponding   member, Académie d'Agriculture de France; Co-founder, 1948, Secretary, 1948–63, Pres., 1981–, Soc. Française d'Economie Rurale.

Principal Contributions   Explaining American agricultural economic thinking to French readers; advocating economic approaches to the study of agricultural problems (as opposed to agrarian sentiments); recommending expansion of production in French agriculture, increased productivity, and structural reform instead of excessive price supports.

Publications *Books:* 1. *Politique agricole*, 3 vols (INRA, 1972, 1975, 1977).

Articles: 1. 'Background thoughts and elements for a discussion on agricultural structures in Europe 1980–1990', *Europe. Review Agric. Econ.*, 2(4), 1975–6; 2. 'Agricultural policies in the EEC and their external implications', *WD*, 5(5–7), 1977.

BERGSON, Abram

Born 1914, Baltimore, Maryland, USA.

Current Post George F. Baker prof. Econ., Harvard Univ., 1971–.

Recent Posts Prof. Econ., Harvard Univ., 1956–71; Dir., Russian Res. Center, Harvard Univ., 1964–8, 1977–80; Member, Social Science Advisory Board, US Arms Control and Disarmament Agency, 1966–73, Chairman, 1971–3.

Degrees BA Johns Hopkins Univ., 1933; MA, PhD, Harvard Univ., 1935, 1940; LLD (*Hon. causa*) Univ. Windsor, 1979.

Offices and Honours Member, AEA, Amer. Philosophical Soc., NAS; Fellow, AAAS, Em Soc; Benjamin F. Fairless Memorial lecturer, Carnegie-Mellon Univ., 1967; John and Dora Haynes Foundation Short lecturer, Univ. Cal., Santa Barbara, 1970; Moskowitz lecturer, NYU, 1972; Knut Wicksell lecturer, Univ. Stockholm, 1974; Award, Disting. contribution, AAAS, 1975; John R. Commons lecturer, 1979.

Principal Contributions Welfare economics, particularly the underlying ethical premises, and consumer surplus analysis; the theory of socialist economics; and the nature and performance of actual socialist systems.

Publications *Books:* 1 *The Structure of Soviet Wages: A Study in Socialist Economics* (Harvard Univ. Press,

1944); 2. *Real National Income of Soviet Russia* (Harvard Univ. Press, 1961); 3. *The Economics of Soviet Planning* (Yale Univ. Press, 1964); 4. *Essays in Normative Economics* (Harvard Univ. Press, 1966); 5. *Productivity and the Social System – the USSR and the West* (Harvard Univ. Press, 1978).

Articles: 1. 'Real income, expenditure proportionality and Frisch's *New methods of measuring marginal utility*', *REStud*, 4, Oct. 1936; 2. 'A reformulation of certain aspects of welfare economics', *QJE*, 52, Feb. 1938; 3. 'Socialist economics', in *A Survey of Contemporary Economics*, ed. H. Ellis, (Blakiston, 1949); 4. 'Market socialism revisited', *JPE*, 75, Oct. 1967; 5. 'On monopoly welfare losses', *AER*, 63(5), Dec. 1973.

BERKELEY, George*

Dates and Birthplace 1685–1753, Kilkenny, Ireland.

Post Held Bishop Cloyne, Ireland, 1734–52.

Degrees BA, MA, Trinity Coll., Dublin, 1704, 1707.

Career Best known as a philosopher and critic of Hobbes and Locke, his work on economic questions is largely contained in *The Querist* in which the problems of Ireland are discussed as a series of some 900 questions. The originality of his method is its application of moral and theological concepts to the question of economic development. He argued that Irish development needed positive government intervention and the creation of an appropriate moral and social environment through the efforts of the Church. His work in economics, as distinct from his philosophical writings, seems to have had little impact on later thinkers.

Publications *Books:* 1. *An essay Towards Preventing the Ruine of Great Britain* (1721, 1953); 2. *The Querist* (1735–7, 1953); 3. *A Word to the Wise* (1749, 1953); 4. *The works of George Berkeley*, 9 vols, eds A.A. Luce and T.E. Jessop (1948–57).

Secondary Literature I.D.S. Ward, 'Berkeley, George', *IESS*, vol. 2.

BERNHOLZ, Peter

Born 1929, Bad Salzuflen, West-phalia, Germany.

Current Post Prof., Dir., Inst. Sozial-wissenschaften, Univ. Basle, Switzerland.

Recent Posts Dozent, Univ. Frank-furt, 1964–6; Prof., Technische Univ., Berlin, 1966–71; Vis. prof., MIT (1969), Virginia Polytechnic Inst. (1974, 1978), Stanford Univ. (1981); Prof., Inst. Sozialwissenschaften, Univ. Basle, 1971–.

Degrees Diplom-Volkswirt, Dr rer. pol., Univ. Marburg, 1953, 1955; (Habilitation) Univ. Frankfurt, 1962.

Offices Rockefeller Fellow, Harvard Univ., Stanford Univ., 1962–3; Member, Verein Sozialpolitik; Member, Public Choice Soc. (Pres., European section, 1974–80, Board member, 1980–); Member, Mont Pelerin Soc.; Member, Scientific Advisory Board, W. German Econ. Minister, 1974–.

Principal Contributions Proof that vote-trading agreements which are profitable to majorities imply cyclical social preferences with separable individual preferences; later demonstrated that the latter is true for particular non-oligarchic social systems, which provides an institutional interpretation of Arrow's Impossibility Theorem. Development of neo-Austrian capital theory by using von Neumann's model but not the average period of production. Derivation of intertemporal money demand (with transaction costs). Explanation of exchange-rate fluctuations in historical perspective.

Publications *Books:* 1. *Mehrergie-bigkeit Laengerer Produktionswege und Neue Kapitaltheorie* (Marburg Dissertation, 1955); 2. *Aussenpolitik und Internationale Wirtschaftsbeziehungen* (Klostermann, 1966); 3. *Grundlagen der Politischen Oekonomie*, 3 vols (Siebeck, 1972–9); 4. *Waehrungskrisen und Waehrungsordnung* (Hoffman & Campe, 1974).

Articles: 1. 'Log-rolling Arrow-paradox and cyclical majorities', *Public Choice*, 15, Summer, 1973; 2. 'A neo-Austrian two-period multi-sector model of capital' (with M. Faber and W.

Reiss), *JET*, 17(1), March 1978; 3. 'Freedom and constitutional economic order', *ZGS*, 135(3), Sept. 1979; 4. 'A general social dilemma: profitable exchange and intransitive group preferences', *ZN*, 40(2), 1980; 5. 'An empirical model of the short-run fluctuations of exchange rates. The case of the Deutschmark and the Swiss franc', *Kredit und Kapital*, Beiheft 6, 1980.

BERNOULLI, Daniel*

Dates and Birthplace 1700–82, Switzerland.

Posts Held Prof. Maths, St Petersburg, 1725–33; Prof. Medicine and Botany, Basle, 1733–50; Prof. Physics, Basle, 1750.

Degree Graduate in medicine.

Offices and Honours 10 prizes, French Academy of Sciences.

Career Member of the second generation of the remarkable Swiss family which produced nine mathematicians of the highest ability in three generations. His chief interests were in theoretical physics, mechanics and probability. The *Specimen* . . . arises from his discussion of the so-called 'Petersburg paradox', mentioned earlier by Nikolaus Bernoulli, in which the expected value of the probability of winning a game of chance is shown to be infinite. Daniel introduced the notion of 'moral' expectation or marginal utility, whose decline, as the winnings of the game increase, resolved the paradox.

Publications 1. *Specimen Theoriae Novae de Mensura Sortis* (1738), reprinted as 'Exposition of a new theory on the measurement of risk', *Em*, 22, 1954.

Secondary Literature O. Ore, 'Bernoulli family', *IESS*, vol. 2.

BERNSTEIN, Blanche

Born 1912, New York City, NY, USA.

Current Post Dir., Social Pol. Res. Inst., New School Social Res., New York City.

Recent Posts Chief, Social Pol. Branch, Office Econ. Social Affairs,

Bureau Internat. Organization Affairs, US State Dept, 1961–8; Dir. Res., Center for NYC Affairs, New School Social Res., 1969–75; Dep. Commissioner, NYC Dept Social Services, 1975–7; Admin., NYC Human Resources Admin., 1978–9.

Degrees BA Hunter Coll., 1933; MA (Econ.), PhD (Econ.) Columbia Univ., 1936, 1940.

Offices and Honour Member, Board Dirs, Grad. Faculty Alumni, Columbia Univ., 1974–; Hunter Coll. Hall of Fame, 1978; Member, Board Trustees, City Univ., 1980–5.

Principal Contributions Analysis of the nature of the welfare problem in New York City and other urban areas in the US, and the analysis of population trends in New York City with its implications for social policy.

Publications *Books:* 1. *Income-tested Social Benefits in New York* (with A.N. Shkuda and E.M. Burns), US Congress, *Subcommittee on Fiscal Policy of the Joint Economic Committee*, Paper no. 8 (US Govt Printing Office, 1973); 2. *Obstacles to Employment of Employable Welfare Recipients* (with M. Rowan and A.N. Shkuda), (NYC Board Social Welfare, 1974); 3. *Foster-Care Needs and Alternatives to Placement: A Projection for 1975–85* (with D.A. Snider and W. Meezan), (NYC Board Social Welfare, 1975); 4. *The Impact of Welfare on Family Stability* (with W. Meezan), (NYC Board Social Welfare, 1975).

BERNSTEIN, Eduard*

Dates and Birthplace 1850–1932, Berlin, Germany.

Post Held Bank employee; political exile in Switzerland and England, 1878–1901.

Career Leading Marxist socialist, personal friend of Friedrich Engels, and an important theoretician of the German Social Democratic Party (SPD) in the closing decade of the nineteenth century. His observation of the discrepancies between socialist doctrine and the economic development of Western Europe led him to break with orthodox Marxism. In *Evolutionary Socialism* . . ., he used statistical data to show how capitalism was differentiating rather than polarising classes, and then moved from this exposure of specific Marxist predictions to an attack on the theory of the economic determinism of the historical process. His 'revisionism' was condemned by the SPD in 1903, but its recent post-war policy has incorporated many of his ideas.

Publications *Books:* 1. *Evolutionary Socialism: A Criticism and Affirmation* (1899, 1909, 1963); 2. *Wie ist Wissenschaftlicher Socialismus Möglich?* (1901).

Secondary Literature P. Gay, *The Dilemma of Democratic Socialism: Eduard Bernstein's Challenge to Marx* (Collier Books, 1952, 1962); C. Gneuss, 'Bernstein, Eduard', *IESS*, vol. 2.

BERRY, Albert

Born 1937, Stratford, Ontario, Canada.

Current Post Prof. Econ., Univ. Toronto, Canada.

Recent Posts Assoc. prof. Econ., Yale Univ., 1967–72; Assoc. prof. Econ., Univ. Western Ontario, 1972–4.

Degrees BA Univ. Western Ontario, 1959; PhD Princeton Univ., 1963.

Offices Member, AEA, CEA, LASA.

Principal Contributions Analysis of the relative efficiency of small farms in developing countries, with special focus on Colombia, but also on a cross-country basis. Analysis of income distribution trends in developing countries.

Publications *Books:* 1. *Income Distribution in Colombia* (with M. Urrutia), (Yale Univ. Press, 1976); 2. *Agrarian Structure and Productivity in Developing Countries* (with W. Cline), (Johns Hopkins Univ. Press, 1978). *Articles:* 1. 'Some welfare aspects of international migration' (with R. Soligo), *JPE*, 77(5), Sept./Oct. 1969; 2. 'Land distribution, income distribution, and productive efficiency of Colombian agriculture', *Food Res. Inst. Stud.*, 12(3), 1973; 3. 'Open unemployment as a social problem in urban Colombia: myth and reality', *EDCC*, 23(2), Jan. 1975; 4. 'A positive interpretation of the expansion of urban services in Latin America, with some Colombian evidence', *Dev. Stud.*, 14(2), Jan. 1978; 5. 'Labour market performance in developing countries: a survey' (with R.H. Sabot), *WD*, 6(11–12), Nov./Dec. 1978.

BERRY, Arthur*

Dates and Birthplace 1862–1929, Croydon, England.
Posts Held Lecturer, Univ. Camb., 1889–1929; Vice-provost, King's Coll., Univ. Camb., 1924–9.
Degree MA Univ. Camb.
Offices Sr Wrangler, Univ. Camb; Vice-pres., London Math. Society, 1908, 1909.
Career Worked chiefly as a mathematician at Cambridge. Made significant but neglected contributions, first to the theory of exchange in *Giornale degli economisti*, June 1891, and then to the theory of distribution (paper to Section F, BAAS, 1890). In both of these his name is closely linked to that of Edgeworth, whose similar contributions were also little noticed.
Publications *Books:* 1. *A short History of Astronomy* (1898).
Secondary Literature G.J. Stigler, *Production and Distribution Theories* (Macmillan, 1941).

BERTRAND, Joseph Louis François*

Dates and Birthplace 1822–1900, Paris, France.
Posts Held Teacher Maths, Collège St Louis, 1841–8, Lycée Henri IV, 1852–6; Prof. Maths, L'Ecole Polytechnique, 1856–95, Collège de France, 1862–1900.
Degrees BA 1838, Dr Science 1839.
Offices Member, Académie des Sciences, 1856; Ed., *Journal des savants*, 1865–1900.
Career An eminent mathematician who in a review of Cournot and Walras launched an attack on current mathematical economics. His remarks were chiefly directed against Cournot whose argument he can be said to have grasped only imperfectly. Though he treated

Walras more kindly, the latter struggled with Bertrand's objections to the concept of 'tâtonnement' for the rest of his career. Bertrand's article was treated as an authoritative refutation of the mathematical approach by opponents of mathematical economics.
Publications *Articles:* 1. 'Review of Walras, *Théorie mathématique de la richesse sociale*, and Cournot, *Recherches sur les principes mathématiques de la théorie de richesses, Journal des Savants*, Sept. 1883.'
Secondary Literature G.H. Bryan, 'Joseph Bertrand', *Nature*, 61, 1899–1900.

BEVERIDGE, William Henry*

Dates and Birthplace 1879–1963, Bengal, India.
Posts Held Fellow, Univ. Coll., Univ. Oxford, 1902–9; Civil servant, 1908–19; Director, LSE, 1919–37; Master, Univ. Coll., Univ. Oxford, 1937–44.
Degrees Classics (first), Bachelor of Civil Law, Univ. Oxford, 1902, 1904.
Offices and Honours Knighted, 1919; created peer, 1945.
Career His early economic work on unemployment, his work as a civil servant, his directorship of the London School of Economics (1932–7), and his scholarly work on the history of wages and prices, all are dwarfed by the wartime investigations on social insurance which resulted in the Beveridge Report of 1942. This document was the blueprint for the Labour government's social legislation after 1945. Beveridge's work was the culmination of efforts begun by Beatrice Webb, with Beveridge's assistance, in the Minority Report of the Royal Commission on the Poor Laws of 1909.
Publications *Books:* 1. *Unemployment: A Problem of Industry* (1909); 2. *Prices and Wages in England from the Twelfth to the Nineteenth Century* (1939); 3. Interdepartmental committee on social insurance and allied services, *Social Insurance and Allied Services* Cmnd 6352 (The Beveridge Report) (1942); 4. *Full Employment in a Free Society* (1944); 5. *Voluntary Action: A*

Report on Methods of Social Advance (1948).

Secondary Literature M. Cole, 'Beveridge, William Henry', *IESS*, vol. 2.

BHAGWATI, Jagdish N.

Born 1934, Bombay, India.
Current Post Arthur Lehman prof. Econ., Columbia Univ., New York City, USA.
Recent Posts Prof. Econ., MIT, 1968–78; Ford Internat. Prof. Econ., MIT, 1978–80.
Degrees BCom. Univ. Bombay, 1954; BA, MA, Univ. Camb., 1956, 1962; PhD MIT, 1967.
Offices and Honours Frank Graham Memorial lecture, Princeton Univ., 1967; Lal Bahadur Shastri lectures, 1973; V.K. Ramaswami Memorial lecture, 1979; Member, Ed. Boards, *WD, JDE, AER*, 1968–71; Founding ed., *J Int E*, 1971–; Fellow, Em Soc, 1973; Mahalanobis Memorial medal, Indian Em Soc, 1974.
Principal Contributions Theoretical writings in international trade, education, migration and public finance. In international economics, principal theoretical contributions include the theory of immiserising growth, and the theory of policy intervention in the presence of distortions. Developed the theory of education based on the job-ladder model and fairness-in-hiring rule. Raised and analysed the theoretical public-finance problem of appropriate tax jurisdiction in the presence of international mobility of people. Developed the general theory of directly-unproductive, profit-seeking activities to analyse the welfare effects of lobbying, tax-evading and other such activities. Important policy work relates to efficient trade regimes for development.
Publications *Books:* 1. *Trade, Tariffs and Growth* (Weidenfeld & Nicolson, MIT Press, 1969); 2. *Planning for Industrialisation: India* (with P. Desai), (MIT, 1970, 1979); 3. *Illegal Transactions and International Trade: Theory and Measurement* (N-H, 1974, 1975); 4. *The Brain Drain and Taxation: Theory and Empirical Analysis* (N-H, 1976); 5. *Foreign Trade Regimes and Economic Development: The Anatomy of Exchange Control and its Consequences* (Ballinger Co., 1978).

Articles: 1. 'Domestic distortions, tariffs and the theory of optimum subsidy' (with V.K. Ramaswami), *JPE*, 71, Feb. 1963; 2. 'Distortions and immiserizing growth: a generalization', *REStud*, 35, Oct. 1968; 3. 'The generalized theory of distortions and welfare', in *Trade, Balance of Payments and Growth: Essays in Honor of C.P. Kindleberger*, eds J. Bhagwati *et al.* (N-H, 1971); 4. 'Education in a "job ladder" model and the fairness-in-hiring rule' (with T.N. Srinivasan), *J Pub E*, 7(1), Feb. 1977; 5. 'Shadow prices for project selection in the presence of distortions: effective rates of protection and domestic resource costs' (with T.N. Srinivasan), *JPE*, 86(1), Feb. 1978.

BICKERDIKE, Charles Frederick*

Dates and Birthplace 1876–1961, England.
Posts Held Lecturer, Univ. Manchester, 1911–12; Civil servant, UK Board of Trade, UK Ministry of Labour, 1912–41.
Degrees BA, MA, Univ. Oxford, 1899, 1910.
Honours OBE, 1937.
Career His chief work was done during the free trade controversies at the turn of the century. He was a protégé of Edgeworth, who said of him that he was the only person since Mill who had found something original and worthwhile to say on the protectionist side of the case. He also worked with Edgeworth on mathematical treatments of economic questions. His last article foreshadows Harrod-Domar-type problems.
Publications *Articles:* 1. 'The theory of incipient taxes', *EJ*, 16, Dec. 1906; 2. 'Relation of the general supply curve to a "particular expenses" curve', *EJ*, 17, Dec. 1907; 3. 'Monopoly and differential prices', *EJ*, 21, March 1911; 4. 'A non-monetary cause of fluctuations in employment', *EJ*, 24, Sept. 1914; 5. 'The instability of foreign exchange', *EJ*, 30, March 1920; 6. 'Saving and the monetary system', *EJ*, 35, Sept. 1925.
Secondary Literature G. Reid, 'Obit-

uary: C.F. Bickerdike', *Times*, 16 February 1961.

BIENAYME, Alain

Born   1934, Toulon, France.
Current Post   Prof. Econ., Univ. Paris IX Dauphine, Paris, 1969–.
Recent Posts   Member, 1974–, Prés., Section des problèmes écon. généraux et de la conjoncture, 1980–, Conseil Econ. et Social; Prés., Conseil d'Admin. l'Office Nat. d'Information sur les Enseignements et les Professions, 1979–.
Degrees   CPE British Inst., 1957; Doctorat d'écon., 1957; Agrégation d'écon., 1964.
Offices and Honours   Chevalier de l'Ordre National du Mérite; Commandeur de l'Ordre d'Alphonse X el Sabio, Spain; Econ. adviser Prés. Edgar Fauré, 1966–78; Médaille d'argent du CNRS, (Econ.), 1977.
Principal Contributions   Evidence on intersectoral transfers of productivity gains; theory explaining why the supply of money is determined by the private sector's demand of money; analyses focusing on the growth of enterprises and on the competitive constraint; and miscellaneous articles and reports on industrial economics, higher education and school systems.
Publications   *Books:* 1. *Croissance et monnaie en plein emploi* (Cujas, 1964); 2. *Politique de l'innovation et répartition des revenus* (Cujas, 1966); 3. *Croissance des entreprises*, 2 vols, (Bordas, 1971–3); 4. *Higher education systems: France* (with K. Bourricaud and S. Quiers), (ICED, 1978); 5. *Stratégies de l'entreprise compétitive* (Masson, 1980).
Articles: 1. 'Le rôle du Plan dans la restructuration de l'appareil de production', *REP*, Aug. 1974; 2. 'L'application de la théorie des organisations aux universités', *RE*, March 1976; 3. 'L'offre compétitive', *Econ. et Stat. INSEE*, Dec. 1976; 4. 'Le principe des transfers croissants', *REP*, 3, 1977; 5. 'Resource allocation and planning in formal education', in *The Future of Formal Education*, ed. T. Husen (Almqvist & Wicksell Internat., 1980).

BISH, Robert Lee

Born   1942, Seattle, Washington, USA.
Current Post   Prof. Econ. Public Admin., Univ. Victoria, British Columbia, Canada, 1981–.
Recent Posts   Ass. prof. Econ. Public Affairs, Univ. Washington, 1968–72; Assoc. prof. Econ. Urban Stud., Univ. Southern Cal., 1972–5; Assoc. prof. Urban Stud., Univ. Maryland, 1976–81.
Degrees   BA Univ. Southern Cal., 1964; MA, PhD, Indiana Univ., 1966, 1968.
Offices   Member, AEA, Amer. Polit. Science Assoc., Amer. Soc. Public Admin., Public Choice Soc., NTA; Ed. Boards, *Urban Affairs Quarterly, State and Local Govt Review*.
Principal Contributions   Development and application of micro-economic theory for analysis of institutional arrangements, with a focus on the structure of governments in urban areas, coastal resource governance and the operation of federal systems.
Publications   *Books:* 1. *The Public Economy of Metropolitan Areas* (Rand-McNally, 1971); 2. *Understanding Urban Government: Metropolitan Reform Reconsidered* (With V. Ostrom), (Amer. Enterprise Inst., 1973); 3. *Urban Economics and Policy Analysis* (with H.O. Nourse), (McGraw-Hill, 1975); 4. *Coastal Resource Use: Decisions on Puget Sound* (with R. Warren *et al.*), (Univ. Washington Press, 1975); 5. *Governing Puget Sound* (Univ. Washington, 1981).
Articles: 1. 'Scale and monopoly problems in urban government services' (with R. Warren), *Urban Affairs Quarterly*, 8, 1972; 2. 'The assumption of knowledge in policy analysis', *Policy Stud. J*, 3, 1975; 3. 'Fiscal equalization through court decisions: policy making without evidence', *Sage Urban Affairs Annual Reviews*, 10, 1976; 4. 'Intergovernmental relations in the United States: concepts and implications from a public choice perspective', in *Inter-organizational Policy Making: Limits to Coordination and Central Control*, eds K. Hanf and F.W. Scharpf (Sage, 1979).

BISHOP, Robert Lyle

Born 1916, St Louis, Missouri, USA.
Current Post Prof. Econ., MIT, Cambridge, USA.
Recent Posts N.e.
Degrees BA, MA, PhD, Harvard Univ., 1937, 1942, 1949.
Principal Contributions Demand theory and consumer's surplus; monopolistic competition – market classification and welfare aspects; bargaining theory as applied to both bilateral monopoly and oligopoly; miscellaneous problems of micro-equilibrium involving taxes, vertical relationships, factor demand and monopsony.
Publications *Articles:* 1. 'Elasticities, cross-elasticites, and market relationships', *AER*, 42, Dec. 1952; 2. 'Duopoly: collusion or warfare?', *AER*, 50, Dec. 1960; 3. 'Game-theoretic analyses of bargaining', *QJE*, 77, Nov. 1963; 4. 'The effects of specific and ad valorem taxes', *QJE*, 82, May 1968; 5. 'Monopoly', *IESS*, 10 (1968).

BLACK, Fischer

Born 1938, Washington, DC, USA.
Current Post Prof. Fin., MIT, Mass., USA, 1975–.
Recent Posts Prof. Fin., Univ. Chicago, 1971–5.
Degrees BA Harvard Coll., 1959; PhD Harvard Univ., 1964.
Principal Contributions Application of general equilibrium theory to realistic models of the pricing of options; expected returns on stocks; business cycles; monetary policy; and international trade and investment.
Publications *Articles:* 1. 'Banking and interest rates in a world without money: the effects of uncontrolled banking', *J Bank Res*, 1, Autumn 1970; 2. 'The pricing of options and corporate liabilities' (with M. Scholes), *JPE*, 81, May/June 1973; 3. 'The effects of dividend yield and dividend policy on common stock prices and returns' (with M. Scholes), *J Fin Econ*, 1(1), May 1974; 4. 'Global monetarism in a world of national currencies', *Columbia J World Bus.*, 13, Spring 1978; 5. 'The magic in earnings: economic earnings versus accounting earnings', *Fin. Analysis J*, 36, Nov./Dec. 1980.

BLACK, Stanley Warren III

Born 1939, Charlotte, N. Carolina, USA.
Current Post Prof. Econ., Vanderbilt Univ., Nashville, Tennessee, 1977–.
Recent Posts Ass. prof. Econ., Princeton Univ., 1966–71; Assoc. prof. Econ., Vanderbilt Univ., 1972–6; Res. Fellow, Inst. Internat. Econ. Stud., Stockholm, Sweden, 1975–6; Special ass. Undersecretary State Econ. Affairs, US Dept. State, 1977–8; Vis. prof. Econ., Yale Univ., 1980–1.
Degrees BA (Hons Econ.) Univ. N. Carolina, 1961; MA (Econ.), PhD, Yale Univ., 1963, 1965.
Offices Member, AEA, Em Soc; Board Eds., *SEJ*, 1980–3.
Principal Contributions Extension of the theory of spot and forward exchange markets; econometric study of Euro-dollar markets; introduction of rational expectations concept into foreign exchange theory and development of asset market theory of exchange rates, together with an empirical application; development of an intertemporal rational expectations model of capital asset pricing with stochastic equilibrium; comparative study of monetary and fiscal policies and exchange rate policies in open economies, with emphasis on political and institutional as well as economic differences between countries.
Publications *Books:* 1. *International Money Markets and Flexible Exchange Rates*, Stud. Internat. Fin. no. 32 (Princeton Univ. Press, 1973); 2. *Floating Exchange Rates and National Economic Policy* (Yale Univ. Press, 1977).
Articles: 1. 'Theory and policy analysis of short-term movements in the balance of payments', *YEE*, 8(1), 1968; 2. 'An econometric study of Euro-dollar borrowing by New York banks and the rate of interest on Euro-dollars', *J Fin*, 26(1), March 1971; 3. 'Rational response to shocks in a dynamic model of capital asset pricing', *AER*, 66(5), Dec. 1976; 4. 'Exchange policies for less developed countries in a world of float-

ing rates', *Princeton Essays Internat. Fin.*, 119, 1976; 5. 'Strategic aspects of the political assignment problem in open economies', in *The Political Economy of Domestic and International Monetary Relations*, eds R. Lombra and W. Witte (Iowa State Univ. Press, 1981).

BLACKORBY, Charles

Born 1938, N. Dakota, USA.
Current Post Prof., Univ. British Columbia, Vancouver, Canada.
Recent Posts N.e.
Degrees BA Harvard Univ., 1960; PhD Johns Hopkins Univ., 1965.
Publications *Books:* 1. *Duality, Separability, and Functional Structure: Theory and Economic Applications* (with D. Primont and R. Russell), (Elsevier, N-H, 1978).
Articles: 1. 'Degrees of cardinality and aggregate partial ordering', *Em*, 43(5–6), Sept./Nov. 1975; 2. 'On testing separability restrictions with flexible functional forms' (with D. Primont and R. Russell), *J Em*, 5(2), March 1977; 3. 'Utility versus equity: some plausible quasi-orderings' (with D. Donaldson), *J Pub E*, 7(3), July 1977; 4. 'Expenditure functions, local duality, and second order approximations' (with W.E. Diewert), *Em*, 47(3), May 1979; 5. 'Ethical indices for the measurement of poverty' (with D. Donaldson), *Em*, 49(4), May 1980.

BLANC, Jean Joseph Louis*

Dates and Birthplace 1811–82, Madrid, Spain.
Posts Held Journalist, ed., professional writer. Exiled in England, 1848–70.
Offices Member, prov. govt of France, 1848; Member, National Assembly, Chamber of Deputies, 1870–82.
Career His reputation as a leading socialist writer was made by his articles in *La Revue du progrès social* which were collected as *L'organisation*. The 1848 Revolution (which overthrew the French monarchy) enabled him to become president of a *Commission du gouvernement pour les travailleurs* in which he spoke in favour of extreme socialist programmes. He advocated the takeover of bankrupted factories and shops by the state in which profits would be divided according to the needs of the workers; he later proposed equal shares for all members of these producer co-operatives. His writings have been attacked as impractical and imprecise, but his philanthropic character is recognised even by his critics; in fact the major role he assigned to the state in his schemes made them more practical than those of Owen and St-Simon.
Publications *Books:* 1. *L'organisation du travail* (1839).
Secondary Literature L.A. Loubère, *Louis Blanc* (1961).

BLANQUI, Jerome Adolphe*

Dates and Birthplace 1798–1854, France.
Posts Held Head, Ecole de Commerce, Paris, 1830–54; Prof. Polit. Econ., Conservatoire des Arts et Métiers, Paris, 1833–54.
Offices Member of Chamber of Deputies representing Gironde; Member, Académie des Sciences Morales et Polit., 1838.
Career Brother of Auguste Blanqui the revolutionist, with whom he is sometimes confused. He was an inspiring lecturer and diligent researcher whose studies involved him in extensive travel throughout Europe. His chief concern was with labour economics, but his work on the history of economics enjoyed international success and remained useful for many years. He was Say's successor at the Conservatoire des Arts et Métiers.
Publications *Books:* 1. *Résumé de l'histoire du commerce et de l'industrie* (1826); 2. *Précis élémentaire d'économie politique* (1826); 3. *Histoire de l'économie politique en Europe* (1837).

BLAU, Julian H.

Born 1917, New York City, NY, USA.

• **Current Post** Prof. Maths, Antioch Coll., Yellow Springs, Ohio, 1952–.

Recent Posts Res. mathematician, Mental Health Res. Inst., Univ. Michigan, 1963; Co-dir, SSRC Res. Training Inst., Stanford Univ., 1964.

Degrees BS City Coll. NY, 1938; MS NYU, 1939; PhD Univ. N. Carolina, 1948.

Offices Em Soc; Amer. Math. Soc.; Math. Assoc. Amer.; Vis. lecturer, Math. Assoc. Amer., 1964–5; NSF Faculty Fellow, 1966–7.

Principal Contributions Studies of social choice and social welfare functions. Two proofs of Arrow's Theorem; several strengthenings of Arrow's Theorem. Studies of independence of irrelevant alternatives. Implications of acyclic social choice for neutral monotonic aggregation. Study of Sen's Liberal Paradox. Proportional representation with infinite populations.

Publications *Articles:* 1. 'The existence of social welfare functions', *Em*, 25, April 1957, reprinted in *Selected Readings in Economic Theory from Econometrica*, ed. K.J. Arrow (MIT Press, 1971); 2. 'Transformation of probabilities', *Proc. Amer. Math. Soc.*, 12, 1961; 3. 'Arrow's Theorem with weak independence', *Ec*, N.S. 38, Nov. 1971; 4. 'A direct proof of Arrow's Theorem', *Em*, 40(1), Jan. 1972; 5. 'Semiorders and collective choice', *JET*, 21(1), Aug. 1979.

BLINDER, Alan S.

Born 1945, New York City, NY, USA.

Current Post Prof. Econ., Princeton Univ., NJ, 1979–.

Recent Posts Instructor Fin., Rider Coll., Trenton, NJ, 1968–9; Instructor Econ., Boston State Coll., 1969; Assistant prof. Econ., 1971–6, Assoc. prof. Econ., 1976–9, Princeton Univ.

Degrees BA (Econ., *Summa cum laude*) Princeton Univ., 1967; MSc. (Econ.) LSE, 1968; PhD (Econ.) MIT, 1971.

Offices Member, AEA; Dep. ass. Dir, Fiscal Analysis Div., Congressional Budget Office, 1975; Fellow, Inst. Advanced Stud., Hebrew Univ., Jerusalem, 1976–7; Res. assoc., NBER, 1978–; Member, Brookings Panel Econ. Activity, 1981.

Principal Contributions Labour supply in the light of human capital theory. Monetary and fiscal policy under stagflation. Uncertainty and general equilibrium analysis.

Publications *Books:* 1. *Toward an Economic Theory of Income and Policy* (MIT Press, 1974); 2. *Natural Resources, Uncertainty and General Equilibrium: Essays in Memory of Rafael Lusky*, ed. (with P. Friedman) (Academic Press, 1977); 3. *Economic Policy and the Great Stagflation* (Academic Press, 1979); 4. *Economics: Principles and Policy* (with W.J. Baumol), (Harcourt Brace Jovanovich, 1979).

Articles: 1. 'Does fiscal policy matter?' (with R.M. Solow), *J Pub E*, 2(4), Nov. 1973; 2. 'Human capital and labor supply: a synthesis' (with Y. Weiss), *JPE*, 84(3), June 1976; 3. 'New measures of monetary and fiscal policy, 1958–1973' (with S.M. Goldfeld), *AER*, 66(5), Dec. 1976; 4. 'Market wages, reservation wages, and retirement decisions' (with R. Gordon), *J Pub E*, 10(2), Oct. 1980; 5. 'Temporary income taxes and consumer spending', *JPE*, 89(1), Feb. 1981.

BLISS, C.J.

N.e.

BOBKIN, M.J.

N.e.

BOHM, Peter Jan Gunnar

Born 1935, Stockholm, Sweden.

Current Post Prof. Econ., Univ. Stockholm.

Degrees PhD (Econ.), Docent (Econ.) Univ. Stockholm, 1964, 1971; Docent Stockholm School Econ., 1970.

Offices Ed., *Swed JE*, 1968–72; Judge, Market Court, Sweden, 1971–.

Principal Contributions Contributions to externality theory and to the analysis of environmental policy. Public goods; theory, methods for revealing preferences and experimental applications. Comprehensive analysis of deposit-refund systems: theory and applications. Concise introductory textbook on welfare theory. Contributions to second-best theory. Analysis of price stabilisation schemes. Allocative efficiency of different ways of organising the credit market. Cost-benefit analysis of industrial projects and policy proposals in Sweden. Economic theory of transportation policy for Sweden.

Publications *Books:* 1. *External Economies in Production* (Almqvist & Wiksell, 1964, 1967); 2. *Resource Allocation and the Credit Market* (Almqvist & Wiksell, 1967); 3. *Pricing of Copper in International Trade – A Case Study of the Price Stabilization Problem* (Norstedts, 1968); 4. *Social Efficiency – A Concise Introduction to Welfare Theory* (Macmillan, Halsted Press, 1973, 1977); 5. *Deposit-refund Systems: Theory and Applications to Environmental, Conservation, and Consumer Policy* (Johns Hopkins Univ. Press, 1981).

Articles: 1. 'On the theory of second best', *REStud*, 34(3), July 1967; 2. 'An approach to the problem of estimating demand for public goods', *Swed JE*, 73(1), March 1971; 3. 'Pollution: taxation or purification?', *Kyklos*, 25(3), 1972; 4. 'Estimating demand for public goods: an experiment', *Europ ER*, 3(1), April 1972; 5. 'Estimating willingness to pay: Why and how?', *Scand JE*, 81(2), 1979.

BÖHM-BAWERK, Eugen Von*

Dates and Birthplace 1851–1914, Austria.
Posts Held Prof. Econ., Univ. Innsbruck, 1881–9; Civil servant, Ministry of Fin., 1889–1904; Minister of Fin., 1895, 1897, 1900; Prof. Econ., Univ. Vienna, 1904–14.
Degree Graduate in Law, Univ. Vienna.
Career One of the greatest figures of the Austrian school, who expanded and reworked Menger's marginal utility theory. His theory of interest, based on the 'three reasons' for interest, was his major personal contribution. Other significant

influences were Von Thünen and John Rae, whose ideas on roundabout production he developed as an element of his capital theory. This aroused furious controversy with fellow economists, into which he entered enthusiastically, writing almost as much in defence of the theory as in its original formulation. Even today there is less than total agreement as to the meaning and significance of his theory of capital and interest. Böhm-Bawerk's considerable polemical skills were further demonstrated by *The Close of the Marxian System* (1896), which remains one of the most powerful attacks on Marxist economics ever written. In his government service he participated in the introduction of a gold currency. His resignation as Minister of Finance came when military expenditure threatened to unbalance the budget.

Publications *Books:* 1. *Capital and Interest*, 3 vols (1884–1912, 1959); 2. *Gesammelte Schriften*, 2 vols, ed. F.X. Weiss (1924–6).

Secondary Literature J. Schumpeter, 'Eugen von Böhm-Bawerk', in *Ten Great Economists from Marx to Keynes* (OUP, 1951); E. Kauder, 'Böhm-Bawerk, Eugen von', *IESS*, vol 2.

BOISGUILBERT, Pierre Le Pesant, Sieur de*

Dates and Birthplace 1646–1714, Normandy, France.
Posts Held Landowner and member, Noblesse de la robe.
Career Though much concerned with workaday economic facts and policy, he soon developed deeper theoretical interests. From his country home in Normandy he developed the idea, which was to take on central importance for the physiocrats, that agriculture was the most essential sector of the economy and should be given preference over the demands of manufacturing. To this end he advocated high prices for agricultural products, leading to a rural population with a greater capacity to consume goods and a swifter circulation of money. His policy propositions were probably easy to disregard because of his exaggerated claims for them, but he

can be seen with hindsight as a major contributor to the development of macro-economic theory in the early eighteenth century.

Publications *Books:* 1. *Le détail de la France* (1695); 2. *Factum de la France* (1706).

Secondary Literature J.J. Spengler, *et al.*, *Pierre de Boisguilbert et la naissance de l'économie politique*, 2 vols (1966).

BOITEUX, Marcel Paul

Born 1922, Niort, Deux Sèvres, France.

Current Post Pres., Chairman of Board, Electricité de France, Paris.

Recent Posts Directeur général, Electricité de France, 1967–78.

Degrees Aggregation, Ecole Normale Supérieure, Sciences Section, 1943, 1946; Grad. Inst. d'Etudes Politiques, Econ. Section, 1947.

Offices Member, Atomic Energy Comm.; Member, Board Dir, Ecole Normale Supérieure, Inst. Pasteur, Ecole Nationale d'Administration; Chairman, Em Soc, 1959; Chairman, Europ. section, Inst. Management Science, TIMS, 1962; Chairman, Internat. Federation Operational Res. Soc., IFORS, 1965, 1966.

Principal Contributions Marginal cost pricing in practice; second best pricing solutions, particularly in regulated industries.

Publications *Articles:* 1. 'Marginal cost pricing of electricity', in *Marginal Cost Pricing in Practice*, ed. J.R. Nelson (Prentice-Hall, 1964).

BONAR, James*

Dates and Birthplace 1852–1941, Perth, Scotland.

Post Held Civil servant, 1881–1919.

Degrees BA Univ. Oxford, 1877; LLD Univ. Glasgow, 1886; DLitt (Hon.) Univ. Camb., 1935.

Offices Founder, vice-pres., RES; Vice-pres., RSS; Pres., Section F, BAAS, 1898; FBA, 1930.

Career An historian of economics, concentrating on the work of Smith, Malthus and Ricardo. He also introduced the work of the Austrian economists to a largely unaware English-speaking public. His *Philosophy and Political Economy* was much appreciated in continental Europe. He contributed extensively to Palgrave's *Dictionary of Political Economy* and published many articles in the *Economic Journal*.

Publications *Books:* 1. *Malthus and His Work* (1885, 1924); 2. *Philosophy and Political Economy* (1893, 1922); 3. *Elements of Political Economy* (1903).

Secondary Literature G.F. Shirras, 'Obituary: James Bonar', *EJ*, 51, April 1941.

BORCH, Karl Henrik

Born 1919, Sarpsborg, Norway.

Current Post Prof. Insurance, Norwegian School Bus., Bergen, 1963–.

Recent Posts Administrator, OEEC, Paris, 1954–9; Res. Fellow, Norwegian School Bus., 1959–62; Res. assoc., Princeton Univ., 1962–3.

Degrees MA (Actuarial Science), PhD (Maths) Oslo Univ., 1947, 1962.

Offices Fellow, Em Soc, 1963; Internat. Stat. Inst., 1968.

Principal Contributions The economic theory of insurance, with extensions to the theory of decisions and equilibrium under uncertainty.

Publications *Books:* 1. *The Economics of Uncertainty* (Princeton Univ. Press, 1968); 2. *Risk and Uncertainty*, ed. (with J. Mossin), (Macmillan, 1968); 3. *The Mathematical Theory of Insurance* (D.C. Heath, 1974); 4. *The Three Markets for Private Insurance* (Geneva Assoc., 1981).

BORTKIEWICZ, Ladislaus Von*

Dates and Birthplace 1868–1931, St Petersburg, Russia.

Posts Held Lecturer, Univs Strasburg and St Petersburg; Prof., Univ. Berlin, 1901–31.

Degrees Graduate Univ. St Petersburg; Doctorate, Univ. Gottingen, 1893.

Offices Member, Internat. Stat. Inst., Swedish Academy of Sciences.

Career A mathematical statistician and mathematical economist. Perhaps his outstanding economic work was an analysis of the so-called 'Transformation problem' in Marxist economics, which attempted to fill the gaps in Marx's own arguments; it went largely unnoticed in Marxist circles until P.M. Sweezy rediscovered it in his *Theory of Capitalist Development* (1942). He also wrote notably on the concept of price index numbers. Vigorous controversy with Böhm-Bawerk on the role of time preference in the theory of interest and with Alfred Weber on the geometrical representation of the location of industries was typical of his many contributions to economics, most of which appeared in articles and reviews.

Publications *Articles:* 1. 'On the correction of Marx's fundamental theoretical construction in the third volume of *Capital',* (in E. von Böhm-Bawerk,) *Karl Marx and the Close of his System*, ed. P.M. Sweezy (1949); 2. 'Value and price in the Marxian system', *Internat. Econ. Papers*, 2 (1952).

Secondary Literature J.A. Schumpeter, 'Ladislaus von Bortkiewicz: 1868–1931', in *Ten Great Economists from Marx to Keynes* (OUP, 1951); E.J. Gumbel, 'Bortkiewicz, Ladislaus von', *IESS*, vol 2.

BORTS, George Herbert

Born 1927, New York City, NY, USA.

Current Post Prof. Econ., Brown Univ., Providence, Rhode Island, USA, 1960–.

Recent Post Ford Foundation Faculty Res. Fellow, LSE, 1960–1.

Degrees BA Columbia Univ., 1947; MA, PhD, Univ. Chicago, 1949, 1953.

Offices Managing ed., *AER*, 1969–80; Guggenheim Memorial Foundation Fellow, 1975–6.

Principal Contributions Analysis of rail-road cost functions, and statistical estimation of production functions; regional economic growth and development in the United States, including regional cycles of employment; and international and inter-regional long-run capital movements.

Publications *Books:* 1. *Economic Growth in a Free Market* (with J.L. Stein), (Columbia Univ. Press, 1964). *Articles:* 1. 'Increasing returns in the railway industry', *JPE*, 62, Aug. 1954; 2. 'The estimation of rail cost functions', *Em*, 28, Jan. 1960; 3. 'The equalization of returns and regional economic growth', *AER*, 50, June 1960; 4. 'The recent controversy over resale price maintenance', *JRSS*, 124, Pt 2, 1961; 5. 'A theory of long-run international capital movements', *JPE*, 73, Aug. 1964.

BOS, Hendricus C.

Born 1926, The Hague, The Netherlands.

Current Post Prof. Development Planning and Econ. Centrally Planned Systems, Erasmus Univ., Rotterdam, 1965–.

Recent Posts Dir., Centre Development Planning, Erasmus Univ., 1968–78; Dir., Netherlands Econ. Inst., 1968–78.

Degrees MA (Econ.), PhD (Econ.), Netherlands School Econ., Rotterdam, 1953, 1964.

Offices and Honours Member, 1968–, Vice-chairman, 1978–, Nat. Advisory Council Development Aid, Netherlands Minister Development Co-op.; Member, UN Comm. Development Planning, 1974–; Knight, Order of the Netherlands' Lion, 1980.

Principal Contributions Mathematical models of economic growth; quantitative models for education planning; theoretical analysis of spatial dispersion of economic activity; methodology of estimating costs and benefits of economic industrial co-operation among developing countries (applied to southeast Asia); quantitative evaluation of some macro-economic effects of private foreign direct investments in developing countries; policy analysis of global economic issues in North-South relations; global modelling of economic relations between developing and developed countries.

Publications *Books:* 1. *A Discussion on Methods of Monetary Analysis and Norms for Monetary Policy* (Rotterdam

Univ. Press, 1956, 1965); 2. *Mathematical Models of Economic Growth* (with J. Tinbergen), (McGraw-Hill, 1962; French and Spanish transls.); 3. *Econometric models of education planning* (with J. Tinbergen), (OECD, 1965); 4. *Spatial Dispersion of Economic Activity* (Rotterdam Univ. Press, 1965; Italian and Russian transls.); 5. *Private Foreign Investment in Developing Countries. A Quantitative Study on the Evaluation of the Macro-economic Effects* (with M. Sanders and C. Secchi), (D. Reidel, 1974).

BOULDING, Kenneth Ewart

Born 1910, Liverpool, England.
Current Post Dir. Program Res. General Social Econ. Dynamics, Inst. Behavioral Science, Univ. Colorado, Boulder, USA, 1967–; Disting. prof. Econ. Emeritus, Univ. Colorado, 1980–.
Recent Posts Prof. Econ., Univ. Michigan, 1949–67; Co-dir., 1961–4, Res. dir., 1964–5, Dir., 1965–6, Center Res. Conflict Resolution, Univ. Michigan; Prof. Econ., 1968–77, Disting. prof. Econ., 1977–80, Univ. Colorado.
Degrees BA (First class hons., PPE), MA, Univ. Oxford, 1931, 1939.
Offices and Honours John Bates Clark medal, AEA, 1949; Amer. Council Learned Socs. prize disting. scholarship Humanities, 1962; Pres., AEA, 1968; Frank E. Seidman disting. award Polit. Econ., 1976; pres., AAAS, 1979.
Principal Contributions Synthesised neo-classical and Keynesian economic theory into a coherent whole in *Economic Analysis*, especially fourth edition (1966). Urged economics down a new path, in *The Reconstruction of Economics* (1949), with emphasis on stocks rather than flows and a macro-theory of functional distribution. In work on evolutionary economics, have urged an integration of economic with biological concepts of ecological equilibrium and dynamics and genetic production. Exchange is only one of three major organisers of social life, the others being the threat system and the integrative system; in work on Grants Economics, argued that one-way transfers should be integrated into the body of economic theory. In work on normative studies, took position that economic policy cannot be judged by economic criteria alone and that a larger normative theory of evaluative judgement is possible. In work in international systems, applied many economic principles to international systems.
Publications *Books:* 1. *Economic Analysis* (Harper, 1941, 1966); 2. *The Reconstruction of Economics* (Wiley, 1950); 3. *The Image* (Univ. Michigan Press, 1956); 4. *Conflict and Defense* (Harper, 1962); 5. *Ecodynamics* (Sage, 1978).
Articles: 1. *Collected Papers*, vols I, II, ed. F.R. Glahe (Colorado Assoc. Univ. Press, 1971), vols III, IV, V, ed. L. Singell (1973, 1974, 1975); 2. *Beasts, Ballads, and Bouldingisms: A Collection of Writings by Kenneth Boulding*, ed. R.P. Beilock (Transaction Books, 1980).

BOUSQUET, Georges H.*

Dates and Birthplace 1900–78, France.
Posts Held Prof., Univ. Algiers; Prof., Univ. Bordeaux, 1962.
Offices Member, Mont. Pelerin Soc.
Career Biographer of Pareto and editor of his works.
Publications *Books:* 1. *Essai sur l'évolution de la pensée économique* (1927); 2. *La Restauration monétaire et financière de l'Autriche* (1927); 3. *Cours d'économie pure* (1928); 4. *Vilfredo Pareto, sa vie et son oeuvre* (1928); 5. *Institutes de science économique*, 2 vols, (1930–2); 6. *Vilfredo Pareto (1848–1923). Le savant et l'homme* (1960); 7. *Esquisse d'une histoire de la science économique en Italie* (1960).

BOWLES, Samuel

Born 1939, New Haven, Conn. USA.
Current Post Prof. Econ., Univ. Massachusetts, Amherst, USA.
Recent Post Assoc. prof. Econ., Harvard Univ., 1971–4.
Degrees BA Yale Univ., 1960; PhD Harvard Univ., 1965.

Offices   Member, Union Radical Polit. Economics, 1969–; Member, Ed. Board, *Review Radical Polit. Econ.*, 1974–6; Member, Steering Comm. Center Popular Econ., 1978–; Guggenheim Memorial Foundation Fellow, 1978–9.

Principal Contributions   Textbook in advanced micro-economic theory, and principal writings in the economics of human resources (particularly education) and in Marxist economic theory. In both areas focused on the processes whereby systems of power and privilege are perpetuated over time and may be modified or overcome. In recent years, turned to the interface of political and economic theory.

Publications   *Books:* 1. *Planning Educational Systems for Economic Growth* (Harvard Univ. Press, 1969); 2. *Notes and Problems in Microeconomic Theory* (with D. Kendrick and P. Dixon), (Markham Publishing Co., 1970, N-H, 1980); 3. *Schooling in Capitalist America* (with H. Gintis), (Basic Books, 1976; German, Spanish, Japanese and Italian transls.).

Articles: 1. 'The efficient allocation of resources in education', *QJE*, 81, May 1967; 2. 'Schooling and inequality from generation to generation', *JPE*, 80(3), Pt 2, May/June 1972; 3. 'The "inheritance of IQ" and the intergenerational reproduction of economic inequality' (with V. Nelson), *REStat*, 56(1), Feb. 1974; 4. 'Heterogeneous labor and the Marxian theory of value: a critique and a reformulation' (with H. Gintis), *Camb JE*, 1(2), 1977; 5. 'Structure and practice in the labor theory of value', *Review Radical Polit. Econ.*, 13(1), March 1981.

BOWLEY, Arthur Lyon*

Dates and Birthplace   1869–1957, Bristol, England.

Posts Held   Part-time Reader Stats, 1895–1919; Full-time prof. Stats, 1919–36, LSE; Lecturer, Maths and Econ., Univ. Extension Coll., Reading, 1900–19.

Degree   Maths, Univ. Camb., 1891.

Offices and Honours   Various offices in BAAS, RSS, and Internat. Stat. Inst.; Ed., London and Camb. Econ. Service, 1925–45; Knighted, 1950.

Career   Began his career as a mathematician but turned to economics because of its relevance to problems of social reform. His early work on wages and prices made extensive use of historical and statistical data and he remained an applied statistician rather than an economist or economic historian. Nevertheless, his advocacy over many years of the use of statistics and mathematics in economics, though unspectacular, influenced generations of economists. He was a constant critic of government statistics and the inadequate sampling techniques used. His various outstanding publications on wages were an important contribution to questions of the distribution of national income.

Publications   *Books:* 1. *A Short Account of England's Foreign Trade in the Nineteenth Century* (1893); 2. *Livelihood and Poverty* (with A.R. Bennett-Hurst), (1915); 3. *The Mathematical Groundwork of Economics* (1924); 4. *Has Poverty Diminished?* (with M.H. Hogg), (1925); 5. *Wages and Income in the United Kingdom Since 1860* (1937); 6. *Studies in the National Income*, ed. (1942).

Secondary Literature   R.G.D. Allen, 'Bowley, Arthur Lyon', *IESS*, vol. 2; A. Darnell, 'A.L. Bowley', *Pioneers of Modern Economics in Britain*, eds D.P. O'Brien and J.R. Presley (Macmillan,1981).

BOWMAN, Mary Jean

Born   1908, New York City, NY, USA.

Current Post   Consultant, World Bank; post-retirement, Prof. Econ. and Education, Univ. Chicago.

Recent Posts   Contract res., Resources for the Future, 1956–7; Res. assoc., Prof. Econ. and Education, Univ. Chicago, 1958–74; Vis. lecturer, Uppsala Univ., Sweden, 1974, LSE, 1975.

Degrees   BA Vassar Coll., 1930; MA Radcliffe Coll., 1932; PhD Harvard Univ., 1938.

Offices and Honours   Phi Beta Kappa, 1930; Virginia Swinburne Brownell prize, Econ., 1930; Nominating

Comm., 1953, Exec. Comm., 1969–71, AEA; Conference Income and Wealth, 1970–, (Nominating Comm., 1971, 1973); Trustee, TIAA, 1973–6; Guggenheim Memorial Foundation Fellow, 1974.

Principal Contributions Analyses of the economics of post-school learning and the development and utilisation of human resources in contexts of change: relations to schooling, interactive effects of labor-market institutions, modes of international transfer of know-how. Integrated applications of economic decision theory and 'information-field' theories from human geography in the explanation of human-investment decisions. Application of theories of business decision-making to analysis of expectations and uncertainty in human investments. Analyses of measures and meanings of inequality in the distributions of income and of opportunity.

Publications *Books:* 1. *Economic Analysis and Public Policy* (with G.L. Bach), (Prentice-Hall, 1943, 1949); 2. *Expectations, Uncertainty, and Business Behavior* (SSRC, 1958); 3. *Resources and People in East Kentucky* (with W.W. Haynes), (Johns Hopkins Univ. Press, 1963); 4. *Where Colleges Are and Who Attends* (with C.A. Anderson and V. Tinto), (McGraw Hill, 1973); 5. *Educational Choice and Labor Markets in Japan* (Univ. Chicago Press, 1981).

Articles: 1. 'A graphical analysis of personal income distribution in the United States', *AER*, 35(4), Sept. 1945, reprinted in *Readings in the Theory of Income Distribution*, eds W. Fellner and B.F. Haley (Blakiston, 1946); 2. 'From guilds to infant training industries', in *Education and Economic Development*, eds C.A. Anderson and M.J. Bowman (Aldine, 1965); 3. 'The assessment of human investments as growth strategy', US Congress, Joint Econ. Comm., *Compendium on Human Resources* (US Govt Printing Office, 1968); 4. 'Expectations, uncertainty, and investment in human beings', in *Uncertainty and Expectations in Economics*, eds C.F. Carter and J.L. Ford (Blackwell, 1972); 5. 'Human resources and the contours of development', in *The Social Context of Education; Essays in Honor of J.P.*

Naik, ed. A.B. Shah (Allied Publishers Pvt Ltd, 1978).

BRAY, John Francis*

Dates and Birthplace 1809–97, Washington, DC, USA.
Posts Held Printer, photographer, farmer.
Career During a lengthy period of residence in England 1822–42 he wrote his chief work, *Labour's Wrongs*, which owed much to his own experience of working conditions in the printing industry. His argument is in the Ricardian socialist tradition, claiming that the employer takes the whole product of a worker's labour and returns only a fraction to him as wages. He argued in favour of communal property organised through the medium of corporations, owned and founded by the workers and issuing money representing labour-time.
Publications *Books:* 1. *Labour's Wrongs and Labour's Remedy* (1839, 1931); 2. *A Voyage from Utopia*, ed. M.F. Lloyd-Prichard (1957).
Secondary Literature H.J. Carr, 'John Francis Bray', *Ec*, N.S. 7, Nov. 1940.

BRECHLING, Frank Paul Richard

Born 1931, Wismar, Germany.
Current Post Prof., Univ. Maryland, College Park, USA.
Recent Posts Northwestern Univ., 1966–79.
Degree BA Trinity Coll., Dublin, 1955.
Principal Contributions Empirical investigation of employment and investment decisions. Analysis of the unemployment insurance system.
Publications *Books:* 1. *The Theory of Interest Rates*, ed. (with F.H. Hahn), (Macmillan, 1965); 2. *Investment and Employment Decisions* (Manchester Univ. Press, 1975).
Articles: 1. 'A note on bond-holding and the liquidity preference theory of interest', *REStud*, 24, June 1957; 2. 'Trade credit and monetary policy' (with R.G. Lipsey), *EJ*, 73, Dec. 1963; 3. 'The relationship between output and

employment in British manufacturing industries', *REStud*, 32, July, Oct. 1965; 4. 'Wage inflation and the structure of regional unemployment', *JMCB*, Pt II, 5(1), Feb. 1973; 5. 'The incentive effects of the US unemployment insurance tax', in *Research in Labor Economics*, ed. R.G. Ehrenberg (JAI Press, 1977).

BREMS, Hans J.

Born 1915, Viborg, Denmark.
Current Post Prof. Econ., Univ. Illinois, Urbana-Champaign, USA 1954–.
Recent Posts Vis. prof., Univs. UCLA (1953), Michigan (1957), Berkeley (1959), Harvard (1960), Kiel (1961), Colorado (1963), Göttingen (1964), Hamburg (1967), Uppsala (1968), Lund (1970), Kiel (1972), Göteborg (1972), Copenhagen (1975), Lund (1975) and Stockholm (1980).
Degrees PhD Univ. Copenhagen, 1950; Dr (*Hon. causa*) Svenska handelshögskolan, Helsinki, 1970.
Offices (Foreign) member, Royal Danish Academy Sciences Letters, 1979.
Principal Contributions Early work gave attention to the determination of optimal product quality under monopolistic competition. Later work centred on international economics and tried to marry the elasticity and the absorption approaches and to come to grips with international direct investment. The last book tries to apply modern growth theory to inflation, unemployment, dwindling natural resources, and international trade.
Publications *Books:* 1. *Product Equilibrium Under Monopolistic Competition* (Harvard Univ. Press, 1951); 2. *Output, Employment, Capital, and Growth* (Harper, 1959, Greenwood, 1973); 3. *Quantitative Economic Theory* (Wiley, 1968); 4. *Inflation, Interest, and Growth: A Synthesis* (D.C. Heath, 1980); 5. *Dynamische Makrotheorie – Inflation, Zins und Wachstum* (J.C.B. Mohr, Paul Siebeck, 1980).
Articles: 1. 'Input-output coefficients as measures of product quality', *AER*, 47(2), March 1957; 2. 'Devaluation, a marriage of the elasticity and the absorption approaches', *EJ*, 67, March 1957; 3. 'A growth model of international direct investment', *AER*, 60(3), June 1970; 4. 'Ricardo's long-run equilibrium', *HOPE*, 2(2), Fall, 1970; 5. 'Alternative theories of pricing, distribution, saving, and investment', *AER*, 69(2), March 1979.

BRENTANO, Lujo*

Dates and Birthplace 1844–1931, Frankfurt-am-Main, Germany.
Posts Held Prussian Stat. Office, 1867–71; Prof. Univs. Berlin (1871–2), Breslau (1872–82), Strasbourg (1882–8), Vienna (1888–9), Leipzig (1889–91) and Munich (1891–1931).
Degrees Dr Law Univ. Heidelberg; Dr Econ. Univ. Göttingen, 1867.
Offices Founder member, Verein für Sozialpolitik.
Career Economic historian whose works are notable for clarity of exposition. He was also an inspiring teacher in his various university posts. His interest in economics began after the completion of his law studies and his work under Ernst Engel in the Prussian Statistical Office turned his interest towards trade unions. He was an advocate of unions as a means of improving the living standards of the worker. Economic liberalism and an attachment to English institutions were other consistent features of his work.
Publications *Books:* 1. *On the History and Development of Guilds, and the Origins of Trade Unions* (1870); 2. *The Relation of Labour to the Law of Today* (1877); 3. *Hours and Wages in Relation to Production* (1894); 4. *Die Deutschen Getreidezölle* (1911); 5. *Mein Leben in Kampf um die Soziale Entwicklung Deutschlands* (1931).
Secondary Literature J.J. Sheehan, *The Career of Lujo Brentano* (Chicago, Univ. Press, 1966); H. Kisch, 'Brentano, Lujo', *IESS*, vol. 2.

BRESCIANI-TURRONI, Constantino*

Dates and Birthplace 1882–1963, Verona, Italy.

Posts Held   Prof. Stats and Econ. various Italian univs. and Univ. Cairo; Pres., Banco di Roma, 1945; Exec. dir. IBRD, 1947–53; Minister Foreign Trade, Italy, 1953.

Degree   Graduate, Univ. Verona.

Career   The last great representative of the Italian classical school, he nevertheless moved beyond the conventional classical methodology in his studies of monetary theory and policy. His work for the Reparations Commission in Germany after World War I resulted in his great work on inflation (1931) and confirmed his opinion that monetary methods were necessary to control inflation. He was a major architect of Italy's post-World War II reconstruction and his later publications concentrated on policy advice.

Publications   Books: 1. *The Economics of Inflation* (1931, 1937); 2. *Le previsioni economiche* (1932); 3. *Economic Policy for the Thinking Man* (1942, 1950); 4. *Il Programma Economico-Sociale del Liberalismo* (1946); 5. *Saggia di economia* (1961).

Secondary Literature   F.M. Tamagna, 'Bresciani-Turroni', Constantino *IESS*, vol. 2.

BRETON, Albert

Born   Montmartre, Sask., Canada.

Current Post   Prof. Econ., Univ. Toronto, Canada, 1970–.

Recent Posts   Reader Public Fin., LSE, 1966–9; Vis. prof. Canadian Stud., Harvard Univ., 1969–70.

Degrees   BA St Boniface Coll., Univ. Manitoba, 1951; PhD Columbia Univ., 1965.

Offices   CEA, AEA, RES; Fellow, Royal Soc. Canada, 1976–.

Principal Contributions   Development of a model of representative government, formulated within the framework of neo-classical economics, in which each group of actors – citizens, political parties and bureaucrats – interact to determine the pattern and volume of public policies. Extension of this basic model to allow for interaction between many representative governments in the context of a federal structure which itself takes shape as part of the analysis.

A further extension incorporating the interaction of governments and government bodies (such as crown corporations) with private institutions provides the basis of a theory of the government sector.

Publications   Books: 1. *The Economic Theory of Representative Government* (Aldine, 1974); 2. *The Economic Constitution of Federal States* (with A. Scott), (Univ. Toronto Press, 1978); 3. *The Design of Federations* (with A. Scott), (Inst. Res. Public Pol., 1980); 4. *The Logic of Bureaucratic Conduct* (with R. Wintrobe), forthcoming.

Articles: 1. 'The economics of nationalism', *JPE*, 72, August 1964; 2. 'A theory of government grants', *CJE*, 31, May 1965; 3. 'An economic theory of social movements' (with R. Breton), *AER*, 59(2), May 1969; 4. 'The equilibrium size of a budget-maximizing bureau: a note on Niskanen's theory of bureaucracy' (with R. Wintrobe), *JPE*, 83(1), Feb.1975; 5. 'The economics of bilingualism' (with P. Mieszkowski), in *The Political Economy of Fiscal Federalism*, ed. W.E. Oates (D.C. Heath, 1977).

BRITTAN, Samuel

Born   N.e.

Current Posts   Econ. commentator, 1966–, Ass. ed., 1978–, *Financial Times* London.

Recent Posts   Econ. ed., *Observer*, 1961–4; Adviser, UK Dept Econ. Affairs, 1965.

Degrees   BA (First class Hon.) Jesus Coll., Univ. Camb.

Offices and Honours   Sr Wincott award for financial journalists, 1971; Res. Fellow, 1973–4, Vis. Fellow, 1974, Nuffield Coll., Univ. Oxford.

Principal Contributions   Pioneering work on interaction between economic doctrine and political influences in British economic policy; critical analysis of the 'left-right' spectrum in relation to economic and other policy. Reinterpretation of free-market doctrines in relation to alternative value systems; systemic weaknesses of democratic political economies; empirical examination of degree of consensus among economists; role of money GDP as ultimate target for financial policy; and property rights in national resources with special reference to North Sea oil.

Publications *Books:* 1. *The Price of Economic Freedom: A Guide to Flexible Rates* (Macmillan, 1970); 2. *Is There an Economic Consensus*? (Macmillan, 1973); 3. *Capitalism and the Permissive Society* (Macmillan, 1973); 4. *The Delusion of Incomes Policy* (with P. Lilley), (Temple Smith, 1977); 5. *The Economic Consequences of Democracy* (Temple Smith, 1977).

Articles: 1. 'How British is the British sickness?', *J Law E*, 21(2), Oct. 1978; 2. 'A people's stake in North Sea oil', *LBR*, 130, April 1978; 3. 'Inflation and democracy', in *The Political Economy of Inflation,* eds J. Hirsch and J.E. Goldthorpe (Martin Robertson, 1978); 4. 'The European monetary system: a compromise that could be worse than either extreme', in *The World Economy* (London, Trade Pol. Res. Centre, 1979); 5. 'Hayek, the New Right, and the crisis of social democracy', *Encounter*, Jan. 1980.

BROCK, W.A.

N.e.

BRONFENBRENNER, Martin

Born 1914, Pittsburgh, Penn., USA.
Current Post Kenan prof. Econ., 1971–, Lecturer Japanese hist., Duke Univ., Durham, N. Carolina.
Recent Posts Assoc. prof., prof., Univ. Wisconsin, Madison, 1947–57; Prof. Econ., Michigan State Univ., East Lansing, 1957–8; Prof. Econ., Univ. Minnesota, 1958–62; Prof. Econ., Grad. School Bus. Carnegie-Mellon Univ., 1962–71.
Degrees BA Washington Univ. (St Louis), 1934; PhD Univ. Chicago, 1939; Certificate, Japanese Language, Univ. Colorado, 1944.
Offices Member, Board Eds., *AER, JEL, EDCC, HOPE*; Vis. Scholar, Center Advanced Study Behavioral Sciences, Stanford Univ., 1966–7, Inst.

Development Stud., Univ. Sussex, 1978–9; Vice-pres., AEA; Pres., SEA, 1978–9, Hist. Econ. Soc., 1981–2.
Principal Contributions Assisted in keeping general economics alive and making Japanological economics respectable. Tried to show that marginal productivity analysis need not be anti-labour, or non-Marxist analysis anti-Marxist, nor academic freedom a cover for activist violence. Labelled crypto-communist in McCarthy days, then Fascist by New Left students.
Publications Books: 1. *Academic Encounter* (Free Press, 1961); 2. *Income Distribution Theory* (Aldine, Macmillan, 1971); 3. *Macroeconomic Alternatives* (AHM, 1979).

Articles: 1. 'The appeal of confiscation in economic development', *EDCC*, 3, April 1955; 2. 'Potential monopsony in labor markets', *ILRR*, 9, July 1956; 3. 'Contribution to the aggregative theory of wages', *JPE*, 64, Dec. 1956; 4. 'A reformulation of naïve profit theory', *SEJ*, 26, April 1960; 5. 'Survey of inflation theory' (with F.D. Holzman), *AER*, 53(4), Sept. 1963.

BROWN, Arthur Joseph

Born 1914, Great Warford, Cheshire, England.
Current Post Emeritus Prof., Univ. Leeds.
Recent Posts Prof. Econ., Univ. Leeds, 1947–79; Pro-vice-chancellor, Univ. Leeds, 1975–7.
Degrees BA, MA, DPhil, Univ. Oxford, 1936, 1939; Hon. DLitt, Univ. Bradford, 1975; Univ. Sheffield, 1979; Kent, 1979; Hon. LlD, Univ. Aberdeen, 1978.
Offices and Honours Jr Webb Medley prize, Sr Webb Medley prize, Univ. Oxford, 1935; 1936; Fellow, All Souls Coll., Univ. Oxford, 1937–46; Pres., Section F, BAAS, 1958; Member, Univ. Grants Committee, 1969–78; Fellow, BA, 1972; CBE, 1974; Pres., RES, 1976–8.
Principal Contributions A statistical demand schedule for money, 1939; statistical comparisons of economic war efforts, 1940–6; elucidation of the price-wage spiral and adumbration of

the Phillips curve, 1955; investigation of the case for customs unions between developing countries with special reference to demand effects and economies of scale; contributions to the economics of disarmament, 1961, 1967; contributions to the economics regional policy with special reference to unemployment and frictions of movement, 1972.

Publications   *Books*: 1. *Applied Economics: Aspects of the World Economy in War and Peace* (A & U, Rinehart, 1947); 2. *The Great Inflation, 1939–51* (OUP, 1955); 3. *Introduction to the World Economy* (A & U, Rinehart, 1959, 1965); 4. *The Framework of Regional Economics in the United Kingdom* (CUP, 1972); 5. *Regional Economic Problems* (with E.M. Burrows), (A & U, Rinehart, 1977).

Articles: 1. 'Interest, prices and the demand schedule for idle money', *OEP*, 2, May 1939; 2. 'Inflation in the British economy', *EJ*, 68, Sept. 1958; 3. 'Economic separatism versus a common market in developing countries, Pt 1–2', *YBESR*, 13, May, Nov. 1961; 4. 'Effects of disarmament on the balance of payments of the UK', in *Disarmament and World Economic Independence* ed. E. Benoit (Columbia Univ. Press, 1967); 5. 'Inflation and the British sickness', *EJ*, 89, March 1979.

BROWN, Harry Gunnison*

Dates and Birthplace   1880–1975, Troy, N.Y., USA.
Posts Held   Prof., Yale Univ., 1909–15; Prof., Univ. Missouri, 1915–50.
Degrees   BA Williams Coll., 1904; PhD Yale Univ., 1909.
Offices   Founder, member, Ed. Council, *Amer. J Econ. and Sociology*.
Career   Academic follower of Henry George who continued to advocate land value taxation throughout a long career. His work on business administration introduced economic principles as a basis for the subject. In retirement, he acted as a consultant to local authorities modernising their tax structures.
Publications   *Books*: 1. *Transportation Rates and their Regulation* (1916); 2. *Principles of Commerce* (1916); 3.

Economics of Taxation 4. *The Economic Basis of Tax Reform* (1932); 5. *Basic Principles of Economics* (1942).
Secondary Literature   W. Lissner, 'In memoriam: H.G. Brown', *Amer. J Econ. Sociology*, 34, 1975.

BRUNNER, K

N.e.

BRUNO, Michael

Born   1932, Hamburg, Germany.
Current Post   Prof. Econ., Hebrew Univ., Jerusalem, 1970–.
Recent Posts   Vis. prof., MIT, 1965–6, 1970–1; Dir. Res., Falk Inst. Econ. Res., Israel, 1972–5; Econ. Pol. Adviser, Israeli Minister Fin., 1975–6; Vis. prof., Harvard Univ., 1976–7.
Degrees   BA King's Coll., Univ. Camb., 1956; PhD Stanford Univ., 1962.
Offices and Honours   Fellow, Em Soc, 1967–; Rothschild prize Social Science, Israel, 1974; Member, Israel Academy Sciences and Humanities, 1975–.
Principal Contributions   The theory of trade and development (developing the concept of domestic resource costs as a positive tool and as an investment criterion of comparative advantage, design and application of input–output and linearised programming models for trade and development planning, and general equilibrium theory of effective protection and of tariff reform). The theory of production, capital and optimal growth (dynamic duality theorems, accumulation in discrete capital models and reswitching of techniques). The design of income tax reform and of family allowance systems. The theory of stabilisation in open industrial and semi-industrial economies in the 1970s, with special reference to stagflation.
Publications   *Books:* 1. *Interdependence, Resource Use and Structural Change in Israel* (Bank of Israel, 1962).
Articles: 1. 'Development alternatives in an open economy: the case of Israel' (with H.B. Chenery), *EJ*, 72, March 1962; 2. 'Optimal patterns of trade and development', *REStat*, 49, Nov. 1967;

3. 'Fundamental duality relations in the pure theory of capital and growth', *REStud*, 36, Jan. 1969; 4. 'Taxes, family grants and redistribution' (with J. Habib), *J Pub E*, 5, 1976; 5. 'Import prices and stagflation in the industrial countries: a cross-section analysis', *EJ*, 90, Sept. 1980.

BUCHANAN, David*

Dates and Birthplace   1779–1848, Montrose, Scotland.

Posts Held   Journalist and ed., *Weekly Register*, 1808–9, *Caledonian Mercury*, 1810–27, *Edinburgh Courant*, 1827–48.

Career   His edition of Smith was an important pre-Ricardian commentary, which criticised various aspects of Smith's work, including the theory of rent, in an able fashion. He developed an argument in favour of progressive taxation in the supplement to the edition. His later *Inquiry . . .* contains a spirited critique of current taxation practices and an attack on the Ricardian theory of rent. He was also a contributor to the *Edinburgh Review* and *Encyclopaedia Britannica*, 7th edn.

Publications   *Books:* 1. *Adam Smith's Wealth of Nations*, 3 vols (with notes and vol. of commentaries) (1814); 2. *Inquiry into the Taxation and Commercial Policy of Great Britain* (1844).

BUCHANAN, James M.

Born   1919, Murfreesboro, Tenn., USA.

Current Post   Univ. disting. prof., General dir., Center Stud. Public Choice, Virginia Polytechnic Inst., Blacksburg, USA, 1969–.

Recent Posts   McIntire prof. Econ., Dir., Thomas Jefferson Center Polit. Econ., Univ. Virginia, 1956–68; Prof. Econ., UCLA, 1968–9.

Degrees   BS Univ. Middle Tennessee, 1940; MA Univ. Tennessee, 1941; PhD Univ. Chicago, 1948.

Offices and Honours   Co-founder (with G. Tullock), Public Choice Soc., 1962; Pres., SEA, 1963; Exec. Comm., 1967–9, Vice-pres., 1972, AEA; Law

Econ. prize, Univ. Miami Law Econ. Center, 1977; Exec. Comm., Mont Pelerin Soc., 1980–1; Vice-pres., WEA, 1982.

Principal Contributions   Integration of the analysis of political decision making (public choice) into the corpus of economic theory, which is the source for what is now called 'public sector economics'. Extension and application of economic analysis to constitutional choices among social-political rules and institutions. Critique of Keynesian macro-economic policy based on analysis of political decision structure. Clarification of theory of opportunity cost. Critique of post-Keynesian theory of public debt.

Publications   *Books:* 1. *Calculus of Consent* (with G. Tullock), (Univ. Michigan Press, 1962); 2. *Cost and Choice* (Markham Publishing, 1969, Univ. Chicago Press, 1979); *The Limits of Liberty* (Univ. Chicago Press, 1975); 4. *Freedom in Constitutional Contract* (Texas A & M Univ. Press, 1978); 5. *The Power to Tax* (with G. Brennan), (CUP, 1980).

Articles: 1. 'Individual choice in voting and the market', *JPE*, 62, Aug. 1954; 2. 'Externality' (with W.C. Stubblebine), *Ec*, N.S. 29, Nov. 1962; 3. 'A contractarian paradigm for applying economic theory', *AER*, 65(2), May 1975; 4. 'Markets, states, and the extent of morals', *AER*, 68(2), May 1978; 5. 'The homogenization of heterogeneous inputs' (with R.D. Tollison), *AER*, 71(1), March 1981.

Secondary Literature   G. Locksley, 'Individuals, contracts and constitutions: the political economy of James M. Buchanan', *Twelve Contemporary Economists*, eds V.R. Shackleton and G. Locksley (Macmillan, 1981).

BUDD, Edward C.

Born   1920, Summit, NJ, USA.

Current Post   Prof. Econ., Pennsylvania State Univ., USA.

Recent Posts   Univ. Illinois, 1949–51; Univ. Oregon, 1951–2; Yale Univ., 1952–61; Consultant, Expert Income Distrib., Bureau Econ. Analysis, US Dept Commerce, 1967–.

Degrees BA, PhD Univ. Cal., Berkeley, 1942, 1954.

Offices AEA; SEA; WEA; IARIW; Phi Beta Kappa, 1942; Exec. Comm., Conference Res. Income Wealth, NBER, 1970–2.

Principal Contributions Historical studies of the US distribution of income by size of income and factor shares. Studies of the effects of inflation, unemployment, and fluctuations in economic activity on the personal distribution of income and wealth. Estimation of the distribution of family personal income for 1964 and 1972 by size and socio-economic characteristics, using microdata files of field surveys and government administrative records.

Publications *Books:* 1. *Inequality and Poverty* (Norton, 1967).

Articles: 1. 'US factor shares', in NBER, *Trends in the American Economy in the 19th Century* (Princeton Univ. Press, 1960); 2. 'The impact of inflation on the distribution of income and wealth' (with D.F. Seiders), *AER*, 61(2), May 1971; 3. 'The creation of a microdata file for estimating the size distribution of income', *RIW*, 17(4), Dec. 1971; 4. 'The BEA and CPS size distributions: some comparisons for 1964' (with D.B. Radner), in *The Personal Distribution of Income and Wealth*, ed. J.D. Smith (Princeton Univ. Press, 1975); 5. 'Macro-economic fluctuations and the size distribution of income and earnings in the US' (with T.C. Whiteman), in *Income Distribution and Economic Inequality*, eds Z. Griliches *et al.* (Halsted Press, Wiley, 1978).

BUKHARIN, Nikolai Ivanovich*

Dates and Birthplace 1888–1938, Moscow, Russia.

Posts Held Ed., *Pravda, Novy Mir* and *Izvestia*; Member, Politburo, Comintern.

Career One of the chief theorists of the Russian Revolution and the Soviet state, he became a revolutionary whilst studying economics. He was an exile with Lenin in the years 1911–17 when he wrote a number of theoretical works including an analysis of imperialism on which Lenin drew repeatedly. For a while, in the 1920s, he was an ally of Stalin who nevertheless had him expelled from his positions of influence in 1929. He argued for a policy of industrialisation at the expense of the peasantry but drew back from Stalin's adoption of an extreme version of his argument. He was indicted in the third round of the Moscow Trials, and was executed in 1938.

Publications *Books:* 1. *The Economic Theory of the Leisure Class* (1914, 1927, 1968); 2. *Imperialism and the World Economy* (1918); 3. *The Economy of the Transitional Period* (1920); 4. *ABC of Communism* (1921, 1969); 5. *The Theory of Historical Materialism* (1921).

Secondary Literature P. Knirsch, *Die Ökonomischen Anschauungen Nikolaj I. Bucharins* (1959); S.F. Cohen, *Bukharin and the Bolshevik Revolution* (Columbia Univ. Press, 1973).

BULLOCK, Charles Jesse*

Dates and Birthplace 1869–1941, Boston, Mass., USA.

Posts Held Instructor Econ., Cornell Univ., 1895–9; Prof., Williams Coll., 1899–1903; Prof. Econ., Harvard Univ., 1903–35.

Degrees BA Univ. Boston, 1889; PhD Univ. Wisconsin, 1895.

Offices Fellow, AAAS.

Career His *QJE* paper of 1902, positing a general law of variation of productive forces, is an important contribution to the theory of substitution, then a neglected field despite Marshall's work on it. He presided over the Harvard Univ. Committee on Econ. Res. which owes its fame to the development of the 'three curve barometer' as an indicator of turning points in the business cycle.

Publications *Books:* 1. *The Finances of the United States 1775–89* (1895); 2. *Introduction to the Study of Economics* (1897); 3. *Essays on the Monetary History of the USA* (1900); 4. *Economic Essays* (1936); 5. *Politics, Finance and Consequences* (1939).

Articles: 1. 'The variation of productive forces', *QJE*, 16, Aug. 1902.

BURMEISTER, Edwin

Born 1939, Chicago, Ill., USA.
Current Post Commonwealth prof. Econ., Univ. Virginia, USA.
Recent Posts Prof. Econ., Univ. Pennsylvania, 1972–6; Vis. prof. Econ., School General Stud., and Vis. Fellow, Dept Econ., Res. School Social Sciences, ANU, 1974–5; Prof. Econ., Member, Center Advanced Stud., Univ. Virginia, 1976–9; Vis. prof. Econ., Univ. Chicago, 1980.
Degrees BA, MA Cornell Univ. 1961, 1962; PhD MIT, 1965.
Offices Fellow, Em Soc; Guggenheim Memorial Foundation Fellow, 1974–5; Ed., *Int ER*, 1971–6; Assoc. ed., *Int ER*, 1976–; Exec. Dir., Thomas Jefferson Center Polit. Econ., Univ. Virginia, 1976–9; Board Eds., *JEL*, 1979–.
Principal Contributions Numerous publications in mathematical economics and economic theory, particularly in the fields of capital theory, economic growth, and macro-economics.
Publications *Books:* 1. *Mathematical Theories of Economic Growth* (with A.R. Dobell), (Macmillan, 1970); 2. *Econometric Model Performance: Comparative Simulation Studies of the US Economy*, ed. (with L.R. Klein), (Univ. Penn. Press, 1976); 3. *Capital Theory and Dynamics* (CUP, 1980).
Articles: 1. 'Capital deepening response in an economy with heterogeneous capital goods' (with S.J. Turnovsky), *AER*, 62(5), Dec. 1972; 2. 'Synthesizing the neo-Austrian and alternative approach to capital theory: a survey', *JEL*, 12(2), June 1974; 3. 'Real Wicksell effects and regular economies', in *Essays in Modern Capital Theory*, eds M. Brown *et al.*, (N-H, 1976); 4. 'Maximin paths of heterogeneous capital accumulation and the instability of paradoxical steady states' (with P.J. Hammond), *Em*, 45(4), May 1977; 5. 'On some conceptual issues in rational expectations modelling', *JMCB*, Nov. 1980.

BURNS, Arthur F.

Born 1904, Stanislau, Austria.
Current Post Disting. Scholar Residence, Amer. Enterprise Inst. Public Pol. Res., Washington, DC.
Recent Posts Prof. Econ., Columbia Univ., 1944–65; Chairman, US President's Council Econ. Advisers, 1953–6; Counsellor, US Pres. 1969–70; Chairman, Board Governors Fed. Reserve System, 1970–8.
Degrees BA, MA, PhD, Columbia Univ. 1925, 1925, 1934; Numerous hon. degrees.
Offices Pres., NBER, 1957–67, AEA, 1959.
Principal Contributions Studies of the process of economic growth, causes of business cycle fluctuations, methods of economic forecasting, and policies for managing national prosperity.
Publications *Books:* 1. *Production Trends in the United States Since 1870* (Princeton Univ. Press, 1934); 2. *Measuring Busness Cycles* (with W.C. Mitchell), (NBER, 1946); 3. *Frontiers of Economic Knowledge* (Princeton Univ. Press, 1954); 4. *The Business Cycle in a Changing World* (Columbia Univ. Press, 1969); 5. *Reflections of an Economic Policy Maker* (Amer. Enterprise Inst. Stud. 217, 1978).
Secondary Literature G.H. Moore, 'Burns, Arthur F.', *IESS*, vol. 18.

BURNS, Arthur Robert*

Dates and Birthplace 1895–1981, London, England.
Posts Held Prof. Econ., Univ. Columbia, New York City, 1933–62; Sr adviser, US Foreign Econ. Admin., 1940–5.
Degrees BSc (Econ.), PhD (Econ.), LSE, 1926, 1928.
Offices AEA, EHA.
Career *The Decline of Competition* was a major influence in the USA in disseminating the theories of Chamberlin and Robinson in undergraduate teaching. After World War II, he turned increasingly to the subject of economic development, once again from the vantage point of institutionalism.
Publications *Books:* 1. *Money and Monetary Policy in Early Times* (1927); 2. *The Decline of Competition* (1936); 3. *Comparative Economic Organisation* (1955).

Articles: 1. 'The quantitative study of recent economic changes in the United States', *WA*, 31, April 1930; 2. 'The process of industrial concentration', *QJE*, 47, Feb. 1933; 3. 'The first phase of the National Industrial Recovery Act, 1933', *Polit. Science Quarterly*, June 1934; 4. 'Has competition declined? Reply', *J Marketing*, 3, April 1939; 5. 'Concentration of production', *Harvard Bus. Review*, 21(3), 1943.

BUTT, Isaac*

Dates and Birthplace   1813–79, Donegal, Ireland.
Posts Held Lawyer; Whately prof., Trinity Coll., Dublin, 1836–41.
Degrees BA, LLB, MA, LLD, Trinity Coll., Dublin, 1835, 1836, 1840, 1840.
Offices MP, 1852–65, 1871–9; Leader, Home Rule party, 1871–9.
Career Politician who, as leader of the Home Rule movement, formulated the programme later adopted by the Irish Nationalist Party. Whilst holding the Whately Chair in Dublin, he contributed to the Irish tradition on value theory, initiated by Longfield. His programme for Ireland included major land reforms.
Publications *Books:* 1. *A Practical Treatise on the New Law of Compensation to Tenants in Ireland* (1871); 2. *Home Government for Ireland* (1874).

BYRON, Ray

Born   1941, Sydney, NSW, Australia.
Current Post Reader Econometrics, ANU, Canberra, Australia.
Recent Post Economist, World Bank, 1976–8.
Degrees BEc., MEC., Univ. Western Australia 1964, 1966; PhD LSE, 1969.
Offices and Honours Member, Em Soc; Bowley prize, LSE, 1969.
Principal Contributions Hypothesis testing in context of demand analysis. Testing for separability. Identifiability tests in the context of systems of simultaneous equations. Estimation of large equation systems. Algorithms for handling large social accounting matrices. Linearised estimation of non-linear equation systems.
Publications *Articles:* 1. 'A simple method for estimating systems of separable demand equations', *REStud*, 37(2), April 1970; 2. 'The restricted Aitken estimation of sets of demand relations', *Em*, 38(6), Nov. 1970; 3. 'Testing structural specification using the unrestricted reduced form', *Em*, 42(5), Sept. 1974; 4. 'Efficient estimation and inference in large econometric systems', *Em*, 45(6), Sept. 1977; 5. 'The estimation of large social account matrices', *JRSS*, 142(4), 1979.

C

CAGAN, Phillip

Born   1927, Seattle, Washington, USA.
Current Post Prof. Econ., Columbia Univ., New York City.
Recent Posts Univ. Chicago, 1955–8, Brown Univ., 1959–64.
Degrees MA, PhD, Univ. Chicago, 1951, 1954.
Offices and Honours AEA; Fellow, Em Soc, 1975–.
Principal Contributions A theory of hyperinflation interrelating the effect of price expectations and monetary growth as a source of government revenue. Empirical analysis of the determinants of US monetary growth and its effects on price movements over the long run and in severe cyclical contractions. Monetary influences on cyclical fluctuations in interest rates. Problems of monetary policy in reducing inflation.
Publications Books: 1. *Determinants and effects of changes in the money stock 1875–1960* (NBER, 1965); 2. *The effect of pension plans on aggregate saving* (NBER, 1965); 3. *The channels of monetary effects on interest rates* (NBER, 1972); 4. *Persistent inflation* (Columbia Univ. Press, 1979).
Articles: 1. 'The monetary dynamics of hyperinflations', in *Studies in the quantity theory of money*, ed. M. Friedman, (Univ. Chicago Press, 1956); 2. 'Why do we use money in open market

operations?', *JPE*, 66, Feb. 1958; 3. 'The demand for currency relative to total money', *JPE*, 66, Aug. 1958; 4. 'Changes in the recession behaviour of wholesale prices in the 1920s and post-World War II, *Explorations Econ. Res.*, 2, Winter 1975; 5. 'The choice among monetary aggregates as targets and guides for monetary policy', *JMCB*, 14(4), Nov. 1982.

CAIN, Glen G.

Born 1933, Chicago, Ill., USA.
Current Post Prof., Univ. Wisconsin, Madison, USA, 1963–.
Degrees BA Lake Forest Coll., 1955; MA Univ. Cal., Berkeley, 1956; PhD Univ. Chicago, 1960.
Offices Ed., *JHR*, 1973–5; Member, Nat. Commission Employment Unemployment Stats, 1977–9.
Publications *Books:* 1. *Married Women in the Labor Force* (Univ. Chicago Press, 1966); 2. *Income Maintenance and Labor Supply: Econometric Studies* (with H. Watts), (Markham Press, 1973). *Articles:* 1. 'Problems in making policy inferences from the Coleman report' (with H. Watts), *Amer. Sociological Review*, April 1970; 2. 'Estimation of a model of labor supply, fertility, and wages of married women' (with M. Dooley), *JPE*, 84(4), Pt 2, Aug. 1976; 3. 'The challenge of segmented labor market theories to orthodox theory: a survey', *JEL*, 14(4), Dec. 1976; 4. 'Issues in the analysis of selection bias' (with B. Barnow and A. Goldberger), in *Evaluation Studies Review Annual*, vol. 5, eds E. Stromsdorfer and G. Farkas (Sage Publications, 1980); 5. 'The effect of unions on wages in hospitals' co-author, in *Research in Labor Economics*, ed. R. Ehrenberg, (JAI Press, 1981).

CAIRNCROSS, Alexander Kirkland

Born 1911, Lesmahagow, Lanarks., Scotland.
Current Post Retired.
Recent Posts Head, UK Govt Econ. Service, 1964–9; Master, St Peter's Coll., Univ. Oxford, 1969–78.

Degrees MA Univ. Glasgow, 1933; PhD Univ. Camb., 1936; Eight hon. degrees, 1962–73.
Offices and Honours Member, Board Governors, LSE, NIESR; Wicksell lecturer, 1960; Hon. foreign member, AAAS; Fellow, BA, 1961–; Pres., Section F, BAAS, 1969; Pres., BAAS, 1970–1; Member of Council, Vice-pres., Pres., 1968–70, RES; Vice-pres., Pres., 1969–71, Scottish Econ. Soc.; Knighted, 1967.
Principal Contributions Early work mainly on historical experience of investment and growth, but including an elementary textbook. Later work concentrated on issues of policy (especially monetary policy), and on problems of economic administration, planning and forecasting.
Publications *Books:* 1. *Introduction to Economics* (Butterworth, 1944, and with P. Sinclair, 1981); 2. *Home and Foreign Investment, 1870–1913* (CUP, 1953, Kelly, 1967); 3. *Factors in Economic Development* (A & U, 1962); 4. *Essays in Economic Management* (A & U, 1971); 5. *Inflation Growth and International Finance* (A & U, 1975). *Articles:* 1. 'The relation between fiscal and monetary policy', Keynes Lecture to British Academy (BA, 1981).

CAIRNES, John Elliott*

Dates and Birthplace 1823–75, Co. Louth, Ireland.
Posts Held Whately Chair Econ., Univ. Dublin, 1856–61; Prof. Polit. Econ. and Jurisprudence, Univ Galway, 1859–70; Prof. Polit. Econ., Univ. Coll., Univ London, 1866–72.
Degrees BA, MA, Trinity Coll., Univ. Dublin, 1848, 1854.
Career Often referred to as 'the last of the classical economists', he was the author of what was the definitive statement of the methodology of the classical school in *The Character and Logical Method* ... He showed his ability to apply this method to particular cases in a number of studies, the most influential of which was *The Slave Power*. This analysis of the social consequences of an economy based on slavery did much to influence British opinion in favour of the

Unionists in the American Civil War. His *Leading Principles* ... was an attempt to restore the strength of the classical structure damaged by his mentor's (J.S. Mill's) abandonment of the wages fund doctrine in 1869. It attempted, among other things, to generalise the concept of non-competing groups to both domestic and international trade.

Publications *Books:* 1. *The Character and Logical Method of Political Economy* (1857, 1875); 2. *The Slave Power* (1862); 3. *Some Leading Principles of Political Economy Newly Expounded* (1874).

Secondary Literature R.D.C. Black, 'Cairnes John Elliott', *IESS*, vol. 2

CAMERON, Rondo

Born 1925, Linden, Texas, USA.
Current Post William Rand Kenan prof., Emory Univ., Atlanta, USA.
Recent Posts Instructor Econ., Yale Univ., 1951–2; Vis. prof. Econ., Univ. Chicago, 1956–7; Prof. Econ. and Hist., Dir., Grad. Program Econ. Hist., Univ. Wisconsin, 1961–9; Rockefeller Foundation, special field rep., Latin Amer., 1965–7.
Degrees BA, MA, Yale Univ., 1948, 1949; PhD Univ. Chicago, 1952.
Offices and Honours AEA; Assoc. française des historiens économistes; Tawney lecturer, EHS; Fulbright Scholar, France, 1950–1; Guggenheim Memorial Foundation Fellow, 1954–5, 1970–1; Fellow, Center Advanced Study Behavioral Sciences, 1958–9; Fulbright res. prof., Univ. Glasgow, 1963–4; Vice-pres., 1970–1, Pres., 1974–5, EHA; Fellow, Woodrow Wilson Internat. Center Scholars, 1974–5; Member, Exec. Comm., Internat. Econ. Hist. Assoc., 1974–82.
Principal Contributions Application of economic principles to the elucidation and understanding of concrete historical events and, conversely, the application of historical knowledge to the improvement and understanding of economic principles.
Publications *Books:* 1. *France and the Economic Development of Europe, 1800–1914* (Princeton Univ. Press, 1961, Octagon Books, 1975; French and Spanish transls., 1971); 2. *Banking in the Early Stages of Industrialization* (with others), (OUP, 1967; Japanese transl. 1973, Spanish, 1974, Italian, 1975); 3. *Essays in French Economic History*, ed. (Richard D. Irwin, 1970); 4. *Banking and Economic Development: Some Lessons of History* (OUP, 1972).

Articles: 1. 'Some lessons of history for developing nations', *AER/S*, 57, May 1967; 2. 'L'Economie française: passé, présent, avenir', *Annales* (Economies, Sociétés, Civilisations), 25, Sept./Oct. 1970; 3. 'The international diffusion of technology and economic development in the modern economic epoch', in *Sixth International Congress of Economic History, 5 Themes* (Copenhagen, 1974); 4. 'Economic history, pure and applied', *JEH*, 36, March, 1976; 5. 'Les Origens historiques du sous-développement économique contemporaine', *Mondes en Développement*, 19, 1977.

CAMPBELL, Robert

Born 1921, San Mateo, Cal., USA.
Current Post Prof. Econ., Univ. Oregon, 1952–.
Degrees BA, PhD, Univ. Cal., Berkeley, 1947, 1953; BS US Merchant Marine Academy, 1960.
Offices AEA; WEA; AAAS; Head, Dept Econ., Univ. Oregon, 1963–77.
Publications *Books:* 1. *People and Markets* (Benjamin/Cummings, 1978).
Articles: 1. *Libraries of the Pacific Northwest*, contributor (Univ. Washington Press, 1960); 2. *The Social Sciences View School Administration*, contributor (Prentice-Hall, 1965); 3. 'The demand for higher education in the US, 1919–1964' (with B.N. Siegel), *AER*, 57, June 1967; 4. 'Economics and health in the history of ideas', *Annales Cisalpines d'Histoire Sociale*, serie I, 1975; 5. 'The Keynesian revolution 1920–1970', in *Fontana Economic History of Europe: The Twentieth Century – 1*, vol. 5, ed. C. Cipolla (Fontana, 1979).

CANARD, Nicolas Francois*

Dates 1750–1833.
Post Held Prof. Maths, Coll. de Moulins.
Career Canard's *Principes. . .*, whilst otherwise unremarkable, had the distinction of being recognised by the French Academy, which failed to notice Cournot and Walras. The book is sometimes claimed to be an early example of mathematical economics, but its use of mathematics is in fact confined to some algebraic formulas.
Publications *Books:* 1. *Principes d'économie politique* (1801); 2. *Mémoires sur les causes qui produisent la stagnation et le décroissement du commerce en France* (1826).

CANNAN, Edwin*

Dates and Birthplace 1861–1935, Madeira, Spain.
Post Held Lecturer, Prof. Econ., LSE, 1895–1926.
Degrees BA, MA, Univ. Oxford, 1884, 1887; LLD (Hon) Univ. Glasgow; Litt.D Univ. Manchester.
Offices Pres., Econ. Section, BAAS, 1902, 1931; Pres., RES, 1932–4.
Career His edition of Smith's *Wealth of Nations* (1904) is perhaps his chief monument because of the outstanding quality of the introduction and explanatory notes. However, his work as a teacher at LSE, where he inspired several generations of students, is another source of his reputation. His teaching was not particularly modern in terms of tools and techniques, but it was based on a deep knowledge of the great writers in the subject which also informs many of his books, including his one undisputed masterpiece, *A History of the Theories of Production and Distribution.* The outspoken and commonsensical style of his various works make them still readable and useful.
Publications *Books:* 1. *Elementary Political Economy* (1888); 2. *A History of the Theories of Production and Distribution in English Political Economy From 1776 to 1848* (1898, 1917, 1953); 3. *The Economic Outlook* (1912); 4. *Wealth* (1914); 5. *Money* (1918); 6. *Review of Economic Theory* (1929, 1953); 7. *An Economist's Protest* (1927); 8. *Modern Currency and the Regulation of its Value* (1931).
Secondary Literature A.L. Bowley, 'Obituary: Edwin Cannan', *EJ*, 45, June 1935.

CANTILLON, Richard*

Dates and Birthplace 1680(?)–1734, Ireland(?)
Post Held Banker.
Career Little definite is known about Cantillon except that he was Irish and turned briefly from a successful banking career, mainly in France, to write one of the most outstanding works in the history of the subject – the *Essai . . . .* This was circulated in manuscript for many years after his death and was extremely influential, at least throughout the eighteenth century. However, it was necessary for Jevons to rediscover it in 1881 after a prolonged neglect. His ideas on population, determination of prices, wages and interest, the role of the entrepreneur, banking, and the influence of money supply on the economy are increasingly quoted and appreciated.
Publications *Books:* 1. *Essai sur la nature du commerce en général* (1755, 1952).
Secondary Literature J.J. Spengler, 'Cantillon, Richard', *IESS*, vol. 2.

CARAVALE, Giovanni Alfredo

Born 1935, Rome, Italy.
Current Post Prof. Econ., Faculty Polit. Sciences, Univ. Rome.
Recent Posts Lecturer, Econ. Pol., Univ. Pescara, 1964–5; Lecturer Econ., 1968–72, Prof. Econ., 1972–9, Univ. Perugia.
Degrees Dottorato Univ. Rome, 1957; Libera Docenza Universitaria, 1963; Prof. Straordinario Econ. Polit., 1972; Prof. Ordinario Econ. Polit., 1975.
Offices Member, Societa' Italiana degli Economisti.
Principal Contributions The analysis of the economic effects of consumer credit especially with reference to the cyclical behaviour of the economy. The

formulation of a comprehensive scheme for the interpretation of cycles and growth. The analytical definition (1967) of a dynamic 'wages function' (relation between rate of increase in wages and unemployment) in terms later repeated in the literature. The formulation of a dynamic model of a Ricardo-type economy in which the central problem of Ricardo's investigation – the determination of the rate of profit – finds a satisfactory and general solution. The rigorous clarification of the relationship between Ricardo's theory of value and P. Sraffa's theory of prices and distribution. The methodologically relevant explicit development of the analysis of growth problems in terms of 'disequilibrium dynamics'.

Publications   *Books:* 1. *Il Credito al Consumo* (Utet, 1960); 2. *Cicli Economici e Trend* (Giuffre, 1961); 3. *Fluttuazioni e Sviluppo Nella Dinamica di Equilibrio* (Iscona, 1967); 4. *Un Modello Ricardiano di Sviluppo Economico* (with D. Tosato) (Boringhieri, 1974); 5. *Ricardo and the Theory of Value, Distribution and Growth* (with D. Tosato), (Routledge & Kegan Paul, 1980).

Articles: 1. 'Oligopolio differentiato e processo di sviluppo', *Econ Int*, 18, 1965; 2. 'Aspetti economici dell'evolutione tecnologica', *Annali della Fac. di Econ. e Commercio di Perugia*, 1977; 3. 'Politica dei redditi', *Enciclopedia Italiana*, 4, Appendice, 1977; 4. 'Saggio di profitto e merce tipo nella teoria di Ricardo' (with D. Tosato), *Rivista Politica Econ.*, 1, 1978; 5. 'L'economia italiana nel commercio internationale', *Annali della Fac. di Econ. e Commercio di Perugia*, 1978.

CARDOZO, Jacob Newton*

Dates and Birthplace   1786–1873, Georgia, USA.
Posts Held   Journalist and newspapers ed.
Career   A critic of both Malthus and Ricardo, chiefly on the grounds that their theories did not fit American circumstances. In his view the Ricardian theory of distribution did not sufficiently take into account the potential for

expansion of manufacturing, and the Malthusian tendency of population growth to outstrip the food supply was merely a product of the imperfect social conditions of the Old World. He was a strong supporter of free trade.

Publications   *Books:* 1. *Notes on Political Economy* (1826).
Secondary Literature   M.M. Leiman, *Jacob N. Cardozo* (Columbia Univ. Press, 1966).

CAREY, Henry Charles*

Dates and Birthplace   1793–1879, Philadelphia, Penn., USA.
Posts Held   Publisher and other business interests.
Career   A businessman-economist with a distinctly American view of the subject, his prolific writings concentrated on the harmony of economic interests. This involved a break with Malthus' and Ricardo's ideas on free trade, population, rent and wages. He became an increasingly committed protectionist, arguing in *The Slave Trade* that protection would end slavery in the South by stimulating industry and fostering economic links with the North. His works made extensive use of historical and statistical data, the latter frequently presented in graphic terms. His long-term influence on economics has been slight despite the wide currency of his writings on his own time.

Publications   *Books:* 1. *Essay on the Rate of Wages* (1835); 2. *Principles of Political Economy*, 3 vols. (1837–40); 3. *The Past, the Present and the Future* (1848); 4. *The Slave Trade* (1853); 5. *Principles of Social Science*, 3 vols. (1858–60).
Secondary   Literature   A.D.H. Kaplan, *Henry Charles Carey: A Study in American Economic Thought* (Johns Hopkins Univ. Press, 1931); H.W. Spiegel, 'Carey, Henry C', *IESS*, vol. 2.

CARLSON, John Allyn

Born   1933, Boston, Mass., USA.
Current Post   Prof. Econ., Purdue Univ., West Lafayette, Indiana, USA, 1962–.

Recent Posts Vis. assistant prof., Cornell Univ., 1961–2; Guest Scholar, Brookings Inst. 1967–8; Res. Fellow Econ. Stats., Univ. Manchester, 1971–2; Hon. Res. Fellow, Univ. Coll., London, 1980.

Degrees BS (Maths) Denison Univ., 1955; PhD (Polit. Econ.) Johns Hopkins Univ., 1961.

Offices and Honours AEA; Phi Beta Kappa, 1955.

Principal Contributions Critical analyses of the use of survey data to obtain information about economic phenomena, particularly data on expectations. Identification of empirical regularities between expectations and various manifestations of economic activity. Currently analysing unemployment statistics and data on consumer search behaviour.

Publications *Books:* 1. *Macroeconomic Adjustments* (Holt, Rinehart & Winston, 1970).

Articles: 1. 'Forecasting errors and business cycles', *AER*, 57, June 1967; 2. 'Inflation expectations' (with M. Parkin), *Ec*, 42, May 1975; 3. 'Are price expectations normally distributed?', *JASA*, 70, Dec. 1975; 4. 'A study of price forecasts', *Annals Econ. Social Measurement*, 6, Winter 1977; 5. 'Money demand responsiveness to the rate of return on money' (with J. Frew), *JPE*, 88(3), June 1980.

CARTER, A.P.

N.e.

CARVER, Thomas Nixon*

Dates and Birthplace 1865–1961, Kirkville, Iowa, USA.

Posts Held Prof. Econ. and Sociology, Oberlin Coll., 1894–1900; Prof. Econ., Harvard Univ., 1900–32; Taught at Univ. Southern Cal. after retirement from Harvard.

Degrees BA Univ. Southern Cal., 1891; PhD Cornell Univ., 1894.

Offices Pres., AEA, 1916.

Career A social philosopher of a down-to-earth kind, befitting his early years as a farmer. Free enterprise capitalism was equated in his economic the-

ory with moral virtue as well as national prosperity. His chief work was on the distribution of income and wealth, but he also did pioneering work in the economics of agriculture. A vigorous controversialist, he continued to present his views in articles and through teaching to the end of his life.

Publications *Books:* 1. *The Distribution of Wealth* (1904, 1918); 2. *Principles of Rural Economics* (1911); 3. *The Present Economic Revolution in the United States* (1925).

Secondary Literature O.H. Taylor, 'Carver, Thomas Nixon', *IESS*, vol. 2.

CASAROSA, Carlo

Born 1942, Calcinaia, Pisa, Italy.

Current Post Prof. straordinario Polit. Econ., Univ. Pisa.

Recent Posts Prof. incaricato stabilizzato Polit. Econ., Univ. Florence, 1973–5, Pisa, 1972–80.

Degrees Dr in Law Univ. Pisa, 1964; Libero Docente Econ. Fiscal Pol., 1970.

Offices Member, Società italiana degli economisti.

Principal Contributions Challenged the established view of the Ricardian theory of distribution and presented an alternative reconstruction of this theory, centred on the notion of dynamic equilibrium. Also explored the micro-foundations of Keynes' aggregate supply and expected demand analysis and showed that such analysis is an extension of the Marshallian theory of the competitive firm to the system as a whole: Keynes' macro-economic propositions do not depend on the type of entrepreneurial behaviour which is usually assumed.

Publications *Books:* 1. *Macroeconomia*, in A. Pesenti *et al.*, *Manuale di Economia Politica*, vol. 11, appendix 4 (Editori Riuniti, 1970).

Articles: 1. 'Il problema dell'esistenza dell'equilibrio temporaneo nei modelli monetari', *Rivista di Politica Econ.*, 53, Oct. 1973; 2. 'La teoria Ricardiana della distribuzione e dello sviluppo economico', *Rivista di Politica Econ.*, 64, Aug./Sept. 1974; 3. 'A new formulation of the Ricardian system', *OEP*, 30(1), March 1978; 4. 'Un contributo all'analisi dei fondamenti microeconomici della teoria keynesiana della domanda effet-tiva', *Rivista di Politica Econ.*, 68, Nov. 1978; 5. 'The microfoundations of Keynes' aggregate supply and expected demand analysis', *EJ*, 91, March 1981.

CASS, David

Born   1937, Honolulu, Hawaii.
Current Post   Prof. Econ., Co-dir., Center Analytic Res. Econ. Social Sciences, Univ. Pennsylvania, USA.
Recent Post   Prof. Econ., Carnegie-Mellon Univ., 1970–4.
Degrees   BA Univ. Oregon, 1958; PhD Stanford Univ., 1965.
Offices and Honours   Amer. ed., *REStud*, 1968–72; Assoc. ed., *JET*, 1969–; Guggenheim Memorial Foundation Fellow, 1970–1; Fellow, Em Soc, 1973; Morgan prize excellence in econ., Dept Econ., Univ. Chicago, 1976; Sherman Fairchild Disting. Scholar, Cal. Inst. Technology, 1978–9.
Principal Contributions   The pure theory of capital, especially to the characterisation of efficient or optimal growth and the normative analysis of decentralised intertemporal allocation.
Publications   *Books:* 1. *The Hamiltonian Approach to Economic Dynamics*, ed. (with K. Shell) (Academic Press, 1976).
Articles: 1. 'Optimum growth in an aggregative model of capital accumulation', *REStud*, 22, July 1965; 2. 'A re-examination of the pure consumption loans model' (with M.E. Yaari), *JPE*, 74, Aug. 1966; 3. 'The structure of investor preferences and asset returns, and separability in portfolio allocation: a contribution to the pure theory of mutual funds' (with J.E. Stiglitz), *JET*, 2(2), June 1970; 4. 'On capital over-accumulation in the aggregative, neo-classical model of economic growth: a complete characterization', *JET*, 4(2), April 1972; 5. 'The role of money in supporting the Pareto optimality of competitive equilibrium in consumption-loan type models' (with M. Okuno and I. Zilcha), *JET*, 20(1), Feb. 1979, reprinted in *Models of Monetary Economies*, eds J. Kareken and N. Wallace (Fed. Reserve Bank Minneapolis, 1979).

CASSEL, Karl Gustav*

Dates and Birthplace   1866–1945, Stockholm, Sweden.
Post Held   Prof., Stockholm Univ.
Degree   Dr (Maths) Uppsala Univ., 1895.
Career   Studied economics in Germany and gained his chief fame from *The Theory of Social Economy*, which was widely sold and translated. This textbook was based on his earlier published papers and presents a simplified version of Walrasian general equilibrium theory. Whilst rejecting utility theory and even marginalism, he still gave his work a thoroughly neo-classical emphasis. He was an important figure in the discussion of German reparations after World War I, wrote extensively on fiscal and monetary problems, and examined the problems of unemployment. He stood out against Keynesian remedies for the depression and rejected the *General Theory* in a very critical review.
Publications   *Books:* 1. *Sozialpolitik* (1902); 2. *The Nature and Necessity of Interest* (1903); 3. *The Theory of Social Economy* (1918, 1932); 4. *The World's Monetary Problems* (1921).
Articles: 1. 'Keynes' *General Theory*', *Int Lab Rev*, 36, 1937.
Secondary Literature   K. Wicksell, *Lectures on Political Economy*, vol. 1, App. 1 (Macmillan, 1934). K.G. Landgren, 'Cassel, Karl Gustav', *IESS*, vol. 2.

CAVES, Richard Earl

Born   1931, Akron, Ohio, USA.
Current Post   Prof. Econ., Harvard Univ., Mass., USA.
Recent Posts   Ass. prof., 1957–60, Assoc. prof. Econ., 1960–2, Univ. Cal. Berkeley.
Degrees   BA Oberlin Coll., 1953; MA, PhD, Harvard Univ., 1956, 1958.
Honours   Wells, prize, Harvard Univ., 1957–8; Henderson prize, 1962.
Principal Contributions   Intersection between the fields of international trade and industrial organisation, including the effect of international trade on the structure and performance of national

markets and on industrial policy, the structure and behaviour of multi-national enterprises, export-led growth of national industries and economies, and transnational comparisons of industrial organisation. Other research areas include the effects of regulation on industrial structure and behaviour, the consequences of resource commitments that create barriers to entry and exit, and the effect of market structure on the internal organisation and thus the behaviour of firms.

Publications *Books:* 1. *Trade and Economic Structure* (Harvard Univ. Press, 1960); 2. *Air Transport and its Regulators* (Harvard Univ. Press, 1962); 3. *Capital Transfers and Economic Policy: Canada, 1951–1962* (with G.L. Reuber), (Harvard Univ. Press, 1971); 4. *Industrial Organization in Japan* (with M. Uekusa), (Brookings Inst., 1976); 5. *Competition in the Open Economy* (with M.E. Porter and A.M. Spence), (Harvard Univ. Press, 1980).

Articles: 1. 'International corporations: the industrial economics of foreign investment', *Ec*, N.S. 38, Feb. 1971; 2. 'Causes of direct investment: foreign firms' shares in Canadian and United Kingdom manufacturing industries', *REStat*, 56(3), Aug. 1974; 3. 'From entry barriers to mobility barriers' (with M.E. Porter), *QJE*, 91(2), May 1977; 4. 'Monopolistic export industries, trade taxes, and optimal competition policy' (with A.A. Auquier), *EJ*, 89, Sept. 1979; 5. 'Industrial organization, corporate strategy and structure', *JEL*, 18(1), March 1980.

CHALMERS, Thomas*

Dates and Birthplace 1780–1847, Fife, Scotland.

Posts Held Clergyman, Church of Scotland; Prof. Moral Philosophy and Polit. Econ., Univ. St. Andrews, 1823–8; Prof. Theology, Univ. Edinburgh, 1828–43; Prof. Divinity, New Coll. (Free Church), Edinburgh, 1843.

Degrees DD Univ. Glasgow, 1816; DCL Univ. Oxford, 1835.

Offices Fellow and Vice-pres., Royal Soc. Edinburgh.

Career Successful evangelical preacher and church leader whose interest in pauperism and other economic problems began with his parish work. His successful organisation of a system of poor relief in his parish helped to make him a confirmed opponent of poor laws. His *Political Economy* was not a systematic theory, but an attempt to show how moral improvement could stem from the adoption of particular economic policies. His enthusiasm for the theory of population and the theory of general gluts made him more Malthusian than Malthus. His remedy for over-population was self-restraint, enjoined by Christian education. His gift for describing economic phenomena in telling phrases, of which 'the margin of cultivation' is perhaps the best known, was much greater than the originality of his analysis.

Publications *Books:* 1. *Enquiry into the Extent and Stability of National Resources* (1808); 2. *Political Economy* (1832).

CHAMBERLAIN, Neil Wolverton

Born 1915, Charlotte, N. Carolina, USA.

Current Post Retired. Armand G. Erpf prof. Modern Corp. Emeritus.

Recent Posts Dir. Program Econ. Development, Ford Foundation, 1957–60; Dept. Econ., Yale Univ., 1960–7; Grad. School Bus., Columbia Univ., 1967–80.

Degrees BA, MA, Western Reserve Univ., 1937, 1939; PhD (Econ.) Ohio State Univ., 1942.

Offices Brookings Res. Fellow, 1940; Ford Foundation Res. Fellow, 1957; Trustee, Salzburg Seminar Amer. Stud., 1957–79; Board Eds., *AER*, 1959–62; Pres., IRRA, 1967.

Principal Contributions The development and elaboration of certain concepts permitting the blending of institutional and social analysis with economic theory. These include aspects of collective bargaining and bargaining power; economic counterpoint (the necessary simultaneous tendencies towards equilibrium and disequilibrium, within both firm and economy); the interplay between technical-economic and political-organisation co-ordination within the firm and economy; ingredients of economic planning, and the nature and role of social values in economic systems.

Publications *Books:* 1. *Collective Bargaining* (McGraw-Hill, 1951, 1965); 2. *A General Theory of Economic Process* (Harper, 1955); 3. *The Firm: Micro-economic Planning and Action* (McGraw-Hill, 1962); 4. *Private and Public Planning* (McGraw-Hill, 1965); 5. *Forces of Change in Western Europe* (McGraw-Hill, 1980).

Articles: 1. 'The nature and scope of collective bargaining', *QJE*, 58, May 1944; 2. 'The organized business in America', *JPE*, 52, June 1944; 3. 'Collective bargaining and the concept of contract', *Columbia Law Review*, 48, Sept. 1948; 4. 'The union challenge to management control', *ILRR*, 16, Jan. 1963; 5. 'Some second thoughts on the concept of human capital', *Proceedings of the Twentieth Annual Winter Meeting: the Development and Use of Manpower* (IRRA, 1967).

CHAMBERLIN, Edward Hastings*

Dates and Birthplace 1899–1967, La Conner, Washington, USA.

Post Held Prof., Harvard Univ., 1927–67.

Degrees Grad. Univ. Iowa; MA Univ. Michigan, 1922; PhD Harvard Univ., 1927.

Offices Ed., *QJE*, 1948–58; Disting. Fellow, AEA, 1965.

Career *The Theory of Monopolistic Competition* and Joan Robinson's *Economics of Imperfect Competition* were independent contributions to the theory of limited competition published in the same year. Chamberlin's book was based on his 1927 thesis, and his later work was essentially concerned with elaborating and buttressing his theory. The book turned attention from the analysis of an industry to the examination of the role of the firm. He saw markets as involving the whole range of variables from pure competition to monopoly with competition and monopoly blended in between the two extremes. Subsequent writers were enabled to

abandon models of pure competition and discuss a more complex market in which firms competed through non-price means, such as physical characteristics of the product. The theory of monopolistic competition continues to create controversy even today and there is little doubt that Chamberlin must be regarded as one of the half-dozen most influential economists of the twentieth century.

Publications *Books:* 1. *The Theory of Monopolistic Competition* (1933, 1937, 1938, 1942, 1946); 2. *Towards a More General Theory of Value* (1957).

Secondary Literature R.E. Kuenne, ed., *Monopolistic Competition Theory: Studies in Impact* (Wiley & Sons, 1967); J.W. Markham, 'Chamberlin, Edward H.', *IESS*, vol. 18; R. Robinson, *Edward H. Chamberlin* (Columbia University Press, 1971).

CHAMPERNOWNE, David Gawen

Born 1912, Oxford, England.

Current Post Prof. Fellow Emeritus, Trinity Coll., Univ. Camb.

Recent Posts Prof. Stats, Univ. Oxford, 1949–59; Reader Econ., 1959–69, Prof. Econ. Stats, 1969–78, Emeritus Prof., 1976–, Univ. Camb.

Degrees MA Univ. Camb., 1938; MA Univ. Oxford, 1945.

Offices Fellow, BA; Co-ed., *EJ*, 1971–5.

Principal Contributions Explanation of economic inequality of various types. The unequal experience during the 1930s of different regions and of different types of industry in the UK. Models of personal distribution of income and wealth, using stochastic variables to represent miscellaneous influences. Estimation from time-series and other economic statistics. Bayesian methods. Effects of ignorance and disagreement about the economic future on the working of market mechanisms.

Publications *Books:* 1. *Uncertainty and Estimation in Economics*, 3 vols, (Oliver & Boyd, Holden Day, 1969); 2. *Distribution of Income between Persons* (CUP, 1973).

Articles: 1. 'A model of income distribution', *EJ*, 63, June 1953; 2. 'Income distribution and egalitarian policy: the outlook in 1980', in *Inkomensverdeling en Openbare Financien*, eds P.J. Eijgelshoven and L.J. van Gemerden (Het Spectrum, 1981).

CHAPMAN, Sydney John*

Dates and Birthplace 1871–1951, Wells, Norfolk, England.
Posts Held Lecturer, Univ. Coll., Cardiff, 1899–1901; Prof., Univ. Manchester, 1901–17; Secretary, UK Board of Trade, 1918–27; Chief econ. adviser, UK Govt, 1927–32.
Degrees BA Univ. London, 1891.
Offices and Honours Pres., Section F, BAAS, 1909; Vice-pres., RSS, 1916; Member and chairman of many UK Govt and League of Nations Committees; Knighted, 1920.
Career His early career included successful publications and the building up of a thriving commerce faculty at Manchester. War-time government service drew him from academic life into the Civil Service. His wide knowledge of industry and his theoretical ability enabled him to handle such matters as the return to tariff protection in 1932.
Publications *Books:* 1. *The Lancashire Cotton Industry* (1904); 2. *Work and Wages*, 3 vols (1904–14); 3. *The Cotton Industry and Trade* (1905); 4. *Outlines of Political Economy* (1911).

CHARNES, A.

N.e.

CHENERY, Hollis Burley

Born 1918, Richmond, Virginia, USA.
Current Post Vice-pres., Development Pol., World Bank, Washington DC, 1972–.
Recent Posts Ass. Admin., US Agency Internat. Devel., Washington, DC, 1961–5; Prof. Econ., Member, Center Internat. Affairs, Harvard Univ., 1965–70; Econ. adviser to pres., World Bank, 1970–2.
Degrees BS (Maths) Univ. Arizona, 1939; BS (Engineering), Univ. Okla-

homa, 1941; MA (Econ.) Univ. Virginia, 1947; PhD (Econ.) Harvard Univ., 1950; Hon. PhD Netherlands School Econ., 1968.
Offices Fellow, Council member, Em Soc; Fellow, AAAS; Guggenheim Memorial Foundation Fellow, 1960–1.
Principal Contributions Comparative analysis of patterns of development and systematic changes in the structure of production; estimation of production functions (including the original CES production function). Allocation of resources in developing countries, effect of interdependence and economies of scale, planning models for different types of country. International economic development, the 'two-gap model', effects of limited foreign exchange, role of international capital flows, and international aspects of industrialisation. Distributional aspects of development policy, relations between efficiency and equity.
Publications *Books:* 1. *Interindustry Economics* (with P. Clark), (Wiley, 1959); 2. *Studies in Development Planning* (Harvard Univ. Press, 1971); 3. *Redistribution with Growth: An approach to Policy* (with others), (OUP, 1974); 4. *Patterns of Development, 1950–1970* (with R. Syrquin), (OUP, 1975); 5. *Structural Change and Development Policy* (OUP, 1979).
Articles: 1. 'Overcapacity and the acceleration principle', *Em*, 20, Jan. 1952; 2. 'Patterns of industrial growth', *AER*, 50(4), Sept. 1960; 3. 'Capital-labor substitution and economic efficiency' (with K. Arrow *et al.*), *REStat*, 43, Aug. 1961; 4. 'Comparative advantage and development policy', *AER*, 51(1), March 1961; 5. 'Foreign assistance and economic development' (with A. Strout), *AER*, 56(4), Sept. 1966.

CHERBULIEZ, Antoine Elisee*

Dates and Birthplace 1797–1869, Geneva, Switzerland.
Posts Held Lawyer and magistrate; Prof. Law and Polit. Econ., Univ. Geneva, 1833; Prof. Polit. Econ., Univ. Zürich, 1851.
Career Turning to the study of economics when past the age of 40, he

produced one of the best textbook expositions of classical economics. Though containing no original contribution of his own, the *Précis* . . . enjoyed widespread and justified success. Cherbuliez was also known as an opponent of Proudhon and the socialists.

Publications   *Books:* 1. *Riche ou pauvre* (1840); 2. *Précis de la science économique* (1862).

CHETTY, V.K.

N.e.

CHEUNG, Steven N.S.

Born   1935, Hong Kong.
Current Post   Prof. Econ., Univ. Washington, USA.
Recent Posts   Ass. prof., Cal. State Coll., Long Beach, 1965–7; Ass. prof., Univ. Chicago, 1968–9; Assoc. prof., Univ. Washington, 1969–72.
Degrees   BA, MA, PhD, UCLA, 1961, 1962, 1967.
Offices and Honours   Member, AEA, Mont Pelerin Soc.; Trustees Cal. State Coll. disting. teaching award, 1966; Post-doctoral Fellow Polit. Econ., Univ. Chicago, 1967–8.
Principal Contributions   A conviction about the importance of property rights in affecting economic behaviour has led to an almost exclusive focus on various aspects of transaction costs. Research interests comprise the economic explanation of pricing and contractual arrangements, including sharecropping, bee-keeping rentals, ticket pricing, rent and price controls, patent and trade-secret licensing, and the pricing and contractual structures of various industries.
Publications   *Books:* 1. *The Theory of Share Tenancy* (Univ. Chicago Press, 1969); 2. *Contractual Arrangements and the Capturability of Returns in Innovation: Report of a Pilot Investigation* (Nat. Technical Info. Service, 1976); 3. *The Myth of Social Cost* (Inst. Econ. Affairs, 1978; Spanish transl., 1980).

Articles: 1. 'Private property rights and sharecropping', *JPE*, 76, Nov./Dec. 1968; 2. 'Transaction costs, risk aversion, and the choice of contractual arrangements', *J Law E*, 12(1), April 1969; 3. 'The structure of a contract and the theory of a non-exclusive resource', *J Law E*, 13(1), April 1970; 4. 'The fable of the bees: an economic investigation', *J Law E*, 16(1), April 1973; 5. 'A theory of price control', *J Law E*, 17(1), April 1974.

CHEVALIER, Michel*

Dates and Birthplace   1806–79, Limoges, France.
Post Held   Prof., Collège de France, Paris, 1940–79.
Offices and Honours   Councillor of State, 1838; Deputy, 1845; Senator; Grand Officier, Légion d'Honneur; Member, Académie des Sciences Morales et Politiques.
Career   In his youth a St-Simonian (experiencing imprisonment in 1832), he was, in later life, a respectable professor frequently employed by the French government. The Cobden-Chevalier commercial treaty between Britain and France (1860) is the best known product of this work. His factual work is of the highest standard, much of it derived from his government service. However, his *Cours* . . ., based on his lectures at the Collège, is analytically unremarkable. His later politics were anti-socialist and included determined attacks on the ideas of Louis Blanc, collected as *L'organisation* . . . and *Questions* . . . .
Publications   *Books:* 1. *Cours d'économie politique*, 3 vols (1842–50); 2. *L'organisation du travail* (1848); 3. *Questions politiques et sociales* (1852).

CHEYSSON, Jean-Jacques Emile*

Dates and Birthplace   1836–1910, France.
Posts Held   Prof. polit. economy, Ecole libre des sciences politiques, Paris, 1882, Ecole des Mines, Paris, 1885.
Offices   Member, Paris Institut, Société de Statistique de Paris, Société

International de Statistique, Société d'Economie Sociale.

Career   Engineer-economist in the Ecole des Mines tradition laid down by Dupuit, whose greatest work is probably his published lecture of 1887, *Statistique géometrique*. This is a highly developed series of analytical arguments, touching on a wide range of topics. It overflows with original and striking ideas on statistical demand, revenue and cost curves, location and transportation rates, wages, profit maximisation, market supply areas, etc.

Publications   *Books:* 1. *Oeuvres choisies* (1911).

Secondary Literature   C. Colson, 'Notice sur la vie et les travaux de M. Emile Cheysson', Académie des sciences morales et politiques, *Seances et travaux* (1913); R.F. Hébert, 'The theory of input selection and supply areas in 1887: Emile Cheysson', *HOPE*, 6(1), 1974.

CHIPLIN, Brian

Born   1945, Bournemouth, England.

Current Post   Sr lecturer Industrial Econ., Univ. Nottingham.

Recent Posts   Vis. prof., Dept Econ., State Univ. New York, Buffalo, USA, 1979–80.

Degree   BA (Industrial Econ.) Univ. Nottingham, 1967.

Principal Contributions   Main research and publications have been in the area of labour economics and particularly the analysis and measurement of sex discrimination.

Publications   *Books:* 1. *The Cotton and Allied Textiles Industry* (Moodies Services, 1973); 2. *Acquisitions and Mergers: Government Policy in Europe* (Wilton House, *Financial Times*, 1975); 3. *Sex Discrimination in the Labour Market* (with P.J. Sloane), (Macmillan, 1976); 4. *The Economics of Advertising* (with B. Sturgess), (Holt Saunders, 1981).

Articles: 1. 'Sexual discrimination in the labour market', *BJIR*, 12, Nov. 1974; 2. 'Personal characteristics and sex differences in professional employment' (with P.J. Sloane), *EJ*, 86, Dec. 1976; 3. 'Non-convexity of indifference

surfaces in the case of labour market discrimination', *AER*, 66(5), Dec. 1976; 4. 'An evaluation of sex discrimination: some problems and a suggested re-orientation', in *Women in the Labor Market*, eds C.S. Lloyd *et al.* (Columbia Univ. Press, 1979); 5. 'Some economic issues of a workers' co-operative economy', in *The Political Economy of Co-operation and Participation*, ed. A. Clayre (OUP, 1980).

CHIPMAN, John S.

Born   1926, Montreal, Canada.

Current Post   Prof. Econ., Univ. Minnesota, USA, 1960–.

Recent Posts   Post-doctoral Fellow in Polit. Econ., Univ. Chicago, 1950–1; Ass. prof. Econ., Harvard Univ., 1951–5; Assoc. prof. Econ., Univ. Minnesota, 1955–60; Vis. prof. Econ., Harvard Univ., 1966–7.

Degrees   BA (Econ. and Political Science), MA (Econ. and Political Science), McGill Univ., 1947, 1948; PhD (Polit. Econ.), Johns Hopkins Univ., 1951.

Offices and Honours   Assoc. ed., *Em*, 1956–69; Fellow, Member Council, Em Soc, 1957, 1976–7, 1981–; Co-ed., ed. *J Int E*, 1971–6, 1977–; Fellow, Center Advanced Study Behavioral Sciences, Stanford, Cal., 1972–3; Fellow, ASA, 1974; Fellow, AAAS, 1979; Assoc. ed., *Canadian J Stats*, 1980–; Simon Guggenheim Foundation Fellow, 1980–1; James Murray Luck award NAS, 1981.

Principal Contributions   Multi-sectoral extension of Keynesian multiplier. Contributions to utility and portfolio theory. Synthesis of international trade theory. Development of the theory of international capital movements and their effects on terms of trade and exchange rates. A model of competitive equilibrium under increasing returns to scale with accompanying tax-subsidy scheme. Analysis of internal-rate-of-return criterion in the context of a renewal model of economic growth. Derivation of conditions for aggregation of preferences and (with J.C. Moore) for validity of conventional welfare measures. Introduction of minimum-bias and minimum-mean-square error estimation and the theory of best approximate aggregation, with application to econometric models of international trade.

Publications *Books:* 1. *The theory of Intersectoral Money Flows and Income Formation* (Johns Hopkins Univ. Press, 1951); 2. *Preferences, Utility and Demand* (with L. Hurwicz *et al.*), (Harcourt Brace Jovanovich, 1971); 3. *Flexible Exchange Rates and the Balance of Payments: Essays in Memory of Egon Sohmen*, ed. (with C.P. Kindleberger), (N-H, 1980).
Articles: 1. 'On least squares with insufficient observations', *JASA*, 59, 1964; 2. 'A survey of the theory of international trade: Pts 1–3', *Em*, 33–34, July, Oct. 1965, Jan. 1966; 3. 'External economies of scale and competitive equilibrium', *QJE*, 84(3), Aug. 1970; 4. 'A renewal model of economic growth: the discrete case', in *Mathematical Topics in Economic Theory and Computation*, eds R.H. Day and S.M. Robinson (SIAM Publications, 1972); 5. 'Estimation and aggregation in econometrics: an application of the theory of generalized inverses', in *Generalized Inverses and Applications*, ed. M.Z. Nashed (Academic Press, 1976).

CHISWICK, Barry R.

Born 1942, New York City, NY, USA.
Current Post Res. prof., Dept. Econ., Survey Res. Laboratory, Univ. Illinois, Chicago, USA, 1978–.
Recent Posts Ass. prof., Assoc. prof., UCLA, 1966–71; Assoc. prof., Columbia Univ., 1969–71; Res. analyst, NBER, 1970–3; Prof., Grad. Center, Queens Coll., NY, 1971–5; Sr staff economist, US President's Council Econ. Advisers, 1973–7; Sr Fellow, Hoover Inst., Stanford Univ., 1977–8.
Degrees BA Brooklyn Coll., 1962; MA, PhD (with distinction), Columbia Univ., 1964, 1967.
Offices and Honours Member, ASA, 1962–, ASA Nat. Council, 1976–7, ASA Census Advisory Comm., 1980–3; Member, AEA, 1965–; Ford Foundation Doctoral Dissertation Fellowship, 1964–5.

Principal Contributions Instrumental in development and application of 'human capital earnings function', a standard technique for analysis of earnings. Pioneering research on relationship between human capital and the distribution of earnings. Pioneering research on determinants of earnings and occupational mobility of immigrants and their impact on the labour market. Analyses of the relative economic position of racial and ethnic minorities. Developed first model of supply and demand for nursing home care. Analyses of effects of public policies (labour market programmes, income transfers, health, immigration) on earnings, employment and 'induced unemployment'.

Publications *Books:* 1. *Income Inequality: Regional Analyses Within a Human Capital Framework* (NBER, 1974); 2. *Statistics and Econometrics* (with S. Chiswick), (Univ. Park Press, 1975); 3. *Human Resources and Income Distribution: Issues and Policies*, ed. (with J. O'Neill), (Norton, 1977); 4. *US Immigration Issues and Policies*, ed. (Amer. Enterprise Inst., 1981).
Articles: 1. 'Time series changes in income inequality in the United States since 1939, with projections to 1985' (with J. Mincer), *JPE*, Pt 2, 80(3), May/June 1972; 2. 'Racial discrimination in the labor market: a test of alternative hypotheses', *JPE*, 81(6), Nov./Dec. 1973; 3. 'The demand for nursing home care: an analysis of the substitution between institutional and non-institutional care', *JHR*, 11(3), Summer 1976; 4. 'The effect of Americanization on the earnings of foreign-born men', *JPE*, 86(5), Oct. 1978; 5. 'The economic progress of immigrants: some apparently universal patterns' in *Contemporary economic problems*, ed. W. Fellner, (Amer. Enterprise Inst., 1979).

CHOW, Gregory

Born 1929, Macau, S. China.
Current Post Prof. Econ., Dir., Econometric Res. Program, Princeton Univ., NJ, USA.
Recent Posts Staff member, Manager Econ. Models, IBM Res. Center,

Yorktown Heights, New York, 1962–70; Vis. prof., Cornell Univ., 1964–5; Adjunct prof., Columbia Univ., 1965–71; Academia Sinica, Lecturer, Taiwan Univ., 1966; Vis. prof., Harvard Univ., 1967.

Degrees BA (Econ.) Cornell Univ., 1951; MA (Econ.), PhD, Univ. Chicago, 1952, 1955.

Offices Fellow, Em Soc, ASA, Academia Sinica; Adviser, Econ. Planning Council, Taiwan; Chairman, AEA Comm. Exchanges with People's Republic China; Board Eds., *AER*, 1970–2; Assoc. ed., *REStat*, 1972–, *Int ER*, 1972–; Member, Ed. Board, *Annals Econ. Social Measurement* 1972–8; Co-ed., *JED*, 1978–; Pres., Soc. Econ. Dynamics Control, 1979–; Chief ed. econ., *Science Technology Review* (in Chinese), 1980–.

Principal Contributions Pioneered in the study of the demand for consumer durables (including automobiles) and for computers. Conducted empirical studies in macro-economics, including the demand for money and the modelling of the macro-economy of the United States. Contributed to econometric methods, including the 'Chow-test' of stability of regression coefficients; methods to estimate systems of simultaneous equations; an information criterion for the selection of econometric models; and the estimation of econometric models under rational expectations. Developed stochastic control methods and pioneered in the study of stabilisation policies and economic planning using these methods.

Publications *Books:* 1. *Demand for Automobiles in the United States: A Study in Consumer Durables* (N-H, 1957; Spanish transl., 1965); 2. *Analysis and Control of Dynamic Economic Systems* (Wiley, 1975); 3. *Econometric Analysis by Control Methods* (Wiley, 1981).
Articles: 1. 'Tests of equality between sets of coefficients in two linear regressions', *Em*, 28, July 1960; 2. 'Multiplier, accelerator, and liquidity preference in the determination of national income in the United States', *REStat*, 44(1), Feb. 1967; 3. 'Technological change and the demand for computers', *AER*, 57(5), Dec. 1967; 4. 'Effect of uncertainty on

optimal control policies', *Int ER*, 14(3), Oct. 1973; 5. 'Estimation of rational expectations models', *JED*, 2, 1980.

CHRIST, Carl Finley

Born 1923, Chicago, Ill., USA.
Current Post Abram G. Huttler prof. Econ., Johns Hopkins Univ., Baltimore, USA.

Recent Posts Assoc. prof., Univ. Chicago, 1955–61; Vis. prof., Univ. Tokyo, 1959; Keynes vis. prof., Univ. Essex, 1966–7; Prof., Johns Hopkins Univ., 1961–; Consultant, Fed. Reserve System, 1979.

Degrees BA Colorado Coll., 1942; BS (Physics), PhD (Econ.), Univ. Chicago, 1943, 1950.

Offices and Honours Phi Beta Kappa, 1943; US-SSRC Fellow, 1948–50; Senior Fulbright Res. Scholar, Univ. Camb., 1954–5; Fellow, Center Advanced Study Behavioral Sciences, 1960–1; Fellow, 1967–, Council member, 1976–, Em Soc; Fellow, ASA, 1970–; Member, Board, NBER, 1975–; Vice-pres., AEA, 1980.

Principal Contributions Econometrics, including a textbook; the testing and evaluation of econometric equations and models, especially by checking how well they describe subsequent data; macro-economic theory, especially the role of the government budget restraint in affecting the stability and equilibrium of macro-economic models under various types of policy change; and the evaluation of US macro-economic policy since World War II.

Publications *Books:* 1. *Econometric Models and Methods* (Wiley, 1966).
Articles: 1. 'Judging the performance of econometric models of the US economy', *Int ER*, 16, Feb. 1975, reprinted in *Econometric Model Performance: Comparative Simulation Studies of the US Economy*, eds L.R. Klein and E. Burmeister (Univ. Penn. Press, 1976); 2. 'Economic models aggregate', *Internat. Encyclopedia of Stats*, vol. 1 (Free Press, 1978), reprinted with postscript from *IESS*, vol. 4 (1968); 3. 'On fiscal and monetary policies and the government budget restraint', *AER*, 69(4), Sept. 1979; 4. 'Regression when each of

two variables is dependent some of the time', in *Quantitative Economics and Development*, eds L.R. Klein *et al.* (Academic Press, 1980); 5. 'Changes in the financing of the Federal Debt and their impact on the US economy, 1948–90', in US Congress, Joint Econ. Comm., *Special Study on Economic Change, vol. 6, Federal Finance: the Pursuit of American Goals* (US Govt Printing Office, 1980).

CHRISTALLER, Walter*

Dates and Birthplace 1893–1969, Bavaria, Germany.

Post Held City planner, Municipality of Berlin, 1921–30.

Degrees Student, Univ. Heidelberg, 1913–14; PhD Univ. Erlangen, 1933.

Offices and Honours Gold medal, Sweden; Hon. Fellow, Assoc. Amer. Geographers.

Career Following in the footsteps of Thünen and Alfred Weber, Christaller developed an abstract theory of the location of cities, emphasising tertiary activities (whereas Thünen and Weber had focused on the primary and secondary sectors), which reached the conclusion that cities tend to be located in the centre of hexagonal market areas. This theory has had a major impact on economic geography and even as Thünen has been called 'the father of location theory', Christaller has been dubbed 'the father of theoretical geography'.

Publications *Books:* 1. *Central Places in Southern Germany* (1933, 1966).

Articles: 1. 'How I discovered the theory of central places' (1968), in *Man, Space and Environment*, eds P.W. English and R.C. Mayfield (1972).

Secondary Literature B.J.L. Berry and A. Pred, *Central Place Studies: A Bibliography of Theory and Applications* (Regional Science Res. Inst., 1965); B.J.L. Berry and W.L. Garrison, 'Recent developments of central place theory', in *Urban Economics. Theory, Development and Planning*, eds W.H. Leahy *et al.* (Free Press, 1970).

CICCHETTI, Charles J.

Born 1943.

Current Post Prof. Econ. Environmental Stud., Univ. Wisconsin, Madison, USA, 1979–.

Recent Posts Resources for the Future, Washington DC, 1969–72; Assoc. lecturer, assoc. prof., Univ. Wisconsin, 1972, 1974–9; Dir., Wisconsin Energy Office, 1975–6; Chairman, Commissioner, Public Service Commission, Wisconsin, 1977–9, 1977–80.

Degrees BA (Econ.) Colorado Coll., 1965; PhD Rutgers Univ., 1969.

Offices Member Board Eds, *J Environmental Econ., Energy Systems and Policy, J Law E*; Special energy counsellor to Governor P.J. Lucy, State of Wisconsin, 1975–6.

Publications *Books:* 1. *A Primer for Environmental Preservation* (MSS Modular Publications, 1973); 2. *Studies in Electric Utility Regulation* (with J. Jurewitz), (Ballinger Books, 1975); 3. *Energy System Forecasting, Planning and Pricing*, ed. (with W. Foell), (Univ. Wisconsin Monograph, 1975); 4. *The Measurement of Congestion Costs: A Case Study of the Spanish Peaks Primitive Area* (with K. Smith), (Ballinger Books, 1976); 5. *The Marginal Cost and Pricing of Electricity: An Applied Approach* (with W. Gillen and P. Smolensky), (Ballinger Books, 1977).

Articles: 1. 'Benefits or costs' in *Benefit Cost and Policy Analysis 1972*, eds W. Nishkanen *et al.* (Aldine Press, 1972); 2. 'An economic analysis of the Trans-Alaska Pipeline', in *Benefit Cost and Policy Analysis 1973*, eds R. Haveman *et al.* (Aldine Press, 1974); 3. 'Some institutional and conceptual thoughts on the measurement of indirect and intangible benefits and costs', in *Benefit Cost Analysis and Water Pollution Control Policy*, eds H. Peskin and E. Seskin (Urban Inst., 1974); 4. 'Congestion, optimal use and benefit estimation: a case study of wilderness recreation' (with V.K. Smith), in *Social Experiments and Social Program Evaluation*, eds J.G. Albert and M. Kamrass (Ballinger Publishing Co., 1974); 5. 'Public utility pricing: a synthesis of marginal cost, regulatory constraints,

Averch-Johnson bias, and peak load pricing' (with J. Jurewitz), in *Studies in Electric Utility Regulation*, eds C. Cicchetti and J. Jurewitz (Ballinger Press, 1975).

CLAPHAM, John Harold*

Dates and Birthplace   1873–1946, Salford, England.
Posts Held   Fellow, King's Coll., Univ. Camb., 1898–1904; Prof. Econ., Univ. Leeds, 1902–8; UK Board of Trade, 1916–18; Dean, then Vice-provost, King's Coll., 1908–46, Prof. Econ. Hist., Univ. Camb., 1928–46.
Degree   BA Univ. Camb., 1895.
Offices and Honours   Pres. EHS, BA; Knighted, 1943.
Career   Originally an historian, he turned to British economic history under the guidance of Marshall. Both as a writer of broad surveys of economic history and as a teacher he was a major influence on the development of the discipline in Britain. His technique remained that of the historian, but he was nevertheless very much aware of developments in economic theory. By providing what he felt were neutral accounts of the development of institutions and changes in economic circumstances, he provided a basis for future work on themes and problems in economic history.
Publications   *Books:* 1. *The Woollen and Worsted Industries* (1907); 2. *The Economic Development of France and Germany 1815–1914* (1921, 1961); 3. *An Economic History of Modern Britain*, 3 vols, (1926–38, 1950–2); 4. *The Bank of England*, 2 vols, (1944); 5. *A Concise Economic History of Britain* (1949, 1957).
Articles: 1. 'Of empty economic boxes', *EJ*, 32, Sept. 1922, 32, Dec. 1922.
Secondary Literature   P. Mathias, 'Clapham, John Harold', *IESS*, vol. 2.

CLARK, Colin Grant

Born   1905, London, England.
Current Post   Dept Econ. Res. consultant, Univ. Queensland, St Lucia, Australia.
Recent Posts   Under-secretary, Labour and Industry, Fin. adviser, Treasury, State of Queensland, Australia, 1938–52; Vis. prof., Univ. Chicago, 1952; Dir., Agricultural Econ. Inst., Oxford Univ., 1953–69; Fellow, Monash Univ., Australia, 1969–78; Inst. Pol. Stud., London, 1976–7.
Degrees   MA Univ. Oxford, 1931; MA Univ. Camb., 1935; PhD Sacro Cuore Univ., Milan, 1955; PhD (Econ.) Tilburg Univ., The Netherlands, 1962; Dr Letters Univ. Oxford, 1971.
Offices   Fellow, Brasenose Coll., Univ. Oxford, 1961; Member, Academy Agric. France, 1964; Corresp. Fellow, BA, 1978.
Principal Contributions   Quantitative international studies of national products. Questioning of capital investment as determining factor in growth. Study of limitations of taxation and proposals for its reduction. Agriculture in developing countries. Beneficial effects of population growth.
Publications   *Books:* 1. *Conditions of Economic Progress* (Macmillan, 1940, 1957); 2. *Growthmanship* (Inst. Econ. Affairs, 1961); 3. *Economics of Subsistence Agriculture* (with M.R. Haswell), (Macmillan, 1964); 4. *Population, Growth and Land Use* (Macmillan, 1967, 1977); 5. *Poverty before Politics* (Inst. Econ. Affairs, 1977).
Articles: 1. 'Public finance and changes in the value of money', *EJ*, 55, Dec. 1945.
Secondary Literature   H.W. Arndt, 'Clark, Colin', *IESS*, vol. 18.

CLARK, John Bates*

Dates and Birthplace   1847–1938, Providence, Rhode Island, USA.
Posts Held   Prof., Smith Coll., 1881–93; Amherst Coll., 1893–5, Columbia Univ., 1895–1923.
Degree   BA, Amherst Coll., 1872.
Offices   Founder, Pres., AEA, 1888; Head, Econ. and Hist. Div., Carnegie Endowment Internat. Peace, 1911–23.
Career   His earlier articles show the influence of his German academic socialist teachers and show him as a critic of capitalism. His *Philosophy*

. . . was a reworking of these articles. At Columbia his intellectual position gradually shifted towards wholehearted support for capitalism. His *Distribution . . .* again reworked previously published material into treatise form and contains the marginal· productivity theory of distribution, which he developed in response to certain writings of Henry George. It also contained his theory of capital, in which capital goods are distinguished from social capital, with the marginal productivity of social capital, not of specific capital goods, determining the role of interest. This involved him in lively controversy with various contemporaries, particularly Böhm-Bawerk. His later *Essentials* ... contained his attempt to move from what he considered the static analysis of his earlier work to a more dynamic model.

Publications *Books:* 1. *The Philosophy of Wealth* (1885); 2. *The Distribution of Wealth* (1899); 3. *Essentials of Economic Theory* (1907).

Secondary Literature A.H. Clark and J.M. Clark, *John Bates Clark: A Memorial* (Columbia Univ. Press, 1938); G.J. Stigler, *Production and Distribution Theories* (Macmillan, 1941); J.M. Clark, 'Clark, John Bates', *IESS*, vol. 2.

CLARK, John Maurice*

Dates and Birthplace 1884–1963, Massachusetts, USA.

Posts Held Assoc. prof. Econ., Amherst, 1910–5; Prof., Univ. Chicago, 1915–26; Prof. Econ., Columbia Univ., 1926–57.

Degrees BA, Amherst Coll., 1905; MA, PhD, Columbia Univ., 1906, 1910.

Offices and Honours Pres., AEA, 1922; F.A. Walker medal, AEA, 1952.

Career Son of John Bates Clark and his successor in the search for an understanding of the dynamic elements in economics. Despite his thorough acquaintance with the techniques of abstract analysis, he chose to express his arguments in purely verbal terms. His interests ranged widely within economics and he published on the business cycle (inventing the acceleration principle), economic costs of war, public works, the labour market and many other topics. The chief problem to which he addressed himself was the implications of competition on welfare and public policy. He considered perfect competition both theoretically and practically unattainable and sought to distinguish it from a realistic concept of 'workable competition'.

Publications *Books:* 1. *Standards of Reasonableness in Local Freight Discriminations* (1910); 2. *Studies in the Economics of Overhead Costs* (1923); 3. *Social Control of Business* (1926, 1939); 4. *The Costs of the World War to the American people* (1931); 5. *Strategic Factors in Business Cycles* (1934); 6. *Preface to Social Economics* (1936); 7. *Alternative to Serfdom* (1948, 1960); 8. *The Ethical Basis of Economic Freedom* (1955); 9. *Competition as a Dynamic Process* (1961).

Articles: 1. 'Toward a concept of workable competition', *AER*, 30, June 1940.

Secondary Literature J.W. Markham, 'Clark, John Maurice', *IESS*, vol. 2.

CLIFFE LESLIE, Thomas Edward*

Dates and Birthplace 1827–82, Wexford, Ireland.

Post Held Prof. Jurisprudence and Polit. Econ., Queen's Univ., Belfast, 1853–82.

Degrees Trinity Coll., Dublin.

Career Leslie's published work was entirely in the form of essays, most of which were later collected in book form. Much of his work concerned the problems of Ireland. He rejected Home Rule as a solution, preferring land reform in favour of small proprietorship. The different circumstances he observed in his studies of land systems led him to reject classical methodology in favour of an emphasis on the historical approach and the importance of economic institutions. He was, however, an independent critic and not part of an organised historical school such as that of Germany.

Publications *Books:* 1. *Land Systems and Industrial Economy of Ireland, England and Continental*

Countries (1870); 2. *Essays in Political and Moral Philosophy* (1879); 3. *Essays in Political Economy* (1879, 1888).

Secondary Literature F.W. Fetter, 'Leslie, T.E. Cliffe', *IESS*, vol. 9.

CLOWER, Robert Wayne

Born 1926, Pullman, Washington, USA.

Current Post Prof. Econ., UCLA.

Recent Posts Assoc. prof. Econ., 1957–62, Prof. Econ., 1963–71, Northwestern Univ.; Dir., Econ. Survey of Liberia, 1961–2; John Maynard Keynes vis. prof. Econ., Univ. Essex, 1965–6; Vis. prof. Econ., Makerere Coll., Kampala, Uganda (1965), Univ. Western Ontario (1974, 1977), Monash Univ. (1972), Bank Italy Res. Staff Seminar, Perugia, Italy (1973), Inst. Advanced Study, Vienna (1974), Washington State Univ. (1978–80).

Degrees BA (Econ.), MA (Econ.), Washington State Univ., 1948, 1949; MLitt. (Econ.), DLitt., Univ. Oxford, 1952, 1978.

Offices and Honours Phi Beta Kappa; Member, RES, AEA, Amer. Assoc. Rhodes Scholars; Rhodes scholarship, 1949–52; Guggenheim Memorial Foundation Fellow, 1965–6; Managing ed., *EI*, 1973–80, *AER*, 1981–; Exec. Comm., AEA, 1978–81; Fellow, Em Soc, 1978–.

Principal Contributions Central focus on foundations of standard economic theory. Principal writings worth mention includes early pieces on stock-flow analysis, microdynamics of business behaviour (ignorant monopolists), microfoundations of monetary theory and, perhaps most important, microfoundations, or rather the absence thereof, of macro-economics.

Publications *Books:* 1. *Introduction to Mathematical Economics* (with D.W. Bushaw), (Richard D. Irwin, 1957); 2. *Growth Without Development, an Economic Survey of Liberia* (with G. Dalton *et al.*), (Northwestern Univ. Press, 1966); 3. *Monetary Theory*, ed. (Penguin Books, 1969; Italian transl., 1972); 4. *Microeconomics* (with J.F.

Due), (Richard D. Irwin, 1972; Spanish transl., 1978).

Articles: 1. 'An investigation into the dynamics of investment', *AER*, 44(1), March 1954; 2. 'The Keynesian counter-revolution: a theoretical appraisal', in *The Theory of Interest Rates*, eds F.H. Hahn and F. Brechling (Macmillan, 1965), reprinted in R. Surrey, *Macroeconomic Themes* (OUP, 1976), in *La Nueva Teoria Monetaria*, ed. J. Saltes (Madrid Libres, 1978), and in T. Korliras and R. Thorn, *Modern Macroeconomics* (Harper & Row, 1979); 3. 'Reflections on the Keynesian perplex', *ZN*, 35(1–2), July 1975; 4. 'The anatomy of monetary theory', *AER*, 67(2), May 1977; 5. 'The transactions theory of the demand for money: a reconsideration' (with P.W. Howitt), *JPE*, 88(3), June 1978.

COASE, Ronald Harry

Born 1910, Middlesex, England.

Current Post Retired. Prof. Emeritus Econ., Sr Fellow Law Econ., Univ. Chicago Law School.

Recent Posts Prof., Univ. Buffalo, 1951–8, Univ. Virginia, 1958–64, Univ. Chicago, 1964–.

Degrees BCom., DSc. (Econ.), Univ. London, 1932, 1951.

Offices Fellow, AAAS, 1978; Disting. Fellow, AEA, 1979.

Principal Contributions n.e.

Publications *Books:* 1. *British Broadcasting, A Study in Monopoly* (Longmans Green, Harvard Univ. Press, 1950).

Articles: 1. 'The nature of the firm', *Ec*, N.S. 4, Nov. 1937, repr. in *Readings in Price Theory*, eds G.J. Stigler and K.E. Boulding (Richard D. Irwin, 1952); 2. 'The marginal cost controversy', *Ec*, N.S. 13, Aug. 1946; 3. 'The problem of social cost', *J Law E*, 3, Oct. 1960; 4. 'The lighthouse in economics', *J Law E*, 17(2), Oct. 1974; 5. 'Marshall on method', *J Law E*, 18(1), April 1975.

Secondary Literature K.G. Elzinga, 'Coase, R.H.', *IESS*, vol. 18.

COATS, Alfred W.

Born 1924, Southall, England.
Current Post Prof., Head Dept. Econ. Social Hist., Univ. Nottingham.
Recent Posts Vis. prof., Univ. Texas, 1978, Emory Univ., Atlanta, 1979, Univ. Western Australia, 1980.
Degrees BA (Intermediate) Univ. London External, 1947; BSc (Econ.) 1948, Univ. London External; MSc. (Econ.) 1950, Univ. Exeter; PhD Johns Hopkins Univ., 1953.
Offices and Honours Member, AEA; RES; EHS; EHA; Assoc. Evolutionary Econ.; Member, Ed. Board, *HOPE*; Phi Beta Kappa, 1953; Rockefeller Foundation Fellow, 1958–9; Fellow, Netherlands Inst. Advanced Stud., 1972–3.
Principal Contributions Work on borderlines of history of economics, methodology, and the sociology of the professions. Studies of economic thought and policy and the role of economists in government.
Publications *Books:* 1. *Essays in American Economic History*, ed. (with R.M. Robertson) (Arnold, 1969); 2. *Classical Economists and Economic Policy*, ed. (Methuen, 1971); 3. *The Marginal Revolution in Economics*, ed. (with R.D.C. Black and C.D. Goodwin), (Duke Univ. Press, 1972); 4. *Revista Española de Economia, El Papel del Economista en la Administracion Publica*, ed. (Liberos, 1979); 5. *Economists in Government: an International Comparative Study*, ed. (Duke Univ. Press, 1981).
Articles: 1. 'Changing attitudes to labour in the mid-eighteenth century', *EHR*, 2(11), Aug. 1958, reprinted in *Essays in Social History*, eds M.W. Flinn and T.C. Smout (OUP, 1974); 2. 'The American Economic Association, 1904–1929', *AER*, 54(3), June 1964; 3. 'Political economy and the tariff reform campaign of 1903', *J Law E*, 11, April 1968; 4. 'The role of scholarly journals in the history of economics: an essay', *JEL*, 9(1), March 1971; 5. 'The culture and the economists: American-British differences', *HOPE*, 12(4), 1980.

COBDEN, Richard*

Dates and Birthplace 1804–65, Sussex, England.
Posts Held Businessman; MP for Stockport, West Riding and Rochdale.
Career Self-made and largely self-educated, his campaign for free trade in corn through the Anti-Corn Law League (founded 1838) made him the most famous advocate of *laissez faire* policies. His activities in parliament and public lectures helped towards the repeal of the Corn Laws in 1846. He was an outspoken opponent of aggressive foreign policy and involvement in war, arranging the 1860 trade treaty with France and supporting the case of the North in the American Civil War. He has no claim as a contributor to the development of economic ideas but a great claim as a populariser and political user of economic concepts. The Manchester base of the League led to the use of the phrase 'Manchester School' (coined by Disraeli) for free trade liberalism in politics and economic thought.
Publications *Books:* 1. *Speeches on Questions of Public Policy* (1870).
Secondary Literature W.D. Grampp, *The Manchester School of Economics* (Stanford Univ. Press, 1960).

CODDINGTON, Alan*

Dates and Birthplace 1941–82, Doncaster, England.
Posts Held Sir Ellis Hunter Memorial Fellow Econ., Univ. York, 1965–6; Ass. lecturer Econ., 1966–7, Lecturer Econ., 1967–75; Sr lecturer Econ., 1975–7, Reader Econ., 1977–9, Prof. Econ., 1981–82, Queen Mary Coll.; Hallsworth Fellow Polit. Econ., Univ. Manchester, 1974–5.
Degrees BSc. Univ. Leeds, 1963; DPhil. Univ. York, 1966.
Offices Member, RES, 1972–82, Inst. Fiscal Stud., 1979–82.
Career Development of the theory of bargaining processes; assessment of the influence of positivist ideas on methodological discussion in economics; assessment of the methodological status of the theory of general competitive equilib-

rium; and investigation of the analytical foundations of Keynesian economics.

Publications Books: 1. *Theories of the Bargaining Process* (A & U, 1968). *Articles:* 1. 'Positive economics', *CJE*, 5(1), Feb. 1972; 2. 'Creaking semaphore and beyond', *British J Philosophy Science*, 26, 1975; 3. 'The rationale of general equilibrium theory', *EI*, 13(4), Dec. 1975; 4. 'Keynesian economics: the search for first principles', *JEL*, 14(4), Dec. 1976; 5. 'Hicks' contribution to Keynesian economics', *JEL*, 17(3), Sept. 1979.

COEN, Robert M.

Born 1939, Columbus, Ohio, USA.
Current Post Prof. Econ., Northwestern Univ., Evanston, Ill., USA.
Recent Posts Ass. prof. Econ., Stanford Univ., 1965–71; Assoc. prof. Econ., Northwestern Univ., 1971–5; Vis. assoc. prof. Econ., Univ. Massachusetts, 1974; Vis. lecturer, Inst. Advanced Stud., Vienna, 1975, 1977.
Degrees BA, Harvard Univ., 1961; MA, PhD, Northwestern Univ., 1964, 1967.
Offices AEA; Em Soc; NTA; Brookings Inst. Res. Fellow, 1964–5; Executive Comm., NBER Conference Res. Income and Wealth, 1973–6.
Principal Contributions Empirical study of the effects of taxation on capital formation. Determination of average service lives and depreciation patterns of plant and equipment. Evaluations of tax depreciation policy. Construction of a medium-term econometric model of the US to study potential and actual growth over a 10–20 year horizon.
Publications Books: 1. *An Annual Growth Model of the US Economy* (with B.G. Hickman), (N-H, 1976). *Articles:* 1. Effects of tax policy on investment in manufacturing', *AER/S*, 58, May 1968; 2. 'Investment behavior, the measurement of depreciation, and tax policy', *AER*, 65(1), March 1975; 3. 'Alternative measures of capital and its rate of return in United States manufacturing', in *The Measurement of Capital*, ed. D. Usher (Univ. Chicago Press, 1980); 4. Investment and growth in an econometric model of the United States'

(with B.G. Hickman), *AER*, 70(2), May 1980.

COHEN STUART, Arnold Jacob*

Dates and Birthplace 1855–1921, The Hague, The Netherlands.
Posts Held Supervisor Waterworks, Java, Dutch East Indies, 1878; Lawyer in Amsterdam; Employee, 1900, then managing dir. of Royal Dutch Petroleum Co., 1906–21.
Degree Dr Law, Univ. Amsterdam.
Offices Member, RES.
Career His attention was turned whilst a student of law to the question of the distribution of the burden of taxation. He reinterpreted J.S. Mill's principle (that justice is achieved when each taxpayer incurs an equal sacrifice) to mean that the sacrifice of each taxpayer should be in the same ratio to the total satisfaction which each taxpayer derives from his income. This permits a higher rate of progression in taxes than Mill's own version of the principle, and was widely accepted in the Edwardian era.
Publications Books: 1. *Bijdrage Tot de Theorie der Progressieve Inkomstenbelasting* (1889).
Secondary Literature F.Y. Edgeworth, 'Obituary: Arnold Jacob Cohen Stuart', *EJ*, 31, Sept. (1921); *Classics in The Theory of Public Finance*, eds R.A. Musgrave and A.T. Peacock (Macmillan, 1958).

COHN, Gustav*

Dates and Birthplace 1840–1919, Germany.
Posts Held Teacher, Riga Polytechnic, 1869–72; Prof., Zürich Polytechnic, 1875–84; Prof., Univ. Göttingen, 1884–1919.
Career His chief contributions were on transportation economics and public finance. On the former, his studies of English railway economics laid the foundations for future treatises on railway theory and policy. He was one of the founders of the modern discipline of public finance. He wrote particularly tellingly on equity in taxation.
Publications Books: 1. *Untersuchun-*

gen Über die Englische Eisenbahnpolitik, 2 vols (1874–5); 2. *Finanzlage der Schweiz* (1877); 3. *Volkswirtschaftliche Aufsätze* (1882); 4. *System der Natiönalokonomie*, 3 vols (1885–98); 5. *Nationalokonomische Studien* (1886); 6. *Zur Geschichte und Politik des Verkehrwesens* (1900); 7. *Zur Politik des Deutschen Finanz- Verkehrs- und Verwaltungswesens* (1905).

Secondary Literature E.R.A. Seligman, 'Cohn, Gustav', *ESS*, vol. 3.

COLE, George Douglas Howard*

Dates and Birthplace 1889–1959, London, England.

Posts Held Fellow, Magdalen, University, All Souls and Nuffield Colls., Univ. Oxford; Chichele Prof. of Social and Polit. Theory, Univ. Oxford, 1944–57.

Degree BA, Univ. Oxford.

Offices Pres., 1952–9, Chairman, 1939–46, 1948–50, Fabian Soc.

Career Developed a brand of socialism, known as 'guild socialism', which sought to reconcile syndicalism and state socialism. As a teacher he inspired several generations among whom were numbered many leaders of emergent Third World countries. His actual involvement in politics was less successful than his voluminous writings. These fell into three categories: factual surveys of world politics and economics, works on economic theory, and historical works. He was also consulted as an adviser by all sections of the labour and trades union movements.

Publications *Books:* 1. *The World of Labour* (1913, 1919); 2. *Self Government in Industry* (1917, 1920); 3. *Life of Robert Owen* (1925, 1930); 4. *Gold Credit and Employment* (1930); 5. *What Marx Really Meant* (1934, 1937); 6. *Principles of Economic Planning* (1935); 7. *The Common People 1746–1946* (with R. Postgate), (1938, 1956); 8. *Money: Its Present and Future* (1944, 1947); 9. *History of Socialist Thought*, 5. vols (1953–60).

Secondary Literature R. Postgate, 'Cole, G.D.H.', *IESS*, vol. 2.

COLQUHOUN, Patrick*

Dates and Birthplace 1745–1820, Dumbarton, Scotland.

Post Held Businessman.

Offices Lord Provost of Glasgow, 1782–3; City Magistrate, London, 1792–1818.

Career Social reformer whose works contain schemes for improved policing, savings banks, boards of education and a national poor rate. He is best known for the very carefully calculated estimate of national income contained in his 1814 work. Arguing that all wealth is produced by labour, his figures showed that the labouring population only received one-fifth of what it produced. His figures were widely quoted by socialist writers.

Publications *Books:* 1. *Treatise on the Police of the Metropolis* (1795); 2. *A New and Appropriate System of Education for the Labouring Poor* (1806); 3. *Treatise on Indigence* (1806); 4. *Treatise on the Population, Wealth, Power, and Resources of the British Empire* (1814, 1815).

Secondary Literature M. Beer, 'Colquhoun, Patrick', *ESS*, vol. 3.

COLSON, Clement-Leon*

Dates and Birthplace 1853–1939, Versailles, France.

Posts Held Lecturer, L'Ecole Polytechnique, L'Ecole des Ponts et Chaussées, L'Ecole Libre des Sciences Politiques, Paris; Inspecteur-général des Ponts et Chaussées, 1908.

Degree Lic. en Droit, 1878.

Offices Vice-pres., Conseil Supérieur de Statistique; Member, Académie des Sciences Morales, 1910; Member, Chairman of Econ. Stat. section, 1923–9, Internat. Stat. Inst.

Career An engineer-economist who published his lectures in book form over a period of years. His economic and statistical views developed in close relationship to each other and railway statistics naturally figured heavily in his total output. He was an important adviser to the French government after 1914 on transport, exchange, commerce and other economic matters. Among the important decisons on which he advised was the devaluation of the franc.

Publications *Books:* 1. *La Garantie d'intérêts et son application en France* (1888); 2. *Transports et tarifs* (1890); 3. *Cours d'économie politique* (1901–7); 4. *Organisme et desordre social* (1912); 5. *L'Outillage économique de la France* (1921).

Secondary Literature 'Obituary: Clément-Léon Colson', *JRSS*, 102, 1939.

COLWELL, Stephen*

Dates and Birthplace 1800–71, Virginia, USA.

Posts Held Lawyer; Iron merchant.

Offices Member, US Revenue Commission, 1865.

Career American protectionist whose analysis of the credit system is probably his chief achievement. He produced a series of reports for the government on taxation and other economic questions.

Publications *Books:* 1. *The Relative Position in our Industry of Foreign Commerce, Domestic Production and Internal Trade* (1850); 2. 'Introduction' to F List, *National System of Political Economy* (1856); 3. *The Ways and Means of Commercial Payment* (1858); 4. *The Claims of Labour* (1861); 5. *Gold, Banks and Taxation* (1864); 6. *State and National Systems of Banks* (1864).

Secondary Literature H.C. Carey, *Memoir of Stephen Colwell* (1871).

COMANOR, William S.

Born 1937, Philadelphia, Penn., USA.

Current Post Prof. Econ., Univ. Cal., Santa Barbara, USA.

Recent Posts Assoc. prof. Econ., Grad. School Bus., Stanford Univ., 1968–73; Vis. assoc. prof. Econ., Harvard Univ., 1973–4; Prof. Econ., Univ. Western Ontario, 1974–5; Dir., Bureau Econ., Fed. Trade Commission, 1978–80.

Degrees BA (Econ.) Haverford Coll., Penn., 1959; PhD (Econ.) Harvard Univ., 1963.

Offices and Honours High Hons Econ., 1959; Phi Beta Kappa, 1959; Harvard Univ. Fellow, 1959; NSF Fellow, 1963; Sloan Foundation Res. Grant, 1968; Fulbright Fellow, 1972.

Principal Contributions The determinants and effects of restrictions on competition, both generally and in specific industries. This has led to studies of the implications of both advertising and research expenditures for various dimensions of efficiency, as well as various aspects of public policies dealing with competition.

Publications *Books:* 1. *Advertising and market power* (with T.A. Wilson), Harvard Univ. Press, 1974); 2. *National Health Insurance in Ontario: the Effects of a Policy of Cost Control* (Amer. Enterprise Inst., 1980).
Articles: 1. 'Advertising market structure and performance' (with T.A. Wilson), *REStat*, 49 Nov., 1967; 2. 'The cost of planning, the FCC and cable television' (with B.M. Mitchell), *J Law E*, 15(1), April 1972; 3. 'Racial discrimination in American Industry', *Ec*, N.S. 40, Nov. 1973; 4. 'Monopoly and the distribution of wealth' (with R.H. Smiley), *QJE*, 89(2) May 1975; 5. 'The effect of advertising on competition: a survey' (with T.A. Wilson), *JEL*, 17(2) June 1979.

COMMONS, John Rogers*

Dates and Birthplace 1862–1945, Hollandsburg, Ohio, USA.

Posts Held Teacher Econ. Univ Wesleyan, Oberlin, Indiana and Syracuse 1890–9; Prof. Univ. Wisconsin, 1904.

Degree BA Oberlin Coll., 1888.

Offices Pres., AEA.

Career Both a theorist and a successful maker of economic policy. His early interest in both the German historical school and marginalism was the inspiration for *The Distribution of Wealth*. In his later theoretical works he developed an analysis of collective action by the state, and a wide range of other institutions, which he saw as essential to understanding economic life. This institutional theory was closely related to his remarkable successes in fact-finding and drafting legislation on a wide range of social issues for the State of Wisconsin. The State became a laboratory for progressive innovations, whose success later gave Commons a similar role at federal level. Indeed, his practical work has been remembered more favourably than his theory which reached its fullest form in *Institutional Economics*. He was also a major historian of American labour.

Publications *Books:* 1. *The Distribution of Wealth* (1893); 2. *A Documentary History of American Industrial Society*, 10 vols (1910–11, 1958); 3. *History of Labor in the United States*, 4 vols (1918–35); 4. *Legal Foundations of Capitalism* (1924, 1959); 5. *Institutional Economics* (1934, 1959); 6. *The Economics of Collective Action*, ed. K.H. Parsons (1950, 1956).

Secondary Literature J. Dorfman, 'Commons, John R', *IESS*, vol. 3; L.G. Harter, *John R. Commons: His Assault on laissez-faire* (Corvallis, 1962).

CONDILLAC, Etienne Bonnot De*

Dates and Birthplace 1714–80, Grenoble, France.

Post Held Private income; Tutor of Duke of Parma, 1758–67.

Offices Member of Academy of Berlin, 1752; Member of French Academy, 1768.

Career Philosopher, educationalist and economist. His philosophical work was based on Locke and Newton, preferring reliance on observation and experience to Descartes' emphasis on fixed principles. His educational work arose from his tutorship of the young Duke of Parma for whom he prepared a systematic course of study. His economics were in his own time, and immediately afterwards, neglected. He stressed the economic interdependence of all occupations and classes, the role of national and international markets, and the significance of competition and the price system when not impaired by monopoly and other restrictions on trade. All this was expressed in the simplest terms he could achieve without losing the capacity for analysis. He was rediscovered by the late nineteenth-century utility theorists as a forerunner.

Publications *Books:* 1. *La commerce*

et le gouvernement considérés relativement l'un à l'autre (1776); 2. *Oeuvres philosophique de Condillac*, 2 vols, ed. G. Le Roy (1947–51).

Secondary Literature J.J. Spengler, 'Condillac, Etienne Bonnot de', *IESS*, vol. 3.

CONDORCET, Marie Jean Antoine Nicolas Caritat, Marquis de*

Dates and Birthplace 1743–94, Ribemont, Picardy, France.

Posts Held Ass. Secretary, French Académie des Sciences, 1769; Inspecteur des Monnaies, 1774.

Offices Member, French Legislative Assembly and Convention; Member, Académie Française, 1782.

Career Distinguished as a writer, administrator and politician, he sought to combine mathematics and philosophy in his writings. Thus he applied the calculus of probabilities to social phenomena including voting patterns. His social philosophy was one of progress, based on a programme of public education. His works include statistical descriptions of different societies and economic analysis, which moved somewhat beyond physiocratic theories to absorb current concepts of collective welfare. His association with the Girondins in the Convention directly led to his death in prison. His application of mathematics to social and economic questions was later taken up by Poisson and Cournot.

Publications *Books:* 1. *Essai sur l'application de l'analyse à la probabilité des décisions rendues à la pluralité des voix* (1785); 2. *Esquisse d'un tableau historique des progrès de l'esprit humain* (1795), transl. as *Sketch for a Historical Picture of the Progress of the Human Mind* (1955); 3. *Oeuvres*, 12 vols, eds A. Condorcet O'Connor and M.F. Arago (1847–9).

Secondary Literature G.G. Granger, 'Condorcet', *IESS*, vol. 3.

COOLEY, Thomas F.

Born 1943, Rutland, Verm., USA.

Current Post Prof. Econ., Univ. Cal., Santa Barbara, USA.

Recent Posts Ass. prof. Econ., Tufts Univ., Medford, Mass., 1970–5; Res. assoc., NBER, 1973–7; Faculty assoc., Joint Center Urban Stud., MIT, Harvard Univ., 1976–80.

Degrees BS Rensselaer Polytechic Inst., 1965; PhD Univ. Pennsylvania, 1971.

Offices AEA; Em Soc; ASA; Assoc. ed., *AER*, 1981–.

Principal Contributions N.e.

Publications *Articles:* 1. 'Tests of an adaptive regression model', *REStat*, 55(2), April 1973; 2. 'An adaptive regression model' (with E.C. Prescott), *Int ER*, 14(2), June 1973. 'Estimation in the presence of stochastic parameter variation' (with E.C. Prescott), *Em*, 44(1), Jan. 1976; 4. 'Rational expectations in American agriculture 1867–1914' (with S.J. DeCanio), *REStat*, 59(1), Feb. 1977; 5. 'Identification and estimation of money demand' (with S.J. LeRoy), *AER*, 71(5), Dec. 1981.

COOPER, Richard

Born 1934, Seattle, Washington, USA.

Current Post Maurits C. Boas Prof. Internat. Econ., Harvard Univ., USA.

Recent Posts Frank Altshul Prof. Internat. Econ., Yale Univ., 1966–77; Provost, Yale Univ., 1972–4; Under-secretary State Econ. Affairs, US State Dept, 1977–81.

Degrees BA, LLD, Oberlin Coll., 1956, 1978; MSc. (Econ.), LSE, 1958; PhD, Harvard Univ., 1962; MA (Hon.), Yale Univ., 1966.

Offices and Honours AEA; RES; Council Foreign Relations; Marshall scholarship, 1956–8; Brookings Inst. Fellow, 1960–1; Ford Foundation Faculty Fellow, 1970–1; Fellow, AAAS, 1974; Fellow, Center Behavioral Sciences, 1975–6.

Principal Contributions The interplay among economic policies of different nations, and the bearing of international market structure on the effectiveness of economic policies showed that as economies became more open, traditional monetary and fiscal instruments of policy became less effective, and 'structural' policies aimed at encouraging investment became more effective in influencing aggregate demand.

Publications *Books:* 1. *The Economics of Interdependence* (McGraw-Hill, 1968, Columbia Univ. Press, 1979); 2. *Sterling, European Monetary Unification and the International Monetary System* (British-N. American Comm., 1972); 3. *A Re-ordered world; Emerging International Economic Problems*, ed. and contributor (Potomac Associates, 1973); 4. *Economy Mobility and National Economic Policy* (Almqvist & Wiksell, 1974); 5. *Towards a Renovated International System* (with K. Kaiser and M. Kosaka), (Trilateral Commission, 1977).

Articles: 1. 'Macroeconomic policy adjustment in interdependent economies', *QJE*, 83(1), Feb. 1969; 2. 'Eurodollars, reserve dollars, and asymmetries in the international monetary system', *J Int E*, 2(4), Sept. 1972; 3. 'An analysis of currency devaluation in developing countries', in *International Trade and Money*, eds M. Connally and A. Swoboda (A & U, 1973); 4. 'Prolegomena to the choice of an international monetary system', in *World Political and International Economics*, eds C.F. Bergsten and L.B. Krause (Brookings Inst., 1975); 5. 'Worldwide versus regional integration: is there an optimal size of the integrated area?', in *Economic Integration: Worldwide, Regional, Sectional*, ed. F. Machlup (Macmillan, 1976).

COPELAND, Morris A.

Born 1895, Rochester, NY, USA.

Current Post Robert Throne Prof. Emeritus, Cornell Univ., USA.

Recent Posts Prof., Cornell Univ. 1942–65; Univ. Missiouri, 1965–8; State Univ. New York, 1969–71.

Degrees BA, DHL, Amherst Coll. 1917, 1957; PhD, Univ. Chicago, 1921.

Offices Fellow, ASA; Pres., AEA, 1957.

Principal Contributions Development of money flows (theory, method and use) now used by almost all national banks all over the world. Other contributions include cross-disciplinary work, early history of economics, psychological studies, etc.

Publications *Books:* 1. *A Study of Money Flows in the United States* (NBER, 1952); 2. *Fact and Theory in Economics: The Testament of an Institutionalist, Collected Papers of Morris A. Copeland,* ed. C. Morse (Cornell Univ. Press, 1958); 3. *Trends in Government Financing* (Princeton Univ. Press, 1961); 4. *Our Free Enterprise Economy* (Macmillan, 1965, Sunshine Press, 1980); 5. *Toward Full Employment in Our Free Enterprise Economy* (Fordham Univ. Press, 1966).

Articles: 1. 'Communities of economic interest and the price system', in *Trend of Economics,* ed. R.G. Tugwell (Alfred A. Knopf, 1924); 2. 'National income and its distribution', in NBER, *Recent Economic Changes,* vol. 2, (McGraw-Hill, 1938); 3. 'On the scope and method of economics', in *Thorstein Veblen: A Critical Appraisal,* ed. D. Dowd (Cornell Univ. Press, 1958).

Secondary Literature 1. J. Cohen, 'Copeland's money flows after twenty-five years; a survey', *JEL,* 10(1), March 1972; 2. J. Millar, 'Institutionalism from a natural science point of view; an intellectual profile of Morris A. Copeland', in *Institutional Economics* (Nijhoff Publishing, 1974).

CORDEN, Max

Born 1927, Breslau, Germany.
Current Post Prof. Econ., ANU, Canberra, Australia.
Recent Posts Lecturer Econ., Univ. Melbourne, 1958–62; Professional Fellow, ANU, 1962–7; Nuffield Reader Internat. Econ., Fellow, Nuffield Coll., Univ. Oxford, 1967–76.
Degrees MComm., Univ. Melbourne, 1953; PhD, Univ. London, 1956; MA, Univ. Oxford, 1967.
Offices Pres., Econ. Soc. Australia and New Zealand, 1977–80.
Principal Contributions Helped to develop the theory of tariffs, especially the theory of the cost of protection, of effective protection, and the relationship between tariffs and subsidies.

Publications *Books:* 1. *Recent Developments in the Theory of International Trade,* Princeton Internat. Fin. Section (Princeton Univ., 1965); 2. *The Theory of Protection* (OUP, 1971); 3. *Trade Policy and Economic Welfare* (OUP, 1974); 4. *Inflation, Exchange Rates and the World Economy* (OUP, Univ. Chicago Press, 1977, 1981).

Articles: 1. 'The calculation of the cost of protection', *ER,* 33, April 1957; 2. 'Tariffs, subsidies and the terms of trade', *Econ,* N.S. 24, Aug. 1957; 3. 'The geometric representation of policies to attain internal and external balance', *REStud,* 28, Oct. 1960; 4. 'The structure of a tariff system and the effective protective rate', *JPE,* 74, June 1966; 5. 'Economies of scale and customs union theory', *JPE,* 80(3), May/June 1972.

COSSA, Luigi*

Dates and Birthplace 1831–96, Milan, Italy.
Post Held Prof. Polit. Econ., Univ. Pavia, 1858–96.
Career Known chiefly for inspiring teaching which formed a generation of Italian economists into a school. He had studied in Germany with Roscher and this encouraged him to take up work in the history of economics. His emphasis was not on any particular view of the discipline but on sound methods. The *Guida* . . . is effectively a history of economics, and for its time it was a remarkable achievement.

Publications *Books:* 1. *Primi Elementi d'Economia Politica* (1860); 2. *Primi Elementi di Scienza Delle Finanze* (1868); 3. *Guida Allo Studio Dell' Economia Politica* (1876); 4. *Saggia d'Economia Politica* (1878).

Secondary Literature A. Loria, 'Obituary – Luigi Cossa', *EJ,* 6, Sept. 1896.

COTTA, Alain

Born 1933, Nice, France.
Current Post Prof. Sciences Econ., Univ. Paris, 1968–.
Recent Post Prof. Sciences Econ., l'Ecole des Hautes Etudes, Paris, 1962–.
Degrees Diplôme de l'Ecole des Hautes Etudes, Paris, 1954; Dr Sciences

Econ., 1957; Agrégé de Sciences Econ., 1960.

Offices Dir. Faculté Sciences Organisations, Univ. Paris IX; 1968–75; Dir. Centre Recherches Pures Appliquées, Univ. Paris IX; 1975–.

Principal Contributions The starting point has been an insistence on the significance of the classical theory of capital. The functioning of the national economy, the global economy and the strategies of large firms and groups have been considered as three stages of a theoretical construction. Recent articles on power concentrate on the way in which decisions within organisations are governed by power conflicts, which intensify in importance as they affect the functioning of national and global economies.

Publications *Books:* 1. *Théorie générale du capital, de la croissance et des fluctuations* (Dunod, 1967); 2. *Les Choix économiques de la Grande Entreprise* (Dunod, 1969); 3. *Croissance et inflation en France depuis 1962* (Presses Univ. de France, 1974); 4. *Le Capitalisme* (Presses Univ. de France, 1977, 1979); 5. *Réflexions sur la grande transition* (Presses Univ. de France, 1979).

Articles: 1. 'Pouvoir et stratégie de la grande firme multinationale', in *The Growth of the Large Multinational Corporation* (CNRS, 1972); 2. 'La Baisse tendancielle du taux de l'intérêt réel', in *Le capital de la fonction de production* (CNRS, 1976); 3. 'Pouvoir et optimum', *REP*, 1974; 4. 'Les Aspects financiers du redéploiement mondial', *REP*, 1, 1981.

COURBIS, Raymond

Born 1937, Alger, Algeria.

Current Post Prof. Ecole Polytechnique, 1972–, Univ. Paris X-Nanterre, 1974–.

Recent Posts Chargé de mission, French Ministry Fin., 1961–71; Prof. Univ. Tours, 1972–3; Dir, Group Applied Macroecon. Analysis, 1972–; Econ. Adviser, Nat. School Admin., 1972–.

Degrees Mining Engineer, Ecole des Mines de Paris, 1961; Diploma Centre Stud. Econ. Programming, 1961–2; Diploma Higher Stud. Econ. Sciences, Univ. Paris, 1969; Dr Econ. Sciences,

Univ. Paris I, 1971; Agrégé des Facultés de Sciences Econ., 1971.

Offices and Honours Prize French Econ. Assoc., 1971; Member, jury 'Concours d'agrégation', 1978–9; Member, Consultative Comm. Univs., 1978–80; Member, CNRS, 1980–.

Principal Contributions Macro-economic theory: introduced into French planning the differentiation between 'exposed' and 'sheltered' sectors, proposed the theory of 'competitive economies' for open economies, leading to the supply-oriented policies of the French 6th and 7th Plans. Recently proposed a dynamic generalisation which unifies demand and supply-oriented approaches. Regional theory: analysis of national impact of regional factors and role of supply in determination of regional growth. Modelling: national and multi-regional models for French economy. National accounting: integration of national and regional accounts.

Publications *Books:* 1. *La Détermination de l'équilibre général en economie concurrencée* (CNRS, 1971, 1980); 2. *Le Modèle FIFI*, 2 vols (with M. Aglietta *et al.*), (INSEE, 1973, 1975); 3. *Compétitivité et croissance en économie concurrencée*, 2 vols (Dunod, 1975); 4. *Les Modèles de prix* (Dunod, 1977); 5. *Construction d'un tableau d'échanges inter-industriels et inter-régionaux de l'économie française* (with C. Pommier), (Editions Economica, 1979, Documentation française, 1980).

Articles: 1. 'Prévision des prix et étude sectorielle des entreprises pendant la préparation du Ve Plan', *Etudes et conjoncture*, 23, 1968; 2. 'Comptabilité nationale à prix constants et à productivité constante', *RIW*, 15(1), March 1969; 3. 'Développement économique et concurrence étrangère', *RE*, 20, 1969; 4. 'The REGINA model: a regional-national model of the French economy', *Econ. Planning*, 12(3), 1972; 5. 'Une reformulation dynamique de la théorie des économies concurrencées', *Econ App*, 33, 1980.

COURCELLE-SENEUIL, Jean-Gustave*

Dates and Birthplace 1813–92, Vauxains, Dordogne, France.
Posts Held Journalist, businessman, and government employee; Prof. Polit. Econ., Univ. Santiago, Chile, 1852–62; retired in France, re-entering journalism and politics.
Offices and Honours Officer, Légion d'Honneur; Councillor of State, France, 1879; Member, Académie des Sciences Morales, 1882.
Career A writer of able works of a practical and factual kind, but with no claims as a theorist. He did attempt some simple graphical presentations which are of interest and used his own distinctive terminology – plutology for theory and ergonomy for applied economics – which gained no currency. His work in government gave him considerable opportunity for the application of his economic ideas, which remained of the liberal, free trade variety.
Publications *Books:* 1. *Le Crédit et la banque* (1840); 2. *Traité des opérations de banque* (1853); 3. *Traité des entreprises industrielles, commerciales et agricoles* (1855); 4. *Traité théoretique et pratique d'économie politique* (1858); 5. *Cours de comptabilité*, 4 vols (1867); 6. *Liberté et socialisme* (1868); 7. *Adam Smith* (1888).

COURNOT, Antoine Augustin*

Dates and Birthplace 1801–77, Gray, Haute-Saône, France.
Posts Held Literary adviser, tutor, household of Marshall St-Cyr, 1823–33; Prof. Maths, Univ. Lyons, 1830–1; Admin. posts, Académie de Grenoble, 1835, Univ. and Académie, Dijon, 1854–62.
Degrees Licentiate sciences, Paris, 1823; Dr sciences, 1829.
Career Beginning as a mathematician, he applied mathematics first to economic questions and then to a general philosophy of the world. His theory of markets and prices and his 'law of demand' in *Recherches . . .* is so devised as to be empirically testable, and is hence a genuine contribution to econometrics. By retaining the element of uncertainty in his argument, he avoided the pitfall of seeming to give economics too great a precision by its expression in mathematical terms. His theory of markets was revolutionary in that it began with the consideration of monopoly and moved by successive stages through duopoly and oligopoly to perfect competition. In this, and numerous other features, his work could only be truly appreciated long after his death.
Publications *Books:* 1. *Recherches sur les principes mathématiques de la théorie des richesses* (1838), Eng. transl., ed. I. Fisher, (1929, 1960); 2. *Principes de la théorie des richesses* (1863); 3. *Revue sommaire des doctrines économiques* (1877).
Secondary Literature F.Y. Edgeworth, 'Antoine Augustin Cournot', *Palgrave's Dictionary Polit. Econ.*, vol 1, ed. R.H.I. Palgrave (Kelley, 1963); H. Guitton, 'Cournot, Antoine Augustin', *IESS*, vol 3.

CRAGG, John G.

Born 1937, Toronto, Canada.
Current Post Prof., Head, Dept Econ., Univ. British Columbia, Canada.
Recent Posts Ass. prof., Univ. Chicago, 1964–7; Dir. Res., Canadian Prices and Incomes Commission, 1969–71.
Degrees BA McGill Univ., 1958; BA Univ. Camb., 1960; PhD Princeton Univ., 1965.
Principal Contributions Showed by Monte Carlo investigation of the small sample properties of simultaneous equations estimators that only weak general rankings were evident and even these depend on exact structure used. Participated in initial application of discrete choice models and multi-nominal logic model to the issue of financial securities and selection of durable goods. Developed some models for limited dependent variables widening the scope of tobit-type models. Examined nature of security analysts' forecasts and their role in security valuation.
Publications *Books:* 1. *Wage Changes and Labor Flows in Canada* (Information Canada, 1973).

Articles: 1. 'On the sensitivity of simultaneous-equation estimators to the stochastic assumptions of the models', *JASA*, 61(1), March 1966; 2. 'On the relative small-sample properties of several structural-equation estimators', *Em*, 35(1), Jan. 1967; 3. 'Expectations and the structure of share prices' (with B.G. Malkiel), *AER*, 60(4), Sept. 1970; 4. 'The issuing of corporate securities' (with N.D. Baxter), *JPE*, 78(6), Dec. 1970; 5. 'Some statistical models for limited dependent variables with application to the demand for durable goods', *Em*, 39(5), Sept. 1971.

CULBERTSON, John M.

Born 1921, Detroit, Mich., USA.
Current Post Prof. Econ., Univ. Wisconsin, Madison, USA.
Recent Posts N.e.
Degrees BA, MA, PhD, Univ. Michigan, 1946, 1947, 1956.
Principal Contributions The development of a scientific economics that explains the performances of economies within a cause-and-effect framework as determined by their circumstances, structures, and processes. Scientific economics contrasts with the now-dominant 'economic theory', which uses assumptions and hypothetical cases to define 'principles' and 'optimal equilibrium positions' that implicitly derive from preconception and ideology.
Publications *Books:* 1. *Full Employment or Stagnation?* (McGraw-Hill, 1964); 2. *Macroeconomic Theory and Stabilization Policy* (McGraw-Hill, 1968); 3. *Economic Development: An Ecological Approach* (Knopf, 1971); 4. *Money and Banking* (McGraw-Hill, 1972, 1977); 5. *Public Finance and Stabilization Policy: Essays in Honor of Richard A. Musgrave*, ed. (with W. Smith), (N-H, 1974).
Articles: 1. 'The term structure of interest rates', *QJE*, 71, Nov. 1957; 2. 'A positive debt management program', *REStat*, 41, May 1959; 3. 'The interest rate structure; towards completion of the classical system', in *The Theory of Interest Rates*, eds F.H. Hahn and F.P.R. Brechling (Macmillan, 1965); 4. 'Ecology, economics, and the quality of life', in *Historical Ecology; Essays on Environment and Social Change*, ed. L.J. Bilsky, (Kennikat Press, 1980); 5. 'Interest rates in a naturalistic economics', *Economies et sociétés*, 19(2,3,4), Feb./April 1980.

CULYER, Anthony John

Born 1942, Croydon, England.
Current Post Prof., dep. dir., Inst. Social Econ. Res., Univ. York.
Recent Posts Reader, Econ., Univ. York, 1976-9; Senior res. assoc., Ontario Econ. Council, 1976; Vis. prof., Queen's Univ., Ontario, 1976; William Evans vis. prof., Univ. Otago, New Zealand, 1979; Vis. Fellow, ANU, 1979.
Degree BA Univ. Exeter, 1964.
Offices RES; Internat. Inst. Public Finance; Ed. Board, *Bull. Econ. Res*; Co-ed., *JHE*; Chairman, UK SSRC Health Economists' Study Group; Chairman, European Workshop Health Indicators; Hon. adviser, US Office Health Econ.; Scientific Adviser, Chief Scientist, UK Dept Health and Social Security.
Principal Contributions Development of economic theory applicable to social questions in general and health in particular.
Publications *Books:* 1. *The Economics of Social Policy* (Martin Robertson, 1973); 2. *Need and the National Health Service* (Martin Robertson, 1976); 3. *An Annotated Bibliography of Health Economics* (with J. Wiseman and A. Walker), (Martin Robertson, 1977); 4. *Measuring Health: Lessons for Ontario* (Toronto Univ. Press, 1978); 5. *The Political Economy of Social Policy* (Martin Robertson, 1980).
Articles: 1. 'The nature of the commodity "health care" and its efficient allocation', *OEP*, 23(2), July 1971; 2. 'Medical care and the economics of giving', *Ec*, N.S. 38, Aug. 1971; 3. 'Merit goods and the welfare economics of coercion', *PF*, 26(4), 1971; 4. 'Health indicators' (with A. Williams and R.J. Lavers), in *Social Indicators and Social Policy*, eds A. Shonfield and S. Shaw (Heinemann, 1972); 5. 'Externality models and health' (with H. Simpson), *ER*, 56(153), June 1980.

CUNNINGHAM, William*

Dates and Birthplace   1849–1919, Edinburgh, Scotland.

Posts Held Univ. extension lecturer, 1874–8; Lecturer, Fellow, Univ. Camb., 1878–91; Prof. Econ., King's Coll., Univ. London, 1891–7; Lecturer, Harvard Univ., 1899, 1914.

Degree BA Univ. Camb., 1872.

Offices Member, officer, BA, Royal Hist. Soc.; Pres., Econ. section, BAAS, 1891, 1905.

Career He established economic history as an independent discipline in British universities by outlining its subject matter, establishing its methods, and stimulating teaching and research. His advocacy of the historical method in economics caused some controversy and influenced Marshall to revise the economic history sections in his *Principles*. Cunningham initiated a revision of opinion on mercantilism and advocated protectionism as a current policy. In addition to his considerable volume of academic achievement, he was also a practising clergyman.

Publications *Books:* 1. *The Growth of English Industry and Commerce* (1882); 2. *Outlines of English Industrial History* (with E.A. McArthur), (1895); 3. *Modern Civilisation in Some of its Economic Aspects* (1896); 4. *Rise and Decline of the Free Trade Movement* (1905); 5. *The Case Against Free Trade* (1911); 6. *The Progress of Capitalism in England* (1916).

Articles: 1. 'The perversion of economic history', *EJ*, 2, Sept. 1892.

Secondary Literature H.S. Foxwell, 'Archdeacon Cunningham (obituary)', *EJ*, 29, Sept. 1919; R.M. Hartwell, 'Cunningham, William', *IESS*, vol 4.

CYERT, Richard Michael

Born 1921, Winona, Minn., USA.

Current Post Pres., Carnegie-Mellon Univ., Pittsburgh, USA, 1972–.

Recent Posts Assoc. prof. Econ., Industrial Admin., Head, Industrial Management Dept, 1955–60, Prof. Econ. Industrial Admin., 1960–2, Dean, Grad. School Industrial Admin., 1962–72, Carnegie-Mellon Univ.

Degrees BS (Econ.) Univ. Minnesota, 1951; PhD Columbia Univ., 1951; Hon. degrees, Univs Gothenburg, Sweden (1972), Leuven, Belgium (1973); Hon. Dr Law, Waynesburg Coll., Penn. (1979), Allegheny Coll., Penn. (1980); Hon. Dr Science, Westminster Coll., Penn., 1979.

Offices and Honours Phi Beta Kappa; Beta Gamma Sigma; Past-pres., Inst. Management Sciences; Member, Board Eds, *Behavioral Science*; Trustee, Comm. Econ. Development; Ford Foundation Faculty Res. Fellow, 1959–60; Guggenheim Memorial Foundation Fellow, 1967–8; Medal, Hofstra Univ., 1973; Outstanding achievement award, Univ. Minnesota, 1975; Fellow, Em Soc, 1977, AAAS, 1980.

Principal Contributions Development of the behavioural theory of the firm. This work merged organisation theory and economic theory and included significant empirical work. Early user of the computer and procedures for simulating the firm. More recently, involved in the application of Bayesian analysis to economic theory; in the process, new methods for dealing with duopoly have been discovered and the concept of adaptive utility has been developed.

Publications *Books:* 1. *Sampling for Accounting Information* (with H.J. Davidson), (Prentice-Hall, 1962); 2. *A Behavioral Theory of the Firm* (with J.G. March), (Prentice-Hall, 1963); 3. *Theory of the Firm: Resource Allocation in a Market Economy* (with K.J. Cohen), (Prentice-Hall, 1965); 4. *Management of Non-profit Organizations: With Emphasis on Universities* (Heath & Co., 1975).

Articles: 1. 'Organizational structure and pricing behavior in an oligopolistic market' (with J.G. March), *AER*, 45, March 1955, reprinted in *Price Policies and Practices*, eds R. Mulvihill and N. Paranka (Wiley, 1967); 2. 'Computer models in dynamic economics' (with K.J. Cohen), *QJE*, 75(1), Feb. 1961, reprinted in *Price Theory*, ed. H. Townsend, (Penguin Books, 1971); 3. 'Multi-period decision models with alternating choice as a solution to the duopoly problem' (with M.H. DeGroot), *QJE*, 84(3), Aug. 1970; 4. 'Bayesian analysis and duopoly theory' (with M.H. DeGroot), *JPE*, 78(5), Sept./Oct. 1970, reprinted in *Studies in Bayesian Econometrics and Statistics*, eds S.E. Fienberg and A. Zellner (N-H, 1974); 5. 'An analysis of co-operation and learning in a duopoly context' (with M.H. DeGroot), *AER*, 63(1), March 1973.

D

DARBY, Michael R.

Born 1945, Dallas, Texas, USA.
Current Post Prof. Econ., UCLA, 1978–.
Recent Posts Ass. prof., Ohio State Univ., 1970–3; Assoc. prof., UCLA, 1973–8; Res. assoc., NBER, 1976–.
Degrees BA Dartmouth Coll., 1967; MA, PhD, Univ. Chicago, 1968, 1970.
Offices Book review ed., *JMCB*, 1973–4; Harry Scherman Res. Fellow, NBER, 1974–5; Vis. Fellow, Hoover Inst., Stanford Univ., 1977–8.
Principal Contributions Early work reformulated Friedman's permanent income hypothesis into a general model of adjustment in asset stocks and pure consumption. Also introduced the effect of income taxes on nominal interest rates under inflation and formulated a dynamic model for analysis of the full adjustment to monetary, fiscal and autonomous shocks. Uncovered a major data error which accounted for the previously inexplicably slow decline in US unemployment after 1933. Recent empirical and analytical work has challenged the short-run validity for industrial countries of the monetary approach to the balance of payments.
Publications *Books:* 1. *Macroeconomics: The Theory of Income, Employment and the Price Level* (McGraw-Hill, 1976); 2. *Have Controls Ever Worked? The Post-war Record* (with M. Parkin), (Fraser Inst., 1976); 3. *The Effects of Social Security on Income and the Capital Stock* (Amer. Enterprise Inst., 1979); 4. *Intermediate Macro-economics* (McGraw-Hill, 1979; Japanese transl. 1981); 5. *The International Transmission of Inflation* (with J. Lothian *et al.*), (NBER, 1981).

Articles: 1. 'The allocation of transitory income among consumers' assets', *AER*, 62(5), Dec. 1972; 2. 'Free competition and the optimal amount of fraud' (with E. Karni), *J Law E*, 16(1), April 1973; 3. 'The permanent income theory of consumption – a restatement', *QJE*, 88(2), May 1974; 4. 'The financial and tax effect of monetary policy on interest rates', *EI*, 13(2), June 1975; 5. 'Three-and-a-half million US employees have been mislaid: or, an explanation of unemployment, 1934–41', *JPE*, 84(1), Feb. 1976.

DASGUPTA, Partha Sarathi

Born 1942, Dacca, India (now Bangladesh).
Current Post Prof. Econ., LSE, England.
Recent Posts Vis. prof., Stanford Univ., 1974–5, Delhi School Econ., 1978; Reader Econ., LSE, 1975–8.
Degrees BSc (Physics, Hons) Univ. Delhi, 1962; BA (Maths), PhD (Econ.), Univ. Camb., 1965, 1968.
Offices Fellow, Em Soc, 1975.
Principal Contributions Economic theory with major bias towards normative issues, dealing with capital and optimal growth theory, taxation and trade, development planning, welfare and justice, natural resources, industrial structure and technical change, and incentive compatibility in planning mechanisms.
Publications *Books:* 1. *Guidelines for Project Evaluation* (with S.A. Marglin and A.K. Sen), (UN, 1972); 2. *Economic Theory and Exhaustible Resources* (with G.M. Heal), (CUP, James Nisbet, 1979); 3. *The Social Management of Environmental Resources* (UN, 1981).
Articles: 1. 'On the concept of optimum population', *REStud*, 36, July 1969; 2. 'The optimal depletion of exhaustible resources' (with G.M. Heal), *REStud*, Symposium, 1974; 3. 'Benefit cost analysis and trade policies' (with J.E. Stiglitz), *JPE*, 82(1), Jan./Feb. 1974; 4. 'The implementation of social choice rules' (with P.J. Hammond and E.S. Maskin), *REStud*,

46(2), April 1979; 5. 'Industrial structure and the nature of innovative activity' (with J.E. Stiglitz), *EJ*, 90, June 1980.

DAVENANT, Charles*

Dates and Birthplace 1656–1714, England.

Posts Held Commissioner of Excise, 1678–89; political pamphleteer; Inspector general of exports and imports, 1702–14; MP, 1698–1707.

Career A political and economic writer of considerable literary skill and with a firm grasp of Petty's political arithmetic. The exigencies of financial survival as a pamphleteer give some of his work an apparent inconsistency which lays him open to the charge of writing solely for immediate advantage. His main original contributions were in the theories of money, international trade and finance, and public finance. These were not, however, isolated insights, for they sprang from an unusually coherent view of the relations between the elements of economic life.

Publications *Books:* 1. *A Memorial Concerning the Coyn of England* (1695), and *A Memorial Concerning Creditt* (1696), in *Two Manuscripts by Charles Davenant*, ed. A.P. Usher (1942); 2. *The Political and Commercial Works of That Celebrated Writer Charles D'Avenant*, 5 vols, ed. C. Whitworth (1771).

Secondary Literature D.A.G. Waddell, 'Davenant, Charles', *IESS*, vol 4.

DAVENPORT, Herbert Joseph*

Dates and Birthplace 1861–1931, Wilmington, Verm., USA.

Posts Held Teacher Econ., Univ. Chicago, 1902–8; Prof., Dean, Univ. Missouri, 1908–16; Prof., Cornell Univ., 1916–29.

Degree PhD (Econ.) Univ. Chicago, 1898 (after study in S. Dakota, Harvard, Leipzig and Paris).

Offices Pres., AEA, 1920.

Career A pupil and admirer of Veblen, although his conviction that most economic doctrines were relative did not lead him to the study of institutions. He sought a theory based on prices and excluding the psychological elements of Marshall and the Austrians. He used the concept of opportunity cost and in his avoidance of utility theory pointed in the direction of the indifference curve approach. In many other respects, his writings bristle with indications of later developments in economics.

Publications *Books:* 1. *Outlines of Economic Theory* (1896); 2. *Value and Distribution* (1908); 3. *Economics of Enterprise* (1913); 4. *The Economics of Alfred Marshall* (1935).

Secondary Literature H.W. Spiegel, 'Davenport, Herbert J.', *IESS*, vol 4.

DAVID, Paul A.

Born 1935, New York City, NY, USA.

Current Post W. Robertson Coe prof. Amer. Econ. Hist., Chairman, Dept Econ., Stanford Univ., USA.

Recent Posts Vis. Fellow, All Souls Coll., Univ. Oxford, 1967–8; Vis. prof. Econ., Harvard Univ., 1972–3; Pitt. prof. Amer. Hist. Inst., Professorial Fellow, Churchill Coll., Univ. Cambridge, 1977–8; Fellow, Center Advanced Stud. Behavioral Sciences, 1978–9.

Degrees BA (Econ. *Summa cum laude*) Harvard Coll., 1956; PhD Harvard Univ., 1973.

Offices and Honours Detur prize, Harvard Coll., 1952–3; Phi Beta Kappa, Harvard Univ., 1956; Sheldon Prize Fellow, 1956; Fulbright Scholar, 1956–8; Guggenheim Memorial Foundation Fellow, 1975–6; Fellow, Internat. Em Soc, 1976; Member, AAAS, 1978; Vicepres., EHA, 1978.

Principal Contributions Furthering the development of quantitative economic history. A wide range of topics have been studied, drawn primarily from the experience of the US in the nineteenth and twentieth centuries: the sources of technological change and diffusion of innovations, savings and the accumulation of capital, the economic consequences of slavery, the impact of tariff policies on industrial growth, trends and fluctuations in wages and the cost of living, changes in contraceptive technology, and the spread of family limitation.

Publications   *Books:* 1. *Households and Nations in Economic Growth*, ed. (with M.W. Reder), (Academic Press, 1974); 2. *Technical Choice, Innovation and Economic Growth: Essays on American and British Experience in the Nineteenth Century* (CUP, 1975); 3. *Reckoning with Slavery: A Critical Study in the Quantitative History of American Negro Slavery* (OUP, 1976). *Articles:* 1. 'Biased efficiency growth and capital-labor substitution in the US 1899–1960' (with T. van de Klundert), *AER*, 55(3), June 1965; 2. 'The mechanization of reaping in the antebellum Midwest', in *Industrialization in two systems*, ed. H. Rosovsky, (Wiley, 1965); 3. 'The growth of real product in the United States before 1840: new evidence, controlled conjectures', *JEH*, 22(2), June 1967; 4. 'Private savings: ultrarationality, aggregation and "Denison's law"' (with J. Scadding), *JPE*, 82(2), Pt 1, March/April 1974; 5. 'The effectiveness of nineteenth-century contraceptive practices: an application of microdemographic modelling approaches' (with W.C. Sanderson), *Proceedings Seventh Internat. Econ. Hist. Congress, 1978*.

DAVIDSON, David*

Dates and Birthplace   1854–1942, Sweden.

Post Held   Prof. Econ., Uppsala Univ., 1890.

Degree   PhD (Law) Uppsala Univ., 1877.

Offices   Ed., founder, *Ekon. Tids.*, 1899–1939.

Career   One of the founders of neoclassical economics in Sweden, frequently engaged in controversies with Cassell and Wicksell. His published thesis, *Bidrag . . .*, was both an analysis of capital along classical lines, and an economic theory based on the structure of wants. The book established his reputation and in later years he became an enthusiastic student of Ricardo's writings and editor of Scandinavia's premier economic journal.

Publications   *Books:* 1. *Bidrag Till Läran om de Ekonomiska Lagarna för Kapitalbildringen* (1878); 2. *Bidrag Till Jordränteteoriens Historia* (1880); 3. *Europas Centralbanker* (1886); 4. *Om Beskattningsnormen Vid Inkomstskatten* (1889).

Secondary   Literature   E.F. Heckscher, 'David Davidson', *Internat. Econ. Papers*, 2 (Macmillan, 1952); K.G. Landgren, 'Davidson, David', *IESS*, vol. 4.

DAVIDSON, Paul

Born   1930, New York City, NY, USA.

Current Post   Prof. Econ., Assoc. Dir., Bureau Econ. Res., Rutgers Univ., NJ, USA.

Recent Posts   Ass. Dir., Econ. Div., Continental Oil Co., 1960–1; Assoc. prof., Univ. Pennsylvania, 1961–6; Vis. lecturer, Univ. Bristol, 1964–5; Sr vis. Univ. Camb., 1970–1, Bank of England, 1979; Vis. prof., Inst. Advanced Stud., Vienna, 1980.

Degrees   BS, Brooklyn Coll., New York, 1950; MBA, City Coll. New York, 1955; PhD, Univ. Pennsylvania, 1959.

Offices and Honours   Consumer Expenditure Study Fellow, Ford Foundation, 1956–7; Fulbright-Harp Fellow, 1964–5; Rutgers Faculty Res. Fellow, 1970–1; George Miller disting. lecturer, Univ. Illinois, 1972; Brookings Econ. Panel, 1974; Lindbeck award res., 1975; Bernardin disting. lecturer, Univ. Missouri, 1979; Co-ed., *J Post Keyn E*, 1978–.

Principal Contributions   Development of the concepts and the analysis of aggregate supply and aggregate demand, money and liquidity, the role of financial and goods markets, and the use of time-related spot and forward contracts for organising production activities in a world of uncertainty. The use of these concepts for analysing inflation and unemployment phenomena in open and closed economies. The development of the concepts of user costs and the importance of economic and monopoly rents to analyse the economics of natural resources, e.g. oil and water use and production flow decisions.

Publications *Books:* 1. *Theories of Aggregate Income Distribution* (Rutgers Univ. Press, 1960); 2. *Aggregate Supply and Demand Analysis* (Harper & Row, 1964); 3. *The Demand and Supply of Outdoor Recreation* (Bureau Outdoor Recreation, US Dept. Interior, 1969); 4. *Money and The Real World* (Macmillan, Halsted, 1972, 1978); 5. *International Money and the Real World* (Macmillan, 1982).

Articles: 1. 'Public policy problems of the domestic crude oil industry', *AER* 53, March 1963; 2. 'A Keynesian view of Friedman's theoretical framework for monetary analysis', *JPE*, 80(5), Sept./Oct. 1972; 3. 'Oil: its time allocation and project independence', *Brookings Papers Econ. Activity*, 2, 1974; 4. 'Money as a factor of production: ultimate neoclassical heresy or Keynesian insight?', *J Post Keyn E*, 2(2), Winter 1979–80; 5. 'Post Keynesian economics: solving the crisis in economic theory', *Public Interest*, Special Issue, 1980.

DAVIS, Kingsley

Born 1908–, Tuxedo, Texas, USA.

Posts Held Chairman, Sociology Dept., Pennsylvania State Univ., 1937–42; Prof., Princeton Univ., 1942–8, Columbia Univ., 1948–55, Univ. Cal., Berkeley, 1955–77.

Degrees BA Univ. Texas, 1930; MA, PhD, Harvard Univ., 1933, 1936.

Offices Member, Chairman, Behavioral Sciences Div., Nat. Res. Council, USA; Member, NAS; Pres., Amer. Sociological Assoc., 1959.

Principal Contributions Social demography with an emphasis on the links between demography and economics. The originator of such concepts as 'the population explosion', 'demographic transition', and 'zero population growth'. Latterly, have approached problems like urbanisation from an increasingly statistical vantage point.

Publications *Books: 1. Human Society* (Macmillan, 1949); 2. *The Population of India and Pakistan* (Russell Sage, 1951, 1968); 3. *World Urbani-zation 1950–1970*, 2 vols (Univ. of California, 1969–72).

Secondary Literature W. Petersen, 'Davis, Kingsley', *IESS*, vol. 18.

DAVIS, Otto Anderson

Born 1934, Florence, S. Carolina, USA.

Current Post Prof. Econ., Public Pol., Carnegie-Mellon Univ., Pittsburgh, Penn., USA.

Recent Posts Assoc. prof. Econ., 1965–7, Prof. Econ., 1967–8, Carnegie-Mellon Univ.; Prof. Polit. Econ., 1969–81, Assoc. Dean, 1968–75, Dean, 1975–81, School Urban Public Affairs, Carnegie-Mellon Univ.

Degrees BA (Econ. and Hist.) Wofford Coll., 1956; MA (Econ.), PhD (Econ.), Univ. Virginia, 1957, 1960.

Offices Pres., Public Choice Soc., 1970–2; Fellow, Center Advanced Study Behavioral Sciences, 1974–5; Fellow, Em Soc, 1978; Member, Pol. Council, Assoc. Public Pol. Analysis and Management, 1979.

Principal Contributions Both theoretical and empirical work on imperfect markets especially where externalities are important. A second area has been concerned with public choices including contributions to the theory of public choice and the study of institutions in which such choices are made. A third area has been the evaluation of public policies including contributions to benefit-cost analysis and urban problems. Finally, there have been contributions in the field of public finance both in a theoretical and empirical sense as well as at a practical level where tax and expenditure decisions are made.

Publications *Articles:* 1. 'The economics of urban renewal' (with A. Whinston), *Law Contemporary Problems*, 26, Winter 1961, repr. in *Economics, Readings, Issues, and Cases*, ed. E. Mansfield, (Norton, 1974); 2. 'Welfare economics and the theory of second best' (with A. Whinston), *REStud*, 32, Jan. 1965; 3. 'A theory of the budgetary process' (with M.A.H. Dempster and A. Wildavsky), *Amer. Polit. Science Review*, 60, Sept. 1966, repr. in *Dimensions of Macroeconomics*, ed. S. Mittra,

(Random House, 1971); 4. 'Social preference orderings and majority rule' (with M.H. DeGroot and M.J. Hinich), *Em*, 40(1), Jan. 1972; 5. 'A simultaneous equations model of the educational process' (with A.E. Boardman and P.R. Sanday), *J Pub E*, 7(1), Feb. 1977.

DEANE, Phyllis

Born 1918, Hong Kong.
Current Post Prof. Econ. Hist., Univ. Camb., 1981–.
Recent Posts Sr res. officer, Dept. Applied Econ., Univ. Camb., 1950–61; Lecturer, 1961–71, Reader, 1971–81, Faculty Econ., Univ. Camb.
Degrees MA (Econ. Science) Univ. Glasgow, 1940; MA Univ. Camb., 1950.
Offices Vis. Fellow, 1956, Soc. Scholars, 1974–, Johns Hopkins Univ.; Chairman, IARIW, 1967–9; Ed., *EJ*, 1968–75; Vis. prof., Univ. Pittsburgh, 1969; Fellow, Royal Hist. Soc. 1971–; Vis. prof., Queen's Univ. Ontario, 1975; Fellow, BA, 1980–; Pres., RES, 1980–2.
Principal Contributions Social accounting for developing countries; regional social accounting for the UK; British economic growth; and history of economic thought.
Publications *Books:* 1. *Colonial Social Accounting* (CUP, 1953); 2. *British Economic Growth* (with W.A. Cole), (CUP, 1962, 1968); 3. *The First Industrial Revolution* (CUP, 1965, 1980); 4. *The Evolution of Economic Ideas* (CUP, 1978).
Articles: 1. 'Contemporary estimates of national income in the nineteenth century', *EHR*, II, 8(3), 1956, 9, April 1957; 2. 'New estimates of GNP for the United Kingdom 1830–1914', *RIW*, 14, June 1968; 3. 'The role of capital in the industrial revolution', *Explorations Econ. Hist.*, 10(4), Summer 1973; 4. 'Relevance of new trends in economic history to the information needs of research workers', in *Organisation and Retrieval of Economic Knowledge*, ed. M. Perlman, (Macmillan, 1977); 5. 'Inflation in history', in *Perspectives on Inflation*, ed. J. Heathfield, (Longman, 1979).

DEATON, Angus Stewart

Born 1945, Edinburgh, Scotland.
Current Post Prof. Econometrics, Univ. Bristol, England, 1976–.
Recent Posts Res. officer, Dept. Applied Econ., Univ. Camb., 1969–76; Vis. prof., Princeton Univ., 1979–80.
Degrees BA, MA, PhD, Univ. Camb., 1967, 1971, 1974.
Offices and Honours Ass. ed., *REStud*, 1975–80; First recipient of Em Soc Frisch medal, 1978; Assoc. ed., 1978–80, Co-ed., 1980–, *Em*; Fellow, Em Soc, 1979–.
Principal Contributions The theory of consumer behaviour and the econometric methods for its implementation. Particularly concerned with the comparative evaluation of competing models and the development of relevant statistical criteria in non-standard cases. Applied work on the consumption function, especially with regard to the effects of inflation, on the analysis of rationing, and on consumer behaviour in developing countries. Also worked on aspects of duality with particular reference to the theory of optimal taxation.
Publications *Books:* 1. *Models and Projections of Demand in Post-war Britain* (Chapman & Hall, Halstead Press, 1972); 2. *Economics and Consumer Behavior* (with J. Muellbauer), (CUP, 1979).
Articles: 1. 'The analysis of consumer demand in the United Kingdom 1900–1970', *Em*, 42(2), March 1974; 2. 'Involuntary saving through unanticipated inflation', *AER*, 67(5), Dec. 1977; 3. 'Testing non-nested non-linear regression models' (with M.H. Pesaran), *Em*, 46(3), May 1978; 4. 'An almost ideal demand system' (with J. Muellbauer), *AER*, 70(3), June 1980; 5. 'Optimal taxation and the structure of preferences', *Em*, 49, 1981.

DEBREU, Gerard

Born 1921, Calais, France.
Current Post Prof. Econ. and Maths, Univ. Cal., Berkeley, USA.
Recent Posts Res. Assoc. CNRS, Paris, 1946–8; Res. assoc., Cowles Commission Res. Econ., Univ. Chicago,

1950–5; Assoc. prof. Econ., Cowles Foundation Res. Econ., Yale Univ., 1955–60.

Degrees Agrégé, DSc. Univ. Paris, 1946, 1956; Dr rer.pol.h.c. Univ. Bonn, 1977; Dr Sciences Econ. h.c. Univ. Lausanne, 1980.

Offices and Honours Vice-pres., pres., Em Soc, 1969–71; Fellow, AAAS, 1970–; Chevalier, Légion d'Honneur, 1976; Member, NAS, 1977.

Principal Contributions Measurement of under-utilisation of resources. Characterisation of Pareto optima. Existence theorems for economic and social equilibrium with contingent commodities. Representation theorems for preferences by means of (continuous, additively decomposed, differentiable, or least concave) utility functions. Theorems on the convergence of the core for a sequence of large economies. Topologies on the set of preferences. Characterisation of the excess demand function of an economy.

Publications *Books:* 1. *Theory of Value, an Axiomatic Analysis of Economic Equilibrium* (John Wiley, 1959, Yale Univ. Press, 1971; French transl., 1966, Spanish transl., 1973, German transl., 1976, Japanese transl., 1977); 2. *Mathematical Economics. Twenty Papers of G. Debreu*, ed. W. Hildenbrand (CUP, 1981).

Articles: 1. 'Existence of an equilibrium for a competitive economy' (with K.J. Arrow), *Em*, 22, July 1954; 2. 'A limit theorem on the core of an economy' (with H. Scarf), *Int ER*, 4, Sept. 1963; 3. 'Economies with a finite set of equilibria', *Em*, 38(3), May 1970; 4. 'Excess demand functions', *J Math E*, 1, 1974; 5. 'The rate of convergence of the core of an economy', *J Math E*, 2, 1975.

DE LEEUW, Frank

Born 1930, Amsterdam, The Netherlands.

Current Post Chief Stat., US Dept. Commerce, Bureau Econ. Analysis, Washington, USA.

Recent Posts Sr res. assoc., Urban Inst., 1969–75; Ass. Dir., US Congressional Budget Office, 1975–7.

Degrees BA Harvard Coll., 1951; MPA, PhD, Harvard Univ., 1953, 1965.

Offices Member, AEA, ASA; Chairman, Conference Res. Income and Wealth, 1971–3.

Principal Contributions Empirical investigations of business investment, capacity utilisation, financial markets, metropolitan housing markets, and fiscal and monetary policies.

Publications *Books:* 1. *Operating Costs in Public Housing* (Urban Inst., 1970); 2. *The Web of Urban Housing* (with R. Struyk), (Urban Inst., 1975).

Articles: 1. 'A model of financial behavior', in *The Brookings Quarterly Econometric Model of the US*, eds J. Duesenberry *et al.*, (Rand McNally, N-H, 1965); 2. 'The channels of monetary policy' (with E. Gramlich), *Fed. Reserve Bull.*, 55(6), June 1969; 3. 'The supply of rental housing' (with N.F. Ekanem), *AER*, 61(5), Dec. 1971; 4. 'The growth of materials capacity and the outlook for its utilization', *Survey Current Bus.*, 58(9), Sept. 1978; 5. 'The impact of the Federal income tax on investment in housing' (with L. Ozanne), *Survey Current Bus.*, 59(12), 1979.

DEL VECCHIO, Gustavo*

Dates and Birthplace 1883–1972, Lugo, Italy.

Posts Held Prof. Polit. Econ., Univs. Trieste, 1920–6, Bologna, 1926–48, Rome, 1948; Rector, Univ. Borconi di Milano, 1934–48.

Degree Grad. Law Univ. Bologna, 1904.

Offices Italian Ministry Treasury, 1947–8; Governor, IMF, 1948–50; Member, Nat. Econ. Council, Italy, 1958; Member, Accademia dei Lincei.

Career Monetary theorist whose ideas had a base in the Walrasian theory of money. Published his views first in a series of papers beginning in 1909 and summed them up in the *Ricerche . . .* and *Capitale e Interesse*.

Publications *Books:* 1. *La Teoria Dello Sconte* (1914); 2. *Ricerche Sopra La Teoria Generale Della Moneta* (1932); 3. *Vecchie e Nove Teorie Economiche* (1933); 4. *Progressi Della Teo-*

ria Economica (1934); 5. *Lezioni di Economia Politica*, 5 vols, (1937–54); 6. *La Sintesi Economica e La Teoria Del Reddito* (1950); 7. *L'Introduzione Alla Finanza* (1954); 8. *Capitale e Interesse* (1956).

Secondary Literature L. dal Pane, 'Commemorazione di Gustavo del Vecchio', in G. Busino *et al.*, *Studi inediti in memoria di Gustavo del Vecchio* (1974).

DEMSETZ, Harold

Born 1930, Chicago, Ill., USA.
Current Post Prof., UCLA, USA.
Recent Post Prof., Univ. Chicago, 1963–71.
Degrees BS Univ. Illinois, 1953; MBA, MA, PhD, Northwestern Univ., 1954, 1955, 1959.
Offices Mont Pelerin Society, 1955–; AEA, 1958–; Sr Res. Fellow, Hoover Inst, Stanford, 1972–7; Chairman, Econ. Dept., UCLA, 1978–80.
Principal Contributions Theoretical and empirical contribution to the literature of industrial organisation, particularly on structural matters, property rights, including a theory of the emergence of property rights, transaction costs and monopolistic competition.
Publications *Articles:* 1. 'Toward a theory of property rights', *AER*, 57, May 1967; 2. 'Why regulate utilities?', *J Law E*, 11, April 1968; 3. 'Information and efficiency, another viewpoint', *J Law E*, 12(1), April 1969; 4. 'Production, information costs, and economic organization' (with A.A. Alchian), *AER*, 62(5), Dec. 1972; 5. 'Industry structure, market rivalry and public policy', *J Law E*, 16(1), April 1973, reprinted in *The Impact of Large Firms on the U.S. Economy*, eds J.F. Weston and S.I. Ornstein (Heath & Co., 1973); 6. 'Accounting for advertising as a barrier to entry', *J Bus*, July 1979.

DENIS, Hector*

Dates and Birthplace 1842–1913, Belgium.
Post Held Prof., Univ. Brussels.
Offices Member, Belgian Chamber of Representatives.

Career Idealistic socialist who sought an inductive basis for his viewpoint. Some of his work on taxation was done as a basis for legislation and showed the necessary increase in public expenditure that would follow the expansion of government activity. His work on the history of economic ideas was probably his most significant contribution.
Publications *Books:* 1. *L'Impôt sur le revenu* (1881); 2. *L'Impôt* (1889); 3. *La dépression économique et sociale et l'histoire des prix*, 2 vols (1895); 4. *Histoire des systèmes économiques et socialistes* (1897); 5. *Discours philosophiques d'Hector Denis* (1919).
Secondary Literature L. Bertrand, 'Denis, Hector', *ESS*, vol. 5.

DENISON, Edward Fulton

Born 1915, Omaha, Neb., USA.
Current Post Assoc. Dir. Nat. Econ. Accounts, US Dept. Commerce, Bureau Econ. Analysis, Washington.
Recent Posts Economist, Ass. Dir. Office Bus. Econ., US Dept. Commerce, 1941–62; Economist and Assoc. Dir. Res., Comm. Econ. Development, 1956–62; Sr Fellow, Div. Econ. Stud., Brookings Inst., 1962–78.
Degrees BA (Econ.), Oberlin Coll., 1936; MA (Econ.), PhD (Econ.), Brown Univ., 1938, 1941; Grad. Nat. War Coll., 1951.
Offices and Honours Sr Fellow Emeritus, Brookings Inst.; Former Chairman Exec. Comm., Conference Res. Income and Wealth; Former vicepres., AEA; Fellow, AAAS; IARIW; Nat. Economists Club; W.S. Woytinsky Lectureship award, Univ. Michigan; Fellow, Former Chairman, Comm. on Comms., ASA.
Principal Contributions Developed growth accounting (sources-of-growth analysis) and applied it to the study of growth in ten advanced countries and to the study of differences in their levels of output. Contributed to the theory and practice of measurement of capital stock, especially with respect to quality changes. Demonstrated unreality of embodiment models. Showed stability of total private saving rate. Participated

in development of concepts and estimates for the national income accounts of USA. Measured and analysed professional incomes.

Publications *Books:* 1. *The Sources of Economic Growth in the United States and the Alternatives Before Us* (Comm. for Econ. Development, 1962); 2. *Why Growth Rates Differ: Post-war Experience in Nine Western Countries* (Brookings Inst., 1967, Russian transl., 1971); 3. *Accounting for United States Economic Growth, 1929–1969* (Brookings Inst., 1974); 4. *How Japan's Economy Grew so Fast* (with W.K. Chung), (Brookings Inst., 1976); 5. *Accounting for Slower Economic Growth: the United States in the 1970s* (Brookings Inst., 1979).

Articles: 1. 'National income and product statistics of the United States, 1929–46' (with M. Gilbert *et al.*), *Survey of Current Bus.*, 27, Suppl., July 1947; 2. 'Theoretical aspects of quality change, capital consumption and net capital formation', *Problems of Capital Formation: Concepts, Measurement, and Controlling Factors*, Studies in Income and Wealth, 19 (Princeton Univ. Press, 1957); 3. 'A note on private saving', *REStat*, 40, Aug. 1958; 4. 'The unimportance of the embodied question', *AER*, 54, March 1964; 5. 'Effects of selected changes in the institutional and human environment upon output per unit of input', *Survey of Current Bus.*, 58, Jan. 1978.

DE QUINCEY, Thomas*

Dates and Birthplace 1785–1859, Manchester, England.
Post Held Professional essayist.
Career Chiefly known for the famous *Confessions of an English Opium Eater* (1821) and for his voluminous writings in the periodical literature on a wide range of subjects, including political economy. The content of his economic writing is purely Ricardian, but his expositional style was so striking that he proved to be one of Ricardo's most effective disciples. J.S. Mill quoted frequently from *The Logic . . .*, and thus ensured De Quincey's economic work such lasting interest as it retains.

Publications *Books:* 1. *The Logic of Political Economy* (1841); 2. *Collected Writings, of Thomas De Quincey*, ed. D. Masson, vol. 9. *Political Economy and Politics* (1897, 1970).

DESTUTT DE TRACY, Antoine-Louis-Claude*

Dates and Birthplace 1754–1836, Paris, France.
Posts Held Army officer and politician.
Offices and Honours Commandant, Légion d'Honneur; Member, L'Inst. de France, 1794; Member, Académie française, 1808.
Career Wrote a treatise on economics as part of a series of *Eléments d'idéologie* begun 1801. As a philosopher in the eighteenth-century mould, he brought to economic ideas a logical rigour which was not matched with equal originality. His insistence that value should be measured in invariant units just as other quantities are measured in given units was taken up by Ricardo. His concept of 'ideology' was taken up and transformed by Marx and Engels.
Publications *Books:* 1. *Traité d'économie politique* (1823).

DHRYMES, Phoebus J.

Born 1932, Ktima, Cyprus.
Current Post Prof. Econ., Colombia Univ., NY, USA.
Recent Posts Prof., assoc. prof. Econ., Univ. Pennsylvania, 1964–73; Founding co-ed., *J Em*, 1973–7.
Degrees BA (Highest hons.) Univ. Texas, Austin, 1957; PhD MIT, 1961; Hon. MA Univ. Pennsylvania, 1971.
Offices Member, Em Soc, AEA, ASA; Fellow, Em Soc, 1967, ASA, 1970.
Principal Contributions In simultaneous equations theory: elucidation of the relationship between the classical methods such as least squares, and simultaneous equations methods such as two and three stage least squares. Applications of asymptotic theory to econometric problems. Solution of the

problem of predictive efficiency when predicting with a simultaneous equations model. Development of the theory of estimation of distributed lags. Development of the theory of estimation of CES production functions. Derivation of the contemporary theory of the demand for labour as derived from microprinciples and applications to major sectors of the US economy.

Publications   *Books:* 1. *Econometrics: Statistical Foundations and Applications* (Harper & Row, 1970, Springer-Verlag, 1974); 2. *Distributed Lags: Problems of Estimation and Formulation* (Holden-Day, 1971, N-H, 1981); 3. *Introductory Econometrics* (Springer-Verlag, 1978); 4. *Mathematics for Econometrics* (Springer-Verlag, 1978); 5. *Domestic Consequences of an Overvalued Currency* (Center of Planning and Econ. Res., Athens, 1978).

Articles: 1. 'On the theory of the monopolistic multiproduct firm under uncertainty', *Int ER*, 5, Sept. 1964; 2. 'Some extensions and tests of the CES class of production functions', *REStat*, 47, Nov. 1965; 3. 'Efficient estimation of distributed lags with auto-correlated errors', *Int ER*, 10(1), Feb. 1969; 4. 'Alternative asymptotic tests of significance and related aspects of 2SLS and 3SLS estimated parameters', *REStud*, 36, April 1969; 5. 'Restricted and unrestricted reduced forms: asymptotic distribution and relative efficiency', *Em*, 41(1), Jan. 1973.

DIAMOND, Peter

Born   1940, New York City, NY, USA.

Current Post   Prof. Econ., MIT, USA.

Recent Posts   Prof., 1963–5, acting assoc. prof., 1965–6, Univ. Cal. Berkeley.

Degrees   BA Yale Univ., 1960; PhD MIT, 1963.

Offices and Honours   AEA; Fellow, 1968–, Council, 1981–4, Em Soc; Fellow, AAAS, 1978–; Mahalanobis Memorial award, 1980.

Principal Contributions   The theory of optimal taxation. Uncertainty and general equilibrium theory.

Publications   *Books:* 1. *Uncertainty in Economics, Readings and Exercises* (with M. Rothschild), (Academic Press, 1978).

Articles: 1. 'National debt in a neoclassical growth model', *AER*, 55, Dec. 1965; 2. 'The role of a stock market in a general equilibrium model with technological uncertainty', *AER*, 57, Sept. 1967; 3. 'Optimal taxation and public production, II: tax rules' (with J.A. Mirrlees), *AER*, 61(3), June 1971; 4. 'A model of price adjustment', *JET*, 3(2), June 1971; 5. 'An equilibrium analysis of search and breach of contract I: steady states' (with E. Maskin), *Bell JE*, 10, 1979.

DÍAZ-ALEJANDRO, Carlos F.

Born   1937, La Habana, Cuba.

Current Post   Prof. Econ., Yale Univ., Conn., USA, 1969–.

Recent Posts   Ass. prof., Econ. Growth Center, Yale Univ., 1961–5; Economist, Staff Comm. Nine, Alliance for Progress, Organisation Amer. States, 1962–3; Assoc. prof. Econ., Univ. Minnesota, 1965–9; Consultant, Interamer. Comm. Alliance Progress, Pan Amer. Union, 1965–6, MIT/ODEPLAN (Santiago) Project Andean Common Market, 1967–8, Commission Internat. Development ('Pearson Commission'), 1968–9; Vis. prof. Econ., Pontificia Univ. Catolica Rio de Janeiro, 1971; Vis., Nuffield Coll., Univ. Oxford, 1975–6.

Degrees   BS (Bus.) Miami Univ., Ohio, 1957; PhD (Econ.) MIT, 1961.

Offices   Member, Ed. Board, *WD* (UK), *Economia* (Portugal); Consultant, Commission US-Latin Amer. Relations ('Linowitz Commission'), 1975; Co-ed., JDE, 1976–; Chairman, Joint Comm. Latin Amer. Stud., US SSRC, 1976–9; Member, Council Foreign Relations, New York, 1977–; Member, AEA Pol. Advisory Board, Econ. Inst., Boulder, Colorado, 1977–80; Member, Academic Panel Consultative Group Internat. Econ. Monetary Affairs, Rockefeller Foundation, 1978–.

Principal Contributions   Analysis of trade and payments problems of semi-industrialised countries. Analytical economic history of Latin America.

Publications *Books:* 1. *Exchange Rate Devaluation in a Semi-Industrialized Country: The Experience of Argentina, 1955–1961* (MIT Press, 1966), Spanish transl., *Devaluacion de la Tasa de Cambio en un Pais Semi-industializado* (Amorrortu, 1975); 2. *Essays on the Economic History of the Argentine Republic* (Yale Univ. Press, 1970), Spanish transl., *Ensayos Sobre la Historia Economica Argentina* (Amorrortu, 1975); 3. *Foreign Trade Regimes and Economic Development: Colombia* (Columbia Univ. Press, 1976); 4. *Politica Economica en Centro y Periferia: Ensayos en Homenaje e Felipe*, ed. (with S. Teitel and V.E. Tokman), (Fondo de Cultura Economica, 1976).

Articles: 1. 'Less developed countries and the post-1971 international financial system', *Princeton Essays in International Finance, no. 108* (Princeton Univ., 1975), Spanish transl., *Los Paises Menos Desarrollados y el Sistema Financiero Internacional Despues de 1971* (Cuadernos de Economia, 12, 35, 1975); 2. 'The post-1971 international financial system and the less developed countries', in *A World Divided: The Less Developed Countries in the International Economy*, ed. G.K. Helleiner, (CUP, 1975); 3. 'Tariffs, foreign capital and immiserizing growth' (with R. Brecher), *J Int E*, 7(4), Nov. 1977; 4. 'International markets for exhaustible resources, less developed countries, and multinational corporations', in *Research in International Business and Finance*, vol. 1, *The Economic Effects of Multinational Corporations*, ed. R.G. Hawkins, (JAI Press, 1979); 5. 'The less-developed countries and transnational enterprises', in *The World Economic Order: Past and Prospects*, eds S. Grassman and E. Lundberg (Macmillan, 1981).

DICKINSON, Henry Douglas*

Dates and Birthplace 1899–1968, England.
Posts Held Res., LSE, 1922–4; Ass. lecturer, Reader, Univ. Leeds, 1924–47; Sr lecturer, Prof., Univ. Bristol, 1947–64.
Degree BA Univ. Camb., 1922.
Career Historian of economic thought, whose interest in both the Austrian school and Marx is revealed in *Institutional Revenue*. This developed into his work on the socialist economy which involved an original model of 'market socialism'.
Publications *Books:* 1. *Institutional Revenue* (1932); 2. *Economics of Socialism* (1939).
Articles: 1. 'Price formation in a socialist community', *EJ*, 43, 1933.
Secondary Literature M.H. Dobb, 'Obituary: H.D. Dickinson', *Hist. Econ. Thought Newsletter*, 3, 1968.

DICKS-MIREAUX, Leslie

Born 1924, England.
Current Post Spec. adviser (Econ. and Industry), Bank of England.
Recent Posts Sr res. officer, NIESR, London, 1956–62; Sr economist, Nat. Econ. Development Office, London, 1962–6; Head, Short-term Forecasting Div. Econ. Stats. Dept, OECD, Paris, 1966–7.
Degrees BSc. (First class hons) King's Coll., Univ. London, 1948.
Principal Contributions The determinants of general wage and price inflation, in particular quantitative attempts to distinguish for Britain between the separate roles of cost factors and demand factors in the inflationary process.
Publications *Articles:* 1. 'The excess demand for labour: a study of conditions in Great Britain, 1946–1956' (with J.C.R. Dow), *OEP*, N.S. 10, Feb. 1956; 2. 'The determinants of wage inflation, United Kingdom, 1946–1956' (with J.C.R. Dow), *JRSS*, 122, Pt 2, 1959; 3. 'The interrelationship between cost and price changes, 1946–1959: a study of inflation in post-war Britain', *OEP*, N.S. 13, Oct. 1961; 4. 'The wages structure and some implications for incomes policy' (with J.R. Shepherd), *Nat. Inst. Econ. Review*, 22, 1962; 5. 'Cost-push or demand-pull: a study of inflation in the UK', *Woolwich Econ. Papers*, 1963.

DIEHL, Karl*

Dates and Birthplace 1864–1943, Frankfurt-am-Main, Germany.
Posts Held Prof., Univ. Rostock, 1898, Univ. Königsberg, 1899; Prof. Econ., Univ. Freiburg, 1908–43.
Career Studied in Berlin, Halle and Vienna. His tenure of the Freiburg Chair further enhanced its prestige. Teaching by the seminar method, he attracted and held a large number of students. His views were largely of an institutionalist type, though he relied very much on the English classics as a starting point. *Theoretische National-ökonomie* reveals his theoretical ability and his willingness to turn theory to the solving of practical problems. He also was a Proudhon scholar of considerable note.
Publications *Books:* 1. *P.J. Proudhon, seine Lehre und sein Leben*, 3 vols (1888–96); 2. *Sozialwissenschaftliche Erläuterungen zu David Ricardos Grundgesetzen*, 2 vols (1905); 3. *Theoretische Nationalökonomie*, 4 vols (1916–33).
Secondary Literature A. Hesse, 'Diehl, Karl', in *Handwörterbuch der Sozialwissenschaften*, vol. 2, eds E.V. Beckerath *et al.* (Gustav Fischer, 1959).

DIETZEL, Carl August*

Dates and Birthplace 1829–84, Germany.
Posts Held Privatdozent, Heidelberg Univ.; Prof., Marburg Univ., 1867.
Degree Dr Heidelberg Univ., 1856.
Career German writer on finance who overturned the accepted idea that public credit is inherently different from private credit. His legitimisation of public credit was reflected in many subsequent German writers.
Publications *Books:* 1. *Das System der Staatsanleihen im Zusammenhang der Volkswirtschaft betrachtet* (1855); 2. *Die Besteuerung der Aktiengesellschaften im Verleindung mit der Gemeindebesteuerung* (1859); 3. *Die Volkswirtschaft und ihr Verhältnis zu Gesellschaft und Staat* (1864).
Secondary Literature F. Meisel, 'Dietzel, Karl August', *ESS* 5.

DIETZEL, Heinrich*

Dates and Birthplace 1857–1935, Germany.
Posts Held Prof., Univ. Dorpat, 1885–90, Univ. Bonn, 1890–1935.
Career A representative of classical economics in Germany opposed to the mainstream dominated by the Historical School and popular Marxism. His pupils held a number of university chairs and high government posts by the time of his death. He wrote illuminatingly on the methods of economic research and a wide variety of questions, such as free trades unions, public loans and taxation. He also wrote a good deal on Rodbertus and the early socialists. Throughout his career he was an enthusiastic, though seldom victorious, propagandist for free trade.
Publications *Books:* 1. *Karl Rodbertus* (1886–8); 2. *Theoretische Sozialökonomik* (1895).
Secondary Literature P. Arndt, 'Heinrich Dietzel' (obituary), *EJ*, 45, Dec. 1935.

DIEWERT, W. Erwin

Born 1941, Vancouver, Canada.
Current Post Prof., Univ. British Columbia, Vancouver, Canada, 1970–.
Recent Posts Univ. Chicago, 1968–70.
Degrees BA, MA, Univ. British Columbia, 1963, 1965: PhD Univ. Cal., Berkeley, 1969.
Offices and Honours Univ. Cal. best thesis in econ. award, 1969; Fellow, Em Soc, 1975; Assoc. ed., *J Em*, 1975–, *AER*, 1979–.
Principal Contributions Assisted in the development of flexible functional forms in the development of duality theory and applied it to various areas of economics including comparative statistics of general equilibrium systems, public finance, international trade theory, economic theory of index numbers (including the idea of superlative index number formulae), the measurement of total factor productivity, and cost-benefit analysis. Also worked on generalisations of concavity and quasiconcavity with applications to economics.

Publications *Articles:* 1. 'An application of the Shepherd duality theorem: a generalised Leontief production function', *JPE*, 79(3), May/June 1971; 2. 'Exact and superlative index numbers', *J Em*, 4(2), June 1976; 3. 'Generalized Slutsky conditions for aggregate consumer demand functions', *JET*, 15(2), Aug. 1977; 4. 'The economic theory of index numbers: a survey', in *Essays in The Theory and Measurement of Consumer Behavior in Honor of Sir Richard Stone*, ed. A. Deaton, (CUP, 1981); 5. 'Duality approaches to microeconomic theory', in *The Handbook of Mathematical Economics*, vol. 2, eds K.J. Arrow and M.D. Intriligator (N-H, 1982).

DIVISIA, François*

Dates and Birthplace 1889–1964, Tizi-Ouzou, Algeria.

Posts Held Govt. engineer, 1919; Res. and teaching, French Ministry Nat. Education; Prof., l'Ecole Nationale des Ponts et Chaussées, 1932–50.

Offices and Honours Chevalier, Légion d'Honneur; Pres., Soc. d'Econométrie, 1935; Pres., Soc. de Statistique de Paris, 1939; Foreign member, Accademia Nazionale dei Lincei, 1951.

Career Originally trained as an engineer, his part-time economic work was recognised by his appointment to a teaching post with the Ministry of National Education. His first major publication, *'L'indice ...*, contained the monetary index known as the Divisia index. *Economique Rationelle* made his reputation with its concise and practical statement of his views. He was moved by what he saw as lack of precision in Keynes' *General Theory* to offer a micro-economic alternative in the form of *Traitement économétrique ...* His work was a major contribution to the development of econometrics.

Publications *Books:* 1. *L'indice monétaire de la théorie de la monnaie* (1926); 2. *Economique rationelle* (1928); 3. *L'épargne et la richesse collective* (1928); 4. *Expositions d'économique*, 3 vols (1951–65); 5. *Traitement économétrique de la monnaie, l'intérêt, l'emploi* (1962).

Secondary Literature R. Roy, 'Divisia, François', *IESS*, vol. 4.

DIXIT, Avinash K.

Born 1944, Bombay, India.
Current Post Prof. Econ. Internat. Affairs, Princeton Univ., USA.
Recent Posts Fellow, Balliol Coll., Univ. Oxford, 1970–4; Prof. Econ., Univ. Warwick, England, 1974–80.
Degrees BSc., Univ. Bombay, 1963; BA, Univ. Camb., 1965; PhD, MIT, 1968.
Offices Assoc. ed., *JET*, 1972–5; Ass. ed., *REStud*, 1975–8; Fellow, Em Soc, 1977; Assoc. ed., *Em*, 1978–81; Co-ed., *Bell JE*, 1981–.
Principal Contributions Theoretical developments in the areas of economic growth and development, public finance, industrial economics and international economics.

Publications *Books:* 1. *Optimization in Economic Theory* (OUP, 1976); 2. *The Theory of Equilibrium Growth* (OUP, 1976); *Theory of International Trade* (with V. Norman), Cambridge Economic Handbooks (Nisbets, CUP, 1980).
Articles: 1. 'Models of dual economies', in *Models of Economic Growth*, eds J.A. Mirrlees and N.H. Stern (Macmillan, 1973); 2. 'Welfare effects of tax and price changes', *J Pub E*, 4(2), Feb. 1975; 3. 'Monopolistic competition and optimum product diversity' (with J.E. Stiglitz), *AER*, 67(3), June 1977; 4. 'The balance of trade in a model of temporary equilibrium with rationing', *REStud*, 45(2), Oct. 1978; 5. 'The role of investment in entry-deterrence', *EJ*, 90, March 1980.

DMITRIEV, Vladimir Karpovich*

Dates and Birthplace 1868–1913, Smolensk, Russia.
Post Held Excise controller, 1896–9.
Degree Grad. Polit. Econ., Univ. Moscow, 1896.
Career The first Russian mathematical economist, his work was influenced by Ricardo and Cournot. During his lifetime and up to the Russian Revolu-

tion, his work received some favourable notice, mainly from outside Russia but also from within. Nevertheless, his writings were literally rediscovered in the 1960s when the work of Sraffa on Ricardo illuminated Dmitriev's pioneering interpretation of Ricardo. Since his ideas, though not Marxian, are compatible with Marxian ideas, it has proved possible to use his precedents to legitimise the introduction of mathematical methods into Russian economics.

Publications *Books:* 1. *Ekonomicheskiye Ocherki* (1904), transl. as *Economic Essays*, ed. D.M. Nuti (1974).

Secondary Literature D.M. Nuti, 'Introduction' to V.K. Dmitriev, *Economic Essays* (CUP, 1974).

DOBB, Maurice Herbert*

Dates and Birthplace 1900–76, England.

Posts Held Lecturer, Reader Econ., Univ. Camb., 1924–67.

Degrees BA Univ. Camb.; PhD LSE, 1924.

Career Marxist economist whose greatest efforts were directed towards developing a theoretical framework for the analysis of capitalism. This led him inevitably into the examination of theories of value and eventual complete rejection of the neo-classical theory. His sympathetic examination of Soviet economic experience under Stalin was later applied to the economic development of the Third World, which became one of his main interests in later life. His work in Marxist economics made few concessions to new interpretations, but this did not prevent him from obtaining considerable influence and respect worldwide. Among his many contributions to the history of ideas was his editorship of Ricardo's *Works and Correspondence* with Piero Sraffa.

Publications *Books:* 1. *Capitalist Enterprise and Social Progress* (1925); 2. *Soviet Economic Development Since 1917* (1928, 1966); 3. *Marx as an Economist* (1943, 1975); 4. *Studies in the Development of Capitalism* (1946); 5. *An Essay on Economic Growth and Planning* (1960, 1969); 6. *Theories of Value and Distribution since Adam Smith* (1973).

Secondary Literature J. Eatwell, 'Dobb, Maurice H.', *IESS*, vol. 18; Maurice Dobb memorial issue, *Camb JE*, 2, March 1978.

DOLBEAR, F. Trenery, Jr

Born 1935, Scranton, Penn., USA.

Current Post Prof., Chairman, Dept Econ., Brandeis Univ., Waltham, Mass., USA.

Recent Posts Ass. prof., Carnegie Inst. Technology, 1963–6; Vis. ass. prof., Stanford Bus. School, 1966–7; Brookings Econ. Pol. Fellow, at US Bureau Budget, 1967–8; Vis. assoc. prof. Econ., Univ. Essex, England 1975–6.

Degrees BA Williams Coll., 1957; MA, PhD, Yale Univ., 1958, 1963.

Offices AEA.

Principal Contributions Clarification of conceptual difficulties in allocation theory relating to externalities, public goods and social risk. Also a continuing interest in experimental economics which dates to doctoral dissertation on the problem of choice under uncertainty. Finally, recent efforts have been devoted to designing computer exercises for more effective teaching of difficult concepts. Currently working on computer teaching materials for intermediate courses in macro-economics, statistics and micro-economics.

Publications *Articles:* 1. 'Individual choice under uncertainty: an experimental study', *YEE*, 3(2), Fall 1963; 2. 'The possibility of oversupply of local "public" goods: a critical note' (with W. Brainard), *JPE*, 75, Feb. 1967; 3. 'On the theory of optimum externality', *AER*, 57(1), March 1967; 4. 'A simulation policy game for teaching macroeconomics' (with R. Attiyeh and W. Brainard), *AER*, 58(2), May 1968; 5. 'Collusion in oligopoly: an experiment on the effect of numbers and information' (with L. Lave *et al.*), *QJE*, 82, May 1968.

DOMAR, Evsey D.

Born 1914, Lodz, Russia (now Poland).

Current Post Ford Internat. Prof. Econ., MIT, USA, 1972–.

Recent Posts Economist, Board Governors Fed. Reserve System, 1943–6; Ass. prof. Econ., Carnegie Inst. Technology, 1946–7; Ass. prof. Econ., Univ. Chicago, 1947–8; Assoc. prof. Polit. Econ., 1948–55, Prof. Polit. Econ., 1955–8, Johns Hopkins Univ.; Prof. Econ., MIT, 1958–72.

Degrees BA (Econ.) UCLA, 1939; MA (Math. Stats, Univ. Michigan, 1941; MA (Econ.), PhD (Econ.), Harvard Univ., 1943, 1947.

Offices and Honours Member, Exec. Comm., 1962–5, Vice-pres., 1970, AEA; Fellow, AAAS, 1962–; Fellow, Center Advanced Study Behavioral Sciences, 1962–3; Recipient, John R. Commons award Omicron Delta Epsilon, 1965; Fellow, Em Soc, 1968–; Pres., Assoc. Comparative Econ., 1970.

Principal Contributions Effects of taxation on risk-taking; models of economic growth; models in economic history, particularly of slavery and serfdom; and socialist theory and models.

Publications *Books:* 1. *Essays in the Theory of Economic Growth* (OUP, 1957).

Articles: 1. 'On the measurement of technological change', *EJ*, 71, Dec. 1961; 2. 'The Soviet collective farm as a producer co-operative', *AER*, 56, Sept. 1966; 3. 'An index-number tournament', *QJE*, 81, May 1967; 4. 'The causes of slavery or serfdom: a hypothesis', *JEH*, 30(1), March 1970; 5. 'On the optimal compensation of a socialist manager', *QJE*, 88(1), Feb. 1974.

DONGES, Juergen B.

Born 1940, Seville, Spain.

Current Post Dir. Prof., Head Development Econ. Dept., Kiel Inst. World Econ., Univ. Kiel, 1972–.

Recent Posts Res. ass., Univ. Saar, 1966–9; Div. Chief. Univ. Kiel, 1969–72.

Degrees Diplom-Volkswirt Univ. Saar, 1966; Dr rer. pol. Univ. Saar, 1969.

Offices Verein für Sozialpolitik; AEA; RES; Member, Scientific Advisory Board, German Federal Ministry Econ. Co-op.; Adviser, Madrid Center Econ. Studies; Consultant, various international orgs.

Principal Contributions Testing development and trade theories, with emphasis on developing countries. Analyses of the impact of economic policies on growth, resource allocation, international trade flows and foreign investment.

Publications *Books:* 1. *Protektion und Branchenstruktur der Westdeutschen Wirtshaft* (with others), (J.C.B. Mohr, 1973); 2. *La Industrialización en España* (Oikos-Tau, 1976); 3. *Aussenwirtschaftsstrategien und Industrialisierung in Entwicklungsländern* (with others), (J.C.B. Mohr, 1978); 4. *Aussenwirtschafts- und Entwicklungspolitik* (Springer-Verlag, 1981).

Articles: 1. 'Shaping Spain's export industry', *WD*, 1(9), Sept. 1973; 2. 'A comparative survey of industrialization policies in fifteen semi-industrial countries', *WA*, 112(4), 1976; 3. 'The Third World demand for a new international economic order', *Kyklos*, 30(2), 1977; 4. 'Muster der industriellen Arbeitsteilung im Rahmen einer erweiterten Europäischen Gemeinschaft' (with others), *Die Weltwirtschaft, 1980, 1*; 5. 'Foreign investment in Portugal', *Fundação Calouste Gulbenkian*, 1980.

DORFMAN, Robert

Born 1916, New York City, NY, USA.

Current Post David A. Wells prof. Polit. Econ., Harvard Univ., USA, 1972–.

Recent Posts Sr Stat., Office Price Admin., 1941–3; Operations Analyst, US Air Force, 1943–50; Assoc. prof. Econ., Univ. Cal., Berkeley, 1950–5; Prof. Econ., Harvard Univ., 1955–72.

Degrees BA, MA, Columbia Univ., 1936, 1937; PhD Univ Cal., 1950.

Offices Council member, ORSA, 1959–62; Fellow, Center Advanced Study Behavioral Sciences, 1960–1; Council member, Em Soc, 1962–4; Pres., Inst. Management Science, 1965–6; Fellow, AAAS, 1967–; Exec.

Comm., AEA, 1968–71; Guggenheim Memorial Foundation Fellow, 1970–1; Environmental Stud. Board, Nat. Res. Council, 1974–7; Vice-pres., Assoc. Environmental Resource Economists 1980–1.

Principal Contributions Early work applied the operations research-systems analysis point of view to economic problems and economics theorising. Thereafter, worked increasingly on applications of economic principles to assessing natural resource and environmental programmes, and on adapting those principles to increase their applicability in practice.

Publications *Books:* 1. *Linear Programming and Economic Analysis* (with P.A. Samuelson and R.M. Solow), (McGraw-Hill, 1958); 2. *Design of Water Resource Systems* (with A. Maass *et al.*), (Harvard Univ. Press, 1962); 3. *Prices and Markets* (Prentice-Hall, 1967, 1978); 4. *Economics of the Environment, Selected Readings* (with N.S. Dorfman), (Norton, 1972, 1977).

Articles: 1. 'Mathematical, or "linear" programming; a non-mathematical exposition', *AER*, 43(5), Dec. 1953; 2. 'General equilibrium with public goods', in *Public Economics*, eds J. Margolis and H. Guiton (Macmillan, 1969); 3. 'An economic interpretation of optimal control theory', *AER*, 59(5), Dec. 1969; 4. 'Forty years of cost-benefit analysis', in *Econometric Contributions to Public Policy*, eds R. Stone and W. Peterson (Macmillan, 1978); 5. 'A formula for the Gini coefficient', *REStat*, 61(1), Feb. 1979.

DORNBUSCH, Rudiger

Born 1942, Krefeld, Germany.
Current Post Prof. Econ., MIT., USA.
Recent Posts Ass. prof., Univ. Rochester, 1972–3; Assoc. prof., Univ. Chicago, 1974.
Degrees Licence de sciences politiques Univ. Geneva, Switzerland, 1966; MA (Econ.), PhD (Econ.), Univ. Chicago, 1969, 1971.
Offices Fellow, Em Soc, 1979; Fellow, AAAS, 1980.

Principal Contributions Work on exchange-rate problems and open economy macro-economics.

Publications *Books:* 1. *International Economic Policy*, ed. (with J. Frenkel), (Johns Hopkins Univ. Press, 1979); 2. *Open Economy Macroeconomics* (Basic Books, 1980); 3. *Macroeconomics* (with S. Fisher), (McGraw Hill, 1981).

Articles: 1. 'Devaluation, money and non-traded goods', *AER*, 63(5), Dec. 1973; 2. 'Expectations and exchange rate dynamics', *JPE*, 84(6), Dec. 1976; 3. 'Comparative advantage, trade and payments in a Ricardian model with a continuum of goods' (with S. Fischer and P.A. Samuelson), *AER*, 67(5), Dec. 1977.

DOUGLAS, Paul Howard*

Dates and Birthplace 1892–1976, Salem, Mass., USA.
Posts Held Teacher Econ., Univ. Illinois, 1916–7, Reed Coll., 1917–18, Univ. Washington, 1919–20; Prof., Univ. Chicago 1920–49, Amherst Coll., 1924–7, New School Social Res., New York City, 1967–9.
Degrees BA Bowdoin Coll., 1913; MA, PhD, Columbia Univ., 1915, 1921.
Offices Senator, Illinois, 1948–66; Pres., AEA, 1948.
Career A pioneer econometrician whose work had as its starting point the marginal productivity theory of his teacher John Bates Clark. In co-operation with Charles W. Cobb, he was responsible for the now famous Cobb-Douglas production function. His work at Chicago as a teacher enabled him to organise research projects designed to test the marginal productivity theory of distribution. *The Theory of Wages* contains his main contribution to this field. As Senator for Illinois for almost 20 years, he drafted and fought for the passage of a number of important pieces of economic legislation.
Publications *Books:* 1. *Real Wages in the United States* (1930, 1966); 2. *The Theory of Wages* (1934, 1964); 3. *Ethics in Government* (1952, 1972).
Articles: 1. 'Are there laws of production?', *AER*, 38, March 1948; 2. 'Comments on the Cobb-Douglas pro-

duction function', in *The Theory and Empirical Analysis of Production*, ed. M. Brown (1967); 3. 'The Cobb-Douglas production function once again: its history, its testing, and some empirical values', *JPE*, 84(3), Oct. 1976.

Secondary Literature G.C. Cain, 'Douglas, Paul H.', *IESS*, vol. 18; P.A. Samuelson, 'Paul Douglas' measurement of production functions and marginal productivities', *JPE*, 87(5), Pt 1, Oct. 1979.

DOWNS, Anthony

Born 1930, Evanston, Ill., USA.
Current Post Sr Fellow, Brookings Inst., Washington DC, USA, 1977–.
Recent Post Chairman, Real Estate Res. Corp., 1959–77.
Degrees BA (Polit. Theory and Internat. Relations) Carleton Coll., 1948–52; MA (Econ.), PhD (Econ.) Stanford Univ., 1952, 1956.
Offices and Honours Lambda Alpha; AEA; AAAS; Nat. Academy Public Admin.
Principal Contributions Application of economic analysis to political theory concerning democratic political parties and bureaucratic organisations, including analysis of impacts of uncertainty and ignorance. Analysis of racial segregation in US cities, its causes and effects. Analysis of dynamics of urban development as related to neighbourhood change and falling population in large US cities.
Publications *Books:* 1. *An Economic Theory of Democracy* (Harper & Row, 1957); 2. *Inside Bureaucracy* (Little Brown, 1967); 3. *Urban Problems and Prospects* (Rand McNally, 1970, 1976); 4. *Racism in America* (US Civil Rights Commission, 1970); 5. *Federal Housing Subsidies* (Heath-Lexington, 1973).
Articles: 1. 'Alternative futures for the American ghetto', *Daedalus*, Fall 1968; 2. 'Up and down with ecology', *Public Interest*, Summer 1972; 3. 'The automotive population explosion', *Traffic Quarterly*, July 1979; 4. 'Too much capital for housing?', *Brookings Bull.*, Summer, 1980; 5. 'Inflation and mortgage interest rates', *Real Estate Review*, Winter 1981.

DUESENBERRY, J.S.

N.e.

DÜHRING, Eugen Karl*

Dates and Birthplace 1833–1921, Berlin, Germany.
Posts Held Prof., Univ. Berlin, 1863–77; then independent scholar and writer.
Degree Dr Phil. Univ. Berlin, 1861.
Career Though blind from an early age, he sought to master a vast range of intellectual disciplines, and in fact made original contributions to several, including economics. His philosophy of life, which he called 'personalism', and his system of social reform, called 'societary', were unifying elements. His aggressive style of disputation earned him enemies and limited the recognition of his work, whilst analytical weaknesses flawed many of his writings. In economics, his greatest contribution was an anti-Marxist theory which explained many of the property relations of capitalist society by political rather than economic causation. Chiefly remembered today as the subject of one of Engels' popular expositions of Marxism in a book known by its abbreviated title, *Anti-Dühring*.
Publications *Books:* 1. *Carey's Umwälzung der Volkswirtschaftslehre und Socialwissenschaft* (1865); 2. *Capital und Arbeit* (1865); 3. *Kritische Grundlegung der Volkswirtschaftslehre* (1866); 4. *Kritische Geschichte der Nationalökonomie und des Socialismus* (1871); 5. *Cursus* (1873).
Secondary Literature G. Albrecht, *Eugen Dühring* (1927).

DUNBAR, Charles Franklin*

Dates and Birthplace 1830–1900, Abington, Mass., USA.
Posts Held Journalist, ed., 1859–69, *Boston Daily Advertiser*; Prof. Polit. Econ., Harvard Univ., 1871–1900.
Degrees BA Harvard Univ., 1851.
Offices Ed., *QJE*, 1886–96.
Career As a journalist he wrote influentially on current financial ques-

tions – paper currency, a national banking system and the National Debt. His publications during his academic career were mainly on currency banking, international trade, taxation and finance, but it was through his editorship of *QJE* that he exercised his greatest influence. He was an organiser and a teacher rather than an original theorist.

Publications *Books:* 1. *Theory and History of Banking* (1891); 2. *Economic Essays*, ed. O.M.W. Sprague (1904).

Secondary Literature F.W. Taussig, (obituary) 'Charles Franklin Dunbar', *EJ*, 10, March 1900.

DUNLOP, John Thomas

Born 1914, Placerville, Cal., USA.
Current Post Lamont Univ. Prof., Harvard Univ., USA.
Recent Posts Prof. Econ., 1950–, Dean, Faculty Arts Sciences, 1969–73, Harvard Univ.; Dir., Cost Living Council, 1973–4; US Secretary Labor, 1975–6; Chairman, Board Trustees, Center Advanced Study Behavioral Sciences, 1976–; Chairman, US Pay Advisory Comm., 1979–80.
Degrees BA, PhD, Univ. Cal., 1935, 1939; LLD, Univ. Chicago, Univ. Pennsylvania.
Offices Pres., IRRA, 1961, IIRA, 1973–6.
Principal Contributions Sought to help bridge the gap between economic analysis and the understanding of labour market institutions and that between economic analysis and actual economic policy making in private institutions and in government.
Publications *Books:* 1. *Wage Determination Under Trade Unions* (Macmillan, 1944, 1950); 2. *Industrial Relations Systems* (Henry Holt, 1958); 3. *Industrialism and Industrial Man* (with C. Kerr *et al.*), (Harvard Univ. Press, 1960); 4. *Labor and the American Community* (with D.C. Bok), (Simon & Schuster, 1970); 5. *The Lessons of Wage and Price Controls – The Food Sector*, ed. (Harvard Univ. Press, 1977).
Articles: 1. 'The movement of real and money wages', *EJ*, 48, Sept. 1938; 2. 'The task of contemporary wage theory', in *The Theory of Wage Determi-*

nation, ed. J.T. Dunlop, (Macmillan, 1957); 3. 'Job vacancy measures and economic analysis', in *The Measurement and Interpretation of Job Vacancies* (NBER, 1966); 4. 'Past and future tendencies in American labor organisations', *Daedalus*, Winter 1978; 5. 'Growth, unemployment and inflation', *Internat. Chamber Commerce*, 26th Congress, 1978.

DUNNING, John H.

Born 1927, Sandy, Bed., England.
Current Post Esmée Fairbairn prof. Internat. Investment and Bus. Stud., Head Dept Econ., Univ. Reading.
Recent Posts Lecturer, Sr lecturer Econ., Univ. Southampton, 1952–64; Prof. Econ., Univ. Reading, 1964–75; Vis. prof. Econ. Internat. Bus., Univ. Western Ontario, 1968–9, Univ. Cal., Berkeley, 1969, Univ. Boston, 1976, HEC Univ. Montreal, 1980; Walker Ames prof., Univ. Washington, Oct. 1981–.
Degrees BSc. (Econ.) Univ. London, 1951; PhD Univ. Southampton, 1957; Hon. PhD Univ. Uppsala, 1975.
Offices Fellow, Academy Internat. Bus., 1978.
Principal Contributions Written extensively in the field of international investment and the multinational enterprise. Also published on industrial, regional and urban economics. Currently working on the theory of international production and the multinational enterprise.
Publications *Books:* 1. *American Investment in British Manufacturing Industry* (A & U, 1958, 1976); 2. *British Industry, Change and Development in the 20th Century* (with C.J. Thomas), (Hutchinson, 1961, 1963); 3. *Studies in International Investment* (A & U, 1970); 4. *The City of London in the National Economy* (with E.V. Morgan), (A & U, 1971); 5. *International Production and the Multinational Enterprise* (A & U, 1981).
Articles: 1. 'The determinants of international production', *OEP*, 25(3), Nov. 1973; 2. 'Theories of business behaviour and the distribution of surplus profits', *Kyklos*, 31(4), 1978; 3.

'Towards an eclectic theory of international production: some empirical tests', *JI Bus Stud*, 11, Spring/Summer 1980; 4. 'Explaining changing patterns of international production; in support of the eclectic theory', *OBES*, 41(4), Nov. 1980; 5. 'Explaining the international direct investment position of countries; towards a dynamic approach', *WA*, 117(2), 1981.

DUNOYER, Charles*

Dates and Birthplace 1786–1862, Carennac, France.
Posts Held Prefect, Allier, 1830–2, Somme, 1832–8; Counsellor of State, 1838–51.
Offices Member, French Inst., 1832; Pres., Soc. Polit. Econ., 1845.
Career Considered during the nineteenth century as a great economist, his ideas are contained in one evolving work which began as a course of lectures at the Paris Athenaeum and appeared successively, though with considerable additions, as *L'Industrie ...*, *Nouveau traité ...* and *De la liberté ...* His theory of 'immaterial wealth' is perhaps the chief individual element of his ideas.
Publications *Books:* 1. *L'Industrie et la morale considerées dans leurs rapports avec la liberté* (1825); 2. *Nouveau traité d'économie sociale*, 2 vols (1830); 3. *De la liberté du travail*, 3 vols (1845); 4. *Le Second empire et une nouvelle restauration*, 2 vols (1865).

DUPONT DE NEMOURS, Pierre Samuel*

Dates and Birthplace 1739–1817, Paris, France.
Posts Held Various official posts in France.
Offices Member, French Estates-General, 1789; Secretary, French provisional govt, 1814.
Career One of the ablest of the physiocrats and their chief publicist, editing the *Ephémérides du citoyen* to which he contributed articles, including a history of economics. In addition to writing voluminously he held a variety of important official posts and eventually emigrated to America where he founded the famous industrial dynasty of Dupont.
Publications *Books:* 1. *Physiocratie* (1768).
Secondary Literature G. Schelle, *Dupont de Nenours et l'école physiocratique* (1888); H.W. Spiegel ed., *Pierre Samuel Dupont de Nemours on economic curves* (Johns Hopkins Univ. Press, 1955).

DUPUIT, Arsene Jules Etienne Juvenal*

Dates and Birthplace 1804–66, Fossano, Piedmont, Italy.
Posts Held Official, Corps des Ponts et Chaussées, Chief engineer, Paris, 1850; Inspector-general, Corps, 1885.
Degree Student l'Ecole Polytechnique and l'Ecole des Ponts et Chaussées.
Offices Member, Soc. d'Econ. Polit.
Career Whilst an enthusiastic supporter of *laissez faire* arguments, he is most remembered for his work on public utilities. His engineering career led him to consider the question of the conditions under which the construction of bridges and public works could be justified. He used a rigorous cost-benefit approach and developed the concept of the demand curve in the process. To measure the utility of works, he examined the benefits discernible over and above the costs or tolls paid by the user. This is the notion which Marshall later named consumer's surplus. Although frequently hailed as the founder of the concept of marginal cost pricing, Dupuit did not in fact carry the argument to its logical conclusion.
Publications *Books:* 1. *La liberté commerciale* (1861).
Articles: 1. 'Memoire sur le tirage de voiture et sur le frottement de roulement', *Annales des Ponts et Chaussées*, Pt 2, 3, 1842, (transl. as 'On tolls and transport charges', *Internat. Econ. Papers*, 1(1962); 2. 'La mesure de l'utilité des traveaux', *Annales des Ponts et Chaussées*, II, 8, 1844, (transl. as 'On the measurement of the utility of public works', *Internat. Econ. Papers*, 2 (1952)); 3. 'De l'utilité et de sa mesure',

J des Economistes, I, 35, July/Sept. 1853.

Secondary Literature W.S. Vickrey, 'Dupuit, Jules', *IESS*, vol. 4; R.B. Ekelund Jr and R.F. Hebert, 'Public economics at the Ecole des Ponts et Chaussées: 1830–1850', *J Pub E*, 2, July 1973.

DURAND, David

Born 1912, Ithaca, NY, USA.
Current Post Prof. Emeritus, Sloan School Management, MIT, USA.
Recent Posts Prof. Management, Sloan School Management, MIT, 1958–72.
Degrees BA Cornell Univ., 1934, MA, PhD, Columbia Univ., 1938, 1941.
Offices Member, Inst. Advanced Study, Princeton Univ., 1941.
Principal Contributions Developed series *Basic Yields of Corporate Bonds* to show term structure of interest rates; experimentation with uses of statistical methods in economics; critical analysis of the cost of capital; and investigation of the importance of measuring time in investment analysis.
Publications *Books: 1. Risk Element in Consumer Instalment Financing* (NBER, 1941); 2. *Basic Yields of Corporate Bonds: 1900–1942*, (NBER, 1942); 3. *Mortgage Lending Experience in Agriculture* (with L.A. Jones), (NBER, Princeton Univ. Press, 1954); 4. *Bank Stocks and the Bank Capital Problem* (NBER, 1957); 5. *Stable Chaos: An Introduction to Statistical Control* (A.D.H. Mark, General Learning Press, 1971).
Articles: 1. 'Bank stocks and the analysis of covariance', *Em*, 23, Jan. 1955; 2. 'Modifications of the Rayleigh test for uniformity in analysis of two-dimensional orientation data' (with J.A. Greenwood), *J Geology*, 66, 1958; 3. 'The cost of capital, corporation finance, and the theory of investment: comment', *AER*, 49, Sept. 1959; 4. 'Indices of profitability: aids to judgement in capital budgeting', *J Bank Res*, 3(4), Winter 1973; 5. 'Payout period, time spread and duration: aids to judgement in capital budgeting', *J Bank Res*, 5(1), Spring 1974.

DURBIN, Evan Frank Mottram*

Dates and Birthplace 1906–48, England.
Posts Held Lecturer, New Coll., Univ. Oxford; Lecturer, LSE; Civil Servant, World War II; MP, 1945–8; Parliamentary secretary, UK Ministry of Works, 1947–8.
Degree BA (PPE, First class hons.) Univ. Oxford.
Offices and Honours Jr, Sr Webb Medley Scholar; Ricardo Fellow.
Career Coming to economics from the natural sciences, he brought to it a formidable logical ability. His perception of the need for state planning led him into Labour politics, as did the ethical values of his non-conformist family background. He favoured a devolved and responsive planning system, but just when his elevation to ministerial rank made it possible to realise his views, he was killed in a swimming accident.
Publications *Books: 1. Purchasing Power and Trade Depression* (1933); 2. *The Problem of Credit Policy* (1935); 3. *Personal Aggressiveness and War* (with J. Bowlby), (1938); 4. *The Politics of Democratic Socialism* (1940); 5. *What Have We To Defend?* (1942); 5. *Problems of Economic Planning* (1949).
Secondary Literature E.H. Phelps Brown, 'Evan Durbin 1906–1948', *Ec*, N.S. 18, Feb. 1951.

E

EASTERLIN, Richard A.

Born 1926, New Jersey, USA.
Current Post William R. Kenan Prof. Econ., Univ. Pennsylvania, USA.
Recent Posts Univ. Pennsylvania, 1953–.
Degrees ME (Distinction) Stevens Inst. Technology, 1945; MA, PhD, Univ. Pennsylvania, 1949, 1953.
Offices AEA; Board Eds., *AER*, 1965–7; *JEL*, 1968–70; Fellow, AAAS, 1978; Pres., PAA, 1978, EHA, 1979–80.
Principal Contributions The application of economics to demographic behaviour: empirically, in regard to the interpretation of trends and long-term

fluctuations in the populations of developed countries and of the demographic transition in developing countries; theoretically, in regard to the role in determining childbearing behaviour of endogenous preferences and 'supply' constraints (reproduction functions). Analysis of the role of 'relative income' in family and social behaviour (marriage, childbearing, women's work, divorce, suicide, crime, etc.). The relation of formal schooling to long-term economic growth, and the implications of economic growth for human welfare.

Publications *Books:* 1. *Population Redistribution and Economic Growth, United States, 1870–1950*, 2 vols (with others), (Amer. Philosophical Soc., 1957, 1960); 2. *Population, Labor Force, and Long Swings in Economic Growth: the American Experience* (Columbia Univ. Press, 1968); 3. *American Economic Growth: an Economist's History of the United States*, co-ed. (Harper & Row, 1972); 4. *Population and Economic Change in Developing Countries*, ed. (Univ. Chicago Press, 1980); 5. *Birth and Fortune: the Impact of Numbers on Personal Welfare* (Basic Books, 1980).

Articles: 1. 'Economic growth: an overview', *IESS*, vol. 4; 2. 'Does economic growth improve the human lot?', in *Nations and Households in Economic Growth: Essays in Honor of Moses Abramovitz*, eds P.A. David and M.W. Reder (Academic Press, 1974); 3. 'Population change and farm settlement in the northern United States', *JEH*, 36(1), March 1976; 4. 'The economics and sociology of fertility: a synthesis', in *Historical Studies of Changing Fertility*, ed. C. Tilly (Princeton Univ. Press, 1978); 5. 'Why isn't the whole world developed?', *JEH*, 41(1), March 1981.

ECKAUS, Richard

Born 1926, Kansas City, Miss., USA.
Current Post Ford Internat. Prof. Econ., MIT, USA.
Recent Posts Instructor Econ., Babson Inst., 1948–50; Instructor Econ., 1951–4, Ass., Assoc. prof. Econ.,

1954–62, Brandeis Univ.; Assoc. prof. Econ., 1962–5, Prof. Econ., 1965–77, MIT.
Degrees BS (Electrical Engineering) Iowa State Univ., 1944; MA (Econ.) Washington Univ., 1946; PhD (Econ.) MIT, 1954.
Offices AEA; Em Soc.
Principal Contributions In the field of economic development constructed both general equilibrium and multisector dynamic linear programming models for analytical purposes; the models have been applied to policy problems in India and Egypt. Also developed hypotheses of unemployment and of financial market imperfections leading to credit rationing. In the field of the economics of education, developed methods for estimating the requirements for both general education and specific skills in the US economy and calculated and compared the returns to education in a large number of occupations.

Publications *Books:* 1. *Planning for Growth* (with K. Parikh), (MIT Press, 1968); 2. *Estimating the Returns to Education* (Carnegie Commission Higher Education, 1973); 3. *Development and Planning*, ed. (with J. Bhagwati) (A & U, 1973); 4. *Appropriate Technologies for Developing Countries* (NAS, 1977). *Articles:* 1. 'The factor proportions problem in economic development', *AER*, 45, Sept. 1955, repr. in *The Economics of Underdevelopment*, eds A.A. Agarwal and S.P. Singh (OUP, 1958); 2. 'The stability of dynamic models', *REStat*, 39, May 1957; 3. 'The north-south differential in Italian economic development', *JEH*, 21(3), Sept. 1961; 4. 'Economic criteria for education and training', *REStat*, 46(2), May 1964; 5. 'Absorptive capacity as a constraint due to maturation processes', in *Development and Planning*, eds J. Bhagwati and R.S. Eckaus (A & U, 1973).

ECKSTEIN, Otto

Born 1926, Ulm, Germany.
Current Post Paul M. Warburg prof. Econ., Harvard Univ.; Pres., Data Resources, Inc., Lexington, Mass., USA.
Recent Posts Technical Dir., Joint Econ. Comm., 1959–60; Member, US

President's Council Econ. Advisers, 1964–6.

Degrees BA, Hon. degree, Princeton Univ., 1951, 1966; MA, PhD, Harvard Univ., 1952, 1955; Hon. degree, Free Univ. Brussels, 1975.

Offices Fellow, ASA, Em Soc, National Assoc. Bus. Economists; Exec. Comm., 1967–70, Vice-pres., 1981, AEA.

Principal Contributions Focused largely on the study of the US economy, using econometric models for forecasting policy analysis, and historical analysis. The Data Resources Economic Information System has been main tool, and is also used by various public, private and academic groups for macromicro analysis. Inflation analysis has also been a continuing topic, beginning with econometric papers on wages, productivity and prices, and more recently core inflation. Earlier worked in the fields of public expenditure analysis and public finance. These included studies of the technique of cost benefit analysis for public works and taxation.

Publications *Books:* 1. *Water Resource Development: The Economics of Project Evaluation* (Harvard Univ. Press, 1958); 2. *Staff Report on Employment, Growth, and Price Levels* (with others), US Congress, Joint Econ. Comm. (US Govt Printing Office, 1959); 3. *The Great Recession* (N-H, 1978); 4. *Public Finance* (Prentice Hall, 1979); 5. *Core Inflation* (Prentice Hall, 1981).

Articles: 1. 'Investment criteria for economic development and the theory of intertemporal welfare economics', *QJE*, 71, Feb. 1957; 2. 'The determination of money wages in American industry' (with T.A. Wilson), *QJE*, 76, Aug. 1972; 3. 'A theory of the wage-price process in modern industry', *REStud*, 31, Oct. 1964; 4. 'The price equation' (with G. Fromm), *AER*, 58, Dec. 1968; 5. 'The data resources model: uses, structure and the analysis of the US economy' (with E. Green and A. Sinai), *Int ER*, 15(3), Oct. 1974.

EDEN, Frederick Morton*

Dates and Birthplace 1766–1809, England.

Posts Held Founder and chairman of the Globe Insurance Co.

Degrees BA, MA, Univ. Oxford, 1787, 1789.

Career His *State of the Poor* is the result of a major social investigation involving travel and correspondence on his part and the employment of a full-time researcher. It contains great quantities of factual information, parish by parish, including family budgets. His conclusions were in favour of friendly societies and against poor laws or minimum wages.

Publications Books: 1. *The State of the Poor*, 3 vols (1797); 2. *Estimate of the Number of Inhabitants in Great Britain and Ireland* (1800); 3. *Address on Maritime Rights* (1808).

Secondary Literature D.W. Douglas, 'Eden, Sir Frederick Morton', *ESS*, vol. 5.

EDGEWORTH, Francis Ysidro*

Dates and Birthplace 1845–1926, Edgeworthstown, Co. Longford, Ireland.

Posts Held Lecturer Logic, Tooke prof. Polit. Econ., King's Coll., Univ. London; Drummond prof. Polit. Econ., Fellow, All Souls Coll., Univ. Oxford, 1891–1922.

Degree BA (First class hons.) Univ. Oxford.

Offices Fellow, BA; Vice-pres., RES; Pres., RSS; Pres., Econ. Section, BAAS, 1889, 1922; Ed., *EJ*, 1891–1926.

Career His earliest writings are concerned with the application of mathematics to social science questions and in *Mathematical Psychics* he worked out practical aspects of utilitarian ethics in mathematical form. The insights on exchange equilibrium, welfare economics and the theory of barter are still valuable. His chief output was in article form on topics such as taxation, monopoly, index numbers and value of money. His exposition was obscure and his personality was retiring, with the result that his ideas are continually being rediscovered by those who arrive at them in their own way. Though his work was never drawn together into a comprehensive scheme, he is still valued for his various precedents in mathematical economics and statistics. His ideas on the 'contract curve' and the 'core' of an exchange economy have recently attracted considerable attention. His editorship of the *EJ* was of major value to the British economics community.

Publications *Books:* 1. *New and Old Methods of Ethics* (1877); 2. *Mathematical Psychics* (1881, 1953); 3. *Metretike* (1887); 4. *Papers Relating to Political Economy*, 3 vols (1891–1921, 1963).

Secondary Literature J.M. Keynes, 'Francis Ysidro Edgeworth: 1845–1926', in *Essays in Biography* (Macmillan 1933, 1972); C. Hildreth, 'Edgeworth, Francis Ysidro', *IESS*, vol. 4; J. Creedy, 'F.Y. Edgeworth', *Pioneers of Modern Economics in Britain*, eds D.P. O'Brien and J.R. Presley (Macmillan, 1981).

EHRLICH, Isaac

Born 1938, Tel-Aviv, Israel.

Current Post Prof. Econ., State Univ. New York, Buffalo, USA.

Recent Posts Univ. Chicago, 1970–7; Tel-Aviv Univ., 1971–2.

Degrees BA (*Cum laude*, Econ., Hist. Muslim People), Hebrew Univ. Jerusalem, 1964; PhD (Econ., Distinction), Columbia Univ., 1970.

Offices Member, AEA; Sr res. assoc., NBER, 1970–7; Melvin H. Baker Chair Amer. Enterprise, State Univ. New York, Buffalo, 1981.

Principal Contributions Applications of general economic theory in the study of diversified human conduct, and an analysis of the role of information, time and uncertainty in guiding that conduct. The most provocative illustration concerns illegitimate activities. Use of optimisation and equilibrium analysis to explain the rate and direction of all legal infractions challenges received theories in criminology. Work on behaviour under uncertainty provides a framework for studying both time allocation into risky endeavours, and the demand for all forms of insurance. Work on asset management and information further emphasises the role of individual enterprise and objective opportunities in explaining productive and consumptive choices.

Publications *Articles:* 1. 'Market insurance, self-insurance, and self-protection' (with G.S. Becker), *JPE*, 80(4), July/Aug. 1972; 2. 'Participation in illegitimate activities – a theoretical and empirical investigation', *JPE*, 81(3), May/June 1973; 3. 'The deterrent effect of capital punishment – a question of life and death', *AER*, 65(3), June 1975; 4. 'Capital punishment and deterrence: some further thoughts and additional evidence', *JPE*, 85(4), Aug. 1977; 5. 'On the usefulness of controlling individuals: an economic analysis of rehabilitation, incapacitation, and deterrence', *AER*, 71(3), June 1981.

EINAUDI, Luigi*

Dates and Birthplace 1874–1961, Carrù, Italy.

Posts Held Fellow Polit. Econ., 1899, Prof. Fin. Science, 1907, Univ. Turin; Governor, Bank of Italy, 1945.

Offices Deputy, Italian Constituent Assembly, 1945; Minister of Budget, 1947; Senator, 1948; Pres., Italian Republic, 1948–55.

Career An economist of the classical school, he was also a liberal in politics. In addition to his writings on finance and taxation, he contributed to economic history and history of economic thought. His personal library of economic works was legendary. Probably his outstanding economic work is *Principi ...* (1932) but his editorial and journalistic work with *La Riforma Sociale* and *Rivista di Storia Economica* were also important. Forced to flee to Switzerland in 1943, his return to Italy was followed by a period of outstanding achievement as a statesman.

Publications *Books:* 1. *Studi Sugli Effetti Delle Imposte* (1902); 2. *La Terra e l'Imposta* (1924); 3. *Principi di Scienza della Finanza* (1932); 4. *I Problemi Economici della Federazione Europea* (1945); 5. *Lezioni di Politica Sociale* (1949).

Secondary Literature U. Papi, 'Einaudi, Luigi', *IESS*, vol. 4.

EISNER, Robert

Born 1922, New York City, NY, USA.

Current Post William R. Kenan prof. Econ., Northwestern Univ., Ill., USA.

Recent Posts Ass. prof., Prof. Econ., Northwestern Univ., 1952–74; Sr res. assoc., NBER, 1969–78; Vis. disting. prof. Econ., State Univ. New York, Binghamton, 1971.

Degrees BSC City Coll. New York, 1940; MA Columbia Univ., 1942; PhD Johns Hopkins Univ., 1951.

Offices Guggenheim Memorial Foundation Fellow, 1960; Fellow, Em Soc, 1962–; Member, Board Eds., *AER*, 1966–76; Assoc. ed., *REStat*, 1970–; AAAS, 1975–; Vice-pres., Acting pres.-elect, 1977–8; Pres.-elect, MEA, 1981.

Principal Contributions Demonstrated the role of distributed lag investment function influenced by acceleration principle, expectations and adjustment costs. Related rates of economic growth to employment and unemployment, gross and net investment and depreciation. Related permanent income hypothesis of consumption to varying proportions of transitory income variants and to limitations in the use of temporary income tax changes in stabilisation policies. Also prepared extended measures of national income and product, including non-market economic activity, and demonstrated the dimensions of capital formation broadly defined.

Publications *Books:* 1. *Determinants of Capital Expenditures: An Interview Study* (Univ. Illinois, 1956).

Articles: 1. 'On growth models and the neo-classical resurgence', *EJ*, 68, Dec. 1958; 2. 'A permanent income theory for investment: some empirical explorations', *AER*, 57(8), June 1967; 3. 'Investment behavior and neo-classical theory' (with M.I. Nadiri), *REStat*, 50, Aug. 1968; 4. 'Total income, total investment and growth', *AER*, 70(2), May 1980; 5. 'Limitations and potentials of countercyclical fiscal and monetary policies', in *The Business Cycle and Public Policy*, US Congress, Joint Econ. Comm., Compendium of Papers (US Govt Printing Office, 1980).

ELCHMAN, W.F.

N.e.

ELLET, Charles Jr*

Dates and Birthplace 1810–62, Penn's Manor, Penn., USA.

Post Held Civil engineer.

Career His career as a civil engineer was a distinguished one, including the building of a suspension bridge of record length over the Ohio, and many other major works. The question of appropriate tariffs for a canal he was constructing, and a period of study at l'Ecole des Ponts et Chaussées in Paris, led to his *Essay . . . .* In this and subsequent works he developed an economic analysis of transportation, involving questions of tariff-fixing and monopoly pricing, in mathematical terms.

Publications *Books:* 1. *An Essay on the Laws of Trade in Reference to the Works of Internal Improvement in the United States* (1839); 2. *The Laws of Trade Applied to the Determination of the Most Advantageous Fares for Passengers on Railroads* (1840).

Secondary Literature C.D. Calsoyas, 'The mathematical theory of monopoly in 1839: Charles Ellet Jr', *JPE*, 58, April 1950; R.B. Ekelund and D.L. Hooks, 'Joint demand, discriminating two-part tariffs and location theory: an early American contribution', *WEJ*, 10, March 1972.

ELTON, Edwin J.

Born 1939, Milwaukee, Wisc., USA.

Current Post Prof. Fin., NYU, USA, 1972–.

Recent Posts Ass. prof., 1965–70, Assoc. prof., 1970–2, NYU; Sr Res. Fellow, Internat. Inst. Management, 1972–4.

Degrees BA Ohio Wesleyan Univ., 1961; MS, PhD, Carnegie Mellon Univ., 1965, 1970.

Offices Assoc. ed., 1974– Dir.,

1979–80, AFA; Assoc. ed., Inst. Management Sciences, 1977–.

Principal Contributions Developed a simple algorithm for solving portfolio problems. The algorithm gives exact solutions, is so simple to solve that it does not require computers, and clarifies for the first time why a security is included or excluded. Demonstrated the presence of tax effects in security returns and measured its importance. Pioneered in the use of mathematical models for analysing financial problems.

Publications *Books:* 1. *Security Evaluation and Portfolio Analysis* (Prentice-Hall, 1972); 2. *Finance as a Dynamic Process* (Prentice-Hall, 1975); 3. *International Capital Markets* (N-H, 1975); 4. *Portfolio Management: Twenty-five Years Later* (N-H, 1979); 5. *Modern Portfolio Theory* (Wiley, 1980.

Articles: 1. 'Marginal stockholder tax rates and the clientele effect' (with M.J. Gruber), *REStat*, 52(1), Feb. 1970; 2. 'Estimating the dependence structure of share prices – implications for portfolio selection' (with M.J. Gruber), *J Fin*, 28(5), Dec. 1973; 3. 'Simple criteria for optimal portfolio selection' (with M.J. Gruber and M.W. Padberg), *J Fin*, 31(5), Dec. 1976; 4. 'Risk reduction and portfolio size: an analytical solution' (with M.J. Gruber), *J Bus*, 50(4), Oct. 1977; 5. 'Taxes and portfolio composition in efficient markets', *J Fin E*, 8(4), Dec. 1980.

ELY, Richard Theodore*

Dates and Birthplace   1854–1943, Ripley, NY, USA.

Posts Held   Lecturer Econ., Johns Hopkins Univ., 1881–92; Prof., Univ. Wisconsin, 1892–1922.

Degree   BA, Columbia Coll., 1876.

Offices   Founder and pres., 1900–2, AEA; Founder, Inst. Res. Land Econ. and Public Utility Econ., 1920.

Career   His advocacy of reform movements and in particular his account of labour organisations caused the early part of his career to be embroiled in controversy over strikes, and the issue of socialism. The University of Wisconsin 'trial' in 1894 exonerated him and

resulted in a classic statement in favour of academic freedom. The school he founded at Wisconsin provided a link between German historical economics and institutionalism, and became famous because of its collaboration with the progressive state government of Wisconsin. *Property and Contract* (1914) was his main published contribution, but was only part of a massive output of articles and editorial work. His teaching and founding work for the AEA made him one of the most influential economists of his time.

Publications *Books:* 1. *The Past and Present of Political Economy* (1884); 2. *The Labor Movement in America* (1886); 3. *An Introduction to Political Economy* (1889); 4. *Outlines of Economics* (1893, with R.H. Hess, 1937); 5. *Property and Contract in their Relation to the Distribution of Wealth* (1914).

Secondary Literature   A.W. Coats, 'Ely, Richard T.', *IESS*, vol. 5.

ENGEL, Ernst*

Dates and Birthplace   1821–96, Germany.

Posts Held   Dir. Stat. Bureaux, Saxony, 1850–8, Prussia, 1861–82.

Degree   Student, l'Ecole des Mines, Paris.

Offices   Founder, Internat. Stat. Inst., 1886.

Career   An official statistician who was involved in social reform movements and devised Engel's Law: the proportion of a consumer's budget spent on food tends to decline as the consumer's income rises. The law is remarkable as probably the first quantitative law derived from empirical economic data; moreover it has been confirmed by innumerable surveys around the world. He also wrote on labour, industry, taxation, insurance, banking and war.

Publications *Books:* 1. *Der Kostenwerth des Menschen* (1883).

Articles: 1. 'Die Productions- und Consumtionsverhaltnisse des Königsreichs Sachsen', *Zeitschrift des Statistischen Bureaus des Königlich Sachischen Ministeriums des Innern*, 3, 1857.

Secondary Literature H.S. Houthakker, 'Engel, Ernst', *IESS*, vol. 5.

ENGELS, Friedrich*

Dates and Birthplace 1820–95, Barmen, Germany.

Posts Held Cotton manufacturer and journalist.

Career Revolutionary and Marx's close collaborator and friend. After their first meeting in 1844 to discuss Engels' early economic writings, Engels gradually left theoretical work to Marx and concentrated on polemical and journalistic writing. He wrote extensively on military topics and the military aspects of revolution. After Marx's death, he organised the editing and publication of Marx's works, including the unpublished second and third volumes of *Kapital*, and provided them with important introductions. Because of the close association in which he and Marx worked it is almost impossible to distinguish their individual contributions to any aspect of theory on which they wrote, including the subject of economics.

Publications *Books:* 1. *Die Lage der Arbeitenden Klasse in England* (1845), transl. as *The Condition of the Working Class in England* (1958); 2. *The Holy Family* (with K. Marx), (1845, 1956); 3. *The German Ideology* (with K. Marx), (1845, 1939); 4. *The Peasant War in Germany* (1850, 1956); 5. *Anti-Dühring* (1878, 1959); 6. *Socialism: Utopian and Scientific* (1880, 1935); 7. *The Origin of the Family, Private Property and the State* (1884, 1942); 8. *Ludwig Feuerbach and the Outcome of Classical German Philosophy* (1886, 1941).

Secondary Literature G. Mayer, *Friedrich Engels: a Biography* (Chapman, 1936); T. Ramm, 'Engels, Friedrich', *IESS*, vol. 5.

ENGERMAN, Stanley L.

Born 1936, New York City, NY, USA.

Current Post Prof. Econ. and Hist., Univ. Rochester, NY, USA, 1963–.

Recent Posts Ass. prof. Econ., Yale Univ., 1962–3.

Degrees BS, MBA, New York Univ., 1956, 1958; PhD Johns Hopkins Univ., 1962.

Offices Member, AEA, AHA, EHA.

Principal Contributions The economics of slavery in the American South and elsewhere.

Publications *Books:* 1. *The Reinterpretation of American Economic History*, ed. (with R.W. Fogel), (Harper & Row, 1971); 2. *Time on the Cross*, 2 vols (with R.W. Fogel), (Little Brown, 1974); 3. *Race and Slavery in the Western Hemisphere: Quantitative Studies*, ed. (with E.D. Genovese), (Princeton Univ. Press, 1975).

ENTHOVEN, Alain

Born 1930, Seattle, Washington, USA.

Current Post Marriner S. Eccles, prof. Public Private Management, Grad. School Bus., Prof. Health Care Econ., School Medicine, Stanford Univ.

Recent Posts Instructor Econ., MIT, 1955–6; Economist, 1956–60, Consultant, 1969–, Rand Corp.; Consultant, Brookings Inst., 1956–60; Vis. assoc. prof. Econ., Univ. Washington, 1958; Operations res. analyst, US Office Dir. Defense Res. Engineering, 1960; Dep. comptroller, Dep. Ass., US Secretary Defense, 1961–5; Ass. Secretary, Defense Systems Analysis, 1965–9; Vice-pres. Econ. Planning, Litton Industries, 1969–71; Pres., Litton Medical Products, 1971–3; Special consultant, US Secretary Dept. Health, Education, Welfare, on Nat. Health Insurance, 1977–8; Member, Health Pol. Advisory Group to Pres.-elect R. Reagan, 1980.

Degrees BA (Econ.) Stanford Univ., 1952; BPhil. (Econ.) Univ. Oxford, 1954; PhD (Econ.) MIT, 1956.

Offices and Honours Phi Beta Kappa; Rhodes Scholarship; AEA; Amer. Assoc. Rhodes Scholars; Sierra Club; Council Foreign Relations; US President's award disting. fed. civilian service, 1963; Dept. Defense medal disting. public service, 1969; Council member, Inst. Medicine, NAS, 1975–7.

Principal Contributions Economics of defence. Economics and public policy in health care.

Publications *Books:* 1. 'Introduction', *A modern design for Defense decision, a McNamara-Hitch-Enthoven anthology*, ed. S.A. Tucker (Industrial Coll. of the Armed Forces, 1966); 2. *How Much is Enough? Shaping the Defense Program 1961-1969* (with K.W. Smith), (Harper & Row, 1971, Kraus Reprint, 1980); 3. *Pollution, Resources and the Environment*, ed. (with A.M. Freeman III), (Norton, 1973); 4. *Health Plan: The Only Practical Solution to the Soaring Cost of Medical Care* (Addison-Wesley, 1980). *Articles:* 1. 'A theorem on expectations and the stability of equilibrium' (with K.J. Arrow), *Em*, 24(3), July 1956; 2. 'The simple mathematics of maximization', in *The Economics of Defense in the Nuclear Age*, eds C.J. Hitch and R.N. McKean (Harvard Univ. Press, 1960); 3. 'A neo-classical model of money, debt, and economic growth', in *Money in a Theory of Finance*, eds J.G. Gurley and E.S. Shaw (Brookings Inst., 1960); 4. 'Does anyone want competition? The politics of NHI', in *New Directions in Public Health Care: A Prescription for the 1980s*, ed. C.M. Lindsay, (Inst. Contemporary Stud., 1980); 5. 'How interested groups have responded to a proposal for economic competition in health services', *AER*, 70(2), May 1980.

ERHARD, Ludwig*

Dates and Birthplace 1897-1977, Fürth, Germany.
Post Held Ass., Nuremberg Inst. for Econ. Observation, 1928-42.
Degree Dr rer. pol. Univ. Frankfurt-am-Main.
Offices Econ. Minister, Bavaria, 1945-6; Dir., Advisory Comm. for Money and Credit, 1947-8; Dir., Econ. Council, Anglo-American Occupation District, 1848-9; Econ. Minister, 1949-63; Vice-chancellor, 1957-63, Chancellor, 1963-6, Bundesrepublik.
Career Professional economist who was entrusted with reconstruction work by the Allies in post-war Germany. The German 'economic miracle' was based on his 'social market system'. His achievement led to his appointment as German Chancellor.
Publications *Books:* 1. *Deutschlands Rückkehr zum Weltmarkt* (1953); 2. *Wohlstand für Alle* (1957); 3. *Deutsche Wirtschaftspolitik* (1962).

EUCKEN, Walter*

Dates and Birthplace 1891-1950, Jena, Germany.
Posts Held Prof. Univ. Tübingen, 1925-7, Univ. Freiburg, 1927-50.
Career A neo-liberal who attempted to integrate the Historical School's approach with that of standard, neo-classical theory. In his *Foundations . . .*, he attempted to develop a taxonomic approach to comparative economic systems. He was influential in post-World War II Germany in the movement to liberalise the German economy.
Publications *Books:* 1. *Kapitaltheoretische Untersuchungen* (1934); 2. *The Foundations of Economics* (1940, 1950).
Articles: 'On the theory of the centrally administered economy: an analysis of the German experiment, Pts I-II', *Ec*, N.S. 15, May/Aug. 1948.
Secondary Literature T.W. Hutchison, 'Walter Eucken and the German social-market economy', in *The Politics and Philosophy of Economics* (Blackwell, 1981); F.A. Lutz, 'Eucken, Walter', *Handwörterbuch der Sozialwissenschaften*, vol. 3, eds E.V. Bekerath et al. (Gustav Fisher, 1959).

EVANS, M.K.

N.e.

F

FABRICANT, S.

N.e.

FAMA, E.

N.e.

FANNO, Marco*

Dates and Birthplace 1878–1965, Italy.

Post Held Prof., Univ. Padua.

Career Writer on cycles who analysed the proportions of factors of production and emphasised the relation between direct and capital goods in a given economic system. He was highly respected as a teacher.

Publications *Books:* 1. *L'Espansione Commerciale e Coloniale Degli Stati Moderni* (1906); 2. *Le Banche e il Mercato Monetario* (1912); 3. *I Transferimenti Anormali dei Capitali e le Crisi* (1935); 4. *Introduzione Allo Studio della Teoria Economica del Corporativismo* (1935); 5. *Principii di Scienza Economica* (1938).

FAWCETT, Henry*

Dates and Birthplace 1833–84, Salisbury, England.

Posts Held Fellow, Trinity Hall, 1856–84, Prof. Polit. Econ., 1863–84, Univ. Camb.

Degree BA Univ. Camb., 1856.

Offices MP for Brighton, 1865–74, Hackney, 1874–84; UK Postmaster-General, 1880–4; Fellow, Royal Soc., 1882.

Career Blinded in a shooting accident at the age of 25, he nevertheless enjoyed a most distinguished career as member of parliament, cabinet minister and professor of economics. His *Manual* ... is in effect a popularisation of the ideas of his friend J.S. Mill, and as such enjoyed great success as a textbook throughout the second half of the nineteenth century. The level of analysis is, however, unremarkable, with a dogmatic presentation of *laissez-faire* and a strict adherence to the wages fund theory. He was the first salaried professor of political economy at Cambridge University, and was Marshall's predecessor in the Chair.

Publications *Books:* 1. *Manual of Political Economy* (1863).

Secondary Literature L. Stephen, *Life of Henry Fawcett* (1885).

FARRELL, Michael J.*

N.e.

FEIGE, Edgar L.

Born 1937, Berlin, Germany.

Current Post Fellow, Vis. Scholar, Netherlands Inst. Advanced Study, 1979–82; Cleveringa Chair Prof., Univ. Leiden, Netherlands, 1981–2.

Recent Posts Prof. Econ., Univ. Wisconsin, Madison, 1963–81; Vis. reader, Univ. Essex, England, 1967–8; Vis. Fulbright Scholar, Autonomous Univ. Madrid, 1971, 1972; Vis. prof., Univ. Leiden, 1980–1.

Degrees BA (Econ.) Columbia Univ., 1958; PhD (Econ.) Univ. Chicago, 1963.

Offices and Honours Eli Lilley Fellow; Earhart Foundation Fellow; Fed. Reserve Bank Chicago Fellow; Ford Foundation Doctoral Dissertation award, 1963; Leonardo Scholar, Univ. Wisconsin, 1977–8.

Principal Contributions Theory and empirical estimates of the demand for money. Theory of the optimal quantity of money. Protection of privacy through partial aggregation. Wage and price controls. Causal testing in economics. Efficient markets – stock prices and exchange rates. Federal Reserve monetary policy. International inflation. Resource scarcity and the Hotelling principle. Peace in the Middle East.

Publications *Books:* 1. *The Demand for Liquid Assets: A Temporal Cross-section Analysis* (Prentice-Hall, 1964).

Articles: 1. 'The optimal quantity of money, bonds, commodity inventories and capital' (with M. Parkin), *AER*, 61(3), June 1971, reprinted in *Teoria de la Demanda de Dinero*, ed. C. Lluch (Spain, 1975); 2. 'Economically rational expectations: are innovations in the rate of inflation independent of measures of innovations in monetary and fiscal policy?' (with D. Pearce), *JPE*, 84(3), June 1976; 3. 'The casual causal relationship between money and income: some caveats from the time-series analyst' (with D. Pearce), *REStat*, 61(4), Nov. 1979; 4. 'Efficient foreign exchange markets and the monetary approach to exchange rate determination' (with D. Caves), *AER*, 70(1), March 1980; 5. 'Multinational inflation under fixed exchange rates; some empirical evidence from latent variable models' (with K. Singleton), *REStat*, 63(1), Feb. 1981.

FEINSTEIN, Charles

Born 1932, Johannesburg, S. Africa.
Current Post Prof. Econ. and Social Hist., Univ. York, England.
Recent Posts Lecturer Econ., Univ. Camb., Fellow, Clare Coll., Univ. Camb., 1963–78.
Degrees BComm., Univ. Witwatersrand, 1950; PhD, Univ. Camb., 1958.
Offices Council, RES, 1980–; Council, EHS, 1980–; Ed., *EJ*, 1980–.
Principal Contributions Estimates of national income and capital formation in the UK.
Publications *Books:* 1. *Domestic Capital Formation in the United Kingdom 1920–1938* (CUP, 1965); 2. *Socialism, Capitalism and Economic Growth, Essays Presented to Maurice Dobb,* ed. (CUP, 1967); 3. *National Income, Expenditure and Output of the United Kingdom, 1855–1965* (CUP, 1972); 4. *British Economic Growth 1856–1973* (with R.C.O. Matthews and J. Odling-Smee), (Stanford Univ. Press, 1981).
Articles: 1. 'Capital formation in Great Britain, 1760–1860', in *Cambridge Economic History of Europe,* vol. 7, eds P. Mathias and M.M. Postan (CUP, 1978); 2. 'Population, occupations and economic development, 1831–1981', in *York, 1831–1981,* ed. C. Feinstein, (Sessions, 1981).

FELDSTEIN, Martin

Born 1939, New York City, NY, USA.
Current Post Prof. Econ., Harvard Univ., 1967–; Pres., NBER, Cambridge, Mass., 1977–.
Recent Posts Fellow, Nuffield Coll., Univ. Oxford, 1965–7.
Degrees BA Harvard Univ., 1961; BLitt., MA, DPhil., Univ. Oxford, 1963, 1964, 1967.

Offices and Honours Fellow, 1970, Council member, 1977–, Fisher-Schultz Lecture, 1980, Em Soc; John Bates Clark medal, AEA, 1977.
Principal Contributions Quantitative studies in public economics, including tax, transfer and spending programmes. More specifically, the effects of these fiscal programmes on capital formation and employment. Studies of social insurance programmes (social security pensions, unemployment insurance, health insurance). Analyses of the interaction between fiscal structure and macroeconomic policy. Studies of capital formation.
Publications *Books:* 1. *Economic Analysis for Health Service Efficiency* (N-H, 1967); 2. *Hospital Costs and Health Insurance* (Harvard Univ. Press, 1981); 3. *Capital Taxation* (Harvard Univ. Press, 1981); 4. *Inflation, Tax Rules and Capital Formation* (Chicago Univ. Press, 1981); 5. *Behavioral Simulation Methods in Tax Policy Analysis* (Chicago Univ. Press, 1981).

FELLNER, William John

Born 1905, Budapest, Hungary.
Current Post Res. Scholar, Project Dir. Contemporary Econ. Problems Series, Amer. Enterprise Inst., Washington, DC.
Recent Posts Sterling Prof. Econ., Yale Univ., 1951–73 (Emeritus thereafter); Member, US President's Council Econ. Advisers, 1973–5.
Degrees Dipl. Ing. Chem. Fed. Inst. Technology, Zürich, 1927; PhD Univ. Berlin, 1929.
Offices and Honours Hon. member, Phi Beta Kappa; Fellow, AAAS; Corresponding member, Bavarian Academy Science; Pres., AEA, 1969.
Principal Contributions Effect of long-run policies on price expectations and cost trends. Influence of relative resource scarcities on the character of innovations. Effect of uncertainty on market results in general and on oligopolistic behaviour in particular.
Publications *Books:* 1. *Monetary Policies and Full Employment* (Univ. Cal. Press, 1946); 2. *Competition Among the Few* (Alfred A. Knopf,

1949); 3. *Trends and Cycles in Economic Activity* (Henry Holt, 1955); 4. *Probability and Profit* (Richard D. Irwin, 1965); 5. *Towards a Reconstruction of Macroeconomics* (Amer. Enterprise Inst., 1976).

Articles: 1. 'Prices and wages under bilateral monopoly', *QJE*, 61, Aug. 1947; 2. 'Average-cost pricing and the theory of uncertainty', *JPE*, 56, June 1948; 3. 'Two propositions in the theory of induced innovations', *EJ*, 71, June 1961; 4. 'Lessons from the failure of demand-management policies', *JEL*, 14(1), March 1976; 5. 'The valid core of rationality hypotheses in the theory of expectations', *JMCB*, 12(4), Pt 2, Nov. 1980.

FELS, Rendigs

Born 1917, Cincinnati, Ohio, USA.
Current Post Prof. Econ., Vanderbilt Univ., Nashville, USA.
Degrees BA, PhD, Harvard Univ., 1939, 1948; MA Columbia Univ., 1940.
Offices Secretary-Treasurer, 1970–5, Treasurer, 1976–, AEA; Pres., SEA, 1968.
Principal Contributions Chiefly responsible for preparing the Test of Understanding in College of Economics, which has been used in over 70 published research studies.
Publications *Books:* 1. *Wages, Earnings and Employment, Nashville, Chattanooga and St Louis Railway, 1866–1896* (Vanderbilt Univ. Press, 1953); 2. *American Business Cycles, 1865–1897* (Univ. N. Carolina Press, 1959); 3. *Challenge to the American economy: An Introduction to Economics* (Allyn & Bacon, 1961, 1966); 4. *Forecasting and Recognizing Business-Cycle Turning Points* (with C.E. Hinshaw), (Columbia Univ. Press, 1968); 5. *Casebook of Economic Problems and Policies* (with R.G. Uhler and S.G. Buckles), (West Publishing Co., 1974, 1981).
Articles: 1. 'The US downturn of 1948', *AER* 55, Dec. 1965; 2. 'A new test of understanding in college economics', *AER/S*, 57, May 1967; 3. 'Multiple choice questions in elementary econom-

ics', in *Recent Research in Economics Education*, ed. K.G. Lumsden (Prentice-Hall, 1970); 4. 'Developing independent problem-solving ability in elementary economics', *AER*, 64(2), May 1974; 5. 'Research on teaching college economics: a survey' (with J.J. Siegfried), *JEL*, 17(3), Sept. 1979.

FERBER, Robert

Dates and Birthplace 1922–1981, New York City, NY, USA.
Posts Held Res. prof. Econ., Bureau Econ. Bus. Res., Prof. Econ. Bus. Admin., 1955–, Dir., Survey Res. Laboratory, 1964–, Univ. Illinois, Urbana-Champaign; Prof. Marketing, Univ. Illinois, Chicago Circle, 1979–81.
Degrees BS (Maths.), City Coll., NY, 1942; MA (Econ. Stats), PhD (Econ. Stats), Univ. Chicago, 1945, 1951.
Offices and Honours Master Scholar award, Ford Foundation, 1963; Hall of Fame Distribution, 1964; Ed., *J Marketing Res.*, 1964–9; Pres., Amer. Marketing Assoc., 1969–70; Ed., *JASA*, 1969–76; Charles Coolidge Parlin award, 1972; Ed., *J Consumer Res.*, 1977–; Chairman Publications Comm., ASA, 1977–; Chairman, Comm. Publications, AEA, 1978–.
Principal Contributions Studies on the reliability of economic data obtained in household surveys and ways of improving these data; investigations of consumer savings and spendings patterns and their determinants in industrialised and in less developed countries; and studies of the roles of expectations in consumer and business behaviour.
Publications *Books:* 1. *A Study of Aggregate Consumption Functions* (NBER, 1953); 2. *Research Methods in Economics and Business* (with R. Ferber and P.J. Verdoorn), (Macmillan, 1962); 3. *The Reliability of Consumer Reports of Financial Assets and Debts*, Studies in Consumer Savings No. 6, (Bureau Econ. and Bus. Res., Univ. Illinois, 1966); 4. *Determinants of Investment Behavior*, ed. (NBER, 1967); 5. *Consumption and Income Distribution in Latin America: Selected*

Topics, ed. (Organization of Amer. States, 1980).

Articles: 1. 'Measuring the accuracy and structure of businessmen's expectations', *JASA*, 48, Sept. 1953; 2. 'The accuracy of aggregate savings functions in the postwar years', *REStat*, 37, May 1955; 3. 'Consumer economics, a survey', *JEL*, 11(4), Dec. 1973; 4. 'Finding the poor' (with P. Musgrove), *RIW*, 24, Sept. 1978; 5. 'Social experimentation and economic policy: a survey' (with W.Z. Hirsch), *JEL*, 16(4), Dec. 1978.

FERGUSON, Adam*

Dates and Birthplace   1723–1816, Perthshire, Scotland.

Posts Held   Military chaplain; Keeper, Advocate's Library, Edinburgh; Prof. Nat. Phil., 1759–64, Prof. Moral Phil., 1764–85, Univ. Edinburgh.

Degree   BA Univ. Edinburgh.

Offices and Honours   Founder member, Royal Soc. Edinburgh; Hon. member, Berlin Academy Sciences.

Career   Scottish moral philosopher whose *History of Civil Society* has been identified as an early example of sociological method. His work is of interest to economists because of the clear exposition of the principle of the division of labour in economy and society, which almost certainly had a major influence on Adam Smith.

Publications   *Books:* 1. *An Essay on the History of Civil Society* (1767, 1978); 2. *Institutes of Moral Philosophy* (1769, 1800); 3. *History of the Progress and Termination of the Roman Republic*, 3 vols (1783, 1841); 4. *Principles of Moral and Political Science*, 2 vols (1792).

Secondary Literature   D. Kettler, *The Social and Political Thought of Adam Ferguson* (Ohio State Univ. Press, 1965); W.C. Lehmann, 'Ferguson, Adam', *IESS*, vol. 5.

FERGUSON, Charles E.*

N.e.

FERRARA, Francesco*

Dates and Birthplace   1810–1900, Palermo, Italy.

Posts Held   Dir. Stats, Palermo region, 1834; Prof. Polit. Econ., Univ. Turin, ?–1859; Controller Customs, Palermo, 1862; Italian Minister Fin., 1867; Dir., School of Commerce, Venice, 1881.

Career   His varied career in the public service, politics and education involved periods of imprisonment and exile as well as periods in government. He founded the *Giornale di Statistica* and was responsible for the *Biblioteca dell'Economista* (1850–70) which collected translations of notable foreign and Italian economic literature. His doctrinaire free-trade liberalism became unfashionable during his later years, when he became an increasingly isolated figure.

Publications   *Books:* 1. *Esame Storico-critico di Economisti e Dottrine Economiche* (1889–92); 2. *Oeuvres économiques choisies* eds G.H. Bousquet and J. Crisafulli (1938).

Secondary Literature   A Loria, 'Francesco Ferrara' (obituary), *EJ*, 10, March 1900; G.H. Bousquet, 'Un grand économiste Italien, Francesco Ferrara', *Revue d'histoire econ. et sociale*, 14, 1926.

FETTER, Frank Albert*

Dates and Birthplace   1863–1949, Peru, Ind., USA.

Posts Held   Prof., Univ. Indiana, 1895–8, Stanford Univ., 1898–1901, Cornell Univ., 1901–11, Princeton Univ., 1911–33.

Degrees   BA Univ. Indiana, 1891; MPhil. Cornell Univ., 1892; PhD Univ. Halle, Germany, 1894.

Offices and Honours   Council member, Amer. Philosophical Soc.; Pres., AEA, 1912; Karl Menger medal, Austrian Econ. Soc., 1927.

Career   His interest in bringing economics into line with new trends in psychology led him to concentrate on theories of value. His work on value theory in turn brought him into friendly contact with Böhm-Bawerk and Wieser, whilst his distaste for the preservation of 'outdated' theory made him an opponent of Marshall. Welfare economics was a major concern, and he turned economic theory to public questions, for instance, in 1923–4 he was a member of a group which placed evidence before the Federal Trade Commission on pricing practices in the steel industry. The concept of 'psychic income', taken up by Irving Fisher, was one of his best known contributions.

Publications *Books:* 1. *The principles of Economics with Applications to Practical Problems* (1904); 2. *Economic Principles* (1915); 3. *Modern Economic Problems* (1917); 4. *Capital, Interest, and Rent. Essays in the Theory of Distribution*, ed M.N. Rothbard (1977).

Secondary Literature S.E. Howard and E.W. Kemmerer, 'Frank Albert Fetter. A birthday note', *AER*, 33, March 1943.

FETTER, Frank Whitson

Born 1899, San Francisco, Cal., USA.

Current Post Retired.

Recent Posts Instructor, Ass. prof. Econ., Princeton Univ., 1924–34; Assoc. prof., Prof. Econ., Haverford Coll., 1934–48; Prof. Econ., Northwestern Univ., 1948–67; Vis. prof. Econ., Dartmouth Coll., 1967–8.

Degrees BA Swarthmore Coll., 1920; MA, PhD, Princeton Univ., 1922, 1926; MA Harvard Univ., 1924.

Offices and Honours Phi Beta Kappa, 1920; Guggenheim Memorial Foundation Fellow, 1937–8; Exec. Comm., AEA, 1944–6; Pres., MEA, 1952; Dir., 1950–73, Chairman, 1965–7, NBER.

Principal Contributions Development of British monetary and banking policy between 1797 and 1875; economic opinion in the British reviews up to 1850; role of economist in parliament between Adam Smith and J.S. Mill; relation of British economic thought to the spirit of the Enlightenment; and the transfer problem.

Publications *Books:* 1. *Monetary Inflation in Chile* (Princeton Univ. Press, 1931; Spanish transl., 1937); 2.

The Irish Pound (A & U, Northwestern Univ. Press, 1955); 3. *Development of British Monetary Orthodoxy* (Harvard Univ. Press, 1965, Augustus M. Kelley, 1978); 4. *Monetary and Financial Policy in 19th-Century Britain*, co-author, (Irish Univ. Press, 1973); 5. *The Economist in Parliament* (Duke Univ. Press, 1980).

Articles: 1. 'The life and writings of John Wheatley', *JPE*, 50, June 1942; 2. 'Does America breed depressions?', *Three Banks Review*, 27, Sept. 1955; 3. 'Economic controversies in the British reviews', *Ec*, 32, Nov. 1965; 4. 'The transfer problem: formal elegance or historical realism?', in *Essays in Money and Banking in Honour of R.S. Sayers* (OUP, 1968); 5. 'The rise and decline of Ricardian economics', *HOPE*, 1(1), Spring 1969.

FINEGAN, T. Aldrich

Born 1929, Long Beach, Cal., USA.

Current Post Prof. Econ., Vanderbilt Univ., Nashville, USA, 1970–.

Recent Posts Ass. prof. Econ., Princeton Univ., 1960–4; Assoc. prof. Econ., Vanderbilt Univ., 1965–70.

Degrees BA Claremont Men's Coll., 1951; MA, PhD, Univ. Chicago, 1953, 1960.

Offices and Honours Member, AEA, IRRA; Lawrence R. Klein award, 1972; Chair, Econ. Dept., 1974–7, Ellen Gregg Ingalls teaching award, 1975, Vanderbilt Univ.; Member, Vice-pres., 1978, SEA.

Principal contributions Economic aspects of labour force participation in the USA.

Publications *Books:* 1. *Economics of Labor Force Participation* (with W.G. Bowen), (Princeton Univ. Press, 1969).

Articles: 1. 'Labor force growth and the return to full employment', *MLR*, 95, Feb. 1972; 2. 'Should discouraged workers be counted as unemployed?', *Challenge*, Nov./Dec. 1978; 3. 'Discouraged workers and economic fluctuations', *ILRR*, 35(1), Oct. 1981.

FISCHER, Stanley

Born 1943, Lusaka, N. Rhodesia (now Zambia).

Current Post   Prof. Econ., MIT, USA, 1977–.

Recent Posts   Ass. prof. Econ., Univ. Chicago, 1970–3; Assoc. prof. Econ., MIT, 1973–7; Fellow, Inst. Advanced Stud., Hebrew Univ. Jerusalem, 1976–7.

Principal Contributions   Work in monetary theory and policy, and international monetary economics.

Publications   *Books:* 1. *Macroeconomics* (with R. Dornbusch), (McGraw-Hill, 1978, 1981); 2. *Rational Expectations and Economic Policy*, ed. (Univ. Chicago Press, 1980).

Articles: 1. 'The demand for index bonds', *JPE*, 83(3), June 1975; 2. 'Long-term contracts, rational expectations and the optimal money supply rule', *JPE*, 85(1), Feb. 1977; 3. 'Comparative advantage, trade, and payments in a Ricardian model with a continuum of goods' (with R. Dornbusch and P.A. Samuelson), *AER*, 67(5), Dec. 1977; 4. 'Towards an understanding of the real effects and costs of inflation' (with F. Modigliani), *WA*, 114(4), 1978; 5. 'Exchange rates and the current account' (with R. Dornbusch), *AER*, 70(5), Dec. 1980.

FISCHER, Wolfram

Born   1928, Weigelsdorf-Tannenberg, Germany.

Current Post   Prof. Econ. and Social Hist., Free Univ. Berlin.

Degrees   Dr Phil. Univ. Tübingen, 1951; Dr rer. pol. Free Univ. Berlin, 1954.

Offices   Chairman, *Berliner Wissenschaftliche Gesellschaft*, 1973–81.

Principal Contributions   Economic history of industrialisation. Economic history of the twentieth century.

Publications   *Books:* 1. *Handwerksrecht und Handwerkswirtschaft um 1800. Studien zur Sozial- und Wirtschaftsverfassung vor der Industriellen Revolution* (Duncker & Humblot, 1955); 2. *Die Wirtschaftspolitik Deutschlands 1918–1945. Schriftenreige der Niedersächsischen Landeszentrale für Politische Bildung* (Hannover, 1961); 3. *Der Staat und die Anfänge der Industrialisierung in Baden. Bd. I: Die staatliche Gewerbepolitik* (Duncker & Humblot, 1962); 4. *Wirtschaft und Gesellschaft im Zeitalter der Industrialisierung. Vorträge, Aufsätze, Studien* (Vandenhoeck & Ruprecht, 1972); 5. *Die Weltwirtschaft im 20. Jahrhundert* (Vandenhoeck & Ruprecht, 1979).

Articles: 1. 'The German Zollverein. A case study in customs union', *Kyklos*, 12, 1960; 2. 'Government activity and industrialization in Germany (1815–1870)', in *The Economics of Take-off into Sustained Growth*, ed. W.W. Rostow (Macmillan, 1963); 3. 'Rural industrialization and population change', *CSSH*, 15, 1973; 4. 'The recruitment and training of administrative and technical personnel (with P. Lundgreen), in *The Formation of National States in Western Europe*, ed. C. Tilly (Princeton Univ. Press, 1975); 5. 'The strategy of public investment in XIXth century Germany', *J Eur EH*, 6, 1977.

FISHER, Franklin M.

Born   1934, New York City, NY, USA.

Current Post   Prof. Econ., MIT, USA 1965–.

Recent Posts   Ass. prof. Econ., Univ. Chicago, 1959–60; Assistant prof., 1960–2, Assoc. prof. Econ., 1962–5, MIT.

Degrees   BA (*Summa cum laude*) MA, PhD, Harvard Univ., 1956, 1957, 1960.

Offices and Honours   Irving Fisher lecturer, 1968; Ed., *Em*, 1968–77; AEA John Bates Clark award, 1973; Vicepres., 1977–8, Pres., 1979, Em Soc.

Principal Contributions   Analysis of identification and simultaneous equation problems in econometrics; existence of aggregate production functions; stability of general equilibrium with full arbitrage; economic theory of price indices; monopoly in American antitrust policy; and empirical studies of various industries.

Publications   *Books:* 1. *A Priori Information and Time-Series Analysis: Essays in Economic Theory and Measurement* (N-H, 1962); 2. *A Study in Econometrics: The Demand for Elec-*

tricity in the United States (with C. Kaysen), (N-H, 1962); 3. *Supply and Costs in the United States Petroleum Industry: Two Econometric Studies*, (Johns Hopkins Univ. Press, 1964); 4. *The Identification Problem in Econometrics* (McGraw-Hill, 1966); 5. *The Economic Theory of Price Indices* (with K. Shell), (Academic Press, 1972).

Articles: 1. 'On the cost of approximate specification in simultaneous equation estimation', *Em*, 29(2), April 1961; 2. 'The costs of automobile model changes since 1949', *JPE*, 70(5), Oct. 1962; 3. 'The existence of aggregate production functions', *Em*, 37(4), Oct. 1969; 4. 'Diagnosing monopoly', *QREB*, 19(2), Summer 1979; 5. 'Stability, disequilibrium awareness, and the perception of new opportunities', *Em*, 49(2), March 1981.

FISHER, Irving*

Dates and Birthplace 1867–1947, Saugerties, NY, USA.

Posts Held Teacher Maths, 1892–5, Prof. Econ., 1895–1935, Yale Univ., Businessman, directorships, including Remington Rand, 1926–47.

Degrees BA, PhD, Yale Univ., 1898, 1891.

Offices Pres., ASA, Internat. Em Soc, Nat. Inst. Social Sciences, Amer. Assoc. Labor Legislation, and active in a host of other societies.

Career One of the greatest, if not the greatest, and certainly one of the most colourful American economists. A writer and teacher of prodigious scope and output, whose business career included the earning of a fortune from the invention of a visible card index system. He campaigned for a great number of causes, including world peace, prohibition, preventive medicine, eugenics, and 100 per cent deposit reserve money. His works are distinguished by their unusual clarity of exposition and contain major contributions to mathematical economics, the theory of value and prices, capital theory, monetary theory, and statistics. The now familiar distinction between stocks and flows is almost entirely due to his brilliant book on *The Nature of Capital and Income*.

His ability in theoretical work was allied to a deep concern with the observation of facts: the Fisher 'ideal index' of prices is only one of his contributions to statistics.

Publications *Books:* 1. *Mathematical Investigations in the Theory of Value and Prices* (1892, 1961); 2. *The Nature of Capital and Income* (1906, 1927); 3. *The Purchasing Power of Money* (1911, 1920); 4. *Elementary Principles of Economics* (1912); 5. *Stabilizing the Dollar* (1920); 6. *The making of Index Numbers* (1922, 1927); 7. *The Money Illusion* (1928); 8. *The Theory of Interest* (1930, 1961); 9. *Booms and Depressions* (1932); 10. *Inflation* (1933).

Secondary Literature J.A. Schumpeter, 'Irving Fisher 1867–1947', in *Ten great Economists from Marx to Keynes* (OUP, 1948); M. Allais, 'Fisher, Irving', *IESS*, vol. 5.

FISHLOW, Albert

Born Philadelphia, Penn., USA.

Current Post Prof. Econ., Dir. Concilium Internat. Area Stud., Yale Univ., USA.

Recent Posts Acting ass. prof. Econ., 1961–3, Assoc. prof. Econ., 1963–6, Prof. Econ., 1966–77, Univ. Cal. Berkeley.

Degrees BA (Econ.) Univ. Pennsylvania, 1956; PhD Harvard Univ., 1963.

Offices and Honours Ed. Board, *Foreign Pol., Internat. Organization, Latin Amer. Res. Review*; David Wells prize, Harvard Univ., 1963; Arthur H. Cole prize, EHA, 1966; Joseph Schumpeter prize, Harvard Univ., 1971; Vice-pres., EHA, 1975; Chairman, SSRC-ACLS Comm. Latin Amer., 1979–81.

Principal Contributions Application of more explicit theoretical and statistical models to historical processes of long-term economic growth in search of rigorous and fresh interpretations of the past; empirical analysis of the influence of politics and policies on contemporary processes of economic growth and distribution, particularly in Latin American countries; clarification of economic issues underlying policy discussions surrounding such current international questions as North-South relations, developing country indebtedness, etc.

Publications   *Books:* 1. *American Railroads and the Transformation of the Ante-bellum Economy* (Harvard Univ. Press, 1965); 2. *Rich and Poor Nations in the World Economy* (with others), (McGraw-Hill, 1978); 3. *Trade in Manufactured Products with Developing Countries: Reinforcing North-South Partnership* (with others), (Trilateral Commission, 1981).

Articles: 1. 'Productivity and technological change in the railroad sector, 1840–1910', *Stud. Income and Wealth,* 30, (NBER, 1965); 2. 'Origins and consequences of import substitution in Brazil', in *International Economics and Development,* ed. L. DiMarco (Academic Press, 1972); 3. 'Brazilian size distribution of income', *AER,* 62(2), May 1972; 4. 'Some reflections on post-1964 Brazilian economic policy', in *Authoritarian Brazil,* ed. A. Stepan (Yale Univ. Press, 1973); 5. 'The mature neighbor policy: a proposal for a United States economic policy for Latin America', in *Latin America and World Economy,* ed. J. Grunwald (Sage Publishers, 1978).

FITOUSSI, Jean-Paul

Born 1942, La Goulette, Tunisia.
Current Post Prof. Econ., Head Econ. Dept., Europ. Univ. Inst., Florence, Italy; Dir. Bureau d'Econ. Théorique et Appliquée, Univ. Louis Pasteur, Strasbourg.
Recent Posts Prof. Econ., Univ. Louis Pasteur, Strasbourg, 1974–9.
Degrees Licencié (Econ.), Diplômé d'études supérieures (Econ.), Dr d'État (Econ.), Strasbourg Univ., 1966, 1967, 1971; Agrégé (Econ.) Univ. Paris, 1973.
Offices and Honours French Econ. Assoc.; AEA; Internat. Assoc. Applied Econometrics; Prize French Econ. Assoc., 1972; Prize Académie des Sciences Morales et Politiques, 1974; Dean, Hon. Dean, Faculty Econ., Univ. Louis Pasteur, 1974–7; Consultant, Comm. Europ. Communities, 1978–80; Member, High Council, French Univs., 1980–; Member, Scientific Advisory Comm. UN World Climate Impact Programme, 1980–.

Principal Contributions The study of disequilibrium theories. Developed a theory of stagflation, built up from micro-economic foundations and an explicit aggregation procedure. Stagflation has been analysed as the result of the interaction of two effects – a global effect, which is the outcome of aggregate disequilibrium, and a structural effect, which works through the dispersion of market disequilibria around their mean. Contributed to the theory and empirical analysis of a consumption function with micro-economic foundations.

Publications   *Books:* 1. *Inflation, équilibre et chômage* (Cujas, 1973); 2. *Le Fondement microéconomique de la théorie Keynésienne* (Cujas, 1974); 3. *Unemployment in Western Countries,* ed. (with E. Malinvaud), (Macmillan, 1980).

Articles: 1. 'Inflation d'équilibre et chômage', *Revue Science Financiere,* 64, 1972; 2. 'De l'inflation d'équilibre à la stagflation: théorie et vérification empirique', *Econ App,* 28(1), 1974; 3. 'Emploi, structure et régulation', *REP,* 89(1), 1979; 4. 'Inflazione e disoccupazione: l'impossibile controllo congiunturale di uno squilibrio strutturale', *RISE,* 26(7), 1979; 5. 'Structure and involuntary unemployment' (with N. Georgescu-Roegen), in *Unemployment in Western Countries,* eds E. Malinvaud and J.P. Fitoussi (Macmillan, 1980).

FLEISHER, B.M.

N.e.

FLEMMING, John Stanton

Born 1941, Reading, England.
Current Post Chief Adviser (Econ.), Bank of England.
Recent Posts Official Fellow Econ., Nuffield Coll., Univ. Oxford, 1965–80.
Degrees BA (PPE), MA, Univ. Oxford, 1962, 1966.
Offices Ass. ed., *OEP,* 1967–72; Assoc. ed., *REStud,* 1972–5; Managing ed., *EJ,* 1975–80; Member, Council RES, 1980–; Member, Council Inst. Fiscal Stud., 1980–.

Principal Contributions Aspects of capital theory, intertemporal decisions, and decisions under uncertainty, together with some empirical and policy applications. Theoretical work has emphasised the implications of capital market imperfection for the utility of windfalls, the consumption function, and the distribution (and transmission) of wealth. Empirical work (with others), on profitability, cost of capital and investment, stressing effects of taxation and inflation. Policy applications in the field of wealth taxation, social security, and adjustment for inflation. Macroeconomic implications of wealth, capital markets, and expectations.

Publications *Books:* 1. *Why We Need a Wealth Tax* (with M.D. Little), (Methuen, 1974); 2. *Inflation* (OUP, 1976).

Articles: 1. 'Portfolio choice and liquidity preference: a continuous time treatment', in *Issues in Monetary Economics*, eds H.G. Johnson and A.R. Nobay (OUP, 1974); 2. 'Wage rigidity and employment adjustment', in *Contemporary Issues in Economics*, eds M. Parkin and A.R. Nobay (Manchester Univ. Press, 1975); 3. 'What discount rate for public expenditure?', in *Public Expenditure*, ed. M.V. Posner (CUP, 1977); 4. 'Aspects of optimal unemployment insurance', *J Pub E*, 10(3), Dec. 1978; 5. 'Effects of earnings inequality, imperfect capital markets, and dynastic altruism on the distribution of wealth and life cycle models', *Ec*, 46, Nov. 1979.

FLÓREZ ESTRADA, Alvaro*

Dates and Birthplace 1765–1854, Spain.

Posts Held Civil servant; Attorney-General, Asturias, 1798; Chief Justice, Seville, 1813.

Offices Corresponding member, Académie des Sciences Morales et Politiques 1851.

Career First distinguishing himself by his opposition to Napoleon and his criticism of Spanish colonial administration, much of his writing was done whilst in exile. His *Curso* . . . is the first systematic economic treatise by a Span-iard, and is largely based on Smith and Ricardo, but diverges from orthodoxy in advocating the common ownership of land. In *La cuestión social* . . . he developed a fully-fledged programme for the nationalisation of land. Subsequent Spanish economists built on his work, without, however, accepting his most original contributions.

Publications *Books:* 1. *Examen Imparcial de las Disensiones de América y Medios de Conciliación* (1814); 2. *Efectos Producidos en Europa por la Baja en el Producto de las Minas de Plato* (1824); 3. *Examen de la Crisis Comercial de la Inglaterra en 1826* (1827); 4. *Curso de Economía Política*, 2 vols (1828); 5. *La Cuestión Social; Origin, Latitud y Efectos del Derecho de Propriedad* (1839).

Secondary Literature G. Bernacer, 'Flórez Estrada, Alvaro', *ESS*, vol. 6.

FLUX, Alfred William*

Dates and Birthplace 1867–1942, Portsmouth, England.

Posts Held Cobden lecturer, 1893–8, Jevons prof., 1898–1901, Univ. Manchester; Prof., McGill Univ., 1901–8; Civil servant, 1908–32, including UK Stat. Dept., Board of Trade.

Degree BA (Maths.) Univ. Camb., 1887.

Offices and Honours Knighted; Pres., RSS; Hon. member, Internat. Inst. Stats; Marshall prize, Univ. Camb., 1889.

Career After an academic career which did not quite fulfil expectations, his official work, particularly in directing the Censuses of Production 1912, 1924 and 1930, was of outstanding quality. His published papers in the field of applied economic statistics covered topics such as wholesale price index numbers, the index of production and national income. He was frequently consulted by the government as an economic adviser.

Publications *Books:* 1. *Economic Principles* (1904); 2. *Swedish Banking System* (1910); 3. *Foreign Exchanges* (1924).

Secondary Literature S.J. Chapman,

'Sir Alfred Flux' (obituary), *EJ*, 52, Dec. 1942.

FOGEL, Robert William

Born 1926.
Current Post Dir., Walgreen Foundation, Dir., Center Population Econ., Univ. Chicago, Chicago, Illinois.
Recent Posts Instructor, Johns Hopkins Univ., 1958–9; Ass. Prof., 1960–4, Prof., 1968–75, Univ. Rochester; Assoc. Prof., 1964–5, Prof., 1965–75, 1981–, Univ. Chicago; Prof., Harvard Univ., 1975–81.
Degrees BA Cornell Univ., 1948; MA Columbia Univ., 1960, Univ. Camb., 1975, Harvard Univ., 1976; PhD Johns Hopkins Univ., 1963.
Offices and Honours Member, Chairman, Hist. Advisory Comm. Math. Social Science Board, 1965–72; Assoc. Columbia Univ. Seminar Econ. Hist., 1969–; Member, Ed. Board, *Explorations Econ. Hist.*, 1970–, *Social Science Hist.*, 1976–80, *Southern Stud.*, 1977–; General ed., MSSB, *Princeton series on Quantitative studies in history*, 1971–6; Member, Board of Trustees, 1972–, Pres., 1977–8, EHA; Chairman, Ad Hoc Comm. Quantitative methods in history, Univ. Chicago, 1974–5; Res. Assoc., Program Dir., NBER, 1978–; NAS Comm. on Aging, 1978–81; General ed., (with S. Thernstrom) CUP series *Interdisciplinary perspectives in modern history*, 1979–; Pres., Social Science Hist. Assoc., 1980–1.
Principal Contributions The application of economic models and statistical methods to the analysis of long-term trends in economic development. Much of the research has focused on the retrieval of data capable of illuminating the relationship between the current and past behaviour of households. Data sets linking together up to ten generations have been constructed to analyse the interaction of economic and cultural factors on such variables as the savings rate, the female participation rate, fertility and mortality rates, economic and social mobility, and migration rates.
Publications Books: 1. *The Union Pacific railroad: a case in premature enterprise* (Johns Hopkins Univ. Press, 1960); 2. *Railroads and American economic growth: essays in econometric history* (Johns Hopkins Univ. Press, 1964; Spanish transl., 1972); 3. *The reinterpretation of American economic history* (with S.L. Engerman et al.), (Harper & Row, 1971; Italian transl., 1975); 4. *Time on the cross: the economics of American negro slavery* (with S.L. Engerman), (Little, Brown, 1974; Braille transcr. 1974; Italian transl., 1978, Japanese transl., 1980, Spanish transl., 1981); 5. *'Scientific' history and traditional history* (with G.R. Elton), Yale Univ. Press, 1982).

FOLEY, Duncan K.

Born 1942, Columbus, Ohio, USA.
Current Post Prof. Econ., Barnard Coll., Columbia Univ., NY, USA, 1977–.
Recent Posts Ass. prof. Econ., 1966–8, Assoc. prof. Econ., 1968–73, MIT; Assoc. prof. Econ., Stanford Univ., 1973–9.
Degrees BA, Central High School, Philadelphia, 1960; BA (Maths), Swarthmore Coll., 1964; PhD (Econ.), Yale Univ., 1966.
Offices and Honours NSF Grant Fellow in Econ., 1964–6; Baker award for superior teaching, MIT Undergraduate Assoc., 1969; Ford Foundation Faculty res. prof., 1969–70.
Principal Contributions Development of methods for extending set theoretic methods and equilibrium analysis to public goods economies. Development of methods (with M. Sidrauski) for studying temporary equilibrium paths of growth in economies with asset market equilibrium structures. Critical study of stock-flow interactions in macro-economic models. Reformulation of the labour theory of value as a basis for macro-economic theory.
Publications Books: 1. *Monetary and fiscal policy in a growing economy* (with M. Sidrauski), (Macmillan, 1970). *Articles:* 1. 'Resource allocation and the public sector', *YEE*, 7(1), Spring 1967; 2. 'Lindahl's solution and the core of an economy with public goods', *Em*, 38(1), Jan. 1970; 3. 'On two specifications of asset equilibrium in macro-economic

models', *JPE*, 83(2), April 1975; 4. 'Problems versus conflicts: economic theory and ideology', *AER*, 65(2), May 1975; 5. 'State expenditure from a Marxist perspective', *J Pub E*, 9(2), April 1978.

FORBONNAIS, François Veron de*

Dates and Birthplace   1722–1800, Mons, France.
Posts Held   Businessman and civil servant.
Offices   Member, Inst. de France, 1794.
Career   Not a great theorist nor rigid adherent of any particular school, he nevertheless wrote sound and realistic economics. The chief policy recommendation with which his name is associated was an *ad valorem* import duty of 15 per cent. He published extremely able analyses of financial data relating to France and Spain, and in his more ambitious works, such as the *Principes...*, achieved an extremely consistent level of accuracy and good sense.
Publications   *Books:* 1. *Recherches et considérations sur les finances de France* (1750); 2. *Considérations sur les finances d'Espagne* (1753); 3. *Eléments du commerce* (1754, 1766); 4. *Principes et observations économiques* (1767).

FOSTER, C.D.

N.e.

FOURIER, Charles*

Dates and Birthplace   1772–1837, Besançon, France.
Posts Held   Businessman and civil servant until 1816, then private income.
Career   Socialist thinker who sought to prescribe a social order in harmony with natural order. His description of the 'phalanstery', a social unit whose numbers and organisation were based on his understanding of the order of the cosmos, led to various Fourierist experiments. His system was non-revolutionary, was believed to be able to flourish within any type of political system, and had some influence on later co-operative movements. Achieved subsequent notoriety as a 'utopian socialist' scorned by the founders of 'scientific socialism', Marx and Engels.
Publications   *Books:* 1. *The Social Destiny of Man* (1808, 1857); 2. *Oeuvres complètes de Ch. Fourier*, 6 vols (1841–5).
Secondary Literature   E. Poulat, *Les cahiers manuscrits de Fourier* (Entente Communautaire, 1957); E. Poulat, 'Fourier, Charles', *IESS*, vol. 5.

FOXWELL, Herbert Somerton*

Dates and Birthplace   1849–1936, Shepton Mallet, England.
Posts Held   Fellow, St John's Coll., Univ. Camb., 1874–98, 1905–36; Prof., Univ. Coll., Univ. London, 1881–1922.
Degrees   BA Univ. London, 1867; BA Univ. Oxford, 1870.
Offices   Fellow, BA; Member, Polit. Econ. Club, 1881–1936; Founder, Pres., 1929–31, RES.
Career   Played an important role in the fostering of economic studies in Britain through his teaching, his work with the Royal Economic Society and other organisations, and his prodigious book collecting. Foxwell was probably the greatest collector of economic literature and over 70,000 books passed through his possession, most of them to form the present collection of the Goldsmith's Library, London University and the Kress Library, Harvard University. His publications were mainly articles or introductions to books, most notably the masterly article on the 'Ricardian socialists' presented as the introduction to Menger's *The Right of the Whole Produce of Labour*.
Publications   *Articles:* 1. 'Introduction' to A. Menger, *The Right of the Whole Produce of Labour* (1899); 2. *Papers on Current Finance* (1919).
Secondary Literature   J.M. Keynes, 'Herbert Somerton Foxwell', in *Essays in Biography* (Macmillan, 1933, 1972).

FRANK, Charles Raphael, Jr

Born   1937, Pittsburgh, Penn., USA.
Current Post   Vice-pres., Salomon Brothers, New York City, USA.

Recent Posts Prof. Econ. Internat. Affairs, Princeton Univ., 1967–74; Sr Fellow, Brookings Inst., 1972–4; Sr economist, Pol. Planning Staff, US State Dept. 1974–7; Dep. ass. Secretary State, US State Dept., 1977–8.

Degrees BS (Maths) Rensselaer Polytechnic Inst., 1959; PhD (Econ.) Princeton Univ., 1963.

Offices AEA; Em Soc; Member, Council Foreign Relations; Member, Res. Advisory Comm. US Agency Internat. Development; Consultant, US Agency Internat. Development, US Treasury, World Bank, UN, Conference Board.

Principal Contributions Generalisations of welfare theory and theory of production with increasing returns to scale; debt servicing problems of developing countries, theory and policy; theory and policy concerning unemployment problems in less developed countries; theory and policy regarding income distribution in less developed countries; analysis of national policies designed to facilitate adjustments required by shifting patterns of international trade; and foreign trade and economic development in S. Korea.

Publications *Books:* 1. *Production Theory and Indivisible Commodities* (Princeton Univ. Press, 1969); 2. *Debt and Terms of Aid* (Overseas Development Council, 1970), repr. in C.R. Frank, Jr *et al. Assisting Developing Countries, Problems of Debts, Burden Sharing, Jobs and Trade* (Overseas Development Council Stud. 1, 1970); 3. *Foreign Trade Regimes and Economic Development: South Korea* (with K.S. Kim and L. Westphal), (NBER, 1975); 4. *Foreign Trade and Domestic Aid: US Trade Adjustment Assistance and Other Adjustment Programs* (with S. Levinson), (Brookings Inst., 1977); 5. *Income Distribution: Problems and Policies in Developing Countries*, ed. (with R. Webb), (Brookings Inst., 1981).

Articles: 1. 'Urban unemployment and economic growth in Africa', *OEP*, 20(2), July 1968, reprinted in *Third World Employment*, ed. R. Jolly *et al.* (Penguin Books, 1973), and in *The Study of Africa*, eds P.J.M. McEwan and R.B. Sutcliffe (Methuen, 1974); 2. 'A generalization of the Koopmans-Gale theorem on pricing and efficiency', *Int ER*, 10(4), Oct. 1969; 3. 'Optimal terms of foreign assistance', *JPE*, 78(5), Sept/Oct. 1970; 4. 'Measurement of debt service capacity: an application of discriminant analysis', *J Int E*, 1(3), Oct. 1971; 5. 'The problem of urban unemployment in Africa', in *Employment and Unemployment Problems of the Near East and South Asia*, vol. 2, eds R.G. Ridker and H. Lubell (Vikas Publications, 1971).

FRANKEL, Sally Herbert

Born 1904, Johannesburg, S. Africa.
Current Post Prof. Emeritus, Univ. Oxford.

Recent Posts Prof. Econ. Underdeveloped Countries, Univ. Oxford, 1946–71; Vis. prof. Econ., Univ. Virginia, 1967, 1969–74.

Degrees MA, Hon. DLitt., Rand Univ. Johannesburg, 1926, 1970; PhD DSc. (Econ.) Univ. London, 1928, 1938; MA Univ. Oxford, 1946; Hon. DSc. (Econ.) Rhodes Univ., Grahamstown, 1969.

Offices Member, Mont Pelerin Soc., 1928–, Econ. Soc. S. Africa, 1928, RES, 1930–, Royal Inst. Internat. Affairs, 1930–, Royal African Soc., 1930–, AEA, 1930–; Member, Union SA Treasury Advisory Council, 1941–2; Member, Miners' Phtisis Commission, 1941–2; Chairman, Enquiry Mining Industry Southern Rhodesia, 1945; Joint ed., *SAJE*, to 1946; Member, East Africa Royal Commission, 1953–5.

Principal Contributions Originated first official calculations of the national income of the Union of South Africa; economic analysis of fundamental factors affecting capital investment and economic growth of African countries; analysis of theories and policies relating to economic growth and decline of underdeveloped societies in relation to advanced economies; analysis of yield to capital investment in gold mining in relation to that obtained on industrial investments and government banks, 1887–1965; analysis of the economic roots of racial conflict; contribution to theory and practice of monetary policies;

and analysis of philosophies of money and the relation of money to liberty.

Publications *Books:* 1. *Capital Investment in Africa: Its Course and Effects* (OUP, 1938); 2. *The Economic Impact on Underdeveloped Societies: Essays on International Investment and Social Change* (OUP, 1953); 3. *Investment and the Return to Equity Capital in the South African Gold-mining Industry. 1887–1965: An International Comparison* (OUP, Harvard Univ. Press, 1967); 4. *Two Philosophies of Money: The Conflict of Trust and Authority* (St Martins Press, Blackwell, 1978); 5. *Money and Liberty* (Amer. Enterprise Inst., 1980).

Articles: 1. 'The position of the native as a factor in the economic welfare of the European population of South Africa', *J Econ. Soc.*, July 1927; 2. 'The tyranny of economic paternalism in Africa', *Optima*, suppl., Dec. 1960; 3. 'Economic change in Africa in historical perspective', in *Economic Development in the Long Run*, ed. A.J. Youngson (Macmillan, 1972); 4. 'The roots of economic progress', in *Science and Ceremony: The Institutional Economics of C.E. Ayres*, eds W. Breit and W.P. Culbertson Jr (Austin, 1975).

FRANKLIN, Benjamin*

Dates and Birthplace 1706–90, Boston, USA.

Posts Held Printer and journalist, 1718–36; Official of Colony and State of Pennsylvania; Missions to England, 1757, 1764–75; Diplomat in France, 1776–85.

Offices Three times Pres. of Pennsylvania; Framer of US Declaration of Independence, 1776; Delegate to US Constitutional Convention, 1787.

Career This great statesman and scientist not only contributed popular treatments of economic topics to periodicals, such as his own *Poor Richard's Almanack*, but also wrote able economic tracts. The position he adopted was broadly that of *laissez-faire*.

Publications *Books:* 1. *Modest Inquiry into the Nature and Necessity of Paper Currency* (1729); 2. *Observations Concerning the Increase of Mankind* (1751); 3. *Positions to be Examined Concerning National Wealth* (1769); 4. *Reflections on the Augmentation of Wages.*

Secondary Literature W.A. Wetzel, *Benjamin Franklin as an Economist* (1895).

FREEMAN, Richard B.

Born 1945, Newburgh, NY, USA.
Current Post Prof., Harvard Univ.
Degrees BA, Dartmouth Coll., 1964; PhD, Harvard Univ., 1969.
Offices Dir., Labor Stud., NBER.

Principal Contributions Empirical findings: students' supply responsiveness is very sizeable; high-level job markets are subject to cobweb-type fluctuations; return to college training in the West has dropped in era of educational expansion; minorities have progressed in era of anti-bias activity in US; slow economic progress of Blacks in US is due to loss of voting rights and consequent governmental discrimination at turn of century; and trade unions have a sizeable non-wage effect, best analysed in 'exit-voice' framework (effects include reduced turnover, greater fringe benefits, reduced inequality).

Publications *Books:* 1. *Labor Market for College-trained Manpower* (Harvard Univ. Press, 1971); 2. *Black Elite* (McGraw-Hill, 1976); 3. *Labor Economics* (Prentice-Hall, 1978); 4. *What Do Unions Do?* (with J. Medoff), (Basic Books, 1982).

Articles: 1. 'Labor market discrimination: a survey of findings and problems', in *Frontiers of Quantitative Economics*, ed. M. Intriligator (N-H, 1974); 2. 'Supply and salary adjustments to the changing science manpower market: physics, 1948–1975', *AER*, 65(1), March 1975; 3. 'Individual mobility and union voice in the labor market', *AER*, 66(2), May 1976; 4. 'The exit-voice tradeoff in the labor market, unionism job tenure, quits, and separations', *QJE*, 94, June 1980; 5. 'The effect of unionism on the dispersion of wages' *ILRR*, 33(5), Oct. 1980.

FRENKEL, Jacob A.

Born 1943, Tel-Aviv, Israel.
Current Post Prof. Econ., Univ. Chicago, USA, 1979–.
Recent Posts Ass. prof. Internat. Econ. Fin., Univ. Chicago, 1970–1; Sr lecturer, Tel-Aviv Univ., 1971–3; Ass. prof. Econ., 1973–4, Assoc. prof. Econ., 1974–8, Univ. Chicago.
Degrees BA (Econ. and Political Sciences), MA ABD (Econ.) Hebrew Univ., Jerusalem, 1966, 1967; MA (Econ.), PhD (Econ.), Univ. Chicago, 1969, 1970.
Offices and Honours Ford Foundation Grants, 1975–6; Ed., *JPE*, 1975–; Carnegie-Rochester Conference Series Advisory Council on Public Pol., 1977–; Recipient, NSF Grants, 1978–80; Res. assoc., NBER, 1978–; Ed. Board, *J Mon E*, 1978–; Advisory ed., *Econ. Letters*, 1980–; Member, NSF Econ. Advisory Panel, 1980–.
Principal Contributions The relation between economic growth and the balance of payments, the developments of the monetary approach to the balance of payments and the asset market approach to exchange rate determination. Developed a methodology for estimating transactions costs in the market for foreign exchange and studied the operation of covered interest arbitrage. Studied the economics of hyperinflation and analysed the use of forward exchange rates as measures of expectations. Studied the purchasing power parity theory and the relation between spot and forward exchange rates, and contributed to the theory and the empirical research on the demand for international reserves.
Publications *Books:* 1. *The Monetary Approach to the Balance of Payments*, ed. (with H.G. Johnson) (A & U, Univ. Toronto Press, 1976); 2. *The Economics of Exchange Rates: Selected Studies*, ed. (with H.G. Johnson), (Addison-Wesley, 1978); 3. *International Economic Policy: Theory and Evidence*, ed. (with R. Dornbusch), (Johns Hopkins Univ. Press, 1978); 4. *Collected Papers of Harry G. Johnson*, ed. (with D. Laidler), (MIT Press, 1981).

Articles: 1. 'A theory of money trade and the balance of payments in a model of accumulation', *J Int E*, 1(2), May 1971; 2. 'Portfolio equilibrium and the balance of payments: a monetary approach' (with C. Rodriguez), *AER*, 65(4), Sept. 1975; 3. 'The forward exchange rate, expectations and the demand for money: the German hyperinflation', *AER*, 67(4), Sept. 1977; 4. 'Transaction costs and interest arbitrage: tranquil versus turbulent periods' (with R. Levich), *JPE*, 85(6), Dec. 1977; 5. 'Flexible exchange rates, prices and the role of "News": lessons from the 1970s', *JPE*, 89(4), Aug. 1981.

FRIEDMAN, Milton

Born 1912, New York City, NY, USA.
Current Post Sr Res. Fellow, Hoover Inst., Stanford, USA.
Recent Posts Prof. Econ., Univ. Chicago, 1948–; Member Res. Staff, NBER, 1948–; columnist, contributing ed., *Newsweek*, 1966–.
Degrees BA Rutgers Univ., 1932; MA Univ. Chicago, 1933; PhD Columbia Univ., 1946; LLD St Paul's Univ., Tokyo, 1963, Kalamazoo Coll., 1968, Rutgers Univ., 1968, Lehigh Univ., 1969, Loyola Univ., Chicago, 1971, Univ. New Hampshire, 1975, Harvard Univ., 1979, Brigham Young Univ., 1980, Dartmouth Coll., 1980; LHD Rockford Coll., 1969; Roosevelt Univ., 1975; LittD, Bethany Coll., 1971; DSc. Univ. Rochester, 1971; Hon. PhD Hebrew Univ., Jerusalem, 1977; DCS Francisco Marroquin Univ., Guatemala, 1978.
Offices and Honours John Bates Clark medal AEA, 1951; Exec. Comm. 1955–7, Pres. 1967, AEA; Board Eds., *AER*, 1951–3; Fellow, Em Soc; Board of Eds., *Em*, 1957–69; Amer. Secretary, 1957–62, Member Council, 1962–5, Vice-pres., 1967–70, Pres., 1970–2, Vice-pres., 1972, Mont Pelerin Soc.; Nobel Prize for Econ., 1976.
Principal Contributions Permanent income theory of consumption; understanding the role of money in determining the course of events, in particular the monetary source of the US great depression; analysis of inflation, its

sources, consequences, and possible cures; concept of natural rate of unemployment and accelerationist theory of Phillips curve; role and operation of monetary policy; theory of capital.

Publications *Books:* 1. *A Theory of the Consumption Function* (Princeton Univ. Press, 1957); 2. *Price Theory* (Aldine, 1962, 1976); 3. *A Monetary History of the United States, 1867–1960* (with A.J. Schwartz), (Princeton Univ. Press, 1963); 4. *Monetary Statistics of the United States* (with A.J. Schwartz), (Columbia Univ. Press, 1970); 5. *Monetary Trends of the United States and the United Kingdom* (with A.J. Schwartz), (Univ. Chicago Press, 1981).

Articles: 1. 'The use of ranks to avoid the assumption of normality implicit in the analysis of variance', *JASA*, 32, Sept. 1937; 2. 'A monetary and fiscal framework for economic stability', *AER*, 38, June 1948; 3. 'The utility analysis of choices involving risk' (with L.J. Savage), *JPE*, 56, Aug. 1948; 4. 'Choice, chance, and personal distribution of income', *JPE*, 61, Aug. 1953; 5. 'The role of monetary policy' (Presidential Address, 1967), *AER*, 58, March 1968.

Secondary Literature N. Thygesen, 'The scientific contributions of Milton Friedman', *Scand JE*, 79, 1979.

FLORENCE, Philip Sargant*

Dates and Birthplace 1890–1982, Nutley, NJ, USA.

Posts Held Lecturer, Univ. Camb., 1921–9; Prof. Commerce, 1929–55, Dean Commerce and Social Sciences, 1947–50, Univ. Birmingham.

Offices and Honours Pres., Section F, BAAS, 1937; CBE, 1952; Vice-pres., RES, 1972–82.

Career Applied economist whose move from Cambridge to Birmingham enabled him to pursue research in the organisation of trade and industry and, as Dean, to foster a broad, interdisciplinary approach in the Faculty of Commerce and Social Sciences. He had an important role in the post-war reconstruction and subsequent planning of the West Midlands.

Publications *Books:* 1. *Economics of Fatigue and Unrest* (1924); 2. *Overpopulation, Theory and Statistics* (1926); 3. *Economics and Human Behaviour* (1927); 4. *The Statistical Method in Economics and Political Science* (1929); 5. *The Logic of Industrial Organisation* (1933); 6. *Industry and the State* (1957); 7. *Economics and Sociology of Industry* (1964); 8. *The Roots of Inflation* (1975).

FRIEND, I.

N.e.

FRISCH, Ragnar Anton Kittil*

Dates and Birthplace 1895–1973, Oslo, Norway.

Posts Held Lecturer at various univs. including Yale, Privatdocent, 1923, Docent, 1928, Prof., 1931–65, Univ. Oslo; Rockefeller Scholar, 1926–8; Vis. prof., Yale Univ., 1930–1.

Degrees BA (Econ.), PhD, Univ. Oslo, 1919, 1926.

Offices and Honours Founder, Em Soc, 1930; Ed., *Em*, 1933–55; Nobel Prize for Econ., 1969.

Career A pioneer of the application of mathematical and statistical methods to economics, which he himself named 'econometrics'. Only part of his wide-ranging work has ever been formally published, but many of the papers he did publish are regarded as classics. He not only exercised a dominating influence over economic thought, but also over economic policy in Norway. Adviser to developing countries such as Egypt and India. The 'decision models' he developed in the 1940s and other models for government planning were widely used. Consumer behaviour, production theory, macro-economic problems and a range of other topics occupied him at different times.

Publications *Books:* 1. *New Methods of Measuring Marginal Utility* (1932); 2. *Statistical Confluence Analysis by Means of Complete Regression Systems* (1934); 3. *Theory of Production* (1965); 4. *Economic Planning Studies: A Collection of Essays* (1976).

Articles: 1. 'Propagation problems and impulse problems in dynamic economies', in *Economic Essays in Honor of Gustav Cassel* (1933), reprinted in *Readings in Business Cycles*, eds R.A. Gordon and L.R. Klein (1965).

Secondary Literature L. Johansen, 'Frisch, Ragnar', *IESS*, vol. 18; L. Johansen, 'Ragnar Frisch's scientific contributions to economics', *Swed JE*, 71(4), Dec. 1969.

FULLARTON, John*

Dates and Birthplace 1780(?)-1849, Scotland.

Posts Held Surgeon and banker, 1813–, in India.

Offices Fellow, Royal Asiatic Soc.

Career Wrote on theory and policy of banking in his retirement from business. *Regulation . . .* was a considerable success and frequently drawn on by later writers including Marx. The book arose from the controversy over Peel's Act of 1844, but the general soundness and accessibility of its argument ensured its long term success. His argument was that of the 'Banking school', in which convertibility of notes was the only requirement for the stability of currency.

Publications *Books:* 1. *On the Regulation of Currencies* (1844).

FURTADO, C.

N.e.

FURUBOTN, Eirik G.

Born 1923, New York City, NY, USA.

Current Post Prof. Econ., Texas A & M Univ., College Station, USA.

Recent Posts Prof. Econ., State Univ. New York, Binghamton, 1963–7; Vis. prof., Tulane Univ., 1965.

Degrees BA Brown Univ., 1948; MA, PhD, Columbia Univ., 1951, 1959.

Offices and Honours Francis Wayland Scholar, Brown Univ., 1948, Phi Beta Kappa; Member, AEA, RES, Em Soc, SEA, Exec. Comm., SEA, 1975–7; Ed. Advisory Board, *Applied Econom-*ics, 1971–2; Board Eds., *SEJ*, 1979–80, *J Law Polit. Econ.*, 1981–.

Principal Contributions Redefining and broadening the concept of the production function and incorporating the behavioural effects of property relations into standard micro-economic theory. By applying 'property-rights' or 'entitlements' approach to problems in the area of comparative systems, it is possible to achieve improved understanding of the behaviour of diverse types of business organisations, including the socialist labour-managed firm, the Soviet firm, the codeterminationist firm, etc.

Publications *Books:* 1. *The Evolution of Modern Demand Theory* (with R.B. Ekelund and W.P. Gramm), (D.C. Heath & Co., 1972); 2. *The Economics of Property Rights* ed. (with S. Pejovich), (Ballinger Publishing Co., 1974).

Articles: 1. 'Engineering data and the production function', *AER*, 55, June 1965; 2. 'The orthodox production function and the adaptability of capital', *WEJ*, 3(3), 1965; 3. 'Property rights and economic theory: a survey of recent literature' (with S. Pejovich), *JEL*, 10(4), Dec. 1972; 4. 'Property rights, economic decentralization, and the evolution of the Yugoslav firm, 1965–1972' (with S. Pejovich), *J Law E* 16(2), Oct. 1973; 5. 'The long-run analysis of the labor-managed firm: an alternative interpretation', *AER*, 66(1), March 1976.

G

GABOR, André

Born 1903, Budapest, Hungary.

Current Post Pricing consultant, Dir., Pricing Res. Ltd, London, England.

Recent Posts Sr lecturer, Univ. Nottingham, 1947–69; Sr lecturer, Univs. Sheffield (1969–70), Leeds (1970–1), York (1971–2), Essex (1972–3), Newcastle upon Tyne (1973–4); Vis. prof., Univ. Clermont, France, 1980, 1981.

Degrees BA (Applied Econ.) School Econ., Berlin, 1928; BSc. (Econ., Hons.) Univ. London, 1944.

Offices and Honours Fellow, RSS; Leverhulme Emeritus Res. Fellow,

1974–6; Edouard Gaudy prize, Société de Géographie Commerciale, Paris, 1977.

Principal Contributions The field of pricing, specifically in relation to consumer behaviour. The research methods developed by study group at Univ. Nottingham are constantly applied everywhere to the pricing problems of the manufacturers of consumer goods.

Publications *Books:* 1. *Pricing: Principles and Practices* (Heinemann Educational Books, 1977, 1980); 2. *Economics papers* (MCB Publications, 1979); 3. *Pricing Decisions* (MCB Publications, 1979).

Articles: 1. 'A new approach to the theory of the firm' (with I.F. Pearce), *OEP*, N.S. 4, Oct. 1952; 2. 'An essay on the mathematical theory of freedom' (with D. Gabor), *JRSS*, A, 117(1), 1954; 3. 'A note on block tariffs', *REStud*, 23(1), 1955; 4. 'Price as an indicator of quality: report on an enquiry' (with C.W.J. Granger), *Ec*, N.S. 33, Feb. 1966; 5. 'The effect of price on choice: a theoretical and empirical investigation' (with C.W.J. Granger and A.P. Sowter), *Applied Econ*, 3(3), Sept. 1971.

GÄFGEN, Gerard

Born 1925, Luxembourg.
Current Post Prof. Econ., Univ. Constance, W. Germany, 1969–.
Recent Posts Prof. Econ., Univ. Karlsruhe, 1962–5; Prof. Econ., Univ. Hamburg, 1965–9; Dean, Faculty Econ. Stat., Univ. Constance, 1979–80.
Degrees Diploma Econ. Dr Econ. Science (Dr rer. pol.), Venia legendi (assoc. to the faculty) econ., Univ. Cologne, 1953, 1955, 1961.
Offices Member, AEA, Gesellschaft Wirtschafts- und Sozialwissenschaften, List-Gesellschaft; Nominated member, 1971, Vice-chairman, 1976–80, Academic Council to the German Ministry of Econ. Affairs.
Principal Contributions Inquiry into the logical structure of rational action, clarification of its importance for the explanation of economic behaviour, especially reformulation of procedures for social choice and of a general strat-

egy for rational decisions. Applications of decision theory, formal ethics, and related methodological conceptions to the theory of economic policy and to political economy. Application of theories of economic behaviour and of methods of evaluation to social issues, especially to health economics, production of ideologies, research policy of the state, and workers' participation.

Publications *Books:* 1. *Theorie der Wirtschaftlichen Entscheidung* (Mohr-Siebeck, 1963, 1974); 2. *Grundlagen der Wirtschaftspolitik* (Kiepenheuer & Witsch, 1966, 1972).

Articles: 1. 'Zur Theorie Kollektiver Entscheidungen in der Wirtschaft', *JNS*, 173, 1961; 2. 'Formale Theorie des Politischen Handelns: Wissenschaftliche Politik als Rationale Wahl von Strategien', in *Politik und Wissenschaft*, eds H. Maier *et al.* (Munich, 1970); 3. 'On the methodology and political economy of Galbraithian economics', *Kyklos*, 27(4), 1974; 4. 'Zur Ökonomie der Ideologiebildung', in *Wirtschaftsrecht und Wirtschaftsordnung*, eds J. Mestmäcker *et al.* (Tübingen, 1975); 5. 'Politische Ökonomie und Lehre von der Wirtschaftspolitik: Zur Realisierbarkeit Wirtschaftspolitischer Vorschläge', in *Wirtschaftspolitik – Wissenschaft und Politische Aufgabe*, eds H. Körner *et al.* (Bern, Stuttgart, 1976).

GAITSKELL, Hugh Todd Naylor*

Dates and Birthplace 1906–63, London, England.
Posts Held Lecturer Econ., Workers' Educational Assoc.; Reader Polit. Econ., Univ. London, 1938; UK Ministry of Econ. Warfare and Board of Trade, 1939–45.
Degree BA Univ. Oxford, 1927.
Offices MP for Leeds South, 1945–63; UK Minister for Fuel and Power, 1946; UK Chancellor of the Exchequer, 1950–1; Leader, Labour Party, 1955.
Career Moving into government service from academic economics during World War II, he quickly established his practical abilities. Membership of parliament, ministerial office and the leadership of his party followed quickly.

His position regarding the economic policy of the Labour Party was that the traditional aim of common ownership of the means of production, distribution and exchange was not sacrosanct. He preferred a version of socialism more adapted to modern society and defended it ably in the Party. His early death frustrated this clarification of economic aims as it did his work on other issues such as disarmament. In the 1930s he studied in Vienna and published a remarkable draft of an unfinished PhD thesis on the Austrian theory of capital.

Publications *Books:* 1. *Chartism* (1929); 2. *Money and Everyday Life* (1939); 3. *The Challenge of Co-existence* (1957).

Articles: 1. 'Notes on the period of production Pts I-II', *ZN*, 7, Dec. 1936, 9, July 1938.

Secondary Literature P. Williams, *Hugh Gaitskell: A Political Biography* (1979).

GALBRAITH, John Kenneth

Born 1908, Iona Station, Ontario, Canada.

Recent Posts Instructor, prof., Harvard Univ. 1935, 1946–75; Deputy Admin., US Office Price Admin., 1941–3; Dir., US Strategic Bombing Survey, 1945–6; US Ambassador to India, 1961–3.

Degrees BA Ontario Coll. Agriculture, Guelph, 1930; PhD (Agricultural Econ.) Univ. Cal., Berkeley, 1934.

Offices Chairman, Amer. Democratic Action, 1967–9; Pres., AEA, 1972.

Principal Contributions N.e.

Publications *Books:* 1. *American Capitalism: The Concept of Countervailing Power* (Houghton Mifflin, 1952, 1956, 1962); 2. *The Great Crash, 1929* (Houghton Mifflin, 1954, 1961, 1972); 3. *The Affluent Society* (Houghton Mifflin, 1958, 1971, 1976); 4. *The New Industrial State* (Houghton Mifflin, 1967, 1972, 1978); 5. *The Age of Uncertainty* (Houghton Mifflin, 1977).

Articles: 1. *A Contemporary Guide to Economics, Peace and Laughter*, ed. A.D. Williams (Houghton Mifflin, 1971).

Secondary Literature M.E. Sharpe, 'Galbraith, John Kenneth', *IESS*, vol. 18; C.H. Hession, *John Kenneth Galbraith and his Critics* (New Amer. Library, 1972).

GALE, Douglas Maxwell

Born 1950, Ottawa, Canada.

Current Post Reader Econ., LSE.

Recent Posts Res. Fellow, Churchill Coll., Univ. Camb., 1975–8; Lecturer Econ., LSE, 1978–81.

Degrees BSc Univ. Trent, 1970; MA Carleton Coll., 1972; PhD Univ. Camb., 1975.

Offices Ass. ed., *REStud*, 1980–.

Principal Contributions Initiated the study of general, manipulable and stochastic rationing schemes and the use of the Nash equilibrium of a generalised game to analyse effective demands under trading uncertainty. Principal contributions have been to the foundations of monetary economics, using game theoretic methods to rationalise the theory of sequence economies and the use of money.

Publications *Books:* 1. *Money in General Equilibrium* (Nisbet, CUP, 1981).

Articles: 1. 'The core of monetary economy without trust', *JET*, 21(3), Dec. 1978; 2. 'Large economies with trading uncertainty', *REStud*, 47(3), April 1980; 3. 'Money, information and equilibrium', *JET*, 23(1), Aug. 1980.

GALENSON, Walter

Born 1914, New York City, NY, USA.

Current Post Jacob Gould Schurman prof., Cornell Univ., NY, USA.

Recent Posts Prof. Econ., Univ. Cal., Berkeley 1951–66; Pitt prof., Univ. Camb., 1970–1.

Degrees BA, PhD, Columbia Univ., 1934, 1940; MA Univ. Camb., 1971.

Offices Guggenheim Memorial Foundation Fellow, 1955–6; Chairman, Center Chinese Stud. Univ. Cal., Berkeley, 1965–9; Adviser, ILO, 1969–72; Pres., Assoc. Comparative Econ. Stud., 1973.

Principal Contributions   Analysis of labour markets in less developed countries; comparative economic studies.

Publications   *Books:* 1. *The Danish System of Labor Relations* (Harvard Univ. Press, 1952); 2. *Labor Productivity in Soviet and American Industry* (Columbia Univ. Press, 1955; Russian transl., 1957, Japanese transl., 1957); 3. *The CIO Challenge to the AFL* (Harvard Univ. Press, 1960); 4. *The Chinese Economy Under Communism* (Aldine Publishing Co., 1971; Japanese transl., 1971); 5. *The International Labor Organization: An American View* (Univ. Wisconsin Press, 1981).

Articles: 1. 'Investment criteria, productivity and economic development' (with H. Leibenstein), *QJE*, 69, Aug. 1955, 70, Nov. 1956; 2. 'Economic development and the sectoral expansion of employment', *Int Lab Rev*, June 1963; 3. 'Earnings and employment in Eastern Europe' (with A. Fox), *QJE*, 81, May 1967; 4. 'The Japanese labor market', in *Asia's New Giant* (Brookings Inst., 1976); 5. 'Economic growth, poverty, and the international agencies', *J Pol. Modelling*, 1(2), 1979.

GALIANI, Ferdinando*

Dates and Birthplace   1728–87, Chieti, Italy.

Posts Held   Secretary, Neapolitan embassy, Paris, 1759–69; Civil servant, mainly in econ. depts, 1769–87.

Career   His economic ideas were eclectic, and despite his long residence in France, he largely rejected physiocracy. He developed a value theory with a considerable subjective element. His discussion of interest did not concern its morality, but explored the reasons why it is paid: he described it as a payment for the lender's risk in parting with his money. Policy prescriptions are largely confined to his *Dialogue* ... which recognises the need to adjust economic principle in accordance with historical and geographical circumstances.

Publications   *Books:* 1. *Della Moneta* (1750); 2. *Dialogue sur le commerce des blés* (1770).

Secondary Literature   G. Arias, 'Ferdinando Galiani et les physiocrates',

Revue sciences polit., 45, 1922; P.R. Toscano, 'Galiani, Ferdinando', *IESS*, vol. 6.

GALLAWAY, Lowell Eugene

Born   1930, Toledo, Ohio, USA.

Current Post   Disting. prof. Econ., Ohio Univ., Athens, Ohio (Prof., 1967–).

Recent Posts   Ass. prof., Colorado State Univ., 1957–9, San Fernando Valley State Coll., 1959–62; Vis. assoc. prof., Univ. Minnesota, 1962–3; Chief, Analytic Stud. Section, US Social Security Admin., 1963–4; Assoc. prof., Univ. Pennsylvania, 1964–7; Vis. prof., Univs. Texas, Arlington (1976), New South Wales (1978), N. Carolina, 1980.

Degrees   BSc Northwestern Univ., 1951; MA, PhD, Ohio State Univ., 1955, 1959.

Principal Contributions   Empirical testing of hypotheses concerning the functioning of labour markets, both contemporary and historical, in a variety of countries. Out of the process of testing emerges a general conclusion to the effect that the evidence is consistent with neo-classical predictions of labour market behaviour. In recent years, there also has been an interest in problems of capital theory. The major conclusion of that work is that it is possible, under a reasonable set of conditions, to specify a well-ordered aggregate production function that possesses standard neo-classical properties.

Publications   *Books:* 1. *The Retirement Decision: an Exploratory Essay*, Social Security Admin., Res. Report no. 9 (US Govt Printing Office, 1965); 2. *Interindustry Labor Mobility in the United States, 1957–1960*, Social Security Admin., Res. Report no. 18 (US Govt Printing Office, 1967); 3. *Geographic Labor Mobility in the United States, 1957–1960*, Social Security Admin., Res. Report no. 28 (US Govt Printing Office, 1969); 4. *Manpower Economics* (Richard D. Irwin, 1971); 5. *Poverty in America* (Grid Inc., 1973).

Articles: 1. 'The North-South wage differential', *REStat*, 45, Aug. 1963; 2. 'Labor mobility, resource allocation, and structural unemployment', *AER*,

53, Sept. 1963, 54, March 1964; 3. 'The foundations of the "war on poverty"', *AER*, 55, March 1965; 4. 'Mobility of native Americans' (with R.K. Vedder), *JEH*, 31(3), Sept. 1971; 5. 'On the specification of the aggregate production function', *RISE*, 28(7), July 1981.

GAREGNANI, Pierangelo

Born 1930, Milan, Italy.
Current Post Prof. Econ., Univ. Rome, 1974–.
Recent Posts Prof. Econ., Univ. Pavia, 1966–9; Prof. Econ., Univ. Florence, 1969–73; Fellow, Trinity Coll., Univ. Camb., 1973–4.
Degrees Doctorate Univ. Pavia, 1953; PhD (Econ.) Univ. Camb., 1959.
Principal Contributions Work along three strictly connected lines: clarification and development of the approach to value and distribution of the English classical economists brought to light by Sraffa in his edition of Ricardo; critique of the notion of capital underlying the subsequent 'marginalist' theories which explain distribution in terms of the 'demand and supply' for factors of production, based on the mutual 'substitutability' between such factors; and use of results under these for an analysis of the possibility of deficiencies of aggregate demand in the long period.
Publications *Books:* 1. *Il Problema della Domanda Effettiva Nello Sviluppo Economico Italiano* (SVIMEZ, 1962); 2. *Il Capitale Nelle Teorie della Distribuzione* (Giuffré, 1978; French transl., Maspéro, 1980); 3. *Valore e Domanda Effettiva* (Einaudi, 1979); 4. *Marx e Gli Economisti Classici* (Einaudi, 1981).
Articles: 1. 'Switching of techniques', *QJE*, 80, Nov. 1966; 2. 'Heterogeneous capital, the production function and the theory of distribution', *REStud*, 37(3), July 1970, reprinted in *A Critique of Economic Theory*, eds G.K. Hunt and J.G. Schwartz (Penguin Books, 1972); 3. 'On a change in the notion of equilibrium in recent work on value: a comment on Samuelson', in *Essays in Modern Capital Theory*, eds M. Brown *et al.* (N-H, 1976); 4. 'Notes on consumption, investment and effective demand', *Camb*

JE, 2, Dec. 1978, 3, March 1979; 5. 'Notes on consumption, investment and effective demand, a reply to Joan Robinson', *Camb JE*, 3, June 1979.

GARNIER, Germain*

Dates and Birthplace 1754–1821, Auxerre, France.
Post Held Prefect, Seine et Oise, France, 1799.
Offices and Honours Created Count, 1804; Pres., Napoleonic Senate, 1809–11; Member of Royal Council of State, 1814; created Marquis.
Career French translator of Smith's *Wealth of Nations*, who emphasised the elements in Smith sympathetic to physiocracy and played down Smith's views on industrialisation. This version of Smith was heartily rejected by Say and his followers, who can be seen as reacting against Garnier almost as much as in favour of Smith. His political career revealed considerable powers of adaptation to the dominant trend of the day.
Publications *Books:* 1. *De la propriété dans ses rapports avec le droit politique* (1792); 2. *Abrégé élémentaire des principes de l'économie politique* (1796); 3. *Théorie des banques d'escompte* (1806); 4. *Appel à tous les propriétaires en Europe* (1818); 5. *Histoire de la monnaie*, 2 vols, (1819).
Secondary Literature E. Teilhac, 'Garnier, Germain', *ESS*, vol 6.

GARNIER, Joseph Clement*

Dates and Birthplace 1813–81, Beuil, Alpes Maritimes, France.
Posts Held Prof., l'Ecole Supérieure de Commerce, Athenée, l'Ecole Nat. des Ponts et Chaussées, Paris.
Offices A founder of Soc. d'Econ. Polit., 1842; Ed., *J des Economistes*, 1845–81; Member, Inst. de France, 1873.
Career Though not remarkable for any theoretical contribution, he achieved a position of considerable influence in the French economic community, chiefly through his editorship of the *Journal des economistes*. Rigidly orthodox in his *laissez faire* beliefs.

Publications *Books:* 1. *Eléments de l'économie politique* (1845); 2. *Richard Cobden, les ligueurs et la ligue* (1846); 3. *Du principe de la population* (1857); 4. *Traité des finances* (1862).

Secondary Literature E. Teilhac, 'Garnier, Joseph Clément', *ESS*, vol 6.

GASTWIRTH, Joseph Lewis

Born 1936, New York City, NY, USA.

Current Post Prof. Stat. Econ., George Washington Univ.

Recent Posts Vis. assoc. prof. Stats, Harvard Univ., 1970–1; Vis. faculty adviser US Office Management and Budget, 1971–2; Vis. prof., MIT, 1979.

Degrees BS (*Summa cum laude*) Yale Univ., 1958; PhD Columbia Univ., 1963.

Offices and Honours Member, Em Soc, AEA, RSS, IRRA; Fellow, ASA, Inst. Math. Stats, Amer. Assoc. Advancement Science; Recipient of NSF research grants; Washington Stat. Soc. prize for young statisticians, 1969; Assoc. ed., *JASA*, 1977–.

Principal Contributions The measurement and estimation of indices of inequality, e.g. the Lorenz curve, from complete and/or grouped data; the use of labour statistics in defining labour market areas and available labour pools with application to employment discrimination cases; and the theory and application of order statistics to robust estimation and search theory.

Publications *Articles:* 1. 'On robust procedures', *JASA*, 61, 1966; 2. 'The estimation of the Lorenz curve and Gini index', *REStat*, 54(3), Aug. 1972; 3. 'On the large sample theory of some measures of income inequality', *Em*, 42(1), Jan. 1974; 4. 'On probabilistic models of consumer search for information', *QJE*, 90(1), Feb. 1976; 5. 'Defining the labour market for equal employment standards' (with S. Haber), *MLR*, 99(3), March 1976.

GAYER, Arthur David*

Dates and Birthplace 1903–51, Poona, India.

Posts Held Lecturer, Ass. prof. Econ., Columbia Univ., 1931–40; Assoc. prof. Econ., Queen's Coll., New York City, 1940–51.

Degrees BA, MA, DPhil Univ. Oxford.

Offices Sr Medley Res. Fellow Econ., Univ. Oxford, 1925–7; Adviser, US Govt comms., 1932–; Sr economist, Fed. Reserve Board, 1936.

Career His work for Roosevelt's Commission on Economic Reconstruction (1932–4) was the ideal complement to his academic study of economic fluctuations. This and the experience of other official work was crystallised in his *Monetary Policy* (1935), his best-known book. He was quick to take up Keynes' message, having arrived at Keynesian policy views well before Keynes. The data and analysis in *Growth and Fluctuation* (1953) is also frequently cited by economic historians.

Publications *Books:* 1. *Monetary Policy and Economic Stabilisation* (1935); 2. *Public Works in Prosperity and Depression* (1935); 3. *Public Works and Unemployment Relief in the United States* (1936); 4. *The Sugar Economy of Puerto Rico* (with P.T. Homan and E.K. James), (1938); 5. *The Growth and Fluctuation of the British Economy 1790–1850*, 2 vols (with W.W. Rostow and A.J. Schwartz), (1953).

Secondary Literature (Obituary) 'Professor A.D. Gayer: problems of economic stability', *Times*, 24 Nov. 1951.

GEARING, F.R.

N.e.

GENOVESE, Eugene D.

Born 1930, New York City, NY, USA.

Current Post Prof. Hist., Univ. Rochester, NY, USA, 1969–.

Degrees BA Brooklyn Coll., NY, 1953; MA, PhD, Columbia Univ., 1955, 1959.

Offices and Honours Fellow, AAAS; Exec. Council, AHA, 1971–5; Bancroft award, 1975 (for *Roll, Jordan, Roll*); Literary award, Amer. Academy Arts,

1975; Pres., Org. Amer. Historians, 1978–9.

Principal Contributions The political economy of European expansion and plantation slavery in a historical and social context. Have tried to demonstrate the usefulness of Marxist methods.

Publications *Books:* 1. *The Political Economy of Slavery* (Pantheon, 1965); 2. *The World the Slaveholders Made* (Pantheon, 1969); 3. *Red and Black* (Pantheon, 1971); 4. *Roll, Jordan, Roll* (Pantheon, 1974); 5. *From Rebellion to Revolution* (Louisiana State Univ. Press, 1979).
Articles: 1. 'The political crisis of social history' (with E. Fox-Genovese), *J Social Hist.*, 1976; 2. 'The slave economies in political perspective' (with E. Fox-Genovese), *J Amer. Hist.*, 1979.

GENOVESI, Antonio*

Dates and Birthplace 1712–69, Salerno, Italy.
Posts Held Teacher Metaphysics, 1741–54, Prof. Commerce, 1754–69, Univ. Naples.
Career A great teacher and founder of a distinct Neapolitan school. His published lectures have been criticised for lack of rigour and system, however, they cover the range of utilitarian ideas current at the time and present a balanced view of trade questions which gives credit to mercantilist ideas.
Publications *Books:* 1. *Lezioni di Commercio Ossiadi Economia Civile* (1765).
Secondary Literature A. Cutolo, *Antonio Genovesi* (1926).

GEORGE, Henry*

Dates and Birthplace 1839–97, Philadelphia, USA.
Posts Held Journalist and political campaigner.
Career Developed the idea that ownership of land by a minority was the chief cause of poverty, and advocated taxation of the 'unearned increment' of rental values. He also favoured public ownership of railways and other mono-polies such as telegraphs, but stopped well short of socialism. His arguments at first received some academic acceptance in Europe but later his enormously successful speaking tours in Britain caused Fawcett, Marshall and others forcibly to reject his ideas. In the 1880s he seized on the term 'single tax' as his main object and formed a major political movement in its favour. To this day he has disciples around the world, particularly in Australia and New Zealand, who generally favour 'site value taxation' of land as the kernel of Georgism.
Publications *Books:* 1. *Our Land and Land Policy* (1871); 2. *Progress and Poverty* (1879, 1936, 1948, 1960); 3. *The Land Question* (1881); 4. *The Condition of Labor* (1891); 5. *The Science of Political Economy* (1897).
Secondary Literature S.B. Cord, *Henry George: Dreamer or Realist?* (Univ. Pennsylvania Press, 1965); C.A. Barker, 'George, Henry', *IESS*, vol. 6.

GEORGESCU-ROEGEN, Nicholas

Born 1906, Constanza, Romania.
Current Post Disting. prof. Emeritus, 1976–.
Recent Posts Prof. Stats, Univ. Bucharest, 1932–46; Lecturer, Res. assoc., Harvard Univ., 1948–9; Prof., 1949–69, Disting. prof., 1969–76, Vanderbilt Univ.
Degrees Lic. Math. Univ. Bucharest, 1926; DStat. Univ. Paris (Sorbonne), 1930; Hon. degrees, Univs. Louis Pasteur (1976), Strasbourg (1976), Florence (1980).
Offices and Honours Co-ed., *Enciclopedia Romaniei*, 1935–47; Fellow, Em Soc, 1950, Internat. Inst. Sociology, 1960, AAAS, 1973, Accademia Toscana di Scienze e Lettere, 1977, Disting. Fellow, AEA, 1971; Assoc. ed., *Em*, 1951–68; Branscomb disting. prof., 1967; Richard T. Ely lectureship, 1969; Member, Internat. Inst. Stats, 1970; Earl Sutherland prize Achievement in Res., 1976.
Principal Contributions Solution of non-integrability paradox in utility theory; proof that deriving a utility function from revealed preference alone is impossible. Stochastic choice, hierarchical

choice (lexicographic). Nature of expectation, risk versus uncertainty. First and most general substitutability theorem for Leontief systems. Minimum necessary conditions for feasible Leontief systems. General theory of relaxation phenomena, applications to Leontief and Hansen-Samuelson models. A flow-fund model for production, factory vs farming. Fallacy of dynamic growth models. Agrarian economics vs neo-classical and Marxist; zero marginal labour productivity. Thermodynamic aspects of economics. Bioeconomies.

Publications *Books:* 1. *Activity Analysis of Production and Allocation* (with T.C. Koopmans *et al.*), (Wiley, 1951); 2. *Analytical Economics: Issues and Problems* (Harvard Univ. Press, 1966); 3. *The Entropy Law and the Economic Process* (Harvard Univ. Press, 1971); 4. *Energy and Economic Myths: Institutional and Analytical Economic Essays* (Pergamon Press, 1976); 5. *Demain la décroissance* (Pierre-Marcel Favre, 1979).

Articles: 1. 'The pure theory of consumer's behavior', *QJE*, 50, Aug. 1936; 2. 'Leontief's system in the light of recent results', *REStat*, 32, Aug. 1950; 3. 'The nature of expectation and uncertainty', in *Expectations, Uncertainty, and Business Behavior*, ed. J.M. Bowman (US SSRC, 1958); 4. 'The steady state and ecological salvation: a thermodynamic analysis', *Bioscience*, 27, April 1977; 5. 'Energy analysis and economic valuation', *SEJ*, 44, April 1979.

GERSCHENKRON, Alexander*

Dates and Birthplace 1904–78, Odessa, Russia.

Posts Held Assoc., Austrian Inst. Bus. Cycle Res.; Res. ass., Lecturer Econ., Univ. Cal., Berkeley, 1938–44; Res. staff, Governors Fed. Reserve System, 1944–8; Prof., Harvard Univ., 1948–74.

Degree Dr rer. pol. Univ. Vienna, 1928.

Career Originally concentrated on Soviet economic history and economics. Examining the swift movement of indices of industrial growth in Russia, he discovered the 'Gerschenkron effect' whereby the choice of base year for such indices influenced their subsequent progress. Among his many other breakthroughs was his account of how the more backward countries of nineteenth-century Europe were able to develop at much greater speed than the earlier industrial countries.

Publications *Books:* 1. *Bread and Democracy in Germany* (1943); 2. *Economic Relations with the USSR* (1945); 3. *A Dollar Index of Soviet Machinery Output 1927–8 to 1937* (1951); 4. *Economic Backwardness in Historical Perspective* (1962); 5. *Continuity in History and Other Essays* (1968); 6. *Europe in the Russian Mirror* (1970); 7. *An Economic Spurt that Failed* (1977).

Secondary Literature A. Erlich, 'Gerschenkron, Alexander', *IESS*, vol. 18.

GERVAISE, Isaac*

Dates and Birthplace 1700s, Paris, France.

Career Eighteenth-century Huguenot merchant in London known only for his *System*. This was a general equilibrium treatment of international trade containing an analysis of the various causes of disequilibrium. It is also unusual for its clear statement of the case for free trade at a time when such ideas were almost unheard of. The quality of Gervaise's argument and his intimate practical understanding of economic phenomena are both remarkable.

Publications *Books:* 1. *The System or Theory of the Trade of the World* (1720).

Secondary Literature J.M. Letiche, 'Gervaise, Isaac', *IESS*, vol. 6.

GESELL, Silvio*

Dates and Birthplace 1862–1930, Belgium.

Posts Held Merchant, Buenos Aires, 1887–1914; Germany after 1914.

Career Monetary writer, considered a crank until Keynes rehabilitated him and others of the 'brave army of heretics' in the *General Theory*. His plan for stamped money was designed to discourage hoarding by requiring that stamps be bought and fixed to money to preserve its value. His chief emphasis was on the velocity of money circulation.

Publications *Books:* 1. *Die Verstaatlichung des Geldes* (1891).

Secondary Literature L. Weden 'Gesell, Silvio', in *Handwörterbuch der Sozialwissenschaften*, vol 3, eds E.V. Beckerath *et al.* (Gustav Fischer, 1959).

GIDE, Charles*

Dates and Birthplace 1847–1932, Uzès, France.

Posts Held Prof., Univs. Bordeaux, Montpellier, Paris.

Offices Founder, *REP*, 1887.

Career He was one of the professors of economics appointed to the Faculties of Law in French universities in 1876. These appointments broke the hold of the *laissez faire* liberal school in French economics and Gide's 1883 *Principes* ... was a means of spreading a more open-minded attitude towards historical and other approaches. Economics was only part of his general interest in social philosophy and he was an enthusiastic and successful advocate of the co-operative movement.

Publications *Books:* 1. *Principes d'économie politique* (1883); 2. *Economie sociale* (1905); 3. *Cours d'économie politique* (1909); 4. *A History of Economic Doctrines* (with C. Rist), (1909, 1948); 5. *Les Colonies Communistes et Co-operatives* (1930).

Secondary Literature C. Rist, 'Charles Gide' (obituary), *EJ*, 42, June 1932; C. Rist, *Charles Gide, sa vie et son oeuvre* (1933).

GIERSCH, Herbert

Born 1921, Reichenbach, Eulengebirge, Germany.

Current Post Prof. Econ., Univ. Kiel, 1969–, Pres., Inst. für Weltwirtschaft, Univ. Kiel, 1969–.

Recent Posts Counsellor, General Secretariat OEEC, Paris, 1953–4; Prof. Econ., Univ. Saar, 1955–69; Vis. prof., Yale Univ., 1962–3; Member, German Econ. Expert Council, 1964–70; Dean Acheson vis. prof., Yale Univ., 1976.

Degree Hon Dr Univ. Erlangen, 1977.

Offices and Honours Grosskreuz des Verdienstordens der Bundesrepublik Deutschland; British Council Fellow, LSE, 1948–9.

Principal Contributions Application of the principle 'redistribute now, grow later' to West Germany (doctoral dissertation, 1948); application of the acceleration principle to explain the demand for imports (1953); application of location theory to predict some effects of European economic integration (1949–50) and to explain the regional distribution of incomes (1959); principles of a national wage policy for a constant cost level in an open economy (1967); proposals for policy assignment in a concerted strategy in an open economy (1965); exchange rates and the location of economic activities (1965); contributions to the theory of flexible exchange rates (1970); German economic policy problems (1970); contributions to the theory of indexation; and elements of a theory of world economic growth (1979).

Publications *Books:* 1. *Allgemeine Wirtschaftspolitik-Grundlagen*, vols 1, 9 (Gabler, 1960); 2. *Growth, Cycles and Exchange rates – The Experience of West Germany* (Almqvist & Wiksell, 1970); 3. *Kontroverse Fragen der Wirtschaftspolitik* (Piper, 1971).

Articles: 1. 'Acceleration principle and propensity to import', *WA*, 70(2), 1953; 2. 'The trade optimum', in *Internat. Econ. Papers*, 7 (Macmillan, 1957).

GIFFEN, Robert*

Dates and Birthplace 1837–1910, Strathaven, Scotland.

Posts Held Journalist, 1860–71; Official, Stat. Section, UK Board of Trade, 1871–97.

Offices Founder, RES; Pres., RSS, 1882–4.

Career Through his frequent contributions to the press and learned journals he was able to disseminate knowledge of the use of official statistics. He was not a theoretical statistician, but nevertheless achieved important progress in difficult fields such as the measurement of national income. The so-called 'Giffen Paradox' was an exception to the general law of demand for which Marshall gave him credit, apparently without warrant. Giffen also wrote on the quantity theory of money. Despite his official post he was an enthusiastic public campaigner for free trade and against bimetallism.

Publications *Books:* 1. *Essays in Finance*, 1st series (1880), 2nd series (1886); 2. *Economic Inquiries and Studies*, 2 vols (1869–1902); 3. *Stock Exchange Securities* (1877); 4. *The Growth of Capital* (1889).

Secondary Literature G.J. Stigler, 'Notes on the history of the Giffen Paradox', *Essays in the History of Economics* (Univ. Chicago Press, 1965); K.J. Penney, 'Giffen, Robert', *IESS*, vol. 6.

GILBERT, Milton*

Dates and Birthplace 1909–79, USA.

Posts Held Ed., *Survey Current Bus.*, US Dept. Commerce, 1938–41; Chief, Nat. Income Div., US Dept. Commerce, 1941–51; Dir., Stats and Nat. Accounts, OEEC, 1951–5; Dir., Econ. and Stats, OEEC, 1955–60; Adviser, 1960–75, Head, Monetary and Econ. Dept., 1975–9, Bank Internat. Settlements, Basle, Switzerland.

Degrees MA Temple Univ; PhD Univ. Penn.

Offices Fellow, ASA.

Career Developed the earliest national accounts in the USA. Worked on international monetary problems, in particular, the analysis of the workings and breakdown of the Bretton Woods par value system.

Publications *Books:* 1. *US National Income Supplements* (with others), (US Govt Printing Office, 1947); 2. *An International Comparison of National Products and the Purchasing Power of Currencies* (with I.B. Kravis), (OECD, 1954); 3. *The Gold Dollar System: Conditions of Equilibrium and the Price of Gold* (Princeton Univ. Press, 1968); 4. *The Discipline of the Balance of Pay-*

ments and the Design of the International Monetary System (OECD, 1970); 5. *Quest for World Monetary Order*, eds P. Oppenheimer and M.G. Dealtry (Wiley, 1980).

GODWIN, William*

Dates and Birthplace 1756–1836, Wisbech, England.

Posts Held Nonconformist clergyman, 1777–82; Professional writer and publisher.

Career His *Enquiry* ... was a great success, with its emphasis on the perfectability of man. His vision of a prosperous society in which equality reigned provoked Malthus into raising the difficulty caused by increasing population. Godwin's role in stimulating Malthus' *Essay* is better remembered than his positive contribution. His belated attempt to refute Malthus in *Of Population* was a pathetic failure, despite the good arguments available to him.

Publications *Books:* 1. *Enquiry Concerning Political Justice* (1793); 2. *Of Population* (1820).

GOLDBERGER, Arthur Stanley

Born 1930, New York City, NY, USA.

Current Post Vilas res. prof. Econ., Univ. Wisconsin, Madison, USA.

Recent Posts Acting ass. prof., Stanford Univ., 1956–9; Assoc. prof., 1960–3, Prof., 1963–70, Groves prof., 1970–9, Res. assoc., Inst. Res. Poverty, Univ. Wisconsin, 1972–.

Degrees BS New York Univ., 1951; MA, PhD, Univ. Michigan, 1952, 1958.

Offices Fellow, Em Soc, 1964–, ASA, 1968–; Guggenheim Memorial Foundation Fellow, 1972; Council member, Em Soc, 1975–80; Fellow, Center Advanced Study Behavioral Sciences, 1976–7, 1980–1; Fellow, AAAS, 1977–.

Publications *Books:* 1. *An Econometric Model of the United States 1929–52* (with L.R. Klein), (N-H, 1955); 2. *Impact Multipliers and Dynamic Properties* (N-H, 1958); 3. *Econometric Theory* (Wiley, 1964); 4. *Topics in Regression Analysis* (Mac-*

millan, 1968); 5. *Structural Equation Models in the Social Sciences*, ed. (with O.D. Duncan), (Seminar Press, 1973).

Articles: 1. 'Best linear unbiased prediction in the generalized linear regression model', *JASA*, 57, 1962; 2. 'Econometrics and psychometrics: a survey of communalities', *Psychometrika*, 36, 1971; 3. 'Structural equation methods in the social sciences', *Em*, 40(6), Nov. 1972; 4. 'The non-resolution of IQ inheritance by path analysis', *Amer. J Human Genetics*, 30, 1978; 5. 'Heritability', *Ec*, 46, Nov. 1979.

GOLDFELD, Stephen M.

Born 1940, New York City, NY, USA.
Current Post Prof. Econ., Princeton Univ., USA.
Recent Posts Vis. res. prof., CORE, Catholic Univ. Louvain, 1970–1; Ford vis. prof., Univ. Cal. Berkeley, 1975–6; Vis. prof., Technion, Haifa, 1980; Member, US President's Council Econ. Advisers, 1980–1.
Degrees BA, Harvard Coll., 1960; PhD, MIT, 1963.
Offices Fellow, Em Soc; Member, Sr adviser, Brookings Panel Econ. Activity, 1972–; Assoc. ed., *Int ER*, 1971–, *J Em*, 1972–, *AER*, 1973–5, *REStat*, 1973–, *JMCB*, 1980–.
Principal Contributions Econometrics, including both methodology and applied work, and macro-economics, with special emphasis on monetary and fiscal factors. Within econometrics focused on non-linear models, problems of aggregation, models of structural change, and disequilibrium models. Research in macro- and monetary economics has included studying the portfolio behaviour of financial institutions and individuals as well as topics in monetary and fiscal policy.
Publications *Books:* 1. *Commercial Bank Behavior and Economic Activity: A Structural Study of Monetary Policy in the Postwar United States* (N-H, 1966); 2. *Precursors in Mathematical Economics: An Anthology* (with W.J. Baumol), (LSE, 1968); 3. *Nonlinear Methods in Econometrics* (with R.E. Quandt), (N-H, 1972); 4. *Studies in Nonlinear Estimation* (with R.E. Quandt), (Ballinger Publishing Co., 1976); 5. *The Economics of Money and Banking* (with L.V. Chandler), (Harper & Row, 1981).

Articles: 1. 'The determinants of member-bank borrowing: an econometric study' (with E.J. Kane), *J Fin*, 21(3), Sept. 1966; 2. 'An econometric model for evaluating stabilization policies' (with A. Ando), in *Studies in Economic Stabilization*, eds A. Ando *et al.* (Brookings Inst., 1968); 3. 'The demand for money revisited', *Brookings Papers Econ. Activity*, 3, 1973; 4. 'New measures of fiscal and monetary policy, 1958–1973' (with A.S. Blinder), *AER*, 66(5), Dec. 1976; 5. 'A model of FHLBB advances: rationing or market clearing?' (with D. Jaffee and R. Quandt), *REStat*, 62(3), Aug. 1980.

GOLDSMITH, Raymond W.

Born 1904, Brussels, Belgium.
Current Post Prof. Econ. Emeritus, Yale Univ., USA.
Recent Post Prof. Econ., Yale Univ., 1960–74.
Degree PhD Univ. Berlin, 1927.
Offices Member Council, Chairman, IARIW, 1950s.
Principal Contributions Development of statistics of saving for US and of estimates of national balance sheets for many countries, using perpetual inventory method. Comparative analysis of financial structure and development.
Publications *Books:* 1. *Kapitalpolitik* (Junker & Dünnhaapt, 1933); 2. *A Study of Saving in the United States*, 3 vols (Princeton Univ. Press, 1955–6); 3. *Studies in the National Balance Sheet of the United States*, 2 vols (with R. Lipsey and M. Mendelson), (Princeton Univ. Press, 1963); 4. *Financial Structure and Development* (Yale Univ. Press, 1969); 5. *The Financial Development of India and Japan 1860–1977* (Yale Univ. Press, 1981).

Articles: 1. 'A century of financial development in Latin America', in *Memoria de la X reunion de Tecnicos de Bancos Centrales del Continente Americano* (1972).

GONNARD, René*

Dates and Birthplace 1874–1966, Chamay les Maçon, France.
Post Held Prof., Univ. Lyons, 1901–44.
Degree Agrégé Econ. 1901.
Offices and Honours Correspondent member, Institut de France; Chevalier, Légion d'Honneur, 1935.
Career Distinguished French historian of economic ideas in the inter-war period.
Publications *Books:* 1. *L'Émigration européenne au XIXe siècle* (1906); 2. *Histoire des doctrines économiques* (1921); 3. *Histoire des doctrines de la population* (1923); 4. *Histoire des doctrines monétaires* (1935); 5. *La Propriété dans la doctrine et dans l'histoire* (1943).

GONNER, Edward Carter Kersey*

Dates and Birthplace 1862–1922, England.
Post Held Prof., Univ. Liverpool, 1891–1922.
Degree MA Univ. Oxford.
Offices Pres., Section F, BAAS, 1897, 1914; Knighted, 1921.
Career His writings range widely from commercial geography to socialist ideas and economic history. He was a successful wartime civil servant in the Ministry of Food.
Publications *Books:* 1. *The Socialist State* (1895); 2. *The Social Philosophy of Rodbertus* (1899); 3. *Interest and Saving* (1906); 4. *Germany in the Nineteenth Century* (1912); 5. *Common Land and Inclosure* (1912).
Secondary Literature L.L. Price, 'Gonner, Sir Edward Carter Kersey', *ESS*, vol. 5.

GOODHART, Charles A.E.

Born 1936, London, England.
Current Post Chief adviser, with particular reference to monetary policy, Bank of England (Adviser, 1969–).
Recent Posts Ass. lecturer, Univ. Camb., 1963–5; Econ. adviser, UK Dept. Econ. Affairs, 1965–7; Lecturer Monetary Econ., LSE, 1967–9.

Degrees BA (Econ. Tripos first) Univ. Camb., 1960; PhD (Econ.) Harvard Univ., 1963.
Offices and Honours Adam Smith prize, Univ. Camb., 1959; Prize Fellowship, Trinity Coll., Univ. Camb., 1963; Dir., UK SSRC Money Study Group, 1979–.
Principal Contributions After two books on banking history, concentrated on monetary theory, application and policy, first as an academic, then as adviser to Bank of England. More widely known for two less serious pieces, first as one of the earliest researchers into the relationship between macro-economic developments and political popularity, and second as the author of 'Goodhart's law': any statistical regularity, notably in the monetary area, will break down when pressure is placed upon it for control purposes.
Publications *Books:* 1. *The New York Money Market and the Finance of Trade, 1900–13* (Harvard Univ. Press, 1969); 2. *The Business of Banking, 1891–1914* (Weidenfeld & Nicolson, 1972); 3. *Money, Information and Uncertainty* (Macmillan, 1975).
Articles: 1. 'Political economy', *Polit. Stud.*, 18, March 1970; 2. 'The importance of money', *Bank of England Quarterly Bull.*, 10, June 1970; 3. 'Monetary policy in the United Kingdom', in *Monetary Policy in Twelve Industrial Countries* (Fed. Reserve Bank Boston, 1973); 4. 'Analysis of the determination of the stock of money', in *Essays in Modern Economics*, eds M. Parkin and A.R. Nobay (Longman, 1973); 5. 'Problems of monetary management: the UK experience', in *Papers in Monetary Economics* (Reserve Bank Australia, 1975).

GORDON, Donald Flemming

Born 1923, Saskatoon, Saskatchewan, Canada.
Current Post Prof., Dir. Center Study Bus. Govt, Baruch Coll., City Univ. NY, USA.
Recent Posts Ass. prof., Assoc. prof., Prof. Econ., Univ. Washington, 1950–66; Prof., Grad. School Management, Univ. Rochester, 1966–74; Prof.,

Exec. Officer PhD Program Econ., City Univ. New York, 1974–6; Prof. Simon Fraser Univ., British Columbia, 1976–8.

Degrees BA Univ. Saskatchewan, 1944; MA Univ. Toronto, 1946; PhD Cornell Univ., 1949.

Offices and Honours AEA; Award, best article 1974 in *EI*; Vice-pres., Pres., WEA, 1978–80.

Principal Contributions A search model of employment with an argument for the invalidity of dynamic equations which depend on expectations (with A.J. Hynes); the distinction between relative and absolute value in classical and Marxian economics: the latter is a definition and not subject to empirical, logical or normative refutation; the methodological position that operational propositions cannot be derived from the maximising calculus, but stem from the hypothesis of stable tastes; a test of the proposition that rapid economic growth in Canada in 1901–10 was primarily due to staple exports (with E.J. Chambers); and an independent development of implicit contracts as an explanation for lay-offs, job-rationing and unemployment.

Publications *Articles:* 1. 'Operational propositions in economic theory', *JPE*, 63, April 1955; 2. 'What was the labor theory of value?', *AER/S*, 49(2), May 1959; 3. 'Primary products and economic growth: an empirical measurement' (with E. Chambers), *JPE*, 74, Aug. 1966; 4. 'On the theory of price dynamics' (with A. Hynes), in *The Microeconomic Foundations of Employment and Inflation Theory*, ed. E.S. Phelps (Norton, 1970); 5. 'A neoclassical theory of Keynesian unemployment', *EI*, 12(4), Dec. 1974.

GORDON, Myron J.

Born 1920, New York City, NY, USA.

Current Post Prof. Fin., Faculty of Management Stud., Univ. Toronto.

Recent Posts Carnegie-Mellon Univ., 1947–52; MIT, 1952–62; Univ. Rochester, 1962–70; Visitor, Univ. Cal., Berkeley, 1966–7; Hebrew Univ., Jerusalem, 1973, Wharton School, Univ. Pennsylvania, 1977.

Degrees BA (Econ.) Univ. Wisconsin, 1941; MA (Econ.), PhD (Econ.), Harvard Univ., 1947, 1952.

Offices Vice-pres., AFA, 1974; Pres., AFA, 1975; Various comms, AFA, AAA, Inst. Management Science.

Principal Contributions The development of capital theory under uncertainty and aversion to risk. The impact of the investment and financing policies of a corporation on the value and the security of the firm under perfectly competitive capital markets and under market imperfections. The macro-implications of micro-policies to survive under uncertainty.

Publications *Books:* 1. *The Investment, Financing and Valuation of the Corporation* (Richard D. Irwin, 1962); 2. *The Cost of Capital to a Public Utility* (Michigan State Univ., 1974); 3. *Accounting: A Management Approach* (with G. Shillinglaw and J. Ronen), (Richard D. Irwin, 1979).

Articles: 1. 'A portfolio theory of the social discount rate and the public debt', *J Fin*, 3(2), May 1976; 2. 'Bond share yield spreads under uncertain inflation' (with P.J. Halpern), *AER*, 66(4), Sept. 1976; 3. 'The cost of equity capital: a reconsideration' (with L.I. Gould), *J Fin*, 33(3), June 1978; 4. 'Debt maturity, default risk, and capital structure', *J Bank Fin*, 3, 1979; 5. 'Growth and survival in a capitalist system', *J Post Keyn E*, 2(4), Summer 1980.

GORDON, Robert James

Born 1940, Boston, Mass., USA.

Current Post Prof. Econ., Northwestern Univ., Ill., USA; Res. assoc., NBER.

Recent Posts Ass. prof., Harvard Univ., 1967–8; Ass. Prof., Univ. Chicago, 1968–73.

Degrees BA Harvard Univ., 1962; BA, MA, Oxford Univ., 1964, 1969; PhD MIT, 1967.

Offices Member, Sr adviser, Brookings Panel Econ. Activity, 1970–1; Co-ed., *JPE*, 1970–3; Board Eds., *AER*, 1975–7; Fellow, Treasurer, 1975–, Em Soc; Organiser, Internat. Seminar Macroecon., 1978– Guggenheim Memorial Foundation Fellow, 1980–1; Exec. Comm., AEA, 1981–3.

Principal Contributions Demonstrated that inflation depends both on demand pressure and supply shocks: excess demand stems from pressures on the central bank to accommodate wage push, supply shocks, and fiscal deficits; oil shocks, price controls, payroll taxes, the minimum wage, and foreign exchange rates have been sources of variance in the US inflation rate, while changes in corporation and personal income tax rates have not had inflationary consequences. Work on price measurement for durable goods has developed new techniques to adjust for improvements in performance and energy efficiency, as well as 20,000 new data observations that yield radically different estimates of changes in aggregate prices and productivity, and in the industry allocation of productivity gains.

Publications *Books:* 1. *Milton Friedman's Monetary Framework: A Debate With His Critics*, ed. (Univ. Chicago Press, 1974; Japanese transl. 1978); 2. *Macroeconomics* (Little Brown, 1978, 1981); 3. *Challenges to Interdependent Economies: The Industrial West in the Coming Decade* (with J. Pelkmans), (McGraw-Hill, 1979); 4. *The Measurement of Durable Goods Prices* (Univ. Chicago Press, 1982).

Articles: 1. 'The incidence of the corporation income tax in US manufacturing', *AER*, 57, Sept. 1967; 2. '$45 billion of US private investment has been mislaid', *AER*, 59, June 1969; 3. 'The welfare cost of higher unemployment', *Brookings Papers Econ. Activity*, 1, 1973; 4. 'The demand for and supply of inflation', *J Law E*, 18(3), Dec. 1975; 5. 'Output fluctuations and gradual price adjustment', *JEL*, 19(2), June 1981.

GORMAN, William

Born 1923, Kesh, Co. Fermanagh, N. Ireland.

Current Post Official Fellow, Nuffield Coll., Univ. Oxford.

Recent Posts Ass. lecturer, Lecturer, Sr lecturer, Dept. Econometrics and Social Stats., Univ. Birmingham,

1949–62; Professorial Fellow, Nuffield Coll., Prof. Econ., Univ. Oxford, 1962–7; Prof. Econ., LSE, 1967–79; Hinkley vis. prof., Johns Hopkins Univ., 1979–80.

Degrees BA, MA, Trinity Coll., Dublin, 1948, 1949; MA Univ. Oxford, 1962; DSoc. Sc. Univ. Birmingham, 1973; DSc. Univ. Southampton, 1974.

Offices Fellow, BA; Past-pres., Europ. Chairman, Em Soc; Chairman, Econ. Study Soc.

Principal Contributions Work on aggregation and consumer theory.

Publications *Articles:* 1. 'Community preference fields', *Em*, 21, June 1953; 2. 'Measuring the quantities of fixed factors', in *Value Capital and Growth: Essays in Honour of Sir John Hicks*, ed. J.N. Wolfe (OUP, 1968); 3. 'The structure of utility functions', *REStud*, 35, Oct. 1968; 4. 'A possible procedure for analysing quality differentials in the egg market', *REStud*, 47, June 1980; 5. 'Some Engel curves', in *Essays on the Theory and Measurement of Demand in Honour of Sir Richard Stone*, ed. A. Deaton (CUP, 1981).

GOSCHEN, George Joachim*

Dates and Birthplace 1831–1907, London, England.

Posts Held Businessman, 1853–66; Dir. Bank of England, 1858.

Degree BA Univ. Oxford, 1853.

Offices and Honours MP, 1863–86, 1887–1900; Cabinet minister, 1866–74, 1887–92, 1895–1900; Chancellor, Univ. Oxford, 1903–7; Created Viscount, 1900.

Career Statesman economist whose early work on foreign exchanges was his only major publicaton. This was the first systematic theory of international price adjustments and was for long the standard work on the subject. A convinced supporter of *laissez faire* policies, he followed non-interventionist policies during his long periods of government office. His major achievements are regarded as the reorganisation of local government finance and the conversion of part of the National Debt.

Publications *Books:* 1. *Theory of the Foreign Exchanges* (1861); 2. *Reports*

and Speeches on Local Taxation
(1872); 3. *Addresses on Educational
and Economical Subjects* (1885); 4.
*Essays and Addresses on Economic
Questions* (1905).

Secondary Literature L.M. Fraser
'Goschen, First Viscount', *ESS*, vol. 6.

GOSSEN, Hermann Heinrich*

Dates and Birthplace 1810–58,
Düren, Germany.

Posts Held Civil servant and
businessman.

Career Gossen's only known publication on economics was ignored by his
contemporaries both because of the
dominance of the views of the Historical
School and the pretentious presentation
of his ideas. Thus, both Jevons and
Walras were forced to recognise that
their work on marginal utility had been
substantially anticipated by Gossen;
indeed, Gossen's exact anticipation of
Jevons' theory of labour supply is almost
uncanny. Gossen's book is, in general,
a working out of the hedonistic calculus
using mathematical methods.

Publications *Books:* 1. *Entwicklung
der Gesetze des Menschlichen Verkehrs
und der Daraus Fliessenden Regeln für
Menschliches Handeln* (1854, 1927).

Secondary Literature H. Riedle,
Hermann Heinrich Gossen 1810–1858
(Keller, 1953); H.W. Spiegel, 'Gossen,
Hermann Heinrich', *IESS*, vol. 6.

GOTTL-OTTLILIENFELD, Friedrich von*

Dates and Birthplace 1868–1958,
Vienna, Austro-Hungary.

Posts Held Prof., Technical High
School, Brünn, 1902–8, Munich,
1908–20; Prof. Theoretical Econ., Univ.
Berlin, 1926–41.

Honours Goethe-Medaille für Kunst
und Wiss.

Career As much a sociologist as an
economist, Gottl is chiefly known for his
constant advocacy and exposition of
Weberian 'Verstehen' doctrine in the
social sciences.

Publications *Books:* 1. *Wirtschaft
als Leiben. Eine Sammlung Erkennt-*
niskritischer Arbeiten (1925); 2. *Wirtschaft als Wissen, Tat und Wehr über
Volkswirtschaftslehre, Autarkie und
Wehrwirtschaft* (1940).

Secondary Literature G. von Haber-
ler, 'Kritische Bemerkungen zu Gottls
Methodologischen Schriften', *ZN*, 1,
June 1930; G. Weippert, 'von Gottl-
Ottlilienfeld, Friedrich', *Handwörter-
buch der Sozialwissenschaften*, vol. 4,
eds E.V. Beckerath *et al.* (Gustav
Fisher, 1960).

GOULD, John P.

Born 1939, Chicago, Ill., USA.

Current Post Prof. Econ., Grad.
School Bus., Univ. Chicago, USA,
1965–.

Recent Posts Special ass., Econ.
Affairs, US Dept. Labor, 1969–70; Con-
sultant econ. affairs to Dir. US Office
Management and Budget, Exec. Office
of Pres., 1970; Vis. prof. Econ., Grad.
Inst. Econ., Nat. Taiwan Univ., 1978.

Degrees SB (Highest distinction)
Northwestern Univ., 1960; PhD Univ.
Chicago, 1966.

Offices and Honours AEA, WEA,
Em Soc; Ed., *J Bus*; Assoc. ed., *J Fin.
Econ, J Accounting Econ; Wall Street
Journal* award, 1960; Earhart Fellow,
1963–4; NSF Grant, 1974–5.

Principal Contributions Earliest
research concentrated on the dynamic
theory of the firm with particular reference to the role of adjustment costs in
capital accumulation and the effect of
diffusion processes in advertising. Subsequent work dealt with the effects of
information and uncertainty in a variety
of circumstances including the resolution of legal conflicts, the demand for
insurance, the effect of risk on the value
of information, and the nature of equilibrium in industries facing stochastic
demand.

Publications *Books:* 1. *Microeconomic Theory* (with C.E. Ferguson),
(Richard D. Irwin, 1975; Japanese
transl., 1977, Spanish transl., 1978).

Articles: 1. 'Adjustment costs in the
theory of investment of the firm',
REStud, 35, Jan. 1968; 2. 'Diffusion
processes and optimal advertising policy', in *Micro-economic Foundations of*

Employment and Inflation Theory, ed. E. Phelps (Norton, 1970, 1973; Macmillan, 1971); 3. 'The economics of legal conflicts', *J Legal Stud.*, June 1973; 4. 'Risk, stochastic preference and the value of information', *JET*, 8(1), May 1974; 5. 'Inventories and stochastic demand: equilibrium models of the firm and industry', *J Bus*, 15(1), Jan. 1978.

GRAHAM, Frank Dunstone*

Dates and Birthplace 1890–1949, Halifax, Nova Scotia, Canada.

Posts Held Instructor Econ., Rutgers Coll., 1917–20; Ass. prof., Dartmouth Coll., 1920–1; Prof., Princeton Univ., 1921–49.

Degrees MA, PhD, Harvard Univ., 1917, 1920.

Offices Econ. adviser, US Fed. Farm Board, 1930–1.

Career Attacked the classical international trade theory, particularly the two-country, two-commodity approach and the assumption of comparative-advantage statically conceived. Rejection of Graham's criticisms was for years the litmus-paper test of orthodoxy in trade theory. Served on the special US War Dept Commission on the conduct of the War in 1945.

Publications *Books:* 1. *Exchange, Prices and Production in Hyper-inflation, Germany 1920–3* (1930); 2. *The Abolition of Unemployment* (1932); 3. *Protective Tariffs* (1934); 4. *Golden Avalanche* (with C.R. Whittlesey) (1939); 5. *Social Goals and Economic Institutions* (1942); 6. *Planning and Paying for Full Employment* (with A.P. Lerner *et al.*) (1946); 7. *The Theory of International Values* (1948).

GRAMLICH, Edward M.

Born 1939, Rochester, NY, USA.
Current Post Prof. Econ., Dir., Inst. Public Pol. Stud., Univ. Michigan, USA.
Recent Posts Dir., Res. Div., US Office Econ. Opportunity; Sr Fellow, Brookings Inst., 1973–6.
Degrees BA Williams Coll.; MA, PhD Yale Univ.

Offices Ed. Board, *Nat. Tax J, J Assoc. Public Pol. and Management, Evaluation Quarterly*; Member, Sr adviser, Brookings Panel Econ. Activity; Econ. Panel, NSF.

Principal Contributions Evaluating government programmes. Earlier, focused on problems of fiscal and monetary stabilisation. Recently, focus has switched to social programmes. Textbook on evaluation tries to straighten out some issues that arise in applying the logic of evaluation to social programmes, such as minimum wages and federal grants.

Publications *Books:* 1. *Savings Deposits, Mortgages, and Housing in the FMP Model*, ed. (with D. Jaffee), (Health-Lexington, 1972); 2. *Educational Performance Contracting: An Evaluation of an Experiment* (with P. Koshel), (Brookings Inst., 1975); 3. *Setting National Priorities: the 1975 Budget* (with B. Blechman and R. Hartman), (Brookings Inst., 1975); 4. *Benefit-cost Analysis of Government Programs* (Prentice-Hall, 1981).
Articles: 1. 'State and local fiscal behavior and Federal grant policy' (with H. Galper), *Brookings Papers Econ. Activity*, 1, 1973; 2. 'The distributional effects of higher unemployment', *Brookings Papers Econ. Activity*, 2, 1974; 3. 'The impact of minimum wages on other wages, employment, and family incomes', *Brookings Papers Econ. Activity*, 2, 1976; 4. 'Macro-policy responses to price shocks', *Brookings Papers Econ. Activity*, 1, 1979; 5. 'Public employee market power and the level of Government spending' (with P. Courant and D. Rubinfeld), *AER*, 69(5), Dec. 1979.

GRANDMONT, Jean-Michel

Born 1939, Toulouse, France.
Current Post Maître de Recherche au CNRS, Paris.
Degrees Licence ès-Sciences Univ. Paris, 1961; Ingénieur l'Ecole Polytechnique, 1962; Ingénieur l'Ecole Nationale des Ponts et Chaussées, 1965; PhD (Econ.) Univ. Cal., Berkeley, 1971.
Offices Assoc. ed., *Em, JET, J Math E.*; Fellow, Em Soc, 1974; Member,

Council of Em Soc, 1977–; Maître des Conférences, l'Ecole Polytechnique, Paris, 1977–.

Principal Contributions Introduction of money in general equilibrium theory; introduction of time and expectations in equilibrium theory (temporal general equilibrium theory); contributions to disequilibrium theory and its relation to macroeconomics; and generalisation of existing results on the aggregation of preferences by the majority rule, using the notion of intermediate preferences.

Publications *Articles:* 1. 'On the short-run equilibrium in a monetary economy', in *Allocation under Uncertainty, Equilibrium and Optimality*, ed. J. Drèze (Macmillan, 1974); 2. 'On money and banking' (with G. Laroque), *REStud*, 42(2), April 1975; 3. 'On temporary Keynesian equilibria' (with G. Laroque), *REStud*, 43, Feb. 1976; 4. 'Temporary general equilibrium theory', *Em*, 45(3), April 1977; 5. 'Intermediate preferences and the majority rule', *Em*, 46(2), March 1978.

GRANGER, Clive William John

Born 1934, Swansea, Wales.
Current Post Prof. Econ., Univ. Cal., San Diego, La Jolla, USA.
Recent Posts Prof. Applied Stats and Econometrics, Univ. Nottingham, 1965–74.
Degrees BA (Maths), PhD (Stats), Univ. Nottingham, 1955, 1959.
Offices Fellow, Em Soc.
Principal Contributions The use of time series methods in econometrics and the improvement of econometric practice. Helped to introduce spectral techniques, bivariate time series models, a testable definition of causality, and the combining of forecasts. Worked on the analysis of data from speculative markets, particularly stock and commodity markets, and on consumers' attitudes towards prices.
Publications *Books:* 1. *Spectral Analysis of Economic Time Series* (with M. Hatanaka), (Princeton Univ. Press, 1964); 2. *Predictability of Stock Market Prices* (with O. Morgenstern), (Heath & Co., 1970); 3. *Speculation, Hedging and Forecasts of Commodity*

Prices (with W.C. Labys), (Heath & Co., 1970); 4. *Forecasting Economic Time Series* (with P. Newbold), (Academic Press, 1977); 5. *Forecasting in Business and Economics* (Academic Press, 1980).
Articles: 1. 'The typical spectral shape of an economic variable', *Em*, 34, Jan. 1966; 2. 'Investigating causal relations by econometric models and cross-spectral methods', *Em*, 37(3), July 1969; 3. 'Spurious regressions in econometrics' (with P. Newbold), *J Em*, 2(2), 1974; 4. 'Forecasting transformed variables' (with P. Newbold), *JRSS*, B, 38, 1976; 5. 'Testing for causality: a personal viewpoint', *J Ec Dyn*, 2, 1980.

GRAY, Alexander*

Dates and Birthplace 1882–1968, Dundee, Scotland.
Posts Held Civil servant, 1905–21, Prof. Polit. Econ., Univ. Aberdeen, 1921–35, Univ. Edinburgh, 1935–56.
Degree BA Univ. Edinburgh, 1902.
Offices and Honours Council member, RES, 1929–55; Knighted, 1947; Pres., Section F, BAAS, 1949.
Career Historian of economic thought whose work was authoritative and distinctive for its elegant style, but who was prevented by diffidence from publishing in economics proper.
Publications *Books:* 1. *The Development of Economic Doctrine* (1931); 2. *The Socialist Tradition* (1946).

GRAY, John*

Dates and Birthplace 1799–1883, England.
Posts Held Businessman and publisher.
Career His early experiences as a clerk in a London wholesale house led him to become a bitter critic of competition. The first remedy which he proposed was producer-co-operatives, but he later changed his emphasis to planning and monetary reform.
Publications *Books:* 1. *Lecture on Human Happiness* (1825, 1931); 2. *The Social System, a Treatise on the Principle of Exchange* (1831); 3. *Remedy*

for the Distress of Nations (1842); 4. *Money* (1848).

Secondary Literature J. Kimball, *The Economic Doctrines of John Gray* (Catholic Univ. of America Press, 1948).

GRAY, Simon*

Dates and Birthplace c. 18th century, England.

Post Held War Office employee.

Career A virulently anti-Malthusian writer who published two works under the pseudonym George Purves, praising his own work (a practice that was not uncommon in the nineteenth century). His *Happiness of States . . .* (1815) contains a clear statement that bread is what has come to be called a 'Giffen good'.

Publications *Books:* 1. *The Essential Principles of the Wealth of Nations* (1797); 2. *The Happiness of States: Or an Inquiry Concerning Population* (1815, 1819); 3. [G. Purves], *All Classes Productive of National Wealth* (1817); 4. [G. Purves], *Gray Versus Malthus: The Principles of Population and Production Investigated* (1818); 5. *Remarks on the Production of Wealth* (1820).

Secondary Literature E. Masuda and P. Newman, 'Gray and Giffen goods', *EJ*, 91, Dec. 1981.

GREEN, Harold Alfred John*

Dates and Birthplace 1923–76, Birmingham, England.

Posts Held Lecturer Econ., Univ. Keele, 1955–8; Ass. prof. Econ., Univ. Cal., Santa Barbara, 1958–9; Ass. prof., Prof. Econ., 1959–72; Prof. Econ. Theory, Univ. Kent, 1972–6.

Degrees BA, MA, Univ. Oxford, 1947, 1948; PhD MIT, 1954.

Offices Simon vis. prof., Univ. Manchester, 1965–6; Vis. prof., Univ. Essex, 1971–2.

Career Principal contribution to economics lay in the careful exposition and evaluation of propositions in economic theory. His earlier work was in the theories of growth and distribution, but the majority of his publications, including his well-known book on consumer theory, were largely concerned with aspects of consumer and social choice under various constraints. His final published paper on optimal taxation brought together apparently different results within a single framework, and many of his earlier works were similarly concerned to survey and reconcile different approaches to a topic.

Publications *Books:* 1. *Aggregation in Economic Analysis* (Princeton Univ. Press, 1964); 2. *Consumer Theory* (Penguin Books, 1971, Macmillan, 1976).
Articles: 1. 'Some logical relations in revealed preference theory', *Ec*, N.S. 24, Nov. 1957; 2. 'The social optimum in the presence of monopoly and taxation', *REStud*, 29, Oct. 1961; 3. 'Embodied progress, investment and growth', *AER*, 56, March 1966; 4. 'Uncertainty and the "expectations hypothesis" ', *REStud*, 34, Oct. 1967; 5. 'Two models of optimal pricing and taxation', *OEP*, 27(3), Nov. 1975.

GREENHUT, Melvin L.

Born 1928, New York City, NY, USA.

Current Post Alumni Disting. prof. Econ., Texas A & M Univ., USA, 1980–.

Recent Posts Prof., Florida State Univ., 1956–9, 1962–6; Prof., Head of Dept., 1966–9, Disting. prof., 1969–80, Texas A & M Univ.; Vis. prof., Univ. Cape Town, 1971, Univ. Pittsburgh, 1976.

Degrees BA Hofstra Univ., 1940; MA, PhD, Washington Univ., 1947, 1951.

Offices and Honours Exec. Comm., 1961–3, First vice-pres., 1965–6, SEA; Ed., *SEJ*, 1966–8; Councillor, RSA, 1967–70; Dir., Region VI, Univ. Profs for Academic Order, 1972–3.

Principal Contributions The area of spatial micro-economics. Earliest writings on plant location theory, integrating spatial duopoly theory with plant location theory. 1956 book on plant location theory combined the 'demand' factor of location with the classical cost theory in an integrated framework. More recently, extended writings comparing f.o.b. pricing with discriminatory delivered pricing schedules, leading to theorems in spatial micro-economics which contradict many of those of classical theory. Articles and a book on the subject have included evaluation of welfare effects under the alternative spatial pricing systems.

Publications *Books:* 1. *Plant Location in Theory and in Practice* (Univ. N. Carolina Press, 1956; Japanese transl., 1972); 2. *Intermediate Income and Growth Theory* (with F. Jackson), (Prentice-Hall, 1961); 3. *A Theory of the Firm in Economic Space* (Lone Star Publishing Co., 1974); 4. *Theory of Spatial Prices and Market Areas* (with F. Ohta), (Duke Univ. Press, 1975); 5. *Economics for the Voter* (with C. Stewart), (Lone Star Publishing Co., 1981).

Articles: 1. 'Related market conditions and interindustrial merger' (with H. Ohta), *AER*, 66(2), June 1976; 2. 'Impact of distance on micro-economic theory', *MS*, 46, 1978; 3. 'Vertical integration of successive oligopolists' (with H. Ohta), *AER*, 69(1), March 1979; 4. 'Spatial pricing patterns in the United States' (with J. Greenhut and S. Li), *QJE*, 96(1), March 1980; 5. 'Spatial pricing in the USA, West Germany, and Japan', *Ec*, 48, Feb. 1981.

GREENWOOD, Michael

Born 1939, Chicago, Ill., USA.
Current Post Prof. Econ., Univ. Colorado, USA.
Recent Posts Assoc. prof. Econ., Kansas State Univ., 1965–73; Brookings Econ. Pol . Fellow, 1971–2; Prof. Econ., Arizona State Univ., 1973–80; Sr Res. economist, Econ. Development Admin. US Dept. Commerce, 1977.
Degrees BS De Paul Univ., 1962; MA, PhD, Northwestern Univ., 1965, 1967.
Offices Member, AEA, WEA, RSA, WRSA, PAA; Assoc. ed., *Review Social Econ.*, 1976–, *J Reg S*, 1977–; Arizona State Univ. Grad. Coll., Disting. res. prof., 1977–8.
Principal Contributions Assessment of the magnitudes of various influences on inter-regional migration to determine

the impacts of origin and destination regions, and to explain intra-urban location patterns of employment, housing and labour force. Other work has focused on the determinants and consequences of international migration.

Publications *Books:* 1. *Migration and Economic Growth in the United States: National, Regional and Metropolitan Perspectives* (Academic Press, 1981).

Articles: 1. 'An analysis of the determinants of geographic labor mobility in the United States', *REStat*, 51(2), May 1969; 2. 'A regression analysis of migration to urban areas of a less developed country: the case of India', *J Reg S*, 11(2), Aug. 1971; 3. 'Research on internal migration in the United States: a survey', *JEL*, 13(2), June 1975; 4. 'A simultaneous-equations model of urban growth and migration', *JASA*, 70, Dec. 1975; 5. 'Metropolitan growth and the intrametropolitan location of employment, housing, and labor force', *REStat*, 62(3), Aug. 1980.

GREGORY, Theodore Emanuel Gugenheim*

Dates and Birthplace 1893–1971, England.
Posts Held Assistant lecturer, LSE, 1913–19; Prof. Econ., Univ. London, 1927–37.
Honours Knighted, 1942.
Career An inspiring though difficult teacher with a deep interest in theory and a strong sense of history. His lectures at LSE on the history of currency and banking carried on a tradition inaugurated by Foxwell. He was frequently called upon as an adviser by overseas governments.
Publications *Books:* 1. *Tariffs: A Study in Method* (1921); 2. *An Introduction to Tooke and Newmarch's 'A History of Prices'* (1928, 1962); 3. *Select Statutes, Documents and Reports Relating to British Banking 1832–1928*, 2 vols (1929); 4. *An Introduction to Finance* (1932); 5. *The Westminster Bank Through a Century*, 2 vols (1936).

GRIFFIN, Keith Broadwell

Born 1938, Colon, Panama.
Current Post Pres., Magdalen Coll., Univ. Oxford, 1979–.
Recent Posts Fellow, Magdalen Coll., Univ. Oxford, 1965–79; Chief, Rural Urban Employment Policies Branch, ILO, 1975–6; 3. Warden, Queen Elizabeth House, Univ. Oxford, 1977–9; Dir., Inst. Commonwealth Studies, Univ. Oxford, 1977–9; Dir., Contemporary China Centre, Univ. Oxford, 1980–.
Degrees BA, Hon. DLitt. Williams Coll., 1960, 1978; BPhil., DPhil., Univ. Oxford, 1962, 1965.
Offices Pres., Development Studies Assoc., 1978–80.
Principal Contributions Rural issues: the effects of new technology (the 'Green Revolution'), land reform, trends in rural poverty, the analysis of Chinese communes. Development strategies: alternative paths combining growth with a more equal distribution of income, including the meeting of 'basic needs'. International economic issues: the effects of foreign aid on domestic savings, consumption, the composition of investment and the rate of growth.
Publications *Books:* 1. *Underdevelopment in Spanish America* (A & U, 1969, MIT Press, 1969; Spanish transl., 1972); 2. *Planning development* (with J. Enos), (Addison-Wesley, 1970, Spanish transl., 1975); 3. *The Political Economy of Agrarian Change* (Macmillan, 1974, 1979, Harvard Univ. Press, 1979); 4. *International Inequality and National Poverty* (Macmillan, 1978, Holmes & Meier, 1978); 5. *Land Concentration and Rural Poverty* (Macmillan, 1979, Holmes & Meier, 1979).
Articles: 1. 'Financing development plans in Pakistan', *PDR*, 5(4), Winter 1965; 2. 'Foreign assistance: objectives and consequences' (with J. Enos), *EDCC*, 18(3), April 1970; 3. 'Problems of transition to egalitarian development' (with J. James), *MS*, 47(3), Sept. 1979; 4. 'Rural poverty and development alternatives in south and southeast Asia: some policy issues' (with A. Ghose), *Development and Change*, Oct. 1980; 5. 'The pattern of income inequality in rural China' (with A. Saith), *OEP*, 33(1), March 1981.

GRILICHES, Zvi

Born 1931, Kaunas, Lithuania.
Current Post Prof. Econ., 1969–, Chairman, Dept. Econ., 1980–, Harvard Univ., USA.
Recent Posts Ass. prof. Econ., 1956–9, Assoc. prof. Econ., 1960–4, Prof. Econ., 1964–9, Univ. Chicago.
Degrees BS, MS, Univ. Cal., Berkeley, 1953, 1954; MA, PhD, Univ. Chicago, 1955, 1957.
Offices and Honours John Bates Clark medal, AEA, 1965; Co-ed., *Em*, 1968–78; Pres., Em Soc, 1975; NAS, 1975; Member, Exec. Comm., AEA, 1979–82.
Principal Contributions The analysis of the economics of diffusion of new technology. Computation of the social rate of return to public research investments. Development of 'hedonic' regression methods for the adjustment of price indices for quality change. Analyses of the returns to education and their interaction with ability and family background. Contribution to the 'sources of growth' methodology and estimation. Estimates of production functions, returns to scale, and returns to private research investments. Contributions to the econometric methodology of specification analysis, distributed lags, models with unobservable components, and sample selection bias.
Publications *Books:* 1. *Economies of Scale and the Form of the Production Function* (with V. Pingstad), (N-H, 1971); 2. *Price Indexes and Quality Charge*, ed. (Harvard Univ. Press, 1971); 3. *Patents, Invention and Economic Change*, by J. Schmookler, ed. (with L. Hurwicz), (Harvard Univ. Press, 1972); 4. *Income Distribution and Economic Inequality*, ed. (with W. Krelle *et al.*), (Campus Verlag, 1978); 5. *Handbook of Econometrics*, ed. (with M. Intriligator), (N-H, 1981).
Articles: 1. 'Hybrid corn: an exploration in the economics of technological change', *Em*, 25(4), Oct. 1957; 2. 'The sources of measured productivity growth: US agriculture, 1940–1960',

JPE, 71, Aug. 1963; 3. 'Distributed lags: a survey', *Em*, 35, Jan. 1967; 4. 'Estimating the returns to schooling: some econometric problems', *Em*, 45(1), Jan. 1977; 5. 'Returns to research and development expenditures in the private sector', in *New Developments in Productivity Measurement*, eds J. Kendrick and R. Vaccar, *Stud. in Income and Wealth, 44* (NBER, 1980).

GRONAU, Reuben

Born   1937, Tel Aviv, Israel.
Current Post   Assoc. prof., Hebrew Univ., Jerusalem.
Recent Posts   Res. supervisor, Maurice Falk Inst. Econ. Res. Israel, 1968–71, 1972–4; Post-doctoral Fellow, Univ. Chicago, 1971–2; Res. assoc., NBER, 1972–; Vis. prof., UCLA, 1972, MIT, 1980–1; Vis. assoc. prof., Stanford Univ., 1975–6.
Degrees   BA, MA, Hebrew Univ., Jerusalem, 1960, 1963; PhD Columbia Univ., 1967.
Principal Contributions   The analysis of the economic activity in the home sector: the analysis and estimation of the value people assign to their time, the analysis of the factors determining the allocation of time in the home sector, and the evaluation of the output of this sector. This analysis led to improved estimates of the factors determining wives' labour force participation and their earnings, allowing for selectivity biases.
Publications   *Books:* 1. *The Value of Time in Passenger Transportations* (Columbia Univ. Press, 1970); 2. *The Supply of Labor and Wages of Israeli Married Women* (Maurice Falk Inst. Econ. Res., 1979) (in Hebrew).
Articles: 1. 'The effect of children on the housewife's value of time', *JPE*, 81(2), Pt 2, March/April 1973); 2. 'The intrafamily allocation of time: the value of housewives' time', *AER*, 65(4), Sept. 1973; 3. 'Wage comparisons – a selectivity bias', *JPE*, 82(6), Nov./Dec. 1974; 4. 'Leisure, home production and work – the theory of the allocation of time revisited', *JPE*, 85(6), Dec. 1977; 5. 'Home production – a forgotten industry', *REStat*, 62(3), Aug. 1980.

GROSSMAN, Gregory

Born   1921, Kiev, USSR.
Current Post   Prof. Econ., Univ. Cal., Berkeley, USA.
Degrees   BS (Commerce), MA (Econ.), Univ. Cal., Berkeley 1942, 1943; PhD (Econ.) Harvard Univ., 1953.
Offices   AEA; Guggenheim Memorial Foundation Fellow, 1964–5; Fellow, Center Advanced Study Behavioral Science, Stanford, Cal., 1969–70; Pres., Western Slavic Assoc., 1971–2; Pres., Assoc. Comparative Econ. Stud., 1972; Member, Academic Council, Kennan Inst. Advanced Russian Stud., 1975–; Pres., Amer. Assoc. Advancement Slavic Stud., 1980–1.
Principal Contributions   Institutional analysis of the Soviet economy and other command economies, of their evolution, and of their reforms. Lately, analysis of the second economy in communist countries.
Publications   *Books:* 1. *Soviet Statistics of Physical Output of Industrial Commodities* (Princeton Univ. Press, 1960); 2. *Value and Plan*, ed. (Univ. Cal. Press, 1960); 3. *Economic Systems* (Prentice-Hall, 1967, 1974).
Articles: 1. 'The structure and organization of the Soviet economy', *Slavic Review*, 21(2), June 1962; 2. 'Notes for a theory of the command economy', *Soviet Stud.*, 15(2), Oct. 1963, repr. in *Comparative Economics Systems: Models and Cases*, ed. M. Bornstein (Richard D. Irwin, 1965); 3. 'Price control, incentives, and innovation in the Soviet economy', in *The Socialist Price Mechanism*, ed. A. Abouchar (Duke Univ. Press, 1977); 4. 'The "second economy" of the USSR', *Problems Communism*, 26(5), Sept./Oct. 1977.

GROSSMAN, Henryk*

Dates and Birthplace   1881–1950, Cracow, Austro-Hungary.
Posts Held   Prof. Polit. Science, Free Polish Univ., Warsaw, 1922–5; Inst. Social Res., Univ. Frankfurt, 1925–30; Prof., Univ. Frankfurt, 1930–3, Univ. Leipzig, 1949–50.
Career   Marxist scholar whose writ-

ings include one of the many attempts to work out the Marxian theory of business cycles. His theory of capitalist breakdown roused a storm of controversy among Marxist theorists in the inter-war period.

Publications *Books:* 1. *Simonde de Sismondi et ses théories économiques* (1924); 2. *Das Akkumulations- und Zusammenbruchsgesetz des Kapitalistischen Systems* (1929).

Articles: 1. 'The evolutionist revolt against classical economics', *JPE*, 51, Oct., Dec. 1943.

Secondary Literature P.M. Sweezy, *The Theory of Capitalist Development,* (OUP, 1942), ch. 11.

GROSSMAN, Herschel I.

Born 1939, Philadelphia, Penn., USA.

Current Post Merton P. Stolz prof. Social Sciences, Prof. Econ., Brown Univ., Providence, USA.

Degrees BA (Highest hons), Univ. Virginia, 1960; BPhil. Univ. Oxford, 1962; PhD Johns Hopkins Univ., 1965.

Offices Simon Sr Res. Fellow, Univ. Manchester, 1971; Ed. Board, *J Mon E*, 1977–; Vis. Scholar, State Univ. New York, Buffalo, 1978; Vis. prof., Inst. Advanced Studies, Vienna, 1979; Simon Guggenheim Foundation Fellow, 1979–80; Res. assoc., NBER, 1979–; Board Eds., *AER*, 1980–; Vis. prof., European Univ. Inst., Florence, 1980.

Principal Contributions Construction of micro-economic foundations for macro-economic analysis, involving the study of non-market-clearing models, models of the sharing of risk between workers and employers, and, most recently, models that involve incomplete information and the postulate of 'rational expectations' in the attempt to discover a theory of fluctuations in aggregate output and employment that is consistent both with maximising behaviour and with empirical evidence.

Publications *Books:* 1. *Money, Employment, and Inflation* (with R.J. Barro), (CUP, 1976; Japanese transl. McGraw-Hill Kogakusha Ltd, Italian transl. Cedam, Chinese transl. Bank of Taiwan Classics in Econ., Spanish transl. Tesis Libreria Editorial).

Articles: 1. 'A general disequilibrium model of income and employment' (with R.J. Barro), *AER*, 61(1), March 1971; 2. 'Money, interest, and prices in market disequilibrium', *JPE*, 75(5), Sept./Oct. 1971; 3. 'Suppressed inflation and the supply multiplier' (with R.J. Barro), *REStud*, 41(1), Jan. 1974; 4. 'Risk shifting, layoffs, and seniority', *J Mon E*, 4(4), 1978; 5. 'Rational expectations, business cycles, and government behavior', in *Rational Expectations and Economic Policy*, ed. S. Fischer (Univ. Chicago Press, 1980).

GROVES, Theodore

Born 1941, Whitehall, Wisc., USA.

Current Post Prof. Econ., Univ. Cal., San Diego, La Jolla, USA, 1978–.

Recent Posts Ass. prof. Econ., Univ. Wisconsin, Madison, 1969–73; Assoc. prof. Managerial Econ., 1973–6, Prof. Managerial Econ., 1976–8, Northwestern Univ.; Vis. prof. Econ., Stanford Univ., 1977–8.

Degrees BA (Econ., *Cum laude*) Harvard Coll., 1964; MA (Theoretical Stats), PhD (Econ.), Univ. Cal., Berkeley, 1966, 1970.

Offices Member, AEA; Fellow, Em Soc, 1977.

Principal Contributions Discovery of the general class of mechanisms (Groves mechanisms) with the property that agents have an incentive to reveal truthfully their preferences among collective choices, thus enabling an optimal group choice to be made. Developed (with M. Loeb) a specific member of the class and solved the partial equilibrium 'free rider' problem with public inputs. Co-discovery (with J. Ledyard) of the first general equilibrium mechanism (the Groves-Ledyard mechanism) for solving the general 'free rider' problem with public goods. The mechanism provides consumers with sufficient incentives to reveal their true preferences for public goods at an equilibrium.

Publications *Books:* 1. *Adaptive Economic Models*, ed. (with R. Day), (Academic Press, 1975).

Articles: 1. 'Incentives in teams', *Em*,

41(4), July 1973; 2. 'Incentives and public inputs' (with M. Loeb), *JPE*, 4(3), Aug. 1975; 3. 'Optimal allocation of public goods: a solution to the "free rider problem" ' (with J. Ledyard), *Em*, 45(4), May 1977; 4. 'Efficient collective choice when compensation is possible', *REStud*, 46(2), April 1979; 5. 'The existence of efficient and incentive compatible equilibria with public goods', *Em*, 48(6), Sept. 1980.

GRUBEL, Herbert

Born 1934, Frankfurt-am-Main, Germany.
Current Post Prof. Econ., Simon Fraser Univ., Vancouver, Canada.
Recent Posts Ass. prof., Stanford Univ., 1962–3; Ass. prof., Univ. Chicago, 1963–6; Assoc. prof., Univ. Penn., 1966–70; Vis. Res. Fellow, ANU, 1969; Sr pol. analyst, US Treasury, 1970; Vis. Res. Fellow, Nuffield Coll., Univ. Oxford, 1974–5; Vis. prof., Univ. Nairobi, 1978–9.
Degrees BA (Bus. Admin., Econ.) Rutgers Univ., 1958; PhD (Econ) Yale Univ., 1962.
Offices Member, AEA.
Principal Contributions Study of foreign exchange markets; intra-industry trade; economics of the 'brain drain'; international diversification benefits; moral hazard and unemployment insurance; milk marketing boards; the international monetary system and disposal of seigniorage; theory of free trade and activity zones; and the theory of optimum exchange rate stability.
Publications *Books:* 1. *Forward Exchange* (Stanford Univ. Press, 1967); 2. *Brain Drain* (with A.D. Scott), (Wilfred Laurier Univ. Press, 1971); 3. *Intra-industry Trade* (with P.J. Lloyd), (Macmillan, 1975); 4. *International Monetary System* (Penguin, 1977); 5. *International Economics* (Irwin, 1981). *Articles:* 1. 'The international flow of human capital' (with A.D. Scott), *AER*, S, 56(2), May 1966; 2. 'Internationally diversified portfolios: welfare gains and capital flows', *AER*, 58, Dec. 1968; 3. 'The case for optimum exchange rate stability', *WA*, 109(3), 1973; 4. 'Taxation and the rates of return from some

US asset holdings abroad, 1960–1969', *JPE*, 82(3), May/June 1974; 5. 'Real and insurance-induced unemployment in Canada' (with D.R. Maki and S. Sax), *CJE*, 8(2), May 1975.

GRUBER, W.H.

N.e.

GUALEY, J.G.

N.e.

GUITTON, Henri

Born 1904, St-Etienne, Loire, France.
Current Post Prof. d'Analyse Econ. et de Statistique, Univ. Paris I, Panthéon-Sorbonne.
Degree Dr (*Hon. causa*) Univ. Liège, 1930.
Offices Member, l'Inst. de France; Pres., l'Académie des Sciences Morales et Politiques; Member, l'Académie Nationale dei Lincei, Rome; Ed., *REP*; Former member, Section de Conjonctur, Conseil Econ. et Social; Past-pres., Commission des Etudes Economiques du CNRS.
Principal Contributions A wide variety of topics of both micro- and macro-economics.
Publications *Books:* 1. *Essai sur la loi di King* (Sirey, 1938); 2. *Les Fluctuations économiques* (Sirey, 1951); 3. *L'Objet de l'économie politique* (Rivière, 1951); 4. *A la recherche du temps économique* (Fayard, 1970); 5. *De l'imperfection en économie* (Calmann Levy, 1979).

GUTOWSKI, Armin F.

Born 1930, Nürnberg, Germany.
Current Post Pres., HWWA – Inst. für Wirtschaftsforschung-Hamburg; Prof. Econ. (Internat. Econ. Pol.), Univ. Hamburg.
Recent Posts Prof. Econ. Development, Univ. Giessen, 1967–70; Chief econ. adviser, Kreditanstalt für Wiederaufbau, Frankfurt, 1969–78; Prof.

Econ. (Money and Internat. Fin.), Univ. Frankfurt, 1970–8.

Degrees Diploma Volkswirt (MA), Dr rer. pol., Venia legendi (Habilitation), Univ. Mainz. 1952, 1957, 1967.

Offices Rockefeller Post-doctoral Fellow, USA, 1960–1; Member, German Council Econ. Experts, 1970–8; Member, Board Advisers, German Fed. Econ. Ministry, 1970–; Member, Joint Comm. Staff Issues, World Bank and IMF, 1977–8; Member, Consultative Group, Internat. Econ. and Monetary Affairs (Group of Thirty), 1978–; Adviser, Govt People's Republic of China, 1979–; 'Bundesverdienstkreuz I Klasse', Fed. Republic Germany, 1979.

Principal Contributions Development of a theory of economic power. Contributions to the theory of flexible exchange rates and of various mixed international monetary systems. Contribution to the foundation of an operational quantitative monetary policy.

Publications *Books:* 1. *Konstruktions- und Entwicklungsaufträge. Ein Beitrag zur Beschaffungspolitik der öffentl. Hand* (Quelle & Meyer, 1960); 2. *Wirtschaftliche Weinbaupolitik. Ein Beispiel Angewandter Agrarwirtschaftslehre und Aussenhandelstheorie* (Quelle & Meyer, 1962); 3. *Konglomerate Unternehmensgrösse und Wirtschaftliche Macht, Vorträge und Aufsätze* (J.C.B. Mohr, Paul Siebeck, 1971).

Articles: 1. 'Theoretical approaches to a concept of supplier's power', *German Econ. Review*, 11(3), 1973; 2. 'Brauchen Wir Neue Instrumente der Kreditpolitik?', in *Währungsstabilität in Einer Integrierten Welt. Beitrage zur Geldtheorie und Geldpolitik* (Verlag Kohlhammer, 1974); 3. 'Chances for price-level stability in various international monetary systems', in *The Phenomenon of Worldwide Inflation*, eds D.I. Meiselman and A.B. Laffer (Washington, 1975); 4. 'How can the world afford OPEC oil?' (with K. Farmanfarmaian *et al.*), *Foreign Affairs*, 53(2), Jan. 1975; 5. 'Realer Wechselkurs, Wettbewerbsfähigkeit und Beschäftigung – Zur Schlüsselrolle der Geldpolitik', in *Theorie und Politik der Internationalen Wirtschaftsbeziehungen*, eds K. Borchard and F. Holzheu (Gustav Fischer Verlag, 1980).

H

HABAKKUK, Hrothgar John

Born 1915, Barry, S. Wales.

Current Post Principal, Jesus Coll., Univ. Oxford.

Recent Posts Prof. Econ. Hist., Univ. Oxford, 1950–67; Vice-chancellor, Univ. Oxford, 1973–7; Pres., Univ. Coll. Swansea, Wales, 1975–.

Degrees MA Univ. Oxford, 1937; MA Univ. Camb., 1938.

Offices Fellow, BA; Council member, RES, 1950–69; Pres., Royal Hist. Soc., 1976–80.

Principal Contributions A restatement of the hypothesis that fertility changes were a major factor in population growth 1750–1830; an exploration of the hypothesis that differences in technology between Britain and USA during nineteenth century were due to differences in factor proportions; in particular that abundance of natural resources in America (a higher land/labour ratio) stimulated substitution of capital for labour and that this substitution was favourable to invention of new methods of production, especially of more mechanised capital-intensive techniques; an attempt to argue that the long swings in investment in America and Britain before 1914 were not inversely related in a systematic way; and studies in English land ownership 1500–1800.

Publications *Books:* 1. *American and British technology in the Nineteenth Century: The Search for Labour-saving Inventions* (CUP, 1962); 2. *Industrial Organisation Since the Industrial Revolution* (Univ. Southampton, 1968); 3. *Population Growth and Economic Development since 1750* (Leicester Univ. Press, 1971).

Articles: 1. 'Free trade and commercial expansion 1853–1870', in *Cambridge History of the British Empire*, vol. 2 (CUP, 1940); 2. 'English population in the eighteenth century', *EHR*, 6(2), 1953; 3. 'Fluctuations in house-building in Britain and the United States in the nineteenth century', *JEH*, 22, June 1962; 4. 'The rise and fall of English landed families, 1600–1800', *Royal Hist. Soc. Transactions*, 29–31, 1979–81.

HABERLER, Gottfried

Born 1900, Vienna, Austria.
Current Post Res. Scholar, Amer. Enterprise Inst., Washington, DC, 1971–; Prof. Emeritus, Harvard Univ., USA.
Recent Posts Rockefeller Foundation Fellow, Univ. London, Harvard Univ., 1927–9; Lecturer, Prof. Econ. Stats, Univ. Vienna, 1928–36; Vis. lecturer, Harvard Univ., 1931–2; Expert, Fin. section, League Nations, Geneva, 1934–6; Prof. Econ., 1936–57, Galen L. Stone Prof. Internat. Trade, 1957–71, Harvard Univ.; Expert, Board Governors Fed. Reserve System, Washington, DC, 1943–4.
Degrees Dr rer. pol., Dr Law, Univ. Vienna, 1923, 1925; Hon. PhD Univs. St Gallen, Switzerland (1949), Saarland (1967), Innsbruck (1970), Econ. Univ., Vienna (1980).
Offices Member, AEA, RES; Pres., 1950–1, Hon. pres., 1953–, IEA; Pres., NBER, 1955; Pres., AEA, 1963; Consultant, US Dept Treasury, Washington, DC, 1965–78.
Principal Contributions Clarification of the concept of the 'price level' (value of money) and the methods of measuring its change by price index numbers. Reformulation of the basic theory of classical international trade, the theory of comparative cost, in terms of the modern general equilibrium theory. Derivation of the welfare implications of the reformulated theory of comparative cost which permits the precise formulation of advantages and disadvantages of free trade and protection. The theory of international transfers of reparations and capital. Clarification of the theory of purchasing power parity. Analysis of the advantages and disadvantages of the systems of fixed and fluctuating exchange rates. Synthesis of the major theories of the business cycle.

Theoretical analysis of causes and cures of inflation.
Publications *Books:* 1. *Der Sinn der Indexzahlen* (J.C.B. Mohr, Paul Siebeck, 1927); 2. *Der Internationale Handel* (Verlag Springer, 1933); 3. *The Theory of International Trade, With its Application to Commercial Policy* (William Hodge, Macmillan, 1936); 4. *Prosperity and Depression* (League of Nations, 1937, Harvard Univ. Press, 1958); 5. *Economic Growth and Stability* (Nash Publishing, 1974).
Articles: 1. 'The market for foreign exchange and the stability of the balance of payments', *Kyklos*, 3(3), 1949; 2. 'Some problems in the pure theory of international trade', *EJ*, 60, June 1950; 3. 'International trade and economic development', *Nat. Bank of Egypt, 50th Anniversary Commemoration Lectures*, (1959); 4. 'Integration and growth of the world economy in perspective', *AER*, 54, March 1964; 5. 'The world economy, money and the great depression 1919–1939' (Amer. Enterprise Inst., 1976).

HADLEY, Arthur Twining*

Dates and Birthplace 1856–1930, New Haven, Conn., USA.
Posts Held Prof., 1879, Dean, Graduate School, 1892–5, Pres., 1899–1921, Yale Univ.
Degree BA Yale Univ., 1876.
Offices Chairman, various govt comms and comtts; Pres., AEA, 1898–9.
Career University administrator whose *Economics* was a very effective introduction to the subject, but also an effective apologia for current economic institutions. He was led to seek justifications for his opposition to social change in ethical and political arguments. His major work on railroads (1885) stands at the forefront of the rich literature on railway rates in the nineteenth century.
Publications *Books:* 1. *Railroad Transportation: Its History and Laws* (1885); 2. *Economics* (1896); 3. *The Relation Between Freedom and Democracy in the Evolution of Democratic Government* (1903); 4. *Standards of*

Public Morality (1907); 5. *Economic Problems of Democracy* (1923).

Secondary Literature M. Lerner, 'Hadley, Arthur Twining', *ESS*, vol. 7; M. Cross and R.B. Ekelund Jr, 'A.T. Hadley on monopoly theory and railway regulation: an American contribution to economic analysis and policy', *HOPE*, 12(2), 1980.

HAGEN, Everett Einar

Born 1906, Holloway, Minn., USA.
Current Post Retired. Self-employed econ. consultant.
Recent Posts Prof. Econ., Univ. Illinois, 1948–51; Econ. adviser, Govt Burma, 1951–3; Prof. Econ., MIT, 1953–72; Dir., Center Internat. Stud., MIT, 1970–2.
Degrees BA St Olaf Coll., 1927; MA, PhD, Univ. Wisconsin, 1932, 1941; Hon. LLD Michigan State Univ., 1974.
Offices Member, AEA, RES, AAAS, Phi Beta Kappa; Guggenheim Memorial Foundation Fellow, 1963–4; Pres., Assoc. Comparative Econ., 1967; Sr Fellow, Center Cultural Exchange between East and West, Honolulu, Hawai, 1972–3.
Principal Contributions Presentation of a theory of social change which explains the initiation of technical progress in less developed countries. Clarification of the roles of technological disemployment and the speed of economic growth in the distribution of income during economic growth. Contributions to the theory of population and to tariff theory.
Publications *Books:* 1. *On the Theory of Social Change* (Dorsey Press, 1962); 2. *Planning Economic Development*, ed. and contributor (Richard D. Irwin, 1963); 3. *The Economics of Development* (Richard D. Irwin, 1968, 1980).
Articles: 1. 'Capital theory in a system with no agents fixed in quantity', *JPE*, 50, Dec. 1942; 2. 'An economic justification of protectionism', *QJE*, 72, Nov. 1958; 3. 'Population and economic growth', *AER*, 49(3), June 1959; 4. 'Analytical models in the study of social systems', *American J Sociology*, 67,

1961; 5. 'Why economic growth is slow', *WD*, 8(4), April 1980.

HAHN, Frank

Born 1925, Berlin, Germany.
Current Post Prof., Univ. Camb., England.
Recent Posts Reader, Math. Econ., Univ. Birmingham, 1957–60; Lecturer, Univ. Camb., 1960–7; Prof., LSE, 1967–72.
Degrees BSc. (Econ.), PhD, Univ. London, 1945, 1950; MA Univ. Camb., 1960; DSoc. Science (Hon.), Univ. Birmingham, 1981.
Offices Managing ed., *REStud*, 1963–7; Pres., Em Soc, 1968; Corresponding Fellow, AAAS, 1971; Fellow, BA, 1975.
Principal Contributions First macro-model of income distribution without abandoning rational choice. Money in general equilibrium: problem of existence and stability. First general equilibrium study of monetary problems in balance of payments. A number of theorems in *tâtonnement* stability. Non-*tâtonnement* processes and a general stability theorem (with Negishi). Transaction costs in general equilibrium. Heterogeneous capital goods and growth – a demonstration that myopically self-fulfilling paths can diverge from steady state. Non-Walrasian analysis, particularly conjectural equilibria. Stability of duopoly. Short period equilibria.
Publications *Books:* 1. *The Share of Wages in National Income* (Heinemann, 1969); 2. *General Competitive Analysis* (with K.J. Arrow), (Oliver & Boyd, 1971).
Articles: 1. 'The share of wages in national income', *OEP*, N.S. 3, June 1951; 2. 'Gross substitutes and the dynamic stability of general equilibrium', *Em*, 26, Jan. 1958; 3. 'The balance of payments in a monetary economy', *REStud*, 26, Feb. 1959; 4. 'A theorem on non-*tâtonnement* stability' (with T. Negishi), *Em*, 30, July 1962; 5. 'Equilibrium with transaction costs', *Em*, 39(3), May 1971.

HAITOVSKY, Y.

N.e.

HAKANSSON, Nils H.

Born 1937, Norway.
Current Post Prof., Univ. Cal.,
Berkeley, USA.
Recent Posts Ass. prof., UCLA,
1966–7, Yale Univ., 1967–9.
Degrees BS Univ. Oregon, 1958;
MBA, PhD, UCLA, 1960, 1966.
Principal Contributions Financial
economics, particularly optimal investment and consumption strategies; economics of information.
Publications *Articles:* 1. 'Optimal
investment and consumption strategies
under risk, an uncertain lifetime and
insurance', *Int ER*, 10(3), Oct. 1969; 2.
'Optimal investment and consumption
strategies under risk for a class of utility
functions', *Em*, 38(5), Sept. 1970; 3.
'Capital growth and mean variance
approach to portfolio selection', *J Fin
Quantitative Analysis*, 6(1), Jan. 1971;
4. 'Optimal myopic portfolio policies
with and without social-correlation of
yields', *J Bus*, 44(3), July 1971; 5.
'Multi-period mean-variance analysis:
toward a general theory of portfolio
selection', *J Fin Quantitative Analysis*,
26(4), Sept. 1971.

HALDI, John

Born 1931, Ann Arbor, Mich., USA.
Current Post Pres., Haldi Assoc.
Inc., New York City, USA.
Degrees BA Emory Univ. 1952; MA,
PhD Stanford Univ., 1953, 1957.
Offices AEA; RES.
Principal Contributions The role of
economies of scale in investment deci-
sions and economic development; appli-
cation of economic principles to
governmental budgeting; and evaluation
of public programmes.
Publications *Books:* 1. *Simulated
Economic Models – A Laboratory
Guide to Economic Principles of Mar-
ket Behavior* (with H. Wagner),
(Richard D. Irwin, 1963); 2. *The Med-
ical Malpractice Insurance Market*,

appendix to *Report of Secretary's Commission on Medical Malpractice* (US
Dept. Health, Education & Welfare,
1973); 3. *Postal Monopoly: An Assessment of the Private Express Statutes*
(Amer. Enterprise Inst. Public Pol. Res.,
1974); 4. *Financing the New Jersey
Unemployment Insurance Program* (US
Dept. Labor & Industry, 1975).
Articles: 1. 'Applications of program
budgeting to environmental problems',
in *Social Sciences and the Environment*
(Univ. Colorado Press, 1967); 2. 'Prom-
ises and pitfalls of PPB', in *Analysis
for Planning-Programming-Budgeting*
(Washington Operations Res. Council,
1968).

HALÉVY, Elie*

Dates and Birthplace 1870–1937,
Etretat, France.
Post Held Prof., l'Ecole Libre des
Sciences Polit.
Degree Agrégé de Phil. Sorbonne,
1900.
Career Historian of England whose
work is best known for its emphasis on
the role of Methodism as a reason why
England escaped the French Revolution.
His account of philosophical radicalism
is a major contribution to the history of
the utilitarian idea and his account of
Thomas Hodgskin rescues an important
early socialist writer from undeserved
obscurity.
Publications *Books:* 1. *La Théorie
platonicienne des sciences* (1896); 2.
*The Growth of Philosophical Radical-
ism*, 3 vols (1901–4, 1928, 1949); 3.
Thomas Hodgskin (1903, 1956); 4. *History of the English People in the Nineteenth Century*, 3 vols (1913–23), 5 vols,
(1926, 1961); 5. *Sismondi* (1933); 6.
Histoire du socialisme européen (1948).

HALL, Charles*

Dates and Birthplace c.
1740–c.1820, England.
Post Held Physician.
Degree Medical grad.(?), Univ.
Leyden.
Career Early critic of capitalism
whose estimate that the poor retained

only the product of one hour's work out of eight made a considerable impression on pre-Marxist socialist writers.

Publications *Books:* 1. *The Effects of Civilisation* (1805).

Secondary Literature M. Beer, 'Hall, Charles', *ESS*, vol. 7.

HALL, Robert Ernest

Born 1943, Palo Alto, Cal., USA.

Current Post Prof. Econ., Sr Fellow, Stanford Univ., USA.

Recent Post Prof. Econ., MIT, 1974–8.

Degrees BA Univ. Cal., Berkeley, 1964; PhD MIT, 1967.

Offices Fellow, 1973, Program Chairman, 1981. Em Soc; Dir., Res. Program Econ. Fluctuations, NBER, 1977–.

Principal Contributions Empirical investigations of labour supply, turnover, and unemployment; general equilibrium analysis of taxation, especially investment incentives; and testing of rational expectations implications for consumption.

Publications *Articles:* 1. 'Why is the unemployment rate so high at full employment?', *Brookings Papers Econ. Activity*, 3, 1970; 2. 'Wages, income, and hours of work in the US labor force', in *Income Maintenance and Labor Supply: Econometric Studies*, eds H. Watts and G. Cain (Rand McNally, 1973); 3. 'Stochastic implications of the life cycle-permanent income hypothesis: theory and evidence', *JPE*, 86(5), Dec. 1978; 4. 'Efficient wage bargains under uncertain supply and demand' (with D. Lilien), *AER*, 69(5), Dec. 1979; 5. 'Employment fluctuations and wage rigidity', *Brookings Papers Econ. Activity*, 1, 1980.

HALL, R.H.

N.e.

HAMADA, Robert S.

Born 1937, San Francisco, Cal., USA.

Current Post Prof. Fin., Dir., Center Res. Security Prices, Grad. School Bus, Univ. Chicago, USA.

Recent Posts Vis. assoc. prof. Fin., Univ. Washington, 1971–2; Baring Brothers Vis. prof. Fin., London Grad. School Bus. Stud., 1973, 1979–80; Leslie Wong Disting. Faculty Res. Fellow, Univ. British Columbia, 1976.

Degrees BA Yale Univ., 1959; MS, PhD, MIT, 1961, 1969.

Offices and Honours AFA, AEA; McKinzie Prize Outstanding Teaching, 1981.

Principal Contributions Theoretical and empirical research on the effects of the capital structure decision. Also, the effects of risk and taxes on the financing and capital budgeting decisions within the firm, on portfolio selection, and on the pricing of multi-period capital assets. Incidence and risk-taking effects of various taxes.

Publications *Articles:* 1. 'Portfolio analysis, market equilibrium and corporation finance', *J Fin*, 24(1), March 1969; 2. 'The effects of leverage and corporate taxes on the shareholders of regulated utilities', in *Rate of Return under Regulation: New Directions and Perspectives*, eds H.M. Trebing and R. Howard (Michigan State Univ. Press, 1969); 3. 'Investment decision with a general equilibrium mean-variance approach', *QJE*, 85(4), Nov. 1971; 4. 'The effect of the firm's capital structure on the systematic risk of common stocks', *J Fin*, 27(2), May 1972; 5. 'Financial theory and taxation in an inflationary world: some public policy issues', *J Fin*, 34(2), May 1979.

HAMBURGER, M.J.

N.e.

HAMERMESH, Daniel

Born 1943, Cambridge, Mass., USA.

Current Post Prof. Econ., Michigan State Univ., USA; Res. assoc., NBER.

Recent Posts Ass. prof., Princeton Univ., 1969–73; Dir. Res., Office US Secretary of Labor, 1974–5; Vis prof., Harvard Univ., 1981.

Degrees BA Univ. Chicago, 1965; PhD Yale Univ., 1969.

Offices and Honours AEA; IRRA; Phi Beta Kappa; Ed. Board, *QREB*.

Principal Contributions Detailed analysis of all aspects of the effects of unemployment insurance on the economy. Demonstration of the importance of understanding the details of social programmes in order to analyse their economic effects. The study of the demand for labour, with particular emphasis on demonstrating the usefulness of such study for the evaluation of labour-market policies. The most comprehensive and detailed estimates of skill substitution in the labour force.

Publications *Books:* 1. *Labor in the Public and Non-profit Sectors* (Princeton Univ. Press, 1975); 2. *Jobless Pay and the Economy* (Johns Hopkins Univ. Press, 1977).
Articles: 1. 'Wage bargains, threshold effects and the Phillips curve', *QJE*, 84(3), Aug. 1970; 2. 'An economic theory of suicide' (with N.M. Soss), *JPE*, 82(1), Jan./Feb. 1974; 3. 'Interdependence in the labour market', *Ec*, 42, Nov. 1975; 4. 'Econometric studies of labor-labor substitution and their implications for policy' (with J. Grant), *JHR*, 14(4), Fall 1979; 5. 'Labor-market competition among youths, white women and others', *REStat*, 63, 1981.

HANCOCK, William Neilson*

Dates and Birthplace 1820–88, Lisburn, Ireland.

Posts Held Lawyer; Prof., Trinity Coll., Dublin, 1846–51, Queen's Coll., Belfast, 1849–51.

Degrees BA, LLB, LLD Trinity Coll., Dublin, 1843, 1846, 1849.

Offices Secretary to various govt comms; Founder, pres., Stat. and Social Inquiry Soc. Ireland 1847, 1881–2.

Career Economist and reformer, whose Statistical and Social Inquiry Society was a means for both investigation and the propagation of reformist ideas. He regarded the problem of Irish agricultural distress as arising from restrictions on the free exchange of land imposed by existing laws. He also wrote on the Poor Laws and published statis-tical reports in connection with his work for government commissions.

Publications *Books:* 1. *Tenant-right of Ulster Considered Economically* (1845); 2. *On Laissez-faire and the Economic Resources of Ireland* (1848); 3. *Impediments to the Prosperity of Ireland* (1850).

Secondary Literature G. O'Brien, 'Hancock, William Neilson', *ESS*, vol. 7.

HANOCH, Giora

Born 1932, Haifa, Israel.

Current Post Prof. Econ., Hebrew Univ. Jerusalem, Israel.

Recent Posts Vis. lecturer, Harvard Univ., 1970, 1974; Vis. prof., UCLA, 1975; Consultant, Rand Corp., 1975–6; Chairman, Dept. Econ., Hebrew Univ., 1977–9; Sr res. assoc., Center Social Sciences, Columbia Univ., 1977–80, 1980–1.

Degrees BA, MA Hebrew Univ., 1960, 1961; PhD Univ. Chicago, 1965.

Offices and Honours Res. assoc., Maurice Falk Research Inst., Israel, 1959–61, 1966–72; Bareli award, Israel Labour Org., 1960; Univ. Fellow, Univ. Chicago, 1964; Consultant, Bank Israel Res. Dept, 1972–; Fellow, Em Soc, 1975–; Member, Israeli Commission Wages Public Sector, 1977–80.

Principal Contributions Topics in the fields of human resources, income distribution, production theory and duality, portfolio selection and uncertainty, panel data analysis, and theory and estimation of labour supply and retirement. Recently been engaged in a research project on labour market behaviour of older persons in the US, using panel data, and a multivariate model of participation, wages, hours and weeks of work, with emphasis on separating age, period and cohort effects.

Publications *Articles:* 1. 'An economic analysis of earnings and schooling', *JHR*, 2(3), Summer 1967; 2. 'Testing the assumptions of production theory: a non-parameter approach' (with M. Rothschild), *JPE*, 80(2), March/April 1972; 3. 'The labor supply curve under income maintenance programs' (with M. Honig), *J Pub E*, 9(1),

Feb. 1978; 4. 'Symmetric duality and polar production functions', in *Production Economics: A Dual. Approach to Theory and Applications*, eds M. Fuss and D. McFadden (N-H, 1978); 5. 'Hours and weeks in the theory of labor supply', in *Female Labor Supply*, ed. J.P. Smith (Princeton Univ. Press, 1980).

HANSEN, Alvin Harvey*

Dates and Birthplace 1887–1975, Viborg, S. Dakota, USA.

Posts Held Schoolteacher and headmaster, 1910–13; Instructor Econ., Univ. Wisconsin, 1915–16, Brown Univ., 1916–19, Univ. Minnesota, 1919–27; Prof. Polit. Econ., Harvard Univ., 1937–62.

Degrees BA Yankton Coll., 1910; MA, PhD Univ. Wisconsin, 1915, 1918.

Offices Vice-pres., ASA, 1937; Pres., AEA, 1938.

Career The chief propagator of Keynesian ideas in America, he was also very frequently called on as a government adviser. Advisory posts held included Director of Research for the 1933–4 Committee on Policy in International Economic Relations, membership of the Advisory Council on Social Security, 1941–3 and special economic adviser to the Federal Reserve Board, 1940–5. From an early preference for deflationary policies, he came to favour policies based on the stimulation of demand. It was in this context he worked out aspects of Keynes' ideas and presented them in more acceptable form for students' consumption. He also made a number of original contributions, for instance, to the theory of the multiplier.

Publications *Books:* 1. *Business-cycle Theory* (1927); 2. *Economic Stabilisation in an Unbalanced World* (1932); 3. *Fiscal Policy and Business Cycles* (1941); 4. *State and Local Finance in the National Economy* (with H.S. Perloff), (1944); 5. *Monetary Theory and Fiscal Policy* (1949); 6. *A Guide to Keynes* (1953); 7. *The Dollar and the International Monetary System* (1965).

Secondary Literature S.E. Harris, 'Hansen, Alvin', *IESS*, vol. 6; P.A. Sam-uelson, 'Alvin Hansen as a creative economic theorist', *QJE*, 90, Feb. 1976.

HANSEN, Bent

Born 1920, Ildved, Hvejsel, Denmark.

Current Post Prof., Chairman Dept., Univ. Cal. Berkeley, USA, 1967–.

Recent Posts Prof., Dir., Konjunkturinstitutet, Stockholm, 1955–64; Consultant, INP, Cairo, 1961–5; Consultant, OECD, Paris, 1965–7.

Degrees Cand. Polit Univ. Copenhagen, 1946; Fil. Lic., Fil. Dr Univ. Uppsala, Sweden, 1950, 1951.

Offices and Honours Fellow, Em Soc; Fellow, Amer. Middle East Stud. Assoc.; Univ. Copenhagen gold medal, 1945; Armbergska priset, vetenskapsakademim, Stockholm, 1955.

Principal Contributions Developed inflation theory in terms of excess demand analysis and the notion of quasi-equilibrium. An early example of disequilibrium theory. Developed fiscal theory in terms of target instrument analysis and suggested use of tax policy for wage control. Initiated studies of wage-drift as a function of excess demand for labour. Studied rural wages in Egypt and used results as evidence against the surplus labour hypothesis.

Publications *Books:* 1. *A Study in the Theory of Inflation* (A & U, 1951); 2. *The Economic Theory of Fiscal Policy* (Stockholm, 1955, A & U, 1958); 3. *Development and Economic Policy in the UAR (Egypt)* (with C. Marrouk), (N-H, 1965); 4. *A Survey of General Equilibrium Theory* (McGraw-Hill, 1971); 5. *Foreign Exchange Regimes and Economic Development* (with R. Nashashibi), (Columbia Univ. Press, 1975).

Articles: 1. 'On wage drift. A problem of money-wage dynamics' (with G. Rehn), in *25 Economic Essays, in Honour of Erik Lindahl* (Stockholm, 1956); 2. 'Employment and wages in rural Egypt', *AER*, 59(3), June 1969; 3. 'Excess demand, unemployment, vacancies, and wages', *QJE*, 84(1), Feb. 1970; 4. 'A theoretical analysis of smuggling' (with J.N. Bhagwati), *QJE*, 87(2), 1973; 5. 'The profitability of the Suez

Canal as a private enterprise' (with K. Tourk), *JEH*, 38(4), Dec. 1978.

HANSEN, W. Lee

Born 1928, Racine, Wisc., USA.
Current Post Prof. Econ. Educational Pol. Stud., Univ. Wisconsin, USA.
Recent Posts UCLA, 1958–65; Sr staff economist, US President's Council Econ. Advisers, 1964–5; Vis. prof., Univ. Minnesota, 1975.
Degrees BA, MA Univ. Wisconsin, 1950, 1955; PhD Johns Hopkins Univ., 1958.
Offices Res. Fellow, Brookings Inst., 1957–8; Postdoctoral Fellow Polit. Econ., Univ. Chicago, 1961–2; Guggenheim Memorial Foundation Fellow, 1969–70.
Principal Contributions Diverse research interests largely centred on the operation of labour markets, the economics of education, and to a lesser degree economics education. Work with B. Weisbrod on the income redistribution effects of financing higher education. Also worked on the labour markets for scientists and engineers. Currently working on the economics of higher education, namely, the determinants of retirement and changes in academic remuneration.
Publications *Books:* 1. *Benefits, Costs and Finance of Public Higher Education* (with B.A. Weisbrod), (Markham, 1969); 2. *Education, Income and Human Capital*, ed. (NBER, 1970); 3. *The Labor Market for Scientists and Engineers* (with G.C. Cain and R.B. Freeman), (Johns Hopkins Univ. Press, 1973); 4. *Basic Concepts in Economics: A Framework for Teaching Economics in the Nation's Schools* (with G.L. Bach *et al.*), (Joint Council Econ. Education, 1977); 5. *Resource Manual for Teacher-Training Programs in Economics* (with P. Saunders and A.L. Welsh), (Joint Council Econ. Education, 1978).
Articles: 1. 'New approaches to teaching the principles course', *AER*, 65(2), May 1975; 2. 'Earnings and individual variations in postschool human investment' (with C.B. Knapp), *JPE*, 84(2), April 1976; 3. 'Modelling the earnings and research productivity of academic economists' (with R.P. Strauss and B. Weisbrod), *JPE*, 86(4), Aug. 1978; 4. 'An era of continuing decline', *Academe: Bull. AAUP*, Sept. 1979; 5. 'Forecasting the market for new PhD economists' (with H.B. Newburger *et al.*), *AER*, 70(1), March 1980.

HARBERGER, Arnold Carl

Born 1924, Newark, NJ, USA.
Current Post Gustavus F. and Ann M. Swift disting. service prof., Univ. Chicago, USA.
Recent Posts Ass. prof. Polit. Econ., Johns Hopkins Univ., 1949–53; Assoc. prof., 1953–9, Prof. Econ., 1959–77, Univ. Chicago; Vis prof., MIT Center Internat. Studies, 1961–2, Harvard Univ., 1971–2, Princeton Univ., 1973–4.
Degrees MA, PhD Univ. Chicago, 1947, 1950; DHC Univ. Tucuman, 1979.
Offices Fellow, Em Soc, AAAS; US SSRC Faculty Res. Fellow, 1951–3, 1954–5; Simon Guggenheim Foundation Fellow, Univs. London, Camb., 1958; Member, Board Eds., *AER*, 1959–61, Exec. Comm. AEA, 1970–2; Member, Res. Advisory Comm., Office Scientific Personnel, NAS, 1961–5; Member, Res. Advisory Board, Comm Econ. Development, 1966–8; Ford Foundation Faculty Res. Fellow, 1968–9; Member, Board Eds., *JEL*, 1969–70.
Principal Contributions Analysis of currency devaluation using two-country macro-economic models. Long-term projections of macro-economic magnitudes and of raw materials demand. Measurement of the efficiency costs of distortions (monopoly, the corporation income tax, etc.) in a general-equilibrium setting. General equilibrium analysis of the incidence of the corporation income tax. Empirical study of the dynamics of inflation. Development of a coherent system of social project evaluation based on the traditional framework of applied welfare economics. Evaluation of methods of incorporating distributional considerations into the

social evaluation of projects and programmes.

Publications *Books:* 1. *The Demand for Durable Goods* (Univ. Chicago Press, 1960); 2. *Project Evaluation* (Macmillan, Univ. Chicago Press, 1972); 3. *Taxation and Welfare* (Little, Brown & Co., Univ. Chicago Press, 1974).

Articles: 1. 'Currency depreciation, income, and the balance of trade', *JPE*, 58, Feb. 1950; 2. 'Monopoly and resource allocation', *AER/S*, 44, May 1954; 3. 'The incidence of the corporation income tax', *JPE*, 70, June 1962; 4. 'The measurement of waste', *AER/S*, 54, May 1964; 5. 'On the use of distributional weights in social cost-benefit analysis', *JPE*, 86(2), Pt 2, April 1978.

HARCOURT, Geoffrey Colin

Born 1931, Melbourne, Australia.
Current Post Prof. Econ., Univ. Adelaide, Australia.
Recent Posts Lecturer Econ. Politics, Fellow and Dir. Stud. Econ., Trinity Hall, Univ. Camb., 1964–6; Vis. Fellow, Clare Hall, Univ. Camb., 1972–3; Vis. prof., Scarborough Coll., Univ. Toronto, 1977, 1980.
Degrees BCom. (Hons.), MCom. Univ. Melbourne, 1954, 1956; PhD Univ. Camb., 1960.
Offices Fellow, 1971, Exec. Comm., 1974–7, Academy Lecturer, 1978, Academy Social Sciences Australia; Pres., Econ. Soc. Australia and New Zealand, 1974–7; Wellington-Burnham Lecturer, Tufts Univ., 1975; Edward Shann Memorial Lecturer, Univ. Western Australia, 1975; Newcastle lecturer Polit. Econ., Univ. Newcastle, 1977.
Principal Contributions Tried to make clear in a fair and good-humoured way to students and colleagues alike the issues involved in the Cambridge controversies over capital theory. Also made contributions to post-Keynesian theory, especially to the theory of pricing and the investment decision, and to the theory of the distribution of income and the level of activity in the short run. Finally, by sketching the intellectual biographies of some leading economists, tried to make the subject more alive and humane.

Publications *Books:* 1. *Economic Activity* (with P.H. Karmel and R.H. Wallace), (CUP, 1967; Italian transl., 1969); 2. *Some Cambridge Controversies in the Theory of Capital* (CUP, 1972; Italian transl., 1973, Polish transl., 1975, Spanish transl., 1975, Japanese transl., 1980); 3. *Theoretical Controversy and Social Significance: An Evaluation of the Cambridge Controversies* (Univ. W. Australia Press, 1975); 4. *The Microeconomic Foundations of Macroeconomics* ed. (Macmillan, 1977); 5. *The Social Science Imperialists and Other Essays, Selected Essays of G.C. Harcourt*, ed. P. Kerr (Routledge & Kegan Paul, 1981).

Articles: 1. 'The accountant in a golden age', *OEP*, N.S. 17, March 1965, reprinted in *Readings in the Concept and Measurement of Income*, ed. (with R.H. Parker) (CUP, 1969); 2. 'A two-sector model of the distribution of income and the level of employment in the short run', *ER*, 41, March 1965; 3. 'Investment-decision criteria, investment incentives and the choice of technique', *EJ*, 78, March 1968; 4. 'Robinson, Joan', in *IESS, Biographical Supplement*, vol. 18; 5. 'Some Cambridge controversies in the theory of capital', *JEL*, 7(2), June 1969, reprinted in *Teori dello Sviluppo Economico*, eds G. Nardozzi and V. Valli, (Etas Kompass, 1971).

HARDY, Charles Oscar*

Dates and Birthplace 1884–1948, Island City, Missouri, USA.
Posts Held Prof., Univ. Ottawa, Kansas, 1910–18; Lecturer, Univ. Chicago, 1918–22; Prof., Univ. Iowa, 1922–4; Member, res. staff, Brookings Inst.
Degrees BA Univ. Ottawa, Kansas, 1904; PhD Univ. Chicago, 1916.
Offices Vice-pres., Fed. Reserve Bank, Kansas City.
Career Mathematician who brought a meticulous concern for accuracy to economic questions. His best-known contribution was on the question of gold, where he argued that there was too

much gold available, and that this permitted an undue volume of credit expansion. Whilst at Brookings he was a frequent adviser to government.

Publications *Books:* 1. *Risk and Risk Bearing* (1923); 2. *Credit Policies of the Federal Reserve System* (1932); 3. *Is There Enough Gold?* (1936); 4. *War-time Control of Prices* (1940).

HARRIS, John Rees

Born 1934, Rockford, Ill., USA.

Current Post Dir., African Stud. Center, Prof. Econ., Boston Univ., Mass., USA 1975–.

Recent Posts Instructor Econ., Northwestern Univ., 1964–6; Ass. prof. Econ., 1966–70, Assoc. prof. Econ. Urban Planning, 1970–4, MIT.

Degrees BA Wheaton Coll., Ill., 1955; MA (Econ.), PhD (Econ.), Northwestern Univ., 1964, 1967.

Offices African Stud. Assoc., 1964–; AEA, 1965–.

Principal Contributions Understanding rural-urban migration in developing countries in terms of expected incomes (the Harris-Todaro model). Recently, incorporated more understanding of the role of labour-market institutions and social networks (particularly extended families) in affecting the pace and selectivity of migration.

Publications *Articles:* 1. 'Migration, employment and development: a two-sector analysis' (with M. Todaro), *AER*, 60(2), March 1970; 2. 'Urban and industrial deconcentration in developing economies: an analytical framework', *Regional Urban Econ.*, 1, Aug. 1971; 3. 'Migration, employment and earnings' (with B. Aklilu), in *The Indonesian Economy*, ed. G.F. Papanek (Praeger, 1980); 4. 'Urban unemployment in developing countries: towards a more general search model' (with R. Sabot), in *Essays on Migration and the Labor Market in Developing Countries*, ed. R. Sabot (Westview Press, 1981).

HARRIS, Joseph*

Dates and Birthplace 1702–64, England.

Post Held Assay master, 1748.

Career Monetary writer who placed his theory of money firmly in a framework of economic principles, in contrast to the common practice of divorcing discussions of money from the analysis of prices. He advocated monometallism, and held views on foreign trade on which Adam Smith may have drawn.

Publications *Books:* 1. *Essay upon Money and Coins*, 2 pts (1757, 1758).

Secondary Literature A.E. Monroe, 'Harris, Joseph', *ESS*, vol. 7.

HARRIS, Seymour Edwin*

Dates and Birthplace 1897–1975, New York City, NY, USA.

Posts Held Instructor, lecturer, prof., Harvard Univ., 1922–64; Chairman, Econ. Dept, Univ. Cal., San Diego, USA, 1964–.

Degrees BA, Phd, Harvard Univ., 1920, 1926.

Offices Member of numerous official commissions and comms.; Ed., *REStat*, 1943.

Career Prolific author and editor of whom F.A. Lutz said that he 'couldn't hold his ink'. His chief concern was with the practical relevance of what he wrote or edited. During his tenure of office *REStat* increased its circulation greatly and published large numbers of papers of immediate relevance. Along with Hansen and Samuelson, he was one of the chief disseminators of Keynesian ideas in America. His publications included books on the economics of health care, education, social security, international monetary policy, central bank policy, monetary history and various other subjects.

Publications *Books:* 1. *The New Economics. Keynes' Influence on Theory and Public Policy*, ed. with introductions (1947); 2. *Keynes Economist and Policy Maker* (1955); 3. *Higher Education in the United States: The Economic Problem* (1960); 4. *Higher Education: Resources and Finance* (1962); 5. *Economics of the Kennedy Years* (1964).

HARRISON, Bennett

Born 1942, Jersey City, NJ, USA.
Current Post Assoc. prof. Econ. Urban Stud., MIT, USA.
Recent Posts Lecturer Econ., New School Social Res., 1967–8; Ass. prof. Econ., Univ. Maryland, 1968–72; Vis. prof., Urban Stud. Program, Univ. Pennsylvania, 1972.
Degrees BA (Hons. Polit. Science), Brandeis Univ., 1965; MA (Econ.), PhD (Econ.), Univ. Pennsylvania, 1966, 1970.
Offices and Honours William Polk Carey prize Econ., Univ. Pennsylvania, 1970; Union Radical Polit. Econ., 1970–.
Principal Contributions Among the first to conduct both theoretical and empirical research in four areas: inner city economic structure and development, public service employment, dual or segmented labour markets, and inter-regional and international capital restructuring (focusing on plant closures).
Publications *Books:* 1. *The Economic Development of Harlem* (Praeger, 1970); 2. *Education, Training, and the Urban Ghetto* (Johns Hopkins Univ. Press, 1972); 3. *The Political Economy of Public Service Employment* (D.C. Heath, 1972); 4. *Urban Economic Development* (Urban Inst., 1974); 5. *Capital and Communities: The De-Industrialization of America* (Basic Books, 1982).
Articles: 1. 'Education and underemployment in the urban ghetto', *AER*, 62(5), Dec. 1972; 2. 'The political economy of state job-creation business incentives', *J Amer. Inst. Planners*, Oct. 1978; 3. 'Welfare payments and the reproduction of low-wage workers and secondary jobs', *Review Radical Polit. Econ.*, 11(2), Summer 1979; 4. 'The theory of "dual" or segmented labour markets', *JEI*, 13(3), Sept. 1979; 5. 'The incidence and regulation of plant closings', *Pol. Stud. J*, Fall 1981.

HARROD, Roy Forbes*

Dates and Birthplace 1900–78, Norfolk, England.
Posts Held Lecturer, Fellow, Christ Church Coll., Univ. Oxford, 1922.
Degree BA Univ. Oxford.
Offices Co-ed., *EJ*.
Career Made major contributions to the conceptualisation of imperfect competition theory, international trade and business cycle theory. His model of economic growth, demonstrating the conditions under which growth is possible at a steadily sustained rate, is his major achievement. Because Evsey Domar produced a later but similar version of the same theory, it has come to be known as 'Harrod-Domar Growth Theory'. He was also the first biographer of Keynes and a major promoter of Keynesian economics. He was a frequent adviser to government and international organisations.
Publications *Books:* 1. *The Trade Cycle* (1936); 2. *Towards a Dynamic Economics* (1948); 3. *Life of John Maynard Keynes* (1951); 4. *Economic Essays* (1952); 5. *Foundations of Inductive Logic* (1956); 6. *Reforming the World's Money* (1965); 7. *Money* (1969); 8. *Economic Dynamics* (1973).
Secondary Literature I.C. Johnson, 'Harrod, Roy F.', *IESS*, vol. 18; H. Phelps-Brown, 'Sir Roy Harrod: A Biographical Memoir', *EJ*, 30, March 1980.

HARSANYI, J.C.

N.e.

HART, Albert Gailord

Born 1909, Oak Park, Ill., USA.
Current Post Prof. Emeritus Econ., Columbia Univ., USA.
Recent Posts Prof. Econ., 1946–78, Special lecturer, 1979, Columbia Univ.
Degrees BA Harvard Univ., 1930; PhD Univ. Chicago, 1936.
Offices Life Fellow, RES; Chairman, Dept. Econ., Columbia Univ., 1959–62, 1977–8; Vice-pres., AEA, 1962; Fulbright prof., Paris, 1962–3, Frankfurt, 1967; UN Technical Assistance Mission, Chile, 1962–3.
Principal Contributions 'Flexibility' as decision-response to uncertainty, dat-

ing from 1936; persuading Congress of merits of current taxation of income, 1941; abatement of 'linkage of risk' as motive for cash-balance demand and insurance (substance of 'factor-of-production' view of money), from 1946; and reformulation of national accounts to show, for example, Venezuelan private economy ex-petroleum.

Publications *Books:* 1. *Anticipations, Uncertainty and Dynamic Planning* (Univ. Chicago Press, 1940, 1951); 2. *Paying for Defense* (with E.D. Allen et al.), (Blakiston, 1942); 3. *Social Framework of the American Economy* (with J.R. Hicks), (OUP, 1945, 1953); 4. *Money, Debt and Economic Activity* (later edns with P.B. Kenen and A.D. Entine), (Prentice-Hall, 1948, 1953, 1961, 1969); 5. *An Integrated System of Tax Information* (Columbia Univ. Press, 1967).

Articles: 1. ' "Model-building" and fiscal policy', *AER*, 35, Sept. 1945; 2. 'Risk, uncertainty, and the unprofitability of compounding probabilities', in *Studies in Mathematical Economics and Econometrics*, eds O. Lange et al. (Univ. Chicago Press, 1942); 3. 'The case for an international commodity reserve currency' (with N. Kaldor and J. Tinbergen), in N. Kaldor, *Essays on Economic Policy*, vol. 2 (Duckworth, 1964); 4. 'Venezuelan national income: a reformulation' (Universidad Central de Venezuela, 1981); 5. 'Regaining control over an open-ended money supply', in *Stagflation Compendium*, US Congress, Joint Econ. Comm. (US Govt Printing Office, 1981).

HART, Peter E.

Born 1928, London, England.
Current Post Prof. Econ., Univ. Reading, 1967–.
Recent Posts Lecturer, Sr lecturer, Univ. Bristol, 1961–7.
Degree BSc (Econ), LSE, 1949.
Offices RSS; Em Soc; Ed. Board, *REStud*, 1963–73; Consultant, NIESR, 1965–80; Ed., *J Ind E*, 1975–; Council, RES, 1980; UK SSRC, Econ. Comm., 1980, Industry Panel, 1981.
Principal Contributions Compiled and explained time series of the factor

distribution of income in the UK 1870–1962 and of the rate of return on capital 1920–62. Analysed the comparative statics and dynamics of personal income distributions, including life cycles of income, and changes in business concentration in individual industries and in manufacturing as a whole. Other work includes spatial economics (regional and international differences in productivity, population densities and optimal aircraft flight paths) and statistical measurements of inequality (the reduction of general entropy measures to moments-of-moment distributions).

Publications *Books:* 1. *Studies in Profit, Business Saving and Investment in the United Kingdom 1920–62*, 2 vols (A & U, 1965, 1968); 2. *Mergers and Concentration in British Industry* (with M.A. Utton and G. Walshe), (CUP, 1973); 3. *Concentration in British Industry 1935–75* (with R. Clarke), (CUP, 1980).

Articles: 1. 'Population densities and optimal aircraft flight paths', *Regional Stud.*, 6, 1973; 2. 'Moment distributions in economics: an exposition', *JRSS*, Pt 3, 138, 1975; 3. 'The comparative statics and dynamics of income distributions,' *JRSS*, Pt 3, 139, 1976; 4. 'The dynamics of earnings, 1963–73', *EJ*, 86, Dec. 1976; 5. 'The statics and dynamics of income distributions: a survey', in *The Statics and Dynamics of Income*, eds N.A. Klevmarken and J.A. Lybeck (Tieto, 1981).

HARTZ, L.

N.e.

HAVEMAN, Robert H.

Born 1936, Grand Rapids, Mich., USA.
Current Post Prof. Econ., Univ. Wisconsin, USA, 1970–.
Recent Posts Prof. Econ., Grinnell Coll., Iowa, 1965–70; Fellow, Netherlands Inst. Advanced Study, 1975–6.
Degrees BA Calvin Coll., 1958; PhD Vanderbilt Univ., 1963.
Offices AEA.
Principal Contributions Applied wel-

fare economics (benefit-cost analysis), micro-data simulation modelling, regional modelling, measuring economic well-being, analysis of income distribution, poverty and its determinants, and analysis of social policy.

Principal Contributions *Books:* 1. *Unemployment, Idle Capacity and the Evaluation of Public Expenditures* (with J.V. Krutilla), (Johns Hopkins Univ. Press, 1968); 2. *The Economics of the Public Sector* (Wiley, 1970, 1976); 3. *The Economic Impacts of Tax-transfer Policy: Regional and Distributional Effects* (with F. Golladay), (Academic Press, 1977); 4. *Earnings Capacity, Poverty, and Inequality* (with I. Garfinkel), (Academic Press, 1978); 5. *Microeconomic Simulation Models for Public Policy Analysis*, ed. (with K. Hollenbeck), (Academic Press, 1980).

Articles: 1. 'Unemployment, excess capacity, and benefit-cost investment criteria' (with J.V. Krutilla), *REStat*, 49, Aug., Nov. 1967; 2. 'Common property, congestion, and environmental pollution', *QJE*, 87(2), May 1973; 3. 'Regional and distributional effects of a negative income tax' (with F. Golladay), *AER*, 66(4), Sept. 1976; 4. 'Congestion, quality deterioration, and heterogenous tastes' (with A.M. Freeman III), *J Pub E*, 8(2), Oct. 1977; 5. 'Earnings capacity and its utilization' (with I. Garfinkel), *QJE*, 42, Aug. 1978.

HAWLEY, Frederick Barnard*

Dates and Birthplace 1843–1929, USA.
Post Held Cotton broker.
Degrees Grad. Williams Coll.
Career Businessman whose economics concentrate on the significance of the entrepreneur. His methodology was the deductive one of the English classics but his material was confined to activities in which motivation was individualistic.
Publications *Books:* 1. *Capital and Population* (1882); 2. *Enterprise and the Productive Process* (1907).
Secondary Literature K.W. Bigelow, 'Hawley, Frederick Barnard', *ESS*, vol. 7.

HAWTREY, Ralph George*

Dates and Birthplace 1879–1971, England.
Posts Held Civil servant, UK Treasury, 1904–45; Price prof. Internat. Econ., Royal Inst. Internat. Affairs, 1947–52.
Degree BA (Maths.) Univ. Camb.
Offices and Honours Fellow, BA; Pres., RES, 1946–8; Knighted, 1956.
Career One of the British economists responsible for the rethinking of monetary theory after 1919, he also pioneered the 'income' approach in Britain. The value of his contribution was in clarifying the operation of the banking system and the role of money in the twentieth-century economy. His views on topics, such as the futility of public works as a method of avoiding slumps, underwent considerable modification as circumstances changed, but the fundamental ideas on the role of the Bank Rate and the influence of the credit system remained consistent.
Publications *Books:* 1. *Good and Bad Trade* (1913, 1962); 2. *Currency and Credit* (1919, 1950); 3. *The Art of Central Banking* (1932, 1962); 4. *Capital and Employment* (1937, 1952); 5. *Economic Destiny* (1944).
Secondary Literature C.W. Guillebaud, 'Hawtrey, R.G.', *IESS*, vol. 6; E.G. Davis, 'R.G. Hawtrey', *Pioneers of Modern Economics in Britain*, eds D.P. O'Brien and J.R. Presley (Macmillan, 1981).

HAYEK, Friedrich A. Von

Born 1899, Vienna, Austria.
Current Post Prof. Emeritus Univs. Chicago and Freiburg im Breisgau, W. Germany.
Degrees Dr jur., Dr rer. pol., Univ. Vienna, 1921, 1923; DSc (Econ.) Univ. London, 1940.
Offices and Honours FBA, 1945; Nobel Prize for Econ. 1974.
Principal Contributions Exploration of the guiding function of prices in determining the accumulation of capital, industrial fluctuations, and the productivity of the economy generally, making a free competitive order the

essential condition for the sustenance of the present numbers of mankind.

Publications *Books:* 1. *Prices and Production* (Routledge & Kegan Paul, 1931, 1935); 2. *The Pure Theory of Capital* (Macmillan, Routledge & Kegan Paul, Univ. Chicago Press, 1941); 3. *The Road to Serfdom* (Routledge & Kegan Paul, Univ. Chicago Press, 1944); 4. *The Constitution of Liberty* (Routledge & Kegan Paul, Univ. Chicago Press, 1960); 5. *Law, Legislation and Liberty*, 3 vols (Routledge & Kegan Paul, Univ. Chicago Press, 1973, 1976, 1979).

Articles: 1. *Profits, Interest and Investment* (Routledge & Kegan Paul, 1939); 2. *Individualism and Economic Order* (Routledge & Kegan Paul, Univ. Chicago Press, 1949); 3. *Studies in Philosophy, Politics and Economics* (Routledge & Kegan Paul, Univ. Chicago Press, 1967); 4. *New Studies in Philosophy, Politics, Economics and the History of Ideas* (Routledge & Kegan Paul, Univ. Chicago Press, 1978).

Secondary Literature F. Machlup, 'Freidrich von Hayek's contributions to economics', *Swed JE*, 76(4), Dec. 1974; N.P. Barry, *Hayek's Economic and Social Philosophy* (Macmillan, 1979).

HAZELL, P.B.R.

N.e.

HEAD, J.G.

N.e.

HEAL, Geoffrey Martin

Born 1944, Bangor, Wales.
Current Post Prof. Econ., Univ. Essex, England.
Recent Posts Prof. Econ., Univ. Sussex, 1973–80; Vis. prof., Yale Univ., 1975, Stanford Univ., 1976; Wesley Mitchell Vis. prof., Columbia Univ., 1979.
Degrees BA, PhD (Econ.), Univ. Camb., 1966, 1969.
Offices Pres.-elect, Assoc. Environmental Resource Economists; Fellow, Em Soc; Assoc. ed., *Em, Econ. Letters,*

Energy Resources; Managing ed., *REStud*, 1969–74.
Principal Contributions To assist in the development of a theoretical basis for the study of alternative economic systems; to contribute to bringing the study of economics with increasing returns to scale in production within the scope of formal resource allocation theory; and to help in the development of theoretical and empirical frameworks for the analysis of economic issues relating to extractive resources.

Publications *Books:* 1. *The Theory of Economic Planning* (N-H, 1973; Spanish, Italian transls.); 2. *Linear Algebra and Linear Economics* (with J. Hughes and R. Tarling), (Macmillan, Elsevier, 1977); 3. *Economic Theory and Exhaustible Resources* (with P. Dasgupta), (Nisbet, CUP, 1979); 4. *Public Policy and the Tax System*, ed. (with J. Hughes), (A & U, 1980).

Articles: 1. 'Planning, prices and increasing returns', *REStud*, 38(3), July 1971; 2. 'Optimal depletion of exhaustible resources' (with P.S. Dasgupta), *REStud*, Symposium 1974; 3. 'Equity efficiency and increasing returns', *REStud*, 46(4), Oct. 1979; 4. 'Metal price movements and interest rates', *REStud*, 47(1), Jan. 1980; 5. 'Marginal cost pricing, two part tariffs and increasing returns in a general equilibrium framework', *J Pub E*, 13, Feb. 1980.

HEARN, William Edward*

Dates and Birthplace 1826–88, Co. Cavan, Ireland.
Posts Held Prof. Greek, Queen's Coll., Univ. Galway, 1849–54; Prof., Dean, Chancellor, Univ. Melbourne, 1854–86.
Degrees BA Trinity Coll., Dublin.
Offices Member, Australian Legislative Council, 1878–88.
Career Hearn's *Plutology* ... is one of those major contributions to economics which have sometimes come from Australia. It is notable for its emphasis on the demand side, its biological analogies, and its capable treatment of capital and production. Hearn had read unusually widely and incorporated the ideas of Longfield and Rae.

Publications *Books:* 1. *Plutology: The Theory of the Efforts to Satisfy Human Wants* (1863).

Secondary Literature J.A. La Nauze, 'Hearn and economic optimism', in *Political Economy in Australia* (1949).

HEATON, Herbert*

Dates and Birthplace 1890–1972, Silsden, Yorks., England.
Posts Held Lecturer, Univs. Birmingham (1912–14), Tasmania (1914–17), Adelaide (1917–25); Prof. Econ., Queen's Univ., Canada, 1925–7; Prof. Econ. Hist., Univ. Minnesota, 1927–.
Degrees MA, DLitt. Univ. Leeds; MCom. Univ. Birmingham.
Offices Pres., EHA, 1948–50.
Career British economic historian, specialising in the seventeenth and eighteenth centuries and in the colonial history of Australia and Canada. His masterly review of Heckscher's great book on mercantilism displays his powers to best advantage.
Publications *Books:* 1. *The Yorkshire Woollen and Worsted Industries* (1920); 2. *Modern Economic History with Special Reference to Australia* (1920); 3. *History of Trade and Commerce with Special Reference to Canada* (1928); 4. *The British Way to Recovery* (1934); 5. *Economic History of Europe* (1936).
Articles: 1. 'Heckscher on mercantilism: review', *JPE*, 45, June 1937.

HECKMAN, James Joseph

Born 1944, Chicago, Ill., USA.
Current Post Prof. Econ., Univ. Chicago, 1974–.
Recent Posts Ass. prof., 1970–3, Assoc. prof., 1973–4, Columbia Univ.
Degrees BA Colorado Coll., 1965; MA, PhD Princeton Univ., 1968, 1971.
Offices Member, AEA, ASA; Assoc. ed., *J Em*; Hescherman Fellow, 1972–3; US SSRC Fellow, 1978–9; Guggenheim Memorial Foundation Fellow, 1979–80; Fellow, Em Soc., 1980.
Principal Contributions Sample selection bias and the economics and econometrics of self-selected samples; the econometrics of panel data; the econometrics of dummy endogenous variables in simultaneous equation systems; the economics of the life cycle (especially work on estimating life-cycle labour supply and the effect of unobservables such as human capital on labour supply); the evaluation of government programmes (especially anti-discrimination programmes); and the economics of heterogeneous individuals.
Publications *Books:* 1. *The Analysis of Longitudinal Labour Market Data*, co-ed. (Academic Press, 1981).
Articles: 1. 'Shadow prices, market wages and labour supply', *Em*, 42(4), July 1974; 2. 'Sample selection bias as a specification error', *Em*, 44(1), Jan. 1976; 3. 'A life-cycle model of earnings, learning and consumption', *JPE*, 84(4), Pt 2, Aug. 1976; 4. 'Dummy endogenous variables in a simultaneous equation system', *Em*, 46(4), July 1978; 5. 'Statistical models for discrete panel data', in *Structural Analysis of Discrete Data*, eds C. Manski and D. McFadden (MIT Press, 1981).

HECKSCHER, Eli Filip*

Dates and Birthplace 1879–1952, Sweden.
Posts Held Prof. Econ. Stats, Stockholm Bus. School, 1909–29; Prof., Stockholm Inst. Econ. Hist., 1929.
Career His work on economic history was that of an economist and statistician. His only real contribution to economic theory was an argument in favour of free trade, which, elaborated as it was by Ohlin, has become known as the 'Heckscher-Ohlin theorem'. However, his prodigious output of articles and pamphlets led him into many historical fields. His work on Swedish population movements and his masterly treatment of mercantilism are perhaps his best-known achievements.
Publications *Books:* 1. *The Continental System: An Economic Interpretation* (1922); 2. *Mercentilism*, 2 vols (1931, 1955); 3. *An Economic History of Sweden* (1954).

Secondary Literature G. Ohlin, 'Heckscher, Eli', *IESS*, vol. 6.

HEILBRONER, Robert L.

Born 1919, New York City, NY, USA.
Current Post Norman Thomas Prof. Econ., New School Social Res., New York City.
Degrees BA Harvard Univ., 1940; PhD New School Social Res., 1963; LLD Lasalle Univ., 1968, Ripon Coll., 1977, Long Island Univ., 1980.
Offices AEA, Exec. Comm., 1976–7.
Principal Contributions Investigations into the nature of contemporary capitalist systems, with special emphasis on historical and social elements. Also the history of economic thought, particularly Adam Smith and classical political economy.
Publications *Books:* 1. *The Worldly Philosophers* (Simon & Schuster, 1952, 1980); 2. *The Future as History* (Harper & Bros., 1960); 3. *An Inquiry into the Human Prospect* (Norton, 1975, 1980); 4. *Marxism: For and Against* (Norton, 1980).
Articles: 1. 'Adam Smith', *Encyclopedia Britannica*, 15th edn (Helen Hemingway Beaton, 1974); 2. 'The paradox of progress: decline and decay in the *Wealth of Nations*', in *Essays on Adam Smith*, eds A.F. Skinner and T.A. Wilson (OUP, 1975); 3.'Modern economics as a chapter in the history of economic thought', *HOPE*, 11(2), Summer 1979; 4. 'Was Schumpeter right?', *Social Res.*, 85(3), Summer 1981.

HELLEINER, Gerald K.

Born 1936, St Pölten, Austria.
Current Post Prof., Univ. Toronto, Canada.
Recent Posts Dir., Econ. Res. Bureau, Univ. Dar es Salaam, 1966–8; Vis. Fellow, Inst. Development Studies, Univ. Sussex, 1971–2; Vis. Fellow, Queen Elizabeth House, Univ. Oxford, 1979.
Degrees BA Univ. Toronto, 1958; PhD Yale Univ., 1962.
Offices Fellow, Royal Soc. Canada; Vice-chairman, North-South Inst., Simon Guggenheim Foundation Fellow, 1971–2; Res. Fellow, Internat. Development Res. Centre, 1975–6; Member, Ed. Boards, *JDE, WD, Internat. Organization*.
Principal Contributions In two general areas: economic development problems in tropical Africa, with particular emphasis upon agricultural marketing and international trade; international aspects of economic development, particularly the impact of various Northern policies in the trade and financial spheres upon the developing countries.
Publications *Books:* 1. *Peasant Agriculture, Government and Economic Growth in Nigeria* (Richard D. Irwin, 1966); 2. *International Trade and Economic Development* (Penguin Books, 1972); 3. *A World Divided, The Less Developed Countries in the International Economy*, ed., (CUP, 1976, 1979); 4. *International Economic Disorder, Essays in North-South Relations* (Macmillan, Univ. Toronto, 1981); 5. *Intra-firm Trade and the Developing Countries* (Macmillan, St Martins, 1981).

HELLER, Heinz Robert

Born 1940, Cologne, Germany.
Current Post Vice-pres., Internat. Econ., Bank of Amer., San Francisco, USA.
Recent Posts Econ. Dept., UCLA, 1965–71; Econ. Dept., Univ. Hawaii, 1971–4; Chief, Fin. Stud. Div., IMF, 1974–8.
Degrees MA Univ. Minnesota, 1962; PhD Univ. Cal., Berkeley, 1965.
Offices AEA; RES; Exec. Council, WEA, 1979–82.
Principal Contributions Attempted to follow a three-step sequence of first building a solid theoretical foundation, then embodying it with empirical content, and finally drawing relevant policy conclusions for business or government. Focused on optimal international reserve holdings for central banks; the relationship between international reserves, money, and global inflation; the international monetary system; the role of the IMF; determinants of

exchange rate practices; country risk analysis; the debt paying capacity of developing countries; the demand for money; and the world money supply.

Publications *Books:* 1. *International Trade: Theory and Empirical Evidence* (Prentice-Hall, 1968, 1973; Japanese transl., 1970, Spanish transl., 1970, Taiwan edn, 1974, German transl., 1975); 2. *The Economic System* (Macmillan, 1972; Portuguese transl., 1977); 3. *International Monetary Economics* (Prentice-Hall, 1974, Taiwan edn, 1978, Spanish transl., 1978, Japanese transl., 1980); 4. *Japanese Investment in the United States* (with E. Heller), (Praeger, 1974); 5. *The Monetary Approach to the Balance of Payments*, ed.(IMF, 1977).

Articles: 1. 'Optimal international reserves', *EJ*, 76, June 1966; 2. 'International reserves and worldwide inflation', *IMF Staff Papers*, March 1976; 3. 'The world money supply: concept and measurement' (with W.H.L. Day), *WA*, 113(4), 1977; 4. 'Determinants of exchange rate practices', *JMCB*, 10(3), Aug. 1978; 5. 'The demand for money and the term structure of interest rates' (with M.S. Khan), *JPE*, 87(1), Feb. 1979.

HELLER, Walter W.

Born 1915, Buffalo, NY, USA.

Current Post Regents' Prof. Econ., Univ. Minnesota, USA.

Recent Posts Fiscal economist, consultant, US Treasury, 1942–53; Member, Econ. Faculty, Univ. Minnesota, 1946–; Chief Internal Fin., US Military Govt, Fed. Republic Germany, 1947–8; Member, ECA Mission German Fiscal Problems, 1951; Chairman, US President's Council Econ. Advisers, 1961–4; Consultant, Exec. Office US President, 1965–9, 1974–7; Consultant, US Congressional Budget Office, 1975–.

Degrees BA, Hon. LLD Oberlin Coll. 1935, 1964; MA, PhD (Econ.) Hon. LLD, Univ. Wisconsin 1938, 1941, 1969; Hon. DLitt. Kenyon, 1965; LLD Ripon, 1967, Long Island Univ., 1968; LHD Coe, 1967, Loyola Univ., 1970, Roosevelt Univ., 1976.

Offices and Honours Phi Beta Kappa, Beta Gamma Sigma; Dir. 1960–, Chairman, 1971–4, NBER; Fellow, AAAS, 1963–; Vice-pres., 1967–8, Pres.-elect, 1973, Pres., 1974, AEA; US Treasury Disting. service award, 1968; Fellow, Amer. Philosophical Soc., 1975–; Disting. Fellow, AEA, 1975.

Principal Contributions Translation of economic analysis and research into public policy and wider dissemination of economic ideas and findings to informed policy makers in business, finance, and government.

Publications *Books:* 1. *State Income Tax Administration* (with C. Penniman), (Public Admin. Service, 1959); 2. *New Dimensions of Political Economy* (Harvard Univ. Press, 1966); 3. *Monetary vs. Fiscal Policy, a Dialogue with Milton Friedman* (Norton, 1969); 4. *Economic Growth and Environmental Quality: Collision or Co-existence?* (General Learning Press, 1973); 5. *The Economy: Old Myths and New Realities* (Norton, 1976).

Articles: 1. 'CED's stabilizing budget policy after ten years', *AER*, 47(4), Sept. 1957; 2. 'Economics and the applied theory of government expenditures', prepared for Subcomm. Fiscal Pol., Congressional Joint Econ. Comm. compendium, *Federal Expenditure Policy for Economic Growth and Stability* (US Govt Printing Office, 1957); 3. 'Economics of the race problem', *Social Res.*, 74(4), Winter 1970; 4. 'What's right with economics?', *AER*, 63(1), March 1975; 5. 'Economic policy for inflation', in *Reflections of America* (US Bureau Census, 1981), reprinted in *Challenge*, Jan./Feb. 1981.

HELMSTÄDTER, Ernst

Born 1924, Mannheim, Germany.

Current Post Prof. Econ., Univ. Münster.

Recent Posts Prof. Econ., Univ. Bonn, 1965–9; Dean, Faculty Econ. and Social Sciences, Univ. Münster, 1974–5; Expert consultant, Deutsche Forschungsgemeinschaft, 1976–.

Degrees Dr rer. pol., Univ. Heidelberg, 1956; Habilitation, Univ. Bonn, 1965.

Offices Board member, List Soc.,

1975–; Board member, Verein für Sozialpolitik, 1978–.

Principal Contributions Input-output analysis: triangulation; theory of technical progress; and theory of income distribution.

Publications *Books:* 1. *Der Kapitalkoeffizient. Eine kapitaltheoretische Untersuchung* (G. Fischer Verlag, 1969); 2. *Wirtschaftstheorie I* (Verlag F. Vahlen, 1974, 1980); 3. *Wirtschaftstheorie II* (Verlag F. Vahlen, 1976, 1981).

Articles: 1. 'Produktionsstruktur und Wachstum', *JNS*, 169, 1957–8; 2. 'Linearität und Zirkularität des volkswirtschaftlichen Kreislaufs', *WA*, 94(1), 1965; 3. 'Investitionsquote und Wachstumsrate bei Harrod-neutralem Fortschritt', *JNS*, 178, 1965; 4. 'Wachstumstheorie I: Uberblick', *Handwörterbuch der Wirtschaftswissenschaft*, vol. 18 (Gustav Fischer, 1979).

HENDERSON, Hubert Douglas*

Dates and Birthplace 1890–1952, Beckenham, England.

Posts Held Statistician, UK Board of Trade, 1914–18; Lecturer Econ., Univ. Camb., 1918–23; Ed., *Nation*, 1923–30; Secretary UK Econ. Advisory Council, 1930–4; Res. Fellow, All Souls Coll., 1934–52, Drummond Prof., 1945–52, Univ. Oxford.

Degrees BA Univ. Camb., 1912.

Offices Member, UK Commissions on the West Indies, Unemployment, Insurance, Population; Knighted, 1942; Pres., Section F, BAAS, 1948–9; Pres., RES, 1950–2.

Career Deeply involved in public affairs through his membership of various official commissions and committees; his economic writings were invariably directed towards contemporary practical questions. His early experience on Keynes' liberal weekly, the *Nation*, involved him in political issues, though he later rejected much of Keynes' *General Theory*. Though in many ways an old-fashioned orthodox economist, his teaching at Oxford was successful in an era during which Keynes' ideas and other more recent developments were dominant.

Publications *Books:* 1. *Supply and Demand* (1922); 2. *The Agricultural Dilemma* (1935); 3. *The Inter-war Years* (1955).

Secondary Literature D.H. Robertson, 'Obituary: Sir Hubert Henderson 1890–1952', *EJ*, 63, Dec. 1953.

HENDERSON, J.M.

N.e.

HERMANN, Friedrich Benedict Wilhelm von*

Dates and Birthplace 1795–1868, Dinkelsbühl, Germany.

Posts Held Prof. Kameralwissenschaften, Univ. Munich, 1827; Dir., Bavarian Stat. Bureau, 1839.

Offices Member, Frankfurt parliament, 1848.

Career Author of one of the few non-Smithian economic works of the period in Germany. He began with consideration of supply and demand, and went on to consider the factors influencing it. His thought is unusually uncluttered by methodological preoccupations and his analysis was both able and influential.

Publications *Books:* 1. *Staatswirthschaftliche Untersuchungen* (1832).

Secondary Literature M. Palyi, 'Hermann, F.B.W. von', *ESS*, vol. 7.

HERTZ, D.B.

N.e.

HESSE, Helmut

Born 1934, Gadderbaum, W. Germany.

Current Post Prof. Econ., Dir., Ibero-Amer. Inst. Econ. Res., Univ. Göttingen.

Degree Dr. rer. pol. Univ. Münster, 1958.

Offices Pres., Verein für Sozialpolitik (German Econ. Assoc.), 1979–; Chairman, Council Econ. Advisers to Fed. Ministry Econ., Fed. Republic Germany, 1980–; Member, German Assoc. Club Rome.

Principal Contributions International division of labour and international trade; structural changes in world trade; the economic development of the Third World and its integration into the world economy; and industrial redeployment. Contributions to the theory of cost-benefit analyses with applications to development and traffic projects.

Publications *Books:* 1. *Der Aussenhandel in der Entwicklung Unterentwickelter Länder Unter Besonderer Berücksichtigung Lateinamerika* (J.C.B. Mohr, Paul Siebeck, 1961); 2. *Strukturwandlungen im Welthandel 1950–1960/61* (J.C.B. Mohr, Paul Siebeck, 1967); 3. *Gesamtwirtschaftliche Produktionstheorie, Teil I und Teil II* (with R. Linde), (Physica-Verlag, 1976); 4. *RIO: Reshaping the International Order. A Report to the Club of Rome* (with J. Tinbergen *et al.*), (E.P. Dutton, 1976); 5. *Einführung in die Entwicklungstheorie und Politik, Teil I: Entwicklungstheorie* (with H. Sautter), (J.C.B. Mohr, Paul Siebeck, Werner Verlag, 1977).

Articles: 1. 'Die Bedeutung der reinen Theorie des internationalen Handels für die Erklärung des Aussenhandels in der Nachkriegszeit', *ZGS*, 122(2), April 1966; 2. 'Importsubstitution und Entwicklungspolitik', *ZGS*, 124(4), Oct. 1968; 3. 'Hypotheses for the explanation of trade between industrial countries 1953–1970', in *The International Division of Labour: Problems and Perspectives*, ed. H. Giersch (J.C.B. Mohr, Paul Siebeck, 1974); 4. 'Zum Konzept einer Handelsanpassungspolitik', in *Probleme der Wettbewerbstheorie und -Politik*, eds G.Bombach *et al.* (Tübingen, 1976); 5. 'Industrial redeployment: opportunity, threat, or illusion?' in *The Role of Europe in the New International Economic Order* (Edns de l'Univ. Bruxelles, 1979).

HEWINS, William Albert Samuel*

Dates and Birthplace 1865–1931, Wolverhampton, England.

Posts Held Univ. extension lecturer, 1887–95; Dir., LSE 1895–1903; Secretary, UK Tariff Commission, 1903–17.

Degrees BA, Univ. Oxford, 1887.

Offices MP for Hereford, 1912–18; Under-secretary of State Colonies, 1917–19.

Career Apart from his successful first directorship of the LSE, the chief reason he is remembered is for his advocacy of trade protection. He maintained this thoroughly unfashionable line in lectures, articles and through his association with Joseph Chamberlain's Tariff Commission.

Publications *Books:* 1. *English Trade and Finance in the 17th Century* (1892); 2. *Imperialism and its Probable Effects on the Commercial Policy of the UK* (1901); 3. *Trade in the Balance* (1924); 4. *Empire Restored* (1927); 5. *Apologia of an Imperialist* (1929).

HICKMAN, Bert George

Born 1924, Los Angeles, Cal., USA.

Current Post Prof. Econ., Stanford Univ., USA, 1966–.

Recent Posts Sr Staff, Brookings Inst., 1956–66; Vis. prof., Univ. Cal., Berkeley, 1960–1; NSF Sr Fellow, Netherlands School Econ., 1964–5; Vis. prof., London Bus. Schl, 1972–3, Kyoto Univ., 1977.

Degrees BS, PhD Univ. Cal., Berkeley 1947, 1951.

Offices Member, AEA; Member, Fellow, 1977, Em Soc; Chairman, Com. Econ. Stability and Growth, US SSRC, 1962–; Member, 1962–6, Chairman, 1968–71, Census Advisory Comm., AEA; Chair, Exec. Comm. Project LINK, 1969–; Chair, CEME Seminar Global Modelling, 1975–.

Principal Contributions Early contributions (1957–63) were to the quantitative-historical analyses of business cycles, long swings in growth, and the relationship between cyclical diffusion and the acceleration principle. Turned next to econometric analyses of investment behaviour and systems of factor demand and production functions (1964–70). Then pursued two parallel and continuing interests: the Hickman-Coen annual growth model of the US (an econometric model combining neo-classical growth theory and Keynesian effective demand theory); and international transmission of economic fluctuations, as a founding member of Project LINK and through specific studies of matrix models of world trade and international income and price multipliers.

Publications *Books:* 1. *Growth and Stability of the Postware Economy* (Brookings Inst., 1960); 2. *Investment Demand and US Economic Growth* (Brookings Inst., 1965); 3. *Quantitative Planning of Economic Policy*, ed. (Brookings Inst., 1965); 4. *Econometric Models of Cyclical Behavior*, ed. (Columbia Univ. Press, 1972); 5. *An Annual Growth Model of the US Economy* (with R.M. Coen), (N-H, 1976).

Articles: 1. 'Diffusion, acceleration, and business cycles', *AER*, 49, Sept. 1959; 2. 'The postware retardation: another long swing in the rate of growth?', *AER/S*, 53, May 1963; 3. 'Constrained joint estimation of factor demand and production functions' (with R.M. Coen), *REStat*, 52(3), Aug. 1970; 4. 'Elasticities of substitution and export demands in a world trade model' (with L.J. Lau), *Europ ER*, 4(4), Dec. 1973; 5. 'The interdependence of national economies and the synchronization of economic fluctuations: evidence from the LINK Project' (with S. Schleicher), *WA*, 114, 1978.

HICKS, John

Born 1904, Warwick, England.

Current Post Prof. Emeritus, Univ. Oxford (retired 1965).

Offices and Honours Fellow, BA, 1943; Knighted, 1966; Nobel Prize for Econ., 1972.

Principal Contributions Many branches of economics, in chronological order: wages, money, general equilibrium, welfare economics, social accounting, cycles, internation trade, consumer theory, growth theory, methodology, and capital theory (three vols at different dates). Used mathematical methods but also interest in historical application of economic concepts.

Publications *Books:* 1. *Theory of Wages* (Macmillan, 1932); 2. *Value and*

Capital (OUP, 1939); 3. *A Contribution to the Theory of the Trade Cycle* (OUP, 1950); 4. *Capital and Growth* (OUP, 1965); 5. *The Crisis in Keynesian Economics* (Blackwell, 1975).

Secondary Literature G.C. Reid and J.N. Wolfe 'Hicks, John R.', *IESS* vol 18; W.J. Baumol 'John R. Hicks' contribution to economics', *Swed JE* 74, Dec. 1972; B. Morgan 'Sir John Hicks' contributions to economic theory', *Twelve Contemporary Economists*, eds J.R. Shackleton and G. Locksley (Macmillan, 1981).

HIGGINS, Benjamin Howard

Born 1912, London, Ontario, Canada.

Current Post Dir., Centre Applied Stud. Development, Univ. South Pacific, UN Centre Regional Development; Consultant, Nagoya, Japan.

Recent Posts Vis. Fellow, Centre Res. Fed. Fin. Relations, Development Stud. Centre, ANU, Canberra; Development Economist, CIDA/Lower Uva Project, Sri Lanka, 1980–1.

Degrees BA Univ. Western Ontario, 1933; MSc. LSE, 1935; MPA Harvard Univ., 1939; PhD Univ. Minnesota, 1941; MA (Hon.) Univ. Melbourne, 1948.

Offices Fellow, Royal Soc. Canada; Member, Ed. Board, *Growth and Change*; Chairman Exec. Comm., AEA Econ. Development Inst., Boulder, Colorado, 1965–7; Chairman, Advisory Comm., UNCRD, 1979–.

Principal Contributions Combined academic research and advisory services to governments. Taught at McGill, Melbourne, Texas, MIT, Montreal, Ottawa, California-Berkeley, Yale, Monash, Murdoch and ANU. Served as adviser to the governments of Australia, Canada, the US and some two dozen countries in Asia, Africa and Latin America. Began career in micro-economics and methodology, moved to macro-economics, and recent years have concentrated on economic development and urban and regional development and planning.

Publications *Books:* 1. *What Do Economists Know?* (Melbourne Univ. Press); 2. *Indonesia's Economic Stabi-*

lisation and Development (Inst. Pacific Relations, 1957); 3. *Social Aspects of Economic Development of Latin America* (with J.M. Echavarria), (UNESCO, 1959); 4. *Economic Development: Principles, Problems, Policies* (Norton, 1959, 1968); 5. *Economic Development of a Small Planet* (with J.D. Higgins), (Norton, 1979).

Articles: 1. 'Interactions of cycles and trends', *EJ*, 65, Dec. 1955; 2. 'Economic development and cultural change: seamless web or patchwork quilt?', in *Essays on Economic Development and Cultural Change in Honour of Bert Hoselitz*, ed. M. Nash (Univ. Chicago Press, 1977); 3. 'The disenthronement of basic needs? Twenty questions', in *Regional Development Dialogue*, 1(1), Spring 1980; 4. 'Growth and stagnation in a world of shifting trade-off curves: homage to Alvin Hansen', in *Développement, croissance, progrès, Economies et sociétés*, Série F, special issue (Dunod, 1981); 5. 'Multilevel planning: a new liberal philosophy', in *Humanizing Development. Essays on People, Space and Development in Honour of Masahiko Honjo*, ed. R.P. Misra (Maruzen, 1981).

HIGGS, Henry*

Dates and Birthplace 1864–1940, Cornwall, England.

Posts Held Civil servant, 1881–1921, including private secretary to Prime Minister Campbell-Bannerman.

Degree LLB Univ. London, 1890.

Offices Founder member, Secretary, RES, 1890, 1892–1905.

Career His long and devoted service to RES in various offices make him an important figure in the history of the British economics profession. His research on Cantillon and French economics was a result of Foxwell's lectures at University Coll., London, which also first aroused his interest in economics. His publications on financial matters gained from his intimate acquaintance with their management at the highest levels, but it is not for his writings but for his more general services to economics that he is remembered.

Publications *Books:* 1. *The Physiocrats* (1897); 2. *The Financial System of the United Kingdom* (1914); 3. *Financial Reform* (1926).

Secondary Literature C.E. Collet and J.M. Keynes, 'Henry Higgs' (obituary), *EJ*, 50, Dec. 1940.

HILDEBRAND, Bruno*

Dates and Birthplace 1812–78, Naumburg, Germany.

Posts Held Prof. Hist., Univ. Breslau, 1839–41; Prof. Govt, Univs. Marburg, Zürich, Bern, Jena.

Degree PhD Univ. Breslau, 1836.

Offices Deputy in the Frankfurt Nat. Assembly, 1848; Founder, *JNS*, 1863.

Career Originally an historian and political radical, he turned increasingly to economic and then statistical questions. His economics was analytically unremarkable but his teaching, particularly his Jena seminar, inspired many economists of the Historical School. His achievements in the statistical field include the founding of the Thuringian Statistical Office in 1864.

Publications *Books:* 1. *Die Nationalökonomie der Gegenwart und Zukunft* (1848, 1922); 2. *Statische Mitteilungen über die Volkswirtschaftlichen Zustände Kurhessens* (1853); 3. *Statistik Thüringens*, 2 vols, (1866–78).

Secondary Literature H. Kisch, 'Hildebrand, Bruno', *IESS*, vol 6.

HILDENBRAND, Werner

Born 1936, Göttingen, Germany.

Current Post Prof. Econ., Rheinische Friedrich-Wilhelms-Univ. Bonn, W. Germany.

Degrees Dr rer. nat., Diploma (Maths.), Habilitation, Univ. Heidelberg, 1964, 1968, 1968.

Offices Fellow, Em Soc, 1971; Member, Rheinisch-Westfälische Akademie Wissenschaften, 1981.

Principal Contributions General equilibrium theory, in particular the analysis of the core of a large economy.

Publications *Books:* 1. *Equilibria and Core of Large Economies* (Princeton Univ. Press, 1974); 2. *Lineare*

Ökonomische Modelle (with K. Hildenbrand), (Springer-Verlag, 1975); 3. *Introduction to Equilibrium Analysis* (with A. Kirman), (N-H, 1976).

Articles: 1. 'Existence of equilibria for economics with production and a measure space of consumers', *Em*, 38(5), Sept. 1970; 2. 'On economies with many agents', *JET*, 2(2), June 1970; 3. 'Limit theorems on the core of an economy', in *Frontiers of Quantitative Economics*, vol 3A, ed. M.D. Intriligator, (N-H, 1977); 4. 'On the uniqueness of mean demand for dispersed families of preferences', *Em*, 48(5), Aug. 1980; 5. 'Short-run production functions based on micro-data', *Em*, 49(5), Sept. 1981.

HILFERDING, Rudolf*

Dates and Birthplace 1877–1941, Vienna, Astro-Hungary.
Posts Held Practised as doctor, 1901–6, 1915–19; Lecturer and ed., German Social Democratic Party.
Degree Dr medicine, Vienna, 1901.
Offices German Minister Fin., 1923, 1928–9; Member, Reichstag, 1924–33.
Career A Marxist and leader of the German Social Democratic Party. His *Finanzkapital* is a classic of Marxist economics; Bukharin and Lenin were both influenced by his analysis of imperialism. The book concentrates on capitalist production in the twentieth century with particular attention to questions of money. He was kidnapped by the Nazis from unoccupied territory in Vichy France and died in unexplained circumstances.
Publications *Books:* 1. *Böhm-Bawerk's Criticism of Marx* (1904, 1949); 2. *Finance Capital* (1910, 1981).
Articles: 1. 'Das Historische Problem', *Zeitschrift für Politik*, 1, 1954.
Secondary Literature T. Bottomore, 'Introduction' to R. Hilferding, *Finance Capital* (Routledge & Kegan Paul, 1981).

HINES, Albert G.

Born 1935, Milk River, Clarendon, Jamaica.
Current Post Prof. Econ., Birkbeck Coll., Univ. London.

Recent Posts Ass. lecturer, Univ. Bristol, 1962–4; Lecturer, Univ. Coll., London, 1964–8; Prof., Univ. Durham, 1968–71; Vis. prof., MIT, 1971–2.
Degree BSc. (Econ.) LSE, 1961.
Offices Chairman, Commission Econ. Stabilisation, Jamaica, 1975–6; Council member, RES, 1977–.
Principal Contributions Empirical and theoretical analyses of the part trade unions play in the process of inflation seen as the outcome of their role in the labour process, in the distribution of income and in the determination of output and employment; in particular, there is the demonstration that trade unions influence wages independently of the demand for labour. Interpretation and development of the reappraisal of Keynesian economics, including the theory of interest rates and the theory of unemployment.
Publications *Books:* 1. *On the Reappraisal of Keynesian Economics* (Martin Robertson, 1971).
Articles: 1. 'Trade unions and wage inflation in the United Kingdom: 1893–1961', *REStud*, 31, Oct. 1964; 2. 'Unemployment and the rate of change of money wage rates in the United Kingdom 1862–1963: a reappraisal', *REStat*, 50, Feb. 1968; 3. 'Investment in UK manufacturing industry 1956–67' (with G. Catephores), in *The Econometric Study of the United Kingdom*, eds K. Hilton and D. Heathfield (Macmillan, 1970); 4. 'The determinants of the rate of change of money wage rates and the effectiveness of incomes policy', in *The Current Inflation*, eds H.G. Johnson and R. Nobay (Macmillan, 1971); 5. 'Involuntary unemployment', in *Unemployment in Western Countries*, eds E. Malinvaud and J. Fitoussi (Macmillan, 1980).

HINSHAW, Randall

Born 1915, La Grange, Ill., USA.
Current Post Prof. Econ., Claremont Grad. School, 1960–, (Chairman Dept., 1967–9, 1977–9).
Recent Posts Economist, Bureau Foreign Domestic Commerce, US Dept. Commerce, 1942; Teaching Fellow Econ., Harvard Univ., 1942–3; Econo-

mist, Div. Internat. Fin., Fed. Reserve Board, 1943–6, 1947–52; Ass. prof. Econ., Amherst Coll., 1946–7; Special adviser, internat. monetary problems, US Mission to Nato and Europ. Regional Orgs., Paris, 1952–7; Deputy US Representative, Europ. Payments Union, Paris, 1952–3; Adviser, US Delegation UN meetings East-West payments problems, Geneva, 1955–7; Vis. prof. Econ., Yale Univ., 1957–8; Oberlin Coll., 1958–9, Univ. S. Cal., 1963–4, Johns Hopkins Univ., Bologna Center, 1965–8, 1971, UCLA, 1968.

Degrees BA, MA, Occidental Coll., 1937, 1938; PhD Princeton Univ., 1944.

Offices Member, Phi Beta Kappa, AEA, WEA, Em Soc, Council Foreign Relations.

Principal Contributions The first to make an estimate of the average price elasticity of the US demand for (merchandise) imports; low figure of −0.5, published in 1945, led to a considerable body of literature on 'elasticity pessimism'.

Publications *Books:* 1. *International Trade and Finance: Essays in Honour of Jan Tinbergen*, ed. (with W. Sellekaerts), (Macmillan, 1973); 2. *Key Issues in International Monetary Reform*, ed. (Marcel Dekker, 1975); 3. *Inflation Trade and Taxes: Essays in Honor of Alice Bourneuf*, ed. (with D.A. Belsley *et al.*), (Ohio State Univ. Press, 1976); 4. *Stagflation: An International Problem*, ed. (Marcel Dekker, 1977); 5. *Domestic Goals and Financial Interdependence: The Frankfurt Dialogue*, ed. (Marcel Dekker, 1980).

Articles: 1. 'American prosperity and the British balance-of-payments problem', *REStat*, 27, Feb. 1945; 2. 'Currency appreciation as an anti-inflationary device', *QJE*, 65, Nov. 1951, 66, Feb. 1952; 3. 'Statement by Randall Hinshaw', in *The United States Balance of Payments: Statements by Economists, Bankers, and Others*, US Congress, Joint Econ. Comm. (US Govt Printing Office, 1963); 4. 'European integration and American trade policy', *Atlantic Community Quarterly*, Spring 1965; 5. 'Non-traded goods and the balance of payments: further reflections', *JEL*, 13(2), June 1975.

HIRSCH, Werner Zvi

Born 1920, Linz, Germany.
Current Post Prof. Econ., UCLA, USA.
Recent Posts Univ. Cal., Berkeley, 1949–51; UN, 1951–2; Brookings Inst., 1952–3; Washington Univ., 1953–63.
Degrees BS (Highest hons.), PhD, Univ. Cal., Berkeley, 1947, 1949.
Offices and Honours Phi Beta Kappa, 1947; Sigma Xi, 1955; Vice-pres., MEA, 1960–1; Citation Cal. Senate, 1970; Pres., Town Hall West, 1978–9; Pres., WRSA.

Principal Contributions Application of micro-economic theory and econometric methods to progress functions, questions of scale economies, regional economics, urban public sector markets and urban housing. Also, the development of methods for the analysis of laws and legal institutions.

Publications *Books:* 1. *Introduction to Modern Statistics* (Macmillan, 1957); 2. *The Economics of State and Local Government* (McGraw-Hill, 1970); 3. *Urban Economic Analysis* (McGraw-Hill, 1973); 4. *Law and Economics: An Introductory Analysis* (Academic Press, 1979); 5. *Social Experimentation and Economic Policy* (with R. Ferber), (CUP, 1981).

Articles: 1. 'Manufacturing progress functions', *REStat*, 34, May 1952; 2. 'Expenditure implications of metropolitan growth and consolidation', *REStat*, 41, Aug. 1959; 3. 'Interindustry relations of a metropolitan area', *REStat*, 41, Nov. 1959; 4. 'Social experimentation and economic policy: a survey (with R. Ferber), *JEL*, 16(4), Dec. 1978; 5. 'Habitability laws and the welfare of indigent tenants', *REStat*, 63, 1981.

HIRSHLEIFER, Jack

Born 1925, New York City, NY, USA.
Current Post Prof. Econ., UCLA, USA, 1962–.
Recent Posts Assoc. prof., Univ. Chicago, 1958–60; Assoc. prof., UCLA, 1960–2.
Degrees BA, MA, PhD, Harvard Univ., 1945, 1948, 1950.

Offices Fellow, AAAS, 1975; Vice-pres., AEA, 1979.

Principal Contributions Theory of optimal investment decisions. Theory of equilibrium in speculative markets. Biological analogies in economics.

Publications *Books:* 1. *Water Supply: Economics, Technology and Policy* (with J.C. DeHaven and J.W. Milliman), (Univ. Chicago Press, 1960, 1969); 2. *Investment, Interest, and Capital* (Prentice-Hall, 1970); 3. *Price Theory and Applications* (Prentice-Hall, 1976, 1980).

Articles: 1. 'On the economics of transfer pricing', *J Bus*, 29, July 1956; 2. 'On the theory of optimal investment decision', *JPE*, 66, Aug. 1958; 3. 'The private and social value of information and the reward to inventive activity', *AER*, 61(4), Sept. 1971; 4. 'Speculation and equilibrium: information, risk and markets', *QJE*, 89(4), Nov. 1975; 5. 'Economics from a biological viewpoint', *J Law E*, 20(1), April 1977.

HOBSON, John Atkinson*

Dates and Birthplace 1858–1940, Derby, England.

Posts Held Schoolmaster, 1880–7; Univ. extension lecturer, 1887–97; Journalist and professional writer.

Degree MA Univ. Oxford.

Career Hobson was essentially a humanistic critic of current economics, rejecting exclusively materialistic definitions of value. With A.F. Mummery he developed the theory of oversaving which was given generous tribute by Keynes. His second major contribution was his analysis of capitalism on which Lenin freely drew. Critics have drawn attention to the technical inadequacies of his arguments, but his influence was significant in at least the two examples cited.

Publications *Books:* 1. *The physiology of industry* (with A.F. Mummery), (1889, 1956); 2. *The Evolution of Modern Capitalism* (1894, 1949); 3. *Imperialism: A Study* (1902, 1948); 4. *The Industrial System* (1909, 1910); 5. *Work and Wealth* (1914, 1933); 6. *Confessions of an Economic Heretic* (1938).

Secondary Literature H.N. Brailsford, *The Life-work of J.A. Hobson* (OUP, 1948); R. Lekachman, 'Hobson, John A.', *IESS*, vol 6.

HOCH, Irving

Born 1926, Chicago, Ill., USA.

Current Post Fellow, Sr Fellow, Resources for the Future, Washington, DC, 1967–.

Recent Posts Economist, Chicago Area Transport Study, Chicago, 1956–9; Ass. prof., Assoc. prof., Agric. Econ., Univ. Cal., Berkeley, 1959–67.

Degrees PhB Liberal Arts (Hons.), 1945, MA (Econ.), PhD (Econ.), Univ. Chicago, 1951, 1957.

Offices and Honours Member, AEA, AAEA, RSA, ASA; Member, Ed. Board, *JUE*; Sr Lecturer, Fulbright-Hays Program, New Autonomous Univ., Madrid, Spain, 1970; Member, NATO Review Panel Council Internat. Exchange of Scholars, 1975–; Moore Lecture Environmental Science, Univ. Virginia, 1975; Scholar in Residence, Agric. Econ., Penn. State Univ., 1978.

Principal Contributions Pioneer applications of analysis of co-variance in estimating production functions. Examined simultaneous equation bias in Cobb-Douglas functions, showing tendency to constant returns to scale. Early developer of regional input-output model, variant with household sector endogenous. Developed formulae for optimal spacing of highways. Early study of economics of wilderness areas. Reviewed state of urban economics as field became established. Developed empirical evidence on quality of life as function of scale of settlement (population size and density); related wage rates to scale and climate. Developed compendium of energy statistics and related population shifts to changes in energy prices.

Publications *Books:* 1. *Forecasting Economic Activity for the Chicago Region: Final Report* (Chicago Area Transportation Study, 1959); 2. *Production Functions and Supply Applications for California Dairy Farms*, Monograph 36, Giannini Foundation (Univ. Cal., 1976); 3. *Energy Use in the*

United States by State and Region: A Statistical Compendium of 1972 Consumption, Prices and Expenditures (Resources for the Future, 1978, 1979).

Articles: 1. 'Simultaneous equation bias in the context of the Cobb-Douglas production function', *Em*, 26(4), Oct. 1958; 2. 'Estimation of production function parameters combining time series and cross-section data', *Em*, 30(1), Jan. 1962; 3. 'The three-dimensional city: contained urban space', in *The Quality of the Urban Environment*, ed. H.S. Perloff (Johns Hopkins Univ. Press, 1969); 4. 'City size effects, trends and policies', *Science*, 193 (4256), Sept. 1976; 5. 'Role of energy in the regional distribution of economic activity', in *Alternatives to Confrontation: A National Policy Toward Regional Change*, ed. V.L. Arnold (D.C. Heath & Co, 1980).

HOCHMAN, Harold M.

Born   1936, New Haven, Conn., USA.

Current Post   Prof. Econ. Public Admin., Baruch Coll. and Grad. Center, City Univ. NY, 1975–, Dir. Center Study Bus. Govt, Baruch Coll., 1981–.

Recent Posts   Dir. Stud. Urban Public Fin., Sr res. assoc., Urban Inst., Washington, DC, 1969–75; Vis. lecturer, Grad. School Public Pol., Univ. Cal., Berkeley 1973–4; Lady Davis Vis. prof. Econ., Hebrew Univ. Jerusalem, 1980–1.

Degrees   BA, MA, PhD, Yale Univ., 1957, 1959, 1965.

Offices   Member, AEA, Public Choice Soc.; Phi Beta Kappa, 1957; Gerard Swope Fellow, General Electric Foundation, 1960–1.

Principal Contributions   Principal contributions in public sector and urban economics. A series of papers (many co-authored with J.D. Rodgers) traced out the relationship between utility interdependence and the logic of redistribution, indicating the conditions under which transfers are required to achieve a Pareto optimum (in contrast to the then-prevailing view that redistribution must be justified by an external value judgement). Subsequent papers examined the empirical underpinnings of redistribution through public choice, examining charitable contributions and voter attitudes toward welfare spending, and developed the concept of transitional equity, which is central to the problem of sustaining fairness in rule change.

Publications   *Books:* 1. *Readings in Microeconomics*, ed. (with W. Breit), (Holt, Rinehart & Winston, 1968, 1971); 2. *Redistribution Through Public Choice*, ed. (with G.E. Peterson), (Colombia Univ. Press, 1974); 3. *The Urban Economy*, ed. (Norton, 1976).

Articles: 1. 'Some aggregative implications of depreciation acceleration', *YEE*, 6(1), Spring 1966; 2. 'Pareto optimal redistribution' (with J.D. Rodgers), *AER*, 59(4), Sept. 1969; 3. 'Rule change and transitional equity', in *Redistribution through Public Choice*, eds H.M. Hochman and G.E. Peterson (Columbia Univ. Press, 1974); 4. 'The simple politics of distributional preference' (with J.D. Rodgers), in *The Distribution of Economic Well-being*, ed. T. Juster (NBER, 1977); 5. 'The optimal tax treatment of charitable contributions' (with J.D. Rodgers), *Nat. Tax J*, March 1977.

HODGSKIN, Thomas*

Dates and Birthplace   1787–1869, England.

Posts Held   Naval officer; Journalist.

Career   Disgusted by the horrors of naval discipline, he first made a name by his attack on this, and established what was essentially an anarchist criticism of society. Turning to writing, he travelled extensively in Germany for the purposes of his book on that country. His economic writings were based on the idea that labour is the sole source of wealth, and that the workers were deprived of their true share of the wealth they produced. His *Popular Political Economy* was derived from his controversial lectures to the London Mechanics Institute and constituted the first textbook of socialist economics. In later life he was a frequent contributor to the *Economist*.

Publications   *Books:* 1. *An Essay on*

Naval Discipline (1813); 2. *Travels in the North of Germany* (1820); 3. *Labour Defended Against the Claims of Capital* (1825, 1964); 4. *Popular Political Economy* (1827); 5. *The Natural and Artificial Right of Property Contrasted* (1832).

Secondary Literature E. Halévy, *Thomas Hodgskin 1787–1869* (Ernest Benn, 1903, 1956).

HOFFMAN, Lutz

Born 1934, Flensburg, Germany.
Current Post Prof. Econ., Dir. Econ. Inst., Univ. Regensburg, W. Germany, 1975–.
Recent Posts Dean Econ. Dept., Univ. Regensburg, 1979–81.
Degrees Diploma examination (Econ.), PhD, Univ. Kiel, 1959, 1962; Habilitation Univ. Saarbrücken, 1969.
Offices Verein für Sozialpolitik, 1964–; RES, 1966–; Verein Deutscher Wissenschaftler, 1981–; Pres., German Section, Internat. Assoc. Energy Economists, 1981–.
Principal Contributions Analysis of the relative merits of import substituting and export-orientated industrialisation policies with reference to Argentina, Brazil, Chile, Colombia and Malaysia. First study (1970) demonstrated that import substitution is an indispensable phase of any industrialisation process, whether promoted by policy measures or not. Later study (1980) emphasised the redundancy of various policy measures used in developing countries for the promotion of industrialisation. Development of new approaches for the estimation and projection of energy demand in developing countries. Major innovation is the introduction of structural variables into the demand equations and a successful demonstration of their statistical significance. Development of methods for the economic evaluation of renewable energy sources and their application to wind energy.
Publications *Books:* 1. *Importsubstitution und Wirtschaftliches Wachstum in Entwicklungsländern – Unter Besonderer Berücksichtigung von Argentinien, Brasilien, Chile und Kolumbien* (J.C.B. Mohr, 1970); 2. *Faktoren der*

Standortwahl für Kernkraftwerke in Ausgewählten Industriestaaten, Schriftenreihe des Bundesministeriums für Raumordnung, Bauwesen und Städtebau (with G. Obermair *et al.*), (Bonn, 1978); 3. *Industrial Growth, Employment and Foreign Investment in Peninsular Malaysia* (with T.S. Fe), (OUP, 1980); 4. *Wind-energy – An Assessment of the Technical and Economic Potential, a Case-study for the Federal Republic of Germany* (with L. Jarass and A. Jarass), (Springer-Verlag, 1981).
Articles: 1. 'Pattern of growth and structural change in West Malaysia's manufacturing industry' (with T.T. Nee), *Kajian Ekonomi Malaysia*, 8(2), 1971, reprinted in *Readings in Malaysian Economic Development*, ed. D. Lim (OUP, 1975); 2. 'Import substitution – export expansion and growth in an open developing economy: the case of West Malaysia', *WA*, 109(3), 1973; 3. 'Employment creation through export growth: a case study of West Malaysia's manufacturing industries' (with T.S. Fe), in *The International Division of Labour – Problems and Perspectives*, ed. H. Giersch (Kiel, 1974), reprinted in *Readings in Malaysian Economic Development*, ed. D. Lim (OUP, 1975); 4. 'Der Einfluss Ausländischer Direktinvestitionen auf den Strukturwandel in Entwicklungsländern – Empirie contra Prophetie?' in *Probleme des Strukturwandels in der Strukturpolitik*, eds G. Bombach *et al.* (J.C.B. Mohr, 1977); 5. 'Energy demand in the developing world: estimations and projections to 1990 by region and country' (with M. Mors), World Bank Monograph on Commodity Models, 1982.

HOLLANDER, Jacob Harry*

Dates and Birthplace 1871–1940, Baltimore, Maryland, USA.
Posts Held Assoc. prof., prof., Johns Hopkins Univ., 1894–1940.
Degrees BA, PhD, Johns Hopkins Univ., 1981, 1894.
Offices Pres., AEA, 1921.
Career A great collector and publisher of material on the history of economics, he also served in numerous

official positions and wrote on economic theory. His government work included reforming the revenue system of Puerto Rico and advising the government of Santo Domingo on its public debt. He also was an official arbitrator in various labour disputes. His contributions to Ricardo scholarship are considerable and he initiated a famous series of *Reprints of Economic Tracts* in 1903.

Publications *Books:* 1. *Studies in State Taxation* (1900); 2. *Report on the Debt of Santo Domingo* (1906); 3. *David Ricardo: A Centenary Estimate* (1911); 4. *The Abolition of Poverty* (1914); 5. *War Borrowing* (1919); 6. *Economic Liberation* (1925); 7. *Want and Plenty* (1932).

Secondary Literature Anon., 'Jacob Harry Hollander', *AER*, 38, June 1948.

Publications *Books:* 1. *The Sources of Increased Efficiency: A Case Study of Dupont Rayon Plants* (MIT Press, 1965); 2. *The Economics of Adam Smith* (Univ. Toronto Press, Heinemann Educational Books, 1973); 3. *The Economics of David Ricardo* (Univ. Toronto Press, Heinemann Educational Books, 1979;.

Articles: 1. 'Adam Smith and the self-interest axiom', *J Law E*, 20, April 1977; 2. 'Mr. Ricardo and the moderns' (with Sir J. Hicks), *QJE*, 41, Aug. 1977; 3. 'On Prof. Samuelson's canonical classical model', *JEL*, 18(2), June 1980; 4. 'The post-Ricardian dissension: a case study in economics and ideology', *OEP*, 32(4), Nov. 1980; 5. 'Marxian economics as general-equilibrium theory', *HOPE*, 13(1), Spring 1981.

HOLLANDER, Samuel

Born 1937, London, England.

Current Post Prof. Econ., Univ. Toronto, Canada.

Recent Posts Vis. prof., Univ. Florence, Italy, 1973–4, LSE, 1974–5, Hebrew Univ., Jerusalem, 1979–80.

Degrees BSc. (Econ.) LSE, 1959; MA, PhD, Princeton Univ., 1961, 1963.

Offices Member, Ed. Board, *HOPE, Collected Works of J.S. Mill*; Guggenheim Memorial Foundation Fellow, 1968–9; Killam Res. Fellow, (Canada Council), 1973–5; Fellow, Royal Soc. Canada, 1976–.

Principal Contributions The primary outcome of research on eighteenth- and nineteenth-century economics is the demonstration of the existence of a 'core' of analytics – essentially allocation via the price mechanism in terms of general equilibrium – common to various representations of the capitalist exchange system. This holds true of works of the most disparate ideological intent – those of Marx and Ricardo as well as of Adam Smith and the late 'neo-classical' economists. Any notion of a dual development of nineteenth-century analysis, involving systems centred upon demand-supply or embryonic general-equilibrium versus systems wherein distribution is solved prior to pricing, is suspect.

HOLTHROP, Marius W.

Born 1902, Amsterdam, The Netherlands.

Current Post Retired.

Recent Posts Pres., De Nederlandsche Bank N.V., 1946–67; Pres., Chairman of Board, Bank for Internat. Settlements, Basle, 1958–67.

Degrees Dr (Econ.) Univ. Amsterdam, 1928; Dr h.c. Netherlands School Econ. (now Erasmus Univ.), Rotterdam, 1963; Dr h.c. Univ. Basle, 1967.

Offices and Honours Knight Order Netherlands Lion; Grand Cross Order Orange-Nassau; Grand Cross Order, Crown, Belgium; Member, Social Econ. Council, 1948–67; Member, Royal Netherlands Academy Sciences, 1950–; Governor, IMF, 1954–67.

Principal Contributions Consistent defence of a quantitative approach to monetary analysis and monetary policy. Widening of the concept of money by inclusion of specific short term claims on government and the banking system in the concept of 'liquidity'. Elaboration of a monetary model in which domestic and external monetary impulses are presented as the determinants of changes in national income and net balance of payments position. Use of this model in annual reports of the Nederlandsche Bank. Introduction in the Netherlands of quantitative credit controls as an instrument of cental bank monetary policy.

Publications *Books:* 1. *De Omloopssnelheid van het Geld* (*The Velocity of Circulation of Money*), (J.H. Paris, 1928); 2. *Analyse en Beleid* (*Analysis and Policy*), 21 annual reports of De Nederlansche Bank 1946–1966 (Nederlandsche Bank, 1970); 3. *Money in an Open Economy: Selected Papers on Monetary Policy, Monetary Analysis and Central Banking* (with G.A. Kessler and F.J. de Jong), (Stenfert Kroese, 1972).

Articles: 1. 'Theories of the velocity of circulation of money in earlier economic literature', *EJ*, 39 Jan. 1929; 2. 'Die Umlaufsgeschwindigkeit des Geldes', in *Beiträge zur Geldtheorie*, ed. F.A. Hayek (Julius Springer, 1933); 3. 'The relative responsibility of government and central banks in controlling aggregate demand', in *Inflation*, ed. D.C. Hague (Macmillan, 1962); 4. 'Monetary policy in an open economy, its objectives, instruments limitations, and dilemmas', in *Essays in International Finance, 43* (Princeton Univ. Press, 1963); 5. 'The balance of payments adjustment process, its asymmetry, and possible consequences for the international payments system,' in *Approaches to Greater Flexibility of Exchange Rates. The Bürgenstock Papers*, ed. G.N. Halm (Princeton Univ. Press, 1970).

HOMAN, Paul Thomas*

Dates and Birthplace 1893–1969, Indianola, Iowa, USA.

Posts Held Prof., Cornell Univ., 1929–47, UCLA, 1950–69, Southern Methodist Univ., Dallas, Texas, 1953–63; US President's Council Econ. Advisers, 1947–50.

Degrees BA Williamette Univ., 1914; BA Univ. Oxford 1919; PhD Brookings Inst., 1926.

Offices Adviser, to UNRRA, UNESCO, etc.; Ed. *AER*, 1941–52.

Career A student of Herbert Davenport at Cornell where he later held a Chair of economics. His discussion of current theory in *Contemporary Economic Thought* was both sympathetic

to heterodoxy and the current orthodox school. His editorship of *AER* was instrumental not only in raising its own standards but those of economics journals in the US generally. His work on public policy involved membership at various times of the Brookings Institute, the War Production Board, UNRRA, UNESCO, and the President's Council of Economic Advisers.

Publications *Books:* 1. *Contemporary Economic Thought* (1928); 2. *Current Economic Problems*, ed. (1932–); 3. *The Sugar Economy of Puerto Rico* (with A.D. Gayer), (1938).

HOPKINS, A.C.

N.e.

HORNER, Francis*

Dates and Birthplace 1778–1817, Edinburgh.

Posts Held Lawyer and politician.

Offices Founder, *Edinburgh Review*, 1802; MP for St. Ives (1806–7), Wendover (1807–12), St Mawes (1813–17); Chairman, UK Bullion Comm., 1810–11.

Career Whig politician whose association with the Bullion Committee made his name as an economic expert, despite the Committee's recommendation for the resumption of cash payments by the Bank of England failing to gain legislative support. He was an opponent of the corn duties and spoke tellingly in parliament on a number of other issues.

Publications *Books:* 1. *The Economic Writings of Francis Horner in the Edinburgh Review 1802–6*, ed. F.W. Fetter, (LSE, 1957).

HÖRNIGK, Philipp Wilhelm Von*

Dates and Birthplace 1638–1712, Austro-Hungary.

Posts Held Civil servant, with Cardinal Lamberg of Passau, 1690.

Degree Grad. Law Univ. Ingolstadt.

Career Brother-in-law of the rather more famous Johann Joachim Becher, he also put forward mercantilist views. His book is a programme for fostering the economic development of Austria by exploitation of waste lands, training of labour, favouring of domestic industry by such means as encouraging export of manufactures and import of raw materials. The analytical content is not prominent. His other writings were political tracts stating the German case against the territorial claims of France.

Publications *Books:* 1. *Oesterreich über Alles wann es nur will* (1684).

Secondary Literature K. Zielenziger, 'Hörnigk, Philipp Wilhelm von', *ESS*, vol. 7.

HORTON, Samuel Dana*

Dates and Birthplace 1844–95, USA.

Post Held Lawyer.

Offices Secretary, Internat. Monetary Congress, Paris, 1878; Amer. representative, Paris Conference, 1881.

Career With F.A. Walker, one of the leading advocates of an international bimetallic coinage. He argued the effectiveness of bimetallism from historical evidence and disregarded the success of Britain with its single standard as an exceptional example. In his later years he abandoned his legal practice and devoted himself entirely to the cause of bimetallism.

Publications *Books:* 1. *Silver and Gold and their Relation to the Problem of Resumption* (1876); 2. *Silver: An Issue of International Politics* (1886); 3. *The Silver Pound and England's Monetary Policy since the Restoration* (1887); 4. *Silver in Europe* (1890); 5. *Confidential Notes on Silver Diplomacy* (1891).

Secondary Literature H.L. Reed, 'Horton, Samuel Dana', *ESS*, vol. 7.

HORVATH, Janos

Born 1921, Cece, Hungary.

Current Post John W. Arbuckle prof. Econ., Butler Univ., Indianapolis, USA.

Recent Posts Sr Fellow, Res. Inst. Internat. Change, Columbia Univ., 1972–3; Vis. prof. Econ., Univ. Colorado, 1980.

Degree PhD (Econ.) Columbia Univ., 1967.

Offices AEA: Assoc. Study of Grants Economy (Program Chairman); Member parliament, Hungary, Econ. and Fin. Comm., 1945–7; Chief economist, Hungarian Farmers' Assoc.; Pres., NOSTRA Nat. Warehouse Center Ltd; Chief Delegate for Hungary, UNRRA: Dir. Amer.-Hungarian Relief; Pres., Hungarian Reconstruction Council, 1956.

Principal Contributions Developed the 'theory of institutional inflation', explaining price increases as consequences of supply constraints rooted in rigidities, primarily cumbersome governmental regulations and excessive market power. Thus, no workable trade off exists between inflation and unemployment; supply constraints *ipso facto* reduce employment while causing inflation. Co-founder, with K.E. Boulding and M. Pfaff, of the 'school of grants economics', a conceptual framework which identifies exchange (*quid pro quo*) vs grant elements (mostly implicit) in all transactions in order to trace their leverage over allocative efficiency and distributive equity. Designed a 'comprehensive concentration index' which consistently reflects horizontal, vertical, and conglomerate mergers.

Publications *Books:* 1. *Chinese Technology Transfer to the Third World: A Grants Economy Analysis* (Praeger, 1976); 2. *The Grants Economics Series* (with K.E. Boulding), (Praeger, 1978–82).

Articles: 1. 'On the evaluation of international grants policy', *PF*, 26(2), 1971; 2. 'Grants economics: a simple introduction' (with K.E. Boulding and M. Pfaff), *Amer. Econ*, 16(1), Spring 1972; repr. in *Recent Advances in Economics*, eds R. Fels and J.J. Siegfried (Richard D. Irwin, 1974); 3. 'Recording actual grant flows in the balance of international payments: an analytical clarification', *QREB*, 14(1), Spring 1974; 4. 'The scope of international grants economy: the case of Eximbank', in *Frontiers in Social Thought: Essays in Honor of Kenneth E. Boulding*, ed. M. Pfaff (N-H, 1976); 5. 'Toward a theory of institutional inflation', in *Stagflation: The Causes, Effects, and Solutions*, US Congress Joint Econ. Comm. (US Govt Printing Office, 1980).

HOSELITZ, Bert F.

Born 1913, Vienna, Austria.
Current Post Prof. Emeritus Econ. Social Science, 1978–.
Recent Posts Instructor Econ., Manchester Coll., Indiana, 1940–1; Res. ass. Econ. Internat. Relations, Inst. Internat. Stud., Yale Univ., 1943; Instructor Social Sciences, 1945–6, Ass. prof. Econ., 1946–7, Assoc. prof. Social Science, 1948–53, Prof. Econ. Social Science, 1954–78; Univ. Chicago; Assoc. prof. Econ., Carnegie Inst. Technology, 1947–8; Vis. prof. Econ., Univ. Frankfurt, 1953–4, MIT, 1963–4, Univ. Cal., Santa Cruz, 1967, Univ. Hawaii, East-West Center, 1971.
Degrees Dr Juris (Econ.) Univ. Vienna, 1936; MA (Econ.) Univ. Chicago, 1945.
Offices Member, AEA, RES, EHA, Royal Econ. Hist. Soc.; Univ. Chicago: Cowles Commission Fellow (1942), Encyclopedia Britannica Fellow (1943–5), Dir. Stud., Comm. Internat. Relations (1948–58), Founder, Dir. Res. Center Econ. Development Cultural Change, (1951–74); Acting Dir., RADIR Project, Hoover Library, Stanford Univ., 1949; Consultant, UNESCO, 1954, 1960–1, US Senate Comm. Foreign Relations, 1956 Internat. Social Science Council, 1960–1; Ed. *EDCC*, 1953–61, 1966–, Ed., *ESS*, 1961; Fellow, Center Advanced Study Behavioral Science, Stanford, Cal., 1955–6; Guggenheim Memorial Foundation Fellow, 1961–2.
Principal Contributions As writer, researcher, and teacher, is most proud of teaching skills from 1940–63. Many students of that period have done and are still doing important work in the field of international relations and economic development.
Publications *Books:* 1. *The Economics of Military Occupation* (with H.S. Bloch), (Univ. Chicago Press, 1944); 2. *The Progress of Underdeveloped Areas*, ed. (Univ. Chicago Press, 1952); 3. *Reader's Guide to the Social Sciences*, ed. (Free Press, 1959, 1970); 4. *Sociol-*

ogical Aspects of Economic Growth (Free Press, 1960; transl. into approximately 25 languages).
Articles: 1. 'Socialist planning and international economic relations', *AER*, 33(4), Dec. 1943; 2. 'The role of cities in the economic growth of underdeveloped countries', *JPE*, 56(3), June 1953; 3. 'Non-economic factors in economic development', *AER*, 47(2), May 1957; 4. 'Tradition and economic growth', in *Tradition, Values, and Socio-economic Development*, eds R. Braibanti and J.J. Spengler (Duke Univ., 1961); 5. 'Entrepreneurship and traditional élites', *Explorations Entrepreneurial Hist.*, 2nd series, 1(1), Fall 1963.

HOTELLING, Harold*

Dates and Birthplace 1895–1973, Fulda, Minn., USA.
Posts Held Journalist and school-teacher; Prof. Econ., Columbia Univ., 1931–46; Prof. Math. Stats, Univ. N. Carolina, 1946–66.
Degrees BA, MA, Univ. Washington, 1919, 1921; PhD Princeton Univ., 1924.
Offices Disting. Fellow, AEA; Pres., Em Soc, 1936–7.
Career A pioneer of mathematical economics and statistical theory whose fame rests on a comparatively small number of published papers, and his success as a teacher. His contributions were mainly in the areas of demand theory, welfare economics, optimisation over time, location theory under conditions of monopolistic competition, and the incidence of taxation.
Publications *Articles:* 1. 'Stability in competition', *EJ*, 39, March 1929, reprinted in *Readings in Price Theory*, eds G.J. Stigler and K.E. Boulding (Richard D. Irwin, 1953); 2. 'Economics of exhaustible resources', *JPE*, 39, April 1931; 3. 'Edgeworth's taxation paradox and the nature of demand and supply functions', *JPE*, 40, Oct. 1932; 4. 'Demand functions with limited budgets', *Em*, 3, Jan. 1935; 5. 'The general welfare in relation to problems of taxation and of railway and utility rates', *Em*, 6, July 1938, reprinted in *Readings in Welfare Economics*, eds K.J. Arrow

and T. Scitovsky (Richard D. Irwin, 1969); 6. 'Multivariate analysis: III Correlation', *IESS*, vol. 10.

Secondary Literature P.A. Samuelson, 'Harold Hotelling as mathematical economist', *Amer. Statist.*, 14(3), 1960; R.W. Pfouts and M.R. Leadbetter, 'Hotelling, Harold', *IESS*, vol. 18.

HOUGH, J.

N.e.

HOUTHAKKER, Hendrick

Born 1924, Amsterdam, The Netherlands.

Current Post Henry Lee, prof. Econ., Harvard Univ., USA.

Recent Posts Prof. Econ., Harvard Univ., 1960–; Member, US President's Council Econ. Advisers, 1968–71.

Degrees Doctorandus, Univ. Amsterdam, 1949; Hon. Dr Univ. Amsterdam, Univ. Fribourg.

Offices and Honours Member, NAS, AAAS, Internat. Stat. Inst., AEA; John Bates Clark medal, 1963, Vice-pres., 1972, AEA; Fellow, pres., 1967, Em Soc; Corresponding member, Netherlands Academy Sciences.

Principal Contributions Empirical research on consumption directed at the forms of Engel curves and at dynamic phenomena; theoretical research on that subject dealing with axiomatics and with special assumptions to improve applicability. Suggested a novel micro-foundaton for the production function; have also explored the price-output behaviour of industries. In international economics demonstrated the importance of income elasticities and presented a computerised extension of the Ricardian model. Publications on commodity markets dealt with the theory of normal backwardation with the efficiency of futures markets and with the conditions under which futures markets can exist. In energy, participated in the development of worldwide models and in research on mineral economics. In addition, contributed to various areas of economic policy, particularly regulation.

Publications *Books: 1. The Analysis of Family Budgets* (with S.J. Prais), (CUP, 1955, 1971); 2. *Consumer Demand in the United States* (with L.D. Taylor), (Harvard Univ. Press, 1966, 1970); 3. *Economic Policy for the Farm Sector* (Amer. Enterprise Inst., 1967); 4. *The World Price of Oil: A Medium-term Analysis* (Amer. Enterprise Inst. Public Pol. Res., 1976).

Articles: 1. 'Revealed preference and the utility function', *Ec*, N.S. 17, May 1950; 2. 'The Pareto distribution and the Cobb-Douglas production function in activity analysis', *REStud*, 23(1), 1955; 3. 'Income and price elasticities in world trade' (with S.P. Magee), *REStat*, 51(2), May 1969; 4. 'Growth and inflation: analysis by industry', *Brookings Papers Econ. Acitivity*, 1, 1979; 5. 'The use and management of North Sea oil', in *Britain's Economic Performance*, eds R.E. Caves and L.B. Krause (Brookings Inst., 1980).

HOXIE, Robert Franklin*

Dates and Birthplace 1868–1916, Edmeston, NY, USA.

Post Held Prof., Univ. Chicago.

Career Labour economist who sought to instil general economic theory with a more accurate vision of the complexity of industrial life. Thus his studies of trade unionism stress its diversity. An outstanding teacher, much of whose best work was heard in the classroom rather than appearing in print.

Publications *Books:* 1. *Scientific Management and Labor* (1915); 2. *Trades Unionism in the United States* (1917).

Articles: 1. 'On the empirical method of economic instruction', *JPE*, 9, Sept. 1901.

Secondary Literature C. Goodrich, 'Hoxie, Robert Franklin', *ESS*, vol. 7.

HUFBAUER, Gary Clyde

Born 1939, San Diego, Cal., USA.

Current Post Deputy Dir., Internat. Law Inst., Georgetown Law Center, Washington, DC; Counsel, Chapman, Duff & Paul, Washington, DC.

Recent Posts Prof. Econ., Univ. New

Mexico, 1970–4; Dir., Internat. Tax Staff, US Treasury, 1974–7; Dep. ass. secretary, Internat. Trade Investment Pol., US Treasury, 1977–80; Adjunct prof., Georgetown Law School, 1980–.

Degrees BA Harvard Coll., 1960; PhD King's Coll., Univ. Camb., 1963; JD Georgetown Law School, 1980.

Offices and Honours Marshall Scholar, 1960–3; Cosmos Club, 1975.

Principal Contributions Study of the relationship between technological change, international trade, and direct investment; study of the balance of payments consequences of multinational enterprise; and study of the economic effects of international tax and trade laws.

Publications *Books:* 1. *Synthetic Materials and the Theory of International Trade* (Duckworth, Harvard Univ. Press, 1966); 2. *Overseas Manufacturing Investment and the Balance of Payments* (with F.M. Adler), (US Treasury Dept, 1968).

Articles: 1. 'The impact of national characteristics and technology on the commodity composition of trade in manufactured goods', in *The Technology Factor in International Trade*, ed. R. Vernon (Columbia Univ. Press, 1970); 2. 'The taxation of export profits', *Nat. Tax J*, March 1975; 3. 'The multinational corporation and direct investment', in *International Trade and Finance*, ed. P.B. Kenen (CUP, 1975); 4. 'US taxation of the undistributed income of controlled foreign corporations' (with D. Foster), US Treasury Dept, *Essays in International Taxation: 1976* (US Govt Printing Office, 1976); 5. 'The GATT codes and the unconditional most-favored-nation principle' (with J.S. Erb and H.P. Starr), *Law Pol. Internat. Bus.*, 1, 1980.

HUME, David*

Dates and Birthplace 1711–76, Edinburgh, Scotland.

Posts Held Tutor, 1745; Diplomat, 1746, 1763–6; Keeper, Advocate's Library, Edinburgh, 1752; Under-secretary State, Home Dept., 1767–8.

Career Primarily known as a philosopher, he also wrote substantial histories, and in his essays dealt with political, sociological and economic topics. All these fields were illuminated by his basic philosophy which involved the analysis of human nature and the examination of the way in which environmental forces act on that nature to produce particular forms of behaviour. The economic essays chiefly deal with money, trade and taxes and have a quality that still makes them refreshing to read. On such topics as monetary theory, international trade and population growth, he was not equalled even by Adam Smith, a close friend on whom he had an enormous influence.

Publications *Books:* 1. *Treatise on Human Nature* (1739–40, 1958, 1969); 2. *Essays Moral and Political*, 2 vols (1741–2, 1912); 3. *Inquiry Concerning Human Understanding* (1748); 4. *Political Discourses* (1752); 5. *History of England*, 3 vols (1754–62, 1894); 6. *Writings on Economics*, ed. E. Rotwein (1955).

Secondary Literature E.C. Mossner, *Life of David Hume* (Univ, Texas Press, 1954); E. Rotwein, 'Hume, David', *IESS*, vol. 6.

HURWICZ, Leonid

Born 1917, Moscow, Russia.

Current Post Regents' Prof. Econ., Univ. Minnesota, USA.

Recent Posts Res. assoc., Cowles Commission, Univ. Chicago, 1944–6; Assoc. prof., Prof., Iowa State Coll., 1946–9; Prof. Econ., Maths, Stats, Univ. Illinois, 1949–51; Univ. Minnesota, 1951–; Vis. prof., Stanford Univ., 1955–6, 1958–9, Harvard Univ., 1969–71, Univ. Cal., Berkeley, 1976–7.

Degrees LLM Univ. Warsaw, 1938; Hon. Dr Science Northwestern Univ., 1980.

Offices Fellow, 1949, Pres., 1969, Em Soc; Fisher (Em Soc) lecturer, Univ. Copenhagen, 1963; Member, AAAS, 1965; Ely (AEA) Lecturer, Univ. Toronto, 1972; Member, NAS, 1974; Disting. Fellow, AEA, 1977.

Principal Contributions Looking at economic systems from a 'designer's point of view', regarding the economic mechanism as the unknown of the problem rather than a datum, the problem being to construct mechanisms satisfying specified desiderata (e.g. informational decentralisation, efficiency, individual rationality). Constructing formal models useful in analysing and designing economic systems; formulating rigorous definitions of informational decentralisation and incentive-compatibility. Using the framework of non-cooperative game theory to study the incentive-compatibility properties of economic mechanisms. Results on stability of competitive equilibrium (with K.J. Arrow and H.D. Block), programming in infinite-dimensional spaces, least squares bias in autoregressive time series. Analysis of the concept of causality.

Publications *Books:* 1. *Studies in Linear and Non-linear Programming* (with K.J. Arrow and H. Uzawa), (Stanford Univ. Press, 1958); 2. *Preferences, Utility and Demand* (with J.S. Chipman *et al.*), (Harcourt, Brace Jovanovich, 1971); 3. *Studies in Resource Allocation Processes* (CUP, 1977).

Articles: 1. 'The theory of economic behavior', *AER*, 35, Dec. 1945; 2. 'On the stability of the competitive equilibrium, I-II' (with K.J. Arrow and H.D. Block), *Em*, 26-27, Oct. 1958, Jan. 1959; 3. 'Optimality and informational efficiency in resource allocation processes', in *Mathematical Methods in the Social Sciences*, eds K.J. Arrow *et al.* (Stanford Univ. Press, 1960); 4. 'Outcome functions yielding Walrasian and Lindahl allocations at Nash equilibrium points', *REStud*, 46(2), April 1979; 5. 'On allocations attainable through Nash equilibria', *JET*, 21, Aug. 1979.

HUTCHESON, Francis*

Dates and Birthplace 1694-1746, Co. Down, Ireland.
Posts Held Presbyterian minister; Prof. Moral Philosophy, Univ. Glasgow, 1729-46.
Career Adam Smith's teacher, whose philosophy had a basis in utilitarian ideas. To him virtue and natural law were both grounded in utility. His *System . . .* incorporates material which was given in his lectures, and the div-

isions of the subject he used are very similar to those later adopted by Smith. He laid great stress on the division of labour, and his ideas on the value of money and whether corn or labour afforded the most stable standard of value resemble those of Smith.

Publications *Books:* 1. *Inquiry into the Origin of our Ideas of Beauty and Virtue* (1720); 2. *Essay on the Passions* (1728); 3. *Introduction to Moral Philosophy* (1753); 4. *A System of Moral Philosophy* (1755).

Secondary Literature W.L. Taylor, *Francis Hutcheson and David Hume as Predecessors of Adam Smith* (Duke Univ. Press, 1965).

HUTCHISON, Terence W.

Born 1912, Bournemouth, England.
Current Post Retired.
Recent Posts Mitsui Prof. Econ., Univ. Birmingham, 1956-78.
Degrees BA, MA, Univ. Camb., 1934, 1937.
Offices Vis. prof., Columbia Univ., 1954-5, Univ. Virginia, 1960, Univ. Saarland, 1962, 1980, Yale Univ., 1963-4, ANU, 1967, Dalhousie Univ., 1970, Univ. Western Australia, 1975, Univ. Cal., Davis, 1978.
Principal Contributions Areas of the method and history of economics.

Publications *Books:* 1. *The Significance and Basic Postulates of Economic Theory* (Macmillan, 1938, Kelley, 1960); 2. *A Review of Economic Doctrines 1870-1929* (OUP, 1953, Greenwood Press, 1975); 3. *Economics and Economic Policy 1946-1966* (A & U, 1968); 4. *Knowledge and Ignorance in Economics* (Blackwell, 1977); 5. *Revolutions and Progress in Economic Knowledge* (CUP, 1978).

Articles: 1. 'A note on tautologies and the nature of economic theory', *REStud*, 2(2), Feb. 1935; 2. 'Theoretische Ökonomie als Sprachsystem', *ZN*, 8(1), 1937; 3. 'Methodological prescriptions in economics: a reply', *Ec*, N.S. 27, May 1960; 4. *Markets and the Franchise*, IEA Occasional paper (Inst. Econ. Affairs, 1966).

HYMER, Stephen*

N.e.

HYNDMAN, Henry Mayers*

Dates and Birthplace 1842–1921, London, England.

Posts Held Journalist and political leader.

Degree BA Univ. Camb., 1863.

Offices Member of Sussex Cricket XI, 1863–8; Founder, Social Democratic Federation, 1881, Nat. Socialist Party, 1916; Founder and ed., *Justice*, 1884.

Career Converted to socialism whilst a wealthy young man by his reading of Marx's *Capital*, he became Britain's first important socialist political leader. His various books expounded Marxism in a readable style to the British public. He was a determined advocate of Indian self-government and an opponent of British imperialist policy.

Publications Books: 1. *England For All* (1881); 2. *The Historical Basis of Socialism* (1883); 3. *A Summary of the Principles of Socialism* (with W. Morris), (1884); 4. *Commercial Crises of the Nineteenth Century* (1892); 5. *Economics of Socialism* (1896); 6. *Record of an Adventurous Life* (1911); 7. *Further Reminiscences* (1912).

I

IJIRI, Yuji

Born 1935, Kobe, Japan.

Current Post Robert M. Trueblood Prof. Accounting and Econ., Carnegie-Mellon Univ., Pittsburgh, USA, 1967–.

Recent Posts Ass., assoc. prof. Bus. Admin., Stanford Univ., Grad. School Bus., 1963–7.

Degrees CPA Japan, 1956; LLB Ritsumeikan Univ., Japan, 1956; MS Univ. Minnesota, 1960; PhD Carnegie-Mellon Univ., 1963.

Offices Member, 1963–, Academic Vice-pres., 1974–5, AAA.

Principal Contributions Aggregation theory, firm size distributions, accounting measurement theory, and quantitative models in business and economics.

Publications *Books:* 1. *Management Goals and Accounting for Control, Studies in Mathematical and Managerial Economics*, ed. H. Theil, vol. 3 (N-H, 1965; Japanese transl. 1970; French transl. 1970; Spanish transl. 1976); 2. *The Foundations of Accounting Measurement: A Mathematical, Economic, and Behavioral Inquiry* (Prentice-Hall, 1967, Scholars Book, 1978; Japanese transl., 1968); 3. *Theory of Accounting Measurement* (American Accounting Assoc., 1975; Japanese transl., 1976); 4. *Skew Distributions and the Sizes of Business Firms* (with H.A. Simon), (N-H, 1977); 5. *Recognition of Contractual Rights and Obligations: An Exploratory Study of Conceptual Issues* (Fin. Accounting Standards Board, 1980).

Articles: 1. 'The linear aggregation coefficient as the dual of the linear correlation coefficient', *Em*, 36(2), April 1968; 2. 'Fundamental queries in aggregation theory', *JASA*, 66(336), Dec. 1971; 3. 'Interpretations of departures from the Pareto curve in firm-size distributions' (with H.A. Simon), *JPE*, 82(2), March-April 1974; 4. 'Distributions associated with Bose-Einstein statistics' (with H.A. Simon), *NAS Proceedings*, 72(5), May 1975; 5. 'Cost flow networks and generalized inverses', in *Extremal Methods and Systems Analysis*, eds A.V. Fiacco and K.O. Kortanek (Springer-Verlag, 1980).

ILCHMAN, Warren F.

Born 1933, Denver, Col., USA.

Current Post Vice-pres. Res. Grad. Stud., State Univ. New York, USA.

Recent Posts Prof. Polit. Science, Univ. Cal., Berkeley, 1965–73; Dean, Coll. Liberal Arts, Grad. School, Prof. Polit. Sciences Econ., Boston Univ., 1974–6; Program Adviser, Internat. Div., Ford Foundation, 1976–80.

Degrees BA Brown Univ., 1955; PhD Univ. Camb., 1959.

Offices and Honours Phi Beta Kappa; Marshall Scholar; contributing author White House Library; Amer. Soc. Public Admin. Burchfield Award,

1965; Fulbright-Hays Sr res. prof., India, 1968–9; Danford Foundation Harbison prize outstanding teaching, 1969–70.

Principal Contributions Early work applied to developing a theoretical capacity to consider political and economic resources in the same calculus. Thereafter, worked increasingly on applying this perspective to the public policy issues of employment, education, land reform and population, and to evaluating the productivity of social science knowledge for public choice.

Publications *Books:* 1. *New Men of Knowledge and the New States: Planners and the Polity* (with A.S. Ilchman), (Univ. Cal. Press, 1968); 2. *The Political Economy of Change* (with N.T. Uphoff), (Univ. Cal. Press, 1969); 3. *The Political Economy of Development: Theory and Contributions* (with N.T. Uphoff), (Univ. Cal. Press, 1972); 4. *Policy Sciences and Population* (with H.D. Lasswell *et al.*), (Heath-Lexington Books, 1975); 5. *Employment and Education: The Policy Nexus* (with A.S. Ilchman and T.N. Dhar), (South Asia Books, 1976).

Articles: 1. 'Balanced thought and economic growth', *EDCC*, 14(4), July 1966; 2. 'The political economy of foreign aid: the case of India', *Asian Survey*, Oct. 1967; 3. 'People in plenty: educated unemployment in India', *Asian Survey*, Oct. 1969; 4. 'Beyond the economics of labor-intensive development: politics and administration', *SEADAG Occasional Papers*, 1973; 5. 'Preserving the cosmopolitan research university in the United States', *Annals AAAS*, 449, May 1980.

INADA, Ken-Ichi

Born 1925, Kiryu, Gunma, Japan.
Current Post Dir. Inst., Prof. Math. Econ., Inst. Social Econ. Res., Osaka Univ., Yamadaoka, Suita, Osaka, Japan, 1969–.
Recent Posts Prof. Econ., Tokyo Metropolitan Univ., 1969–.
Degree BA (Maths) Tokyo Univ., 1947.
Offices Fellow, Council, 1968–75,

Em Soc; Pres., Japanese Assoc. Theoretical Econ., 1980–1.
Principal Contributions In the field of economic growth and development: two sector growth model, turnpike theorem and economic development model. In the field of welfare economics: the existence problem of the social welfare function; the necessary and sufficient condition for the simple majority decision rule to be transitive; and non-existence theorems of social welfare functions where the individuals' preference are expressed as the ordinary indifference fields in the commodity space.
Publications *Books:* 1. *New Economics* (in Japanese, *Nihon Keizai Shinbun-sha*, 1965, 1974); 2. *Mechanism of Economic Development* (in Japanese, *Sobun-sha*, 1972).

Articles: 1. 'Economic growth under neutral technical progress', *Em*, 32(1–2), Jan./April 1964; 2. 'On the economic welfare function', *Em*, 32(3), July 1964; 3. 'On neo-classical models of economic growth', *REStud*, 32(2), April 1965; 4. 'Development in monocultural economies', *Int ER*, 12(2), June 1971; 5. 'Social welfare function and social indifference surfaces', *Em*, 39(3), May 1971.

INGRAM, John Kells*

Dates and Birthplace 1823–1907, Temple Carne, Donegal, Ireland.
Posts Held Fellow, 1846, Prof. Oratory, 1852, Regius Prof. Greek, 1866–77, Librarian, 1879–87, Vice-provost, 1898–9, Trinity Coll., Dublin.
Degree BA Trinity Coll., Dublin, 1843.
Offices Founder, Stat. and Social Enquiry Soc. Ireland; First ed., *Hermathena*.
Career A firm adherent of Comte and spokesman for historical economics in Britain, who also shone in the fields of law, literature, the classics and mathematics. His attack on classical economics encompassed its methodology and its conclusions. The latter he characterised as apologies for the employing classes. His *History* . . . was extremely successful, being frequently translated and serving as a textbook till the 1920s. Its

polemical Comtist tone now renders it obsolete. In it Ingram is drawn into extreme positions, such as his condemnation of mathematical economics as completely sterile.

Publications *Books:* 1. *A History of Political Economy* (1888).

Secondary Literature C.L. Falkiner, *Memoir of John Kells Ingram* (1907).

INNIS, Harold Adams*

Dates and Birthplace 1894–1952, Otterville, Ontario, Canada.

Posts Held Prof. and Dean, Univ. Toronto.

Degrees BA, MA McMaster Univ, 1916, 1918; PhD Univ. Chicago, 1923.

Offices Pres., Canadian Polit. Science Assoc., 1937; Pres., EHA, 1942; Pres., Royal Soc. Canada, 1946; Pres., AEA, 1951.

Career Canada's most famous economic historian who sought a distinctively New World approach. His books on the fur and fishery trades of Canada re-oriented opinions on Canadian history in dramatic fashion. His later work concentrated on the economic and political aspects of communications and communications media. This work, though not fully worked out at the time of his death, was intended to combat the anti-cultural implications of modern communications monopolies.

Publications *Books:* 1. *The Fur Trade in Canada: An Introduction to Canadian Economic History* (1930); 2. *The Cod Fisheries: The History of an International Economy* (1940); 3. *Political Economy in the Modern State* (1946); 4. *Empire and Communications* (1950); 5. *The Bias of Communications* (1951); 6. *Changing Concepts of Time* (1952).

Secondary Literature J.B. Brebner, 'Obituary: Harold Adams Innis', *EJ*, 63, Sept. 1953.

INTRILIGATOR, Michael D.

Born 1938, New York City, NY, USA.

Current Post Prof. Econ., UCLA, USA.

Recent Posts Ass. prof. Econ., 1963–6, Assoc. prof. Econ., 1966–72, UCLA.

Degrees SB (Econ.), PhD (Econ.), MIT, 1959, 1963; MA (Econ.) Yale Univ., 1960.

Offices and Honours Disting. teaching awards, UCLA, 1966, 1976, 1979; Ford Faculty Res. Fellow, 1967–8; Member, AEA WEA; Member, Em Soc, (Member, Program Comm., 1968, 1969, 1970, 1975, Chairman, Program Comm., 1969; Member, Visitors Selection Comm., 1969–71).

Principal Contributions The theory and applications of quantitative economics, including mathematical economic theory and econometrics and their applications to health economics and strategic arms control. Produced several applications of control theory in economics; formulated a probabilistic model of social choice; made contributions to adaptive control and to the Nash bargaining problem; participated in the development of econometric models of industrial organisation and macroeconometric and micro-simulation models of the health care system; and developed models of arms races and related phenomena, including military strategy, proliferation, and arms limitation agreements.

Publications *Books:* 1. *Mathematical Optimization and Economic Theory* (Prentice-Hall, 1971); 2. *Frontiers of Quantitative Economics*, vols. 1–3, ed. (N-H, 1971, 1974, 1977); 3. *Econometric Models, Techniques, and Applications* (Prentice-Hall, N-H, 1978); 4. *Handbook of Mathematical Economics*, vols 1–3 ed. (with K.J. Arrow), (N-H, 1981, 1982); 5. *Handbook of Econometrics* vols 1–3, ed. (with Z. Griliches), (N-H, 1982, 1983).

Articles: 1. 'Generalized comparative statics with applications to consumer and producer theory' (with P.J. Kalman), *Int ER*, 14(2), June 1973; 2. 'A probalistic model of social choice', *RE Stud*, 40(4), Oct. 1973; 3. 'Strategic considerations in the Richardson model of arms races', *JPE*, 83(2), April 1975; 4. 'A new approach to the Nash bargaining problem' (with D.L. Brito and A.M. Buoncristiani), *Em*, 45(5), July 1977; 5. 'Income redistribution: a probabilistic approach', *AER*, 69(1), March 1979.

ISARD, Walter

Born 1919, Philadelphia, Penn.
Current Post Prof. Econ. (Regional Science & Peace Science), Cornell Univ., Ithaca, NY.
Recent Posts Chairman, Dept. Regional Science, Univ. Penn., 1956–79; Assoc., Center Internat. Affairs, Harvard Univ., 1974–.
Degrees BA (with distinction) Temple Univ., 1939; MA 1941, PhD 1943, Harvard Univ.; Hon. PhD Poznan Academy Econ., 1976, Erasmus Univ, Rotterdam, 1978, Univ. Karlsruhe, 1979, Umea Univ., 1980, Univ. Illinois, 1982.
Principal Contributions Extension and development of location theory, interregional input-output analysis and integrated multi-regions models.
Publications *Books:* 1. *Location and space economy* (Technology Press, Wiley, 1956); 2. *Methods of regional analysis*, (with others), (MIT Press, Wiley, 1960); 3. *Regional input-output study*, (with T. Langrord), (MIT Press, 1971); 4. *Introduction to regional science* (Prentice-Hall, 1975); 5. *Spatial dynamics and optimal space-time development*, (with P. Liossatos *et al.*), (Elsevier, N-H, 1979).

ISNARD, Achylle-Nicolas*

Dates and Birthplace 1749–1803, Paris, France.
Posts Held Civil engineer, Arbois, Evreux, Le Havre, Carcassonne, Lyons.
Degree Grad. L'Ecole des Ponts et Chaussées, Paris.
Offices Member of the Tribunate, 1800.
Career Engineer-economist whose chief work is his *Traité* ... Whilst having some affinity to the physiocratic philosophy, this work rejected the doctrine that the soil alone produces a 'produit net'. It is remarkable for its mathematical treatment of production, capital, money and the theory of exchange. The latter is sufficiently similar to that of Walras to suggest that Walras was influenced by Isnard.
Publications *Books:* 1. *Traité des richesses*, 2 vols (1781); 2. *Catechisme sociale ou instructions élémentaires sur la morale sociale è l'usage de la jeunesse* (1784); 3. *Observations sur le principe qui a produit les révolutions* (1789); 4. *Les Devoirs de la deuxième législature*, 4 vols (1791); 5. *Considérations théoriques sur les Caisses d'amortissement de la dette publique* (1801).
Secondary Literature W. Jaffé, 'A.N. Isnard, progenitor of the Walrasian general equilibrium model', *HOPE*, 1(1), Spring 1969.

J

JAFFÉ, William*

Dates and Birthplace 1898–1980, New York City, NY, USA.
Posts Held Ass. prof., 1928–36, Assoc. prof., 1936–56, Prof. Econ., 1956–66, Prof. Emeritus, 1966–80, Northwestern Univ.; Prof. Econ., York Univ., Ontario, 1970–80.
Degrees City Coll., New York, 1918; MA Columbia Univ., 1919; Dr Droit ès sciences écon. et polit., Univ. Paris, 1924; Hon. LLD York Univ., 1974.
Offices and Honours Em Soc; AEA; RES; Hist. Econ. Soc.; Res. fellowships: Guggenheim Memorial Foundation Fellow, 1958–9, Ford Foundation, 1963–4, NSF, 1965–9, Canada Council, 1972–80, Killam Foundation, 1975–7; Foreign member, Royal Netherlands Academy Sciences Letters, 1968; Corresponding Fellow, BA, 1977; Chevalier, Légion d'Honneur, 1978; Fellow, Royal Soc. Canada, 1979; Hist. Econ. Soc. Disting. Fellow, 1980
Career First, in his translation of Walras' *Eléments d'économie politique pure*, Jaffé furnished English-speaking economists with access to Walras' major theoretical work. Second, in his edition of Walras' *Correspondence*, he provided a sourcebook of bibliographical, biographical, scientific, social and economic information about Walras and his century that is relevant for understanding the genesis of Walras' work and the development of neo-classical economics.

Third, in his many essays on Walras, he treated most of the themes that are important in Walras' work, and many of the questions that can be asked about his life and impact on economic thought. Thus he provided an exposition and evaluation of Walras' theories, and a history of the circumstances and sources that were important in their development.

Publications *Books:* 1. *Les Théories economiques et sociales de Thorstein Veblen* (1924); 2. *The Economic Development of Post-war France* (with W.F. Ogburn), (1929); 3. L. Walras, *Elements of Pure Economics*, transl. and ann. (1954); 4. *Correspondence of Léon Walras and Related Papers*, 3 vols, ed. and ann. (N-H, 1965).

Articles: 1. 'New light on an old quarrel. Barone's unpublished review of Wicksteed's *Essay on the co-ordination of the Laws of Distribution* and related documents', *Cahiers Vilfredo Pareto*, 3, 1964; 2. 'Walras' theory of *tâtonnement:* a critique of recent interpretations', *JPE*, 75, Feb. 1967; 3. 'Reflections on the importance of Léon Walras', in *P. Hennipman Festschrift, Schaarste en Welvaart*, eds A. Heertje *et al.* (Stenfert Kroese, 1971); 4. 'Walras' economics as others see it', *JEL*, 18(2), June 1980; 5. 'Another look at Léon Walras' theory of *Tâtonnement'*, *HOPE*, 13(2), Summer 1981.

Secondary Literature D.A. Walker, 'William Jaffé, historian of economic thought, 1898–1980', *AER*, 71(5), Dec. 1981; V.J. Tarascio, 'William Jaffé, 1898–1980', *HOPE*, 13(2), Summer 1981.

JAFFEE, Dwight M.

Born 1943, Chicago, Ill., USA.
Current Post Prof. Econ., Princeton Univ., NJ, USA, 1968–.
Recent Posts N.e.
Degrees BA Northwestern Univ., 1964; Phd MIT, 1968.
Offices Assoc. ed., *JMCB*, 1973–5, *J Fin*, 1974–, *J Mon E*, 1975–8, *Housing Fin. J*, 1980–.
Principal Contributions Developed theories and tests of the existence and rationality of non-price credit rationing by lenders. Analysed alternative meth-

ods of estimating market demand and supply for markets in disequilirbium, and carried out various applications of these techniques. Carried out a variety of theoretical and empirical studies relating to thrift institution, mortgage market developments and innovation, the impact of mortgage finance on housing, and financial reform. Other work includes contributions to portfolio theory, the risk structure of interest rates, and international finance.

Publications *Books:* 1. *Credit Rationing and the Commercial Loan Market* (Wiley, 1971); 2. *Savings Deposits, Mortgages and Residential Construction*, ed. (with E. Gramlich), (D.C. Heath, 1972); 3. *Economic Implications of an Electronic Monetary Transfer System* (with M. Flannery), (D.C. Heath, 1973).

Articles: 1. 'A theory and test of credit rationing' (with F. Modigliani), *AER*, 59(5), Dec. 1969; 2. 'Methods of estimation for markets in disequilibrium' (with R.C. Fair), *Em*, 40(3), May 1972; 3. 'On the application of portfolio theory to depository financial intermediaries' (with O.D. Hart), *REStud*, 41(1), Jan. 1974; 4. 'Imperfect information, uncertainty, and credit rationing' (with T. Russell), *QJE*, 40(4), Nov. 1976; 5. 'Mortgage credit availability and residential construction activity' (with K. Rosen), *Brookings Papers Econ. Activity*, 2, 1979.

JAMES, P.M. Emile

Born 1899, Riom, France.
Current Post Prof. honoraire de l'Univ. Paris.
Degrees Dr (en sciences econ.) Prof. agrégé Sorbonne, 1922, 1926.
Offices and Honours Officier, Légion d'Honneur; Member, l'Institut de France (Académie des sciences morales et politiques).
Principal Contributions n.e.
Publications *Books:* 1. *Problèmes monetaires d'aujourd'hui* (Grey, 1954); 2. *Histoire de la pensée économique au XX siècle* (PVP, 1955); 3. *Histoire sommaire de la pensée économique* (Darmert, 1956).

JASZI, George

Born 1915, Budapest, Hungary.
Current Post Dir., Bureau Econ. Analysis, US Dept. Commerce, Washington, DC, 1963–.
Degrees BSc. LSE, 1936; PhD Harvard Univ., 1946.
Offices and Honours Chairman, Conference Res. Income and Wealth, 1955–6, Chairman, Internat. Assoc. Res. Income and Wealth, 1973; Fellow, ASA, 1965; Fellow, Nat. Assoc. Bus. Economists, 1972; Rockefeller public service award, 1974; Disting. exec., Sr Elec. Service, 1980; Hon. Fellow, LSE, 1980.
Principal Contributions Contributed to the development of macro-economic accounts: national income and product, input-output, saving and investment, etc., and their use in economic analysis.
Publications *Articles:* 1. 'The conceptual basis of the accounts', *Income and Wealth*, 22, 1958; 2. 'The measurement of aggregate economic growth: a review of key conceptual and statistical issues as suggested by the United States experience', *REStat*, 63(4), Nov. 1961; 3. 'An improved way of measuring quality change', *REStat*, 64(3), Aug. 1962; 4. 'Taking care of soft figures: reflections on improving the accuracy of the GNP', *Stat. News*, 18, Aug. 1972; 5. 'A framework for the measurement of economic and social performance', in *The Measurement of Economic and Social Performance*, ed. M. Milton (Columbia Univ. Press, 1973).

JENCKS, Christopher

Born 1936, Baltimore, Maryland, USA.
Current Post Prof. Sociology Urban Affairs, Northwestern Univ., Evanston, Ill., USA, 1979–.
Recent Posts Prof. Sociology, Harvard Univ., 1973–9; Vis. prof., Univ. Cal., Santa Barbara, 1977–8.
Degrees BA Harvard Coll., 1958.
Offices and Honours Guggenheim Memorial Foundation Fellow, 1968; Amer. Sociological Assoc. Sorokin prize, 1974.
Principal Contributions Research on the role of family background, genes, academic aptitude and school experience in determining both individual economic success and the overall level of economic success in the USA.
Publications *Books:* 1. *The Academic Revolution* (with D. Riesman), (Doubleday, 1968, Univ. Chicago Press, 1980); 2. *Inequality* (Basic Books, 1972); 3. *Who Gets Ahead?* (Basic Books, 1979).

JENKIN, Henry Charles Fleeming*

Dates and Birthplace 1833–85, Kent, England.
Posts Held Engineer; Prof. Engineering, Univ. Coll., Univ. London, 1866–8, Univ. Edinburgh, 1868–.
Degree MA Univ. Genoa, 1850.
Offices Fellow, Royal Soc., 1865.
Career A successful engineer, inventor, and scientific journalist, he turned to economics in 1868 with an article on trade unions. Two subsequent published papers on 'The graphic representation of the laws of supply and demand' (1870) and 'Principles which regulate the incidence of taxes' (1871) constitute the sum of his economic publications. His application of mathematics was related to the partial equilibrium analysis of individual markets which Marshall later developed. His work was little noticed, even by Jevons and Marshall, and had little effect on the subsequent course of economic thought despite its striking quality and originality.
Publications *Books:* 1. *Graphic representations and other essays on Political Economy* (1887, 1931).
Secondary Literature A.D. Brownlie and M.F. Lloyd Prichard, 'Professor Fleeming Jenkin, 1833–1885; pioneer in engineering and political economy', *OEP*, 15, Nov. 1963.

JENSEN, Michael C.

Born 1939, Rochester, Minn., USA.
Current Post Prof., Dir., Managerial Econ. Res. Center, Grad. School Management, Univ. Rochester, USA.
Recent posts Instructor, Northwestern Univ., 1967; Ass. prof., 1967–71, Assoc. prof., 1972–9, Univ. Rochester.

Degrees BA Macalester Coll., 1962; MA, PhD, Univ. Chicago, 1964, 1968.

Offices and Honours Member, AEA; Founding ed., *J Fin E*, 1973–; Assoc. ed., *J Accounting Econ.*, 1978–; Advisory ed., *Econ. Letters*, 1978–; Recipient Leo Melamed prize (with W.H. Meckling), 1978; Recipient Graham and Dodd plaque (with W.H. Meckling), 1978; Member exec. comm., WEA, 1981–4.

Principal Contributions In finance, primarily to asset pricing theory, portfolio theory, efficient market theory, and the measurement of portfolio performance. In economics, primarily to the theory of property rights, agency theory, corporate control and organisation theory, and law and economics.

Publications *Books:* 1. *Studies in the Theory of Capital Markets*, ed. (Praeger, 1972).

Articles: 1. 'The adjustment of stock prices to new information' (with E. Fama *et al.*), *Int ER*, 10, Feb. 1969; 2. 'Risk, the pricing of capital assets, and the evaluation of investment portfolios', *J Bus*, 42(2), April 1969; 3. 'The capital asset pricing model: some empirical tests (with F. Black and M. Scholes), in *Studies in the Theory of Capital Markets*, ed. M.C. Jensen (Praeger, 1972); 4. 'Capital markets: theory and evidence', *Bell JE*, 3(2), Autumn 1972; 5. 'Rights and production functions: an application to labor-managed firms and codetermination' (with W.H. Meckling), *J Bus*, 52(4), Oct. 1979.

JEVONS, Herbert Stanley*

Dates and Birthplace 1975–1955.

Posts Held Lecturer, Prof. Econ., Univ. Wales, Cardiff, 1905–11; Prof. Econ., Univ. Allahabad, India 1914–23, Univ. Rangoon, Burma 1923–30.

Degree BSc., MA Univ. London.

Offices Ed., *Indian J Econ.*, 1916–22; Council member, RSS, 1932–7.

Career Originally a geologist (like his father), his switch to economics at Cardiff also brought him involvement in housing reform. Temporarily abandoning his academic career, he spent the years 1911–14 directing various housing

schemes. In India, too, he was involved in practical matters, particularly on behalf of the cotton industry. His work on the coal trade and economics of tenancy law was well received and influential. In his later years, he was an adviser to the Emperor of Ethiopia and organised the Abyssinian Association and the Anglo-Ethiopian Society.

Publications *Books:* 1. *Essays on Economics* (1905); 2. *The British Coal Trade* (1915) 3. *Economics of Tenancy Law and Estate Management* (1921); 4. *Money, Banking and Exchange in India* (1922): 5. *The Future of Exchange and the Indian Currency* (1922); 6. *Economic Equality in the Co-operative Commonwealth* (1933).

Secondary Literature (Obituary) 'Prof. Stanley Jevons: friend of Ethiopia', *Times*, 29 June 1955.

JEVONS, William Stanley*

Dates and Birthplace 1835–82, Liverpool, England.

Posts Held Assayer of Australian Mint, 1854–8; Tutor, lecturer, prof. Logic and Moral Philosophy, Owens Coll., Manchester, 1863–76; Prof. Polit. Econ., Univ. Coll., London, 1876–81.

Degrees BA, MA, Univ. Coll., London, 1860, 1862.

Offices Pres., BAAS, 1870.

Career With Menger and Walras he was one of the three co-discoverers of marginal utility theory, but was also widely known for his textbooks on logic, and his applied economic studies. In *The Coal Question*, he treated coal as the essential resource for the British industrial economy and argued that it was an exhaustible resource. His other quantitative studies, collected posthumously in *Investigations*, were largely concerned with economic fluctuations, which he examined through statistics on seasonal movements, business cycles and secular trends. His later work included the heroic but doomed attempts to trace business cycles to sunspot activity. His discovery of the marginal utility concept in 1860 aroused no interest, and not until *Theory of Political Economy* was published in 1871 was it properly made public. The root of his inspiration was

Bentham's 'felicific calculus' of pleasure and pain. Although *Theory of Political Economy* provides only half the entire field of micro-economics – the theory of consumer behaviour – the book, along with the treatises of Menger and Walras, must be considered as opening up a new period in economic theorising. The preface to the second edition, together with a bibliography of works on mathematical economics dating back to 1711, did much to teach the generation that came after him about the long history of marginal analysis and utility theory in the century before 1871.

Publications *Books:* 1. *Investigations in Currency and Finance* (1863–84); 2. *The Coal Question* (1865); 3. *The Theory of Political Economy* (1871, 1957, 1970); 4. R.D. Collison Black, ed. *Papers and correspondence of William Stanley Jevons*, 7 vols (1972–81).

Secondary Literature J.M. Keynes, *Essays in Biography* (Macmillan, 1933, 1972); T.W. Hutchison, 'Jevons, William Stanley', *IESS*, vol. 8; R.D. Collison Black, 'W.S. Jevons', *Pioneers of Modern Economics in Britain*, eds D.P. O'Brien and J.R. Presley (Macmillan, 1981).

JOHANNSEN, Nicolaus August Ludwig Jacob*

Dates and Birthplace 1844–1928, Germany.

Post Held Businessman.

Career German-American economic 'crank' whose theories were taken seriously by Hobson, Wesley Mitchell and other unorthodox economists. His earlier works were pseudonymous but the *Neglected Point* ... appeared under his own name, and argued that depressions were caused by an 'impaired' form of savings. His subsequent works put forward various methods by which depressions might be avoided, including a form of taxed currency similar to Gesell's stamped money.

Publications *Books:* 1. *Cheap Capital* (pseud. A. Merwin), (1878); 2. *Depressions-Perioden* (pseud. J.J.O. Lahne), (1903); 3. *A Neglected Point in Connection with Crises* (1908); 4. *Die*

Steuer der Zukunft (1913); 5. *The True Way for Deflation* (1920); 6. *Business Depressions* (1925).

Secondary Literature J. Dorfman, 'N.A.L.J. Johannsen: the "amateur economist" ', in *The Economic Mind in American Civilisation*, vol. 3 (The Viking Press, 1949).

JOHANSEN, Leif

Born 1930, Eidsvoll, Norway.

Current Post Prof. Econ., Inst. Econ., Univ. Oslo, Norway, 1965–.

Recent Posts Assoc. prof. Public Fin., Univ. Oslo, 1959–65.

Degrees Candidate Econ., PhD, Univ. Oslo, 1954, 1962.

Offices and Honours Member, Norwegian Academy Sciences, Royal Swedish Academy Sciences; Foreign hon. member, AEA; Fellow, Em Soc, 1966–, Council member, Em Soc, for several periods; Co-ed., assoc. ed., *J Pub E*; Member Ed. Boards of various scientific journals; Fridtjof Nansen award sciences (Norwegian Academy Sciences), 1979.

Principal Contributions Development of a fairly large multi-sectoral growth model (the MSG-model), which includes input-output relationships, factor substitution in production, income generation, price-dependent consumer-demand relations, and other relations for the Norwegian economy. The model has been extensively used in Norwegian long-term planning and projections, and was probably the first empirical elaboration and application of a general equilibrium model (for a moving equilibrium) with endogenous prices and substitution effects. Production economics: the development of a production model in which there are *ex ante* substitution possibilities, but factor proportions rigidities *ex post* (later called 'putty-clay theory'), first in the context of economic growth theory, and later as a contribution to general theory of production. Various contributions to public economics, especially the formal elaboration of the Lindahl theory of public expenditure and the interpretation of this theory on the basis of modern welfare theory. The synthesising of various approaches to theory and methodology of economic policy and planning; more special contributions in such fields as complete systems of demand functions, dynamic input-output analysis, etc.

Publications *Books:* 1. *A multi-sectoral Study of Economic Growth* (N-H, 1960, 1974); 2. *Public Economics* (N-H, Oslo Univ. Press, 1965); 3. *Production Functions. An Integration of Micro- and Macro, Short-run and Long-run Aspects* (N-H, 1972); 4. *Lectures on Macro-economic Planning*, 2 vols (N-H, 1977–8).

Articles: 1. 'Substitution versus fixed production coefficients in the theory of economic growth: a synthesis', *Em*, 27, April 1959; 2. 'Rules of thumb for the expansion of industries in a process of economic growth', *Em*, 28, April 1960; 3. 'Some notes on the Lindahl theory of determination of public expenditures', *Int ER*, 4, Sept. 1963; 4. 'On the theory of dynamic input-output models with different time profiles of capital construction and finite life-time of capital equipment', *JET*, 19(2), Dec. 1978; 5. 'The bargaining society and the inefficiency of bargaining', *Kyklos*, 32(3), 1979.

JOHNSON, David Gale

Born 1916, Vinton, Iowa, USA.

Current Post Eliakim Hastings Moore Disting. service prof. Econ., Chairman, Dept. Econ., 1980–, Univ. Chicago, USA.

Recent Posts Dean, Div. Social Sciences, 1960–70, Chairman, Dept. Econ., 1971–4, Provost, 1975–80, Univ. Chicago.

Degrees BS, PhD, Iowa State Coll., 1938, 1945; MS Univ. Wisconsin, 1939.

Offices Dir., US SSRC, 1953–6; Agric. Board Nat. Res. Council, NAS, 1958–61; Pres., 1964–5, Fellow, 1968–, AAEA; Member, Exec. Comm., Div. Behavioral Sciences, Nat. Res. Council, NAS, 1969–73; Fellow, AAAS, 1976–.

Principal Contributions Showing the ineffectiveness of agricultural price policies in increasing the incomes of low-income farmers and proving incomes in rural areas are increased primarily through the transfer of labour resources out of agriculture. Showing that institutional arrangements, such as share renting of agricultural land, that survive over the centuries are almost certainly efficient, even though economists often argue to the contrary, and that programmes that result in stable prices of food products in a given country or region result in increased price instability in international markets for the same products. For many agricultural products the primary source of price instability is the actions of man and not variability in production.

Publications *Books:* 1. *Forward Prices for Agriculture* (Univ. Chicago Press, 1947, Arno Press, 1976); 2. *Agriculture and Trade: A Study of Inconsistent Policies* (Wiley, 1950); 3. *World Agriculture in Disarray* (Macmillan, 1973); 4. *World Food Problems and Prospects* (Amer. Enterprise Inst., 1975); 5. *The Soviet Impact on World Grain Trade* (British-North American Comm. 1977).

Articles: 1. 'The nature of the supply function for agricultural products', *AER*, 40, Sept. 1950; 2. 'Resource allocation under share contracts', *JPE*, 58, April 1950; 3. 'Output and income effects of reducing the farm labor force', *JFE*, 62, Nov. 1960; 4. 'Increased stability of grain supplies in developing countries: optimal carryovers and insurance', in *The New International Economic Order: the North-South debate*, ed. J. Bhagwati (MIT Press, 1977); 5. 'International prices and trade in reducing the distortions of incentives', in *Distortions of Agricultural Incentives*, ed. T.W. Schultz (Indiana Univ. Press, 1978).

JOHNSON, G.E.

N.e.

JOHNSON, Harry G.*

Dates and Birthplace 1923–79, Toronto, Canada.

Posts Held Acting prof., St Francis Xavier Univ., 1943–4; Instructor, Univ. Toronto, 1946–7; Ass. lecturer, 1949, Lecturer, 1950–6, Univ. Camb.; Prof.,

Univ. Manchester, 1956–9; Prof., 1959–, Charles F. Grey Disting. service prof., 1974–, Univ. Chicago; Prof., LSE, 1966–74; Prof., Grad. Inst. Internat. Stud., Geneva, 1976–.

Degrees BA, MA, Univ. Toronto, 1943, 1947; BA, MA, Univ. Camb., 1946, 1951; MA, PhD, Harvard Univ. 1948, 1958; MA, DSc. Univ. Manchester, 1960, 1972; Hon. LLD St Francis Xavier Univ., 1965, Univ. Windsor, 1966, Queen's Univ., Ontario, 1967, Univ. Sheffield, 1969, Carleton Univ., 1970, Univ. Western Ontario, 1973.

Offices and Honours Fellow, AAAS, 1962, BA, 1969, Em Soc, 1972, Royal Soc. Canada, 1976; Pres., Canadian Polit. Science Assoc., 1965–6; Chairman, UK AUTE, 1968–71; Pres., Section F, BAAS, 1972–3; Pres., EEA, 1976–7; Vice-pres., AEA, 1976; Officer, Order Canada, 1976.

Career As one of the most prolific economists of his generation, he contributed to the formulation and development of the theory of effective protection, the concept of the 'scientific' tariff, the monetary approach to balance-of-payments problems, and the two-factor, two-sector model of general equilibrium, both in the context of comparative statics and economic growth. Also his writings helped to lead macro-economists to a new and continually evolving synthesis of Keynesian thinking with the neo-classical tradition of micro-economics. Finally, he wrote expertly on a wide variety of special topics, such as brain drain, the economics of R & D, and the economics of higher education.

Publications Books: 1. *International Trade and Economic Growth: Studies in Pure Theory* (A & U, 1958); 2. *Economic Policies Toward Less Developed Countries* (Brookings Inst., 1967); 3. *Essays in Monetary Economics* (A & U, 1967, 1969); 4. *Aspects of the Theory of Tariffs* (A & U, 1971); 5. *On Economics and Society* (Univ. Chicago Press, 1975).

Articles: 1. 'Optimum tariffs and retaliation', *REStud*, 21(2), 1954; 2. 'The cost of protection and the scientific tariff', *JPE*, 68(4), Aug. 1960; 3. 'Monetary theory and policy', *AER*, 52(3), June 1962; 4. 'The monetary approach to balance-of-payments theory', *J Fin Quantitative Analysis*, 7, March 1972.

Secondary Literature J.N. Bhagwati and J.A. Frankel, 'Johnson, Harry G.', *IESS*, vol. 18.

JOHNSON, Robert W.

Born 1921, Denver, Col., USA.

Current Post Prof. Management, Krannert Grad. School Management, Purdue Univ., West Lafayette, Indiana, USA.

Recent Posts Lecturer, Prof. Fin., Univ. Buffalo, 1950–9; Prof. Fin. Admin., Michigan State Univ., 1959–64.

Degrees MBA Harvard Bus. School, 1946; PhD Northwestern Univ., 1950.

Offices Vice-pres., Dir., AFA, 1969; Pres., Fin. Management Assoc., 1971.

Principal Contributions Research on the costs and benefits of various types of government regulations in the area of consumer and mortgage credit. Studies of pricing policies, industry structure, and anti-trust issues in the consumer credit field. In the area of finance, most research and publication has been in the area of capital investment and financial management.

Publications Books: 1. *Financial Management* (Allyn & Bacon, 1959, 1971, with R. Melicher, 1982); 2. *Self-correcting Problems in Finance* (with R.I. Robinson), (Allyn & Bacon, 1971, 1976); 3. *Capital Budgeting* (Kendall/Hunt Publishing Co., 1977).

Articles: 1. 'Regulation of finance charges on consumer instalment credit', *Michigan Law Review*, 66, 1967; 2. 'Better way to monitor accounts receivable', *Harvard Bus. Review*, 50, 1972; 3. 'Denial of self-help repossession: an economic analysis', *Southern Cal. Law Review*, 47, 1973; 4. 'Consumer credit regulation: illusion or reality', *Bus. Lawyer*, 33, 1978; 5. 'Pricing of bank card services', *J Retail Banking*, 1, 1979.

JOHNSON, Thomas

Born 1934, Halletsville, Texas, USA.

Current Post Prof. Econ. and Stats., N. Carolina State Univ., USA.

Recent Posts Ass. prof. Econ. and Stats., Southern Methodist Univ., 1969–74, Assoc. prof., 1974; Assoc. prof., Econ. and Stats., N. Carolina State Univ., 1974–8.

Degrees AA (Maths.) Navarro Coll., 1955; BA (Maths.) Univ. Texas, 1957; MA (Maths.) Texas Christian Univ., 1962; MES (Experimental Stats.), PhD (Econ. and Stats.), N. Carolina State Univ., 1967, 1969.

Offices and Honours Member, AEA, Em Soc, ASA; Phi Theta Kappa, 1955; Pi Mu Epsilon, 1961; Phi Kappa Phi, 1967; Outstanding Young Men in Amer., 1972; Amer. Men and Women of Science, 1973.

Principal Contributions Economic research has focused on the economics of renewable resources with particular emphasis on human capital. Econometric research has focused on models with qualitative and limited dependent variables. Also concerned with improving the teaching of economics.

Publications *Books:* 1. *Toward Economic Understanding* (with P. Heyne), (Science Res. Assoc., 1976); 2. *A Student's Guide to Economic Understanding* (Science Res. Assoc., 1976).

Articles: 1. 'A model for returns from investment in human capital', *AER*, 60(4), Sept. 1970; 2. 'Qualitative and limited dependent variables in economic relationships', *Em*, 40(3), May 1972; 3. 'Selection without (unfair) discrimination', *Communications in Statistics – Theory and Methods*, A7(11), 1978; 4. 'Time in school: the case of the prudent patron', *AER*, 68(5), Dec. 1978; 5. 'Allocation of time by married couples approaching retirement' (with R.L. Clark and A.A. McDermed), *Social Security Bull.*, 43(4), April 1980.

JOHNSON, William Ernest*

Dates and Birthplace 1859–1931, Cambridge, England.

Posts Held Sidgwick Lecturer, 1886–1931, Fellow, King's Coll., 1902–31, Univ. Camb.

Degrees BA, MA, Univ. Camb., 1882, 1885.

Offices Fellow, BA, 1926.

Career Logician who, seemingly unaware of Fisher and Pareto, took the indifference curves in Edgeworth's *Mathematical Psychics* and turned them upside down. He called these 'iso-utility' curves, and they have been used in this form ever since. However, Johnson's work, and that of Slutsky, was independently rediscovered by Hicks and Allen to whom its use must be attributed.

Publications *Books:* 1. *Logic*, 3 vols (1921–4).

Articles: 1. 'On certain questions connected with demand' (with C.P. Sanger), *Camb. Econ. Club*, 1894; 2. 'The pure theory of utility curves', *EJ*, 23, Dec. 1913, repr. in *Precursors in Mathematical Economics: An Anthology*, eds W.J. Baumol and S.M. Goldfeld (LSE 1978).

JOHNSTON, Bruce Foster

Born 1919, Lincoln, Nebraska, USA.

Current Post Prof., Economist, Food Res. Inst., Stanford Univ., USA.

Recent Posts Consultant, Amer. Development Bank, 1976, ILO, 1977, World Bank, 1978, 1980, 1981, FAO, 1980; Vis. Res. Scholar, Internat. Inst. Applied Systems Analysis, Vienna, Austria, 1978–9.

Degrees BA (Polit. Science) Cornell Univ., 1941; MA (Econ.), PhD (Agric. Econ.), Stanford Univ., 1950, 1953.

Offices Guggenheim Memorial Foundation Fellow, 1962; Joint FAO/WHO Expert Comm. Nutrition, 1974–5.

Principal Contributions Analysis of the agricultural development experience of Japan and Taiwan; elucidation of the role of agriculture in economic development and of agriculture-industry interactions in the development process; description and analysis of the food and agricultural economies of sub-Saharan Africa; and study of health, nutrition, and family planning programmes as components of a rural development strategy.

Publications *Books:* 1. *The Staple Food Economies of Western Tropical Africa* (Stanford Univ. Press, 1958); 2. *Agricultural Development and Eco-*

nomic Growth, ed. (with H.M. Southworth), (Cornell Univ. Press, 1967); 3. *Agriculture and Structural Transformation: Economic Strategies in Late-developing Countries* (with P. Kilby), (OUP, 1975); 4. *Agricultural Change in Tropical Africa* (with K.R.M. Anthony *et al.*), (Cornell Univ. Press, 1979); 5. *Redesigning Rural Development: A Strategic Perspective* (with W.C. Clark), (Johns Hopkins Univ. Press, 1981).

Articles: 1. 'The seed-fertilizer revolution and labor force absorption' (with J. Cownie), *AER*, 59(4), Pt 1, Sept. 1969; 2. 'The Japanese "model" of agricultural development: its relevance to developing nations', in *Agriculture and Economic Growth: Japan's Experience*, ed. (with K. Ohkawa and H Kaneda), (Tokyo Univ. Press, 1969); 3. 'Agriculture and structural transformation in developing countries: a survey of research', *JEL*, 8(2), June 1970; 4. 'Food, health, and population in development', *JEL*, 15(3), Sept. 1977.

JOHNSTON, Jack

Born 1923, Belfast, N. Ireland.
Current Post Prof. Econ., Univ. Cal., Irvine, USA.
Recent Posts Prof. Econometrics, 1959–67, Stanley Jevons Prof. Econometrics 1967–78, Univ. Manchester, England.
Degrees BComSc. Queen's Univ., Belfast, 1947; PhD Univ. Wales, 1957; Hon. MA (Econ.) Univ. Manchester, 1962.
Offices AEA, ASA, RES, RSS; Fellow, Em Soc, 1963.
Principal Contributions A series of studies in applied econometrics, especially in the areas of statistical cost functions and labour productivity; the clarification and exposition of econometric methods; and theoretical and empirical studies of wage and price inflation.
Publications *Books:* 1. *Statistical Cost Analysis* (McGraw-Hill, 1960, Spanish transl., 1961); 2. *Econometric methods* (McGraw-Hill, 1963, 1972, Japanese, Spanish, Portuguese, Italian and Hindi transls.).

Articles: 1. 'An econometric study of the production decision', *QJE*, 75, May 1961; 2. 'The productivity of management consultants', *JRSS*, 126(2), 1963; 3. 'A model of wage determination under bilateral monopoly', *EJ*, 82, Sept. 1972; 4. 'A macro-model of inflation', *EJ*, 85, June 1975; 5. 'The elusive Phillips curve', *J Macroecon*, 2(4), Fall 1980.

JONES, Richard*

Dates and Birthplace 1790–1855, Tunbridge Wells, England.
Posts Held Clergyman; Prof. Polit. Econ., King's Coll., Univ. London, 1833–5, Haileybury Coll., 1835–55.
Degree MA Univ. Camb., 1819.
Offices Member, UK Tithe Commission and Charity Commission.
Career As a member of the Cambridge circle, which included Whewell and Herschel, he became a devotee of the inductive method in the sciences and was determined to apply it to political economy. His volume on rent was the only part of his *Essay* ... which he completed, and consisted of a categorisation of forms of rent extending much beyond that described by Ricardo. This form of attack on Ricardian economics met with little success, but he is now widely looked on as a precursor of the historical school in Britain.
Publications *Books:* 1. *Essay on the Distribution of Wealth and on the Sources of Taxation*, vol. 1, *Rent* (1831); 2. *Literary Remains*, ed. W. Whewell (1859, 1964).
Secondary Literature L.G. Johnson, *Richard Jones Reconsidered* (1955); W.L. Miller, 'Richard Jones's contribution to the theory of rent', *HOPE*, 9(3), Fall 1977.

JONES, R.W.

N.e.

JOPLIN, Thomas*

Dates and Birthplace 1790(?)-1847, Newcastle upon Tyne, England.
Posts Held Timber merchant and banker.

Career His *Essay* ... attacked the monopoly of the Bank of England and proposed the setting up of joint stock banks. This attracted considerable notice and his ideas were at the root of the.system initiated in 1828. Joplin's own banking ventures brought him little profit and he died in some obscurity. His subsequent writings were largely ignored.

Publications *Books:* 1. *An Essay on the General Principles and Present Practices of Banking in England and Scotland* (1822); 2. *Outlines of a System of Political Economy* (1823); 3. *Views on the Subject of Corn and Currency* (1826); 4. *An Analysis and History of the Currency Question* (1832); 5. *The Cause and Cure of our Commercial Embarrassments* (1841).

JORGENSON, Dale W.

Born 1933, Bozeman, Montana, USA.

Current Post Frederick Eaton Abbe Prof. Econ., Harvard Univ., USA.

Recent Posts Ass. prof., Assoc. prof., Prof. Econ., Univ. Cal., Berkeley, 1959–69; Prof. Econ., Harvard Univ., 1969–.

Degrees BA Reed Coll., 1955; MA, PhD, Harvard Univ., 1957, 1959.

Offices and Honours Fellow, Em Soc, 1964, ASA, 1965, AAAS, 1969; John Bates Clark medal, AEA, 1971; Member, NAS, 1978.

Principal Contributions Originator of the neo-classical theory of investment, based on the rental price of capital services, and the application of this theory to the analysis of tax policy and the explanation of productivity change. Originator of the neo-classical theory of development of a dual economy. Originator of rational distributed lag functions and their application to the econometric modelling of investment. Originator of transcendental logarithmic production and cost functions and direct and indirect utility functions. Originator of dynamic general equilibrium models for the analysis of energy and economic growth.

Publications *Articles:* 1. 'Capital theory and investment behavior', *AER*, 53(2), May 1963, repr. in *Readings in Business Cycles*, eds R.A. Gordon and L.R. Klein (Richard D. Irwin, 1965); 2. 'The embodiment hypothesis', *JPE*, 74(1), Feb. 1966; 3. 'Testing alternative theories of the development of a dual economy', in *The Theory and Design of Economic Development*, eds I. Adelman and E. Thorbecke (Johns Hopkins Univ. Press, 1966), repr. in Bobbs-Merrill Reprint Series in Economics, Econ.-168, and in *Development Digest*, 4(2), July 1966; 4. 'The explanation of productivity change' (with Z. Griliches), *REStud*, 34(99), July 1967, repr. in *Growth Economics*, ed. A.K. Sen (Penguin Books, 1970), and *Survey Current Bus.*, 52(5), Pt 2, May 1972; 5. 'Econometric studies of investment behavior: a review', *JEL*, 9(4), Dec. 1971.

JOSKOW, Paul L.

Born 1947, New York City, NY, USA.

Current Post Prof. Econ., Dept Econ., MIT, USA.

Recent Posts Vis. prof., Harvard Univ., 1979–80.

Degrees BA Cornell Univ., 1968; MPhil., PhD, Yale Univ., 1971, 1972.

Offices AEA, Em Soc; Nat. Econ. Res. Assoc., Special Consultant; Admin. Conference US.

Principal Contributions Research work has focused on the interrelationships between private firms and government. Theoretical and empirical work on the behaviour of firms subject to regulatory constraints and the behaviour of regulatory commissions. Industries studied include the electric power industry, the property/liability insurance industry, the uranium industry, the nuclear power industry and the hospital system. In addition research contributions have been made in the areas of peak load pricing, anti-trust policy, econometric models of fuel use, financial modelling and oligopoly theory.

Publications *Books:* 1. *Electric Power in the United States: Models and Policy Analysis* (with M. Baughman and D. Kamat), (MIT Press, 1979); 2. *Controlling Hospital Costs: the Role of*

Government Regulation (MIT Press, 1981).

Articles: 1. 'Inflation and environmental concern: structural change in the process of public utility price regulation', *J Law E,* 17(2), Oct. 1974; 2. 'Firm decision-making processes and oligopoly theory', *AER*, 65(2), May 1975; 3. 'Electric utility fuel choice behavior in the United States' (with F.S. Mishkin), *Int ER*, 18(3), Oct. 1977; 4. 'The effects of learning by doing on nuclear power plant operating reliability', *REStat*, 61(2), May 1979; 5. 'The effects of competition and regulation on hospital bed supplies and the reservation quality of the hospital', *Bell JE*, 11(2), Autumn 1980.

JUGLAR, Clement*

Dates and Birthplace 1819–1905, France.

Posts Held Physician; Teacher Stats, L'Ecole Libre des Sciences Polit.

Offices Founder, Soc. de Stat. de Paris; Pres., Soc. d'Econ. Sociale; Member, Académie des Sciences Morales et Polit., 1892.

Career From his early background in medicine he brought to the study of economics a scientific training and an interest in demographic phenomena. He turned immediately to the question of commercial crises of which he became the first theorist. He saw these in the context of economic cycles which occur naturally, cannot be avoided, but can be predicted. His use of statistics was able and imaginative and he proved to be a remarkably accurate predictor of the turning points in business cycles.

Publications *Books:* 1. *Des crises commerciales et de leur retour périodique* (1862); 2. *Du change et de la liberté d'émission* (1868); 3. *Les Banques de dépôt d'escompte et d'émission* (1884).

Articles: 1. 'Des crises commerciales', *Annuaire de l'écon. polit.*, 13, 1856.

Secondary Literature A. Marchal, 'Juglar, Clément', *IESS*, vol. 8.

JUSTER, F. Thomas

Born 1926, Hollis, NY, USA.

Current Post Prof. Econ., Dir., Inst. Social Res., Univ. Michigan, USA.

Recent Posts Vice-pres. Res., NBER, 1968–72; Program Dir., Survey Res. Center, 1973–5.

Degrees BS (Education) Rutgers Univ., 1949; PhD (Econ.), Columbia Univ., 1956.

Offices AEA, 1956–; Member, 1960–, Fellow, 1967–, ASA; AFA, 1965–72; Chairman, Bus. Econ. Section, ASA, 1971; ASA Advisory Comm. US Census Bureau, 1973–9; Chairman, NAS Comm. Data Needs for Energy Consumption, 1975–6; Advisory Comm., US Congressional Budget Office, 1976–; Chairman, Exec. Comm. Conference RIW, 1979–.

Principal Contributions The methodology of measuring behavioural phenomena, and the use of such behavioural measurements in modelling household behaviour; these include analyses of the role of finance rates and charges on consumer-borrowing decisions, and of the role of uncertainty in consumer-saving decisions. In recent years, principal contributions have been the development of social accounting systems focused on the use of non-market time for the production of various types of household outputs. Analysis has focused on the joint contributions of wealth, defined very broadly to include non-economic states of being, and of time in the production of societal well-being.

Publications *Books:* 1. *Anticipations and Purchases: An Analysis of Consumer Behavior* (Princeton Univ. Press, 1964); 2. *Consumer Sensitivity to Finance Rates: An Empirical and Analytical Investigation* (with R.P. Shay), (Columbia Univ. Press, 1964); 3. *Household Capital Formation and Financing: Growth and Cyclical Behavior, 1897–1962* (Columbia Univ. Press, 1966); 4. *Education, Income and Human Behavior*, ed. and contributor (Columbia Univ. Press, 1975); 5. *The distribution of economic well-being*, ed. (Columbia Univ. Press, 1978).

Articles: 1. 'Consumer buying intentions and purchase probabilities: an experiment in survey design', *JASA*, 61, Sept. 1966; 2. 'Microdata, economic research, and the production of economic knowledge', *AER*, 60(2), May 1970; 3. 'Inflation and the consumer' (with P. Wachtel), *Brookings Papers Econ. Activity*, 1, 1972; 4. 'A framework for the measurement of economic and social performance', in *The Measurement of Economic and Social Performance*, ed. M. Moss (Columbia Univ. Press, 1973); 5. 'A theoretical framework for the measurement of well-being' (with P. Courant and G.K. Dow), *IRIW*, 1981.

K

KAHN, Alfred E.

Born 1917, Paterson, NJ, USA.
Current Post Robert Julius Thorne Prof. Econ., Cornell Univ., 1967–; Special consultant, Nat. Econ. Res. Assocs, New York.
Recent Posts Chairman, Dept. Econ., 1958–63, Dean, Coll. Arts, Sciences, 1969–74, Cornell Univ.; Chairman, NY State Public Service Commission, 1974–7; Chairman, Civil Aeronautics Board, 1977–8; Chairman, US Council Wage Price Stability, 1978–80; Adviser to US President on Inflation, 1978–80.
Degrees BA (*Summa cum laude*), MA NYU 1936, 1937; PhD Yale Univ., 1942; Hon. LLD Colby Coll., 1978, Univ. Massachusetts, 1979, Ripon Coll., 1980.
Offices and Honours NYU Alumni achievement award; Fellow, AAAS; Member, Board Eds., *AER*, 1961–4; Board Econ. Advisers, Amer. Telephone Telegraph, 1968–74; Exec. Comm. Nat. Assoc. Regulatory Utility Commissioners, 1974–8.
Principal Contributions Anti-trust policy and industrial regulation of public utilities, particularly the oil industry.
Publications *Books:* 1. *Great Britain in the World Economy* (Columbia Univ. Press, 1946, 1968); 2. *Fair Competition: The Law and Economics of Anti-trust Policy* (with J.B. Dirlam), (Cornell Univ. Press, 1954, 1970); 3. *Integration and Competition in the Petroleum Industry* (with M.G. DeChazeau), (Yale Univ. Press, 1959, Kennikat Press, 1973); 4. *The Economics of Regulation*, 2 vols (Wiley, 1970, 1971).
Articles: 1. 'Investment criteria in development programs', *QJE*, 65, Feb. 1951; 2. 'Standards for anti-trust policy', *Harvard Law. Review*, 67, Nov. 1953, reprinted in AEA, *Readings in Industrial Organization and Public Policy*, eds R.B. Heflebower and G.W. Stocking (Richard D. Irwin, 1958); 3. 'The depletion allowance in the context of cartelization', *AER*, 54, June 1964; 4. 'Market power inflation: a conceptual framework', in *The New Inflation in Industrial Economies*, ed. J. Blair (Lenox Hill Publishing Co., 1974); 5. 'Applications of economics to an imperfect world', *AER*, 69(2), May 1979.

KAHN, Richard

Born 1905, London, England.
Current Post Emeritus Prof. Econ., Univ. Camb.; Fellow, King's Coll., Univ. Camb.
Recent Posts Prof. Econ., Univ. Camb.
Degrees BA, MA Univ. Camb., 1927, 1931.
Offices and Honours Fellow, BA. Created life peer 1974.
Principal Contributions As a member of the Cambridge group of economists, worked with Keynes, and helped to develop Keynesian thought and theory of growth. Worked on application of economic theory to national and international practical economic problems, including that of inflation.
Publications *Books:* 1. *Selected Essays on Employment and Growth* (CUP, 1972); 2. *The Making of Keynes' General Theory* (CUP, 1981).
Articles: 1. 'Some aspects of the development of Keynes's thought', *JEL*, 16(3), June 1978.

KAIN, John F.

Born 1935, Fort Wayne, Ind. USA.
Current Post Prof. Econ., 1969–,

Prof. City Regional Planning, Grad. School Design (Chairman Dept 1975–80), Kennedy School Govt, 1980–, Harvard Univ.

Recent Posts Sr staff member, Rand Corp., Santa Monica, 1961–2; Assoc. prof., Dept. Econ., US Air Force Academy, 1962–4.

Degrees BA Bowling Green State Univ., 1957; MA, PhD Univ. Cal., Berkeley, 1961, 1961; Hon. MA Harvard Univ., 1964.

Offices AEA; Em Soc; Amer. Planning Assoc.; Amer. Inst. Certified Planners; Urban Land Inst.

Principal Contributions Author of several papers identifying links between housing market segregation, discrimination and low levels of Black home-ownership and wealth. Head of 10–year project to develop NBER Urban Simulation Model and to apply it to the analysis of housing and urban development programs and policies.

Publications 1. *The Urban Transportation Problem* (with J.R. Meyer and M. Wohl), (Harvard Univ. Press, 1965); 2. *Empirical Models of Urban Land Use* (with H.J. Brown *et al.*), (NBER, 1971); 3. *The Detroit Prototype of the NBER Urban Simulation Model* (with G.K. Ingram and J.R. Ginn), (NBER, 1972); 4. *Housing Markets and Racial Discrimination: A Micro-economic Analysis* (with J.M. Quigley), (NBER, 1975); 5. *Essays on Urban Spatial Structure* (Ballinger Publishing Co., 1975).

Articles: 1. 'Housing segregation, Negro employment, and metropolitan decentralization', *QJE*, 82(2), May 1968; 2. 'How to improve transportation at practically no cost', *Public Pol.*, 20(3), Summer 1972; 3. 'Housing market discrimination, homeownership, and savings behaviour' (with J.M. Quigley), *AER*, 62(3), June 1972; 4. 'Cumulative urban growth and urban density functions' (with D. Harrison Jr), *JUE*, Jan. 1974; 5. 'Simulation of housing market dynamics' (with W.C. Apgar), *Amer. Real Estate Urban Econ. Assoc. J*, 7(4), Winter 1980.

KALDOR, Nicholas

Born 1908, Budapest, Hungary.
Current Post Prof. Emeritus, Fellow, King's Coll., Univ. Camb.
Recent Posts Ass. lecturer, Reader Econ., LSE, 1932–47; Res. assoc., Nat. Inst. Econ. Planning and Social Res., 1943–5; Chief, Econ. Planning Staff, US Strategic Bombing Survey, 1945; Dir., Res. and Planning Div., ECE, Geneva, 1947–9; Member, UN group of experts on internat. measures for full employment, 1949; Fellow, King's Coll., 1949–, Reader Econ., 1952–65, Prof. Econ., 1966–75, Univ. Camb.; Member, UK Royal Commission on Taxation of Profits and Income, 1951–5; Adviser on tax reform, Govt India, 1956; Econ. adviser, UN ECLA, Santiago, Chile, 1956; Fiscal adviser, Govs Ceylon (1958), Mexico (1960), British Guiana (1961), Turkey (1962), Iran (1966), Venezuela (1976); Ford vis. res. prof., UCLA, 1959–60; Econ. adviser, Govt Ghana, 1961; Vis. economist, Reserve Bank Australia, 1963; Special adviser, UK Chancellor of the Exchequer, 1964–8, 1974–6.

Degrees BSc. (Econ., First class hons) LSE, 1930; Hon. Dr Univ. Dijon.

Offices and Honours Fellow, BA, 1963; Hon. Fellow, LSE, 1970; Pres., Section F, BAAS, 1970; Pres., RES, 1974–6; Created life peer, 1974; Hon. member, AAAS, AEA, RES of Belgium, Hungarian Academy of Sciences, 1979.

Principal Contributions See introductions to *Collected economic essays*, particularly vols 1 and 3.

Publications *Books:* 1. *Statistical Analysis of Advertising Expenditure and Revenue of the Press* (with A. Silberston), (NIESR, CUP, 1948); 2. *National and International Measures for Full Employment*, principal author (UN, 1949); 3. *An Expenditure Tax* (A & U, 1955); 4. *Indian Tax Reform* (Indian Dept Econ. Affairs, 1956); 5. *Reports on Taxation*, 2 vols (Duckworth, 1979).

Articles: 1. *Essays on Value and Distribution* (Duckworth, Free Press, 1960); 2. *Essays on Economic Stability and Growth* (Duckworth, Free Press,

1960); 3. *Essays on Economic Policy*, 2 vols (Duckworth, Norton, 1964, 1965); 4. *Further Essays on Economic Theory* (Duckworth, 1978); 5. *Further Essays on Applied Economics* (Duckworth, 1978).

Secondary Literature L.L. Pasinetti, 'Kaldor, Nicholas', *IESS*, vol. 18.

KALECKI, Michal*

Dates and Birthplace 1899–1970, Lodz, Russia (now Poland).
Posts Held Econ. journalist; Employee, Polish Res. Inst. Bus. Cycles and Prices, 1929–37; Oxford Inst. Stats, 1940–5; Economist, UN, 1946–54; Govt economist, teacher of econ., Poland, 1955–67.
Degree Student Gdansk Polytechnic.
Offices Member, Polish Academy Sciences, 1966.
Career Acknowledged posthumously as an independent creator of many of the elements of the 'Keynesian' system. A Marxist of an individual kind, he worked in capitalist and socialist countries and was critical of both economic systems. He used statistics and mathematical methods extensively, first to make his theorising congruent with current circumstances and second, to give it the quality of precision. Along with Oskar Lange, he was responsible for the introduction of modern Western methods in economics into the Eastern bloc. He did not undertake broad economic surveys but concentrated on a number of precise and detailed studies. His most outstanding contributions were in the theory of macroeconomic dynamics.
Publications *Books:* 1. *Essays in the Theory of Economic Fluctuations* (1939); 2. *Studies in Economic Dynamics* (1943); 3. *Studies in the Theory of Business Cycles 1933–9* (1966); 4. *Introduction to the Theory of Growth in a Socialist State* (1969); 5. *Selected Essays on the Dynamics of the Capitalist Economy 1933–70* (1971); 6. *The Last Phase in the Transformation of Capitalism* (1972); 7. *Selected Essays on the Economic Growth of the Socialist and Mixed Economy* (1972).
Secondary Literature G.R. Feiwel,

'Kalecki, Michal', *IESS*, vol. 18; G.R. Feiwel, *The Intellectual Capital of Michal Kalecki* (Univ. of Tennessee Press, 1975).

KAMERSCHEN, David R.

Born 1937, Chicago, Ill., USA.
Current Post Disting. prof. Econ. and Chair Public Utilities, Univ. Georgia, USA 1980–.
Recent Posts Ass. prof., Washington Univ., 1964–6; Assoc. prof., 1966–8, Prof., 1968–74, Univ. Missouri; Dept Head, Prof., Univ. Georgia, 1974–80.
Degrees BS, MA Miami (Ohio) Univ., 1959, 1960; PhD Michigan State Univ., 1964.
Offices Exec. Comm., SEA, 1974–6; Ed., Board Eds, of numerous economic journals.
Principal Contributions Major work has been in applied micro-economics theory and development-population economics. Recent years, particularly active in hypothesis testing in anti-trust and public utility economics, so as to aid society in using its scarce resources more effectively in the formulation of public policy. Tried to keep non-specialists and non-economists informed about what is happening in these areas by pedagogical notes on consulting and testifying experiences.
Publications *Books:* 1. *Readings in Microeconomics* (World Publishing Co., 1967, Wiley, 1969); 2. *Macroeconomics: Selected Readings* (with W.L. Johnson), (Houghton Mifflin Co., 1970); 3. *Economics* (with G.M. Vredeveld), (Cliff Notes, 1975); 4. *Money and Banking* (South-Western Publishing Co., 1980); 5. *Intermediate microeconomic theory* (with L. Valentine), (South-Western Publishing Co., 1981).
Articles: 1. 'An estimation of the "welfare losses" from monopoly in the American economy', *WEJ*, 4(3), Summer 1966; 2. 'Market growth and industry concentration', *JASA*, 63, March 1968; 3. 'The influence of ownership and control of profit rates', *AER*, 58(3), Pt 1, June 1968, 'Corrections', *AER*, 58(5), Dec. 1968; 4. 'Literacy and socioeconomic development', *Rural Sociology*, 33(2), June 1968; 5. 'An economic

approach to the detection and proof of collusion', *Amer. Bus. Law J*, 17(2), Summer 1979.

KAMIEN, Morton I.

Born 1938, Warsaw, Poland.
Current Post Harold L. Stuart Prof. Managerial Econ., J.L. Kellogg Grad. School Management, Northwestern Univ., Evanston, Ill., USA, 1970–.
Recent Posts Carnegie-Mellon Univ., 1963–70.
Degrees BA City Coll. New York, 1960; PhD Purdue Univ., 1964.
Principal Contributions Dynamic models of monopoly behaviour under uncertainty, especially in connection with limit pricing (with N.L. Schwartz). Dynamic models of technical advance especially in regard to the relationship between market structure and the pace of innovative activity (with N.L. Schwartz). Probability of the voting paradox.
Publications *Books:* 1. *Dynamic Optimization* (with N.L. Schwartz), (N-H, 1981); 2. *Market Structure and Innovation* (with N.L. Schwartz), (CUP, 1982).
Articles: 1. 'Limit pricing and uncertain entry' (with N.L. Schwartz), *Em*, 39(3), May 1971; 2. 'Timing of innovations under rivalry' (with N.L. Schwartz), *Em*, 40(1), Jan. 1972; 3. 'Market structure and innovative activity: a survey' (with N.L. Schwartz), *JEL*, 13(1), March 1975; 4. 'On the degree of rivalry for maximum innovative activity' (with N.L. Schwartz), *QJE*, 90(2), May 1976; 5. 'Potential rivalry, monopoly profits and the pact of inventive activity' (with N.L. Schwartz), *REStud*, 45(1), Feb. 1978.

KANTOROVICH, Leonid Vitalievich

Born 1912, St Petersburg, Russia.
Current Post Chief, Laboratory, Inst. System Stud., Academy Science, State Comm. Science and Technique, Moscow, USSR, 1976–.
Recent Posts Chief, Laboratory, Inst. Maths Academy Science, Leningrad, 1940–60; Vice-dir. Siberian Inst. Maths, 1960–71; Chief, Laboratory Inst. Nat. Econ. Management, Moscow, 1971–6.
Degrees Leningrad State Univ. 1930; Full prof. 1934, Dr Sciences 1935, Leningrad Univ.; Hon. Dr Univ. Glasgow, 1966, Univ. Grenoble, 1967, Univ. Helsinki, 1971, Univ. Paris (Sorbonne), 1975, Univ. Camb., 1976, and others.
Offices and Honours Order of Lenin; State premia (Maths) 1949; Lenin premia (Econ.), 1965; Corresponding member, 1958–64, Member, 1964–, Academy Science, USSR; Hon. member, Hungarian Academy Science, 1967, AAAS, 1969, Jugoslav Academy Arts Sciences, 1979; Corresponding member, Engineering Academy, Mexico, 1976; Nobel Prize for Econ., 1975.
Principal Contributions From 1929 in many branches of mathematical analysis: set theory, function theory, functional analysis, numerical mathematics, and computer-technique. Developed the outlines of linear programming in 1939: effective algorithms, objectively determined valuations (shadow prices), many fields of applications. Particularly potential method for transportation problem. Introduced static and dynamic models of current and perspective planning. Considered general problem of optimal use of resources. Applied the optimisation models in the problem of planning, price theory, theory of rent, effectiveness theory of investments, amortisation theory, technical progress, and other problems of a socialist economy.
Publications *Books:* 1. *The Mathematical Method of Production Planning Organisation* (USSR State Publishing House, 1939; English transl., *Management Science*, 1960); 2. *The Best Uses of Economic Resources* (in Russian) (USSR State Publishing House, 1959); 3. *Optimal Solution in Economics* (in Russian) (USSR State Publishing House, 1972); 4. *Essays in Optimal Planning*, ed. J. Smolinski (Wiley, 1976); 5. *Functional Analysis* (USSR State Publishing House, 1977; English transl., 1981).
Articles: 1. 'Functional analysis and applied mathematics', *Uspechi Math. Nauk*, 1949 (in Russian); 2. 'On the

translocation of masses', *Management Science*, 1, 1958; 3. 'Estimating the effectiveness of capital expenditures' (with V.N. Bogachev and V.L. Makarov), *Matekon*, 8(1), Fall 1971; 4. 'Economic problems of science and technical progress', *Scand JE*, 78(5), 1976; 5. 'Mathematical economic modelling of science and technical progress', in *Optimisation and Technical Progress*, 9th IFIP Conference (Springer, 1979).

Secondary Literature L. Johansen, 'L.V. Kantorovich's contribution to economics', *Scand JE*, 78(1), 1976.

KATONA, G.

N.e.

KATZNER, Donald Wahl

Born 1938, Baltimore, Maryland, USA.

Current Post Prof., 1975–, Chairman Dept. Econ., 1976–, Univ. Mass.

Recent Posts Ass. prof., Univ. Pennsylvania, 1965–71; Assoc. prof., 1970–1, Prof., 1971–3, Univ. Waterloo; Lecturer, Univ. Cal., San Diego, 1973–5.

Degrees BA (Maths) Oberlin Coll., 1959; MA (Maths), PhD (Econ.) Univ. Minnesota, 1962, 1965.

Offices AEA, Em Soc.

Principal Contributions Organisation and unification of the subject matter of the theory of demand. Exploration of the problems arising from the introduction of non-quantifiable elements into economic analysis of specific non-quantifiable phenomena.

Publications *Books:* 1. *Static Demand Theory* (Macmillan, 1970); 2. *Choice and the Quality of Life* (SAGE, 1979).

Articles: 1. 'A note on the differentiability of consumer demand functions', *Em*, 36, April 1968; 2. 'A simple approach to existence and uniqueness of competitive equilibria', *AER*, 62(3), June 1972; 3. 'On not quantifying the non-quantifiable', *J Post Keyn E*, 1(2), 1978–9; 4. 'Profits, optimality and the social division of labor in the firm' (with H. Gintis), in *Sociological Economics*, ed. L. Levy-Garboua (SAGE, 1979); 5.

'The formal structure of argument in Professor Apter's *Choice and the Politics of Allocation*', *Pol Meth*, 6, 1979.

KAUTSKY, Karl*

Dates and Birthplace 1854–1938, Prague, Austro-Hungary.

Offices Founder, ed., *Die Neue Zeit*, 1883–1917; German Secretary State Foreign Affairs, 1918.

Career Socialist theorist who in his early career was closely associated with Engels, and was later involved in all the major theoretical and political debates within the German Social Democratic Party and the socialist movement generally. His journalism spread Marxist ideas, he drafted political programmes, opposed Soviet Bolshevism' and in later life did non-Marxian social science research. His considerable output includes historical works, polemical tracts and a major examination of the materialist conception of history.

Publications *Books:* 1. *The Economic Doctrines of Karl Marx* (1887); 2. *The Class Struggle (Erfurt Program)* (1892); 3. *Die Agrarfrage* (1899); 4. *The Road to Power* (1909); 5. *The Dictatorship of the Proletariat* (1918); 6. *Terrorism and Communism* (1919); 7. *Die Materialistische Geschichtsanffassung*, 2 vols (1927).

Secondary Literature J.H. Kautsky, 'Kautsky, Karl', *IESS*, vol. 8.

KEENEY, Ralph Lyons

Born 1944, Lewistown, Montana, USA.

Current Post Head Decision Analysis Group, Woodward-Clyde Consultants, San Francisco, USA.

Recent Posts Ass. assoc. prof. Civil Engineering Management, MIT, 1969–74; Res. Scholar, Internat. Inst. Applied Systems Analysis, Laxenburg, Austria, 1974–6.

Degrees BSc (Engineering) UCLA, 1966; SM (Electrical Engineering) 1967, EE (Electrical Engineering), PhD (Operations Res.) MIT, 1968, 1969.

Offices and Honours Lanchester prize for best English language publication operations res. (*Decisions with Multiple Objectives*) 1976; Council member, ORSA, 1979–82.

Principal Contributions Structuring models of value-judgements for complex situations. Specifically, von Neumann-Morgenstern utility functions are derived from various assumptions. Many applications of these utility functions have been illustrated and used in practical decision situations. Contributions to structuring preferences for groups.

Publications *Books:* 1. *Decisions with Multiple Objectives* (with H. Raiffa), (Wiley, 1976); 2. *Conflicting Objectives in Decisions* ed. (with D. Bell and H. Raiffa), (Wiley, 1977); 3. *Decision Analysis. A Videotape Course* with *Study Guide for Decision Analysis* (with A. Drake), (MIT Center Advanced Engineering Study, 1978); 4. *Siting Energy Facilities* (Academic Press, 1980); 5. *Acceptable risk* (with B. Fischhoff *et al.*), (CUP, 1981).

Articles: 1. 'Multiplicative utility functions', *Operations Res.*, 22, 1974; 2. 'A group preference axiomatization with cardinal utility', *Management Science*, 23, 1976; 3. 'The art of assessing multiattribute utility functions', *Organizational Behavior Human Performance*, 19, 1977; 4. 'Decision analysis – how to cope with increasing complexity', *Management Review*, 68, 1979; 5. 'Evaluating alternatives involving potential fatalities', *Operations Res.*, 28, 1980.

KEESING, Donald B.

Born 1933, London, England.
Current Post Sr economist, World Bank, Washington, DC.
Recent Posts Ass. prof. Econ., Columbia Univ., 1964–8; Assoc. prof. Econ., Stanford Univ., 1968–72; Prof. Econ., Univ. N. Carolina, 1972–5; Development Econ. Dept, World Bank, 1975–.
Degrees BA (Hist.), MA (Econ.), PhD (Econ.) Harvard Univ., 1954, 1956, 1961.
Principal Contributions Explored causes of international trade in manufactures – labour skills, R & D, scale economies, country size and national policies. Also studied education, human resources, and employment in Mexico over long periods; issues relating to income distribution and national development policy; and trade in textile products under the Multi-Fibre Arrangement. At the World Bank worked primarily on manufactured exports from developing countries and surrounding policy issues. Took charge of work on industry and energy demand in first economic report on China.

Publications *Books:* 1. *Trade Policy for Developing Countries* (World Bank Staff Working Paper no. 353, 1979); 2. *Textile Quotas against Developing Countries* (with M. Wolf), (UK Trade Pol. Res. Centre, 1980).

Articles: 1. 'Labor skills and comparative advantage', *AER*, 56(2), May 1966; 2. 'The impact of research and development on United States trade', *JPE*, 75, Feb. 1967; 3. 'Outward-looking policies and economic development', *EJ*, 77, June 1967; 4. 'Structural change early in development: Mexico's changing industrial and occupational structure from 1895 to 1950', *JEH*, 29(4), Dec. 1969; 5. 'Economic lessons from China', *JDE*, 2(1), March 1975.

KELLEY, Allen Charles

Born 1937, Everett, Washington, USA.
Current Post Prof., Duke Univ., N. Carolina, USA.
Recent Posts Univ. Wisconsin, Madison, 1964–71; Vis. prof., Monash Univ., Australia, 1972; Esmee Fairbairn Res. prof., Heriot Watt Univ., Edinburgh, 1978; Res. Scholar, Internat. Inst. Applied Systems Analysis, Laxenburg, Austria, 1979.
Degrees BA PhD Stanford Univ., 1959, 1964.
Offices Member, AEA, Internat. Union Scientific Study Population, Pop. Assoc., Amer.,; Vice-pres., SEA; Phi Beta Kappa, Stanford Univ.; Trustee, Exec. member, Joint Council Econ. Res., New York City.
Principal Contributions Research has focused on the interplay of economic and demographic change. Micro-eco-

nomic studies have revealed the way households in LDCs finance child costs. Macro-economic studies have demonstrated the importance of general equilibrium feedbacks in accounting for the impact of demographic change. Research in economic education has established a benefit-cost methodology for evaluating changes in instructional technology, and has illustrated this methodology with reference to TIPS (Teaching Information Processing System). Research in economic history has utilised the counterfactual method using a general-equilibrium macroeconomic model to gain insights into the impacts of major historical events.

Publications *Books:* 1. *Dualist Economic Development: Theory and History* (with J.G. Williamson and R. Cheetham), (Univ. Chicago Press, 1972); 2. *Lessons from Japanese Development: An Analytical Economic History* (with J.G. Williamson), (Univ. Chicago Press, 1974); 3. *Modelling Urbanization and Economic Growth* (with J.G. Williamson), (Internat. Inst. Applied Systems Analysis, 1980).

Articles: 1. 'Population growth, the dependency rate, and the pace of economic development', *Pop. Stud.*, 27(3), Nov. 1973; 2. 'The role of population in models of economic growth', *AER* 64(2), May 1974; 3. 'Demographic change and the size of the government sector', *SEJ*, 43(2), Oct. 1976; 4. 'Interactions of economic and demographic household behavior', in *Population and Economic Change in Less Developed Countries*, ed. R.A. Easterlin (Univ. Chicago Press, 1979); 5. 'Demographic impacts on demand patterns in the low-income setting', *EDCC*, 30(1), Oct. 1981.

KEMMERER, Edwin Walter*

Dates and Birthplace 1875–1945, Scranton, Penn., USA.
Posts Held Prof. Econ., Cornell Univ., 1906–12; Prof., Princeton Univ., 1912–43.
Degrees Grad., Wesleyan Univ., 1899; PhD Cornell Univ., 1903.
Offices Adviser on currency systems to the Philippines, Mexico, Guatemala, Colombia, South Africa, Chile, Poland, Ecuador, Bolivia, Peru, China and Turkey.
Career A tenacious defender of the gold standard who first made his name as an international economist. He gave frequent service to foreign governments on questions of currency. His interest in money problems began with his Cornell thesis and ended with his determined attacks on the Bretton Woods Agreement. His attachment to the gold standard strengthened with his advancing years and is the theme of most of his writings.
Publications *Books:* 1. *Money and Credit Instruments in their Relation to General Prices* (1907); 2. *Modern Currency Reforms* (1916); 3. *The ABC of the Federal Reserve* (1919); 4. *The Principles of Money* (1935); 5. *ABC of Inflation* (1942); 6. *Gold and the Gold Standard* (1944).
Secondary Literature G.F. Shirras, 'Obituary: Edwin Walter Kemmerer (1875–1945)', *EJ*, 56, June 1946.

KEMP, Murray C.

Born 1926, Melbourne, Australia.
Current Post Res. prof. Econ., Univ. New South Wales, Australia.
Recent Posts Vis. prof., Univs Cal., Berkeley (1969–70), Paris (1976–7), Western Ontario (1977).
Degrees BCom., MA Univ. Melbourne 1947, 1949; PhD Johns Hopkins Univ., 1955.
Offices Fellow, Em Soc, 1964; Keynes Prof., Univ. Essex, 1967–8.
Principal Contributions Has contributed to the pure theory of international trade, to the economic theory relating to exhaustible resources and to the inter-relationships between the two.
Publications *Books:* 1. *The Pure Theory of International Trade* (Prentice-Hall, 1964); 2. *A Contribution to the General Equilibrium Theory of Preferential Trading* (N-H, 1969); 3. *Variational Methods in Economics* (with G. Hadley), (N-H, 1971); 4. *Three Topics in the Theory of International Trade* (N-H, 1976); 5. *Exhaustible Resources, Optimality,*

and trade, ed. (with N.V. Long), (N-H, 1980).

KENDRICK, J.W.

N.e.

KENEN, Peter B.

Born 1932, Cleveland, Ohio, USA.
Current Post Walker Prof. Econ. Internat. Fin., Dir. Internat. Fin. Section, Princeton Univ., NJ, 1971–.
Recent Posts Instructor Econ., 1957–8, Ass. prof., 1958–61, Assoc. prof., 1961–4, Prof. 1964–71, Chairman, Dept. Econ., 1967–9, Provost, 1969–70, Columbia Univ.
Degrees BA Columbia Univ., 1954; MA, PhD, Harvard Univ., 1956, 1958.
Offices and Honours David A. Wells prize, Harvard Univ., 1958–9; Ford Foundation Faculty Res. Fellow, 1962–3; US SSRC Fellow, 1966–7; Fellow, Center Advanced Study Behavioral Sciences, 1971–2; Guggenheim Memorial Foundation Fellow, 1975–6; Univ. medal, Columbia Univ., 1977; Vis. res. prof., Univ. Cal., Berkeley, 1980.
Principal Contributions Research on the pure theory of international trade, with special attention to the measurement of the gains from trade and the role of human capital in the determination of trade patterns. Research on international monetary theory and policy, including contributions to the theory of optimum currency areas, the concept and measurement of the demand for international reserves, the reserve-asset preferences of central banks, and the theory of the balance of payments and exchange-rate determination.
Publications *Books:* 1. *British Monetary Policy and the Balance of Payments, 1951–57* (Harvard Univ. Press, 1960); 2. *International Economics* (Prentice-Hall, 1964, 1971); 3. *A Model of the US Balance of Payments* (D.C. Heath & Co, 1978); 4. *Asset Markets, Exchange Rates, and Economic Integration* (with P.R. Allen), (CUP, 1980); 5. *Essays in International Economics* (Princeton Univ. Press, 1980).

KENNEDY, Charles

Born 1923, London, England.
Current Post Self-employed; Hon. prof. Econ. Theory, Univ. Kent.
Recent Posts Prof. Econ., Univ. West Indies, 1961–6; Prof. Econ. Theory, Univ. Kent, 1966–9.
Degrees BA, MA Univ. Oxford, 1942, 1948.
Offices Dean, Faculty Social Sciences, Univ. West Indies, 1962–4; Dir., Bank Jamaica, 1963–6.
Principal Contributions Welfare economics, the macro-economic analysis of open economies, monetary theory, growth theory, technical progress, warrant theory; most widely recognised contribution has been the development of the theory of induced bias in technical progress. Contributed to the debate leading to the development of inflation accounting in the UK.
Publications *Articles:* 1. 'Concerning utility', *Ec*, N.S. 21, Feb. 1954; 2. 'Induced bias in innovation and the theory of distribution', *EJ*, 74, Sept. 1964; 3. 'Keynesian theory in an open economy', *Social and Econ. Stud.*, 15(1), March 1966; 4. 'A generalisation of the theory of induced bias in technical progress', *EJ*, 83, March 1973; 5. 'Inflation accounting: retrospect and prospect', Univ. Camb. Dept. Applied Econ., *Econ. Pol. Review*, 4, 1978.

KESSEL, Reuben A.*

N.e.

KEYNES, John Maynard*

Dates and Birthplace 1883–1946, Cambridge, England.
Posts Held Civil servant, UK India Office, 1906–8, UK Treasury, 1915–19, 1940–5; Teacher Econ., Univ. Camb., 1908–42; Businessman, including Chairman, Nat. Mutual Life Insurance Co., 1921–38; Journalist for various papers including *The Nation* (Chairman, 1923–9).
Degree MA Univ. Camb., 1905.
Offices and Honours Fellow, BA; Pres., RES; Governor, Internat. Bank

Reconstruction and Development; Dir, Bank of England; Ed., *EJ*, 1911–44; created viscount, 1942.

Career Unquestionably the major figure in twentieth-century British economics and one of the major world figures in the discipline. His reputation does not purely rest on the *General theory*, which initiated the so-called 'Keynesian revolution', but also on his other writings, most notably the *Treatise on Money*, his immensely influential work for government, and his prominent place in the cultural and intellectual life of his day. His trenchant criticism of the 1919 treaty with Germany first raised him to national prominence and effectively undermined support for the treaty. During World War II, he was the chief architect of British economic policy and his contribution to post-war economic reconstruction through his contribution to the Bretton Woods Conference and the founding of the IMF was immense. His early economic work was very much within the Marshallian tradition, but during the crises of the 1920s he came increasingly to identify deflationary policies as the cause of much of the problem. From this beginning he developed his new theory of employment and his theories of interest, wages and money. The gradual, but increasingly widespread, acceptance of all or part of his views raised Keynesianism for a while to the position of a prevailing orthodoxy. In recent years, his star has begun to wane. Even so he remains to this day one of the three or four most influential economists that ever lived.

Publications *Books:* 1. *Indian Currency and Finance* (1913), vol. 1 of *Collected writings of John Maynard Keynes*, eds E. Johnson and D. Moggridge (1971); 2. *The Economic Consequences of the Peace* (1919), vol. 2 of *Collected writings* (1971); 3. *A Treatise on Probability* (1921), vol. 8 of *Collected writings* (1973); 4. *A Tract on Monetary Reform* (1923), vol. 4 of *Collected writings* (1971); 5. *A treatise on Money*, 2 vols, (1930), vols 5, 6 of *Collected writings* (1971); 6. *Essays in Biography* (1933), vol. 10 of *Collected writings* (1972); 7. *The General Theory of Employment, Interest and Money*

(1936), vol. 7 of *Collected writings* (1973).

Secondary Literature R.F. Harrod, *The Life of John Maynard Keynes* (Macmillan 1951), 'Keynes, John Maynard', *IESS*, vol. 8; D.E. Moggridge, *Keynes* (Fontana, 1976).

KEYNES, John Neville*

Dates and Birthplace 1852–1949, Salisbury, England.

Posts Held Fellow, Pembroke Coll., 1876, Registrar, 1910–25, Univ. Camb.

Degrees BSc., MA, DSc. Univ. Camb., 1876, 1891, 1891.

Career Logician and political economist who first made his name with his textbook on logic, which remained much-used both because of the clarity of its exposition and its avoidance of mathematical symbolism. His influential methodological book on economics followed Marshall in somehow reconciling the historical and the abstract deductive method. He was the father of John Maynard Keynes and outlived his son.

Publications *Books:* 1. *Studies and Exercises in Formal Logic* (1884); 2. *The Scope and Method of Political Economy* (1891, 1955).

Secondary Literature C.D. Broad and A.C. Pigou, 'Dr J.N. Keynes (1852–1949)' (obituary), *EJ*, 60, June 1950; D. Dillard, 'Keynes, John Neville', *IESS*, vol. 8.

KEYSERLING, Leon H.

Born 1908, Charleston, S. Carolina, USA.

Current Post Self-employed economist.

Recent Posts Chairman, US President's Council Econ. Advisers, 1949–53; Consulting economist, 1953–71; Voluntary work on US economy, 1971–.

Degrees BA Columbia Univ., 1928; LLB Harvard Law School, 1931; Hon. Dr Bus. Science Bryant Coll., 1965; Hon. Dr Humane Letters Univ. Missouri, 1978.

Offices and Honours Member, AEA, Amer. Polit. Science Assoc.; Phi Beta Kappa, 1928; $10,000 prize, Pabst essay contest, 1944; Hon. member faculty, Industrial Coll. Armed Forces, 1965–.

Principal Contributions Author of important economic and social legislation for the 1933–46 period, also the Humphrey Hawkins Full Employment and Balanced Growth Act, 1978. Prepared economic studies, speeches and articles, congressional testimony and committee reports. Top expert to the Senate Committee on Banking and Currency, 1935–7, and consultant to Congressional Committees, 1937–46, and 1953–.

Publications *Books:* 1. *Taxation of Whom and For What* (Conference on Econ. Progress, 1969); 2. *Prices, Wages and Profits* (Conference on Econ. Progress, 1971); 3. *Full Employment Without Inflation* (Conference on Econ. Progress, 1975); 4. *'Liberal' and 'Conservative' National Economic Policies and their Consequences, 1919–1979* (Conference on Econ. Progress, 1979); 5. *Money, Credit and Interest Rates: Their Gross Mismanagement by the Federal Reserve System* (Conference on Econ. Progress, 1980).

Articles: 1. 'Federal finances and the economy', *Annals Amer. Acad. Pol. Soc. Sci.*, 1–12, Sept. 1968; 2. 'The Keynesian revolution and its pioneers: discussion', *AER*, 62(2), May 1972; 3. 'Toward more realism and relevance in national economic policy', *Atlantic Econ. J*, March 1980; 4. 'Should the President and the Congress obey the law? A case study based upon the 1978 Humphrey Hawkins Act', *Univ. Toledo Coll. Law Review*, March 1981.

KILLINGSWORTH, C.C.

N.e.

KINDLEBERGER, Charles P.

Born 1910, New York City, NY, USA.

Current Post Vis. prof. Econ., Middlebury Coll., Vermont; Prof. Emeritus Econ., MIT, USA.

Recent Posts Prof. Econ., MIT, 1948–81.

Degrees BA Univ. Penn., 1932; MA,

PhD Columbia Univ.; 1934, 1937; D.h.c., Univ. Paris (Sorbonne), 1966; D.h.c., Univ. Ghent, 1971.

Offices and Honours Member, RES, AAAS, EHS, AEA; Vice-pres., AEA, 1966; Disting. Fellow, AEA, 1980; Harms prize, Inst. für Weltwirtschaft, Kiel, 1978.

Principal Contributions Textbook on international economics, now in 6th edn, (with E. Despres and W.S. Salant). Developed theory of US as a bank, conducting international financial intermediation to provide world with liquidity. Interested in hierarchical structure of world financial system, with leading country as lender of last resource. Contributed to the theory of financial crises, their propagation, and halting by last-resort lending. In addition, *Europe's Postwar Growth* applies the Lewis model of growth with unlimited supplies of labour to Europe after World War II. Currently engaged in work on a financial history of Western Europe.

Publications *Books:* 1. *International Short-term Capital Movements* (Columbia Univ. Press, 1937); 2. *Economic Growth in France and Britain, 1851–1950* (Harvard Univ. Press, 1964); 3. *The World in Depression, 1929–1939* (Allen Lane, The Penguin Press, 1973); 4. *Manias, Panic and Crashes* (Basic Books, 1978); 5. *International Money* (A & U, 1981).

Articles: 1. 'Group behavior and international trade', *JPE*, 59, Feb. 1951; 2. 'The formation of single financial centers', *Princeton Studies in International Finance no. 34* (Princeton Univ., 1974); 3. 'Keynesianism vs monetarism in eighteenth- and nineteenth-century France', *HOPE*, 12(4), Winter 1980; 4. 'The rise and fall of the United States in the world economy', in *The Business Cycle and Public Policy, 1929–80, Papers Submitted to the Joint Economic Committee, Congress of the United States* (US Govt Printing Office, 1980).

KING, A. Thomas

Born 1944, Emporia, Kans., USA.

Current Post Economist, Fed. Home

Loan Bank Board, Washington, DC, 1978–.

Recent Posts Lecturer, Ass. prof. Econ., Univ. Maryland, 1970–8; Res. assoc., Bureau Bus. Econ. Res., Univ. Maryland, 1970–8; Brookings Econ. Pol. Fellow, 1976–7.

Degrees BA Stanford Univ., 1966; MPhil., PhD Yale Univ., 1969, 1972.

Offices and Honours Member, Phi Beta Kappa, AEA; Paul Baran award for Sr Essay, 1966; Hon. Woodrow Wilson Fellow, 1966; NSF Fellow, 1966–70; Brookings Econ. Pol. Fellow, 1976–7; Board Eds., *Land Econ*, 1978; Ed., *Housing Fin. Review*, 1980–.

Principal Contributions Investigated the reasons for housing price variations, including the effects of property taxes, local amenities and racial discrimination, showing how these and other characteristics of urban areas could be analysed using computational methods for general equilibrium analysis. A notable paper showed that the household's demand for housing could be analysed in the framework of the Lancastrian 'new demand theory'. Most recently studied institutional and economic influences on mortgage markets.

Publications *Books:* 1. *Property Taxes, Amenities, and Residential Land Values* (Ballinger Press, 1973); 2. *Discrimination in Mortgage Lending: A Study of Three Cities* (NYU, 1981).

Articles: 1. 'Racial discrimination, segregation, and the price of rental housing' (with P. Mieszkowski), *JPE*, 81(3), May/June 1973; 2. 'The demand for housing: a Lancastrian approach', *SEJ*, 43(2), Oct. 1976; 3. 'Computing general equilibrium prices for spatial economics', *REStat*, 53(3), Aug. 1977; 4. 'General equilibrium with externalities: a computational method and urban applications', *JUE*, 7(1), Jan. 1980; 5. 'Socially responsible mortgage lending: some perspectives on HMDA and CRA', *J Amer. Real Estate and Urban Econ. Assoc.*, Spring 1980.

KING, B.F.

N.e.

KING, Gregory*

Dates and Birthplace 1648–1712, Lichfield, England.

Posts Held Surveyor, mapmaker and accountant.

Career Political arithmetician whose only work in this field was his first publication of 1695. This broadsheet summarised the duties payable under the Act of 1694, but King also looked at the demographic implications of the information arising from the assessment of the duties. His estimates of population were not published in his lifetime but were widely known and quoted. His two later tracts include his estimates of family income and expenditure in England, and comparisons of estimated national income and expenditure for England, France and Holland. His estimates were meticulously calculated and internally consistent. His calculations of the price of wheat in relation to variations in the size of the wheat harvest have become known as 'Gregory King's Law'.

Publications *Books:* 1. *A Scheme of the Rates and Duties Granted to His Majesty upon Marriages Births and Burials* (1695); 2. *Two Tracts by Gregory King*, ed. G.E. Barnett (1936), includes 'Natural and political observations and conclusions' (1696), and 'Of the naval trade of England' (1697).

Secondary Literature D.V. Glass, 'Gregory King's estimate of the population of England and Wales 1695', *Population Stud.*, 3, 1950; P. Deane, 'King, Gregory', *IESS*, vol. 8.

KLEIN, Lawrence R.

Born 1920, Omaha, Neb., USA.

Current Post Benjamin Franklin Prof. Econ. Fin., Univ. Pennsylvania, USA.

Degrees BA Univ. Cal., Berkeley, 1942; PhD MIT, 1944.

Offices and Honours Phi Beta Kappa, 1942; Fellow, 1948, Pres., 1960, Em Soc; John Bates Clark medal, AEA, 1959; Member, AAAS, 1961, Amer. Philosophical Soc., 1970, NAS, 1973; William Butler award, 1975; Pres., EEA, 1975; Pres., AEA, 1977; Fellow,

Nat. Assoc. Bus. Economists, 1979; Nobel Prize for Econ., 1980.

Principal Contributions Mathematical modelling of economic systems based on received economic doctrine, with empirical estimation from live data of the actual economy, application of estimated systems to problems of theoretical economic analysis and public policy, including cyclical studies, stochastic fluctuations, dynamic multiplier response, scenario analysis, and prediction. Models studied include developing and centrally planned economies, as well as industrial market economies, together with their international trade and financial inter relationships.

Publications *Books: 1. The Keynesian Revolution* (Macmillan, 1947, 1966); 2. *Economic Fluctuations in the United States, 1921–1941* (Wiley, 1950); 3. *A Textbook of Econometrics* (Row, Peterson, 1953, 1974); 4. *An Econometric Model of the United States, 1929–1952* (with A.S. Goldberger), (Wiley, 1955); 5. *An Introduction to Econometrics* (Row, Peterson, 1962). *Articles: 1.* 'Macroeconomics and the theory of rational behavior', *Em*, 14, April 1946; 2. 'Theories of effective demand and employment', *JPE*, 55, April 1947; 3. 'A comparison of eleven econometric models of the United States' (with G. Gromm), *AER*, 63(2), May 1973; 4. 'Research contributions of the SSRC-Brookings econometric model project – a decade in review', in *The Brookings Model*, eds G. Fromm and L.R. Klein (N-H, 1975).

Secondary Literature R.V. Ball, 'On Lawrence Klein's Contributions to Economics', *Scand JE*, 83(1), 1981.

KLEVORICH, A.K.

N.e.

KLOTEN, Norbert Wilhelm

Born 1926, Sinzig, Rhein, Germany.
Current Posts Pres., Landeszentralbank, Baden-Würtemberg, Stuttgart.
Recent Posts Prof. Econ., Univ. Tübingen, 1960–76; Scholarly expert, Planning Staff, Fed. Chancellory, Bun-

desrepublik, 1967–9; Council Econ. Experts, Bundesrepublik, 1969–76 (Chairman, 1970–6).
Degrees Diploma Polit. Econ., Dr rer. pol. Univ. Bonn, 1948, 1951; Dr rer. pol. h.c. Univ. Karlsruhe, 1980.
Offices Member, Central Bank Council of the Deutsche Bundesbank; Advisory Council, Fed. Econ. Ministry; Kuratorium Fritz Thyssen Foundation; Board of Dirs, Adolf Weber Foundation; Assoc. Econ. Social Res./Soc. Social Politics; Listgesellschaft; Internat. Inst. Public Fin.; Hon. Prof. Econ., Univ. Tübingen, 1976.
Principal Contributions The theory of economic order, the theory of transport, especially of railroad tariffs, major aspects of the history and the methods of economic thought, decision making and planning in economic policy, and monetary and fiscal policy.

Publications *Books: 1. Die Eisenbahntarife im Güterverkehr. Versuch einer Theoretischen Grundlegung* (J.C.B. Mohr, P. Siebeck, 1959); 2. *Zur Entwicklung des Geldwertes in Deutschland* (with H-J. Barth *et al.*), (J.C.B. Mohr, P. Siebeck, 1980); 3. *Das Europäische Währungssystem. Eine Europapolitische Grundentscheidung im Rückblick* (Rheinisch-Westfälische Akademie der Wissenschaften, 1980). *Articles: 1.* 'Wirtschaftswissenschaft: Methodenlehre, Teil II', in *Handwörterbuch der Sozialwissenschaften* (G. Fischer, J.C.B. Mohr, Vandenhoek & Ruprecht, 1952); 2. 'Der Methodenpluralismus und das Verstehen', in *Systeme und Methoden in den Wirtschafts- und Sozialwissenschaften. Erwin von Beckerath zum 75. Geburtstag*, ed. (with W. Krelle *et al*), (J.C.B. Mohr, P. Siebeck, 1964); 3. 'Utopie und Leitbild im wirtschaftspolitischen Denken', *Kyklos*, 20, 1967; 4. 'Wissenschaftliche Erkenntnis – politische Entscheidung', in *Verhandlungen auf der Arbeitstagung des Vereins für Socialpolitik* (Gesellschaft für Wirtschafts- und Sozialwissenschaften, 1977); 5. 'Wirtschaftsdemokratie – eine ordnungspolitische Alternative?', in *Die Demokratie im Spektrum der Wissenschaften*, ed. K. Hartmann (Freiburg, 1978).

KMENTA, Jan

Born 1928, Prague, Czechoslovakia.
Current Post Prof. Econ. and Stats,
Univ. Michigan, USA.
Recent Posts Ass. prof., Univ. Wisconsin, 1963–5, Prof., Michigan State
Univ., 1965–73.
Degrees BEc. (First class hons)
Sydney Univ., 1955; MA (Econ.), PhD
(Econ.) Stanford Univ., 1959, 1964.
Offices and Honours Member, AEA;
Fellow, Em Soc, ASA; Czechoslovak
Soc. Arts and Sciences in USA; Assoc.
ed., *JASA*, 1973–9, *REStat*, 1975–;
Alexander von Humboldt prize, Fed.
Republic of Germany, 1979.
Principal Contributions Areas of
research include macro-econometric
models, production function models, and
econometric methods.
Publications *Books:* 1. *Elements of
Econometrics* (Macmillan, 1971;
Spanish transl., 1977; Portuguese
transl., 1978); 2. *Evaluation of Econometric models*, ed. (with J.B. Ramsey),
(Academic Press, 1980).
Articles: 1. 'An econometric model of
Australia', *AEP*, 5, Dec. 1966; 2.
'Formulation and estimation of Cobb-
Douglas production function models'
(with A. Zellner and J. Drèze), *Em*, 37,
Oct. 1966; 3. 'On estimation of the CES
production function', *Int ER*, 8, June
1967; 4. 'Autonomous expenditures versus money supply: an application of
dynamic multipliers' (with P.E. Smith),
REStat, 55(3), Aug. 1973; 5. 'The
dynamics of household budget allocation to food expenditures' (with J. Benus
and H. Shapiro), *REStat*, 58(2), May
1976.

KNAPP, Georg Friedrich*

Dates and Birthplace 1842–1926,
Giessen, Germany.
Posts Held Head, Leipzig City Stat.
Office; Teacher, Univ. Leipzig,
1867–74, Univ. Strassburg, 1874–1919.
Career Statistician, economic historian and economic theorist whose first
published work was a systematic theory
of mortality measurement. He developed his application of mathematical
methods to demographic problems in
later publications. At Strassburg he
switched his attention to agricultural
history, identifying landed estates as a
special form of capitalism. His final
phase produced his controversial work
on money which emphasised the role of
the state in preserving the value of
money.
Publications *Books:* 1. *Über die
Ermittlung der Sterblichkeit aus den
Aufzeichnungen der Bevölkerungs-
statistik* (1868); 2. *Die Neueren Ansichten über Moralstatistik* (1871); 3.
Theorie des Bevölkerungs-wechsels
(1874); 4. *Die Bauernbefreiung und der
Uroprung der Landarbeiter*, 2 vols
(1887); 5. *The State Theory of Money*
(1905).
Secondary Literature J.A. Schumpeter, 'Georg F. Knapp', *Ten Great
Economists from Marx to Keynes*
(OUP, 1951).

KNEESE, Allen V.

Born 1930, Fredricksburg, Texas,
USA.
Current Post Sr Fellow, Resources
for the Future, Washington, DC.
Recent Posts Royer Vis. prof. Polit.
Econ., Univ. Cal., Berkeley, 1971; Dir.,
Quality of the Environmental Program,
Resources for the Future, 1967–74;
Prof. Econ., Univ. New Mexico, 1974–8.
Degree PhD (Econ.) Indiana Univ.,
1956.
Offices Member, Commission Natural Resources, NAS, 1974–80; Chairman, Board Minerals and Energy, NAS,
1975–80; Pres., Assoc. Environmental
and Resource Economists, 1978.
Principal Contributions One of the
first economists to undertake a sustained
programme of research on environmental economics. Helped to establish this
area as a legitimate field of economic
inquiry which is now taught in most
universities.
Publications *Books:* 1. *Managing
Water Quality: Economics, Technology, Institutions* (with B.T. Bower),
(Johns Hopkins Univ. Press, 1968; German transl., 1972); 2. *Economic Theory
of Natural Resources* (with O.C.
Herfindahl), (Charles E. Merrill Publishing, 1974); 3. *Pollution, Prices, and*

Public Policy (with C.L. Schultze), (Brookings Inst., 1975; Spanish transl., 1976); 4. *Economics and the Environment* (Penguin Books, 1976); 5. *Environmental Quality and Residuals Management: Report of a Research Program on Economic, Technological, and Institutional Aspects* (with B.T. Bower), (Johns Hopkins Univ. Press, 1979).

Articles: 1. 'Production, consumption, and externalities' (with R. Ayres), *AER*, 59(3), June 1969; 2. 'Environmental pollution: economics and policy', *AER*, 61(2), May 1971; 3. 'Natural resources policy 1975–1985', *J Environmental Econ. Management*, 3(4), Dec. 1976; 4. 'Environment, health, and economics – the case of cancer' (with W. Schulze), *AER*, 67(1), Feb. 1977; 5. 'The Southwest – a region under stress' (with F.L. Brown), *AER*, 68(2), 1978.

KNETSCH, Jack L.

Born 1933, Kalamazoo, Mich., USA.

Current Post Prof. Econ., Simon Fraser Univ., British Columbia, Canada, 1974–.

Recent Posts Economist, US Tennessee Valley Authority, 1956–61; Res. assoc., Resources for the Future, 1961–6; Prof. Econ., George Washington Univ., 1966–70; Sr economist, US Environment Council, 1970–1; Adviser Malaysia Project, Harvard Development Service, 1971–3.

Degrees BS, MS Michigan State Univ., 1955, 1956; MPA, PhD Harvard Univ., 1959, 1963.

Offices AEA; CEA; Member, Board Dirs, WRSA; Assoc. Environmental and Resource Economists.

Principal Contributions Improvements in methods of assessing non-market economic values, particularly of outdoor recreation and environmental quality. Other efforts have resulted in development of recreation benefit and demand estimates, and contributions to compensation policy assessments and definitions of property entitlements.

Publications *Books:* 1. *Economics of Outdoor Recreation* (with M. Clawson), (Johns Hopkins Univ. Press, 1967, 1974); 2. *Outdoor Recreation and Water Resources Planning* (Amer. Geophysical Union, 1974).

Articles: 1. 'The influence of reservoir projects on land values', *JFE*, 46, Feb. 1964; 2. 'A recreation site demand and benefit model' (with F. Cesario), *Regional Stud.*, 10, 1976; 3. 'Displaced facilities and benefit calculations', *Land Econ.*, 53, Feb. 1977; 4. 'Expropriation of private property and the basis of compensation' (with T.E. Borcherding), *Univ. Toronto Law J*, 1978; 5. 'Consumers' surplus measures and the evaluation of resources' (with I.M. Gordon), *Land Econ.*, 55, Feb. 1979.

KNIES, Karl*

Dates and Birthplace 1821–98, Marburg, Germany.

Posts Held Docent, Univ. Marburg, 1846; Prof. Politics, Univ. Freiburg, 1855; Dir., Board Education, Baden, 1862–5; Prof., Univ. Heidelberg, 1865–96.

Degree Dr Univ. Marburg, 1846.

Career Historical economist, whose early political involvement forced his exile in Switzerland after 1848. He returned to academic success at Freiburg and Heidelberg. His economics was essentially nationalistic, and a source of his objection to the cosmopolitanism of the classical school. Knies was an able teacher and his Heidelberg seminar achieved a pre-eminent position in Austro-German economics.

Publications *Books:* 1. *Die Statistik als Selbständige Wissenschaft* (1850); 2. *Die Eisenbahnen und ihre Wirkungen* (1853); 3. *Die Politische Ökonomie von Geschichtlichen Standpunkte* (1853); 4. *Der Telegraph als Verkehrsmittel* (1857); 5. *Geld und Credit*, 3 vols, (1873–9).

Secondary Literature H. Kisch, 'Knies, Karl', *IESS*, vol. 8.

KNIGHT, Frank Hyneman*

Dates and Birthplace 1885–1972, McLean County, Ill., USA.

Posts Held Taught Univs Cornell, Chicago, Iowa, (and again) Chicago, 1928–55.

Degrees BA Milligan Coll., 1911; BA, MA Univ. Tennessee, 1913; PhD Cornell Univ., 1916.

Offices and Honours Pres., 1950, Francis Walker medal, AEA, 1957.

Career His published work is chiefly in article form, and is usually concerned with clarifying some particular problem and assessing possible solutions. This remained at the level of analysis and he was loath to propose specific social reforms. His earliest and most fundamental contribution was a clarification of profit theory, developing the crucial distinction between risk and uncertainty. He then turned to capital theory and in the process launched a vigorous attack on the Austrian theory of capital. Other writings concern methodological and philosophical questions in relation to economics. His unwillingness to commit himself wholly to any single approach or answer deprived him of disciples but his deep effect on students and readers is well documented.

Publications *Books:* 1. *Risk, Uncertainty and Profit* (1921); 2. *The Economic Organisation* (1933); 3. *The Economic Order and Religion* (with T.W. Merriam), (1945); 4. *Freedom and Reform* (1947); 5. *The Ethics of Competition and Other Essays* (1951); 6. *On the History and Method of Economics* (1956); 7. *Intelligence and Democratic Action* (1960).

Secondary Literature J.M. Buchanan, 'Knight, Frank H', *IESS*, vol. 8.

KOMIYA, Ryutaro

Born 1928, Kyoto, Japan.

Current Post Prof. Econ., Univ. Tokyo.

Recent Posts Dean, Faculty Econ., Univ. Tokyo, 1978–80.

Principal Contributions Analysis of various aspects of contemporary Japanese economy and policy issues. In international economics, monetary or general equilibrium approach to the balance of payments theory and the theory of direct investment. Recently, theoretical and historical analysis of developments in the yen-dollar exchange market, Japanese government's foreign exchange pol-

icies, and short-term capital movements under the floating exchange rate system since 1973.

Publications *Books:* 1. *Postwar Economic Growth in Japan*, ed. (Univ. Cal. Press, 1966); 2. *International Economics* (with A. Amano), (in Japanese, *Iwanami-Shoten*, 1972); 3. *Theory of Corporate Finance* (with K. Iwata), (in Japanese, *Nihon Keizai Shimnunsha*, 1973); 4. *Studies on the Contemporary Japanese Economy* (in Japanese, 1975); 5. *Studies in International Economics* (in Japanese, *Iwanami-Shoten*, 1975).

Articles: 1. 'Monetary assumptions, currency depreciation and the balance of trade', *ESQ*, 17(2), Dec. 1966; 2. 'Non-traded goods and the pure theory of international trade', *Int ER*, 8(2), June 1967; 3. 'Economic growth and the balance of payments: a monetary approach', *JPE*, 77(1), Jan./Feb. 1969; 4. 'Planning in Japan', in *Economic Planning East and West*, ed. M. Bornstein (Ballinger Publishing Co., 1975), reprinted in *Comparative Economic Systems: Models and Cases*, ed. M. Bornstein (Richard D. Irwin, 1975); 5. 'Inflation in Japan' (with Y. Suzuki), in *World-wide Inflation: Theory and Recent Experience*, eds L. Krause and W.S. Salant (Brookings Inst., 1977).

KONDRATIEFF, Nikolai Dmitrievich*

Dates and Birthplace 1892–(?), Russia.

Posts Held Founder, Dir., Moscow Business Conditions Inst., 1920–8.

Offices Dep. Minister for Food, Kerensky govt., 1917.

Career Russian economist and statistician whose work on agricultural statistics included the devising of the so-called 'peasant indices' of the products bought and sold by farmers. He was one of the authors of the first Soviet five-year plan for agriculture. His analysis of the phenomenon of 'long-cycles' (or as he called them, 'long-waves') is the work with which his name is most usually associated. Coming into conflict with official policies on the question of planning he was imprisoned and died at some unknown date in the 1930s.

Publications *Books:* 1. *Mirovoe Khoziaistro i Ego Kon'iunktury Vo Vremia i Posle Voiny* (The World Economy and its Condition During and After the War) (1922); 2. *Bol'shie Tsikly Kon'iunktury* (Major Economic Cycles) (1928).

Articles: 1. 'The long-waves in economic life', *REStat*, 17 (pt 12), Nov. 1935, (transl. of 1925 article).

Secondary Literature G. Garvy, 'Kondratieff, N.D.', *IESS*, vol. 8.

KOOPMANS, Tjalling C.

Born 1910, 's Graveland, Netherlands.

Current Post Alfred Cowles Prof. Emeritus Econ., Yale Univ., USA.

Recent Posts Res. assoc., Cowles Comm., 1944–54, Assoc. prof. Econ., 1946–8, Dir. res., Cowles Comm., 1948–54, Prof. Econ., 1948–55, Univ. Chicago; Prof. Econ., Yale Univ., 1955–81; Dir., Cowles Foundation Res. Econ., Yale Univ., 1961–7.

Degrees MA (Physics, Maths) Univ. Utrecht, 1933; PhD Univ. Leiden, 1936; Hon. PhD (Econ.) Netherlands School Econ., 1963, Catholic Univ. Louvain, 1967; Hon. PhD (Science) Northwestern Univ., 1975; Hon. PhD (Law) Univ. Pennsylvania, 1976.

Offices and Honours Member, 1934–, Fellow, 1940–, Vice-pres., 1949, Pres., 1950, Council member, 1949–55, 1966–71, 1973–8, Em Soc; Member, 1941–, Pres., 1978, AEA; Correspondent, Royal Netherlands Academy Sciences, 1950–; Member, Amer. Math. Soc., 1952–, Inst. Management Sciences, 1954–, ORSA, 1954–, AAAS, 1960–, NAS, 1969–, Math. Programming Soc., 1972–, Internat. assoc. Energy Economists, 1979. Nobel Prize for Econ. 1975

Principal contributions Applications of mathematical statistics to econometrics. Economic dynamics. Exposition and evaluation of methods of economics. Allocation of resources, activity analysis. Models of transportation. Best allocation of resources over time. Choice of criteria for allocation over time.

Publications *Books:* 1. *Linear Regression Analysis of Economic Time Series* (Netherlands Econ. Inst., 1937); 2. *Tanker Freight Rates and Tankship Building* (Netherlands Econ. Inst., 1939); 3. *Statistical Inference in Dynamic Economic Models*, co-ed. (Yale Univ. Press, 1950); 4. *Activity Analysis of Production and Allocation*, co-ed. (Yale Univ. Press, 1951); 5. *Studies in Econometric Method*, co-ed. (Yale Univ. Press, 1953); 6. *Three Essays on the State of Economic Science* (McGraw-Hill, 1957); 7. *Scientific Papers of Tjalling C. Koopmans* (Springer-Verlag, 1970).

Articles: 1. 'Intertemporal distribution and "optimal" aggregate economic growth', in W. Fellner *et al. Ten Economic Studies in the Tradition of Irving Fisher* (Wiley, 1967); 2. 'Examples of production relations based on microdata', in *The Microeconomic Foundations of Macroeconomics*, ed. G.C. Harcourt (Macmillan, 1977.

Secondary Literature L. Werin and K.G. Jungenfelt, 'Tjalling Koopman's contribution to economics', *Scand JE*, 78(1), 1976.

KORNAI, János

Born 1928, Budapest, Hungary.

Current Post Prof. Econ., Head Res. Dept., Inst. Econ., Hungarian Academy Sciences, Budapest, Hungary, 1967–.

Recent Posts Head Dept., Computing Centre, Hungarian Academy Sciences, Budapest, 1963–7.

Degrees CSc. (candidate sciences), Dr Sc. Hungarian Academy Sciences 1956, 1966; Dr Oec. (Econ.) Karl Marx Univ. Econ., Budapest, 1961; Hon. Dr Univ. Paris, 1978, Univ. Posnan, Poland, 1978.

Offices Fellow, Em Soc, 1968, Pres., 1978; Hon. member, AAAS, 1972, AEA, 1976; Vice-chairman, Comm. Development Planning, UN, 1972–7; Corresp. member, Hungarian Academy Sciences, 1976, BAAS, 1978; Foreign member, Royal Swedisih Academy, 1980.

Principal Contributions Theory: contributions to the theory of socialism and planning, in particular models of multi-level planning and hierarchical control, centralisation and decentralis-ation, non-price signals and quantity adjustment, long-term growth, elabo-ration of a general theory of the shortage economy. *Dogmengeschichte* and meth-odology: critical appraisal of Walrasian general equilibrium theory; contribu-tions to the theoretical foundations, methodology and conceptual framework of non-Walrasian economics. Reforms: among the first economists in Eastern Europe suggesting decentralisation reforms and extended use of market forces; directed pioneering projects introducing mathematical programming into planning in socialist countries.

Publications *Books:* 1. *Overcentral-ization in Economic Administration* (OUP, 1959, Hungarian edn, 1957); 2. *Mathematical planning of Structural Decisions* (N-H, 1967, 1975, Hungarian transl., 1965, 1973); 3. *Anti-equilibrium* (N-H, 1971, 1975, Hungarian transl., 1971); 4. *Rush Versus Harmonic Growth* (N-H, 1972, Hungarian transl., 1972); 5. *Economics of Shortage* (N-H, 1980, Hungarian transl., 1980).

Articles: 1. 'Two-level planning' (with T. Lipták), *Em*, 33, Jan. 1965; 2. 'Multi-level programming – a first report on the model and on the experi-mental computations', *Europ ER*, 1. 1969; 3. 'The normal state of the market in a shortage economy: a queue model' (with J.W. Weibull), *Scand JE*, 80, 1978; 4. 'Resource-constrained versus demand constrained systems', *Em*, 47(4), July 1979; 5. 'The dilemmas of a socialist economy: the Hungarian experience', *Camb JE*, 4, 1980.

KRAUS, Alan

Born 1939, Schenectady, NY, USA.
Current Post Prof. Fin., Univ. British Columbia, Canada.
Recent Posts Ass. prof., Stanford Univ., 1968–73; Economist, Inst. Inves-tor Study, US Securities Exchange Commission, 1969–70; Assoc. prof., Univ. British Columbia, 1973–4, Univ. Washington, 1975–6.
Degrees BA, PhD Cornell Univ. 1961, 1969; MBA Stanford Univ., 1963.
Offices AEA; AFA; Assoc. ed., *J Fin*, 1977–, *J Fin Econ.*, 1977–; Pol.

Advisory Comm., *J Fin Quantitative Analysis*, 1979–; Exec. Comm., W. Fin. Assoc., 1979–81.
Principal Contributions Various studies in the theory of general and partial equilibrium in financial securities markets under uncertainty, focusing on the implications of particular individual preference functions and security return probability distributions, the conditions for aggregation of individual security demand functions, and the rational use by market participants of information signalled by equilibrium prices. Addi-tional contributions in financial eco-nomics include empirical research on the effects on stock prices of trading by large financial institutions.
Publications *Articles:* 1. 'Price impacts of block trading on the New York Stock Exchange' (with H.R. Stoll), *J Fin*, 27(3), June 1972; 2. 'Mar-ket equilibrium in a multiperiod state preference model with logarithmic util-ity' (with R.H. Litzenberger), *J Fin*, 30(5), Dec. 1975; 3. 'Skewness prefer-ence and the valuation of risk assets' (with R.H. Litzenberger), *J Fin*, 31(4), Sept. 1976; 4. 'Necessary conditions for aggregation in securities markets' (with M.J. Brennan), *J Fin. Quantitative Analysis*, 13(3), Sept. 1978; 5. 'Distin-guishing beliefs in equilibrium prices' (with G.A. Sick), *J Fin*, 35(2), May 1980.

KRAVIS, Irving Bernard

Born 1916, Philadelphia, Penn., USA.
Current Post Prof. Econ., Univ. Pennsylvania, USA.
Recent Posts Ass. prof., Assoc. prof., Prof. Econ., 1949–, Chairman, Dept. Econ., 1955–7, 1962–7, Assoc. Dean, Wharton School, 1958–60, Univ. Pennsylvania.
Degrees BS, AM, PhD Univ. Penn-sylvania, 1938, 1939, 1947.
Offices Fellow, Em Soc, AAAS; Ford Faculty Res. Fellow, 1960–1; Res. Staff, NBER, 1962–; Guggenheim Memorial Foundation Fellow, 1967–8; Member, 1975–9, Chairman, 1978–81, Council IARIW.

Principal Contributions Research interests are concerned with the structure of world economy. Within this broad area, worked on various aspects of international trade and on the measurement of real product and income of the countries of the world. The international trade aspects have included efforts to explain the reasons for trade flows, particularly the role of prices. The work on product and income comparisons provides comparable data not only for the aggregate GDP and overall price levels of different countries but also for the structure of quantities and prices for various categories of final expenditures on GDP. The methodology developed has been used to produce estimates for more than 30 countries and is being applied to other countries by the UN Statistical Office.

Publications *Books:* 1. *An International Comparison of National Products and the Purchasing Power of Currencies* (with M. Gilbert), (OEEC, 1954); 2. *The Structure of Income: Some Quantitative Essays* (Univ. Penn. Press, 1962); 3. *Price Competitiveness in World Trade* (with R. Lipsey), (NBER, 1971); 4. *A System of International Comparisons of Gross Product and Purchasing Power* (with Z. Kenessey et al.), (Johns Hopkins Univ. Press, 1975); 5. *International Comparisons of Real Product and Purchasing Power* (with A. Heston and R. Summers), (Johns Hopkins Univ. Press, 1978).

Articles: 1. ' "Availability" and other influences on the commodity composition of trade', *JPE*, 64, April 1956; 2. 'Trade as a handmaiden of growth: similarities between the nineteenth and twentieth centuries', *EJ*, 80, Dec. 1970; 3. 'Price behavior in the light of balance of payments theories' (with R. Lipsey), *J Int E*, 8(2), May 1978; 4. 'Real GDP per capita for more than one hundred countries' (with A. Heston and R. Summers), *EJ*, 88, June 1978; 5. 'An approximation of the relative real per capita GDP of the People's Republic of China', *J Comp Econ*, 5(1), March 1981.

KREGEL, Jan Allen

Born 1944, Dallas, Texas, USA.
Current Post Prof. Econ. Rutgers Univ., NJ, USA, and Gewoon Hoogleraar, Rijksuniv., Groningen, The Netherlands.

Recent Posts Lecturer Econ., Univ. Bristol, 1969–72; Lecturer, Sr Lecturer, Univ. Southampton, 1973–8.

Degrees BA Beloit Coll., Wisconsin, 1966; PhD Rutgers Univ., 1970.

Offices RES; AEA.

Principal Contributions An attempt to formulate a coherent framework for economic analysis on the basis of the work of Keynes, Kalecki, and the classical economists, which has come to be called the 'post-Keynesian' approach.

Publications *Books:* 1. *Rate of Profit, Distribution and Growth: Two Views* (Macmillan, Aldine, 1971); 2. *Theory of Growth* (Macmillan, 1972); 3. *The Reconstruction of Political Economy* (Macmillan, 1973, 1975, Halsted, 1973; Italian transl. 1975); 4. *Theory of Capital* (Macmillan, 1976).

Articles: 1. 'Economic methodology in the face of uncertainty', *EJ*, 86, June 1976; 2. 'On the existence of expectations in English neoclassical economics', *JEL*, 15(2), June 1977; 3. 'I fondamenti Marshalliani del principio della domanda effettiva di Keynes', *Giornale degli Economisti e Annali di Economia*, 39, March/April 1980; 4. 'Economic dynamics and the theory of steady growth', *HOPE*, 12(1), Spring 1980; 5. 'Markets and institutions as features of a capitalistic production system', *J Post Keyn E*, 3, Fall 1980.

KREININ, Mordechai E.

Born 1930, Tel-Aviv, Israel.
Current Post Prof. Econ., Michigan State Univ., USA.

Recent Posts Ass. prof., Assoc. prof., Prof., Michigan State Univ., 1957–; Vis. prof., Univs. Toronto, Hawaii, NYU, UCLA; Adviser, UNCTAD, Geneva, 1971–5; Res. consultant, IMF, Washington, 1976; Vis. scholar, Inst. Internat. Econ., Univ. Stockholm, 1978–80.

Degrees BA (Econ.) Univ. Tel-Aviv, 1951; MA (Econ.), PhD (Econ.) Univ. Michigan, 1952, 1955.

Offices and Honours Member, AEA, MEA, AAUP: Disting. faculty award,

Michigan State Univ., 1968; Disting. Educator of America, 1970.

Principal Contributions In addition to contributions to the theory of commercial policy, developed means of measuring the effects of various commercial policy measures on trade flows, welfare, and employment; these were then applied to a variety of policy situations, such as customs unions, multilateral tariff reductions, exchange rate changes, optimum currency areas, and the like. Work in the area of trade and development evaluated critically the proposals for a new international economic order, individual economies, and related issues. Work on balance of payments theory evaluated critically the monetary approach to the balance of payments. Developed and applied techniques to measure elasticities in international trade.

Publications *Books:* 1. *Israel and Africa: A Study of Technical Co-operation* (Praeger, 1964); 2. *Alternative Commercial Policies: Their Effects on the American Economy* (Michigan State Univ. Bureau Bus. Econ. Res., 1967); 3. *International Economics: A Policy Approach* (Harcourt, Brace Jovanovich, 1971, 1979); 4. *Trade Relations of the EEC: An Empirical Investigation* (Praeger, 1974); 5. *The Monetary Approach to the Balance of Payments: A Survey* (with L. Officer), Princeton Special Stud. in Internat. Econ., No. 43 (Princeton Univ., 1978). *Articles:* 1. 'Trade liberalization under the "Kennedy Round": the static effects' (with B. Balassa), *REStat*, 49, May 1967; 2. 'Factor substitution and effective protection reconsidered' (with J.B. Ramsey and J. Kmenta), *AER*, 61(5), Dec. 1971; 3. 'Disaggregated import demand functions – further results', *SEJ*, 40(1), July 1973; 4. 'A new international economic order? – a critical survey of the issues' (with others), *J World Trade Law*, Dec. 1976, reprinted in *World trade and payments*, ed. B. Balassa (Norton, 1978), and in *International Business 1977*, ed. D. Hanley (Michigan State Univ. Bureau Bus. Econ. Res., 1977); 5. 'Effect of exchange rate changes on the prices and volume of trade', *IMF Staff Papers*, 24(2), July 1977.

KRUEGER, Anne O.

Born 1934, Endicott, NY, USA.
Current Post Prof. Econ., Univ. Minnesota, Minneapolis, USA, 1959–.
Recent Posts Univ. Wisconsin, 1955–9; Sr res. Staff, NBER, 1976–; Vis. prof., Univs. Monash, MIT, Northwestern, Aarhus, Paris, ANU.
Degrees BA (Econ.) Oberlin Coll., 1953; MS (Econ.), PhD (Econ.) Univ. Wisconsin, 1956, 1958.
Offices Dir., member, Exec. Comm., ODC: Member, Res. Comm., Comm. Econ. Development; Consultant, USIA, AID, US Dept Treasury, NSF, Harvard Inst. Internat. Development, Korean Development Inst., Pres., MEA, 1974–5; Vice-pres. AEA, 1977.

Principal Contributions Application of economic theory to the analysis of trade and related policies in developing countries.

Publications *Books:* 1. *Foreign Trade Regimes and Economic Development: Turkey* (Columbia Univ. Press, 1974); 2. *The Benefits and Costs of Import Substitution in India: A Microeconomic Study* (Univ. Minnesota Press, 1975); 3. *Trade and Development in Korea*, ed. (with W. Hong), (Korea Development Inst., 1975); 4. *Growth, Distortions and Patterns of Trade Among Many Countries*, Princeton Stud. in Internat. Fin., no. 40 (Princeton Univ., 1977); 5. *Foreign Trade Regimes and Economic Development: Liberalization Attempts and Consequences* (Ballinger, 1978). *Articles:* 1. 'Some economic costs of exchange control: the Turkish case', *JPE*, 74(5), Oct. 1966; 2. 'Balance of payments theory', *JEL*, 7(1), March 1969; 3. 'The political economy of the rent-seeking society', *AER*, 64(3), June 1974; 4. 'Trade policy as an input to development', *AER*, 70(2), May 1980; 5. 'Protectionist pressures, imports, and employment in the United States', *Scand JE*, 82(2), 1980.

KRUTILLA, John Vasil

Born 1922, Tacoma, Washington, USA.
Current Post Sr Fellow, Resources for the Future, Washington, DC.

Recent Posts Industrial economist, 1952–4, Principal economist, 1954–5, Tennessee Valley Authority; Fellow, 1955–75, Assoc. Dir., Water Resources Program, 1960–7, Dir., Natural Environments Program, 1968–75, Resources for the Future.

Degrees BA Reed Coll., 1949; MA, PhD Harvard Univ., 1951, 1952; Hon. Dr Laws Reed Coll., 1978.

Offices and Honours Phi Beta Kappa Soc.; Amer. Inst. Biological Sciences; AEA; Amer. Assoc. Advancement Science; Assoc. Environmental/Resource Economists (Vice-pres., 1978, Pres.-elect, 1979, Pres., 1980); NAS Comm. on Biological Effects of Ionizing Radiation; Consultancies for US Govt: US Bureau Budget, Dept Commerce, Dept Agriculture, Fed. Power Commission; Consultant, UNECLA, UNECAFE, UN Development Programme, UN Environmental Programe; Amer. Motors conservation award, 1977.

Principal Contributions Pioneered work in the field of natural resource and environmental economics, viewing the latter as a resource allocative issue involving the interrelation of private and common property resources and natural-resource-related public goods. Applied relevant concepts from welfare economic theory to public sector planning, programming and budgeting, criteria for investment and operating decisions to improve efficiency in the provision of non-priced resource services and related public goods, addressing the special problems associated with long-run ecological consequences and technical irreversibilities.

Publications *Books:* 1. *Multiple Purpose River Development: Studies in Applied Economic Analysis* (with O. Eckstein), (Johns Hopkins Univ. Press, 1958); 2. *Unemployment, Idle Capacity and the Evaluation of Public Expenditures: National and Regional Analysis* (with R. Haveman), (Johns Hopkins Univ. Press, 1968); 3. *Natural Environments: Studies in Theoretical and Applied Analysis*, ed. (Johns Hopkins Univ. Press, 1972); 4. *The Economics of Natural Environments: Studies in the Valuation of Commodity and Amenity Resources* (with A. Fisher), (Johns Hopkins Univ. Press, 1975); 5. *Explorations in Natural Resource Economics* ed. (with V.K. Smith), (Johns Hopkins Univ. Press, 1981).

Articles: 1. 'Welfare aspects of benefit cost analysis', *JPE*, 69(3), June 1961; 2. 'Conservation reconsidered', *AER*, 57(4), Sept. 1967; 3. 'The economics of environmental preservation: a theoretical and empirical analysis' (with C. Cicchetti and A. Fisher), *AER*, 62(4), Sept. 1972; 4. 'Resource conservation, environmental preservation, and the rate of discount' (with A. Fisher), *QJE*, 89, Aug. 1975; 5. 'Resource and environmental constraints to growth' (with V.K. Smith), *AJAE*, 61(3), Aug. 1979.

KUCZYNSKI, Jürgen Peter

Born 1904, Elberfeld, Germany.
Current Post Academy of Sciences, German Democratic Republic.
Recent Posts Dir. Inst. Econ. Hist., Academy Sciences, GDR; Prof. Econ. Hist. Humboldt-Univ., Berlin.
Degrees Dr Phil. Univ. Erlangen, 1924; Hon. Dr rer. oec. Humboldt-Univ., Berlin; Hon. Dr rer. nat. Technische Univ. Dresden.
Offices and Honours Member, Academies Sciences, GDR, USSR; Fellow, RSS; Member, Exec. Council, Internat. Assoc. Econ. Historians; Various orders, medals and prizes.
Principal Contributions Collection and publication of the first regular unemployment statistics in US. Computation and publication of the first regular net real wage statistics in Germany.
Publications *Books:* 1. *History of Labour Conditions in Germany, Great Britain and the British Empire, France and the United States*, 40 vols, (Akademie Verlag, 1960–80); 2. *Studies in the History of Social Sciences*, 10 vols (Akademie Verlag, 1970); 3. *History of the Everyday Life of the German People 1600–1945*, 5 vols (Akademie Verlag, 1974).

KUENNE, Robert E.

Born 1924, St Louis, Missouri, USA.
Current Post Prof. Econ., Princeton Univ., USA.

Recent Posts   Vis. prof. Military Systems Analysis, US Army War Coll., 1967–; Consultant, Inst. Defense Analyses, 1968–; Consultant, Inst. Energy Analyses, 1977–.

Degrees   B Journalism Univ. Missouri, 1947; BA, MA Washington Univ., 1948, 1949; MA, PhD Harvard Univ., 1951, 1953.

Offices   AEA, RSA; Defense Orientation Conference Assoc; US Naval Inst.; Bicentennial Preceptor, Princeton Univ., 1957–60; Sr Fellow, Council Humanities, Princeton Univ., 1962–5; Ford Foundation Faculty Fellow, 1968; Member, Scientific and Management Advisory Comm., US Army Computer Systems Command, 1971–4.

Principal Contributions   Updating Walrasian general equilibrium theory, especially in the area of integrating money; innovating new techniques for the analysis of oligopolistic industries, and for their inclusion in operational general equilibrium models; and analysing spatial structure of economic phenomena, especially in devising algorithms for the solution of locational patterns and for the nature of spatial oligopoly.

Publications   *Books:* 1. *The Theory of General Economic Equilibrium* (Princeton Univ. Press, 1963); 2. *The Attack Submarine: A Study in Strategy* (Yale Univ. Press, 1965); 3. *The Polaris Missile Strike: A General Economic Systems Analysis* (Ohio State Univ. Press, 1967); 4. *Microeconomic Theory of the Market Mechanism* (Macmillan, 1968); 5. *Eugen von Böhm-Bawerk* (Columbia Univ. Press, 1971).

Articles: 1. 'Towards a usable general theory of oligopoly', *DE*, 122(6), 1974; 2. 'Spatial oligopoly: price-location interdependence and social cost in a discrete market space', *Regional Science Urban Econ*, 7, 1977; 3. 'Money, capital, and interest in intertemporal general equilibrium theory', *Econ App*, 30(4), 1977; 4. 'Rivalrous consonance and the power structure of OPEC' *Kyklos*, 32(4), 1979; 5. 'Duopoly reaction functions under crippled optimization regimes', *OEP*, 32(2), June 1980.

KUH, Edwin

Born   1925, Chicago, Ill., USA.

Current Post   Prof. Econ. Finance, Dir., Center Computational Res. Econ. Management Science, MIT.

Degrees   BA Williams Coll., 1949; PhD Harvard Univ., 1955.

Offices and Honours   Wells prize, Harvard Univ., 1955; Fellow, Em Soc, 1965; Fellow, AAAS, 1968.

Principal Contributions   Worked on three principal topics: investment behaviour, cyclical productivity and income distribution, and diagnostics for econometric model reliability. Early endeavour was sorting out the influence of (*ex-post*) profits and output on investment; later, studied observed regularities in cyclical income arising from labour demand function dynamics. More recently, work on model reliability has been on aggregation conditions under which aggregates improve estimation efficiency. Work on diagnostics concerns detection of influential subsets of data in regression that can dominate and contaminate estimates, and parameter sensitivity analysis for complete econometric models.

Publications   *Books:* 1. *The investment decision: an empirical study* (with J.R. Meyer), (Harvard Univ. Press, 1957); 2. *Capital Stock Growth: a Micro-econometric Approach* (N-H, 1963); 3. *The Brookings Quarterly Econometric Model of the United States* ed. (with J.S. Duesenberry *et al.*), (Rand McNally, N-H, 1965); 4. *An Introduction to Applied Macroeconomics* (with R. Schmalensee), (N-H, 1972); 5. *Diagnostics in the Linear Regression Model: Identifying Influential Data and Sources of Collinearity* (with D. Belsley and R. Welsch), (John Wiley, 1980).

Articles: 1. 'Income distribution and employment over the business cycle', in *The Brookings Quarterly Econometric Model of the United States*, ed, (with J.S. Duesenberry *et al.*), (Rand McNally, N-H, 1965); 2. 'Unemployment, production functions, and effective demand', *JPE*, 74, June 1966; 3. 'A productivity theory of wage levels – an alternative to the Phillips curve', *REStud*, 34(4), Oct. 1967; 4. 'An essay on aggregation theory and practice', in *Essays in Honour of Jan Tinbergen* ed. W. Sellekaerts (Macmillan, 1974); 5. 'The variances of regression coefficient estimates using aggregate data' (with R. Welsch), *Em*, 44(2), March 1976.

KURZ, Mordecai

Born 1934, Nathanya, Israel.
Current Post Prof. Econ., Stanford Univ.; Dir., Inst. Math. Stud. Social Sciences (Econ. Section), 1969–.
Degrees BA (Econ. Polit. Science) Hebrew Univ., Jerusalem, 1954–7; MA (Econ.), PhD (Econ.) Yale Univ. 1958, 1961; MS (Stat.) Stanford Univ., 1960.
Offices Member, AEA; Fellow, Em Soc; Consultant, World Bank; Special econ. adviser, Health and Welfare, Govt Canada; Special Econ. Adviser, US President's Commission on Pension Pol.; Res. Assoc., NBER; Ford Foundation Faculty Fellow, 1973; Fellow, Inst. Advanced Stud., Hebrew Univ., Jerusalem, 1979–80.
Principal Contributions Economic growth and optimal public policy. Since 1970 have studied general equilibrium problems with transaction costs and more recently concentrating on the study of the effects of power on economic allocation problems with emphasis on the behaviour of the public sector in a democratic economy. Also competed research on income distribution, welfare policy, social security and pension programmes.
Publications *Books:* 1. *Public Investment, The Rate of Return, and Optimal Fiscal Policy* (with K.J. Arrow), (Johns Hopkins Univ. Press, 1970).
Articles: 1. 'The general instability of a class of competitive growth processes', *REStud*, 35, April 1968; 2. 'Equilibrium in finite sequence of markets with transaction cost', *Em*, 42(1), Jan. 1974; 3. 'Altruistic equilibrium', in *Economic Progress, Private Values and Public Policy, Essays in Honor of William Fellner*, eds B. Balassa and R. Nelson (N-H, 1977); 4. 'Distortion of preferences, income distribution and the case for a linear income tax', *JET*, 14(2), April 1977; 5. 'Unemployment equilib-

rium in an economy with linked prices', *JET*, 1982.

KUZNETS, Simon

Born 1901, Russia.
Current Post Retired.
Recent Posts Prof. Polit. Econ., Johns Hopkins Univ., 1954–60; Prof. Econ., Harvard Univ., 1960–71.
Degrees: BSc, MA, PhD Columbia Univ., 1923, 1924, 1926.
Offices and Honours Pres., ASA, 1949, AEA, 1954; Nobel Prize for Econ., 1971.
Principal Contributions Study of types of economic change (cyclical fluctuations, secular movements, seasonal variations); clarification and quantification of the concepts of national economic product and its structure; attempt to apply the concepts and measures of national economic product to the study of economic growth of nations; and the bearing of demographic trends and structures on economic growth and income distribution.
Publications *Books:* 1. *Secular Movements in Production and Prices* (Houghton-Mifflin, 1930); 2. *Seasonal Variations in Industry and Trade* (NBER, 1933); 3. *National Income since 1869* (NBER, 1946); 4. *Modern Economic Growth* (Yale Univ. Press, 1966); 5. *Economic Growth of Nations* (Harvard Univ. Press, 1971).
Articles: 1. 'Equilibrium economics and human cycle theory', *QJE*, 44, May 1930; 2. 'National income: a new version', *REStat*, 30, Aug. 1948; 3. 'Long swings in the growth of populations and in related economic variables', *Amer. Philosophical Soc. Proceedings*, 102, Feb. 1952; 4. Economic growth and income inequality', *AER*, 45(1), March 1955; 5. 'Demographic aspects of the size distribution of income', *EDCC*, 25, Oct. 1976.
Secondary Literature R.A. Easterlin, 'Kuznets, Simon', *IIES*, vol. 18.

L

LAFFONT, Jean-Jacques Marcel

Born 1947, Toulouse, France.
Current Post Prof. Econ., Univ.
Sciences Sociales, Toulouse, France.
Recent Posts Researcher, CNRS,
Paris, 1975–7; Prof. Econ., Univ.
Amiens, 1977–9; Dir., d'Etudes à l'Ecole
des Hautes Etudes en Sciences Sociales,
Paris, 1980; Maître de Conférences à
l'Ecole Polytechnique, 1975–81.
Degrees Diplomé ENSAE Paris,
1970; Doctorat 3° cycle (Math.
Appliquées) Univ. Paris VI, 1972; PhD
(Econ.) Harvard Univ. 1975.
Offices and Honours Fellow, Em Soc;
Member Comité Dir de l'Assoc.
Française Sciences Econ.; Assoc. ed.,
JET, Econ. Letters, J Math E; Wells
prize, Harvard Univ.
Principal Contributions Theory of
incentives with a characterisation of
incentive compatible mechanisms and a
study of their properties. Econometrics
of disequilibrium, ranging from an early
applied paper to the development of
estimation methods in disequilibrium
simultaneous equations systems. Various contributions in theoretical public
finance, general equilibrium theory, the
economics of uncertainty, and the econometrics of non-linear systems.
Publications *Books:* 1. *Effets
externes et théorie économique* (CNRS,
1977); 2. *Incentives in Public Decision
Making* (with J. Green), (N-H, 1979);
3. *Essays in the Economics of Uncertainty* (Harvard Univ. Press, 1980).
Articles: 1. 'First order certainty
equivalence with instrument dependent
randomness', *REStud*, 42(4), Oct. 1975;
2. 'Optimism and experts against
adverse selection in a competitive economy', *JET*, 10(3), Sept. 1975; 3. 'Disequilibrium econometrics for business
loans' (with R. Garcia), *Em*, 45(5), July
1977; 4. 'Characterization of satisfactory mechanisms for the revelation of
preferences for public goods' (with J.
Green), *Em*, 45(2), March 1977; 5.
'Taxing price makers' (with R.
Guesnerie), *JET*, 19(2), Dec. 1979.

LAIDLER, David Ernest William

Born 1938, Tynemouth, England
Current Post Prof. Econ., Univ.
Western Ontario, Canada.
Recent Posts Ass. prof. Econ., Univ.
Cal., Berkeley, 1963–6; Lecturer Econ.,
Univ. Essex, 1966–9; Prof. Econ., Univ.
Manchester, 1969–75.
Degrees BSc.(Econ.) LSE, 1959;
MA Univ. Syracuse, 1960; PhD Univ.
Chicago, 1964; MA Univ. Manchester,
1973.
Offices Member, AEA; Member ed.
boards, *MS*, 1969–75, *REStud*, 1970–5,
AER, 1976–9, *CJE*, 1977–80, *JEL*,
1978–; Secretary, Soc. Econ. Analysis
Ltd., 1971–5; List lecturer, BAAS,
1972; Member Exec. Comm., CEA,
1980–.
Principal Contributions First published work dealt with the aggregate
demand for money function. Also work
on the economics of inflation. Concerned
with integrating the analysis of
inflation-output interaction into monetary models of the inflationary process
in closed and open economies. Though
generally 'monetarist' in tone, work does
not rely on the assumption of market
clearance as does most American monetarist economics.
Publications *Books:* 1. *The Demand
for Money, Theories and Evidence*
(Internat. Textbook Co., 1969, T.Y.
Crowell, 1976; 2. *Introduction to
Microeconomics* (Philip Allan, 1975,
1981); 3. *Essays on Money and Inflation* (Univ. Manchester Press, Univ.
Chicago Press, 1975).
Articles: 1. 'The rate of interest and
the demand for money – some empirical
evidence', *JPE*, 74, Dec. 1966; 2. 'The
definition of money – theoretical and
empirical problems', *JMCB*, 1(3), Aug.
1969; 3. 'Inflation – a survey (with J.M.
Parkin), *EJ*, 85, Dec. 1975; 4. 'Money
and money income – an essay on the
transmission mechanism', *J Mon E*, 4,
April 1978; 5. 'Monetarism – an interpretation and an assessment', *EJ*, 91,
March 1981.

LAL, Deepak Kumar

Born 1940, Lahore, India.
Current Post Reader Polit. Econ., Univ. Coll., Univ. London, England.
Recent Posts Lecturer, Christ Church, Univ. Oxford, 1966–8; Res. Fellow, Nuffield Coll., Univ. Oxford, 1968–70; Lecturer, Polit. Econ., Univ. Coll., 1970–9.
Degrees BA (Hons.) Delhi School Econ., 1959; BA (Hons.) BPhil., MA Univ. Oxford, 1962, 1965, 1966.
Offices Consultant, OECD Development Centre, 1967–8, World Bank, 1971–, ILO, 1973–4, UNIDO, 1975–7, OECD, 1975–7, LADB, 1976–7; Full-time consultant, Indian Planning Commission, New Delhi, 1973–4; Adviser, Ministry Planning, S. Korea, 1977; Adviser, Ministry Fin. Planning, Sri Lanka, 1978; Vis. Fellow, Res., School Pacific Stud., ANU, 1978.
Principal Contributions Development and application of modern 'second best' welfare economics, in the form of cost-benefit analysis, in the design of public policies, particularly in developing countries; the theory of trade and development, and the political economy of both real and monetary international economics; a critical examination of the philosophical, political and economic bases of alternative policies concerning poverty, distribution and growth in developing countries, and critical appraisals of the new macro-economics, including an on-going study of labour market evolution during different stages of development.
Publications *Books:* 1. *Wells and Welfare – An Exploratory Cost-benefit Study of Small-scale Irrigation in Maharashtra* (OECD Development Centre, 1972); 2. *Methods of Project Appraisal* (Johns Hopkins Univ. Press, 1974); 3. *Appraising Foreign Investment in Developing Countries* (Heinemann Educational Books, 1975); 4. *Unemployment and Wage Inflation in Industrial Economies* (OECD, 1977); 5. *Prices for Planning – Towards the Reform of Indian Planning* (Heinemann Educational Books, 1980).
Articles: 1. 'The foreign exchange bottleneck revisited: a geometric note', *EDCC*, 20(4), July 1972; 2. 'Disutility of effort, migration and the shadow wage rate', *OEP*, 25(1), March 1973; 3. 'Distribution and development', *WD*, 4(9), Sept. 1976; 4. Poverty, power and prejudice – the North-South confrontation', *Fabian Res. Series*, No. 340, Dec. 1978; 5. 'A liberal international economic order: the international monetary system and economic development', *Princeton Essays in Internat. Fin., no. 139*, (Princeton Univ., 1980).

LAMBIN, Jean-Jacques

Born 1933, Brussels, Belgium.
Current Post Prof. ordinaire, Univ. Catholique de Louvain; Prof. ordinaire, Faculté Univ. Catholique de Mons; Dir. Res., Center Socio-Econ. Stud. Advertising Marketing (CESAM).
Degrees Dr Law, PhD (Applied Econ.) Univ. Catholique de Louvain, 1957, 1965; MBA Univ. Cal., Berkeley, 1961.
Offices Vis. prof., Cornell Univ., Sherbrooke Univ., Laval Univ.; Member, Ed. boards, *J Marketing Res., J Forecasting*, Presses Universitaires de France (Collection Systèmes et Décisions), *J Advertising*; Member, Amer. Marketing Assoc.
Principal Contributions Analysis measurement and forecasting of demand; measuring advertising sales effectiveness; sales forecasting; price quality ratios evaluation; product portfolio analysis; company- and band-image study; computerised marketing information system (microcomputer); marketing expenditures allocation system; feasibility study.
Publications *Books:* 1. *La Décision commerciale face à l'incertain* (Dunod, 1965); 2. *Modèles et programmes de marketing* (Presses Universitaires de France, 1970); 3. *Advertising, Competition and Market Conduct* (N-H, 1976); 4. *La Gestion marketing des entreprises*, Tome 1, *Analyse* (with R. Peeters), (Presses Univs. de France, 1977).

LAMPMAN, Robert J.

Born 1920, Plover, Wisc., USA.
Current Post Prof. Econ., Univ. Wisconsin, USA.
Recent Posts Ass. prof., Assoc. prof., Univ. Washington, 1948–58.
Degrees BA, PhD Univ. Wisconsin, 1942, 1950.
Offices IRRA, NTA; Exec. Comm., AEA, 1976–9.
Principal Contributions Studies of distribution of income and wealth. Analysis of income re-distribution programmes.
Publications *Books:* 1. *The Share of Top Wealth-holders in National Wealth, 1922–56* (Princeton Univ. Press, 1962); 2. *Washington Medical Service Corporations* (with G.A. Shipman and S.F. Miyamoto), (Harvard Univ. Press, 1962); 3. *Ends and means of Reducing Income Poverty* (Academic Press, 1971).
Articles: 1. 'Recent thought on egalitarianism', *QJE*, 71, May 1957; 2. 'Transfer approaches to distribution policy', *AER*, 60(2), May 1970; 3. 'What does it do for the poor?', *Public Interest*, Jan. 1974; 4. 'Social welfare benefits and labor supply', National Commission on employment and unemployment statistics (US Govt Printing Office, 1979).

LANCASTER, Kelvin John

Born 1924, Sydney, Australia.
Current Post John Bates Clark Prof. Econ., Columbia Univ., USA.
Recent Posts Reader Econ., Univ. London, 1959–62; Prof. Polit. Econ., Johns Hopkins Univ., 1962–6; Prof. Econ., Columbia Univ., 1966–.
Degrees BSc, BA, MA Univ. Sydney, 1948, 1949, 1953; BSc (Econ.), PhD Univ. London, 1953, 1958.
Offices Member, AEA; Fellow, Em Soc.
Principal Contributions The best-known are the theory of second best (with R. G. Lipsey), the analysis of qualitative systems, the 'characteristics' approach to consumer theory (product variety and differentiation), and the analysis of perfect monopolistic competition.

Publications *Books:* 1. *Mathematical Economics* (Macmillan, 1968); 2. *Introduction to Modern Microeconomics* (Rand McNally, 1969, 1974); 3. *Consumer Demand: A New Approach* (Columbia Univ. Press, 1971); 4. *Variety, Equity, and Efficiency* (Columbia Univ. Press, 1979).
Articles: 1. 'The general theory of second best' (with R.G. Lipsey), *REStud*, 24(1), 1956; 2. 'The theory of qualitative linear systems', *Em*, 33, April 1965; 3. 'A new approach to consumer theory', *JPE*, 74, April 1966; 4. 'Socially optimal product differentiation', *AER*, 65(4), Sept. 1975; 5. 'Intra-industry trade under perfect monopolistic competition', *J Int E*, 10(4), Nov. 1980.

LANDES, William Martin

Born 1939, New York City, NY, USA.
Current Post Clifton R. Musser Prof. Econ., Univ. Chicago Law School, USA.
Recent Posts Prof., Univ. Chicago Law School, 1974–.
Degrees BA Columbia Coll., 1960; PhD Columbia Univ., 1966.
Offices Res. Staff, NBER, 1968–; Ed., *J Law E*, 1974–.
Principal Contributions The application of economic theory and quantitative methods to law. Early work concerned the impact of laws (e.g. fair employment laws) and legal institutions (e.g. courts) on behaviour. More recently, developed models to test the hypothesis that common law rules in torts, contracts and property are best explained as efforts by courts to promote efficient resource allocation.
Publications *Articles:* 1. 'An economic analysis of the courts', *J Law E*, 14(1), April 1971; 2. 'Legal precedent: a theoretical and empirical analysis' (with R. Posner), *J Law E*, 19(2), Aug. 1976; 3. 'An economic study of US aircraft hijacking, 1961–1976', *J Law E*, 21(1), April 1978; 4. 'Salvors, finders, Good Samaritans, and other rescuers: an economic study of law and altruism' (with R. Posner), *J Legal Stud.*, 7, Jan. 1978; 5. 'Joint and multiple tortfeasors: an economic analysis' (with R. Posner), *J Legal Stud.*, 9, June 1980.

LANDRY, Michel Auguste Adolphe*

Dates and Birthplace 1874–1956, Ajaccio, Corsica.

Posts held Prof., l'Ecole Pratique des Hautes Etudes, 1907; Conseiller Générale de Calvi, 1920–51.

Degrees Agrégé de philosophie, Dr ès lett., l'Ecole Normale Supérieure, Paris.

Offices Deputy, 1910–46; Senator, Corsica, 1946; Minister, Marine et Travail.

Career *L'intérêt* ... is still remembered as a restatement of Böhm-Bawerk's theory of time-preference in the language of utility theory. Subsequent work was largely in economic and particularly demographic history.

Publications *Books:* 1. *L'Utilité sociale de la propriété individuelle* (1901); 2. *L'intérêt du capital* (1904); 3. *Manuel d'économique* (1980); 4. *Les Mutations des monnaies dans l'ancienne France* (1910); 5. *La Révolution démographique* (1934); 6. *Traité de démographie* (1945).

Secondary Literature R. Courtin, 'Nécrologie: Adolphe Landry', *REP*, Jan./Feb. 1957.

LANGE, Oskar*

Dates and Birthplace 1904–65, Tomaszow, Pland.

Posts Held Lecturer, Krakow Univ., 1931–5, Univ. Michigan, 1936–43; Prof., Univ. Chicago, 1943–5; Prof., Univ. Warsaw, 1955–65.

Degrees LIM, LLD, Univ. Krakow, 1927, 1928.

Offices Polish ambassador to USA, 1945, UN, 1946–9; Chairman, Polish State Econ. Council.

Career His economic work can be divided between his early period and his return to Poland. During the former his main concern was with analytical questions, and during the latter his interest lay in propagating an undogmatic version of Marxism. His paper 'On the economic theory of socialism', first published in 1936–7, not only made a major contribution to the bourgeois theory of socialism but also influenced the 'new' welfare economics emerging at the time. His war-time book, *Price Flexibility and Employment*, was one of the first of many later attempts to provide a micro-economic underpinning to Keynesian macroeconomics. His post-war *Political Economy* was an important event in the communist countries, accepting as it did basic Marxian premises, but incorporating modern economic techniques. His personal contributions to the fields of econometrics and growth theory are minor in comparison to this introduction of modern economics to Poland and the other countries of the Soviet bloc.

Publications *Books:* 1. *On the Economic Theory of Socialism*, ed. B.E. Lippincott (1938); 2. *Price Flexibility and Employment* (1944); 3. *The political Economy of Socialism* (1958); 4. *Introduction to Econometrics* (1958); 5. *Ekonomia Polityczna* (Political Economy) (1959); 6. *Pisnia Ekonomiczne i Spoleczne 1930–1960* (Economic and Social Essays 1930–1960) (1961).

Articles: 1. 'Marxian economics and modern economic theory', *REStud*, 2, June, 1935, reprinted in D. Horowitz, ed., *Marx and Modern Economics* (1968).

Secondary Literature S. Wellisz, 'Lange, Oskar', *IESS*, vol. 8.

LARDNER, Dionysius*

Dates and Birthplace 1793–1859, Dublin, Ireland.

Posts Held Ed. of encyclopaedic works, and miscellaneous writer; Prof. Natural Philosophy, Univ. London, 1827.

Degrees BA, MA, LLB, LLD Trinity Coll., Dublin, 1817, 1819, 1827, 1827.

Offices Fellow, Royal Soc.; Hon. Fellow, Stat. Soc., Paris.

Career As a scientific populariser and editor, his greatest achievement was probably the *Cabinet Cyclopaedia*, 133 vols (1829–49), which included numerous distinguished contributors. Only *Railway Economy* from amongst his many writings is a contribution to economics. In this work he examined various economic questions both mathematically and graphically in a way which Jevons acknowledged as an influence on his own thinking. This included hints of a profit-maximising theory of the firm and an account of monopoly price discrimination. Marshall labelled Lardner's conjecture that cost reductions in transport are likely to increase by the square of the distance over which goods are transported as 'Lardner's Law of Squares'.

Publications *Books: Railway Economy* (1850, 1968).

Secondary Literature D.L. Hooks, 'Monopolistic price discrimination in 1850: Dionysius Lardner', *HOPE*, 3(1), Spring 1971.

LASPEYRES, Etienne*

Dates and Birthplace 1834–1913, Germany.

Post Held Teacher, Univ. Giessen, 1874–1900.

Degree BA Univ. Heidelberg.

Career Statistician and advocate of quantitative economics, chiefly known for his work on index numbers. He published various comprehensive price studies based on German data. Lack of statistical data prevented him from testing his important ideas on index numbers.

Publications *Books:* 1. *Geschichte der Volkswirtschaftlichen Anschauungen der Niederländer* (1863); 2. *Der Einfluss der Wohnung auf die Sittlichkeit* (1869).

Articles: 1. 'Die Kathedersocialisten und die statistischen Congresse', *Deutsche Zeit- und Streit-Fragen*, 52, 1875; 2. 'Statistischen Untersuchungen zur Frage der Steuerüberwälzung', *Finanz Archiv*, 18, 1901.

Secondary Literature R. Meerworth, 'Laspeyres, Etienne', *ESS*, vol. 9.

LASSALLE, Ferdinand*

Dates and Birthplace 1825–64, Breslau, Germany.

Posts Held Journalist and politician.

Degrees Student at Breslau, Berlin and Paris.

Career Prussian socialist leader who organised the first German workers' party, the *Allgemeiner Deutscher Arbeiterverein*, in 1863. Joined with Marx in 1848 but retained his Hegelian belief that ideas were to some extent independent of economic circumstances. His version of socialism was one in which the state would grant workers capital or credit to form co-operatives; the co-ops would enable the workers to enjoy profits as well as wages and thus escape what he called 'the iron law of wages', i.e. subsistence wages. His opposition to *laissez-faire* liberalism led him into an unlikely alliance with Bismarck, which he hoped would result in the granting of universal suffrage. He was killed in a duel before this alliance came to fruition.

Publications *Books:* 1. *Gesammelte Reden und Schriften*, 12 vols (1919–20).

Secondary Literature E. Bernstein, *Ferdinand Lassalle as a Social Reformer* (Swann Sonnenschein, 1893); G. Mayer, 'Lassalle, Ferdinand', *ESS*, vol. 9.

LASUEN, José, Ramon

Born 1932, Alcañiz, Spain.

Current Post Dir., Dept. Econ. Resources, Univ. Autónoma de Madrid (UAM).

Recent Posts Prof., Univ. Barcelona, 1960; Res. assoc., RFF, Washington, DC, 1967; Dean, School Econ., UAM, 1969; Gen. Sec. Social Democracy Federation, 1976; Member of parliament, Pres., 1977, Econ. adviser to Pres., 1978, Aragon Assembly.

Degrees BA, PhD (Econ.) Madrid Univ. 1954, 1959; MA (Econ.) Stanford Univ., 1957; PhD Hon. Causa World Academy of Scholars, 1965.

Offices RSA, 1963; Ekistics, 1965; General Systems Assoc., 1968; Assepelt, 1970; Club of Rome, 1977.

Principal Contributions In the 1960s showed that regional income disparities create sectoral demands inimical to development as they require small, local, anti-competitive supplies or excessive imports. In the 1970s demonstrated that growth poles are adoption and diffusion centres of innovations; their stable historical ordering is due to the stability of the market and business organisational traits which determine innovation diffusion and adoption patterns. In the 1980s argued that economic centres create, through political dominance, regional income differentials but foster national development through their innovation creation or adoption. Politically weak economic centres and politically strong economic peripheries (the inverted case) result in regional disparities and in national underdevelopment.

Publications *Books:* 1. *Sectores Prioritarios del Desarollo Español* (Guadiana, 1973); 2. *Miseria y Riqueza* (Alianza Editorial, 1974); 3. *Ensayos de Economia Reigonal y Urbana* (Ariel, 1976); 4. *Le España Mediocrática* (Planeta, 1979).

Articles: 1. 'Regional income inequalities and the problems of growth in Spain', *J Reg S*, 8, 1962; 2. 'On growth poles', *Urb Stud*, 6(2), 1969; 3. 'Urbanisation and development', *Urb Stud*, 10, 1973; 4. 'Spain's regional prospects', in *Regional Development in Spain. Experiences and Prospects* (Mouton, 1981).

LATANE, Henry A.

Born 1907, Buchanan, Virg., USA.
Current Post Chairman, Latane Morris Investment Assoc. N. Carolina, USA 1980–.
Recent Posts Willis Prof. Investment Banking, Univ. N. Carolina, 1969–80.
Degrees BA Univ. Richmond, 1928; MBA Harvard Univ., 1930; PhD Univ. N. Carolina, 1959.
Offices AEA; AFA; Inst. Chartered Fin. Analysts; Assoc. ed., *J Fin*, 1970–; Dir, SEA, 1973–4.
Principal Contributions The development of a seasonal adjustment model to minimise the difference of each period from the average of the two adjacent periods. Tests of the relationship between interest and income velocity. Justification of the geometric mean as a criterion for choosing among risky ventures to maximise the likelihood of long-run success. Development of a portfolio balance strategy, including money bonds and stocks. Investigation and tests of capital market anomalies. Errors in *ex-post* tests of *ex-ante* probability beliefs on assets pricing.

Publications *Books:* 1. *Security Analysis and Portfolio Management* (with D.L. Tuttle), (Ronald Press, 1970, 1975).

Articles: 1. 'Seasonal factors determined by difference from average of adjacent months', *JASA*, 37, Dec. 1942; 2. 'Cash balances and the interest rate – a pragmatic approach', *REStat*, 36(4), Nov. 1954; 3. 'Criteria for choice among risky ventures', *JPE*, 67(2), April 1959; 4. 'Investment criteria: a three asset portfolio balance model', *REStat*, 45(4), Nov. 1963; 5. 'Standardized unexpected earnings – a progress report (with C.P. Jones), *J. Fin*, 32(5), Dec, 1977.

LAUDERDALE, James Maitland 8th Earl of*

Dates and Birthplace 1759–1839, Scotland.
Post Held Landowner.
Career His major economic work was the *Inquiry . . .*, a work cast in the Smithian mould, which nevertheless deviated from classical orthodoxy in several ways. He emphasised the role of utility in determining relative prices and also argued that over-saving was a possibility. His later works are on monetary questions and, paradoxically for a writer who feared under-consumption, took the Bullionist position.

Publications *Books:* 1. *An Inquiry into the Nature and Origin of Public Wealth* (1804, 1819); 2. *Thoughts on the Alarming State of the Circulation* (1805); 3. *Three Letters to the Duke of Wellington* (1829).
Secondary Literature B. Corry, 'Lauderdale, James Maitland', *IESS*, vol. 9.

LAUGHLIN, James Laurence*

Dates and Birthplace 1850–1933, USA.
Posts Held Taught at Harvard Univ., and Cornell Univ., 1873–92; Founder, Head Dept Polit. Econ., Univ. Chicago, 1892–1916.

Offices Founder of *JPE*, 1892.

Career As the founder of the Chicago department, he made a major contribution to American economics as a teacher and colleague. His career included enthusiastic campaigning against the free-silver agitation and in favour of the federal reserve system. His publications chiefly concern monetary topics: *Money, Credit and Prices* (1931) is his major achievement in this field.

Publications *Books:* 1. *The Study of Political Economy* (1885); 2. *History of Bimetallism in the United States* (1886); 3. *Principles of Money* (1903); 4. *Credit of the Nations* (1918); 5. *Money and Prices* (1919); 6. *A New Exposition of Money, Credit and Prices.* 2 vols (1931); 7. *The Federal Reserve Act* (1933).

Secondary Literature J.U. Nef, 'James Laurence Laughlin (1850–1933)', *JPE*, 42, Feb. 1934.

LAUNHARDT, Carl Friedrich Wilhelm*

Dates and Birthplace 1832–1918, Hanover, Germany.

Posts Held Prof. Engineering Science and Rector, Polytechnic Coll., Hanover, Germany, 1869–1918.

Honours Hon. Dr Dresden Inst. Technology, 1903.

Career A civil engineer who applied mathematical techniques to economic problems. His writing on railway pricing virtually discovered the theory of marginal cost pricing as well as its implication of deficits for decreasing-cost industries, and continues to influence current thinking on railway tariffs. He also made significant contributions to industrial location theory, particularly market area analysis. A version of the pole principle for finding plant locational equilibrium points is to be found in the seminal 1882 article. His *Mathematische Begründung* is, among other things, the first ever text of mathematical economics; in addition to original results on location, it taught the doctrines of Jevons and Walras.

Publications *Books:* 1. *The theory of the Trace: being a discussion of the Principles of Location* (1872, 1900); 2. *Mathematische Begründung der Volkswirtschaftslehre* (1885, 1976).

Articles: 1. 'Die Bestimmung des Zweckmässigsten Standortes einer Gewerblichen Anlage', *Zeitschrift des Vereines Deutscher Ingenieure*, 26, 1882.

Secondary Literature E.M. Fels, 'Launhardt, Wilhelm', *IESS*, vol. 9; J.V. Pinto, 'Launhardt and location theory: rediscovery of a neglected book', *J Reg S*, 17(1), 1977.

LAVELAYE, Emile Louis Victor de*

Dates and Birthplace 1822–92, Bruges, Belgium.

Posts Held Lawyer and writer; Prof., Univ. Liège, 1864.

Career Belgian academic socialist whose prolific writings made many contributions to the journals, in addition to his books. His topics included money, international law, agricultural economics and many others, economic and non-economic. He saw political economy as an art not a science, accepted the role of the state in economic life, and judged economic questions in terms of moral standards.

Publications *Books:* 1. *Etudes historiques et critiques sur le principe et les conséquences de la liberté du commerce international* (1857); 2. *De la propriété et de ses formes primitives* (1873); 3. *Le socialisme contemporaine* (1880); 4. *Eléments d'économie politique* (1882); 5. *La Monnaie et le bimétallisme international* (1891).

Secondary Literature E. Mahaim, 'Obituary: Emile de Lavelaye', *EJ*, 2, March, 1892.

LAVIGNE, Marie

Born 1935, Strasbourg, France.

Current Post Prof. Econ., Univ. Paris I Panthéon-Sorbonne, France, 1974–.

Recent Posts Ass. prof. Econ., Univ. Strasbourg, 1959–69; Ass. prof. Econ., Univ. Paris I, 1969–73; Prof. Econ., Univ. Paris XII, 1973–4.

Degrees MA (Law), MA (Russian language and literature), PhD (Econ.) Univ. Strasbourg, 1955, 1956, 1960.

Offices and Honours Sec. gen. Res. Centre USSR and Eastern European Countries, Univ. Strasbourg, 1959–69; Silver medal (Econ.) CNRS, 1963; Dir. Centre Internat. Econ. Socialist countries, Univ. Paris I, 1973–.

Principal Contributions Economic theory of socialism (analysis and critique of Soviet views); planning and management in the Eastern European countries; money and finance (international and domestic) in socialism; and international economic relations of Eastern European countries (Comecon integration and East-West relations).

Publications *Books:* 1. *Le Capital dans l'économie soviétique* (SEDES, 1962); 2. *Le Problème des prix en Union Soviétique* (with H. Denis), (Cujas, 1965); 3. *Les Économies socialistes soviétiques et européenes* (Armand Colin, 1970); English ed., *The Socialist economies of USSR and Eastern Europe* (Martin Robertson, 1974; revd. French edn, 1979); 4. *Le Comecon* (Cujas, 1974); 5. *Les Relations Economiques Est-Ouest* (PUF, 1979).

Articles: 1. 'The problem of the multinational socialist enterprise', *ACES Bull*, 17(1), Summer 1975; 2. 'Economic reforms in Eastern Europe: ten years after', in *Economic Development in Soviet Union and Eastern Europe*, vol.1, ed. Z. Fallenbuchl (Praeger, 1975); 3. 'The creation of money by the State Bank of the USSR', *Econ. and Society*, 7(1), Feb. 1978; 4. 'The International Monetary Fund and the Soviet Union', in *Internationale Wirtschafts Vergleiche und Interdependenzen: Festschrift für Franz Nemschak*, ed. F. Levcik (Springer-Verlag, 1978); 5. 'L'URSS dans le Comecon face à l'Ouest', in *Stratégies des pays socialistes dans l'échange international*, ed. M. Lavigne (Economica, 1980).

LAVINGTON, Frederick*

Dates and Birthplace 1881–1927, England.

Posts Held Bank employee, 1897–1908; UK Board of Trade, 1912; Fellow, Emmanuel Coll., Univ. Camb., 1922.

Degree BA Univ. Camb., 1911.

Honours Adam Smith prize, 1912.

Career An economist of the most orthodox, classical kind, seeing his work on the capital market as a mere application of Marshall's ideas to an individual case. This reliance on authority disguised the considerable originality of his major study of the British capital market.

Publications *Books:* 1. *The English Capital Market* (1921); 2. *The Trade Cycle* (1922).

Secondary Literature 'Frederick Lavington (obituary)', *EJ*, 37, 1927.

LAW, John*

Dates and Birthplace 1671–1729, Edinburgh, Scotland.

Posts Held Banker, merchant and statesman.

Offices Minister of Fin., France, 1720.

Career Promoted various schemes for banks, beginning in 1702 with a proposal for a Bank of France. The schemes involved the creation of paper money backed by land holdings, which he argued would stimulate economic activity. In 1716 he was permitted to set up his General Bank in France, and in the following year his Company of the West began to sell stock in France's North American possession of Louisiana and Mississippi. His financial influence grew to a peak with his appointment as Minister of Finance in 1720. His belief that shares of stock were identical with money led to mistakes in the management of the speculative 'bubble' which followed. Law's system collapsed and he was permanently discredited, his name becoming almost synonymous with cranky monetary panaceas.

Publications *Books:* 1. *Money and Trade Considered* (1705, 1966); 2. *Oeuvres complètes*, 3 vols (1934).

Secondary Literature E.J. Hamilton, 'Law, John', *IESS*, vol. 9.

LAZEAR, Edward Paul

Born 1948, New York City, NY, USA.

Current Post Prof. Industrial Relations, Univ. Chicago, Grad. School Bus., Chicago, Res. assoc., NBER.

Recent Posts Res. assoc., NORC; Ass. prof. Econ., 1974–8, Assoc. prof. Industrial Relations, 1978–81, Univ. Chicago.

Degrees BA (Econ.), MA (Econ.) UCLA, 1971; PhD (Econ.) Harvard Univ., 1974.

Offices AEA: Em Soc; Grad. Fellow, 1971–4, Fellow, 1979–81, NSF; Fellow, Inst. Advanced Study, Hebrew Univ. Jerusalem, 1978–9.

Principal Contributions Analysis of the effect of compensation schemes on productivity; a general theory of labour union behaviour; work on income distribution, analysis of wage differentials by race and sex, and the cause of such differentials; general studies on the relationship between wages and schooling, productivity, and demographic characteristics; and examination of labour institutions such as pensions, severance pay, and mandatory retirement.

Publications *Articles:* 1. 'Education: consumption or production?', *JPE*, 85(2), June 1977; 2. 'Why is there mandatory retirement?', *JPE*, 87(6), Dec. 1979; 3. 'The narrowing of black-white wage differentials is illusory', *AER*, 69(4), Sept. 1979; 4. 'Family background and optimal schooling decisions', *REStat*, 62(1), Feb. 1980; 5. 'Agency, earnings profiles, productivity and hours restrictions', *AER*, 71(4), Sept. 1981.

LEAVITT, H.J.

N.e.

LEDERER, Emil*

Dates and Birthplace 1882–1939, Pilsen, Austro-Hungary.

Post Held Prof., New School Social Res., New York City, USA.

Career A leading academic socialist in the Weimar Republic. Emigrated to the USA in early 1930s where he continued to work on problems of business cycles and technological unemployment at the New School with Adolph Lowe and Hans Neisser.

Publications *Books:* 1. *Die Privatan-*

gestellen in der Modernen Wirtschaftsentwicklung (1912); 2. *Die Wirtschaftlichen Organisationen* (1913); 3. *Grundzüge der Ökonomischen Theorie* (1922); 4. *Aufriss der Theoretischen Oekonomie* (1933); 5. *Technical Progress and Unemployment* (1938); 6. *The State of the Masses: The Threat of the Classless Society* (1939).

Secondary Literature H. Neisser, 'Emil Lederer 1882–1939: I The sociologist', 'II The economist', *Social Res.*, 7, 1940, 8, 1941.

LEE, Tong Hun

Born 1931, Seoul, Korea.

Current Post Prof. Econ., 1967–, Chairman Dept., 1978–, Univ. Wisconsin, USA.

Recent Posts Res. assoc., Social Systems Res. Inst., Univ. Wisconsin, Madison 1960–2; Ass. prof. Econ., 1962–4, Assoc. prof. Econ., 1964–7, Univ. Tennessee; UN Mission to Korea, 1977.

Degrees BS (Commerce) Yonsei Univ., Seoul, 1955; BA (Econ.) Northeast Missouri State Univ., 1956; MA (Econ.) Univ. Wisconsin, Madison, 1958; PhD (Econ.) Univ. Wisconsin, Milwaukee, 1961.

Offices and Honours Member, AEA: Fellow, Em Soc; NSF Grant, 1965–8, 1973–6.

Principal Contributions Using mathematical and statistical methods, contributed in several areas of economics: a joint estimation procedure for estimating a set of probability functions; provided the first evidence showing that, although permanent income has a unique role in housing, the permanent income elasticity is still less than unity; provided the first set of empirical evidence supporting the Gurley-Shaw hypothesis that non-bank financial intermediary liabilities are close substitutes for cash and demand deposits at commercial banks; and developed a methodology for interregional interindustry analysis that requires data only on interindustry sales flows.

Publications *Books:* 1. *Regional and Interregional Intersectoral Flow Analysis* (with D.P. Lewis and J.R. Moore), (Univ. Tennessee Press, 1973).

Articles: 1.'Income, wealth, and the demand for money', *JASA*, 59, Sept. 1964; 2. 'Joint estimation of relationships involving discrete random variables' (with A. Zellner), *Em*, 33, April 1965; 3. 'Alternative interest rates and the demand for money: the empirical evidence', *AER*, 57, Dec. 1967; 4. 'Housing and permanent income: tests based on a three-year re-interview survey', *REStat*, 50, Nov. 1968; 5. 'More on windfall income and consumption', *JPE*, 83(2), April 1975.

LEFF, Nathaniel H.

Born 1938, New York City, NY, USA.

Current Post Prof. Bus. Econ., Internat. Bus., Grad. School Bus., Columbia Univ., USA.

Degrees BA Harvard Univ., 1959; MA Columbia Univ., 1962; PhD MIT, 1966.

Offices and Honours Member, AEA, RES, EHA; Awards US SSRC, Tinker Foundation, IBM Fellowship.

Principal Contributions Clarification of the economics of developing countries, including aspects of trade and development, macro-economic adjustment, industrial organisation and entrepreneurship.

Publications *Books:* 1. *The Brazilian Capital Goods Industry 1929–1964* (Harvard Univ. Press, 1968); 2. *Economic Policy-Making and Development in Brazil, 1947–1964* (Wiley, 1968).

Articles: 1. 'Long-term Brazilian economic development', *JEH*, 29(3), Sept. 1969; 2. 'Development and regional inequality in Brazil', *QJE*, 86(2), May 1972; 3. 'Entrepreneurship & economic development: the problem revisited', *JEL*, 17(1), March 1979; 4. 'Macroeconomic adjustment in developing countries' (with K. Sato), *REStat*, 62(2), May 1980.

LEFTWICH, Richard H.

Born 1920, Burden, Kan., USA.

Current Post Regents Prof. Econ., Oklahoma State Univ., Stillwater, USA, 1976–.

Recent Posts Ass. prof. Econ., 1948–51, Assoc. prof. Econ., 1951–5, Prof. Econ., 1955–76, Oklahoma State Univ.; Vis. prof. Econ., Univ. Católica de Chile, Santiago, 1962–3, Tunghai Univ., Taichung, Taiwan, 1981.

Degrees BA (Econ.) Southwestern Coll., 1941; MA (Econ.), PhD (Econ.) Univ. Chicago 1948, 1950.

Offices and Honours AEA; Past-pres., SEA, MEA, Western Social Science Assoc.; Beta Gamma Sigma Disting. Scholar, 1976.

Principal Contributions Carried out research and work in restructuring the principles course to increase student interest in economics. Also work in applied economic development (Chile, Taiwan etc.).

Publications *Books:* 1. *The Price System and Resource Allocation* (Dryden Press, 1955, 1979); 2. *An Introduction to Economic Thinking* (Holt, Rinehart & Winston, 1969); 3. *Elementary Analytics of a Market System* (General Learning Press, 1972); 4. *The Economics of Social Issues*, (with A.M. Sharp), (Bus. Publications, 1974, 1980); 5. *A Basic Framework for Economics* (Bus. Publications, 1980).

Articles: 1. 'Organized labor and national economic objectives', *SEJ*, 32, April 1966; 2. 'Exchange rate policies, balance of payments, and trade restrictions in Chile', *EDCC*, 14, July 1966; 3. 'Syllabus for an "issues approach" to teaching economic principles', *J. Econ. Educ.*, Special Issue, Winter 1974; 4. 'Objectives of the college-level principles of economics course', in *Goals and Objectives of the Introductory College-level Course in Economics* (Fed. Reserve Bank Minneapolis, 1976); 5. 'Productivity', in *Encyclopedia Americana* (1977).

LEHFELDT, Robert Alfred*

Dates and Birthplace 1868–1927, Birmingham, England.

Posts Held Prof. Physics, East London Coll., S. Africa, 1896; Prof. Physics, 1906, Prof. Econ., 1916–27, South African School of Mines and Technology.

Degrees BSc Univ. London, 1889; BA Univ. Camb., 1890.

Offices Pres., Section F, South African Assoc. Advancement Science, 1920; Founder and vice-pres., Econ. Soc. South Africa.

Career After an early successful career as a physicist, began to turn his mathematical skills to economic and sociological problems. Many of his studies were of South African questions and his appointment in 1917 to the Statistical Council of South Africa enabled him to encourage the national collecting of statistics. He was convinced that economic pressures would eventually oblige South Africa to recognise the non-white population as full citizens. Outside South Africa he was chiefly known for his work on currency, particularly in the light of South African gold production.

Publications *Books:* 1. *Economics in the Light of War* (1916); 2. *Gold Prices and the Witwatersrand* (1919); 3. *The National Resources of South Africa* (1922); 4. *Restoration of the World's Currencies* (1923); 5. *Money* (1926); 6. *Controlling the Output of Gold* (1926); 7. *Descriptive Economics* (1927).

Secondary Literature S.H. Frankel, 'Obituary, Professor Robert Alfred Lehfeldt', *EJ*, 38, March, 1928.

LEIBENSTEIN, Harvey

Born 1922.

Current Post Andelot Prof. Econ. Pop., Harvard Univ., USA, 1967–.

Recent Posts Ass. prof., 1951–60, Prof., 1960–7, Univ. Cal., Berkeley; Vis. prof., Harvard Univ., 1966–7.

Degrees BS, MA Northwestern Univ. 1945, 1946; PhD Princeton Univ., 1951.

Offices and Honours Social affairs officer, Pop. Div., UN, 1949; US SSRC Fellow, 1950–1; Consultant, Rand Corp., 1954–5; Faculty Res. Fellow, Univ. Cal., Berkeley, 1956–9; Guggenheim Memorial Foundation Fellow, 1963; Member, Inst. Advanced Stud., Princeton Univ., 1978–9.

Principal Contributions The microeconomics of human fertility, and X-efficiency theory (the non-allocative aspects of inefficiency). The latter attempts to develop a mode of analysis which relaxes the maximisation assumption of conventional micro-theory and substitutes postulates under which individuals are non-maximisers when there is little pressure on them, approaching maximising behaviour as external pressure increases. Behaviour according to convention is an important aspect of this approach. Also, current research involves the application of the prisoner's dilemma paradigm to normal economic behaviour.

Publications *Books:* 1. *Economic Backwardness and Economic Growth: Studies in the Theory of Economic Development* (Wiley, 1957); 2. *Economic Theory and Organisational Analysis* (Harper, 1960); 3. *Beyond Economic Man* (Harvard Univ. Press, 1976); 4. *General X-efficiency Theory and Economic Development* (OUP, 1978); 5. *Inflation, Income Distribution and X-efficiency Theory* (Croom Helm, 1980).

Articles: 1. 'Bandwagon, snob and Veblen effects in the theory of consumers' demand', *QJE*, 64, May 1950, repr. in *Readings in Microeconomics*, ed. D.R. Kamerschen (World Publishing, 1967); 2. 'Allocative efficiency vs "X-efficiency"', *AER*, 56, June 1966; 3. 'Allocative efficiency, X-efficiency, and the measurement of welfare losses' (with W.S. Comanor), *Ec*, N.S. 36, Aug. 1969; 4. 'An interpretation of the economic theory of fertility: promising path or blind alley?' *JEL*, 12(2), June 1974; 5. 'A branch of economics is missing: micro-micro theory', *JEL*, 17(2), June 1979.

LEIJONHUFVUD, Axel

Born 1933, Stockholm, Sweden.

Current Post Prof., Chairman, Dept. Econ., UCLA, USA.

Recent Posts Assoc. prof., UCLA, 1964–71; Prof. Econ., 1971–; Vis. prof. Stockholm School Econ., 1969, Inst. Advanced Studies, Vienna, 1976, Inst. Advanced Studies, Jerusalem, 1978, Nihon Univ., Tokyo, 1980, Univ. Louis Pasteur, Strasbourg, 1980.

Degrees Fil. kand. Univ. Lund, 1960;

MA Univ. Pittsburgh, 1961; PhD Northwestern Univ., 1967.

Offices Member, AEA, WEA; Marshall Lecturer, Univ. Camb., 1974–5; Member, Board, Econ. Inst., Boulder, Colorado, 1980–.

Principal Contributions Reassessment of Keynesian economics, particularly its relationship to micro-economic theory. Clarification of some of the issues in the monetarist debate. Challenge to the widespread professional opinion that inflation is relatively harmless.

Publications *Books:* 1. *On Keynesian Economics and the Economics · of Keynes: A Study in Monetary Theory* (OUP, 1968); 2. *Information and Co-ordination: Essays in Macroeconomic Theory* (OUP, 1981).

Articles: 1. 'Theories of stagflation', *UCLA Working Paper* no. 176, Aug. 1980; 2. 'What was the matter with IS-LM?', *UCLA Working Paper* no. 186, Oct. 1980.

LEKACHMAN, Robert

Born 1920, New York City, NY, USA.

Current Post Disting. Prof., City Univ., New York, USA.

Recent Posts Prof., Barnard Coll., Columbia Univ., 1948–65; Prof., State Univ. New York, Stonybrook, 1965–73.

Degrees BA, PhD Columbia Univ., 1942, 1954.

Offices AEA.

Principal Contributions *History of Economic Ideas*, published in 1959, and still in print.

Publications *Books:* 1. *History of Economic Ideas* (Harper, 1959); 2. *Ages of Keynes* (Random, 1966); 3. *Inflation* (Vintage, 1973); 4. *Economists at Bay* (McGraw-Hill, 1976); 5. *Capitalism for Beginners* (Pantheon, 1981).

LELAND, Hayne E.

Born 1941, Boston, Mass., USA.

Current Post Prof., School Bus. Admin., Univ. Cal., Berkeley, USA.

Recent Posts Ass. prof., Stanford Univ., 1968–74; Assoc. prof., Univ. Cal., Berkeley, 1974–8.

Degrees BA, PhD Harvard Univ. 1963, 1968; MSc (Econ.) LSE, 1965.

Offices Assoc. ed., *Int ER* 1973–8, *JET*, 1976–9.

Principal Contributions Integration of production and financial theory; savings and investment under uncertainty; theory of markets with asymmetric information; regulation under uncertainty; optimal nonlinear pricing; optimal risk sharing; and theory of portfolio insurance.

Publications *Articles:* 1. 'Savings and uncertainty: the precautionary demand for saving', *QJE*, 82, Aug. 1968, reprinted in P. Diamond and M. Rothschild eds, *A Book of Readings* (Univ. Chicago Press, 1979); 2. 'Theory of the firm facing uncertain demand', *AER*, 62(3), June 1972; 3. 'Production theory and the stock market', *Bell JE*, 5(1), Spring 1974; 4. 'Information asymmetrics, financial structure, and financial intermediation' (with D. Pyle), *J Fin*, 31(2), May 1976; 5. 'Quacks, lemons, and licensing: a theory of minimum quality standards', *JPE*, 87(6), Dec. 1979.

LENIN, Vladimir Illich*

Dates and Birthplace 1870–1924, Simbirsk, Russia.

Posts Held Organiser of the Russian Communist Party; Leader of Russia after the 1917 Revolution.

Degrees Grad. Law Univ. St Petersburg, 1891.

Career His writings, though revered in Soviet Russia, are not remarkable for their originality. *Imperialism . . .* owes much to the writings of Hobson, Bukharin, and Hilferding, and even the earlier *Development of Capitalism in Russia*, his only genuine contribution to economics, is derivative of the work of others. This latter work, while presented as an application of the theory of Marx's *Capital* to Russian conditions, is in fact a radically unorthodox work which abandons many of the central ideas of Marxism, such as the progressive role of industrialisation in the countryside.

Publications *Books:* 1. *The Development of Capitalism in Russia* (1899, 1960); 2. *What is to be done?* (1901,

1961); 3. *Imperialism, the Highest Stage of Capitalism* (1916, 1964); 4. *The State and Revolution* (1917, 1964); 5. *Selected Works*, 12 vols (1935–8).

Secondary Literature A. Nove, 'Lenin as an economist', in *Lenin: the Man, the Theorist, the Leader*, eds L. Shapiro and P. Reddaway (Weidenfeld & Nicolson, 1967); J.D. Clarkson, 'Lenin', *IESS*, vol. 9.

LEONTIEF, Wassily

Born 1906, St Petersburg, Russia.
Current Post Prof. Econ., NYU, 1975–; Dir., Inst. Econ. Analysis, NYU, USA.
Recent Posts Res. assoc., Inst. World Econ., Univ. Kiel, 1927–8; Econ. adviser, Chinese govt., Nanking, 1928–9; Res assoc., NBER, 1931; Instructor, 1932–3, Ass. prof., 1933–9, Assoc. prof., 1939–46, Prof. Econ., 1946–53, Henry Lee Chair Political Econ., 1953–75, Harvard Univ.; Part-time gen. consultant, US Dept. Labor, 1941–7, 1961–5; Part-time econ. consultant, Chief, Russian Econ. Sub-division, US Office Strategic Services, 1943–5; Consultant, UN Secretary General's Consultative Group Econ. and Social Consequences of Disarmament, 1961–2; Part-time gen. consultant, US Dept Commerce, 1966–; Member, Exec. Board, Environmental Protection Agency, 1975–80; Part-time general consultant, Office Technology Assessment, 1980–; Consultant, UN Development Programme, 1980–.
Degrees MA (Social sciences), Univ. Leningrad, 1921–5; PhD (Econ.) Univ. Berlin, 1925–8; Hon. degrees: Univs. Pisa (1953), Brussels (1962), York (1967), Louvain (1971), Paris (Sorbonne) (1972), Penn. 1976, Lancaster (1976), Toulouse (1980), Louisville (1980), Vermont (1980), C.W. Post Center, Long Island (1980.
Offices and Honours Member, Amer. Philosophical Soc., Internat. Stat. Inst.; Hon. member, Japan Econ. Res. Center, Tokyo; Hon. Fellow, RSS; Corresp. Fellow, Inst. de France, 1968; Officer, French Legion d'Honneur, 1968; Corresp. Fellow, BA, 1970; Bernard-Harms Prize Econ., W. Germany, 1970; Pres.,

AEA, 1970; Nobel Prize for Econ., 1973; Member, NAS, 1974; Accademia Nazionale dei Lincie, Italy, 1975; American Comm. East-West Accord, 1975; Hon. member, Royal Irish Academy, 1976; Pres., Section F, BAAS, 1976; Fellow, AAAS, 1977; Commission to Study Organization of Peace, 1978; Comm. National Security, 1980; Russian-American Hall of Fame, 1980.
Principal Contributions Input-output analysis. Theory of international trade and its empirical implementation.
Publications *Books:* 1. *The Structure of the American Economy, 1919–1929* (OUP, 1941, 1953); 2. *Studies in the Structure of the American Economy* (OUP, 1953); 3. *Input-output Economics* (OUP, 1966); 4. *Essays in Economics* (OUP, 1966); 5. *The Future of the World Economy* (OUP, 1977).
Articles: 1. 'The use of indifference curves in the analysis of foreign trade', *QJE*, 47(2), May 1933, repr. in H.S. Ellis and L.A. Metzler, eds, *Readings in the Theory of International Trade* (Blakiston Co., 1949); 2. 'Implicit theorizing: a methodological criticism of the neo-Cambridge School', *QJE*, 51(1), Feb. 1937; 3. 'Postulates: Keynes' General theory and the classicists', in *The New Economics*, ed. S. Harris (Knopf, 1948); 4. 'Sails and rudders, ship of state', *New York Times*, 16 March 1973; 5. 'Is technological unemployment inevitable?', *Challenge*, Sept/Oct. 1979.
Secondary Literature W.H. Miernyk, 'Leontief, Wassily', *IESS*, vol. 18; R. Dorfman, 'Wassily Leontief's contributions to economics', *Swed: JE*, 79, 1977

LERNER, Abba P.

Born 1903, Russia.
Current Post Retired.
Recent Posts Ass. lecturer, LSE, 1935–7; Ass. prof., Univ. Kansas City, 1940–2; Assoc. prof., 1942–6, Prof. Econ., 1946–7, New School Social Res.; Prof. Econ., Roosevelt Univ., 1947–59, Michigan State Univ., 1959–65, Univ. Cal., Berkeley 1965–71; Disting. prof. Econ., Queen's Coll., New York, 1971–8, Florida State Univ., 1978–80.

Degrees BSc (Econ.), PhD (Econ.) Univ. London, 1932, 1943; Hon. DSc Northwestern Univ., 1978.

Offices and Honours Tooke Scholarship, 1930; Gonner prize, 1932; Gladstone Memorial prize, 1932; LSE Res. Fellowship, 1932–4; Leon Fellowship, Univ. London, 1934–5; Rockefeller Fellow, US, 1938–9; Consultant, Rand Corp., 1949; Econ. Commission Europe, Geneva, 1950–1, Econ. Advisory Staff, Jerusalem, 1953–5; Adviser, Treasury, Govt Israel, Bank Israel, 1955–6; Fellow, Center Advanced Study Behavioral Sciences, 1960–1; Vice-pres., 1963, Disting. Fellow, 1966, AEA; Hon. Fellow, LSE, 1970–; Fellow, AAAS, 1971–; Pres., Univ. Center Rational Alternatives, 1973–; Member, NAS, 1974–; Pres., Atlantic Econ. Soc., 1980.

Principal Contributions See P.A. Samuelson, 'A.P. Lerner at sixty', *REStud*, 31, June 1964. Later contributions include a plan for controlling inflation by taxing wage increases.

Publications *Books:* 1. *The Economics of Control* (Macmillan, 1944); 2. *The Economics of Employment* (McGraw-Hill, 1951); 3. *Essays in Economic Analysis* (Macmillan, 1953); 4. *Flation* (Quadrangle, 1972, Penguin Books, 1973); 5. *MAP – A Market Anti-inflation Plan* (with D. Colander), (Harcourt Brace Jovanovich, 1980).

LEROY-BEAULIEU, Paul*

Dates and Birthplace 1843–1916, France.

Posts Held Journalist, ed., 1867–72; Prof. Public Fin., Ecole Libre des Sciences Polit., 1872; Prof. Polit. Econ., Collège de France, Paris, 1880.

Degree Studied in Paris.

Offices Ed., *Journal des débats*, 1871; Founder and ed., *Economiste français*, 1873.

Career Liberal economist who largely followed the principles of classical economics. However, he rejected Ricardo's rent theory and Lassalle's 'iron law of wages' in favour of a more optimistic view. He modified his opposition to state intervention in the case of state encouragement of large families. He was a large landowner and his suc-cess in agricultural management led to his frequent consultation as an adviser by firms.

Publications *Books:* 1. *L'État moral et intellectual des classes ouvrières* (1868); 2. *Traité de la science des finances*, 2 vols (1877); 3. *Essai sur la répartition des richesses* (1881); 4. *Traité théoretique et pratique d'économie politique*, 4 vols, (1895).

Secondary Literature E.R.A. Seligman, 'Leroy-Beaulieu, Paul', *ESS*, vol. 9; *Classics in the Theory of Public Finance*, eds R.A. Musgrave and A.T. Peacock (Macmillan, 1958).

LESCURE, Jean*

Dates and Birthplace 1882–1947, France.

Posts Held Prof., Univs. Poitiers, Bordeaux, Paris.

Degree Agrégé, 1910.

Career Writer on cycles whose methodology was derived from that of Juglar. His emphasis was on the role of rising prices of cost items in creating losses for manufacturers newly entering a buoyant market, as well as the time-lags resulting from the manufacture and setting up of new plant and equipment.

Publications *Books:* 1. *Des crises générales et périodiques de surproduction* (1906); 2. *L'Épargne en France* (1914); 3. *Hausses et baisses des prix de longue durée* (1933); 4. *Etude sociale comparée des régimes de liberté et des régimes authoritaires* (1939); 5. *Principes d'économie rationelle* (1947). *Articles:* 1. 'Hausses et baisses générales des prix', *REP*, 1912.

LESOURNE, Jacques

Born 1928, La Rochelle, France.

Current Post Prof. Econ., Conservatoire Nat. des Arts et Métiers, Paris, Dir. Stud., Inst. Auguste Comte, Paris.

Recent Posts Managing Dir., Chairman, Sema Metra Group, 1958–75; Dir. Interfutures Project, OECD, 1976–9.

Degrees L'Ecole Polytechnique, 1948–51; L'Ecole des Mines de Paris, 1951–3.

Offices Fellow, Em Soc; Member,

Internat. Stat. Inst.; Council member, Futuribles; Chairman, Assoc. Française d'Informatique et de Recherche Opérationnelle; Vice-chairman, Assoc. Française pour le Développement de l'Analyse de Systèmes, 1973–9; Council member, TTMS, 1977–9; Chairman, Assoc. Française de Sciences Econ., 1981–.

Principal Contributions Research concentrated on applied economics in three main fields: business economics and OR; cost-benefit analysis; and long-term studies (prospective analysis) and systems analysis. Other contributions concern the theory of investment, dynamics of the firm, and the methodology of prospective analysis.

Publications *Books:* 1. *Economic Technique and Industrial Management* (Prentice-Hall, 1962); 2. *Modèles de croissance de l'entreprise* (Dunod, 1972); 3. *Cost-benefit Analysis – Theory and Applications* (N-H, 1975); 4. *A Theory of the Individual for Economic Analysis* (N-H, 1977); 5. *Facing the Future: Mastering the Probable and Managing the Unpredictable* (with Interfutures), (OECD, 1979).

LESTER, Richard A.

Born 1908, Blasdell, NY, USA.
Current Post Assoc., Industrial Relations Section, Princeton Univ., NJ, USA.
Recent Posts Prof. Econ., 1948–74, Dean Faculty, 1968–73, Princeton Univ.
Degrees PhB Yale Univ., 1929; AM, PhD Princeton Univ., 1930, 1936.
Offices and Honours Exec. board member, 1950–2, Pres., 1956, IRRA; Exec. comm. member, 1951–3, Vice-pres., 1961, AEA; Chairman Subcomm. Res. Nat. Manpower Advisory Comm., 1962–8; US Dept. Labor award of merit, 1968.
Principal Contributions Initiated reform in the theory of the firm in the 1940s. Made contributions to the theory of wage differentials and to analysis of the adjustments that firms make to wage changes and labour shortages. Developed a system for the study of professional and managerial work careers and pay and for analysing sex and race dis-

crimination in such employment. Drew a new set of conclusions from analysis of the experience with paper money in the American colonies.

Publications *Books:* 1. *Monetary Experiments* (Princeton Univ. Press, 1939); 2. *Economics of Labor* (Macmillan, 1941, 1964); 3. *Hiring Practices and Labor Competition* (Industrial Relations Section, Princeton Univ., 1954); 4. *Economics of Unemployment Compensation* (Industrial Relations Section, Princeton Univ., 1962); 5. *Reasoning about Discrimination* (Princeton Univ. Press, 1980).
Articles: 1. 'Shortcomings of marginal analysis for wage-employment problems', *AER*, 36, March 1946; 2. Southern wage differentials: developments, analysis, and implications', *SEJ*, 13, April 1947; 3. 'Reflections on the "labour monopoly" issue', *JPE*, 55, Dec. 1947; 4. 'A range theory of wage differentials', *ILRR*, 5, July 1952; 5. 'Reflections on collective bargaining in Britain and Sweden', *ILRR*, 10, April 1957.

LEVASSEUR, Emile*

Dates and Birthplace 1828–1911, Paris, France.
Posts Held Teacher Rhetoric, Alençon, Besançon; Teacher Econ. Hist., Collège de France, Paris, 1868–71; Prof., Conservatoire des Arts et Métiers, Paris, 1871; Founder teacher, L'Ecole Libre des Sciences Polit., 1871–1911.
Degrees Agrégé des Lettres, L'Ecole Normale Supérieure.
Career The founder of modern economic history in France, he sought to introduce the lessons of social and economic science into history. He also introduced the historical method into the largely abstract world of French political economy. He described his own area of work as 'economic art' in contrast to pure theory, which he typified as 'economic science'.
Publications *Books:* 1. *Recherches historiques sur le système de Law* (1854); 2. *Histoire des classes ouvrières et de l'industrie en France avant 1789* (1959); 3. *Histoire des classes ouvrières*

et de l'industrie en France de 1789 à 1870 (1867); 4. *Rapport sur le commerce et le tonnage relatifs au canal interocéanique* (1879); 5. *La Population française*, 3 vols (1889–92).

Secondary Literature C. Fohlen, 'Levasseur, Emile', *IEES*, vol. 9.

LEVHARI, David

Born 1935, Ramat-Gan, Israel.
Current Post Prof. Econ., Hebrew Univ. Jerusalem, 1964–.
Recent Posts Vis. prof., Univs. Stanford, Pennsylvania, Illinois, Amsterdam.
Degrees BA (Econ. Stats.), MA (Econ.) Hebrew Univ. 1959, 1961; PhD MIT, 1964.
Offices Fellow, Em Soc, 1970–; Chairman, Dept Econ., 1975–7.
Principal Contributions The fields of capital theory, growth models, and dynamic models of optimisation. Studied growth models with various kinds of technological change and their economic implications. More recently studied exploitation of exhaustible or renewable resources, optimal accumulation under uncertainty, inflation and indexed bonds markets.
Publications *Articles:* 1. 'Extension of Arrow's "Learning by doing"', *REStud*, 33(2), Jan. 1966; 2. 'Optimal savings under uncertainty' (with T. Srinivasan), *REStud*, 36, April 1969; 3. 'The relation between the rate of return and the rate of technical progress' (with E. Sheshinski), *REStud*, 36, July 1969; 4. 'Risk and the theory of indexed bonds' (with N. Liviatan), *AER*, 67(3), June 1977; 5. 'The great fish war: an example using a dynamic Cournot-Nash equilibrium' (with L. Mirman), *Bell JE*, 11(1), Spring 1980.

LEVITAN, Sar A.

Born 1914, Shiauliai, Lithuania.
Current Post Dir., Res. Prof. Econ., George Washington Univ. Center Social Pol. Stud., Washington, DC, 1967–.
Recent Posts Chairman, Nat. Commission Employment Unemployment Stats, 1977–9.
Degrees BS Coll. City New York,

1937; MA, PhD Columbia Univ., 1939, 1949.
Offices Chairman, Exec. Comm., Nat. Council Employment Pol., USA; Chairman, Center Employment Pol. Stud., USA.
Principal Contributions Major interest has been to assess the impact of government policies in the field of employment and social welfare. As an institutional economist, work has drawn on the insights of other disciplines in examining major policy issues concerning labour market operations and measurements, poverty and manpower programmes, and the status of minorities.
Publications *Books:* 1. *Still a Dream: The Changing Status of the Blacks since 1960* (Harvard Univ. Press, 1975); 2. *The Promise of Greatness* (Harvard Univ. Press, 1976); 3. *Evaluating Federal Social Programs: An Uncertain Art* (W.E. Upjohn Inst. Employment Res., 1979); 4. *Programs in Aid of the Poor* (Johns Hopkins Univ. Press, 1980); 5. *Human Resources and Labor Markets* (Harper & Row, 1981).

LEVY, Haim

Born 1939, Jerusalem, Israel.
Current Post Prof. Fin., Hebrew Univ., Jerusalem.
Recent Posts Vis. prof., Univ. Cal., Berkeley, 1972; Dir., School Bus., Hebrew Univ., 1973–5; Vis. prof., Univ. Penn., 1979, Univ. Florida, 1980.
Degrees BA, MA, PhD Hebrew Univ., 1963, 1966, 1969.
Offices AEA.
Principal Contributions In the areas of stochastic dominance; international diversification of portfolios; mergers (portfolios approach); the capital asset pricing model and an imperfect market; and the investment horizon, and decision making.
Publications *Books:* 1. *Investment and Portfolio Analysis* (with M. Sarnat), (Wiley, 1972); 2. *Financial Decision Making under Uncertainty* (with M. Sarnat), (Academic Press, 1977); 3. *Corporate Investment and Financing Decisions* (with M. Sarnat), (Prentice-Hall International, 1977); 4. *The Israeli*

Stock Market (with M. Smith and M. Sarnat), (Schoken 1978); 5. *Statistics: Decisions and Applications in Business and Economics* (Random House, 1981).

Articles: 1. 'The efficiency analysis of choices involving risk' (with G. Hanoch), *REStud*, 36, July 1969; 2. 'Stochastic dominance, efficiency criteria and efficient portfolios: the multiperiod case', *AER*, 63(5), Dec. 1973; 3. 'Stochastic dominance with riskless assets' (with Y. Kroll), *J Fin*, 11, 1976; 4. 'Equilibrium in an imperfect market: a constraint on the number of securities in the portfolio', *AER*, 68(4), Sept. 1978; 5. 'Approximating expected utility by a function of mean and variance' (with H.M. Markovitz), *AER*, 69(3), June 1979.

LEWIS, W.A.

N.e.

LEXIS, Wilhelm*

Dates and Birthplace 1837–1914, Eschweiler, Germany.

Posts Held Res. in Chemistry, Univ. Heidelberg, 1859–61; Prof., Univs. Strassburg (1872), Dorpat (1874), Freiburg (1876), Breslau (1884), Göttingen (1887).

Degree Grad. Univ. Bonn, 1859.

Career Having studied a wide range of subjects, he turned to the social sciences and brought his statistical expertise to economic questions. He was a strong critic of contemporary mathematical economics as having an inadequate quantitative base. His considerable contributions to population theory and economic time series are probably less well-known than his achievements in the theory of statistics and its application. In an interesting critique of the second volume of Marx's *Capital* in 1885, he correctly predicted the 'transformation problem' that emerged in vol. 3 of *Capital* (not published until 1894); Engels commented extensively on Lexis' solution in his preface to *Capital*, vol. 3.

Publications *Books:* 1. *Die Französischen Ausfahrprämien im* *Zusammenhange mit der Tarifgeschichte und Handelsentwicklung Frankreichs* (1870); 2. *Einleitung in die Theorie der Bevölkerungsstatistik* (1875); 3. *Erörterungen über die Währungsfrage* (1881); 4. *Abhandlungen zur Theorie der Bevölkerungs- und Moralstatistik* (1903); 5. *Das Kredit und Bankswesen* (1914).

Articles: 1. 'The concluding volume of Marx's *Capital*', *QJE*, 10, Oct. 1895.

Secondary Literature K-P. Heiss, 'Lexis, Wilhelm', *IESS*, vol. 9.

LIEBEN, Richard*

Dates and Birthplace 1842–1919, Austrio-Hungary.

Post Held Banker.

Offices Vice-pres., Handels-Akademie and Court Arbitration, Stock Exchange.

Career He advocated the adoption of the gold standard to the inquiry into the reform of the Austrian currency in 1892. For an account of his writings, see Auspitz, Rudolf.

Publications *Books:* 1. *Untersuchungen über die Theorie des Preises* (with R. Auspitz), (1889).

Secondary Literature O. Weinberger, 'Lieben, Richard', *ESS*, vol. 9.

LIEBHAFSKY, Herbert Hugo

Born 1919, Shiner, Texas, USA.

Current Post Prof. Econ., Univ. Texas, Austin, USA, 1956–.

Recent Posts Economist, US Dept of State, 1949–53; Univ. Michigan, 1953–6.

Degrees BA, MA Texas A & M Univ., 1940, 1941; Juris Dr Univ. Michigan Law School, 1949; PhD Univ. Michigan, 1956.

Offices and Honours Member, Michigan Bar, 1949; Fred M. Taylor award Econ. Theory, Michigan, 1955; Board Eds., *SEJ*, 1962–6; Omicron Delta Epsilon, *Amer. Economist*, 1964–9; Life membership, Indian Inst. Econ. Res. (Bhartiya Arthik Shodh Sansthan), 1980; Board Supervisors, Indian Inst. Econ. Res. Journal, *Varta*, 1980.

Principal Contributions Interpretations of the Marshallian constancy assumption; limitations of empirical studies of demand; ideological basis and limitations of the economic theory of law emanating from the Chicago School of economists. Epistomological and ethical preconceptions of economic theory and analysis.

Publications *Books:* 1. *The Nature of Price Theory* (Dorsey Press, 1963, 1968; Hindi transl. 2 vols., 1977); 2. *American Government and Business* (Wiley, 1971).

Articles: 1. 'Marshall's industry and trade: a curious case of neglect', *CJE*, 21, Aug. 1955; 2. 'The rational consumer's demand for psychiatric help: a preference function generating a perfectly price-inelastic demand function', *JPE*, 80(4), July/Aug. 1972; 3. 'Additive preference functions, price elasticities, and empirical studies of demand', *Indian Econ J*, 20, 1973; 4. 'The problem of social cost: an alternative approach', *Natural Resources J*, 13(4), Oct. 1973; 5. 'Price theory as jurisprudence: law and economics, Chicago style', *JEI*, 10, March 1976.

LINDAHL, Erik Robert*

Dates and Birthplace 1891–1960, Stockholm, Sweden.

Posts Held Ass. prof., Univs. Lund (1920–4), Uppsala (1924); Prof., Univs. Göteborg (1932), Lund (1939–58).

Degree Dr. Univ. Lund, 1919.

Career One of the so-called 'Stockholm School' of Swedish economists who, along with Myrdal and Ohlin, developed Wicksell's monetary theory by applying it to conditions of less than full employment. He began in the field of public finance using marginalist principles to produce a value-of-service theory. His work was essentially an attempt to reconcile economic analysis with the concept of equity. The result was to be an economic policy which could anticipate threats to equilibrium and avert them by appropriate monetary adjustments.

Publications *Books:* 1. *Die Gerechtigkeit der Besteuerung* (1919); 2. *Scope and Means of Monetary Policy* (1929);

3. *Studies in the Theory of Money and Capital* (1939).

Articles: 'Some controversial questions in the theory of taxation' (1928), reprinted in *Classics in the Theory of Public Finance*, eds R.A. Musgrave and A.T. Peacock (1958).

Secondary Literature B.B. Seligman, 'Erik Lindahl: money and capital', in *Main Currents in Modern Economics* (The Free Press 1962).

LINDBECK, Assar

Born 1930, Umeå, Sweden.

Current Post Prof., Dir., Inst. Internat. Econ. Studies, Univ. Stockholm, Sweden.

Recent Posts Prof. Econ., Stockholm School Econ., 1964–71; Vis. prof., Columbia Univ. 1968–9, Univ. Cal., Berkeley 1969, ANU, 1970, Yale Univ. 1976, Stanford Univ. 1977.

Degrees MS (Social Sciences), PhD (Econ.) Univ. Stockholm, 1953, 1963.

Offices Member, Nobel Prize Comm. Econ.; Member, Board Swedish Telecommunications; Expert consultant, OECD, UN, World Bank; Fellow, Em. Soc; Hon. member, AEA.

Principal Contributions Attempts to contribute to the micro-foundations of monetary and macro-theory, emphasising the effects on behaviour of firms, households and credit institutes of various instruments of monetary and fiscal policy. Have studied how policies are actually pursued, by endogenising the behaviour of politicians, rather than confining analysis to the effects of hypothetical policies.

Publications *Books:* 1. *A Study in Monetary Analysis* (Acta Universitatis Stockholmiensis, 1963); 2. *The Political Economy of the New Left* (Harper & Row, 1971, 1977); 3. *The Economics of the Agriculture Sector* (Almqvist & Wiksell, 1973); 4. *Swedish Economic Policy* (Univ. Cal. Press, 1974, Macmillan, 1975); 5. *Inflation – Global, International and National Aspects* (Leuven Univ. Press, 1980).

Articles: 1. 'The method of isolation in economic statics – a pedagogical note', *Swed JE*, 68, Sept. 1966; 2. 'The changing role of the national state', *Kyk-*

los, 28(1), 1975; 3. 'Stabilization policy in open economies with endogenous politicians', *AER*, 66(2), May 1976; 4. 'Economic dependence and interdependence in the industrialized world', in *From Marshall Plan to Global Interdependence* (OECD, 1978); 5. 'Imported and structural inflation and aggregate demand – the Scandinavian model reconstructed', in *Inflation and Employment in Open Economies*, ed. A. Lindbeck (N-H, 1979).

LINDBLOM, Charles Edward

Born 1917, Turlock, Cal., USA.
Current Post Sterling Prof. Econ. Polit. Science, Yale Univ., USA.
Degrees BA (Econ.), BA (Polit. Science)Stanford Univ., 1937; PhD (Econ.) Univ. Chicago, 1945; Dr Humane Letters Univ. Chicago, 1973.
Offices and Honours Pres., assoc. Comparative Econ. Stud., 1975–6; Pres., American Polit. Science Assoc., 1980–1.
Principal Contributions Comparative studies of market systems and centrally administered systems.
Publications *Books:* 1. *Politics, Economics and Welfare* (with R.A. Dahl), (Harper Bros., 1953); 2. *A Strategy of Decision* (with D. Braybrooke), (The Free Press, 1963); 3. *The Intelligence of Democracy* (The Free Press, 1965); 4. *Politics and Markets: The World's Political-economic Systems* (Basic Books, 1977); 5. *Usable Knowledge: Social Science and Social Problem Solving* (with D.K. Cohen), (Yale Univ. Press, 1979).
Articles: 1. 'In praise of political science', *World Politics*, Jan. 1957; 2. 'The science of "muddling through" ', *Public Admin. Review*, Spring 1959; 3. 'Still muddling, not yet through', *Public Admin. Review*, Winter 1979.

LINDSAY, Cotton M.

Born 1940, Atlanta, Georgia, USA.
Current Post Prof. Econ., Emory Univ., Atlanta, Georgia, 1981–.
Recent Posts Ass. prof. Econ., 1969–75, Assoc. prof. Econ., 1975–80, Prof. Econ., 1980–1, UCLA.

Degrees BA Univ. Georgia, 1962; PhD Univ. Virginia, 1968.
Offices AEA; SEA; Public Choice Soc.; Mont Pelerin Soc.; NATO Postdoctoral Fellow, 1968–9; Nat. Fellow, Hoover Inst. War, Revolution, Peace, 1975–6.
Principal Contributions Markets for medical care and economic issues in medical education. The theory of human capital. The theory of government enterprises.
Publications *Books:* 1. *Canadian National Health Insurance: Lessons for the US* (Roche Labs, 1978); 2. *National Health Issues: The British experience* (Roche Labs, 1980); 3. *New Directions in Public Health Care*, ed. (Inst. Contemporary Stud., 1980); 4. *Equal Pay for Comparable Work: An Economic Analysis of a New Antidiscrimination Doctrine* (Law Econ. Center Occasional Paper, 1980).
Articles: 1. 'Measuring human capital returns', *JPE*, 79(6), Nov./Dec. 1971; 2. 'A theory of government enterprise', *JPE*, 84(5), Oct. 1976; 3. 'How do human capital investors form earnings expectations?', *SEJ*, 46, Oct. 1979; 4. 'Medical schools: producers of what? Suppliers to whom?', *J Law E*, 23, April 1980; 5. 'Markets for medical care and medical education: an integrated long-run structural approach' (with K.B. Leffler), *JHR*, 16(1), Winter 1981.

LINTNER, John

Born 1916, Lone Elm, Kansas, USA.
Current Post George Gund Prof. Econ. Bus. Admin., Harvard Univ., USA, 1964–.
Recent Posts Ass., assoc., prof., Harvard Bus. School, 1945–64.
Degrees BA (Econ.) Univ. Kansas, 1939; MA (Econ.), PhD (Econ.) Harvard Univ., 1942, 1946.
Offices and Honours AEA; Amer. Assoc. Advancement Science; Harvard Soc. Fellows, 1942–5; Fellow, AAAS, 1961–; Fellow, Em Soc, 1971–; Disting. service citation, Univ. Kansas, 1973; Pres., AFA, 1974.
Principal Contributions Early work on the development of modern portfolio theory, and the so-called 'capital asset

pricing model', Later work incorporated diverse information sets and probability assessments, restrictions on short selling and the absence of a riskless asset. Also identified an important risk-eliminating as well as a risk-sharing function of capital markets. Earlier work on corporate savings behaviour developed the model of dividend policy which is still standard, and examined the effects of taxes on corporate growth and merger activity. Later work includes both theoretical and empirical studies of inflation on security returns.

Publications   *Books:* 1. *Effects of Federal Taxes on Growing Enterprises* (with J.K. Butters), (Harvard Univ. Press, 1945); 2. *Mutual Savings Banks in the Savings and Mortgage Markets*, (Harvard Univ. Press, 1948); 3. *Effects of Taxation on Corporate Mergers* (with J.K. Butters and W.L. Cary), (Harvard Univ. Press, 1951).

Articles: 1. 'Distribution of incomes of corporations among dividends, retained earnings, and taxes', *AER*, 46(2), May 1956; 2. 'The valuation of risk assets and the selection of risky investments in stock portfolios and capital budgets', *REStat*, 47, Feb. 1965; 3. 'The aggregation of investor's diverse judgements and preferences in purely competitive securities markets', *J Fin. Quant. Analysis*, 4(4), Dec. 1969; 4. 'The market price of risk, size of market, and investor's risk aversion', *REStat*, 52, Feb. 1970; 5. 'Inflation and security returns', *J Fin*, 30(2), May 1975.

LIPPMAN, Steven A.

Born   1943, Los Angeles, Cal., USA.
Current Post   Prof., Grad. School Management, UCLA, 1967–.
Degrees   BA. Univ. Cal., Berkeley, 1964; MS, PhD Stanford Univ., 1967, 1968.
Offices   Assoc. ed., *Management Science*, 1972–81.
Principal Contributions   Introduced the most useful conditions in the theory underlying Markov decision processes with unbounded rewards. Introduced the idea of phantom transitions in continuous time, finite horizon dynamic programming. Wrote the most up-to-

date survey of work on job search (with J.J. McCall). Many results in the economics of uncertainty.

Publications   *Books:* 1. *Elements of Probability and Statistics* (Holt, Rinehart & Winston, 1971); 2. *Studies in the Economics of Search* (with J.J. McCall), (N-H, 1979).

Articles: 1. 'On dynamic programming with unbounded rewards', *Management Science*, 21 1975; 2. 'Applying a new device in the optimization of exponential queueing systems', *Operations Res.*, 23, 1975; 3. 'The economics of job search: a survey, Pts I-II' (with J.J. McCall), *EI*, 14(2, 3), June, Sept. 1976; 4. 'The economics of uncertainty: selected topics and probabilistic methods' (with J.J. McCall), in *Handbook of Mathematical Economics*, eds K.J. Arrow and M. Intriligator (N-H, 1981).

LIPSEY, Richard

Born   1928, Victoria, Canada.
Current Post   Sir Edward Peacock Prof. Econ., Queen's Univ., Ontario, Canada.
Recent Posts   Prof. Econ., LSE, 1961–4; Vis. prof., Univ. Cal., Berkeley, 1963–4; Prof. Econ., Chairman Dept. Econ., Dean, School Social Studies, Univ. Essex, 1964–9; Vis. prof., Univ. British Columbia, 1969–70, Univ. Colorado, 1974–5; Simon Vis. prof., Univ. Manchester, 1972; Irving Fisher Vis. prof., Yale Univ., 1979–80.
Degrees   BA Univ. British Columbia, 1951; MA Univ. Toronto, 1953; PhD Univ. London, 1957.
Offices and Honours   Ed., *REStud*, 1962–4; Member, Governing Council and Board, NIESR, 1964–70; Chairman, Econ. Study Society, 1965–9; Member, UK SSRC, 1966–9; Fellow, Em Soc, 1974; Fellow, Royal Society Canada, 1980; Queen's prize University-wide Excellence in Res., inaugural prize, 1980; Chairman, CEA, 1980–1.
Principal Contributions   Welfare economics: the general theory of second best and customs union theory; monetary and value theory; early sorting out of stocks and flows and temporary and full equilibrium in Patinkin's first-edi-

tion model; theoretical and empirical analysis of trade credit. Inflation theory: theory and empirical work on Phillips curves and profits as a determinant of wage inflation and incomes policies. Location theory: demonstration that Hotelling's model is not a major explanation of clustering of firms, while comparison and multi-purpose shopping is. Industrial organisation; work on how the durability and divisibility of capital affects its ability to act as an entry barrier.

Publications *Books:* 1. *An Introduction to Positive Economics* (Weidenfeld & Nicolson, 1963, 1979; Portuguese, Spanish, German, Italian, Greek, Hebrew, Gujurati, Sinhali and Tamil transls); Australian edn (with P. Langley and D. Mahoney), (1982); 2. *Economics* (with P.O. Steiner), (Harper & Row, 1966, 1981; French, Spanish and Bhasa transls); Canadian edn (with G.R. Sparks and P.O. Steiner), (1973, 1979); 3. *An Introduction to a Mathematical Treatment of Econòmics* (with G.C. Archibald), (Weidenfeld & Nicolson, 1967, 1977; Spanish, Portuguese and German transls); 4. *The Theory of Customs Unions: A General Equilibrium Analysis* (Weidenfeld & Nicolson, 1973); 5. *Mathematical Economics: Methods and Applications* (with G.C. Archibald), (Harper & Row, 1976).

Articles: 1. 'The general theory of second best' (with K. Lancaster), *REStud*, 24, June 1957; 2. 'The relation between unemployment and the rate of change of money wage rates in the United Kingdom, 1862–1957: a further analysis', *Ec*, N.S. 27, Feb. 1960; 3. 'The principle of minimum differentiation reconsidered: some new developments in the theory of spatial competition' (with B.C. Eaton), *REStud*, 42(1), Jan. 1975; 4. 'Capital, commitment and entry equilibrium' (with B.C. Eaton), *Bell JE*, 1981; 5. 'An economic theory of central places' (with B.C. Eaton), *EJ*, 91, Dec. 1981.

LIST, Friedrich*

Dates and Birthplace 1789–1846, Reutlingen, Germany.
Posts Held Prof. Polit. Econ., Univ.

Tübingen, 1817–9; Journalist and businessman in the USA, 1825–32; Amer. Consul, Leipzig and Baden.
Offices Member, Legislature of Württemberg, 1820; Founder, *Das Zollvereinsblatt*, 1843.
Career Whilst a political exile in US he was encouraged by a protectionist organisation to write the *Outlines . . . in* which he drafted the national system of political economy that was more completely realised in his 1841 book. His emphasis was on political factors, and particularly the significance of the nation. His enthusiastic promotion of railways was partially because of their role in the economic integration of the German states of the Zollverein. His advocacy of protection has been treated as if it were general, rather than a recognition of the need for protection in certain stages of political and economic development; he was in fact no doctrinaire protectionist.

Publications *Books:* 1. *Outlines of Political Economy* (1827, 1931); 2. *The National System of Political Economy* (1841, 1928); 3. *Schriften, Reden, Briefe*, 10 vols (1927–36).

Secondary Literature E. Salin and R.L. Frey, 'List, Friedrich', *IESS*, vol 9.

LITTLE, Ian Malcom David

Born 1918, Rugby, England.
Current Post Retired.
Recent Posts Fellow, Nuffield Coll., Univ. Oxford, 1952–76; Dep. Dir., Econ. Section, UK Treasury, 1953–5; Vice-pres., OECD Development Centre, 1965–7; Prof., Univ. Oxford, 1972–6; World Bank, 1976–8.
Degrees BA, DPhil. Univ. Oxford, 1947, 1949.
Offices Board member, British Airports Authority, 1969–74; Member, UN Comm. Development Planning, 1972–5; Fellow, BA, 1973–.
Principal Contributions 1950 book which analysed the normative nature of welfare economics and the theory of consumers' behaviour underlying it, while drawing attention to the dubious validity of optimal solutions. In 1960s wrote on international aid and instituted

research on the failings of the industrialisation policies of developing countries. In the 1970s suggested and developed methods of cost-benefit analysis appropriate to developing countries.

Publications *Books:* 1. *A Critique of Welfare Economics* (OUP, 1950, 1957); 2. *The Price of Fuel* (OUP, 1953); 3. *International Aid* (with J.M. Clifford), (A & U, Basic Books, 1965); 4. *Industry and Trade in Some Developing Countries* (with T. Scitovsky and M.F.G. Scott), (OUP, 1970); 5. *Project Appraisal and Planning for Developing Countries* (with J.A. Mirrlees), (Heinemann, 1974).

Articles: 1. 'A reformulation of the theory of consumers' behaviour', *OEP*, N.S. 1, Jan. 1949; 2. 'Direct versus indirect taxes', *EJ*, 61, Sept. 1951; 3. 'Social choice and individual values', *JPE*, 60, Oct. 1952; 4. 'The real cost of labour, and the choice between consumption and investment', *QJE*, 75, Feb. 1961; 5. 'Higgledy-piggledy growth', *BOIS*, 24, Nov. 1962.

LIU, Ben-Chieh

Born 1938, Chungking, China.
Current Post Manager, Energy Environmental Econ. Projects, Argonne Nat. Laboratory, Ill., USA.
Recent Posts Adjunct prof., Univ. Missouri, 1969–78; Sr Economist, 1972–4, Principal economist, 1974–80, Sr adviser Econ., 1980, Midwest Res. Inst., Kansas City.
Degrees BA Nat. Taiwan Univ., 1961; MA Memorial Univ., Newfoundland, 1965; MA, PhD Washington Univ., 1968, 1971.
Offices Constitution Comm. member, ASA; AEA; Pol. Comm. member, Assoc. Social Econ.; Em Soc; Internat. Inst. Stats.
Principal Contributions Developed quality of life models for US by state and by metropolitan areas; developed physical and economic damage functions for air pollution and provided regional damage estimates; developed physical and economic damage functions for earthquake related natural hazard; developed benefit-cost cross-impact probabilistic approach model for public

investment project cost-effectiveness evaluation; contributed to urban and regional planning and development in the fields of health, transportation, retail trades, migration and industrial growth.

Publications *Books:* 1. *Quality of Life in US* (Midwest Res. Inst., 1972); 2. *Quality of Life Indicators in US Metropolitan Areas* (US Govt Printing Office, 1976, Praeger, 1977); 3. *Air Pollution Damage Functions and Regional Damage Estimates* (Technomic Publishing, 1978); 4. *Physical and Economic Damage Functions for Earthquakes* (Westview Press, 1981).

Articles: 1. 'Determinants of retail sales in large metropolitan areas, 1954 and 1963', *JASA*, 65, Dec. 1970; 2. 'Differential net migration rates and the quality of life', *REStat*, 57(3), Aug. 1975; 3. 'Economic and non-economic quality of life indicators in large metropolitan areas', *American J Econ. Sociology*, 1977; 4. 'Air pollution and material damage functions', *J Environmental Management*, 1978; 5. 'An integrated model for earthquake risk and damage assessment', *J Math. Social Science*, 1981.

LIU, Ta-Chung*

Dates and Birthplace 1914–75, China.
Posts Held Ass. Commercial Counsellor, Chinese Embassy, Washington DC, 1942–5; Economist, IMF, 1945–55; Prof. Econ., Cornell Univ., 1955–75.
Degrees BS, MS (Engineering), PhD (Econ.) Cornell Univ., 1936, 1937, 1940.
Offices and Honours Secretary, Chinese delegation, Bretton Woods Conference, 1946; Chairman, Taiwan Commission on Tax Reform, 1968–70; Order of Bright Star with Grand Cordon, 2nd class, Republic of China, 1970.
Career First attempt to construct national accounts for China. First monthly econometric model of the US economy. Estimates of manufacturing production functions using cross-section data (with G. Hildebrand). Theoretical analysis of the econometric problems of underidentification, structural estima-

tion and forecasting, and the effects of aggregation over time.

Publications *Books:* 1. *China's National Income, 1931–36* (Brookings Inst., 1946); 2. *Measuring Production Functions in the United States, 1957: An Inter-industry and Interstate Comparison of Productivity* (with G.H. Hildebrand), (Cornell Univ. Press, 1965); 3. *The Economy of the Chinese Mainland: National Income and Economic Development, 1933–39* (with K.C. Yeh), (Princeton Univ. Press, 1965); 4. *Economic Trends in Communist China*, ed. (with W. Galenson and A. Eckstein), (Aldine, 1968); 5. *Statement in Economic Development in Mainland China: Hearings Before the Joint Economic Committee* (US Govt Printing Office, 1972).

Articles: 1. 'The elasticity of US import demand: a theoretical and empirical appraisal', *IMF Staff Papers*, 3, Feb. 1954; 2. 'Under-identification, structural estimation and forecasting', *Em*, 28, Oct. 1960, reprinted in *Selected Readings in Econometrics from Econometrica*, eds J.W. Hooper and M. Nerlove (MIT Press, 1970); 3. 'A monthly recursive econometric model of United States: a test of feasibility', *REStat*, 51(1), Feb. 1969; 4. 'The covariance matrix of the limited information estimator and identification test' (with W. Breen), *Em*, 37(2), April 1969; 5. 'Chinese and other Asian economies: a quantitative evaluation' (with K.C. Yeh), *AER*, 63(2), May 1973.

Secondary Literature L.R. Klein *et al.*, 'Ta-Chung Liu, 1914–1975', *Em*, 45(2), March 1977.

LIVIATAN, N.

N.e.

LLOYD, Cynthia B.

Born 1943, New York City, NY, USA.

Current Post Pop. affairs officer, UN, New York, 1979–.

Recent Posts Ass. prof., Barnard Coll, Columbia Univ., 1972–9; Co-dir., Program Sex Roles Social Change, Center Social Sciences, Columbia Univ., 1977–9.

Degrees BA Bryn Mawr Coll., 1964; MA, PhD Columbia Univ., 1967, 1972.

Offices Member, AEA, PAA; Acting Chairman, Econ. Dept, Barnard Coll., 1976–7.

Principal Contributions Leader in bringing the study of women in the labour market into the mainstream of economic analysis. Most recent book is addressed to the question why such radical change in women's roles in the labour market have taken place without any concomitant improvement in their relative economic status. What follows is a critical analysis within a dynamic framework of the interaction of supply and demand in the market to produce differential outcomes. The net impact of various aspects of government policy are also included in the analysis.

Publications *Books:* 1. *Sex Discrimination and the Division of Labor*, ed. and contributor (Columbia Univ. Press, 1975); 2. *Women in the Labor Market*, ed. (with E. Andrews and C. Gilroy), (Columbia Univ. Press, 1979); 3. *The Economics of Sex Differentials* (with B. Niemi), (Columbia Univ. Press, 1979).

Articles: 1. 'An economic analysis of the impact of government on fertility: some examples from the developed countries', *Public Pol.*, 22(4), Fall 1974; 2. 'Sex differentials in labor supply elasticity: the implications of sectoral shifts in demand' (with B. Niemi), *AER*, 68(2), May 1978; 3. 'Female labor supply in the context of inflation' (with B. Niemi), *AER*, 71(2), May 1981.

LLOYD, William Forster*

Dates and Birthplace 1795–1852, Bradenham, England.

Posts Held Student, Christ Church Coll., Univ. Oxford, 1812–37; Drummond Prof., Univ. Oxford, 1832–7.

Degree MA Univ. Oxford, 1818.

Offices Fellow, Royal Soc., 1834.

Career During his tenure of the Drummond Chair, he published some of his lectures, as provided for under the terms attached to the appointment. The lectures generally have a policy orientation, except in the case of the one of

1833 on value. This more purely theoretical lecture contains a very clear description of the principle of diminishing marginal utility. Lloyd's work was largely forgotten until this early statement of the principle was rediscovered by Seligman in 1903.

Publications *Books:* 1. *Prices of Corn in Oxford* (1830); 2. *Lectures on Population, Value, Poor Laws and Rent* (1837).

Secondary Literature R.M. Romano, 'William Forster Lloyd – a non-Ricardian?', *HOPE*, 9(3), Fall 1977.

LOASBY, Brian J.

Born 1930, England.

Current Post Prof. Management Econ., Univ. Stirling, 1971–.

Recent Posts Lecturer, 1967, Sr lecturer, 1968, Univ. Stirling.

Degrees BA, MLitt Univ. Cambridge, 1952, 1957.

Principal Contributions The analysis of decision processes in organisations, extending and applying the work of Simon, Cyert and March, also relating behaviour in organisation to the theory of knowledge; the development of economic theory, especially the theory of the firm, and the value and limitations of models in a world of complexity and ignorance: an attempt to provide some answers to problems emphasised by Shackle of rational behaviour in the face of an unknowable future.

Publications *Books:* 1. *The Swindon Project* (Pitman, 1973); 2. *Choice, Complexity and Ignorance* (CUP, 1976). *Articles:* 'Long-range forward planning in perspective', *JMS*, 4, Oct. 1967; 2. 'The decision maker in the organization', *JMS*, 5, Oct. 1968; 3. Hypothesis and paradigm in the theory of the firm', *EJ*, 81, Dec. 1971; 4. An analysis of decision processes', *R & D Management*, 4, 1974; 5. 'Whatever happened to Marshall's theory of value', *SJPE*, 25(1), Feb. 1978.

LOCKE, John*

Dates and Birthplace 1632–1704, Somerset, England.

Posts Held Sr Student, Christ Church Coll., Univ. Oxford, 1658–83; Political adviser, Lord Shaftesbury and other Whig politicians; held various minor official positions after 1689.

Offices Member, Council of Trade and Plantations; Fellow, Royal Soc., 1688.

Career One of England's greatest philosophers whose wide interests included economics. His two specifically economic publications of 1691 and 1695 advocate maintaining the interest rate and not devaluing the currency. He distinguished between value and price, related market value to supply and demand, and saw price as determined by the amount of money available in relation to supply and demand.

Publications *Books:* 1. *Two Treatises of Government* (1690); 2. *An Essay Concerning Human Understanding*, 2 vols (1690); 3. *Some Considerations of the Consequences of the Lowering of Interest and Raising the Value of Money* (1691); 4. *Further Considerations* (1695).

Secondary Literature R.L. Colie, 'Locke, John', *IESS*, vol. 9; K.I. Vaughn, *John Locke Economist and Social Scientist* (Univ. of Chicago Press, 1980).

LONGE, Francis Davy*

Dates and Birthplace 1831–1910, Suffolk, England.

Posts Held Ass. commissioner Children's Employment Commission; Inspector local govt board.

Degrees BA Univ. Oxford.

Career Author of the first decisive refutation of the wages fund theory which was, however, ignored by Mill whose recantation seems to have been entirely due to Thornton's independent treatment of the doctrine.

Publications *Books:* 1. *An Inquiry into the Law of Strikes* (1860); 2. *A Refutation of the Wage-Fund Theory* (1866, 1903).

Secondary Literature J.H. Hollander, 'Longe, Francis Davy', *ESS*, vol. 9.

LONGFIELD, Samuel Mountifort*

Dates and Birthplace 1802–84, Ireland.

Posts Held Barrister and judge; Prof. Polit. Econ., 1832–6, Regius Prof. Law, 1834–84, Trinity Coll., Dublin.

Degrees BA, MA, LLD Trinity Coll., Dublin, 1823, 1829, 1831.

Offices Pres., Stat. Social Enquiry Soc., Ireland, 1863–7.

Career Better known for his legal career, he nevertheless during his period as first holder of the Whately Chair published various lectures which included remarkable economic insights. His analysis of the determinants of value, distribution of income, and nature of capital are all in advance of contemporary thinking. The marginalist aspects of his writings possibly owe something to his considerable ability as a mathematician.

Publications *Books:* 1. *Four Lectures on Poor Laws* (1834); 2. *Lectures on Political Economy* (1834, 1931); 3. *Three Lectures on Commerce and One on Absenteeism* (1835).

Secondary Literature E. McKinley, 'Longfield, Samuel Mountifort', *IESS*, vol. 9; L.S. Moss, *Mountifort, Longfield: Ireland's First Professor of Political Economy* (Green Hill Publishers, 1976).

LORIA, Achille*

Dates and Birthplace 1857–1943, Mantua, Italy.

Posts Held Prof. Polit. Econ., Univ. Siena, 1881–91, Univ. Padua, 1891–1903, Univ. Turin, 1903–32.

Degrees Laurea Law, Univ. Bologna, 1877.

Offices Member, Academia dei Lincei, 1901; Senator, 1919.

Career Developed his own quasi-Marxian, deterministic theory of economic development based on the relationship of the productivity of land to the density of population: land scarcity leads to the subjugation of some parts of society by others, this subjugation taking such forms as feudalism or high capitalism. His interest in land-labour ratios encouraged him to develop some ideas on the location of industry independently of Alfred Weber. Frequent use of data from the Americas and the relevance of some of his ideas to American circumstances gave his writings a certain currency in US.

Publications *Books:* 1. *La Legge di Popolazione ed il Sistema Sociale* (1882); 2. *The Economic Foundations of Society* (1886, 1904); 3. *Contemporary Social Problems* (1894, 1911); 4. *Il Movimento Operaio: Origine, Forme, Sviluppo* (1903); 5. *The Economic Synthesis: A Study of the Laws of Income* (1909, 1914); 6. *The Economic Causes of War* (1912, 1918); 7. *Dinamica Economica* (1935).

Secondary Literature L. Einaudi, 'Achille Loria 1857–1943', *EJ*, 56, 1946; S.B. Clough, 'Loria Achille', *IESS*, vol. 9.

LOVELL, Michael C.

Born 1930, Cambridge, Mass., USA.

Current Post Prof. Econ., Wesleyan Univ., Middletown Conn., USA, 1969–.

Recent Posts Ass. prof., Yale Univ., 1959–63; Assoc. prof., 1963–6, Prof. Econ., 1966–9, Carnegie-Mellon Univ.

Degrees BA Reed Coll., 1952; MA Stanford Univ., 1954; PhD Econ. Harvard Univ., 1959.

Offices and Honours Assoc. ed., *Em*, 1965–8; Foreign ed., *REStud*, 1968–70; First prize, Joint Council Econ. Education for the teaching of econ., 1973–4; Sr adviser, Brookings Panel Econ. Activity, 1974–; Comm. Publications, AEA, 1974–8, Chairman, 1976–8; Assoc. ed., *JASA*, 1975–7; Fellow, Em Soc, 1980.

Principal Contributions Contributions range from a statistical study of the early history of the Bank of England to an examination of the role of inventories and expectational errors in the generation of business cycles. Developed a least squares procedure for seasonally adjusting economic time series, devised a CPI Futures Market and investigated pre-testing bias. Also studied the impact of the minimum wage on teenage unemployment, and demonstrated that the distribution of income influences the provision of public goods.

Publications *Books:* 1. *Sales Anticipations and Inventory Behavior* (with A. Hirsch), (Wiley, 1969); 2. *Macroeconomics: Measurement, Theory and Policy* (Wiley, 1975; Spanish transl., 1979).

Articles: 1. 'Buffer stocks, sales expectations, and stability: a multi-sector analysis of inventory cycle', *Em*, 30, April 1962; 2. 'Seasonal adjustment of economic time series and multiple regression analysis', *JASA*, 58, Dec. 1963; 3. 'Product differentiation and market structure', *WEJ*, 82(2), June 1970; 4. 'The production of economic literature, an interpretation', *JEL*, 11(1), March 1973; 5. 'Spending for education, the exercise of public choice', *REStat*, 60(4), Nov. 1978.

LOWE, Adolph

Born 1893, Stuttgart, Germany.
Current Post Retired.
Recent Posts Prof. Econ. Theory Sociology, Univ. Kiel, 1926–31; Prof. Polit. Econ. Emeritus, Goethe Univ., Frankfurt-am-Main, 1931–3; Hon. special lecturer, Econ. Polit. Science, Univ. Manchester, 1933–40; Alvin Johnson Prof. Econ. Emeritus, Grad. Faculty, New School Social Res., New York City, 1941–63.
Degrees LLB, LLD Univ. Tübingen, 1915, 1918.
Offices and Honours Dir. Res., Inst. World Econ., Univ. Kiel, 1926–30; Dir. Res., Inst. World Affairs, New School Social Res., 1942–51; Hon. member, German Soc. Sociology, 1975; Veblen-Commons award, 1979.
Principal Contributions Main interest: elaboration of a political economics. In contrast with traditional approaches – classical, neo-classical, Marxian – which base their explanatory and predictive analyses on some maximisation hypothesis, political economics tries to derive the means – behaviour, motivations, public controls – suitable to attain one or more politically stipulated macro-goals. Other concerns: a theory of growth with emphasis on disequili-

brium paths; a theory of process innovations; a three-sector model as basis of capital theory; and spontaneous conformity on political essentials as a precondition of political liberty.

Publications *Books:* 1. *Economics and Sociology*, (A & U, 1915); 2. *The Price of Liberty* (Hogarth Press, 1937); 3. *On Economic Knowledge* (Harper & Row, 1965, M.E. Sharpe, 1977); 4. *The Path of Economic Growth* (CUP, 1977); 5. *The Dielmma of Freedom* (Columbia Univ. Press, 1982).

Articles: 1. 'A structural model of production', *Social Res.*, 19(2), 1952; 2. 'The classical theory of economic growth', *Social Res.*, 21(2), 1954; 3. 'Structural analysis of real capital formation', in NBER, *Capital Formation and Economic Growth* (Princeton Univ. Press, 1955); 4. 'Technological unemployment reexamined', in *Wirtschaft und Kultursystem* (Eugen Rentsch Verlag, 1955); 5. 'Toward a science of political economics', in *Economic Means and Social Ends*, ed. R.L. Heilbroner (Prentice-Hall, 1969).

LOWE, Joseph*

Dates and Birthplace N.e.
Career Improved the technique of index numbers and recommended their use for measuring the variations of money over time. The 'tabular standard' as he called it was intended for voluntary use in stabilising long run contracts. It constitutes a major step forward in monetary analysis.
Publications *Books:* 1. *An Inquiry into the State of the British West Indies* (1807); 2. *The Present State of England in Regard to Agriculture, Trade and Finance* (1822, 1823).

LUCAS, Robert E. Jr

Born 1937, Yakima, Washington, USA.
Current Post John Dewey Disting. service prof. Econ., Univ. Chicago, USA.

Recent Posts Prof. Econ., Carnegie-Mellon Univ., 1970–4; Ford Foundation Vis. res. prof. Econ., Univ. Chicago, 1974–5; Prof. Econ., Vice-chairman, Econ. Dept., Univ. Chicago, 1975–.

Degrees BA (history), PhD (Econ.) Univ. Chicago, 1959, 1964.

Offices Fellow, Em Soc, 1976; Ed., *JPE*, 1978–; Member, Exec. Comm., AEA, 1979–; Member, NAS, 1980; Fellow, AAAS, 1980; Marion O'Kellie McKay Lecturer, Univ. Pittsburgh, 1980; *JMCB* Lecturer, Ohio State Univ., 1980.

Principal Contributions Econometric studies of capital-labour substitution and variations in capacity utilisation; theory of investment and technological change at the firm and industry level; theoretical and econometric work on labour supply; business-cycle theory, and capital theory.

Publications *Books:* 1. *Studies in Business-cycle Theory* (MIT Press, 1981); 2. *Rational Expectations and Econometric Practice*, ed. (with T.J. Sargent), (Univ. Minnesota Press, 1981).

Articles: 1. 'Adjustment costs and the theory of supply', *JPE*, 75(4), Pt 1, Aug. 1967; 2. 'Real wages, employment, and inflation' (with L.A. Rapping), *JPE*, 77(5), Sept./Oct. 1969; 3. 'Investment under uncertainty' (with E.C. Prescott), *Em*, 39(5), Sept. 1971; 4. 'Expectations and the neutrality of money', *JET*, 4(2), April 1972, repr. in *Uncertainty in Economics: A Book of Readings*, eds P. Diamond and M. Rothschild (Univ. Chicago Press, 1974); 5. 'Econometric policy evaluation: a critique', in *The Phillips Curve and Labor Markets*, eds K. Brunner and A. Meltzer (N-H, 1975).

LUCE, Robert Duncan

Born 1925, Scranton, Penn., USA.

Current Post Alfred North Whitehead Prof. Psychology, Harvard Univ., USA.

Recent Posts Ass. prof. Sociology Math. Stats, Columbia Univ., 1954–7; Lecturer, Social Relations, Harvard Univ., 1957–9; Prof. Psychology, 1959–68, Benjamin Franklin Prof., 1968–9, Univ. Penn.; Vis. prof., Inst. Advanced Study, Princeton Univ., 1969–72; Prof. Social Science, Univ. Cal., Irvine, 1972–6.

Degrees BS (Aeronautical Eng.) 1945, PhD (Maths) 1950, MIT.

Offices and Honours AAAS, 1966; Amer. Psychological Assoc. Disting. Scientific Contributions award, 1970; NAS, 1972; Pres., Psychometric Soc., 1976–7; Pres., Soc. Math. Psychology, 1979.

Principal Contributions Exposition of game theory; probabilistic models of choice; theory of semi-orders; conjoint measurement; conditional expected utility theory (with D.H. Krantz, 1971); and exposition of axiomatic measurement theory.

Publications *Books:* 1. *Games and Decisions* (with H. Raiffa), (Wiley, 1959); 2. *Individual Choice Behavior* (Wiley, 1959); 3. *Handbook of Mathematical Psychology* 3 vols, ed. (with R.R. Bush and E. Galanter), (Wiley, 1963, 1965); 4. *Foundations of Measurement* (with D.H. Krantz *et al.*), (Academic Press, 1971); 5. *Contemporary Developments in Mathematical Psychology* ed. (with D.H. Krantz *et al.*), (Freeman, 1974).

Articles: 1. 'Semi-orders and a theory of utility discrimination', *Em*, 24, April 1956; 2. 'Simultaneous conjoint measurement: a new type of fundamental measurement' (with J.W. Tukey), *J Math. Psychology*, 1, 1964; 3. 'A neural timing theory for response times and the psychophysics of intensity' (with D.M. Green), *Psychological Review*, 79, 1972; 4. 'The algebra of measurement' (with L. Narens), *J Pure Applied Algebra*, 8, 1976; 5. 'Dimensionally invariant laws correspond to meaningful qualitative relations', *Philosophy of Science*, 45, 1978.

LUNDBERG, Erik Filip

Born 1907, Stockholm, Sweden.

Current Post Scientific adviser,

Skandinaviska Enskilda Banken, Stockholm.

Recent Posts Dir. Govt Econ. Res. Inst. (Konjunkturinstitutet), 1937–55; Member, State Power Board, 1946–77; Prof. Univ. Stockholm, 1946–65; Member, Govt Planning Council, 1961–; Prof. Stockholm School Econ., 1965–70.

Degree PhD (Econ.) Univ. Stockholm, 1937.

Offices and Honours Pres., Royal Swedish Academy Science, 1973–6; Chairman, Nobel Comm. Econ., 1975–80; Söderström's medal Econ. Science, 1980; Bernhard Harms prize, Weltwirtschaftliches Inst., Kiel, 1980.

Principal Contributions Theory of business cycles, particularly models of unstable growth based on the multiplier and acceleration principles. Studies of inflation based on excess demand gaps for goods and labour. Analysis of wage inflation, including effects of marginal and other taxes (tax multiplier effects). Analysis of relations between capital investment and productivity growth in Swedish industry. Discovery of the 'Horndal effect': how labour productivity can go on rising over a long period without new investment. In this connection carried out some empirical analysis of relations between *ex-ante* and actual *ex-post* returns on investment. Comparative studies of stabilisation policies in Sweden from 1920–80.

Publications *Books:* 1. *Studies in the Theory of Economic Expansion* (P.S. Kinga Son, 1937, 1956); 2. *Business Cycles and Economic Policy* (A & U, 1957); 3. *Produktivitet och Räntabilitet* (Productivity and profitability) (Norstedt and Söner, 1961); 4. *Instability and Economic Growth* (Yale Univ. Press, 1968); 5. *Inflation och Arbetslöshet* (Inflation and unemployment) (with L. Calmfors), (SNS, 1974).

Articles: 1. 'The profitability of investment', *EJ*, 69, Dec. 1959; 2. 'Studier i monetär analys' ('Studies in monetary analysis'), *Ekon Tids*, 2, 1963; 3. 'Productivity and structural change – a policy issue in Sweden', *EJ*, Supplement, 82, March 1972; 4. 'World inflation and national policies', Inst. International Econ. Studies, Stockholm,

Seminar paper no. 80, 1977; 5. 'Fiscal and monetary policies in Taiwan', Inst. Internat. Econ. Stud., Stockholm, Seminar paper no. 90, 1977.

LUTZ, Friedrich August*

Dates and Birthplace 1901–75, Sarrebourg, France.

Posts Held Privatdozent, Univ. Freibourg/Br, 1932–8; Instructor, Prof., Princeton Univ., 1938–53; Prof., Univ. Zürich, 1953.

Degree Dr ès sc. pol.

Offices Member, Mont. Pélerin Soc.

Career Writer in the Austrian tradition, whose *Zinstheorie* was a masterful survey of the history of interest theory and whose *Theory of Investment of the Firm* was a major modern restatement of Austrian capital theory in micro-economic terms.

Publications *Books:* 1. *Das Konjunkturproblem in der Nationalökonomie* (1932); 2. *Rebuilding the World Economy* (with N.S. Buchanan), (1947); 3. *Theory of Investment of the Firm* (with V. Lutz), (1951); 4. *Zinstheorie* (1956).

LUXEMBOURG, Rosa*

Dates and Birthplace 1870–1919, Zamosc, Russia.

Posts Held Polit. leader, German Social Democratic Party; Lecturer, Party School, Berlin, 1907–.

Degree Dr Univ. Zürich, 1898.

Career A founder of the Social Democratic Party of Poland, the leader of the Left Wing of the German Social Democrats and a prominent Marxist economic theoretician. In *Accumulation of Capital* she argued that capitalism must expand into underdeveloped countries and non-capitalist areas, because of the inherent insufficiency of aggregate demand. In this way capitalism is an essential cause of the international tensions and instabilities that characterise the modern world. She was murdered whilst in military custody during the 1919 German Revolution.

Publications   *Books:* 1. *Die Indus-trielle Entwicklung Polens* (1898); 2. *The Accumulation of Capital* (1913, 1956); 3. *Gesammelte Werke*, vols 3, 4 and 6 only (1922–8); 4. *Ausgewählte Reden und Schriften*, 2 vols (1951).

Secondary Literature   J.P. Nettl, *Rosa Luxembourg*, 2 vols (OUP, 1966); T. Kowalik, 'Luxembourg, Rosa', *IESS*, vol. 9.

LYDALL, Harold F.

Born 1916, Pretoria, S. Africa.
Current Post Retired. Emeritus Prof. Econ., Univ. East Anglia; Hon. res. assoc., Inst. Econ. Stats, Univ. Oxford.
Recent Posts Prof. Econ., Univ. Adelaide, 1962–7; UN, Geneva, 1967–70; Prof. Econ., Univ. East Anglia, 1970–8.
Degrees BA Univ. S. Africa, 1935; MA Univ. Oxford, 1950.
Offices Fellow, Em Soc; Member, Exec. Comm., NIESR.
Principal Contributions Empirical studies of distributions of income and wealth with international comparisons. Theory of earnings inequality. Theory of factor shares. The role of small firms in economic development. Employment effects of expansion of trade in manufactures between developed and developing countries.
Publications   *Books:* 1. *British Incomes and Savings* (Blackwell, 1955); 2. *The Role of Small Enterprises in Indian Economic Development* (with P.N. Dhar), (Asia Publishing House, 1961); 3. *The Structure of Earnings* (OUP, 1968); 4. *Trade and Employment* (ILO, 1975); 5. *A Theory of Income Distribution* (OUP, 1979).
Articles: 1. 'The life cycle in income, saving, and asset ownership', *Em*, 23, April 1955; 2. 'A comparison of the distribution of income and wealth in Britain and the United States' (with J.B. Lansing), *AER*, 49, March 1959; 3. 'The long-term trend in the size distribution of income', *JRSS*, A, 122, Pt 1, 1959; 4. 'A theory of distribution and growth with economies of scale', *EJ*, 81, March 1971; 5. 'Theories of the distribution of earnings', in *The Personal Distribution of Incomes*, ed. A.B. Atkinson (A & U, 1976).

M

MADDALA, Gangadharrao S.

Born 1933, Hyderabad, India.
Current Post Grad. res. prof. Econ., Univ. Florida, USA, 1975–.
Recent Posts Ass. prof. Econ., Stanford Univ., 1963–7; Prof. Econ., Univ. Rochester, 1967–75.
Degrees BA (Maths) Andhra Univ., India, 1955; MA (Stats) Bombay Univ., 1957; PhD (Econ.) Univ. Chicago, 1963.
Offices Assoc. ed., *Em*, 1971–80; Fellow, Em Soc, 1975; Vice-pres., Atlantic Econ. Soc., 1981–2.
Principal Contributions International diffusion of technical change. Analysis of pooled cross-section and time series data. Flexible functional forms for Lorenz curves and income distributions. Analysis of disequilibrium models and models involving individual self-selection.
Publications   *Books:* 1. *Econometrics* (McGraw-Hill, 1977).
Articles: 1. 'International diffusion of technical change – a case study of the oxygen steelmaking process (with P.T. Knight), *EJ*, 77, Sept. 1977; 2. 'The use of variance components models in pooling cross-section and time series data', *Em*, 39(2), March 1971; 3. 'Maximum likelihood methods for models of markets in disequilibrium' (with F.D. Nelson), *Em*, 42(6), Nov. 1974; 4. 'A function for size distribution of incomes', *Em*, 44(5). Sept. 1976; 5. 'Returns to college education: an investigation of self-selection bias based on project talent data', *Int ER* 19(3), Oct. 1978.

MALINVAUD, E.

N.e.

MALKIEL, Burton G.

Born 1932, Boston, Mass., USA.
Current Post Chairman, Econ. Dept., Prof., Princeton Univ., USA.
Recent Posts N.e.
Degrees BA Harvard Coll., 1953; MBA Harvard Grad. School Bus. Admin., 1955; PhD Princeton Univ., 1964.
Offices Dir., Vanguard Group Investment Companies, Prudential Insce Co. Amer.; Pres., AFA; Governor, Amer. Stock Exchange; Gordon S. Rentschler Memorial Prof., 1969; US President's Council Econ. Advisers, 1975–7.
Principal Contributions In the area of finance and capital markets, theoretical and empirical work on the interest rate structure and stock market valuations; also problems of corporation finance, including such issues as the capital structure decision of corporations.
Publications *Books:* 1 *The Term Structure of Interest Rates* (Princeton Univ. Press, 1966); 2. *Strategies and Rational Decisions in the Securities Options Market* (with R. Quandt), (CUP, 1969); 3. *A Random Walk Down Wall Street* (McGraw-Hill, 1973, 1975, 1981); 4. *The Inflation Beater's Investment Guide* (Norton, 1980); 5. *Expectations and the Valuation of Shares* (with J. Cragg), (Univ. Chicago Press, 1981).
Articles: 1. 'Equity yields, growth, and the structure of share prices', *AER*, 53(5), Dec. 1963; 2. 'Expectations and the structure of share prices' (with J. Cragg), *AER*, 60(4), Sept. 1970; 3. 'Male-female pay differentials in professional employment' (with J. Malkiel), *AER*, 63(4), Sept. 1973; 4. 'Taxation and corporation finance' (with R. Gordon), *NBER Working Paper, 576*, Nov. 1980.

MALTHUS, Thomas Robert*

Dates and Birthplace 1766–1834, Surrey, England.
Posts Held Clergyman, 1797–1834; Prof. Polit. Econ., East India Coll., Haileybury, 1805–34.
Degree BA Univ. Camb., 1788.
Offices Fellow, Jesus Coll., Univ. Camb., 1793.
Career His *Essay* ... was conceived as a reply to the optimistic view of society put forward by Godwin, Condorcet and others. The essential argument that population growth can and will outstrip the food supply has led to 'Malthusian' entering the language to express this and related concepts. The *Essay* in its first edition was a closely-argued tract of 50,000 words, but in its second (1803) and subsequent editions Malthus added a great deal of extra material from his reading and travels, developing it into a full-scale demographic treatise. In his *Principles* ... he revealed the differences with Ricardo on questions of theory which had already been closely examined in their private correspondence with each other. His stress on the inadequacy of aggregate demand, the theory of 'general gluts', is his chief divergence from Ricardo. This first received a sympathetic reception in the twentieth century, largely as a result of Keynes' favourable comments. Such was Malthus' fame in his own lifetime, and indeed throughout the nineteenth and twentieth centuries, that he may well be described as the most famous social scientist that ever lived.
Publications *Books:* 1. *An Essay on the Principal of Population* (1798, 1963); 2. *An Inquiry into the Nature and Progress of Rent* (1815, 1970); 3. *Principles of Political Economy* (1820, 1834, 1964).
Secondary Literature J.M. Keynes, *Essays in Biography* (Macmillan, 1933, 1972); D.V. Glass, ed. *Introduction to Malthus* (Watts & Co., 1953); G.F. McCleary, *The Malthusian Population Theory* (Faber & Faber, 1953); M. Blaug, 'Malthus, Thomas Robert', *IESS*, vol. 9; P. James, *Population Malthus: His Life and Times* (Routledge & Kegan Paul, 1979).

MANDELBROT, Benoit

Born 1924, Warsaw, Poland.
Current Post IBM Fellow, IBM

Thomas J. Watson Res. Center, USA.
Recent Posts Vis. prof. Econ.,
1962–3, Applied Sciences, 1963–4,
Maths, 1979–80, Harvard Univ.; Visitor, Inst. Hautes Etudes Scientifiques,
Bures, France, 1980.
Degrees Ecole Polytechnique, 1947;
PhD (Maths) Univ. Paris, 1952.
Offices and Honours Fellow, Inst.
Math. Stats, Em Soc, ASA, Inst. Electrical Electronics Engineers, Amer.
Assoc. Advancement Science; Rockefeller Foundation Scholar, 1953–4;
Guggenheim Memorial Foundation Fellow, 1968; Trumbull Lecturer, Yale
Univ., 1970; Abraham Wald Memorial
Lecturer, Columbia Univ., 1974;
Samuel Wilks Memorial Lecturer, Princeton Univ., 1974.
Principal Contributions Advanced
a radical modification of the random
walk model of commodity and security
prices in 1963, combining the short and
the long run, and implying correctly that
price variation mostly results from
jumps – the variance of price change is
infinite, hence a new econometrics is
needed. The model is based on the 'scaling principle', which was later extended
to account for non-periodic cycles, and
then to a general theory of fractals. Also
concerned with efficient markets not
ruled by random walks, and with income
distributions.
Publications *Books:* 1. *Logique, language et théorie de l'information* (with
L. Apostel), (Presses Univ. France,
1957); 2. *Les Objets fractals: forme,
hasard et dimension* (Flammarion,
1975); 3. *Fractals: Form, Chance and
Dimension* (W.H. Freeman & . Co.,
1977); 4. *Fractal Geometry of Nature*
(W.H. Freeman & Co., 1981).
Articles: 1. 'The Pareto-Lévy law and
the distribution of income', *Int ER*, 1,
May 1960; 2. 'New methods in
statistical economics', *JPE*, 71, Oct.
1963; 3. 'The variation of certain speculative prices', *J Bus*, 36, Oct. 1963,
repr. in *The Random Character of
Stock Market Prices*, ed. P.H. Cootner
(MIT Press, 1964); 4. 'Forecasts of
future prices, unbiased markets and
"martingale" models', *J Bus*, 39, Jan.
1966; 5. 'Statistical methodology for non
periodic cycles: from the covariance to

R/S analysis', *Annals Econ. Social
Measurement*, 1, 1972.

MANDEVILLE, Bernard*

Dates and Birthplace 1670(?)-1733,
Rotterdam, The Netherlands.
Post Held Physician, England, 1699.
Degree MD Univ. Leyden, 1691.
Career Satirical writer whose *Grumbling Hive* ... introduced the concept
of a public benefit which was derived
from the sum of what might be regarded
as private vices. He developed this into
the more substantial *Fable of the Bees*
... The vices he describes – luxury,
pride, greed, envy, avarice – all stimulate commercial and manufacturing
activity. This amounts to a description
of a *laissez faire* economic system,
though Mandeville also favoured judicious state management to promote
trade, agriculture, etc. His paradox
offended many, but his book was widely
read and its lesson was taken by Hume
and Smith.
Publications *Books:* 1. *The Grumbling Hive: or Knaves Turn'd Honest*
(1705); 2. *The Fable of the Bees: Or,
Private Vices, Publick Benefits* (1714,
1970); 3. *Free Thoughts on Religion,
the Church and National Happiness*
(1720); 4. *A Modest Defence of Publick
Stews* (1724); 5. *An Enquiry into the
Origin of Honour* (1732).
Secondary Literature N. Rosenberg,
'Mandeville and *Laissez-faire*', *J Hist.
Ideas*, 24, 1963; M.M. Goldsmith,
'Mandeville, Bernard', *IESS*, vol. 9.

MANGOLDT, Hans Karl Emil Von*

Dates and Birthplace 1824–68, Dresden, Germany.
Posts Held Official, Ministry of
Foreign Affairs, 1847–50; Ed., *Weimarer Zeitung*, 1852; Teacher, Polit.
Econ., Univ. Göttingen, 1858–62; Prof.
Polit. Econ., Univ. Freibourg (Breisgau), 1862–8.
Degree Dr Polit. Science, Univ.
Tübingen.
Career His theoretical achievements
were much better appreciated in Britain

than in Germany during his own lifetime. His theory of international values was discussed by Edgeworth, and Marshall approved of his theory of entrepreneurial profit. His price theory is probably his greatest contribution, going beyond the determination of an equilibrium price to show that there could be several equilibrium prices. He also analysed price formation in the case of joint demands, joint supplies, or both; this last achievement was taken up by Marshall.

Publications *Books:* 1. *Die Lehre vom Unternehmergewinn* (1855); 2. *Grundriss der Volkswirthschaftslehre* (1863).

Secondary Literature E. Schneider 'Mangoldt, Hans Karl Emil von', *IESS*, vol. 9.

MANN, H. Michael

Born 1934, Camden, NJ, USA.
Current Post Prof., Boston Coll., USA.
Recent Posts Special econ. ass., Ass. Attorney-General, Anti-trust Div., US Dept. Justice, 1968–9; Dir., Bureau Econ., US Fed. Trade Commission, 1971–3.
Degrees BA Haverford Coll., 1956; PhD Cornell Univ., 1962.
Offices Managing ed. (USA), *J Ind E*, 1977–.
Principal Contributions Established, through replication, the consistency of Bain's findings that entry barriers matter importantly in affecting the ability of firms to price persistently in monopolistic fashion. As part of ongoing research with J.A. Henning, attempting to demonstrate that the notion of causal priority provides a potentially significant means by which to uncover causal relationships among industrial organisation variables.
Publications *Books:* 1. *Industrial Concentration: The New Learning*, ed. (with H.J. Goldschmid *et al.*) (Little, Brown & Co., 1974).
Articles: 1. 'Seller-concentration, barriers to entry, and rates of return in 30 industries, 1950–1960', *REStat*, 48, Aug. 1966; 2. 'Advertising and concen-

tration: an empirical investigation' (with J.A. Henning and J.W. Meehan, Jr), *J Ind E*, 16, Nov. 1967; 3. 'Asymmetry, barriers to entry, and rates of return in twenty-six concentrated industries, 1948–1957', *WEJ*, 8(1), March 1970; 4. 'Advertising and oligopoly: correlations in search of understanding' (with J.A. Henning), in D.G. Tuerck, *Issues in Advertising: The Economics of Persuasion* (Amer. Enterprise Inst., 1978); 5. 'An appraisal of model building in industrial organisation' (with J.A. Henning), *Res. Law Econ.*, 3, 1981.

MANSFIELD, Edwin

Born 1930, Kingston, NY, USA.
Current Post Prof. Econ., Univ. Penn., USA.
Recent Posts Assoc. prof. Econ., Carnegie-Mellon Univ., 1960–3; Prof. Econ., Harvard Univ., 1963–4; Prof. Econ., Cal. Inst. Technology, 1967–8; Fellow, Center Advanced Study Behavioral Sciences, Stanford, 1971–2.
Degrees BA Dartmouth Coll., 1951; MA, PhD Duke Univ., 1953, 1955; Diploma RSS, 1955; MA (Hon.) Univ. Penn., 1971.
Offices Fullbright Fellow, 1954–5; Fellow, Em Soc, 1969–; Fellow, Center Advanced Study Behavioral Sciences, 1971–2; US Chairman, US-USSR Working party Science and Technology, 1974–5; Fellow, AAAS, 1978–; Certificate of Appreciation, US Secretary of Commerce, 1979; First US economist to lecture in People's Republic of China under Sino-American scientific agreements, 1979; Member, Comm. Science, Engineering and Public Policy, AAAS, 1981–.
Principal Contributions Interested for many years in the economics of technological change. Research has been directed at the process of innovation, the factors that influence the rate of innovation, and the effects of technological change on firms, industries, and the entire economy. Also concerned with international technology transfer, industrial organisation, the theory of the firm, operations research, and econometrics. Written several leading textbooks on

elementary economics, intermediate microeconomics, and statistics.

Publications *Books:* 1. *Industrial Research and Technological Innovation (Norton, 1968); 2. Research and Innovation in the Modern Corporation* (Norton, 1971); 3. *Economics: Principles, Problems, Decisions* (Norton, 1974, 1980); 4. *The Production and Application of New Industrial Technology* (Norton, 1977); 5. *Statistics for Business and Economics* (Norton, 1980).

Articles: 1. 'Technical change and the rate of imitation', *Em*, 29, Oct. 1961; 2. 'Entry, Gilrat's law, innovation, and the growth of firms', *AER*, 52, Dec. 1962; 3. 'Foreign trade and US research and development' (with A. Romeo and S. Wagner), *REStat*, 61(1), Feb. 1979; 4. 'Basic research and productivity increase in manufacturing', *AER*, 70(5), Dec. 1980.

MANTOUX, Paul Joseph*

Dates and Birthplace 1877–1956, Paris, France.

Posts Held Prof. French Hist., London, 1913; League of Nations Secretariat, 1920–7; Founder, Dir., Inst. des Hautes Etudes Internat., Geneva, 1927; Prof., Conservatoire Nat. des Arts et Métiers, Univ. Paris, 1934–44.

Degree Dr ès lettres, Univ. Paris, 1906.

Honours Officer, Légion d'Honneur.

Career His work as an economic historian was largely in the earlier part of his career. After World War I, he was concerned first with the affairs of the League of Nations and then with the Institut des Hautes Etudes Internationales. He was instrumental in founding the latter as a means of fostering world co-operation to fill the gap created by the inadequacies of the league.

Publications *Books:* 1. *La Crise du trade-unionisme* (with M. Alfassa), (1903); 2. *The Industrial Revolution of the Eighteenth Century* (1906, 1961); 3. *Notes sur les comptes rendus des séances du parlement anglais au XVIII siècle* (1906).

Secondary Literature (Obituary), 'M. Paul Mantoux: worker for world peace', *Times*, 18 December 1956.

MANUILOV, Aleksandr Apollonovich*

Dates and Birthplace 1861–1929, Russia.

Posts Held Teacher and rector, Univ. Moscow, 1888–1911; Member, Board of State Banks, 1924.

Degree Grad. Law Univ. Odessa, 1883.

Offices Minister of Education, Russian provisional govt., 1917.

Career A critic of the czarist government, his 1905 document on agrarian reform became the basis of the Cadet Party's agrarian programme. Exiled after 1917, he returned and adopted an orthodox Leninist position.

Publications *Books:* 1. *Arenda Zemli v Irlandii* (1895); 2. *Poniatie o Tsennosti Po Ucheniiu Ekonomistov Klassicheskoi Shkoly* (1901); 3. *Arenda Zemli v Rossii v Ekonomicheskom Otnoshenii* (1903); 4. *Pozemel'nyi Vopros v Rossii* (1905); 5. *Politicheskaia Ekonomiia* (1914).

MARCET, Jane*

Dates and Birthplace 1769–1858, London, England

Post Held Writer.

Career Writer of popular educational works on a range of topics which included political economy. These were widely read and praised by various distinguished economists. *Conversations* ... sums up the economic doctrines current before the publication of Ricardo's *Principles* including the just discovered theory of differential rent. Ricardo was a personal friend and so was Malthus, who looms larger in the *Conversations* ... than Adam Smith.

Publications *Books:* 1. *Conversations in Political Economy* (1816); 2. *John Hopkins' Notions on Political Economy* (1833); 3. *Rich and Poor* (1851).

Secondary Literature L.M. Fraser, 'Marcet, Jane', *ESS*, vol. 10.

MARCHAL, Jean-Marie Paul

Born 1905, Colombey-les-Belles, France.

Current Post Prof. honoraire, Inst. France (Académie des Sciences Morales et Politiques), Univ. Paris I, Panthéon, Sorbonne, Paris.

Recent Posts Prof. Sciences Econ., Univ. Paris I, 1947–71; Prof. invité, Dept. Econ. Politique, Univ. Geneva, 1972–75; Inst. France, Paris, 1980.

Degrees Dr Droit (Sciences Econ.), Prof. titulaire, Univ. Nancy, 1929, 1935; Agrégé Sciences Econ. Paris, 1934; Univ. Paris, 1946; Prof. Ecole Pratique Hautes Etudes Sorbonne, 1957; Dr (Hon. causa) Univ. Geneva, 1959, Univ. Thessalonika, 1965, Univ. Liège, 1965.

Offices and Honours Member, Conseil Econ., 1947–50; Founder-member, *RE*; Chevalier (1953), Officier (1963), Commandeur (1977) Lègion d'Honneur; Hon. member Socété d'Econ. Politique de Belgique, 1953; Assoc. corresp. Académie Stanislas, Nancy, 1953; Foreign assoc. Academia Nazionale Lincei, Rome, 1965; Member, Comité Patronage, *ZN*, Vienna; Member Comité Executif, IEA, 1965–71.

Principal Contributions Research has been orientated towards price theory, public finance, evolution of French system of national accounting, distribution of national income, wage and profit theory, money and banking problems, credit multipliers, and the international monetary system.

Publications *Books:* 1. *Le Mécanisme des prix et la structure de l'économie* (Librairie de Médicis, 1946, Ed. Génin, 1966); 2. *Cours d'économie politique* (Librairie de Médicis, 1950, 1957); 3. *La Répartition du revenue national*, 4 vols (with P. Lecaillon), (Edn Génin, 1955–70); 4. *Monnaie et crédit* (Ed. Cujas, 1964, 1981); 5. *Théorie des flux monétaires* (with P. Lecaillon), (Edn Cujas, 1967).
Articles: 1. 'The construction of a new theory of profit', *AER*, 41, Sept. 1951; 2. 'Is the income of the 'cadres' a special class of wages?' (with J. Lecaillon), *QJE*, 72, May 1958; 3. 'Le multiplicateur de crédit généralisé (with P.

Poulon), *RE*, 1977; 4. 'Effet d'encaisse réelle et inflation (with P. Poulon), *Banque*, Sept. 1977; 5. 'The spreading progress of incomes in an economy: a reassessment of the multiplier theory through the probabilistic approach' (with P. Poulon), in *Pioneering Economics, in Honour of Demaria* (Edn Cedam, 1978).

MARCZEWSKI, Jean

Born 1908, Warsaw, Poland.

Current Post Retired Hon. prof., Univ. Paris I, Panthéon-Sorbonne, Paris.

Recent Posts Polish Ministry Foreign Affairs, posted in Strasburg, Bucharest, Warsaw, Brussels, 1926–40; Consultant, OECD, Paris, 1949–52; Prof., Univ. Caën, 1950–9; Prof., Inst. Polit. Stud., Paris, 1952–8; Prof., Univ. Paris I, 1959–77.

Degrees MA (Law and Econ.) Univ. Strasburg, 1929; PhD (Law and Econ.) Univ. Paris, 1941; Agrégé de Science Econ. Paris, 1950.

Offices and Honours Hon. Chairman, Soc. d'Economie Politique, Assoc. Française de Science Econ., Académie de Comptabilité; IARIW; Soc. Littéraire et Hist. Polonnaise; Prix de la Faculté de Paris, 1941; Prix Vouters, 1941; Prix de l'Académie des Sciences Morales et Politiques, 1973.

Principal Contributions Theory of quantitative history (1961). Theory of planning and its implementation into the critical analysis of Soviet-type systems (1948–76). Theory of inflationary and deflationary circuits. Theoretical explanation of stagflation as a result of an uncompleted inflationary circuit. Determination of inflationary factors and measurement of their contribution to the total inflationary gap (1977–81).

Publications *Books:* 1. *Politique monétaire et financière du IIIᵉ Reich* (Sirey, 1941); 2. *Planification et croissance économique des démocraties populaires* (Presses Univ. France, 1956); 3. *Crisis in Socialist Planning* (Praeger, 1974); 4. *Inflation and Unemployment in France: A Quantitative Analysis* (Praeger, 1978); 5. *Vaincre l'inflation et le chômage* (Economica, 1978).

Articles: 1. 'Some aspects of the economic growth of France, 1660–1958', *EDCC*, 9(3), April 1961; 2. 'Histoire quantitative – buts et méthodes', *Cahiers de l'Inst. de Science Econ. Appliquée*, Série AF, 1, July 1961; 3. 'The take-off hypothesis and French experience', in *The Economics of Take-off into Sustained Growth*, ed. A.E. Robinson (Macmillan, 1963); 4. 'The role of prices in a command economy', *Soviet Stud.*, 23(1), July 1971; 5. 'Inflation, redistribution of factors and unemployment, illustrated in the case of France', *RIW*, 24(3), Sept. 1978.

MARKHAM, Jesse William

Born 1916, Richmond, Virg., USA.
Current Post Charles Wilson Prof. Bus. Econ., Harvard Univ., USA.
Recent Posts Ass. prof., 1948–52, Assoc. prof. Econ., 1952–3, Vanderbilt Univ.; Assoc. prof., 1953–7, Prof. Econ., 1957–68, Princeton Univ.
Degrees BA Univ. Richmond, 1941; MA, PhD Harvard Univ., 1947, 1949.
Offices and Honours Phi Beta Kappa; AEA; SEA; Julius Rosenwald Fellow, 1941, 1946; Ford Foundation Res. prof., 1958–9.
Principal Contributions Subjecting the micro-economic models of oligopoly and imperfect competition to comprehensive empirical tests. Sought to erect better models through empirical inquiry to the micromodels of Cournot, Stackelberg and Edgeworth, as amended and embellished by Professors Joan Robinson and Edward Chamberlin.
Publications *Books:* 1. *Competition in the Rayon Industry* (Harvard Univ. Press, 1952; Japanese transl., 1955); 2. *The Fertilizer, Industry: Study of an Imperfect Market* (Vanderbilt Univ. Press, 1958); 3. *The Common Market: Friend or Competitor* (with C. Fiero and H. Piquet), (New York Univ. Press, 1964); 4. *Conglomerate Enterprise and Public Policy* (Div. Grad. School Bus. Admin., Harvard Univ., 1973); 5. *Horizontal Divestiture and the Petroleum Industry* (with T. Hourihan and F. Sterling), (Ballinger Publishing Co., 1977).
Articles: 1. 'An alternative approach to the concept of workable competition', *AER*, 40(3), June 1950; 2. 'The nature and significance of price leadership', *AER*, 41(5), Dec. 1951; 3. 'Oligopoly', *IESS*, vol.11; 4. 'Concentration: a stimulus or retardant to innovation?', in *Industrial Concentration: The New Learning*, eds H.J. Goldschmid *et al.* (Little, Brown & Co., 1974); 5. 'The role of competition in the American economy', *ZGS*, 136(3), Sept. 1980.

MARSCHAK, Jacob*

Dates and Birthplace 1898–1977, Kiev, Russia.
Posts Held Privatdozent, Univ. Heidelberg, 1930–3; Lecturer, Reader Stats., 1933–9, Dir. Oxford Inst. Stats, 1935–9, Univ. Oxford; Prof., Grad. Faculty, New School Social Res., 1940–2; Dir., Cowles Commission Res. Econ., 1943–8; Prof. Econ., Univ. Chicago, 1943–55, Yale Univ., 1955–60; Prof. Econ., Dir., Western Management Science Inst., UCLA.
Degrees PhD Univ. Heidelberg, 1922, Hon. degrees: Univs. Bonn (1968), Cal. (1971), Heidelberg (1972), Northwestern Univ. (1977).
Offices and Honours NAS; Fellow, AAAS; Council member, Inst. Management Science; Pres., Em Soc, 1946; Vice-pres., ASA, 1947; Fellow, Inst, Math. Stats, 1953; Fellow, Center Advanced Study Behavioral Sciences, 1955–6; Hon. Foreign Fellow, RSS, 1963; Disting. Fellow, 1967, Pres., 1977, AEA.
Career Pioneered the development of economic theories of information, organisation and decision under uncertainty. Starting with studies of money and liquidity, he gradually edged towards a systematic theory of the economic value of information. With R. Radner, developed the theory of teams, concerning efficient use of information in decentralised organisations, and proposed and elaborated the theory of stochastic decision. This latter work (done partly with Block, Davidson, Becker and DeGroot) linked theories of rational economic choice to psychological measurement in the attempt to pro-

vide a basis of statistical studies for individual choice.

Publications *Books:* 1. *Elaztizität der Nachfrage* (1931); 2. *Economic theory of teams* (with R. Radner) (1972); 3. *Economic information, decision, and prediction* (1974).

Articles: 1. 'Random simultaneous equations and the theory of production' (with W.H. Andrews), *Em*, 12, July/Oct. 1944, 13, Jan. 1945; 2. 'Role of liquidity under complete and incomplete information', *AER/S*, 39, May 1949; 3. 'Towards an economic theory of organization and information', in *Decision Processes*, eds R.M. Thrall *et al.* (1954); 4. 'Binary-choice constraints and random utility indicators', in *Mathematical Methods in the Social Sciences*, eds K.J. Arrow *et al.* (1959); 5. 'Economics of information systems', in *Frontiers of Quantitative Economics*, ed. M. Intriligator (1971).

Secondary Literature K.J. Arrow, 'Marschak, Jacob,' *IESS*, vol. 18.

MARSHALL, Alfred*

Dates and Birthplace 1842–1924, London, England.

Post Held Fellow, St John's Coll., Univ. Camb., 1865–77, 1885–1908; Principal, Univ. Coll., Bristol, 1877–82; Lecturer, Fellow, Balliol Coll., Univ. Oxford, 1883–4; Prof. Polit. Econ., Univ. Camb., 1885–1908.

Offices Fellow, BA; Vice-pres., RES.

Career The dominant figure in British economics of the late nineteenth and early twentieth centuries, whose *Principles . . .* still has the power to fascinate and excite the reader. Though he wrote infrequently, his influence by his teaching at Cambridge was a major source of influence on his contemporaries. One of the ablest mathematicians of his generation, he sought to expression in the simplest language possible, adding the mathematical and quantitative material as appendices and footnotes. His partial equilibrium analysis – the chief element of his methodology – was designed to be appropriate to a dynamic or biological view of economic life. The chief achievement of the *Principles* is his working out of the economics of the stationary state. Independently discovered the marginal utility theory, though typically he did not publish until he had fully integrated this into his system. His welfare economics was of central importance since his decision to take up economics originated in a moral purpose, and his general conclusion was that a redistribution of income from rich to poor would increase total satisfaction. Keynes was among his pupils and the 'Keynesian revolution' can be seen as remaining within the Marshallian tradition.

Publications *Books:* 1. *The Economics of Industry* (with M.P. Marshall), (1879); 2. *Principles of Economics* (1890), Ninth variorum ed. C.W. Guillebaud, 2 vols (1961); 3. *Industry and Trade* (1919); 4. *Money Credit and Commerce* (1923); 5. *Official Papers* (1926).

Secondary Literature J.M. Keynes, 'Alfred Marshall', in *Essays in biography* (Macmillan, 1933, 1972); B. Corry, 'Marshall, Alfred', *IESS*, vol. 10; D.P. O'Brien, 'A. Marshall' *Pioneers of modern Economics in Britain*, eds D.P. O'Brien and J.R. Presley (Macmillan, 1981).

MARSHALL, Mary Paley*

Dates and Birthplace 1850–1944, Stamford, England.

Posts Held Lecturer, Univ. Camb., 1875, then Univs. Bristol, Oxford and Camb.

Career Great-granddaughter of William Paley and wife of Alfred Marshall, her abilities as an economist deserve mention in their own right. As the first woman lecturer in economics at Cambridge and joint-author of a good economic text, she might have had an outstanding career. However, on marriage to Marshall she submerged her career in his.

Publications *Books:* 1. *The Economics of Industry* (with A. Marshall), (1879) 2. *What I Remember* (1947).

Secondary Literature J.M. Keynes, 'Mary Paley Marshall', in *Essays in biography* (Macmillan, 1933, 1972).

MARTIN, Henry*

Dates and Birthplace ?-1721, Wiltshire, England.

Posts Held Lawyer and journalist, *Spectator* and *British Merchant*, 1713–14; Inspector-general imports exports, 1715.

Career *Consideration* ... was published anonymously; sometimes attributed to Sir Dudley North, it was attributed to Martin by McCulloch. The tract is one of the first to espouse wholeheartedly a free trade system, justified on grounds of the benefits to be derived from international specialisation. The monopolistic chartered trading companies are attacked on the basis of this principle. His intervention via the *British Merchant* is credited with causing the rejection of the commercial treaty with France at the Treaty of Utrecht.

Publications *Books:* 1. *Considerations on the East India Trade* (1701), reprinted in *Early English Tracts on Commerce*, ed. J.R. McCulloch (1856, 1954).

Secondary Literature M. Arkin, 'A neglected forerunner of Adam Smith', *SAJE*, 23, Dec. 1955.

MARTINEAU, Harriet*

Dates and Birthplace 1802–76, Norwich, England.

Posts Held Writer.

Career Wrote on various subjects to earn a living. Mrs Marcet's *Conversations* inspired her to try stories to illustrate principles of political economy. These sold in tens of thousands, provided her with literary celebrity, and probably introduced more early nineteenth-century readers to basic economic ideas than any other contemporary source. Their content was based on a journalistic interpretation of the classical economists, chiefly Smith and Malthus. She also played a major part in popularising the ideas of Comte in Britain.

Publications *Books:* 1. *Illustrations of Political Economy*, 9 vols (1832–4); 2. *Poor Laws and Paupers Illustrated* (1833); 3. *Illustrations of Taxation* (1834); 4. *Society in America* (1837); 5. *History of England during the Thirty Years Peace* (1849); 6. *The Philosophy of Comte, Freely Translated and Condensed* (1853).

Secondary Literature R.K. Webb, *Hariet Martineau. A Radical Victorian* (Heinemann, 1960).

MARX, Karl*

Dates and Birthplace 1818–83, Trier, Germany.

Posts Held Writer and political leader; lived in exile in France, Belgium and England, with financial support from Friedrich Engels.

Degree Phd Univ. Jena, 1841.

Career Best known as the founder of international communism, he was a philosopher, social scientist and one of the major economists of his or any other age. Already deeply involved in socialist politics, his *Communist Manifesto* may be described as the most important political pamphlet of the nineteenth century. His life was spent in London, writing and organising, the former taking increasing precedence over the latter. The comprehensiveness of his studies and the difficulties of his personal circumstances meant that many of his major projects remained unfinished at his death. His masterpiece *Das Kapital* is only partially complete; the first volume appeared during his lifetime, and further material was edited by Engels. Much other material has been published posthumously including the important *Grundrisse* and *Theorien über den Mehrwert*. Using Hegel's dialectical method, but abandoning his political philosphy, he attempted to show both how society was progressing through successive stages towards the ultimate goal of communism and how that process might be accelerated. To this end he absorbed as much as possible of the existing social and economic thought; for example, his knowledge of previous writings in political economy was as nearly comprehensive as was possible at the time. His ideas have inspired both political Marxism and a very large body of social science grounded in his theoretical schema.

Publications *Books:* 1. *The Poverty of Philosophy* (1847, 1956); 2. *Com-*

munist manifesto (1848, 1972); 3. *The Class Struggles in France* (1950, 1976); 4. *A contribution to the critique of Political Economy* (1859, 1971); 5. *Capital,* vol. 1, (1867, 1976), vols. 2 and 3, ed. F. Engels, (1885–94, 1909, 1978); 6. *Theories of surplus value,* 3 vols (1905–10, 1963); 7. *Collected works,* 12 vols (1927–35); 8. *Foundation of the critique of Political Economy* (1939–41, 1973).

Secondary Literature E. Mandel, *Marxist Economic Theory* (Merlin Press, 1962); M. Rubel, 'Marx, Karl', *IESS,* vol. 10; D. McLellan, *Karl Marx. His Life and Thought* (Macmillan, 1973); L. Kolakowski, *Main Currents of Marxism,* 3 vols (OUP, 1978).

MAS-COLELL, Andreu

Born 1944, Barcelona, Spain.
Current Post Prof. Econ., Harvard Univ., USA.
Recent Posts Ass. prof. Econ. Maths, 1975–7; Assoc. prof. Econ. Maths, 1977–9, Prof. Econ. Maths, 1979–81, Univ. Cal., Berkely.
Degrees Licenciado en Ciencias Econ. Univ. Bilbao, 1967; PhD (Econ.) Univ. Minnesota, 1972.
Offices Assoc. ed., *JET,* 1975–80, *SIAM J Applied Maths,* 1976–9, *J Math E,* 1977–, *Em,* 1978–; Fellow, Em Soc. 1978–; Sloan Fellow, 1978–80.
Principal Contributions General field of research: mathematical economics and economic theory. Main contributions have been to several foundational aspects of demand and general equilibrium theory. In particular extension of the Walras-Arrow-Debreu-McKenzie model to situations with differentiated commodities or with agents not satisfying some of the traditional rationality or convexity postulates; use and development of calculus and differential topological tools for the examination of the structure of price equilibria (uniqueness, local uniqueness, comparative statics, index of equilibria, etc.); relationships between the notion of price-taking equilibrium and a variety of solution concepts (descendant from Cournot and Edgeworth) incorporating strategic interdependences.

Publications *Articles*; 1. 'Continuous and smooth consumers: approximation theorems', *JET,* 8(3), July 1974; 2. 'An equilibrium existence theorem without complete or transitive preference', *J Math E,* 1(3), 1974; 3. 'A model of equilibrium with differentiated commodities', *J Math E,* 2, 1975; 4. 'On the recoverability of consumers' preferences from market demand behavior', *Em,* 45(6), 1977; 5. 'Notes on the smoothing of aggregate demand', *J Math E,* 5, 1978.

MASON, Edward S.

Born 1899, Clinton, Iowa, USA.
Current Post Retired.
Recent Posts Dept. Econ., Harvard Univ., 1969; Consultant, World Bank, 1978.
Degrees BA Univ. Kansas, 1919; MA, PhD LLD, Harvard Univ., 1920, 1925, 1957; BLitt. Univ. Oxford, 1923; DLitt. Williams Coll., 1946; LLD Yale Univ., 1956.
Offices US President's Comm. Foreign Aid, 1947; US President's Materials Pol. Commission, 1952; Pres., AEA, 1962; Board Dirs., Overseas Development Council, Resources for the Future, 1965–; US President's Task Force Internat. Development, 1970.
Principal Contributions Study of the relations between the structure of industry and the behaviour and performance of firms.
Publications *Books:* 1. *The Street Railway in Massachusetts* (Harvard Univ. Press, 1932); 2. *Controlling World Trade* (McGraw-Hill, 1946); 3. *Economic Concentration and the Monopoly Problem* (Harvard Univ. Press, 1959); 4. *The World Bank since Bretton Woods* (with R.E. Asker), (Brookings Inst., 1973); 5. *The Economic and Social Development of the Republic of Korea* (with others), (Harvard Univ. Press, 1981).
Articles: 1. 'Monopoly in law and economics', *Yale Law J,* 47(1), Nov. 1939; 2. 'The current status of the monopoly problem in the United States', *Harvard Law Review,* 62(8), June 1949; 3. 'Raw materials, rearmament, and economic development', *QJE,* 66, Aug.

1952; 4. 'On the appropriate size of a development program', *Harvard Center Internat. Affairs, Occasional paper*, 1964; 5. 'Economic development in India and Pakistan', *Harvard Center Internat. Affairs, Occasional paper*, 1966.

MASSELL, B.F.

N.e.

MAYER, Thomas

Born 1927, Vienna, Austria.
Current Post Prof. Econ., Univ. Cal. Davis, USA.
Recent Posts Economist, US Govt., 1951–3; Vis. ass. prof., West Virginia Univ., 1953–4; Ass. prof., Notre Dame Univ., 1954–6; Ass. prof., Assoc. prof., Michigan State Univ., 1956–61; Vis. assoc. prof., Univ. Cal., Berkeley, 1961–2.
Degrees BA Queen's Coll., New York, 1948; MA, PhD Columbia Univ., 1949, 1953.
Offices Member, AFA, AEA, RES; Pres., WEA, 1978–9.
Principal Contributions Dealt mainly with the empirical testing of hypotheses, particularly about consumption functions. Raised some questions about the applicability of standard econometric procedures and have also tried to clarify the nature of monetarism and evaluate the evidence for it.
Publications *Books*; 1. *Monetary Policy in the United States* (Random House, 1968); 2. *Intermediate Macroeconomics* (with D.C. Rowan), (Norton, 1972); 3. *Permanent Income, Wealth and Consumption* (Univ. Cal. Press, 1972); 4. *The Structure of Monetarism* (with others), (Norton, 1978); 5. *Money, Banking and the Economy* (with J. Duesenberry and R. Aliber), (Norton, 1981).
Articles: 1. 'The inflexibility of monetary policy', *REStat*, 40, Nov. 1958; 2. 'The distribution of ability and earnings', *REStat*, 42, May 1960; 3. 'Liquidity functions in the American economy' (with M. Bronfenbrenner), *Em*, 28, Oct. 1960; 4. 'Selecting economic hypotheses by goodness of fit', *EJ*, 85, May 1975; 5. 'Economics as an exact science', *EI*, 18(2), April 1980.

MAZZOLA, Ugo*

Dates and Birthplace 1863–99, Italy.
Posts Held Teacher, Univ. Camerino; Prof. Public Fin., 1887, Polit. Econ., 1896, Univ. Pavia.
Degree Grad. law Univ. Naples.
Career Specialised in the study of public finance, seeing the state as a co-operative and the finances of the state as a co-operative activity on the part of the citizens. This co-operation is to enable citizens to purchase certain services at a lower cost than if they were obtained privately. He saw no clash between public and private needs, both equally needing to be satisfied for the sake of general welfare. In his *I Dati Scientifici . . .*, he described for the first time the characteristics of what is now known as 'public goods'.
Publications *Books:* 1. *L'Assicurazione degli Operaî Nella Scienza e Nella Legislazione Germanica* (1885); 2. *I Dati Scientifici Della Finanza Pubblica* (1890); 3. *L'Imposta Progressiva in Economia Pura e Sociale* (1895); 4. *La Colonizzazione Interna in Prussia* (1900).
Secondary Literature C. Pagin, 'Mazzola, Ugo', *ESS*, vol. 10; *Classics in the theory of Public Finance*, eds R.A. Musgrave and A.T. Peacock (Macmillan 1958).

MACAVOY, Paul Webster

Born 1934, Haverhill, Mass., USA.
Current Post Milton Steinbach Prof. Organization Management Econ., Yale Univ., 1978–.
Recent Posts Ass. prof. Econ., Grad. School Bus., Univ. Chicago, 1960–3; Ass. prof. Econ., 1963–5, Assoc. prof., Prof. Management, 1966–74, MIT; Henry R. Luce Prof. Public Pol., MIT, 1974–5; Member, US President's Council Econ. Advisers, 1975–6; Prof. Organisation Management Econ., Yale Univ., 1976–8.
Degrees BA (Phi Beta Kappa), Hon.

LLD Bates Coll., 1955, 1976; MA, PhD Yale Univ., 1956, 1960.

Offices Sr. Staff Economist, US President's Council Econ. Advisers, Exec. Office President, 1965–6; Member, Council Econ. Advisers, State Govt NY, 1969–72; Sr Fellow, Brookings Inst., 1970–1; Mass. Public Power Study Commission, 1974–5; Board Dirs, New Haven Water Co., 1976–7, Columbia Gas System, 1977–8, Amer. Cyanamid Co., 1977–80, AMAX Corp., 1978–, Combustion Engineering, Inc., 1980–.

Principal Contributions Regulatory problems in the energy field, particularly the natural gas industry.

Publications *Books:* 1. *Price Formation in Natural Gas Fields: A Study of Competition Monopsony and Regulation* (Yale Univ. Press, 1962); 2. *Economic Strategy for Developing Nuclear Breeder Reactors* (MIT Press, 1969); 3. *The Economics of the Natural Gas Shortage 1960–1980* (with R.S. Pindyck), (N-H, 1975); 4. *The Regulated Industries and the Economy* (Norton, 1979); 5. *The Decline of Service in the Regulated Industries* (with A.S. Carron), (Amer. Enterprise Inst., 1980).

Articles: 1. 'The effectiveness of the Federal Power Commission', in *The Crisis of the Regulatory Commissions*, ed. P.W. MacAvoy (Norton, 1970); 2. 'The regulation-induced shortage of natural gas', *J Law E*, 14(1), April 1971; 3. 'Economic prescriptions for developing the regulated industries', *Review Social Econ.*, 24(1), March 1971; 4. 'The natural gas shortage and the regulation of natural gas producers' (with S. Breyer), *Harvard Law Review*, April 1973, repr. in *Energy Supply and Government Policy*, eds R.S. Kalter and W. Vogeley (Cornell Univ. Press, 1976); 5. 'The Natural gas policy act of 1978', *Natural Resources J*, Dec. 1979.

McCALL, John J.

Born 1933, Chicago, Ill., USA.
Current Post Prof. Econ., UCLA, 1968–.
Recent Posts Rand Corp., 1959–66; Univ. Chicago, 1967.
Degrees BA Univ. Notre Dame; PhD Univ. Chicago.

Offices Member, AEA.
Principal Contributions Systematic study of the economics of search and its applications to labour economics, microeconomics, macroeconomics, industrial organisation and econometrics. Also research on the competitive firm under uncertainty and general problem of information and uncertainty in economics.

Publications *Books:* 1. *Optimal Replacement Policy* (with D.W. Jorgenson and R. Radner), (N-H, 1967); 2. *Income Mobility, Racial Discrimination and Economic Growth* (D.C. Heath & Co, 1973); 3. *Studies in the Economics of Search*, ed. (with S.A. Lippman), (N-H, 1979).

Articles: 1. 'Competitive production for constant risk utility functions', *REStud*, 34, Oct. 1967; 2. 'Simple economics of incentive contracting', *AER*, 60(5), Dec. 1970; 3. 'Economics of information and job search', *QJE*, 84(1), Feb. 1970; 4. 'Probabilistic microeconomics', *Bell JE*, 2, 1971.

McCLOSKEY, Donald N.

Born 1942, Ann Arbor, Mich., USA.
Current Post Prof., Chairman Econ., Prof. Hist., Univ. Iowa, Iowa City.
Recent Posts Ass. prof., 1968–73, Assoc. prof. Econ., 1973–80, Assoc. prof. Hist., 1979–80, Univ. Chicago.
Degrees BA Harvard Coll., 1964; PhD (Econ.) Harvard Univ., 1970.
Offices and Honours NSF grants; David A. Wells prize, Harvard Univ., 1970–1; Ed. Board, *Explorations Econ. Hist.*, 1974–; Ed., *JEH*, 1980–.
Principal Contributions Introduction of economics to British economic history and history to economics, and teaching in texts on intermediate microeconomics and on British economic history.

Publications *Books:* 1. *Essays on a Mature Economy: British after 1840*, ed. (Methuen, Princeton Univ. Press, 1971); 2. *Economic Maturity and Entrepreneurial Decline: British Iron and Steel, 1870–1914* (Harvard Univ. Press, 1973); 3. *Enterprise and Trade in Victorian Britain: Essays in Historical Economics* (A & U, 1981); 4. *The Economic History of Britain,*

1700–present, ed. (with R. Floud), (CUP, 1981); 5. *The applied Theory of Price* (Macmillan, 1982).

Articles: 1. 'Did Victorian Britain fail?', *EHR*, 23(3), Dec. 1970; 2. 'The persistence of English common fields', in *European Peasants and their Markets*, eds E.L. Jones and W.N. Parker (Princeton Univ. Press, 1975); 3. 'How the gold standard worked, 1880–1914' (with J.R. Zecher), in *The Monetary Approach to the Balance of Payments*, eds J.A. Frenkel and H.G. Johnson (A & U, 1976); 4. 'English open fields as behavior towards risk', *Res. in Econ. Hist.*, ed. P. Uselding (JAI Press, 1976); 5. 'Does the past have useful economics?', *JEL*, 14(2), June 1976.

McCULLOCH, John Ramsay*

Dates and Birthplace 1789–1864, Scotland.

Posts Held Journalist and ed., *The Scotsman*, 1818–20; Private tutor of econ., 1820–8; Prof. Polit. Econ., Univ. Coll., London, 1828–32; Comptroller, HMSO, 1838–64.

Offices Chief reviewer of economic books for the *Edinburgh Review*, 1817–; Delivered Ricardo memorial lectures, 1823–4.

Career Traditionally regarded as the most loyal and dogmatic of Ricardo's followers, recent examination of his writings has shown more clearly the Smithian flavour of many of his views, and the shifts in his opinions over time. He was, however, a tireless propagandist for his version of Ricardo's ideas and for political economy generally, the two of which he tended to identify with each other. His statistical, encyclopaedic and bibliographical works were extremely successful and were better suited to his abilities than questions of pure theory. He also contributed in *A discourse* ... the first serious history of economic thought anywhere.

Publications *Books:* 1. *A Discourse on the Rise, Progress, Peculiar Objects and Importance of Political Economy* (1824); 2. *Principles of Political Economy* (1825, 1886); 3. *A Dictionary, Practical, Theoretical and Historical of Commerce and Commercial Navigation*

(1832, 1882); 4. *Descriptive and Statistical Account of the British Empire*, 2 vols (1837, 1854); 5. *The Literature of Political economy* (1845, 1938); 6. *A Treatise on the Principles and Practical Influence of Taxation and the Funding System* (1845, 1975).

Secondary Literature M. Blaug, 'McCulloch, John Ramsay', *IESS*, vol. 9; D.P. O'Brien, *J.R. McCulloch: A Study in Classical Economics* (A & U 1970).

MACDOUGALL, George Donald Alastair

Born 1912, Glasgow, Scotland.

Current Post Chief econ. adviser, Confederation British Industry, London, 1973–.

Recent Posts Ass. lecturer, Univ. Leeds, 1936–9; Winston Churchill's Stat. Branch, 1939–45, 1951–3; Fellow, Wadham Coll., 1945–50, Nuffield Coll., 1947–64, Univ. Oxford; Econ. Dir. OEEC, Paris, 1948–9; Econ. Dir., UK Nat. Econ. Development Office, 1962–4; Dir. General, UK Dept. Econ. Affairs, 1964–8; Head UK Govt Econ. Service, Chief Econ. Adviser, UK Treasury, 1969–73.

Degrees BA, MA Univ. Oxford, 1935, 1938, Hon LLD Univ. Strathclyde, 1968; Hon. DLitt Univ. Leeds, 1971, Hon DSc. Univ. Aston, Birmingham, 1979.

Offices and Honours OBE, 1942; CBE, 1945; Knighted, 1953; Pres., RES, 1972–4; Chairman, Exec. Comm., NIESR, 1974–; Pres., Soc. Long Range Planning, 1977–; Vice-pres., Soc. Bus. Economists, 1978.

Principal Contributions The use of economic analysis, and usually a quantitative approach, to illuminate real problems of policy that have arisen during the past half-century in the UK and elsewhere, including Western Europe, the United States, Venezuela, India and Australia. The attempt to educate students, civil servants, politicians, businessmen and others.

Publications *Books:* 1. *The World Dollar Problem* (MacMillan, 1957); 2. *The Dollar Problem: A Reappraisal* (Princeton Univ. Press, 1960); 3.

Studies in Political Economy, 2 vols. (Macmillan, 1975); 4. *The Role of Public Finance in European Economic Integration*, Chairman (EEC, 1977). *Articles:* 1. 'The British trade cycle 1929–37', in *Britain in Recovery* (BAAS, 1938); 2. 'Britain's foreign trade problem', *EJ*, 57, March 1947; 3. 'British and American exports: a study suggested by the theory of comparative costs', *EJ*, 61, Dec. 1951, 62, Sept. 1952; 4. 'Inflation in the United Kingdom', *ER*, 35, Dec. 1959; 5. 'The benefits and costs of private investment from abroad: a theoretical approach', *ER*, 36, March, Aug. 1960.

McFADDEN, Daniel L.

Born   1937, Raleigh, N. Carolina, USA.
Current Post   Prof. Econ., MIT, USA.
Recent Posts   Vis. assoc. prof., Univ. Chicago, 1966–7; Prof. Econ., Univ. Cal. Berkeley, 1968–79; Vis. Scholar, MIT, 1970–1; Vis. prof., Yale Univ., 1977–8.
Degrees   BS (Physics), PhD (Econ.) Univ. Minnesota, 1957, 1962.
Offices and Honours   Mellon Post-doctoral Fellow, 1962–3; Ford Faculty Res. Fellow, 1966–7; Fellow, Em Soc, 1969; John Bates Clark medal, AEA, 1975; AAAS, 1977; Irving Fisher Res. Prof., 1977–8; Outstanding teacher award, MIT Econ. Dept, 1981; NAS, 1981.
Principal Contributions   Primary concern of research is integration of the theory and measurement of economic behaviour. One research area is the reformulation of production theory, using duality, in terms of market data; a second is the development of empirical consumer theory for unconventional budget sets, such as discrete alternatives, with applications in the demand for transportation and the demand for energy using appliances.
Publications   *Books:* 1. *Urban Travel Demand: A Behavioral Analysis* (with T. Domencich), (N-H, 1975); 2. *Production Economics: A Dual Approach to Theory and Applications*, ed. (with M. Fuss) (N-H, 1978); 3. *Structural*

Analysis of Discrete Data with Econometric Applications, ed. (with C.F. Manski), (MIT Press, 1981). *Articles:* 1. 'Conditional logit analysis of qualitative choice behavior', in *Frontiers of Econometrics*, ed. P. Zarembka (Academic Press, 1973); 2. 'On the existence of optimal development programs in infinite horizon economies', in *Models of Economic Growth*, eds J. Mirrlees and H. Stern (N-H, 1973); 3. 'Modelling the choice of residential location', in *Proceedings of the Conference on Spatial Interaction Theory and Planning Models* (N-H, 1978); 4. 'Determinants of the long-run demand for electricity' (with C. Puig and D. Kirshner), *ASA Proceedings*, 1978; 5. 'Pareto optimality and competitive equilibrium in infinite horizon economies' (with M. Majumdar and T. Mitra), *J Math E*, 7(1), March 1980.

McKENZIE, Lionel Wilfred

Born   1919, Montezuma, Georgia, USA.
Current Post   Wilson Prof. Econ., Univ. Rochester, NY, USA.
Recent Posts   Instructor Econ., MIT, 1946; Ass. prof., Assoc. prof., Duke Univ., 1948–57; Prof. Econ., Chairman Dept. Econ., 1957–66, John Munro Prof. Econ., 1964–7, Univ. Rochester.
Degrees   BA Duke Univ., 1939; MA, PhD Princeton Univ. 1942, 1956; BLitt. Oxford Univ., 1949.
Offices and Honours   Rhodes Scholar, 1939; Fellow, Em Soc, 1958; Fellow, AAAS, 1967; Guggenheim Memorial Foundation Fellow, 1973–4; Fellow, Center Advanced Study Behavioral Sciences, 1973–4; Member, NAS, 1978; Taussig Res. Prof., Harvard Univ., 1980–1.
Principal Contributions   On existence of competitive equilibrium: one of the two first rigorous proofs of existence under general conditions, followed by several generalisations of the theorem to include external economies and weaker assumptions of interiority. On stability of equilibrium: a theorem on stability with weak gross substitutes and the weakest form of *tâtonnement*. On international economics: a general

theorem on factor price equalisation, a general theorem on specialisation in production in the Graham model of world trade. On optimal growth: various turnpike theorems in the context of Von Neumann's model and a multi-sector Ramsey model, with and without a discount factor.

Publications *Articles:* 1. 'On equilibrium in Graham's model of world trade and other competitive systems', *Em*, 22, April 1954; 2. 'Specialisation and efficiency in world production', *REStud*, 21(3), June 1954; 3. 'Equality of factor prices in world trade', *Em*, 23, July 1955; 4. 'On the existence of general equilibrium for a competitive market', *Em*, 27, Jan. 1959; 5. 'Stability of equilibrium and the value of positive excess demand', *Em*, 28, July 1960.

MCKINNON, Ronald

Born 1935, Edmonton, Canada.
Current Post Prof. Econ., Stanford Univ., USA, 1961–.
Degrees BA Univ. Alberta, 1956; PhD Univ. Minnesota, 1960.
Principal Contributions Working out the logic of the international dollar standard. Exchange rate policies for large and small countries including the US itself. Establishing the importance of financial liberalisation in less developed countries in parallel with liberalising foreign trade. How to maintain monetary control during the liberalisation processes.

Publications *Books:* 1. *Money and Capital in Economic Development* (Brookings Inst., 1973); 2. *Money in International Exchange: The Convertible Currency System* (OUP, 1979). *Articles:* 1. 'The exchange rate and macro-economic policy: changing postwar perception', *JEL*, 19(2), June 1981; 2. 'Currency substitution and instability in the world dollar standard', *AER*, 72(3), June 1982.

MACLEOD, Henry Dunning*

Dates and Birthplace 1821–1902, Edinburgh, Scotland.
Posts Held Lawyer; Employed by govt to prepare digest of laws on bills of exchange, 1868–70.
Degrees BA, MA Univ. Camb., 1843, 1863.
Career Whilst his work on banking was widely appreciated in his day, as an economist he was shunned by the establishment and failed to obtain any university Chair. (His implication in the failure of the Royal British Bank had brought him a conviction for conspiracy to defraud, which partially explains his isolation.) Though an original thinker, particularly on the theory of value, his frequently restated views failed to be accepted as the new departure which he claimed them to be. He was responsible for the invention of the term 'Gresham's Law'.

Publications *Books:* 1. *The Theory and Practice of Banking*, 2 vols (1855); 2. *The Elements of Political Economy* (1858); 3. *On the Modern Science of Economics* (1887); 4. *The Theory of Credit*, 2 vols (1889–91); 5. *Bimetallism* (1894); 6. *History of Economics* (1896).
Secondary Literature F.A. Hayek 'Macleod, Henry Dunning', *ESS*, vol. 10.

MACVANE, Silas Marcus*

Dates and Birthplace 1842–1914, Prince Edward Island, Canada.
Posts Held Instructor, Ass. prof., Prof., Harvard Univ., 1875–1911.
Degrees BA Acadia Coll., 1865; Harvard Univ., 1873.
Career Teacher of history, law, politics and government and writer of able works on economics. His criticisms of the writings of F.A. Walker in *QJE* were effective in identifying weaknesses in Walker's ideas. His *Working Principles* ... achieved some success as a textbook and was a clear exposition of current orthodoxy.
Publications *Books:* 1. *The Working Principles of Political Economy* (1890). *Articles:* 1. 'The Austrian theory of value', *Amer. Academy Polit. and Social Science Annals*, 4, 1893–4.
Secondary Literature F.W. Taussig, 'MacVane, Silas Marcus', *ESS*, vol. 10.

McVICKAR, John*

Dates and Birthplace 1787–1868, New York City, NY, USA.

Posts Held Ordained Clergyman, 1812; Teacher, Columbia Coll., New York City, 1817–64.

Degree BA Columbia Coll., 1804.

Career He was one of the earliest, if not the earliest, professors of political economy in US, treating the subject as a branch of moral philosophy. Whilst on a year's sabbatical he was enrolled as a member of the Political Economy Club in London, and met many of the leading economists of the day.

Publications *Books:* 1. *Outlines of Political Economy* (1825); 2. *Hints on Banking* (1827); 3. *First Lessons in Political Economy* (1837).

Secondary Literature J.B. Langstaff, *The Enterprising Life: John McVickar 1787–1868* (Columbia Univ. Press, 1961).

MACHLUP, Fritz

Born 1902, Wiener Neustadt, Austria.

Current Post Prof. Econ., NYU USA.

Recent Posts Goodyear Prof. Econ., Univ. Buffalo, 1935–47; Hutzler Prof. Polit. Econ., Johns Hopkins Univ., 1947–60; Walker Prof. Econ. Internat. Fin., Princeton Univ., 1960–71.

Degrees Dr Rer. Pol., Dr Rer. Pol. 50 Year Renewal, Univ. Vienna, 1923, 1973; Hon. LLD Lawrence Coll., 1956, Lehigh Univ., 1967, LaSalle Coll., 1968; Hon. Dr Sc. Pol. Univ. Kiel, 1965; Hon. Dr oecon. Univ. St Gallen, 1972; Hon. LHD Case Inst. Technology, 1967.

Offices and Honours Hon. member, Phi Beta Kappa, 1937; Pres., SEA, 1959–60; AAAS, 1961; Pres., AAUP, 1962–4; Amer. Philosophical Soc., 1963; Nat. Academy Education, 1965; Fellow, Amer. Assoc. Advancement Science, 1966; Pres., AEA, 1966; Hon. senator, Univ. Vienna, 1971; Pres., 1971–4, Hon. pres., 1974–, IEA; Bernhard Harms prize, Univ. Kiel, 1974; Academia Nazionale dei Lincei, Rome, Foreign member, 1974.

Principal Contributions Work in international economics in 17 books and nearly 100 articles. In the field of economic organisation, major work on competition and monopoly embodied in a 1952 book and, especially, work on knowledge production in the book of 1962 and the series started in 1980. Also work in methodology, most of which is collected in a 1978 volume.

Publications *Books:* 1. *International Trade and the National Income Multiplier* (Blakiston, 1943); 2. *The Economics of Sellers' Competition* (Johns Hopkins Univ. Press, 1952); 3. *Essays on Economic Semantics* (Prentice-Hall, 1963, NYU Press, 1967); 4. *Methodology of Economics and Other Social Sciences* (Academic Press, 1978); 5. *Knowledge: its Creation, Distribution, and Economic Significance,* vol. 1, *Knowledge and Knowledge Production* (Princeton Univ. Press, 1980).

Articles: 1. 'The theory of foreign exchange, Pt I-II', *Ec*, N.S. 6, Nov. 1939, 7, Feb. 1940; 2. 'Marginal analysis and empirical research', *AER*, 36, Sept. 1946; 3. 'Another view of cost-push and demand-pull inflation', *REStat*, 42, May 1960; 4. 'The supply of inventors and inventions', *WA*, 85(2), 1960; 5. 'Theories of the firm: marginalist, behavioral, managerial', *AER*, 57(1), March 1967.

Secondary Literature J.S. Chipman, 'Machlup, Fritz', *IESS*, vol. 18; *Breadth and depth in economics: Fritz Machlup – the man and his ideas*, ed. J.S. Dreyer (D.C. Heath & Co., 1978).

MACKAY, R. Ross

Born 1940, Delhi, India.

Current Post Sr lecturer, Dir. Inst. Econ. Res., Univ. Coll. N. Wales, Wales.

Recent Posts Lecturer Econ., Univ. Newcastle, 1965–79.

Degree MA Aberdeen Univ., 1963.

Offices Member, Ed. Board, *Regional Stud.*; Member, UK SSRC Urban and Regional Econ. Seminar Group.

Principal Contributions Started research programme in the early 1970s designed to identify the nature and extent of the regional policy impact in

Britain. As research progressed two important themes emerged: present performance can only be understood in the context of an extended historical perspective; the very nature of economics, its essential reliance on imprecise relationships, its dependence on human rather than mechanical reactions, suggests that we must devise methods of policy evaluation which can highlight differences in the forms of response.

Publications *Articles:* 1. 'The impact of the regional employment premium', in *Economics of Industrial Subsidies*, ed. A. Whiting (HMSO, 1976); 2. 'Regional policy', in *Scotland 1980*, ed. D.I. MacKay (Q Press, 1977); 3. 'The death of regional policy – or resurection squared?', *Regional Stud.*, 13, 1979; 4. 'Important trends in regional policy and regional employment – a modified interpretation' (with L. Thompson), *SJPE*, 26, 1979; 5. 'Regional policy and regional employment – the UK experience', in *Planning in Stagnating Regions*, eds W. Buhr and P. Friedrich (Baden-Baden, 1981).

MEADE, James Edward

Born 1907, Oxford, England.
Current Post Retired.
Recent Posts Member, Econ. Section League of Nations, 1938–40; Econ. ass., Dir. Econ. Section, UK Cabinet offices, 1940–5, 1946–7; Prof. Commerce, LSE, 1947–57; Fellow, Christ's Coll., 1957–64, Prof. Polit. Econ., 1957–68, Univ. Camb.; Nuffield Res. Fellow, Nuffield Coll., Univ. Oxford, 1969–74.
Degrees BA (First class), MA Univ. Camb, 1928, 1957; BA (First class), MA Univ. Oxford, 1930, 1933 Hon. Dr. Univs. Basle, Bath, Essex, Hull, Oxford.
Offices and Honours Hon. Fellow, LSE, Oriel Coll., Hertford Coll., Univ. Oxford, Christ's Coll., Univ. Camb.; Pres., Section F, BAAS, 1957; Hon. member, Soc. Royale d'Econ. Polit. de Belgique, 1958, AEA, 1962, AAAS, 1966; Chairman, Econ. Survey Mission, Mauritius, 1960; Pres., 1964–6, Vicepres., 1966–, RES; Chairman, Comm. Inst. Fiscal Stud., 1975–7; Nobel Prize for Econ. 1977.

Principal Contributions Mainly concerned to apply economic theory to the formulation of economic policies.
Publications *Books:* 1. *National Income and Expenditure* (with R. Stone), (Macmillan, 1944); 2. *Theory of International Economic Policy*, 2 vols (OUP, 1951, 1955); 3. *A Neo-classical Theory of Economic Growth* (A & U, 1960); 4. *Principles of Political Economy*, vol. 1, *The Stationary Economy* (A & U, 1965), vol. 2, *The Growing Economy* (A & U, 1968), vol. 3, *The Controlled Economy* (A & U, 1972), vol. 4, *The Just Economy* (A & U, 1976); 5. *The Intelligent Radical's Guide to Economic Policy* (A & U, 1975).
Secondary Literature W.M. Corden and A.B. Atkinson 'Meade, James E.' *IESS* vol. 18; H.G. Johnson, 'James Meade's Contribution to economics', *Scand JE*, 80(1), 1978.

MEANS, G.C.

N.e.

MEEK, Ronald Lindley*

Dates and Birthplace 1917–78, New Zealand.
Posts Held Lecturer, Univ. Glasgow, 1948–63; Prof. Econ., Univ. Leicester, 1963–78.
Degrees LlM, MA New Zealand, 1939, 1946; PhD Univ. Camb., 1949.
Career Outstanding scholar of physiocracy, Turgot, and Adam Smith, whose work on the eighteenth century culminated in his painstaking edition of Smith's *Lectures on Jurisprudence* (1977). He also made a major contribution to the recent revival of Marxian economics by his patient and undogmatic exposition of Marx's ideas during the cold-war period of the 1940s and 1950s.
Publications *Books:* 1. *Studies in the Labour Theory of Value* (1956); 2. *Economics of Physiocracy* (1962); 3. *Economics and Ideology* (1967); 4. *Turgot on Progress, Sociology and Economics* (1973); 5. *Social Science and the Ignoble Savage* (1976); 6. *Smith, Marx and After* (1977).

Secondary Literature Obituaries, *UK Hist. Econ. Thought Newsletter*, 21, 1978, 23, 1979, 24, 1980.

MEIER, Gerald Marvin

Born 1923, Tacoma, Washington, USA.

Current Post Prof. Internat. Econ., Stanford Univ., USA, 1963–.

Recent Posts Ass. prof., Prof. Econ., 1954–9, Chester D. Hubbard Prof. Econ., 1959–63, Wesleyan Univ.; vis. assoc. prof., 1956–7, 1958–9, Vis. prof., 1959–61, Yale Univ.; Vis. prof., Stanford Univ., 1962.

Degrees BA (Social Science) Reed Coll., 1947; BLitt. (Econ.) Univ. Oxford, 1952; PhD (Econ.) Harvard Univ., 1953; MA (*Hon causa*) Wesleyan Univ., 1959.

Offices and Honours Phi Beta Kappa, 1947; Rhodes Scholar, 1948–50, 1951–2; Res. Student, Nuffield Coll., Univ. Oxford, 1949–52; Guggenheim Memorial Foundation Fellow, 1957–8; Brookings Nat. Res. Prof. Econ., 1961–2; SSRC Grant, 1968; Internat. Legal Center Res. Grant, 1970; Rockefeller Foundation Res. Grant, 1974–5; Russell Sage Resident Fellow, Law/Social Science, Yale Univ., 1976–7.

Principal Contributions Attempted to establish economic development as a standard course for undergraduates by writing first textbook in the subject (1957). Later emphasised the relations between international trade and economic development, with particular attention to issue of 'gains from trade' vs 'gains from growth'. Special focus on theory of policy, with effort to integrate some of the other questions of political economy with modern techniques of policy analysis.

Publications *Books:* 1. *Economic Development* (with E. Baldwin), (Wiley, Chapman & Hall, 1957); 2. *International Trade and Development* (Harper & Row, 1963, USIA, 1965); 3. *Leading Issues in Development Economics* (OUP, 1964, 1976); 4. *Problems of a World Monetary Order*, (OUP, 1974, 1981); 5. *International Economics: Theory of Policy* (OUP, 1980).

Articles: 1. 'The trade matrix: a further comment on Professor Frisch's paper', *AER*, 38, Sept. 1948; 2. 'A note on the theory of comparative costs and long period developments', *Econ Int*, 5, Aug. 1952; 3. 'The poverty of nations', *WA*, 78(1), 1957; 4. 'UNCTAD proposals for international economic reform', *Stanford Law Review*, 19, June 1967; 5. 'Externality law and market safeguards', *Harvard Internat. Law J*, 18, Summer 1977.

MEISELMAN, David I.

Born 1924, Boston, Mass., USA.

Current Post Prof. Econ., Dir., Grad. Econ. Program Northern Virginia, Virginia Polytechnic Inst., State Univ., Northern Campus, Dulles Internat. Airport, Washington, DC.

Recent Posts Ass. prof. Econ., Univ. Chicago, 1958–62; Sr economist, US Treasury, 1964–6; Sr consultant, World Bank, 1966; Vis. prof. Econ., Univ. Minnesota, 1966–8; Prof. Econ., Macalester Coll., 1966–71.

Degrees BA Boston Univ., 1947; MA, PhD Univ. Chicago, 1951, 1961.

Offices and Honours Winner, Ford Foundation doctoral dissertation competition, 1962; Member, Mont Pelerin Soc., 1964–; Ed. Board, *JMCB*, 1968–72, Chairman, Ed. Board, *Pol. Review*, 1978–; Miles B. Lane Lecturer, Georgia Inst. Technology, 1969; Pres., Philadelphia Soc., 1974.

Principal Contributions Demonstrated that markets reflect anticipations and the discounting of future events (such as interest rates and inflation); that the quantity of money is the main actor in the inflation drama; that mismanagement of money is the principal cause of economic fluctuations; and that market participants are systematically more astute than central bankers and government officials.

Publications *Books:* 1. *The Term Structure of Interest Rates* (Prentice-Hall, 1962); 2. *The Measurement of Corporate Sources and Uses of Funds* (with E. Shapiro), (NBER, 1964); 3. *Varieties of Monetary Experience*, ed. (Univ. Chicago Press, 1970); 4. *The Phenomenon of Worldwide Inflation,* co-ed. (Amer. Enterprise Inst., 1975); 5. *Welfare Reform and the Carter Public Service Employment Program: A Critique* (Law Econ. Center, Univ. Miami School Law, 1978).

Articles: 1. 'The relative stability of monetary velocity and the investment multiplier in the United States, 1897–1958' (with M. Friedman), in *Stabilization Policies*, Commission Money and Credit (Prentice-Hall, 1963); 2. 'Bond yields and the price level: the Gibson paradox regained', in *Banking and Monetary Essays in Commemoration of the Centennial of the National Banking System* (Prentice-Hall, 1963); 3. 'More inflation – more unemployment', *Tax Review*, Jan. 1976; 4. 'Money, factor proportions, and real interest rates', in *Hearings on the Impact of the Federal Reserve's Money Policies on the Economy*, 94th Congress, 2nd Session, 9 June 1976 (US Govt Printing Office, 1976).

MELLOR, John Williams

Born 1928, Paris, France.

Current Post Dir., Internat. Food Pol. Res. Inst., Washington DC.

Recent Posts Prof. Agric. Econ., Econ., Asian Stud., Cornell Univ., 1952–76; Chief economist, Agency Internat. Development, US Dept. of State, 1976–7.

Degrees BSc (distinction), MSc (Agric. Econ.) Cornell Univ., 1950, 1951; Diploma (Agric. Econ., distinction) Univ. Oxford, 1952; PhD Cornell Univ., 1954.

Offices and Honours Member, AEA; AAEA award for best published research, 1967; Fellow, AAAS, 1977; AAEA award for publication of enduring quality, 1978; Member, Fellow, 1980, AAEA.

Principal Contributions Delineation of the role of the agricultural sector in the economic growth of low-income countries. Particular emphasis given to documenting and conceptualising the level and composition of intersectoral resource transfers. For these purposes two sector models have been explored: critiques of standard growth theory drawn and social accounting methods applied. A variant of this work has been analysis of the links between growth in agricultural production and income and small-scale non-agricultural estimates in rural market towns. Work on labour transfers has conceptualised the basis of peasant labour allocations, the role of marketings of food in determining intersectoral labour transfers, and the interaction of change in technology with these processes. Work on agricultural price policy has dealt with the interaction of income distribution and production effects.

Publications *Books:* 1. *The Economics of Agricultural Development* (Cornell Univ. Press, 1966); 2. *Developing Rural India: Plan and Practice* (with T.F. Weaver *et al*.), (Cornell Univ. Press, 1968); 3. *The New Economics of Growth – A Strategy for India and the Developing World* (Cornell Univ. Press, 1976); 4. *India: a rising middle power*, ed. (Westview Press, 1979).

Articles: 1. 'The role of agriculture in economic development' (with B.F. Johnston), *AER*, 51(4), Sept. 1961; 2. 'The use and productivity of farm family labor in early stages of agricultural development', *JFE*, 45(3), Aug. 1963; 3. 'Accelerated growth in agricultural production and the intersectoral transfer of resources', *EDCC*, 22(1), Oct. 1973; 4. 'Food price policy and income distribution in low-income countries', *EDCC*, 27(1), Oct. 1978; 5. 'Technological change, distributive bias and labor transfer in a two sector economy (with U. Lele), *OEP*, 1982.

MELMAN, Seymour

Born 1917, New York City, NY, USA.

Current Post Prof. Industrial Engineering, Columbia Univ.

Recent Posts Faculty Columbia Univ., 1948–; Consultant UN, Group Governmental Experts Relationship between Disarmament and Development, 1979–80.

Degrees BSS Coll. City New York, 1939; PhD Columbia Univ., 1949.

Offices and Honours Vice-pres., NY Academy Sciences, 1974–5; Pres., Assoc. Evolutionary Econ., 1975; 1980

Sarah L. Poiley Memorial award, NY Academy Sciences, 1980; Great Teacher award, Soc. Older Graduates Columbia Univ., 1981; Hon. Member Faculty, Industrial Coll. Armed Forces, 1981; Rolex Award for Enterprise, 1981.

Principal Contributions On the development of decision making in industrial microeconomy: from cost minimising to cost passing-along, and cost maximising. Dynamics of productivity growth: relation between management and worker decision making and effects on productivity. How decision-making criteria have controlling effect on design and selection of technology. Mechanism and magnitudes of growth of managerial decision making, independently of productivity. Micro- and macro-characteristics of military economy and effects on civilian economy: productivity, inflation, unemployment, depletion of industries. Consequences of evolving civilian and military micro-economics for diminishing production capability.

Publications *Books:* 1. *Dynamic Factors in Productivity* (Blackwell, Wiley, 1956); 2. *Decision Making and Productivity* (Blackwell, Wiley, 1958); 3. *Our Depleted Society* (Holt, Rinehart & Winston, Dell Books, 1965); 4. *Pentagon Capitalism* (McGraw-Hill, 1970); 5. *The Permanent War Economy* (Simon & Schuster, 1974).

Articles: 1. 'The rise of administrative overhead in the manufacturing industries of the United States, 1899–1947', *OEP*, 3, Feb. 1951; 2. 'Managerial vs. co-operative decision making in Israel', *Stud. Comparative Econ. Development*, 6, 1970–1; 3. 'Ten propositions on the war economy', *AER*, 62(2), May 1972; 4. 'The impact of economics on technology', *JEI*, 9(1), March 1975; 5. 'Decision making and productivity as economic variables', *JEI*, 10(1), March 1976.

MELTZER, Allan H.

Born 1928, Boston, Mass., USA.
Current Post John M. Olin Prof. Polit. Econ. Public Pol., Carnegie-Mellon Univ., Pittsburgh, USA.

Recent Posts Prof. Econ., 1964–, Vis. prof., Yugoslav Inst. Econ. Res., 1968, Harvard Univ., 1967–8, Maurice Falk Prof. Econ. Social Science, 1970–80, Carnegie-Mellon Univ.; vis. prof. City Univ., London, 1979, Vargas Inst., Rio de Janeiro, 1976–7, 1978–9.

Degrees BA (Econ.) Duke Univ., 1948; MA (Econ.), PhD (Econ.) UCLA, 1955, 1958.

Offices AEA, AFA; Board Eds, *JEL*, 1973–5; Assoc. ed., *J Fin*, 1974–80; Advisory Board, *J Mon E*, 1974–; Ed. Board, *Pol. Review*, 1978–.

Principal Contributions The theory of the relation of money to economic activity and prices; the theory of the supply of money in closed and open economies; the development of economic policies based on applicable economic theory; and theories of the size and growth of government.

Publications *Books:* 1. *A Study of the Dealer Market for US Government Securities* (US Congress Joint Econ. Comm., 1960); 2. *An Analysis of Federal Reserve Monetary Policymaking* (US Congress Banking and Currency Comm., 1964); 3. *The Carnegie-Rochester Conference Series*, ed. (with K. Brunner), (N-H, 1976–); 4. *Carnegie Papers on Political Economy*, vol. 1, ed. (with P. Ordeshook and T. Romer), (Martinus Nijhoff, 1981).

Articles: 1. 'The demand for money: the evidence from the time series', *JPE*, 71, June 1963; 2. 'A credit market theory of the money supply and an explanation of two puzzles in US monetary policy' (with K. Brunner), *RISE*, 13(5), May 1966; 3. 'Liquidity traps for money, bank credit and interest rates' (with K. Brunner), *JPE*, 76, Jan./Feb. 1968; 4. 'Money, debt and economic activity' (with K. Brunner), *JPE*, 80(5), Sept./Oct. 1972; 5. 'A rational theory of the size of government', *JPE*, 88(5), Oct. 1981.

MENDERSHAUSEN, H.

N.e.

MENGER, Anton*

Dates and Birthplace 1841–1906, Maniow, Austro-Hungary.

Posts Held Prof. Civil Procedure, Univ. Vienna, 1877.

Degree Grad. Law Univ. Vienna, 1872.

Career Brother of Carl Menger; lawyer, he examined the juridical theory of socialism as a counterpart to the more usual interest in its economic theory. This enabled him to detect antecedents of Marx in the early socialists and provided him with a critique of Marx as an ethical theory about entitlements to a share in the national product. He was able to influence the compilers of the German Civil Code (1896) to reflect the needs of poorer citizens, advocating a form of state socialism in which the rights of consumers were to be defended against those of producers.

Publications *Books:* 1. *The Right to the Whole Produce of Labour* (1886, 1889); 2. *Das Bürgerliche Recht und die Besitzlosen Volksklassen* (1890); 3. *Uber die Sozialen Aufgaben der Rechtswissenschaft* (1895); 4. *Neue Staatslehre* (1903).

Secondary Literature G. Gurvitch, 'Menger, Anton', *ESS*, vol. 9.

MENGER, Carl*

Dates and Birthplace 1840–1921, Neu Sandec, Austro-Hungary.

Posts Held Member, press section, Austrian Prime Minister's office; Lecturer, Extraordinary prof., 1873, Full prof., 1879–1903, Univ. Vienna; Tutor, Archduke Rudolf, 1876.

Degree Dr Law, Univ. Cracow, 1867.

Career The founder of the Austrian school of marginal analysis whose international influence was wider than that of his co-discoverers, Walras and Jevons. The *Principles* is a detailed account of the relations between utility, value and price. He was also the initiator and a major participant in the 'Methodenstreit' with the German Historical School. He argued that a 'compositive method' of analysing society was more effective than the use of history to discover empirical laws about society. His contribution to the 1892 dispute on the reform of the Austrian currency was the basis of later Austrian theory on the value of money.

Publications *Books:* 1. *Principles of Economics* (1870, 1934, 1950); 2. *Problems of Economics and Sociology* (1883); 3. *Die Irrthümer des Historismus in der Deutschen Nationalökonomie* (1884); 4. *Collected Works of Carl Menger*, 4 vols (1934–6).

Secondary Literature F.A. von Hayek, 'Menger, Carl', *IESS*, vol. 10. J.A. Schumpeter, 'Carl Menger, 1840–1921', in *Ten Great Economists from Marx to Keynes (OUP, 1951)*.

MERCIER DE LA RIVIÈRE, Pierre Paul*

Dates and Birthplace 1720–93, Saumur, France.

Posts Held Member, Parlement de Paris, 1747–59, 1764–; Intendant, Martinique.

Career His *Ordre naturel ...* concentrated on the political aspects of physiocracy in which he argued that there is a natural law of property which is based on the physical order of nature, and which underlies all other laws. Taxation and the use of public revenue by the ruler are both governed by the natural law of property. His *De l'instruction publique* outlined the system of education which would eventually bring about the ideal society in which nations are at peace, and men cease to profit at the expense of others.

Publications *Books:* 1. *L'Ordre naturel et essentiel des sociétés politiques* (1767); 2. *L'Intérêt général de l'état* (1770); 3. *De l'instruction publique* (1775); 4. *Essais sur les maximes et lois fondamentales de la monarchie française* (1789); 5. *Palladium de la constitution politique* (1790).

Secondary Literature F. Mauro, 'Mercier de la Rivière', *IESS*, vol. 10.

MEYER, John Robert

Born 1927, Pasco, Washington, USA.

Current Post Prof. Transportation, Logistics and Distribution, Harvard Univ., USA, 1970.

Recent Posts Prof. Econ., Harvard Univ., 1959–68; Prof. Econ., Yale Univ., 1968–73; Pres., NBER, 1967–77.
Degrees BA Univ. Washington, 1950; PhD Harvard Univ., 1955.
Offices and Honours Fellow, Em Soc, AAAS; Exec. Comm., AEA; David A. Wells prize, Harvard Univ., 1955.
Principal Contributions Pioneered the development and use of large-scale data bases and computers for testing various economic hypotheses concerning business investment decisions, urban location trends, transportation costs, regional migration patterns, the impact of transportation on economic development, etc. Conducted early investigations into the profitability of slavery in the ante-bellum US South and other quantitative issues in economic history. Recent work on evaluating the benefits and costs of government regulation of US business activities.
Publications *Books:* 1. *The Investment Decision: An Empirical Inquiry* (with E. Kuh), (Harvard Univ. Press, 1957); 2. *Economics of Competition in the Transportation Industries* (with M.J. Peck *et al.*), (Harvard Univ. Press, 1959); 3. *The Urban Transportation Problems* (with J.F. Kain and M. Wohl), (Harvard Univ. Press, 1965); 4. *Techniques of Transport Planning*, 2 vols (with D. Kresge *et al.*), (Brookings Inst., 1970); 5. *The Economics of Competition in the Telecommunications Industry* (with others), (Oelgeschlager, Gunn and Hain, 1979).
Articles: 1. 'Acceleration and related theories of investment: an empirical inquiry' (with E. Kuh), *REStat*, 37, Aug. 1955; 2. 'Correlation and regression estimates when the data are ratios' (with E. Kuh), *Em*, 23, Oct. 1955; 3. 'Economic theory, statistical inference and economic history' (with A.H. Conrad), *JEH*, 17, Dec. 1957; 4. 'The economics of slavery in the ante-bellum South' (with A.H. Conrad), *JPE*, 66, April 1958, 66, Oct. 1958; 5. 'Regional economics: a survey', *AER*, 53(1), March 1963, reprinted in *Regional analysis*, ed. L. Needleman (Penguin Books, 1968).

MIESZKOWSKI, Peter Michael

Born 1936, Pelplen, Poland.
Current Post Prof. Econ., Chairman Dept., Univ. Houston, Texas.
Recent Posts Ass. prof., 1962–7, Assoc. prof., 1967–71, Yale Univ.; Prof. Econ., Queen's Univ., Ontario, 1971–4.
Degrees BSc, MA McGill Univ., 1957, 1959; PhD Johns Hopkins Univ., 1963.
Offices Member, AEA.
Principal Contributions Applied income distribution problems with special emphasis on tax incidence theory. Also, general equilibrium effects of trade unions on income distribution, and the importance of peer group effects on educational achievement. In urban economics, analysis of racial discrimination in housing, related work on the determinants of real estate values and the effects of externalities on property values. Also contributions on the efficiency aspects of migration across regions and the theory of capitalisation. Work on the theory of taxation includes analysis of the implementation of an expenditure tax system, foreign trade aspects of taxation, and the relative efficiency of tariffs as a means of protecting domestic production and raising revenue.
Publications *Books:* 1. *Current Issues in Urban Economics* (with M. Straszhem), (Johns Hopkins Univ. Press, 1979); 2. *Fiscal Federalism and Grants-in-aid* (with W. Oakland), (Urban Inst., 1979).
Articles: 1. 'The effects of unionization of the distribution of income: a general equilibrium approach' (with H.G. Johnson), *QJE*, 84(4), Nov. 1970; 2. 'The property tax: excise tax or profits tax?', *J Pub E*, 1(1), April 1972; 3. 'Public goods, efficiency, and regional fiscal equilization' (with F. Flatters and V. Henderson), *J Pub E*, 3(2), May 1974.

MIKESELL, Raymond F.

Born 1913, Eaton, Ohio, USA.
Current Post W.E. Miner Prof. Econ., Univ. Oregon, USA, 1957–.
Recent Posts Ass. prof. Econ., Univ.

Washington, 1937–42; Economist, US Dept. Treasury, 1942–6; Prof. Econ., Univ. Virginia, 1946–56; Member Sr Staff, US President's Council Econ. Advisers, Exec. Office US President, 1955–6.

Degrees BA, MA, PhD Ohio State Univ., 1935, 1935, 1939.

Offices Econ. adviser, Bretton Woods Internat. Monetary Fin. Conference, 1944; Member Board Eds., *AER*, 1953–5; Sr res. assoc., NBER, 1970–4; Member, Advisory Council, Overseas Private Investment Corp., 1971–4; Vice-pres., Academy Internat. Bus., 1971–2; Co-chairman, Res. Council, Georgetown Univ. Center Strategic and Internat. Stud., 1973–80; Member, Nat. Materials Advisory Board, 1981–2.

Principal Contributions Analysis of the impacts of foreign exchange policies and practices on international trade and the balance of payments; effects of operations of Eurocurrency market on US balance of payments; the contribution of foreign aid and foreign private investment on economic development; and the economic structure of the world copper industry.

Publications *Books:* 1. *Foreign Exchange in the Post War World* (Twentieth Century Fund, 1954); 2. *The Economics of Foreign Aid* (Aldine Press, 1968); 3. *Foreign Investment in the Petroleum and Mineral Industries* (Johns Hopkins Univ. Press, 1974); 4. *Foreign Dollar Balances and the International Role of the Dollar* (with J.H. Furth), (NBER, 1974); 5. *The World Copper Industry: Structure and Economic Analysis* (Johns Hopkins Univ. Press, 1979).

Articles: 1. 'The role of international monetary agreements in a world of planned economies', *JPE*, 55(6), Dec. 1947, repr. in *Readings in the Theory of International Trade*, eds H.S. Ellis and L.A. Metzler (Blakiston, 1949); 2. 'The theory of common markets as applied to regional arrangements among developing countries', in *International Trade Theory and the Developing World*, eds R. Harrod and D. Hague (Macmillan, 1963); 3. 'The nature of the savings function in developing countries: a survey of the theoretical and empirical literature' (with J.E. Zinser),

JEL, 11(1), March 1973; 4. 'Rules for floating exchange rates' (with H.N. Goldstein), *Essays in International Finance*, No. 109 (Princeton Univ., 1975); 5. 'The rate of exploitation of exhaustible resources: the case of an export economy', *Natural Resources Forum*, 1, 1976.

MILL, James*

Dates and Birthplace 1773–1836, Forfar, Scotland.

Posts Held Preacher, 1798–1802; Professional writer, 1802–19; Officer, East India Company, 1819–36.

Degrees BA Univ. Edinburgh.

Career The disciple and promoter of Jeremy Bentham, he developed the economic side of utilitarian analysis and incorporated the ideas of Malthus and Ricardo. It was through James Mill that a group of followers of Bentham, the so-called 'philosophical radicals' was formed. His *Elements* ... is the first English textbook of economics.

Publications *Books:* 1. *History of British India*, 3 vols (1817); 2. *Elements of Political Economy* (1821); 3. *Analysis of the Phenomena of the Human Mind*, 2 vols (1928).

Secondary Literature A. Bain, *James Mill* (Macmillan, 1882); D. Winch, *Selected Economic Writings of James Mill* (Oliver & Boyd, 1966).

MILL, John Stuart*

Dates and Birthplace 1806–73, London, England.

Posts Held Officer, East India Company, 1823–58.

Offices MP for Westminster, 1865–8.

Career The dominant figure of mid-nineteenth-century British political economy, he was educated by his father James as an ardent Benthamite utilitarian, but his mental crisis of 1826 induced serious modifications of his views. Saint-Simon, Comte and other writers can be counted as influences subsequent to this period, as can his friendship with his future wife, Harriet Taylor. His *System of Logic* established his reputation as a major thinker, and it is his philosophical and political writings, most notably *On Liberty,* that are the chief source of his continuing fame. However, the *Principles* is almost equally remembered, becoming the leading economic textbook in the English-speaking world for the rest of the century. It was intended to modify the abstract and sometimes cold-hearted classical political economy. Though his introduction of an historical method did not advance the subject greatly, his perception of the limits to the applicability of abstract-deductive analysis was important. His attacks on the cult of wealth, his concern with the problems of growth and development, his treatment of the question of population and his sympathy with the working man all reflect his humanitarian approach. His analytical ideas on money, international trade and the dynamics of distribution have all been highly praised. On the role of the state in economic life, he struck a judicious balance between his defence of individual freedom and the recognition of a need for some state intervention, in cases such as that of infant industries. The dominance of Mill in subsequent years was such that Jevons felt it necessary to attack him in order to win a favourable hearing for marginal utility economics.

Publications *Books: 1. A system of Logic* (1843); 2. *Essays on Some Unsettled Questions of Political Economy* (1844); 3. *Principles of Political Economy* (1848, 1903); 4. *On Liberty* (1859); 5. *Utilitarianism* (1861); 6. *Autobiography* (1973); 7. *J.S. Mill, Collected Works,* 9 vols. ed. J.M. Robson (Univ. of Toronto Press, 1963–74).

Secondary Literature V.W. Bladen, 'Mill, John Stuart: economic considerations' *IESS,* vol. 10; P. Schwartz, *The New Political Economy of J.S. Mill* (Weidenfeld and Nicolson, 1972).

MILLER, Herman P.

Born 1921, New York City, NY, USA.

Current Post Pres., H.P. Miller Inc., Silver Spring, Maryland, USA.

Recent Posts Chief, Popul. Div., Bureau Census, 1972–; Adjunct prof. Econ., Temple Univ., Philadelphia, Penn., 1974–.

Degrees BA City Coll. New York, 1942; MA George Washington Univ., 1950; PhD American Univ., 1954.

Offices and Honours Fellow, ASA; Gold medal for meritorious service, US Dept. Commerce, 1964.

Principal Contributions Study of income distribution and the valuation of human capital. At the Bureau of the Census (1946–72), pioneered the development of household surveys of income and the concepts of income inequality, provety, and lifetime income. Since establishing his own consulting firm (1972), has worked on the application of the concept of human capital to law.

Publications *Books: 1. Income of the American People* (Wiley, 1954); 2. *Historical Statistics of the US, Colonial Times to 1957,* ed. (US Govt Printing Office, 1960); 3. *Income Distribution in the United States* (US Govt Printing Office, 1966); 4. *Earnings* (with R. Hornseth), (US Govt Printing Office, 1967); 5. *Rich man, poor man* (T.Y. Crowell, 1971).

Articles: 1. 'Annual and lifetime income in relation to education', *AER,* 50, Dec. 1960; 2. 'Lifetime income and economic growth', *AER,* 55, Sept, 1965; 3. 'State differentials in income concentration' (with A. Al-Samarrie), *AER,* 57, March 1967.

MILLER, Marcus Hay

Born 1941, Darjeeling, India.

Current Post Prof. Econ., Univ. Warwick, England.

Recent Posts Lecturer, LSE, 1967–76; Economist, Bank England, 1972–3; Vis. prof. Internat. Fin., Univ. Chicago, 1976; Prof. Econ. Univ. Manchester, 1976–8; Chairman, Academic Panel, UK Treasury, 1979–80; Specialist adviser, House of Commons Select Comm. Treasury Civil Service, 1980–1.

Degrees BA (First class) Univ. Oxford, 1963; PhD (Econ.) Yale Univ., 1971.

Offices UK SSRC Money Study Group Comm., 1970–; Ed. Board, *REStud,* 1971–6; Joint ed., *Ec,* 1973–6;

AUTE Exec. Comm., 1975–80; UK Treasury Academic Panel, 1976–80; Exec. Comm., NIESR, 1980–; Houblon-Norman Fellow, Bank England, 1981–2.
Principal Contributions N.e.
Publications *Books:* 1. *Monetary Policy and Economic Activity in West Germany*, ed. (with A.S. Courakis and S. Frowen), (Intertext Publishing Co., 1977); 2. *Essays on Fiscal and Monetary Policy*, ed. (with M.J. Artis), (OUP, 1981).
Articles: 1. 'Estimates of the static balance of payments and welfare costs of UK entry in the Common Market', *Nat. Inst. Econ. Review*, 57, Aug. 1971; 2. 'Can a rise in import prices be inflationary and deflationary? Economists and UK inflation 1973–4', *AER*, 68(4), Sept. 1976; 3. 'The static economic effects of the UK joining the EEC: a general equilibrium approach' (with J. Spencer), *REStud*, 44(1), Feb. 1977; 4. 'The precautionary demand for narrow and broad money' (with C. Sprenkel), *Ec*, N.S. 47, Nov. 1980; 5. 'Monetary control in the UK', *Camb JE*, 5(1), March 1981.

MILLER, Merton H.

Born 1923, Boston, Mass., USA.
Current Post Leon Carroll Marshall Disting. service prof., Grad. School Bus., Univ. Chicago, USA.
Recent Posts Edward Eagle Brown Prof. Banking Fin., Grad. School Bus., Univ. Chicago, 1965–81.
Degrees BA Harvard Univ., 1944; PhD Johns Hopkins Univ., 1952.
Offices Fellow, Em Soc; Co-ed., *J Bus*; Pres., AFA, 1976.
Principal Contributions Co-author of the Modigliani-Miller theorems and other applications of economic theory to the field of finance.
Publications *Books:* 1. *The Theory of Finance* (with E. Fama), (Holt, 1972); 2. *Macro-economics: A Neoclassical Introduction* (with C. Upton), (Richard D. Irwin, 1974).
Articles: 1. 'The cost of capital, corporation finance and the theory of investment' (with F. Modigliani), *AER*, 48, June 1958, 49, Sept. 1959; 2. 'Dividend Policy, growth and the valuation of shares' (with F. Modigliani), *J Bus*, 34, Oct. 1961, 36, Jan. 1963; 3. 'Debt and taxes', *J Fin*, 32(2), May 1977.

MILLS, Edwin Smith

Born 1928, Collingswood, NJ, USA.
Current Post Prof. Econ., Princeton Univ., USA.
Recent Posts Prof. Polit. Econ., Johns Hopkins Univ., 1963–70.
Degrees BA Brown Univ., 1951; PhD Univ. Birmingham, 1956.
Offices Member, AEA, RES, Em Soc.
Principal Contributions Interactions among price, output and inventory movements in firms and markets; market processes in urban areas; benefits, costs and government intervention in presence of polluting discharges; and industrial organisation and anti-trust programmes.
Publications *Books:* 1. *Studies in the Structure of the Urban Economy* (Johns Hopkins Univ. Press, 1972); 2. *Urban Economics* (Scott, Foresman, 1972, 1980); 3. *The Economics of Environmental Quality* (Norton, 1978); 4. *Urbanization and Urban Problems, Studies in the Modernization of the Republic of .Korea: 1945–1975* (with B.N. Song), (Harvard Univ. Press, 1979); 5. *Measuring the Benefits of Water Pollution: A Statement* (with D. Greenberg), (Academic Press, 1980).
Articles; 1. 'An aggregative model of resource allocation in a metropolitan area', *AER*, 57(2), May 1967, repr. in *Urban Analysis*, eds A. Page and W. Seyfried (Scott, Foresman, 1970), *Readings in Urban Economics*, eds M. Edel and J. Rothenberg (Macmillan, 1972), and *Urban Economics Readings and Analysis*, ed. R. Grieson (Little, Brown, 1973); 2. 'The Tiebout hypothesis and residential income segregation' (with B. Hamilton and D. Puryear), in *Fiscal Zoning and Land Use Controls*, eds E.S. Mills and W.E. Oates (D.C. Heath & Co., 1975); 3. 'Urbanization and urban problems' (with K. Ohta), in *Asia's New Giant*, eds H. Patrick and H. Rosovsky (Brookings Inst., 1976); 4. 'Planning and market processes in urban

models', in *Public and Urban Economics: Essays in honor of William S. Vickrey*, ed. R. Grieson (D. C. Heath & Co., 1976); 5. 'Economic analysis of urban land-use controls', in *Current Issues in Urban Economics*, eds P. Mieszkowski and M. Straszheim (Johns Hopkins Univ. Press, 1979).

MINCER, Jacob

Born 1922, Tomaszow, Poland.
Current Post Joseph L. Buttenwieser Prof. Econ., Columbia Univ., NY, USA.
Recent Posts Res. Staff, NBER, 1960–; Prof. Econ., Columbia, 1962–; Vis. prof., Univ. Chicago, Hebrew Univ. Jerusalem, Stockholm School Econ.
Degrees BA Emory Univ., 1950; PhD Columbia Univ., 1957.
Offices Postdoctoral Fellow, Univ. Chicago, 1957–8; Fellow, ASA, 1967–, Em Soc. 1973–; Guggenheim Memorial Foundation Fellow, 1970; Member, AEA Advisory Comm. US Census, 1972–6; Member, AAAS, 1974–, Nat. Academy Education, 1974–; Assoc. ed., *REStat*, 1977–, *Econ. Education Review*, 1979–.
Principal Contributions Research has attempted to integrate non-market (household) economic behaviour with behaviour in the labour market, thus producing one of the first impulses for the development of modern human capital analysis of wage structures, including a first formulation and application of the human capital earnings function; the initial development of the theory of labour supply in the family context, as well as initial formulation and application of empirical labour supply functions; development and formulation of empirical fertility (family size) functions in economic demography focused on opportunity costs in non-market behaviour. Current research is in the economics of labour mobility and of wage floors.
Publications *Books:* 1. *Economic Forecasts and Expectations*, ed. (Columbia Univ. Press, 1969); 2. *Schooling, Experience and Earnings* (Columbia Univ. Press, 1974).
Articles: 1. 'Labor force participation of married women', in *Aspects of Labor Economics*, ed. H.G. Lewis (Princeton Univ. Press, 1962); 2. 'The distribution of labor incomes', *JEL*, 8(1), March 1970; 3. 'Family investment in human capital: earnings of women' (with S. Polachek), *JPE*, 82(2), Pt II, March/April 1974; 4. 'Family migration decisions', *JPE*, 86(5), Oct. 1978; 5. 'Labor mobility and wages' (with B. Jovanovic), in *Studies in labor markets*, ed. S. Rosen (Chicago Univ. Press, 1981).

MIRABEAU, Victor Riquetti, Marquis De*

Dates and Birthplace 1715–89, France.
Posts Held Army officer and landowner.
Career From 1765 his Paris salon was the meeting place for the 'économistes'. Mirabeau came to be known as 'l'ami des hommes' after his 1756 publication in which he anticipated much of Quesnay's system. His starting point is the dependence of all aspects of the state on agriculture; then prescribes reforms which would both revive agriculture and the state itself. His son, Honoré Gabriel, was a major figure in the early years of the Revolution, and also wrote on economic questions.
Publications *Books:* 1. *Mémoire concernant l'utilité des états provinciaux* (1750); 2. *L'Ami des hommes, ou traité de la population* (1756); 3. *Théorie de l'impôt* (1760); 4. *Lettres sur les corvées* (1760); 5. *Philosophie rurale*, 3 vols (with F. Quesnay), (1764).
Secondary Literature P. Sagnac, 'Mirabeau, Marquis de', *ESS*, vol. 10.

MIRRLEES, James A.

Born 1936, Minnigaff, Scotland.
Current Post Edgeworth Prof. Econ., Univ. Oxford.
Recent Posts Ass. lecturer, Lecturer Econ., Univ. Camb., Fellow, Trinity Coll., Univ. Camb., 1963–8; Vis. prof., Dept. Econ., MIT, 1968, 1970, 1976.
Degrees MA (Maths) Univ. Edinburgh, 1957; Math. Tripos, Pt II (wrangler) Math. Tripos, Pt III (dis-

tinction), PhD (Econ.) Univ. Camb., 1958, 1959, 1963.

Offices and Honours Stevenson prize Econ., Univ. Camb., 1962; Adviser, MIT Center Internat. Stud., India Project, New Delhi, 1962–3; Adviser, Pakistan Inst. Development Econ., Karachi, 1966–8; Member, UK Treasury Comm. Pol. Optimization (Ball Comm.), 1976–8; Vice-pres., Em Soc, 1980–.

Principal Contributions Utilitarian analysis of economic policy, especially growth theory: influence of uncertainty on optimum growth; non-substitution theorems with durable goods; definition and theory of 'agreeable plans'; exhaustible resources; growth with indivisibilities. Optimal tax theory: commodity taxes and public-sector production decision rules; theory and calculation of optimum income-tax schedules; theory of mixed linear/non-linear tax systems; taxation of urban location; taxation of family size. Development economics: methods of cost-benefit analysis; rigorous models of low-income economies; aid policies. Incentive systems and social insurance: solutions of moral hazard problems; legal liability; pay structures in hierarchies; theory of retirement pensions; incentives for inventive activity.

Publications *Books*: 1. *Models of Economic Growth*, ed. (with N.H. Stern), (Macmillan, 1973); 2. *Project Appraisal and Planning for Developing Countries* (with I.M.D. Little), (Heinemann, Basic Books, 1974).

Articles: 1. 'Optimal taxation and public production I: Production efficiency', and 'II: Tax rules' (with P.A. Diamond), *AER*, 61(2,3), March, June 1971; 2. 'Notes on welfare economics, information, and uncertainty', in *Essays in Equilibrium Behavior Under Uncertainty*, eds M. Balch *et al*. (N-H, 1974); 3. 'Optimum saving with economies of scale' (with A.K. Dixit and N.H. Stern), *REStud*, 42(3), July 1975; 4, 'A pure theory of underdeveloped economies, using a relationship between consumption and productivity', in *Agriculture in Development Theory*, ed. L.G. Reynolds (Yale Univ. Press, 1975); 5. 'Optimal tax theory: a synthesis', *J Pub E*, 6(4), Nov. 1976.

MISES, Ludwig Edler Von*

Dates and Birthplace 1881–1973, Lemberg, Austro-Hungary.

Posts Held Prof., Univ. Vienna, 1913–38; Prof., Grad. Inst. Internat. Stud., 1934–40; Prof., NYU, 1945–69.

Degree Dr Univ. Vienna, 1906.

Offices Founder, Mont Pelerin Soc.; Adviser, Austrian Chamber of Commerce, 1909–34; Founder, Austrian Inst. Bus. Cycle Res., 1926.

Career The leading twentieth-century figure of the Austrian School, he developed a once widely accepted theory of business cycles in which booms result from bank credit expansion. His other main contribution was the demonstration that socialist planning could not achieve a rational allocation of resources because of its lack of a true price system. He extended this argument to a general critique of government intervention in a private enterprise economy. He was deeply interested in epistemological questions and developed his own methodology, known as praxeology, which laid heavy stress on individual choices and purposive human action as the *a priori* foundation of valid economic reasoning. He is today hailed as the founding father of the 'new' Austrian School.

Publications *Books*: 1. *The Theory of Money and Credit* (1912, 1953, 1981); 2. *Socialism: An Economic and Sociological Analysis* (1922, 1959); 3. *The Free and Prosperous Commonwealth* (1927, 1962); 4. *Die Ursachen der Wirtschaftskrise* (1931); 5. *Epistemological Problems of Economics* (1933, 1960); 6. *Nationalökonomie: Theorie des Handelns und Wirtschaftens* (1940); 7. *Human Action* (1949, 1966); 8. *The Ultimate Foundation of Economic Science* (1962).

Secondary Literature M.N. Rothbard, 'Von Mises, Ludwig', *IESS*, vol. 16; L.S. Moss, ed., *The Economics of Ludwig von Mises* (Sheed & Ward, 1974).

MISHAN, Ezra

Born 1917, Manchester, England.

Current Post Hon. Fellow, City Univ., London, England.

Recent Posts LSE, 1956–77.

Degrees BA Univ. Manchester, 1946; MSc (Econ.) Univ. London, 1949; PhD Univ. Chicago, 1951.

Honours The De Vries Lectures, Netherlands School Econ., 1969.

Principal Contributions Over 100 articles, a large proportion of which are contributions to theory of allocation and welfare. Textbooks on normative economics and cost benefit analysis. Popular books on economic fallacies and the economic growth debate. Popular articles on social topics.

Publications *Books:* 1. *The Costs of Economic Growth* (Penguin Books, 1967); 2. *Welfare Economics: An Assessment* (N-H, 1969); 3. *Cost-benefit Analysis* (A & J, 1971, 1975, 1981); 4. *Introduction to Normative Economics* (OUP, 1980); 5. *Economic Efficiency and Social Welfare* (A & J, 1981).

Articles: 1. 'Rent as a measure of welfare change', *AER*, 49(3), June 1959; 2. 'A proposed normalization procedure for public investment criteria', *EJ*, 77, Dec. 1967, 81, March 1971; 3. 'The postwar literature on externalities', *JEL*, 9(1), March 1971; 4. 'Evaluation of life and limb: a theoretical approach', *JPE*, 79(4), July/Aug. 1971; 5. 'Welfare criteria: resolution of a paradox', *EJ*, 83, Sept. 1973.

MITCHELL, Wesley Clair*

Dates and Birthplace 1874–1948, Rushville, Ill., USA.

Posts Held Prof., Univ. Cal., 1903–13, Columbia Univ., 1913–19, 1922–44; Dir., New School Social Res., 1919–31.

Degrees BA, PhD Univ. Chicago, 1896, 1899.

Offices Dir., NBER, 1920–45; Member, Res. Comm. Social Trends, 1929–33; Member, Nat. Planning Board, 1933.

Career Leading authority on business cycles, who devoted himself chiefly to economic research. He helped to found NBER in 1920 to further the development of quantitative studies of the US economy. He regarded his central task as the study of the 'money economy' and consistently sought a dynamic theory of social change. Though other contemporaries, such as Aftalion and Spiethoff, achieved similar results in business cycle theory, his work on cycles was unique in its breadth and continuity.

Publications *Books:* 1. *A History of the Greenbacks* (1903); 2. *Gold Prices and Wages Under the Greenback Standard* (1908); 3. *Business Cycles* (1913, 1959); 4. *The Making and Uses of Index Numbers* (1915, 1938); 5. *Business Cycles: The Problem and Its Setting* (1927); 6. *The Backward Art of Spending Money* (1937, 1950); 7. *Measuring Business Cycles* (with A.F. Burns), (1946); 8. *What Happens During Business Cycles* (1951).

Secondary Literature V. Zarnowitz, 'Mitchell, Wesley C.', *IESS*, vol. 10.

MODIGLIANI, Franco

Born 1918, Rome, Italy.

Current Post Inst. prof., Prof. Econ. Fin., MIT, USA.

Recent Posts Instructor, Assoc. Econ. Stats., Bard Coll., Columbia Univ., 1942–4; Lecturer, Ass. prof. Math. Econ. Em., New School Social Res., 1943–4, 1946–8; Assoc. prof., 1949, Prof. Econ., 1950–2, Univ. Illinois; Prof. Econ. Industrial Admin., Carnegie Inst. Technology, 1952–60; Prof. Econ., Northwestern Univ., 1960–2.

Degrees D (Jurisprudence) Univ. Rome, 1939; D (Social Science) New School Social Res., 1944; LLD (Ad Hon.) Univ. Chicago, 1967; Dr (*Hon. causa*) Univ. Catholique de Louvain, 1974, Istituto Univ. di Bergamo, 1979.

Offices Pres., Em Soc, 1962, AEA, 1976, AFA, 1981; Academic consultant, Board Governors, Fed. Reserve System, 1966–; Sr adviser, Brookings Panel Econ. Activity, 1971–; Member, NAS, 1973–; Vice-pres., IEA, 1976–81.

Principal Contributions Contributed to clarifying the relation between the Keynesian 'revolution', classical economics and monetarism, and implications for monetary and fiscal stabilisation policies. Had major responsibility for building model of US economy (MPS) for Federal Reserve System. Originated the life-cycle hypothesis of saving which has found wide applications in the study of family and national saving. Author (with M. Miller) of two theorems basic to modern finance to the effect that underefficient, rational markets and abstracting from tax effects, the market value of a firm and its cost of capital are independent of the debt – equity ratio and of the dividend – payout ratio.

Publications *Books:* 1. *National Incomes and International Trade* (with H. Neisser), (Univ. Illinois Press, 1953); 2. *Planning Production, Inventories and Work Forces* (with others), (Prentice-Hall, 1960); 3. *New Mortgage Designs for Stable Housing in Inflationary Environment,* ed. (with D. Lessard), (Fed. Reserve Bank Boston, Conference series 14, 1975); 4. *Collected Papers of Franco Modigliani:* vol. 1, *Essays in Macroeconomics;* vol. 2, *Life Cycle Hypothesis of Saving;* vol. 3, *Theory of Finance and Other Essays* (MIT Press, 1980).

Articles: 1. 'Towards an understanding of the real effects and costs of inflation' (with S. Fischer), *WA*, 114(4), 1978; 2. 'Optimal demand policies against stagflation' (with L. Papademos), *WA*, 114(4), 1978; 3. 'Inflation, rational valuation and the market' (with R.C. Cohn), *Fin Analysis J*, March/April, 1979; 4. 'The structure of financial markets and the monetary mechanism' (with L. Papademos), in *Controlling Monetary Aggregates III* (Fed. Reserve Bank Boston, Conference series 23, 1980); 5. 'The trade-off between real wages and employment in an open economy (Belgium)' (with J. Dreze), *Europ ER*, 15(2), 1981.

MOLINARI, Gustave de*

Dates and Birthplace 1819–1912, Liège, Belgium.
Posts Held Journalist and propagandist in Paris, 1840–52; Prof. Polit. Econ., Royal Brussels Museum Industry, 1852–60; Ed., *Journal des Débats*, 1867–76; Ed., *Journal des Economistes*, 1881–1909.

Offices A founder and later Hon. Pres., Soc. d'Econ. Polit.
Career Determined advocate of free trade liberalism and opponent of socialism, first as a journalist in Paris and then in academic and editorial capacities. He related liberty and property to the economic phenomena of value, arguing that the object of liberty is value and that value is the substance of property.

Publications *Books:* 1. *L'Organisation de la liberté industrielle* (1846); 2. *Les Soirées de la rue St Lazare* (1849); 3. *Le Mouvement socialiste et les réunions publiques* (1870); 4. *Les Problèmes du XXᵉ siécle* (1901); 5. *L'Economie de l'histoire, théorie du progrès* (1908).

Secondary Literature Y. Guyot, 'Obituary: Gustave de Molinari', *EJ*, 22, March 1912.

MÖLLER, Hans

Born 1915, Berlin, Germany.
Current Post Prof., Ludwig-Maximilians-Univ. München, Bundesrepublik.
Recent Posts Economist, Bank Deutscher Länder, 1948–50; Member, German Delegation OEEC, Paris, 1950–4; Prof. Univ. Frankfurt, 1954–8.
Degrees Diplom-Vokswirt, Dr rer. pol., Dr rer. pol. habil., Univ. Berlin, 1936, 1938, 1942.
Offices Member, Bayerische Akademie Wissenschaften; Part-time adviser EEC Commission, 1958–70; Chairman, Advisory Council Fed. Ministry Econ., Bundesrepublik, 1970–7.
Principal Contributions Reception of neo-classical theory in Germany during and after World War II, in particular the development of modern price theory along the lines set by Chamberlin, Robinson and von Stackelberg; integration of real and monetary theory with special reference to international economics; and in the economic policy field, promotion of applications of regional and environmental economics and work on international economic organisations and the world economic order.
Publications *Books:* 1. *Internationale Wirtschaftsorganisationen*

(Wiesbaden, 1960); 2. *Aussenwirtschaftspolitik* (Wiesbaden, 1961); 3. *Zur Vorgeschichte der Deutschmark* (Tubingen, 1961); 4. *Kalkulation, Absatzpolitik und Preisbildung* (Wiesbaden, 1962); 5. *Das Ende einer Weltwährungsordnung* (München, 1972).

Articles: 1. 'Die Formen und Grundlagen einer Theorie der regionalen Preisdifferenzierung', *WA*, 57, 1943; 2. 'H. von Stackelberg und sein Beitrag für die Wirtschaftswissenschaft', *ZGS*, 105, 1949; 5. 'Urpsrungs- und Bestimmungslandprinzip', *Finanzarchiv*, 27, 1968.

MONDLAK, Y.

N.e.

MONRING, H.

N.e.

MONSEN, R. Joseph Jr

Born 1931, Payson, Utah, USA.
Current Post Prof., Chairman, Dept Bus. and Govt, Univ. Washington, 1973–.
Recent Posts Vis. prof., Stanford Univ., 1971–2.
Degrees BS Univ. Utah, 1953; MA Stanford Univ., 1954; PhD Univ. Cal., Berkeley, 1961.
Offices and Honours Annual res. award, Land Econ. Foundation, 1958; Guggenheim Memorial Foundation Fellow, 1968–9; General Electric res. award, 1976, 1977, 1978.
Principal Contributions Research on ideologies and theories of capitalism, effects of ownership-type control on performance of large firms, and on performance of state owned firms.
Publications *Books:* 1. *Modern American Capitalism: Ideologies and Issues* (Houghton Mifflin Co., 1963); 2. *The Makers of Public Policy: American Power Groups and their Ideologies* (McGraw-Hill, 1965); 3. *Business and the Changing Environment* (McGraw-Hill, 1973).
Articles: 1. 'The effect of separation of ownership and control on the performance of the large firm', *QJE*, 82, Aug. 1968; 2. 'Public goods and private status', *Public Interest*, Spring 1971; 3. 'The unrecognized social revolution', *Cal. Management Review*, Winter 1971; 4. 'State owned business abroad: new competitive threat', *Harvard Bus. Review*, March 1979; 5. 'The state-owned firm: a review of data and issues', in *Business Environment and Public Policy*, ed. L. Preston (JAI Press, 1980).

MOORE, Henry Ludwell*

Dates and Birthplace 1869–1958, USA.
Posts Held Prof., Smith Coll., 1896–1902, Columbia Univ., 1902–29.
Degree PhD Johns Hopkins Univ., 1896.
Career A pioneer of econometrics who produced quantitative estimates of elasticities of demand and supply, of productivity changes, of cost curves and the determinants of wage rates. After his early work on wages, he turned to the search for a fundamental explanation of economic fluctuations. His explanation was that 8-year cycles of rainfall governed cycles of the whole economy. Later attempts to relate cycles to the transits of Venus failed by his own admission. His final book was an attempt to devise a research programme to estimate Walras' equations of general equilibrium.
Publications *Books:* 1. *Laws of Wages: An Essay in Statistical Economics* (1911); 2. *Economic Cycles: Their Law and Cause* (1914); 3. *Forecasting the Yield and Price of Cotton* (1917); 4. *Generating Economic Cycles* (1923); 5. *Synthetic Economics* (1929).
Secondary Literature G.J. Stigler, 'Henry L. Moore and statistical economics', in *Essays in the History of Economics* (Univ. of Chicago Press, 1965), 'Moore, Henry L.', *IESS*, vol. 10.

MORELLET, André*

Dates and Birthplace 1727–1819, Lyons, France.
Post Held Abbé of the Catholic Church.

Offices Member, Napoleonic Corps Législatif.

Career One of the *encyclopaedistes* and a contributor to Peuchet's *Dictionnaire universel de la géographie commercante* (1799–1800). He was an ardent free trader, arguing that since man is naturally free, any interference with his buying and selling is a violation of natural law. His *Mémoire* ... was responsible for the suspension of the Compagnie des Indes (1769). His translation of the *Wealth of Nations* into French remained unpublished.

Publications *Books:* 1. *Réflexions sur les avantages de la libre fabrication et de l'usage des toiles peintes en France* (1758); 2. *Manuel des inquisiteurs* (1762); 3. *Fragment d'une lettre sur la police des grains* (1764); 4. *Mémoire sur la situation actuelle de la Compagnie des Indes* (1769); 5. *Réfutation d'un écrit intitulé Dialogues sur le commerce des blés* (1770).

Secondary Literature L. Strachey, *Portraits in Miniature* (1931); H. Hauser, 'Morellet, Abbé André', *ESS*, vol. 11.

MORGAN, James N.

Born 1918, Corydon, Ind., USA.

Current Post Res. Scientist, Inst. Social Res., Prof. Econ., Univ. Michigan, USA.

Recent Posts Ass. prof., Brown Univ., 1947–9.

Degrees BA Northwestern Univ., 1939; PhD Harvard Univ., 1947.

Offices Member, NAS; Fellow, ASA; Member, Board Dirs, Consumers Union USA.

Principal Contributions Consumer behaviour studied through survey research, survey data collection and analysis methods. Survey research on the poor, the wealthy, car accident victims, injured workers, and businessmen. A major study in its 14th year has followed all the members of an original sample of families, forming a self-replacing panel and allowing studies of the dynamics of change in income and in family composition.

Publications *Books:* 1. *Income and Welfare in the United States* (with M.

David *et al.*), (McGraw-Hill, 1962); 2. *The Economic Behaviour of the Affluent* (with R. Barlow and H. Brazer), (Brookings Inst., 1966); 3. *Productive Americans* (with I. Sirageldin and L. Baerwaldt), (Inst. Social Res., Ann Arbor, 1966); 4. *The Economics of Personal Choice* (with G. Duncan), (Univ. Michigan Press, 1980); 5. *Five Thousand American Families: Patterns of Economic Progress* 9 vols, ed. and co-author (Inst. Social Res., Ann Arbor, 1972–81).

Articles: 1. 'The anatomy of income distribution', *REStat*, 44, Aug. 1962; 2. 'Problems in the analysis of survey data, and a proposal' (with J. Sonquist), *JASA*, 58, June 1963; 3. 'Education and income' (with M. David), *QJE*, 77, Aug. 1963; 4. 'Some pilot studies on communication and consensus in the family', *Public Opinion Quarterly*, Spring 1968; 5. 'Trends in planned early retirement' and 'Trends in satisfaction with retirement' (with R. Barfield), *The Gerontologist*, 1978.

MORGENSTERN, Oskar*

Dates and Birthplace 1902–77, Goerlitz, Germany.

Posts Held Privatdozent, Prof., Univ. Vienna, 1929–38; Prof., Univ. Princeton, 1938–70.

Degree Dr Univ. Vienna, 1925.

Offices Disting. Fellow, AEA, 1976.

Career With von Neumann, introduced games theory into economics. The problem of prediction was his starting point, and the use of formal mathematical models of games was merely suggested as a helpful approach. The burgeoning popularity of games theory has, however, resulted in a rich literature, spanning economics, sociology, and political science. Also wrote on the economics of defence and developed von Neumann's ideas on growth theory.

Publications *Books:* 1. *Wirtschaftsprognose* (1928); 2. *Die Grenzen der Wirtschaftspolitik* (1934); 3. *Theory of Games and Economic Behaviour* (with J. von Neumann), (1944, 1964); 4. *On the Accuracy of Economic Observations* (1950); 5. *The Question of National Defense* (1959); 6. *Predictability of*

Stock Market Prices (with C.W.J. Granger), (1970); 7. *Mathematical Theory of Expanding and Contracting Economies* (with G.L. Thompson), (1976).

Articles: 'Ten critical points in contemporary economic theory: an interpretation', *JEL*, 10(4), Dec. 1972.

Secondary Literature M. Shubik, 'Morgenstern, Oskar', *IESS*, vol. 18.

MORISHIMA, Michio

Born 1923, Osaka, Japan.
Current Post Chairman, Internat. Centre Econ. and Related Disciplines, LSE.
Recent Posts Ass. prof., Univ. Kyoto, 1950–1, Univ. Osaka, 1951–69; Rockefeller Foundation Fellow, Univ. Oxford and Yale Univ., 1956–8; Vis. Sr Fellow, All Souls Coll., Univ. Oxford, 1963–4; Prof. Econ., Univ. Essex, 1968–70; Prof. Econ., LSE, 1970–.
Degrees Keizai Gakushi (BA) Univ. Kyoto, 1946; MA Univ. Oxford, 1958.
Offices and Honours Vice-pres., 1964, Pres., 1965, Em Soc; Assoc. ed., *Em*, 1969–70; Co-ed. and ed., *Int ER*, 1969–70; Ed. Board, *Ec*, 1974–; *JEL*, 1975–80; Foreign hon. member, AAAS, 1975; Hon. member, AEA, 1976; *Bunka Kunsho* (Cultural Order of Japan) 1976.
Principal Contributions Multi-sectoral theory of growth: simultaneous optimisation of population and capital. Econometric growth model for the US economy. Marx and Walras in the light of modern economic theory. Input-output analysis of disguised unemployment in Japan and of de-industrialisation in the UK. Role played by ethical doctrines in the creation of Japanese capitalism.
Publications *Books:* 1. *Theory of Economic Growth* (OUP, 1969); 2. *Marx's Economics: A Dual Theory of Value and Growth* (CUP, 1973); 3. *The Economic Theory of Modern Society* (CUP, 1975); 4. *Walras' Economics* (CUP, 1977); 5. *Value, Exploitation and Growth* (with G. Catephores), (McGraw-Hill, 1978).

MORRIS, Cynthia Taft

Born 1928, Cincinnati, Ohio, USA.
Current Post Prof. Econ., Amer. Univ., Washington, DC, 1972–.
Degrees BA Vassar Coll., 1949; MSc (Econ.) LSE, 1951; PhD Yale Univ., 1959.
Offices and Honours EHA; NSF Grants, 1965, 1968, 1970, 1979.
Principal Contributions Co-author with Irma Adelman of innovative quantitative studies of influence of institutional influences on economic development.
Publications *Books:* 1. *Evolution of Wage Structure* (with L.G. Reynolds), (Yale Univ. Press, 1956); 2. *Society, Politics, and Economic Development* (with I. Adelman), (Johns Hopkins Univ. Press, 1967); 3. *Economic Growth and Social Equity in Developing Countries* (with I. Adelman), (Stanford Univ. Press, 1973).
Articles: 1. 'A factor analysis of the interrelationship between social and political variables and per capita gross national product' (with I. Adelman), *QJE*, 74, Nov. 1965; 2. 'An econometric model of socio-economic and political change in underdeveloped countries' (with I. Adelman), *AER*, 78(5), Dec. 1968; 3. 'The derivation of cardinal scales from ordinal data: an application of multi-dimensional scaling to measure levels of national development' (with I. Adelman), in *Economic Development and Planning. Essays in Honour of Jan Tinbergen*, ed. W. Sellekaerts (Internat. Arts and Sciences Press, 1974); 4. 'The role of institutional influences in patterns of agricultural development in the nineteenth and early twentieth centuries: a cross-section quantitative study' (with I. Adelman), *JEH*, 39, March 1979; 5. 'Patterns of industrialization in the latter nineteenth and early twentieth centuries: a cross-section quantitative study' (with I. Adelman), in *Research in Economic History*, vol. 5, ed. P. Uselding (JAI Press, 1980).

MOSES, Leon N.

Born 1924, New York City, NY, USA.

Current Post Prof. Econ., Northwestern Univ., Evanston, USA.
Recent Posts Dir., 1974–9, Dir., Academic Program, 1979–, Transportation Center, Northwestern Univ.
Degrees BA Ohio State Univ., 1947; MA, PhD Harvard Univ., 1951, 1953.
Offices AEA; Ford Foundation Fellow, 1967–8; Rockefeller Foundation Fellow, 1969–70; Pres., RSA, 1975.
Principal Contributions The spatial and temporal aspects of decisions by firms and the influence of factor prices and transport costs on those decisions. The influence of changes in the regulatory environment, especially in transportation, on firms' spatial choices. The development and growth of cities and regions and the interregional trade and factor relationships between regions under the influence of changes in the technology and costs of production, transportation and communication.
Publications Articles: 1. 'A general equilibrium model of production, interregional trade, and location of industry', REStat, 42, Nov. 1960; 2. 'The location of economic activity in cities' (with H.F. Williamson Jr), AERS, 57, May 1967; 3. 'Outputs and prices in inter-industry models', RSA Proceedings, 1973; 4. 'Interdependence and the location of economic activities' (with G.S. Goldstein), JUE, 2, 1975; 5. 'Dynamics and land use: the case of forestry' (with J. Ledyard), in Public Finance and Urban Economics: Essays in honor of William S. Vickrey, ed. R.E. Grieson (Lexington Books, 1975).

MUELLBAUER, John N.J.

Born 1944, Kempten, Allgäu, W. Germany.
Current Post Official Fellow Econ., Nuffield Coll., Univ. Oxford, 1981–.
Recent Posts Lecturer, Warwick Univ., 1969–72; Lecturer, 1972–5, Reader, 1975–7, Prof., 1977–81, Birkbeck Coll., London.
Degrees BA (First class hons.) Univ. Camb., 1965; PhD Univ. Cal., Berkeley, 1975.
Offices and Honours Wrenbury Fellow Polit. Econ., Univ. Camb., 1964–5; Flood Fellow Econ., Univ. Cal.,

Berkeley, 1965–6, 1967–8; Board member, REStud, 1973–; Assoc. ed., Em, 1979–; Medallion, Helsinki Univ., 1979; Fellow, Em Soc, 1979–.
Principal Contributions The relationship of theory to applied economics: thus each theoretical contribution arises out of a problem in applied economics; and conversely, each applied piece is placed within a tight theoretical framework. The main areas are: aggregation theory, particularly in the context of consumer demand and labour supply; index numbers and quality measurement with applications to consumer and producer durables; prices and inequality: the distribution impact of different structures of relative prices; theory and measurement of equivalence scales and hence of welfare comparisons across households; non-Walrasian macro-economics; and employment functions.
Publications Books: 1. Economics and Consumer Behaviour (with A. Deaton), (CUP, 1980).
Articles: 1. 'Household production theory, quality and the "hedonic technique" ', AER, 64(6), Dec. 1974; 2. 'Aggregation, income distribution and consumer demand', REStud, 42(4), Oct. 1975; 3. 'Macro-economic models with quantity rationing' (with R. Portes), EJ, 88, Dec. 1978; 4. 'The estimation of the Prais-Houthakker model of equivalence scales', Em, 48(1), Jan. 1980; 5. 'Unemployment, employment and exports: a non-clearing markets approach' (with D. Winter), Europ ER, 13(3), May 1980.

MUELLER, Dennis C.

Born 1940, USA.
Current Post Prof. Econ., Univ. Maryland, USA.
Recent Posts Assoc. prof., Cornell Univ., 1970–6; Sr Res. Fellow, Internat. Inst. Management, Berlin, 1974–7; Consultant, Fed. Trade Commission, 1978–.
Degrees BS (Maths, Magna cum laude) Colorado Coll., 1962; PhD (Econ.) Princeton Univ., 1066.
Offices AEA; Public Choice Soc.
Principal Contributions Study of

corporate decision making, allocation of corporate cash flows among competing uses. Determinants and effects of advertising, R & D, and mergers. Social costs of monopoly and its persistence. Study of effects of various collective decision rules. Development of voting by veto procedure. Surveys of public choice literature.

Publications *Books:* 1. *Public Choice* (CUP, 1979); 2. *The Determinants and Effects of Mergers: An International Comparison*, ed. (Oelgeschlager, Gunn, and Hain, 1980); 3. *The Political Economy of Growth*, ed. (Yale Univ. Press, 1981).

Articles: 1. 'The firm decision process: an econometric investigation', *QJE*, 81, Feb. 1967, reprinted in *Readings in the Economics of Industrial Organization*, ed. D. Needham (Holt, Rinehart & Winston, 1970), and in *Readings in Managerial Economics*, ed. K.S. Paldo (Prentice-Hall, 1973); 2. 'A theory of conglomerate mergers', *QJE*, 83, Nov. 1969; 3. 'Life-cycle effects on corporate returns on retentions' (with H.G. Grabowski), *REStat*, 57(4), Nov. 1975; 4. 'The persistence of profits above the norm', *Ec*, 44, Nov. 1977; 5. 'Voting by veto', *J Pub E*, 10, Aug. 1978, reprinted in J.J. Laffont, ed., *Aggregation and the Revelation of Preferences* (N-H, 1979).

MÜLLER, Adam Heinrich*

Dates and Birthplace 1779–1829, Berlin, Germany.
Posts Held Tutor, Prince Bernhard of Saxe-Weimar, Dresden, 1806–9; Civil servant, Austria, 1813.
Career German Catholic economist of the Romantic school, who rejected the individuality and emphasis on material values of contemporary political economy. He was closely associated with Metternich and the reactionary politics of the post-Napoleonic period. He favoured an organic view of society in which the state would act to unite all social elements. The implications of this were nationalist and protectionist. He had some influence on the Historical School and inspired Spann's 'universalism'.
Publications *Books:* 1. *Die Elemente*

der Staatskunst, 2 vols (1809, 1920); 2. *Ausgewählte Abhandlungen* (1812, 1931); 3. *Die Theorie der Staatshaushaltung und Ihre Fortschritte* (1812); 4. *Versuche einer Neuen Theorie des Geldes* (1816, 1922); *Zwölf Reden uber die Beredsamkeit und Deren Verfall in Deutschland* (1817, 1920).
Secondary Literature J. Baxa, *Adam Müller* (Fischer, 1930); H.R. Bowen, 'Müller, Adam Heinrich', *IESS*, vol. 10.

MUNDELL, R.A.

N.e.

MUNS, Joaquín

Born 1935, Barcelona, Spain.
Current Post Exec. dir., World Bank, Washington, DC.
Recent Posts Economist, Western Hemisphere, IMF, 1965–8; Prof. Internat. Econ. Organisation, Univ. Barcelona, 1971–; Exec. dir., IMF, representing Costa Rica, El Salvador, Guatemala, Honduras, Mexico, Nicaragua, Spain and Venezuela, 1978–80.
Degrees Licenciado en Derecho (LIMO) 1958, Licenciado en Ciencias Económicas (MSc.), PhD (Econ. *Summa cum laude*), Univ. Barcelona, 1959, 1972.
Offices Member, AEA.
Principal Contributions In the field of industrial economics, PhD thesis *(Industrialisation and Growth of Developing Countries)* proved the overall negative balance of the schemes of import substituting industrialisation practised since the 1930s; and in international economic organisation, has devised a methodological approach to its study.
Publications *Books:* 1. *Input-output Table of the Catalan Economy For the Year 1967* (in Spanish, Cocin, 1972); 2. *Industrialisation and Growth in the Developing Countries* (in Spanish, Ariel, 1972); 3. *The European Option for the Spanish Economy. White Book on the Repercussions of the Entry of Spain into the European Common Market* (in Spanish, Guadiana, 1973); 4. *Crisis and Reform of the International Monetary system*, ed. (in Spanish, Inst. de Estudios Fiscales, 1975, 1978).

Articles: 1. 'The SDR and the future of international liquidity', *Revista Española Economía* (in Spanish) Jan./April 1973; 2. 'Economists and the international economic system', *Revista Española Economía* (in Spanish) Sept./Dec. 1976; 3. 'While the Spanish economy waits for the elections', *The Banker*, April 1977; 4. 'International financing in Latin America. Concluding remarks', in *Proceedings of an International Conference on Financing in Latin America* (1980).

MUSGRAVE, Richard Abel

Born 1910, Königstein, Germany.
Current Post H.H. Burbank Prof. Polit. Econ., Harvard Univ., USA.
Recent Posts Prof. Econ., Univ. Michigan, 1948–58; Prof. Econ., Johns Hopkins Univ., 1958–61; Prof. Econ., Princeton Univ., 1962–5.
Degrees Diplom Volkswirt Univ., Heidelberg, 1933; PhD Harvard Univ., 1937; Dr Laws (*Hon. causa*), Allegheny Coll., 1979.
Offices Member, AAAS; Vice-pres., 1962, Disting. Fellow, 1978, AEA; Ed., *QJE*, 1969–75; Hon. Vice-pres., Internat. Inst. Public Fin., 1978.
Principal Contributions Incorporation of the economics of public finance into the larger body of economic theory, with special concern for the role of the public sector in a democratic society.
Publications *Books:* 1. *The Theory of Public Finance* (McGraw-Hill, 1958); 2. *Classics in the Theory of Public Finance* (with A.T. Peacock), (Macmillan, 1958); 3. *Fiscal Systems* (Yale Univ. Press, 1969); 4. *Public Finance in Theory and Practice* (with P. Musgrave), (McGraw-Hill, 1973); 5. *Fiscal Reform in Colombia* (Harvard Univ. Press, 1979).
Articles : 1. 'The voluntary exchange theory of public economy', *QJE*, 53, Feb. 1939; 2. 'Proportional income taxation and risk taking' (with E. Domar), *QJE*, 58, May 1944; 3. 'Distribution of tax payments by income groups: a case study for 1948', *National Tax J*, 5, March 1951, 5, March 1952; 4. 'Tax reform: growth with equity', *AER/S*, 53, May 1963; 5. 'Maximin, uncertainty,

and the leisure trade-off', *QJE*, 88(4), Nov. 1974.

MUTH, John Fraser

Born 1930, Chicago, Ill., USA.
Current Post Prof. Production Management, School Bus., Indiana Univ., USA, 1969–.
Recent Posts Carnegie-Mellon Univ., 1956–64; Michigan State Univ., 1964–9.
Degrees BSIE Washington Univ., 1952; MS, PhD Carnegie-Mellon Univ., 1954, 1962.
Offices AEA; ORSA; Inst. Management Sciences; Amer. Inst. Decision Sciences; Amer. Inst. Industrial Engineers; Fellow, Em Soc.
Principal Contributions Rational expectations in certain dynamic economic models.
Publications *Books:* 1. *Planning Production, Inventories, and Work Force* (with C.C. Holt *et al.*), (Wiley, 1960); 2. *Operations Management: Analysis for Decisions* (with G.K. Groff), (Wiley, 1972).
Articles: 1. 'Rational expectations and the theory of price movements', *Em*, 29, July 1961.

MUTH, Richard F.

Born 1927, Chicago, Ill., USA.
Current Post Prof. Econ., Stanford Univ., USA.
Recent Posts Assoc. prof., Grad. School Bus., Univ. Chicago, 1959–64; Economist, Inst. Defense Analyses, 1964–6; Prof. Econ., Washington Univ., 1966–70.
Degrees BA, MA Washington Univ., 1949, 1950; PhD Univ. Chicago, 1958.
Offices AEA; Em Soc; Vice-pres., RSA, 1975–6.
Principal Contributions Principal work in housing, especially housing demand, the spatial pattern of urban housing markets, and government housing programmes.
Publications *Books:* 1. *Regions, Resources and Economic Growth* (with others), (Johns Hopkins Univ. Press, 1960); 2. *Cities and Housing* (Chicago

Univ. Press, 1969); 3. *Public Housing* (Amer. Enterprise Inst., 1974); 4. *Urban Economic Problems* (Harper & Row, 1975).

Articles: 1. 'The demand for non-farm housing', in *The Demand for Durable Goods*, ed. A.C. Harberger (Chicago Univ. Press, 1960); 2. 'Household production and consumer demand functions', *Em*, 34, July 1966; 3. 'A vintage model of the housing stock', *RSA Papers*, 1973; 4. 'Numerical solution of urban residential land-use models', *JUE*, 2, 1975; 5. 'The allocation of households to dwellings', *J Reg S*, 18(2), Aug. 1978.

MYINT, H.L.A.

Born 1920, Bassein, Burma.
Current Post Prof. Econ., LSE, England.
Recent Posts Lecturer Econ. Underdeveloped Countries, Univ. Oxford, 1950–65; Rector, Rangoon Univ., 1958–61.
Degrees BA Rangoon Univ., 1939; PhD (Econ.) Univ. London, 1943; MA Univ. Oxford, 1950.
Offices Member, RES.
Principal Contributions The theory of underdeveloped economies especially the effect of external economic forces on the internal economic organisation of these countries; the relationship between economic theory including the history of economic thought and development economics; the development and application of a theory of economic organisation and institutions to the underdeveloped countries.
Publications *Books:* 1. *Theories of Welfare Economics* (Longman, Harvard Univ. Press, 1948); 2. *The Economics of the Developing Countries* (Hutchinson, 1964, Praeger, 1980); 3. *Economic Theory and the Underdeveloped Countries* (OUP, 1971); 4. *South-east Asia's Economy, Development Policies in the 1970s* (Penguin Books, Praeger, 1972).
Articles: 1. 'An interpretation of economic backwardness', *OEP*, N.S. 6, June 1954, repr. in *The Economics of Underdevelopment*, eds A.N. Agarwala and S.P. Singh (OUP, 1958); 2. 'The

"classical theory" of international trade and the underdeveloped countries', *EJ*, 68, June 1958, repr. in *Development Economics and Policy Readings*, ed. I. Livingstone (A & U, 1981); 3. 'Economic theory and the underdeveloped countries', *JPE*, 73, Oct. 1965; 4. 'Dualism and the internal integration of underdeveloped economies', *BNLQR*, 93, June 1970; 5. 'Adam Smith's theory of international trade in the perspective of economic development', *Ec*, N.S. 44, Aug. 1977.

MYRDAL, Gunnar

Born 1898, Gustafs Parish, Sweden.
Current Post Retired, Prof. Emeritus, Univ. Stockholm, Sweden.
Recent Posts Assoc. prof., Post-Grad. Inst. Internat. Stud., Univ. Geneva, 1931–2; Lars Hierta Chair Polit. Econ., Univ. Stockholm, 1933–9; Exec. Secretary, UNECE, 1947–57; Prof. Internat. Econ., Univ. Stockholm, 1961–5; Disting. vis. prof., NY City Univ., 1974–5.
Degrees Dr juris, econ., Univ. Stockholm, 1927; Hon. degrees: Harvard Univ., 1938, and 30 others.
Offices and Honours Senator, Swedish parliament, 1934–6, 1942–6; Chairman, Post-War Planning Commission, Sweden, 1945–7; Minister of Commerce, Sweden, 1945–7; Malinowsky Award, Soc. Applied Anthropology, 1950; Dir., Inst. Internat. Econ. Stud., Univ. Stockholm, 1961–; Chairman, Board, Stockholm Internat. Peace Res. Inst., 1962–; Nobel Prize Econ., 1974.
Principal Contributions N.e.
Publications *Books:* 1. *Monetary Equilibrium* (William Hodge & Co., 1939); 2. *The Political Element in the Development of Economic Theory* (Routledge & Kegan Paul, 1953); 3. *Economic Theory and Underdeveloped Regions* (Duckworth, Methuen, 1957, 1963); 4. *Asian Drama. An inquiry into the Poverty of Nations*, 3 vol. (Twentieth Century Fund, Pantheon Books, 1968); 5. *The Challenge of World Poverty. A World Anti-poverty Program in Outline* (Random House, 1972).
Secondary Literature E. Lundberg, 'Gunnar Myrdal's contribution to eco-

nomic theory', *Swed JE*, 76(4), Dec. 1974.

N

NECKER, Jacques*

Dates and Birthplace 1732–1804, Geneva, Switzerland.
Post Held Banker, 1750–72.
Offices Representative to the French Court, 1768; Dir.-general, French Royal Treasury, 1776; Dir.-general Fin., 1777–81, 1788–9, 1789–90.
Career Banker-economist whose protectionist ideas went against the physiocratic norms of the 1770s and 1780s. His attempts to cope with the financial morass in which *ancien régime* France found herself, though largely ineffective, led to his re-appointment to his previous post as finance minister in the first year of the Revolution. Administrative reforms in the provinces were his main achievement.
Publications *Books:* 1. *Eloge de Jean-Baptiste Colbert* (1773); 2. *Sur la législation et le commerce des grains* (1775); 3. *Compte rendu présenté au roi* (1781); 4. *De l'administration des finances de la France*, 3 vols (1784); 5. *Oeuvres complètes*, 15 vols (1820).
Secondary Literature P. Harsin, 'Necker, Jacques', *ESS*, vol. 9.

NEGISHI, Takashi

Born 1933, Tokyo, Japan.
Current Post Prof. Econ., Univ. Tokyo, Japan.
Recent Posts Vis. lecturer, LSE, 1975; Canadian Council Vis. prof., Univ. British Columbia, 1977.
Degrees Keizaigakuhakushi (PhD Econ.) Univ. Tokyo, 1965.
Offices and Honours Fellow, Em Soc; Assoc. Ed., *Em*, *J Int E*; Nikkei prize Best Books Econ., 1973; Matsunaga Science Foundation Prize Social Science, 1977.
Principal Contributions Analysis of existence, optimality, stability and dichotomy of general economic equilibrium. Applications of general equilibria

theory to international economics (gains from trade, infant industry, customs union, foreign exchanges) and to public economics (second best, public goods). Considerations of micro-economic foundations of macro-economics.
Publications *Books:* 1. *Kakaku to Haibun no Riron* (Theory of Price and Allocation), (Toyokeizai, 1965); 2. *Boekirieki to Kokusaishushi* (Gains from Trade and Balance of Payments), (Sobunsha, 1971); 3. *General Equilibrium Theory and International Trade* (N-H, 1972); 4. *Micro-economic Foundations of Keynesian Macro-economics* (N-H, 1979).
Articles: 1. 'Monopolistic competition and general equilibrium', *REStud*, 28, June 1961; 2. 'A theorem on non-*tâtonnement* stability' (with F.H. Hahn), *Em*, 30, July 1962; 3. 'Protection of the infant industry and dynamic internal economy', *ER*, 44, March 1968; 4. 'The excess of public expenditures on industries', *J Pub E*, 2(3), July 1973; 5. 'Foreign exchange gains in a Keynesian model of international trade', *Econ App*, 32(4), May 1979.

NELSON, Charles R.

Born 1942, Milwaukee, Wisc., USA.
Current Post Prof. Econ., 1975–, Chairman, Dept Econ., 1979–, Univ. Washington.
Recent Posts Assoc. prof. Bus. Econ., Univ. Chicago, 1973–5.
Degrees BA Yale Univ., 1963; MA, PhD Univ. Wisconsin, 1967, 1969.
Offices and Honours Irving Fisher Graduate Monograph Award, 1972; Program Chairman, Bus. Econ. Section, ASA, 1981.
Principal Contributions Use of time series methods to test hypotheses in monetary and financial economics and to evaluate econometric models.
Publications *Books:* 1. *The Term Structure of Interest Rates* (Basic Books, 1972); 2. *Applied Time Series Analysis for Managerial Forecasting* (Holden-Day, 1973).
Articles: 1. 'The prediction performance of the FRB-MIT-PENN model of the US economy' *AER*, 62(5), Dec. 1972; 2. 'The stochastic structure of the

velocity of money' (with J.P. Gould), *AER*, 64(3), June 1974; 3. 'On testing the hypothesis that the real rate of interest is constant' (with G.W. Schwert), *AER*, 67(3), June 1977; 4. 'Recursive structure in US income, prices, and output', *JPE*, 87(6), Dec. 1979; 5. 'Adjustment lags vs information lags: a test of alternative explanations of the Phillips curve phenomenon', *JMCB*, 12(1), March 1981.

NELSON, Richard R.

Born 1930, New York City, NY, USA.
Current Post Prof. Econ., Yale Univ., USA.
Degrees BA Oberlin Coll., 1952; PhD Yale Univ., 1956.
Offices Member, AEA.
Principal Contributions Contribution to the understanding of forces influencing the rate and direction of technological advance; analysis of the organisation of R & D activity and the role of private and public funding agencies; development of a general theoretical structure capable of treating economic growth fuelled by technological advance as an evolutionary process.
Publications *Books:* 1. *Technical Change, Economic Growth and Public Policy* (with M.T. Peck and E.D. Kalachek), (Brookings Inst., 1968); 2. *Structural Change in a Developing Economy* (with T.P. Schultz and R. Slighton), (Princeton Univ. Press, 1970); 3. *The Moon and the Ghetto* (W.W. Norton, 1977); 4. *An Evolutionary Theory of Economic Capabilities and Behavior* (with S.G. Winter), (Harvard Univ. Press, 1981).

NERLOVE, Marc

Born 1933, Chicago, Ill., USA.
Current Post Cook Prof. Econ., Northwestern Univ., USA, 1974.
Recent Posts Assoc. prof. Econ. and Agric. Econ., Univ. Minnesota, 1959–60; Prof. Econ., Stanford Univ., 1960–5; F.W. Taussig Res. prof., Harvard Univ., 1967–8; Prof. Econ., Yale Univ., 1965–9; Prof. Econ., Univ. Chicago, 1969–74.

Degrees BA Univ. Chicago, 1952; MA, PhD Johns Hopkins Univ., 1955, 1956, MAH Yale Univ., 1965.
Offices and Honours Fellow, Em Soc, 1960–; Fellow, ASA, 1964–; John Bates Clark medal, AEA, 1969; Fellow, AAAS, 1971–; P.C. Mahalinobis medal, Indian Em Soc, 1975; Exec. Comm., AEA, 1977–9; Member, NAS, 1979–; Pres. Em Soc, 1981.
Principal Contributions Development of econometric methods for the analysis of economic time series, especially distributed lags and cross-sections over time; agricultural supply analysis; production and cost function estimation; demand analysis; population and economic growth.
Publications *Books:* 1. *The Dynamics of Supply: Estimation of Farmers' Response to Price* (Johns Hopkins Univ. Press, 1958); 2. *Distributed Lags and Demand Analysis* (US Govt Printing Office, 1958); 3. *Estimation and Identification of Cobb-Douglas Production Functions* (Rand McNally, N-H, 1965); 4. *Analysis of Economic Time Series: A Synthesis* (Academic Press, 1979).
Articles: 1. 'Spectral analysis of seasonal adjustment procedures', *Em*, 32, July 1964; 2. 'Lags in economic behavior', *Em*, 40(2), March 1972; 3. 'Household and economy: toward a new theory of population and economic growth', *JPE*, 82(2), Pt 2, March–April 1974; 4. 'The dynamics of supply: retrospect and prospect', *AJAE*, 61(2), June 1979; 5. 'On the formation of price expectations: an analysis of business test data', *Europ ER*, 14, Feb. 1981.

NEUBERGER, Egon

Born 1925, Zagreb, Yugoslavia.
Current Post Prof. Econ., Dir. Grad. Stud., State Univ., New York, Stony Brook, USA, 1967–.
Recent Posts Econ. analyst, US Dept. State, 1949–54; Econ. officer, US Embassy, Moscow, 1952–3; Amherst Coll., 1957–60; Rand Corp., 1960–66; Univ. Michigan, 1965–66.
Degrees BA Cornell Univ., 1947; MA, PhD Harvard Univ., 1949, 1958.
Offices and Honours Ed., Irving Fisher and Frank W. Taussig Compe-

titions, 1969–; Exchange Fellow, AAAS, 1972; Exec. Comm., Assoc. Comparative Econ. Stud., 1974–6; Winner, Ford Foundation Internat. Competition on Res. on Soviet Union and Eastern Europe, 1975; Pres., Omicron Delta Epsilon, Internat. Honor Soc. Econ., 1980–2.

Principal Contributions Development of a conceptual framework for analysing economic systems, the DIM (decision-making, information, motivation) framework. This has been applied by a variety of scholars to analyses of economic systems of many countries, as well as to the Mormon Church, the East German *Kombinat*, the Israeli kibbutz, the Yugoslav self-managed enterprise, and many others. Provided seminal contributions to the study of Yugoslav investment auctions, the division of labour in the Council for Mutual Economic Assistance, the economics of worker managed organisations, and the transmission of international economic disturbances.

Publications *Books:* 1. *International Trade and Central Planning: an Analysis of Economic Interactions*, co-ed. and contributor (Univ. Cal. Press, 1968); 2. *Perspective in Economics: Economists Look at their Fields of Study*, co-ed. and contributor (McGraw-Hill, 1971); 3. *Comparative Economic Systems: A Decision-making Approach* (Allyn & Bacon, 1976); 4. *Internal Migration: A Comparative Perspective*, co-ed. and contributor (Academic Press, 1977); 5. *The Impact of International Economic Disturbances on the Soviet Union and Eastern Europe: Transmission and Response*, co-ed. and contributor (Pergamon Press, 1980).

Articles: 1. 'The Yugoslav investment auctions', *QJE*, 73, Feb. 1959; 2. 'International division of labor in CEMA: limited regret strategy', *AER/S*, 54, May 1964, reprinted in P.M. Mayor, *Economia 1964–66* (Aguilar, 1966); 3. 'Is the USSR superior to the West as a market for primary products?', *REStat*, 46, Aug. 1964; 4. 'The Yugoslav self-managed enterprise: a systemic approach', in *Plan and Market: Reform in Eastern Europe*, ed. M. Bernstein (Yale Univ. Press, 1973); transl. in *Ekonomska Misao*, 3, 1972; 5. 'The university department as a non-profit labor co-operative', in *Collective Choice in Education*, ed. M.J. Bowman (Martinus Nijhoff, 1981).

NEUMANN, John Von*

Dates and Birthplace 1903–57, Budapest, Austro-Hungary.

Posts Held Privatdozent, Univ. Berlin, 1926–9, Univ. Hamburg, 1929–30; Prof., Princeton Univ., 1931–3; Prof., Inst. Advanced Study, Princeton Univ., 1933–57.

Degrees PhD Univ. Budapest, 1926; Dip Zürich Technische Hochschule, 1926.

Offices and Honours Member, NAS; Enrico Fermi award, 1956.

Career Outstanding creative mathematician whose interests ranged from pure mathematics, to computing and mathematical physics. He also introduced innovations in mathematical economics, using game theory to model economic and social phenomena. His book on game theory (with Oskar Morgenstern) is one of the classics of twentieth-century social science. In 1973 he analysed the steady-state equilibrium properties of a uniformly-expanding closed economy under conditions of constant returns to scale in production and an unlimited supply of natural resources. This amazingly early article, which only became famous when it was translated in 1945, initiated an entire era in modern growth theory.

Publications *Books:* 1. *Theory of Games and Economic Behavior* (with O. Morgenstern), (1944, 1964); 2. *Collected Works* 6 vols, ed. A.H. Taub (1961–3).

Articles: 1. 'A model of general economic equilibrium', *REStud*, 13(1), 1945, repr. in *Readings in the Theory of Growth*, ed. F.H. Hahn (1971).

Secondary Literature O. Morgenstern, 'Von Neumann, John', *IESS*, vol. 16.

NEVIN, Edward T.

Born 1925, Pembroke Dock, Wales.
Current Post Prof. Econ., Univ. Coll., Swansea, Wales.

Recent Posts Sr res. officer, Econ. Res. Inst., Dublin, 1961–3; Prof. Econ., Univ. Coll. Wales, Aberystwyth, 1963–8.

Degrees BA, MA Univ. Wales, 1948, 1950; PhD Univ. Camb., 1952.

Offices Member, Council RES, 1970–3; Chairman, AUTE, 1972–4; Econ. adviser, Police Federation England and Wales, 1976–; Pres., Section F, BAAS, 1977.

Principal Contributions Analysis of origins and impact of British monetary policy; distribution and effects of UK National Debt; first application of input-output analysis to regional social accounting in UK.

Publications *Books:* 1. *The Problem of the National Debt* (Univ. Wales Pess, 1954); 2. *The Mechanics of Cheap Money* (Univ. Wales Press, 1955); 3. *Textbook of Economic Analysis* (Macmillan, 1958, 1981); 4. *Capital Funds in Underdeveloped Countries* (Macmillan, 1961; Spanish transl., 1963); 5. *The London Clearing Banks* (with E.W. Davis), (Elek Books, 1970). *Articles:* 1. 'The burden of the public debt: a survey', *Riv Intern*, 16(11), Nov. 1969; 2. 'Europe and the regions', *Three Banks Rev.*, June 1972; 3. 'How not to get a first', *EJ*, 82, June 1972; 4. 'The economics of devolution' (BAAS, 1978); 5. 'Regional policy', in *The Economics of the European Community*, ed. A.M. El-Agraa (1980).

NEWCOMB, Simon*

Dates and Birthplace 1835–1909, Nova Scotia, Canada.

Posts Held Prof. Maths, US Navy, 1861–97; Prof. Maths Astronomy, Johns Hopkins Univ., 1884–93.

Degrees BS Univ. Harvard, 1858.

Offices Member, NAS, 1869.

Career Scientist and astronomer, and America's first mathematical economist. He was an opponent of labour unions, attacked inconvertible paper money and generally adhered to an orthodox political economy. However, his *Principles* . . . contains a number of original mathematical contributions.

Publications *Books:* 1. *A Critical Examination of our Financial Policy* *during the Southern Rebellion* (1865); 2. *ABC of Finance* (1878); 3. *Plain Man's Talk on the Labor Question* (1886); 4. *Principles of Political Economy* (1886).

Secondary Literature A.W. Coates, 'Newcomb, Simon', *IESS*, vol. 11.

NEWHOUSE, Joseph P.

Born 1942, Waterloo, Iowa, USA.

Current Post Sr Economist, Rand Corp., USA.

Recent Posts Economist, Rand Corp., 1968–72.

Degrees BA, PhD Harvard Univ., 1963, 1969.

Offices AEA; RES; Em. Soc; Ed., *JHE*; Inst. Medicine, NAS, 1977.

Principal Contributions Designed and directed a major social experiment in health financing policy in US, 1971–81. The project enrolled nearly 8000 individuals in six geographic areas and randomised them to insurance plans that varied their price of medical services. This project greatly improved knowledge of demand for medical care services and health care financing, as well as the technology of social experimentation.

Publications *Books:* 1. *An Economic Analysis of Public Library Services* (with A.D. Alexander), (D.C. Heath & Co., 1972); 2. *The Economics of Medical Care: A Policy Perspective* (Addison-Wesley, 1978). *Articles:* 1. 'Toward a theory of non-profit institutions: an economic model of a hospital', *AER*, 60(1), March 1970, repr. in *Heatlh Economics*, eds M. Cooper and A. Culyer (Penguin Books, 1973); 2. 'The economics of group practice', *JHR*, 8(1), Winter 1973; 3. 'Deductibles and demand: a theory of the consumer facing a variable price schedule under certainty' (with E.B. Keeler, and C.E. Phelps), *Em*, 45(3), April 1977; 4. 'On having your cake and eating it too: econometric problems in estimating the demand for health services' (with C.E. Phelps and M.S. Marquis), *J Em*, 13(3), Aug. 1980; 5. 'The demand for medical care services: a retrospect and prospect', in *The Pro-*

ceedings of the World Congress on Health Economics (N–H, 1981).

NEWMAN, Peter Kenneth

Born 1928, London, England.
Current Post Prof., 1966–, Chairman, 1973–, Dept. Polit. Econ., Johns Hopkins Univ., USA.
Recent Posts Prof. Econ., Univ. Michigan, 1961–; Econ. adviser, Eastern African Common Services Organisation, UN Technical Assistance Admin., 1963–4; Vis. prof. Johns Hopkins Univ., 1964–5; Sr assoc., Robert R. Nathan Assoc., 1965–6.
Degrees BSc (Econ.), MSc (Econ.), DSc (Econ.) Univ. London, 1949, 1951, 1962.
Offices AEA; RES; Em Soc.
Principal Contributions Mathematical formulations of price theory; economics of malaria eradication; the socio-economic problems of ethnically-divided societies.
Publications *Books:* 1. *Cost in Alternative Locations: The Clothing Industry* (with D.C. Hague), (CUP, 1952); 2. *British Guiana: Problems of Cohesion in an Immigrant Society* (OUP, 1964); 3. *The Theory of Exchange* (Prentice-Hall, 1965); 4. *Malaria Eradication and Population Growth, with Special Reference to Ceylon and British Guiana* (Univ. Michigan, 1965); 5. *Readings in Mathematical Economics*, 2 vols., ed. (Johns Hopkins Univ. Press, 1968).
Articles: 1. 'The erosion of Marshall's theory of value', *QJE*, 74, Nov. 1960; 2. 'Approaches to stability analysis', *Ec*, N.S. 28, Feb. 1961; 3. 'Production of commodities by means of commodities', *Schweizerische Zeitschrift Volkswirtschaft Statistik*, 98, March 1962, Dec. 1962; 4. 'Some properties of concave functions', *JET*, 1(3), Oct. 1969; 5. 'Malaria and mortality', *JASA*, 72, 1977.

NEWMARCH, William*

Dates and Birthplace 1820–82, Thirsk, England.
Posts Held Employee, later dir., insurance and banking houses.

Offices Pres., RSS, 1869–71.
Career Statistician and economist, and leading critic of Peel's Bank Act, 1844. His continuation of Tooke's *History of Prices* to cover the period 1847–56 was designed to refute the theories of the currency school which lay behind Peel's Act. He denied that an increase in the volume of money in circulation had the effects that were alleged.
Publications *Books:* 1. *The new Supplies of Gold* (1853); 2. *On the Loans Raised by Mr Pitt During the First French war* (1855); 3. *History of Prices*, vols 5 and 6 (1857).
Secondary Literature L.M. Fraser, 'Newmarch, William', *ESS*, vol. 11.

NICHOLSON, Joseph Shield*

Dates and Birthplace 1850–1927, Wrawby, Lincs., England.
Posts Held Prof. Polit. Econ., Univ. Edinburgh, 1880–1925.
Degrees MA Univ. London; Sc.D Univ. Camb.
Offices Fellow, BA.
Career His published work was largely directed at students, while his articles, collected in volumes such as *War Finance*, at the general public. His economics was inspired by Adam Smith and by moral and philosophical considerations. His later works make use of statistical and historical data and are mainly concerned with contemporary issues.
Publications *Books:* 1. *Money and Monetary Problems* (1888); 2. *Principles of Political Economy*, 3 vols (1893–1901); 3. *Strikes and Social Problems* (1896); 4. *History of the English Corn Laws* (1904); 5. *War Finance* (1918); 6. *Inflation* (1919); 7. *The Revival of Marxism* (1920).
Secondary Literature W.R. Scott, 'Obituary: Joseph Shield Nicholson', *EJ*, 37, Sept. 1927.

NISKANEN, William Arthur

Born 1933, Bend, Oregon, USA.
Current Post Member, US President's Council Econ. Advisers, Washington, D.C.

Recent Posts Dir. Special Stud., US Office Secretary of Defense, 1962–4; Dir. Econ., Inst. Defense Analyses, 1964–70; Ass. Dir., US Office Management and Budget, 1970–2; Prof., Grad. School Public Pol., Univ. Cal., Berkeley, 1972–5; Dir. Econ., Ford Motor Co., 1975–80; Prof. Grad. School Management, UCLA, 1980–1.

Degrees BA Harvard Coll., 1954; MA, PhD Univ. Chicago, 1955, 1962.

Offices Founder, Nat. Tax Limitation Comm., 1976; Member, Census Advisory Comm., AEA, 1977–81.

Principal Contributions The economics of bureaucracy. Early contributions to demand for alcoholic beverages, defence analysis, and government management; recent contributions to structure of local government, economics of car industry, and selected topics in public choice.

Publications *Books:* 1. *Bureaucracy and Representative Government* (Aldine-Atherton, 1971); 2. *Structural Reform of the Federal Budget Process* (Amer. Enterprise Inst., 1973).

Articles: 1. 'The defense resource allocation process', *Defense Management*, 1966; 2. 'The peculiar economics of bureaucracy', *AER/S*, 58, May 1968; 3. 'Bureaucrats and politicians', *J Law Econ*, 18(3), Dec. 1975; 4. 'The prospect for liberal democracy', *Fiscal Responsibility in Constitutional Democracy* (1978); 5. 'Economic and fiscal effects on the popular vote for the President', *Public Policy and Public Choice*, 1979.

NORDHAUS, William D.

Born 1941, Albuquerque, New Mexico, USA.

Current Post John Musser Prof. Econ., Yale Univ., 1979–.

Recent Posts Ass. prof. Econ., 1967–70, Assoc. prof. Econ., 1970–3, Prof. Econ., 1973–, Yale Univ.; Member, US President's Council Econ. Advisers, 1977–9.

Degrees Certificat, Inst. d'Etudes Politiques, Paris, 1962; BA Yale Univ., 1963; PhD (Econ.) MIT, 1967.

Offices Assoc. ed., *AER, J Conflict Resolution, Energy Econ.*

Principal Contributions Major research has been in economic growth and natural resources, including studies of the long-run efficient allocation of resources (especially energy), as well as the question of the extent to which resources constrain economic growth. Also research in wage and price behaviour, stressing the behavioural aspects of corporate pricing.

Publications *Books:* 1. *Invention, Growth and Welfare: A Theoretical Treatment of Technological Change* (MIT Press, 1969); 2. *Industrial Pricing in the United Kingdom* (with W. Godley and K. Coutts), (CUP, 1978); 3. *International Studies in the Demand for Energy*, ed. (with others), (N-H, 1978); 4. *The Efficient Use of Energy Resources* (Yale Univ. Press, 1979).

Articles: 1. 'Some sceptical thoughts on the theory of induced innovations', *QJE*, 87(2), May 1973; 2. 'World dynamics: measurement without data', *EJ*, 83, Dec. 1973; 3. 'Resources as a constraint on growth', *AER*, 64(2), May 1974; 4. 'The political business cycle', *REStud*, 42(2), April 1975; 5. 'Thinking about carbon dioxide: theoretical and empirical aspects of optimal control strategies' (US Dept of Energy, 1980).

NORMAN, George Warde*

Dates and Birthplace 1793–1882, Bromley, England.

Posts Held Member of family timber firm, 1810–30; Dir., Bank of England, 1821–72; Dir., Sun Insurance Office, 1830–64.

Offices Gave evidence before numerous official commissions; Founder member, Polit. Econ. Club, 1821.

Career His *Remarks . . .*, which produced criticism from Torrens and Overstone, developed his theory of cycles, which came close to being a purely monetary one, but he did admit other causal factors. He gave extensive evidence to the committee inquiring into the working of the Bank Charter Act; his *Letter to Sir C. Wood . . .* also deals with this.

Publications *Books:* 1. *Remarks upon some Prevalent Errors with Respect to Currency and Banking* (1833); 2. *Letter to Sir C. Wood, Bart* on *Money and the Means of Economising the Use of it* (1841); 3. *An Examination of some Prevailing Opinions as to the Pressure of Taxation* (1849); 4. *Remarks on the Incidence of Import Duties* (1860); 5. *Papers on Various Subjects* (1869).

NORTH, Douglass C.

Born 1920, Cambridge, Mass., USA.

Current Post Prof. Econ., Univ. Washington, USA.

Recent Posts Grad. Teaching Fellow, Univ. Cal., 1946–9; Prof. Econ., 1950–61, Dir., Inst. Econ. Res., 1961–6, Chairman, Dept Econ., 1967–79, Univ. Washington; Peterkin Prof. Polit. Econ., Rice Univ., 1979; Pitt Prof., Univ. Camb., 1981–2.

Degrees BA, PhD Univ. Cal., Berkeley, 1942, 1952.

Offices Co-ed., *JEH*, 1960–6; Member, Board Dirs, NBER, 1967; Member, Board Trustees, Econ. Inst., 1968, 1971, 1978; Pres., EHA, 1972–3; Vis. assoc. Dir., Centre de Recherche Historique, Ecole Pratique des Haute Etudes, Paris, 1973; Pres., WEA, 1975–6.

Principal Contributions Development of a model of the growth of the American economy from 1790–1860; usefulness of applying simple neo-classical theory to problems in American economic history; and development of a general model of institutional change and applying it to economic history of the Western world. Empirical contributions have been development of the balance of payments from 1790–1860; development of export/import price indices of the US from 1790–1860; and development of an index of the productivity of ocean shipping from 1600–1914.

Publications *Books:* 1. *The Economic Growth of the United States 1790 to 1860* (Prentice-Hall, 1961); 2. *Growth and Welfare in the American Past: A New Economic History* (Prentice-Hall, 1966); 3. *Institutional Change and American Economic Growth* (with L.E. Davis), (CUP, 1971); 4. *The Rise of the Western World: A New Economic History* (with R.P. Thomas), (CUP, 1973, Dutch, Italian, Japanese, Spanish and French transls., 1975–80); 5. *Structure and Change in Economic History* (Norton, 1981).

Articles: 1. 'Economic history', *IESS*, vol 4, 1968; 2. 'Sources of productivity change in ocean shipping 1600–1850', *JPE*, 76, Oct. 1968; 3. 'An economic theory of the growth of the western world' (with R.P. Thomas), *EHR*, 23(1), April 1970; 4. 'The first economic revolution' (with R.P. Thomas), *EHR*, 30(2), May 1977; 5. 'Structure and performance: the task of economic history', *JEL*, 16(3), Sept. 1978.

NOVE, Alexander

Born 1915, St Petersburg, Russia.

Current Post Bonar Prof. Econ., Univ. Glasgow, 1963–.

Recent Posts Reader, Russian social econ. stud., Univ. London, 1958–63; Dir., Inst. Soviet East European Stud., Univ. Glasgow 1963–79.

Degrees BSc Econ. Univ. London, 1936; DAg (*Hon causa*) Giessen, Germany, 1977.

Offices Fellow, BA, 1978.

Principal Contributions The evolution of the USSR and of Soviet-type economies; economics of socialism; efficiency criteria of nationalised industries in East and West; the USSR as a model of development; planning methods in USSR and in developing countries; socialist agriculture; Russian and Soviet economic thought; comparative systems; the interaction of political, economic and historical factors in Soviet history.

Publications *Books:* 1. *The Soviet Economy* (A & U, 1961, many transls.); 2. *Was Stalin Really Necessary?* (A & U, 1963); 3. *Economic History of the USSR* (Allen Lane, Penguin Press, 1969); 4. *Efficiency Criteria for Nationalized Industries* (A & U, 1973); 5. *The Soviet Economic System* (A & U, 1977, 1981).

NOVOZHILOV, Viktor Valentinovich*

Dates and Birthplace 1892–1970, Kharkov, Russia.

Degree Grad. Univ. Kiev, 1915.

Honours Honoured scientist of the USSR, 1957; Lenin prize, 1965.

Career His work was mainly concerned with the balance between expenditure and performance in the Soviet economy. In this he used mathematical methods and was largely responsible for making mathematical economics quasi-respectable in the USSR after World War II. His later work included a model for the optimisation of resources of production.

Publications *Books:* 1. *Problemy Izmerenii Zatrat i Rezul'tatov Pri Optimal'nom Planirovanii* (1967).

NUTI, Domenico Mario

Born 1937, Arezzo, Italy.

Current Post Prof. Polit. Econ., Dir., Centre Russian East European Stud., 1980–, Univ. Birmingham, England.

Recent Posts Fellow, King's Coll., Univ. Camb., 1966–79, Res. fellow, 1966–1969, Tutor, 1969–73, Dir. Stud. Econ., 1973–6; Lecturer, 1976–9; Ass. lecturer, 1971–3, Lecturer Econ., 1973–9, Faculty Econ. Polit., Univ. Camb.

Degrees Dottore Giurisprudenza Univ. Rome, 1962; MA, PhD Univ. Camb., 1966, 1970.

Offices and Honours Stevenson prize, Univ. Camb., 1965; Exec., British Nat. Assoc. Soviet East Europe. Stud., 1980–.

Principal Contributions An exploration and development of the Austrian theory of capital and time (steady-state relationships between wage, interest, consumption and growth; valuation of capital and income per man) leading to criticism of aggregate production functions. A detailed investigation of official instructions for the selection of investment projects in the Soviet Union and East-European countries. An analysis of recent reforms of industrial organisation in Eastern Europe, their connection with macro-economic policies and in particular the over-accumulation bias of socialist economies, with special reference to Poland.

Publications *Books:* 1. *Socialist Economics*, ed. (with A. Nove), (Pen-

guin Books, 1972, 1976); 2. Edition of V.K. Dmitriev, *Economic Essays on Value Competition and Utility* (CUP, 1974).

Articles: 1. 'Capitalism, socialism and steady growth', *EJ*, 80, March 1970; 2. 'On the truncation of production flows', *Kyklos*, 26(3), 1973; 3. 'The evolution of Polish investment planning', *Jahrbuch Wirtschaft Osteuropas*, 3, 1973; 4. 'The transformation of labour values into production prices and the Marxian theory of exploitation', in *The Subtle Anatomy of Capitalism*, ed. J. Schwartz (Goodyear, 1977); 5. 'The contradictions of socialist economies – a Marxian interpretation', in *The Socialist register*, eds R. Miliband and J. Saville (Merlin Press, 1979).

O

OATES, Wallace Eugene

Born 1937.

Current Post Prof. Econ., Univ. Maryland, College Park, USA, 1979–.

Recent Posts Prof. Econ., Princeton Univ., 1965–79.

Degrees MA (Econ.), PhD (Econ.) Stanford Univ., 1959, 1965.

Offices and Honours AEA; RES; NTA; Guggenheim Memorial Foundation Fellow, 1974–5; Senior Fulbright-Hays Res. Scholar, 1974–5.

Principal Contributions In public finance, major contribution to the development of fiscal federalism; in environmental economics, has written and worked with public agencies on the design and implementation of pricing incentives for protection of the environment.

Publications *Books:* 1. *Fiscal Federalism* (Harcourt, Brace Jovanovich, 1972); 2. *Introduction to Econometrics* (with H. Kelejian), (Harper & Row, 1974, 1981); 3. *The Theory of Environmental Policy* (with W. Baumol), (Prentice-Hall, 1975); 4. *The Political Economy of Fiscal Federalism* (Heath-Lexington, 1977); 5. *Economics, Environmental Policy, and the Quality of Life* (with W. Baumol), (Prentice-Hall, 1979).

Articles: 1. 'The theory of public finance in a federal system', *CJE*, 1, Feb. 1968; 2. 'The effects of property taxes and local public spending on property values: an empirical study of tax capitalization and the Tiebout hypothesis', *JPE*, 77(6), Nov./Dec. 1969; 3. 'The analysis of revenue sharing in a new approach to collective fiscal decisions' (with D. Bradford), *QJE*, 85(3), Aug. 1971; 4. 'The use of standards and prices for protection of the environment' (with W. Baumol), *Swed JE*, 73(1), March 1971.

O'BRIEN, Denis

Born 1939, Knebworth, Herts., England.

Current Post Prof. Econ., Durham Univ., England.

Recent Posts Lecturer, Sr lecturer, 1963–70, Reader, 1970–2, Queen's Univ., Belfast.

Degrees BSc (Econ.) Univ. London, 1960; PhD Queen's Univ., Belfast, 1969.

Offices Council member, RES, 1978–83.

Principal Contributions Re-evaluation of the economic thought of the nineteenth-century economist J.R. McCulloch. Discovery and editing of the papers of the influential nineteenth-century monetary economist S.J. Loyd, Lord Overstone. The pursuit of empirical studies of competition policy (including the large-scale use of nonparametric statistical methods) in an attempt to resolve the inconclusive nature of *a priori* argument in this area. The combination of (non-parametric) statistical techniques with literary and historical detection to solve authorship puzzles.

Publications *Books:* 1. *Information Agreements, Competition and Efficiency* (with D. Swann), (Macmillan, 1969); 2. *J.R. McCulloch: A Study in Classical Economics* (A & U, 1970); 3. *The Correspondence of Lord Overstone*, 3 vols (CUP, RES, 1971); 4. *The Classical Economists* (OUP, 1975); 5. *Competition Policy, Profitability and Growth* (with others), (Macmillan, 1979).

Articles: 1. 'Patent protection and competition in polyamide and polyester fibre manufacture', *J Ind E*, 12, July 1964; 2. 'The transition in Torrens' monetary thought', *Ec*, N.S. 32, Aug. 1965; 3. 'Customs unions: trade creation and trade diversion in historical perspective', *HOPE*, 8(4), Winter 1976; 4. 'The longevity of Adam Smith's vision: paradigms research programmes and falsifiability in the history of economic thought', *SJPE*, 23(2), June 1976; 5. 'Torrens, McCulloch and the "Digression on Sismondi": whose digression?' (with A. Darnell), *HOPE*, 12(3), Fall 1980.

O'BRIEN, George Augustine Thomas*

Dates and Birthplace 1892–1973, Dublin, Ireland.

Posts Held Barrister, 1913–16; Journalist, 1916–26; Prof., Univ. Coll., Dublin, 1926–61.

Degrees BA, DLitt. Univ. Coll., Dublin, 1912, 1919.

Offices Member of Seanad of Ireland, 1948–65; Pres., Stat. Soc. Ireland, 1942.

Career Perhaps best known outside Ireland for his discovery of Ricardo's letters to James Mill, he was Ireland's major economic historian and most influential teacher of economics during his long tenure of the University College Chair. He also sat on numerous commissions of inquiry, and wrote at length on current economic matters in the British and Irish periodical press. His economics, though avowedly taking the conventional deductive, non-mathematical form he learnt in his youth, was non-doctrinaire and responsive to trends. He held a place of unique respect and influence in Irish economics.

Publications *Books:* 1. *The Economic History of Ireland in the Eighteenth Century* (1918); 2. *The Economic History of Ireland in the Seventeenth Century* (1919); 3. *The Economic History of Ireland from the Union to the Famine* (1921); 4. *Agricultural Economics* (1929); 5. *Notes on the Theory of Profit* (1929); 6. *The Four Green Fields* (1936); 7. *The Phantom of Plenty* (1948).

Secondary Literature J. Meenan, *George O'Brien: A Biographical Memoir* (1980).

OFFICER, Lawrence H.

Born 1940, Montreal, Canada.
Current Post Prof. Econ., Michigan State Univ., USA, 1970–.
Recent Posts Instructor Econ., 1964–5, Ass. prof. Econ., 1965–70, Harvard Univ.; Vis. prof. Econ., Grad. School Bus. Univ. Chicago, 1980–1.
Degrees BA (Econ. and Polit. Science), (First class hons.) McGill Univ., 1960; MA, PhD Harvard Univ., 1962, 1965.
Offices and Honours Honourable mention 18th annual awards program for the teaching of Econ., Joint Council Econ. Education; Assoc. ed., *QJE*, 1966–71, *REStat*, 1968–; Member, Board Eds., *CJE*, 1971–4.
Principal Contributions Analysis of the market structure of the international shipping industry. Development of an econometric model of the Canadian economy under floating exchange rates. Surveys of purchasing-power-parity theory and of monetary approach to the balance of payments. Various empirical investigations of the purchasing-power-parity theory. Empirical studies of the demand for international reserves.
Publications *Books*: 1. *An Econometric Model of Canada under the Fluctuating Exchange Rate* (Harvard Univ. Press, 1968); 2. *The International Monetary System: Problems and Proposals* (with T.D. Willett), (Prentice-Hall, 1969); 3. *Issues in Canadian Economics* (with L.B. Smith), (McGraw-Hill, 1974); 4. *The Monetary Approach to the Balance of Payments: A Survey* (with M.E. Kreinin), (Internat. Fin. Section, Princeton Univ., 1978); 5. *So You Have to Write an Economics Term Paper* ... (with D.H. and J.A. Saks), (Michigan State Univ., 1980).
Articles: 1. 'The purchasing-power-parity theory of exchange rates: a review article', *IMF Staff Papers*, 23(1), March 1976; 2. 'The demand for international liquidity: a test of the square-root law', *JMCB*, 8(3), Aug. 1976; 3. 'The productivity bias in purchasing power parity: an econometric investigation', *IMF Staff Papers*, 23(3), Nov. 1976; 4. 'The relationship between absolute and relative purchasing power parity', *REStat*, 60(4), Nov. 1978: 5. 'Effective exchange rates and price ratios over the long run: a test of the purchasing-power-parity theory', *CJE*, 13(2), May 1980.

OHLIN, Bertil Gotthard*

Dates and Birthplace 1899–1979, Klippan, Sweden.
Posts Held Prof. Econ., Univ. Copenhagen, 1925–30; Prof., Stockholm School Econ. Bus., 1930–65.
Degrees BA, Dr., Univ. Stockholm, 1919, 1924.
Offices and Honours Member, Swedish parliament, 1938–70; Leader, Folkpartiet, 1944–67; Swedish Minister Trade, 1944–5; Nobel Prize for Econ., 1977.
Career A successful political career as leader of Sweden's main opposition party probably limited the quantity of his output. International trade was his main subject from his published dissertation of 1924 onwards, and *Interregional and International Trade* was his masterpiece. In this he developed Cassel's simplified Walrasian equilibrium model in a manner similar to Heckscher's 1919 article and produced what is nowadays known as the 'Heckscher-Ohlin theorem', which accounts for the commodity composition of international trade entirely by the relative factor endowments of countries. He also made major contributions to theory of money, employment and economic fluctuations, though much of this work has not appeared in English. In his application of the concept of aggregate demand, and his distinction between expected and realised saving and investment, Ohlin anticipated some aspects of Keynes' *General Theory*.
Publications *Books:* 1. *Handelns Teori* (the Theory of Trade) (1924); 2. *The Course and Phases of the World Economic Depression* (1931, 1972); 3. *Interregional and International Trade* (1933, 1967); 4. *The Problem of*

Employment Stabilisation (1949, 1977).

Secondary Literature H. Dickson, 'Ohlin, Bertil', *IESS*, vol. 18; R.E. Caves, 'Bertil Ohlin's contribution to economics', *Scand JE*, 80(1), 1978; O. Steiger, 'Bertil Ohlin, 1899–1979', *HOPE*, 13(2), Summer 1981.

OI, Walter Y.

Born 1929, Los Angeles, Cal., USA.
Current Post Elmer B. Milliman Prof. Econ., Chairman Dept. Econ., Univ. Rochester, NY, USA.
Recent Posts Assoc. prof. Econ., 1962–5, Prof. Econ., 1965–7, Univ. Washington; Prof., Grad. School Management, Univ. Rochester, 1967–75; Staff Economist, US President's Commission on an All-Volunteer Armed Force, Washington, DC, 1969–70; Emma and Carol Roush Disting. Vis. Scholar, Hoover Inst., Stanford Univ., 1970–1; Vis. sr res. economist, Industrial Relations Section, Princeton Univ., 1973–4.
Degrees BS, MA UCLA, 1952, 1954; PhD Univ. Chicago, 1961.
Offices Fellow, Em Soc.
Principal Contributions Application of economic theory to problems in labour economics and industrial organisation that have potential policy implications. The quasi-fixed factor paper extends the overhead cost analysis of J.M. Clark to explain the cyclic behaviour of labour markets, while basic economic principles are used to analyse the merits of conscription versus voluntarism in employing military personnel. The Disneyland and product safety papers represent applications of price theory. Use of the basic tools of neo-classical economics to analyse problems.
Publications *Books:* 1. *The Economic Value of the United States Merchant Marine* (with A.R. Ferguson et al.), (Transportation Center, 1961); 2. *Economics of Private Truck Transportation* (with A.P. Hurter), (William C. Brown Co., 1965); 3. *Demand Analysis for Air Travel by Supersonic Transport*, 2 vols (with N.S. Asher et al.), (Inst. Defense Analyses, 1966).
Articles: 1. 'Labor as a quasi-fixed factor', *JPE*, 70, Dec. 1962; 2. 'The costs and implications of an all-volunteer force', in *The Draft, A Handbook of Facts and Alternatives*, ed. S. Tax (Univ. Chicago Press, 1967); 3. 'On the relationship among different members of the k-class', *Int ER*, 10(1), Feb. 1969; 4. 'A Disneyland dilemma: two-part tariffs for a Mickey Mouse monopoly', *QJE*, 85, Feb. 1971; 5. 'The economics of product safety', *Bell JE*, 4, Spring 1973.

ONCKEN, August*

Dates and Birthplace 1844–1911, Heidelberg, Germany.
Posts Held Farmer, 1865–71; Lecturer, agric. coll., Vienna; Prof. Econ., Univ. Berne, 1910.
Degrees Studied at Heidelberg, Berlin and Munich.
Career Agricultural economist and historian of economic ideas who advocated the industrialisation of agriculture and turned to the study of the physiocrats because of their preoccupation with agriculture. He also defended Adam Smith against German economists of the Historical School and attempted to harmonise the ideas of Smith and Kant.
Publications *Books:* 1. *Adam Smith in der Kulturgeschichte* (1874); 2. *Adam Smith und Immanuel Kant* (1877); 3. *Der Ältere Mirabeau und die Ökonomische Gesellschaft in Bern* (1886); 4. *Die Maxime: Laissez-faire et Laissez-passer* (1886); 5. *Oeuvres économiques et philosophiques de François Quesnay* (1888); 6. *Was Sagt die Nationalökonomie als Wissenschaft über die Bedautung Löher und Niedriger Getreidepreise?* (1901); 7. *Die Geschichte der Nationalökonomie. Erster Teil: Die Zeit vor Adam Smith* (1902).
Secondary Literature S. Bauer, 'Oncken, August', *ESS*, vol. 11.

OPIE, Roger G.

Born 1927, Adelaide, Australia.
Current Post Fellow, lecturer Econ., New Coll., Univ. Oxford, 1961–.
Degrees MA Univ. Adelaide, 1950; MPhil, MA Univ. Oxford, 1954, 1961.

Offices Member, UK Monopolies and Mergers Commission, 1968–81; Member, UK Price Commission, 1977–80; CBE, 1976.

Principal Contributions Contributed intensively and extensively to the preparation and writing of the UK National Plan (1965) as Ass. Dir., UK Dept of Economic Affairs. Later professional work (1967–70) has been to advise the Chairman of the UK National Board for Prices and Incomes and to participate in numerous investigations carried out by the Monopolies and Mergers Commission and the Price Commission.

Publications *Articles:* Chapters in 1. *Banking in Western Europe*, ed. R. Sayers (OUP, 1961); 2. *Economic Growth in Britain*, ed. J.M. Henderson *et al.* (Weidenfeld & Nicolson, 1964); 3. *Unfashionable Economics*, ed. P. Streeten (Weidenfeld & Nicolson, 1969); *The Labour Government's Economic Record*, ed. W. Beckerman (Butterworth, 1971).

OPPENHEIMER, Franz*

Dates and Birthplace 1864–1943, Berlin, Germany.

Posts Held Lecturer, Univ. Berlin, 1909–19; Prof., Univ. Frankfurt, 1919–29.

Degrees MD Univ. Berlin, 1885; PhD Univ. Kiel, 1908

Career Sociologist who used theoretical models to explain social change. Gossen's marginal utility theory and von der Goltz's theorem – the volume of migration from rural areas is directly related to the proportion of agricultural land in large estates – were major influences on his thinking. His attack on monopoly control of land traced land monopoly through successive social and economic systems. His agrarian socialism led him to oppose dogmatic Marxism whilst accepting aspects of Marx's analysis.

Publications *Books:* 1. *Die Siedlungsgenossenschaft* (1896, 1922); 2. *Das Grundgesetz der Marxschen Gesellschaftslehre* (1903, 1926); 3. *The State: Its History and Development Viewed Sociologically* (1907, 1926); 4. *Die Soziale Frage und der Sozialismus* (1912, 1925); 5. *Kapitalismus- Kommunismus- wissenschaftlicher Sozialismus* (1919); 6. *System der Soziologie*, 4 vols (1922–35); 7. *Erlebtes, Erstrebtes, Erreichtes: Lebenserinnerungen* (1931, 1964).

Secondary Literature H.H. Gerth, 'Oppenheimer, Franz', *IESS*, Vol. 11.

ORCUTT, Guy Henderson

Born 1917, Wyandotte, Mich., USA.

Current Post Prof. Econ., A. Whitney Griswold Prof. Urban Stud., 1970–, Prof. Stats, 1980–, Yale Univ., USA.

Recent Posts Ass. prof., Assoc. prof. Econ., 1949–58, Vis. prof., 1965–6, Harvard Univ.; Brittingham Prof. Econ., Univ. Wisconsin, 1958–69; Sr adviser, World Bank, 1967–8; Dir. Poverty Inequality Project, Urban Inst., 1968–75; Irving Fisher Vis. prof., Yale Univ., 1969–70.

Degrees BS (Physics, Hons.), MA (Econ.), PhD (Econ.) Univ. Michigan, 1939, 1940, 1944.

Offices Fellow, Em Soc, 1956–; Fellow, 1959–, Vice-pres., 1959–61, ASA; Member, Exec. Comm., AEA, 1972–5; Board Dirs, 1975–8, Treasurer, 1976–8, US SSRC.

Principal Contributions Demonstration of importance of auto-correlation for econometric research and devising of methods to take account of autocorrelation in estimation and testing. Work on the measurement of price elasticities in international trade. Demonstrations of the importance of micro-entity time series data for effective testing of economic hypotheses. Conceptualisation and development of quantitative, micro-analytic, system modelling in economics. Work on the conceptualisation and implementation of research on measurement of air pollution.

Publications *Books:* 1. *Microanalysis of Socioeconomic Systems: A Simulation Study* (with M. Greenberger *et al.*), (Harper, 1961); 2. *Forecasting on a Scientific Basis* (with H. Wold *et al.*), (Inst. Gulbenkian de Ciencia, 1967); 3. *Policy Exploration Through Microanalytic Simulation* (with S. Caldwell *et al.*), (Urban Inst., 1976); 4. *Microsimulation-models, Methods and*

Applications, ed. (with B. Bergman and G. Eliasson), (Almqvist & Wiksell, 1980).

Articles: 1. 'A study of the autoregressive nature of the time series used for Tinbergen's model of the economic system of the United States, 1919–1932', *JRSS*, Series B, 10(1), 1948; 2. 'Measurement of price elasticities in international trade', *REStat*, 32, May 1950, reprinted in R.E. Caves and H.G. Johnson, eds, *Readings in International Economics* (Richard D. Irwin, 1968); 3. 'Actions, consequences, and casual relations', *REStat*, 34, Nov. 1952; 4. 'Incentive and disincentive experimentation for income maintenance policy purposes' (with A.G. Orcutt), *AER*, 58, Sept. 1968; 5. 'Data aggregation and information loss' (with H. Watts and J. Edwards), *AER*, 58, Sept. 1968.

OREZE, J.

N.e.

ORTES, Giammaria*

Dates and Birthplace 1713–90, Venice, Italy.

Posts Held Clergyman.

Career His idiosyncratic system has something in common with that of Steuart whom he may have read. His starting point was that consumption was the limiting factor on total output. He attacked the view that money and wealth were identical, arguing that money was merely a symbol of wealth, and expressly excluding it from his list of items that constitute wealth. He drew attention to the disparity between the potential growth of population and the increase of subsistence. He set an absolute limit to population of three billion, suggesting that when the limit was reached parents would eat their children.

Publications *Books:* 1. *Economia Nazionale* (1774); 2. *Reflections on Population* (1790).

Secondary Literature J.J. Spengler, 'Ortes, Giammaria', *ESS*, vol. 11.

OTT, Alfred E.

Born 1929, Kassel, Germany.

Current Post Ordentlicher Universitätsprof., Univ. Tübingen, Baden-Württemberg, W. Germany, 1963–.

Recent Posts Prof. Univ. Saarlandes, Saarbrücken, 1960–3.

Degrees Diplom-Volkswirt, Dr rer. pol., Univ. Heidelberg, 1952, 1954; Habilitation Univ. München, 1958.

Offices Dir., Inst. Angewandte Wirtschaftsforschung Tübingen; Mitglied, Theoretischen Ausschusses für Unternehmenstheorie und -politik des Vereins für Sozialpolitik; Stellvertretender Vorsitzender des Kuratoriums des Inst. Systemtechnik und Innovationsforschung Karlsruhe; Mitglied, Kuratoriums des Ifo-Instituts für Wirtschaftsforschung München, Kuratoriums des Bundes der Steuerzahler Landesverband Baden-Württemberg; Vorsitzender Pädagogischen Arbeitsstelle für Erwachsenenbildung Baden-Württemberg.

Principal Contributions Concerned with problems of price theory: market structures in static and dynamic contexts, oligopoly pricing, monopolistic competition, price differences; technical progress; cycles and growth: theory and evidence of growth cycles; determination of growth. Further concerned with dynamic growth theory, Marxian economics, selected problems of political economy (demand management, regional policy etc.).

Publications *Books:* 1. *Marktform und Verhaltensweise* (Gustav Fischer Verlag, 1959); 2. *Einführung in die Dynamische Wirtschaftstheorie* (Vandnehoeck & Ruprecht, 1963, 1970); 3. *Vertikale Preisbildung und Preisbindung* (Vandenhoeck & Ruprecht, 1966); 4. *Grundzige der Preistheorie* (Vandenhoeck & Ruprecht, 1968, 1976). 5. *Der EDV-Markt in der Bundesrepublik Deutschland* (with N. Kloten *et al.*), (J.C.B. Mohr, Paul Siebeck, 1976).

Articles: 1. 'Technischer Fortschritt', in *Handwörterbuch der Sozialwissenschaften*, vol. 10 (1959); 2. 'Produktionsfunktion, technischer Fortschritt und Wirtschaftswachstum', in *Einkom-*

mensverteilung und Technischer Fortschritt, ed. E. Schneider (Berlin, 1959; English transl., *Internat. Econ. Papers*, no. 11, Macmillan, 1962); 3. 'Preistheorie', *JSW*, 13, 1962; 4. 'Les systèmes de classification des marchés et l'ologopole', *Econ App*, 15, 1962; 5. 'Wachstumszyklen und technischer Fortschritt', in *Technischer Fortschritt – Ursache und Auswirkung Wirtschaftlichen Handelns* (Inst. für Wirtschaftsforschung, 1974).

OVERSTONE, Samuel Jones Loyd*

Dates and Birthplace 1796–1883, England.
Post Held Banker.
Degrees BA, MA Univ. Camb., 1818, 1822.
Offices and Honours MP for Hythe, 1819–26; Created Baron Overstone, 1860.
Career Influential authority on British banking and finance who favoured convertibility of banknotes. The view he expressed to parliamentary committees in 1833 and 1840 was subsequently embodied in the Bank Act, 1844. Further evidence to committees in 1848 and 1857 was published by him afterwards.
Publications *Books:* 1. *Tracts and other Publications on Metallic and Paper Currency* (1858).
Secondary Literature *The Correspondence of Lord Overstone*, ed. D.P. O'Brien, 3 vols (CUP, RES, 1971).

OWEN, Robert*

Dates and Birthplace 1771–1858, Newtown, Wales.
Post Held Cotton manufacturer.
Career Successful businessman and critic of industrialism who preached co-operative organisation. His New Lanark Mills in Scotland were organised as a model factory community. He developed this idea further to advocate villages in which collective working would be the basis for social regeneration. In 1824 he set up New Harmony, Indiana as a model community. On his return to Britain in 1829, he was drawn into workers' politics and promoted the

Grand National Consolidated Trades Union in 1833 and 1834. This, like his other experiments, failed, but he soon came to be regarded as the father of the co-operative movement.
Publications *Books:* 1. *Observations on the Effect of the Manufacturing System* (1815); 2. *A New View of Society* (1816, 1956); 3. *Two Memorials on Behalf of the Working Classes* (1818); 4. *Report to the County of Lanark* (1821); 5. *Lectures on an Entire New State of Society* (1830).
Secondary Literature G.D.H. Cole, *The Life of Robert Owen* (Macmillan, 1925); A. Briggs, 'Owen, Robert', *IESS*, vol. 11.

OZAWA, Terutomo

Born 1935, Yokohama, Japan.
Current Post Prof. Econ., Colorado State Univ., Fort Collins, USA.
Recent Posts Vis. res. assoc., Center Pol. Alternatives, MIT, 1975–6; Consultant, UNITAR, 1970–1, World Bank, 1971–2, UN-ESCAP, 1979–80; OECD, 1981–2.
Degrees BA Tokyo Univ. Foreign Stud., 1958; MBA, PhD Columbia Univ, 1962, 1966.
Offices AEA.
Principal Contributions Exploration of the two major post-war phenomena of the Japanese economy: technology absorption and R & D; and overseas investment activities of Japanese corporations.
Publications *Books:* 1. *Japan's Technological Challenge to the West, 1950–74: Motivation and Accomplishment* (MIT Press, 1974); 2. *Multinationalism, Japanese Style: The Political Economy of Outward Dependency* (Princeton Univ. Press, 1979).
Articles: 1. 'Japan's resource dependency and overseas investment', *J World Trade Law*, 11, Jan./Feb. 1977; 2. 'Japan's multinational enterprise: the political economy of outward dependency', *World Politics*, 30, July 1978; 3. 'International investment and industrial structure: new theoretical implications from the Japanese experience', *OEP*, 31(1), March 1979; 4. 'Japan's new resource diplomacy: government-

backed group investment', *J World Trade Law*, 14, Jan/Feb. 1980; 5. 'Government control over technology acquisition and firms' entry into new sectors: the experience of Japan's synthetic-fibre industry', *Camb JE*, 4, June 1980.

P

PALGRAVE, Robert Harry Inglis*

Dates and Birthplace 1827–1919, Westminster, England.
Post Held Banker.
Offices and Honours Ed., *The Economist*, 1877–83; Fellow, Royal Soc., 1882; Pres., Section F, BAAS, 1883; Knighted, 1909.
Career Writer on banking from the point of view of a practitioner rather than a theoretician. His interest in the discipline of economics proper is represented by the substantial *Dictionary of Political Economy,* a basic reference work until recent times.
Publications *Books:* 1. *Notes on Banking in Great Britain, Ireland, Sweden, Denmark and Hamburg* (1872); 2. *Analysis of the Transactions of the Bank of England 1844–72* (1873); 3. *Bank Rate and the Money Market* (1903); 4. *Dictionary of Political Economy,* 3 vols (1894–1908).
Secondary Literature A.W. Kiddy, 'Obituary: Sir Inglis Palgrave', *EJ*, 29, 1919.

PANTALEONI, Maffeo*

Dates and Birthplace 1857–1924, Frascati, Italy.
Posts Held Prof. at various Italian univs; Prof., Univ. Rome, 1901–.
Degree Dr Law Univ. Rome, 1881.
Offices Member, Chamber of Deputies, 1901; Senator, 1923.
Career Italian economist who attempted to avoid being identified with any of the contemporary schools. He wrote studies of price fluctuations, discriminatory pricing, industrial cartels and banking, and sought to develop a dynamic theory of economics. In the latter he attempted a synthesis of mar-

ginal utility theory with Ricardian value theory. His considerable involvement in quantitative work led him eventually to doubt the usefulness of utility theory in macro-economic questions; he also rejected the work of the marginalists in public finance.
Publications *Books:* 1. *Teoria Della Traslazione Dei Tributi* (1882, 1958); 2. *Dall'ammontare probabile Della Ricchezza Privata in Italia* (1884); 3. *Pure Economics* (1889, 1957); 4. *Note in Margine Della Guerra* (1917); 5. *Tra le Incognite* (1917); 6. *Politica* (1918); 7. *Erotemi di Economia*, 2 vols (1925).
Articles: 1. 'Contribution to the theory of the distribution of public expenditure' (1883, 1904), repr. in *Classics in the Theory of Public Finance*, eds R.A. Musgrave and A.T. Peacock (Macmillan, 1958).
Secondary Literature P. Sraffa and A. Loria, 'Maffeo Pantaleoni', *EJ*, 34, Dec. 1924; L. Frey, 'Pantaleoni, Maffeo', *IESS*, vol. 11.

PAPANEK, Gustav

Born 1926, Vienna, Austria.
Current Post Prof., Chair, Dept. Econ., Boston Univ., USA.
Recent Posts Dir., Development Advisory Service, Harvard Univ., 1965–70; Dir. Harvard Advisory Group Planning Commission and Ministry Fin., Govt Indonesia, 1971–3; Interim Dir. Center Asian Development Stud., Boston Univ., 1977–80.
Degrees BA (Agric. Econ.) Cornell Univ., 1947; MA (Econ.), PhD (Econ.) Harvard Univ., 1949, 1951.
Offices Council, Soc. Internat. Development, 1970–3; Member Exec. Comm., 1971–3, Vice-pres., Pres.-elect, 1980–2, Assoc. Comparative Econ. Stud.; Vice-pres., 1975–6, Pres., 1976–7, Assoc. Asian Stud., New England Conference.
Principal Contributions Work has centred on the use of the market mechanism as a tool to achieve the planned goals of a society, particularly in less developed countries. Specifically, analysis of the possibility of achieving both high rates of growth and greater equality; and the contribution of foreign aid

to growth. In teaching: the use of the case method to encourage the application of theory and methodology to the solution of actual problems.

Publications *Books:* 1. *Pakistan's Development: Social Goals and Private Incentives* (Harvard Univ. Press, 1967, OUP Karachi, 1968, 1971); 2. *Development Policy – Theory and Practice*, ed. (Harvard Univ. Press, 1968); 3. *Decision Making for Economic Development*, co-author (Houghton-Mifflin, 1971); 4. *Development Policy – the Pakistan Experience*, co-ed. (Harvard Univ. Press, 1971); 5. *The Indonesian Economy*, ed. and contributor (Praeger, 1980).

Articles: 1. 'The effect of aid and other resource transfers on savings and growth in less developed countries', *EJ*, 82, Sept. 1972; 2. 'Aid, foreign private investment, savings and growth in less developed countries', *JPE*, 81(1), Jan./Feb. 1973; 3. 'Development theory – the earnest search for a mirage', *EDCC*, 25, Suppl., 1977, repr. in *Essays in Economic Development and Cultural Change*, ed. M. Nash (Univ. Chicago Press, 1977); 4. 'Economic growth, income distribution and the political process in less developed countries', in *Income Distribution and Economic Inequality*, eds Z. Griliches *et al.* (Campus Verlag, 1978); 5. '*Laissez-faire*, growth and equity: Hong Kong', *EJ*, 91, June 1981.

PAPI, Giuseppe Ugo

Born 1906, Capua, Italy.
Current Post Prof. Emeritus Econ., Univ. Rome.
Recent Posts Gen. sec. Internat. Inst. Agric., 1939–48; 'Socio Nazionale' Accademia dei Lincei, Rome, 1945–; Rector, Univ. Rome, 1953–66; Pres., Food Agriculture Comm., OEEC, 1959.
Degrees Dr (*hon. causa*), Law Faculties, Univs. Grenoble (1955), Salonica (1957), Bordeaux (1957), Frankfurt (1958), Paris (1958), Marseilles (1960), Glasgow (1961), Lille (1965).
Offices and Honours Assoc. member Inst. de France, Académie des Sciences Morales et Politiques; Légion d'Honneur: Great Cross Merito Republica Italiana; Cavaliere ordinecivile, Savoie.

Principal Contributions Argued that rational production-competition as far as possible in international markets represents an inflexible condition for the solution of social and political problems, in every country; a reversal of such a logical sequence implies, in each country, inflation, unemployment and stagnation.

Publications *Books:* 1. *Escape from Stagnation* (King & Son, 1933); 2. *Theory of Economic Behaviour of the Government* (Giuffre, 1956); 3. *Principles of Economics*, 3 vols (Cedam, 1956–66); 4. *International Economics* (UTET, 1960); 5. *Inflation* (Buffetti, 1974).

Articles: 1. 'The importance of the method in Pantaleoni's work', *Rivista Polit. Econ.*, 1976; 2. 'Vie verso il communismo', *Rivista Italiana di Demografiae Statistica*, 31, 1977; 3. 'Rational production, first condition of a social order', *Giornale degli Economisti*, Oct. 1980.

PARETO, Vilfredo*

Dates and Birthplace 1848–1923, Paris, France.
Posts Held Engineer, 1870–92; Prof., Univ. Lausanne, 1893–1900.
Degree Engineering, Polytechnic Inst., Turin, 1869.
Offices Senator.
Career Italian engineer economist, whose mathematical ability led to his appointment as Walras' successor at Lausanne. In the *Manual* . . . he worked out an improved version of general equilibrium theory and demonstrated the restricted sense in which perfect competition achieved an optimal solution. He made important contributions to the discussion of the methodology of economics and the place of the discipline in the social sciences as a whole. His distinction between cardinal and ordinal utility and between an individual and a collective optimum were major theoretical contributions.
Publications *Books:* 1. *Cours d'économie politique* (1896–7, 1964); 2. *Systèmes socialistes* (1902–3, 1965); 3.

Manual of political economy, (1906, 1909, 1971); 4. *The Mind and Society: a Treatise on General Sociology*, 4 vols (1916, 1963).

Secondary Literature J.A. Schumpeter, 'Vilfredo Pareto', *Ten Great Economists from Marx to Keynes* (OUP, 1951); M. Allais, 'Pareto, Vilfredo: contributions to economics', *IESS*, vol. 11.

PARKIN, John Michael

Born 1939, Birdwell, Yorks., England.
Current Post Prof. Econ., Univ. Western Ontario, Canada.
Recent Posts Ass. lecturer Applied Econ., Univ. Sheffield, 1964–5; Lecturer Econ., Univ. Leicester, 1965–7; Lecturer, Sr lecturer Econ., Univ. Essex, 1967–70; Prof. Econ., Univ. Manchester, 1970–5.
Degrees BA (First class hons) Univ. Leicester, 1963; MA Econ (Hon.) Univ. Manchester, 1970.
Offices Ed., *MS*, 1974–5; Member Ed. Boards, *REStud*, 1969–75, *JMCB*, 1973–4, *J Mon E*, 1975–, *AER*, 1980–.
Principal Contributions Joint director of research project on inflation (Manchester, 1970–5) and joint editor/author of four vols on UK and world inflation. Specific contribution covered the effects of incomes policies on wages and prices; the measurement and modelling of the determinants of inflation expectations; the relationship between domestic inflation and domestic and world monetary action; the causes of worldwide inflation in the late 1960s; the political economy of inflation. Theoretical and empirical work on the portfolio behaviour of banks, non-bank financial institutions and the non-financial sector.
Publications *Books:* 1. *Incomes Policy and Inflation*, ed. (with M.T. Sumner), (Manchester Univ. Press, 1972); 2. *Inflation in the World Economy*, ed. (with G. Zis), (Manchester Univ. Press, Univ. Toronto Press, 1976); 3. *Inflation in Open Economies*, ed. (with G. Zis), (Manchester Univ. Press, Univ. Toronto Press, 1977); 4. *Inflation in the United Kingdom*, ed. (with M.T. Sumner), (Manchester Univ. Press, Univ. Toronto Press, 1978).
Articles: 1. 'Incomes policy: a reappraisal' (with R.G. Lipsey), *Ec*, N.S. 37, May 1970; 2. 'Discount house portfolio and debt selection', *REStud*, 37(4), Oct. 1970; 3. 'The optimal quantity of money, bonds, commodity inventories and capital' (with E.L. Feige), *AER*, 61(3), June 1971; 4. 'Inflation: a survey' (with D.E.W. Laidler), *EJ*, 85, Dec. 1975; 5. 'A comparison of alternative techniques of monetary control under rational expectations', *MS*, 46(3), Sept. 1978.

PARNELL, Henry Brooke*

Dates and Birthplace 1776–1842, Ireland.
Post Held Politician.
Offices and Honours MP, 1797–1801; Member, UK Bullion Comm., 1810; MP for Queen's County, 1802, Portarlington, 1802–3, Queen's County, 1806–32, Dundee, 1833–41; Created 1st Baron Congleton, 1841.
Career Whig financial expert whose parliamentary speeches and pamphlets on economic questions were widely respected. He was an enthusiastic defender of the report of the Bullion Committee and attacked the corn laws. His treatise, *On Financial Reform*, laid out the basic principles which were adopted with success by Peel and Gladstone.
Publications *Books:* 1. *Observations upon the State of the Currency of Ireland* (1804); 2. *The Principles of Currency and Exchange* (1805); 3. *Treatise on the Corn Trade* (1809); 4. *Observations on Paper Money* (1827); 5. *On Financial Reform* (1830); 6. *A Plain Statement of the Power of the Bank of England* (1832).

PARSONS, Donald O.

Born 1944, Pittsburgh, Penn., USA.
Current Post Prof. Econ., Ohio State Univ., USA.
Recent Posts Ass. prof., 1970–3, Assoc. prof., 1973–7, Ohio State Univ.; Res. Fellow, NBER, 1975–6.

Degrees BA Duke Univ., 1966; PhD Univ. Chicago, 1970.

Offices AEA, Em Soc.

Principal Contributions Research in three areas: the mobility of labour, specifying job turnover as a joint employer-employee decision; the economics of education, developing family aspects, including bequest motives, of schooling choice in a human capital framework; and the determinants of male labour-force participation in the US as the interaction of health, market wages, and transfer or welfare incentives.

Publications *Books:* 1. *Poverty and the Minimum Wage* (Amer. Enterprise Inst., 1980).

Articles: 1. 'Specific human capital: an application to quit rates and layoff rates', *JPE*, 80(6), Nov./Dec. 1972; 2. 'Quit rates over time: a search and information approach', *ER*, 63(3), June 1973; 3. 'Intergenerational wealth transfers and the educational decisions of male youth', *QJE*, 89(4), Nov. 1975; 4. 'The decline in male labor force participation', *JPE*, 88(1), Feb. 1980; 5. 'Racial trends in male labor force participation', *AER*, 70(5), Dec. 1980.

PASINETTI, Luigi Lodovico

Born 1930, Bergamo, Italy.

Current Post Prof. Econ., Univ. Cattolica del Sacro Cuore, Milan, Italy,

Recent Posts Res. Fellow, Nuffield Coll., Univ. Oxford, 1960–1; Fellow, Lecturer Econ., King's Coll., Univ. Camb., 1961–73; Lecturer, Reader Econ., Univ. Camb., 1961–76; Wesley Clair Mitchell Vis. res. prof. Econ., Columbia Univ., 1971, 1975; Vis. res. prof., Indian Stat. Inst., Calcutta and New Delhi, 1975.

Degrees Laurea (Econ.) Univ. Cattolica del Sacro Cuore, Milan, 1953–4; PhD (Econ.) Univ. Camb., 1962.

Offices and Honours Fellow, Em Soc, 1978–; St Vincent prize Econ., 1979; Council member, Exec. Comm., IEA, 1980–.

Principal Contributions Capital, rate of profit, rate of interest, income distribution and multi-sector economic growth. Name associated with the Pasinetti theorem which states the independence of the rate of profit from the saving propensities of the working class, and with the debate on the switching of techniques.

Publications *Books:* 1. *A multi-sector Model of Economic Growth* (King's Coll., Univ. Camb., 1963); 2. *Growth and Income Distribution – Essays in Economic Theory* (CUP, 1974); 3. *Lectures on the Theory of Production* (Columbia Univ. Press, Macmillan, 1977); 4. *Essays on the Theory of Joint Production*, ed. (Macmillan, 1980); 5. *Structural Change and Economic Growth* (CUP, 1981).

Articles: 1. 'A mathematical formulation of the Ricardian system', *REStud*, 27, Feb. 1960; 2. 'Rate of profit and income distribution in relation to the rate of economic growth', *REStud*, 29, Oct. 1962; 3. 'Changes in the rate of profit and switches of technique', *QJE*, 80, Nov. 1966; 4. 'The notion of vertical integration in economic analysis', *Metroecon*, 25, 1973; 5. 'Rate of profit and income distribution in a pure labour economy', *J Post Keyn E*, 2(4), Winter 1980.

PATINKIN, Don

Born 1922, Chicago, Ill., USA.

Current Post Prof. Econ., Hebrew Univ. Jerusalem, Israel, 1949–.

Degrees BA, MA, PhD, Hon. DHL, Univ. Chicago, 1943, 1945, 1947, 1976.

Offices and Honours Phi Beta Kappa, 1943; Fellow, 1953, Pres., 1974, Em Soc; Rothschild prize, 1959; Member, Israel Academy Sciences Humanities, 1963; Foreign hon. member, AAAS, 1969; Israel prize, 1970; Hon. member, AEA, 1975; Pres., Israel Econ. Assoc., 1976.

Principal Contributions Contributed primarily to monetary theory and its history, 1870–1940. Developed an integration of value theory and monetary theory by means of a general-equilibrium, micro-economic analysis which shows that there is a direct effect of real money balances on demand functions in all markets, including those for commodities. Developed a corresponding macro-economic model which also provides for a disequilibrium theory of unemployment. Traced and analysed the development of Keynes' monetary thought, as well as the relationship between this and the Stockholm School and Kalecki. Wrote a history of the first decade of the Israeli economy.

Publications *Books:* 1. *Money, Interest, and Prices: an Integration of Monetary and Value Theory* (Row Peterson, 1956, 1965; Spanish transl., 1959; Japanese transl., 1971; French transl., 1972; Italian transl., 1978); 2. *The Israel Economy: The First Decade* (Maurice Falk Inst. Econ. Res. Israel, 1959); 3. *Studies in Monetary Economics* (Harper & Row, 1972); 4. *Keynes' Monetary Thought: A Study of its Development* (Duke Univ. Press, 1976, 1978; German transl., 1979; Japanese transl., 1980; Italian transl., 1982); 5. *Anticipations of the 'General Theory' and other Essays on Keynes* (Univ. Chicago Press, 1982).

Articles: 1. 'Some reflections on the brain drain', in *The Brain Drain*, ed. W. Adams (Macmillan, 1968); 2. 'The collected writings of John Maynard Keynes: from the *Tract* to the *General Theory*', *EJ*, 85, June 1975; 3. 'What advanced countries can learn from the experience with indexation', *Explorations Econ. Res.*, 4(1), Winter 1977.

PATTANAIK, Prasanta Kumar

Born 1943, Cuttack, Orissa, India.
Current Post Prof. Math. Econ., Univ. Birmingham, England.
Recent Posts Prof. Econ., La Trobe Univ., Australia, 1975–7; Vis. Fellow, ANU; Prof. Econ., Southern Methodist Univ., Texas, 1977–8.
Degrees BA (Hons.) Utkal Univ., 1963; MA, PhD Univ. Delhi, 1965, 1968.
Offices Assoc. ed., *JET*, 1975–; Fellow, Em Soc, 1979–; Member, Ed. Board, *REStud*, 1980–.
Principal Contributions Mainly in the area of collective choice and welfare economics: investigation of various restrictions on individual preferences to ensure consistency of different democratic group decision rules; and exploration of the problem of strategic misrevelation of preferences.

Publications *Books:* 1. *Voting and Collective Choice* (CUP, 1971); 2. *Strategy and Group Choice* (N-H, 1978).

Articles: 1. 'A note on democratic decision and the existence of choice sets', *REStud*, 35, Jan. 1968; 2. 'Necessary and sufficient conditions for rational choice under majority decision' (with A.K. Sen), *JET*, 1(2), Aug. 1969; 3. 'On some suggestions for having non-binary social choice functions' (with R.N. Batra), *Theory and Decision*, 1972; 4. 'Counter-threats and strategic manipulation under voting schemes', *REStud*, 43, Feb. 1976; 5. 'On nicely consistent voting systems' (with B. Dutta), *Em*, 46(1), Jan. 1978.

PATTEN, Simon Nelson*

Dates and Birthplace 1852–1922, Sandwich, Ill., USA.
Posts Held Schoolteacher, 1882–8; Prof. Polit. Econ., Univ. Pennsylvania, 1888–1917.
Degrees MA, PhD Univ. Halle, 1878.
Offices Pres., AEA, 1908.
Career Social philosopher who never limited himself to the traditional field of economic inquiry. Frequently involved in intellectual controversy, but his ability to stimulate discussion made him a very successful teacher. He favoured protectionism and nationalism in economic policy.

Publications *Books:* 1. *Premises of Political Economy* (1885); 2. *Theory of Social Forces* (1896); 3. *Development of English Thought* (1899); 4. *Theory of Prosperity* (1902); 5. *Heredity of Social Progress* (1903); 6. *New Basis of Civilisation* (1907).

Secondary Literature H.R. Seager, 'S.N. Patten', in *Essays in Economic Theory*, ed. R.G. Tugwell (Alfred A. Knopf, 1924).

PAULY, W.V.

N.e.

PEACOCK, Alan Turner

Born 1922, Ryton-on-Tyne, England.

Current Post Principal, Univ. Coll., Bucks. England.

Recent Posts Prof. Econ. Science, Univ. Edinburgh, 1956–62; Prof. Econ., Univ. York, 1962–78; Chief econ. adviser, UK Dept. Trade and Industry, 1973–6.

Degrees MA (Econ. and Polit. Science, First class) Univ. St Andrews, 1947; Dr Univ. (*Hon. causa*) Univ. Stirling, 1974.

Offices Member, Advisory Council, Inst. Econ. Affairs, 1961–; Member, UK Royal Commission Constitution, 1971–3; Hon. pres., Internat. Inst. Public Fin., 1975–; Fellow, BA, 1979–; Hon. Fellow, LSE, 1980–.

Principal Contributions Appear to have a knack of hitting on interesting problems in public sector economics and the economic analysis of government for which others find more elegant solutions.

Publications *Books:* 1. *Economics of National Insurance* (William Hodge, 1952); 2. *Growth of Public Expenditure in the United Kingdom 1890–1955* (with J. Wiseman), (Princeton Univ. Press, OUP, 1961, 1967); 3. *Economic Theory of Fiscal Policy* (with G.K. Shaw), (A & U, 1971, 1976); 4. *Welfare Economics: A Liberal Reinterpretation* (with C.K. Rowley), (Martin Robertson, 1975); 5. *Economic Analysis of Government* (Martin Robertson, 1979).

Articles: 1. 'Consumption taxes and compensatory finance' (with J.H. Williamson), *EJ*, 77, March 1967; 2. 'Welfare economics and public subsidies to the arts', *MS*, 37(4), Dec. 1969, reprinted in M. Blaug, ed., *The Economics of the Arts* (Martin Robertson, 1976); 3. 'International linkage models and the public sector' (with M. Ricketts), *Public Fin.*, 30(3), 1975; 4. 'Approaches to the analysis of government expenditure growth' (with J. Wiseman), *Public Fin. Quarterly*, 7(1), 1979; 5. 'On the anatomy of collective failure', *PF*, 35(1), 1980.

PEARCE, Ivor Frank

Born 1916, Bristol, England.

Current Post Prof. Econ., Univ. Southampton, 1961–.

Recent Posts Vis. prof., Univ. Pennsylvania, 1965, 1969, Univ. Cal., Berkeley, 1972, 1980, Inst. Advanced Stud., ANU, 1972, St Hilda's Coll., Univ. Melbourne, 1977–8.

Degrees BA Univ. Bristol, 1949; PhD Univ. Nottingham, 1953.

Offices Fellow, Em Soc; Council member, Inst. Econ. Affairs, London.

Principal Contributions International balance of payments and money market theory; the theory of value in international trade; the theory of capital and economic growth; general equilibrium and income distribution theory; the theory of consumer behaviour; the theory and practice of large-scale econometric model-building; the theory and measurement of social welfare, and the mathematisation of economics.

Publications *Books:* 1. *A Contribution to Demand Analysis* (OUP, 1964); 2. *International Trade*, 2 vols (Macmillan, Norton, 1970); 3. *A Model of Output, Employment, Wages and Prices in the United Kingdom* (CUP, 1976).

Articles: 1. 'The place of money capital in the theory of production' (with A. Gabor), *QJE*, 72, Nov. 1958; 2. 'The problem of the balance of payments', *Int ER*, 2, Jan. 1961; 3. 'An exact method of consumer demand analysis', *Em*, 29, Oct. 1961; 4. 'Matrices with dominating diagonal blocks', *JET*, 9(2), Oct. 1974; 5. 'The incredible Eurodollar', *The Banker*, June 1980.

PECHMAN, Joseph A.

Born 1918, New York City, NY, USA.

Current Post Dir., Econ. Stud., Brookings Inst., Washington, DC, 1962–.

Recent Posts Ass. dir., Tax Advisory Staff, US Treasury, 1946–53; Assoc. prof. Fin., MIT, 1953–4; Economist, US President's Council Econ. Advisers, 1954–6; Economist, Comm. Econ. Development, 1956–60; Exec. Dir.,

Stud. Govt Fin., Brookings Inst., 1960–70.

Degrees BS Coll. City New York, 1937; MA, PhD, LLD (Hon.) Univ. Wisconsin, 1938, 1942, 1978.

Offices and Honours Phi Beta Kappa; Irving Fisher Res. Prof., Yale Univ., 1966–7; Time Board of Economists, 1970–; Pres., AFA, 1971; Fellow, AAAS, 1973–; Fellow, Center Advanced Stud. Behavioral Sciences, 1975–6; Vice-pres., AEA, 1978; Pres., EEA, 1979.

Principal Contributions Research concerned mainly with the impact of taxation on the economy and on the distribution of income. Developed a microdata set of family units which provides the basis for preparing estimates of the distribution of tax burdens under alternative incidence assumptions. Considerable work on methods of broadening the individual income tax base so that it will be consistent with an economic definition of income.

Publications *Books:* 1. *Social Security: Perspectives for Reform* (with H.J. Aaron and M.K. Taussig), (Brookings Inst., 1968); 2. *Who Bears the Tax Burden?* (with B. Okner), (Brookings Inst., 1974); 3. *Federal Tax Reform: The Impossible Dream* (with G. Break), (Brookings Inst., 1975); 4. *Federal Tax Policy* (Brookings Inst., 1977); 5. *Setting National Priorities: The 1982 Budget* (Brookings Inst., 1981).

Articles: 1. 'Individual income tax erosion by income classes' (with B.A. Okner), *Compendium of Papers on the Economics of Federal Subsidy Prorams*, Joint Econ. Comm., US Congress (Govt Printing Office, 1972); 2. 'Responsiveness of the Federal individual income tax to changes in income', *Brookings Papers Econ. Activity*, 2, 1973; 3. 'International trends in the distribution of tax burdens: implications for tax policy', (Inst. Fiscal Stud., 1973); 4. 'Making economic policy: the role of the economist', in *Handbook of Political Science*, vol. 6, *Policies and Policymaking* (Addison-Wesley Publishing, 1975); 5. 'Taxation', in *Britain's Economic Performance*, eds R.E. Caves and L.B. Krause (Brookings Inst., 1980).

PECK, Merton Joseph

Born 1925, Cleveland, Ohio, USA.

Current Post Prof. Econ., 1963–, Chairman Econ. Dept., 1969–74, 1978–, Yale Univ.

Recent Posts Assoc. prof., Harvard Bus. School, 1956–61; Dept. Ass. Comptroller, Dir. Systems Analysis, US Office Secretary Defense, 1961–2; Member, US President's Council Econ. Advisers, Exec. Office Pres., 1968–9.

Degrees BA Oberlin Coll., 1949; MA, PhD Harvard Univ., 1951, 1954.

Offices Member, AEA, Assembly Engineering, NAS, Connecticut Academy Science Engineering.

Principal Contributions Concerned with the application of economic theory and quantitative methods to the understanding of particular industries and sectors, illustrated by texts on the weapons industry, US railroad industry, and federal regulation of television. The works attempts in each case to conclude with policy recommendations, but principal objective is to illustrate ways of understanding the diverse industries that make up an industrial economy.

Publications *Books:* 1. *Weapons Acquisition: An Economic Analysis* (with F.M. Scherer), (Harvard Bus. School, 1962); 2. *Technology, Economic Growth and Public Policy*, ed. (with R. Nelson and E. Kalachek), (Brookings Inst., 1967); 3. *Economic Aspects of Television Regulation* (with R. Noll and J. McGowan), (Brookings Inst., 1973); 4. *Unsettled Questions on Regulatory Reform*, ed. (with P. MacAvoy), (Amer. Enterprise Inst., 1978).

Articles: 1. 'The single-entity proposal for international telecommunications', *AER*, 60(2), May 1970; 2. 'Television: old theories, current facts, and future policies' (with J. McGowan), *AER*, 61(2), May 1971; 3. 'Technology', in *Asia's New Giant: How the Japanese Economy Works*, eds H. Patrick and H. Rosovsky (Brookings Inst., 1976); 4. 'Technology and economic growth: the case of Japan' (with A. Goto), *Res. Pol.*, 1981.

PENNINGTON, James*

Dates and Birthplace 1777–1862, Kendal, England.
Post Held Businessman.
Offices Member, Polit. Econ. Club, 1828.
Career Expert on currency who was frequently consulted by the British government in the regulation of the currency of the West Indies after 1833. His *Letter to Kirkman Finlay* . . . advocated the restriction of Bank of England note issues. Peel consulted him on the framing of the Bank Act 1844 but moved beyond his recommendations by separating the Bank's banking and issue departments.
Publications *Books:* 1. *The Currency of the British Colonies* (1848); 2. *A Letter to Kirkman Finlay on the Importation of Foreign Corn* (1840).

PERLMAN, Selig*

Dates and Birthplace 1888–1959, Bialystok, Poland.
Posts Held Student, res. ass., Prof., Univ. Wisconsin, 1908–59.
Offices Member, Wisconsin Commission Human Rights, 1947.
Career Labour historian and theoretician, whose theory of the labour movement he called the Commons-Perlman theory in tribute to his mentor at Wisconsin. The theory was not abstract but was based on his encyclopaedic knowledge of labour history. He believed that job security and not wage bargaining or workers' control was the true explanation of the rise of trade unions.
Publications *Books:* 1. *History of Trade Unionism in the United States* (1922); 2. *Theory of the Labor Movement* (1928, 1956).
Secondary Literature E.E. Witte, 'Selig Perlman', *ILRR*, 13, April 1960.

PERROUX, François

Born 1903, Lyons, France.
Current Post Pres., Inst. Sciences Math. Econ. Appliquées, Paris; Hon. Prof., Collège de France, 1975–.

Recent Posts Prof. Coll. de France, 1925–75; Prof., Univ. Lyons, 1926–8; Prof., Univ. Paris (1938–55), Ecole des Hautes Etudes, Sorbonne, Paris.
Degrees Licence et Diplôme d'Etudes Supérieures des Lettres, 1923–4, Doctorat de Sciences Econ., 1932, Univ. Lyons, Agrégé des Sciences Econ., Univ. Paris, 1928; Hon. Dr Univs. Sao-Paulo (1936), Coimbra (1937), Liège (1955), Frankfurt-am-Main (1957), Lisbon (1960), Cordoba, (1963), Montevideo (1963), Georgetown, Washington (1963), ICA, Peru (1964), Lima (1964–8), Chile (1967), Barranquilla (1967–8), Bogota (1968), Quebec (1968), Barcelona (1969), Bucharest (1969), Ottawa (1974).
Offices and Honours G.O. de l'Ordre Nat. du Mérite; Commandeur Légion d'Honneur; Commandeur Palmes Académiques; Conseil Nat. Services Publics, 1945; Conseil Supérieur Comptabilité, 1947; Pres., Congrès Internat. de la Comptabilité, 1948; Pres., Sous-Commission Méthodes, Commission Comptes Budgets Econ., Ministère Fin., 1952; French Co-dir. Europ. Soc. Culture, Venice, 1956; Member, Conseil Internat. Sciences Sociales, 1960; Foreign member, Accademia Nazionale dei Lincei, 1960; Corresponding Fellow, BA, 1961; Hon. member, AEA, 1962; CNRS, 1963; Medaille d'Or 'C.C. Söderström', Royal Academy Sciences, Stockholm, 1971; Member, Royal Academy Barcelona.
Principal Contributions After thorough study of the static general equilibrium theory, was led to develop a generalised equilibrium theory based on the concept of active units, capable of modifying their environment: asymmetrical actions in the irreversible time are combined in a whole whose temporary equilibria engender, under specified conditions, a general 'equilibrium', characterised by the exhaustion of the agent's energy for change. This state provides a framework, in terms of pretopology, for the active units to hold together and to react on each other through market operations and organisational processes.
Publications *Books:* 1. *Le Problème du profit* (Edns Marcel Giard, 1926); 2. *La Valeur* (Presses Univ. de France,

1943); 3. *Théorie générale du progrès économique* (Cahiers de l'ISEA, 1956–7, Greek transl., 1962); 4. *L'Économie du XXème siècle* (Presses Univ. de France, 1961, 1969); 5. *Unités actives et mathématiques nouvelles. Révision de la théorie de l'équilibre général* (Dunod, 1975).

Articles: 1. 'Economic spaces: theory and application', *QJE*, 64(1), Feb. 1950, repr. in *Readings in Regional Development*, ed. J. Friedmann (CUP, 1965); 2. 'Prises de vue sur la croissance de l'économie française 1780–1950', *Income and Wealth*, vol. 5 (NBER, 1956); 3. 'L'équilibre des unités passives et l'équilibration générale des unités actives', *Econ App*, 3–4, 1978.

PESCH, Heinrich*

Dates and Birthplace 1854–1926, Germany.
Posts Held Mainz Theological Seminary, 1892–1900.
Degrees Grad. Univ. Bonn, 1875, Univ. Berlin, 1903.
Offices Member, Soc. of Jesus.
Career Catholic economist who stressed the moral basis of economics, arguing that economic phenomena should be evaluated in terms of welfare, and called the social system he advocated 'Christian solidarism'. This involved stressing the interdependence of groups within society and the necessity of subordinating private economic interests to the collective welfare of the people.
Publications *Books:* 1. *Liberalismus, Sozialismus und Christliche Gesellschaftsordnung*, 2 vols (1893–1900); 2. *Lehrbuch der Nationalökonomie*, 5 vols (1905–23).
Secondary Literature G. Briefs, 'Pesch, Heinrich', *ESS*, vol. 12.

PESTON, Maurice

Born 1931, London, U.K.
Current Post Prof. Econ., Queen Mary Coll., Univ. London, England.
Recent Posts Special adviser, UK Secretary of State Education and Science, 1974–5; Sr special adviser, UK Secretary of State Prices and Consumer Protection, 1976–9; Chairman, Econ. Board, UK SSRC, 1976–9.
Degrees BSc (Econ. First class hons.) LSE, 1952.
Offices and Honours Chairman, UK Comm. Nat. Academic Awards, 1967–73; Ed., *Applied Econ.*, 1972–; Council member, RES, 1978–.
Principal Contributions Microeconomics: clarification of the analysis of returns to scale, the interpretation of the objectives sought by the firm, the theory of forward markets and the analysis of changes in preferences. Macroeconomics: elaboration of a number of aspects of the balanced budget multiplier, the need for interventionist macro-economic policy, and the nature of macro-economics itself.
Publications *Books:* 1. *Public Goods and the Public Sector* (Macmillan, 1972); 2. *Theory of Macroeconomic Policy* (Philip Allan, 1974); 3. *Whatever Happened to Macroeconomics?* (Manchester Univ. Press, 1980).
Articles: 1. 'Random variations risk and returns to scale' (with T.M. Whitin), *QJE*, 68, Nov. 1954; 2. 'Generalising the balanced budget multiplier', *REStat*, 40, Aug. 1958; 3. 'On the sales maximisation hypothesis', *Ec*, N.S. 26, May 1959; 4. 'The correlation between targets and instruments', *Ec*, N.S. 39, Nov. 1972; 5. 'Monetary policy and incomes policy. Complements or substitutes?', *Applied Econ.*, Dec. 1980.

PFOUTS, Ralph William

Born 1920, Atchison, Kans., USA.
Current Post Prof. Econ., Univ. N. Carolina, USA.
Recent Posts Assoc. prof. Econ., 1952–7, Chairman, Dept. Econ., 1962–8, Univ. N. Carolina.
Degrees BA, MA Univ. Kansas, 1942, 1947; PhD Univ. N. Carolina, 1952.
Offices PAA; Pres., N. Carolina Chapter, ASA, 1952–3; US SSRC Fellow, Univ. Camb., 1953–4; Program Comm., Em Soc, 1961; Vice-pres., 1961–2, Pres., 1965–6, SEA; Ford Foundation Faculty res. Fellow, MIT 1962–3; Vice-pres., 1973–6, Pres.,

1977–8, Atlantic Econ. Soc.; Nominating Comm., AEA, 1977.

Principal Contributions Research interests have included urban and regional economics; and an attempt to develop a more realistic prototype of the consumer by including wages, hours of work, savings and income from earning assets. Also, the theory of difference equations in the development of a duopoly model which included learning processes in collaboration with the late C.E. Ferguson. A continuing interest has been the theory of the multiproduct firm; and index numbers viewed not as indicators of utility, but as indicators of price and quality changes.

Publications *Books:* 1. *Techniques of Urban Economic Analysis*, ed. (Chandler-Davis Co., 1960); 2. *Essays in Economics and Econometrics: a Volume in Honor of Harold Hotelling*, ed. (Univ. N. Carolina Press, 1960); 3. *Elementary Economics: A Mathematical Approach* (Wiley, 1972).

Articles: 1. 'A theory of the responsiveness of hours of work to changes in wage rates' (with F. Gilbert), *REStat*, 40, May 1958; 2. 'A matric general solution of linear difference equations with constant coefficients' (with C.E. Ferguson), *Maths Magazine*, 33, 1960; 3. 'The theory of cost and production in the multi-product firm', *Em*, 29, Oct. 1961; 4. 'Learning and expectations in dynamic duopoly behavior' (with C.E. Ferguson), *Behavioral Science*, 7, 1962; 5. 'A note on systems of simultaneous difference equations with constant coefficients', *Naval Res. Logistics Quarterly*, 12, 1965.

PHELPS, Edmund S.

Born 1933, Evanston, Ill., USA.
Current Post Prof. Econ., Columbia Univ., NY, USA.
Recent Posts Vis. assoc. prof., MIT, 1962–3; Assoc. prof., Yale Univ. and Cowles Foundation, 1963–6; Prof., Univ. Penn., 1966–71; Prof., NYU, 1978–9.
Degrees BA Amherst Coll., 1955; MA, PhD Yale Univ., 1957, 1959.
Offices Fellow, AAAS, Em Soc; Fellow, US SSRC, 1966; Fellow, Center

Advanced Study Behavioral Sciences, 1969–70; Exec. Comm., AEA, 1976–8; Guggenheim Memorial Foundation Fellow, 1978.

Principal Contributions Initiated the expectational reformulation of macro-economic theory, beginning with an algebraic statement of the 'natural rate' hypothesis (1967, 1968) and continuing with the earliest constructions of non-Walrasian micro-macro models of expectational equilibrium and disequilibrium without complete information: a model of firms' wage competition to retain their experienced employees (1968), a model of the impact of inventories on labour supply through the expected real rate of interest (1969), the 'island parable' of search unemployment (1969), and a model of firms' price competition for customers (1970). Subsequent research considered employer commitments, the question of their indexation, and the effects of their non-synchronisation (1977, 1978, 1979).

Publications *Books:* 1. *Fiscal Neutrality Toward Economic Growth* (McGraw-Hill, 1965); 2. *Golden Rules of Economic Growth*, ed. and contributor (with others), (Norton, N-H, 1966); 3. *Microeconomic Foundations of Employment and Inflation Theory*, ed. and contributor (with others), (Norton, Macmillan, 1970); 4. *Inflation Policy and Unemployment Theory*, ed. and contributor (with others), (Norton, 1972); 5. *Economic Justice: A Reader*, ed. (Penguin Books, 1973).

Articles: 1. *Studies in Macroeconomic Theory:* Vol. 1: *Employment and Inflation*, Vol. 2 *Redistribution and Growth* (Academic Press, 1979, 1980).

PHELPS BROWN, Ernest Henry

Born 1906, Calne, England.
Current Post Retired.
Recent Posts Fellow, New Coll., Univ. Oxford, 1930–47; Prof. Econ. Labour, Univ. London, 1947–68.
Degrees MA Univ. Oxford, 1931; Hon. DLitt Heriot-Watt Univ., 1972.
Offices Pres., RES, 1970–2.
Principal Contributions Study of the movement of money and real wages over

time; the relation between real wages and productivity in the course of economic development and changes in population. Factors in economic development indicated by historical and comparative studies. Pay, profits and productivity in five western economies, 1860–1960. The pay structure, social and economic influences on differentials. Industrial relations in the light of economic and social history. Contemporary incomes policy.

Publications *Books:* 1. *The Framework of the Pricing System* (Chapman & Hall, 1936); 2. *The Growth of British Industrial Relations* (Macmillan, 1959, Papermac, 1965); 3. *The Economics of Labor* (Yale Univ. Press, 1962); 4. *A Century of Pay* (with M.H. Browne), (Macmillan, 1968); 5. *The Inequality of Pay* (OUP, 1977).

Articles: 1. 'The share of wages in national income' (with P.E. Hart), *EJ*, 62, June 1952; 2. 'Seven centuries of the prices of consumables, compared with builders' wage-rates' (with S.V. Hopkins), *Ec*, N.S. 23, Nov. 1956; 3. 'The meaning of the fitted Cobb-Douglas function', *QJE*, 71, Nov. 1957; 4. 'The underdevelopment of economics', *EJ*, 83, March 1972. 5. 'New wine in old bottles: reflections on the changed working of collective bargaining in Great Britain', *BJIR*, 11, Nov. 1973.

PHILIPPOVICH VON PHILIPPS-BERG, Eugen*

Dates and Birthplace 1858–1917, Vienna, Austro-Hungary.

Posts Held Privatdozent, Univ. Vienna; Prof., Univ. Freiburg, 1885–93, Univ. Vienna, 1893–1917.

Offices Member, Upper House, Austrian parliament, 1907.

Career Early career influenced by the German Historical School, but his later leanings were toward Austrian theory. His *Grundriss* . . . was the leading German textbook on general economics for 25 years, and reconciled the ideas of the two Schools. His political influence, through a group known as the Austrian Fabians, has had a considerable effect on Austrian social legislation.

Publications *Books:* 1. *Die Bank von England im Dienste der Finanzverwaltung des Staates* (1885); 2. *Über Aufgabe und Methode der Politischen Ökonomie* (1886); 3. *Der Badische Staatshaushalt in den Jahren 1868–89* (1889); 4. *Grundriss der Politischen Ökonomie*, 2 vols (1893–1907); 5. *Die Entwicklung der Wirtschaftspolitischen Ideen im Neunzehnten Jahrhundert* (1910).

Secondary Literature F.A. Hayek, 'Philippovich von Philippsberg, Eugen', *ESS*, vol. 12.

PHILLIPS, Alban William Housego*

Dates and Birthplace 1914–75, Te Rehunga, Dannevirke, New Zealand.

Posts Held Tooke Prof. Econ. Science and Stats., Univ. London, 1958–67; Prof. Econ., Res. School Social Sciences, ANU, 1967–70.

Degrees BSc (Econ.), PhD Univ. London, 1949, 1952.

Offices and Honours Member, UK Inst. Electrical Engineers, 1938; Vis. prof., MIT, 1965–6; Walras-Bowley Lectures, Em Soc, San Francisco, 1966.

Career The originator of the Phillips curve relating the rate of change of money wage rates to the level of unemployment. Pioneered the application of optimal control and control engineering techniques to econometric models. Developed econometric estimation techniques for models with autoregressive, moving average errors.

Publications *Articles:* 1. 'Stabilisation policy in a closed economy', *EJ*, 64, June 1954; 2. 'The relation between unemployment and the rate of change of money wage rates in the United Kingdom, 1861–1957', *Ec*, N.S. 25, Nov. 1958; 3. 'The estimation of parameters in systems of stochastic differential equations', *Biometrika*, 461, 1959; 4. 'Employment, inflation and growth', *Ec*, N.S. 29, Feb. 1962; 5. 'Estimation of systems of difference equations with moving average disturbances', Walras-Bowley Lecture, Em Soc, 1966.

Secondary Literature K. Lancaster, 'Phillips, A. William', *IESS*, vol. 18.

PIERSON, Nicolaas Gerard*

Dates and Birthplace 1839–1909, The Netherlands.

Posts Held Cotton merchant and banker; Dir., 1866, Pres., 1885–91, Nederlandsche Bank; Prof., Univ. Amsterdam, 1877.

Offices Dutch Minister Fin., 1891–4; Prime Minister and Minister Fin., 1897–1901; Member, Dutch Second Chamber, 1905–.

Career As a statesman he sought to reform the Dutch tax system according to the principle of the ability to pay – indirect taxes were reduced, and an income tax introduced. His *Leerboek* . . . was his chief publication, and places the emphasis on ecomics as a means for improving material welfare, rather than on pure theory. His position in Dutch economics was pre-eminent and substantially influenced the progress of the subject in Holland.

Publications *Books:* 1. *Grondbeginselen der Staathuishoudkunde*, 2 vols (1875–6); 2. *Leerboek der Staathuishoudkunde*, 2 vols (1884–90); 3. *Verspreide Economische Geschriften*, 6 vols (1910–11).

Secondary Literature H.W.C. Bordewijk, 'Pierson, Nicolaas Gerard', *ESS*, vol. 12.

PIGOU, Arthur Cecil*

Dates and Birthplace 1877–1959, Ryde, Isle of Wight, England.

Posts Held Lecturer, 1901, Fellow, 1902, King's Coll., Prof. Polit. Econ., 1908–43, Univ. Camb.

Degree MA Univ. Camb., 1900.

Offices and Honours Adam Smith prize, 1903; Fellow, BA, 1927.

Career Marshall's successor to the Cambridge chair and devoted expositor of Marshall's economics during his tenure of the chair. Pioneered welfare economics in *Wealth and Welfare*, which embodied his own concerns for justice and the protection of the interests of the poor. Singled out by Keynes in *The General Theory* as the leading advocate of the classical views which Keynes rejected, he came to accept much of Keynes' thinking in his later years. The quality of all his books is outstanding, but he has only slowly won a place as an underrated economist of first distinction.

Publications *Books:* 1. *Principles and Methods of Industrial Peace* (1905); 2. *Wealth and Welfare* (1912), subsequently *The Economics of welfare* (1920, 1960); 3. *Unemployment* (1914); 4. *Industrial fluctuations* (1927, 1929); 5. *A Study in Public Finance* (1928, 1956); 6. *The Theory of Unemployment* (1933); 7. *The Economics of Stationary States* (1935); 8. *Employment and Equilibrium* (1941, 1949); 9. *Keynes' 'General Theory': A Retrospective View* (1950).

Secondary Literature A. Robinson, 'Pigou, Arthur Cecil', *IESS*, vol. 12; D. Collard, 'A.C. Pigou', *Pioneers of Modern Economics in Britain*, eds D.P. O'Brien and J.R. Presley (Macmillan, 1981).

PIORE, Michael Joseph

Born 1940, New York City, NY, USA.

Current Post Mitsui Prof., Problems Contemporary Technology, MIT, USA, 1981–.

Recent Posts Ass. prof., 1966–70, Assoc. prof., 1970–5, Prof. Econ., 1975–81, MIT; Res. Fellow, Kennedy School Govt, Harvard Univ., 1968–9, 1969–70; Res. coordinator/acting exec. dir., Governor's Advisory Council (Dept. Govt Programs), Puerto Rico, 1970–1; Consultant Labor, Manpower, Income Maintenance, Puerto Rico, 1970–2.

Degrees BA (Econ., *Magna cum laude*) Harvard Coll., 1962; PhD (Econ., special field: Labor) Harvard Univ., 1966.

Offices AEA; IRRA; Union Radical Political Economics.

Principal Contributions One of the originators of the dual labour market hypothesis, explaining the problems of poor and disadvantaged groups in industrial society by their segregation in a distinct set of jobs with little access to other employment opportunities. Subsequent work recognised broader patterns of division among jobs and workers into several labour market segments, each associated with distinct processes of wage determination and job allocation. Also concerned with understanding the impact of such a segmented labour market upon such macro-economic indices as inflation, unemployment and labour productivity. More recent work has focused on the variation in labour market structures across countries, and the clues which such variation provides for the understanding of the causes of segmentation and its precise impact upon economic performance and social welfare. Recent work has focussed on international migration from underdeveloped to industrial countries.

Publications *Books:* 1. *Internal Labor Markets and Manpower Adjustment* (with P.B. Doeringer), (D.C. Heath & Co., 1971); 2. *Birds of Passage, Migrant Labor and Industrial Societies* (CUP, 1979); 3. *Unemployment and Inflation: Institutionalist and Structuralist views*, ed. (Sharpe Press, 1979); 4. *Dualism and Discontinuity in Industrial Society* (with S. Berger), (CUP, 1980).
Articles: 1. 'On-the-job training in a dual labor market: public and private responsibilities in on-the-job training of disadvantaged workers', in *Public-private Manpower Policies*, eds A. Weber et al. (IRRA, 1969); 2. 'Fragments of a sociological theory of wages', *AER*, 63(2), May 1973, and *Proceedings of IRRA*, 63(2), 1972; 3. 'Conceptualization of labor market reality', in *Manpower Research and Labor Economics*, eds G.I. Swanson and J. Michaelson (Sage Publications, 1979); 4. 'Union and politics', in *The Shrinking Perimeter, Unionism and Labor Relations in the Manufacturing Sector*, eds H.A. Jarvis and M. Roomkin (D.C. Heath & Co., 1980).

PIROU, Gaëtan*

Dates and Birthplace 1886–1945, France.
Posts Held Prof., Univ. Paris.
Offices Ed., *REP*; Chef de Cabinet to Pres., French Senate, 1927–30.
Career Teacher of economics who introduced much foreign economic thinking to French universities. His works on general economics make a very precise distinction between descriptive economics, theoretical economics and economic doctrine. The lack of mathematical content in his work rendered it a little behind the trend of the times but his grasp of the history of economics was broad and firm.

Publications *Books:* 1. *Les Doctrines économiques* (1925); 2. *Introduction à l'étude de l'économie politique* (1929); 3. *Le Corporatisme* (1935); 4. *La Monnaie française de 1936 à 1938* (1938); 5. *L'utilité marginale de C. Menger à J.B. Clark* (1938); 6. *Traite d'économie politique* (1942).
Secondary Literature H.S. Bloch, 'Memorial: Gaëtan Pirou', *AER*, 37, March 1947.

PLANT, Arnold*

Dates and Birthplace 1898–1978, London, England.
Posts Held Prof., Univ. Cape Town, SA, 1923–30; Prof. Commerce, LSE, 1930–65.
Degrees BCom., BSc (Econ.) Univ. London, 1922, 1923.
Offices and Honours Adviser to comms on raw materials allocation, 1940–6; Knighted, 1947; Chairman, UK SSRC, 1955–62.
Career Remembered as a teacher, university administrator, official adviser, and expert on the economics of patents.
Publications *Books: Selected Economic Essays and Addresses* (1974).

POLAK, Jacques Jacobus

Born 1914, Rotterdam, The Netherlands.
Current Post Exec. dir., Cyprus, Israel, Netherlands, Romania, Yugoslavia, IMF, Washington, DC, 1981–.
Recent Posts Dir., Res. Dept., IMF, 1958–79, Econ. counsellor, IMF, 1966–79.
Degrees MA (Econ.), PhD (Econ.) Univ. Amsterdam, 1936, 1937; PhD (Hon.) Erasmus Univ., Rotterdam, 1937.
Offices Fellow, Em Soc; Professorial

Lecturer, Johns Hopkins Univ., 1949–50, George Washington Univ., 1950–5.

Principal Contributions Econometric models of world economy; monetary theory of the balance of payments; development of Special Drawing Rights provision under the IMF.

Publications *Books:* 1. *The Dynamics of Business Cycles* (with J. Tinbergen), (Univ. Chicago Press, CUP, 1950); 2. *An International Economic System* (Univ. Chicago Press, A & U, 1954); 3. *The New International Monetary System*, ed. (with R.A. Mundell), (Columbia Univ. Press, 1977).

Articles: 1. 'Balance of payments problems of countries reconstructing with the help of foreign loans', *QJE*, 57, Feb. 1943; 2. 'European exchange depreciation in the early twenties', *Em*, 11, April 1943; 3. 'Monetary analysis of income formation and payments problems', *IMF Staff Papers*, 6, Nov. 1957; 4. 'Some reflections on the nature of Special Drawing Rights', *IMF Pamphlet* no. 16, 1971; 5. 'Coordination of national economic policies', Group of Thirty, 1981.

POLLAK, Robert A.

Born 1938, New York City, NY, USA.

Current Post Prof. Econ. Public Pol., Univ. Pennsylvania, USA.

Recent Posts Ass. prof. Econ., 1964–8, Assoc. prof. Econ., 1968–72, Univ. Pennsylvania; Economist, Bureau Labor Stats, US Dept. Labor, 1968–9.

Degrees BA Amherst Coll., 1960; PhD MIT, 1964.

Offices Fellow, Em Soc; Ed., *Int ER*; Consultant, US Bureau Labor Stats; Principal investigator, numerous grants, NSF.

Principal Contributions Research has centred on three areas: (1) household behaviour, focused on the structure of preferences (e.g., conditional demand functions, generalised separability) and on the specification and estimation of complete demand systems from time series and household budget data (with J.J. Wales). This work has led to the development of new functional forms (e.g. the quadratic expenditure system, and the generalised translog) and the specification and analysis of tractable dynamic structures (e.g. habit formation, price dependent preferences, interdependent preferences). (2) Index number theory: developed the concept of 'subindexes'. (3) Social choice theory: characterised the class of collective choice rules (with D.H. Blair) which satisfy Arrow's three axioms and yield acyclic social preferences.

Publications *Articles:* 1. 'Generalized separability', *Em*, 40(3), May 1972; 2. 'The relevance of the household production function and its implications for the allocation of time' (with M.L. Wachter), *JPE*, 83(2), April 1975; 3. 'Estimation of complete demand systems from household budget data: the linear and quadratic expenditure system' (with T.J. Wales), *AER*, 68(3), June 1978; 4. 'Collective rationality and dictatorship: the scope of the Arrow Theorem' (with D.H. Blair), *JET*, 21(1), Aug. 1979; 5. 'Theory and time series estimation of the quadratic expenditure system' (with H. Howe and T.J. Wales), *Em*, 47(5), Sept. 1979.

PONSARD, Claude

Born 1927, Dijon, France.

Current Post Prof., Univ. Dijon.

Degrees PhD (Econ) Univ. Dijon, 1953; Diploma High Stud. Practical School, Sorbonne, Paris, 1957; Aggregate (Econ.) 1958.

Offices and Honours Vouters prize, 1954; Dir., Inst. Econ. Maths, assoc. with NCSR, 1969–; Chevalier, Légion d'Honneur, 1980.

Principal Contributions Integration of space in economic analysis; formal representations of space and analytic implications: application of graph theory and topology in spatial economic theory; subjective spaces and their analysis with the fuzzy subsets theory; history of spatial economic theories; mathematical models in location and space-economy.

Publications *Books:* 1. *Economie et espace* (SEDES, 1955); 2. *Histoire des théories économiques spatiales* (Armand Colin, 1958); 3. *Un modèle*

topologique d'équilibre économique interregional (Dunod, 1969); 4. *Une révision de la théorie des aires de marché* (Sirey, 1974).
Articles: 1. 'Hiérarchie des places centrales et graphes phi-flous', *Environment and Planning*, A, 9, 1977; 2. 'Economie urbaine et espaces métriques', *Sistemi Urbani*, 1(1), 1979; 3. 'On the imprecision of consumers' spatial preferences', *RSA Papers*, 42, 1979; 4. 'Fuzzy economic spaces', *Document de Travail, IME*, 43, 1980; 5. 'L'équilibre spatial du consommateur dans un contexte imprécis', *Sistemi Urbani*, 3(1), 1981.

PORTES, Richard

Born 1941, Chicago, Ill., USA.
Current Post Prof. Econ., 1972–, Head Dept., Birkbeck Coll., Univ. London.
Recent Posts Fellow, tutor Econ., Balliol Coll., Univ. Oxford, 1965–9; Ass. prof. Econ. Internat. Affairs, Princeton Univ., 1969–72; Co-dir., Centre d'Economie Quantitative Comparative, EHESS, Paris, 1978–.
Degrees BA Yale Univ., 1962; MA, DPhil. Univ. Oxford, 1965, 1969.
Offices and Honours Member, AEA, RES, Council Foreign Relations, Em Soc, Royal Inst. Internat. Affairs; Rhodes Scholarship; Ed. Board, *REStud*, 1967–9, 1972–80, *J Comparative Econ.*, 1980–; Vis. prof., Inst. Internat. Econ. Stud., Univ. Stockholm, 1973, 1974, 1976, 1978, Harvard Univ., 1977–8; Guggenheim Memorial Foundation Fellow, 1977–8; BA Overseas Vis. Fellow, 1977–8; Res. assoc., NBER, 1980–.
Principal Contributions Analysis of enterprise behaviour under central planning; developing macro-economic theory of closed and open centrally planned economies; macro-econometrics of labour market, consumption goods market and foreign trade under central planning; assessment of economic reforms in CPEs and of East-West economic and financial relations; analysis of macro-economic models with quantity rationing and inventories; and hypothesis testing with disequilibrium estimation methods.
Publications *Books:* 1. *Planning and Marketing Relations*, ed. (with M. Kaser), (Macmillan, 1971); 2. *The Polish Crisis: Western Economic Policy Options* (Royal Inst. Internat. Affairs, 1981).
Articles: 1. 'The enterprise under central planning', *REStud*, 36, April 1969; 2. 'The strategy and tactics of economic decentralisation', *Soviet Stud.*, 23(4), April 1972; 3. 'The control of inflation: lessons from East European experience', *Ec*; 44, May 1977, repr. in *Comparative Economic Systems*, ed. M. Bornstein (Richard D. Irwin, 1978); 4. 'Macroeconomic models with quantity rationing' (with J. Muellbauer), *EJ*, 88, Dec. 1978; 5. 'Disequilibrium estimates for consumption goods markets in centrally planned economies' (with D. Winter), *REStud*, 47(1), Jan. 1980.

POSNER, Richard A.

Born 1939, USA.
Current Post Lee Brena Freman Prof. Law, Univ. Chicago Law School, USA.
Degrees BA Yale Univ., 1959; LLB Harvard Univ., 1962.
Offices Amer. Laws Inst.; Amer. Bar Assoc.; NBER.
Principal Contributions Use of economic theory to explain the common law; economic analysis of antitrust law; and economic analysis of the state.
Publications *Books:* 1. *Economic Analysis of Law* (Little, Brown Co., 1973, 1977); 2. *Antitrust Law: An Economic Perspective* (Univ. Chicago Press, 1976); 3. *The Economics of Justice* (Harvard Univ. Press, 1981).
Articles: 1. 'Taxation by regulation', *Bell JE*, 2(1), Spring 1971; 2. 'A theory of negligence', *J Legal Stud.*, 1(1), Jan. 1972; 3. 'The social costs of monopoly and regulation', *JPE*, 83(4), Aug. 1975.

POSTLETHWAYT, Malachy*

Dates and Birthplace 1707–67, England.
Posts Held Businessman.

Career Writer on British trade, and the means for improving it, who is chiefly remarkable for the way in which his books conveyed, without acknowledgement, Cantillon's unknown ideas to a British readership. *The Universal Dictionary* ... though in large part a translation from the French of Savary des Bruslons, was a successful compendium of practical information for eighteenth-century merchants.

Publications *Books:* 1. *The African Trade* (1745); 2. *The National and Private Advantage of the African Trade Considered* (1746); 3. *The Universal Dictionary of Trade and Commerce* (1751); 4. *Great Britain's True System* (1757).

Secondary Literature E.A.J. Johnson, 'Malachy Postlethwayt', in *Predecessors of Adam Smith* (1937).

PREBISCH, Raúl

Born 1901, Tucumán, Argentina.
Current Post Dir., CEPAL Review, UNECLA, Santiago, Chile, 1976–.
Recent Posts Exec. sec., UNECLA, 1950–63; Sec.-Gen., UNCTAD, 1963–9.
Degrees BA (Econ.) Univ. Buenos Aires; *Hon. causa* degrees: Univs. Columbia Los Andes, Colombia; Penjab, India; Bar Ilan, Israel; Complutense, Spain; Montevideo, Edinburgh.
Offices and Honours Jawaharlal Nehru award Internat. Understanding, 1974; Dag Hammarskjold hon. medal German UN Assoc., 1977; Third World prize, Third World Foundation, 1981.
Principal Contributions The development of the countries of the world economic periphery, particularly those of Latin America, both in the field of theory and in that of the implementation of ideas. In theory, propounded original interpretations respecting relations between the industrial centres and the periphery and the specific internal processes which characterise the development of the latter; proposals for action have had great influence, in particular these relating to the creation of the New International Economic Order.
Publications *Books:* 1. *Introducción a Keynes*, ed. (Fondo de Cultura Económica, 1947); 2. *Una Nueva Politica Commercial Para el Desarrollo* (Fondo de Cultura Económica, 1964); 3. *Transformación y Desarrollo* (Fondo de Cultura Económica, 1965); 4. *Interpretación del Proceso de Desarrollo Latino-Americano en 1949*, UN Serie conmemorativa del XXV Aniversario de la CEPAL, Santiago, (UN, 1973), and in *Estudio Económico de América Latina, 1949* (1950); 5. *Capitalismo Periférico. Crisis y Transformación* (Fondo de Cultural Económica, 1981).
Articles: 1. 'Commercial policy in the underdeveloped countries', *AER/S*, 49, May 1959; 2. 'El desarrollo económico della América Latina y algunos de sus principales problemas', *Boletín Económico América Latina*, 7(1), Feb. 1962.

PREOBRAZHENSKI, Evgeni*

Dates and Birthplace 1886–1937, Russia.
Career Participant in the Soviet economic debate of the late 1920s. He was a leading spokesman of the left-wing opposition, and his writings, though often concerned with particular current issues, contain insights of high quality. His starting point was the 'goods famine' of 1925 which he explained in terms of fundamental flaws in the running of the Soviet economy. He favoured a high rate of economic expansion at the expense of the agricultural sector. The defeat of his viewpoint led inevitably to his disappearance in the purges of the 1930s.
Publications *Books:* 1. *Novaia Ekonomika* (1926); 2. *Zakat Kapitalizma* (1931).
Secondary Literature A. Erlich, 'Preobrazhenski and the economics of Soviet industrialization', *QJE*, 64, Feb. 1950.

PREST, Alan Richmond

Born 1919, York, England.
Current Post Prof. Econ. (with special reference to Public Sector), LSE.
Recent Posts Lecturer Econ., Univ. Camb., 1949–64; Prof. Econ., Univ. Manchester, 1964–70.

Degrees BA, MA, PhD Univ. Camb., 1940, 1944, 1948; MSc (Econ.) Univ. Manchester, 1967.

Offices Pres., Section F. BAAS, 1967.

Principal Contributions Publications in fields of public finance and related subjects, mainly of an applied character.

Publications *Books:* 1. *Public Finance in Theory and Practice* (Weidenfeld & Nicolson, 1960; with N.A. Barr, 1979); 2. *Public Finance in Developing Countries* (Weidenfeld & Nicolson, 1962, 1972; 3. *Self Assessment for Income Tax* (with N.A. Barr and S.R. James), (Heinemann, 1977); 4. *Intergovernmental Fiscal Relations in the UK* (Australian National Univ. Press, 1978); 5. *The Taxation of Urban Land* (Manchester Univ. Press, 1981).

Articles: 1. 'National income of the United Kingdom', *EJ*, 58, March 1948; 2. 'The expenditure tax and saving', *EJ*, 69, Sept. 1959; 3. 'Cost-benefit analysis: a survey' (with R. Turvey), *EJ*, 75, Dec. 1965; repr. in RES and AEA, *Surveys of Economic Theory* vol. 3 (Macmillan, St Martin's Press, 1966); 4. 'The budget and interpersonal distribution', *PF*, 23(1–2), 1968; 5. 'The structure and reform of direct taxtion', *EJ*, 89, June 1979.

PROUDHON, Pierre Joseph*

Dates and Birthplace 1809–65, Besançon, France.

Posts Held Printer and political writer.

Career Socialist writer whose doctrine 'property is theft' is self-explanatory. He believed that the current forms of the state had to be replaced by a mutualist organisation of the economy which included free credit and the exchange of services; society would then become a federation of territorial and occupational groups. One of Marx's earliest publications, *The Poverty of Philosophy* (1847), is a polemic against Proudhon.

Publications *Books:* 1. *What is Property?* (1840); 2. *Du principe fédératif* (1863); 3. *De la capacité politique des classes ouvrières* (1865); 4. *Oeuvres complètes*, 20 vols (1923–).

Secondary Literature M. Prélot, 'Proudhon, Pierre Joseph', *IESS*, vol. 12.

PRYOR, Frederic L.

Born 1933, Owusso, Mich., USA.

Current Post Prof. Econ., Swarthmore Coll., Penn., USA.

Degrees BA (Chemistry) Oberlin Coll., 1955; PhD (Econ.) Yale Univ., 1962.

Principal Contributions The empirical and theoretical comparison of economic systems, in which two basic questions inform such analyses: what are the causal forces underlying the origin and development of different economic institutions? And what is the impact of such different economic institutions on the performance of the economy?

Publications *Books:* 1. *The Communist Foreign Trade System* (A & U, 1963); 2. *Public Expenditures in Communist and Capitalist Nations* (A & U, 1968); 3. *Property and Industrial Organization in Communist and Capitalist Nations* (Indiana Univ. Press, 1973); 4. *The Origins of the Economy: A Comparative Study of Distribution in Primitive and Peasant Economies* (Academic Press, 1977).

Q

QUANDT, Richard E.

Born 1930, Budapest, Hungary.

Current Post Hughes-Rogers Prof. Econ., Princeton Univ., USA.

Recent Posts Prof., 1964–, Chairman, Dept. Econ., 1968–71, Princeton Univ.

Degrees BA Princeton Univ., 1952; MA, PhD Harvard Univ., 1955, 1957.

Offices and Honours Guggenheim Memorial Foundation Fellow, 1958–9; Member, AEA, SEA, WEA; Fellow, Em Soc. 1968, ASA, 1979; Assoc. ed., *Bell JE, REStat, JASA*, 1974–80, *J Reg S*, 1973–9, *Em*, 1975–80.

Principal Contributions Development of stochastic utility theory; development of abstract mode model of transport demand; switching regression models; development of optimisation algorithms; development of non-linear estimation; econometrics of disequilibrium and quantity rationing models; game against nature approach to securities option markets; and statistical analysis of linear programming solution methods.

Publications *Books:* 1. *Microeconomic Theory: A Mathematical Approach* (with J.M. Henderson), (McGraw-Hill, 1958, 1980); 2. *Strategies and Rational Decisions in the Securities Option Market* (with B.J. Malkiel), (MIT Press, 1969); 3. *The Demand for Travel*, ed. (D.C. Heath & Co., 1970); 4 *Nonlinear Methods in Econometrics* (with S.M. Goldfeld), (N-H, 1972); 5. *Studies in Nonlinear Estimation* (with S.M. Goldfeld), (Ballinger, 1976).

Articles: 1. 'A probabilistic theory of consumer behavior', *QJE*, 70, Nov. 1956; 2. 'The estimation of the parameters of a linear regression system obeying two separate regimes', *JASA*, 53, June 1958; 3. 'Estimation of modal splits', *Transportation Science*, 2, 1968; 4. 'A new approach to estimating switching regressions', *JASA*, 67, June, 1972; 5. 'A comparison of methods for testing non-nested hypotheses', *REStat*, 56 (1), Feb. 1974.

QUESNAY, François*

Dates and Birthplace 1694–1774, Méré, France.

Posts Held Doctor; Consulting physician to Louis XV.

Career The founder of the physiocratic school, he did not write on economics until he was in his sixties. His two *Encyclopédie* articles introduced the characteristic argument that only agriculture could produce a 'produit net'. Despite his position close to the seat of power, he wrote articles critical of the regime, some of which were collected in *Physiocratie*. Arguing from a concept of natural laws, in effect a description of the elements of a free enterprise system, he developed a version of society in which a strong mon-

arch regulates affairs so that the natural order of things can operate freely. Because farmers and landowners were considered the truly productive classes in the physiocratic system, there was a counterbalancing disregard for the contributions of the merchant and industrialist. The criticism of privileged and unproductive groups, which were closely associated with the monarchy as it existed, was what made physiocracy a somewhat subversive doctrine. His *Tableau économique* was first hailed by Marx, and has since come to be regarded as a crude version of input-output analysis, pointing towards general equilibrium theory.

Publications *Books:* 1. *Tableau économique* (1758, 1972); 2. *La Physiocratie*, 2 vols (1768); 3. *Oeuvres économiques et philosophiques* (1888).

Articles: 1. 'Fermiers', *Encyclopédie*, 6, 1756; 2. 'Grains', *Encyclopédie*, 7, 1957.

Secondary Literature R.L. Meek, *The Economics of Physiocracy* (Harvard Univ. Press, 1963); B.F. Hoselitz, 'Quesnay, François', *IESS*, vol. 13.

R

RADNER, Roy

Born 1927, Chicago, Ill., USA.

Current Post Member, Technical Staff, Bell Laboratories, Murray Hill, NJ, USA.

Recent Posts Ass. prof., Cowles Commission, Univ. Chicago, 1954–5; Ass. prof. Econ., Res. assoc., Cowles Foundation, Yale Univ., 1955–7; Assoc. prof., Prof. Econ. Stats, Univ. Cal., Berkeley, 1957–79.

Degrees PhB, BS (Maths), MS (Maths), PhD (Math. Stats) Univ. Chicago, 1945, 1950, 1951, 1956.

Offices and Honours Member, AEA; Inst., Math. Stats; Amer. Assoc. Advancement Science; Fellow, Center Advanced Study Behavioral Sciences, 1955–6; Guggenheim Memorial Foundation Fellow, 1961–2, 1965–6; Overseas Fellow, Churchill Coll., Univ. Camb., 1969–70; AAAS, 1970; Vice-pres., Pres̀., Em Soc, 1971–3; NAS,

1975; Commission Human Resources, 1976–9; Assembly, Behavioral Social Science, Nat. Res. Council, USA, 1979–.

Principal Contributions Contributions to the theory of decision making in decentralised organisations: the theory of teams (developed with J. Marschak); game-theoretic analyses of incentives for efficient decision-making in long-lasting organisations; bounded rationality; and existence and optimality of market equilibria under uncertainty including equilibria with private information, equilibrium of plans, prices, and price-expectations, and rational expectations equilibrium. Characterisation of optimal investment strategies: optimal capital accumulation under certainty (turnpike theory) and uncertainty; and optimal strategies for inspection and maintenance of stochastically failing equipment. Empirical studies of demand and supply in higher education.

Publications *Books:* 1. *Optimal Replacement Policy* (with D.W. Jorgenson and J.J. McCall), (N-H, Rand-McNally, 1967); 2. *Decision and Organization* (with C.B. McGuire), (N-H, 1972); 3. *Economics Theory of Teams* (with J. Marschak), (Yale Univ. Press, 1972); 4. *Demand and Supply in US Higher Education* (with L.S. Miller), (McGraw-Hill, 1975); 5. *Mathematicians in Academia* (with C.V. Kuh), (Conference Board Math. Sciences, 1980).

Articles: 1. 'Paths of economic growth that are optimal with regard only to final states: a "turnpike theorem"', *REStud*, 28, Feb. 1961; 2. Equilibre des marchés à terme et au comptant en cas d'incertitude', *Cahiers d'Econometrie*, 9, 1967; 3. 'Satisficing', *J Math E*, 2, 1975; 4. 'Monitoring cooperative agreements in a repeated principal-agent relationship', *Em*, 49(5), Sept. 1981; 5. 'Equilibrium under uncertainty', in *Handbook of Mathematical Economics*, eds K.J. Arrow and M. Intriligator (N-H, 1981).

RAE, John*

Dates and Birthplace 1796–1872, Scotland.

Posts Held Schoolmaster in Canada, California and Hawaii.

Career Though working in near complete isolation, he succeeded in creating a theory of capital to which Böhm-Bawerk and others were indebted; in his lifetime some small recognition from J.S. Mill was almost the only notice he obtained. In addition to his capital theory, he discussed the formation of saving, the importance of inventions, and the role of government in redirecting money from luxury expenditure into education, and other forms of public expenditure.

Publications *Books:* 1. *Statement of Some New Principles on the Subject of Political Economy* (1834).

Secondary Literature R.W. James, *John Rae, Political Economist*, 2 vols (Univ. of Toronto Press, 1965); J.J. Spengler, 'Rae, John', *IESS*, vol 13.

RAMSAY, George*

Dates and Birthplace 1800–71, Banff, Scotland.

Post Held Landowner.

Degrees BA, MA Univ. Camb., 1823, 1826.

Career Though an isolated and uninfluential figure, Ramsay's *Essay ...* shows an unusually good grasp of contemporary French economic thought. His grasp of the distinction between capitalist and entrepreneur ('master') is particularly strong.

Publications *Books:* 1. *Essay on the Distribution of Wealth* (1836).

Secondary Literature J.S. Prybyla, 'The economic writings of George Ramsay, 1800–1871', *SJPE*, 10, Nov. 1963.

RAMSEY, Frank Plumpton*

Dates and Birthplace 1903–30, Cambridge, England.

Post Held Fellow, Kings Coll., Univ. Camb.

Degree BA Univ. Camb., 1923.

Career In a short but fruitful life he made major contributions to mathematical logic and philosophy. From his undergraduate days, Cambridge economists had tested their theories against his logical abilities and in his two published papers he showed analytical ability of the highest level. Keynes regarded his 1928 article as 'one of the most remarkable contributions to mathematical economics ever made'.

Publications *Books:* 1. *Foundations of Mathematics and Other Essays* (ed. R.B. Braithwaite) (1931).

Articles: 1. 'A contribution to the theory of taxation', *EJ*, 37, March 1927 repr. in *Precursors in Mathematical Economics: An Anthology*, eds. W.J. Baumol and S.M. Goldfeld (LSE, 1968); 2. 'A mathematical theory of saving', *EJ*, 38, Dec. 1928.

Secondary Literature J.M. Keynes, 'F.P. Ramsey', *Essays in Biography* (Macmillan, 1933, 1972).

RANIS, Gustav

Born 1929, Darmstadt, Germany.

Current Post Prof. Econ., Yale Univ., USA, 1964–.

Recent Posts Ass. Admin. Program, US Agency Internat. Development, 1965–7; Dir., Econ. Growth Center, Yale Univ., 1967–75.

Degrees BA Brandeis Univ., 1952; MA, PhD Yale Univ., 1953, 1956.

Offices US SSRC Fellow, Japan, 1955–6; Member, Board Trustees, Brandeis Univ., 1968–; Member, Council Foreign Relations, 1969–; Ford Foundation Faculty Fellow, Mexico, 1971–2; Ford Foundation supported Vis. prof., Colombia, 1976–7.

Principal Contributions Overall theory of development with particular reference to the labour-surplus type of developing economy. With John Fei, responsible in opening up a major area of theoretical and policy research relevant to a large family of developing countries. Recent work on a rigorous formulation of the relationship between growth and the distribution of income and the likelihood of the existence of real world complementarities or trade-offs among these objectives; the method is based on a linear decomposition of the Gini coefficient, permitting a direct linkage between changes in the distribution of income and such growth-related variables as the functional shares, the relative size of the agricultural and non-agricultural sectors in a dual economy context, saving, education, and other labour-market related phenomena. Relationship between decision-making on fertility at the family level and the distribution of family income.

Publications *Books:* 1. *Development of the Labor Surplus Economy: Theory and Policy* (with J. Fei), (Richard D. Irwin, 1964); 2. *The Gap Between Rich and Poor Nations*, ed. (Macmillan, St Martin's Press, 1972); 3. *Sharing in Development: A Programme of Employment, Equity and Growth for the Philippines*, chief of mission and ed. (ILO, 1974); 4. *Growth with Equity: the Taiwan Case* (with J. Fei and S. Kuo), (OUP, 1979); 5. *Science, Technology and Economic Development: A Historical and Comparative Study*, ed. (with W. Beranek), (Praeger, 1979).

Articles: 1. 'A theory of economic development' (with J. Fei), *AER*, 51, Sept. 1961; 2. 'Investment criteria, productivity and economic development: an empirical comment', *QJE*, 76, May 1962; 3. 'Production functions, market imperfections and economic development', *EJ*, 72, June 1962; 4. 'Growth and the family distribution of income by factor components' (with J. Fei and S. Kuo), *QJE*, 42, Feb. 1978, reprinted in *El Trimestre Economico*, July 1980; 5. 'Equity with growth in Taiwan: how "special" is the "special case"?', *WD*, 6(2), March 1978.

RAU, Karl Heinrich*

Dates and Birthplace 1792–1870, Germany.

Posts Held Prof., Univ. Erlangen, 1816–22, Univ. Heidelberg, 1822.

Career The author of the most successful mid-nineteenth-century textbook of economics in Germany. The 3-volume treatment (economic laws, economic policy and public finance) exercised a lasting influence on the structure of German economics teaching. Following the success of the Historical School, his emphasis on classical economic principles caused his reputation to decline.

Publications *Books:* 1. *Ansichten der*

Volkswirtschaft (1821); 2. *Über die Kameralwissenschaft* (1825); 3. *Lehrbuch der Politischen Ökonomie*, 3 vols (1826–37); 4. *Über Beschränkungen der Freiheit in der Volkswirtschaftspflege* (1847).

Secondary Literature K. Pribram, 'Rau, Karl Heinrich', *ESS*, vol 13.

RAYMOND, Daniel*

Dates and Birthplace 1786–1849, Connecticut, USA.

Post Held Lawyer.

Career First American author of formal treatise on political economy. He favoured an element of government intervention, particularly in the case of protective tariffs. On currency, he supported a gold-backed government issue, and strongly opposed the issue of bank notes by private banks. He denounced slavery on both economic and moral grounds and, like many American writers, did not accept Malthus on population.

Publications *Books:* 1. *The Missouri Question* (1819); 2. *Thoughts on Political Economy* (1820), 2nd edn, *The Elements of Political Economy*, 2 vols (1823).

Secondary Literature A.D.H. Kaplan, 'Raymond, Daniel', *ESS*, vol. 13.

READ, Samuel*

Dates and Birthplace N.e.

Career His *Political Economy*, his chief work, led the anti-Ricardian spirit of the times, and bears affinities to the work of Samuel Bailey. The analysis of profit and interest exercised some influence on his contemporaries.

Publications *Books:* 1. *On Money and the Bank Restriction Laws* (1816); 2. *The Problem Solved in the Explication of a Plan of a Safe Steady and Secure Government Paper Currency* (1818); 3. *Exposure of Certain Plagiarisms of J.R. McCulloch* (1819); 4. *General Statement of an Argument on the Subject of Population* (1821); 5. *Political Economy* (1829).

Secondary Literature E.R.A.

Seligman, 'On some neglected British economists, Pts I-II', *EJ*, 13, Sept., Dec. 1903.

REAGAN, Barbara Benton

Born 1920, San Antonio, Texas, USA.

Current Post Prof. Econ., Southern Methodist Univ., Texas, 1967–.

Recent Post Disting. vis. prof. Kenyon Coll., 1978–9.

Degrees BS Univ. Texas, 1941; MA (Stats) Amer. Univ., 1947; PhD (Econ.) Harvard Univ., 1952.

Offices and Honours Phi Beta Kappa; Nat. Advisory Food Drug Council, US Office Health, Education, Welfare, 1968–71; Chair, AEA Comm. Status Women Econ. Profession, 1974–8; Advisory Board, Amer. Council Life Insurance, 1977–; Board Eds, *JEL*, 1977–9; Advisory Comm., White House Conference Balanced Nat. Growth Econ. Development, 1977–8; Advisory Board, Texas Coastal Management Program, 1977–8; Pres., Southwestern Social Science Assoc., 1978–9; Board Dirs, Fed. Home Loan Bank, Little Rock, 1981–.

Principal Contributions Analysed factors affecting women's surge into the labour market, occupational segregation by sex, and labour market discrimination against women. Extended human capital model in examining male-female wage differences, and criticised misuse of residual method of measuring discrimination. Quantified the 'revolving-door' effect on hiring and replacing academic faculty, which is disproportionately greater for women. Analysis of labour migration of Blacks and Mexican Americans emphasised effects of retraining programmes.

Publications *Books:* 1. *Women in the Workplace: Implications of Occupational segregation*, co-ed. (Univ. Chicago Press, 1976); 2. *Issues in Federal Statistical Needs Relating to Women*, ed. (US Bureau Census, 1979); 3. *Economic Foundations of Women in the Labor Force* (1981).

Articles: 1. 'Condensed versus detailed schedule in expenditure surveys', *Agric. Econ. Res.*, 6(2), 1954; 2. 'Sex discrimination in universities: an approach through internal labor market analysis', *AAUP Bull*, March 1974; 3. 'Two supply curves for economists? Implications of mobility and career attachment of women', *AER*, 67(2), May 1975; 4. *'De facto* job segregation', in *American Women Workers in a Full Employment Economy*, US Congress, Joint Econ. Comm. (US Govt Printing Office, 1977); 5. 'Stocks and flows of academic economists', *AER*, 69(2), May 1979.

RECKTENWALD, Horst Claus

Born 1920, Spiesen, Germany.
Current Post Prof. Econ., Dir. Inst. für Volkswirtschaftslehre, Friedrich-Alexander-Univ. Erlangen-Nürnberg, W. Germany.
Recent Posts Dean Faculty, 1965; Rector Univ., 1968; Pres. Wirtschafts- und Sozialwissenschaftlichen Fakultätentag, 1969–73.
Degrees Dr rer. pol., Venia legendi Univ. Mainz, 1954, 1957.
Offices and Honours Pres. Inst. Internat. Fin. Publiques, Paris; Member Board Dirs, Internat. Inst. Management Verwaltung, Berlin; Member, Advisory Councils Bundesministerien; Member, Foundation Council New Univ. Regensburg, Augsburg, Munich (Hochschule der Bundeswehr) and Passau; Award for *Tax Incidence and Income Redistribution*, 'Outstanding academic book', USA, 1972; Order Fed. Republic Germany (Bundesverdienstkreuz First class), 1976.
Principal Contributions Methodological and analytical aspects of tax shifting and incidence; analytical and empirical research on income redistribution; concepts of cost-benefit analysis; anatomy and causes of R- and Q-Inefficiency in the public sector. Research on Adam Smith's works and translation of *Wealth of Nations* into German.
Publications *Books:* 1. *Steuerinzidenztheorie* (Duncker & Humblot, 1958); 2. *Nutzen-Kosten-Analyse und Programmbudget* (Mohr-Siebeck, 1970); 3. *Tax Incidence and Income Redistribution* (Wayne State Univ. Press, 1971); 4. *Political Economy*

(Macmillan, 1973); 5. *Markt und Staat* (Vandenhoeck & Ruprecht, 1979).
Articles: 1. 'Effizienz und Innere Sicherheit', *Kyklos*, 20(2), 1967; 2. 'Zur Lehre von den Marktformen', *WA*, 67(2), reprinted in *Preistheorie*, ed. A.E. Ott (Cologne, 1968); 3. 'Grundlagen einer Integrierten Wirtschafts- une Finanzpolitik', *ZN*, 29, repr. in *Finanzpolitik*, ed. H.C. Recktenwald (Duncker & Humblot, 1969); 4. 'Staatsausgaben in Säkularer Sicht – Versuch einer Beschreibung', in *Theorie und Praxis des Finanzpolitischen Interventionismus, Festschrift für Fritz Neumark*, eds H. Haller *et al.* (Mohr-Siebeck, 1970); 5. 'An Adam Smith renaissance anno 1976? A reappraisal of his scholarship', *JEL*, 16(1), 1978.

REDDAWAY, W. Brian

Born 1913, Cambridge, England.
Current Post Retired.
Recent Posts Lecturer, Univ. Camb., 1939–55; Statistician, Board of Trade, UK, 1941–7; Econ. Dir., OEEC, Paris, 1951–2; Dir., Dept Applied Econ., 1955–70, Prof. Polit. Econ., 1969–80, Univ. Camb.
Degrees BA, MA Univ. Camb., 1934, 1938.
Offices Fellow, BA, 1967; Member, Nat. Board Prices and Incomes, 1967–71; CBE, 1971; Ed., *EJ*, 1971–6.
Principal Contributions Attempts to bring together theory and practice and to distinguish what is really important in practical problems.
Publications *Books:* 1. *Russian Financial System* (Macmillan, 1935); 2. *Measurement of Production Movements* (CUP, 1948, 1965); 3. *Development of the Indian Economy* (A & U, 1962); 4. *Effects of UK direct investment overseas*, 2 vols (CUP, 1967, 1968); 5. *Effects of the Selective Employment Tax*, 2 vols (CUP, HMSO, 1970, 1973).
Articles: 1. 'General theory of employment, interest and money', *ER*, 12, June 1936; 2. 'Wage flexibility and the distribution of labour', *LBR*, 54, Oct. 1959; 3. 'The economics of under-developed countries', *EJ*, 73, March 1963; 4. 'Rising prices for ever?', *LBR*, 81, July 1966;

5. 'Can Mrs Thatcher do it?', *MBR*, 62, Autumn 1980.

REDER, Melvin W.

Born 1919, San Francisco, Cal., USA.
Current Post Isidore and Gladys Brown Prof. Urban Labor Econ., Univ. Chicago, 1974–.
Recent Posts Prof. Econ., Stanford Univ.; Disting. prof. Econ., Grad. Center, City Univ. New York, 1971–4.
Degrees BA Univ. Cal., Berkeley, 1939; PhD Columbia Univ., 1946.
Offices AEA.
Principal Contributions Incompatibility of assuming parametric prices simultaneously with a dynamic price adjustment mechanism to excess demand; showed (with G.R. Neumann) that strikes vary inversely with intertemporal substitutability of output; and showed that cyclical variability of skill differentials was related to variations in living standards.
Publications *Books:* 1. *Studies in the Theory of Welfare Economics* (Columbia Univ. Press, 1947); 2. *Labor in a Growing Economy* (Wiley, 1957). *Articles:* 1. 'The theoretical problems of a national wage-price policy', *CJE*, 14, Feb. 1948; 2. 'The theory of union wage policy', *REStat*, 34, Feb. 1952; 3. 'The theory of occupational wage differentials', *AER*, 45(5), Dec. 1955; 4. 'Job scarcity and the nature of union power', *ILRR*, 13, April 1960; 5. 'Conflict and contract: the case of strikes' (with G.R. Neumann), *JPE*, 88(5), Oct. 1980.

REES, Albert

Born 1921, New York City, NY, USA.
Current Post Pres., Alfred P. Sloan Foundation, New York.
Recent Post Prof. Econ., Princeton Univ., 1966–79.
Degrees BA Oberlin Coll., 1943; MA, PhD Univ. Chicago, 1947, 1950.
Principal Contributions Contributed to the understanding of the influence of trade unions on wages, the sources of wage differences within occupations, and the historical measurement of changes in real wages. Also participated in one of the first uses of experimental methods to measure economic behaviour.
Publications 1. *Real Wages in Manufacturing, 1890–1914* (Princeton Univ. Press, 1961); 2. *The Economics of Trade Unions* (Univ. Chicago Press, 1962, 1977); 3. *Workers and Wages in an Urban Labor Market* (with G.P. Schultz), (Univ. Chicago Press, 1970); 4. *The Economics of Work and Pay* (Harper & Row, 1973, 1979).

REIFFERS, Jean-Louis

Born 1941, Paris, France.
Current Post Prof., Dir. du Centre d'Econ. et des Finances Internationales, Univ. d'Aix-Marseille, France.
Recent Posts Doyen, Faculté des Sciences Econ. 1973–6; Doyen honoraire 1977; Dir., Conseil scientifique de la Faculté des Sciences Econ., Univ. d'Aix-Marseille, 1979–81.
Degrees Licence ès Sciences Econ., Diplome d'Etudes Supérieures Sciences Econ., Dr d'Etat, Faculté de Droit et des Sciences Econ., Univ. d'Aix-Marseille 1964, 1965, 1969; Agrégation de Sciences Econ. et de Gestion Concours National, Paris, 1970.
Offices Pres., Groupe d'Aix; Member, Conseil d'Administration, Vicepres. chargé de la recherche, Bureau Méridional de Planification Agricole, 1976–; Member, Comité Scientifique des Editions Dunod en Economie, 1977–; Member, Comité de Direction de la *Revue Mondes en Développement*, 1981; Correspondant, *RE*.
Principal Contributions The analysis of Customs Union by application to EEC; analysis of the effect of immigrant workers on growth in the Federal German Republic; links between the international specialisation of France, US, GDR, Japan. More generally, economic and sociological analysis of the capacity of a nation to develop a specific path to take advantage of the international division of labour.
Publications *Books:* 1. *L'Union douanière européenne et l'avantage col-*

lectif mondial, diffusée avec le concours de la Commission de la CEE (Thèse d'Etat), (Univ. d'Aix-Marseille, 1969); 2. *Le Rôle de l'immigration des travailleurs étrangers dans la croissance de la République Fédérale Allemande* (BIT, 1970); 3. *L'Occident en désarroi, ruptures d'un système économique* (with X. Greffe), (Dunod, 1978); 4. *Activités des sociétés transnationales et développement endogine: effets sur la culture, les communications, l'éducation, la science et la technologie* (with A. Cartadanis *et al.*), (UNESCO, 1981).

Articles: 1. 'Réflexions sur le paradoxe de léontief', *Econ App*, 25(1), 1972; 2. 'Les difficultés de méthode liées à l'explication des flux d'investissements directs à l'étranger', *Revue monde en développement*, Dec. 1974; 3. 'Effets de la structuration du système productif sur l'emploi en Côte d'Ivoire' (with J. Brossier and D. Peguin), (BIT, 1980); 4. 'Insertion dans la DIT et espace social du travail', *Revue Economie Industrielle*, 4, 1980; 5. 'Division internationale du travail et qualification: une comparaison France-Allemagne' (with A. Lebahar), in *Economie internationale: la recherche en France*, ed. J-L. Reiffers (Dunod, 1981).

REYNOLDS, Lloyd G.

Born 1910, Alberta, Canada.

Current Post Sterling prof. Econ., Yale Univ., USA.

Recent Posts Instructor Econ., Harvard Univ., 1936–9; Ass. prof. Econ., Johns Hopkins Univ., 1939–45.

Degrees BA, Hon. LLD Univ. Alberta, 1931, 1957; MA McGill Univ., 1933; PhD Harvard Univ., 1936; Hon. MA Yale Univ., 1948.

Offices Exec. Comm., 1952–5, Vice-pres., 1959, AEA; Pres., IRRA, 1955.

Principal Contributions Price theory; the theory of labour markets and wage determination; the applicability of western economic theory to centrally planned economies and developing economies; and development theory and development experience.

Publications *Books:* 1. *The Struc-*

ture of Labor Markets (Harper & Bros., 1951); 2. *The Evolution of Wage Structure* (with C.T. Morris), (Yale Univ. Press, 1956); 3. *The Three Worlds of Economics* (Yale Univ. Press, 1972); 4. *Agriculture in Development Theory* (Yale Univ. Press, 1975); 5. *Image and Reality in Economic Development* (Yale Univ. Press, 1977).

RICARDO, David*

Dates and Birthplace 1772–1823, London, England.

Posts Held Stockjobber and loan contractor, 1793–1814; Country landowner, 1814–23.

Offices Founder member, Geological Soc.; MP for Portarlington, Ireland, 1819–23; Founder of the Polit. Econ. Club, 1821.

Career Successor to Adam Smith's pre-eminent position in British economics, his influence continued to dominate the aims and methods of the discipline throughout the nineteenth century. Despite his own considerable practical experience, his writings are severely abstract and frequently difficult. His chief emphasis was on the principle of diminishing returns in connection with the rent of land, which he believed also regulated the profits of capital. He attempted to deduce a theory of value from the application of labour, but found it difficult to separate the effects of changes in distribution from changes in technology. The questions thus raised about the labour theory of value were taken up by Marx and the so-called 'Ricardian socialists' as a theoretical basis for criticism of established institutions. Ricardo's law of rent was probably his most notable and influential discovery. It was based on the observation that the differing fertility of land yielded unequal profits to the capital and labour applied to it. Differential rent is the result of this variation in the fertility of land. This principle was also noted at much the same time by Malthus, West, Anderson, and others. His other great contribution, the law of comparative cost, or comparative advantage, demonstrated the benefits of international specialisation, while furnishing an explanation of the commodity composition of international trade. This was at the root of the free trade argument which set Britain firmly on the course of exporting manufactures and importing foodstuffs. His success in attaching other economists, particularly James Mill and McCulloch, to his views largely accounted for the remarkable dominance of his ideas long after his own lifetime. Though much of this was eventually rejected, his abstract method and much of the theoretical content of his work became the framework for economic science at least until the 1870s.

Publications *Books:* 1. *The High Price of Bullion* (1810); 2. *Essay on the Influence of a Low Price of Corn on the Profits of Stock* (1814); 3. *On the Principles of Political Economy and Taxation* (1817); 4. *On Protection to Agriculture* (1822); 5. *Plan for the Establishment of a National Bank* (1824); 6. *David Ricardo: Works and Correspondence*, 11 vols, eds. P. Sraffa and M.H. Dobb (CUP, 1951–73).

Secondary Literature M. Blaug, *Ricardian economics. A historical study* (Greenwood Press, 1973); M. Blaug, 'Ricardo, David', *IESS*, vol. 13.

RICCI, UMBERTO*

Dates and Birthplace 1879–1946, Chieti, Italy.

Posts Held Statistician, Internat. Inst. Agric., 1910; Prof., Univs Macerta, Parma, Pisa, Bologna, Rome (1924–8), Cairo (1929–40) and Istanbul (1942–6).

Career Beginning his career as an administrator he rose, via his work on agricultural economics, to become a major theoretician. He wrote on capital, supply and demand curves, theory of wants, savings and taxation, and dealt with applied economics in various journals. One of these articles was the immediate cause of the Fascist government depriving him of his Rome Chair.

Publications *Books:* 1. *Reddito e Imposta* (1914); 2. *Les Bases théoretiques de la statistique agricole internationale* (1914); 3. *Politica ed Economia* (1920); 4. *Dal Protezionismo al Sindacalismo* (1926); 5. *La Politica Annonaria dell'Italia Durante la Grande Guerra* (1939); 6. *Eléments d'économie politique pure: théorie de la valeur* (1951).

Secondary Literature L. Einaudi, 'Obituary: Umberto Ricci', *AER*, 36, Sept. 1946.

RIDKER, Ronald G.

Born 1931, Chicago, Ill., USA.
Current Post Sr economist, World Bank, Washington, DC.
Recent Posts Econ. adviser, Agency Internat. Development, 1966–70; Sr Fellow, Resources for the Future, 1970–80.
Degrees BA Univ. Cal., Berkeley, 1952; MA Fletcher School Law and Diplomacy, 1953; PhD Univ. Wisconsin, 1958.

Principal Contributions Efforts to measure economic costs of environmental damages; development of practical programmes to reduce desired family size in developing countries; and contributions to long-run planning.

Publications *Books:* 1. *Economic Costs of Air Pollution, Studies in Measurement* (Praeger, 1967); 2. *Employment in South Asia: Problems, Prospects, and Prescriptions* (Overseas Development Council, 1971); 3. *Research Reports of the Commission on Population Growth and the American future*, vol. 3, *Population, Resources, and the Environment* (with H.W. Herzog), (US Govt Printing Office, 1972); 4. *Population and Development: The Search for Selective Interventions* (John Hopkins Univ. Press, 1976); 5. *To Choose a Future: Resource and Environmental Consequences of Alternative Growth Paths* (with W.D. Watson), (Johns Hopkins Univ. Press, 1980).

Articles: 1. 'The economic determinants of discontent, an empirical investigation', *J Dev Stud*, 4, Jan. 1968; 2. 'Economic, energy, and environmental consequences of alternative energy regimes, an application of the RFF/SEAS modeling system' (with W. Watson and A. Shapanka), in *Modeling Energy-economic Interaction: Five Approaches*, ed. C. Hitch (Resources for the Future, 1977); 3. 'The effects of slowing population growth on long-run economic growth in the US during the next half century', in *The Economic Consequences of Slowing Population growth*, eds T.J. Espenshade and W.J. Serow (Academic Press, 1978); 4. 'Resource, and environmental consequences of economic growth, 1975–2025', in *World Population and Development: A Look Forward*, ed. P. Hauser (Syracuse Univ. Press,1979); 5. 'The no-birth bonus scheme – an evaluation of the use of savings accounts for family planning in south India', *Population and Development Review*, 1980.

RIST, Charles*

Dates and Birthplace 1874–1955, Lausanne, Switzerland.

Post Held Prof. Polit. Econ., Univs. Montpellier, Paris, 1913–33; Dep. Governor, Bank of France, 1926; Pres., Banque Ottomaine.

Degrees Lic. és Lett., Dr en droit, Univ. Paris.

Offices and Honours Officer, Légion d'Honneur; Pres., Assoc. Française des Sciences, Econ.; Member, Inst. de France.

Career Invited by Charles Gide to co-operate in his history of economics when he succeeded Gide to the Montpellier Chair. In addition to this work, he was also a successful adviser to foreign governments, undertaking financial missions in Romania, Turkey, Spain and Austria.

Publications *Books:* 1. *A History of Economic Doctrines* (with C. Gide), (1915, 1948); 2. *La Déflation en pratique* (1923); 3. *Histoire des doctrines relatives au crédit et la monnaie* (1938); 4. *Précis des mécanisme économique élémentaires* (1946).

Secondary Literature 'Charles Rist: l'homme – la pensée – l'action', *REP*, Nov./Dec. 1955.

RIVLIN, Alice Mitchell

Born 1931, Philadelphia, Penn., USA.

Current Post Dir., US Congressional Budget Office, Washington, DC.

Recent Posts Brookings Inst., 1957–66; Dep. ass. secretary, Ass. secretary, US. Dept Health, Education and Welfare, 1966–9; Sr Fellow, Brookings Inst., 1969–75.

Degrees BA Bryn Mawr Coll., 1952; PhD Radcliffe Coll., Harvard Univ., 1958.

Offices and Honours W.S. Woytinsky lectureship award, Univ. Michigan, 1972; Gladys M. Kammerer award, 1972, Charles E. Merriam award, 1977, Amer. Polit. Science Assoc.; Ely Lecture award, AEA, 1973; Member, Exec. Comm., 1979, Vice-pres., 1981, AEA.

Principal Contributions Academic career devoted to policy analysis of federal budgetary problems in US and two tours of duty in the government, managing analytical staffs devoted to improving the budgetary decision process – principal contribution, the organisation of the Congressional Budget Office to improve the analysis and information available to Congress for budget decisions.

Publications *Books:* 1. *Setting National Priorities*, co-author (Brookings Inst., 1971, 1972, 1973); 2. *Systematic Thinking for Social Action* (Brookings Inst., 1971); 3. *Ethical and Legal Issues of Social Experiments*, co-author (Brookings Inst., 1975); 4. *Income Distribution – Can Economists Help?* (Brookings Inst., 1975); 5. *How Can Experiments be more Useful?* (Brookings Inst., 1976).

ROBBINS, Lionel

Born 1898, Sipson, Middx, England.

Current Post Occasional lecturer Hist. Econ. Thought, LSE.

Recent Posts Prof. Econ., 1929–61, Part-time prof., 1962–7, LSE; Dir., Econ. Section, UK Offices of the War Cabinet, 1941–5; Chairman, *Financial Times*, 1961–70.

Degrees BSc (Econ.), Hon. DSc Univ. London; MA Univ. Oxford; Hon. DLitt Univs. Dunelm, Exeter, Strathclyde, Sheffield, Heriot-Watt; Hon. LHD Univs. Columbia, Pennsylvania; Hon. D Univs. York, Stirling.

Offices and Honours Member, UK

Econ. Advisory Council, 1930–7; Fellow, 1942, Pres., 1962–7, BA; Trustee, Nat. Gallery, 1952–74, Tate Gallery, 1953–9, 1962–7; Pres., RES, 1954–5; Life peer, 1959; Chairman, UK Comm. on Higher Education, 1961–4; Dir., Royal Opera House, 1962–; Member, Chairman, Court Governors, LSE, 1968–74; Chancellor, Stirling Univ., 1968–78.

Principal Contributions The general conception of the nature of economic science and political economy: the economic problem in peace and war; the economic causes of war; and various contributions to the history of economic thought, political economy past and present. Broad outlines of international economic problems – monetary and real.

Publications *Books:* 1. *An Essay on the Nature and Significance of Economic Science* (Macmillan, 1932, 1935, 1969); 2. *The Theory of Economic Policy in English Classical Political Economy* (Macmillan, 1952, 1978); 3. *Robert Torrens and the Evolution of Classical Economics* (Macmillan, 1958); 4. *The Theory of Economic Development in the History of Economic Thought* (Macmillan, 1968); 5. *Autobiography of an Economist* (Macmillan, 1971).

Articles: In 1. *The University in the Modern World* (Macmillan, 1966); 2. *The Evolution of Modern Economic Theory* (Macmillan, 1970); 3. *Political Economy: Past and Present* (Macmillan, 1976); 4. *Higher Education Revisited* (Macmillan, 1980); 5. 'Economics and political economy', *AER*, 71(2), May 1981.

Secondary Literature T.W. Hutchison, 'Robbins, Lionel', *IESS*, vol. 18; M. Peston, 'Lionel Robbins: Methodology, Policy and Modern Theory', *Twelve Contemporary Economists*, eds J.R. Shackleton and G. Locksley (Macmillan, 1981).

ROBERTSON, Dennis Holme*

Dates and Birthplace 1890–1963, Lowestoft, England.

Posts Held Fellow, Trinity Coll., 1914–38, Reader Econ., 1930–8, Prof., 1944–57, Univ. Camb.; Prof. Econ., Univ. London, 1939–44.

Degree MA Univ. Camb.

Offices and Honours Fellow, BA, 1932; Pres., RES, 1948–50; Knighted, 1953.

Career Monetary economist; his work on industrial fluctuations was also very significant. Keynes' pupil and then collaborator, he later became a prominent critic of Keynes' *General Theory*. This did not prevent his return to Cambridge and to the chair of economics, after which he devoted much of his attention to teaching. His major contribution is to the study of business cycles, but his contribution to the development of Keynesian economics, despite his well-known reservations, is also important.

Publications *Books:* 1. *A Study of Industrial Fluctuation* (1915); 2. *Money* (1922); 3. *The Control of Industry* (1923); 4. *Banking Policy and the Price Level* (1926); 5. *Essays in Monetary Theory* (1940); 6. *Britain in the World Economy* (1954); 7. *Growth, Wages, Money* (1961).

Secondary Literature S.R. Dennison, 'Robertson, Dennis Holme', *IESS*, vol. 13; J.R. Presley, *Robertsonian Economics* (Macmillan, 1979).

ROBERTSON, Hector Menteith

Born 1905, Leeds, England.

Current Post Emeritus Prof. Econ., Univ. Cape Town, SA.

Recent Posts Jagger Prof. Econ., Univ. Cape Town, 1950–70; Vis. prof. Econ. Hist., Univ. Melbourne, 1956, 1971.

Degrees BA, MA Univ. Leeds, 1925, 1926; PhD Univ. Camb., 1929.

Offices and Honours Gladstone Memorial prize, 1925; Member, 1927–, Corresp. S. Africa, 1953–, RES; Member, EHS, 1927–; Member, 1930–, Pres., 1950–2, Hon. life member, 1975–, Econ. Soc. S. Africa; Ellen McArthur prize, Univ. Camb., 1932; Member, Econ. Hist. Assoc., 1942–; Joint ed., *SAJE*, 1947–75.

Principal Contributions Lecturing – predominantly in history of economic thought and economic history (particularly S. African). Much remains unpublished, especially studies of 17th–18th centuries economic problems in the Cape as visualised or reported by Dutch East India Company officials. Principal writings on critiques of theories linking economic developments with religious dogmas; interpretations of the classical economists; and studies of economic developments in South Africa.

Publications *Books:* 1. *Aspects of the Rise of Economic Individualism* (CUP, 1933, Augustus M. Kelley, 1968); 2. *South Africa, Economic and Political Aspects* (Duke Univ. Press, 1937); 3. *The Adam Smith Tradition: Inaugural Lecture* (OUP, Cape Town, 1950).

Articles: 1. '150 years of economic contact between Black and White, Pts I-II', *SAJE*, 2, Dec. 1934, 3, March, 1935; 2. 'Economic development of the Cape under Van Riebeeck, Pts I-IV', *SAJE*, 13, March, June, Sept., Dec. 1945; 3. 'Adam Smith's approach to the theory of value' (with W.L. Taylor), *EJ*, 67, June 1957; 4. 'Alfred Marshall's aims and methods illustrated from his treatment of distribution', *HOPE*, 2(1), Spring 1970; 5. 'Euge! Belle! Dear Mr. Smith: *The Wealth of Nations* 1776–1976', *SAJE*, 44, 1976.

ROBINSON, Edward Austin Gossage

Born 1897, Farnham, England.
Current Post Emeritus Prof. Econ., Univ. Camb.
Recent Posts Econ. section, War Cabinet Office, 1939–42; Econ. adviser, Head Programme Div., UK Ministry Production, 1942–5; Econ. adviser, UK Board Trade, 1946; Econ. planning staff, UK Treasury, 1947–8; Prof. Econ., Univ. Camb., 1950–66; Dir. econ., UK Ministry of Power, 1967–8.
Degree MA Univ. Camb., 1922.
Offices Ed., *EJ*, 1934–70; Secretary RES, 1944–70; Chairman Council, NIESR, 1949–62; Treasurer, 1950–9, Pres., 1959–62, IEA; Ed., IEA Publications, 1950–79.
Principal Contributions Early work in the field of the structure of industry and the basis of monopoly power. After

World War II, principally concerned with the applied problems of development economics, especially in Africa and Asia.
Publications *Books:* 1. *The Structure of Competitive Industry* (Nisbet, 1931); 2. Lord Hailey, *African Survey*, contributor (Macmillan, 1937); 3. *Monopoly* (Nisbet, 1941).

ROBINSON, Joan

Born 1903, Camberley, England.
Current Post Emeritus Prof. Econ., Univ. Camb.
Recent Posts Prof. Econ., Univ. Camb., 1965–71.
Degrees MA Univ. Camb., 1927; Hon. LLD Univs. London, Liège.
Principal Contributions Imperfect competition; contributions to development of Keynesian economics; capital theory and growth; theory of international trade; development of economic theory.
Publications *Books:* 1. *Economics of Imperfect Competition* (Macmillan, 1933); 2. *Accumulation of Capital* (Macmillan, 1956, 1969); 3. *Aspects of Development and Underdevelopment* (CUP, 1979); 4. *Collected Economic Papers*, 5 vols (Blackwell, 1979).
Secondary Literature G.C. Harcourt 'Robinson, Joan' *IESS* vol. 18; T. Skouras, 'The economics of Joan Robinson', *Twelve Contemporary Economists*, eds J.R. Shackleton and G. Locksley (Macmillan, 1981).

RODBERTUS, Johann Karl*

Dates and Birthplace 1805–75, Greifswald, Swedish Pomerania.
Post Held Barrister in the Prussian service, 1826–32.
Career German state socialist, particularly associated with Lassalle and Wagner. His programme for relieving the distress of the working classes, attendant on industrialisation, was economic rather than political. The private ownership of land and of the means of production was to be eliminated not by revolution or political organisation, but by a gradual evolutionary process.

While enjoying a considerable reputation in his own lifetime, he is nowadays little read.
Publications *Books:* 1. *Die Forderungen der Arbeitenden Klassen* (1839); 2. *Zur Erkenntnis Unserer Staatswirtschaftlichen Zustände* (1842); 3. *Zur Erklärung und Abhälfe der Heutigen Creditnoth des Grundbesitzes* (1868–9); 4. *Briefe und Socialpolitische Aufsätze*, 2 vols (1882); 5. *Schriften*, 4 vols, ed. A. Wagner (1899).
Secondary Literature B. Fritsch, 'Rodbertus, Johann Karl', *IESS*, vol. 13.

ROGERS, James Edwin Thorold*

Dates and Birthplace 1823–90, W. Meon, Hants., England.
Posts Held C. of E. clergyman, private tutor, Univ. Oxford, 1846–59; Prof. Econ. Stats, King's Coll., Univ. London, 1859–90; Drummond Prof., Univ. Oxford, 1862–8, 1888–90.
Degree BA Univ. Oxford, 1846.
Offices MP, 1880–6.
Career On leaving the Church to pursue economic studies he developed an idiosyncratic system based on the use of empirical evidence, but retaining much of the *laissez faire* liberalism of the classical economists he so despised. His opinionated, anti-establishment views interrupted his Oxford career, but his monumental publications of price data secured his scholarly reputation.
Publications *Books:* 1. *A History of Agriculture and Prices in England*, 7 vols (1866–1902); 2. *A Manual of Political Economy for Schools* (1868); 3. *Six Centuries of Work and Wages* (1884); 4. *The Economic Interpretation of History* (1888); 5. *The Relations of Economic Science to Social and Political Action* (1888); 6. *The Industrial and Commercial History of England*, ed. A.G.L. Rogers (1892).
Secondary Literature A.W. Coats, 'Rogers, James E. Thorold', *IESS*, vol. 13.

ROOSA, R.V.

N.e.

ROPKE, J.

N.e.

RÖPKE, Wilhelm*

Dates and Birthplace 1899–1966, Schwarmstedt, Germany.
Posts Held Privatdozent, Univs Jena and Graz; Prof., Univ. Marburg, 1928–33, Univ. Istanbul, 1933–7, Grad. Inst., Geneva, 1937–66.
Degree PhD Univ. Marburg, 1921.
Career Extremely prolific and wide-ranging writer whose chief aim was the rehabilitation of the market economy. As an opponent of the Nazis he was an exile after 1933; he was equally a critic of socialist economics. Through his close friendship with Ludwig Erhard he was a major architect of the German 'economic miracle'.
Publications *Books:* 1. *Die Lehre von der Wirtschaft* (1937); 2. *Die Gesellschaftskrisis der Gegenwart* (1942); 3. *Civitas Humana* (1944); 4. *Internationale Ordnung* (1945); 5. *Jenseits von Angebot und Nachfrage* (1958).
Secondary Literature P. Boarman, 'Wilhelm Röpke', *German Econ. Review*, 4(2), 1966.

ROSA, Jean-Jacques

Born 1941, Marseilles, France.
Current Post Prof. Econ., Inst. d'Etudes Politiques, Paris.
Recent Posts Prof. Econ., Univ. Paris II, 1975.
Degrees Dr ès Sciences Econ. 1970; Agrégation de Sciences Econ. 1971.
Offices Member, AEA, AFA; Forum member, Board of European Fin. Assoc.; Member, Commission des Comptes de la Nation; Former co-ed., *J Bank Fin*; Ed., *Vie et Sciences Economiques, Politique Economique*; Past-pres., Assoc. Nationale des Docteurs es Sciences Econ., 1974–80.
Principal Contributions Applied policy analysis, especially with respect to the problems of unemployment and social security; a political-economic theory of the trade union as a firm; and a study of complementarity in the growth of markets and states.

Publications *Books:* 1. *L'Economique retrouvée* (with F. Aftalion), (Economica, 1977); 2. *Social Security: An International Perspective*, ed. (JCS & Fnep, 1981).
Articles: 1. 'Rentabilité, risque et équilibre à la Bourse de Paris', *RE*, 27(4), July 1976; 2. Théorie de la firme syndicale', *Vie et Sciences Econ.*, July, 1980; 3. 'Le statut de la fonction publique', *Vie et Sciences Econ.*, Oct. 1981.

ROSCHER, Wilhelm Georg Friedrich*

Dates and Birthplace 1817–94, Germany.
Posts Held Lecturer, Prof., Univ. Göttingen, 1840–8; Prof., Univ. Leipzig, 1848–94.
Career One of the founders of the German Historical School who explicitly excluded normative in favour of positive economics. The value of historical study, he argued, was that it showed that all nations proceed through stages of development and decay. He also wrote on purely historical and philosophical topics, as well as venturing comprehensively into the history of economic thought.
Publications *Books:* 1. *Grundriss zu Vorlesungen über die Staatswirtschaft nach Geschichtlicher Methode* (1843); 2. *System der Volkswirtschaft*, 5 vols (1854–94); 3. *Geschichte der National – Ökonomie in Deutschland* (1874).
Secondary Literature E. Salin, 'Roscher, Wilhelm', *IESS*, vol. 13.

ROSE, Klaus

Born 1928, Bochung, Germany.
Current Post Prof. Volkswirtschaftstheorie; Dir. Instituts Allgemeine Aussenwirtschaftstheorie, Johannes Gutenberg-Univ., Mainz, W. Germany.
Degrees Diplom-Volkswirt, Dr rer. pol. (PhD), Habilitation (inaugural dissertation) Univ. Köln, 1950, 1952, 1957; Ordentlicher Prof., Univ. Mainz, 1961.
Principal Contributions The pure theory of international trade, and the international monetary economics: several problems in these fields have been examined, e.g. optimum tariffs, factor proportions in international trade, problems of exchange rates, and the monetary approach to the balance of payments.
Publications *Articles:* 1. 'Der monetäre Ansatz in der Zahlungsbilanztheorie', *JSW*, 28, 1977; 2. 'Wachtumstheorie', *Handwörterbuch der Wirtschaftswissenschaften*, 7 (Mohr-Siebeck, 1977); 3. 'Wechselkurs', *Handwörterbuch der Wirtschaftswissenschaften*, 8 (Mohr-Siebeck, 1980); 4. 'Freie Wechselkurse, Finanzmarkttheorie und Kaufkraftparität in Politik und Markt', in *Wirtschaftspolitische Probleme der 80er Jahre*, eds D. Duwendag and H. Siebert (G. Fischer, 1980); 5. 'Theorie der Aussenwirtschaft', *Handwörterbuch der Wirtschaftswissenschaften,* 8 (Mohr-Siebeck, 1981).

ROSEN, Sherwin

Born 1938, Chicago, Ill., USA.
Current Post Prof. Econ., Univ. Chicago, USA.
Recent Posts Univ. Rochester, 1964–77 (Kenan Prof. Econ., 1975–7); Sr res. assoc., NBER, 1967–; Sr res. assoc., National Opinion Res. Center, 1980–.
Degrees MA, PhD Univ. Chicago, 1962, 1966.
Offices Fellow, Em Soc, AEA; Board Eds., *AER*, 1970–4; Nominating Comm., *AER*, 1979; Census Advisory Comm., AEA, 1981–.
Principal Contributions Labour economics: the demand for factors of production; the economics of trade unionism; theory and applications of equalising differences, including the value of life, the economics of discrimination and measurement of the quality of life; the theory of human capital; educational choice and the determination of lifetime earnings; determinants of the distribution of income; and models of selection and assignment in economics. Industrial organisation: advertising and information; product differentiation in pure competition; and monopolistic price and quality discrimination with product differentiation.

Publications *Books:* 1. *A Disequilibrium Model of Demand for Factors of Production* (with M.I. Nadiri), (NBER, 1974).

Articles: 1. 'Learning and experience in the labor market', *JHR*, 7(3), Summer 1972; 2. 'Hedonic prices and implicit markets: product differentiation in pure competition', *JPE*, 82(1), Jan.-Feb. 1974; 3. 'The value of saving a life: evidence from the labor market' (with R. Thaler), in *Household Production and Consumption*, ed. N. Terleykyj (Columbia Univ. Press, 1975); 4. 'Education and self-selection' (with R. Willis), *JPE*, 87(5), Pt 2, Oct. 1979; 5. 'Rank-order tournaments as optimum labor contracts' (with E. Lazear), *JPE*, 89(5), Oct. 1981.

ROSENBERG, N.

N.e.

ROSENSTEIN-RODAN, Paul N.

Born 1902.
Posts Held Prof. Polit. Econ., Univ. Coll., Univ. London, 1934–47; Econ. adviser, IBRD, 1947–52; Prof., MIT, 1952–68, Univ. Texas, 1968–72, Univ. Boston, 1972–.
Degree Dr Univ. Vienna.
Principal Contributions Development economics, particularly as an adviser to governments. Writings shifted from purely theoretical approach to development problems towards an applied economics approach. The concepts of complementarity in consumption and production, the time sequence of economic adjustments, and the importance of economies of scale in production, all of which are to be found in early theoretical work, recur in later contributions to the practice of development.
Publications *Books:* 1. *Disguised Unemployment and Under-employment in Agriculture* (MIT Center for Internat. Stud., 1956).

Articles: 1. 'Marginal utility', in *Handwörterbuch der Staatswissenschaften,* 4 (1927), and *Internat. Econ. Papers,* 10 (Macmillan, 1960); 2. 'The role of time in economic theory', *Ec,*

N.S. 1, Feb. 1934; 3. 'Problems of industrialisation of eastern and south-eastern Europe', *EJ,* 53, June/Sept. 1943; 4. 'International aid for underdeveloped countries', *REStat,* 43, May 1961; 5. 'Criteria for evaluation of national development effort', *J Developmental Planning,* 1, Jan. 1969.
Secondary Literature R.S. Eckaus, 'Rosenstein-Rodan, Paul N.', *IESS,* vol. 18.

ROSOVSKY, Henry

Born 1927, Free City of Danzig (now Gdansk, Poland).
Current Post Walter S. Barker Prof. Econ., Dean, Faculty Arts Sciences, Harvard Univ., USA.
Recent Posts Ass. prof., Prof. Econ. and Hist., Univ. Cal., Berkeley, 1958–65; Prof. Econ., Harvard Univ., 1965–; Vis. prof., Univs Hitotsubashi Tokyo, Stanford, Hebrew, Jerusalem.
Degrees BA, Hon. LLD Coll. William and Mary, 1949, 1976; MA, PhD Harvard Univ., 1953, 1959; Hon. LHD Univs Yeshiva (1977), Hebrew Union Coll. (1978), Colgate Univ. (1979).
Offices and Honours Ed., *Explorations in Entrepreneurial Hist.,* 1954–6; Assoc. ed., *JEH,* 1958–61; Chairman, Center Japanese Korean Stud., Univ. Cal., Berkeley, 1962–5; Schumpeter prize, Harvard Univ., 1963; Board Dirs, Assoc. Asian Stud., 1963–6; Chairman, Pol. Advisory Board, Econ. Inst., Boulder, Colorado, 1967–74; Assoc. dir., East Asia Res. Center, Harvard Univ., 1967–9; Chairman, Council Res. Econ. Hist., 1968–71; Fellow, AAAS, 1969.
Principal Contributions As an economic historian, specialised in the study of modern economic growth in 19th-century Japan. Also attempted to consider Japanese economic growth in comparative perspective.
Publications *Books:* 1. *Capital Formation in Japan, 1868–1940* (The Free Press, 1961); 2. *Quantitative Japanese Economic History: An Annotated Bibliography and a Survey of US holdings* (Univ. Cal. Press, 1961); 3. *Japanese Economic Growth: Trend Acceleration*

in the Twentieth Century (with K. Ohkawa), (Stanford Univ. Press, 1973); 4. *Asia's New Giant: How the Japanese Economy Works*, ed. (with H. Patrick), (Brookings Inst., 1975); 5. *The Modernization of Japan and Russia* (with others), (The Free Press, 1975).

Articles: 1. 'The indigenous components in the modern Japanese economy, (with K. Okahawa), *EDCC*, 9, April 1961; 2. 'Japan's transition to modern economic growth, 1868–1885', in *Industrialization in Two Systems*, ed. H. Rosovsky (Wiley, 1966); 3. 'What are the lessons of Japanese economic history?', in *Economic Development in the Long Run*, ed. A.J. Youngson (A & U, 1972).

ROSS, Stephen A.

Born 1944, Boston, Mass., USA.
Current Post Edwin J. Beinecke Prof. Organization Management Fin., Prof. Econ., School Organization Management, Yale Univ., USA, 1977–.
Degrees BS (Maths and Physics, Hons.) Cal. Inst. Technology, 1965; PhD (Econ.) Harvard Univ., 1969.
Offices and Honours Univ. Lindback award nominee for disting. teaching, 1972–5; Guggenheim Memorial Foundation Fellow, 1975–6; NSF Grant, 1978–81.
Principal Contributions Work in financial economics and the economics of uncertainty, focusing on asset pricing, options, corporate finance, statistics in finance, and general agency theories of non-market interactions under uncertainty.
Publications *Articles:* 1. 'A Fisherian approach to trade, capital movements, and tariffs' (with M. Connolly), *AER*, 60(3), June 1970; 2. 'The economic theory of agency: the principal's problem'; *AER*, 63(2), May 1973; 3. 'Portfolio turnpike theorems for constant policies', *J Fin Econ*, 1(2), 1974; 4. 'Pricing and timing decisions in oligopoly industries' (with M.L. Wachter), *QJE*, 89, Feb. 1975; 5. 'A survey of some new results in financial option pricing theory' (with J.C. Cox), *J Fin*, 31(1), May 1976.

ROSSI, Pellegrino Luigi Edoardo*

Dates and Birthplace 1787–1848, Carrara, Italy.
Posts Held Prof. Law, Univ. Bologna, 1813; Prof., Univ. Geneva, 1819; Prof. Econ., then Constitutional Law, Collège de France, 1833; French ambassador to Rome, 1845; Papal Prime Minister, 1848.
Offices and Honours Involved in drafting Swiss constitution, 1832; Member, French Academy, 1836; Peer of France, 1839.
Career Say's successor in the chair at the Collège de France and a member of the school which dominated the chief journals and institutions of economic life in France throughout the nineteenth century. His economics was the conventional Ricardianism of his day but the *Cours* . . . achieved considerable success. His varied academic and political career ended in assassination in Rome.
Publications *Books:* 1. *Traité de droit pénal*, 3 vols (1829); 2. *Cours d'économie politique*, 4 vols (1840–54); 3. *Mélanges d'économie politique, d'histoire et de philosophie*, 2 vols (1857).
Secondary Literature L. Ledermann, 'Rossi, Pellegrino Luigi Edoardo', *ESS*, vol. 13.

ROSTOW, Walt W.

Born 1916, New York City, NY, USA.
Current Post Rex G. Baker Jr prof. Polit. Econ., Univ. Texas, USA.
Recent Posts Dep. special ass. US President Nat. Security Affairs, 1961; Counsellor, Chairman, Pol. Planning Council, Dept. State, 1961–6; US Member Inter-Amer. Comm. Alliance Progress, Rank Ambassador, 1964–6; Special ass. US Pres. Nat. Security Affairs, 1966–9.
Degrees BA, PhD Yale Univ., 1936, 1939; MA Balliol Coll., Univ. Oxford, 1938.
Principal Contributions British economic history with special emphasis on business cycles and trend periods (Kondratieff cycles); a dynamic, disaggregated theory of production and prices

in which change in population, technology, and relative prices of basic commodities are rendered endogenous, applied to both economic development via stages of economic growth and the history of the world economy; the interaction of economic, political, and social change examined in the context of various societies.

Publications *Books:* 1. *Essays on the British Economy of the Nineteenth Century* (OUP, 1948); 2. *The process of Economic Growth* (Norton, 1952, OUP, 1953, 1960); 3. *The Stages of Economic Growth* (CUP, 1960, 1971); 4. *The World Economy: History and Prospect* (Univ. Texas Press, 1978); 5. *British Trade Fluctuations, 1868–1896: A Chronicle and a Commentary* (Arno Press, 1981).

Articles: 1. 'Investment and the great depression', *EHR*, 8, May 1938; 2. 'Trends in the allocation of resources in secular growth', in *Economic Progress*, ed.L.H. Dupriez (Macmillan, 1955); 3. 'The take-off into self-sustained growth', *EJ*, 66, March 1956; 4. 'The interrelation of theory and economic history', *JEH*, 17, Dec. 1957; 5. 'A simple model of the Kondratieff cycle' (with M. Kennedy and F. Nasr), in *Research in Economic History: A Research Annual*, 4, ed. P. Uselding (Macmillan, 1979).

ROTHENBERG, Jerome

Born 1924, New York City, NY, USA.

Current Post Prof. Econ., MIT, USA; 1966–.

Recent Posts Ass. prof., Univ. Cal., Riverside, 1954–7; Ass. prof. Econ., Univ. Chicago, 1957–60; Assoc. prof., Prof. Econ., Northwestern Univ., 1960–6; Vis. Fellow, Nuffield Coll., Univ. Oxford, 1965–6; Academic vis., LSE, 1973–4.

Degrees BA Columbia Coll., 1945; MA, PhD Columbia Univ., 1947, 1954.

Offices and Honours AEA; Em Soc.; Phi Beta Kappa, 1945; Fellow, Nat. Inst. Public Affairs, 1945–6; Fellow, Center Advanced Study Behavioral Sciences, 1956–7; Comm. Urban Econ., 1962–7; Res. Grant Brookings Inst.,

1966–7; Chairman, Comm. Urban Public Econ., 1976–.

Principal Contributions Fields researched: welfare theory, utility theory, health economics, federalism and local public economics, cost-benefit analysis, urban housing and residential location, urban transportation, migration theory, environmental economics, natural resources, regulatory policy, national defence economics, economics of crime. Basic emphases throughout: extend traditional theory to accommodate dimensions, concepts, relationships from other social sciences; enrich traditional theory with a deeper sense of what is special to the particular area studied; and apply economic analysis to areas far from traditional concerns but with due respect for the special complexities inherent in each area.

Publications *Books:* 1. *The Measurement of Social Welfare* (Prentice-Hall, 1961); 2. *Economic Evaluation of Urban Renewal* (Brookings Inst., 1967); 3. *An Approach to the Welfare Analysis of Intertemporal Resource Allocation* (Center Planning and Econ. Res., 1967); 4. *Readings in Urban Economics*, ed. (with M. Edel), (Macmillan, 1972); 5. *Transport and the Urban Environment; The management of Water Quality and the Environment*, ed. (with I.G. Heggie), (Macmillan, 1974).

Articles: 1. 'Non-convexity, aggregation and Pareto optimality', *JPE*, 68, Oct. 1960; 2. 'A model of economic and political decision-making', in *The Public Economy of Urban Communities*, ed. J. Margolis (Resources for the Future, 1965); 3. 'Endogenous city-suburb rivalry through household location', in *The Political Economy of Multi-level Government*, ed. W. Oates (Heath-Lexington, 1976); 4. 'Simultaneous estimation of the supply and demand for housing location in a multizoned metropolitan area' (with K. Bradbury *et al.*), in *Residential Location and Urban Housing Markets*, ed. G.K. Ingram (Ballinger, 1977); 5. 'Urban housing markets and housing policy', in *Selected Readings in Quantitative Urban Analysis*, eds S.I. Bemstein and W.G. Mellon (Pergamon, 1978).

ROTHSCHILD, Kurt Wilson

Born 1914, Vienna, Austria.
Current Post Prof., Johannes Keppler Univ., Austria.
Recent Posts Lecturer Econ., Glasgow Univ., 1940–7; Res. Fellow, Austrian Inst. Econ. Res., Vienna, 1947–66.
Degrees Dr iuris Univ. Vienna, 1938; MA (Econ. and Political Philosophy) Glasgow Univ., 1940.
Offices and Honours National-ökonomische Gesellschaft, Austria; RES; AEA; Verein für Sozialpolitik; Club of Rome; Prize, City of Vienna, contributions to the social sciences, 1980.
Principal Contributions Main interests directed towards problems of wages, employment, income distribution; international economics; and the Austrian economy. Development of 'realistic' theories by taking account of social, sociological, political and psychological factors.
Publications *Books:* 1. *The Austrian Economy since 1945* (Royal Inst. International Affairs, 1950); 2. *The Theory of Wages* (Blackwell, 1954, 1965); 3. *Economic Forecasting* (Springer-Verlag, 1969); 4. *Power in Economics*, ed. (Penguin, 1971); 5. *Introduction to Disequilibrium Theory* (Springer-Verlag, 1981).
Articles: 1. 'The degree of monopoly', *Ec*, N.S. 9, Feb. 1942; 2. 'Price theory and oligopoly', *EJ*, 37, Sept. 1947; 3. 'The Phillips curve and all that', *SJPE*, 18(3), Nov. 1971; 4. 'Export structure, export flexibility and competitiveness', *WA*, 111(2), 1975; 5. 'Arbeitslose: Gibt's die?', *Kyklos*, 31(1), 1978.

ROTHSCHILD, Michael

Born 1942, Chicago, Ill., USA.
Current Post Prof. Econ., Univ. Wisconsin, USA, 1976–.
Recent Posts Instructor Econ., Boston Coll., 1968–9; Ass. prof. Econ., Harvard Univ., 1969–73; Lecturer Econ., 1972–4, Assoc. prof. Econ., 1974–5, Prof. Econ., 1975–6, Princeton Univ.
Degrees BA (Anthropology) Reed Coll., 1963; MA (Internat. Relations) Yale Univ., 1975; PhD (Econ.) MIT, 1969.
Offices and Honours Board Eds., *JEL*; Assoc. ed., *Em*, 1970–3, 1979–, *JET*, 1973–; Fellow, Em Soc, 1974–, Council member, 1979–; Member, NSF Advisory Panel Econ., 1975–7; Romnes Faculty Fellow, Univ. Wisconsin, 1977; Guggenheim Memorial Foundation Fellow, 1978–9.
Principal Contributions Helped to develop techniques which are used to analyse the operation of markets whose participants have incomplete and asymmetric information. Examples are the definition of increasing risk, the appropriate equilibrium concept for markets with self-selection, and the properties of optimal search rules. Have used probabilistic models to examine such topics as the processes by which juries reach decisions, the probability of casting a decisive vote, and the operating characteristics of common bureaucratic rules-of-thumb.
Publications *Books:* 1. *Uncertainty in Economics: Readings and Exercises* (with P.A. Diamond), (Academic Press, 1978).
Articles: 1. 'Increasing risk: I. A definition' (with J.E. Stiglitz), *JET*, 2(3), Sept. 1970; 2. 'Models of market organization with imperfect information: a survey', *JPE*, 81(6), Nov./Dec. 1973; 3. 'Searching for the lowest price when the distribution of prices is unknown', *JPE*, 82(4), July/Aug. 1974; 4. 'On the allocation of effort' (with R. Radner), *JET*, 10(3), June 1975; 5. 'Equilibrium in competitive insurance markets: an essay on the economics of imperfect information' (with J.E. Stiglitz), *QJE*, 90, Nov. 1976.

ROY, Andrew Donald

Born 1920, London, England.
Recent Posts Lecturer, Univ. Camb., Fellow, Sidney Sussex Coll., Univ. Camb. 1951–64; Sr Econ. Adviser, HM Treasury, 1964–9; Joint Head, (Dep. dir., Econ. Section), Econ. Assessment Divisions, HM Treasury, 1969–72; Head (Under-secretary), Econ. and Stats Division 4, UK Dept. Trade and

Industry, 1972–4; Ass. under-secretary of State (Econ.), UK Ministry of Defence, 1974-6; Chief Econ. Adviser (Under-Secetary), UK Dept. Health and Social Security, 1976–80.

Degrees BA (First class Hons. Mathematical Tripos Pt I, 1939, Econ. Tripos Pt II, 1948), MA Univ. Camb., 1948, 1950.

Offices Member, RES, RSS, Em Soc; London and Cambridge Econ. Service, 1949–62.

Principal Contributions Theoretical work on border between economics and statistics in fields of distribution of earnings and portfolio analysis. Applied work as contributor to regular periodical analyses of UK economy as member of London and Cambridge Economic Service. Study of use and requirements of economic statistics for policy purposes. In Government economic service: contributions to development of more systematic government interest in relevant academic economic research; evolution of Treasury's methods of short-term forecasting and including introduction of computable model; establishment of permanent source of professional advice on economic aspects of defence in Ministry of Defence.

Publications *Books:* 1. *British Economic Statistics* (with C.F. Carter), (CUP, 1954).

Articles: 1. 'The distribution of earnings and individual output', *EJ*, 60, Sept. 1950; 2. 'Some thoughts on the distribution of earnings', *OEP*, N.S. 3, June 1951; 3. 'Safety first and the holding of assets', *Em*, 20, July 1952, repr. in *The Theory of Business Finance*, eds S.H. Archer and A. D'Ambrosio (Macmillan, 1976); 4. 'Some notes on pistimetric inference', *JRSS*, B, 22, 1960; 5. 'A Bayesian approach to the control of expenditure', *Government Economic Service working paper no. 9* (HMSO, 1978).

RUEFF, Jacques Leon

Born 1896, Paris, France.
Posts Held Finance Section, League of Nations, 1927–30; Prof., L'Ecole Libre des Sciences Polit., 1930–40; Inspector General of Finances.

Degrees L'Ecole Polytechnique, 1919–21; l'Ecole des Sciences Polit., 1922–3.

Offices and Honours Commander, Légion d'Honneur; Pres., Polit. Econ. Stat. Socs., Paris; Vice-pres., Internat. Inst. Stats.; Croix de Guerre, 1914–8; Member, Inst. de France, 1964.

Career A premature 'monetarist' and thorough-going anti-Keynesian, who emerged in post-war France under de Gaulle as an extremely influential proponent of orthodox monetary policies, including the return to the gold standard.

Publications *Books:* 1. *Des sciences physiques aux sciences morales* (1922); 2. *Théorie des phénomènes Monétaires* (1927); 3. *Epître aux dirigistes* (1949); 4. *The Age of Inflation* (1963); 5. *Balance of Payments* (1965); 6. *La Réforme du système monetaire international* (1973).

Articles: 1. 'L'assurance-chômage cause du chômage permanente', *REP*, April 1931; 2. 'Nouvelle discussion sur la chômage, les salaires et les prix', *REP*, Sept./Oct. 1951.

RUGGLES, Richard

Born 1916, Columbus, Ohio, USA.
Current Post Stanley Rezor Prof. Econ., Yale Univ., USA.

Degrees BA, PhD Harvard Univ., 1939, 1942.

Offices Fellow, ASA, Em Soc; Managing ed., *RIW*, 1975–.

Principal Contributions The development of national economic accounts and their integration with microdata bases for enterprises, households and governments.

Publications *Books:* 1. *National Income Accounts and Income Analysis*, (with N.D. Ruggles), (McGraw-Hill, 1956); 2. *Design of Economic Accounts* (with N.D. Ruggles), (NBER, 1971).

Articles: 1. 'Integrated economic accounts for the United States, 1947–80' (with N.D. Ruggles), *Survey Current Bus.*, 1982.

RUTTAN, Vernon W.

Born 1924, Alden, Mich., USA.
Current Post Prof., Dept. Agric. and

Applied Econ., Econ. Dept., Univ. Minnesota, USA.

Recent Posts Economist, Div. Regional Stud., 1951–3, Gen. manager, Tennessee Valley Authority 1954; Ass. prof., 1955–7, Assoc. prof., 1957–60, Prof., 1960–3, Dept. Agric. Econ., Purdue Univ. 1958–9; US President's Council Econ. Advisers, Exec. Office Pres., Staff Economist, 1961–3; Agricultural Economist, Rockefeller Foundation, Internat. Rice Res. Inst., Philippines, 1963–5; Trustee, 1967–73, Pres., 1973–7, Agric. Development Council Inc.; Prof. and Head, Dept. Agric. Econ., Univ. Minnesota, 1965–70; Prof. and Dir., Econ. Development Center, 1970–3.

Degrees BA Yale Univ., 1948; MA, PhD Univ. Chicago, 1950, 1952; Hon. Dr Laws 1978.

Offices and Honours Publication Award, AAEA, 1956, 1957, 1962, 1966, 1967, 1971, 1979; Fellow, AAEA, 1974; Fellow, AAAS, 1976.

Principal Contributions Theory and measurement of productivity growth; extension and testing of the theory of induced technical change; development of the theory of induced institutional change; and empirical analyses of the rate of technical and institutional change on agricultural development.

Publications *Books:* 1. *The Economic Demand for Irrigated Acreage: New Methodology and Some Preliminary Projections, 1954–1980* (Johns Hopkins Univ. Press, 1965); 2. *Plant Science: An Introduction to World Crops* (with J. Janick *et al.*), (W.H. Freeman, 1969); 3. *Agricultural Development: An International Perspective* (with Y. Hayami), (Johns Hopkins Univ. Press, 1971); 4. *Induced Innovation: Technology, Institutions and Development* (with H.P. Binswanger), (Johns Hopkins Univ. Press, 1978).

Articles: 1. 'The contribution of technological progress to farm output: 1950–75', *REStat*, 38, 1956; 2. 'Agricultural policy in an affluent society', *JFE*, 48(5), Dec. 1966; 3. 'Factor prices and technical change in agricultural development: the United States and Japan, 1880–1960' (with Y. Hayami), *JPE*, 78(5), Sept./Oct. 1970; 4. 'Induced innovation in agriculture'

(with H.P. Binswanger and Y. Hayami), in *Economic Growth and Resources: National Resources,* vol. 3, eds C. Bliss and M. Boserup (Blonden, Macmillan, 1980); 5. 'Three cases of induced institutional innovation', in *Public Choice and Rural Development*, eds C.S. Russell and N.K. Nicholson (Johns Hopkins Univ. Press, 1981).

RYBCZYNSKI, Tadeusz M.

Born 1923, Lwow, Poland.
Current Post Econ. adviser, Lazard Brothers, 1954–, Dir., Lazard Securities Ltd, London, England.
Recent Posts Lloyds Bank Ltd, 1949–53.
Degrees BCom, MSc (Econ.), Univ. London, 1949, 1952.
Offices Fellow, Inst. Bankers; Member, Scientific Comm., Internat. Center Banking and Monetary Stud., Geneva; Chairman, Soc. Bus. Economists, 1962–75; Governor, Member Council Management and Exec. Comm., NIESR; Member, Governing Body, Trade Pol. Res. Centre, London, 1968–; Council member, 1969–74, Treasurer, 1976–, RES; Member, UK Monopolies and Mergers Commission, 1978–.
Principal Contributions An attempt to see when the factor price equalisation theorem, developed by Samuelson and Stolper, holds good.
Publications *Books:* 1. *The Economist in Business*, ed. (Blackwell, 1967); 2. *Value Added Tax – the UK Position and the European Experience*, ed. (Blackwell, 1969); 3. *Towards an Open World Economy – A Report By an Advisory Group* (with others), (Macmillan, 1972); 4. *A New Era in Competition*, ed. (Blackwell, 1973); 5. *The Economics of the Oil Crisis* ed. (Macmillan, 1976).

Articles: 1. 'Factor endowment and relative commodity prices', *Ec*, 84, Nov. 1955, repr. in *Readings in International Economics*, eds, R.E. Caves and H.G. Johnson (A & U, 1968); 2. 'UK financial sector since Radcliffe – non-clearing banks', in *Money in Britain 1959–1969* ed R. Croome and H.G. Johnson (OUP, 1970); 3. 'The cost and sources of capital', in *Problems of Investment*, ed. R. Shone (Blackwell, 1971); 4. 'Economics, economists and industry', in *Users of Economics*, ed. G.D.N. Worswick (Blackwell, 1972); 5. 'Financial decisions and economic policy', in *Financial Management Handbook* (Kluwer-Harrap, 1977).

S

SAINT-SIMON, Claude Henri de Rouvroy*

Dates and Birthplace 1760–1825, Paris, France.

Posts Held Army officer, 1777–81; Businessman and speculator, 1781–1804; Writer and journalist, 1804–25.

Career His influence on Comte and social reformers, rather than his publications, is the source of his fame. His identification of the phenomenon of 'industrialisation', advocacy of a science of society, and 'evolutionary organicist' theory of society are his major contributions. He advocated planned industrialisation and peaceful social change led by engineers, manufacturers and scientists. His last work, *New Christianity*, inspired a movement involving many intellectuals, which eventually split, with Enfantin leading one wing towards mystical religion.

Publications *Books:* 1. *Introduction aux travaux scientifiques du dix-neuvième siècle* (1807); 2. *Mémoire sur la science de l'homme* (1813); 3. *New Christianity* (1825); 4. *Selected Writings*, ed. F.M.H. Markham (1952).

Secondary Literature M.V. Martel, 'Saint-Simon', *IESS*, vol. 13.

SALIN, Edgar*

Dates and Birthplace 1892–1974, Frankfurt-am-Main, Germany.

Posts Held Prof. Univ. Heidelberg, 1924–7; Prof., 1927–74, Rector, 1971, Univ. Basle.

Offices Founder, Friedrich List Gesellschaft.

Career A follower of Otto Spann's 'universalist economics', which enjoyed a brief spell of fame in Germany in the first quarter of this century, being a typical German holistic reaction to the atomism of mainstream anglophone economics. In his *Geschichte* ..., the entire history of economic thought is depicted as a struggle between collectivist and individualist ideas. During this early period, he made a major contribution to the historical understanding of Greek economics. In later years, he turned his attention to modern topics, including atomic energy and international monetary fluctuations.

Publications *Books:* 1. *Platon und die Griechische Utopie* (1921); 2. *Geschichte der Volkswirtschaftslehre* (1923, 1951); 3. *Wirtschaft und Staat* (1932); 4. *Jakob Burkhardt und Nietzsche* (1938); 5. *Ökonomik der Atomkraft* (1955); 6. *Die Entwicklung des Internationalen Verkehrs* (1964).

Articles: 1. 'Economics: romantic and universalist economics', *ESS*, vol. 5.

SALOP, Steven

Born 1946, Reading, Penn., USA.

Current Post Assoc. dir., Special Projects, Bureau Econ., Fed. Trade Commission, Washington, DC.

Recent Posts Economist, Civil Aeronautics Board, 1977–8; Dep. ass. dir. Consumer Protection, Fed. Trade Commission, 1978–9; Ass. dir. Industry Analysis, Fed. Trade Commission, 1979–80.

Degrees BA Univ. Pennsylvania, 1968; MPhil, PhD Yale Univ., 1971, 1972.

Offices and Honours AEA; Em Soc; Assoc. Consumer Res.; Phi Beta Kappa, 1968; Univ. Pennsylvania Schonbaum Prize Econ., 1968.

Principal Contributions Work has focused on two areas: an attempt to explain better the role of imperfect information in the economy; and, more generally, it has tried to integrate various concepts at the frontier of economic theory (e.g. imperfect information and strategic interaction) into fields of applied economics and other social sciences like marketing and law, and to bring insights from these fields into the scope of neo-classical economic theory.

Publications *Articles:* 1. 'Bargains

and rip-offs: a model of monopolistically competitive price dispersion' (with J. Stiglitz), *REStud*, 44(3), Oct. 1977; 2. 'The noisy monopolist: information, price dispersion and price discrimination', *REStud*, 44(3), Oct. 1977; 3. 'A model of the natural rate of unemployment', *AER*, 69(1), March 1979; 4. 'Strategic entry deterrence', *AER*, 69(2), May 1979; 5. 'Efficient regulation of consumer information' (with H. Beales and R. Craswell), *J Law E*, 24(2), Oct. 1981.

SAMUELS, Warren Joseph

Born 1933, New York City, NY, USA.

Current Post Prof. Econ., Michigan State Univ., USA, 1968–.

Recent Post Univ. Miami, 1959–68.

Degrees BBA Univ. Miami, 1954; MSc, PhD Univ. Wisconsin, 1955, 1957.

Offices Ed., *J. Econ Issues*, 1971–81; Pres., Hist. of Econ. Soc., 1981–2.

Principal Contributions Greater clarity of the role of government in economic affairs both in the history of economic thought and in contemporary economics. Particular attention given to role of legal factors obscured by abstract ideological and theoretical formulations. Identification of fundamental areas of choice, and choice processes, not otherwise specified and treated in economic theory, particularly welfare economics and related fields.

Publications *Books:* 1. *The Classical Theory of Economic Policy* (World, 1966); 2. *Pareto on Policy* (Elsevier, 1974).

Articles: 1. 'The history of economic thought as intellectual history', *HOPE*, 6(3), Fall 1974; 2. 'The political economy of Adam Smith', *Ethics*, 87, 1977; 3. 'Normative premises in regulatory theory', *J Post Keyn E*, 1(1), Fall 1978; 4. 'The state, law, and economic organization', *Res. Law and Sociology*, 2, 1979; 5. 'The role and resolution of the compensation problem' (with N. Mercuro), *Res. Law and Econ*, 1, 1979, 2, 1980.

SAMUELSON, Paul Anthony

Born 1915, Gary, Ind., USA.

Current Post Inst. Prof., MIT, USA.

Recent Posts MIT, 1940–.

Degrees BA Univ. Chicago, 1935; MA, PhD Harvard Univ., 1936, 1941; Hon. degrees: LLD, DSci., DLit., DLetters, DEcon., various univs.

Offices and Honours Contributing ed., *Newsweek*; David Wells prize, Univ. Harvard, 1941; John Bates Clark medal, 1947, Pres., AEA, 1961; Pres., Em Soc, 1953; Pres., 1965–8, Hon. pres., 1968–, IEA; Albert Einstein medal, 1970; Nobel Prize for Econ., 1970.

Principal Contributions The theory of consumer's behaviour and capital theory; growth theory; various topics in mathematical economics; welfare economics; international trade theory; fiscal policy and income determination; the pure theory of public expenditure; the methodology of economics; the history of economic thought; portfolio selection and the theory of speculative markets; and the economics of population.

Publications *Books:* 1. *Foundations of Economic Analysis* (Harvard Univ. Press, 1947); 2. *Economics* (McGraw-Hill, 1948, 1980); 3. *Linear Programming and Economic Analysis* (with R. Dorfman and R. Solow), (McGraw-Hill, 1948).

Articles: 1. *Collected scientific papers of Paul A. Samuelson*, vols 1 and 2, ed. J.E. Stiglitz, vol. 3, ed. R.C. Merton, vol. 4, eds H. Nagatani and K. Crowley (MIT Press, 1966, 1972, 1977).

Secondary Literature A. Lindbeck, 'Paul Anthony Samuelson's contributions to economics', *Swed JE*, 72(1), Jan. 1970; A. Kendry, 'Paul Samuelson and the scientific awakening of economics', *Twelve Contemporary Economists*, eds J.R. Shackleton and G. Locksley (Macmillan, 1981).

SANDMO, Agnar

Born 1938, Tønsberg, Norway.

Current Post Prof. Econ., Norwegian School Econ. and Bus Admin., Bergen, Norway.

Recent Posts Ass., assoc. and acting

prof., Norwegian School Econ. and Bus Admin., 1966–71.

Degrees Sivilokønom, licentiat, Dr oecon. Norwegian School Econ. and Bus Admin., 1961, 1966, 1970.

Offices Member, Fellow Em Soc 1976–; Member, AEA.

Principal Contributions Economics of uncertainty, and the theory of public finance. In the first, worked on problems of consumer and firm behaviour under risk aversion; in the second, on public goods theory, public investment criteria, externalities and positive and normative theories of taxation.

Publications *Books:* 1. *Essays on Public Economics: the Kiryat Anavim Papers,* ed. (Lexington Books, 1978); 2. *Aims and Means of Industrial Policy* (Inst. of Industrial Econ., 1978, in Norwegian).

Articles: 1. 'On the theory of the competitive firm under price uncertainty', *AER*, 61(1), March 1971; 2. 'Discount rates for public investment under uncertainty', *Int ER*, 13(2), June 1972; 3. 'Public goods and the technology of consumption', *REStud*, 40(4), Oct. 1973; 4. 'Portfolio theory, asset demand and taxation', *REStud*, 44(2), June 1977; 5. 'Welfare implications of the taxation of savings' (with A.B. Atkinson), *EJ*, 90(1), Sept. 1980.

SARGAN, John Denis

Born 1924, Doncaster, England.
Current Post Prof. Econometrics, LSE, England.
Recent Post Reader, Econometrics, Univ. Leeds, 1961–3.
Degree MA Univ. Camb., 1948.
Offices Pres., Em Soc, 1980.
Principal Contributions Theory and methodology of estimation of simultaneous equation. Econometric models with auto-correlated errors. Estimation of models of price-wage inflation for the UK.
Publications *Articles:* 1. 'The estimation of economic relationships using instrumental variables', *Em*, 26, July 1958; 2. 'The maximum likelihood estimation of economic relationships with autoregressive residuals', *Em*, 29, July

1961; 3. 'Gram-Charlier approximations applied to *t* ratios of *k*-class estimators', *Em*, 43(2), March 1975; 4. 'Econometric estimators and the Edgeworth approximation', *Em*, 44(3), July 1976; 6. 'A model of wage-price inflation', *REStud*, 47, Sept. 1980.

SARGENT, Thomas J.

Born 1943, Pasadena, Cal., USA.
Current Post Prof. Econ., Univ. Minnesota, USA.
Recent Posts Vis. prof., Univ. Chicago, 1976–7; Vis. prof., Harvard Univ., 1981–2.
Degrees BA Univ. Cal., Berkeley, 1964; PhD Harvard Univ., 1968.
Offices and Honours Phi Beta Kappa, 1963; Fellow Em Soc, 1976; Mary Elizabeth Morgan prize, Univ. Chicago, 1979–80.
Principal Contributions Studies of the role of expectations in macro-economic models, and the relationship between dynamic economic theory and time series analysis.
Publications *Books:* 1. *Macroeconomic Theory* (Academic Press, 1979); 2. *Rational Expectations and Econometric Practice,* eds (with R.E. Lucas Jr), (Univ. Minnesota Press, 1981).
Articles: 1. 'Rational expectations and the dynamics of hyperinflation' (with N. Wallace), *Int ER*, 14(2), June 1973; 2. 'Interpreting economic time series', *JPE*, 89(1), Feb. 1981.

SATO, Kazuo

Born 1927, Sapporo, Hokkaido, Japan.
Current Post Prof. Econ., State Univ. New York, Buffalo, USA.
Recent Posts Inst. Soc. Econ. Res., Osaka Univ., 1959–64; Econ. Affairs Officer, UN, 1962–70; Vis. prof., MIT, 1969–70; Univs. Pittsburgh (1976), Tsukuba, (1977), State Univ. New York, Albany (1978), Columbia (1981).
Degrees BA Hokkaido Univ., 1953; MA, PhD Yale Univ., 1956, 1960.
Offices Ed., *Japanese Econ. Stud.*
Principal Contributions Work has been connected with theory of economic

growth (the role of technical progress, relation with income distribution), theory of production functions (aggregation of microunits into a macro-production function), theory of capital (theoretical basis), index number theory (based on production and utility theories), economic development (macro-economic adjustments in developing countries), macro-economic theory (macro-economic equilibrium in developed economies), and studies of the contemporary and inter-war Japanese economy.

Publications *Books:* 1. *Introduction to Sets and Mappings in Modern Economics* (N-H, 1970); 2. *Production Functions and Aggregation* (N-H, 1975); 3. *Essays in Modern Capital Theory*, co-ed. (N-H, 1976); 4. *Industry and Business in Japan* (M.E. Sharpe, Croom Helm, 1980).

Articles: 1. 'The neo-classical postulate and the technology frontier in capital theory', *QJE*, 88(3), Aug. 1974; 2. 'A simultaneous equation model of savings in developing countries' (with N.H. Leff), *JPE*, 83(6), Dec. 1975; 3. 'The meaning and measurement of the real value added index', *REStat*, 58(4), Nov. 1976; 4. 'The demand function for industrial exports: a cross-counter analysis', *REStat*, 59(4), Nov. 1977; 5. 'Macroeconomic adjustment in developing countries: instability, short-run growth, and external dependency' (with N.H. Leff), *REStat*, 62(1), May 1980.

SATO, Ryuzo

Born 1931, Akita Prefecture, Japan.
Current Post Prof. Econ., Brown Univ., 1967–.
Degrees BEcon, Dr Econ Hitotsubashi Univ., 1954, 1969; PhD Johns Hopkins Univ., 1962.
Offices and Honours Ford Foundation Res. Fellow, Univ. Camb., 1970–1; Guggenheim Memorial Foundation Fellow; Visit. prof., Univ. Bonn, Hitotsubashi Univ., 1974–5.
Principal Contributions Invariance problems in economic dynamics by the application of Lie groups. In the foreword to my *Theory of Technical Change* ... Paul A. Samuelson stated 'now Ryuzo Sato of Brown University is mak-

ing a pioneering attempt to apply Lie's theory to modern economics ... [he] is the only scholar who has studied the application of Lie group to economics'.

Publications *Books:* 1. *Theory of Economic Growth* (Keizo Publishing Co., 1968); 2. *Theory of Technical Change and Economic Invariance: Application of Lie Groups* (Academic Press, 1981).

Articles: 1. 'The stability of the competitive system which contains gross complementary goods', *REStud*, 39(4), Oct. 1972; 2. 'The most general class of CES functions', *Em*, 43(5–6), Sept./Nov. 1975; 3. 'The relationship of technological change and the demand for and supply of raw materials' (with R.V. Romachondran), in, *R & D Assessment* (NSF, 1975); 4. 'Homothetic and non-homothetic CES production functions', *AER*, 67(3), June 1977; 5. 'The impact of technological change on the holotheticity of production functions', *REStud*, 47(4), July 1980.

SAUVY, Alfred

Born 1898, Villeneuve de la Raho, France.
Recent Posts UN Commission Pop., 1947–; Conseil Econ. et Social, 1947–74; Prof., Collège de France, 1959–70.
Degrees Ancien élève l'Ecole Polytechnique; Dr h.c. Univs Geneva, Brussels, Liège, Utrecht, Montreal, Palermo.
Offices and Honours Grand Officier, Légion d'Honneur; Commandeur de la Santé Publique; Commandeur d'Académie; Ancien pres. de la Conjoncture et du Plan au Conseil Econ. et Social.
Principal Contributions Short-term economic fluctuations and demographic changes in the world; the effects of technical change on total employment; the struggle for clarity in statistical information bearing on matters of economic policy.
Publications *Books:* 1. *Théorie générale de la population*, 2 vols (PUF, 1954, 1966); 2. *Histoire économique de la France entre les deux guerres*, 4 vols (Fayard, 1965, 1975); 3. *Le Coût et la*

valeur de la vie humaine (Hermann, 1977); 4. *La Tragédie du pouvoir* (Flammarion, 1978); 5. *La Machine et le chômage* (Dunod, 1980).

Secondary Literature J. Bourgeois-Pichat 'Sauvy, Alfred' *IESS* vol. 18.

SAX, Emil*

Dates and Birthplace 1845–1927, Jauernig, Austro-Hungary.
Posts Held Prof., Univ. Prague, 1879–93.
Career Extended the marginal theory of value to public finance and transportation. His *Grundlegung* ... was a major influence on the development of the theory of taxation and *Die Verkehrsmittel* ... a standard work on transportation economics.
Publications *Books:* 1. *Die Verkehrsmittel in Volks- und Staatswirthschaft*, 2 vols (1878–9); 2. *Grundlegung der Theoretischen Staatswirthschaft* (1887); 3. *Der Kapitalzins* (1916).
Articles: 1. 'The valuation theory of taxation' (1924, 1956), reprinted in *Classics in the Theory of Public Finance*, eds R.A. Musgrave and A.T. Peacock, (1958).
Secondary Literature E. Lindahl, 'Sax, Emil', *ESS*, vol. 13.

SAY, Horace Emile*

Dates and Birthplace 1794–1860, France.
Post Held Businessman.
Offices Founder of Soc. d'Econ. Polit. and *J des Economistes*; Member, Tribunal de Commerce; Councillor of State, 1849–51; Member, l'Académie des sciences morales et politiques, 1857.
Career Son of J.B. Say and his father's devoted follower, his work on commercial relations with Brazil arose from his own business experience there. His work on industrial statistics was based on a massive survey conducted under his supervision by the Paris Chamber of Commerce.
Publications *Books:* 1. *Histoire des relations commerciales entre la France et le Brésil* (1830); 2. *Etudes sur l'administration de la ville de Paris* (1846); 3. *Statistique de l'industrie à Paris*.

SAY, Jean-Baptiste*

Dates and Birthplace 1767–1832, Lyons, France.
Posts Held Journalist and ed., *La Décade*, 1793–99; Cotton manufacturer, 1806–13; Prof. Industrial Econ., Conservatoire des Arts et Métiers, Paris, 1817; Prof. Polit. Econ., Collège de France, Paris, 1830–2.
Offices Member, French Tribunate, 1799–1806.
Career Inspired by Smith's *Wealth of Nations*, he wrote his *Treatise* ... which introduced Smithian ideas to France and other European countries. His analysis developed beyond Smith's, including an emphasis on the role of the entrepreneur. The famous law of markets (Say's law) became widely accepted as a statement of the eternal ability of market forces to produce equilibrium of production and demand. His influence dominated officially-taught economics in France for most of the nineteenth century: unorthodox views and different approaches tended to be kept outside the conventional academic world and were confined to such institutions as the écoles which trained engineers.
Publications *Books:* 1. *A Treatise on Political Economy* (1803, 1880, 1971); 2. *Catéchisme d'économie politique* (1815); 3. *Cours complet d'économie politique pratique*, 6 vols (1828–9).
Secondary Literature G. Leduc, 'Say, Jean Baptiste', *IESS*, vol. 14.

SAY, Léon*

Dates and Birthplace 1826–96, France.
Posts Held Politician, financier and journalist.
Offices Member, French Senate and Chamber of Deputies; Member, French Academy; Pres., Senate; Prefect of the Seine; Ambassador to London; French Minister of Fin., 1872–9, 1882.
Career An economist of the *laissez faire* liberal tradition, and a follower of his grandfather, J.-B. Say, on most

issues. Responsible for many major financial transactions, notably the liquidation of the war debt to Germany, and the establishment of redeemable government stock. Despite an association in the 1860s with the co-operative movement, he was a determined opponent of socialism and an anti-protectionist.

Publications *Books:* 1. *Critical Enquiry into the Financial Situation of Paris* (1866); 2. *Ten Days in Upper Italy* (1883); 3. *State Socialism* (1886); 4. *Democratic Solutions of the Problems of Taxation*, (1886).

Secondary Literature C. Gide, 'Léon Say', *EJ*, 6, June 1896.

SAYERS, Richard Sidney

Born 1908, Bury St Edmunds, England.
Current Post Retired.
Recent Posts Econ. adviser, UK Cabinet Office, 1945–7; Cassel Prof. Econ., LSE, 1947–68.
Degrees MA Univ. Camb., 1933; MA Univ. Oxford, 1936; Hon. DLitt Univ. Warwick, 1967; Hon. DCL Univ. Kent, 1967.
Offices and Honours Fellow, 1957–, Vice-pres., BA; Hon. Fellow, St Catharine's Coll., Univ. Camb., 1960; Hon. Fellow, Inst. Bankers, 1960; Pres., Section F, BAAS, 1960; UK Monopolies Commission, 1968; Emeritus Prof., Univ. London, 1968–; Hon. Fellow, LSE, 1972; Pres., 1972–4, Vice-pres., EHS; Vice-pres., RES, 1973.
Principal Contributions English monetary history; relationship between monetary policy and theory and institutions, as exemplified in report of the Committee on the working of the monetary system (Radcliffe Report) 1959.
Publications *Books:* 1. *Modern Banking* (OUP, 1938, 1967); 2. *Financial Policy* (HMSO, Longman, 1956); 3. *Central Banking after Bagehot* (OUP, 1957); 4. *History of Economic Change in England, 1880–1939* (OUP, 1967); 5. *The Bank of England, 1880–1939* (OUP, 1967); 5. *The Bank of England, 1891–1944* (CUP, 1976).
Articles: 1. 'Ricardo's views on monetary questions', *QJE*, 67, Feb. 1953,

reprinted in *Papers in English Monetary History*, eds T.S. Ashton and R.S. Sayers (OUP, 1953); 2. 'The dilemma of central banking', *J Inst Bankers*, 79, 1958; 3. 'Monetary thought and monetary policy in England', *EJ*, 70, Dec. 1960; 4. 'Bank rate in Keynes' century', *BA Proceedings*, 65, 1979.

SCARF, Herbert E.

Born 1930, Philadelphia, Penn., USA.
Current Post Sterling Prof. Econ., Yale Univ., USA.
Recent Posts Rand Corp., 1954–7; Ass. and assoc. prof., Dept. Stats, Stanford Univ., 1957–63.
Degrees BA Temple Univ., 1951; MA, PhD(Maths.) Princeton Univ., 1952, 1954; LHD Univ. Chicago, 1978.
Offices and Honours Fellow, Em Soc, AAAS; Dir., Cowles Foundation Res. Econ., Yale Univ., 1967–71; Dir., Div. Social Sciences, Yale Univ., 1971–2, 1973–4; Lanchester prize, ORSA, 1974; Member, NAS, 1976.
Principal Contributions Proof that optimal policies for the dynamic inventory problem have a simple form (1960); the first counter-example to the conjecture that the Walrasian price adjustment mechanism is globally stable (1960); convergence of the core to the set of competitive equilibria (1963); sufficient conditions for a general n-person game to have a non-empty core (1967); globally convergent algorithms for calculating equilibrium prices (1967); indivisibilities in production (1977).
Publications *Books:* 1. *Studies in the Mathematical Theory of Inventory and Production* (with K. Arrow and S. Karlin), (Stanford Univ. Press, 1958); 2. *Contributions to the Theory of Inventory and Replacement* (with K. Arrow and S. Karlin), (Stanford Univ. Press, 1961); 3. *Multistage Inventory Models and Techniques* (with D.M. Gilford and M.W. Shelley), (Stanford Univ. Press, 1963); 4. *The Computation of Economic Equilibria* (with T. Hansen), (Yale Univ. Press, 1973).
Articles: 1. 'The optimality of (S, s) policies in the dynamic inventory problem', in *First Stanford Symposium on*

Mathematics in Social Sciences (Stanford Univ. Press, 1960); 2. 'Some examples of global instability of the competitive equilibrium', *Int ER*, 1, Sept. 1960; 3. 'A limit theorem on the core of an economy' (with G. Debreu), *Int ER*, 4, Sept. 1963; 4. 'The core of an n-person game', *Em*, 35, Jan. 1967; 5. 'The approximation of fixed points of a continuous mapping', *SIAM J Applied Maths.*, 15(5), 1967.

SCHAFFLE, Albert Eberhard Friedrich*

Dates and Birthplace 1831–1904, Nürtingen, Germany.
Posts Held Journalist with *Schwäbischer Merkur*; Prof. Polit. Econ., Univ. Tübingen, 1860, Univ. Vienna, 1868–71.
Offices Member, Wurttemberg parliament, 1861–5; Austrian Minister of Commerce, 1871.
Career German academic socialist whose *Quintessenz* . . . was widely read and translated. The early theoretical works, and his brief period of ministerial office in Austria, were succeeded by a long period as a writer in Stuttgart, when he produced a large number of works on a wide range of economic and financial topics. His influence, both as an opponent of *laissez faire* liberalism and a reconciler of German philosophy and the inductive method of economic investigation, was considerable.
Publications *Books:* 1. *Hand- und Lehrbuch der Nationalökonomie* (1861); 2. *Über die Theorie der Ausschliessenden Absatzverhältnisse* (1867); 3. *Capitalism and Socialism* (1869); 4. *Quintessenz des Sozialismus* (1874); 5. *Bau und Leben des Sozialen Körpers*, 4 vols (1875–8); 6. *Aussichtslosigkeit der Sozialdemokratie* (1884) 7. *Steuern*, 2 vols (1895–7).
Secondary Literature F.K. Mann, 'Schaffle, Albert Eberhard Friedrich', *ESS*, vol. 13.

SCHELLING, Thomas Crombie

Born 1921, Oakland, Cal., USA.
Current Post Lucius N. Littauer Prof. Polit. Econ., Harvard Univ., USA.

Recent Posts US govt economist, 1948–53; Prof. Econ., Yale Univ., 1953–8.
Degrees BA Univ. Cal., Berkeley, 1944; AM, PhD (Econ.) Harvard Univ., 1948, 1951.
Offices and Honours Member, Inst. Medicine; Fellow, AAAS, Amer. Assoc. Advancement Science; Assembly, Behavioral and Social Sciences, NAS; Chairman, Res. Advisory Board, Comm. Econ. Development; Frank E. Seidman Disting. Award Polit. Econ., 1977.
Principal Contributions The theory of bargaining and conflict management in general, with applications to nuclear strategy and arms control, crime and extortion, addiction and self-control, personal and business ethics, and the legal status of the dying. Contributions to theory of interdependent choice and behaviour, with applications to racial and other segregation, health-related behaviours, mass behaviour, regulation and law enforcement. Specific contributions to policy analysis in energy, health, environmental protection, nuclear proliferation, terrorism, and the valuation of human life. Earlier contributions to theory of economic warfare, strategic trade controls, foreign-aid strategy, international cost sharing, and military alliances.
Publications *Books:* 1. *International Economics* (Allyn & Bacon, 1958); 2. *The strategy of Conflict* (Harvard Univ. Press, 1960, 1980); 3. *Strategy and Arms Control* (with M.H. Halperin), (Twentieth Century Fund, 1961); 4. *Arms and Influence* (Yale Univ. Press, 1966); 5. *Micromotives and Macrobehavior* (Norton, 1978).
Articles: 1. 'The dynamics of price flexibility', *AER*, 39, Sept. 1949; 2. 'Economics and criminal enterprise', *Public Interest*, Spring 1967; 3. 'Game theory and the study of ethical system', *J Conflict Resolution*, 12, March 1968.

SCHERER, Frederic Michael

Born 1932, Ottawa, Ill., USA.
Current Post Prof. Econ., Northwestern Univ., USA, 1976–.
Recent Posts Harvard Univ.,

1958–63; Princeton Univ., 1963–6; Univ. Michigan, 1966–72; Internat. Inst. Management, Berlin, 1972–4; US Federal Trade Commission, Bureau Econ., 1974–6.

Degrees BA Univ. Michigan, 1954; MBA, PhD Harvard Univ., 1958, 1963.

Offices and Honours Lanchester prize, ORSA, 1964; Assoc. ed., *REStat*, 1977–; Board eds., *AER*, 1977–80; Advisory panels, NSF, 1977–81.

Principal Contributions The economics of industrial technology, including theoretical and empirical studies of market structure and innovation, economies of scale, productivity growth, product variety, worker satisfaction, and military research and development; and a graduate-level text providing a comprehensive theoretical and empirical analysis of industrial structure, behaviour and performance.

Publications *Books:* 1. *The Weapons Acquisition Process: An Economic Analysis* (with M.J. Peck), (Harvard Univ. Press, 1962); 2. *The Weapons Acquisition Process: Economic Incentives* (Harvard Univ. Press, 1964); 3. *Industrial Market Structure and Economic Performance* (Rand McNally, Houghton Mifflin, 1970, 1980); 4. *The Economics of Multi-plant Operation: An International Comparisons Study* (with others), (Harvard Univ., 1975).

Articles: 1. 'The theory of contractual incentives for cost reduction', *QJE*, 78, May 1964; 2. 'Firm size, market structure, opportunity, and the output of patented inventions', *AER*, 55, Dec. 1965; 3. 'Research and development resource allocation under rivalry', *QJE*, 81, Aug. 1967; 4. 'The determinants of industrial plant sizes in six nations', *REStat*, 55(2), May 1973; 5. 'The welfare economics of product variety: an application to the ready-to-eat cereals industry', *J Ind E*, 28(2), Dec. 1979.

SCHMALENSEE, Richard Lee

Born 1944, Belleville, Ill., USA.

Current Post Prof. Applied Econ., Sloan School Management, MIT, USA.

Recent Posts Assoc. prof. Econ., Dept Econ., Univ. Cal., San Diego, 1974–7; Assoc. prof. Applied Econ.,

Sloan School Management, MIT, 1977–9.

Degrees SB, PhD MIT, 1965, 1970.

Offices AEA; Ed. Boards, *J Ind E*, *Recherches Economiques de Louvain*; Ed., MIT Press series, Regulation of Econ. Activity; Program Chairman, North Amer. Winter Meeting, World Congress, Em Soc, 1980.

Principal Contributions Major work has focused on the development and use of economic theory to deal with issues in industrial organisation, particularly in the areas of advertising and non-price competition. Study of natural resource markets, price policy, entry deterrence, and various public policy topics.

Publications *Books: The Economics of Advertising* (N–H, 1972); 2. *The Control of Natural Monopolies* (D.C. Heath & Co., 1979).

Articles: 1. 'A note on the theory of vertical integration', *JPE*, 81(2), Pt 1, March/April 1973; 2. 'A model of advertising and product quality', *JPE*, 86(3), June 1978; 3. 'Entry deterrence in the ready-to-eat breakfast cereal industry', *Bell JE*, 1978; 4. 'On oligopolistic markets for nonrenewable natural resources' (with T. Lewis), *QJE*, 95(3), Nov. 1980; 5. 'Economies of scale and barriers to entry', *JPE*, 1982.

SCHMIDT, Kurt

Born 1924, Sobernheim, Germany.

Current Post Prof. Econ., Univ. Mainz, 1968.

Degrees Dr rer.pol., Habilitation (Privatdozent), Diplom-Volkswirt Univ. Bonn, 1952, 1957, 1969.

Offices Rockefeller Fellow, USA, 1960–1; Vis. prof. and res. assoc., Bologna, Italy; Prof. Econ., Technische Hochschule, Berlin, 1963–8; Member, Wissenschaftlicher Beirat beim Bundesministerium für Finanzen; Member, Sachverständigenrat zur Begutachtung der gesamtwirtschaftlichen Entwicklung.

Principal Contributions Early work devoted to a critical review of the arguments in favour of progressive taxation. Later works treat the problem in a political-sociological way.

Publications *Books:* 1. *Die Steuer-*

progession (Mohr-Siebeck, 1960); 2. *Kollektivbedürfnisse und Staatstätigkeit*, in *Theorie und Praxis des Finanzpolitischen Interventionismus (Fritz Neumark zum 70. Geburtstag)* (Mohr-Siebeck, 1970); 3. *Die Mehrjährige Finanzplaung, Wunsch und Wirlichkeit* (with E. Wille), (Mohr-Siebeck, 1970).

Articles: 1. 'Zur Reform der Unternehmungsbesteuerung', *Finanzarchiv*, N.F., 22, 1962–3; 2. 'Entwicklungstendenzen der öffentlichen Ausgaben im demokratischen Gruppenstaat', *Finanzarchiv*, N.F., 25, 1966; 3. 'Zur politischen Reaktion auf Nachfragewogen in der Staatswirtschaft', *Finanzarchiv*, N.F., 33, 1974; 4. 'Grundprobleme der Besteuerung', *Handbuch der Finanzwissenschaft*, 3, 2, (Mohr-Siebeck, 1978); 5. 'Korruption' (with C. Garschagen), *Handwörterbuch der Wirtschaftswissenschaft*, 4, (Mohr-Siebeck, 1978).

SCHMITT, Bernard

Born 1929, Colmar, France.
Current Post Prof., Education Nationale, France.
Recent Posts Maître de Recherche, CNRS, 1964; Prof., Univ. Freibourg, Switzerland, 1964.
Degrees Doctorat d'Etat Paris, 1958; Agrégation, 1977.
Honours Bronze medal, 1964, Silver medal, 1968, CNRS.
Principal Contributions Integration of money and national output; theory of profits; international money; the study of time in economics.
Publications *Books:* 1. *L'Analyse macroéconomique des revenus* (Dalloz, 1971); 2. *Macroeconomic Theory, a Fundamental Revision* (Castella, 1972); 3. *Théorie unitaire de la monnaie nationale et internationale* (Castella, 1975); 4. *La Pensée de Karl Marx, analyse et critique*, 2 vols (with A. Cencini), (Castella, 1975, 1977); 5. *L'Or, le dollar et la monnaie internationale* (Calmann-Levy, 1978).

SCHMOLLER, Gustav*

Dates and Birthplace 1838–1917, Württemberg, Germany.

Posts Held Prof. Staatswissenschaften, Univ. Halle, 1864–72, Univ. Strasbourg, 1872–82, Univ. Berlin, 1882–1913.
Degree Grad. Univ. Tübingen, 1860.
Offices Founder, Verein für Sozialpolitik; Member, Prussian State Council, 1884, Upper House of Parliament, 1889.
Career Founder of the 'younger historical school' ('academic socialists') and promoter of research in the social sciences in Germany. Menger's attack on his ideas inaugurated the famous *Methodenstreit*. Schmoller's major work, the *Grundriss*, is wide in scope but lacks coherence. His political stance – between conservatism and revolutionary socialism – was boldly maintained, and achieved a good deal of public support.
Publications *Books:* 1. *Zur Geschichte der Deutschen Kleingewerke im 19 Jahrhundert* (1870); 2. *Über einige Grundfragen der Sozialpolitik und der Volkswirtschaftslehre* (1874–97); 3. *Grundriss der Allgemeinen Volkswirtschaftslehre* (1900–4).
Secondary Literature W. Fischer, 'Schmoller, Gustav', *IESS*, vol. 14.

SCHMOOKLER, John*

N.e.

SCHNEIDER, Erich*

Dates and Birthplace 1900–70, Germany.
Posts Held Schoolteacher, 1925–36; Prof., Univs. Aarhus, 1936–46, Kiel, 1946–68; Dir., Inst. for World Econ., Univ. Kiel, 1961–9.
Degree Dr rer. pol. Univ. Frankfurt, 1922.
Offices and Honours Pres., Verein für Sozialpolitik, 1963–6; List gold medal, 1965.
Career His contribution to price theory and particularly the theory of monopoly made his name, but his *Einführung* ... was his chief achievement. It gave German students a grounding in modern analysis based on his very wide knowledge of the inter-

national literature of economics. Part 4 is a masterly history of price theory from Smith to Marshall.

Publications *Books:* 1. *Reine Theorie Monopolistischer Wirtschaftsformen* (1932); 2. *Theorie der Produktion* (1934); 3. *Einführung in die Wirtschaftstheorie,* 4 vols (1947–62); 4. *Pricing and Equilibrium* (1952); 5. *Volkswirtschaft und Betriebswirtschaft: Ausgewählte Aufsätze* (1964); 6. *Zahlungsbilanz und Wechselkurs* (1968); 7. *Die Wirtschaft im Schulunterricht* (1968); 8. *Joseph A. Schumpeter: Leben und Werk eines Grossen Sozialökonomen* (1970).
Secondary Literature W. Vogt, 'Erich Schneider and economic theory', *German Econ. Review,* 9(4), 1971.

SCHNEIDER, Helmut

Born 1936, Saarbruecken, Germany.
Current Post Prof., Univ. Zürich, Switzerland.
Recent Posts Prof. Econ., Free Univ. Berlin, 1967–9; Prof. Econ., Univ. Mannheim, 1969–73.
Degrees Diplom Volkswirt Univ. Saarbruecken, 1959; Dr rer. pol. Univ. Muenster, 1963.
Principal Contributions Effects of taxation: in a dynamic context, national tax policy – even an otherwise 'neutral' profits tax – affects production, prices, investment and optimal financing of multi-national enterprises; and taxes may be inappropriate for redistribution of income and wealth in a growing economy with bargaining-determined wages.
Publications *Books:* 1. *Der Einfluss der Steuern auf die Unternehmerischen Investitionsentscheidungen* (J.C.B. Mohr, 1964); 2. *Das Allgemeine Gleichgewicht in der Marktwirtschaft. Eine mikroökonomische Analyse mit Hilfe der Theorie der Strategischen Spiele* (J.C.B. Mohr, 1969); 3. *Mikroökonomie, eine Einführung in die Preis-. Produktions- und Wohlfahrtstheorie* (Vahlen, 1973, 1977).
Articles: 1. 'Staatsaktivität und optimales Wachstum', in H. Haller and W. Albers, eds. *Probleme der Staatsverschuldung, Schriften des Vereins für Sozialpolitik N.F.,* vol. 61 (Duncker

& Humblot, 1975); 2. 'Tarifverhandlungen, wirtschaftliches Wachstum und staatliche Umverteilungspolitik', in *Öffentliche Finanzwirtschaft und Verteilung III,* ed. W. Dreissig, *Schriften des Vereins für Socialpolitik N.F.,* vol. 75/III (Duncker & Humblot, 1975); 3. 'Steuern V: Wirkungslehre' (with H.H. Nachtkamp), in *Handwörterbuch der Wirtschaftswissenschaften* (G. Fischer, 1977); 4. 'Multinationale Unternehmen und nationale Steuerpolitik' (with H.H. Nachtkamp), *Zeitschrift für Wirtschafts- und Sozialwissenschaften,* 100, 1980; 5. 'Preise I: Konkurrenzpreisbildung', in *Handwörterbuch der Wirtschaftswissenschaften* (G. Fischer, 1980).

SCHULTZ, Henry*

Dates and Birthplace 1893–1938, Poland.
Post Held Prof., Univ. Chicago, 1926–38.
Degrees BA City Coll., New York; PhD Columbia Univ., 1926.
Career Econometrician whose early years were spent conducting statistical investigations for various government departments. Inspired by his teacher H.L. Moore, and having a detailed grasp of Cournot, Walras and Pareto, he was able to make a synthesis of theory and empirical work on demand. His work on statistical demand analysis involved several contributions to statistical theory.
Publications *Books:* 1. *Statistical Laws of Demand and Supply* (1928); 2. *The theory of Measurement of Demand* (1938).
Articles: 1. 'Theoretical considerations relating to supply', *JPE,* 35, Aug. 1927; 2. 'Marginal productivity and the general pricing process', *JPE,* 37, Oct. 1929; 3. 'Interrelations of demand', *JPE,* 41, Aug. 1933; 4. 'Interrelations of demand, price and income', *JPE,* 43, Aug. 1935.
Secondary Literature H. Hotelling, 'The work of Henry Schultz', *Em,* 7, April 1939; K.A. Fox, 'Schultz, Henry', *IESS,* vol. 14.

SCHULTZ, Paul T.

Born   1940, Ames, Iowa, USA.
Current Post   Malcolm K. Brachman Prof. Econ., Yale Univ., USA.
Recent Posts   Dir. Pop. Res., Rand Corp., 1968–72; Prof. Econ., Univ. Minnesota, 1972–5; Prof. Econ., Yale Univ., 1974.
Degrees   BA Swarthmore Coll., 1961; PhD MIT, 1966.
Offices   AEA; Em Soc; Member, Internat. Union Scientific Study Pop., 1973–; Dir., PAA, 1979–82; Fellow, AAAS, 1980–.
Principal Contributions   Extended consumer-demand theory to explain interdependent demographic and economic behaviour of individuals and families, in particular, fertility, labour force behaviour, marriage, migration and mortality. Microeconometric analyses of families during economic development estimate the effects of relative prices and opportunities on mortality, fertility and schooling, which provide links between the 'demographic transition' and the onset of modern economic growth. Changes in the age-composition of populations perturb aggregate measures of income inequality and wage structures; when these demographic repercussions are suitably taken into account, evaluation of public welfare programmes and trade/price policies are performed more reliably.
Publications   *Books:* 1. *Love and Life between the Censuses* (with others), (Rand Corp., 1970); 2. *Structural Change in a Developing Economy* (with others), (Princeton Univ. Press, 1971); 3. *Fertility Determinants: A Theory, Evidence and an Application to Policy Evaluation* (Rand Corp., 1974); 4. *Economics of Population* (Addison-Wesley, 1981).
Articles: 1. 'An economic model of family planning and fertility', *JPE*, 77(2), March/April, 1969; 2. 'An economic perspective on population growth', in *Rapid Population Growth* (Johns Hopkins Univ. Press, 1971); 3. 'Explanations of birth-rate change over space and time: a study of Taiwan', *JPE*, Pt 2, 81(2), April 1973; 4. 'Estimating labor supply functions for married women', in *Female Labor Supply*, ed. J.P. Smith (Princeton Univ. Press, 1980); 5. 'Protection and the distribution of personal income by sector', in *Alternative Trade and Employment Strategies*, ed. A. Krueger (Univ. Chicago Press, 1981).

SCHULTZ, Theodore W.

Born   1902, Arlington, S. Dakota, USA.
Current Post   Prof. Emeritus Econ., Univ. Chicago, USA.
Recent Posts   Faculty Econ., 1930–43, Head Dept. Econ. Sociology, 1934–43, Iowa State Coll; Prof. Econ., 1943–, Chairman, Dept. Econ., 1946–61, Charles L. Hutchinson Disting. service prof., 1952–, Univ. Chicago; Consultant to US govt, UN specialised agencies, and private foundations.
Degrees   BS, DSc. S. Dakota State Coll., 1928, 1959; MS, PhD, LLD Univ. Wisconsin, 1928, 1930, 1968; LLD Grinnel Coll., 1949, Michigan State Univ., 1962, Univ. Illinois, 1968, Catholic Univ. Chile, 1979.
Offices and Honours   Trustee, Inst. Current World Affairs, 1935–58, Pop. Council, 1957–78, Internat. Agric. Development Service, 1975–; Board member, active member, 1940–, Nat. Planning Assoc.; Occasional Chairman, member Res. Advisory Board, 1943–, Comm. Econ. Development; NBER: Member, Board Dirs., 1949–67, Vicepres., 1958; Fellow, Center Advanced Study Behavioral Sciences, 1956–7, Amer. Farm Econ. Assoc., 1957–, AAAS, 1958–, Amer. Philosophical Soc., 1962–; Accademia Economico-Agraria dei Georgofili, Florence, 1958–, Accademia Nazionale di Agricoltura, Bologna, 1960–; Guest, Soviet Academy Sciences, 1960; AEA: Pres., 1960, Disting. fellow, 1965–, Francis A. Walker medal, 1972; Founding member, Nat. Academy Education, 1965, member, NAS, 1974–; Disting. service award, Amer. Agric. Eds. Assoc., 1973; Governor, Board Internat. Development Res. Center, Canada, 1973–8; Leonard Elmhirst medal, Internat. Agric. Econ. Assoc., 1976; Nobel Prize for Econ., 1980.

Principal Contributions The economic value of education; analysis of the increases in the value of human time over time; economics of research and its contribution to productivity; the value of the ability to deal with disequilibria; investment in entrepreneurship; understanding the improvements in the quality of physical and human capital as sources of gains in productivity; declining economic importance of land; location effects on economic growth of agriculture; assessment of the economic calculations of farmers in low income countries; and the concept of human capital, investment in this form of capital, its effect on the supply of labour, household production, children and fertility.

Publications *Books:* 1. *Measures for Economic Development of Underdeveloped Countries*, joint author (UN, 1951); 2. *The Economic Value of Education* (Columbia Univ. Press, 1963); 3. *Transforming Traditional Agriculture* (Yale Univ. Press, 1964); 4. *Investment in Human Capital: The Role of Education and of Research* (Free Press, 1971); 5. *Human Resources, Human Capital: Policy Issues and Research Opportunities* (NBER, 1972).

Articles: 1. 'Capital formation by education', *JPE*, 6, Dec. 1960; 2. 'Investment in human capital', *AER*, 51(1), March 1961, reprinted in *Economics of Education 1*, ed. H. Blaug (Penguin Books, 1969); 3. 'The value of the ability to deal with disequilibria', *JEL*, 13(3), Sept. 1975; 4. 'Migration: an economist's view', in *Human Migration*, eds W.H. McNeil and R. Adams (Indiana Univ. Press, 1978); 5. 'Life span, health, savings and productivity' (with R. Ram), *EDCC*, 27(3), April 1979.

Secondary Literature D.G. Johnson, 'Schultz, Theodore W.', *IESS* vol. 18; M.J. Bowman, 'On Theodore Schultz's contributions to economics', *Swed JE* 82(4), 1980.

SCHUMPETER, Joseph Alois*

Dates and Birthplace 1883–1950, Triesch, Austro-Hungary

Posts Held Teacher, Univs. Czernovitz and Graz; Prof., Univ Bonn, 1925–32; Prof., Harvard Univ., 1932–50.

Degree Grad. Univ. Vienna.

Offices Minister of Fin., Austria, 1919–20; Pres., AEA; Founding member, Pres., Em Soc.

Career Great teacher and historian of economics, his own economic theory was complex and wide-ranging. The distinction between statics and dynamics was essential to his account of capitalism – certain periods approximating to equilibrium, and others exhibiting considerable change. His analysis of business cycles started from this point and distinguished the types and behaviour of cycles. The posthumous *History ...* shows a prodigious grasp of the literature of economics. In this, as in his major book *Capitalism, Socialism and Democracy*, he relates economic phenomena and ideas to a wider context of social analysis. The latter, whilst rejecting the Marxian analysis, still envisages capitalism as moving by its own internal forces towards Schumpeter's vision of a socialist society.

Publications *Books:* 1. *Das Wesen und der Hauptinhalt der Theoretischen Nationalokonomie* (1908); 2. *Theory of Economic Development* (1912, 1934, 1949); 3. *Epochen der Dogmen- und Methodengeschichte* (1914); 4. *Die Krise des Steuerstaats* (1918); 5. *Business Cycles*, 2 vols (1939); 6. *Imperialism and Social Classes* (1941, 1951); 7. *Capitalism, Socialism and Democracy* (1942); 8. *Ten Great Economists* (1951); 9. *Essays of J.A. Schumpeter* (1951); 10. *History of Economic Analysis* (1964).

Secondary Literature S.E. Harris, *Schumpeter: Social Scientist* (Harvard Univ. Press, 1951); W.F. Stolper, 'Schumpeter, Joseph A.', *IESS*, vol. 14.

SCHULTZE, C.L.

N.e.

SCITOVSKY, Tibor

Born 1910, Budapest, Hungary.
Current Post Prof. Emeritus, Univ. Cal., Santa Cruz, USA.
Recent Posts Stanford Univ., 1946–58, 1970–6; Univ. Cal., Berkeley, 1958–66; Development Centre, OECD, Paris, 1966–8; Yale Univ., 1968–70; LSE, 1976–8.
Degrees Dr iuris Univ. Budapest, 1932; MSc (Econ) LSE, 1938.
Offices AAAS; AEA; RES; Disting. Fellow, Vice-pres., AEA, 1973.
Principal Contributions Exploring the behaviour of markets where the stock demand for assets is equated with the stock supply; reconsideration of the theory of tariffs; comparing and contrasting the assumption of rational consumer behaviour with empirical evidence and the psychologist's findings.
Publications *Books:* 1. *Welfare and Competition* (Richard D. Irwin, A & U, 1951, 1971); 2. *Economic Theory and Western European Integration* (A & U, 1958); 3. *Papers on Welfare and Growth* (Stanford Univ. Press, A & U, 1964); 4. *Money and the Balance of Payments* (Rand McNally, 1969); 5. *The Joyless Economy* (OUP, 1976).
Articles: 1. 'A study of interest and capital', *Ec*, N.S. 7, Aug. 1940; 2. 'A reconsideration of the theory of tariffs', *REStud*, 9(2), 1942; 3. 'Two concepts of external economies', *JPE*, 62, April 1954; 4. 'Market power and inflation', *Ec*, 45, Aug. 1978; 5. 'Asymmetries in economics', *SJPE*, 25(3), Nov. 1978.

SCOTT, Anthony Dalton

Born 1923, Vancouver, Canada.
Current Post Prof. Econ., 1953–, Head of Dept., 1965–72, Univ. British Columbia, Canada.
Recent Posts Lecturer, LSE, 1950–3; Commissioner, Canadian Section, Internat. Joint Commission under Boundary Water Treaty, 1967–71.
Degrees BComm., BA Univ. British Columbia, 1945, 1947; Harvard Univ., 1949; PhD LSE, 1953; Hon. LLD Guelph Univ., 1980.
Offices and Honours Exec. member, AEA, 1966–70; Pres., Canadian Polit. Science Assoc., 1966–7; Fellow, Royal Soc. Canada, 1969–; Killem Fellow, Canada Council, 1972, 1974; Queen's Jubilee medal, 1978; Reserve Bank of Australia Fellow, 1978–9; Pres., Academy Humanities and Social Sciences, 1979.
Principal Contributions First worked on resource conservation in relation to other aspects of capital theory. Subsequently wrote numerous papers on regulation of fisheries, theory of the mine, benefit-cost analysis, hydro-electric resources, recreation, pollution, and generally on the control of both 'common-property' and exhaustible resources. Simultaneously, started theoretical examination of federal economies, and finance, including intergovernmental grants and interprovincial migration. These two interests have converged in papers and books on international pollution and fisheries, migration of skilled manpower (the brain drain), and on the relation of federal systems to regional endowments of energy and resources.
Publications *Books:* 1. *Natural Resources – The Economics of Conservation* (Univ. Toronto Press, 1955, McClelland & Stewart, 1973); 2. *Output, Labour and Capital in the Canadian Economy* (with W.C. Hood), (Queen's Printer, 1956); 3. *The Common Wealth of Ocean Fisheries* (with F.T. Christy Jr), (Johns Hopkins Univ. Press, 1965, 1972); 4. *The Brain Drain* (with H. Grubel), (Wilfred Laurier Press, 1976); 5. *The Economic Constitution of Federal States* (with A. Breton), (Univ. Toronto Press, 1978).
Articles: 1. 'A note on grants in federal countries', *Ec*, N.S. 17, Nov. 1950; 2. 'Evaluation of federal grants', *Ec*, N.S. 19, Nov. 1952; 3. 'The fishery: the objectives of sole ownership', *JPE*, 63, April 1955; 4. 'The economics of regulating fisheries', in *Economic Effects of Fishery Regulation*, ed. R. Hamlisch (FAO, 1962); 5. 'Theory of mine under conditions of certainty', in *Extractive Resources and Taxation*, ed. M. Gaffney (Madison, 1967).

SCOTT, William Robert*

Dates and Birthplace 1868–1940, Lisnamallard, Northern Ireland.

Posts Held Lecturer, St Andrews Univ., 1896–1915; Adam Smith Prof., Univ. Glasgow, 1915–40.

Degrees BA, MA, DLitt. Trinity Coll., Dublin, 1889, 1891, 1902; DPhil. St Andrews Univ., 1900.

Offices Fellow, BA; Pres., Section F, BAAS, 1915; Pres., EHS, 1928; Pres., RES, 1935–7.

Career Economic historian whose account of joint-stock companies is based on massive scholarship and a sound grasp of business procedures. He did valuable work on contemporary economic problems, some of it for official commissions and much of it published in article form. His work on Smith involved the patient assembly of new factual material.

Publications *Books:* 1. *Francis Hutcheson* (1900); 2. *Constitution and Finance of English, Scottish and Irish Joint-stock Companies to 1720*, 3 vols (1910–12); 3. *Report to the Board of Agriculture for Scotland* (1914); 4. *Economic Problems of Peace after War*, 2 vols (1917–18); 5. *Adam Smith as Student and Professor* (1937).

Secondary Literature J.H. Clapham, 'Obituary: William Robert Scott', *EJ*, 50, June/Sept. 1940.

SCROPE, George Julius Poulett*

Dates and Birthplace 1797–1876, England.

Post held Private income.

Degree BA Univ. Camb., 1821.

Offices Fellow, Royal Soc., 1826; MP for Stroud, 1833–68.

Career He adopted the name Scrope on marrying the heiress of that family, and his interest in the state of the workers on the Scrope family estate turned his attention partially away from geology, in which he had already made a name, to political economy. He wrote many pamphlets on economic questions, opposing the Malthusian theory of population, defending the Poor Laws, advocating unemployment insurance, criticising the gold standard and commenting on other issues. He was, however, more than just a current commentator, attributing business cycles to psychological causes aggravated by monetary phenomena, and using the concept of equilibrium to analyse supply and demand. Despite the high quality of his work and his publication of a systematic treatise, his contribution was largely ignored.

Publications *Books:* 1. *Principles of Political Economy* (1833); 2. *Friendly Societies* (1872).

Articles: 1. 'The political economists', *Quarterly Review*, 1831.

Secondary Literature R. Opie, 'A neglected English economist: George Poulett Scrope', *QJE*, 44, Nov. 1929.

SEAGER, Henry Rogers*

Dates and Birthplace 1870–1930, USA.

Posts Held Prof., Univs Pennsylvania, Columbia.

Offices Pres., AEA, 1922.

Career Labour economist and expert on trusts whose arguments for social insurance were considered highly effective. Through his writings and public activities he achieved some success in changing government attitudes towards corporations and trusts.

Publications *Books:* 1. *Introduction to Economics* (1904); 2. *Social Insurance* (1910); 3. *Principles of Economics* (1913); 4. *Trust and Corporation Problems* (1929); 5. *Labor and other Economic Essays* (1931).

Secondary Literature C.A. Gulick, 'Seager, Henry Rogers', *ESS*, vol. 14.

SEERS, Dudley

Born 1920, London, England.

Current Post Professorial Fellow, Inst. Development Stud., Univ., Sussex, 1973–.

Recent Posts Chief, Survey Section, UN ECLA, 1957–61; Vis. prof., Yale Univ., 1961–3; Dir., Econ. Development Div., UN ECA, 1963–4; Dir., Econ. Development Div., UN ECA, 1963–4; Dir.-general, Econ. Planning Staff, UK Ministry Overseas Development,

1964–7; Dir., Inst. Development Stud., Univ. Sussex, 1967–73.

Degrees BA Univ. Camb., 1941.

Offices and Honours Ed. Board, *J Dev Stud*; Pres., Soc. Internat. Development, 1968–70; Council, RES, 1975–8; Pres., Europ. Assoc. Development Res. and Training Insts., 1975–8; Companion, Order St Michael and St George, 1975.

Principal Contributions Originally stressed the relativism of economics – the danger in particular of transferring economic propositions uncritically from industrial countries to the Third World. More recent work puts more emphasis on the extent to which European countries, and the European economic system as a whole, show problems familiar to those in the development field, suggesting that theory and practical experience in that field may throw light on our problems too. Other main interest has been in criticising the massive transfer of statistical categories and frameworks to the Third World, and suggesting what might be more appropriate.

Publications *Books:* 1. *Towards Full Employment. A programme for Colombia, Prepared by an Inter-agency Team organised by the ILO* (with others), (ILO, 1970); 2. *Matching Employment Opportunities and Expectations. A programme of action for Ceylon*, 2 vols (with others), (ILO, 1971); 3. *Under-developed Europe: Studies in Core-periphery Relations*, ed. (with B. Schaffer and M. Kiljunen), (Harvester Press, 1979); 4. *Integration and Unequal Development: The Experience of the EEC*, ed. (with C. Vaitsos), (Macmillan, 1980); 5. *The Second Enlargement of the EEC: Integration of Unequal Partners*, ed. (with C. Vaitsos), (Macmillan, 1981).

Articles: 1. 'The limitations of the special case', in *The Teaching of Development Economics*, eds K. Martin and J. Knapp (Frank Cass, 1967); 2. 'What are we trying to measure?', *J Dev. Stud.*, 8(3), April 1972; 3. 'The political economy of national accounting', in *Employment, Income Distribution and Development Strategy: Problems of the Developing Countries – Essays in Honour of H.W. Singer*, eds A.K. Cairncross and M. Puri (Macmillan, 1975); 4. 'Life

expectancy as an integrating concept in social and demographic analysis and planning', *RIW*, 23(3), Sept. 1977; 5. 'The congruence of Marxism and other neo-classical doctrines', in *Towards a New Strategy of Development* (Pergamon Press, 1980).

SELDEN, Richard T.

Born 1922, Pontiac, Mich., USA.

Current Post Carter Glass Prof. Econ., Univ. Virginia, USA, 1969–.

Recent Posts Ass. and assoc. prof. Econ., Vanderbilt Univ., 1952–8; Res. Staff, NBER, 1958–64; Assoc. prof. Banking, Columbia Univ., 1959–63; Prof. Econ., Cornell Univ., 1963–9; Fulbright Advanced Res. Scholar, Belgium, 1965; Vis. prof. Econ., Stanford Univ., 1967; Vis. Scholar, Inst. Internat. Econ. Stud., Univ. Stockholm, 1978.

Degrees BA, PhD Univ. Chicago, 1948, 1954; MA Columbia Univ., 1949.

Offices and Honours Member, AEA, AFA, SEA; Consultant, comms. of US Congress, Board Governors Fed. Reserve System; Guggenheim Memorial Foundation Fellow, 1965; Vice-pres., Virginia Assoc. Economists, 1976.

Principal Contributions Main research interests have been in applied monetary and macro-economics, including work on the demand for money as an early member of the modern quantity theory school under Milton Friedman's leadership; extensive empirical tests of alternative theories of inflation; and studies of US financial markets and institutions.

Publications *Books*; 1. *The Postwar Rise in the Velocity of Money, a Sectoral Analysis* (NBER, 1962); 2. *Trends and Cycles in the Commercial Paper Market* (NBER, 1963); 3. *Time Deposit Growth and the Employment of Bank Funds* (with G.R. Morrison), (Assoc. Reserve City Bankers, 1965); 4. *Capitalism and Freedom: Problems and Prospects*, ed. (Univ. Virginia Press, 1975).

Articles: 1. 'Monetary velocity in the United States', in *Studies in the Quantity Theory of Money*, ed. M. Friedman (Univ. Chicago Press, 1956); 2. 'Cost-push versus demand-pull inflation,

1955–57', *JPE*, 67, Feb. 1959; 3. 'Business pricing policies and inflation' (with H.J. DePodwin), *JPE*, 71, April 1963; 4. 'A critique of Dutch monetarism', *J Mon E*, 1(2), April 1975; 5. 'The inflationary seventies: comparisons among selected high-income countries', in *Inflation Through the Ages: Economic, Social, Psychological and Historical Aspects*, ed. E.H. Marcus (Columbia Univ. Press, 1981).

SELIGMAN, Edwin Robert Anderson*

Dates and Birthplace 1861–1939, New York City, NY, USA.

Post Held Lecturer, prof., Columbia Univ., 1885–1931.

Degrees BA, MA, LLB, PhD Columbia Univ., 1879, 1884, 1885.

Offices Founder, pres., 1902–4, AEA; Founder, pres., 1919–20, AAUP; Chief ed., *ESS*, 1927–35.

Career Expert on public finance, member of innumerable tax commissions, and a key figure in the professionalisation of American economics. His work on income tax concentrated on the equity case for a progressive income tax in terms of ability to pay, but he also explored the incidence of taxation and the effects of taxes on production. Also wrote on general economics, where the influence of his earlier German studies is revealed by his high estimation of the value of historical studies. His interest in the history of economic thought was reflected in his remarkable personal library which he bequeathed to Columbia University.

Publications *Books:* 1. *The Shifting and Incidence of Taxation* (1892); 2. *Progressive Taxation in Theory and Practice* (1894, 1908); 3. *Essays in Taxation* (1895, 1928); 4. *Economic Interpretation of History* (1902, 1934, 1961); 5. *Principles of Economics* (1905, 1929); 6. *The Income Tax: A Study of the History, Theory and Practice of Income Taxation at Home and Abroad* (1911, 1914); 7. *Studies in Public Finance* (1925); 8. *Essays in Economics* (1925).

Secondary Literature C.S. Shoup, 'Seligman, Edwin R.A.', *IESS*, vol. 14

SEN, Amartya Kumar

Born 1933, Santiniketan, Bengal, India.

Current Post Drummond Prof. Polit. Econ., Fellow All Souls Coll., Univ. Oxford.

Recent Posts Prof. Econ., Delhi Univ., 1963–71; Prof. Econ., LSE, 1971–7; Prof. Econ., Univ. Oxford, 1977–80.

Degrees BA Calcutta Univ., 1953; BA, PhD Univ. Camb., 1955, 1959; Hon. DLitt Univ. Saskatchewan, 1979.

Offices and Honours Fellow, BA; Fellow, Em Soc; Foreign hon. member, AAAS; Andrew D. White Prof., Cornell Univ.; Chairman, UN Expert Group Role Advanced Skill and Technology, 1968; Mahalanobis Prize, 1976.

Principal Contributions Works in welfare economics and social choice theory, particularly in expanding their informational bases, incorporating considerations of liberty and rights, and exploring problems of collective rationality. Contributions to methods and techniques of economic measurement, particularly of real national income, poverty, inequality, and unemployment. Exploration of the analytic foundations of rational choice and of the behavioural bases of economic theory. Contributions to the choice of technology in developing countries, and to methods of shadow pricing and cost-benefit analysis. Developing a theory of the causation of famines, focusing on entitlement relations and general economic interdependence rather than just on food supply, and application to particular famines in Asia and Africa.

Publications *Books:* 1. *Choice of Techniques* (Blackwell, 1960, 1968, Indian edn, CUP, 1960, Spanish transl., 1969); 2. *Collective Choice and Social Welfare* (Holden-Day, 1970, Oliver & Boyd, 1971, N-H, 1980); 3. *On Economic Inequality* (OUP, Norton,1973; Indian edn, OUP, 1973; German transl., 1975; Japanese transl., 1975; Spanish transl., 1979); 4. *Employment, Technology and Development* (OUP, 1975, Indian edn, OUP, 1975); 5. *Poverty and Famines: An Essay on Entitlement and Deprivation* (OUP, 1981).

Articles: 1. 'Peasants and dualism with or without surplus labour', *JPE*, 74, Oct. 1966; 2. 'The impossibility of a Paretian Liberal', *JPE*, 78(1), Jan./Feb. 1970, reprinted in *Philosophy and Economic Theory*, eds F. Hahn and M. Hollis (OUP, 1979); 3. 'Poverty: an ordinal approach to measurement', *Em*, 44(2), March 1976; 4. 'On weights and measures: informational constraints in social welfare analysis', *Em*, 45(7), Oct. 1977; 5. 'Personal Utilities and public judgments: or what's wrong with welfare economics?', *EJ*, 89, Sept. 1979.

SENIOR, Nassau William*

Dates and Birthplace 1790–1864, Compton Beauchamp, England.

Posts Held Lawyer; Drummond Prof., Univ. Oxford, 1825–30, 1847–52.

Degrees BA, MA Univ. Oxford, 1812, 1815.

Offices Barrister, 1819; Member, Polit. Econ. Club, 1823; Member, numerous govt. comms, including Poor Laws, 1833, Factory conditions, 1837, Popular education, 1857.

Career As an adviser to the Whig party, he exercised a marked influence on social and economic policy during the 1830s. He also made considerable theoretical contributions in the lectures given during his terms as Drummond Professor. His rigorous restatement of the theory of value, his abstinence theory of capital, his treatment of population, money and international trade, and his distinction between the science and art of political economy, all received favourable notice.

Publications *Books:* 1. *An Outline of the Science of Political Economy* (1836, 1838, 1951); 2. *Letters on the Factory Act* (1837); 3. *Lecture on the Production of Wealth* (1847); 4. *Four Introductory Lectures on Political Economy* (1852); 5. *Historical and Philosophical Essays*, 2 vols (1865).

Secondary Literature M. Bowley, *Nassau Senior and Classical Economics* (Kelly, 1949), 'Senior, Nassau William', *IESS*, vol. 14.

SETON, Francis

Born 1920, Vienna, Austria.

Current Post Sr Fellow, Nuffield Coll., Univ. Oxford.

Recent Posts Vis. prof., Univs Osaka, (1958) Columbia (1958), Wharton School, Pennsylvania (1963), Waterloo, Ontario (1970, 1976), La Trobe, Melbourne, (1974).

Degrees MA (Econ.), PhD (Econ.) Univ. Oxford, 1949, 1954.

Offices Ed., *OEP*, 1960–75, *Int ER*, 1965–70; Consultant, UK Nat. Econ. Development Office, Dept. Econ. Affairs, UK Board of Trade, London, 1960–70; Consultant, UN (ECE), 1961–2, UN (Human Rights Commission), 1972; Adviser, Govt Iran, 1966–7, Govt Chile, 1969, 1970, Govt. Indonesia, 1972–3.

Principal Contributions Price and value concepts in the theory and practice of centrally planned economies, e.g. the Marxian 'transformation problem'; economic development and policy in the Soviet Union; problems of planning, trade, and aid for developing countries; shadow pricing for project appraisal.

Publications *Books:* 1. *The Tempo of Soviet Industrial Expansion* (Manchester Stat. Soc., 1957); 2. *The Effect of Fiscal Codes on the Yield of Capital Projects* (UK Board of Trade, 1969); 3. *Shadow Wages in the Chilean Economy* (OECD Development Centre, 1972); 4. *Industrial Management – East and West*, ed. (with A. Silberston), (Praeger, 1973).

Articles: 1. 'The social accounts of the Soviet Union in 1934', *REStat*, 36, Aug. 1954; 2. 'Productivity, trade balance, and international structure', *EJ*, 66, Dec. 1956; 3. 'The transformation problem', *REStud*, 24, June 1957 repr. in *The Economics of Marx*, eds M.C. Howard and J.E. King (Penguin Books, 1976); 4. 'Ideological obstacles to rational price setting in communist countries', in *The Socialist Price Mechanism*, ed. A. Abouchar (Duke Univ. Press, 1977); 5. 'A quasi-competitive price basis for intersystem comparisons of economic structure and performance', *J Comparative Econ.*, 5(4), Dec. 1981.

SHACKLE, George Lennox Sharman

Born 1903, Cambridge, England.
Current Post Retired; Emeritus Prof., Univ. Liverpool.
Recent Post Brunner Prof. Econ. Science, Univ. Liverpool, 1951–69.
Degrees BA, PhD (Econ.) Univ. London, 1931, 1937; DPhil Univ. Oxford, 1940; Hon. DSc New Univ. Ulster, 1974; Hon. DSoc.Sc. Univ. Birmingham, 1978.
Offices Council member, RES, 1955–69; Prof. F. de Vries Lecturer, Rotterdam School Econ., 1957; Vis. prof., Columbia Univ., 1957, Pittsburgh Univ., 1967; Pres. Section F. BAAS, 1966; Fellow, BA, 1967–; Keynes Lecturer, BA, 1976.
Principal Contributions See Publications, below.
Publications *Books:* 1. *Expectations, Investment and Income* (CUP, 1938, 1968); 2. *Expectation in Economics* (CUP, 1949, 1952); 3. *Decision, Order and Time in Human Affairs* (CUP, 1961, 1969); 4. *Epistemics and Economics* (CUP, 1972); 5. *Imagination and the Nature of Choice* (Edinburgh Univ. Press, 1979).
Articles: 1. 'Some notes on monetary theories of the trade cycle', *REStud*, 1(1), Oct. 1933; 2. 'A theory of investment decisions', *OEP*, 6, April 1942; 3. 'Recent theories concerning the nature and role of interest', *EJ*, 71, June 1961; 4. 'Time and choice', The Keynes Lecture (BA, 1976); 5. 'Imagination, formalism and choice', in *Time, Uncertainty and Disequilibrium*, ed. M.J. Rizzo (D.C. Heath & Co., 1979).

SHARPE, W.F.

N.e.

SHELL, Karl

Born 1938, Paterson, NJ, USA.
Current Post Prof. Econ. Public Pol., Univ. Pennsylvania, USA, 1970–.
Recent Posts Ass. prof. Econ., 1964–7, Assoc. prof. Econ., 1967–8,

MIT; Assoc. prof. Econ., Univ. Pennsylvania, 1968–70.
Degrees BA Princeton Univ., 1960; PhD Stanford Univ., 1965.
Offices and Honours Ford Foundation Faculty Res. fellow, 1967–8; Ed., *JET*, 1968–; Fellow, Em Soc, 1973; Co-dir., Center Analytic Res. Econ. and Social Sciences, 1975–; Guggenheim Memorial Foundation Fellow, 1977–8.
Principal Contributions Intertemporal economic theory with some emphasis on the role of money and government debt in dynamic allocation of resources. The economic theory of price indices, beginning with the cost-of-living index and proceeding to the various production price indices. Technological change, the theory of economic growth, and proposals for financing higher education in the United States.
Publications *Books:* 1. *Essays on the Theory of Optimal Economic Growth* (MIT Press, 1967); 2. *The Economic Theory of Price Indices* (with F.M. Fisher), (Academic Press, 1972); 3. *Mathematical Methods in Investment and Finance*, ed. (with G.P. Szegö), (N-H, 1972); 4. *The Hamiltonian Approach to Dynamic Economics*, ed. (with D. Cass), (Academic Press, 1976).
Articles: 1. 'The allocation of investment in a dynamic economy' (with J.E. Stiglitz), *QJE*, 81(4), Nov. 1967; 2. 'Public debt, taxation, and capital intensiveness' (with E.S. Phelps), *JET*, 3(1), Oct. 1969; 3. 'Notes on the economic of infinity', *JPE*, 79(5), Sept./Oct. 1971; 4. 'The structure and stability of competitive dynamical systems' (with D. Cass), *JET*, 12(1), Oct. 1976; 5. 'The overlapping-generations model, I: the case of pure exchange without money' (with Y. Balasko), *JET*, 23(3), June 1981.

SHEPHERD, William Geoffrey

Born 1936, Ames, Iowa, USA.
Current Post Prof. Econ., Univ. Michigan, USA.
Degrees BA Amherst Coll., 1957; MA, PhD Yale Univ., 1958, 1963.
Offices AEA; Ed. Boards, *REStat, Antitrust Bull.*; Chairman, Transpor-

tation and Public Utilities Group AEA, 1976–6.

Principal Contributions Research on the various elements of industrial organisation and public policy: focusing on market share's role in market structure and assessing the trends of actual competition; testing the effects of structure on profits and performance; measuring economies of scale; setting normative criteria for anti-trust actions toward dominance and mergers; defining how the regulation of utilities evolves and assessing regulation's economic effects; and restating the elements of public enterprise and evaluating its economic performance. Throughout, there is a stress on drawing normative lessons both from concepts and from industrial patterns. The applied research deals primarily with the US and UK economies.

Publications *Books:* 1. *Economic Performance under Public Ownership* (Yale Univ. Press, 1965); 2. *The Treatment of Market Power* (Columbia Univ. Press, 1975); 3. *Public Policies Toward Business* (with C. Wilcox), (Richard D. Irwin, 1975, 1979); 4. *Public Enterprise: Economic Analysis of Theory and Practice* (Heath-Lexington, 1976); 5. *The Economics of Industrial Organisation* (Prentice-Hall, 1979).

Articles: 1. 'Trends of concentration in American manufacturing industry, 1947–58', *REStat*, 46, May 1964; 2. 'Marginal-cost pricing in American utilities', *SEJ*, 33, July 1966; 3. 'Alternatives for public expenditure', in R.E. Caves *et al.*, *Britain's Economic Prospects* (Brookings Inst., 1968); 4. 'The elements of market structure', *REStat*, 54, Feb. 1972; 5. 'Managerial discrimination in large firms', *REStat*, 55, Nov. 1973.

SHESHINSKI, Eytan

Born 1939, Haifa, Israel.
Current Post Sir Isaac Wolfson Prof. Public Fin., Hebrew Univ., Jerusalem, Israel.
Recent Posts Vis. prof. Econ., Stanford Univ., 1976; Chairman, Dept. Econ., Hebrew Univ., Jerusalem, 1978; Oskar Morgenstern Disting. Fellow, Mathematica, Princeton Univ., 1980;

Fellow, Center Advanced Study Behavioral Sciences, Stanford Univ., 1981.
Degrees BA (Econ., with distinction), MA (Econ., with distinction) Hebrew Univ., Jerusalem, 1961, 1963; PhD (Econ.) MIT, 1966.
Offices and Honours Fellow, Em Soc; Co-ed., *Em*, 1977–81; Council, Em Soc, 1979–81; Wicksell Lectures, 1980; Walras-Bowley Lecture, Em Soc, 1981.

Principal Contributions Switching of techniques in linear open input-output models; the theory of optimum income taxation; externalities and corrective taxation; firm's optimum behaviour under inflation; and social security and theory of intergenerational transfers.

Publications *Articles:* 1. 'The optimal linear income-tax', *REStud*, 39, July 1972, repr. in *Economic Justice*, ed. E.S. Phelps (Penguin Books, 1973); 2. 'Direct versus indirect remedies for externalities' (with J. Green), *JPE*, Pt 4, 84(4), Aug. 1976; 3. 'Inflation and costs of price adjustment' (with Y. Weiss), *REStud*, 44(2), June 1977; 4. 'Efficiency in the optimum supply of public goods' (with L. Lau and J. Stiglitz), *Em*, 46(2), March 1978.

SHIBATA, Hirofumi

Born 1929, Japan.
Current Post Prof. Econ., Osaka Univ., Japan.
Recent Posts Assoc. prof. Econ., Queen's Univ., Canada, 1965–8; Reader Econ., Univ. York, 1968–71; Vis. assoc. prof. Econ., Univ. Maryland, 1970–1; Prof. Econ., Univ. Kentucky, 1971.
Degrees BA (Econ.) Kobe Univ., 1953; MA (Econ.) McGill Univ., 1962; PhD (Econ.) Columbia Univ., 1965.
Offices Member, AEA, SEA, CEA, Internat. Inst. Public Fin.; Consultant, Canadian Dept. Fin., 1965, Urban Inst., Washington, DC, 1972; Res. Fellow, Private Planning Assoc. Canada (Montreal), 1965–8; Sr economist, UN Dept Econ. Social Affairs, 1973; Ed., *Growth and Change, J Regional Development*, 1977–.
Principal Contributions The first analysis of 'voluntary export control', explaining voluntarism in terms of non-equivalence of tariffs and quotas; intro-

duction of an analytical method of free-trade areas as distinct from customs unions in their economic effects; introduction of a new concept 'the restricted origin principle of taxation' and use of it in analyses of international tax harmonisation; analysis of pure public goods geometrically showing possibilities of overproduction of public goods; clarification of externalities under which a unilaterally imposed Pigovian tax can be successful; analysis of group consumption goods and group formation processes; stability analysis of internalisation of an externality under a corrective tax; and analysis of interactions between control policies of polluters and the victims' defensive activities.

Publications *Books:* 1. *Harmonization of National Economic Policies under Free Trade* (with H.J. Johnson and P. Wonnacott), (Univ. Toronto Press, 1968); 2. *Fiscal Harmonization under Freer Trade: Principles and their Applications to a Canada-US Free Trade Area* (Univ. Toronto Press, 1969).

Articles: 1. 'On the equivalence of tariffs and quotas', *AER*, 58, March 1968; 2. 'A bargaining model of the pure theory of public expenditure', *JPE*, 79(1), Jan./Feb. 1971; 3. 'Pareto optimality, trade and the pigovian corrective tax', *Ec*, N.S. 39, May 1972; 4. 'Pareto optimality and gains from trade: a further elucidation', *Ec*, 41, Feb. 1974; 5. 'A theory of group consumption and group formation', *PF*, 34(3), 1979.

SHONFIELD, Andrew Akiba*

Dates and Birthplace 1917–81, England.

Posts Held Journalist, *Financial Times*, 1947–57, *Observer*, 1958–61; Dir. Stud., 1961–8, Res. Fellow, 1969–71, Dir., 1972–7, Royal Inst. Internat. Affairs; Prof. Econ., European Univ. Inst., Florence, Italy, 1978–81.

Degree BA Univ. Oxford, 1939.

Offices and Honours Chairman, UK SSRC, 1969–71; Knighted, 1978.

Career As a journalist, he put forward a view of British economic and political affairs which was sympathetic to the Left in a non-doctrinaire fashion,

and was concerned with helping Britain rid herself of delusions about her economic strength and political importance. His books carefully related economic problems to his understanding of social problems, and were directed at educating the public rather than solving technical problems. His appointment to a Chair at the European University Institute was a reflection of his own commitment to the idea of European union.

Publications *Books:* 1. *British Economic Policy since the War* (1958); 2. *Attack on World Poverty* (1960); 3. *Modern Capitalism* (1965); 4. *Europe: Journey to an Unknown Destination* (1973).

Secondary Literature (Obituary) 'Sir Andrew Shonfield: distinguished journalist and economist', *Times*, 24 January 1981.

SHOUP, Carl S.

Born 1902, San José, Cal., USA.

Current Post Self-employed consultant.

Recent Posts Member of Faculty, 1928–46, Prof. Econ., 1946–71, Columbia Univ.; Interregional adviser, tax reform planning, UN, 1971–4; Vis. prof., Dalhousie Univ., 1974–5.

Degrees BA Stanford Univ., 1924; PhD Columbia Univ., 1930; Hon. PhD Strasbourg Univ., 1967.

Offices and Honours Dir., Shoup Tax Mission Japan, 1949–50; Hon. member, Pres., 1949–50, NTA; Hon. member, Pres., 1950–3, Internat. Inst. Public Fin.; Dir., Fiscal Survey Venezuela, 1958, Tax Mission Liberia, 1969; Japanese govt Order of the Sacred Treasure, 1967; Disting. Fellow, AEA, 1972.

Principal Contributions Analysing and clarifying concepts, issues and effects of certain taxes (excess profits tax, income tax, and value added tax). Government services (crime deterrence, etc.): choice of level of service, and shifting and incidence of service benefits; role and significance of government outlays and revenues in national income accounting; international aspects of taxation; analysis of Ricardo's economics of taxation.

Publications *Books:* 1. *The Sales*

Tax in France (Columbia Univ. Press, 1930); 2. *Facing the Tax Problem* (with others), (Twentieth Century Fund, 1937); 3. *Principles of National Income Analysis* (Houghton-MIfflin, 1947); 4. *Ricardo on Taxation* (Columbia Univ. Press, 1960); 5. *Public Finance* (Aldine, 1969; Japanese and Spanish transls.).

Articles: 1. 'Taxation of excess profits', *Polit. Science Quarterly*, 55(4), Dec. 1940, 56(1–2), March 1941; 2. 'Taxation aspects of international economic integration', *Internat. Inst. Public Fin. Proceedings*, 1953; 3. 'Theory and background of value added tax', *NTA Proceedings*, 1955; 4. 'Standards for distributing a free governmental service: crime prevention', *PF*, 19(4), 1964; 5. 'Collective consumption and relative size of the government sector', in *Public and Urban Economics, in Honor of William S. Vickrey*, ed. R.E. Grieson (D.C. Heath & Co., 1976).

SHOVE, Gerald Frank*

Dates and Birthplace 1887–1947, England.
Posts Held Fellow, King's Coll., Reader Econ., Univ. Camb.
Degree MA Univ. Camb.
Career A colleague of Keynes who was not, however, a member of the famous 'circus' that criticised Keynes' work. His teaching, and his small number of articles, were inspired by a desire to make a useful contribution to thinking in a wider political and ethical sphere. His chief contribution was towards the restatement of the theories of value and distribution.
Publications *Articles:* 1. 'Varying costs and marginal net profits', *EJ*, 38, 1928; 2. 'The representative firm and increasing returns', *EJ*, 40, 1930; 3. 'The place of Marshall's *Principles* in the development of economic theory', *EJ*, 52, 1942; 4. 'Mrs Robinson on Marxian economics', *EJ*, 54, 1944.
Secondary Literature F. Shove, *Fredegond and Gerald Shove* (CUP, 1952).

SHUBIK, Martin

Born 1926, New York City, NY, USA.

Current Post Seymour H. Knox Prof. Math. Institutional Econ., Yale Univ., USA, 1975–.
Recent Posts Dir., Cowles Foundation Res. Econ., Yale Univ., 1973–6.
Degrees BA (Maths), MA (Polit. Econ.) Univ. Toronto, 1947, 1949; MA (Econ.), PhD (Econ.) Princeton Univ., 1951, 1953.
Offices and Honours Fellow, Center Advanced Study Behavioral Sciences, 1955; Fellow, Em Soc, 1971, World Academy Arts Sciences, 1975; Hon. Prof., Vienna, 1978; Medal, Collège de France, 1978.
Principal Contributions Identification of Edgeworth Contract curve with the core and use of replication to study convergence of the core (1954–9); games of economic survival (1956–9); Shapley value viewed as axioms of cost accounting (1960–3); convergence of Shapley value to competitive equilibrium (1960–4); market games (1966–9) and strategic market games (1971–80), involving the introduction of money, markets and financial institutions into a general equilibrium framework; the money rate of interest (1979–81).
Publications 1. *Strategy and Market Structure* (Wiley, 1959); 2. *The War Game* (with G. Brewer), (Harvard Univ. Press, 1979); 3. *The Aggressive Conservative Investor* (with M.J. Whitman), (Random House, 1979); 4. *Market Structure and Behavior* (with R.E. Levitan), (Harvard Univ. Press, 1980); 5. *Game Theory in the Social Sciences: Concepts and Solutions* (MIT Press, 1981).

Articles: 1. 'Incentives, decentralized control, the assignment of joint costs and internal pricing', *Management Science*, 8(2), April 1962, repr. in A. Bonini *et al., Management Controls: New Directions in Basic Research* (McGraw-Hill, 1964), and *Readings in Management Decision*, ed. L.R. Amey (Longman, 1966); 2. 'On market games' (with L.S. Shapley), *JET*, 1(1), June 1969; 3. 'Commodity money, oligopoly, credit and bankruptcy in a general equilibrium model', *WEJ*, 11(1), March 1973; 4. 'A theory of money and financial institutions', *Econ App*, 31(1–2), 1978; 5. 'Efficiency of Cournot-Nash equilibria in strategic market games: an axiomatic approach' (with P. Dubey and A. Mas-Colell), *JET*, 22(2), April 1980.

SIDGWICK, Henry*

Dates and Birthplace 1838–1900, Skipton, England.

Posts Held Fellow, Trinity Coll., 1859–69, 1885–1900, Lecturer, 1859–75, Praelector Moral Polit. Philosophy, 1875–83, Knightsbridge Prof., 1883–1900, Univ. Camb.

Career Philosopher who taught moral sciences and who was deeply involved in university reform. He is regarded as one of the founder figures of the Cambridge School, despite having written little on economics. His *Principles* ... is largely based on Mill, but includes several innovations such as a clear recognition of market failure due to externalities in production.

Publications *Books:* 1. *The Methods of Ethics* (1874); 2. *Principles of Political Economy* (1883); 3. *The Scope and Method of Economic Science* (1885); 4. *The Elements of Politics* (1891).

Secondary Literature A. and E. Sidgwick, *Henry Sidgwick: A Memoir* (Macmillan, 1906); B. Corry, 'Sidgwick, Henry', *IESS*, vol. 14.

SIEBERT, Horst

Born 1938, Neuwied, Germany.

Current Post Prof. Econ. Internat. Trade, Univ. Mannheim, 1969–.

Recent Posts Vis. prof., NYU (1976), Univs. New Mexico (1977), Aberdeen (1979), MIT (1980–1).

Degrees MA (Econ.) Univ. Cologne, 1963; PhD, Habilitation (Econ.), Univ. Münster, 1965, 1969.

Offices *AER*; RSA; Gesellschaft für Wirtschafts- und Sozialwissenschaften.

Principal Contributions Study of regional economic growth; analysis of environmental allocation in a neo-classical framework; regional environmental allocation; environmental protection and trade.

Publications *Books:* 1. *The Political Economy of Environmental Protection* (with B.A. Antal), (JAI Press, 1979); 2. *Trade and Environment. A Theoreti-*

cal Enquiry (with J. Eichberger *et al.*), (Elsevier, 1980); 3. *Politik und Markt. Wirtschaftspolitische Probleme der 8 Oer Jahre*, ed. (with D. Duwendag), (Fischer-Verlag, 1980); 4. *Erschöpfbare Ressourcen*, ed. (Duncker & Humblot, 1980); 5. *Economic Theory of the Environment* (D.C. Heath & Co., 1981).

SIEGFRIED, John J.

Born 1945, Allentown, Penn., USA.

Current Post Prof. Econ., Chairman Dept, Vanderbilt Univ., Tennessee, USA.

Recent Posts Economist, US Fed. Trade Commission, Washington, DC, 1975–6; Sr Staff economist, US President's Council Econ. Advisers, Washington, DC, 1976–7.

Degrees BS Rensselaer Polytechnic Inst., Troy, NY, 1967; MA Penn. State Univ., 1968; PhD Univ. Wisconsin, 1972.

Offices and Honours Phi Kappa Phi; AEA Comm. Econ. Education. 1976–82.

Principal Contributions A methodology for evaluating hypotheses about corporate political power and firm and market characteristics, using the effectiveness of corporations in lowering tax rates to assist political power. Application of micro-economic principles and empirical measurement to faculty reward structures, the welfare cost of monopoly, investment in PhD training, the determinants of anti-trust activity, the market for lawyers, professional team sports, sub-optimal economic capacity, the income distribution effects of price changes, and various studies of the effectiveness of different methods for teaching economics, including a comprehensive survey of the literature.

Publications *Books:* 1. *Recent Advances in Economics*, ed. (with R. Fels), (Richard D. Irwin, 1974); 2. *Economic Analysis and Anti-trust Law*, ed. (with T. Calvani), (Little, Brown, & Co., 1979); 3. *The Economics of Crime: An Anthology of Recent Work*, ed. (with R.L. Andreano), (Schenkman Publishing Co., 1980); 4. *The Economics of Firm Size, Market Structure and Social*

Performance, ed. (Fed. Trade Commission, 1980); 5. *Research on Teaching College Economics: Selected Readings*, ed. (with R. Fels), (Joint Council Econ. Education, 1981).

Articles: 1. 'Financial rewards to research and teaching: a case study of academic economists' (with K.J. White), *AER*, 63(2), May 1973; 2. 'Economic power and political influence: the impact of industry structure on public policy' (with L.M. Salamon), *Amer. Polit. Science Review*, 71(3), Sept. 1977; 3. 'Research on teaching college economics: a survey' (with R. Fels), *JEL*, 16(3), Sept. 1979; 4. 'Bias in economics education research from random and voluntary selection into experimental and control groups' (with G.H. Sweeney), *AER*, 70(2), May 1980; 5. 'Cost efficiency and monopoly power: a survey' (with E. Wheeler), *QREB*, 21(1), Spring 1981.

SILBERBERG, Eugene

Born 1940, New York City, NY, USA.

Current Post Prof. Econ., Univ. Washington, USA.

Recent Posts Ass. prof., 1967–73, Assoc. prof., 1973–9, Univ. Washington.

Degrees BS City Coll. New York, 1960; PhD Purdue Univ., 1964.

Offices Member, AEA.

Principal Contributions Development of the primal-dual approach to deriving comparative statics theorems, generalisations of a method first presented by Paul Samuelson; formulation and analysis of consumer's surplus as a line integral; identification of the various consumer's surpluses as different paths of integration of demand functions; and general non-existence of functions identifying monetary evaluations of changes in utility.

Publications *Books:* 1. *The Structure of Economics* (McGraw-Hill, 1978).

Articles: 1. 'Duality and the many consumer's surpluses', *AER*, 62(5), Dec. 1972; 2. 'Is the act of voting rational?' (with Y. Barzel), *Public Choice*, 13, Autumn 1973; 3. 'A revision of comparative statics methodology in econom-

ics, or how to do comparative statics on the back of an envelope', *JET*, 7(2), Feb. 1974; 4. 'The theory of the firm in "long-run" equilibrium', *AER*, 64(4), Sept. 1974; 5. 'Shipping the good apples out: the Alchian and Allen substitution theorem reconsidered' (with T. Borcherding), *JPE*, 86(1), Feb. 1978.

SILBERSTON, Zangwill Aubrey

Born 1922, London, England.

Current Post Prof. Econ., Imperial Coll. Science and Technology, Univ. London.

Recent Posts Lecturer Econ., Univ. Camb., 1953–71; Fellow, St John's Coll., Univ. Camb., 1958–71; Chairman, Faculty Board Econ. and Politics, Univ. Camb., 1966–70; Official Fellow Econ., Nuffield Coll., Univ. Oxford, 1971–8; Dean, Nuffield Coll., Univ. Oxford, 1972–8.

Degrees BA, MA Univ. Camb., 1943, 1950; MA Univ. Oxford, 1971.

Offices Member, UK Monopolies Commission, 1965–8; Non-exec. board member, British Steel Corp., 1967–76; Member, Departmental Comm. Patent System, UK Banks Comm., 1967–70; Econ. Adviser, Confederation British Industry, 1972–4; Member, UK Royal Commission on the Press, 1974–7; Sec.-gen., RES. 1979–.

Principal Contributions Industry studies, especially of the motor and steel industries; empirical studies of economies of large-scale production in a number of manufacturing industries; studies of the patent system: law, administration, economic effects of the patent system; empirical studies of the growth of firms and theoretical and applied work on the theory of the firm and the economics of industry.

Publications *Books:* 1. *The Motor Industry* (with G. Maxcy), (A & U, 1959); 2. *Economies of Large-scale Production in British Industry* (with C. Pratten and R.M. Dean), (CUP, 1965); 3. *The Patent System - administration* (with K.H. Boehm), (CUP, 1967); 4. *The Economic Impact of the Patent System* (with C.T. Taylor), (CUP, 1973); 5. *The Steel Industry, International Comparisons of Industrial*

Structure and Performance (with A. Cockerill), (CUP, 1974).

Articles: 1. 'Size of plant, size of enterprise and concentration in British manufacturing industry 1935–58' (with A. Armstrong), *JRSS*, 128(3), 1965; 2. 'Price behaviour of firms, surveys in applied economics', *EJ*, 80, Sept. 1970; 3. 'Economies of scale in theory and practice', *EJ*, 83, Suppl., March 1972; 4. 'Alternative managerial objectives: an exploratory note' (with G.M. Heal), *OEP*, 24(2), July 1972; 5. 'The ownership and control of industry' (with S. Nyman), *OEP*, 30(1), March 1978.

SIMLER, N.J.

N.e.

SIMONS, Henry Calvert*

Dates and Birthplace 1899–1946, Virden, Ill., USA.
Posts Held Prof., Univ. Iowa, 1920–7, Univ. Chicago, 1927–46.
Degree BA Univ. Michigan, 1920.
Career One of the founders of the Chicago School, he set out to redefine the relations between government and a *laissez faire* economy in the context of the considerable government intervention practised during the 1930s depression. He argued that government should provide a framework for the operation of the economy by creating appropriate monetary and competitive conditions; government was not to support monopolies and was to limit the growth of trade union power. His ideas on taxation were most fully worked out and have had long term influence on the federal income tax system.
Publications *Books:* 1. *Personal Income Taxation* (1938); 2. *Economic Policy for a Free Society* (1948); 3. *Federal Tax Reform* (1950).
Articles: 1. 'Some reflections on syndicalism', *JPE*, 52, March 1944.
Secondary Literature H. Stein, 'Simons, Henry C.', *IESS*, vol. 14.

SIMS, Christopher Albert

Born 1942, Washington, USA.
Current Post Prof. Econ., Univ. Minnesota, USA.

Recent Posts Ass. prof., Harvard Univ., 1967–9.
Degrees BA (Maths), PhD (Econ.) Harvard Univ., 1963, 1968.
Offices Co-ed., *Em*, 1977–81; Council member, Em Soc, 1978–.
Principal Contributions Research aimed at urging economists analysing macro-economic time series to avoid rigidly simplified models based on implausible assertions of a priori knowledge. Theoretical econometric work has considered problems arising in the use of densely parameterised, weakly identified models, and presented a test of the standard exogeneity assumption. Applied work has addressed substantive issues in macro-economics with these methods. In early work, the identifying exogeneity assumption of monetarist, distributed lag, money-income relations was confirmed. Recent work: implications of rational expectations monetarism have been shown to be disconfirmed.
Publications *Articles:* 1. 'Discrete approximations to continuous time distributed lags in econometrics', *Em*, 39(3), May 1971; 2. 'Money, income and causality', *AER*, 62(4), Sept. 1972; 3. 'Distributed lags', in *Frontiers of Quantitative Economics II*, eds M.D. Intriligator and D.A. Kendrick (N-H, 1974); 4. 'Seasonality in regression', *JASA*, 69, Sept. 1974; 5. 'Macroeconomic and reality', *Em*, 48(1), Jan. 1980.

SISMONDI, Jean Charles Leonard Simonde De*

Dates and Birthplace 1773–1842, Geneva, Switzerland.
Posts Held Bank clerk, farmer and professional writer.
Career Historian whose economic ideas passed through different phases. The acceptance of free-trade principles in *De la richesse commerciale* was abandoned in favour of a critical posture towards free trade and industrialisation. *Nouveaux principes ...* attacked wealth accumulation both as an end in itself, and for its detrimental effect on the poor. His critique was noticed by Malthus, Ricardo and J.S.

Mill, but despite his favourable attitude towards the poor, he was attacked by Marx, Lenin and other socialists.

Publications *Books:* 1. *Tableau de l'agriculture toscane* (1801); 2. *De la richesse commerciale*, 2 vols (1803); 3. *Histoire des républiques italiennes du moyen âge*, 16 vols (1809–18); 4. *Nouveaux principes d'économie politique*, 2 vols (1819); 5. *Histoire des français*, 31 vols (1821–44).

Secondary Literature G. Sotiroff, 'Simonde de Sismondi, J.C.L.', *IESS*, vol. 14.

SJAASTAD, L.A.

N.e.

SLICHTER, Sumner Huber*

Dates and Birthplace 1892–1959, Madison, Wisc., USA.

Posts Held Instructor, Ass. prof., Prof., Cornell Univ., 1920–30; Prof., Harvard Univ., 1930–59.

Degrees BA, MA Univ. Wisconsin, 1913, 1914; PhD Univ. Chicago, 1918.

Offices Pres., AEA, 1941; Pres., IRRA, 1949.

Career Economic commentator, whose chief concern was with labour relations on which he did extensive field research. His faith in the potential for expansion of the American economy was considerable. He was deeply suspicious of trade unions, and argued that the ability of unions to influence the state of the economy should be restricted by legislation. He wrote extensively for newspapers and magazines, spoke on innumerable public platforms, and did much to popularise economic thinking on labour problems.

Publications *Books:* 1. *The Turnover of Factory Labor* (1919); 2. *Modern Economic Society* (1931); 3. *Union Policies and Industrial Management* (1941); 4. *The Challenge of Industrial Relations* (1947); 5. *The American Economy: Its Problems and Prospects* (1948); 6. *The Impact of Collective Bargaining on Management* (1960); 7. *Potentials of the American Economy: Selected Essays* (1961).

Secondary Literature J.T. Dunlop, 'Sumner Huber Slichter', in S.H. Slichter, *Potentials of the American Economy* (Harvard Univ. Press, 1961).

SLUTSKY, Eugen*

Dates and Birthplace 1880–1948, Yaroslavl, Russia.

Posts Held Teacher of law, technical coll., 1911–18; Prof. Polit. Econ., Kiev Inst. Commerce, 1918–26; Inst. Bus. Cycles, Moscow, 1926–31; Central Inst. Meteorology, 1931–4; Math. Inst., Academy of Sciences, 1934–48.

Degrees Grad. Law, Polit. Econ. Univ. Kiev, 1911, 1918.

Career Mathematician and economist whose main achievement was in consumer behaviour. 'Slutsky's relation' deals with the relationship of the substitution effect and the income effect due to changes in the price of a commodity. Later work was on mathematical statistics and probability theory. His contribution to the theory of stochastic processes reflects on the question of causation of fluctuations or cycles in economic and other phenomena.

Publications *Books:* 1. *Izbrannye Trudy: Teoria Veroiatnostei, Matematicheskaia Statistika* (1960).

Articles: 1. 'On the criterion of goodness of fit of the regression lines and on the best method of fitting them to the data', *JRSS*, 77, 1913; 2. 'On the theory of the budget of the consumer', *Giornale degli Economisti*, 1915, repr. in *Readings in Price Theory*, eds K.E. Boulding and G.J. Stigler (1953); 3. 'The summation of random causes as the source of cyclic processes', *Em*, 5. April 1937.

Secondary Literature R.D.G. Allen, 'The work of Eugen Slutsky', *Em*, 18, July 1950; A.A. Komis, 'Slutsky, Eugen', *IESS*, vol. 14.

SMART, William*

Dates and Birthplace 1853–1915, Renfrewshire, Scotland.

Posts Held Businessman; Lecturer, Univ. Dundee, 1866–7, Univ. Glasgow, 1886–96; Prof., Univ. Glasgow, 1896–1915.

Degree MA Univ. Glasgow.

Offices Pres., Section F, BAAS, 1904; Member, Poor Laws Commission, 1905–9.

Career Translator of the Austrian economists and largely responsible for making their works known in Britain. His own books exhibit a balance between his practical experience of the business world and his enthusiasm for marginal utility theory.

Publications *Books:* 1. *An Introduction to the Theory of Value* (1891); 2. *Studies in Economics* (1895); 3. *The Distribution of Income* (1899); 4. *Taxation of Land Values and the Single Tax* (1900); 5. *The Return to Protection* (1904); 6. *Economic Annals of the Nineteenth Century*, 2 vols (1910–17).

Secondary Literature T. Jones, 'Smart, William', *ESS*, vol. 14.

SMITH, Adam*

Dates and Birthplace 1723–90, Kirkcaldy, Scotland.

Posts Held Prof. Logic, 1751–2, Prof. Moral Philosophy, 1752–63, Univ. Glasgow; Tutor to Duke of Buccleuch, 1764–6; Adviser to Charles Townshend, 1766–7; Commissioner of Customs for Scotland, 1778–90.

Degree MA Univ. Glasgow, 1740.

Career Moral philosopher, often regarded as the founder of modern political economy. Though he wrote and lectured on a wide range of subjects, *Moral Sentiments* and the *Wealth of Nations* were his only full-length treatises, whose underlying philosophy and methodology seems to have been established early in his life, and both, though superficially inconsistent, reflect a single view of the world. In *Moral Sentiments* he explored the ethical conduct of men under the influence of social pressures; the *Wealth of Nations* was concerned with economic processes resulting from the operation of self-interest, and was used to illustrate the nature of economic relations in a market society, including the economic policies appropriate to such an order. Its remarkable success meant that it effectively defined the scope and content of political economy for later generations and was widely cited as an authority in favour of free market, *laissez faire* economics, but is much more than the unsubtle apologia for private enterprise that it has been made to seem, allowing as it does an important regulating function to government.

Publications *Books:* 1. *The Theory of Moral Sentiments* (1759); 2. *An Inquiry into the Nature and Causes of the Wealth of Nations* (1776); 3. *Works of Adam Smith*, various eds, 6 vols (OUP, 1976–81).

Secondary Literature J. Viner, 'Smith, Adam', *IESS*, vol. 14.

SMITH, Vernon Lomax

Born Wichita, Kans., USA.

Current Post Prof. Econ., Univ. Arizona, USA.

Recent Posts Krannert Outstanding Prof., Purdue Univ., 1961–7; Prof. Brown Univ., 1967–8; Prof. Univ. Mass., 1968–75; Vis. prof., Cal. Tech. and Univ. Southern Cal., 1974–5.

Degrees BS Cal. Tech., 1949; MA Univ. Kansas, 1952; PhD Harvard Univ., 1955.

Offices and Honours Ford Foundation Faculty Res. Fellow, 1958–9; Board Eds., *AER*, 1969–72; Fellow, Center Advanced Study Behavioral Sciences, 1972–3; Sherman Fairchild Disting. Scholar, 1973–4.

Principal Contributions Capital theory – integration of capital replacement investment and production theories. Proved neutrality of investment expenditure for tax depreciation purposes. Developed measure of capital based on net wealth added by an establishment (analogous to value added on current account). Developed first model of default risk in corporate finance in which value of firm depends on debt-equity ratio. Natural resource economics – formal modelling of renewable resource harvesting over time. Application of common property hunting model to explanation of pleistocene animal extinctions and the rise of agriculture. Experimental economics – developed laboratory experimental methods for testing microeconomic theories under various institutions of exchange: 1) English, Dutch, double oral, and discriminative and competitive sealed bid auctions; sealed bid-offer auctions; and posted offer (take-it-or-leave-it) pricing.

Publications *Books:* 1. *Economics: An Analytical Approach* (with K. Davidson and J. Wiley), (Richard D. Irwin, 1958, 1962); 2. *Investment and Production* (Harvard Univ. Press, 1961); 3. *Economics of Natural and Environmental Resources* (Gordon and Breach, 1977); 4. *Research in Experimental Economics*, vol. 1, ed. (Johnson & Assoc. Press, 1979); 5. *Research in Experimental Economics*, vol. 2, ed. (JAI Press, 1982).

Articles: 1. 'The theory of investment and production', *QJE*, 73, Feb. 1959; 2. 'An experimental study of competitive market behavior', *JPE*, 70, April 1962; 3. 'Corporate financial theory under uncertainty', *QJE*, 84(3), Aug. 1970; 4. 'Economics of the primitive hunter culture with applications to Pleistocene extinction and the rise of agriculture', *JPE*, 83(4), Aug. 1975; 5. 'Relevance of laboratory experiments to testing resource allocation theory', in *Evaluation of Econometric Models*, eds J. Kmenta and J.B. Ramsey (Academic Press, 1980).

SMITHIES, A.

N.e.

SMOLENSKY, Eugene

Born 1932, New York City, NY, USA.
Current Post Dir., Inst. Res. on Poverty, Univ. Wisconsin, USA.
Recent Posts Prof. Econ., 1969–, Chairman, Dept Econ., 1978–80, Univ. Wisconsin.
Degrees BA Brooklyn Coll., 1952; MA American Univ., 1956; PhD Univ. Penn., 1961.
Principal Contributions The finding that income inequality in the US has been unchanged throughout 20th century, except for a one-time decline during World War II. Expanding the accounting framework to contain regional and sectoral shifts, the growth of the fisc, changing household living arrangements, permanent as opposed to nominal income has all been in vain.

Publications *Books:* 1. *Aggregate Supply and Demand Analyses*, (with P. Davidson), (Harper & Row, 1964); 2. *Public Expenditures, Taxes and the Distribution of Income* (with M. Reynolds), (Academic Press, 1977).

SOLOMON, Ezra

Born 1920, Rangoon, Burma.
Current Post Dean Witter Prof. Fin., Stanford Univ., USA.
Recent Posts Faculty, Univ. Chicago, 1948–61; Grad. School Bus., Stanford Univ., 1961–; Member, US President's Council Econ. Advisers, 1971–3.
Degrees BA (Econ. Hons) Univ. Rangoon, 1940; PhD Univ. Chicago, 1950.
Offices AEA; AFA; Ed., *J Bus*, 1953–7; Board Eds., *J Fin*, 1963–5, *J Quantitative Fin. Analysis*, 1965–6, *J Bus Fin*, 1968–70; Member, US Presidential Commission Fin. Structure Regulation, 1970–1.
Principal Contributions Early work, with others, unified the then descriptive field of corporation finance with the abstractions of capital theory into a modern theory of financial management dealing with the pricing of corporate capital assets and securities under conditions of uncertainty. Later work pioneered exploring systematic differences between conventional accounting rates of return and underlying true rates of return.

Publications *Books:* 1. *The Management of Corporate Capital*, ed. (Free Press, 1959); 2. *Metropolitan Chicago - An Economic Analysis* (with Z. Bilbija), (Free Press, 1960); 3. *The Theory of Financial Management* (Columbia Univ. Press, 1963; Spanish transl., 1965, Portuguese transl., 1969, Turkish transl., 1970, French transl., 1971, Japanese transl., 1971, Italian transl., 1972); 4. *The Anxious Economy* (Stanford Univ. Press, 1975, San Francisco Books, 1976); 5. *Introduction to Financial Management* (with J. Pringle),

(Goodyear Publishing, 1977, 1980; Portuguese transl., 1981).

Articles: 1. 'Measuring a company's cost of capital', *J Bus*, 28, Oct. 1955; 2. 'The arithmetic of capital-budgeting decisions', *J Bus*, 29, April 1956; 3. 'Leverage and the cost of capital', *J Fin*, 18, May 1963; 4. 'Return on investment: the relation of book-yield to true yield', in *Basic research in accounting measurement* (AAA, 1965); 5. 'Alternative rate of return concepts and their implication for utility regulation', *Bell JE*, 1(1), Spring 1970, and in *Bell Yearbook 1*, ed. P.W. MacAvoy (Praeger, 1970).

SOLOW, Robert M.

Born 1924, New York City, NY, USA.

Current Post Inst. Prof., MIT.

Recent Posts Eastman Prof., Univ. Oxford, 1968–9; Member, Board of Dirs, Federal Reserve Bank, Boston, 1975–80, Chairman, 1979–80.

Degrees BA, MA, PhD Harvard Univ., 1947, 1949, 1951; Hon. degrees Univs. Chicago (1967), Brown (1972), Williams (1974), Paris I, (1975), Warwick (1976), Lehigh (1977).

Offices and Honours Member, Amer. Philosophical Soc.; Corresponding member, BAAS; David A. Wells prize, Harvard Univ., 1951; John Bates Clark medal, AEA, 1961; Pres., Em Soc, 1964; Council member, NAS, 1976–9; Pres., AEA, 1980.

Principal Contributions The theory of long-run growth, especially conditions of equilibrium, intertemporal efficiency, the sources of increases in income per capita, and the role of non-renewable resources. Macroeconomic theory, especially systematic analysis of the failure of markets to clear, nature of unemployment, interrelations with inflation, and role of stocks and flows. Theory of capital and interest.

Publications *Books:* 1. *Linear Programming and Economic Analysis* (with R. Dorfman and P.A. Samuelson), (McGraw-Hill, 1958); 2. *Capital Theory and the Rate of Return* (N-H, 1963); 3. *The Nature and Sources of Unemployment in the US* (Almqvist & Wiksell, 1964); 4. *Growth Theory: An Exposition* (OUP, 1969).

Articles: 1. 'A contribution to the theory of economic growth', *QJE*, 70, Feb. 1956, and in *Readings in Mathematical Economics*, 2 vols, ed. P. Newman (Johns Hopkins Univ. Press, 1968); 2. 'Technical change and the aggregate production function', *REStat*, 39, Aug. 1957, and in *Readings in Economic Statistics and Econometrics*, ed. A. Zellner (Nettle, Brown, 1968); 3. 'Output, employment and wages in the short run' (with J. Stiglitz), *QJE*, 82, Nov. 1968; 4. 'Does fiscal policy matter?' (with A Blinder), *J Pub E*, 2(4), Nov. 1973; 5. 'Intergenerational equity and exhaustible resources', *REStud*, Symposium 1974.

SOMBART, Werner*

Dates and Birthplace 1863–1941, Ermsleben, Germany.

Posts Held Syndic with Bremen Chamber of Commerce, 1888–90; Assoc. prof. Polit. Econ., Univ. Breslau, 1890–1906; Prof., Handelshochschule, Berlin, 1906–18, Univ. Berlin, 1918–.

Degree PhD Univ. Berlin, 1888.

Career Writer on capitalism, whose viewpoint swung so sharply from Marxism to ultra-conservatism to national-socialism that he is virtually impossible to categorise. His chief work *Der Moderne Kapitalismus* is eclectic and sometimes unreliable, but presents a historical analysis of capitalism which differs from the Marxian version in regarding modern capitalism as an improvement on early competitive capitalism.

Publications *Books:* 1. *Sozialismus und Soziale Bewegung im 19 Jahrhundert* (1896); 2. *Der Moderne Kapitalismus* (1902); 3. *Die Deutsche Volkswirtschaft im 19 Jahrhundert* (1903); 4. *Die Juden und das Wirtschaftsleben* (1911); 5. *Der Bourgeois* (1913); 6. *Studien zur Entwicklungsgeschichte des Modernen Kapitalismus*, 2 vols (1913); 7. *Deutscher Sozialismus* (1934).

Secondary Literature J. Kuczynski, 'Sombart, Werner', *IESS*, vol. 15.

SOMERS, H.M.

N.e.

SONNENFELS, Joseph von*

Dates and Birthplace 1732–1817, Nikolsburg, Austro-Hungary.

Posts Held Prof. Cameral Science, Univ. Vienna, 1763.

Offices and Honours Served as adviser to Austrian govt on various occasions; Ennobled, 1797; Freiherr, 1804.

Career Neo-cameralist, who advised successive Austrian emperors and advocated enlightened absolutism – e.g. the state had the positive role of ensuring basic standards of life, including hospitals and reformed prisons. He believed in the virtues of a growing population and consequently favoured labour-intensive industries and small land proprietorship. He saw money not merely as a medium of exchange, but as a productive factor. Though many of his views were not particularly original, his ideas were influential, chiefly through the use of his *Grundsätze* ... as a textbook.

Publications *Books:* 1. *Grundsätze der Polizi, Handlung und Finanzwissenschaft*, 2 vols (1763–7); 2. *Betrachtungen über die Neuen Politischen Handlungsgrundsätze der Engländer* (1764); 3. *Leitfaden in den Handlungswissenschaften* (1776); 4. *Gesammelte Schriften*, 10 vols (1783–7).

Secondary Literature K. Zielenziger, 'Sonnenfels, Freiherr Joseph von', *ESS*, vol. 14.

SOWELL, Thomas

Born 1930, Gastonia, N. Carolina, USA.

Current Post Sr Fellow, Hoover Inst., Stanford Univ., USA.

Recent Posts Ass. prof. Econ., Cornell Univ., 1965–9; Assoc. prof. Econ., Brandeis Univ., 1969–70; Project Dir., Urban Inst., Washington DC, 1972–4; Fellow, Center Advanced Study Behavioral Sciences, Stanford Univ., 1976–7; Vis. prof. Econ., Amherst Coll., 1977; Prof. Econ., UCLA, 1974–80.

Degrees BA (Econ. *Magna cum laude*) Harvard Coll., 1958; MA (Econ.) Columbia Univ., 1959; PhD (Econ.) Univ. Chicago, 1968.

Offices AEA, 1960–; US President's Econ. Pol. Advisory Board, 1981–.

Principal Contributions Chief work has been in the history of economic thought, general decision-making theory, and the economic history of racial and ethnic groups.

Publications *Books:* 1. *Black Education: Myths and Tragedies* (David McKay, 1972); 2. *Say's Law: An Historical Analysis* (Princeton Univ. Press, 1972); 3. *Classical Economics Reconsidered* (Princeton Univ. Press, 1974); 4. *Knowledge and Decisions* (Basic Books, 1980); 5. *Ethnic America* (Basic Books, 1981).

Articles: 1. 'Marx's "increasing misery" doctrine', *AER*, 50, March 1960; 2. 'Karl Marx and the freedom of the individual', *Ethics*, Jan. 1963; 3. 'Marx's *Capital* after one hundred years', *CJE*, 33, Feb. 1967; 4. 'The "evolutionary" economics of Thorstein Veblen', *OEP*, N.S. 19, July 1967; 5. 'Sismondi: a neglected pioneer', *HOPE*, 4(1), Spring 1972.

SPANN, Othmar*

Dates and Birthplace 1878–1950, Vienna, Austro-Hungary.

Posts Held Studied in Zürich, Berne and Tübingen; Prof., Technical High School, Berlin, 1909, Univ. Vienna, 1919–38.

Degree Dr Polit. Science, Univ. Tübingen, 1903.

Career German Romantic economist and social theorist who developed a philosophical standpoint known as universalism, the antithesis of the atomism and individualism which was said to characterise Anglo-Saxon economics. His *History of Economics* went through 19 edns and until the 1930s was the most widely read history of economic thought in German-speaking countries.

Publications *Books:* 1. *The History of Economics* (1910, 1930).

Secondary Literature W. Heinrich, 'Spann, Othmar', *Handwörterbuch der Sozialwissenschaft*, 9 (Fischer, 1958);

E. Salin, 'Economics: romantic and universalist economics', *ESS*, vol. 5.

SPENCE, Andrew Michael

Born 1943, Montclair, NJ, USA.
Current Post Prof. Econ. Business Admin., Harvard Univ., USA, 1979–.
Recent Posts Ass. prof. Public Admin., Harvard Univ., 1973–5; Assoc. prof. Econ., Stanford Univ., 1973–6; Prof. Econ., Harvard Univ., 1976–9.
Degrees BA Princeton Univ., 1966; BA Univ. Oxford, 1968; PhD Harvard Univ., 1972.
Offices and Honours Rhodes Scholar, 1966–8; David A. Wells prize, Harvard Univ., 1972. Fellow, Em Soc, 1976–.
Principal Contributions Research in the area of market structure and performance: the informational structure of markets; product differentiation and monopolistic competition; and dynamic aspects of competition, focusing on the evolution of markets, competitive strategies and market performance. Related work deals with price and other forms of discrimination with imperfect and asymmetric information.
Publications *Books:* 1. *Market Signaling* (Harvard Univ. Press, 1974).
Articles: 1. 'Competitive and optimal responses to signals: an analysis of efficiency and distribution', *JET*, 7(3), March 1974; 2. 'Product selection, fixed costs, and monopolistic competition', *REStud*, 43(2), June 1976; 3. 'Nonlinear prices and welfare', *J Pub E*, 8(1), Aug. 1977; 4. 'Entry, capacity, investment and oligopolistic pricing', *Bell JE*, 8(2), Autumn 1977; 5. 'Investment, strategy and growth in a new market', *Bell JE*, 10(1), Spring 1979.

SPENGLER, Joseph J.

Born 1902, Piqua, Ohio, USA.
Current Post James B. Duke Prof. Emeritus Econ., Duke Univ., N. Carolina, USA.
Recent Posts Regional Price Exec., US Office Price Admin., 1942–3; Duke Univ., 1934–72; Univ. N. Carolina, 1972–3.

Degrees BA, MA, PhD, Dr Humane Letters (Hon.) Ohio State Univ., 1926, 1929, 1930, 1965; Hon. Dr Science Alma Coll., 1968; Hon. Dr Law Tulane Univ., 1978.
Offices and Honours Phi Beta Kappa, 1927; US SSRC, 1945–60; Pres., SEA, 1947, PAA, 1957, AEA, 1965, Hist. Econ. Soc., 1975–6 (Disting. Fellow, 1981), Atlantic Econ. Soc., 1976–7; Fellow, ASA, 1950, Amer. Assoc. Advancement Science, 1950, Amer. Philosophical Soc., 1954, AAAS, 1962, Mont Pelerin Soc., 1963, World Academy Arts Science, 1966.
Principal Contributions Study of decline in fertility, and of history of economics; identification and analysis of the interrelations between various population movements and phenomena, and economic phenomena, together with the nature of interrelations between population phenomena and aspects of macro- and micro-economics; ageing effects and changes in the composition of 'economic thought' over time.
Publications *Books:* 1. *France Faces Depopulation* (Duke Univ. Press, 1938, 1979); 2. *Indian Economic Thought* (Duke Univ. Press, 1971); 3. *Population Economics, Selected Essays* (Duke Univ. Press, 1972); 4. *Facing Zero Population Growth, Reactions and Interpretations, Past and Present* (Duke Univ. Press, 1978); 5. *Origins of Economic Thought and Justice* (Southern Illinois Univ. Press, 1980).
Articles: 1. 'Population doctrines in the United States, Pts I-II', *JPE*, 41, Aug., Oct. 1933; 2. 'French population theory since 1800, Pts I-II', *JPE*, 44, Oct., Dec. 1936; 3. 'Monopolistic competition and the use and price of urban land service', *JPE*, 54, Oct. 1946; 4. 'Aspects of the economics of population growth, Pts I-II', *SEJ*, 14, Oct. 1947, Jan. 1948; 5. 'Smith v. Hobbes: economy vs. polity', in *Adam Smith and the Wealth of Nations*, ed. F.R. Glake (Univ. Colorado Press, 1978).

SPIETHOFF, Arthur*

Dates and Birthplace 1873–1957, Germany.

Posts Held Taught at Berlin, Prague and Bonn Univs.

Offices Ass. ed., and Ed., *Schmoller's Jahrbuch*, 1899–1908.

Career Beginning his work on business cycles, he discovered the need for a new general theory of economics to replace the Historical School orthodoxy in which he had been trained. Within the framework of his historical-realistic theory he was then able to pursue his empirical work on cycles. He considered cycles, including the long waves, which he identified independently, as part of the essential pattern of capitalist economics. He also did valuable work on the capital and money market, and on land utilisation and housing, using the same conceptual framework.

Publications *Books:* 1. *Die Wirtschaftlichen Wechsellagen*, 2 vols (1955).
Articles: 1. 'Vorbemerkungen zu einer Theorie der Überproducktion', *Schmoller's Jahrbuch*, 26, 1902; 2. 'The "historical" character of economic theories', *JEH*, 12(2), 1952; 3. 'Business cycles', (1923), repr. in *Internat. Econ. Papers*, 3 (1953); 4. 'Pure theory and economic Gestalt theory', in F.C. Lane and J.C. Riemersma, eds, *Enterprise and Secular Change* (1953).

Secondary Literature G. Clausing, 'Spiethoff, Arthur', *IESS*, vol. 15.

SPULBER, Nicolas

Born 1915, Brasov, Romania.
Current Post Disting. prof. Emeritus Econ., Indiana Univ., USA, 1980–.
Recent Posts Vis. prof. Econ., City Coll. New York, 1963–4; Prof. Econ., 1961–74, Sr res. Scholar, Internat. Development Res. Center, 1967–72, Disting. prof. Econ., 1974–80, Indiana Univ.
Degrees MA, PhD (*Magna cum laude*) Graduate Faculty, New School Social Res., New York, 1950, 1952.
Offices and Honours AEA; Halle Fellow, New School Social Res., 1951–2; Amer. Philosophical Soc. Grant, 1956; Ford Faculty Res. Fellow, 1961; Ford Foundation Grant, Study of Soviet-type economies, 1962.
Principal Contributions The study of

the Soviet strategy of development: its sources, determination, rationale, and the principles and methods of Soviet planning; the actual experiences of socialist planned economies and their attempts at modifying the Soviet-type economic model; the study of quantitative policy and planning and the provision of a single quantitative framework for the formulation of policy decisions, the use of instruments for carrying them out, and the integration of policies and instruments into consistent plans – national, sectoral, or regional.

Publications *Books:* 1. *The Economics of Communist Eastern Europe* (MIT, Wiley, 1957, Greenwood Press, 1976); 2. *The Soviet Economy: Structure, Principles, Problems* (Norton, 1962, 1969); 3. *Socialist Management and Planning* (Indiana Univ. Press, 1971); 4. *Quantitative Economic Policy and Planning*, co-author (Norton, 1976); 5. *Organizational Alternatives in Soviet-type Economies* (CUP, 1979).
Articles: 1. 'Socialism, industrialization and convergence', *Jahrbuch Wirtschaft Osteuropas*, 2, 1971; 2. 'On some issues in the theory of the "socialist economy" ', *Kyklos* 25(4), 1972; 3. 'Is there an economic system based on the sovereignty of each consumer?' (with G.M. von Furstenberg), *ZN*, 33(3–4), 1973; 4. 'Welfare criteria for comparing changes within and between economic systems' (with G.M. von Furstenberg), *WA*, 110(4), 1974; 5. 'On the pioneering stage in input-output economics: the Soviet national economic balance 1923–24, after fifty years' (with K. Moayed-Dadkhah), *REStat*, 57(1), Feb. 1975.

SRAFFA, Piero

Born 1898, Turin, Italy.
Current Post Fellow, Trinity Coll., Univ. Camb.
Recent Posts Prof. Polit. Econ., Univ. Perugia, 1924–6; Prof. Polit. Econ., Univ. Cagliari, 1926–7; Lecturer, Univ. Camb., 1927.
Degree Grad. Univ. Turin.
Principal Contributions Criticism of Marshall's theory of the firm, and the perfect competition model current in the

1920s. Editing of the works and correspondence of Ricardo. Re-examination of classical theories of value and income distribution which has led others to re-examine and sometimes abandon aspects of marginalist economic theory.

Publications *Books:* 1. *Works and Correspondence of David Ricardo*, 11 vols, ed. (with M.H. Dobb) (CUP, 1951–73); 2. *Production of Commodities by Means of Commodities: Prelude to a Critique of Economic Theory* (CUP, 1960, 1975).

Articles: 1. 'The bank crisis in Italy', *EJ*, 32, 1922; 2. 'Sulle relazioni fra costo e quantità prodotta', *Snnali di Economia*, 2, 1925; 3. 'The laws of returns under competitive conditions', *EJ*, 36, Dec. 1926, repr. in *Readings in Price Theory*, eds G.J. Stigler and K.E. Boulding (1953); 4. 'Increasing returns and the representative firm: a symposium', *EJ*, 40, March 1930; 5. 'Dr Hayek on money and capital', *EJ*, 42, March 1932, 42, June 1932.

Secondary Literature L.L. Pasinetti, 'Sraffa, Piero', *IESS*, vol. 18; A. Roncaglia, *Sraffa and the Theory of Prices* (1978).

STACKELBERG, Heinrich von*

Dates and Birthplace 1905–46, Kudinowo, Russia.

Posts Held Privatdozent, Univs. Cologne and Berlin; Prof. Univ. Bonn, 1941–3, Univ. Madrid, 1943–6.

Degree PhD Univ. Cologne, 1932.

Career Mathematical economist whose early economic interest was in pricing under conditions of oligopoly. Later work was on capital theory, and at the time of his death he was attempting a theory of the whole economic process. A stalwart opponent of central planning, he worked out his criticism in a mathematical form.

Publications *Books:* 1. *Grundlagen einer Reiner Kostentheorie* (1932); 2. *Marktform und Gleichgewicht* (1934); 3. *Grundzüge der Theoretischen Volkswirtschaftslehre* (1943).

Secondary Literature W. Eucken, 'Obituary: Heinrich von Stackelberg', *EJ*, 58, March 1948.

STALIN, Joseph*

Dates and Birthplace 1879–1953, Gori, Russia.

Posts Held Commissar for nationalities, 1917–23, and for state control, 1919–23; Sec-gen. of the Party central comm., 1922–53; Head of Soviet govt and supreme commander-in-chief, 1941.

Offices and Honours Too numerous to list comprehensively.

Career Head of the Soviet Communist Party and leader of Russia who was responsible for the intensive industrialisation programme begun in 1928, and the forced collectivisation of agriculture. He published on various subjects including economics, and his 1952 essay sought to re-establish the validity of some economic 'laws' even in a socialist society.

Publications *Books: Economic problems of socialism in the USSR* (1952).

STAMP, Josiah Charles*

Dates and Birthplace 1880–1941, Bexley, England.

Posts Held Civil servant, 1896–1919; Dir., Nobel Industries (1919–26), ICI (1926–8), and other companies. Consultant, British govt, 1935–; Member of many official commissions and comms.

Degrees BSc, DSc Univ. London, 1911, 1916.

Offices and Honours Dir., Bank of England; Pres., Section F, BAAS, 1926; Pres., RSS, 1930–2; Created Baron, 1938.

Career Statistician and expert on taxation who did much to restructure the British tax system. His work was analytical and statistical rather than theoretical. The concept of excess profits, which could be taxed at a higher than normal rate, and the index of profits he developed in 1932, were two of his contributions in this field. His public lectures and articles included expositions of the problems of the national income and capital, as well as taxation questions.

Publications *Books:* 1. *The Fundamental Principles of Taxation* (1921); 2. *Wealth and Taxable Capacity*

(1922); 3. *Some Economic Factors in Modern Life* (1929); 4. *The Calculus of Plenty* (1935); 5. *The Science of Social Adjustment* (1937); 6. *The National Capital and other Statistical Studies* (1937).

Secondary Literature J.H. Jones, *Josiah Stamp: Public Servant* (Pitman, 1964); J. Mogey, 'Stamp, Josiah Charles', *IESS*, vol. 15.

STEIN, Herbert

Born 1916, Detroit, Mich., USA.

Current Post Prof. Econ., Univ. Virginia, USA.

Recent Posts Member, 1969–71, Chairman, 1972–4, US President's Council Econ. Advisers; Sr Fellow, Amer. Enterprise Inst., 1975–.

Degrees BA Williams Coll., 1935; PhD Univ. Chicago, 1958; Hon. LLD, Rider Coll., 1971, Univ. Hartford, 1974, Williams Coll., 1980.

Offices and Honours Member, AEA, SEA; First prize, Pabst Post-war Employment Awards, 1944; Fellow, Center Advanced Study Behavioral Sciences, 1965–6; Co-founder, first Chairman, National Economists' Club, 1967.

Principal Contributions Development of concept and application of built-in economic stabilisers and high-employment budget; history of macroeconomic policy in US, 1929–65; and explanation of economic issues for layman.

Publications *Books:* 1. *The Fiscal Revolution in America* (Univ. Chicago Press, 1969).

Articles: 1. 'Fiscal policy: reflections on the past decade'; 2. 'Spending and getting'; 3. Price fixing as seen by a price fixer: part II'; 4. 'Balancing the budget'; 'Achieving credibility'; all in *Contemporary Economic Problems* (Amer. Enterprise Inst., 1976, 1977, 1978, 1979, 1980).

STEUART, James Denham*

Dates and Birthplace 1712–80, Edinburgh, Scotland.

Post Held Landowner.

Career Jacobite exile, whose continental travels provided abundant material for his *Inquiry* . . . The book is an expression of the Scottish philosophical school of the eighteenth century, couched in sophisticated mercantilist terms. His view of society was dynamic: free nations succeeding slave societies, and states passing through various phases of development; government should intervene when necessary in the operations of the market and little advantage is to be gained from free trade. His ideas were little noticed in Britain but received some attention from the German Historical School.

Publications *Books:* 1. *An Inquiry into the Principles of Political Economy*, 2 vols (1767, 1976); 2. *Works, Political, Metaphysical and Chronological*, 6 vols (1805).

Secondary Literature A.S. Skinner, 'Introduction', J. Steuart, *Inquiry*, vol. 1 (Oliver & Boyd, 1976); W. Stark, 'Steuart, James Denham', *IESS*, vol. 15.

STEWART, Dugald*

Dates and Birthplace 1753–1828, Edinburgh, Scotland.

Posts Held Prof. Moral Philosophy, Univ. Glasgow, 1785–1810.

Career His lectures on political economy were extremely well attended and influential, many future statesmen, including Lord Palmerston, being amongst his students. The content of the lectures was derived very closely from Adam Smith, though differed slightly on some matters – e.g. he was rather more sympathetic towards the physiocrats than Smith. He was the author of the first biography of Smith.

Publications *Books:* 1. *Outlines of Moral Philosophy* (1793); 2. *Account of the Life and Writings of Adam Smith* (1795), repr. in A. Smith, *Essays on Philosophical Subjects*, eds W.P.D. Wightman and J.C. Bryce (1980); 3. *Philosophical Essays* (1810); 4. *Collected Works*, 11 vols (1854–60).

Secondary Literature M. Stewart, *Memoir of the Late Dugald Stewart* (1838).

STIGLER, George Joseph

Born 1911, Renton, Washington, USA.

Current Post Charles R. Walgreen Disting. service prof. Amer. Insts., Univ. Chicago, USA.

Recent Posts Ass. prof., Iowa State Univ., 1936–8; Various ranks, Univ. Minnesota, 1938–46; Prof., Brown Univ., 1946–7; Prof., Columbia Univ., 1947–58; Prof., Univ. Chicago, 1958–.

Degrees BBA Univ. Washington, 1931; MBA, Dr Sci. Northwestern Univ., 1932, 1979; PhD Univ. Chicago, 1938; Dr Sci. Carnegie-Mellon Univ., 1973, Univ. Rochester, 1974, Helsinki School Econ., 1976; LLD Brown Univ., 1980.

Offices NAS; Amer. Philosophical Soc.; Pres., AEA, 1964; Pres., Hist. Econ. Soc., 1977.

Principal Contributions Primary work has been in economic theory, industrial organisation, and history of economic thought.

Publications *Books:* 1. *Production and Distribution Theories* (Macmillan, 1941); 2. *Essays in the History of Economics* (Univ. Chicago Press, 1965); 3. *The Theory of Price* (Macmillan, 1942, 1952, 1966); 4. *The Organization of Industry* (Richard D. Irwin, 1968); 5. *The Citizen and the State. Essays on Regulation* (Univ. Chicago Press, 1975).

Articles: 1. 'The economics of information', *JPE*, 69, June 1961; 2. 'Information in the labor market', *JPE*, 70(5), Pt 2, Oct. 1962; 3. 'A theory of oligopoly', *JPE*, 72, Feb. 1964.

STIGLITZ, Joseph E.

Born 1942, Gary, Ind., USA.

Current Post Prof. Econ., Princeton Univ., USA.

Recent Posts Prof. Econ., Yale Univ., 1968–70; Vis. Fellow, St Catherine's Coll., Univ. Oxford, 1973–4; Prof. Econ., Stanford Univ., 1974–6; Drummond Prof. Polit. Econ., Univ. Oxford, 1976–9; Oskar Morgenstern Disting. Fellow, Vis. prof., Inst. Advanced Stud. Mathematica Inc., 1978–9.

Degrees BA, DHL, Amherst Coll., 1964, 1974; PhD (Econ.) MIT, 1966.

Offices and Honours General ed., Em Soc Reprint Series; Co-ed., *J Pub E*; Amer. ed., *REStud*, 1968–76; Assoc. ed., *Energy Econ.*, *JET*, 1968–73, *AER*. 1972–6; Guggenheim Memorial Foundation Fellow, 1969–70; Fellow, Em Soc, 1972; John Bates Clark medal, AEA, 1979.

Principal Contributions Recent research has been to extend understanding of how imperfect and costly information affects economic behaviour and market equilibrium. This work has shown that the basic existence, characterisation and welfare theorems of perfect competition are not robust (under weak conditions, market equilibrium does not exist; when it does, it is characterised by non-linear price schedules; in equilibrium, demand may not equal supply) and has laid the foundations of a more general theory which explicitly incorporates imperfect information. This work has explored detailed applications of this theory to the behaviour of monopolists and the government, and to equilibrium in labour, capital, and product markets.

Publications *Books:* 1. *Collected Scientific Papers of P.A. Samuelson, I*, ed. (MIT Press, 1965); 2. *Readings in Modern Theory of Economic Growth*, ed. (with H. Uzawa), (MIT Press, 1969); 3. *Lectures in Public Economics* (with A.B. Atkinson), (McGraw-Hill, 1980); 4. *The Theory of Commodity Price Stabilization* (with D.M.G. Newbery), (OUP, 1981).

Articles: 1. 'Increasing risk: I–II' (with M. Rothschild), *JET*, 2(3), Sept. 1970, 3(1), March 1971; 2. 'On the irrelevance of corporate financial policy', *AER*, 64(5), Dec. 1974; 3. 'The design of tax structure: direct versus indirect taxation' (with A.B. Atkinson), *J Pub E*, 6(4), July/Aug. 1976; 4. 'Equilibrium in competitive insurance markets: the economics of markets with imperfect information' (with M. Rothschild), *QJE*, 40(4), Nov. 1976; 5. 'On the impossibility of informationally efficient markets' (with S.J. Grossman), *AER*, 70(3), June 1980.

STONE, John Richard Nicholas

Born 1913, London, England.
Current Post Emeritus Prof., Univ. Camb.
Recent Posts UK Office War Cabinet, Central Stat. Office, 1940–5; Dir., Dept. Applied Econ., Univ. Camb., 1945–55; P.D. Leake Prof. Fin. Accounting, Univ. Camb., 1955–80.
Degrees BA, MA, ScD Univ. Camb., 1935, 1938, 1957; Hon. doctorates: Univs. Oslo, Free Univ. Brussels (1965), Geneva (1971), Warwick (1975), Panthéon-Sorbonne, Paris I (1977), Bristol, 1978.
Offices and Honours Fellow, King's Coll., Univ. Camb., 1945–; CBE, 1946; Member, Internat. Stat. Inst., 1946; Fellow, 1946, Pres., 1955, Em Soc; Hon. member, Soc. Incorporated Accountants Auditors, 1954; Fellow, BA, 1956; Foreign hon. member, AAAS, 1968; Hon. member, AEA, 1976; Hon. Fellow, Gonville and Caius Coll., Univ. Camb., 1976; Knighted, 1978; Pres., RES, 1978–80.
Principal Contributions First official estimates of British national income and expenditure (1941, with J.E. Meade). Standardised systems of national accounts: League of Nations, 1945–7; OEEC, 1950–2 (with M. Gilbert *et al.*); UN, 1953 (with G. Jaszi *et al.*) and 1968 (with A. Aidenoff). Demand analysis with single equations and systems of equations (linear expenditure system); aggregate consumption and saving functions. The 'Cambridge growth project' model of the British economy (with J.A.C. Brown, T.S. Barker, *et al.*). An integrated system of social and demographic statistics: UN, 1975. Application of mathematical and statistical techniques to adjustment of observations; seasonal variation; projection errors; economic control; Markov processes; sigmoid growth; simulation.
Publications *Books:* 1. *National Income and Expenditure* (with J.E. Meade), (OUP, 1944) (with G. Stone), (OUP, Bowes & Bowes, 1977); 2. *The Measurement of Consumers' Expenditure and Behaviour in the United Kingdom, 1920–1938* (with D.A. Rowe *et al.*), CUP, 1954, 1966); 3. *Mathe-matics in the Social Sciences and Other Essays* (Chapman & Hall, 1966); 4. *Mathematical Models of the Economy and Other Essays* (Chapman & Hall, 1970); 5. *Demographic Accounting and Model Building* (OECD, 1971).
Articles: 1. 'Transition and admission models in social demography', *Social Science Res.*, 2(2), 1973, and in *Social Indicator Models* (Russell Sage Foundation, 1975); 2. 'Direct and indirect constraints in the adjustment of observations', in *Nasjonalregnskap, Modeller og Analyse* (Statistisk Sentralbyrå, 1975); 3. 'Sigmoids', *Bull. Applied Stats.*, 8(1), 1980; 4. 'A simple growth process tending to stationarity', *EJ*, 90, Sept. 1980; 5. 'The relationship of demographic accounts to national income and product accounts', in *Social Accounting Systems*, eds. F.T. Juster and K.C. Land (Academic Press, 1982).

STORCH, Heinrich Friedrich Von*

Dates and Birthplace 1766–1835, Riga, Russia.
Posts Held Govt employee, 1789.
Offices Member, Russian Academy of Sciences.
Career His historical-statistical work on Russia and published lectures on political economy were his two sources of fame. Though basically a Smithian, he developed a theory of stages in economic development, with different economic principles needed to explain the workings of each stage. His later work was largely concerned with questions of national income.
Publications *Books:* 1. *Statistische Uebersicht der Staatshalterschaften des Russischen Reiches* (1795); 2. *Historisch-statistisches Gemälde des Russischen Reiches*, 9 vols (1797–1803); 3. *Cours d'économie politique*, 6 vols (1815); 4. *Considérations sur la nature du revenu national* (1824).
Secondary Literature V. Gelesnoff, 'Storch, Heinrich Friedrich von', *ESS*, vol. 14.

STREETEN, Paul

Born 1917, Vienna, Austria.
Current Post Dir., Center Asian

Development Stud., Prof. Econ., Boston Univ., USA.

Recent Posts Dep. dir. General Econ. Planning, UK Ministry Overseas Development, 1964–6; Acting dir., Fellow, Inst. Development Stud., Univ. Sussex, Prof., 1966–8; Warden Queen Elizabeth House, Dir., Inst. Commonwealth Stud., Fellow Balliol Coll., Univ. Oxford, 1968–78; Special adviser World Bank, 1976–8; Dir. Stud., Overseas Development Council, 1978–9.

Degrees MA Aberdeen Univ., 1945; BA, MA, DLitt. Univ. Oxford, 1947, 1951, 1976; Hon. LLD Aberdeen Univ., 1980.

Offices and Honours RES; AEA; Hon. Fellow, Inst. Development Stud., Univ. Sussex; Pres., UK Chapter Soc. Internat. Development; Dir., Commonwealth Development Corp; Member, UK Royal Commission Environmental Pollution.

Principal Contributions Early work was in the area of international trade, public finance and the theory of the firm. For the last 20 years, main work has been in development economics, especially its international aspects, education, industrialisation, human capital formation, employment, technology, income distribution and poverty eradication. Also interest in the philosophical foundations of economics and methodology.

Publications *Books:* 1. *Value in Social Theory*, ed. (Routledge & Kegan Paul, 1958, German transl., 1964); 2. *Economic Integration: Aspects and Problems* (Sythoff, 1961, 1964); 3. *The Frontiers of Development Studies* (Macmillan, 1972); 4. *Foreign Investment, Transnationals and Developing Countries* (with S. Lall), (Macmillan, 1977); 5. *Development Perspectives 1981* (Macmillan, 1981).

Articles: 1. 'Elasticity optimism and pessimism in international trade', *Econ Int*, 7(1), Feb. 1954; 2. 'Programs and prognoses', *QJE*, 68(3), Aug. 1954; 3. 'Growth, the terms of trade and the balance of trade' (with J. Black), *Econ App*, April/Sept. 1957; 4. 'The limits of development research', *WD*, 2(10–12), Oct./Dec. 1974; 5. 'New strategies for development' (with F. Stewart), *OEP*, 28(3), Nov. 1976.

STROTZ, R.H.

N.e.

STRUMILIN, Stanislav Gustavovich*

Dates and Birthplace 1877–1974, Dashkovtsy, Russia.

Posts Held Employed by Soviet State Planning Comm., 1921–37, 1943–51; Taught, Moscow State Univ., 1921–3, Inst. Nat. Econ., 1929–30, Moscow State Inst. Econ., 1931–50, CPSU Academy Social Sciences, 1948–74.

Offices and Honours Member, Soviet Academy, 1931; Lenin Prize, 1958; Hero of Socialist Labour, 1967.

Career His career spanned the entire Stalinist era and covered a wide range of activities; his more than 700 publications range through statistics, social sciences and economic history. He devised an index of labour productivity (the Strumilin index) and until his death he presided over all Soviet debates on economic questions.

Publications *Books:* 1. *Wealth and Labour* (1905); 2. *Problems of the Economics of Labour* (1925); 3. *Essays on the Soviet Economy* (1928); 4. *The Industrial Revolution in Russia* (1944).

Articles: 1. 'The economic significance of national education', *Planovoe Khoziaistvo*, 9–10, 1924, reprinted in *Readings in the Economics of Education*, eds. M.J. Bowman *et al.* (UNESCO, 1968). 2. 'The economics of education in the USSR', *Internat. Social Science J.*, 14(4), 1962.

STUBBLEBINE, William Craig

Born 1936, West Point, NY, USA.

Current Post Von Tobel Prof. Polit. Econ., Dir., Center Study Law Structures, Claremont Men's Coll., Cal., 1966–.

Recent Posts Ass. prof., Univ. Virginia, 1961–3, Univ. Delaware, 1963–6; Nat. Science Fellow, MIT, 1965–6; Fulbright Scholar, Univ. Turin, 1967–8; Vis. prof., Southern Methodist Univ., 1971, Virginia Polytechnic Inst., 1972.

Degrees BS Univ. Delaware, 1958; PhD Univ. Virginia, 1963.

Offices and Honours AEA: Amer. Polit. Science Assoc.; Mont Pelerin Soc; Public Choice Soc.; WEA; Snavely Prize, Univ. Virginia, 1965; Vice-pres., Western Tax Assoc., 1979–81.

Principal Contributions Participated in the rethinking of externality theory, public good theory, and property rights theory, as well as theoretical and practical applications of public choice theory. Contributions to the development of constitutional limits on government taxing and spending has had a major impact, including adoption of constitutional amendments in several American states.

Publications *Articles:* 1. 'Externality' (with J.M. Buchanan), *Ec*, N.S. 29, Nov. 1962; 2. 'Institutional elements in the finance of education', *SEJ*, 32, Nov. 1965; 3. 'On property rights and institutions', in *Explorations in the Theory of Anarchy* (Virginia Polytechnic Inst., 1972); 4. 'California and the finance of education' (with R.K. Teeples), in *Property Taxation and the Finance of Education* (Univ. Wisconsin Press, 1974); 5. 'SJR 56: the Federal limit', Proposed Constitutional amendment to balance the Federal Budget, Hearings, US Senate, series no. 96–41 (US Govt Printing Office, 1980).

SUITS, Daniel B.

Born 1918, St Louis, Miss., USA.

Current Post Prof. Econ., Michigan State Univ., USA.

Recent Posts Assoc. prof. Econ., 1955–9, Prof. Econ., Dir., Res. Seminar Quantitative Econ., 1959–69, Univ. Michigan; Prof., Chairman Econ., Univ. Cal., Santa Cruz, 1969–74; Vis. prof. Econ., Univ. Hawaii, 1973–4.

Degrees BA (Phil.), MA (Econ.), PhD (Econ.) Univ. Michigan, 1940, 1941, 1949.

Offices and Honours AEA; Phi Kappa Phi, 1940; Fellow, Em Soc, 1967; Fellow, ASA, 1968; Fellow, East-West Pop. Inst., 1977–; Disting. Faculty Award, Michigan State Univ., 1980.

Principal Contributions Work in statistical testing of economic theory and in quantitative measurement of economic relationships has involved compilation and extensive application of econometric models for annual forecasts of the US economic outlook, analysis of economic policy, assessment of the economic impact of disarmament, and more recently study of the long-run relationships between economic development and demographic change.

Publications *Books:* 1. *Statistics, an Introduction to Quantitative Economic Research* (Rand McNalley, 1963); 2. *Theory and Application of Econometric Models* (Center Econ. Res., 1963); 3. *An Econometric Model of the Greek Economy* (Center Econ. Res., 1964); 4. *Principles of Economics* (Harper & Row, 1970, 1973); 5. *Gambling in the US*, App. 2, *Final Report of Commission for Review of the National Policy Toward Gambling* (with M. Kallick *et al.*), (US Govt Printing Office, 1977).

Articles: 1. 'Use of dummy variables in regression equations', *JASA*, 52, 1957; 2. 'Forecasting and analysis with an econometric model', *AER*, 52, March 1962; 3. 'The determinants of consumer expenditure', in D.B. Suits *et al.*, *Impacts of Monetary Policy* (Prentice-Hall, 1963); 4. 'Birth control in an econometric simulation' (with W. Mardfin *et al.*), *Int ER*, 16(1), Feb. 1975; 5. 'Measurement of tax progressivity', *AER*, 67(1), Sept. 1977.

SWEEZY, A.R.

N.e.

SWEEZY, Paul M.

Born 1910, New York City, NY, USA.

Current Post Ed., *Monthly Review*, 1949–.

Recent Posts Dept. Econ., Harvard Univ., 1934–46; Vis. prof., Cornell Univ., 1958–9; Stanford Univ., 1960–1, Yale Univ., 1972, New School Social Res., 1975.

Degrees BA, PhD Harvard Univ., 1931, 1937.

Offices and Honours David A. Wells prize, Harvard Univ., 1938; Member, Exec. Comm., AEA, 1964–7.

Principal Contributions N.e.

Publications *Books:* 1. *Monopoly and Competition in the English Coal Trade, 1550–1850* (Harvard Univ. Press, 1938); 2. *The Theory of Capitalist Development* (OUP, 1942, Monthly Review Press, 1969); 3. *Socialism* (McGraw-Hill, 1948); 4. *The Present as History* (Monthly Review Press, 1953); 5. *Monopoly Capital* (with P.A. Baran), (Monthly Review Press, 1966).

T

TAUBMAN, Paul

Born 1939, Fall River, Mass., USA.
Current Post Prof. Econ., Chairman, Univ. Pennsylvania, USA.
Recent Posts Ass. prof., Harvard Univ., 1964–6; Staff member, US President's Council Econ. Advisers, 1965–77; Res. assoc., NBER, 1978–.
Degrees BS (Econ.), PhD (Econ.) Univ. Pennsylvania, 1961, 1964.
Offices Member, AEA, Em Soc; Fellow, Internat. Soc. for Twin Stud., Em Soc.
Principal Contributions Introduced into economics the use of twins to analyse various issues, such as the bias on education coefficients when not controlling for differences in unobserved abilities; the extent to which IQ and observed measures of family background account for this bias; the decomposition of the variance in earnings into genetic, common and non-common environment; and the importance of parental aversion to inequality in the earnings of offspring in the allocation of resources to siblings.
Publications *Books:* 1. *Policy Simulations of the Brookings Model* (with G. Fromm), (Brookings Inst., 1968); 2. *Mental Ability and Higher Educational Attainment in the Twentieth Century* (with T.J. Wales), (NBER, Carnegie Commission on Higher Education, 1972); 3. *Education as an Investment and as a Screening Device* (with T.J. Wales), (NBER, Carnegie Commission on Higher Education, 1974); 4. *Inter- and Intragenerational Determinants of Socio-economic Success with Special Reference to Genetic, Family, and other Environments* (with J. Behrman *et al.*), (N-H, 1980).
Articles: 1. 'User cost, capital utilization, and investment theory' (with M. Wilkinson), *Int ER*, 11(2), June 1970; 2. 'The determinants of earnings: genetics, family and other environments: a study of white male twins', *AER*, 66(5), Dec. 1976; 3. 'Controlling for and measuring the effects of genetics and family environment in equations for schooling and labor market success' (with J.R. Behrman and T.J. Wales), in *Kinometrics: The Determinants of Socioeconomic Success Within and Between Families*, ed. P. Taubman (NBER, 1977); 4. 'Changes in the impact of education and income on mortality' (with S. Rosen), in *Statistical Uses of Administration Records with Emphasis on Mortality and Disability Research by HEW*, eds L. De Bene and F. Scheuren (unpublished, 1979).

TAUSSIG, Frank William*

Dates and Birthplace 1859–1940, St Louis, Miss., USA.
Posts Held Instructor, 1885–92, Prof. Econ., 1892–1935, Harvard Univ.
Degrees BA, PhD, LLB Harvard Univ., 1879, 1883, 1886.
Offices Member, govt commss; Adviser, President Wilson; Ed., *QJE*, 1896–1936.
Career Neo-classical economist who, through his teaching, the *Principles. . . ,* and his editorship of the *QJE*, exercised a considerable influence on successive generations of American economists. International trade was his principal theoretical interest and he devoted much of his attention to the question of tariffs. In his writings on general economic theory he stressed the continuity between classical and neo-classical theory, arguing that there was only one continuous body of ideas which had been subsequently elaborated and refined.
Publications *Books:* 1. *The Tariff History of the United States* (1888, 1931); 2. *Wages and Capital* (1896, 1932); 3. *Principles of Economics*, 2 vols (1911, 1939); 4. *Some Aspects of*

the Tariff Question (1915, 1931); 5. *International Trade* (1927).

Secondary Literature J.A. Schumpeter, *Ten Great Economists from Marx to Keynes* (OUP, 1951); G. Haberler, 'Taussig, Frank W.', *IESS*, vol. 15.

TAWNEY, Richard Henry*

Dates and Birthplace 1880–1962, Calcutta, India.

Posts Held Ass., Univ. Glasgow, 1906–8; Teacher, 1908–14, Fellow, Balliol Coll., 1918–21, Univ. Oxford; Prof. Econ. Hist., LSE, 1931–49.

Degree BA Univ. Oxford, 1903.

Offices and Honours Member, official cmts. and comms; Pres., Workers' Educational Assoc., 1928–44; Fellow, BA, 1935.

Career Economic historian whose *Religion and the Rise of Capitalism*, elaborating the Weber thesis on the Protestant ethic, is a major work of scholarship which has had an inspiring effect on generations of readers. A pioneer member of the Fabian society, his *Acquisitive Society* and *Equality* are fundamental statements of opposition to the moral values of capitalism and class privilege.

Publications *Books:* 1. *The Agrarian Problem in the Sixteenth Century* (1912, 1963); 2. *Studies in the Minimum Wage*, 2 vols (1914); 3. *The Acquisitive Society* (1920, 1948); 4. *Religion and the Rise of Capitalism* (1926, 1963); 5. *Equality* (1931, 1952, 1961); 6. *Land and Labour in China* (1932, 1964); 7. *Business and Politics under James I: Lionel Cranfield as Merchant and Minister* (1958).

Secondary Literature L. Stone, 'Tawney, R.H.', *IESS*, vol. 15.

TAYLOR, Fred Manville*

Dates and Birthplace 1855–1932, Northville, Mich., USA.

Posts Held Prof., Albion Coll., 1879–92; Ass. prof., Prof., Univ. Michigan, 1894–1929.

Degrees BA Northwestern Univ.; PhD Univ. Michigan, 1888.

Offices Pres., AEA, 1928.

Career Originally a political scientist, his early economic interests were in applied and, particularly, monetary questions, however, he developed an increasing interest in theory, and his *Principles of Economics* reflect the development of his ideas through teaching general economics, in which he placed a strong emphasis on theoretical rigour. Many of his pupils became distinguished economists. His theoretical position was a modified version of the doctrines of the Austrian School. His 1929 article was an answer to von Mises' argument that socialism was impractical.

Publications *Books:* 1. *Some Chapters on Money* (1906); 2. *Principles of Economics* (1911).

Articles: 'The guidance of production in a socialist state', *AER*, 19(1), March 1929, repr. in *On the Economic Theory of Socialism*, ed. B.E. Lippincolt (1938).

TAYLOR, Lester D.

Born 1938, Iowa, USA.

Current Post Prof. Econ., Univ. Arizona, USA, 1974–.

Recent Posts Ass. prof., Harvard Univ., 1964–8; Assoc. prof., Univ. Michigan, 1969–74.

Degrees BA (highest distinction) Univ. Iowa, 1960; PhD Harvard Univ., 1963.

Offices and Honours Phi Beta Kappa; AEA; Em Soc.

Principal Contributions Research interests have focused on the theory and measurement of consumer demand, aggregate consumption and saving, pricing policies in the regulated industries, and econometric and statistical techniques.

Publications *Books:* 1. *Consumer Demand in the United States 1929–1970* (with H.S. Houthakker), (Harvard Univ. Press, 1966, 1970); 2. *Probability and Mathematical Statistics* (Harper & Row, 1974); 3. *Telecommunications Demand: A Survey and Critique* (Ballinger Publishing Co., 1980).

Articles: 1. 'On the estimation of

dynamic demand functions' (with D. Weiserbs), *REStat*, 54(4), Nov. 1972; 2. 'Estimation by minimizing the sum of absolute errors', in *Frontiers in Econometrics*, ed. P. Zarembka (Academic Press, 1974); 3. 'The demand for electricity: a survey', *Bell JE*, 6(1), Spring 1975; 4. 'Experiments in seasonal-time-of-day-pricing of electricity to residential users' (with J.T. Wenders), *Bell JE*, 7(2), Fall 1976.

TELSER, Lester G.

Born 1931, Chicago, Ill., USA.
Current Post Prof. Econ., Univ. Chicago, USA.
Recent Posts Univ. Chicago, 1958–.
Degrees BA Roosevelt Coll., 1951; MA, PhD Univ. Chicago, 1953, 1956.
Offices Fellow, ASA, Em Soc; Faculty Res. Fellow, Ford Foundation, 1969–70.
Principal Contributions Analysis of the nature of competition and of the conditions under which some form of co-operation among firms and their customers is necessary in order to have an efficient equilibrium; this material applies the theory of the core to economics in various ways in order to gain better understanding of how a modern economy works. Other contributions include application of core theory to determine the distribution of equilibrium prices, study of the costs and benefits of organised markets, especially futures markets, and development and tests of a theory of the economic effects of advertising.
Publications *Books:* 1. *Functional Analysis in Mathematical Economics* (with R.L. Graves), (Univ. Chicago Press, 1972); 2. *Competition, Collusion and Game Theory* (Aldine, 1972); 3. *Economic Theory and the Core* (Univ. Chicago Press, 1978).
Articles: 1. 'Futures trading and the storage of cotton and wheat', *JPE*, 66, June 1958; 2. 'Why should manufacturers want fair trade', *J Law E*, 3, Oct. 1960; 3. 'Advertising and competition', *JPE*, 72, Dec. 1964; 4. 'Organised futures markets: cost and benefits' (with H.N. Higginbotham), *JPE*, 85(5), Oct.

1977; 5. 'A theory of self enforcing agreements', *J Bus*, 53(1), Jan. 1980.

TEMIN, Peter

Born 1937, Philadelphia, Penn., USA.
Current Posts Prof. Econ., MIT, USA, 1970–.
Recent Posts Woodrow Wilson Fellow, 1959–60, NSF Co-operative Fellow, 1960–1, MIT; Teaching ass., Dept Econ., 1961–2, Ass. prof. Industrial Hist., Sloan School Management, 1965–7, Assoc. prof. Econ. Hist., 1967–70, MIT; Res. Fellow, 1961–2, Jr Fellow, Soc. Fellows, 1962–5, Vis. Fellow, Charles Warren Center Stud. Amer. Hist., 1976–7, Harvard Univ.
Degrees BA (Econ., highest hons.) Swarthmore Coll., 1959; PhD (Econ.) MIT, 1964.
Offices AEA; EHA; EHS.
Principal Contributions A contributor to the 'new economic history'. This analysis typically starts with a formal model of some aspect of economic behaviour, assembles historical data for use in the model, and draws conclusions by joining the data and the model. Work has centred on questions of monetary history, technical change, and industrial organisation in nineteenth- and twentieth-century America.
Publications *Books:* 1. *The New Economic History*, ed. (Penguin Books, 1972); 2. *Causal Factors in American Economic Growth in the Nineteenth Century* (Macmillan, 1975); 3. *Did Monetary Forces Cause the Great Depression?* (Norton, 1976); 4. *Reckoning with Slavery* (with P. David *et al.*), (OUP, 1976); 5. *Taking your Medicine: The Dilemma of Drug Regulations* (Harvard Univ. Press, 1980).

THEIL, Henri

Born 1924, Amsterdam, The Netherlands.
Current Post McKethan-Matherly Prof. Econometrics Decision Sciences, Univ. Florida, USA.
Recent Posts Prof. Em., 1953–66, Dir. Em. Inst., 1956–66, Netherlands

School Econ., Rotterdam; Univ. Prof., Dir. Center Math. Stud. Bus Econ., Univ. Chicago, 1965–81.

Degrees PhD (Econ.) Univ. Amsterdam, 1951; LLD Univ. Chicago, 1964; Dr (*Hon. causa*) Free Univ. Brussels, 1974.

Offices Pres., Em Soc, 1961.

Principal Contributions Econometric methodology; the application of informational measures in economics; and consumption and production theory.

Publications *Books:* 1. *Linear Aggregation of Economic Relations* (N-H, 1954); 2. *Economic Forecasts and Policy* (N-H, 1958, 1961); 3. *Principles of Econometrics* (Wiley, 1971); 4. *Theory and Measurement of Consumer Demand*, 2 vols (N-H, 1975, 1976).

THIRLWALL, Anthony

Born 1941, Workington, England.

Current Post Prof. Applied Econ., Univ. Kent, England.

Recent Posts Vis. prof., W. Virginia Univ., 1967; Econ. Adviser, UK Dept. of Employment, 1968–70; Res. assoc., Princeton Univ., 1971–2; Vis. Scholar, King's College, Univ. Camb., 1979; Vis. prof., Univ. Melbourne, 1981.

Degrees Univ. Leeds, 1962; MA Clark Univ., 1963; PhD Univ. Leeds, 1967.

Offices Council Member, RES; Governor, NIESR.

Principal Contributions The understanding of 'regional' economic differences, the theory of cumulative causation, and the concept of balance of payments constrained growth; the measurement of types of unemployment; the development of models of inflation and growth, and of population and growth.

Publications *Books:* 1. *Growth and Development* (Macmillan, 1972, 1978); 2. *Inflation Saving and Growth in Developing Countries* (Macmillan, 1974); 3. *Regional Growth and Unemployment in the United Kingdom* (with R. Dixon), (Macmillan, 1975); 4. *Financing Economic Development* (Macmillan, 1976; Spanish, Turkish and Greek transls); 5. *Balance of Payments Theory and the United Kingdom Experience* (Macmillan, 1980).

Articles: 1. 'Technical progress: a survey' (with C. Kennedy), *EJ*, 82, March 1972; 2. 'An empirical estimate for Britain of the impact of the real balance effect on income and interest', *SEJ*, 39(2), Oct. 1972; 3. 'A cross-section study of population growth and the growth of output and per capita income in a production function framework', *MS*, 40(4), Dec. 1972; 4. 'A model of regional growth rate differences on Kaldorian lines' (with R. Dixon), *OEP*, 27(2), July 1975; 5. 'The input-output formulation of the foreign trade multiplier' (with C. Kennedy), *AEP*, 18(32), June 1979.

THOMPSON, Thomas Perronet*

Dates and Birthplace 1783–1869, Hull, England.

Posts Held Naval officer, 1803–6; Army officer, 1806–8, 1810–68, (appointed General, 1868); Governor, Sierra Leone, 1808–10.

Degree BA Univ. Camb., 1802.

Offices Fellow, Royal Soc., 1828; MP for Hull, 1836–7, Bradford, 1847–52, 1857–9.

Career Active service in the army terminated in 1822, when he turned to writing, founding the *Westminster Review*, the organ of the 'philosophical radicals'. He was the proprietor of and chief contributor 1829–36. His anti-corn law writings were his most successful publications and he played a major role in the Anti-Corn Law League.

Publications *Books:* 1. *The True Theory of Rent in Opposition to Mr. Ricardo and Others* (1826, 1827); 2. *Catechism on the Corn Laws* (1827, 1940); 3. *Catechism on the Currency* (1848).

THOMPSON, William*

Dates and Birthplace 1775–1833, Cork, Ireland.

Post Held Private income.

Career British 'utilitarian' socialist and feminist. His earliest theoretical concerns were with problems of distribution, which led him to advocate co-operation rather than competition. He rapidly became recognised as the chief theorist of the co-operative movement and concentrated on the attempt to mobilise opinion amongst the labouring classes in favour of consumers' and producers' co-operatives.

Publications *Books:* 1. *An Inquiry into the Principles of the Distribution of Wealth* (1824, 1963); 2. *Appeal of One Half of the Human Race, Women, Against the Pretensions of the Other Half, Men* (1825); 3. *Labour Rewarded* (1827); 4. *Practical Directions for the Establishment of Communities* (1830).

Secondary Literature R.K.P. Pankhurst, *William Thompson: Britain's Pioneer Socialist, Feminist and Co-operator* (Watts, 1954); A. Briggs, 'Thompson, William', *IESS*, vol. 16.

THORNTON, Henry*

Dates and Birthplace 1760–1815, Clapham, England.

Posts Held Banker.

Offices MP for Southwark, 1782–1815; Member of comms and comtts on suspension of cash payments, 1797, Irish currency, 1804, Bullion Comm., 1810, Corn trade, 1813.

Career Monetary theorist who systematised ideas on: money, the velocity of circulation, interest, prices and employment, and international economic relations in his *Enquiry.* . . . These ideas are embedded in a defence of the Bank of England's policy regarding the suspension of cash payments. He later became more critical of the Bank, and favoured a reduced circulation of notes. Though very successful in his own day, the *Enquiry* was gradually forgotten until Hollander, Viner, and others rediscovered it and drew attention to its anticipations of modern monetary theory.

Publications *Books:* 1. *An Enquiry into the Nature and Effects of the Paper Credit of Great Britain* (1802, 1939).

Secondary Literature S. Meacham, *Henry Thornton of Clapham* (Harvard Univ. Press, 1964); T.W. Hutchison, 'Thornton, Henry', *IESS*, vol. 16.

THORNTON, William Thomas*

Dates and Birthplace 1813–80, Burnham, England.

Posts Held Employee, East India Company, 1836–58; Secretary, public works, India Office, 1858–80.

Honours CBE, 1873.

Career Colleague and friend of J.S. Mill, he advocated land reforms as a remedy for rural distress, particularly that of Ireland. It was Thornton's criticism of the wages fund theory that induced Mill's retraction on the subject.

Publications *Books:* 1. *Over-population and its Remedy* (1845); 2. *A Plea for Peasant Proprietors* (1848); 3. *On Labour, its Wrongful Claims and Rightful Dues* (1869); 4. *Indian Public Works and Cognate Topics* (1875).

THÜNEN, Johann Heinrich von*

Dates and Birthplace 1783–1850, Oldenburg, Germany.

Posts Held Landowner and farmer.

Career Founder of location theory, mathematical economist and econometrician whose work, though little appreciated in his own time, has since been re-evaluated as one of the outstanding early contributions to economics. The 'isolated state' refers to an abstract spatial model which he used to develop theories of rent, location, wages and interest. His ideas were built on the meticulous accumulation of data from his farming experiments on his estate. He expressed his ideas verbally, arithmetically and in algebraic terms, making extensive use of calculus. He developed an exact theory of marginal productivity and applied the theory to questions of production and distribution. The *Isolated State* . . . was not a systematic treatise, and his very great number of achievements have to be disinterred from amongst much other material, such as practical discussions of agricultural economics. Despite this it is one of the great economic classics.

Publications *Books:* 1. *Der Isolierte Staat in Beziehung auf Landwirtschaft und Nationalökonomie*, 3 vols (1826–63), (English transl. Pt 1, 1826, selections from Pt 2, 1850; ed. P. Hall, 1966).

Secondary Literature A.H. Leigh, 'Thünen, Johann Heinrich von', *IESS*, vol. 16.

THUROW, L.C.

N.e.

TIEBOUT, C.M.

N.e.

TINBERGEN, Jan

Born 1903, The Hague, The Netherlands.
Current Post Retired.
Recent Posts Prof. Development Planning, Erasmus Univ. Rotterdam (previously Netherlands School Econ.), part-time 1933–55, full-time 1955–73; Dir., Central Planning Bureau, The Hague, 1945–55; Prof. Internat. Co-operation, Univ. Leiden, 1973–5.
Degrees Dr (Physics) Univ. Leiden, 1929; 20 hon. degrees in econ. and social sciences.
Honours Erasmus prize (European Cultural Foundation), 1967; Nobel Prize in Econ., 1969.
Principal Contributions Econometric models of cyclical movements; models of socio-economic growth including education sector; introduction of non-tradables into macro-models; semi-input-output; demand-supply factors in income distribution; production functions with several types of labour.
Publications *Books:* 1. *Business Cycles in the USA, 1921–1933* (League of Nations, 1939); 2. *Business Cycles in the UK, 1870–1914* (N-H, 1956); 3. *Mathematical Models of Economic Growth* (with H.C. Bos), (McGraw-Hill, 1962); 4. *Economic Policy: Principles and Design* (N-H, 1967); 5. *Income Distribution: Analysis and Policies* (N-H, 1975).
Articles: 1. 'The appraisal of road construction: two calculation schemes', *REStat*, 39, Aug. 1957; 2. 'Testing and applying a theory of utility' (with N. Bouma and B.M.S. van Praag), *Europ*

ER 8(2), Aug. 1976; 3. 'How to reduce the incomes of the two labour élites?', *Europ ER* 10(2), Nov. 1977; 4. 'Two approaches to quantify the concept of equitable income distribution?', *Kyklos*, 33(1), 1980; 5. 'Market-determined and residual incomes – some dilemmas' (with J. Kol), *Econ App*, July 1980.
Secondary Literature H.C. Bos, 'Tinbergen, Jan', *IESS*, vol 18.

TOBIN, James

Born 1918, Champaign, Ill., USA.
Current Post Sterling prof. Econ., Yale Univ., 1957–.
Recent Posts Member, US President's Council Econ. Advisers, Washington, DC, 1961–2; Vis. prof., Univ. Nairobi Inst. Development Stud., 1972–3; Chairman, Dept. Econ., Yale Univ., 1968–9, 1974–8.
Degrees BA (*Summa cum laude*), MA, PhD Harvard Univ, 1930, 1940, 1947; LLD (*hon. causa*) Syracuse Univ., 1967, Univ. Illinois, 1969, Dartmouth Coll., 1970, Swarthmore Coll., 1980; Dr Econ. (*hon. causa*) New Univ. Lisbon, 1980.
Offices and Honours Fellow, Vice-pres., 1957, Pres., 1958, Em Soc; Vice-pres., 1964, Pres.-elect, 1970, Pres., 1971, AEA; Member, 1972, Secretary, Class V, Behavioral and Social Sciences, 1974–7, Section Chairman, Econ. Sciences, 1979–82, NAS; Pres., EEA, 1977; Nobel Prize in Econ., 1981.
Principal Contributions Clarification and extension of Keynesian macro-economic models with respect to money wages, inflation, money demand, consumption and saving, and fiscal and monetary policies. Development of theory of portfolio choice under uncertainty, including the separation theorem basic to capital asset pricing model; and application of the theory to macro-economics. Incorporation of money and inflation in growth theory. Empirical studies of consumption, saving, asset demand. Origination of method (TOBIT) for estimating relationships involving limited or truncated dependent variables. Theory of capital investment emphasising importance of ratio of market value to replacement cost, 'q'.

Publications *Books:* 1. *The American Business Creed* (with S.E. Harris *et al.*), (Harvard Univ. Press, 1956); 2. *National Economic Policy* (Yale Univ. Press, 1966); 3. *Essays in Economics: Macroeconomics* (Markham Pub., 1971, N-H, 1974); 4. *The New Economics One Decade Older* (Princeton Univ. Press, 1974); 5. *Essays in Economics: Consumption and Econometrics* (N-H, 1975).

Articles: 1. 'A dynamic aggregative model', *JPE*, 63, April 1955; 2. 'Estimation of relationships for limited dependent variables', *Em*, 26, Jan. 1958; 3. 'Liquidity preference as behavior towards risk', *REStud*, 25, Feb. 1958; 4. 'Money, capital, and other stores of value', *AER/S*, 51, May 1961; 5. 'Money and economic growth', *Em*, 33(4), Oct. 1965.

TODARO, Michael P.

Born 1942, New York City, NY, USA.

Current Post Prof. Econ., NYU, USA.

Recent Posts Assoc. dir., Social Sciences, Rockefeller Foundation, 1972–6; Vis. prof. Econ., Univ. Cal., Santa Barbara 1976; Deputy dir., Sr assoc., Center Pol. Stud., Pop. Council, 1976–8.

Degrees BA (High hons) Haverford Coll., 1964; MPhil, PhD (Econ.) Yale Univ., 1966, 1967.

Offices and Honours Phi Beta Kappa, 1964; Member, Internat. Advisory Comm., Pop. Inst., East-West Center, Hawaii, 1972–4; Member Ed. Board, *Population and Development Review*, 1977–; William Pyle Philips Disting. visitor, Haverford Coll., 1977; Member Ed. Board, *PDR*, 1979–.

Principal Contributions Pioneering theoretical writings on the relationship between rural-urban migration and urban unemployment in less developed countries. 'Expected-income' model first demonstrated the economic rationality of continued migration in the face of rising urban unemployment and inflexible urban wages. An important policy implication of this model is that the creation of more urban jobs would probably worsen rather than relieve the urban unemployment problem, and helped reorient development thinking towards a new emphasis on rural development. Author of an international text on economic development.

Publications *Books:* 1. *Economic Theory* (with P.W. Bell), (OUP, 1969, 1973); 2. *Development Planning: Models and Methods* (OUP, 1972); 3. *Internal Migration in Developing Countries* (ILO, 1976); 4. *Economics for a Developing World* (Longman, 1977, 1982); 5. *Economic Development in the Third World* (Longman, 1977, 1981).

Articles: 1. 'A model of labor migration and urban unemployment in less developed countries', *AER*, 59(1), March 1969; 2. 'Technological transfer, labour absorption, and economic development' (with H. Pack), *OEP*, 21(3), Nov. 1969; 3. 'Migration, unemployment, & development: a two-sector analysis' (with J.R. Harris), *AER*, 60(1), March 1970; 4. 'Urban job expansion, induced migration and rising unemployment: a formulation and simplified empirical test for LDCs', *JDE*, 3(3), Sept. 1976; 5. 'Development policy and population growth: a framework for planners', *Population and Development Review*, 3(1–2), March/June 1977.

TOOKE, Thomas*

Dates and Birthplace 1774–1858, Kronstadt, Russia.

Posts Held Merchant in the Russian trade; Governor, Royal Exchange Insurance Co.

Offices Fellow, Royal Soc., 1821; Founder and member, Polit. Econ. Club, 1821–58; Witness before govt. comms; Member, Commission on Child Employment, 1833, 1840.

Career Major spokesman for free trade, and author of the Merchants' Petition, 1820. Defended the gold standard on many occasions before espousing the Banking Principle that note issues need no rigid controls. Although he rejected the quantity theory of money, he never developed a complete monetary theory. His interest in the effect of monetary policy on prices led him into his life-long work on price data. Though he and his collaborator, William Newmarch, constructed no indices on the basis of the data, the raw material was used by others, including Jevons.

Publications *Books:* 1. *Thoughts and Details on the High and Low Prices of the Thirty years from 1793 to 1822* (1823); 2. *Considerations on the State of the Currency* (1826); 3. *On the Currency in Connexion with the Corn Trade* (1829); 4. *A History of Prices and the State of the Circulation from 1792 to 1856*, 6 vols (with W. Newmarch), (1838–57); 5. *An Inquiry into the Currency Principle* (1844, 1959); 6. *On the Bank Charter Act of 1844* (1856).

Secondary Literature T.E. Gregory, *An Introduction to Tooke and Newmarch's 'A History of Prices'* (LSE, 1962); F.W. Fetter, 'Tooke, Thomas', *IESS*, vol. 16.

TORRENS, Robert*

Dates and Birthplace 1780–1864, Ireland.

Posts Held Army officer, 1797–1835; Proprietor, *Globe* newspaper.

Offices Fellow, Royal Soc., 1818; Founder member, Polit. Econ. Club, 1821; MP for Ashburton, 1831–2, Bolton, 1832–5.

Career Critic of the labour theory of value, and an independent discoverer of the principle of comparative advantage. He wrote extensively on economic questions for over 50 years. As an advocate of the principle of colonisation as a remedy for over-population, he promoted schemes for the colonisation of Australia. His views on international trade were unusual for the day in rejecting unilateral free trade, arguing instead that reciprocal tariffs might be optimal under certain circumstances. Although his early writings had put the case for paper currency, he soon became a major spokesman of the Currency School. Though influential in his day, he had little effect posthumously and was rediscovered only recently.

Publications *Books:* 1. *The Economist Refuted* (1808); 2. *An Essay on Money and Paper Currency* (1812); 3. *An Essay on the External Corn Trade* (1815); 4. *An Essay on the Production of Wealth* (1821, 1970); 5. *Letters on Commercial Policy* (1833, 1958); 6. *The Budget* (1841–2, 1965); 7. *The Principles and Practical Operation of Sir Robert Peel's Bill of 1844* (1848).

Secondary Literature L. Robbins, *Robert Torrens and the Evolution of Classical Economics* (Macmillan, 1958); B. Corry, 'Torrens, Robert', *IESS*, vol. 16.

TOWNSEND, Harry

Born 1925, Blackburn, Lancs., England.

Current Post Prof. Econ., Univ. Lancaster.

Recent Posts Lecturer Econ., Univ. Sheffield, 1950–5; Lecturer, Reader Econ., LSE, 1955–72.

Degrees BSc (Econ.) Univ. London, 1949.

Offices and Honours Leverhulme Scholar, LSE, 1946–9; Knoop Res. Fellow, Univ. Sheffield, 1950–1; Nursey Premium, Soc. Engineers, 1968.

Principal Contributions Application of price theory to industry: analysis of industrial organisation in terms of market, administrative and co-operative integration.

Publications *Books:* 1. *Business Enterprise* (with R.S. Edwards), (Macmillan, 1958; Spanish transl., 1966); 2. *Studies in Business Organisation* (with R.S. Edwards), (Macmillan, 1961); 3. *Business Growth* (with R.S. Edwards), (Macmillan, 1966); 4. *Scale, Innovation, Merger and Monopoly* (Pergamon, 1968; Italian transl., 1970); 5. *Price Theory*, ed. (Penguin Books, 1971, 1980).

Articles: 1. 'Economic theory and the cutlery trades', *Ec*, N.S. 21, Aug. 1954; 2. 'The cutlery trade', in *The Structure of British Industry*, vol. 2, ed. D.L. Burn (Macmillan, 1958); 3. 'Price theory and petrol prices', in *Essays in Honour of Lord Robbins*, eds M.H. Peston and B.A. Corry (Weidenfeld & Nicolson, 1972); 4. 'Big business and big science', *Science Public Pol.*, Dec. 1974; 5. 'Economics of consumerism', Univ. Lancaster, unpublished, 1974.

TOYNBEE, Arnold*

Dates and Birthplace 1852–83, London, England.

Posts Held Lecturer, Tutorial Fellow, Balliol Coll., Univ. Oxford, 1878–83.

Degree BA Univ. Oxford, 1878.

Career Coined the phrase 'industrial revolution' and introduced the concept of a single, decisive transformation of the British economy in the third quarter of the eighteenth century. He turned to economics because of its relevance to social reform, and rejected the deductive in favour of the historical method. He argued that economic policies were appropriate or not, according to historical circumstances, and therefore rejected *laissez-faire* in favour of a kind of municipal socialism for his own time. He is remembered for his inspiring teaching which influenced many Oxford contemporaries to accept a socially-committed version of economics.

Publications *Books:* 1. *The Industrial Revolution* (1884).

Secondary Literature A. Milner, *Arnold Toynbee* (1901); R. Lekachman, 'Toynbee, Arnold', *IESS*, vol. 16.

TRIFFEN, R.

N.e.

TSIANG, Sho-Chieh

Born 1918, Shanghai, China.

Current Post Prof. Econ., Cornell Univ., NY, USA.

Recent Posts Prof. Econ., Nat. Peking Univ., 1946–8; Prof. Econ., Nat. Taiwan Univ., 1948–9; Economist, IMF, 1949–60; Prof. Econ., Univ. Rochester, 1960–9.

Degrees BSc (Econ.), PhD LSE, 1941, 1945; DSc (Econ.) Univ. London, 1975.

Offices and Honours RES; AEA; Member, Academia Sinica, ROC, 1957–; Guggenheim Memorial Foundation Fellow, 1966–7.

Principal Contributions The synthesis of loanable funds and liquidity preference theories of interest, and

contributions to theory of precautionary demand for money, the means-variance approach to portfolio allocation, and theories of foreign exchange, international capital flows and forward exchanges. Noteworthy also is the elucidation of the confusions caused by indiscriminate application of 'Walras Law' to monetary analysis.

Publications *Articles:* 1. 'The theory of forward exchange and effects of government intervention on the forward exchange market', *IMF Staff Papers*, 8, April 1959; 2. 'The rationale of mean-standard deviation analysis, skewness preference, and the demand for money', *AER*, 62, June 1972; 3. 'The dynamics of international capital flows, and internal and external balance', *QJE*, 89(3), May 1975; 4. 'The monetary theoretic foundation of the modern monetarist approach to the balance of payments', *OEP*, 29(3), Nov. 1977; 5. 'Keynes' finance demand for liquidity, Robertson's loanable funds theory, and Friedman's monetarism', *QJE*, 94(3), May 1980.

TSURU, Shigeto

Born 1912, Tokyo, Japan.

Current Post Editorial adviser, Asahi Shimbun, Tokyo, Japan, 1975–.

Recent Posts Vice-minister, Econ. Stabilisation Board, Japan Govt., 1947–8; Prof. Econ., 1948–72, Pres., 1972–5, Hitotsubashi Univ., Tokyo.

Degrees BA Harvard Coll., 1935; MA PhD (Econ.). Harvard Univ. 1936, 1940.

Offices and Honours Vice-pres., Internat. Social Science Council, 1967–73; Member Exec. Comm., 1971–4, Vice-pres., 1974–7, Pres., 1977–80, IEA.

Principal Contributions The resuscitation of political economy, as contrasted to economics, in an attempt to re-appraise the viability of the capitalist system. Have questioned the welfare significance of the national income (or GNP) concept years before it became fashionable (1943) and wrote on development planning and other welfare-related fields of applied economics, such as medical economics, environment, and urban problems.

Publications *Books:* 1. *Has capitalism changed?* (in Japanese), (Iwanami, 1959); 2. *Essays on economic development* (in Japanese), (Kinokuniya, 1968); 3. *Towards a new political economy* (in Japanese), (Kodansha, 1976).

TUCKER, George*

Dates and Birthplace 1775–1861, Bermuda.

Posts Held Prof. Moral Philosophy, Univ. Virginia, 1825–45.

Offices Congressman, 1819–25.

Career Writer on various subjects whose economic work was probably his most significant. He was a critic of Ricardo, and questioned the Malthusian population theory. Though a Southerner, he was critical of slavery on both economic and moral grounds.

Publications *Books:* 1. *Laws of Wages, Profits and Rent Investigated* (1837); 2. *The Theory of Money and Banks Investigated* (1839); 3. *Progress of the United States in Population and Wealth in Fifty Years* (1843); 4. *Banks or No Banks* (1857); 5. *Political Economy for the People* (1859); 6. *Essays Moral and Metaphysical* (1860).

Secondary Literature H.U. Faulkner, 'Ticker, George', *ESS*, vol. 15.

TUCKER, Josiah*

Dates and Birthplace 1712–99, Laugharne, Wales.

Post Held Clergyman, 1737–99.

Degrees BA, MA, DD Univ. Oxford, 1736, 1739, 1755.

Career Pamphleteer, who wrote frequently on economic topics and on the question of the American colonies, whose independence he favoured. His attacks on monopolies and his belief that trade was not benefited by the conflict with the colonies were favourably noticed by subsequent writers, including McCulloch.

Publications *Books:* 1. *A Brief Essay on the Advantages and Disadvantages Which Respectively Attend France and Great Britain with Regard to Trade* (1749); 2. *The Elements of Commerce and Theory of Taxes* (1755); 3. *The Case of Going to War, for the Sake of Procuring, Enlarging or Securing of Trade, Considered in a New Light* (1763); 4. *A Letter from a Merchant in London to his Nephew in North America* (1766); 5. *The True Interest of Great Britain Set Forth in Regard to the Colonies* (1774).

Secondary Literature W.E. Clark, *Josiah Tucker: Economist* (1903); J.F. Rees, 'Tucker, Josiah', *IESS*, vol. 15.

TUGAN-BARANOVSKY, Mikhail Ivanovich*

Dates and Birthplace 1865–1919, Kharkov, Russia.

Posts Held Privatdozent, Univ. St Petersburg, 1894–9, 1905–15; Dean Faculty Law, Univ. Kiev, 1917–19.

Degrees Grad., MA Univ. Kharkov, 1888, 1890.

Offices Member, Ukrainian Academy Sciences; Fin. minister, Ukrainian Republic, 1918.

Career Opponent of the Populists, who argued that Russia could by-pass capitalism and become a peasant socialist country. His study of crises in England was designed to refute this by showing the way capitalism had evolved in England. His critique of Marxism in other works led him to be regarded as a revisionist. His disproportionality theory of crises – in which crises occur because some sectors of industry expand out of proportion to others, – was widely admired by contemporaries. In later years he abandoned Marxism, becoming interested in co-operative movements.

Publications *Books:* 1. *Promyshlennye Krizisy v Sovremennoi Anglii* (1894); 2. *The Russian Factory* (1898); 3. *Modern Socialism in its Historical Development* (1906); 4. *Osnovy Politicheskoi Ekonomii* (1909); 5. *Zemel'naia Reforma i Kooperatsiia* (1918).

Secondary Literature O. Crisp, 'Tugan-Baranovskii', *IESS*, vol. 16; A. Nove, 'M.I. Tugan-Baranovsky (1865–1919)', *HOPE*, 2(2), 1970.

TULLOCK, Gordon

Born 1922, Rockford, Ill., USA.
Current Post Univ. disting. prof., Center Study Public Choice, Virginia Polytechnic Inst. and State Univ., USA, 1972–.
Recent Posts Foreign Service, US State Dept., 1947–56; Ass. and assoc. prof., Univ. S. Carolina, 1959–62; Assoc. prof., Univ. Virginia, 1962–7; Prof. Econ. Polit. Science, Rice Univ., 1967–8; Prof. Econ., Virginia Polytechnic Inst. and State Univ., 1968–72.
Degrees DJ Univ. Chicago Law School, 1947; Yale Univ., 1949–51; Cornell Univ., 1951–2.
Offices Pres., Public Choice Soc., 1965; Pres., SEA, 1980.
Principal Contributions The application of economic methods outside the traditional field of economics, analysing areas which are normally studied by political scientists, now generally referred to as Public Choice. Also worked in the economics of law, biology, social organisation, science, and the economics of conflict.
Publications *Books:* 1. *The Calculus of Consent: Logical Foundations of Constitutional Democracy* (with J.M. Buchanan), (Univ. Michigan Press, 1962; Spanish and Japanese transls, 1980); 2. *The Politics of Bureaucracy* (Public Affairs Press, 1965); 3. *The Social Dilemma: The Economics of War and Revolution* (Center Study Public Choice, 1974; Japanese transl., 1979); 4. *Trials on Trial: The pure Theory of Legal Procedures* (Columbia Univ. Press, 1980).
Articles: 1. 'The welfare costs of tariffs, monopolies and theft', *WEJ*, 5, June 1967; 2. 'The paradox of revolution', *Public Choice*, 11, Fall 1971; 3. 'The edge of the jungle', in *Explorations in the Theory of Anarchy*, ed. G. Tullock (Center Study Public Choice, 1972); 4. 'A new and superior process for making social choices' (with T.N. Tideman), *JPE*, 84(5), Oct. 1976; 5. 'Federalism: problems of scale', in *Economics of Federalism*, eds B.S. Grewal *et al.* (ANU Press, 1981).

TURGOT, Anne Robert Jacques*

Dates and Birthplace 1727–81, Paris, France.
Posts Held Intendant of Limoges, 1761–74; Contrôleur général of France, 1774–6.
Career Reforming administrator and minister whose efforts were cut short by the resistance of the privileged classes. His attempts to rationalise the tax burdens and obligations of French society were justified in theoretical terms of physiocratic variety. His *Reflections* ... is frequently described as one of the most important general treatises on political economy written before Smith's *Wealth of Nations* and there is little doubt that it was a major influence on Adam Smith. His other economic writings have only recently become available in English.
Publications *Books:* 1. *Reflections on the Formation and the Distribution of Wealth* (1769–70, 1973); 2. *Oeuvres de Turgot et documents le concernant*, 5 vols (1913–23).
Secondary Literature W. Stark, 'Turgot, Anne Robert Jacques', *IESS*, vol. 16; R.L. Meek, *Turgot on Progress, Sociology and Economics* (CUP, 1973); P.D. Groenewegen, *The Economics of A.R.J. Turgot* (Martinus Nijhoff, 1977).

TURNOVSKY, Stephen John

Born 1941, Wellington, New Zealand.
Current Post Prof. Econ., ANU, Australia.
Recent Posts Ass. prof. Econ., Univ. Penn., 1968–71; Assoc. prof. Econ., Univ. Toronto, 1971–2; Vis. prof. School Bus. Admin., Univ. Cal., Berkeley, 1975; Vis. prof. Econ., Univ. Paris-Dauphine, 1979, Univ. Minnesota, 1979; Vis. res. assoc., CEPREMAP, Paris, 1979.
Degrees BA, MA (First class hons) Victoria Univ. Wellington, 1962, 1963; PhD Harvard Univ., 1968.
Offices Fellow, Academy Social Science, Australia, 1976; Assoc. ed., *Int ER*, 1972–; Joint ed., *ER*, 1973–7;

Assoc. ed., *JMCB*, 1977–; Assoc. ed., 1978–81, Ed., 1981–, *J Ec Dyn*.

Principal Contributions Worked extensively in macro-economic theory, particularly in the modelling and analysis of consistently specified dynamic systems; emphasis on inflation, inflationary expectations, and their interaction with other macro-economic variables for both closed and open economies. Also, issues pertaining to price stabilisation revolving around the allocation of benefits and losses of various stabilisation schemes.

Publications *Books:* 1. *The Inflationary Process in North American Manufacturing* (with L.D. Taylor and T.A. Wilson), (Prices and Incomes Commission, Ottawa, 1973); 2. *Applications of Control Theory to Economic Analysis*, ed. (with J.D. Pitchford), (N-H, 1977); 3. *Macroeconomic Analysis and Stabilization Policy* (CUP, 1977; Japanese transl., 1980).

Articles: 1. 'Empirical evidence on the formation of price expectations', *JASA*, 65, Dec. 1970; 2. 'The stability properties of optimal economic policies', *AER*, 64(1), March 1974; 3. 'The dynamics of fiscal policy in an open economy', *J Int E*, 6(2), May 1976; 4. 'Expectations and the dynamics of devaluation', *REStud*, 47(4), July 1980; 5. 'The analysis of macroeconomic policies in perfect foresight equilibrium' (with W.A. Brock), *Int ER*, 22, March 1981.

TURVEY, Ralph

Born 1927, Birmingham, England.
Current Post Chief, Bureau Stats, ILO.
Recent Posts LSE, 1948–64; Chief economist, UK . Electricity Council, 1964–7; Dep. Chairman, UK National Board for Prices and Incomes, 1968–71.
Degrees BSc (Econ.), DSc (Econ.) Univ. London, 1947, 1971.
Offices and Honours Swedish govt. scholarship, Uppsala Univ., 1947–8; Council member, RES, 1971–6; Member, Inflation Accounting Comm., 1974–5; Member, UK National Water Council, 1974–5.
Principal Contributions Applied the Stockholm School approach to multiplier theory, expounded the idea of

inflation as resulting from competing efforts to buy, produce and/or earn more than feasible, and approached interest theory in terms of multiple-asset stock equilibrium. Wrote one of the first texts on urban land economics, co-authored a widely read survey of cost-benefit analysis, and contributed to the theory of externalities. Subsequently contributed to applied welfare economics especially through practical work on public enterprise pricing, developing a systems concept of marginal cost applied to electricity in particular, but also to gas, water supply and transport.

Publications *Books:* 1. *The Economics of Real Property* (A & U, 1957); 2. *Interest Rates and Asset Prices* (A & U, 1960); 3. *Optimal Pricing and Investment in Electricity Supply* (A & U, 1968); 4. *Economic Analysis and Public Enterprises* (A & U, 1971); 5. *Electricity Economics* (with D. Anderson), (Johns Hopkins Univ. Press, 1977).

Articles: 1. 'Some aspects of the theory of inflation in a closed economy', *EJ*, 61, Sept. 1951; 2. 'On divergences between social cost and private cost', *Ec.*, N.S. 30, Aug. 1963; 3. 'Optimization and suboptimization in fishery regulation', *AER*, 54, March 1964; 4. 'Cost-benefit analysis: a survey' (with A.R. Prest), *EJ*, 75, Dec. 1965, repr. in AEA-RES, *Surveys of economic theory*, vol. 3 (Macmillan, 1966); 5. 'The treatment of seasonal items in consumer price indices', *ILO Bull Lab Stat*, 4, 1979.

U

ULMAN, Lloyd

Born 1920, New York City, NY, USA.
Current Post Prof. Econ., Dir., Inst. Industrial Relations, Univ. Cal., Berkeley, USA.
Degrees BA Columbia Coll., 1940; MA Univ. Wisconsin, 1941; PhD Harvard Univ., 1950.
Offices and Honours Sr labor economist, US President's Council Econ. Advisers, 1961–2; Guggenheim Memorial Foundation Fellow, Vis. member,

LSE, 1966–7; Vis. Fellow, All Souls Coll., Univ. Oxford, 1973–4; Member, US President's Pay Advisory Comm., 1979–80; McDonald-Currie lecturer, Faculty Arts, McGill Univ., 1980; Bernard Moses Memorial lecturer, 1981.

Principal Contributions The economics of collective bargaining and institutional behaviour in the labour markets of the Western democracies: the impact of social and economic environments in shaping the objectives and instruments of trade union movements and the structural characteristics of collective bargaining. Sought to explore areas of interaction between collective bargaining and competitive forces in determining wages and employment, including activities of trade unions (and employers) to shape their market environment. Has considered the impact and compensatory features of public policies designed to contain the exercise of bargaining power in the interests of stabilisation and growth. More recently, the properties of a model of variable bargaining intensity (in contrast to conventional models of union behaviour), which would admit the direct influence of political and social change on the bargaining process.

Publications *Books:* 1. *The Rise of the National Trade Union* (Harvard Univ. Press, 1955, 1966); 2. *The Government of the Steel Workers' Union* (Wiley, 1962); 3. *Wages and Labour Mobility* (with P. de Wolff *et al.*), (OECD, 1965); 4. *Wage Restraint: A Study of Incomes Policies in Western Europe* (Univ. Cal. Press, 1971). *Articles:* 1. 'Marshall and Friedman on union strength', *REStat*, 37, Nov. 1955; 2. 'The development of trades and labor unions', and 'Unionism and collective bargaining in the modern period', in *American Economic History*, ed. S.E. Harris (McGraw-Hill, 1961); 3. 'Collective bargaining and industrial efficiency', in *Britain's Economic Prospects*, eds. R.E. Caves *et. al* (Brookings Inst., 1968); 4. 'Collective bargaining and competitive bargaining', *SJPE*, 21(2), June 1974; 5. 'Multinational unionism: incentives, barriers, and alternatives', *Industrial Relations*, 14(1), Feb. 1975.

UNWIN, George*

Dates and Birthplace 1870–1925, Stockport, England.

Posts Held Private secretary to Leonard Courtney; Lecturer, 1908–10, Prof. Econ., 1910–25, Univ. Edinburgh.

Career Economic historian, who attributed the success of the industrial revolution to the decline of state intervention in the late eighteenth century. His interpretations were much more in line with those of economists and sociologists than was usual in historical writing and he influenced subsequent generations in this approach, both through his teaching and his writings.

Publications *Books:* 1. *Industrial Organisation in the Sixteenth and Seventeenth Centuries* (1904); 2. *The Guilds and Companies of London* (1908); 3. *Finance and Trade under Edward III* (1918); 4. *Samuel Oldknow and the Arkwrights* (1924); 5. *Studies in Economic History* (1927).

Secondary Literature T.S. Ashton, 'Unwin, George', *IESS*, vol. 16.

USHER, Abbott Payson*

Dates and Birthplace 1883–1965, Lynn, Mass., USA.

Posts Held Prof., Cornell Univ., 1910–20, Univ. Boston, 1920–2; Prof. Econ., Harvard Univ., 1922–49.

Degrees BA, MA, PhD Harvard Univ., 1904, 1905, 1910.

Career Economic historian whose work drew on his knowledge of a range of disciplines, and emphasised the theoretical and statistical elements. His studies of inventions, markets and banking, all drew striking modern parallels.

Publications *Books:* 1. *The History of the Grain Trade in France 1400–1710* (1913); 2. *Introduction to the Industrial History of England* (1920); 3. *A History of Mechanical Inventions* (1929); 4. *The Early History of Deposit Banking in Mediterranean Europe* (1943). *Articles:* 1. 'The industrialization of modern Britain', *Technology and Culture*, 1, 1960.

Secondary Literature J.H. Dales, 'Usher, Abbott P.', *IESS*, vol. 16.

USHER, Dan

Born 1934, Montreal, Canada.
Current Post Prof., Queen's Univ., Ontario, Canada.
Recent Posts UN, 1960–1; Univ. Manchester, 1961–3; Res. Fellow, Nuffield Coll., Univ. Oxford, 1963–6; Columbia Bus School, 1966–7.
Degrees BA McGill Univ., 1956; PhD Univ. Chicago, 1960.
Offices CEA; NBER Conference Income and Wealth.
Principal Contributions Contributions to the theory of national accounting, particularly the comparison of real income among countries and over time; papers on economic theory; and development of the concept of equity as a criterion for economic policy.
Publications *Books:* 1. *The Price Mechanism and the Meaning of National Income Statistics* (OUP, 1969); 2. *The Measurement of Economic Growth* (Blackwell, Mott, 1980); 3. *The Economic Prerequisite to Democracy* (Blackwell, Mott, 1981).

UZAWA, Hirofumi

Born 1928, Yonago, Tottori, Japan.
Current Post Prof. Econ., Dean Faculty Econ., Univ. Tokyo, Japan.
Recent Posts Ass. prof. Econ. Maths, Univ. Cal., Berkeley, 1960–1; Assoc. prof. Econ., Stanford Univ., 1961–4; Prof. Econ., Univ. Chicago, 1964–9.
Degree BS Univ. Tokyo, 1951.
Offices Fellow, Advanced Center Res. Behavioral Sciences, 1961–2, RES, 1961–, AAAS, 1964–; Fellow, 1961, Vice-pres., 1975, Pres., 1976, Em Soc; Overseas Fellow, Churchill Coll., Univ. Camb., 1966–7; Hon. Foreign Fellow, AEA, 1978–.
Principal Contributions The analysis of the processes of economic growth in a capitalistic market economy, emphasis being placed upon the allocation of scarce resources between the production of consumption goods and investment goods. The analysis of the economic processes of market disequilibrium where the demand and supply for each good are necessarily equated; replaces the standard formulation of the Keynesian theory in terms of the Hicksian model of IS-LM analysis by the theory of dynamic disequilibrium where the employment of labour is not determined at the level at which its marginal product is equated with the market real wage. Then, a complete theory of the processes by which a firm in a capitalistic economy is subject to the phenomenon of fluctuations is constructed and its macro-economic implications are fully analysed.
Publications *Books:* 1. *Studies in Linear and Non-linear Programming* (with K.J. Arrow and L. Hurwicz), (Stanford Univ. Press, 1958); 2. *Economic Development and Economic Fluctuations* (with K. Inada), (Iwanami Shoten, 1972); 3. *Social Costs of the Automobile* (in Japanese), (Iwanami Shoten, 1974); 4. *Re-examining Modern Economic Theory* (in Japanese), (Iwanami Shoten, 1977).
Articles: 1. 'On a two-sector model of economic growth', *REStud*, I, II, 29, Oct. 1961; 30, June 1963; 2. 'Production functions with constant elasticities of substitution', *REStud*, 29, Oct. 1962; 3. 'Time preference and the Penrose effect in a two-class model of economic growth', *JPE*, 77(4), Pt II, July/Aug. 1969; 4. 'Towards a Keynesian model of monetary growth', *Models of economic growth*, eds J.A. Mirrlees and N.H. Stern, (Wiley, 1973); 5. 'La théorie économique du capital collectif social', *Cahier d'econometrie et economique*, 1974.

UZTÁRIZ, Gerónimo*

Dates and Birthplace 1670–1732, Spain.
Posts Held Member, Spanish Council of Trade and Council of the Indies.
Career Possibly the best-known Spanish mercantilist whose *Teórica* . . . was translated and widely admired. It is an assemblage of facts and criticism rather than theoretical analysis – even his recognition that economic conditions govern population levels, rather than vice versa, was hardly new. His advocacy of industrialisation and armament for Spain is interesting, since this is presumably the policy he had recommended

to Cardinal Alberoni when he was one of the latter's advisers.

Publications *Books:* 1. *Teórica y Práctica de Comercio y de Marina* (1724).

Secondary Literature E.J. Hamilton, 'The mercantilism of Gerónimo de Uztáriz', in *Economics, Sociology and the Modern World*, ed. N.E. Himes, (Univ. of Chicago Press, 1935).

V

VANDERLINT, Jacob*

Dates and Birthplace ?–1740.
Career English pamphleteer whose one important work was often mentioned favourably during the nineteenth century because it argued for free trade. He called for the cultivation of more land to increase the amounts of food available and to reduce its price, which in turn would give the country a competitive advantage in foreign trade.
Publications *Books:* 1. *Money Answers All Things* (1734).
Secondary Literature J.F. Rees, 'Vanderlint, Jacob', *ESS*, vol. 15.

VANEK, Jaroslav

Born 1930, Prague, Czechoslovakia.
Current Post Prof. Econ., 1966–, Karl Marx Prof. Internat. Stud., 1969–, Dir, Program Participation and Labor-Managed Systems, 1970–, Cornell Univ., USA.
Recent Posts Assoc. dir., Program Comparative Econ. Devel., 1967–70; Consultant, Govt Peru, 1971; Vis. prof., Inst. Econ. Science, Belgrade, 1972, Univ. Catholique de Louvain, Belgium, 1974; Fellow, Netherlands Inst. Advanced Stud., 1975–6; Vis. prof., Res. Fellow, Inst. Social Stud., The Hague, 1978–9; Econ. adviser to Prime Minister, Turkey, 1978–9.
Degrees Gymnasium Diploma, Prague, 1949; Diploma (Stats, Maths, Econ.) Sorbonne, Paris, 1952; Licencia (Econ.) Univ. Geneva, 1954; PhD (Econ.) MIT, 1957.
Offices and Honours Guggenheim

Memorial Foundation Fellow, 1961–2; Ford Foundation Faculty Fellow, 1967–8.
Principal Contributions Major areas: international trade and development; theory of labour-managed firms; solar energy through workers' co-operatives and inexpensive technology; and practical problems of self-managed enterprises.
Publications *Books:* 1. *International Trade: Theory and Economic Policy* (Richard D. Irwin, 1962; Japanese and Spanish transls, 1965); 2. *Maximal Economic Growth* (Cornell Univ. Press, 1968); 3. *The General Theory of Labour-managed Market Economies* (Cornell Univ. Press, 1970); 4. *The Participatory Economy: An Evolutionary Hypothesis and a Development Strategy* (Cornell Univ. Press, 1971; Spanish, German and Swedish transls). 5. *The Labor-managed Economy: Essays by Jaroslav Vanek* (Cornell Univ. Press, 1977).
Articles: 1. 'A rehabilitation of "well-behaved" social indifference curves', *REStud*, 31, Jan. 1964; 2. 'A theory of growth with technological change', *AER*, 57(1), March 1967; 3. 'Towards a better understanding of the incremental capital-output ratio' (with A.H. Studenmund), QJE, 82, Aug. 1968; 4. 'Economic growth and international trade in pure theory', *QJE*, 85, May 1971; 5. 'Tariffs, economic welfare and development potential', *EJ*, 81, Dec. 1971.

VAN PRAAG, Bernard M.S.

Born 1939, Amsterdam, The Netherlands.
Current Post Prof. Econ., Univ. Leyden, The Netherlands, 1972–.
Degree Dr Econ. Amsterdam Univ., 1968.
Principal Contributions Developed the theory of income evaluation, which has been tested empirically in the framework of the Leyden Income Evaluation Project. On the basis of this theory, studies are made about income inequality, poverty, the social reference process, and the evaluation of leisure versus income. In the field of econometric

methodology, developed the model-free method. Also made contributions to the economic theory of social security and health economics.

Publications *Books:* 1. *The Theory of Individual Welfare Functions and Consumer Behavior* (N-H, 1968).

Articles: 1. 'The welfare function of income in Belgium: an empirical investigation', *Europ ER*, 2, 1971; 2. 'The introduction of an old-age pension in a growing economy', *J Pub E*, 4(1), Feb. 1975; 3. 'A new approach to the construction of family equivalence scales' (with A. Kapteyn), *Europ ER*, 7(4), May 1976; 4. 'The poverty line L concept and measurement' (with T. Goedhart *et al.*), *JHR*, 12(4), Fall 1977; 5. 'A dynamic model of interaction between state and private sector' (with F. van Winden), *Economic letters*, 1, 1978.

VAUBAN, Seigneur Sébastien le Prestre de*

Dates and Birthplace 1633–1707, St Léger de Fougeret, France.

Posts Held Professional soldier, 1650; Governor of Lille, 1668; General commissioner fortifications, 1678; Marshal of France, 1703.

Career Soldier and outstanding military engineer, whose examination of the military potential of areas led him to collect quantities of social and economic information. Turning to the economic condition of the country as a whole, he identified the chaotic and burdensome tax system as a major problem. His scheme for a new and justly-apportioned taxation was not received favourably by those in power, but it contributed an important element to the debate on the reform of French society which culminated in the French Revolution.

Publications *Books:* 1. *Projet d'une dixième royale* (1707); 2. *Oisivetés*, ed. A.M. Augoyat, 3 vols (1842–5).

Secondary Literature E.R.A. Seligman, 'Vauban, Seigneur Sébastien le Prestre de', *ESS*, vol. 15.

VEBLEN, Thorstein Bunde*

Dates and Birthplace 1857–1929, Cato, Wisc., USA.

Posts Held Teacher, Univ. Chicago, 1892–1906, Stanford Univ., 1906–9 Univ. Missouri, 1911–18, New School for Social Res., 1918–26.

Degrees BA Carleton Coll., 1880; PhD Yale Univ., 1884.

Career Economist and sociologist who criticised American society from an evolutionary and cosmopolitan viewpoint. His scathing indictment of capitalism did not, however, lead him to involvement with programmes for reform which he saw as ineffective. He saw society as a conflict between an acquisitive and a technocratic instinct. The terms 'conspicuous consumption' and 'pecuniary emulation' have entered the language from Veblen's works. He was little read in his own day, but was highly regarded by some of his pupils, who sustained him through the difficulties of his academic career, and he soon came to be regarded as the founder of an American Institutionalist School, which survives to this day. American Institutionalism, however, owes perhaps more to Mitchell and Commons than to Veblen, who was too idiosyncratic to be capable of imitation and development.

Publications *Books:* 1. *The Theory of the Leisure Class* (1899, 1953, 1959); 2. *The Theory of Business Enterprise* (1904, 1958); 3. *Imperial Germany and the Industrial Revolution* (1915, 1964); 4. *The Higher Learning in America* (1918, 1957); 5. *Absentee Ownership and Business Enterprise in Recent Times* (1923, 1945); 6. *Essays in our Changing Order* (1934); 7. *The Place of Science in Modern Civilisation* (1961).

Secondary Literature J. Dorfman, *Thorstein Veblen and his America* (Kelly, 1961); A.K. Davis, 'Veblen, Thorstein', *IESS*, vol. 16.

VERNON, Raymond

Born 1913, New York City, NY, USA.

Current Post Prof. Internat. Affairs, Harvard Univ., USA.

Recent Post Prof., Harvard Univ., 1959–.

Degrees BA City Coll., New York,

1933; PhD Columbia Univ., 1941; MA (hon.) Harvard Univ., 1959.

Offices Dir., World Peace Foundation; Dir., US/UN Association; Overseer, Florence Heller School, Brandeis Univ.; Ed., *Journal Policy Analysis and Management;* Fellow, AAAS; Member, US Council on Foreign Relations; Fellow, Academy Internat. Bus.

Principal Contributions Various studies of the economics of multinational enterprises, including the international location of industry; work on dynamic factors in changing comparative advantage of nations, including especially product cycle phenomena. Various studies in urban economics.

Publications *Books:* 1. *Metropolis* (Harvard Univ. Press, 1958, 1962); 2. *Dilemma of Mexico's Development* (Harvard Univ. Press, 1964); 3. *Manager in the International Economy* (Prentice-Hall, 1968); 4. *Sovereignty at Bay* (Basic Books, 1971); 5. *Storm over the Multinationals* (Harvard Univ. Press, 1977).

Articles: 1. 'International investment and international trade in the product cycle', *QJE*, 80, May 1968; 2. 'US direct investment in Canada: consequences for the US economy', *J Fin*, 28(2), May 1973; 3. 'The location of economic activity', in *Economic Analysis and the Multinational Enterprise*, ed. J.H. Dunning (A & U, 1974); 4. 'Foreign production of technology-intensive products by US-based multinational enterprise' (with W. Davidson), *Report to NSF*, (1979); 5. 'The product cycle hypothesis in a new international environment', *OBES*, 41(4), Nov. 1979.

VERRI, Pietro*

Dates and Birthplace 1728–97, Milan, Italy.

Posts Held Official, Austrian administration of Milan.

Offices Founder, Società dei Pugni, Milan, ed. of its journal *Il Caffè*, 1764–6.

Career His economic work, though chiefly the underpinning of policy recommendations, was scientifically of the highest standard. His concept of economic equilibrium was based ultimately on the calculus of pleasure and pain, for like his contemporary Beccaria he was a utilitarian. As an administrator he had access to copious supplies of facts and wove them into his argument in the most apposite fashion. His work on the calculation of balance of payments figures is just one of his achievements in the quantitative field, and his other original contributions include a constant-outlay demand curve.

Publications *Books:* 1. *Elementi del Commercio* (1760); 2. *Bilancio del Commercio dello Stato di Milano* (1764); 3. *Riflessioni Sulle Leggi Vincolanti* (1769); 4. *Meditazioni Sull'economia Politica* (1771).

Secondary Literature C. Pagui, 'Verri, Pietro', *ESS*, vol. 15.

VICKERS, Douglas

Born 1924, Rockhampton, Australia.

Current Post Prof. Econ., Univ. Massachusetts, USA.

Recent Posts Prof. Fin., Univ. Pennsylvania, 1957–72; Prof. Econ., Univ. Western Australia, 1972–7.

Degrees BCom Univ. Queensland, Australia, 1949; BSc (Econ.), PhD Univ. London, 1952, 1956; MA Univ. Pennsylvania, 1972.

Offices AEA; RES.

Principal Contributions A re-examination of the development of the theory of money and cognate intellectual history in the eighteenth century, published in *Studies in the Theory of Money*; an integration of the theory of money and the problems of money capital into the theory of the firm, published in *The Theory of the Firm: Production, Capital, and Finance*; and a reconsideration of the relevance of uncertainty, disequilibrium, and time for the theory of finance and the displacement of timeless Walrasian statics, published in *Financial Markets in the Capitalist Process*.

Publications *Books:* 1. *Studies in the Theory of Money 1690–1776* (Chilton, 1959); 2. *The Theory of the Firm: Production, Capital, and Finance* (McGraw-Hill, 1968); 3. *Man in the Malestrom of Modern Thought* (Presbyterian & Reformed Publishing Co.,

1975); 4. *Economics and Man: Prelude to a Christian Critique* (Craig Press, 1976); 5. *Financial Markets in the Capitalist Process* (Univ. Pennsylvania Press, 1978).

Articles: 1. 'Profitability and reinvestment rates: a note on the Gordon paradox', *J Bus*, 39(3), July 1966; 2. 'The cost of capital and the structure of the firm', *J Fin*, 25, March 1970; 3. 'Finance and false trading in non-*tatònnement* markets', *AEP*, 14, Dec. 1975; 4. 'Adam Smith and the status of the theory of money', in *Essays on Adam Smith*, ed. T. Wilson and A. Skinner (Clarendon Press, 1976); 5. 'Uncertainty, choice, and the marginal efficiencies', *J Post Keyn E*, 2(2), Winter 1979.

VICKREY, William

Born 1914, Victoria, British Columbia, Canada.

Current Post McVickar Prof. Polit. Econ., Columbia Univ., NY, USA.

Recent Posts Fellow, Center Advanced Study Behavioral Sciences, Stanford, Cal., 1967–8; Vis. lecturer, Monash Univ., Australia, 1971; Public Fin. Consultant ('Interregional Adviser') UN Center Development Programs, Planning and Pol., 1974–5.

Degrees BS Yale Univ., 1935; MA, PhD Columbia Univ., 1937, 1947; Dr Humane Letters, Univ. Chicago, 1979.

Offices and Honours Chairman, Econ. Dept., Columbia Univ., 1964–7; Chairman, Metropolitan Econ. Assoc. (NYC), 1964–5; Fellow, Em Soc, 1967; Dir., NBER, 1973–; Fellow, AAAS, 1974; Disting. Fellow, AEA, 1978.

Principal Contributions Progressive taxation reform proposals: cumulative averaging assessment, bequeathing power succession tax, age different graduation of succession taxes, taxable tax credit for government interest, rationalization of undistributed profits tax, of earned income credit. Theory and application of marginal cost pricing: responsive pricing, urban congestion charges, simulated futures markets in airline reservations, impacts of inflation on utility regulation, pricing and fare collection methods. Public choice theory: demand revealing procedures, auctions and bidding theory, self-policing imputation sets in game theory, social welfare functions. Land value taxation: short-versus long-term impacts and relationships with marginal cost pricing.

Publications *Books:* 1. *Agenda for Progressive Taxation* (Ronald Press, 1949, 1971); 2. *The Revision of the Rapid Transit Fare Structure of the City of New York* (Finance Project, Mayor's Comm. Management Survey, 1952); 3. *Microstatics* (Harcourt Brace & World, 1964); 4. *Metastatics and Macroeconomics* (Harcourt Brace & World, 1964).

Articles: 1. 'Utility, strategy, and social decision rules', *QJE*, 74, Nov. 1960, reprinted in *Readings in Welfare Economics*, eds K.J. Arrow and T. Scitovsky (Richard D. Irwin, 1969); 2. 'Counter-speculation, auctions, and competitive sealed tenders', *J. Fin*, 16, 1961; 3. 'Responsive pricing of utility services', *Bell JE*, 2, 1971; 4. 'The city as a firm', in *The Economics of Public Services*, eds M.S. Feldstein and R.P. Inman (Macmillan, 1977); 5. 'Optimal transit subsidy policy', *Transportation*, 9, 1980.

VIETORISZ, Thomas

Born 1926, Budapest, Hungary.

Current Post Prof. Econ., New School Social Res., New York City.

Recent Posts Assoc. dir., Econ. Development Training Program, UNECLA, 1957–60; Res. staff member, T.J. Watson Res. Center, IBM Corp., 1961–3; Vis. prof., Univs. Cornell, MIT, 1970–81.

Degrees Absolutorium (Chem. Eng.), Technical Univ., Budapest, 1946; SM (Chem. Eng.) PhD (Econ.) MIT, 1948, 1956.

Offices Consultant, UN, World Bank, OECD, Inter-American Bank, US govt, US state govts, Govts of Mexico and Puerto Rico, and numerous private firms and organisations, 1964–81.

Principal Contributions Methods of strategic planning: industrial planning (chemical industries, engineering industries); regional planning (Third World countries, metropolitan areas); mathematical planning models (linear and integer programming, simulation); political economy of development and planning in industrially advanced countries, Third World areas, and socialist economies.

Publications *Books:* 1. *Industrial Complex Analysis and Regional Development* (with W. Isard and E.W. Schooler), (MIT Press, Wiley, 1959); 2. *Techniques of Sectoral Economic Planning: The Chemical industries* (UN, 1966); 3. *Engineering Industry, Chemical Industry* (UNIDO, 1969); 4. *The Economic Development of Harlem* (with B. Harrison), (Praeger, 1970); 5. *Planning and Programming of Metalworking Industries with Special View to Exports* (with R. Lissak), (UN, 1972).

Articles: 1. 'Locational choices in planning', in *National Economic Planning*, ed. M. Milligan (Columbia Univ. Press, 1967); 2. 'Decentralization and project evaluation under economies of scale and indivisibilities', *UN Industrialization and Productivity Bull.*, 11, 1968; 3. 'Quantized preferences and planning by priorities', *AER*, 60(2), May 1970; 4. 'Indicators of labor market functioning and urban social distress' (with R. Mier and J. Giblin), in *The Social Economy of Cities*, 9, (*Urban Affairs Annual Review*, 1975); 5. 'The use of input-output computer information in programming for chemical processes', in *Advances in Input-output Analysis* (Ballinger Publishing, 1976).

VINCENS, Jean

Born 1926, Figeac, France.
Current Post Prof., Univ. Sciences Sociales, Toulouse, France, 1958–.
Degrees Dr Sciences Econ. Univ. Toulouse, 1954; Agrégé des Sciences Econ. 1958; Dr (*Hon. Câusa*) Univ. Catholique de Louvain, 1981.
Offices Dir., Faculté Sciences Econ., Toulouse, 1969–77; Conseiller Scientifique Centre d'Etudes et de Recherches sur les Qualifications, 1970–; Vice-pres., Univ. Sciences Sociales, Toulouse I, 1980–.
Principal Contributions Effects of

redistribution on the income inequality of working households, the transfers taking place mostly from bachelors, and from couples with more than one working member, towards households having only one working member and bringing up children; elaboration of the concept of 'plants population' applied to manpower forecasting; professional and regional manpower forecasting; study of the relationships between the school system and the production system.

Publications *Books:* 1. *La Prévision de l'emploi* (Presse Univ. de France, 1970); 2. *Etudes des comportements sur le marché du travail* (with D. Robinson), (OCDE, 1974); 3. *La Formation continue et l'emploi* (with A. Cabanis), (Privat, 1980).

Articles: 1. 'Transferts sociaux et pyramide des revenus salariaux', *RE*, 2, March 1957; 2. 'Les prévisions régionales de l'emploi dans l'industrie', *RE*, 6, March 1967; 3. 'Quelques remarques sur les relations entre formations et emplois', *Economies et sociétés. Cahiers de l'ISMEA.* Série emploi Oct./Dec. 1977; 4. 'Les nouveaux aspects du problème de l'emploi', *REP*, 1, 1979; 5. 'Post-secondary education and employment. The French case', *Europ J Education*, 16(1), 1980.

VINER, Jacob*

Dates and Birthplace 1892–1970, Montreal, Canada.
Posts Held Instructor, Prof., Univ. Chicago, 1916–46; Prof., Princeton Univ., 1946–70.
Degrees BA McGill Univ., 1914; MA, PhD Harvard Univ., 1915, 1922.
Offices and Honours Consultant, US Tariff Commission, Treasury Dept., State Dept.; Ed., *JPE*, for 18 years; F.A. Walker medal, AEA; Pres., AEA, 1939–40.
Career His great breadth of scholarship included major contributions to the theory of cost and production, international economics and the history of economic thought. In the first category, his 1921 and 1931 articles, both reprinted in *The Long View and the Short*, are of major importance, the latter including the now famous envelope

cost curve of modern textbooks. His work on international trade is in the Ricardian tradition, and deals mainly with the real side. His work on the history of economics ranges widely, but was latterly concerned with the interplay of theological and economic ideas.

Publications *Books:* 1. *Dumping: A Problem in International Trade* (1923); 2. *Canada's Balance of International Indebtedness* (1924); 3. *Studies in the Theory of International Trade* (1937); 4. *Trade Relations between Free Market and Controlled Economies* (1943); 5. *The Customs Union Issue* (1950); 6. *International Economics* (1951); 7. *International Trade and Economic Development* (1952); 8. *The Long View and the Short* (1958); 9. *The Role of Providence in the Social Order* (1972); 9. 'Religious Thought and Economic Society: Four Chapters of an Unfinished Work', eds J. Melitz and D. Winch, *HOPE*, 10(1), Spring 1978.

Secondary Literature W.J. Baumol and E.V. Seiler, 'Viner, Jacob', *IESS*, vol. 18; L. Robbins, *Jacob Viner: A Tribute* (Princeton Univ. Press, 1970).

VON WEIZSÄCKER, Carl Christian

Born 1938, Berlin, Germany.
Current Post Prof. Econ., Univ. Bonn, W. Germany.
Recent Posts Prof. Univ. Heidelberg, 1965–72; Vis. prof., MIT, 1968–70; Prof. Univ. Bielefeld, 1972–4.
Degrees Dr Phil, Habilitation Univ. Basel, 1961, 1965.
Offices and Honours Fellow, Em Soc, 1969–; Co-ed., *Em*, 1969–74; Wicksell Lecture, Stockholm, 1972; Member, Advisory Board, W. German Ministry Econ. Affairs, 1977–; Foreign hon. member, AAAS, 1979–; First Böhm-Bawerk Lecture, Univ. Innsbruck, 1980.
Principal Contributions Theory of optimal growth: 'golden rule' (1961), 'overtaking criterion' (1965). Theory of technical progress: so-called Kennedy-Weizsäcker theory of induced technical change (1963), book on the economic theory of technical change (1966) and theory of progressive industries (1980). Capital theory: duality relations in cap-

ital theory (1963), book on steady state capital theory (1971) and coefficient of intertemporal substitution (1974). Welfare economics: welfare economics of endogenous change of tastes (1971). Economics of information: the principle of extrapolation (1980). Industrial organisation: a new concept of 'barriers to entry' (1980). And economics of telecommunications: a new definition of the role of government and the market (1981).

Publications *Books:* 1. *Wachstum, Zins und Optimale Investitionsquote* (Mohr, Siebeck, 1962); 2. *Zur Ökonomischen Theorie des Technischen Fortschritts* (Vandenhoek & Ruprecht, 1966); 3. *Steady State Capital Theory* (Springer, 1971); 4. *Barriers to Entry. A Theoretical Treatment* (Springer, 1980); 5. *Die Rolle des Wettbewerbs im Fernmeldebereich* (with G. Knieps and J. Müller), (Baden-Baden, 1981).

Articles: 1. 'Existence of optimal programs of accumulation for an infinite time horizon', *REStud*, 32, April 1965; 2. 'Notes on endogenous change of tastes', *JET*, 3(4), Dec. 1971; 3. 'Substitution along the time axis', *Kyklos*, 27(4), 1974; 4. 'A welfare analysis of barriers to entry', *Bell JE*, 11(2), Autumn 1980; 5. 'Rechte und Verhältnisse in der modernen Wirtschaftslehre', *Kyklos*, 34(3), 1981.

W

WATCHER, Michael L.

Born 1943, New York City, NY, USA.
Current Post Prof. Econ. Management, Univ. Pennsylvania, USA.
Recent Posts Ass. prof. Econ., 1969–73, Assoc. prof. Econ., 1973–6, Univ. Pennsylvania; Res. assoc., NBER, 1978–; Sr adviser, Brookings Panel Econ. Activity, 1976–, Commissioner, 1978–.
Degrees BS Cornell Univ., 1964; MA (Econ.), PhD (Econ.) Harvard Univ., 1967, 1970.
Offices and Honours AEA; Em Soc.; IRRA; Julian and Janice Bers Prof., Univ. Pennsylvania, 1972–3; NSF Grant, 1972–7; Nat. Inst. Child Health

Human Development, 1972–81; General Electric Foundation Grant, 1977–81; Twentieth-Century Fund Grant, 1978–81.

Principal Contributions The endogenous theory of fertility; the household production function in the 'new' economics of the family; the operation of the labour market during slumpflation.

Publications *Articles:* 1. 'Wage determination, inflation, and the industrial structure' (with S.A. Ross), *AER*, 63(4), Sept. 1973; 2. 'The relevance of the household production function and its implications for the allocation of time' (with R.A. Pollak), *JPE*, 83(2), April 1975; 3. 'Intermediate swings in labor-force participation', *Brookings Papers Econ. Activity*, 2, 1977; 4. 'Obligational markets and the mechanics of inflation' (with O.E. Williamson), *Bell JE*, 9(2), Autumn 1978; 5. 'Fertility determination, endogenous preferences and natural fertility' (with R.A. Easterlin and R.A. Pollack), in *Population and Economic Change in Less Developed Countries*, ed. R.A. Easterlin (Univ. Chicago Press, 1980).

WAGNER, Adolph Heinrich Gotthelf*

Dates and Birthplace 1835–1917, Erlangen, Germany.

Posts Held Taught at Vienna, Hamburg, Dorpat, Freiburg im Breisgau, 1858–70; Prof. Polit. Econ., Univ. Berlin, 1870–1917.

Degree Dr Univ. Göttingen, 1857.

Offices Founder, Verein für Sozialpolitik, 1872; Member, Lower House, Prussian Diet, 1882–5; Member, Upper House, 1910–17.

Career Conservative critic of *laissez-faire* economics who sought by the intervention of the state to secure social justice for the working classes. His economics was based on theoretical principles and he was largely on the Austrian side in the 'Methodenstreit'. His greatest contribution was in public finance where he integrated the subject with general economics and gave it strong theoretical principles. He stressed the redistributive potential of taxation and accepted the growth of public expenditure by the modern state. He also made important contributions to monetary and banking policy.

Publications *Books:* 1. *Beiträge zur Lehre von den Banken* (1857); 2. *Die Geld- und Credittheorie der Peel'schen Bankacte* (1862); 3. *Finanzwissenschaft*, 4 vols (1871–2); 4. *Theoretische Sozialökonomik*, 2 vols (1907–9).

Secondary Literature G. Meyer, 'Wagner, Adolf', *IESS*, vol. 16; *Classics in the Theory of Public Finance*, eds R.A. Musgrave and A.T. Peacock (Macmillan, 1958). H. Rubner, ed., *Adolph Wagner, Briefe, Dokumente, Augenzeugenberichte 1851–1917* (Duncker & Humblot, 1978).

WAKEFIELD, Edward Gibson*

Dates and Birthplace 1796–1862, London, England.

Career Colonisation theorist, whose scheme was based on the sale not grant of land to colonists, both to ensure that the purchasers cultivated it properly and also to provide funds for the development of the colonisation process; he also argued for self-government once the colony was sufficiently large. The colony of S. Australia was organised according to his principles, and proved very successful. He also advised Lord Durham on his *Report on the Affairs of British North America* which set Canada on the course towards self-government, and gave similar advice on the colonisation of New Zealand. His defence of colonisation, based on the notion that Britain was suffering from an excess of both capital and labour, influenced the later classical economists, such as J.S. Mill, in taking a more sceptical attitude towards Say's law and the so-called impossibility of general gluts.

Publications *Books:* 1. *Letter from Sydney* (1829); 2. *Facts Relating to the Punishment of Death in the Metropolis* (1831); 3. *View of the Art of Colonisation* (1849).

Secondary Literature R. Lekachman, 'Wakefield, Edward Gibbon', *IESS*, vol. 16.

WALD, Abraham*

Dates and Birthplace 1902–50, Cluj, Romania.

Posts Held Austrian Inst. Bus. Cycle Res., 1932–8; Res. Fellow, Columbia Univ., 1938–50.

Career Mathematical statistician whose work on decision theory and sequential analysis is of outstanding importance. He also did some work in econometrics and mathematical economics, including existence proofs for general equilibrium, seasonal corrections of time series, formulae for index numbers, the Cournot duopoly problem, and stochastic difference equations.

Publications *Books:* 1. *Sequential Analysis* (1947); 2. *Statistical Decision Functions* (1950).

Articles: 1. On some systems of equations of mathematical economics', *ZN*, 7, 1936; 2. 'On the statistical treatment of linear stochastic difference equations (with H.B. Mann), *Em*, 11, July/Oct. 1943.

Secondary Literature H. Freeman, 'Wald, Abraham', *IESS*, vol. 16.

WALKER, Amasa*

Dates and Birthplace 1799–1875, Woodstock Conn., USA.

Posts Held Businessman; Teacher Polit. Econ., Oberlin Coll., 1842–8, and Amherst Coll.

Offices Massachusetts Secretary of State and member of the Legislature; Congressman, 1862.

Career In addition to his public and political life, he taught and wrote on political economy. He was the chief American advocate of the currency school. He illustrated his argument that prices are determined by the quantity of money by the use of charts. His economics was in general orthodox and he was a supporter of free trade. His son Francis, who co-operated on the *Science of Wealth*, attained a similar position of eminence in the discipline.

Publications *Books:* 1. *The Nature and Uses of Money and Mixed Currency* (1857); 2. *Science of Wealth* (with F.A. Walker), (1866).

Secondary Literature H.E. Miller, 'Walker, Amasa', *ESS*, vol. 15.

WALKER, Francis Amasa*

Dates and Birthplace 1840–97, Boston, USA.

Posts Held Chief Treasury Bureau Stats, 1869–70; Superintendent Censuses, 1870, 1880; Prof., Yale Univ., 1872–81; Pres., MIT, 1881–97.

Degree BA Amherst Coll., 1860.

Offices Pres., ASA, 1883–96, AEA, 1886–92.

Career After his experience of statistical work, and under the tutelage of his father, he took up economics and became a chief figure in the discipline. He was concerned to establish economics as a science rather than a branch of practical politics. He developed his own distribution theory, vigorously repudiating the wages fund doctrine, argued for bimetallism and pioneered the use of graphic presentation of data. He also encouraged the creation of permanent census staff and fostered the use of statistics by economists.

Publications *Books:* 1. *The Wages Question* (1876); 2. *Money* (1878); 3. *Money in its Relations to Trade and Industry* (1879); 4. *Land and its Rent* (1883); 5. *Political Economy* (1883); 6. *International Bimetallism* (1896); 7. *Discussions in Economics and Statistics*, 2 vols (1899).

Secondary Literature H.W. Spiegel, 'Walker, Francis A.', *IESS*, vol. 16.

WALLACE, Robert*

Dates and Birthplace 1697–1771, Kincardine, Scotland.

Post Held Clergyman.

Offices Moderator, General Assembly, Church of Scotland, 1743; Royal Chaplain for Scotland, 1744.

Career Pre-Malthusian writer on population who disputed Hume's contention that population had increased since ancient times. However, on returning to the question in *Various Prospects* ..., he argued that the capacity for mankind to reproduce itself would frustrate the prospects for more perfect forms of society. Godwin attempted to refute this, Malthus found it congenial towards his own views. His writings in general are in the traditions of the Scottish Enlightenment.

Publications *Books:* 1. *Dissertation on the Numbers of Mankind* (1753); 2. *Characteristics of the Present State of Great Britain* (1758); 3. *Various Prospects of Mankind, Nature and Providence* (1761).

Secondary Literature J.F. Rees, 'Wallace, Robert', *ESS*, vol. 15.

WALLACE, T.D.

N.e.

WALLICH, Henry C.

Born 1914, Berlin, Germany.
Current Post Governor, Board Governors, Fed. Reserve System.
Recent Post Prof. Econ., Yale Univ., 1951–74.
Degree PhD Harvard Univ., 1944.
Honours Commander's Cross, Order of Merit of Fed. Republic of Germany, 1980.
Principal Contributions Monetary and other policy issues.
Publications *Books:* 1. *Monetary Problems of an Export Economy* (Harvard Univ. Press, 1950); 2. *Public Finance in a Developing Country, El Salvador, A Case Study* (with J.H. Adler), (Harvard Univ. Press, 1951); 3. *Monetary and Banking Legislation of the Dominican Republic, 1947* (with R. Triffin), (Fed. Reserve Bank of New York, 1953); 4. *Mainsprings of the German Revival* (Yale Univ. Press, 1955); 5. *The Cost of Freedom* (Harper & Bros, 1960).

WALLIS, Kenneth F.

Born 1938, Mexborough, Yorks. England.
Current Post Prof. Econometrics, Univ. Warwick.
Recent Posts Lecturer, Reader, Stats with special reference to Econometrics, LSE, 1966–77.
Degrees BSc, MSc Tech. Univ.

Manchester, 1959, 1961; PhD Stanford Univ., 1966.
Offices Council member, RSS, 1972–6; Fellow, Em Soc, 1975; Co-ed., *Em*, 1977–84.
Principal Contributions The development of statistical methods for the econometric analysis of economic time series.
Publications *Books:* 1. *Introductory Econometrics* (with M.B. Stewart), (Blackwell, Halstead Press, 1972, 1981); 2. *Topics in Applied Econometrics* (Blackwell, Univ. Minnesota Press, 1973, 1979).
Articles: 1. 'Wages, prices and incomes policies: some comments', *Ec*, N.S. 38, Aug. 1971; 2. 'Testing for fourth-order autocorrelation in quarterly regression equations', *Em*, 40(4), July 1972; 3. 'Seasonal adjustment and relations between variables', *JASA*, 69, March 1974; 4. 'Multiple time series analysis and the final form of econometric models', *Em*, 45(6), Sept. 1977; 5. 'Econometric implications of the rational expectations hypothesis', *Em*, 48(1), Jan. 1980.

WALRAS, Antoine Auguste*

Dates and Birthplace 1801–66, Montpellier, France.
Post Held Educational administrator.
Career Rejecting utility and labour, he suggested 'rareté' as the true source of value. This placed the emphasis on the quantity of a commodity available, and led him to argue that political economy should be a mathematical science. In the *Théorie* ... he developed a doctrine of property which involved public ownership of land. Not least of his achievements was the formative influence he exercised on the ideas of his son, Léon.
Publications *Books:* 1. *De la nature de la richesse, et de l'origine de la valuer* (1831); 2. *Théorie de la richesse sociale* (1849); 3. *Esquisse d'une théorie de la richesse* (1863).
Secondary Literature E. Antonelli, 'Walras, Antoine Auguste', *ESS*, vol. 15.

WALRAS, Marie-Esprit Léon*

Dates and Birthplace 1834–1910, Evreux, France.
Posts Held Journalist, railway official, bank employee; Prof., Univ. Lausanne, 1870–92.
Degrees Bacc. (lettres), (science), Univ. Paris, 1851, 1853.
Career Co-discoverer with Jevons and Menger of marginal utility theory, he was also the first economist to produce a multi-equational model of general equilibrium. He divided his economic work into three parts; pure, applied and social, the latter being normative and concerned with questions of justice. His first economic publication (1860) was in this area and very much in the tradition of the work of his father, Auguste. On obtaining the Lausanne chair, he concentrated on pure economics and taught himself mathematics. The results appear in the *Elements* ... which, through successive editions, became an increasingly sophisticated version of his general equilibrium model. He also did significant work on monetary reform, concentrating on bimetallism and the question of bank note issue. However, he was never able to produce the systematic treatises on applied and social economics which he had envisaged. Though well known to economists of his time through his voluminous correspondence, true appreciation of his monumental achievements only came posthumously in the 1930s.
Publications *Books:* 1. *L'Économie politique et la justice* (1860); 2. *Recherche de l'idéal social* (1868); 3. *Elements of Pure Economics* (1874–7, 1926, 1954); 4. *Théorie mathématique du bimétallisme* (1881); 5. *Etudes d'éonomie sociale* (1896, 1936); 6. *Etudes d'économie politique appliquée* (1898, 1936); 7. *Correspondence of Léon Walras and Related Papers*, 3 vols; ed. W. Jaffé (1965).
Secondary Literature W. Jaffé, 'Walras Léon', *IESS*, vol. 16.

WALTERS, Alan Arthur

Born 1926, Leicester, England.
Current Post Econ. adviser, UK Prime Minister, Civil Service Dept., 1981–.
Recent Posts Cassel Prof. Econ., LSE, 1968–77; Prof. Polit. Econ., Johns Hopkins Univ., 1977–81.
Degrees BSc (Econ.) Univ. London, 1951; Hon. DLitt Univ. Leicester, 1981.
Offices Council, Inst. Econ. Affairs, 1964–80; Fellow, Em Soc, 1969.
Principal Contributions Developed the ideas of efficient pricing of publicly owned industries, particularly congestion pricing for roads; developed and applied cost-benefit techniques, particularly to problems of airport investment and location, as in the UK Roskill Commission on 3rd London Airport; developed estimates of the demand for money in the UK, and explored the dynamic implications of a permanent income hypothesis, including overshoots, etc.; and studies of monetary dynamics.
Publications *Books:* 1. *The Economics of Road User Charges* (Johns Hopkins Univ. Press, 1968); 2. *An Introduction to Econometrics* (Macmillan, 1968, 1970); 3. *Money in Boom and Slump* (Inst. Econ. Affairs, 1968, 1970); 4. *Microeconomic Theory* (with P.R.G. Layard), (McGraw-Hill, 1978); 5. *Port Pricing and Investment Policies for Developing Countries* (with E. Bennathan), (OUP, 1979).
Articles: 1. 'The theory and measurement of marginal private and social cost of highway congestion', *Em*, 29, Oct. 1961; 2. 'Production and cost functions: an economic survey', *Em*, 31, Jan./April 1963; 3. 'Professor Friedman on the demand for money', *JPE*, 73, Oct. 1965; 4. 'Demand for money in the UK 1877–1961: some preliminary findings' (with N.J. Kavanagh), *OBES*, 28, May 1966; 5. 'Consistent expectations, distributed lags and the quantity theory', *EJ*, 81, June 1971.

WARBURTON, Clark*

Dates and Birthplace 1896–1979, Shady Grove, NY, USA.
Posts Held Instructor, Ewing Christian Coll., 1921–5, Rice Inst., 1925–9; Assoc. prof., Emory Univ., 1929–31; Member, Res. Staff, Fed. Reserve Comm., 1932, Brookings Inst., 1932–4;

Economist, Fed. Deposit Insurance Corp., 1934–65; Vis. prof., Univ. Cal., Davis, 1966–7.

Degrees BA, MA Cornell Univ., 1921, 1928; PhD Columbia Univ., 1932.

Offices Pres., SEA, 1963–4.

Career Pioneer monetarist whose contribution to the modern restatement of the quantity theory of money was long unrecognised. His published papers in the 1940s were unusual in their opposition to the current Keynesian tide. His writings have a strong empirical bias, originally related to his research for the Federal Deposit Insurance Corporation.

Publications *Books:* 1. *Depression, Inflation and Monetary Policy: Selected Papers* 1945–1953 (1966).

Articles: 1. 'Plateaux of prosperity and plains of depression', in *Economic Essays in Honor of Wesley Clair Mitchell* (1935); 2. 'Monetary disturbances and business fluctuations in two centuries of American history', in *In Search of a Monetary Constitution*, ed. L.B. Yeager (1962); 3. 'Monetary disequilibrium in the first half of the twentieth century', *HOPE*, 13(2), Summer, 1981.

Secondary Literature M.D. Bordo and A.J. Schwartz, 'Clark Warburton: pioneer monetarist', *J Mon E*, 5, 1979.

WATTS, Harold Wesley

Born 1932, Salem, Oregon, USA.

Current Post Prof. Econ., Columbia Univ., NY, 1976–; Sr Fellow, Mathematica Pol. Res., Princeton, NJ, 1978–.

Recent Posts Ass. dir., Cowles Foundation Res. Econ., Yale Univ., 1957–61; Dir, Inst. Res. Poverty, Univ. Wisconsin, 1966–7; Prof. Econ., Univ. Wisconsin, 1966–76; Dir., Center Social Sciences, Columbia Univ., 1976–9.

Degrees BA Univ. Oregon, 1954; MA, PhD Yale Univ., 1955, 1957.

Offices and Honours Irving Fisher Res. prof., Yale Univ., 1971–2; Carnegie Council Children, 1972–7; Guggenheim Memorial Foundation Fellow, 1975–6; Fellow, Em Soc, 1979–; Paul F. Lazarsfeld Award, 1980.

Principal Contributions Clarification of conceptual basis of economic poverty, and implementation of alternative concepts in analysing income distributions; analysis of negative income tax and other linear tax and transfer schemes; development and implementation of first major social experiment – the New Jersey negative tax experiment; development of method for optimising experimental designs to estimate functions of linear regression parameters. Analysis of the child development process as a human capital accumulation programme.

Publications *Books:* 1. *Income Maintenance and Labor Supply: Econometric Studies* (with G.C. Cain), (Univ. Wisconsin, Inst. Res. Poverty Monograph Series, 1973); 2. *The New Jersey Income Maintenance Experiment*, vols II and III (with A. Rees), (Academic Press, 1977).

Articles: 1. 'An economic definition of poverty', in *On Understanding Poverty: Perspectives from the Social Sciences*, ed. D.P. Moynihan (Basic Books, 1969); 2. 'Problems in making policy inferences from the Coleman report' (with G. Cain), *Amer. Sociological Review*, 35(2), April 1970; 3. 'The labor-supply response of husbands', *JHR*, 9(2), Spring 1974; 4. 'A model of the endowment of human wealth or Let's look at social policy through the eyes of the 21st century's adults', in *Economic Progress, Private Values and Public Policy, Essays in Honor of William Fellner*, eds B. Belassa and R. Nelson (N-H, 1977); 5. 'Why, and how well, do we analyse inequality', in *Major Social Issues, A Multidisciplinary View*, eds J.M. Yinger and S.J. Cutler (The Free Press, 1978).

WAUD, Roger Neil

Born 1938, Detroit, Mich., USA.

Current Post Prof. Econ., Univ. N. Carolina, USA, 1972–.

Recent Posts Ass. prof. Grad. School Bus., Univ. Chicago, 1964–9; Assoc. prof. Econ., Univ. N. Carolina, 1969–72; Sr economist, Board Governors, Fed. Reserve System, 1973–5.

Degrees BA Harvard Univ., 1960; MA (Applied stats), PhD Univ. Cal., Berkeley, 1962, 1965.

Offices   Member, AEA, SEA, Em Soc; Member, Ed. Board, 1970–3, Exec. Comm., 1977–9, SEA.

Principal Contributions   Examined implications of distributed lag mis-specification which results from failure to recognise that partial adjustment and adaptive expectations models are each special cases of more general model; provided evidence of an 'announcement effect' associated with Federal Reserve discount rate changes in the United States; examined and pointed out pit-falls in use of the Almon lag technique as applied to debate on the relative importance of monetary and fiscal policy in the United States; studied inter-national evidence on the behaviour of the output-inflation trade-off.

Publications   *Books:* 1. *Economics* (Harper & Row, 1980); 2. *Macroeconomics* (Harper & Row, 1980).

Articles: 1. 'Misspecification in the "partial adjustment" and "adaptive expectations" models', *Int ER*, 9, June 1968; 2. 'Public interpretation of Fed-eral Reserve discount rate changes', *Em*, 38(2), March 1970; 3. 'The Almon lag technique and the monetary versus fiscal policy debate' (with P. Schmidt), *JASA*, 68, March 1973; 4. 'Net outlay uncer-tainty and liquidity preference as behav-ior towards risk', *JMCB*, 7(4), Nov. 1975; 5. 'Further international evidence on output-inflation tradeoffs' (with R. Froyen), *AER*, 70(3), June 1980.

WAUGH, F.V.

N.e.

WEBB, Beatrice*

Dates and Birthplace   1858–1943, Gloucester, England.

Posts Held   Social investigator and writer.

Offices   Member, Royal Commission on the Poor Laws, 1905–9; Member, various other comms and comtts, includ-ing Comm. on equal pay, 1919.

Career   Co-operative work with her husband, Sidney, on a multitude of social and political issues. She came from a prosperous but radical back-ground and began her career as a social investigator on Charles Booth's study of London life and labour. Though less in the public eye than her husband, she was fully involved in all his activities, was co-author of all their major publi-cations and a strong influence on innu-merable politicians, social scientists and writers.

Publications   *Books:* 1. *The Co-oper-ative Movement in Great Britain* (1891); 2. *The Wages of Men and Women: Should They be Equal?* (1919); 3. *My Apprenticeship* (1926); 4. *Our Partner-ship* (1948). See also Webb, Sydney.

Secondary Literature   M. Cole, 'Webb, Sidney and Beatrice', *IESS*, vol. 16.

WEBB, Sidney James*

Dates and Birthplace   1859–1947, London, England.

Posts Held   Clerk, 1875–8; Civil ser-vant, 1878–91; Journalist, writer and politician.

Offices and Honours   Member, Exec. Comm., Fabian Soc.; Founder, LSE; Member, London County Council, 1892–1910; MP, 1922–9; Member, Labour govts, 1924, 1929–31; created Lord Passfield, 1929.

Career   Already established as a theorist of the Fabian Society, and a collector of social and economic infor-mation, his marriage in 1892 to Beatrice Potter began the extraordinary partner-ship which achieved so much in research and socialist politics. Their position was basically utilitarian, and they sought to achieve a socialist society by the replace-ment of private ownership with a range of public and co-operative forms of own-ership. Gradual change was to be the means for this, and the trades unions, co-operative movement and Labour Party were amongst the agencies they employed to spread their views. The pamphlets of the Fabian Society best expressed their programme. Much of their research was in economic history, but their efforts on government com-missions, including the minority report of the Commission on the Poor Laws (1909), were extremely influential. They later came to see Soviet communism as a vision of the society they wished for Britain, but violent revolution was never part of their programme.

Publications *Books:* 1. *Facts for Socialists* (1887). The following all jointly with Beatrice Webb: 2. *The History of Trade Unionism* (1894); 3. *Industrial Democracy*, 2 vols (1897); 4. *English Local Government*, 10 vols (1906–29); 5. *The Break-up of the Poor Law* (1909); 6. *The Consumers' Co-operative Movement* (1921); 7. *The Decay of Capitalist Civilisation* (1923); 8. *Methods of Social Study* (1932); 9. *Soviet Communism* (1935).

Secondary Literature M. Cole, 'Webb, Sidney and Beatrice', *IESS*, vol. 16.

WEBER, Alfred*

Dates and Birthplace 1868–1958, Erfurt, Germany.

Posts Held Prof., Univ. Berlin, 1899–1904, Univ. Prague, 1904–7, Univ. Heidelberg, 1907–33.

Degree Dr Univ. Berlin, 1895.

Career Although better known in Germany for his sociological writings, his first book is a landmark in the history of location theory. He developed von Thünen's analysis by his examination of the factors governing the location of industry. His writings were suppressed by the Nazis, but he re-emerged after World War II as a political and intellectual influence on the new German state.

Publications *Books:* 1. *Theory of the Location of Industries* (1909, 1929); 2. *Die Krise des Modernen Staatsgedankens in Europa* (1925); 3. *Kulturgeschichte als Kultursoziologie* (1935); 4. *Abschied von der Bisherigen Geschichte* (1946); 5. *Der Dritte oder der Vierte Mensch* (1953).

Secondary Literature E. Salin, 'Weber, Alfred', *IESS*, vol. 16.

WEBER, Max*

Dates and Birthplace 1864–1920, Erfurt, Germany.

Posts Held Prof. Econ., Univ. Freiburg, 1894–6, Univ. Heidelberg, 1896–1904.

Career One of the major figures in sociology whose system was based on the meaning individuals attach to their actions. This led him to reject various other systems, including the utilitarianism of the marginalists. His famous thesis on Protestantism and capitalism was intended to resolve the paradox of the condemnation of the acquisitive spirit in Protestant theology and the evident economic success of members of Protestant sects. Much of his other work was on the sociology of religion and the methodology of the social sciences. In *Wirtschaft und Gesellschaft* he examined economic activity for what it revealed about the social behaviour of groups. Owing to ill-health, much of his written work is in unfinished fragments which have been edited and published posthumously. Even his finished writings, however, are tortuously written and have created endless controversies.

Publications *Books:* 1. *The Protestant Ethic and the Spirit of Capitalism* (1904–5, 1930); 2. *Wirtschaft und Gesellschaft*, 2 vols (1922, 1956); 3. *The Theory of Social and Economic Organization*, eds A.M. Henderson and T. Parsons (1922, 1957); 4. *General Economic History* (1923, 1950).

Secondary Literature R. Bendix, 'Weber, Max', *IESS*, vol. 16.

WEINTRAUB, Sidney

Born 1914, New York City, NY, USA.

Current Post Prof. Econ., Univ. Pennsylvania; Disting. prof., Univ. South, 1981–.

Recent Posts Grad. Faculty, New School Social Res., 1951–7; Univ. Minnesota, 1959; Univ. Hawaii, 1967; Univ. Waterloo, Canada, 1969–71; Univ. Western Australia, 1974.

Degrees LSE, 1938–9; PhD NYU, 1941.

Offices Consultant, US Treasury, US State Dept., US Forest Service, US Federal Communications Comm., US Federal Power Comm., Prices and Incomes Comm. (Canada), Econ. Council Canada, Univ. Puerto Rico, Council Applied Econ. Res. (India); Co-ed. and co-founder, *J Post Keyn E*; Ed., *Puerto Rico Econ. Quarterly.*

Principal Contributions Still unexploited time and multi-market analyses in price theory; development and integration of aggregate demand, aggregate supply, and macro-distribution; conceptualisation and formalisation of theory of general price level, consumer price level, and the price level in the open economy; theory of growth and distribution in under-employed and unsteady states; generalising Kalecki and simplifying macro-economics; interpreting Keynes; TIP, a tax-based incomes policy as a contribution to economic policy of inflation; a theory of profits; and economic descent from popular orthodoxy for two decades.

Publications *Books:* 1. *Price Theory* (Pitman, 1949, Greenwood Press, 1979); 2. *An Approach to the Theory of Income Distribution* (Chilton Book Co., 1958, Greenwood Press, 1979); 3. *Employment Growth and Income Distribution* (Chilton Press, 1966); 4. *Capitalism's Inflation and Unemployment Crisis* (Addison-Wesley, 1978); 5. *Keynes, Keynesians, and Monetarists* (Univ. Pennsylvania Press, 1978).

WEISBROD, Burton A.

Born 1931, Chicago, Ill., USA.
Current Post Prof. Econ., 1966–, Fellow, Inst. Res. Poverty, Univ. Wisconsin, USA.
Recent Post Vis. prof., Yale Univ., 1976–7.
Degrees BS (Management) Univ. Illinois, 1951; MA (Econ.), PhD (Econ.) Northwestern Univ., 1952, 1958.
Offices Sr Staff Member, US President's Council Econ. Advisers, 1963–4; Exec. Comm., NBER Conference Income and Wealth, 1975–7; Exec. Comm., AER, 1975–7; Member, NAS, Inst. Medicine, 1976–; Sr res. fellow, Brookdale Inst., Jerusalem, 1978–; Member, Board Dirs., NBER, 1979–; Pres., MEA, 1980–1.
Principal Contributions Research has focused on economics of education, health and welfare; the role of government expenditure and regulatory policy in affecting economic efficiency and dis-
tributional equity; and the importance of institutional forms, particularly the place of non-profit organisations in a mixed economy.

Publications *Books:* 1. *Economics of Public Health* (Univ. Pennsylvania Press, 1961); 2. *External Benefits of Public Education* (Princeton Univ. Industrial Relations Section, 1964); 3. *Disease and Economic Development: The case of Parasitic Diseases in St Lucia, West Indies* (with R.L. Andreano et al.), (Univ. Wisconsin Press, 1974); 4. *The Voluntary Nonprofit Sector: An Economic Analysis* (Heath-Lexington, 1978); 5. *Public Interest Law: An Economic and Institutional Analysis* (with J.F. Handler and N.K. Komesar), (Univ. Cal. Press, 1978).

Articles: 1. 'Toward a theory of the voluntary non-profit sector in a three-sector economy', in *Altruism, Morality and Economic Theory*, ed. E.S. Phelps (Russell Sage Foundation, 1975); 2. 'Governmental behavior in response to compensation requirements' (with J. Cordes), *J Pub E*, 11(1), 1979; 3. 'Private goods, collective goods: the role of the nonprofit sector', in *The Economics of Non-proprietary Organizations, Research in Law and Economics*, supplement 1, eds K. Clarkson and D. Martin (JAI Press, 1980); 4. 'A guide to benefit-cost analysis, as seen through a controlled experiment in treating the mentally ill', *JHR*, 16(4), Fall 1981; 5. 'Some economic consequences of technological advance in medical care: the case of a new drug' (with J. Geweke), in *Drugs and Health: Economic Issues and Policy Objectives* (1981).

WEITZMAN, Martin L.

Born 1942, New York City, NY, USA.
Current Post Prof. Econ., MIT, USA.
Recent Posts Ass. prof Econ., 1967–70, Assoc. prof. Econ., 1970–2, Yale Univ.; Assoc. prof. Econ., MIT, 1972–3.
Degrees BA Swarthmore Coll., 1963; MS Stanford Univ., 1964; PhD MIT, 1967.
Offices and Honours Assoc. ed., var-

ious journals; Guggenheim Memorial Foundation Fellow, 1970–1; Fellow, Em Soc, 1976–.

Principal Contributions Theoretical work on comparing the effectiveness of various methods of planning and regulation, e.g. evaluating the effects of different regulatory instruments like prices and quantities; contribution to economic growth, search theory, incentives, R & D, economies of scale, and comparative systems.

Publications *Articles:* 1. 'Optimal growth with economies of scale in the creation of overhead capital', *REStud*, 37(4), Oct. 1970; 2. 'Free access vs. private ownership as alternative systems for managing common property', *JET*, 8(2), June 1974; 3. 'Prices vs. quantities', *REStud*, 41(4), Oct. 1974; 4. 'On the welfare significance of national product in a dynamic economy', *QJE*, 90, Feb. 1976; 5. 'Optimal search for the best alternative', *Em*, 47(3), May 1979.

WELCH, Finis R.

Born 1938, Olney, Texas, USA.
Current Post Prof. Econ., UCLA, USA.
Recent Posts Prof., Exec. Officer, PhD Program Econ., City Univ. New York, 1971–3; Economist, Rand Corp., 1973–8.
Degrees BS Univ. Houston, 1961; PhD Univ. Chicago, 1966.
Offices AEA; Member Ed. Board, *AER*, 1974–7, *JEL*, 1981–; Fellow, Em Soc, 1980.
Principal Contributions Empirical work on relations within the US between income and schooling, race differences in income, and effects of cohort size on lifetime patterns of earnings.
Publications *Articles:* 1. 'Education in production', *JPE*, 78(1), Jan. 1970; 2. 'Education and racial discrimination', in *Discrimination in Labor Markets*, eds O. Ashenfelter and A. Rees (Princeton Univ. Press, 1974); 3. 'Minimum wage legislation in the United States', *EI*, 12(3), Sept. 1974; 4. 'Black-white male wage ratios, 1960–1970' (with J.P. Smith), *AER*, 67(3), June 1977; 5. 'Effects of cohort size on earnings: the

baby-boom babies' financial bust', *JPE*, 87(5), Pt 2, Oct. 1979.

WELLISZ, Stanislaw Henryk

Born 1925, Warsaw, Poland.
Current Post Prof. Econ., Columbia Univ., USA.
Degrees BA, MA, PhD Harvard Univ., 1947, 1949, 1954.
Offices AEA; Indian Econ. Assoc.; Polish Inst. Arts and Sciences in Amer.
Principal Contributions Advanced (simultaneously with but independently of others) the hypothesis that rate of return regulation leads to over-capitalisation of public utilities; demonstrated the limited applicability of the Coase theorem; showed that protected urban wage sectors in developing countries lead to queuing; developed the theory of hierarchic firms (with Calvo), and helped to prove that the optimal wage exceeds the opportunity cost of labour.
Publications *Books:* 1. *The Economies of the Soviet Bloc* (McGraw-Hill, 1964, 1966).
Articles: 1. 'Regulation of natural gas pipeline companies: an economic analysis', *JPE*, 71, Feb. 1963; 2. 'Dual economies, disguised unemployment and the unlimited supply of labour', *Ec*, N.S. 35, Feb. 1968; 3. 'Lessons of twenty years of planning in developing countries', *Ec*, N.S. 38, May 1971; 4. 'Project evaluation, shadow prices and trade policy' (with R. Findlay), *JPE*, 84(3), June 1976; 5. 'Hierarchy, ability, and income distribution' (with G. Calvo), *JPE*, 87(5), Pt 2, Oct. 1979.

WELLS, David Ames*

Dates and Birthplace 1828–98, Springfield, Mass., USA.
Posts Held Chairman, National Revenue Commission, 1865–6; Special Commission Revenue, 1866–70; Chairman, New York State Tax Commission, 1870–6.
Degrees Grad. Williams Univ., 1847, Lawrence Scientific School, 1851.
Career Originally a geologist and chemist, he turned to economics in middle life. He was an able collector of

statistics and his ability to draw worthwhile conclusions from imperfect material was considerable. Tariffs, currency, theory of money and taxation were his chief economic interests. He became a determined free-trader.

Publications *Books:* 1. *Our Burden and Strength* (1864); 2. *Reports of the Special Commissioner of the Revenue* (1866–9); 3. *Recent Economic Changes* (1889); 4. *The Theory and Practice of Taxation* (1900).

Secondary Literature E.R.A. Seligman, 'Wells, David Ames', *ESS*, vol. 15.

WEST, Edward*

Dates and Birthplace 1782–1828, London, England.

Posts Held Fellow, Univ. Coll., Univ. Oxford, 1807; Lawyer, 1814; Chief Justice, Bombay, India, 1823–8.

Degrees BA, MA Univ. Oxford, 1804, 1807.

Honours Knighted, 1822.

Career One of the independent discoverers of the theory of differential rent, more usually associated with Ricardo. His *Essay* . . . (1815) contains a clear statement of the principle of diminishing returns. His writings contain various anticipations of later doctrine, e.g. the idea that international trade tends to equalise factor prices between countries.

Publications *Books:* 1. *Essay on the Application of Capital to Land* (1815); 2. *Treatise of the Law and Practice of Extents in Chief and in Aid* (1817); 3. *The Price of Corn and Wages of Labour* (1826).

Secondary Literature W.D. Grampp, 'West, Edward', *IESS*, vol. 16.

WHATELY, Richard*

Dates and Birthplace 1787–1863, London, England.

Posts Held Fellow, Oriel Coll., 1811, Drummond Prof., 1829–31, Univ. Oxford; Archbishop of Dublin, 1831–63.

Degrees BA, MA, BD, DD Univ. Oxford, 1808, 1812, 1825.

Offices Chairman, Royal Commission on the Irish Poor, 1833–6; Vice-pres., Royal Irish Academy, 1848.

Career A prolific writer (chiefly on religious topics) his writings on political economy derive essentially from the views expressed in his *Elements of Logic*. Here he rejected induction as extra-logical. His economics is abstract and deductive and contributed little that was new. However, by instituting the Whately Chair at Trinity College, Dublin, he made possible a distinguished tradition. His involvement in Irish education led him to write various textbooks, including one on economic topics.

Publications *Books:* 1. *Elements of Logic* (1826); 2. *Introductory Lectures on Political Economy* (1831); 3. *Easy Lessons on Money Matters* (1837); 4. *Miscellaneous Lectures and Reviews* (1861).

Secondary Literature L.M. Fraser, 'Whately, Richard', *ESS*, vol. 15.

WHEATLEY, John*

Dates and Birthplace 1772–1830, Erith, England.

Posts Held Lawyer, 1797; Businessman in the West India trade; Clerk, Supreme Court, Calcutta, India, 1825–30.

Degree BA Univ. Oxford, 1793.

Career Writer on money who stated much of the theory which later came to be associated with Ricardo and the Bullion Report, 1810. He argued that there is an optimum quantity of money in a country which keeps prices in equilibrium with other countries; hence, an issue of paper money in excess of this amount depreciates a currency.

Publications *Books:* 1. *Remarks on Currency and Commerce* (1803); 2. *Thoughts on the Object of the Foreign Subsidy* (1805); 3. *Essay on the Theory of Money and Principles of Commerce*, 2 vols (1807–22); 4. *Letter to Lord Grenville on the Distress of the Country* (1816); 5. *Report on the Reports of the Bank Committees* (1819); 6. *Letter to the Duke of Devonshire on the State of Ireland* (1824).

Secondary Literature F.W. Fetter,

'Life and writings of John Wheatley', *JPE*, 50, June 1942.

WHEWELL, William*

Dates and Birthplace 1794–1866, Lancaster, England.

Posts Held Fellow, tutor, master Trinity Coll., Univ. Camb., 1817–66; Prof. Mineralogy, 1828–32, Prof. Moral Philosophy, Univ. Camb., 1838–55.

Offices A founder, Camb. Philosophical Soc., 1818; Vice-Chancellor, Univ. Camb., 1842–3.

Career Mathematician, philosopher of science and university administrator, who published early papers on economics using mathematical language. There is some dispute as to whether this was genuine mathematical economics or merely economics set out algebraically. In pursuit of the encouragement of the inductive method in economics, he cajoled his friend Richard Jones into completing and publishing at least a part of his projected major work on economics.

Publications *Articles:* 1. 'Mathematical exposition of some doctrines of political economy', *Camb. Phil. Soc. Transactions*, 3, 1830; 2. 'Mathematical exposition of some of the leading doctrines in Mr. Ricardo's *Principles*', *Camb. Phil. Soc. Transactions*, 4, 1831; 3. 'Mathematical exposition of some doctrines of political economy', *Camb. Phil. Soc. Transactions*, 9, 1850.

Secondary Literature R.D. Theocharis, 'Whewell, William', *IESS*, vol. 16.

WICKSELL, Knut*

Dates and Birthplace 1851–1926, Stockholm, Sweden.

Posts Held Lecturer, journalist and pamphleteer; Ass. prof., Univ. Uppsala, 1899; Assoc. prof., 1900, Prof., 1903–17, Univ. Lund.

Degrees Licentiate (Maths), Dr Univ. Uppsala, 1876, 1895.

Offices Pres., Economists Club, Stockholm, 1917.

Career Theorist and political activist whose rigorous work on the marginalist theory of price and distribution and on monetary theory are models of their kind. The *Lectures on Political Economy* have been aptly called a 'textbook for professors'. In an unusually chequered career (including a brief spell of imprisonment) he wrote and lectured tirelessly on radical issues. He was an advocate of social and economic reforms of various kinds, most notably neo-Malthusian population controls. In his later years he was revered by the new generation of economists who became known as the Stockholm School. They developed his ideas on 'the cumulative process' into a dynamic theory of monetary macro-economics simultaneously with but independently of the Keynesian revolution.

Publications *Books:* 1. *Value, Capital and Rent* (1893, 1954); 2. *Finanztheoretische Untersuchungen nebst Darstellung und Kritik des Steuerwesens Schwedens* (1896); 3. *Interest and Prices* (1898, 1936); 4. *Lectures on Political Economy*, 2 vols (1901–6, 1935–51); 5. *Selected Papers on Economic Theory* (1958).

Secondary Literature T. Gårdlund, *The Life of Knut Wicksell* (Almqvist & Wiksell, 1958); C.G. Uhr, *Economic Doctrines of Knut Wicksell* (Univ. of California Press, 1960); T. Gårdlund, 'Wicksell, Knut', *IESS*, vol. 16.

WICKSTEED, Philip Henry*

Dates and Birthplace 1844–1927, Leeds, England.

Posts Held Clergyman, 1867–97; Univ. extension lecturer, 1887–1918.

Degree MA Univ. London.

Career Writer on theology, literature and philosophy, who turned to economics in middle life, influenced by socialist sentiments and his membership of the Fabian Society. He was Jevons' first major follower and wrote on opportunity costs, the reversability of the supply curve and distribution theory. His principle of maximisation, though chiefly valuable in his economic writings, was intended to provide a guide to choices and behaviour in all aspects of life.

Publications *Books:* 1. *The Alphabet of Economic Science* (1888, 1955); 2.

An Essay on the Co-ordination of the Laws of Distribution (1894, 1932); 3. *The Common Sense of Political Economy*, 2 vols (1910, 1950).

Secondary Literature C.H. Herford, *Philip Henry Wicksteed: His Life and Work* (Dent, 1931); W.D. Grampp, 'Wicksteed, Philip Henry', *IESS*, vol. 16.

WIESER, Friedrich, von*

Dates and Birthplace 1851–1926, Vienna, Austro-Hungary.

Posts Held Civil servant, 1872–84; Lecturer, Univ. Vienna, 1883; Prof., Univ. Prague, 1884, Univ. Vienna, 1903.

Offices Minister of Commerce, Austria, 1917.

Career Member of the Austrian School of Economists, whose early interest in sociology was diverted towards economics by the publication of Menger's *Grundsätze*. His early work was on the theory of cost; he later wrote on currency, taxation and social and economic policy. In *Social Economics* he produced the only systematic treatise by any of the older Austrian School. After World War I he returned to sociology, and developed his 'law of small numbers' which described the action of élites.

Publications *Books:* 1. *Über den Ursprung und die Hauptgesetze des Wirtschaftlichen Werthes* (1884); 2. *Natural Value* (1889, 1956); 3. *Social Economics* (1914, 1927); 4. *Das Gesetz der Macht* (1926); 5. *Gesammelte Abhandlungen*, ed. F.A. von Hayek (1929).

Secondary Literature F.A. von Hayek, 'Wieser, Friedrich von', *IESS*, vol. 16.

WILES, Peter John de la Fosse

Born 1919, Rugby, England.

Current Post Prof. Russian Social and Econ. Studies, LSE, 1965–.

Recent Posts Fellow, New Coll., Univ. Oxford, 1948–60; Prof. Econ., Brandeis Univ., 1960–3; Res. assoc., Inst. Internat. Ekonomi, Stockholm, 1963–4; Vis. prof., City Coll. New York, 1964–5.

Degrees Wartime MA in virtue of Distinction in wartime Classical Honour Moderations, 1939; BA Univ. Oxford, 1941.

Principal Contributions Sovietology: demonstration that allocative inefficiency is compatible with rapid economic growth in Soviet-type systems and that economic convergence between East and West is highly improbable. Theory of the capitalist firm: administered prices, cost inflation, extreme insufficiency of orthodoxy. Practical control planning; institutions and motivations, especially military, behind international technology transfer. Human capital: seminal general article and later critique of the rationality assumptions.

Publications *Books:* 1. *Price, Cost and Output* (Blackwell, 1962); 2. *The Political Economy of Communism* (Blackwell, 1962); 3. *Communist International Economics* (Praeger, Blackwell, 1969); 4. *Distribution of Income East and West* (N-H, 1974); 5. *Economic Institutions Compared* (Blackwell, 1978).

Articles: 1. 'Agenda for the age of inflation', *Economist*, Aug./Sept. 1951; 2. 'The Soviet economy outpaces the West', *For Aff*, July 1953; 3. 'The nation's intellectual investment', *BOIS*, 18, Aug. 1956; 4. 'On the CoCom embargo', in *Probleme des Industrialismus Ost und West*, eds W. Gumpel and D. Keese (1973); 5. 'Cost of inflation and the state of economic theory', *EJ*, 83(330), June 1973.

WILLETT, Thomas D.

Born 1942, Staunton, Virginia, USA.

Current Post Horton prof. Econ., Claremont Grad. School, Claremont McKenna Coll., Claremont, Cal., USA.

Recent Posts Ass. prof. Econ., Harvard Univ., 1967–70; Assoc. prof. Econ., Cornell Univ., 1970–2; Dep. ass. sec., Dir. Internat. Monetary Res., US Treasury, 1972–7.

Degrees BA William and Mary Coll., 1964; PhD Univ. Virginia, 1967.

Offices Ed. Boards, *QJE*, 1968–76, *REStat*, 1968–76, *J Econ Bus*, 1970–8,

Pol. Analysis, 1974–80, *SEJ*, 1976–9, *Internat. Stud. Quarterly*, 1980–, *Internat. Organisation*, 1981–; Co-ed., *Public Pol.*, 1969–72.

Principal Contributions International monetary problems: especially the stability and reform of the international monetary system and analysis of flexible exchange rates; applied public choice analysis of various political institutions; analysis of the causes and effects of inflation; and application of public choice theory to the analysis of macroeconomic policy and international economic relations.

Publications *Books:* 1. *The Economic Approach to Public Policy* (Cornell Univ. Press, 1976); 2. *The Theory of Optimum Currency Areas* (Princeton Internat. Fin. Section, 1976); 3. *Floating Exchange Rates and International Monetary Reform* (Amer. Enterprise Inst., 1977); 4. *International Liquidity Issues* (Amer. Enterprise Inst., 1980); 5. *Studies on Exchange Rate Flexibility* (Amer. Enterprise Inst., 1982).

Articles: 1. 'Interest rate policy and external balance' (with F. Forte), *QJE*, 83(2), May 1969; 2. 'Reserve asset preferences and the confidence problem in the crisis zone' (with L.H. Officer), *QJE*, 83(4), Nov. 1969; 3. 'A note on the relation between the rate and variability of inflation' (with D.E. Logue), *Ec*, 43, May 1976; 4. 'Monetarism, budget deficits, and wage push inflation: the case of Italy and the UK', *BNLQR*, 127, Dec. 1978; 5. 'Fiscal federalism: a voting system where spillovers taper off spatially' (with R.D. Tollison), *Public Fin. Quarterly*, 6(3), July 1978.

WILLGERODT, Hans

Born 1924, Hildesheim, Germany.
Current Post Dir., Wirtschaftspolitische Seminar, Univ. Cologne, W. Germany, 1963.
Recent Posts Prof., Univ. Cologne, 1963; Dir., Inst. Wirtschaftspolitik, Univ. Cologne, 1970.
Degrees Diplom-Volkswirt, Doctorate, Habilitation, Privatdozent Univ. Bonn, 1954, 1959.
Offices Member, Mont Pelerin Soc., AEA, Deutsche Gesellschaft für Auswärtige Politik, List-Gesellschaft, Gesellschaft für Wirtschafts- une Sozialwissenschaften (Verein für Sozialpolitik); Member, Ed. Board, Ludwig Erhard-Stiftun, Arbeitsgemeinschaft deutscher wirtschaftswissenschaftlicher Forschungsinst.

Principal Contributions Problems created when using trade barriers as a means of balance-of-payments policy. International monetary order: early analysis and prediction of the economic and political difficulties of a monetary union of the EEC. Proof that convertibility and flexible exchange rates reduce the alleged danger of petro-dollars and political fund transfers. NIEO: criticism of the Corea-Plan and the Report of the North-South Commission; in contrast a liberal economic order is advocated. Proposition of a supply side policy to fight stagflation, and rejection of Keynesian instruments; recommendation to foster private property as a basic element of a sound economic and political order.

Publications *Books:* 1. *Handelsschranken im Dienste der Währungspolitik* (Helmut Küpper, 1962); 2. *Vermögen für alle* (with A. Domsch et al.), (Econ. Verlag, 1971); 3. *Wege und Irrwege zur Europäischen Währungsunion* (Rombach, 1972); 4. *Der 'Gemeinsame Agrarmarkt der EWG'* (J.C.B. Mohr, Paul Siebeck, 1974). 5. *Die Krisenempfindlichkeit des Internationalen Währungssystems* (with K. Bartel and U. Schillert), (Duncker & Humblot, 1981).

Articles: 1. 'Sectoral integration: agriculture, transport, energy and selected industries', in *Economic Integration Worldwide, Regional Sectoral*, ed. F. Machlup (Macmillan, 1976); 2. 'Planning in West Germany: the social market economy', in *The Politics of Planning. A Review and Critique of Centralized Economic Planning* (Inst. Contemporary Stud., 1976); 3. 'Die "motivierte Zahlungsbilanztheorie" – vom "schicksalhaften Zahlungsbilanzdefizit" und der Unsterblichkeit falscher Inflationslehren', in *Internationale Wirtschaftsordnung*, eds H. Gröner and A. Schüller (G. Fischer, 1978); 4. 'Stabilitätsförderung durch marktwirtschaftliche Ordnungspolitik – Notwendigkeit und Grenzen', in *Probleme der Wirt-schaftspolitik*, ed. E. Teichmann (G. Fischer, 1978); 5. 'Wirtschaftsordnung und Staatsverwaltung', *ORDO*, 30, 1979.

WILLIAMS, Alan

Born 1927, Birmingham, England.
Current Post Prof., Univ. York.
Recent Posts Lecturer Econ., Univ. Exeter, 1954–63; Vis. lecturer, Woodrow Wilson School, Princeton Univ., 1963–4; Dir. Econ. Stud., UK Treasury Centre Admin. Stud., London, 1966–8.
Degrees BCom Univ. Birmingham, 1951; Hon. DPhil Univ. Lund, 1977.
Offices Member, UK Nat. Water Council; Member, UK SSRC Health and Health Services Panel; Founder-member, UK SSRC Health Economists Study Group; Member, UK Royal Comm. NHS, UK Dept. Health Social Security Chief Scientist's Res. Comm., UK SSRC Social Science Law Comm., Yorkshire Water Authority, Council Chartered Inst. Public Fin. Accountancy.
Principal Contributions Early work concentrated on the welfare economies of multi-level government but later emphasis shifted to the expenditure side of the budget, and specifically to the problem of economic appraisal of public expenditure, especially in the broad area of social services. Recent work directed at finding theoretically correct, yet operationally feasible ways of valuing the benefits of public services, which do not rely on willingness or ability to pay but on some explicit egalitarian principle other than similar preferences; concentrating on the problems facing the NHS.
Publications *Books:* 1. *Public Finance and Budgeting Policy* (A & U, 1962); 2. *Output Budgeting and the Contribution of Microeconomics to Efficiency in Government* (HMSO, 1967); 3. *Current Issues in Cost-Benefit Analysis* (with H.G. Walsh), (HMSO, 1969); 4. *Efficiency in the Social Services* (with R. Anderson), (Blackwell, Martin Robertson, 1975); 5. *The Principles of Practical Cost Benefit Analysis* (with R. Sugden), (OUP, 1978).

Articles: 1. 'The optimal provision of public goods in a system of local government', *JPE*, 74, Feb. 1966; 2. 'Cost benefit analysis: bastard science? and/or insidious poison in the body politik', *J Pub E*, 1(2), Aug. 1972; 3. 'Measuring the effectiveness of health care systems', *British J Preventive Social Medicine*, 28, Aug. 1974; 4. 'Health service planning', in *Studies in Modern Economic Analysis*, eds M.J. Artis and A.R. Nobay (Blackwell, 1977); 5. 'Welfare economics and health status measurement', in *Health, Economics and Health Economics*, eds M. Perlman and J. van der Graag (N-H, 1981).

WILLIAMS, Anne Douglas

Born 1943, Montreal, Canada.
Current Post Assoc. prof., Bates Coll., Maine, USA.
Recent Posts Ass. prof., Univ. Pennsylvania, 1975–81; Res. dir., US House Representatives, Select Comm. Pop., 1977–8.
Degrees BA Smith Coll., 1965; MA, PhD Univ. Chicago, 1972, 1976.
Offices AEA; Pop. Assoc. Amer.; Internat. Union Scientific Study Pop.; Amer. Assoc. Advancement Science; Descendants of the Illegitimate Sons and Daughters of the Kings of Britain; Univ. Pennsylvania Summer Res. Fellow, 1975, 1977.
Principal Contributions Measurement of the determinants of fertility in US. Emphasis on effects of infant mortality on fertility and statistical biases of these measures with finding of non-linear responses. Analysis of the relative income hypothesis using cross-sectional data of twins to find confirmation of importance of female labour force participation.
Publications *Books:* 1. *Domestic Consequences of United States Population Change, Report for Select Committee on Population, US House of Representatives*, principal author (with others), (US Govt Printing Office, 1978); 2. *Consequences of Changing US Population*, 3 vols, *Demographics of Ageing, Baby Boom and Bust, Population Movement and Planning*, ed. (with

others), Select Comm. Population, US House of Representatives (US Govt Printing Office, 1978).

Articles: 1. 'Bayesian analysis of the Federal Reserve-MIT-Penn model's Almon lag consumption function' (with A. Zellner), *J Em*, 1(3), Oct. 1973, reprinted in *Bayesian Analysis in Econometrics and Statistics*, ed. A. Zellner (N-H, 1980); 2. 'Effects of economic development on fertility', (TEMPO, 1974); 3. 'Determinants of fertility in developing countries: review and evaluation of the literature', in *Population, Public Policy, and Economic Development*, ed. M.C. Keeley (Praeger, 1976); 4. 'Measuring the impact of child mortality on fertility', *Demography*, 14(4), Nov. 1977; 5. 'Comments on Ben Porath *Child Mortality and Fertility: Issues in the Demographic Transition of a Migrant Population*', in *Population and Economic Change in Developing Countries* (NBER, 1980).

WILLIAMSON, Jeffrey G.

Born 1935, New Haven, Conn., USA.

Current Post Prof. Econ., Inst. Res. on Poverty, Univ. Wisconsin, USA.

Recent Posts Ass. prof. Econ., and Assoc. dir., Grad. Program Econ. Development, Vanderbilt Univ., 1961–3; Ass. prof., 1963–4, Assoc. prof., 1964–8, Prof. Econ., Univ. Wisconsin, 1968–; Vis. prof. Econ., Univ. Philippines, 1967–8; Vis. prof. Econ., Harvard Univ., 1972; Vis. prof. Econ. (Guggenheim), Stanford Univ. and NBER, 1976–7; Vis. res. Scholar, Internat. Inst. Applied Systems Analysis, Austria, 1978–80.

Degrees BA (Maths) Wesleyan Univ., 1957; MA (Econ.), PhD (Econ.) Stanford Univ., 1959, 1961.

Offices Consultant, US State Dept, Agency for Internat. Development, 1964–70; Member, ed. board, 1965–80, Co-ed., 1969–73, Assoc. ed., 1974–7, *Explorations in Economic History*; Member, ed. board, *EDCC*, 1969–; Member, AEA Comm. Education and Training of Minority Group Economists, 1969–71; Assoc. ed., *REStat*,

1972–; Member, Council for Res. in Econ. History, EHA, 1972–6; Consultant, World Bank, 1973–.

Principal Contributions The application of cliometric techniques to problems in the economic history of America, Britain and Japan. Emphasis on the understanding of accumulation, distribution and growth from low income levels. Similar analysis of Third World economies, using computable general equilibrium models.

Publications *Books:* 1. *American Growth and the Balance of Payments, 1820–1913: A Study of the Long Swing* (Univ. N. Carolina Press, 1964); 2. *Dualistic Economic Development: Theory and History* (with A. Kelley and R.J. Cheetham), (Univ. Chicago Press, 1972); 3. *Late Nineteenth-century American Development: A General Equilibrium History* (CUP, 1974); 4. *Lessons from Japanese Development: An Analytical Economic History* (with A. Kelley), (Univ. Chicago Press, 1974); 5. *American Inequality: A Macroeconomic History* (with P. Lindert), (Academic Press, 1980).

Articles: 1. 'Regional inequality and the process of national development: a description of the patterns', *EDCC*, 13(4), Pt 2, July 1965, reprinted in *Regional Analysis: Selected Readings*, ed. L. Needleman (Penguin, 1968), and *Economia Regional*, ed. J. Schwartzman (Belo Horizonte, Cedeplar, 1977); 2. 'Capital accumulation, labor-saving and labor absorption once more', *QJE*, 85(1), Feb. 1971; 3. 'Writing history backwards: Meiji Japan revisited' (with A. Kelley), *JEH*, 31(4), Dec. 1971; 4. 'The sources of American inequality, 1896–1948', *REStat*, 58(4), Nov. 1976; 5. 'Inequality, accumulation, and technological imbalance: a growth-equity conflict in American history', *EDCC*, 27(2), Jan. 1979.

WILLIAMSON, Oliver E.

Born 1932, Superior, Wisc., USA.

Current Post Charles and William L. Day Prof. Econ. and Social Science, Univ. Penn., USA.

Recent Post Dir., Center Study of

Organisational Innovation, Univ. Penn., 1976–.

Degrees SB MIT, 1955; MBA Stanford Univ., 1960; PhD Econ., Carnegie-Mellon Univ., 1963.

Offices and Honours Univ. Honours Fellowship, Stanford Univ., 1958–60; Ford Foundation Fellowship, Carnegie Inst. Technology, 1960–2; Alexander Henderson Award Excellence in Econ. Theory, Carnegie Inst. Technology, 1962; Ford Foundation Dissertation Fellow, Carnegie Inst. Technology, 1962–3; Award winner, Ford Foundation Dissertation Competition, 1963; NSF Res. Support, 1964–8, 1972–; Sr Fellow, Brookings Inst., 1967–71; Assoc. ed., *Bell J Es*, 1973–4, 1977–8; Ed. or coed., 1974–7, 1979–; Fellow, Em Soc., 1977; Fellow, Center Advanced Study Behavioural Sciences, 1977–8; Guggenheim Memorial Foundation Fellow, 1977–8.

Principal Contributions The study of managerial discretion in the large corporation and assessing the efficacy of various controls that can be applied; the application of economic and organisational analysis to anti-trust enforcement and regulation; the study of transaction costs and their ramifications for the efficient organisation of economic activity; applications include vertical integration, the employment relation, conglomerate organisation, regulation, and technology transfer. The approach has a bearing on industrial organisation, organisation theory, planning, labour economics, corporate governance, and aspects of the law of contract.

Publications *Books:* 1. *The Economics of Discretionary Behavior: Managerial Objectives in a Theory of the Firm* (Prentice-Hall, 1964, Markham Publishing Co., 1967, Eurospan Ltd., 1974); 2. *Corporate Control and Business Behavior: An Inquiry into the Effects of Organisation Form on Enterprise Behavior* (Prentice-Hall, 1970; Japanese transl. 1978); 3. *Markets and Hierarchies: Analysis and Anti-trust Implications* (The Free Press, 1975; Japanese transl., 1978).

Articles: 1. 'Managerial discretion and business behavior', *AER*, 53, Dec. 1963, repr. in *Economic Theories of International Politics*, ed. B.M. Russett (1968), *The Modern Business Enterprise*, ed. M. Gilbert (Penguin Books, 1972), and *The Economics of Property Rights*, eds E. Furobotn and S. Pejovich (Harvard Univ. Press, 1974). 2. 'Economics as an anti-trust defense: the welfare trade-offs', *AER*, 58, March 1968, repr. in *Readings in Industrial Economics: Private Enterprise and State Intervention*, ed. C.K. Rowley (Macmillan, 1971); 3. 'The vertical integration of production: market failure considerations', *AER*, 61(2), May 1971, repr. in *Journal of Reprints for Anti-trust Law and Economics*, 1974; 4. 'Franchise bidding for natural monopolies – in general and with respect to CATV', *Bell JE*, 7, Spring 1976; 5. 'Transaction cost economics: the governance of contractual relations', *J Law E*, 22, Oct. 1979.

WILLIS, Robert J.

Born 1940, Great Falls, Montana, USA.

Current Post Prof., State Univ. New York, Stony Brook, USA.

Recent Posts Ass. prof., Wesleyan Univ., 1966–71; Ass. prof., Assoc. prof., Grad. Center, City Univ. New York, 1971–4; Res. assoc. NBER, 1971–; Assoc. prof., Stanford Univ., 1974–8; Res. assoc., Econ. Res. Center, Nat. Opinion Res. Center, 1980–.

Degrees BA Dartmouth Coll., 1962; MA, PhD Univ. Washington, Seattle, 1965, 1971.

Offices AEA; PAA; Res. fellow, NBER, 1970–1; Member, Panel Fertility Determinants, Comm. Pop. Demography, NAS, 1979–82.

Principal Contributions Formulation and empirical tests of micro-economic theories of family decision making concerning fertility, contraception, female labour supply and human capital investment in both static and life cycle framework; econometric estimates of measured and unmeasured components of labour force and earnings mobility in panel data; econometric test of comparative advantage model of college attendance with estimates of structural supply function of college enrolment and estimates of rate of return for self-selection; and integration of micro-models of life-cycle family behaviour into overlapping generation model to study the interaction of economic development, institutional change and demographic transition.

Publications *Articles:* 1. 'A new approach to the economic theory of fertility behavior', *JPE*, Pt II, 81(2), March/April 1973; 2. 'A beta-logistic model for the analysis of sequential labor force participation of married women' (with J.M. Heckman), *JPE*, 85(1), Feb. 1977; 3. 'Dynamic aspects of earnings mobility' (with L.A. Lillard), *Em*, 46(5), Sept. 1978; 4. 'Education and self-selection' (with S. Rosen), *JPE*, Pt II, 87(5), Oct. 1979; 5. 'The old age security hypothesis and population growth', in *Demographic Behavior: Interdisciplinary Perspectives*, ed. T.K. Burch (Westview Press, 1980).

WILSON, James*

Dates and Birthplace 1805–60, Hawick, Scotland.

Posts Held Businessman, 1821–44; Proprietor, Chief writer, the *Economist*, 1843–60.

Offices and Honours MP, 1847–59; Fin. Secretary HM Treasury, 1853–8; Fin. member, Council of India, 1859–60.

Career Businessman whose acute comments on current issues were first made public in pamphlet form and then through *The Economist*. In parliament he spoke effectively on economic issues and was a highly regarded financial minister. In India he began a reform of the taxation system and introduced a paper currency. His economic ideas were the conventional orthodoxy of the day – anti-corn law, pro-free trade, and in favour of a sound, convertible currency. His 1840 work, *Fluctuations . . .*, is regarded as one of the first systematic accounts of the phenomenon of business cycles.

Publications *Books:* 1. *Influences of the Corn Laws* (1839); 2. *Fluctuations of Currency, Commerce and Manufactures* (1840); 3. *The Revenue, or What Shall the Chancellor Do?* (1841); 4. *Capital, Currency and Banking* (1847).

WILSON, Robert Bidler

Born 1937, Geneva, Nebraska, USA.

Current Post McBean Prof. Decision Sciences, Stanford Univ., USA.

Degrees BA (Maths), MBA, DBA Harvard Univ., 1959, 1961, 1963.

Offices Fellow, Inst. Math. Stud. Social Sciences, 1971–; Fellow, Assoc. ed., Em Soc., 1976–; Fellow, AAAS, 1981–.

Principal Contributions Computational methods for non-linear optimisation and equilibria of games and economies; theories of risk sharing and incentives, and analyses of information; topics in game theory: competitive bidding, repeated games with incomplete information, extensive-form games; contributions to theories of social choice and voting; theory of the firm.

Publications *Articles:* 1. 'The theory of syndicates', *Em*, 36(1), Jan. 1968; 2. 'A bidding model of "perfect" competition', *REStud*, 44(3), Oct. 1977; 3. 'The bilinear complementarity problem and competitive equilibria of piecewise linear economic models', *Em*, 46(1), Jan. 1978; 4. 'Competitive exchange', *Em*, 46(3), May 1978; 5. 'Information, efficiency, and the core of an economy', *Em*, 46(4), July 1978.

WILSON, Thomas

Born 1916, Belfast, N. Ireland.

Current Post Adam Smith Prof. Polit. Econ., Univ. Glasgow.

Recent Posts Univ. Coll., Univ. Oxford, 1946–58; Faculty Fellow, Nuffield Coll., Univ. Oxford, 1948–58.

Degrees BA Queen's Univ., Belfast, 1938; PhD Univ. London, 1940; MA (by decree) Univ. Oxford, 1946.

Offices General ed., *OEP*, 1948–58, Ed. Board, *J Ind E*, 1960–; Council, 1958–, Pres., 1977–8, Scottish Econ. Soc.; Council, RES, 1964–6; UK SSRC Econ. Comm., 1969–73; Exec. Comm., NIESR, 1971–; Vis. Fellow, All Souls Coll., Univ. Oxford, 1974–5.

Principal Contributions Fluctuations in output and employment with particular reference to the USA and the UK (this was extended in an early study of inflation); exploration of the ground between Keynesianism and monetarism, leading to the revival of interest in Robertson's non-Walrasian monetarism; the relationship between different branches of economics with an extension of work into price theory, regional economics, including fiscal federalism, and international monetary adjustments; the respective roles of the market and the state; the basis in welfare economics of policy recommendations, with welfare programmes in Britain and other countries as one field of application.

Publications *Books:* 1. *Fluctuations in Income and Employment* (Pitman, 1941, Kraus Reprint, 1970); 2. *Inflation* (Blackwell, 1961); 3. *Pensions Inflation and Growth*, ed. and contributor (Heinemann, 1974); 4. *Essays on Adam Smith*, ed. (with A.S. Skinner) and contributor (OUP, 1975); 5. *The Market and the State*, ed. (with A.S. Skinner) and contributor (OUP, 1976).

Articles: 1. 'The political economy of inflation', *BA Proceedings*, 1975; 2. 'Effective devaluation and inflation', *OEP*, 26(1), March 1976; 3. 'Crowding out: the real issues', *BNLQR*, 130, Sept. 1979; 4. 'Robertson, money and monetarism', *JEL*, 18(4), Dec. 1980; 5. 'Welfare economics and the welfare state', *Scand JE*, 83(1), 1981.

WINSTON, Gordon Chester

Born 1929, San Francisco, Cal., USA.

Current Post Prof. Econ., Chairman Econ. Dept Williams Coll., Mass., USA.

Recent Posts Sr res. adviser, Head of Project, Yale Univ. Pakiston Project, 1966–8, 1970–1; member, Inst. Advanced Study, Princeton Univ., 1978–9; Vis. Scholar, Inst. Internat. Econ. Stud., Stockholm, 1979–80.

Degrees BA (Eng. Lit.) Whitman Coll., 1950; MA (Econ.), PhD (Econ.), Stanford Univ., 1961, 1964.

Offices AEA, RES, WEA; Internat. Soc. Study of Time.

Principal Contributions Development of a theory of optimal capital utilisation with its implications for capital productivity, growth, productive capacity, and the meaning and measure-

ment of factor proportions; the analysis of efficient time-shaped production of perishable products; time-specific analysis of household work and consumption activities; a theory of time-shaped markets and peak loads; the theoretical and empirical (international cross-section) analysis of long-run aggregate labour supply based on household work-leisure choices; the integration of these into a time-specific theory that reveals the economic importance of the timing of processes within the analytical 'unit time' of orthodox analysis.

Publications *Books:* 1. *Industrial Capacity and Employment Promotion: Case Studies of Sri Lanka, Nigeria, Morocco and Over-all Survey of other Developing Countries* (with N. Phan-Thuy *et al.*), (Gower Publishing Co., 1981); 2. *The Timing of Economic Activities: Firms, Households and Markets in Time-specific Analysis* (1981).

Articles: 1. 'An international comparison of income and hours of work', *REStat*, 48, Feb. 1966; 2. 'Capital utilization in economic development', *EJ*, 81, March 1971; 3. 'Shift working, employment and economic development: a study of industrial workers in Pakistan' (with G. Farooq), *EDCC*, 26(2), Jan. 1978; 4. 'On measuring factor proportions in industries with different seasonal and shift patterns or did the Leontief paradox ever exist?', *EJ*, 89, Dec. 1979; 5. 'Addiction and backsliding: a theory of compulsive consumption', *JEB*, 1(1), Dec. 1980.

WINTER, Sidney G., Jr

Born 1935, Iowa City, Iowa, USA.

Current Post Prof. Econ., Organization Management, Yale Univ., USA, 1976–.

Recent Posts Res. economist, Rand Corp., 1966–8; Prof. Econ., Res. assoc., Inst. Public Pol. Stud., Univ. Michigan, 1968–76.

Degrees BA Swarthmore Coll., 1956; MA, PhD Yale Univ., 1957, 1964.

Offices Member, AEA; Fellow, Em Soc, 1968–; Assoc. ed., *JET*, 1969–71, *Admin. Science Quarterly*, 1969–72, *Behavioral Science*, 1969–79; Founding co-ed., *J Econ. Behavior Organization*, 1980–.

Principal Contributions Theory of the firm and industry: by constructive example has shown that it is possible to do economic theory without methodological principles that proclaim the irrelevance of facts relating to the behaviour of individual firms. Also explored the connections between these issues and the phenomena of industry structure, technological change and economic growth (with Richard Nelson).

Publications *Books:* 1. *An Evolutionary Theory of Economic Capabilities and Behavior* (with R. Nelson), (Harvard Univ. Press, 1981).

Articles: 1. 'Economic "natural selection" and the theory of the firm', *YEE*, 4, Spring 1964; 2. 'Optimal price policy under atomistic competition' (with E.S. Phelps), in E.S. Phelps *et al.*, *Microeconomic Foundations of Employment and Inflation Theory* (Norton, 1970); 3. 'Satisficing, selection and the innovating remnant' *QJE*, 85, May 1971; 4. 'Optimization and evolution in the theory of the firm', in *Adaptive Economic Models*, eds R. Day and T. Groves (Academic Press, 1975); 5. 'Forces generating and limiting concentration under Schumpeterian competition' (with R.R. Nelson), *Bell JE*, 9, Autumn 1978.

WOLD, Herman

Born 1908, Skien, Norway.
Current Post Prof. invité, Dept Econometrics, Univ. Geneva, Switzerland.
Recent Posts Prof. Stats, Univ. Uppsala, 1942–70; Prof. Stats, Univ. Göteborg, 1970–5 (Prof. Emeritus, 1975–).
Degrees Studentexamen Skara Coll., 1927; Fil. kandidate, Fil. Licentiate, Fil. Dr Univ. Stockholm, 1930, 1933, 1938.
Offices and Honours Vice-pres., Internat. Stat. Inst., 1957–61; Member, Royal Swedish Academy Science, 1961–; Pres., Em Soc, 1966; Hon. Dr, Technical Univ. Lisbon, 1966; Member, Royal Swedish Academy Science Comm. Nobel Prize Econ. Science, 1968–80; Hon. member, AEA, 1979; Hon. foreign member, AAAS, 1979.

Principal Contributions Stationary time series and stochastic processes: decomposition theorem; applications of autoregressive and moving average processes; analysis of consumer demand: synthesis of utility theory, statistical method, and empirical applications; path models with directly observed variables: causal chain systems vs. interdependent (ID) systems; the Fix-Point method for estimation of ID systems; strengthening the philosophical foundations by general definitions of the notions of model and cause-effect relations; systems analysis by path models with indirectly observed variables: soft modelling using PLS (Partial Least Squares) estimation; prediction accuracy vs. parameter accuracy.

Publications *Books:* 1. *A Study in the Analysis of Stationary Time Series* (Almqvist & Wiksell, 1938, 1954); 2. *Demand Analysis: A Study in Econometrics* (with L. Juréen), (Almqvist & Wiksell, 1952, Wiley, 1953); 3. *Forecasting on a Scientific Basis*, ed. (Gulbenkian Foundation, 1967); 4. *The Fix-point Approach to Interdependent Systems*, ed. (N-H, 1980); 5. *Systems under Indirect Observation*, I-II, ed. (with K.G. Jöreskog), (N-H, 1981).

Articles: 1. 'A synthesis of pure demand analysis, I-III', *Skandinavisk Aktuarietidskrift*, 26, 1943, 27, 1944; 2. 'Causal inference from observational data. A review of ends and means', *JRSS*, A, 119, 1956; 3. 'On the consistency of least squares regression', *Sankhyā*, A, 25(2), 1963; 4. 'Cycles', *Internat. Encyclopedia Stats*, vol. 2 (Free Press, 1978); 5. 'Models for knowledge', in *The Making of Statisticians*, ed. J. Gani (Springer, 1982).

WOLFE, P.

N.e.

WONNACOTT, Ronald J.

Born 1930, London, Ontario, Canada.
Current Post Prof. Econ., Univ. Western Ontario, Canada, 1958–.

Degrees BA Univ. Western Ontario, 1955; MA, PhD Harvard Univ., 1959.
Offices Pres., CEA, 1980–1.
Principal Contributions Research on Canada-US economic ties, including a two-country input-output analysis; research on the effects of Canada-US free trade, (with Paul Wonnacott); writings in econometrics, and in statistics (with Tom Wonnacott); a first year university textbook in economics (1979) (with Paul Wonnacott).
Publications *Books:* 1. *Canadian-American dependence: An Inter-industry Analysis of Production and Prices* (N-H, 1961); 2. *Free Trade Between the US and Canada* (with P. Wonnacott), (Harvard Univ. Press, 1967); 3. *Econometrics* (with T.H. Wonnacott), (Wiley, 1970, 1979); 4. *Canada's Trade Options* (Econ. Council Canada, 1975); 5. *Economics* (with P. Wonnacott), (McGraw-Hill, 1979, 1982).
Articles: 1. 'Wage level and employment structure in United States regions: a free trade precedent', *JPE*, 72, Aug. 1964; 2. 'Automotive agreement of 1965' (with P. Wonnacott), *CJE*, 33, May 1967; 3. 'Canada's future in a world of trade blocs: a proposal', *Canadian Public Pol.*, Winter 1975; 4. 'Industrial strategy: a Canadian substitute for trade liberalization?', *CJE*, 84(5), Nov. 1975.

WOOD, Stuart*

Dates and Birthplace 1853–1914, Philadelphia, Penn., USA.
Posts Held Iron founder, cotton merchant, banker and property speculator.
Degree PhD (Econ.) Harvard Univ., 1875
Offices Vice-pres., AEA, 1901.
Career Probably the first American PhD in economics and an independent discoverer of marginal productivity theory. He also published a review article on the history of the wage-fund doctrine.
Publications *Articles:* 1. 'A new view of the theory of wages Pts I-II', *QJE*, 3, Oct. 1888, July 1889; 2. 'The theory of wages', *AEA Publications*, 4, 1889; 3. 'A critique of wages theories', *Annals*

Amer. Academy of Policy and Social Sciences, 1, 1890.
Secondary Literature G.J. Stigler, *Essays in the History of Economics* (Univ. Chicago Press, 1965).

WORSWICK, George David Norman

Born 1916, London, England.
Current Post Dir., NIESR, 1965–.
Recent Posts Fellow, tutor, Econ., Magdalen Coll., Univ. Oxford, 1945–65.
Degrees BA, MA Univ. Oxford, 1937, 1944; DSc (*Hon causa*) City Univ., London, 1975.
Offices Fellow, BA, 1979.
Principal Contributions Pure theory, e.g. rationing and economic growth; applied economics, with special reference to the British economy at war and in peace. Life-time advocate of incomes policy as a means to achieve full employment without inflation.
Publications *Books:* 1. *The British Economy 1945–50,* co-ed. (OUP, 1952); 2. *The British Economy in the 1950s*, co-ed., (OUP, 1962); 3. *Profits in the British Economy 1900–1938*, co-ed., (Blackwell, 1967).
Articles: 1. 'Points, prices and consumer choice', *BOIS*, 6(3), Feb. 1944; 2. 'Stability and flexibility of full employment', in *Economics of Full Employment* (Blackwell, 1944); 3. 'Mrs. Robinson on simple accumulation', *OEP*, 2(2), June 1959; 4. 'Fiscal policy and stabilization in Britain', *JMCB*, 1(3), Aug. 1969; 5. 'Is progress in economic science possible?', *EJ*, 82, March 1972.

WRIGHT, Gavin

Born 1943, New Haven, Conn., USA.
Current Post Prof. Econ., Univ. Michigan, 1978–.
Recent Posts Ass. prof., Yale Univ., 1969–71; Ass. prof., 1972–4, Assoc. prof., 1974–8, Univ. Michigan.
Degrees BA Swarthmore Coll., 1965; PhD Yale Univ., 1969.
Offices and Honours AEA; Cole

prize, 1974, Ed. Board, 1976–, EHA; Guggenheim Memorial Foundation Fellow, 1976; Ed. Boards, *Comparative Stud. Soc. and Hist.*, 1978–, *Explorations Econ. Hist.*, 1979–.

Principal Contributions Applications of econometric methods to American economic history – major work has concerned the regional development of the US South from the slave period to the present. Research in aspects of labour history and in the political economy of government.

Publications *Books:* 1. *Reckoning with Slavery* (with P. Temin), (OUP, 1976); 2. *The Political Economy of the Cotton South* (Norton, 1978).

Articles: 1. 'The effects of pre-Civil War Territorial expansion on the price of slaves' (with P. Passell), *JPE*, 80(6), Nov./Dec. 1972; 2. 'The political economy of New Deal spending: an econometric analysis', *REStat*, 56(1), Feb. 1974; 3. 'Cotton competition and the post-bellum recovery of the American South', *JEH*, 34(3), Sept. 1974; 4. 'The efficiency of slavery', *AER*, 69(1), March 1979; 5. 'Cheap labor and southern textiles, 1880–1930', *QJE*, 1981.

WRIGLEY, Edward Anthony

Born 1931, Manchester, England.
Current Post Prof. Pop. Stud., LSE.
Recent Posts Dir., UK SSRC Group Hist. Pop. and Social Structure, 1974–9.
Degrees BA, MA, PhD Univ. Camb., 1952, 1956, 1957.
Offices and Honours William Volker Res. Fellow, Comm. Social Thought, Univ. Chicago, 1953–4; Fellow, Peterhouse Coll., Univ. Camb., 1958–; Ellen McArthur prize Econ. Hist., 1958; Member, Princeton Inst. Advanced Study, 1970–1; Hinkley vis. prof., Dept Hist., Johns Hopkins Univ., 1975; Pres., British Soc. Pop. Stud., 1977–9; Tinbergen Vis. prof., Erasmus Univ., Rotterdam, 1979; Fellow, BA, 1980–.
Principal Contributions The determinants of levels and trends in fertility, mortality and nuptiality in the past; the interactions between economic and demographic variables; the genesis and course of the industrial revolution; the

nature of the contrasts between pre- and post-industrial societies.

Publications *Books:* 1. *Industrial Growth and Population Change* (CUP, 1961); 2. *An Introduction to English Historical Demography* (Weidenfeld & Nicolson, 1966); 3. *Population and History* (Weidenfeld & Nicolson, 1969); 4. *Nineteenth-century Society*, ed. (CUP, 1972); 5. *The Population History of England: A Reconstruction* (with R.S. Schofield), (Edward Arnold, 1981).

Articles: 1. 'The supply of raw materials in the industrial revolution', *EHR*, II, 15, Aug. 1962; 2. 'Family limitation in pre-industrial England', *EHR*, II, 19, April 1966; 3. 'A simple model of London's importance in changing English society and economy', *Past and Present*, 37, 1967; 4. 'The process of modernization and the industrial revolution in England', *J Interdisciplinary Hist.*, 32, 1972; 5. 'Fertility strategy for the individual and the group', in *Historical Studies of Changing Fertility*, ed. C. Tilly (Princeton Univ. Press, 1978).

Y

YAARI, Menahem E.

Born 1935, Jerusalem, Israel.
Current Post Prof. Econ., Hebrew Univ., Jerusalem.
Recent Posts S.A. Schonbrunn Chair Math. Econ., Hebrew Univ., 1971–; Vis. prof., Univ. Pennsylvania, 1979–80.
Degrees BA Hebrew Univ., 1958; PhD Stanford Univ., 1962.
Offices and Honours Member, AEA, Israel Econ. Assoc.; Co-ed., *Em*, 1968–75; Fellow, Em Soc, 1970; Walras-Bowley Lecture, Em Soc, 1977.
Principal Contributions Studies in consumer theory, economics of uncertainty and moral hazard, changes of tastes, and distributive justice.
Publications *Books:* 1. *Linear Algebra for Social Sciences* (Prentice-Hall, 1971).
Articles: 1. 'A law of large numbers in the theory of consumer's choice under uncertainty', *JET*, 12(2), April 1976; 2.

'Endogenous changes in tastes: a philosophical discussion', *Erkenntnis*, 1977; 3. 'Separably concave utilities, or the principle of diminishing eagerness to trade', *JET*, 18(1), June 1978; 4. 'Rawls, Edgeworth, Shapley, Nash: theories of distributive justice re-examined', *JET*, 23, 1981; 5. 'Consistent utilization of an exhaustible resource, or how to eat an appetite-arousing cake', *Em*, forthcoming, 1982.

YOTOPOULOS, Pan A.

Born 1933, Athens, Greece.
Current Post Prof. Econ., Food Res. Inst., Stanford Univ., USA, 1968–.
Recent Posts Prof., Univ. Wisconsin, 1961–3, 1965–7; Dir. Basic Res., Center Planning Econ. Res., Athens, 1963–5; Prof., Univ. Hawaii, 1967–8.
Degrees Diploma (Polit.Science and Econ.) Univ. Athens, 1956; MA (Econ.) Univ. Kansas, 1957; PhD (Econ.) UCLA, 1962.
Offices and Honours Member, AEA, Em Soc, AAEA, PAA; AAEA award for Professional Excellence, 1969; Sr Fellow award, East-West Center, Honolulu, Hawaii, 1974; Adviser, UN-FAO, 1975–; Consultant, World Bank, 1976–.
Principal Contributions Work on economic development grew around two distictive characteristics of less developed countries: the paramount importance of agriculture within the economy led to research in the theory of production and efficiency; the empirical treatment of multi-period inputs in terms of service flows and the comparison of efficiency in terms of technical, price and economic efficiency were some of the original aspects of that research; and the imbalance between population and resources led to the study of employment and demography; the integration of the demographic decision with the production and consumption behaviour of the household is the novel aspect in that research.
Publications *Books:* 1. *Surplus Labor in Greek Agriculture, 1953–1960* (with A.A. Pepelasis), (Athens Center Planning Econ. Res., 1962); 2. *Allocative Efficiency in Economic Develop-ment: A Cross-section Analysis of Epirus Farming* (Athens Center Planning Econ. Res., 1968); 3. *Economics of Development: Empirical Investigations* (with J.B. Nugent), (Harper & Row, 1976); 4. *The Population Problem and the Development Solution, Food Res. Inst. Stud., 16* (Stanford Univ., 1977); 5. *Resource Use in Agriculture: Applications of the Profit Function in Selected Countries* (with L.J. Lau), *Food Res. Inst. Stud. 17* (Stanford Univ., 1979).
Articles: 1. 'The "wage-productivity" theory of underemployment: a refinement', *REStud*, 32, Jan. 1965; 2. 'From stock to flow capital inputs for agricultural production functions: a micro-analytic approach', *JFE*, 49, May 1967; 3. 'A test for relative efficiency and an application to Indian agriculture' (with L.J. Lau), *AER*, 61(1), March 1971; 4. 'The balanced-growth version of the linkage hypothesis: a test' (with J.B. Nugent), *QJE*, 87, May 1973; 5. 'The linear logarithmic expenditure system: an application to consumption-leisure choice' (with L.J. Lau and W.L. Lin), *Em*, 46(4), July 1978.

YOUNG, Allyn Abbott*

Dates and Birthplace 1876–1929, Kenton, Ohio, USA.
Posts Held Prof., Univs. Leland, Stanford, Washington, Cornell, Harvard and London.
Degree PhD Univ. Wisconsin, 1902.
Offices Various advisory posts, US govt, the League of Nations; Member, Polit. Econ. Club; Pres., Section F, BAAS.
Career His extremely wide qualifications, his practical work for government and his busy academic career left him no time for a major treatise. However, his published articles and his teaching ensured a great reputation for him among his contemporaries. Banking and currency were among the many specific areas on which he had worked, but before his early death he had begun a systematic treatise on economic theory.
Publications *Books:* 1. *Economic Problems New and Old* (1927); 2.

Analysis of Banking Statistics for the United States (1928).

Articles: 1. 'Increasing returns and economic progress', *EJ*, 38, Dec. 1928.

Secondary Literature T.E. Gregory, 'Obituary: Professor Allyn A. Young', *EJ*, 29, June 1939.

Z

ZABEL, Edward

Born 1927, Orange, NJ, USA.

Current Post Prof. Decision Sciences Econ., Univ. Florida, USA.

Recent Posts Rand Corp., Santa Monica, 1958; Dept. Econ., Univ. Rochester, 1958–80.

Degrees BA Syracuse Univ., 1950; MA, PhD Princeton Univ., 1953, 1956.

Offices and Honours AEA; Em Soc; WEA; Inst. Management Sciences; Phi Beta Kappa, 1950; Ford Foundation Faculty Res. Fellow, 1964–5; Assoc. ed., Management Science, 1969–73; Board Eds., *Applied Econ.*, 1973–.

Principal Contributions Early papers analysed firm and consumer behaviour under uncertainty in multi-period models, and considered the competitive firm's search for high prices over time, the monopolistic firm's response to random deviations in demand, and the consumer's commodity and portfolio decisions when portfolio changes incur transaction costs. Later papers attempt to use insights obtained in earlier work to analyse multi-period trading processes when markets need not be cleared each period.

Publications *Articles:* 1. 'Efficient accumulation of capital for the firm', *Em*, 31, Jan./April 1963; 2. 'A dynamic model of the competitive firm', *Int ER*, 8, June 1967; 3. 'Risk and the competitive firm', *JET*, 3(2), June 1971; 4. 'Consumer choice, portfolio decisions and transaction costs', *Em*, 41(2), March 1973; 5. 'Competitive price adjustment without market clearing', *Em*, 49, 1981.

ZAREMBKA, Paul

Born 1942, St Louis, Missouri, USA.

Current Post Prof. Econ., State Univ. Buffalo, NY, 1976–.

Recent Posts Assoc. prof. Econ., State Univ. Buffalo, 1973–6; Sr res. officer, World Employment Programme, ILO, Geneva, 1974–7; Res., Group Study Res. on Science, Louis Pasteur Univ., Strasbourg, 1978, 1979.

Degrees BS (Maths) Purdue Univ., 1964; MS (Econ.), PhD (Econ.) Univ. Wisconsin, 1967, 1967.

Honours Fulbright-Hayes Lecturer, Academy Econ. Stud., Poznań, Poland, 1979.

Principal Contributions Neo-classical theory of economic development, econometric theory of estimation of variables subject to parametric transformation, empirical estimation of the CES production function, capital-theoretic conception of the neo-classical production function, and the Cambridge approach to investment theory. A break in conceptual thinking consisted of a reformation centred on Marx's *Capital* in its a-Hegelian, a-economistic interpretation. Have reinterpreted accumulation of capital in Marx as the process of penetration of non-capitalist forms of production and apply this interpretation to twentieth-century historical developments.

Publications *Books:* 1. *Toward a Theory of Economic Development* (Holden-Day, 1972); 2. *Frontiers in Econometrics*, ed. (Academic Press, 1974); 3. *Essays in Modern Capital Theory*, ed. (with M. Brown and K. Sato), (N-H, 1976); 4. *Research in Political Economy: A Research Annual*, ed. (JAI Press, 1977–81).

Articles: 1. 'Transformation of variables in econometrics', in *Frontiers in Econometrics*, ed. P. Zarembka (Academic Press, 1974); 2. 'Capital heterogeneity, aggregation, and the two-sector model', *QJE*, 89 (1), Feb. 1975; 3. 'The capitalistic mode of production: economic structure', in *Research in Political Economy*, vol. 1, ed. P. Zarembka (JAI Press, 1977); 4. 'Investment and saving in capitalist society: an interpretation of the Cambridge position', in *On the Stability of Contemporary Economic Systems, Proceedings of the Third Reisenburg Symposium*, eds O. Kyn and W. Schrettl (Vandenhoeck & Ruprecht, 1979); 5. 'Accumulation of capital in the periphery', in *Research in Political Economy*, vol. 2, ed. P. Zarembka (JAI Press, 1979).

ZARNOWITZ, Victor

Born 1919, Lańcut, Poland.
Current Post Prof. Econ. Fin., Grad. School Bus., Univ. Chicago, USA, 1965–.
Recent Posts Res. assoc., NBER, 1952–; Assoc. prof. Fin., Grad. School Bus., Univ. Chicago, 1959–64; Dir., Study Cyclical Indicators, 1972–5, Consultant, Bureau Econ. Analysis, US Dept Commerce, 1975–.
Degrees MA, PhD (Econ., *Summa cum laude*) Univ. Heidelberg, 1949, 1951.
Offices Member, AEA, ASA, Em Soc, Centre Internat. Res. Econ. Tendency Surveys: Harvard Univ., US-SSRC Postdoctoral Res. Training Fellow, 1953–4; Ford Foundation Faculty Res. Fellow, 1963–4; Fellow, ASA, 1976.
Principal Contributions Applications of macro-economic theory, especially the study of business cycles, growth, inflation, and forecasting. Work on the cyclical behaviour of prices; orders and production; inventories; and fixed capital investment. Contributions to research on leading, co-incident, and lagging business cycle indicators; forecasting and simulations with econometric models; and evaluation of economic forecasts.
Publications *Books:* 1. *Die Theorie der Einkommensverteilung* (J.C.B. Mohr, Paul Siebeck, 1951); 2. *Unfilled Orders, Price Changes, and Business Fluctuations* (NBER, 1962); 3. *An Appraisal of Short-term Economic Forecasts* (Colombia Univ. Press, 1967); 4. *The Business Cycle Today*, ed. and co-author (Columbia Univ. Press, 1972); 5. *Orders, Production, and Investment: A Cyclical and Structural Analysis* (Columbia Univ. Press, 1973). *Articles:* 1. 'Cause and consequence of changes in retailers' buying' (with R.P. Mack), *AER*, 48(1), March 1958; 2. 'Cyclical aspects of incorporations and the formation of new business enterprises', in *Business Cycle Indicators*, vol. 1, ed. G.H. Moore (NBER, 1960); 3. 'Business cycle analysis of econometric model simulations' (with G.H. Moore and C. Boschan), in *Econometric Models of Cyclical Behavior*, vol. 1, ed. B.G. Hickman (NBER, 1972); 4. 'Cyclical indicators: an evaluation and new leading indexes' (with C. Boschan), *Bus. Conditions Digest*, May 1975; 5. 'An analysis of annual and multiperiod quarterly forecasts of aggregate income, output, and the price level', *J Bus*, 52(1), Jan. 1979.

ZECKHAUSER, Richard Jay

Born 1940, Philadelphia, Penn., USA.
Current Post Prof. Polit. Econ., J.F. Kennedy School Govt, Harvard Univ., 1972–.
Recent Posts Ass. prof., 1968–70, Assoc. prof., 1970–2, Harvard Univ.
Degrees BA (*Summa cum laude*), PhD Harvard Univ., 1962, 1969.
Offices and Honours Current grants and awards: NSF, S.S. Huebner Foundation; US National Commission Employment Pol.; John Williams Award, Harvard Univ., 1962; Founder, Dir., Niederhoffer, Cross and Zeckhauser Inc., New York, 1967–; Res. Assoc., 1981–, NBER, Inst. Poverty, Univ. Wisconsin, Center Health Pol. Management, Harvard Univ.
Principal Contributions Results of theoretical papers: involuntary unemployment is consequence of worker and firm heterogeneity; paying expected externality effectively decentralises multi-stage externality and group decision problems under uncertainty; groups employing Bayesian methods cannot preserve Pareto optimality; need to design incentive-compatible mechanism to assign individuals to positions; fundamental non-convexity if externality leads to shutdown; voting mechanisms inefficient if intensities of preference matter; numerous results in agency theory, insurance, and populations with

heterogeneous risk. Applications studies: regulation; health care; catastrophic illness; valuation of life; and price variability (many co-authored).

Publications *Books:* 1. *Benefit Cost and Policy Analysis Annual 1974*, ed. (Aldine Publishing, 1975); 2. *A Primer for Policy Analysis* (with E. Stokey), (Norton, 1978); 3. *What Role for Government in the 1980s*, ed. (Assoc. Public Pol. Management, 1981); 4. *Demographic Dimensions of the New Republic* (with P. McClelland), (CUP, 1982).

Articles: 1. 'Voting systems, honest preferences and Pareto optimality', *Amer. Polit. Science Review*, Sept. 1973; 2. 'The occupational safety and health administration' (with A.L. Nichols), *US Senate Committee on Government operations* (US Govt Printing Office, 1978); 3. 'The efficient allocation of individuals to positions' (with A. Hylland), *JPE*, 87(2), April 1979; 4. 'Impossibility of Bayesian group decision making with separate aggregation of beliefs and values' (with A. Hylland), *Em*, 47(6), Nov. 1979; 5. 'Long-term effects of interventions to improve survival in mixed populations' (with D. Shepard), *J Chronic Diseases*, 1980.

ZELLNER, Arnold

Born 1927, New York City, NY, USA.

Current Post H.G.B. Alexander Prof. Econ. and Stats., Grad. School Bus., Univ. Chicago, USA, 1966–.

Recent Posts Ass. and assoc. prof. Econ., Univ. Washington, 1955–60; Assoc. prof. and Prof. Econ., Univ. Wisconsin, 1960–6.

Degrees BA (Physics) Harvard Univ., 1949; PhD (Econ.) Univ. Cal., Berkeley, 1957.

Offices Member, AEA, Internat. Stat. Inst., Amer. Assoc. Advancement Science; Founder and Seminar Leader, NBER-NSF Seminar on Bayesian inference in econometrics; Co-ed., *J Em*, 1973–; Fellow, Council member, 1978–, Em Soc; Fellow, Chairman, Bus. & Econ. Stats. Section, 1980, ASA; Board Dirs., NBER, 1980–.

Principal Contributions Worked to develop and apply better econometric methods and models for analysing economic data and policy problems, recently concentrating on Bayesian econometrics and on a structural econometric modelling/time series analysis approach to econometric model-building.

Publications *Books:* 1. *Economic Aspects of the Pacific Halibut Fishery* (with J.A. Crutchfield), (Govt Printing Office, 1963); 2. *Systems Simulation for Regional Analysis: An Application to River-basin Planning* (with H.R. Hamilton *et al.*), (MIT Press, 1969); 3. *Estimating the Parameters of the Markov Probability Model from Aggregate Time Series Data* (with T.C. Lee and G.G.Judge), (N-H, 1970, 1977; Russian transl., 1977); 4. *An Introduction to Bayesian Inference in Econometrics* (Wiley, 1971; Russian transl., 1980); 5. *Bayesian Analysis in Econometrics and Statistics: Essays in Honor of Harold Jeffreys*, ed. (N-H, 1980).

Articles: 1. 'Three-stage least squares: simultaneous estimation of simultaneous equations' (with H. Theil), *Em*, 30, Jan. 1062; 2. 'An efficient method of estimating seemingly unrelated regressions and tests for aggregation bias', *JASA*, 57, June 1962; 3. 'Time series analysis and simultaneous equation models' (with F. Palm), *J Em*, 2, May 1974; 4. 'Bayesian and alternative approaches in econometrics', in *Studies in Bayesian Econometrics and Statistics in Honor of Leonard J. Savage*, ed. (with S.E. Fienberg), (N-H, 1975); 5. 'Statistical analysis of econometric models', *JASA*, 74, Sept. 1979.

ZEUTHEN, Frederik*

Dates and Birthplace 1888–1959, Copenhagen, Denmark.

Posts Held Civil servant, 1912–30; Prof., Univ. Copenhagen, 1928–58.

Degrees Grad. (Econ.), PhD Univ. Copenhagen, 1912, 1928.

Offices Fellow, Em Soc.

Career Economist who made early contributions to the theory of bargaining, the use of inequalities in the Walras system and the theory of monopolistic competition.

Publications *Books:* 1. *Den Ökonomiske Fordeling* (1928); 2. *Problems of Monopoly and Economic Warfare* (1930); 3. *Arbejdslön og Arbejdslöshed* (1939); 4. *Economic Theory and Method* (1955).

Secondary Literature H. Brems, 'From the years of high theory: Frederik Zeuthen (1888–1959)', *HOPE*, 8(3), Fall 1976.

Appendix 1

INDEX OF PRINCIPAL FIELDS OF INTEREST

The full version of the AEA Classification Scheme of Fields of Interest is appended below for reference. This index refers to living economists only.

1. General economics; Theory; History; Systems

Abramovitz, Moses
Ackley, Gardner
Akerlof, George A.
Alchian, Armen A.
Aldcroft, Derek H.
Alexander, Sidney S.
Allen, Roy
Ando, Albert K.
Archibald, George C.
Arrow, Kenneth J.
Artis, Michael J.
Bach, George L.
Bailey, Elizabeth E.
Bailey, Martin J.
Bain, Joe S.
Baron, David P.
Bartoli, Henri
Basmann, Robert L.
Bator, Francis M.
Bauer, Peter T.
Baumol, William
Becker, Gary S.
Beckerman, Wilfred
Beckmann, Martin J.
Ben-Porath, Yoram
Bergson, Abram
Bernholz, Peter
Bishop, Robert L.
Blackorby, Charles
Blau, Julian H.
Blinder, Alan S.
Bohm, Peter J.G.
Boiteux, Marcel P.
Borch, Karl H.
Boulding, Kenneth E.
Bowles, Samuel
Brechling, Frank P.R.
Brems, Hans J.
Breton, Albert
Bronfenbrenner, Martin
Buchanan, James M.
Budd, Edward C.
Burmeister, Edwin
Cameron, Rondo
Campbell, Robert
Caravale, Giovanni A.
Casarosa, Carlo
Cass, David
Chamberlain, Neil W.
Champernowne, David G.

Cheung, Steven N.S.
Clower, Robert W.
Coase, Ronald H.
Coats, A.W.
Coddington, Alan
Cooley, Thomas F.
Copeland, Morris A.
Cotta, Alain
Cragg, John G.
Culbertson, John M.
Culyer, Anthony J.
Cyert, Richard M.
Dasgupta, Partha S.
Davidson, Paul
Deane, Phyllis
Debreu, Gerard
Demsetz, Harold
Dhrymes, Phoebus J.
Diamond, Peter
Diewert, W. Erwin
Dixit, Avinash K.
Dolbear, F. Trenery
Domar, Evsey D.
Dorfman, Robert
Ehrlich, Isaac
Eisner, Robert
Engerman, Stanley
Feinstein, Charles
Fellner, William J.
Fels, Rendigs
Fetter, Frank W.
Fischer, Wolfram
Fishlow, Albert
Fitoussi, Jean-Paul
Flemming, John S.
Foley, Duncan K.
Frankel, S. Herbert
Friedman, Milton
Furubotn, Eirik G.
Gabor, André
Gäfgen, Gérard
Galbraith, John K.
Gale, Douglas M.
Gallaway, Lowell E.
Garegnani, Pierangelo
Genovese, Eugene D.
Georgescu-Roegen, Nicholas
Goodhart, Charles A.E.
Gordon, Donald F.
Gordon, Robert J.

Gorman, William
Gould, John P.
Grandmont, Jean-Michel
Greenhut, Melvin L.
Grossman, Gregory
Grossman, Herschel I.
Groves, Theodore
Grubel, Herbert
Guitton, Henri
Gutowski, Armin F.
Hahn, Frank
Hall, Robert E.
Hansen, Bent
Hansen, W. Lee
Harcourt, Geoffrey C.
Hart, Albert G.
Hayek, Friedrich A.
Heal, Geoffrey M.
Heilbroner, Robert L.
Heller, Walter W.
Helmstadter, Ernst
Hesse, Helmut
Hicks, John
Higgins, Benjamin H.
Hildenbrand, Werner
Hines, Albert G.
Hirshleifer, Jack
Hollander, Samuel
Holtrop, Marius W.
Horvath, Janos
Hoselitz, Bert F.
Hurwicz, Leonid
Hutchison, Terence W.
Inada, Ken-Ichi
Intriligator, Michael D.
James, P.M. Emile
Jaszi, George
Johansen, Leif
Johnston, Jack
Jorgenson, Dale W.
Joskow, Paul L.
Kahn, Alfred E.
Kahn, Richard
Kaldor, Nicholas
Kamerschen, David R.
Katzner, Donald W.
Kemp, Murray C.
Kennedy, Charles
Kindleberger, Charles P.
Kloten, Norbert W.

Kmenta, Jan
Kneese, Allen V.
Komiya, Ryutaro
Kornai, János
Kraus, Alan
Kregel, Jan A.
Kreinin, Mordechai E.
Krutilla, John V.
Kuczynski, Jurgen P.
Kuenne, Robert E.
Kurz, Mordecai
Kuznets, Simon
Laffont, Jean-Jacques M.
Laidler, David E.W.
Lancaster, Kelvin J.
Lavigne, Marie
Lazear, Edward P.
Leftwich, Richard H.
Leibenstein, Harvey
Leijonhufvud, Axel
Lekachman, Robert
Leland, Hayne E.
Leontief, Wassily
Lerner, Abba P.
Levhari, David
Levy, Haim
Liebhafsky, Herbert H.
Lindbeck, Assar
Lindblom, C. Edward
Lindsay, Cotton M.
Lippman, Steven A.
Lipsey, Richard
Little, Ian M.D.
Loasby, Brian J.
Lovell, Michael C.
Lowe, Adolph
Lucas, Robert E.
Lydall, Harold F.
McCall, John J.
McCloskey, Donald N.
McFadden, Daniel L.
McKenzie, Lionel W.
Maddala, Gangadharrao S.
Marchal, Jean M.P.
Markham, Jesse W.
Mas-Colell, Andreu
Mayer, Thomas
Melman, Seymour
Mincer, Jacob
Mirrlees, James A.
Mishan, Ezra
Moller, Hans
Monsen, R. Joseph
Morishima, Michio
Morris, Cynthia T.

Moses, Leon N.
Mueller, Dennis C.
Musgrave, Richard A.
Muth, John F.
Muth, Richard
Negishi, Takashi
Nelson, Richard R.
Neuberger, Egon
Newman, Peter K.
Niskanen, William A.
North, Douglass C.
Nove, Alexander
Nuti, Domenico M.
O'Brien, Denis
Oi, Walter Y.
Ott, Alfred E.
Pasinetti, Luigi L.
Patinkin, Don
Pattanaik, Prasanta K.
Peacock, Alan T.
Pearce, Ivor F.
Pechman, Joseph A.
Perroux, Francois
Peston, Maurice
Pfouts, Ralph W.
Phelps, Edmund S.
Pollak, Robert A.
Portes, Richard
Pryor, Frederic L.
Quandt, Richard E.
Radner, Roy
Recktenwald, Horst C.
Reder, Melvin W.
Robertson, Hector M.
Robinson, Joan
Robbins, Lionel
Rosa, Jean-Jacques
Rosovsky, Henry
Ross, Stephen A.
Rothenberg, Jerome
Rothschild, Kurt W.
Rothschild, Michael
Rybczynski, Tadeusz M.
Salop, Steven
Samuels, Warren J.
Samuelson, Paul A.
Sandmo, Agnar
Sato, Kazuo
Sato, Ryuzo
Sauvy, Alfred
Savers, Richard S.
Scarf, Herbert E.
Scherer, Frédéric M.
Schmalensee, Richard L.
Schmidt, Kurt

Schmitt, Bernard
Scitovsky, Tibor
Seers, Dudley
Sen, Amartya K.
Seton, Francis
Shackle, George L.S.
Shell, Karl
Shepherd, William G.
Sheshinski, Eytan
Shoup, Carl S.
Shubik, Martin
Siebert, Horst
Silberberg, Eugene
Silberston, Z. Aubrey
Smith, Vernon L.
Solow, Robert M.
Sowell, Thomas
Spence, Andrew M.
Spengler, Joseph J.
Stigler, George J.
Stiglitz, Joseph E.
Stubblebine, W. Craig
Suits, Daniel B.
Sweezy, Paul M.
Taylor, Lester D.
Telser, Lester G.
Temin, Peter
Tobin, James
Townsend, Harry
Tullock, Gordon
Turnovsky, Stephen J.
Turvey, Ralph
Ulman, Lloyd
Usher, Dan
Vickers, Douglas
Von Weizsacker, Carl C.
Weintraub, Sidney
Weisbrod, Burton A.
Weitzman, Martin L.
Wellisz, Stanislaw H.
Wiles, Peter J.F.
Willgerodt, Hans
Williamson, Jeffrey G.
Willis, Robert J.
Wilson, Robert B.
Winston, Gordon C.
Winter, Sidney G.
Wold, Herman
Worswick, George D.N.
Wright, Gavin
Yaari, Menahem E.
Zabel, Edward
Zarembka, Paul
Zeckhauser, Richard J.
Zellner, Arnold

2. Economic growth; Development; Planning; Fluctuations

Abramovitz, Moses
Adams, F. Gérard
Adelman, I.
Aldcroft, Derek H.

Allais, Maurice
Allen, Roy
Arndt, Heinz W.
Arrow, Kenneth J. Babeau,

Andre
Baer, Werner
Balassa, Bela
Baldwin, Robert E.

Balogh, Thomas
Bardhan, Praneb K.
Barlow, Robin
Bauer, Peter T.
Behrman, Jere R.
Berry, Albert
Bhagwati, Jagdish N.
Blinder, Alan S.
Bos, Hendricus C.
Bowman, Mary J.
Brems, Hans J.
Bruno, Michael
Burns, Arthur F.
Cairncross, Alexander K.
Cameron, Rondo
Caravale, Giovanni A.
Casarosa, Carlo
Cass, David
Chenery, Hollis B.
Chow, Gregory
Coats, A.W.
Coen, Robert M.
Cotta, Alain
Courbis, Raymond
David, Paul A.
Denison, Edward F.
Diaz-Alejandro, Carlos F.
Domar, Evsey D.
Donges, Juergen B.
Easterlin, Richard A.
Eckaus, Richard
Engerman, Stanley L.
Fels, Rendigs
Fischer, Wolfram
Fishlow, Albert
Fitoussi, Jean-Paul
Frank, Charles R.
Frankel, S. Herbert
Freeman, Richard B.
Furubotn, Erik G.
Galenson, Walter
Giersch, Herbert
Goldsmith, Raymond W.
Gordon, Myron J.
Griffin, Keith B.
Grossman, Gregory
Guitton, Henri
Habakkuk, H. John
Haberler, Gottfried
Hagen, Everett E.
Hansen, Bent

Harberger, Arnold C.
Harris, John R.
Heal, Geoffrey M.
Helleiner, Gerald K.
Helmstadter, Ernst
Hickman, Bert G.
Hicks, John
Higgins, Benjamin H.
Hoffmann, Lutz
Hoselitz, Bert F.
Ilchman, Warren F.
Inada, Ken-Ichi
Johansen, Leif
Johnston, Bruce F.
Kaldor, Nicholas
Kantorovich, Leonid V.
Keesing, Donald B.
Kelley, Allen C.
Keyserling, Léon H.
Klein, Lawrence R.
Koopmans, Tjalling C.
Krueger, Anne O.
Kurz, Mordecai
Kuznets, Simon
Lal, Deepak K.
Lasuen, José R.
Leff, Nathaniel H.
Leibenstein, Harvey
Lerner, Abba P.
Lindblom, C. Edward
Little, Ian M.D.
Lowe, Adolph
Lucas, Robert E.
Lundberg, Erik F.
MacDougall, G. Donald A.
McKenzie, Lionel W.
Mandelbrot, Benoit
Marczewski, Jean
Mas-Colell, Andreu
Mason, Edward S.
Meade, James E.
Meier, Gerald M.
Mellor, John W.
Meltzer, Allan H.
Morishima, Michio
Morris, Cynthia T.
Myint, Hla
Myrdal, Gunnar
Nordhaus, William D.
Nove, Alexander
Nuti, Domenico M.

Ott, Alfred E.
Papanek, Gustav
Papi, G. Ugo
Parkin, John M.
Pasinetti, Luigi L.
Perroux, Francois
Phelps Brown, E. Henry
Portes, Richard
Prebisch, Raul
Prest, Alan R.
Pryor, Frederic L.
Radner, Roy
Ranis, Gustav
Reddaway, W. Brian
Reynolds, Lloyd G.
Ridker, Ronald G.
Robinson, E. Austin G.
Robinson, Joan
Rosovsky, Henry
Roy, Andrew D.
Ruttan, Vernon W.
Sato, Kazuo
Schultz, T. Paul
Schultz, Theodore W.
Seers, Dudley
Selden, Richard T.
Sen, Amartya K.
Seton, Francis
Sims, Christopher A.
Solow, Robert M.
Spulber, Nicolas
Stein, Herbert
Stone, J. Richard N.
Streeten, Paul
Sweezy, Paul M.
Thirlwall, Anthony
Tinbergen, Jan
Todaro, Michael P.
Vanek, Jaroslav
Vietorisz, Thomas
Weitzman, Martin L.
Wiles, Peter J.F.
Williamson, Jeffrey G.
Wilson, Thomas
Winston, Gordon C.
Worswick, George D.N.
Wrigley, Edward A.
Yotopoulos, Pan A.
Zarembka, Paul
Zarnowitz, Victor

3. Quantitative economic methods and data

Adams, F. Gerard
Aigner, Dennis J.
Allais, Maurice
Amemiya, Takishi
Ashenfelter, Orley
Ball, Robert J.
Barten, Anton P.

Basmann, Robert L.
Beckmann, Martin J.
Boiteux, Marcel P.
Budd, Edward C.
Burmeister, Edwin
Byron, Ray
Carlson, John A.

Champernowne, David G.
Chipman, John S.
Chiswick, Barry R.
Chow, Gregory
Christ, Carl F.
Clark, Colin G.
Cooley, Thomas F.

Copeland, Morris A.
Courbis, Raymond
Cragg, John G.
Deane, Phyllis
Deaton, Angus S.
Debreu, Gerard
De Leeuw, Frank
Denison, Edward F.
Dhrymes, Phoebus J.
Dicks-Mireaux, Leslie
Diewert, W. Erwin
Durand, David
Eckstein, Otto
Eisner, Robert
Elton, Edwin J.
Feige, Edgar L.
Feinstein, Charles
Ferber, Robert
Fisher, Franklin M.
Gastwirth, Joseph L.
Goldberger, Arthur S.
Goldfeld, Stephen M.
Goldsmith, Raymond W.
Granger, Clive W.J.
Griliches, Zvi
Gronau, Reuben
Hanoch, Giora
Hart, Peter E.
Heckman, James J.
Hickman, Bert G.
Hoch, Irving
Houthakker, Hendrik
Hurwicz, Leonid
Ijiri, Yuji

Intriligator, Michael D.
Jaffee, Dwight M.
Jaszi, George
Johnson, Thomas
Johnston, Jack
Jorgenson, Dale W.
Juster, F. Thomas
Kain, John F.
Kantorovich, Leonid V.
Keeney, Ralph L.
Klein, Lawrence R.
Kmenta, Jan
Koopmans, Tjalling C.
Kornai, János
Kravis, Irving B.
Kuenne, Robert E.
Kuh, Edwin
Laffont, Jean-Jacques M.
Lambin, Jean-Jacques
Lee, Tong H.
Leontief, Wassily
Liu, Ben-chieh
Lovell, Michael C.
Luce, R. Duncan
Lydall, Harold F.
McFadden, Daniel L.
Maddala, Gangadharrao S.
Mandelbrot, Benoit
Mansfield, Edwin
Marczewski, Jean
Meyer, John R.
Morgan, James N.
Muellbauer, John N.J.
Nelson, Charles R.

Nerlove, Marc
Orcutt, Guy H.
Pfouts, Ralph W.
Pollak, Robert A.
Ponsard, Claude
Quandt, Richard E.
Roy, Andrew D.
Ruggles, Richard
Samuelson, Paul A.
Sargan, John Denis
Sargent, Thomas J.
Sato, Ryuzo
Scarf, Herbert E.
Sims, Christopher A.
Smith, Vernon L.
Smolensky, Eugene
Stone, J. Richard N.
Suits, Daniel B.
Taubman, Paul
Taylor, Lester D.
Theil, Henri
Usher, Dan
Van Praag, Bernard M.S.
Wallis, Kenneth F.
Walters, Alan A.
Watts, Harold W.
Waud, Roger N.
Welch, Finis R.
Wold, Herman
Wonnacott, Ronald J.
Zabel, Edward
Zarnowitz, Victor
Zellner, Arnold

4. Domestic monetary and fiscal theory and institutions

Aaron, Henry
Ackley, Gardner
Akerlof, George A.
Aliber, Robert Z.
Ando, Albert K.
Artis, Michael J.
Atkinson, Anthony B.
Bach, George L.
Bailey, Martin J.
Ball, Robert J.
Barlow, Robin
Barro, Robert J.
Basevi, Georgio
Bernholz, Peter
Bish, Robert L.
Black, Fischer
Black, Stanley W.
Bohm, Peter J.G.
Breton, Albert
Bronfenbrenner, Martin
Brown, Arthur J.
Buchanan, James M.
Burns, Arthur F.

Carlson, John A.
Christ, Carl F.
Coddington, Alan
Coen, Robert M.
Cooper, Richard
Culbertson, John M.
Darby, Michael R.
De Leeuw, Frank
Diamond, Peter
Dicks-Mireaux, Leslie
Dolbear, F. Trenery
Dornbusch, Rudiger
Eckstein, Otto
Feige, Edgar L.
Feldstein, Martin
Fellner, William J.
Fetter, Frank W.
Fischer, Stanley
Flemming, John S.
Foley, Duncan K.
Frenkel, Jacob A.
Friedman, Milton
Gale, Douglas M.

Goldfeld, Stephen M.
Goodhart, Charles A.E.
Gordon, Robert J.
Gramlich, Edward M.
Grandmont, Jean-Michel
Grossman, Herschel I.
Hagen, Everett E.
Hahn, Frank
Hamada, Robert S.
Harberger, Arnold C.
Hart, Albert G.
Haveman, Robert H.
Hayek, Friedrich A.
Heller, H. Robert
Heller, Walter W.
Hirsch, Werner Z.
Hochman, Harold M.
Holtrop, Marius W.
Jaffee, Dwight M.
James, P.M. Emile
Kahn, Richard
King, A. Thomas
Kloten, Norbert W.

Kregel, Jan A.
Kuh, Edwin
Laidler, David E.W.
Lampman, Robert J.
Latane, Henry A.
Leftwich, Richard H.
Leijonhufvud, Axel
Lintner, John
Lipsey, Richard
Lundberg, Erik F.
McKinnon, Ronald
Marchal, Jean M.P.
Mayer, Thomas
Meiselman, David I.
Meltzer, Allan H.
Mieszkowski, Peter M.
Miller, Marcus H.
Miller, Merton H.
Mirrlees, James A.
Modigliani, Franco
Musgrave, Richard A.
Nelson, Charles R.
Nevin, Edward T.

Niskanen, William A.
Nordhaus, William D.
Oates, Wallace E.
Opie, Roger G.
Orcutt, Guy H.
Patinkin, Don
Peacock, Alan T.
Pechman, Joseph A.
Peston, Maurice
Phelps, Edmund S.
Polak, J.J.
Prest, Alan R.
Recktenwald, Horst C.
Reddaway, W. Brian
Rees, Albert
Rivlin, Alice M.
Robbins, Lionel
Rosa, Jean-Jacques
Rose, Klaus
Ruggles, Richard
Samuels, Warren J.
Sandmo, Agnar
Sargent, Thomas J.

Sayers, Richard S.
Schmidt, Kurt
Schneider, Helmut
Scott, Anthony D.
Selden, Richard T.
Shell, Karl
Sheshinski, Eytan
Shibata, Hirofumi
Shoup, Carl S.
Shubik, Martin
Solomon, Ezra
Stein, Herbert
Stubblebine, W. Craig
Tobin, James
Tsiang, Sho-chieh
Vickers, Douglas
Wallich, Henry C.
Walters, Alan A.
Waud, Roger N.
Weintraub, Sidney
Willett, T.D.
Williams, Alan

5. International economics

Adams, Walter
Aliber, Robert Z.
Arndt, Heinz W.
Balassa, Bela
Baldwin, Robert E.
Balogh, Thomas
Bardhan, Pranab K.
Basevi, Giorgio
Bator, Francis M.
Berry, Albert
Bhagwati, Jagdish N.
Black, Fischer
Black, Stanley W.
Borts, George H.
Bos, Hendricus C.
Brown, Arthur J.
Bruno, Michael
Cairncross, Alexander K.
Caves, Richard E.
Chenery, Hollis B.
Chipman, John S.
Cooper, Richard
Corden, Max
Darby, Michael R.
Diaz-Alejandro, Carlos F.
Dixit, Avinash K.
Donges, Juergen B.
Dornbusch, Rudiger
Dunning, John H.
Fischer, Stanley
Frank, Charles R.
Frenkel, Jacob A.

Giersch, Herbert
Griffin, Keith B.
Grubel, Herbert
Gutowski, Armin F.
Haberler, Gottfried
Helleiner, Gerald K.
Heller, H. Robert
Hesse, Helmut
Hoffmann, Lutz
Horvath, Janos
Houthakker, Hendrik
Hufbauer, Gary C.
Johnson, D. Gale
Keesing, Donald B.
Kemp, Murray C.
Kenen, Peter B.
Kindleberger, Charles P.
Komiya, Ryutaro
Kravis, Irving B.
Kreinin, Mordechai E.
Krueger, Anne O.
Lal, Deepak K.
Lancaster, Kelvin J.
Lavigne, Marie
Lesourne, Jacques
Lindbeck, Assar
MacDougall, G. Donald A.
McKinnon, Ronald
Machlup, Fritz
Meade, James E.
Meier, Gerald M.
Meiselman, David I.

Mikesell, Raymond F.
Miller, Marcus H.
Moller, Hans
Muns, Joaquin
Myint, Hla
Negishi, Takashi
Neuberger, Egon
Officer, Lawrence H.
Ozawa, Terutomo
Papi, G. Ugo
Parkin, John M.
Pattanaik, Prasanta K.
Pearce, Ivor F.
Polak, J.J.
Prebisch, Raul
Ranis, Gustav
Reiffers, Jean-Louis
Rose, Klaus
Rybczynski, Tadeusz M.
Schmitt, Bernard
Schneider, Helmut
Scitovsky, Tibor
Shibata, Hirofumi
Siebert, Horst
Thirlwall, Anthony
Tsiang, Sho-hieh
Turnovsky, Stephen J.
Vernon, Raymond
Wallich, Henry C.
Willett, T.D.
Willgerodt, Hans
Wonnacott, Ronald J.

6. Administration; Business finance; Marketing; Accounting

Albach, Horst
Borch, Karl H.
Cyert, Richard M.
Downs, Anthony
Durand, David
Elton, Edwin J.
Fisher, Franklin M.
Gabor, André
Gordon, Myron J.
Groves, Theodore
Haldi, John

Hamada, Robert S.
Ijiri, Yuji
Ilchman, Warren F.
Jensen, Michael C.
Johnson, Robert W.
Keeney, Ralph L.
Kennedy, Charles
Kraus, Alan
Latane, Henry A.
Lesourne, Jacques
Levy, Haim

Liebhafsky, Herbert H.
Lintner, John
Malkiel, Burton G.
Miller, Merton H.
Modigliani, Franco
Muth, John F.
Ross, Stephen A.
Solomon, Ezra
Williamson, Oliver E.

7. Industrial organisation; Technological change; Industry studies

Adams, Walter
Adelman, Morris A.
Albach, Horst
Alchian, Armen A.
Alexander, Sidney S.
Bailey, Elizabeth E.
Bain, Joe S.
Baron, David P.
Baumol, William
Beesley, Michael E.
Bienayme, Alain
Bishop, Robert L.
Borts, George H.
Caves, Richard E.
Cheung, Steven N.S.
Chiplin, Brian
Clower, Robert W.
Coase, Ronald H.
Comanor, William S.
Dasgupta, Partha S.
David, Paul A.
Davis, Otto A.
Demsetz, Harold
Dunlop, John T.
Dunning, John H.
Eckaus, Richard
Galbraith, John K.

Gould, John P.
Griliches, Zvi
Habakkuk, H. John
Haldi, John
Hart, Peter E.
Hollander, Samuel
Jensen, Michael C.
Joskow, Paul L.
Kahn, Alfred E.
Kamerschen, David R.
Kamien, Morton I.
Landes, William M.
Leff, Nathaniel H.
Leland, Hayne E.
Levhari, David
Lippman, Steven A.
Loasby, Brian J.
Machlup, Fritz
Mann, H. Michael
Mansfield, Edwin
Markham, Jesse W.
Mason, Edward S.
Melman, Seymour
Meyer, John R.
Mills, Edwin S.
Mueller, Dennis C.
Muns, Joaquin

Nelson, Richard R.
O'Brien, Denis
Opie, Roger G.
Parsons, Donald O.
Peck, Merton J.
Posner, Richard A.
Robinson, E. Austin G.
Rosen, Sherwin
Salop, Steven
Schelling, Thomas C.
Scherer, Frederic M.
Schmalensee, Richard L.
Shepherd, William G.
Siegfried, John J.
Silberston, Z. Aubrey
Spence, Andrew M.
Stigler, George J.
Stiglitz, Joseph E.
Telser, Lester G.
Townsend, Harry
Turvey, Ralph
Vernon, Raymond
Vietorisz, Thomas
Von Weizsacker, Carl C.
Williamson, Oliver E.
Willis, Robert B.
Winter, Sidney G.

8. Agriculture; Natural resources

Adelman, I.
Adelman, Morris A.
Bergmann, Denis R.
Cicchetti, Charles J.
Clark, Colin G.
Dorfman, Robert
Goergescu-Roegen, Nicholas

Hoch, Irving
Johnson, D. Gale
Johnston, Bruce F.
Kamien, Morton I.
Kneese, Allen V.
Knetsch, Jack L.
Krutilla, John V.

Mellor, John W.
Mikesell, Raymond F.
Oates, Wallace E.
Ruttan, Vernon W.
Schultz, Theodore W.
Scott, Anthony D.
Yotopoulos, Pan A.

9. Manpower; Labour; Population

Ashenfelter, Orley
Atkinson, Anthony B.
Bartoli, Henri
Becker, Gary S.
Behrman, Jere R.
Bell, Carolyn S.
Ben-Porath, Yoram
Bernstein, Blanche
Bienayme, Alain
Bowles, Samuel
Bowman, Mary J.
Brechling, Frank P.R.
Cain, Glen G.
Chamberlain, Neil W.
Chiplin, Brian
Chiswick, Barry R.
Dunlop, John T.
Easterlin, Richard A.
Finegan, T. Aldrich
Freeman, Richard B.
Galenson, Walter
Gallaway, Lowell E.
Gastwirth, Joseph L.
Goldberger, Arthur S.
Gramlich, Edward M.
Greenwood, Michael
Gronau, Reuben

Hall, Robert E.
Hamermesh, Daniel
Hanoch, Giora
Hansen, W. Lee
Harrison, Bennett
Haveman, Robert H.
Heckman, James J.
Hines, Albert G.
Jencks, C.
Johnson, Thomas
Kelley, Allen C.
Kuczynski, Jurgen P.
Lazear, Edward P.
Lester, Richard A.
Levitan, Sar A.
Lloyd, Cynthia B.
McCall, John J.
MacKay, R. Ross
Miller, Herman P.
Mincer, Jacob
Myrdal, Gunnar
Nerlove, Marc
Newhouse, Joseph P.
Newman, Peter K.
Oi, Walter Y.
Parsons, Donald O.
Phelps Brown, E. Henry

Piore, Michael J.
Reagan, Barbara B.
Reder, Melvin W.
Rees, Albert
Reiffers, Jean-Louis
Reynolds, Lloyd G.
Ridker, Ronald G.
Rosen, Sherwin
Rothschild, Kurt W.
Sauvy, Alfred
Schultz, T. Paul
Sowell, Thomas
Spengler, Joseph J.
Taubman, Paul
Tinbergen, Jan
Todaro, Michael P.
Ulman, Lloyd
Vincens, Jean
Wachter, Michael L.
Watts, Harold W.
Welch, Finis R.
Williams, Anne D.
Willis, Robert J.
Wrigley, Edward A.
Zeckhauser, Richard J.

10. Welfare programmes; Consumer economics; Urban and regional economics

Aaron, Henry
Babeau, André
Barten, Anton P.
Beckerman, Wilfred
Beesley, Michael E.
Bell, Carolyn S.
Bernstein, Blanche
Bish, Robert L.
Blackorby, Charles
Boulding, Kenneth E.
Byron, Ray
Culyer, Anthony J.
Davis, Otto A.
Deaton, Angus S.
Downs, Anthony
Enthoven, Alain
Feldstein, Martin
Ferber, Robert
Gäfgen, Gérard
Gorman, William
Greenhut, Melvin L.
Greenwood, Michael

Hamermesh, Daniel
Harris, John R.
Harrison, Bennett
Hirsch, Werner Z.
Hochman, Harold M.
Jencks, C.
Juster, F. Thomas
Kain, John F.
King, A. Thomas
Knetsch, Jack L.
Lambin, Jean-Jacques
Lampman, Robert J.
Landes, William M.
Lasuen, José R.
Lee, Tong H.
Lekachman, Robert
Lester, Richard A.
Levitan, Sar A.
Lindsay, Cotton M.
Liu, Ben-chieh
Lloyd, Cynthia B.
MacKay, R. Ross

Mieszkowski, Peter M.
Miller, Herman P.
Mills, Edwin S.
Morgan, James N.
Moses, Leon N.
Muellbauer, John N.J.
Muth, Richard F.
Nevin, Edward T.
Newhouse, Joseph P.
Piore, Michael J.
Ponsard, Claude
Posner, Richard A.
Reagan, Barbara B.
Rothenberg, Jerome
Schelling, Thomas C.
Smolensky, Eugene
Theil, Henri
Vanek, Jaroslav
Van Praag, Bernard M.S.
Weisbrod, Burton A.
Williams, Alan
Wilson, Thomas

Appendix 2

AMERICAN ECONOMIC ASSOCIATION'S CLASSIFICATION OF FIELDS IN ECONOMICS

000 General Economics: Theory; History; Systems
   010 General Economics
      011 General economics
      012 Teaching of Economics
   020 General Economic Theory
      021 General equilibrium theory
      022 Micro-economic theory
      023 Micro-economic theory
      024 Welfare theory
      025 Social choice; bureaucratic performance
      206 Economics of Uncertainty and Information
   030 History of Economic Thought; Methodology
      031 History of economic thought
      036 Economic methodology
   040 Economic History
      041 Economic history: general
      042 North American (excluding Mexico) economic history
      043 Ancient and medieval economic history until 1453
      044 European economic history
      045 Asian economic history
      046 African economic history
      047 Latin American and Caribbean economic history
      048 Oceanic economic history
   050 Economic Systems
      051 Capitalist economic systems
      052 Socialist and communist economic systems
      053 Comparative economic systems
100 Economic Growth; Development; Planning; Fluctuations
   110 Economic Growth; Development; and Planning Theory and Policy
      111 Economic growth theory and models
      112 Economic development models and theories
      113 Economic planning theory and policy
      114 Economics of war, defence, and disarmament (including product and factor market topics)
   120 Country Studies
      121 Economic studies of less industrialised countries
      122 Economic studies of more industrialised countries
      123 Comparative economic studies involving both more and less industrialised countries; international statistical comparisons
   130 Economic Fluctuations; Forecasting; Stabilisation; and Inflation
      131 Economic fluctuations
      132 Economic forecasting and econometric models
      133 General outlook and stabilisation theories and policies
      134 Inflation and deflation
200 Quantitative Economic Methods and Data
   210 Econometric, Statistical, and Mathematical Methods and Models
      211 Econometric and statistical methods and models

212 Construction, analysis, and use of econometric models
213 Mathematical methods and models
214 Computer programs
220 Economic and Social Statistical Data and Analysis
221 National income accounting
222 Input-output
223 Financial accounts
224 National wealth and balance sheets
225 Social indicators and social accounts
226 Productivity and growth: Theory and data
227 Prices
228 Regional statistics
229 Micro-data
300 Domestic Monetary and Fiscal Theory and Institutions
310 Domestic Monetary and Financial Theory and Institutions
311 Domestic monetary and financial theory and policy
312 Commercial banking
313 Capital markets
314 Financial intermediaries
315 Credit to business, consumer, etc. (including mortgages)
320 Fiscal Theory and Policy; Public Finance
321 Fiscal theory and policy
322 National government expenditures and budgeting
323 National taxation and subsidies
324 State and local government finance
325 Intergovernmental financial relationships
400 International Economics
410 International Trade Theory
411 International trade theory
420 Trade Relations; Commercial Policy; International Economic Integration
421 Trade relations
422 Commercial policy
423 Economic integration
430 Balance of Payments; International Finance
431 Balance of payments; mechanisms of adjustment; exchange rates
432 International monetary arrangements
440 International Investment and Foreign Aid
441 International investment and capital markets
442 International business
443 International aid
500 Administration; Business Finance; Marketing; Accounting
510 Administration
511 Organisation and decision theory
512 Managerial economics
513 Business and public administration
514 Goals and objectives of firms
520 Business Finance and Investment
521 Business finance
522 Business investment
530 Marketing
531 Marketing and advertising
540 Accounting
541 Accounting

900   Welfare Programmes; Consumer Economics; Urban and Regional Economics
   910   Welfare, Health, and Education
      911   General welfare programmes
      912   Economics of education
      913   Economics of health
      914   Economics of poverty
      915   Social security (public superannuation and survivors benefits)
      916   Economics of crime
      917   Economics of minorities; economics of discrimination
   920   Consumer Economics
      921   Consumer economics; levels and standards of living
   930   Urban Economics
      931   Urban economics and public policy
      932   Housing economics (includes non-urban housing)
      933   Urban transportation economics
   940   Regional Economics
      941   Regional economics

Appendix 3

INDEX OF COUNTRY OF RESIDENCE
IF NOT USA

AUSTRALIA
Arndt, Heinz W.
Byron, Ray
Clark, Colin G.
Corden, Max
Harcourt, Geoffrey C.
*Hearn, William E.
Kemp, Murray C.
Turnovsky, Stephen J.

AUSTRIA
Rothschild, Kurt W.

AUSTRO-HUNGARY
*Auspitz, Rudolf
*Bauer, Otto
*Böhm-Bawerk, Eugen
*Hornick, Philipp W.
*Lieben, Richard
*Menger, Anton
*Menger, Carl
*Muller, Adam H.
*Philippovich von Phillipsberg,
Eugen
*Sax, Emil
*Sonnenfels, Joseph
*Spann, Othmar
*Wieser, Friedrich

BELGIUM
Barten, Anton P.
Denis, Hector
Lambin, Jean-Jacques
*Lavelaye, Emile L. V.

CANADA
Archibald, George C.
Berry, Robert J.
Bish, Robert L.
Blackorby, Charles
Breton, Albert
Cragg, John G.
Diewert, W. Erwin
Gordon, Myron J.
Grubel, Herbert
Helleiner, Gerald K.
Hollander, Samuel
*Innis, Harold A.
*Jaffé, William
Knetsch, Jack L.
Kraus, Alan
Laidler, David E.W.
Lipsey, Richard
Parkin, John M.

Scott, Anthony D.
Usher, Dan
Wonnacott, Ronald J.

CHILE
Prebisch, Raúl

DENMARK
*Zeuthen, Frederik

FIJI
Higgins, Benjamin H.

FRANCE
*Aftalion, Albert
Allais, Maurice
*Antonelli, Etienne
*Aupetit, Albert
Babeau, André
Bartoli, Henri
*Bastiat, Frédéric
*Bergmann, Denis R.
*Bertrand, Joseph L.
Bienayme, Alain
*Blanc, J.-J. Louis
*Blanqui, Jerome A.
*Boisguilbert, Pierre P.
Boiteux, Marcel P.
*Bousquet, Georges H.
*Canard, Nicolas F.
*Cantillon, Richard
*Chevalier, Michel
*Cheysson, Jean-Jacques
*Colson, Clement L.
*Condillac, Etienne B.
*Condorcet, M.-J.A.N.C.
Cotta, Alain
Courbis, Raymond
*Courcelle-Seneuil, Jean G.
*Cournot, Antoine A.
*Destutt de Tracy, Antoine L.C.
*Divisia, Francois
*Dunoyer, Charles
*Dupont de Nemours, Pierre S.
*Dupuit, A. Jules E.J.
Fitoussi, Jean-Paul
*Forbonnais, François V.
*Fourier, Charles
*Garnier, Germain
*Garnier, Joseph C.
*Gide, Charles
*Gonnard, René
Grandmont, Jean-Michel
Guitton, Henri

*Halévy, Elie
*Isnard, Achylle-Nicolas
James, P.M. Émile
*Juglar, Clement
Laffont, Jean-Jaques M.
*Landry, Michel A.A.
Lavigne, Marie
*Law, John
*Leroy-Beaulieu, Paul
*Lescure, Jean
Lesourne, Jacques
*Levasseur, Émile
*Mantoux, Paul J.
Marchal, Jean M.-P.
Marczewski, Jean
*Mercier de la Rivière, Pierre
P.
*Mirabeau, Victor R.
*Molinari, Gustave
*Morellet, André
*Necker, Jacques
Perroux, François
Pirou, Gäetan
Ponsard, Claude
*Proudhon, Pierre J.
*Quesnay, François
Reiffers, Jean-Louis
*Rist, Charles
Rosa, Jean-Jacques
*Rossi, Pelegrino L.E.
Rueff, Jacques L.
*Saint-Simon, Claude H.R.
Sauvy, Alfred
*Say, Horace E.
*Say, Jean B.
*Say, Léon
Schmitt, Bernard
*Turgot, A.R. Jacques
*Vauban, Sebastien P.
Vincens, Jean
*Walras, Antoine A.

GERMANY
Albach, Horst
*Bernstein, Eduard
*Bortkiewicz, Ladislaus
*Brentano, Lujo
*Christaller, Walter
*Cohn, Gustav
*Diehl, Karl
*Dietzel, Carl A.
*Dietzel, Heinrich
Donges, Juergen B.
*Duhring, Eugen K.

*Engel, Ernst
*Erhard, Ludwig
*Eucken, Walter
Fischer, Wolfram
Gafgen, Gerard
*Gesell, Silvio
Giersch, Herbert
*Gossen, Hermann H.
*Gottl-Ottlilienfeld, Friedrich
*Grossman, Henryk
Gutowski, Armin F.
Helmstadter, Ernst
*Hermann, Friedrich B.W.
Hesse, Helmut
*Hildebrand, Bruno
Hildenbrand, Werner
*Hilferding, Rudolf
Hoffman, Lutz
*Kautsky, Karl
Kloten, Norbert W.
*Knapp, Georg F.
*Knies, Karl
Kuczynski, Jürgen P.
*Laspeyres, Etienne
*Lassalle, Ferdinand
*Launhardt, C.F. Wilhelm
*Lexis, Wilhelm
*List, Friedrich
*Luxembourg, Rosa
*Mangoldt, Hans K.E.
Moller, Hans
*Oncken, August
*Oppenheimer, Franz
Ott, Alfred E.
*Pesch, Heinrich
*Rau, Karl H.
Recktenwald, Horst C.
*Rodbertus, Johann K.
*Roscher, Wilhelm G.F.
Rose, Klaus
*Schaffle, Albert E.F.
Schmidt, Kurt
*Schmoller, Gustav
*Schneider, Erich
Siebert, Horst
*Soden, Friedrich J.H.
*Sombart, Werner
*Spiethoff, Arthur
*Thünen, Johann H.
Von Weizsäcker, Carl C.
*Wagner, Adolph H.G.
*Weber, Alfred
*Weber, Max
Willgerodt, Hans

HUNGARY
Kornai, János

IRELAND
*Bastable, Charles F.
*O'Brien, George A.T.

ISRAEL
Ben-Porath, Yoram
Bruno, Michael
Gronau, Reuben
Hanoch, Giora
Levhari, David
Levy, Haim
Patinkin, Don
Sheshinski, Eytan
Yaari, Menahem E.

ITALY
*Amoroso, Luigi
*Antonelli, Giovanni B.
*Barone, Enrico
Basevi, Giorgio
*Beccaria, Cesare B.
*Bresciani-Turroni,
    Constantino
Caravale, Giovanni A.
Casarosa, Carlo
*Cossa, Luigi
*Del Vecchio, Gustavo
*Einaudi, Luigi
*Fanno, Marco
*Ferrara, Francesco
*Galiani, Ferdinando
Garegnani, Pierangelo
*Genovesi, Antonio
*Loria, Achille
*Mazzola, Ugo
*Ortes, Giammaria
*Pantaleoni, Maffeo
Papi, G. Ugo
*Pareto, Vilfredo
Pasinetti, Luigi L.
*Ricci, Umberto
*Verri, Pietro

JAPAN
Inada, Ken-Ichi
Komiya, Ryutaro
Negishi, Takashi
Shibata, Hirofumi
Tsuru, Shigeto
Uzawa, Hirofumi

NETHERLANDS
Bos, Hendricus
*Cohen Stuart, Arnold J.
Holtrop, Marius W.
*Pierson, Nicolaas G.
Tinbergen, Jan
Van Praag, Bernard M.S.

NORWAY
Borch, Karl H.
*Frisch, Ragnar A.K.
Johansen, Leif
Sandmo, Agnar

POLAND
*Kalecki, Michal
*Lange, Oskar

RUSSIA
*Bukharin, Nikolai I.
*Dmitriev, Vladimir K.
Kantorovich, Leonid V.
*Kondratieff, Nikolai D.
*Lenin, Vladimir I.
*Manuilov, Aleksandr A.
*Novozhilov, Viktor V.
*Preobrazhenski, Evgeni
*Slutsky, Eugen
*Stalin, Joseph
*Storch, Heinrich F.
*Strumilin, Stanislav G.
*Tugan-Baranovsky, Mikhail I.

SOUTH AFRICA
*Lehfeldt, Robert A.
Robertson, Hector M.

SPAIN
Florez Estrada, Alvaro
Lasuen, José R.
*Stackelberg, Heinrich
*Uztariz, Geronimo

SWEDEN
*Akerman, Gustaf
Bohm, Peter J.G.
*Cassel, Karl G.
*Davidson, David
*Heckscher, Eli F.
*Lindahl, Erik R.
Lindbeck, Assar
Lundberg, Erik F.
Myrdal, Gunnar
*Ohlin, Bertil G.
*Wicksell, Knut

SWITZERLAND
Bernholz, Peter
*Bernouilli, Daniel
*Cherbuliez, Antoine E.
*Lutz, Friedrich A.
*Ropke, Wilhelm
*Salin, Edgar
Schneider, Helmut
*Sismondi, J.C.L.S.
Turvey, Ralph
*Walras, Leon M.E.
Wold, Herman

UNITED KINGDOM
Aldcroft, Derek H.
Allen, Roy
*Anderson, James
Artis, Michael J.
*Ashley, William J.
Atkinson, Anthony B.

*Sidgwick, Henry
Silberston, Z. Aubrey
*Smart, William
*Smith, Adam
*Spence, Thomas
*Spencer, Herbert
Sraffa, Piero
*Stamp, Josiah C.
*Steuart, James D.
*Stewart, Dugald
Stone, J. Richard N.
*Tawney, Richard H.
Thirlwall, Anthony
*Thompson, Thomas P.

*Thompson, William
*Thornton, Henry
*Thornton, William T.
*Tooke, Thomas
*Torrens, Robert
Townsend, Harry
*Toynbee, Arnold
*Tucker, Josiah
*Unwin, George
*Vanderlint, Jacob
*Wakefield, Edward G.
*Wallace, Robert
Wallis, Kenneth F.
Walters, Alan A.

*Webb, Beatrice
*Webb, Sidney J.
*West, Edward
*Whately, Richard
*Wheatley, John
*Whewell, William
*Wicksteed, Philip H.
Wiles, Peter J.F.
Williams, Alan
*Wilson, James
Wilson, Thomas
Worswick, George D.N.
Wrigley, Edward A.

Appendix 4

INDEX OF COUNTRY OF BIRTH IF NOT USA

*Juglar, Clement
Laffont, Jean-Jacques M.
*Landry, Michel A.A.
Lavigne, Marie
*Leroy-Beaulieu, Paul
*Lescure, Jean
Lesourne, Jacques
*Levasseur, Emile
*Lutz, Friedrich A.
*Mantoux, Paul J.
Marchal, Jean M.P.
Mellor, John W.
*Mercier de la Rivière, Pierre P.
*Mirabeau, Victor R.
*Morellet, André
*Pareto, Vilfredo
Perroux, François
*Pirou, Gaëtan
Ponsard, Claude
*Proudhon, Pierre J.
*Quesnay, François
Reiffers, Jean-Louis
Rosa, Jean-Jacques
Rueff, Jacques L.
*Saint-Simon, Claude H.R.
Sauvy, Alfred
*Say, Horace E.
*Say, Jean B.
*Say, Léon
Schmitt, Bernard
*Turgot, A.R. Jacques
*Vauban, Sebastien P.
Vincens, Jean
*Walras, Antoine A.
*Walras, M.E. Léon

GERMANY
Albach, Horst
Arndt, Heinz W.
Baer, Werner
Beckmann, Martin J.
Bernholz, Peter
*Bernstein, Eduard
Brechling, Frank P.R.
*Brentano, Lujo
Bruno, Michael
*Christaller, Walter
*Cohn, Gustav
Corden, Max
*Diehl, Karl
*Dietzel, Carl A.
*Dietzel, Heinrich
Dornbusch, Rudiger
*Duhring, Eugen
Eckstein, Otto
*Engel, Ernst
*Engels, Friedrich
*Erhard, Ludwig
*Eucken, Walter
Feige, Edgar L.
Fischer, Wolfram
Giersch, Herbert
*Gossen, Hermann H.

Grubel, Herbert
Gutowski, Armin F.
Hahn, Frank
Heller, H. Robert
Helmstadter, Ernst
*Hermann, Friedrich B.W.
Hesse, Helmut
*Hildebrand, Bruno
Hildenbrand, Werner
Hirsch, Werner Z.
Hoffman, Lutz
*Johannsen, Nicolaus A.L.J.
Kloten, Norbert W.
*Knapp, Georg F.
*Knies, Karl
Kuczynski, Jürgen P.
*Laspeyres, Etienne
*Lassalle, Ferdinand
*Launhardt, C.F. Wilhelm
*Lederer, Emil
*Lexis, Wilhelm
*List, Friedrich
Lowe, Adolph
*Mangoldt, Hans K.E.
*Marx, Karl
Moller, Hans
*Morgenstern, Oskar
Muellbauer, John N.J.
*Muller, Adam H.
Musgrave, Richard A.
*Oncken, August
*Oppenheimer, Franz
Ott, Alfred E.
*Pesch, Heinrich
Ranis, Gustav
*Rau, Karl H.
Recktenwald, Horst C.
*Rodbertus, Johann K.
*Röpke, Wilhem
*Roscher, Wilhelm G.F.
Rose, Klaus
*Salin, Edgar
*Schaffle, Albert E.F.
Schmidt, Karl
*Schmoller, Gustav
*Schneider, Erich
Schneider, Helmut
*Schulze-Gavernitz, Friedrich G.
Siebert, Horst
*Soden, Friedrich J.H.
*Sombart, Werner
*Spiethoff, Arthur
*Thünen, Johann H.
Von Weizsäcker, Carl C.
*Wagner, Adolph H.G.
Wallich, Henry C.
*Weber, Alfred
*Weber, Max
Willgerodt, Hans

GREECE
Yotopoulos, Pan A.

HONG KONG
Cheung, Steven N.S.
Deane, Phyllis

HUNGARY
Balassa, Bela
Bator, Francis M.
Horvath, János
Kornai, János
Quandt, Richard E.
Vietorisz, Thomas

INDIA
Bardhan, Pranab K.
Bhagwati, Jagdish N.
Dasgupta, Partha S.
Dixit, Avinash K.
*Gayer, Arthur D.
Lal, Deepak K.
McKay, R. Ross
Maddala, Gangadharrao S.
Miller, Marcus H.
Pattanaik, Prasanta K.
Sen, Amartya K.
*Tawney, Richard H.

ISRAEL
Ben-Porath, Yoram
Ehrlich, Isaac
Frenkel, Jacob A.
Gronau, Reuben
Hanoch, Giora
Kreinin, Mordechai E.
Kurz, Mordecai
Levhari, David
Levy, Haim
Sheshinski, Eytan
Yaari, Menahem E.

ITALY
*Amoroso, Luigi
*Antonelli, Giovanni B.
*Barone, Enrico
Basevi, Giorgio
*Beccaria, Cesare B.
*Bresciani-Turroni, Constantino
Caravale, Giovanni A.
Casarosa, Carlo
*Cossa, Luigi
*Del Vecchio, Gustavo
*Einaudi, Luigi
*Fanno, Marco
*Ferrara, Francesco
*Galiani, Ferdinando
Garegnani, Pierangelo
*Genovesi, Antonio
*Loria, Achille
*Mazzola, Ugo
Modigliani, Franco
Nuti, Domenico M.
*Ortes, Giammaria
*Pantaleoni, Maffeo

*Butt, Isaac
Cairncross, Alexander K.
*Cairnes, John E.
*Cantillon, Richard
*Chalmers, Thomas
Champernowne, David G.
*Chapman, Sydney J.
Chiplin, Brian
*Clapham, John H.
Clark, Colin G.
*Cliffe Leslie, Thomas E.
Coase, Ronald H.
Coats, A.W.
*Cobden, Richard
*Coddington, Alan
*Cole, George D.H.
*Colquhoun, Patrick
Culyer, Anthony J.
*Cunningham, William
*Davenant, Charles
Deaton, Angus S.
*De Quincey, Thomas
*Dickinson, Henry D.
Dicks-Mireaux, Leslie
*Dobb, Maurice H.
Dunning, John H.
*Durbin, Evan F.M.
*Eden, Frederick M.
*Edgeworth, Francis Y.
*Fawcett, Henry
*Ferguson, Adam
Flemming, John S.
*Flux, Alfred W.
*Foxwell, Herbert S.
*Fullarton, John
*Gaitskell, Hugh T.N.
*Gervaise, Isaac
*Giffen, Robert
*Godwin, William
*Gonner, Edward C.K.
Goodhart, Charles A.E.
Gorman, William
*Goschen, George J.
Granger, Clive W.J.
*Gray, Alexander
*Gray, John
*Gray, Simon
*Green, Harold A.J.
*Gregory, Theodore E.G.
Habakkuk, H. John
*Hall, Charles
*Hancock, William N.
*Harris, Joseph
*Harrod, Roy F.
Hart, Peter E.
*Hawtrey, Ralph G.
Heal, Geoffrey M.
*Hearn, William E.
*Heaton, Herbert
*Henderson, Hubert D.
*Hewins, William A.S.
Hicks, John
*Higgs, Henry

*Hobson, John A.
*Hodgskin, Thomas
Hollander, Samuel
*Horner, Francis
*Hume, David
*Hutcheson, Francis
Hutchison, Terence W.
*Hyndman, Henry M.
*Ingram, John K.
*Jenkin, Henry C.F.
*Jevons, Herbert S.
*Jevons, William S.
*Johnson, William E.
Johnston, Jack
*Jones, Richard
*Joplin, Thomas
Kahn, Richard
Keesing, Donald B.
Kennedy, Charles
*Keynes, J. Maynard
*Keynes, J. Neville
*King, Gregory
Laidler, David E.W.
*Lardner, Dionysius
*Lauderdale, James M.
*Lavington, Frederick
*Law, John
*Lehfeldt, Robert A.
Little, Ian M.D.
*Lloyd, William F.
Loasby, Brian J.
*Locke, John
*Longe, Francis D.
*Longfield, S. Mountifort
*Lowe, Joseph
*McCulloch, John R.
McDougall, G. Donald A.
*Mcleod, Henry D.
*Malthus, T. Robert
*Marcet, Jane
*Marshall, Alfred
*Marshall, Mary P.
*Martin, Henry
*Martineau, Harriet
Meade, James E.
*Mill, James
*Mill, John S.
Mirrlees, James A.
Mishan, Ezra
Nevin, Edward T.
Newman, Peter K.
*Newmarch, William
*Nicholson, Joseph S.
*Norman, George W.
O'Brien, Denis
*O'Brien, George A.T.
*Overstone, Samuel J.L.
*Owen, Robert
*Palgrave, R.H. Inglis
Parkin, John M.
*Parnell, Henry B.
Peacock, Alan T.
Pearce, Ivor F.

*Pennington, James
Peston, Maurice
Phelps Brown, E. Henry
*Pigou, Arthur C.
*Plant, Arnold
*Postlethwayt, Malachy
Prest, Alan R.
*Rae, John
*Ramsay, George
*Ramsey, Frank P.
*Read, Samuel
Reddaway, W. Brian
*Ricardo, David
Robbins, Lionel
*Robertson, Dennis H.
Robertson, Hector M.
Robinson, E. Austin G.
Robinson, Joan
*Rogers, J.E. Thorold
Roy, Andrew D.
Sargan, John D.
Sayers, Richard S.
*Scott, William R.
*Scrope, George P.
Seers, Dudley
*Senior, Nassau W.
Shackle, George L.S.
*Shonfield, Andrew A.
*Shove, Gerald F.
*Sidgwick, Henry
Silberston, Z. Aubrey
*Smart, William
*Smith, Adam
*Spence, Thomas
*Spencer, Herbert
*Stamp, Josiah
*Steuart, James D.
*Stewart, Dugald
Stone, J. Richard N.
Thirlwall, Anthony
*Thompson, Thomas P.
*Thompson, William
*Thornton, Henry
*Thornton, William T.
*Torrens, Robert
Townsend, Harry
*Toynbee, Arnold
*Tucker, Josiah
Turvey, Ralph
*Unwin, George
*Vanderlint, Jacob
*Wakefield, Edward G.
*Wallace, Robert
Wallis, Kenneth F.
Walters, Alan
*Webb, Beatrice
*Webb, Sidney J.
*West, Edward
*Whately, Richard
*Wheatley, John
*Whewell, William
*Wicksteed, Philip H.
Wiles, Peter J.F.

Williams, Alan
*Wilson, James
Wilson, Thomas
Worswick, George D.N.

Wrigley, Edward A.

YUGOSLAVIA
Neuberger, Egon

ZAMBIA
Fischer, Stanley